Contents

PART II Water-Based Units 327

UNIT 8   Rafting 567

Christopher R. Pelchat and Michael L. Kinziger

PART III   Snow- and Ice-Based Units   623

UNIT 9   Snowshoeing. 625

Briget Tyson Eastep

UNIT 10   Mountaineering. 675

Mat Erpelding and Scott Schumann

UNIT 11   Nordic Skiing 745

Reid Cross

UNIT 12   Ice Climbing 821

Thomas Stuessy and John R. Kascenska

Photo Credits

Preface

The idea for this book stemmed from our experiences as field instructors and managers for various nationally known outdoor adventure programs, most notably Outward Bound and the Wilderness Education Association. Our experiences occurred during our formative years, when we were pursuing dream jobs, working in different outdoor settings with diverse groups, and teaching a variety of outdoor adventure pursuits. We started in a relatively new industry with limited standards, procedures, and curriculum requirements. As the industry matured, greater emphasis was placed on risk management, standards, policies, procedures, and instructor certification, but limited attention was directed toward formalized curriculum.

Over the past two decades, outdoor recreation activities that contain the elements of risk and adventure have exploded in popularity. Many social and economic factors have contributed to this growth, including greater visibility through the media; the development of equipment that is safer, lighter, and more readily available; and an increase in the number of people who seek challenging and adventurous lifestyles. An upsurge in the number of instructional programs, training and instructional guides, and books has also contributed to this growth. To meet this burgeoning demand, professionals today are expected to instruct multiple activities with proficiency. However, although curricula exist for select activities, a comprehensive curriculum guide that systematically addresses all activities in a single resource does not.

To meet this growing interest, a number of human and leisure service agencies and organizations, schools, colleges, and universities provide instruction in a variety of outdoor adventure pursuits. Programs operate within a set of established standard operating procedures, which include a curriculum designed to help the organization meet its educational goals. How we design and present curricula is of fundamental importance to our students and to the development of our field. To prepare adequately, instructors must take the time and energy to seek specific curricula from multiple resources. The amount of support materials needed to teach multiple adventure activities tends to be overwhelming. An all-in-one resource serves an immediate and practical need within the outdoor industry.

Technical Skills for Adventure Programming: A Curriculum Guide is designed to facilitate the instruction of specific outdoor adventure skills. The book organizes these skills into land-based activities (backpacking, rock climbing, caving, and mountain biking), water-based activities (sea kayaking, whitewater kayaking, canoeing, and rafting), and snow- and ice-based activities (snowshoeing, mountaineering, nordic skiing, and ice climbing). These activities constitute mainstream educational and leisure pursuits in elementary schools, middle schools, high schools, colleges and universities, and other institutions. Of course, we could not include all possible adventure-based activities. Instead, we present some of the most common or popular activities and will consider others in future editions.

The primary emphasis of this book is on the instruction of technical skills supported by sound pedagogy and professional experience. College students training to be professional outdoor leaders will find this book an invaluable resource, as will physical educators who integrate adventure activities into their classrooms. Outdoor leaders who teach technical skills will also benefit from the structured lesson plans presented.

The lessons follow a single template and include outcomes with predetermined, logically organized skills and knowledge that all students are to learn. Each lesson features a set of assessment procedures.

To assemble this book, we invited a number of expert outdoor programmers and master instructors to share their knowledge, expertise, and the industry's common practices by contributing lesson plans. We solicited the help of master educators, who dedicated much time and energy to the development of this curriculum guide. We applaud their efforts and humbly thank them for adding to the profession's body of knowledge. Working with this esteemed group of educators was a pleasure.

We wrote the first two chapters. Chapter 1 provides an overview of *Technical Skills for Adventure Programming* and discusses the limitations of the book. Chapter 2 provides an overview of the teaching process in the context of adventure-based activities and addresses key issues—such as national standards, environmental ethics, and inclusion—that we felt should be discussed before diving into the actual lessons.

The CD-ROM bound into the book includes all lessons in an easily accessible PDF format. This tool allows the user to choose specific lessons to print and carry into the field. We acknowledge that some instructors appreciate having hard copies for reference purposes without having to lug the entire volume into the field. We support keeping those loads light whenever possible. Lessons can also be distributed to students or coinstructors if they are going to play a role in the instructional process.

Users of *Technical Skills for Adventure Programming* finally have an all-in-one resource, based on current methods, to support their instructional efforts. We encourage you to provide us with feedback. Our ultimate goal is to improve curricula, thereby raising the standards of our profession. Your feedback will provide us with an avenue to improve this work in future editions. Have fun, be safe, and take care of our environment.

Mark Wagstaff
Radford University
Recreation, Parks and Tourism
P.O. Box 6369
Radford, VA 24142
mwagstaff@radford.edu

Aram Attarian
North Carolina State University
Parks, Recreation & Tourism Mgt.
P.O. Box 8004
Raleigh, NC 27695-8004
aram_attarian@ncsu.edu

CHAPTER 1

How to Use This Book

High-adventure activities hold an important place in modern society. Daily routines that find us confined to an office, going to school, taking care of family, and maintaining basic needs are void of adventure. The innate, thrill-seeking drive to push oneself to mental and physical limits is absent from modern-day life. Those who choose to boat wild rivers, climb mountains, explore wild caves, or mountain bike desert trails reap the benefits of adventure-based activities. Increased self-confidence, physical fitness, stress reduction, positive social interaction, and environmental stewardship are all positive outcomes of participation.

As the adventure sports industry grows, so does the need to educate this new breed of recreationist. Proper training helps participants engage in experiences that are more enjoyable and environmentally sound. In addition, proper skills instruction empowers participants to monitor personal and group safety. *Technical Skills for Adventure Programming: A Curriculum Guide* is designed to promote quality instruction to enhance learning. For clarity in terminology, we refer to instructors of adventure-based activities using two synonymous terms: *adventure-based educators* and *outdoor leaders*.

A new generation of adventure-based educators is emerging to serve the growing population of outdoor enthusiasts. Only a few decades ago, formal training for outdoor leaders was limited to learning by trial and error or mentorship. Today, professional outdoor leaders can find formal training through university degree programs, professional association certification programs, in-house staff training initiatives, and specialized leadership development programs. *Technical Skills for Adventure Programming* is intended to enhance the instructional efforts of this noble group of educators. Specifically, the book focuses on one aspect of teaching and leading outdoor adventures: technical skills instruction.

Technical skills instruction can be defined as facilitating the student's technical ability to engage in an adventure sport with a reasonable degree of competence. For example, the art of teaching a canoeing stroke becomes a complex task when eyed through a critical lens. Adventure-based activities such as canoeing are composed of complex skill sets that the participant must learn and perfect through an experiential learning process. Quality instruction can maximize the skills needed to execute efficient strokes, read moving water, and use specialized equipment. Students engage in the learning process from a variety of approaches based on their preferred learning styles. Professionals who teach technical skills must be well versed in experiential teaching techniques and learning theory. Long gone are the traditional practices in which the learning experience was centered on the teacher rather than the student. Modern learning theory offers adventure-based educators a more diverse, effective approach to skills instruction.

Purpose and Intended Audience

Technical Skills for Adventure Programming offers you a curriculum to teach adventure-based activities using a holistic approach. Although national curricula exist for select adventure sports, this book provides the first comprehensive teaching resource for multiple activities. Its development reflects the growth of the outdoor leadership profession and meets an important need. The lessons in this guide are designed and written for adventure-based educators with background experience in the activity being taught. Therefore, to use this curriculum guide effectively, you should have experience in the specific activity. The authors of each unit have defined basic terms and provided illustrations and diagrams of the basic skills to bring clarity to their written descriptions. We acknowledge that much diversity currently exists in the way these activities are being taught around the world. The goal of this book is to focus on the essential knowledge and skills necessary to facilitate enjoyable, reasonably safe, and environmentally sound outdoor adventure experiences.

The information in this curriculum guide focuses on technical skills as well as related risk management issues and environmental stewardship. We chose not to address other aspects of outdoor instruction related to quality outdoor leadership; that huge topic is beyond the scope of this book.

Outdoor leaders need skill and experience to teach and lead the activities contained in

Technical Skills for Adventure Programming. Effective outdoor instructors know their personal abilities and limitations and avoid leading their students or themselves into dangerous situations. Those who teach adventure-based activities must master the following core competencies of professional outdoor leaders before leading others in adventure-based settings:

◆ Foundational knowledge
◆ Self-awareness and professional conduct
◆ Decision making and judgment
◆ Teaching and facilitation
◆ Environmental stewardship
◆ Program management
◆ Safety and risk management
◆ Technical ability

Figure 1.1 describes those eight core competencies in detail. Although the lessons in this book address many of these competencies, the emphasis remains on technical skills instruction. The primary focus is to assist you in developing the student's technical abilities in select adventure activities. Nevertheless, you should have background training and experience in all eight competency areas.

As an adventure-based educator, you have an obligation to your students to be properly trained and experienced in the art of outdoor leadership. Do not rely solely on this book to instruct adventure-based activities. Our intended audience is the person who has participated in formal outdoor leadership training programs and has taken the time to seek formal training in the specified activity.

Foundational Knowledge

Sense of Purpose

Sense of purpose refers to the general philosophy on which the practice of outdoor leadership is based. Why do we do what we do in the field of outdoor leadership? What value does the practice of outdoor leadership hold for society? What am I as an outdoor leader trying to accomplish through my work? Answers to these questions help us develop a sense of purpose as outdoor leaders and an understanding of the general purpose of the practice of outdoor leadership.

Sense of Heritage

Sense of heritage refers to the history of the profession. In understanding who we are as a profession, we need to understand our origins. Good outdoor leaders know the general roots of the profession, have a sense of future trends in the profession, and feel a sense of place within the tradition of the profession.

Breadth of the Profession

Breadth of the profession refers to the various contexts and ways in which outdoor leadership is practiced. Outdoor leadership is a profession that is broad in scope. It is practiced in a variety of contexts, from traditional wilderness programs to public schools to national parks. Good outdoor leaders are aware of the various professional contexts that constitute the profession, and they are aware of the various organizational contexts in which outdoor leadership is practiced.

Understanding Leadership

One of the primary goals of outdoor leadership is to serve as a source of transformation in the lives of people. This goal can be accomplished only through effective leadership. Consequently, competency in the theory and practice of leadership is essential to outdoor leadership.

Self-Awareness and Professional Conduct

Acting Mindfully

Good outdoor leaders are always mindful in their actions, meaning that they are intentional in all their actions. They always act with regard to the ultimate goals of a group experience. At times, they are attentive to the needs of group members. At times, they are attentive to tasks that must be accomplished. Nonetheless, every leader action involves mindfulness and specific intent.

Knowing Your Abilities and Limitations

One aspect of acting mindfully and intentionally involves having an accurate sense of your abilities

continued ▶

FIGURE 1.1 The eight basic competencies that form the foundation for outdoor leadership development.

Adapted, by permission, from B. Martin et al., 2006, *Outdoor leadership: Theory and practice* (Champaign, IL: Human Kinetics).

and limitations. Without a clear sense of your abilities and limitations, you as an outdoor leader can hardly begin to define appropriate levels of challenge for your program participants. Without a clear sense of your abilities and limitations, you may set the bar too high, thus jeopardizing the emotional or physical safety of your participants. In such cases, you may become a danger to the group or, at the very least, diminish the quality of an experience.

How You Affect Others

Another aspect of acting mindfully and intentionally involves knowing how you affect others. In what ways do you typically influence a group? What effect does your personality typically have on others in a group? Without a clear sense of the influence that you have within a group, you can hardly begin to fashion experiences for the group that are psychologically rewarding. On the contrary, you might come across as a social oaf, serving only to hinder group development.

Personal and Professional Ethics

Yet another aspect of acting mindfully and intentionally is principled behavior. Leaders without moral scruples ultimately serve as negative influences within groups. Having a strong sense of personal and professional ethics is essential to effective leadership. The leader who bends or breaks rules or allows others to bend or break rules undermines the quality and value of an experience.

Decision Making and Judgment

Decision Making as a Conscious Process

Many of the decisions that we make in our lives are snap decisions that we come to without much conscious thought. This approach to decision making is acceptable when the decisions are simple and the consequences are small. In situations when decisions are complex, uncertainty is high, and the difference in consequences may mean the difference between life and death, this approach is unacceptable. Good decision making is a conscious process that involves weighing options as well as the consequences of each of the options in choosing a course of action.

Role of Judgment in Decision Making

Judgment becomes part of the decision-making process when the consequences of a particular decision or course of action are unclear or unknown and you as a leader must make a best guess about a course of action. Judgment is defined as an estimation of the likely consequences of such a decision or course of action. Effective judgment relies on experience and knowledge as a basis for estimating likely consequences.

Awareness of Available Resources in Decision Making

Conducting an inventory of available resources is essential to effective decision making. The inventory includes physical resources available in the surrounding environment; physical resources within the possession of the group, such as equipment; and human resources—knowledge, experience, and expertise—both within and outside the group. Taking an inventory is aimed at ascertaining the resources that are available to you in making a decision or choosing a certain course of action.

Teaching and Facilitation

Facilitation Skills

A common approach to facilitation in the early days of outdoor leadership was to let the experience speak for itself. Outdoor leaders took a hands-off approach when it came to the broader lessons that participants might gain from an experience. Outdoor leaders eventually began to realize, however, that they were forgoing an opportunity to make a difference in the lives of their participants. They eventually began to frame experiences in ways that would help participants gain as much as possible from an experience in a process known as facilitation. Facilitation is intended to enhance the quality of experiences for individuals and groups. It involves assisting individuals and groups in gaining insights from experiences that they may not gain on their own.

Teaching Skills

Outdoor leaders commonly find themselves in situations in which they are offering direct instruction to course participants. Whether they are teaching participants basic wilderness living skills, climbing or paddling techniques, or safety and rescue skills, outdoor leaders are instructors. To become an effective instructor, you must learn how to teach. This means learning how to create lessons and learning activities. It entails developing an understanding of the various instructional and learning styles. It entails learning how to model effective technique and how to coach others in developing effective technique.

Teaching Experientially

Outdoor leaders place a great deal of emphasis on learning by doing. As noted earlier in this chapter, experiential education provides the method by which outdoor leaders deliver their educational content. Every lesson should involve a degree of explanation.

FIGURE 1.1 *(continued)*

Every lesson should involve a degree of demonstration. Every lesson should involve a greater degree of practice. This means giving participants an opportunity to learn skills and dispositions in a hands-on manner. In teaching a group how to operate camp stoves, for instance, you should explain the process of operating a camp stove, demonstrate the process of operating a camp stove, and then give your students the chance to practice operating camp stoves. The same is true for any other skill or lesson in which your students might be engaged.

Environmental Stewardship

Environmental Ethics

Ethics is defined as a moral code, or as rules of conduct. Environmental ethics refers to the moral code or rules of conduct that we follow in our relationship with the natural environment. Outdoor leaders typically follow the principles of Leave No Trace as the basis of their interactions with the natural environment. These principles are aimed at environmental preservation.

Ecological Literacy

As noted earlier, one of the disciplines into which outdoor education is divided is environmental education. The goal of environmental education is to develop environmental or ecological literacy in people so that they can engage in intelligent action with regard to their relationship with the natural environment. Ecological literacy entails thinking and acting critically in an environmental context, especially when it involves making decisions and exercising judgment regarding environmental problems or issues.

Natural Resource Management

Our classroom in the field of outdoor leadership is the outdoors. We rely on natural areas as a setting for teaching and programming. National, state, and municipal agencies manage many of the areas that we use. In using these areas, you must know the rules and regulations under which these areas are managed, as well as the management principles and practices of the managing agencies. You should also know the specific issues that are important to the different areas into which you travel for outdoor education and recreation experiences.

Program Management

Planning Skills

Planning skills are applied in developing a program design or structure. Program design includes program goals and objectives, program procedures and opera-tions, and program activities and services. Planning skills are also applied in developing trips, activities, and lessons. Trip plans include such components as emergency management plans, contingency plans, time control plans, energy control plans, and so forth. Proper planning is essential to effective outdoor leadership.

Organizational Skills

After a plan has been established, its successful implementation depends largely on the organizational skills of the leader. The leader must create a system under which to get things done and orchestrate a variety of plan components that must come together to create a unified, harmonic whole.

Management Skills

Management skills refer primarily to the ability to direct the collective efforts of people in accomplishing program goals and objectives. Management skills include both supervision and administration skills.

Safety and Risk Management

Participant Safety

A primary goal of outdoor leadership is to ensure the safety of people who venture into natural settings for outdoor education and recreation experiences. Both the physical and the psychological safety of program participants are important.

Preparation and Planning

One of the reasons that program planning is considered a core competency in outdoor leadership is the importance of program planning in ensuring the safety of program participants. Poorly planned programs are more prone to mistakes and mishaps than are well-planned trips. In outdoor education and recreation, the slightest mishap can compromise the safety of program participants.

Legal Aspects of Safety and Risk Management

Safety and risk management in outdoor leadership must be considered from a legal perspective as well as a practical perspective. Outdoor leaders can potentially be held liable for any injury or loss that may befall a program participant. To be held liable, the outdoor leader (or the program for which the outdoor leader works) must be proved to have been negligent of his or her duty to provide a certain standard of care to the program participant. In addition, the program participant must show that the injury or loss resulted from the leader's failure to provide that standard of

continued ▶

FIGURE 1.1   (continued)

care. In any case, a leader or program that is shown to be negligent can be held financially responsible for that injury or loss. Program planning is as much about assuring that participants engage in a safe and high-quality experience as it is about ensuring that you as a leader are adhering to the standard of care in the industry.

Assessing Your Abilities and Limitations

As an outdoor leader, you must be able to make accurate assessments of both your own limitations and the limitations of your followers. The safety of your followers is often in your hands. Knowing your and your followers' limitations is crucial to ensuring your safety and the safety of your group.

Technical Ability

Proficiency in Particular Outdoor Activities

Outdoor leaders must possess technical competency in a variety of areas. The most basic of these areas is backcountry living skills, which include stove operation and use, cooking, navigation using a map and compass, animal encounter prevention techniques, latrine construction and use, and so forth. Additionally, outdoor leaders should develop expertise in varying activity areas or varying modes of travel. These may include canoeing, kayaking, rafting, sailing, technical rock climbing, mountaineering, backcountry skiing or snowboarding, and mountain biking. The ability to operate a challenge ropes course represents another set of technical skills that is important to the outdoor leader. Challenge ropes courses are only a small part of the field of outdoor education and recreation, but because they

are common in the industry, all outdoor leaders should be competent in their operation and use.

Experience-Based Competency

Technical proficiency in outdoor activities can be gained only through experience. The more experience that people gain, the more competent they generally become. Many guides introduce themselves to their guests with a short, humorous story to reassure them that they should not worry: "I watched a video about whitewater rafting last night, and I am sure that I can get you down the river safely today." Outdoor leaders who fall out of practice in a given technical activity should refresh themselves before leading people in those activities. A common practice among whitewater rafting companies is to have their guides perform at least two refresher runs on the rivers on which they will be guiding at the beginning of each rafting season. Outdoor leaders should do their best to stay in practice in the areas in which they lead others.

Professional Certification

Professional certifications are one indicator of competence in different areas of expertise. Certifications signify only a minimal level of competence; nonetheless, they do indicate competence. Certifications also typically represent the industry norm or standard of care in various technical activities. Examples of professional certifications in the field of outdoor education and recreation include the American Mountain Guide Association's instructor and guide certifications in rock climbing and mountaineering and the American Canoe Association's instructor certifications in canoeing and kayaking.

FIGURE 1.1   *(continued)*

Keep in mind when using *Technical Skills for Adventure Programming* that information and skills overlap across units. For example, the basic camp knots addressed in unit 1 have application in many other units; that unit teaches the bowline knot, and other units refer to that information. The same concept applies to many other skills. Thus, when necessary, you must refer to other units for detailed information.

Design

We created a template based on a comprehensive lesson format complete with learning objectives

and assessment procedures. Highly experienced and motivated outdoor educators used this template to write the lessons for the activities. Each of them possesses many years of teaching experience, and all are considered experts in their fields. As a result, *Technical Skills for Adventure Programming* presents fundamental adventure activities taught throughout the outdoor profession. The primary focus is on technical skills instruction based on sound pedagogy and professional experience.

In addition, we designed this guide to be field friendly. Rather than carry the entire volume into the field, you can take selected material in your dry bag or backpack. The CD-ROM bound into the book includes electronic versions of all lessons and resources, allowing you to print only what you need to take into the field.

General Organization

Technical Skills for Adventure Programming is divided into three parts: land-based activities, water-based activities, and snow- and ice-based activities. Each part contains several units, and each unit includes a series of lessons that systematically cover a progression of skills.

Part I: Land-Based Units

Units 1 through 4 make up the land-based curriculum, which includes backpacking, rock climbing, caving, and mountain biking.

Unit 1, written by Mick Daniel (Adams State College, Colorado) and Tammie Stenger-Ramsey (Western Kentucky University), outlines the knowledge and skills associated with backpacking. Mick and Tammie guide you through a sequence of basic outdoor living skills used in backpacking. They focus on backpacking in a small group. Much of the information in this unit can be transferred to the other adventure activities in the book. For example, you will find Mick and Tammie's lessons on clothing and equipment useful when teaching students how to dress for other adventure activities. Likewise, the basic camping skills lesson explains knots that can be applied during other adventure activities. Mick and Tammie end their unit with valuable information on creating inclusive adventure-based activities.

Unit 2, written by Shayne Galloway (University of Otago, New Zealand) and Aram Attarian (North Carolina State University), tackles the sport of rock climbing. Shayne and Aram focus primarily on the skills needed to manage a top-rope site. As with the first unit, information found here applies to other adventure activities. For example, the lessons on knot tying and belaying contain information that has application in activities such as ice climbing and mountaineering.

In unit 3 David Goodman (Radford University) provides an excellent curriculum for beginning and intermediate cavers. David supplies you

with the knowledge and skills needed to lead enjoyable and environmentally sound caving experiences. He also addresses the basics of vertical caving and integrates popular activities from a national caving curriculum titled *Project Underground*.

Unit 4, by Josh Whitmore (Western Carolina University), introduces the sport of mountain biking. You will find Josh's work to be an excellent reference when designing a mountain biking curriculum. Josh focuses primarily on beginner riding skills but also addresses select intermediate skills. He also covers topics such as safety and basic bike maintenance.

Part II: Water-Based Units

Units 5 through 8 make up the water-based section of *Technical Skills for Adventure Programming*. These units include sea kayaking, whitewater kayaking, canoeing, and rafting.

Unit 5, written by Tommy Holden (North Carolina State University), provides you with a valuable tool to teach basic sea kayaking skills. Tommy does a superb job introducing the sport and providing information that can be applied to other water-based activities. His lessons on equipment, basic strokes, and rescue techniques have application in other units. The lessons focus on saltwater environments but are applicable to large bodies of fresh water.

In unit 6 Bruce Martin (University of Ohio, Athens) provides an inclusive guide to the art of whitewater kayaking instruction. Bruce skillfully outlines an instructional curriculum for basic whitewater kayaking. He adds to the sea kayaking unit by expanding on specific techniques and knowledge associated with whitewater kayaking. Bruce addresses the kayak roll and how to read moving water, and he expands on rescue techniques. He also introduces the basics of play boating.

Unit 7 provides a comprehensive lesson series for the sports of flatwater and whitewater canoeing. Laurie Gullion (University of New Hampshire) expertly outlines the knowledge and skills needed to teach this popular activity. Laurie focuses on the fundamental skills that you need to cover for both tandem and solo paddling. She adds to the water-based section by discussing the basics of strokes and equipment and other topics such as rescues and inclusive paddling.

Finally, unit 8 describes that skills and knowledge needed to instruct whitewater rafting. Christopher Pelchat (Ithaca College, New York) and Michael Kinziger (University of Idaho) provide a comprehensive curriculum for this growing sport. Besides discussing the specifics of rafting, Christopher and Michael add to the other water-based lessons by expanding on safety and rescue techniques. Christopher and Michael focus primarily on developing paddle captain skills in oar rigs and paddle rafts.

Part III: Snow- and Ice-Based Units

Units 9 through 12 make up the snow- and ice-based section of *Technical Skills for Adventure Programming*. These units include snowshoeing, mountaineering, nordic skiing, and ice climbing.

Unit 9, developed by Briget Tyson Eastep (Southern Utah University), provides you with a valuable tool to teach snowshoeing. Briget designed a curriculum to assist beginner and experienced instructors with knowledge and skills to facilitate snowshoeing instruction. Briget covers the history of the sport and provides a number of activities to make her unit an enjoyable learning experience.

Unit 10, designed by Mat Erpelding (Wilderness Medical Training Center, Inc.) and Scott Schumann (University of Utah), introduces the complex sport of mountaineering. Mat and Scott focus on the essential knowledge and skills to be mastered by beginning mountaineers. They carefully cover basic skills, equipment, and safety considerations. Note that mountaineering is a complex sport, and those who teach this topic must have background knowledge.

Unit 11, written by Reid Cross (California State University at Chico), does an outstanding job of introducing you to the basics of nordic skiing. Reid systematically outlines the knowledge and skills necessary to teach backcountry and telemark skiing techniques. He covers basic equipment needed, basic technique, and safety concerns for the sport.

In unit 12 Thomas Stuessy (Green Mountain College, Vermont) and John Kascenska (Lyndon State College, Vermont) introduce the exciting sport of ice climbing. Thomas and John provide a basic curriculum for outdoor educators who wish to include this sport in their program offerings. Thomas and John expand on the mountaineering chapter and focus on the essential skills needed to instruct safe ice-climbing experiences. They focus on beginner skills and carefully address risk management issues.

Lesson Format

Each unit consists of a series of lessons. The number of lessons per unit varies depending on the complexity of the topic and the author's teaching format. Units reflect distinct personal approaches that the authors take when teaching their topics. You will note throughout this book that units and lessons vary in design and length based on the authors' methods. The diversity reflects a variety of approaches that will not conform to a static lesson formula. For example, the novice instructor attempting to teach a paddle stroke may become confused because the kayaking, canoeing, and rafting units each use a different description of the stroke phases and slightly different terms. We welcome these differences as a way to provide diverse ways to teach a topic. You will find this diversity helpful when expanding your own methods. We all know that being able to teach and explain content in more than one way can help us reach different types of learners.

Each of the authors has tested the lessons and has designed them to provide flexible programming options so that instructors can add or delete information of their choosing. Each of the lessons was developed using a template that we designed. This format can be adapted in traditional education settings such as physical education classes.

Each of the ready-to-use lessons contains the following information.

Overview

This section introduces the topics that will be covered in the lesson. A brief look at this section allows the instructor to determine the specific content of the plan.

Justification

This section explains the need for the activity in terms of educational needs and interests of the students. The justification focuses on how the students will benefit and why.

Goals

Goals determine the purpose, aim, and rationale for what the students will work on during the lesson. The goals are tied into the justification and are typically limited to one or two phrases.

Objectives

Student learning objectives are phrased in terms of intended outcomes that a student should be expected to demonstrate or know as a result of participating in the lesson. To provide a more holistic approach to learning, we chose to use Bloom's taxonomy (Anderson & Krathwohl, 2001) as the model for learning objective development. Objectives describe what learners will be able to do at the end of instruction based on cognitive, psychomotor, and affective domains. The following is a brief overview of Bloom's three domains:

◆ **Cognitive (knowledge)**. These objectives describe the specific knowledge to be developed. Intellectual skills to be developed are understanding, comprehension, application, analysis, synthesis, and evaluation.

◆ **Psychomotor (physical skills)**. Objectives describe what the student can perform in the area of motor skills. Physical skills necessary to master or accomplish the technical skills associated with the lesson can be simple or complex. Attributes of physical mastery involve coordination, speed, precision, and proficiency.

◆ **Affective (attitude)**. Affective objectives describe how the student deals with lesson content on an emotional level, which is driven by values and ethics. Attitudinal attributes to be developed or influenced as a result of the

lesson are appreciation, enthusiasm, motivation, or respect. Affective objectives influence one's values and ethics.

Equipment and Areas Needed

A basic equipment list is supplied for each lesson. The list helps you determine how much preparation time, equipment, and resources will be needed and how much management will be involved. You must determine the quantity of items needed based on your specific group size. If the lesson requires a specific setting or environment, the author recommends a specific area. For example, the author may recommend that the activity take place on a beach at the edge of the water.

Risk Management Considerations

This section notes potential objective risks associated with facilitating the activities developed for the lesson. Of course, risks will vary depending on your specific approach to the lesson. Note that the authors do not repeat risk management information for each lesson. Typically, the first few lessons cover the objective hazards associated with the adventure activity. Unique or additional hazards are listed in subsequent lessons when applicable. We recommend that you revisit this section and adapt as needed.

Lesson Content

The lesson content section provides two important functions. First, it serves as a step-by-step description of how to execute the lesson and achieve objectives. It focuses on what you should have students do during the lesson, how long it will take, and how the transitions between activities should occur.

Second, the lesson content section contains information and facts that make up the body of knowledge associated with learning the skill. You can use these facts and information as a reminder or guide to ensure that you cover critical content.

Some lessons contain Important Terms boxes as a convenient reference and teaching tool for instructors. The definitions found within these

The lesson plans contain hands-on experiences to facilitate learning.

Important Terms boxes may contain additional information beyond what is found in the unit glossary to provide more depth and understanding of a concept or term.

The lesson content is divided into four areas: introduction, main activities, closure activities, and follow-up activities.

Introduction Introductions vary greatly among the units and lessons. Some introductions are simply catchy phrases designed as attention grabbers. Other introductions are in-depth dialogues combined with activities to get students started. The variability reflects the diverse backgrounds and experience bases of the contributing authors. Some authors use training and curriculum from national organizations throughout their lessons, whereas others share techniques and experience gleaned from many years of personal teaching experience.

Main Activities The main activities section reflects the step-by-step sequence or progression of activities that will facilitate learning the content to meet lesson objectives. It includes advice and tips on conveying techniques and reinforcing critical content. This section can contain anywhere from one to seven main activities depending on the complexity of the sport. The main activities also vary in design. Some are simple lectures or demonstrations, whereas others are sophisticated experientially based initiatives.

Closure Activities The closure section includes activities that reinforce learning based on the main activities. Closure activities vary in purpose and design. In some cases, closure activities include additional skills and knowledge that fall into the progression of learning a specific skill. In other cases, this section uses activities to summarize main concepts. Closure activities can also be used to evaluate students or correct misunderstandings. Depending on your needs, you may find these closure activities critical or optional.

Follow-Up Activities The follow-up section is similar to the closure section because it suggests activities or ideas to reinforce or apply newly found skills. This section offers additional activity suggestions for instructors who may need an additional lesson or experience to meet the specific needs of their students. In many cases, follow-up activities are logical activities that would culminate the learning sequence. For example, a follow-up activity might be a trip on a river, an outing to a cave, or an activity on snow to apply skills covered in the lesson.

Assessment

The assessment section describes how you can assess or evaluate outcomes. We purposefully kept the assessment broad and linked outcomes to specific activities within the lesson. You are responsible for taking the next step if you need to conduct a more objective assessment. For example, you may need to develop a tool such as a rubric or checklist to evaluate or measure the articulated outcomes. In other words, the assessment section provides the context or activity suggestion to which you can apply specific measurements.

Teaching Considerations

Although lessons fall in a logical sequence as a whole, this section clarifies various issues. For example, you might want to consider breaking skills and activities into smaller pieces to address timing issues. This section also shares teaching tips related to the teaching environment (such as differences between teaching the skill indoors versus outdoors during a trip), diversity (assisting diverse learners with skill acquisition), and alternatives (such as suggestions for other ways to teach a specific topic).

Unit Features

Units contain several key design features. All units begin with an introductory lesson, which provides a basic overview of the adventure sport. This lesson covers the key terminology, history, and a general overview of the sport.

In addition, some units end with a lesson on inclusion and accessibility. Authors with expertise in this area share their knowledge (see the backpacking, rock climbing, canoeing, snow-shoeing, and nordic skiing units). The authors encourage users of this curriculum guide to take reasonable steps to ensure effective communication with individuals with physical or mental disabilities by providing adapted equipment or modified lessons in order to afford them the opportunity to participate in and enjoy the benefits of the activities outlined in this guide.

All units include a lesson discussing outdoor ethics in relation to Leave No Trace principles. Although some of this information will be redundant, each author attempted to focus on the particulars of the specific activity and designed creative activities to teach the skills.

Following the lessons, all units include a skills checklist designed to help your students gauge their learning and prepare them for an outdoor experience. Each unit also includes a glossary to assist instructors and students with unfamiliar terminology. Unit glossaries reflect terminology used in all lessons contained in a particular unit.

Finally, all units end with a comprehensive resource list. Authors compiled their favorite resources to assist you with the teaching process. You will find that some resources are referred to in specific lessons, whereas others reflect general tools for additional support. The authors provide a brief overview of each resource. This handy guide serves as a valuable resource for instructors of all ability levels.

Conclusion

The authors who contributed to this manual attempted to be as detailed as possible to reduce confusion over terms, techniques, and methods. Those who have little instructional experience with the activities featured in this manual should consult other resources mentioned at the end of each unit. You should pay careful attention to the risk management section of the lessons, but do not rely solely on those sections! Although the contributors outlined potential hazards from their own experience, other hazards will present themselves depending on individual situations. Environmental factors, human factors, instructor experience, organizational policies, and equipment items are issues that will vary. Adventure-based educators must be excellent risk managers.

Good judgment and the ability to make sound decisions are crucial. We realize that a publication such as *Technical Skills for Adventure Programming* provides a canned approach to teaching. To improve your teaching effectiveness, you must exercise creativity and receive feedback. Use this curriculum guide as a resource to support excellent instruction—as one tool in a larger process to foster student learning. We encourage you to develop and maintain your individual creativity and teach at your ability level. Too often instructors and participants become caught up in the glamour and adrenaline rush of the adventure-based activity to the detriment of the environment, personal or group safety, or overall enjoyment of the experience. We urge you to read chapter 2 on teaching as a reminder of why and how adventure educators should practice their craft.

References

Anderson, L.W., & Krathwohl, D.R. (2001). *A taxonomy for learning, teaching, and assessing: A revision of Bloom's taxonomy of educational objectives.* New York: Longman.

Teaching Adventure-Based Activities

Effective adventure-based educators practice their art armed with the knowledge and abilities that all great experiential educators possess. Knowledge of the experiential learning process, an understanding of diverse learning styles, the ability to use various teaching methods, and the ability to exercise basic outdoor leadership competencies represent the primary knowledge and skills needed to instruct outdoor activities successfully. Besides having these skills and abilities, educators need to instill in their students practices that will minimize their effect on the natural resources that support these activities. Also important is the ability to modify or adapt activities that allow people with special needs or challenges the opportunity to participate in these activities. Finally, outdoor educators should be able to use professional and national standards to serve as resources to support programs and lessons.

To maximize the learning that will result from your reading of *Technical Skills for Adventure Programming*, we begin with an in-depth discussion of teaching and learning. This chapter begins with an overview of the theory and practice of effective teaching as it applies to outdoor, adventure-based activities. It culminates with a look at the importance of environmental stewardship, inclusion, and connection to professional and national standards, three special topics to consider when planning and delivering your lessons.

Those not familiar with the body of knowledge associated with adventure-based instruction will find this chapter particularly helpful when preparing and facilitating lessons. The knowledge contained in this chapter will also help reinforce and refine the practices of seasoned outdoor instructors. For the sake of clarity, the terms *educator*, *instructor*, and *leader* will be used synonymously, as will the terms *outdoor* and *adventure-based*.

Three Global Goals

Effective teachers always keep the bigger picture in perspective. In other words, they know where they are going and how to get there effectively. It is easy to get lost in the glamour, thrill, and technical intricacies of adventure-based sports. An effective adventure-based educator keeps three basic goals in mind when engaged in the teaching process.

First, an educator should strive to facilitate engaging educational experiences. Enjoyable educational experiences tend to motivate and energize learners. Having fun while learning fosters active student engagement and promotes personal growth in all domains, such as knowledge, skills, and dispositions. Enjoyable educational experiences also facilitate a functional group process whereby participants experience a richer, more diverse educational experience by being part of a group. In addition, educators strive to create meaningful experiences. Meaningful experiences, in an outdoor education context, translate into a host of benefits. Humans seek adventure-based experiences as a form of leisure activity. Spending one's leisure time rock climbing, kayaking, or caving facilitates physical, psychological, emotional, and, in some cases, spiritual development.

Second, an educator should manage associated risks to create a reasonably safe learning environment. Outdoor educators cannot ensure complete program safety because uncontrollable objective hazards such as lightning, fast-moving water, falling rock, or cold temperatures may occur. Effective outdoor educators, however, can manage objective risks through proper adventure-based risk management techniques. Outdoor leaders apply this awareness and associated techniques during the lesson planning and facilitation process.

Third, educators should strive to facilitate experiences that have a minimal effect on the natural environment. The adventure-based activities found in this text take place in the natural environment. Instructors and students have an ethical obligation to protect the natural resources. Ultimately, all users affect the natural environment. Effective adventure-based instructors know how to minimize that effect to protect the integrity of the natural environment.

Keeping these three global goals in mind will enable adventure-based educators to facilitate meaningful experiences.

Theory and Practice of Adventure-Based Education

Adventure-based education is a subdiscipline of outdoor education. Outdoor education is defined as education about the relationships within the natural environment and between the environment and human societies (Bunting, 2006). Adventure-based education focuses on the development of interpersonal and intrapersonal relationships while participating in outdoor activities that include attributes of risk and challenge. Mastering technical skills is an integral ingredient when developing intrapersonal and interpersonal relationships in an adventure-based context. From an intrapersonal perspective, technical competency enhances self-confidence, self-reliance, self-efficacy, individual wellness, and a host of other personal attributes. Technical skill enhances interpersonal attributes such as teamwork, communication skills, and leadership skills. For example, a group kayaking expedition requires individuals to communicate and confront problems as a team to navigate a body of water successfully. Effective adventure-based educators know how to facilitate technical skills instruction to enhance intrapersonal and interpersonal development. They execute this task based on the theory and practice of adventure-based education.

This chapter is divided into four major sections that embody the theory and practice of adventure-based instruction. First, we discuss and analyze experiential learning by using David Kolb's experiential learning cycle. Second, we analyze the nature of learning through the lens of learning styles within the context of the experiential learning cycle. Not all people learn information and skills the same way. Understanding that each learner has specific learning needs will help ensure success. Third, we discuss the experiential teaching process. Outdoor leaders must engage in a larger process to facilitate experiential learning opportunities. The experiential teaching process described by Bunting (2006) provides the model for this discussion. Finally, we look at the nature of teaching adventure-based activities in the outdoors.

To teach effectively, adventure educators must possess diverse instructional tools and be aware of the physical environment when teaching adventure-based activities outdoors.

Experiential Learning

Students learn in a variety of ways to cope and adapt to their surrounding world. Learning takes place in many ways—by experiencing something directly, listening to a lecture, reading a text, conducting an experiment, or participating in a group activity, among others. Experiential learning and teaching forms the theoretical cornerstone that allows outdoor leaders to teach technical skills effectively. Outdoor leaders embrace experiential education as the means to apply experiential learning theory. "Experiential education is a philosophy and methodology in which educators purposefully engage the learners in direct experience and focused reflection in order to increase knowledge, develop skills, and clarify values" (AEE Web site, n.d.).

John Dewey (1938), a great educator and educational reformist, was one of the first to stress the importance of experience as a meaningful form of education. Dewey perceived experiential learning as a cyclical process that includes three phrases:

◆ Observing a specific situation and surrounding conditions

◆ Recalling past knowledge related to the situation

◆ Making judgments based on observations and past knowledge to determine significance

Dewey's work inspired a number of other models and perspectives that are applied to adventure-based programs (Gibbons & Hopkins, 1980; Pfeiffer & Jones, 1980; Joplin, 1981; Kolb, 1984; Priest, 1990). Each model provides a unique perspective into learning experientially.

David A. Kolb's work is important for the purposes of this manual because his experiential learning model also includes the concept of learning styles. Kolb is a professor of organizational behavior. Kolb's interests in making sense of concrete experiences and different styles of learning inspired him and his colleague Roger Fry to create a model of experiential learning. Kolb makes explicit use of theorists such as Piaget, Dewey, and Lewin. One of the primary goals of this chapter is to help you be an effective educator. Understanding the experiential learning cycle and how it relates to diverse learners is an important ingredient for instructional success.

Kolb's Experiential Learning Cycle

Kolb created a model of experiential learning that consists of four phases. He believed that learning is maximized when the learner moves through all phases during the learning process (see figure 2.1). The four phases are concrete experience, reflective observation, abstract conceptualization, and active experimentation.

In phase 1, concrete experience, the learner directly engages in a new activity to gain an understanding. The learner has a hands-on experience. For example, a whitewater canoeing instructor puts the participants in a canoe on moving water to teach the importance of leaning downstream. The participants are able to experience the lesson through all their senses in an immediate way. They have no time to stop and think about it. If they do not lean correctly, the boat capsizes.

Phase 2, reflective observation, entails participants' reflection on thoughts and feelings about an experience. Participants view the experience from many perspectives. The whitewater instructor schedules time for students to watch the instructor demonstrate a proper boat lean. Instructors then allot time to discuss as a group what the participants are seeing and experiencing. To enrich the discussion and reflection, the

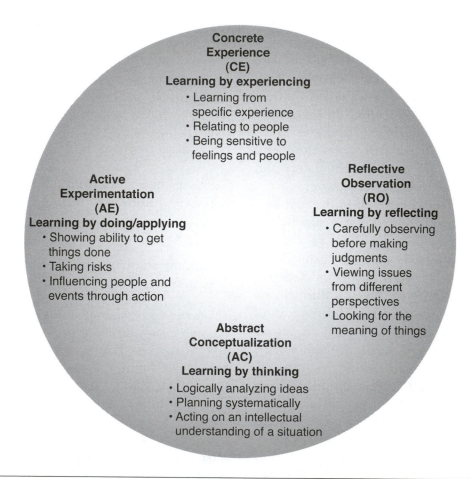

FIGURE 2.1 Kolb's learning cycle demonstrates the four phases of experiential learning.

Reprinted, by permission, from B. Martin et al., 2006, *Outdoor leadership: Theory and practice* (Champaign, IL: Human Kinetics), 173. Adapted, by permission, from D.A. Kolb, © Experience-Based Learning Systems, Inc.

instructor maneuvers a toy canoe in a mock river drawn in the sand to demonstrate boat lean.

Phase 3, abstract conceptualization, is a process to incorporate observations into a "theory" from which new implications for action can be figured out. These implications then become the impetus for establishing new experiences. Applying this phase to the whitewater canoe experience, the instructor facilitates a discussion on a nearby beach to enforce the significance of boat lean. Participants conceptualize the lean to understand the dynamics of the water in relationship to the boat to facilitate different maneuvers.

Phase 4, active experimentation, involves testing theories and concepts through problem solving in different situations. The whitewater instructor facilities an exercise to practice leans in a variety of situations to test the participants' understanding.

Using Diverse Teaching Methods

In the previous description of the learning phases the whitewater instructor moved the students through each phase by integrating different teaching methods or situations to convey information and skills. Note that this model is cyclical and that no formal starting or stopping place exists in the learning process. Teachers must mix up their methods and provide a variety of outlets to maximize learning experientially. To facilitate learning in each of the phases, the following suggestions are offered to guide your teaching efforts (Svinicki & Dixon, 1987; Kolb, 2000):

◆ Concrete experience: Provide new learning experiences such as games, films, role playing, lab work, or fieldwork. Peer feedback and discussion during the experience are helpful techniques to implement. Outdoor leaders serve as coaches or helpers in this phase.

◆ Reflective observation: Have participants take an observer role to see from different perspectives. Lectures, journaling, group discussions, and questioning are effective teaching techniques in this phase. Outdoor leaders serve as guides and taskmasters to foster the reflective process.

◆ Abstract conceptualization: Studying alone, reading about theories, presenting clear and well-constructed ideas, building models, creating analogies, and writing papers are examples of teaching methods that enhance this phase. Outdoor leaders serve as communicators of information in this phase.

◆ Active experimentation: Leaders provide opportunities to practice self-paced learning activities, case studies, or simulations in this phase. Outdoor leaders serve as role models to foster learning during active experimentation.

After reviewing the previous suggestions, you should carefully self-assess your teaching methods. Ask yourself a critical question regarding method: Are your teaching methods diverse enough to move your students through the cycle? For example, do you use only lectures and demonstrations to teach knowledge and skills? If the answer is yes, then students in your groups are probably not learning at their fullest potential. Consider guided discussions, small group exercises, problem-solving exercises, video critiques, and research projects as additional methods to use when teaching. If you use only a few methods, you are unlikely to reach all students. This issue concerns addressing diverse learning styles, which is discussed in the next section.

Learning Styles

A learning style represents the preferred way that a learner perceives or gathers and processes information. Most people tend to exercise their preference when immersed in a challenging learning situation (figure 2.2). Effective outdoor leaders understand that students gather and process information differently. For example, the instructor who relies solely on demonstrations to teach a skill will reach only students who learn best through demonstrations. The remainder of students in the group will struggle to learn. Effective instructors meet diverse learning needs by addressing a variety of learning styles when teaching. A simplistic way to understand learning styles, from an instructional viewpoint, is to divide your students into three distinct learning categories: visual, auditory, and tactile.

Visual learners learn best through visual cues such as reading and writing. They prefer demonstrations and watch closely for the instructor's nonverbal cues. Visual learners tend to take notes so that they can remember and visualize details and pictures. They watch others before acting and need to see the instructor's body language and facial expressions to understand the content fully. These people may think in pictures and learn best from visual displays such as diagrams, photos, drawings, and so on. They like to be encouraged by a smile or expressions of encouragement.

Auditory learners learn best when instructors verbalize information. They prefer listening but also like to talk to process information. They like talking and working with others to discuss the information. Auditory learners talk problems out and tend to repeat themselves. They remember better when they hear information and discuss it orally. They are encouraged by oral praise. They listen to tone of voice, pitch, and speed. Written information may have little meaning until it is heard.

Kinesthetic, or tactile, learners learn best through experience or a hands-on approach. They tend to experiment, touch, and manipulate things. They tend to select options with physical activity, tend not to be as attentive during visual or auditory presentations, and may find it hard to sit still for long periods. If presented something new, they try it as soon as possible and can appear to be impulsive. The kinesthetic learner likes to be called on to try things first as opposed to sitting and waiting.

The challenge for outdoor leaders is to develop teaching situations or lessons that address various learning styles. By acknowledging various learning styles, outdoor educators can eliminate the frustration and difficulty that some learners experience. Many benefits exist if instructors embrace a variety of strategies. Adventure educators capitalize on individual strengths when addressing learning diversity. Participants experience satisfaction, fun, and a sense of accomplishment when successful learning occurs. Knowledge of learning styles helps the leader understand differences exhibited among students. Behaviors such as inattention, boredom, and restlessness may be symptoms of ineffective teaching techniques. Instead of blaming participants, the outdoor leader can take a critical look at personal teaching effectiveness and adapt to improve. Adventure educators must be aware of individual differences and critically examine why individuals have difficulty learning. Many students lean on one style to gather and process information. Outdoor leaders have the opportunity to help participants develop other styles to become more effective learners. Finally, the probability of meeting all program goals will increase if the leader attends to learning styles.

FIGURE 2.2   The dominant learning style will surface when problem solving a tent setup for the first time.

Kolb's Four Styles

Along with his four phases of experiential learning, Kolb delineated four distinct learning styles. His research narrowed down learning styles to four preferred methods (Kolb, 2000). Note that learning styles are referred to as preferences. People maintain the capacity to learn in many different ways. Kolb found that we prefer or resort to one style over others in many situations. Outdoor leaders must not typecast or categorize participants based on learning styles. Learning styles vary according to the situation and shift as people grow, develop, and experience life.

Kolb identified four learning styles that people may choose to exercise in any given situation: diverging, assimilating, converging, and accommodating (see figure 2.3). Each learning style can be identified by characteristics and behaviors exhibited in learning situations. Observing behavioral preferences gives the outdoor leader much insight into the participant's learning abilities. The following are generalized characteristics associated with each learning style. Note how each style connects to the phases of the experiential learning cycle.

◆ Divergers rely on concrete experience and reflective observation; they like being imaginative, understanding people, and recognizing problems. They brainstorm, they are open-minded and emotional, and they generate ideas and have broad cultural interests.

◆ Assimilators rely on reflective observation and abstract conceptualization; they like planning, creating models, defining problems, and developing theories. Assimilators tend to be patient during the problem-solving and planning processes. They tend to be more interested in concepts than in people and relationships.

◆ Accommodators rely on active experimentation and concrete experience; they like getting things done, leading, taking risks, and initiating activities. These people tend to be adaptable and practical, and others may perceive them as impatient. Accommodators carry out plans and solve problems intuitively.

◆ Convergers rely on abstract conceptualization and active experimentation; they like solving problems, making decisions, reasoning deductively, defining problems, being logical, and being unemotional. They prefer to deal with things as opposed to people.

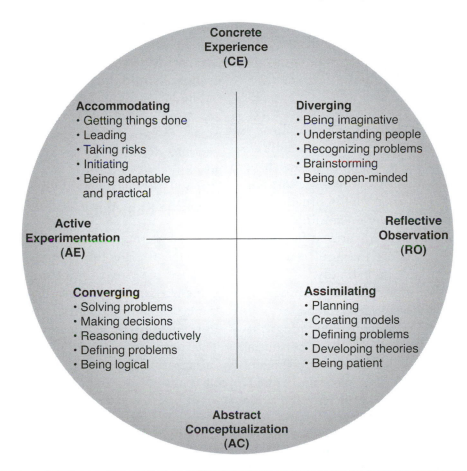

FIGURE 2.3 Kolb's four learning styles.

The following scenario explains Kolb's four learning styles in the context of outdoor skills instruction. A group of 12 is on a weekend backpacking trip. The leaders covered basic map and compass skills using a traditional lecture and demonstration format. The leaders handed over the navigational responsibilities to the hiking group with the educational intention of developing navigational skills after an initial lesson. The instructors plan to sit back and observe the group apply past learning. The group finds itself at a trail junction, confused about their current location and which way to continue. As the instructors observe, the divergers in the group brainstorm ideas and check with group members to ensure that everyone is happy. The accommodators display impatience; they just want to make a decision and deal with the consequences later. The assimilators attempt to define the problem and are more interested in creating an action plan to get out of the situation. The convergers could not care less and show no emotion regarding the ensuing chaos erupting in the group; they focus only on the map and compass to come up with a plan.

As you might imagine, the diversity of approaches creates conflict and frustration within the group. The leaders calmly observe, realizing that diverse learning styles are at work. The leaders are able to intervene and facilitate a solution by meeting the diverse learning styles. The leaders choose to stop the action and encourage the group to debrief the situation and review or clarify any misunderstandings related to navigational skills. With new information provided by the instructors, the group can devise a plan and carry it out immediately.

The concepts of experiential learning and learning styles form the basis for effective teaching in the outdoors. To maximize learning, outdoor leaders must be aware of the experiential learning process. Leaders must also be cognizant of instructional design or the sequence of methods so that all four phases of the learning cycle are addressed. To facilitate this process and meet diverse learning needs, outdoor leaders should carry a large teaching toolbox. As discussed previously, leaders must adjust their teaching styles by guiding, acting as taskmasters, and coaching or role modeling to fit each phase of the learning cycle. Leaders must also integrate a variety of teaching methods or tools into their repertoire to achieve teaching effectiveness. Guided discussions, demonstrations, group projects, lectures, role playing, simulations, stories, self-directed activities, experimentation, analogies, games, and other tools make up the outdoor leader's teaching toolbox.

Experiential Teaching

An understanding of experiential learning and learning styles is not enough. To be an effective adventure-based educator, you must also understand and apply the experiential teaching model. Experiential teaching encompasses a larger process of knowing, planning, implementing, reflecting, evaluating, and adapting. For example, an effective mountain bike instructor or climbing teacher who engages in experiential teaching adheres to a series of steps or stages to reach desired outcomes. Experienced outdoor leaders naturally follow this cycle when focused on specific, desired outcomes. Beginner outdoor leaders should consciously follow models to promote learning. See Bunting's experiential teaching model (figure 2.4) to view the six stages of experiential teaching. The following sections describe the six stages of experiential teaching.

Stage 1: Knowledge

This stage represents the instructor's overall knowledge of the topic. From a technical skills perspective, instructors may know specific standards and objectives associated with the topic. National standards, curricula, and general information will be integrated into the lessons. The instructor's experience and prior training information makes up the knowledge stage. Methods of teaching certain topics, sequencing of activities, and time frames are all considered. The knowledge stage creates the foundation for planning. If instructors do not have adequate knowledge, research, and additional training, assistance from experts may be needed to prepare properly.

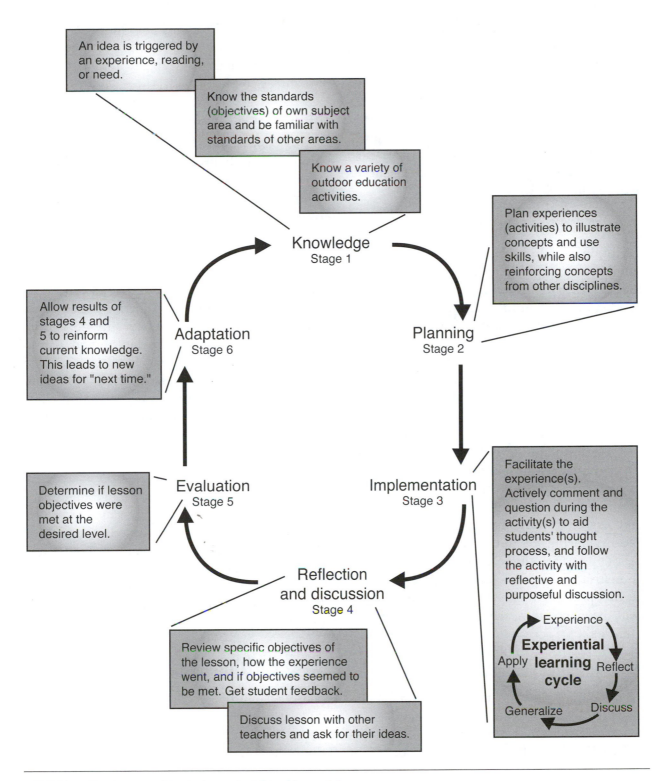

FIGURE 2.4   The six stages of Bunting's experiential teaching model.

Reprinted, by permission, from C. Bunting, 2005, *Interdisciplinary teaching through outdoor education* (Champaign, IL: Human Kinetics), 7.

Stage 2: Planning

Using knowledge and experience, instructors begin designing a formal structure or procedure to teach. This may be in the form of lessons or activities that reflect a specific teaching progression. Instructors take into consideration group size and makeup as they design formal lessons. Equipment, facilities, and the teaching onvironment are all considered as lessons are formulated. Preparing all aspects of the teaching experience in advance allows instructors to be more organized and purposeful in their efforts. This stage is important to targeting specific, articulated learning outcomes. The plans should revolve around a conscious process to achieve intended outcomes. The planning process also includes designing activities that meet the needs of all learning styles.

Stage 3: Implementation

The implementation phase represents the actual activity or student learning experience. In this stage the instructor facilitates the experiential learning cycle. Instructors lead a dynamic process that includes concrete experiences, reflection activities, discussion, and generalizing and applying knowledge and skills. Instructors monitor group safety and environmental impact as they facilitate activities. Instructors constantly adjust their leadership styles by being directive or by taking a hands-off approach depending on the group's ability and intended outcomes. For example, when teaching technical skills, instructors may be directive at first by creating exercises that foster basic skill development. They use a tightly controlled process of information sharing, demonstrations, and guided practice. As the students develop basic skills, the instructor steps back and facilitates activities that promote higher levels of skill development through games, trips, or problem-solving activities.

Stage 4: Reflection and Discussion

Stage 4 actually begins during the implementation stage. Instructors begin to reflect and evaluate progress informally. Instructors ask questions such as "How can this be improved?" or "What about the experience worked, and what did not work?" Feedback from other instructors or the students themselves provides issues for consideration. Instructors develop an overall sense of their successes and failures. This stage is similar to the reflection and generalization of the experiential learning cycle. The instructor begins to process the experience in anticipation of a

more formal evaluation. Seasoned adventure-based educators naturally engage in reflection and discussion as they process and analyze the learning experience.

Stage 5: Evaluation

This stage represents the formal evaluation process. The instructor specifically addresses formal goals and objectives to determine whether they were met. This process reflects a critical analysis of desired outcomes. During the planning stage, formal lesson plans are designed with measurable, specific, realistic objectives. Well-developed objectives help facilitate a meaningful evaluation process. The level of accomplishment for each objective can be determined and documented. As a result, the overall success of the lesson can be determined. Evaluation data provides concrete feedback to assess teaching effectiveness. Also in many instances, organizations and programs use evaluation data as an accountability measure. The evaluation stage is important on many fronts.

Stage 6: Adaptation

All outstanding teachers learn from their experiences. This stage reflects the instructor's efforts to modify and adapt lessons based on reflection, discussion, and formal evaluation. Instructors naturally take this step to improve their future effectiveness. Modifying and improving lessons for future use under diverse conditions helps ensure success.

Outdoor Teaching Tips

Seasoned outdoor adventure educators acknowledge that many participants simply respond better in an outdoor education setting than they do in the traditional classroom. In many ways, an outdoor leader has a unique opportunity to teach resistant learners through the magic of an outdoor experience. Participants do not view the outdoor classroom as they do the familiar four-walled classroom. Some perceive the outdoor classroom as having freedom from rules and daily responsibilities. Others perceive it as an unfamiliar environment that requires focus and attention to guard against the unknown. An effective outdoor leader takes advantage of these perceptions by capitalizing on higher levels of motivation and focus.

Keep in mind that teaching in a dynamic, outdoor environment requires dealing with some practical issues. Simple teaching considerations that address safety, comfort, and fun during the learning process can make a huge difference for the learner. Many of these important considerations are discussed in the following sections.

Environmental Considerations

As outdoor educators know, environmental considerations influence overall learning. Participants become distracted, lose concentration, and disengage when environmental conditions cause discomfort or concern. Outdoor leaders must pay close attention to the immediate environment as they create the ideal outdoor learning situation. If outdoor instructors remember to meet the student's basic needs such as food, water, shelter, warmth, and comfort, learning comes much more easily. Being cognizant of basic needs is particularly important when living outdoors. Instructors should address the following concerns to foster the ideal learning situation.

Sun

If conducting a formal class, place participants' backs to the sun. Participants should not fight the sun's glare while viewing a teaching situation. Position yourself to face the sun. If you need sunglasses, occasionally lower or remove the glasses for eye contact when making critical points or introducing yourself to the group the first time. Whenever possible, form group circles in the shade to protect the group from the sun's harmful effects. Participants who seek the sun always have the option to slide out of the shade into the sunlight.

Foul Weather

Attempting to teach most subjects in the rain, falling snow, and blowing wind usually results in mixed participant reaction. Although some may be able to focus on the lesson, others will be too preoccupied with being wet or cold to

pay attention. Instructors should consider other activities according to weather. Ensure before a lesson starts that participants have extra clothing and water handy to minimize disruptions. Building a classroom shelter out of rain tarps, rafts, or other forms of cover can create a comfortable atmosphere to cover topics.

Noise

Most assume that the outdoors is a serene, quiet environment. On the contrary, outdoor instructors compete with streams, rivers, wind, insects, and other environmental factors. You must be able to project your voice so that all can hear. This must always be a conscious act. If necessary, change locations or the progression of activities or stop speaking until the noise stops or passes.

Terrain

Outdoor classrooms are found on large rocks, forest floors, mountainsides, in caves, and on beaches. Before launching into a lesson, you must choose your location carefully. Find comfortable spots for sitting and standing when appropriate. On a slope or rocky area, attempt to find a level area to gather or circle up so that students are not struggling to find a comfortable spot. Also, remember to insulate students from the cold ground with pads. Be aware of environmentally sensitive areas when gathering a group of people. Follow Leave No Trace principles and search for durable surfaces such as large rocks or sand.

Teaching Props

Adventure educators need instructional aids just as traditional teachers do. Instructional aids allow outdoor educators to mix up their teaching strategies to meet the needs of all learners. Outdoor leaders should be able to provide visual examples, graphic demonstrations, and written information to supplement lectures and direct experience. The following teaching tips address creative aids to be used in the field.

Library

Many outdoor leaders consider carrying a library on extended trips. Instructional books and handouts pertaining to the activity go far in supplementing formal outdoor lessons. Visuals like books allow students to digest information through reading and pictures, either as a group or during personal time. A good outdoor library enhances the learning process by meeting specific learning styles. With a group of 6 to 10 trip participants, dividing the library up among group members prevents one person from being loaded down with too much bulk and weight.

Boards

Although chalkboards and whiteboards do not typically accompany canoeing, climbing, and caving trips, variations do. A large diagram, drawn in sequence, often helps make a point. A nice patch of sand or dirt to draw in can be extremely effective. Props such as sticks and rocks become boats, people, boundaries, and so on to help make the point. Some outdoor leaders carry dry erase markers to draw on sleeping pads or pieces of clear ground plastic as a whiteboard. White garbage bags taped over pads make an excellent writing surface. You can also laminate pieces of white paper (of the desired size) before entering the field.

Concrete Examples

The power of an appropriate, realistic example in an outdoor setting cannot be overestimated. In the traditional classroom, teachers often describe situations with the assumption that students will experience it later. The outdoor educator must take advantage of the rich resources available. For example, when teaching the art of digging a cathole for human waste disposal, consider digging an actual hole for demonstration purposes. Simply describing the proper way to dig a hole and offering appropriate environmental rationale is often not enough. Certain learners will process and apply the skill correctly if you provide a good demonstration or model.

Teaching Tools

Adventure-based educators rely on specific tools and techniques that help direct the outdoor learning experience. These tools help set the tone for the learning environment and assist instructors in managing a group. Learn-

ing occurs in such a dynamic environment that the instructor must take advantage of learning opportunities as they surface. Issues of timing and awareness of participant motivations and physical health play into knowing the tricks of the adventure-based teaching trade. The following sections discuss various tools or issues that you should be aware of when teaching adventure-based activities outdoors.

Challenge by Choice

The nature of adventure-based activities requires that participants have a choice. Facilitating technical skills development is no exception. Students typically experience many perceived emotional, psychological, and physical risks during instruction. An accepted practice in adventure-based education is that leaders give their participants a choice when risk is involved (Wurdinger, 1997). Providing a choice promotes an atmosphere of self-control and personal freedom (figure 2.5). Therefore, participant motivation comes from within rather than from an outside force, offering a form of personal empowerment. Empowerment creates a positive environment for learning and growing. Adventure educators should introduce challenge by choice early in the instructional progression. Framing this concept early on helps set a positive tone to enhance the learning environment.

Full-Value Contract

A traditional tool used in adventure programming is the full-value contract (Schoel, Prouty, & Radcliffe, 1988). Experienced instructors typically manage group behavior and attitudes with a full-value contract (FVC). The FVC serves as a tool to establish healthy group norms. The FVC allows the group to be more self-directive and self-monitoring in an experiential learning context. Technical skills instruction typically includes group activities and facilitates situations in which students must assist and rely on one another. This interdependency can foster healthy or unhealthy group dynamics. Adventure educators use the FVC to promote teamwork, support, respect, patience, and other behavioral norms that promote productive group

FIGURE 2.5 Challenge by choice empowers the participant to set the level of challenge, promoting an atmosphere of self-control and personal freedom.

work. Like challenge by choice, the FVC should be presented early in the instructional progression to help set the tone for a positive learning experience.

Teachable Moments

Teachable moments are lessons taught spontaneously and stimulated by a specific situation or event (Drury, Bonney, Berman, & Wagstaff, 2005). Teachable moments surface constantly during an outdoor experience. As groups encounter unknown situations, outdoor educators have the opportunity to relay information and skills related to the situation. For example, a caving group comes across a hibernating bat hanging on the wall above. The teacher gathers the group away from the bat and in a low voice discusses the dangers to the bat if awoken. Participants learn to respect the bat and conduct themselves appropriately. Another teachable moment finds a participant struggling with a rain tarp. A knot has been cinched so tight that it is impossible to untie. Frustrated, the participant asks for the instructor's help. The instructor takes the

opportunity to teach a more appropriate knot that requires minimal effort to untie.

As one would suspect, teachable moments are numerous during an outdoor experience. The teacher must carefully select appropriate situations to address as formal teachable moments. Instructors who address every situation are asking for trouble. Participants tend to disengage if the action is constantly halted for a lesson. If the lesson requires the entire group's attention, time must be taken to round up and organize the group to ensure that the message is conveyed to everyone. Informal teachable moments include those situations when individuals or small groups within the larger group encounter an opportunity (Drury et al., 2005). The teacher may choose to present a message or skill informally as part of a casual discussion. This approach provides powerful learning opportunities because the timing is immediate and pertinent to the situation. In other words, formal and informal teachable moments take advantage of the participant's desire and motivation to learn.

Creating the Need to Know

One of the most powerful outdoor teaching strategies involves motivating the participant to learn by creating the need to know. Adventure-based instructors can facilitate situations that motivate participants to seek knowledge and skills. The instructor does this by placing the participants in a situation where they seek knowledge and skills to accomplish a task. This approach requires careful timing. Using this technique inappropriately can be a safety factor and can negatively affect participant attitudes. For example, the teacher attempts to teach map-reading skills to a group of teenagers. The group is unruly and has no desire or need to focus on the lesson. The teacher empowers the group to self-navigate for the day. The group becomes hopelessly lost and struggles to interpret the map. At this point, the teacher intervenes with an offer to teach map interpretation. The group members eagerly agree and provide their undivided attention for the 30-minute lesson. This strategy backfires when participants perceive that they were set up to fail because of lack of information. The teacher's choice undermines the group's trust, and the experience becomes negative. Therefore, teachers should make their strategies clear before the trip starts so that students can anticipate and accept consequences more readily.

Timing Based on Needs

Instructors must assess energy levels before presenting a lesson. If energy levels are low after a full day of hiking or paddling, most participants would revolt if forced to participate in a full-blown lesson. For example, after many hours of hiking, the group may not be able to focus on a 20-minute lesson on campsite selection. After a rest period with food and water, the group might be able to focus. Instructor judgment is crucial in these situations. Many times group energy is highest in the morning and lower at night. Instructors should plan lessons around the peak hours and plan alternative activities for down time. Teachers should heed the pitfalls of nighttime activities. Although some activities are appropriate at night, forcing participants to focus in the dark with only candles and flashlights takes away from learning about many topics.

Time Management

Competent outdoor educators adequately inform participants of upcoming events. Materials needed, proper clothing, food needs, and estimated start and ending times are shared up front. Providing this information allows participants to be appropriately prepared. Learning is maximized when formal learning activities balance with all other activities. Finally, aspiring outdoor leaders who push themselves mentally and physically should know that veteran adventure educators include self-care in the time management equation. Adventure educators must be rested, well nourished, hydrated, and properly clothed to meet the rigorous demands of teaching outdoors. Teaching fanatics tend to overextend themselves and the group. As a result, teaching effectiveness decreases.

Gender Awareness

Consider creating diverse learning opportunities for women, especially in the context of techni-

cal skill development. Veteran instructors know that meeting the learning needs of both women and men can be a challenging task. For example, men approach skill development differently from women. Typically, men develop skills by pushing one another and charging into the learning situation with an attitude of authority and confidence. For men, an aggressive approach that fosters competition is great fun, rewarding, and often effective. Women typically require a more nurturing, supportive environment in which cooperation is paramount.

The research suggests that instructors should provide single-gender programs as an alternative (Loeffler, 1996). Single-gender programming creates the supportive environment needed for women to approach learning in a more comfortable way. As a result, learning and skill development is enhanced. If single-gender programming is not feasible, the instructor must be sensitive to the atmosphere present during a lesson. You can control a competitive atmosphere by encouraging supportive behavior. One approach is to have students share their feelings and apprehensions. Curb aggressive, competitive behavior from the start. Ensure that students are supporting one another and taking appropriate turns so that one gender is not always first. Make sure that successes of all sizes are being celebrated. Before jumping right into an activity, allow students to process what is about to happen. The full-value contract and challenge by choice tools will help here.

Additional Teaching Considerations

Adventure-based educators need to consider three additional issues when teaching technical skills. Environmental stewardship, inclusion, and connection to professional and national standards must be considered when planning and delivering lessons. As instructors we have an ethical obligation to be stewards of the outdoor environments used to teach adventure-based skills and a duty to serve people of all abilities. The world of outdoor adventure is open to everyone and is particularly beneficial to those of differing mental and physical abilities. Professional and national standards are an important part of any curriculum because they provide the framework for quality programming, provide guidance for developing state and local standards, and increase the status of our profession.

Note that in addition to the general information in this chapter, specific information related to these three areas is found throughout *Technical Skills for Adventure Programming*. Contributors have addressed environmental, inclusive, or professional standards specific to their activities in their lessons.

Environmental Stewardship

Many of the activities described in this text have their foundation in physical education curriculum and as a result show a strong approach toward physical activity, skill development, and lifetime sports. Participation in adventure activities can also provide participants with opportunities to develop interpersonal relationships and interact with the natural environment.

Parks and natural areas provide the primary resources for conducting adventure programs and activities. Recent reports suggest that the number of adventure programs continues to grow (Attarian, 2001). Resource managers who manage the lands where these activities take place believe that backcountry areas are already being overused by people seeking recreational experiences. They've also expressed concern over the lack of stewardship skills and knowledge possessed by those leading these activities (Gager, Hendee, Kinziger, & Krumpe, 1998). With growing interest and use, many parks and natural areas are beginning to show the effects of overuse. As a result, impacts are becoming more visible and more of a concern to both adventure program providers and resource managers. An impact is defined as an undesirable change in environmental or social conditions of a recreation site or experience (Hammitt & Cole, 1998). Impacts can compromise the objective of preserving the naturalness of an area by making it less attractive, appealing, or functional to the visitor. Impacts can also detract from the recreation experience of visitors through crowding, conflicts between users, dissatisfaction, and

visible human impacts (Hammitt & Cole, 1998). Recreational use in parks and natural areas affects soil, vegetation, and wildlife. Improper disposal of human waste, litter, noise, and potential damage to historical and cultural sites have also been identified as major problems.

As educators, we need to be more aware of our environment, become stewards of the land, and give something back to the settings that support our programs. We need to educate others and ourselves on how to minimize our impact by being effective role models for our students. You and your students need to be aware of these impacts and ways to reduce them. The Leave No Trace Center for Outdoor Ethics has developed a set of principles (appendix A), which are activity and setting specific and provide the foundation for this process to take place (LNT, 2006). Each of the chapter authors identifies and expands on these principles to help you prepare and deliver an environmentally sound outdoor experience.

Inclusive and Accessible Adventure

New technology combined with an increased awareness of the needs and capabilities of people with disabilities has changed the whole concept of access to the outdoors and participation in adventure activities. A variety of lightweight, high-tech, adaptive devices have been developed to help people with disabilities enjoy outdoor sports such as mountain biking, rock climbing, kayaking, sailing, and skiing.

Inclusive and accessible adventure activities can be designed to meet the needs of youth and adults with physical disabilities, developmental disabilities, emotional or behavioral needs, unique medical conditions, and other special needs. To be successful at integrating students with disabilities into standard outdoor adventure programs, educators need to be familiar with the processes that initiate inclusive environments and ways to accommodate individual differences (Dillenschneider, 2007). The primary purpose of these programs is to provide outdoor recreation and education programs that lead to increased health, wellness, and community involvement. The terms *inclusive* and *universal* imply full integration, allowing persons with and without disabilities to participate on an equal basis (Terry, 1995). The Americans with Disabilities Act (ADA) legally provides access to inclusive adventure programs. The act also guarantees that people with disabilities have opportunities similar to those of the rest of the population (Sugarman, 2001). Because of the ADA, providers have the responsibility for including these people in their activities and programs (figure 2.6).

Planning for inclusivity should include six steps:

1. Developing a community resource base and written resource materials

2. Addressing personal attitudes about people with disabilities

3. Dealing with information by starting slowly, gathering relevant information from the participant (for example, through medical history forms or an interview with the participant) to gain an understanding of his or her expectations and ability level

4. Modifying program or activity components by adapting equipment, environment, or skills sequence

5. Implementing the program

6. Evaluating the program (Sugarman, 2001)

You can design each of the activities described in this curriculum guide to accommodate the needs of people with disabilities, although it is beyond the scope of this manual to provide detailed information on adapting programs. You will find, however, that specific units address issues and offer suggestions related to the activity.

When working with people with disabilities, keep in mind a few simple principles. First, keep the normalization principle in mind by providing what the public would normally experience. Focus on abilities rather than disabilities, and stress collaborative participation. Next, design activities based on a skills progression. Begin activities at the highest level exhibited by individuals. When needed, modify or change only what is necessary and in the process allow participant input when modifications or changes

take place, because many participants will have better understanding of their abilities than you will. Finally, raise the level of challenge as skills and confidence increase.

You may also find the following suggestions useful as you plan inclusive activities:

◆ Provide students with an overview of the program or activity in which they are about to participate.

◆ Always have the student with the impairment help you understand her or his actual needs and strengths.

◆ Commit yourself to "possibility thinking"—a belief that outcomes that seem initially impossible are achievable.

◆ Provide appropriate, high-quality, individualized supports.

◆ Do no harm (Dillenschneider, 2007).

Participation in inclusive outdoor adventures should also take into consideration the choice, use, and maintenance of equipment, because equipment plays an important part in the safety and delivery of the technical skills associated with adventure activities. Maintain an inventory that includes equipment for all sizes, especially backpacks, personal flotation devices (PFDs),

FIGURE 2.6   Effective instructors make sure outdoor adventures are accessible by everyone.

harnesses, and helmets. When using equipment, attempt to stay as close to the standard version as possible. For some activities you may have to modify equipment or sites or control the level of difficulty so that students can participate. If you undertake modifications, adapt on an individual level. In some situations, have mats, boards, and other portable flat, hard surfaces available to improve accessibility.

Effective communication is another key concern when working with this population. Good communication focuses on being open and providing feedback between leaders and participants. Participants should be empowered to create and articulate the best options for any given situation. Use inclusive language that is not negative, judgmental, or paternalistic. Paternalistic could mean referring to adults as kids or overemphasizing routine achievements.

To be positive and nonjudgmental, use objective terms to emphasize each person's abilities. For example, use the term *person with a physical disability* as opposed to *crippled*. Avoid the term *normal*; instead use the phrase *people without disabilities*. Never pretend to understand someone if the message is unclear; instead, ask the person to repeat the statement until you understand. In some cases it may be more appropriate to rephrase questions in a yes or no format or, if speaking is a problem, devise another mode of communication such as tapping or blinking. Finally, make sure that you have pencil and paper on hand when an interpreter is not available. Additional information on accessibility and standards for outdoor programs can be found on the National Center on Accessibility Web site (www.ncaonline.org).

Professional and National Standards

Numerous professional and national standards serve as resources to support and even direct this curriculum guide. Detailing and describing all related standards is beyond the scope of this section. Nevertheless, instructors in each of the adventure activities should know of and be able to access related standards. In many cases, you can be certified in a specific activity area. A list of professional associations, certifications, and curriculum that support the adventure activities appears in appendix B.

Beyond the professional groups and national resources listed in appendix B, each of the units described in this curriculum guide can be designed to support and deliver the national standards created by the National Association for Sport and Physical Education (NASPE, 2006). Figure 2.7 lists the NASPE national standards, which direct public educators' efforts to ensure the health and fitness of our nation's youth. Specifically, NASPE drives physical education curriculum in our public schools. NASPE generates the framework for quality adventure pursuits or physical education programs, provides program accountability, and supports professionalism for our programs. Outdoor adventure-based pursuits

Standard 1: Demonstrates competency in motor skills and movement patterns needed to perform a variety of physical activities.

Standard 2: Demonstrates understanding of movement concepts, principles, strategies, and tactics as they apply to the learning and performance of physical activities.

Standard 3: Participates regularly in physical activity.

Standard 4: Achieves and maintains a health-enhancing level of physical fitness.

Standard 5: Exhibits responsible personal and social behavior that respects self and others in physical activity settings.

Standard 6: Values physical activity for health, enjoyment, challenge, self-expression, or social interaction.

FIGURE 2.7 The six NASPE national standards help drive physical education curricula.

Reprinted from *Moving Into the Future: National Standards for Physical Education*, 2nd ed., with permission from the National Association for Sport and Physical Education (2004), 1900 Association Drive, Reston, VA 20191, USA.

play a vital role in improving the quality and diversity of physical education curriculum. Paddling whitewater, rock climbing, mountain biking, snowshoeing, backpacking, and all other activities in this guide offer exciting benefits in the form of health and fitness to our youth. Fighting obesity, promoting lifetime activities, and encouraging general fitness are just a few benefits offered through adventure activities.

Conclusion

This chapter outlined basic knowledge and skills and offered an overview of the importance of environmental stewardship, inclusion, and connection to professional and national standards associated with effective adventure-based instruction.

Whatever the adventure-based activity being taught, the instructor should keep three over-arching goals in mind. Adventure-based skills lessons should be enjoyable and educational, managed for associated risks, and environmentally sensitive. The next step to ensure teaching success requires the instructor to embrace three key concepts in designing and executing lessons. First, effective adventure educators draw from models and theories of experiential education to maximize the outdoor learning process. Second, outdoor leaders must understand learning styles so that they can teach lessons to meet the needs of diverse learners. Third, instructors must be aware of and apply specific teaching tools or techniques that are unique to teaching in the outdoors.

Teaching in the outdoors allows us to use a variety of land- and water-based resources to conduct our programs. In the process, we should be able to instill in our students the appropriate Leave No Trace principles for the activities and environments that we work in and convey to them the importance of stewardship. As educators we need to be more aware of our environment, become stewards of the land, and give something back to the settings that support our programs.

Social integration has become an important part of outdoor programming. As professionals we have an obligation to meet the needs of people with disabilities by developing program activities and initiating effective ways to include people with disabilities into adventure programs and activities.

Professional and national standards serve as goals for teaching and learning. Standards provide guidelines, curriculum, learning objectives, technical information, and risk management protocol to support instructor efforts. Standards are also important because they specify what your students should know and do. When possible, your programs should incorporate the standards established by the organizations that provide guidance for many of the activities presented in this book.

Armed with clear goals, theory and techniques, knowledge, and appropriate resources, adventure-based instructors will have a significant effect on their participants and maximize the powerful benefits of adventure-based activities!

References and Resources

Association for Experiential Education (AEE). (n.d.). AEE Web site. Retrieved from www.aee.org

Attarian, A. (2001). Trends in outdoor adventure education. *Journal of Experiential Education*, *24*(3), 141–149.

Bunting, C.J. (2006). *Interdisciplinary teaching through outdoor education*. Champaign, IL: Human Kinetics.

Buell, L.H. (1981). *Outdoor leadership competency*. Greenfield, MA: Environmental Awareness Publications.

Dewey, J. (1938). *Experience and education*. New York: Collier Books.

Dillenschneider, C. (2007). Integrating persons with impairments and disabilities into standard outdoor adventure education programs. *Journal of Experiential Education*, *30*(1), 70–83.

Drury, J.K., Bonney, B.F., Berman, D., & Wagstaff, M.C. (2005). *The backcountry classroom: Lessons, tools, and activities for teaching outdoor leaders* (2nd ed.). Guilford, CT: Falcon Guides.

Gager, D., Hendee, J.C., Kinziger, M., & Krumpe, E. (August, 1998). What managers are saying and doing about wilderness experience programs. *Journal of Forestry*, *96*(8), 33–37.

Gibbons, M., & Hopkins, D. (1980). How experiential is your experience-based program? *Journal of Experiential Education*, *4*(1), 32–37.

Green, P. (1981). *The content of a college-level outdoor leadership course for land-based outdoor pursuits in the Pacific Northwest: A delphi consensus*. PhD diss., University of Oregon, Portland.

Hammitt, W.E., & Cole, D.N. (1998). *Wildland recreation—ecology and management*. New York: Wiley.

Joplin, L. (1981). On defining experiential education. *Journal of Experiential Education*, 4(1), 17–20.

Kolb, D.A. (1984). *Experiential learning.* Englewood Cliffs, NJ: Prentice-Hall.

Kolb, D.A. (2000). *Facilitator's guide to learning.* Boston: Hay/McBer.

Leave No Trace Center for Outdoor Ethics (LNT). (2006). *Leave No Trace principles.* Retrieved from www.lnt.org

Loeffler, T.A. (1996). Leading the way: Strategies that enhance women's involvement in experiential education careers. In K. Warren (ed.), *Women's voices in experiential education*, 94–106. Dubuque, IA: Kendall Hunt.

Martin, B., Cashel, C., Wagstaff, M., & Breunig, M. (2006). *Outdoor leadership: Theory and practice.* Champaign, IL: Human Kinetics.

McAvoy, L. (1978). Outdoor leadership training. *Journal of Physical Education and Recreation*, 49(4), 42–43.

National Association for Sport and Physical Education. (2006). *NASPE national standards.* Retrieved from www.aahperd.org/NASPE/publications-nationalstandards.html

Pfeiffer, J.W., & Jones, J.E. (1980). *The 1980 annual handbook for group facilitators.* San Diego, CA: University Associates.

Priest, S. (1984). Outdoor leadership down under. *Journal of Experiential Education*, 8, 13–15.

Priest, S. (1990). Everything you always wanted to know about judgment, but were afraid to ask. *Journal of Adventure Education and Outdoor Leadership*, 7(3), 5–12.

Schoel, J., Prouty, D., & Radcliffe, P. (1988). *Islands of healing: A guide to adventure based counseling.* Beverly, MA: Project Adventure.

Sugarman, D. (2001). Inclusive outdoor education: Facilitating groups that include people with disabilities. *Journal of Experiential Education*, 24(3), 166–172.

Svinicki, M.D., & Dixon, N.M. (1987). Kolb model modified for classroom activities. *College Teaching*, 35(4), 141–146.

Swiderski, M. (1981). *Outdoor leadership competencies identified by outdoor leaders in five western regions.* PhD diss., University of Oregon.

Terry, T. (1995). Universal adventure programming: Opening our programs to people with physical disabilities. *Journal of Leisurability*, 22(2), 16–20.

Wurdinger, S.D. (1997). *Philosophical issues in adventure education* (3rd ed.). Dubuque, IA: Kendall Hunt.

PART I

Land-Based Units

Unit 1: Backpacking

Unit 2: Rock Climbing

Unit 3: Caving

Unit 4: Mountain Biking

The first part of *Technical Skills for Adventure Programming: A Curriculum Guide* focuses on popular land-based activities that provide a host of benefits. Backpacking, rock climbing, caving, and mountain biking allow the participant to experience unique environments through specific modes of travel.

Backpacking allows for a self-contained experience to remote regions of our natural world by foot. A backpacker must learn to be self-reliant and be able to exercise a multitude of outdoor living skills such as trip planning, cooking, navigation, first aid, shelter construction, environmental stewardship, and pack packing. A strong skill base allows backpackers to experience parks, trail systems, and vast open spaces safely for a weekend or weeks at a time.

Rock climbers use many of the backpacker's fundamental outdoor living skills but must possess additional skill sets that include the use of specialized equipment needed to scale rock faces found on all continents. Natural rock offers a variety of challenges for people of all skill levels.

Those who cave will tell you that cavers form a tight social network of avid explorers always in search of undiscovered underground passages. Caving encompasses outdoor living skills, shares many technical skills associated with rock climbing, and requires a specific mind-set to explore our underground world.

Finally, mountain bikers are strong athletes who choose to experience forests, deserts, and mountains under the power of foot and pedal. Mountain biking requires specific skills and knowledge to be safe and to protect the environment. Mountain bikers ride to get in shape, explore natural areas, and test themselves. This demanding sport provides all the benefits of a healthy leisure activity.

Outdoor leaders who facilitate any of these four activities are promoting healthy lifetime activities. Although these activities are lumped together in this part of the book, they are distinct sports supported by their own professional organizations. Outdoor leaders have a variety of resources, trainings, and certifications to develop their competencies within these four disciplines.

The contributors in this unit draw from a variety of resources and personal experience to assist the outdoor leader in these four areas. We want to bring your attention to specific information and issues as you plan your land-based lessons.

Inclusion

Two inclusion lessons are featured in part I. In unit 1, the authors address inclusion issues in lesson 15. The lesson begins by defining basic terms and discussing what it means to have a disability. The main portion of the lesson focuses on inclusive techniques that apply to all land-based activities. We recommend that when teaching rock climbing, caving, or mountain biking, you use this lesson as a foundation for the other lessons when discussing inclusion and accessibility. Lesson 15 in unit 2 discusses specific techniques associated with rock climbing that you can apply to the other activities.

Risk Management

Throughout the book, the authors address specific risk management issues associated with their lessons. Lesson 11 in unit 2 gives a brief overview of the Williamson–Meyer matrix (Gookin, 2003), which identifies potential causes of accidents in outdoor settings. You can modify this model for each of the parts in this book, because it provides a foundation for risk management and a great starting point for your discussions on risk management.

Leave No Trace

Each contributor focused on the LNT information specific to her or his activities. Unit 1 touches on each of the seven LNT principles through a series of activities in the context of general outdoor living skills. You can apply these creative activities to the other units by substituting activity-specific information. Units 2, 3, and 4 all focus on LNT information and techniques specific to the activity. Both the rock-climbing unit and the mountain biking unit followed protocol developed by the Leave No Trace National Center for Outdoor Ethics. Much

of the information for the unit on caving was taken from the National Speleological Society's *A Guide to Responsible Caving* (Jones, 2003).

Anchor Systems and Knots

The backpacker, rock climber, and caver use many of the same knots and rope systems. Basic camp knots such as the square knot, bowline, taut line hitch, girth hitch, and clove hitch are covered in unit 1, lesson 9. The overhand knot, figure-eight family, double fisherman's, water knot (ring bend), Prusik, Munter hitch, Munter mule, and coiling rope are covered in unit 2, lesson 3. The rock-climbing unit goes into detail concerning the construction of natural anchors (lesson 6), artificial anchors (lesson 7), and fixed anchors (lesson 8). You will find that tensionless anchors are featured in the caving unit, lesson 5.

Connecting Units

Throughout this and other parts of this book, you'll find that the authors refer to other units if a topic was discussed elsewhere. For example, all units will address proper dress for their respective activities. Unit 1, lesson 6 addresses a universal clothing system for any outdoor activity. When teaching the selection and use of proper outdoor clothing, consider using this lesson as the foundation regardless of the activity that you are facilitating. The same holds true for navigation; unit 1, lessons 11 and 12, discuss basic map and compass use. In general, refer to unit 1 for all basic outdoor living skills.

A final note relates to stretching and warm-ups. Before participating in any physical activity, make sure that you stress warm-ups, which include traditional stretching or simply engaging in the activity at a slow pace initially. You will find that each author recommends specific techniques and reminds you to emphasize this important task.

References

Gookin, J. (2003). *National outdoor leadership school instructors handbook*. Lander, WY: National Outdoor Leadership School.

Jones, C. (2003). *A guide to responsible caving* (3rd ed.). Huntsville, AL: National Speleological Society.

Backpacking

Mick Daniel • **Tammie L. Stenger-Ramsey**

UNIT 1, LESSON 1

▷ Introduction to Backpacking

OVERVIEW

Backpacking is an adventurous way to travel an area and is a common aspect of many other adventure activities such as mountaineering and rock climbing. This lesson defines backpacking and provides a brief overview of how backpacking became a leisure activity. This lesson also introduces organizations that teach and use backpacking from a programmatic standpoint.

JUSTIFICATION

This lesson explores the many facets of backpacking to broaden the students' perception of the sport. Many styles have arisen in recent years from lightweight, fast-moving backpacking trips to long expeditions. Students will find it valuable to understand the broad nature of this popular activity. Students can also expand their skills and participation in the sport by being knowledgeable about available resources.

GOAL

To introduce backpacking as an outdoor activity and provide basic resources to enhance a broader understanding of the sport.

OBJECTIVES

At the end of this lesson, students will be able to

- describe some organizations that teach backpacking skills (cognitive);
- locate and use a variety of training resources available to the beginning backpacker (cognitive);
- appreciate the importance of formal training and learning to be a responsible user (affective);
- discover new trends in the sport of backpacking (affective); and
- demonstrate some physical conditioning exercises to improve strength, endurance, and flexibility necessary for successful backpacking (psychomotor).

EQUIPMENT AND AREAS NEEDED

- Whiteboard and markers
- Publications and brochures from the various programs that you are discussing
- Outdoor magazines
- Current books about backpacking
- Internet access (optional)

RISK MANAGEMENT CONSIDERATIONS

- If you are teaching these classes in an outdoor environment, always survey the area for environmental hazards like bee's nests, widow makers, and so forth.
- Be sure to have everyone dressed appropriately for the weather.

LESSON CONTENT

Introduction (30 Minutes)

This lesson provides a fascinating look into a leisure pursuit now shared by millions of people, from its origins to the current ultralight movement.

Backpacking is a leisure pursuit in which people carry in a backpack various equipment designed to carry out the basic functions of living outdoors. In recent history it is used not only for hiking to and through remote locations in backcountry areas but also for travel around the world. This lesson focuses specifically on traveling in the backcountry.

When did backpacking start? Undoubtedly people have carried equipment that they have needed on their backs since humankind started needing things to be comfortable.

◆ Mountaineers in the Alps from as early as the late 1700s were probably using backpacks to carry their equipment, although most moved from one village to another to spend the night.

◆ John Muir was packing around the Sierra Nevada in the late 1800s, but as a recreational sport, backpacking probably started with the return of the soldiers from World War II.

◆ During World War II soldiers carried backpacks as a form of training and, in combat, to move as a unit through the countryside. Backpacking, then, as leisure pursuit can probably be traced back to the early 1950s. On their return many soldiers brought that experience to the Boy Scouts and other organizations.

Main Activities

Activity 1: Overview of Resources (30 Minutes)

Many organizations, clubs, and colleges are involved in teaching backpacking.

◆ Some of the most prominent are the Outward Bound (OB) schools, the National Outdoor Leadership School (NOLS), the Wilderness Education Association (WEA), Sierra Club, Appalachian Mountain Club (AMC), and the Colorado Mountain Club (CMC). A number of youth organizations also use backpacking for teaching and recreation. For example, the Boy Scouts taught backpacking since early in their history and introduced countless youth to the sport. Today a great number of summer camps and youth programs offer extended backpacking expeditions as part of their summer programming.

◆ OB and NOLS are prominent organizations that teach a variety of backcountry skills including backpacking. Both have their roots in extended backcountry expeditions. They have years of experience and offer a huge number of courses each year. OB and NOLS are equally priced and offer similar programs. In general, an OB course promotes personal growth and development through backpacking experiences. NOLS focuses more on leadership and technical skill development and uses backpacking as a primary mode of travel. Both OB and NOLS curricula teach basic outdoor living skills associated with backpacking.

◆ The WEA affiliates with outdoor organizations and universities throughout the United States and Canada to teach an outdoor leadership curriculum based on a certification process. The WEA includes backpacking in their national curriculum.

- The Sierra Club, AMC, and CMC as well as many other organizations offer a variety of courses based largely on the expertise of volunteer leaders who have been active in the club.
- Many universities and colleges offer full selections of outdoor skills classes, usually culminating in a variety of credit-based and non-credit-based trips. Outdoor recreation majors have become popular, so students seeking outdoor careers receive formal training.
- Concurrently many outdoor retailers like L.L. Bean and REI are beginning to offer skills courses and trips that help educate people about the gear that they need for activities like backpacking.

Visit these Web sites for more detailed information:

- National Outdoor Leadership School, www.nols.edu
- Outward Bound USA, www.outwardbound.com
- Colorado Mountain Club, www.cmc.org
- Appalachian Mountain Club, www.outdoors.org
- Boy Scouts, www.scouting.org
- Girl Scouts, www.girlscouts.org
- REI, www.rei.com
- L.L. Bean, www.llbean.com
- WEA, www.weainfo.org

Activity 2: Ultralight Backpacking (One Hour)

Recommend these resources to students:

- www.backpacking.net/ultralit.html
- www.the-ultralight-site.com
- http://gorp.away.com

Have students research ultralight backpacking as an assignment and then facilitate a class discussion on the topic.

- The newest trend in backpacking is the ultralight movement. The ultralight movement seeks to reduce the overall backpack weight to allow for longer and faster travel days. Traditional backpacking or expedition-style backpacking uses similar equipment but less emphasis is placed on the weight of individual items.
- Ultralight backpacking typically can reduce the overall backpack weight to below 20 pounds (9 kilograms), which is about half of the weight of an expedition backpack. This reduction is achieved by carefully examining equipment based on its weight and function. Most people start reducing their pack weight by first examining the tent, sleeping bag, and the backpack itself. Typically, the equipment is lightened, not the food or water.
- This style of backpacking has influenced equipment manufacturers, and hence equipment is becoming lighter and more durable as time goes by. Overall the weight of backpacks is down significantly from just 20 years ago because of technology—stronger and lighter fabrics, metals, and composites.

Activity 3: Formal Training (One Hour)

Develop an activity in which students research potential resources to obtain formal training. Students should shop around and find training opportunities that would foster their development based on current experience. Have students report to the class their findings, which would include course descriptions, cost, time frame, information on the sponsoring organization, and so forth. Use the following information to support the assignment.

◆ With any outdoor skill, proper training provides better experiences. Backpackers with formal knowledge and training affect the natural environment less and experience fewer serious accidents and incidents. Seeking the correct training and information is a vital step in learning to backpack.

◆ Many resources are available to the new backpacker including guidebooks, instructional books, online resources, seminars, and courses.

◆ Guidebooks are typically designed to educate users about an area that they are interested in backpacking. They provide specific information on sites to see in the area and can provide detailed trail information for the backpacker. They typically bring more people to an area and hence increase use. A guidebook is not a substitute for a map and the skill to use one.

◆ Many specific skill books teach backpacking skills. These books usually cover the gamut of information necessary to start backpacking. Nothing replaces the experience of a trip, so novices must plan the first trip accordingly and be wary of being too ambitious.

◆ Locally, retail stores and clubs may sponsor seminars to teach specific backpacking skills. Topics may include equipment, cooking, use of a map and compass, and so on. These seminars tend to be an inexpensive way to begin to learn some basic skills.

◆ Taking a course dedicated to backpacking is the best way to learn all the information necessary and gain training to allow a safe trip for the participant and the environment. Local community colleges may offer basic backpacking courses. Organizations mentioned in activity 1 offer courses and published curriculum on the topic.

Activity 4: Physical Fitness (30 Minutes)

Begin this activity with a lecture format by covering an overview of fitness and specific information on strength, endurance, and flexibility.

Brief Overview   Backpacking is a rigorous sport. Participants carry heavy packs on their backs while walking on varied, uneven terrain, usually for long periods. Participants burn more calories in a day of backpacking than they consume in a typical day at home. Because of the demanding physical nature of this sport, participants should be physically prepared for the challenge that they will be undertaking. Before beginning any type of physical conditioning program, participants should discuss their plans with their physician and be sure to receive appropriate training from a qualified person.

Strength   The primary muscles that a person should strengthen before any backpacking trip are those in the front of the thigh (quadriceps), back of the thigh (hamstrings), back of the lower leg (calves), buttocks, abdomen, and lower back. Strong muscles help stabilize the joints and prevent premature physical fatigue.

Endurance   The ability to travel for long periods is important in the sport of backpacking. Participants should begin a daily walking program before embarking on a trip. Backpackers should be able to walk at least 3 miles (5 kilometers) at a moderately brisk pace without difficulty before the beginning of the trip. If 3 miles

Is difficult, participants may need to start with lower mileage and increase by .25 miles (.4 kilometers) every few days to build up. When walking 3 miles becomes easy, participants may choose to carry a small backpack with 5 to 10 pounds (3 to 5 kilograms) on their walks and slowly build up to carrying 30 pounds (14 kilograms). Varied terrain on the training route is ideal. If the route does not include hills, participants can walk up and down flights of steps instead.

Flexibility   Stretching is a component of fitness that is often used ineffectively. Participants should warm up their muscles for at least five minutes before stretching. This principle means that during a backpacking trip, or during pretrip training, students should not stretch until the first break. Stretching also works well as a cool-down activity after reaching the destination for the day.

At this point, demonstrate and practice stretches with the participants to ensure that they understand proper stretching techniques. Figure BP1.1 describes and shows the quadriceps stretch, calf stretch, hamstring stretch, lower-back and abdomen stretch, and shoulder stretch.

Closure Activity

Researching Current Trends (One to Two Hours)

Have students research the current trends among backpackers using a variety of media including the Internet, magazines, and current publications. For example, *Backpacker Magazine* features the latest in trends, opinions, and perspectives on the sport of backpacking. Students will be amazed at the diversity and rich activity associated with the sport. Provide an opportunity for the students to have a round-table discussion about current trends that they have identified in the sport. Consider highlighting the ones that may directly affect your class for discussion.

Follow-Up Activity

Additional Training Options (One Hour)

Besides focusing on basic outdoor living skills associated with backpacking, consider introducing more specialized training that would complement a backpacker's skill set. Research and discuss possibilities such as wilderness medicine training and certification, Leave No Trace training and certification, and search and rescue training.

ASSESSMENT

- ◆ Check that students have an understanding of organizations that teach backpacking skills.
- ◆ Verify that students can locate and use training resources available to the beginning backpacker by having them explore what might best suit their needs.
- ◆ Assess whether students appreciate the importance of obtaining training and learning to be a responsible user by having them research training opportunities.
- ◆ Confirm that students can discover new trends in the sport of backpacking by exploring available resources.
- ◆ Ensure that students can execute physical conditioning exercises and stretches to improve strength, endurance, and flexibility necessary for successful backpacking by completing the stretches outlined in activity 4.

Stretching Techniques

Quadriceps Stretch

Stand on the right leg, hold on to a tree or a friend for balance if necessary, and support yourself with the right hand if desired. Keep the knees side by side and bend the left leg. Grasp the ankle with the left hand and gently pull the foot toward the buttock. Stop the movement when the muscle feels a slight resistance and hold for 5 to 10 seconds. Change legs. Repeat two or three times on each side.

Calf Stretch

Find a tree (or other stable object) to lean against, and face the tree. Place the hands on the tree while standing about an arm's length away. Step back with one foot while keeping the back straight. Slightly bend the forward knee, keeping the heel on the ground. Lean forward, keeping the back leg straight and the heel on the ground. You should feel the stretch in the back leg.

Hamstring Stretch

Sit on the ground with the legs extended in front of the torso. Straighten the arms and place the palms of the hands on top of the legs. Keeping the back as straight as possible, bend from the hips and reach the arms forward toward the toes. When you feel slight resistance, grab the legs with the arms and hold for 5 to 10 seconds. Raise back up and repeat two or three times. This stretch can also be done in a standing position, as seen in the photo.

Lower-Back and Abdomen Stretch

Stand facing forward with the feet shoulder-width apart. Place the hands on the hips and slowly rotate to the right. Hold for 10 seconds, and then rotate to the left and hold for 10 seconds. It is important to rotate at the hips while keeping the knees and legs facing forward.

Shoulder Stretch

Stand facing forward with the feet about shoulder-width apart. Raise the arms to the side to shoulder height. Slowly move the arms to the front, keeping them at shoulder height. Clasp the hands in front by intertwining the fingers. Push forward to feel the stretch, and hold for 10 seconds.

FIGURE BP1.1   Stretching improves flexibility and can help prevent injuries.

TEACHING CONSIDERATIONS

- If the course is taking place without Internet access, consider providing popular outdoor magazines as a resource.
- Be clear about the style of backpacking that you are teaching. Emphasize that your approach is only one way of backpacking and that through experience they will discover what style they like best.
- Warn students that not all training opportunities are equal. Help students become critical of training programs and curricula so that they will obtain quality training.

UNIT 1, LESSON 2

▷ Trip Planning

OVERVIEW

Planning prevents poor performance. In this lesson students learn the importance of trip planning and the fundamental skills needed to prepare for an outdoor expedition. During these activities, students learn about establishing a trip rationale or purpose, the importance of determining an appropriate location and route, the need for having contingency plans, and a variety of trip-planning considerations. They will then plan an actual trip.

JUSTIFICATION

Appropriate planning for a backpacking expedition allows for a safer, more comfortable, and more environmentally friendly trip. When all participants are aware of, and buy into, the purpose of the trip, the chances of poor **expedition behavior** resulting from differences of opinion decrease. If the trip is well planned, the route matches the ability and desires of the participants. When the itinerary is shared with friends, family, and land management agencies, a quicker response in the event of an emergency is more likely. Moreover, if all participants have appropriate food, clothing, and gear, they are more likely to be comfortable, safe, and happy in a variety of situations. Appropriate planning allows participants to follow LNT principles more closely, which means that participants and future visitors have a greater opportunity to experience the area in its natural state.

GOAL

To develop students' understanding of the multiple facets of and importance of trip planning and to be able to design their own backpacking trips.

OBJECTIVES

At the end of this lesson, students will be able to

- explain why establishing a trip rationale or purpose is essential (cognitive),
- describe the importance of location and route selection (cognitive),

◆ explain the importance of contingency planning (cognitive),

◆ describe various trip-planning considerations (cognitive),

◆ create an actual trip plan (psychomotor), and

◆ appreciate the need to properly plan (affective).

EQUIPMENT AND AREAS NEEDED

◆ Paper (enough for each small-group brainstorming session)

◆ Pencils or pens

◆ Participant journals

◆ One trip-planning consideration list for each student (figure BP2.1 on page 45)

◆ Trip-planning resources (books from the reference list—enough for each student to have one)

RISK MANAGEMENT CONSIDERATIONS

◆ If you are teaching in the outdoors, be sure to have scanned your teaching area to ensure that it is clear of any hazards such as bees, dead tree limbs, and so on.

◆ Be aware of local weather patterns and be prepared for inclement weather. Consider setting up a tarp as shelter if the situation warrants.

◆ For an outdoor classroom, find a flat, open area that is free of trip hazards (roots, rocks, holes).

LESSON CONTENT

Introduction

"Failing to plan means planning to fail." Without meaningful planning for a backpacking trip, problems great and small can quickly arise. This unit will relate to understanding the importance of trip planning, having a trip purpose, multiple considerations related to pretrip planning, and the importance of creating contingency plans.

Main Activities

Activity 1: Why Plan? (30 Minutes; Longer for a Large Group)

Explain that this activity helps participants understand the importance of trip planning. Divide the group into smaller groups of about four participants each. Ask each group to create a list of problems that can arise if the leader fails to plan or plans inadequately for a backpacking trip.

◆ Ask each group to select one of the problems and create a short skit that reveals the consequences of a poorly planned trip.

◆ Give each group an opportunity to present their skit to the large group.

◆ End with a short discussion of the positive outcomes of appropriate planning (safety, comfort, organization, morale, environmental impact).

Activity 2: Trip Purpose (15 Minutes)

Ask the students if they have ever been on a trip during which people had differing opinions on what should happen. Have students share their experiences. Explain that determining the purpose for the trip should always be the first consideration when planning a trip. Any other decisions regarding the trip should reflect the purposes of that trip so that the participants' needs will be met.

Have the students write for five minutes about why determining a purpose is important to the planning process. Ask the students to create a minimum of three possible trip goals and write them in their journals. At the end of the writing period ask each person to share his or her goals with the larger group. Lead a discussion about differences in goals.

Note: Although the purpose for a trip may be established up front, during the trip individual wants and desires may appear that differ from the original purpose. In that event, the group should discuss the differences of opinion and determine whether they need to redefine the purpose or goals. In that situation, the group must make sound decisions in modifying the trip. Be sure to clarify the differences between leader goals, trip goals, and individual goals. This discussion should make it apparent that a variety of agendas can positively or negatively influence a trip.

Activity 3: Pretrip Planning Considerations (45 to 60 Minutes)

Explain to the participants that after the purpose and corresponding goals have been established, many factors should be considered when planning a trip. Provide each participant with the list of trip-planning considerations (figure BP2.1) and some trip-planning resource books.

Assign one to three trip-planning considerations to each person (depending on the size of group; if the class is large, have the participants form small groups and assign one consideration to each small group). For each planning consideration the participants should

1. explain how the trip purpose can influence that consideration;
2. create a list of additional important responsibilities to be undertaken and additional significant factors; and
3. create an acronym, phrase, or mnemonic device that will help other participants remember the important responsibilities and factors of that consideration.

Ask the participants to share the information with the large group.

Activity 4: Contingency Plans (15 Minutes)

Divide the group into small groups of four or five. Have each group brainstorm situations that may occur during a backpacking trip that cause the original itinerary to change. Have each group share one of those situations with the large group. Ask each group to create at least one possible solution for that situation. Have them share their contingency plan with the large group. Follow with a discussion on creating contingency plans in advance versus creating the plan on the fly. A few examples of situations in which contingency plans might be needed are when a group member is injured and needs to be evacuated, when the group travels more slowly than planned and cannot reach the intended destination, or when another group is already at the planned campsite.

Trip-Planning Considerations

Consider the following items when trip-planning:

- ☐ Location—knowledge of area, availability of maps, type of terrain, types of trails, knowledge of land management agency rules and regulations, permit requirements, weather and climate patterns, short-term and long-term weather forecast.

- ☐ Route—places of interest in the area, teaching sites, campsites, access points, escape routes.

- ☐ Itinerary—duration of trip, dates, travel times (time control plan, or TCP) for all legs of route (include transportation to and from), contingency plans.

- ☐ Participants—physical abilities (including fitness, strength, endurance, coordination), emotional and social maturity level, technical skills, safety skills, environmental skills, age, gender, interests, special needs (dietary, medical). Ensure that participants meet the required criteria for the trip. Keep participants informed.

- ☐ Group size—appropriate for purpose of trip, allowing for optimal learning and relationship growth, minimizing environmental impact, and meeting requirements of governing land management agency.

- ☐ Leadership—number of leaders for the group (at least two for most formal trips), skills, training, knowledge, maturity, communication skills.

- ☐ Clothing and equipment—individual clothing and equipment lists (including what not to bring), group gear lists, emergency or safety lists, inspection of all equipment before trip, weight of packs (about one-third of body weight recommended).

- ☐ Food and water—amount of food, type of food, menu versus TFP, amount of fuel, water treatment methods, availability of water on trail.

- ☐ Accommodations—during travel to and from the site, campsites during the trip, reservations, costs.

- ☐ Transportation—safety, type of vehicles, drivers, appropriate driver's license for vehicle, shuttle services, parking arrangements, rental agreements, trailers to haul equipment, seat belts, maps and driving directions, vehicle inspections, accident procedures, loading and unloading people and equipment, checking of gas gauge, location of last gas station, what to do with keys and valuables.

- ☐ Communication—walkie-talkies, radios, cellular phones, satellite phones, costs, maintenance, battery life, charged batteries, extra batteries, contingency plan if communication fails.

- ☐ Budget (expenses)—vehicle, equipment (purchase, rental, repair), permits and user fees, staff, food, administrative (telephone calls, photocopies, advertising), lodging, facility rental, maps.

- ☐ Income (if any)—carry spare cash and credit cards.

- ☐ Safety and risk management plan—create for every trip; should include 10 items:

  1. Trip rationale
  2. Itinerary (detailed time, location, evacuation routes, emergency agencies, and telephone numbers)
  3. Participant and staff vital information (health information, emergency contact)
  4. Signed legal forms
  5. Budget of expenses
  6. Location of nearest phones, medical facilities, land management ranger office
  7. Procedures and forms (search and rescue procedures, missing-person report forms, crisis and fatality response forms and guidelines, accident response forms and guidelines, blood-borne pathogen handling procedures)
  8. Alcohol and drug policies
  9. Media and information dispersal information
  10. Equipment and clothing lists (individual, group, and safety)

- ☐ Pretrip meetings—introductions, purpose of trip, trip itinerary, hazards and risks, activity requirements (fitness and skills, participant responsibilities, additional costs), equipment requirements, food, expectations for behavior, environmental and sanitation information, travel arrangements, accommodations, tent and cook groups, necessary pretrip skill instruction. Ensure that all legal documents are signed, that you have obtained health and contact information, and that plans are finalized.

- ☐ Posttrip responsibilities—evaluation, location of shower facilities, group debrief, thank-you notes. Clean and store equipment, dispose of food, return vehicles, plan a follow-up meeting (pictures, video, dinner).

- ☐ Promotion and public relations—advertising, participant recruitment, press releases, promotional items (T-shirts, hats, patches, bandannas).

- ☐ Final trip checklist—double- and triple-check each item before departing.

FIGURE BP 2.1   Use this list as a guide to develop a comprehensive trip plan.

Closure Activity

Quick Quiz (20 Minutes)

Quiz the students on the acronyms or mnemonic devices that they created during activity 3, Pretrip Planning Considerations, to see whether they remember important aspects of trip planning. Name the consideration and ask the students to give you the acronym or mnemonic device and then describe what the acronym or device stands for.

- Location
- Route
- Itinerary
- Participants
- Group size
- Leadership
- Clothing and equipment
- Food and water
- Accommodations
- Transportation
- Communication
- Budget
- Income
- Safety and risk management plan
- Pretrip meetings
- Posttrip responsibilities
- Promotion and public relations
- Final trip checklist

Follow-Up Activity

Plan a Trip (Time as Needed)

Have the students plan all or part of a backpacking trip. Break the students up into small groups and have each group come up with a trip plan. The amount of time that you have with the group and the number of trips that you take will determine what type of plan they create. Each group may create a plan for the same trip, or they may each plan for different trips. If you are going to take only one trip with the group, you may want to give each group one or two aspects of the plan to prepare. For example, one group may be responsible for the location and route, another group for the risk management plan, and so on.

ASSESSMENT

- Check that students can explain why establishing a trip rationale or purpose is essential by observing their engagement in the pretrip planning activity that promotes discussion on this topic. During activity 1, Why Plan?, check on each group during brainstorming and skit creation to make sure that all participants are providing appropriate examples. During the second activity, Trip Purpose, evaluate the students' responses during the discussion. Read journals to determine how well participants understood this concept.

◆ Confirm that students can describe the importance of location and route selection by making a checklist of relevant considerations.

◆ Verify that students can explain the importance of contingency planning by observing the group discussion in the fourth activity, Contingency Plans. Ensure that all participants have an opportunity to discuss the topic.

◆ Check that students can describe various trip-planning considerations by asking them to explain the acronym or mnemonic device created by other students in the class during activity 3.

◆ Confirm that students can create an actual trip plan by developing an organized plan for the group's first proposed trip.

◆ Verify that students appreciate the need to plan properly by predicting what could happen if trips are not appropriately planned by presenting the short skit during activity 1.

TEACHING CONSIDERATIONS

◆ Although certain aspects of this lesson may work in an outdoor setting during an expedition, this lesson is best suited to a classroom atmosphere. Because of the length of the activities, you may wish to schedule breaks after writing in journals and between other activities.

◆ An additional activity to develop trip-planning skills involves creating a fantasy trip. Ask students to pick a dream location for a backpacking trip. Have them research that area and develop a plan for a trip to be undertaken by a group of friends. Picking a dream location for a vacation-oriented trip may motivate students and even inspire them to take the trip!

UNIT 1, LESSON 3

▷ Food and Nutrition

OVERVIEW

The phrase "you are what you eat" takes on a whole new meaning in the backcountry. In this lesson students learn the fundamentals of planning and selecting appropriate foods to supply nutrition needs for outdoor expeditions.

JUSTIFICATION

Adequate nutrition and hydration are necessary to keep energy levels high during expeditions. Eating enough of the right kinds of foods helps with thermoregulation, body tissue repair, and maintenance of appropriate energy levels, positive attitudes, and comfort (Gookin, 2003; Pearson, 2004; Petzoldt, 1984; Richard, Orr, & Lindholm, 1991). Selecting appropriate rations for a trip is just as important as having appropriate clothing and gear.

GOAL

To develop the participants' understanding of how to plan for food needs during backpacking trips, how to use different food-rationing processes, how to package food, and how nutrition affects performance during expeditions.

OBJECTIVES

At the end of this lesson, students will be able to

◆ describe the functions of the five different types of nutrients (cognitive),

◆ demonstrate the ability to make sound dietary decisions (cognitive),

◆ select food items to combine to make a nutritious and balanced meal (cognitive),

◆ explain the difference in caloric needs for backpacking trips of varying intensity in varying climates (cognitive),

◆ package food effectively following appropriate LNT principles (psychomotor), and

◆ appreciate nutritional solutions for specific physical conditions (affective).

EQUIPMENT AND AREAS NEEDED

◆ Food bags with a variety of rations (flour, grains, pasta, potatoes, dried milk, nuts, seeds, cheese, oil, margarine, peanut butter, brown sugar, hard candy, dried vegetables, spice kit, and so on)

◆ Physical condition list

◆ Nutrient name list (cut so that each nutrient is on a separate piece of paper)

◆ Nutrient function list (cut so that each function is on a separate piece of paper)

◆ Scissors (for cutting nutrient lists)

◆ Paper or notebook (one for each participant)

◆ Pencil or pen (one for each participant)

◆ Prize for winning team

◆ Plastic bags (enough for packaging all food for the trip)

◆ Gloves

◆ Food scales

RISK MANAGEMENT CONSIDERATIONS

◆ Have gloves available for activities that may include physical contact with food because of food allergies and sanitation.

◆ Have food alternatives available for the expedition (in case of food allergies).

◆ If teaching in the outdoors, pay attention to the risk management concerns detailed in lesson 2.

LESSON CONTENT

Introduction

One of the primary concerns of novice backpackers is what they will eat. Food not only provides energy and vital **nutrients** for the body but also may be a source of comfort. When planning food rations and creating meals during the trip, follow the concept of KLMNOP:

◆ K/calories
◆ Lightweight
◆ Minerals and vitamins
◆ Nutrients
◆ Optimum flexibility and variety
◆ Packaging

There are two ways of planning food choices. For trips shorter than five days, a **menu plan** (determining all the ingredients for each individual meal) is often the most efficient method of determining food needs for a trip. Menu planning involves creating a menu for each meal and then determining all the ingredients for each meal. Figure BP3.1 provides an example of a menu plan.

Using the **total food planning (TFP)** method allows easier pretrip planning, especially for longer expeditions, and permits greater creativity and flexibility while in the field (Pearson, 2004). TFP is a bulk ration system, in which participants select

Sample Menu Plan for One Day for a Two-Person Cook Group

Meal	Menu	Ingredients
Breakfast	Oatmeal	1 1/2 cup (350 milliliters) oats
		1/4 cup (60 milliliters) powdered milk
		1/4 cup (60 milliliters) raisins
		1/4 cup (60 milliliters) dried apples
		1/2 cup (120 milliliters) walnuts
		1 tablespoon (15 milliliters) butter
		1/4 cup (60 milliliters) brown sugar
Lunch and trail food	Peanut butter bagels	2 bagels
		4 tablespoons (60 milliliters) peanut butter
		2 tablespoons (30 milliliters) honey
		1/2 cup (120 milliliters) raisins
	Trail mix	1/4 cup (60 milliliters) raisins
		1/4 cup (60 milliliters) cranberries
		1/4 cup (60 milliliters) peanuts
		1/4 cup (60 milliliters) sunflower seeds
		1/4 cup (60 milliliters) M&Ms
Dinner	Pasta and tomato sauce	8 ounces (220 grams) pasta
		2 tablespoons (30 milliliters) tomato powder
		1/4 cup (60 milliliters) textured vegetable protein (TVP)
		1/4 cup (60 milliliters) parmesan cheese
		1 tablespoon (15 milliliters) butter
		1 teaspoon (5 milliliters) Italian seasoning
		Pinch salt and pepper

FIGURE BP3.1   Menu planning is an efficient way to determine food needs for trips shorter than five days.

specific quantities of foods in appropriate balance without having specific meals in mind. During the trip, the food items are mixed and matched in a variety of ways. Most people carry a recipe book like *The NOLS Cookery* when using the TFP system, because they must do a significant amount of cooking from scratch. Figure BP3.2 provides a sample TFP ration list.

Main Activities

Activity 1: K/calories (15 Minutes)

Ask students what kilocalories (calories) are and how many they usually eat at home each day. **Calories** are units of energy. Average daily consumption is 1,800 to 2,300 calories (Gookin, 2003).

◆ Explain the significant variation in caloric needs between summer and winter backpacking expeditions. An average experience in summer requires 2,500 to 3,200 calories; a strenuous experience or a winter experience requires 3,000 to 4,200 calories. Very strenuous activities in harsh winter weather require 3,700 to 6,000 calories (Pearson, 2004).

◆ Share the approximate caloric intake of varying amounts of dry food: 1.5 pounds (.7 kilograms) = 2,500 calories; 2 pounds (.9 kilograms) = 3,000 calories; 2.25 pounds (1 kilogram) = 3,700 calories; 2.5 pounds (1.1 kilograms) = 4,500 calories (Pearson, 2004).

◆ Explain that foods are selected for backpacking expeditions based on the principles of KLMNOP.

  – K/calories—provide enough calories per person per day; use food low in weight and high in calories.
  – Lightweight—the preference is for less bulky items and those with little or no water content.
  – Minerals and vitamins—cover a variety of nutrition factors.
  – Nutrients—cover a variety of nutrition factors.
  – Optimum flexibility and variety—ease of preparation and having a wide selection of foods to eat are the key points. Menu planning means that participants determine the amount of each ingredient needed to prepare each individual meal during a short trip. Total food planning allows greater flexibility in meal preparation for longer trips. Participants can be creative and eat a variety of meals while minimizing preparation before the expedition. Having recipe books for participants is strongly encouraged with TFP.
  – Packaging—ease of packing is important (amount of mess and waste).

◆ Have participants work with their cook groups to determine how many calories they will need each day and then calculate the total weight of food that they will need for the expedition using this formula:

___ pounds (kilograms) per person per day × ___ number of people in group × ___ number of days in the field

◆ Have each group share their results.

Activity 2: Nutrient Matching (15 Minutes)

Before starting this activity, print out the nutrient name and function list (table BP3.1 on page 53). Cut the list apart so that each strip of paper contains only one item or description. Put the strips with nutrient names in one pile and the nutrient descriptions in another pile.

Total Food Planning Ration List

	Food group members' names	
	Pounds (or kilograms) per person per day (PPPPD) (or KPPPD)	
	Total pounds (or kilograms) = sum PPPPD (or KPPPD) × number of days	
	Requested amount in pounds (kilograms) =	% × total pounds (kilograms)
%	**Item**	
12	Cheese	
	◆ Cheddar	
	◆ Mozzarella	
	◆ Swiss	
	◆ Parmesan	
8	Flour	
	◆ Whole wheat	
	◆ White	
	◆ Cornmeal	
2	Prepared bread (for late rations add to flour)	
	◆ Bagels	
	◆ Tortillas	
4	Cocoa	
	◆ Cocoa powder	
	◆ Hot chocolate	
3	Powdered milk	
3	Protein	
	◆ Pepperoni	
	◆ Tuna	
	◆ Chicken	
	◆ Textured vegetable protein	
3	Beans	
	◆ Lentils	
	◆ Refried beans	
	◆ Black beans	
4	Trail mix	
6	Dried fruit	
	◆ Raisins	
	◆ Cranberries	
	◆ Dates	
	◆ Prunes	
	◆ Apricots	
	◆ Apples	
	◆ Bananas	

continued ▶

FIGURE BP3.2   The total food planning ration list is a helpful tool when cooking from scratch.

3	Fruit drink mix	
	◆ Apple cider	
	◆ Tang	
	◆ Jello	
3	Rice	
12	Grains	
	◆ Hummus	
	◆ Couscous	
	◆ Bulgur wheat	
	◆ Oatmeal	
	◆ Falafel	
	◆ Cream of wheat	
	◆ Tabouli	
5	Pasta	
	◆ Spaghetti	
	◆ Macaroni	
6	Nuts	
	◆ Peanuts	
	◆ Walnuts	
	◆ Almonds	
	◆ Cashews	
	◆ Sunflower seeds	
	◆ Peanut butter	
7	Potato	
	◆ Flakes	
	◆ Diced (hash browns)	
2	Soup bases	
	◆ Veggie broth	
	◆ Chicken broth	
	◆ Beef broth	
1	Dried veggie combo	
1	Tomato base	
8	Sweets	
	◆ Chocolate chips	
	◆ Butterscotch chips	
	◆ Coconut	
	◆ Brown sugar	
	◆ Honey	
	◆ M&Ms	
	◆ Hard candy	
	◆ Maple syrup	
5	Fats	
	◆ Margarine	
	◆ Oil	
2	Baking needs and spices	Do not request on this form.

FIGURE BP3.2   (continued)

Divide participants into two groups. Pass out the nutrient names to the first group and the nutrient functions to the second group. Participants talk to each other to find their match. When the whole group has agreed on the right answers, check to see whether they are correct. When all the nutrients are properly matched, have each pair share the information with the whole group.

Activity 3: Name That Nutrient (20 Minutes)

As the leader, pull an item out of the food bag and tell them what it is. Each group will determine in which nutrient category the item belongs. The first team to answer correctly earns 1 point. At the end of the game, have a prize for the winning team. Be sure to discuss that certain types of food may fall into more than one category; for example most grains are both carbohydrate and protein. Be aware that although plant-based foods have some protein, they often must be used in combination with other foods to obtain a complete protein. One example of getting a complete protein from two plant-based foods is to eat beans with rice.

Activity 4: Food Planning (30 Minutes)

Students will plan their rations for a backpacking trip. They may use either menu planning or TFP. At the end of this activity, students will have a list of food items with the specific quantity of each. For examples, see the sample menu plan and the sample total food planning ration list in the lesson introduction.

Activity 5: Food Packaging (Two to Three Hours)

Either method of food planning (TFP or menu planning) may be used for this activity.

◆ Divide the large group into their individual cook groups.

◆ Have the groups determine how much of each item they will need to bring to satisfy the caloric needs of their group members.

◆ Bring out food scales, measuring cups, and lots of plastic bags. Produce bags from local grocery stores are often the most inexpensive choice, but they are not very sturdy and may need to be doubled up.

TABLE BP3.1 Nutrient Name and Function

Nutrient name	Nutrient function
Carbohydrates	The starches and sugars in foods from plants. They provide short-term energy and are burned during exercise. They should make up about 60 percent of the diet.
Proteins	The 22 amino acids necessary to build and repair body cells. They also deliver oxygen and other nutrients to muscles. Meat, fish, dairy, and soy provide amino acids in the right proportions for the body to use. Most plants lack certain proportions of amino acids; therefore, combining them is necessary (for example, beans and rice). They should make up 15 to 20 percent of the diet.
Fats	Necessary for long-term energy and are eventually burned during exercise. They are calorie dense and provide extra flavor to food. They also help provide a feeling of being full. They should make up 20 to 25 percent of the diet.
Minerals and vitamins	Typically have no calories but are essential for proper physiological function. They occur naturally in food and water. A well-balanced diet should provide all these necessary nutrients.
Water	Makes up half to three-quarters of body weight. Consumption is vital for proper physiological functioning, including digestion and blood circulation. On backpacking trips most people should consume between four and five quarts (liters) each day.

- Explain that most foods have extra packaging that adds weight and trash to a pack after the food is eaten. Even items that do not have extra packaging may not be easily resealed, so most food items will need to be repackaged.

- Foods should be double bagged to keep food from spilling and to prevent moisture from getting to the food if one of the bags tears.

- A simple overhand knot pulled half-way through (quick release) makes the bags easy to tie and untie. For details on tying knots, see lesson 9 (page 94).

- Circulate through the group to check on their progress, answer questions, and assist when necessary.

Leave No Trace (LNT) has seven basic principles (see appendix A for details). Three of those principles relate closely to food planning and packaging.

- Plan ahead and prepare. By planning for nutritional needs and repackaging food before leaving for the trip, participants are following the advice of the first LNT principle. In fact, the LNT curriculum specifically mentions repackaging food as a significant component of "Plan ahead and prepare." Repackaging food helps backpackers minimize the amount of waste that they have in the backcountry, helps protect their food from contamination and spills, and helps protect their food from wildlife.

- Dispose of waste properly. Many food items have extra packaging that must be disposed of (or recycled) after preparation. Repackaging before the trip minimizes the amount of trash that the participants must carry out. Moreover, removing the excess packaging in town is easier because trash and recycling centers are available. A second consideration is that certain types of original food packaging are not waterproof or easy to reseal after opening. Waterproofing food and making sure that all items are sealed minimizes food spillage, waste, or damage from moisture.

- Respect wildlife. Many animals have an extremely sharp sense of smell. Double bagging food and making sure that all food items are securely sealed will help prevent animals from discovering food. Although this method alone will not completely protect the food, it is a good start. For more information on hanging food (bear bagging), see lesson 9 on basic camping skills.

Closure Activity

Physical Condition Role Play (10 Minutes)

Before starting this activity, print out the physical condition examples and remedies (table BP3.2).

Divide the group into five or six smaller groups. Give each group a less-than-optimum physical condition and have them brainstorm possible food and nutrition solutions to remedy the situation. Each group will act out the scenario and their solution for the other participants.

While groups are planning and brainstorming, circulate through the groups and provide assistance when needed. Make sure that each group is providing an appropriate solution to the problem so that they do not provide incorrect information to the group.

TABLE BP3.2   **Physical Condition and Nutritional Solutions**

Physical condition	Nutritional solution
Chronic tiredness or low motivation	Eat more; examine other possible causes.
Low energy on trail	Eat larger breakfast; eat more carbohydrates and less fat while on the trail.
Sore muscles at the end of the day	Consume extra protein at dinner.
Sleeping cold	Eat more fats and consume adequate carbohydrates at dinner.
Muscle cramps after activity and sweating	Drink water with salts; eat fruit.
Dizziness when standing along with dark urine	Drink about two quarts (liters) of water; eat carbohydrates.

Follow-Up Activity

Review the Basics (10 Minutes)

◆ Ask the students what KLMNOP means.

◆ Have the students select items from the food bag that they could use for a meal or trail food that would assist with one of the problem physical conditions.

ASSESSMENT

◆ Check that students can describe the functions of the five different types of nutrients by writing in their journals. By journaling, students will have access to this information later.

◆ Confirm that students have the ability to make sound dietary decisions by looking at the cook groups' menu plans or TFP ration lists. Determine whether each group has an appropriate variety of nutrients before food packaging begins.

◆ Verify that students can determine what is necessary for a nutritious and balanced meal by observing them as they plan a meal with a group before the expedition.

◆ Check that students can select food items to combine to make nutritious and balanced meals. The assessment will occur during the follow-up activity when students select items that will help with problems.

◆ Confirm that students can describe the caloric needs for backpacking trips of varying intensity in varying weather by observing their participation in a large group discussion (for example, moderate intensity in late spring, high intensity in winter).

◆ Verify that students can follow appropriate LNT principles in packaging food for an entire trip by observing them remove excess packaging, double bag food, and tie knots that are easy to untie.

◆ Check that students appreciate nutritional solutions for specific physical conditions by observing them address below-average physical conditions during the closing activity. If the class is part of an expedition, assessment may be done by observing physical condition, energy levels, and dietary intake throughout the trip.

TEACHING CONSIDERATIONS

◆ This lesson may be best taught in stages. Splitting the lesson into two parts is probably a good idea. After the session on calories, participants who have difficulty with math may need a break so that they can be attentive during the remainder of the session when they receive information on nutrients.

◆ Doing this activity pretrip or at the beginning of a course will help minimize some of the performance and group interaction issues that may arise because of poor nutrition.

◆ Consider providing a couple of calculators to assist students with mathematical calculations.

◆ Students can be evaluated and assessed on their ability to plan nutritious meals and eat what their bodies need throughout the trip. You can also do follow-up with reminders throughout the course when people are not feeling well.

UNIT 1, LESSON 4

▷ Food Preparation and Cooking

OVERVIEW

Beginning backpackers often lack the skills and confidence to prepare quality nutritious meals in the backcountry. Students learn in this lesson to prep a kitchen area for safety, cleanliness, cooking, and cleanup. The lesson covers stove safety and preparation of an actual meal.

JUSTIFICATION

Basic food preparation skills and the ability to cook are important to having an enjoyable trip. Student will be able to take pride in a well-cooked meal that is planned and prepared.

GOALS

◆ To develop students' ability to establish and set up a functional, safe kitchen.
◆ To develop students' understanding of basic principles of backcountry cooking.

OBJECTIVES

At the end of this lesson, students will be able to

◆ demonstrate the ability to set up a safe and functional kitchen (cognitive),
◆ assemble and prepare both stoves and cooking sets properly (psychomotor),
◆ prepare a simple backcountry meal (psychomotor), and
◆ appreciate a well-prepared backcountry meal (affective).

EQUIPMENT AND AREAS NEEDED

◆ Backpacking stoves and fuel
◆ Assorted pots and pans
◆ Matches or lighter
◆ Macaroni
◆ Cheese

- Powdered milk
- Butter
- Water
- Food tarp
- Personal bowls and spoons

RISK MANAGEMENT CONSIDERATIONS

- Be sure to use stoves on level, stable surfaces.
- Backpacking stoves present a hazard because typically they are used on the ground where a mishap can result in burned feet, a serious complication on a backpacking trip. Be sure to teach proper cooking etiquette and safety before allowing participants to cook.
- Sometimes picnic tables are used for cooking if available; this arrangement puts the stove at an unsafe height where a burn to the lower torso and genitalia would be serious.
- Be sure to check for food allergies before preparing and consuming food.
- Follow all recommended manufacturer's instructions that accompany each type of stove you use. These guidelines include using gas fuel stoves in well-ventilated areas.
- Have a large metal pot or bucket on hand that can be used to smother an out-of-control burning stove or fire.

LESSON CONTENT

Introduction

Preparing food in the backcountry is one of the most crucial skills that a backpacker can develop. Food provides necessary energy and serves as a source of enjoyment. Many of us value mealtime with friends and families, so why not continue that tradition in the backcountry? When cooking in the backcountry, the first priority is to set up a safe kitchen where participants can cook nutritious, good-tasting food to maintain proper caloric intake. The cleanup of those meals helps to ensure the health of participants as well as the natural environment. The main activities found is this lesson focus on four primary topics: stove safety, kitchen safety, organizing the kitchen, and cooking the meal. You can cover this information through lecture, demonstration, and discussion followed by actual practice.

Main Activities

Activity 1: Stove Safety (30 Minutes)

Carefully cover the following information through discussion and demonstration. Break the class into small groups so that students can practice lighting their stoves. Carefully monitor the groups as they practice. Consider requiring them to inform you before the first lighting so that you can provide proper supervision.

Stoves and Fuels   A backpacking stove should be fairly easy to use and field serviceable. Most modern stoves use either a propane blended cartridge or, more commonly, white gas. These fuels are commonly available within the United States. Discuss the following fuel categories and stove types.

- White gas is probably the most common fuel and stove type found in the United States. The fuel is highly volatile and burns clean and hot. Most white-gas stoves have an external fuel tank that supplies fuel to the burner on the stove.

- Dual-fuel stoves burn multiple kinds of fuel (white gas, unleaded gasoline, and kerosene) and are the best choice for foreign travel. Many require additional accessories to make the switch between fuels.

- Propane canister stoves are typically more common on big double-burner camp stoves. Several backpacking stoves run solely on propane, but these may have problems in cold conditions and environments. Cold conditions can cause the propane to lose pressure until the canisters are heated up, and holding any kind of open flame to a propane canister is not a good idea.

- Blended gas stoves run on a mixture of various gases to achieve a better burn in different conditions. MSR, Primus, and Jetboil have proprietary blends. Most of the stoves themselves will run on any compressed gas, even propane, but each works differently in different environments. The cartridges are seldom refillable and can't be recycled everywhere. Many of these stoves have push-button ignitions, which are a huge convenience in some situations and conditions.

- Alcohol stoves may be the most environmentally friendly and safe stoves available. Unfortunately, most of these stoves produce inadequate BTUs to bring water to a boil quickly and tend not to get hot enough at all at higher altitudes. They are ideal for simple one-person cooking.

- Stoves that use chemical packets tend to be homemade, although several versions are available online (see the resources section at the end of the unit). Several types of chemical fuel tablets are available, but generally they are hexamethylenetetramine or some derivative. Like alcohol stoves, these stoves are most practical for light cooking duty for one or two people. The lightweight movement has embraced this type of fuel and stove.

Cooking Area   Selection of an appropriate cooking area is important. Ideally, the cooking area should be fairly open, flat, and free of combustible items like forest litter and dry grasses.

- Observe Leave No Trace principles and attempt to prevent animal problems. Cooking near your tent and backpack storage is not recommended.

- If the backpacking stove has a detachable fuel canister, check to make sure that gas is not leaking from any of the connections before lighting the stove.

- When lighting the stove you should have room to move quickly away! Backpacking stoves regularly flare up and may catch an unprepared chef by surprise. Be aware of loose-hanging polyester clothes, long hair, beards, and so on that may catch fire or melt.

- Be sure to follow the manufacturer's directions carefully when lighting and using stoves.

- If a stove flares up out of control, the best method for extinguishing the stove is to cover it with a pot to prevent oxygen from feeding the fuel. Dumping water on the stove is not always effective and may cause the stove to flame up even more.

Activity 2: Kitchen Considerations (20 Minutes)

Combine the topics of kitchen safety and kitchen organization by providing a model kitchen for the students. Through discussion and lecture, cover both topics at once. Teach this lesson before the first meal. Have students work as teams to set up their own kitchens. They can report to you after completing the task to discuss their choices. Use the following guidelines for proper management of the kitchen area.

Kitchen Safety Many backcountry meals require some amount of boiling water. Given that the stove is routinely located on the ground, those in the area must guard against accidentally knocking boiling water over onto someone's feet. Practice a few simple kitchen setup rules.

◆ Try to establish a flat cooking area in a low-traffic area of camp.

◆ When using a stove, try to be in a position where you can move to safety or have a barrier (like a camp chair) between you and the hot surface or boiling water.

◆ Provide some sort of cutting board for cutting up vegetables and general food preparation. Examples of cutting surfaces are rollable cutting boards that can be found at grocery stores as well as Frisbees and the tops of pots.

◆ Keep a minimum number of people (one or two) in the kitchen at any given time so that the kitchen and meal are always supervised. This approach will help prevent accidents and burned meals.

Kitchen Organization

◆ Organize your cooking space so that utensils, pots, food, and spices are within easy reach of your kitchen area. Be cautious about placing items where reaching over the stove could cause an accident. An ideal kitchen configuration is a semicircle with food and spices on one side of the stove and utensil and cooking accessories on the other. In group kitchens, spreading the kitchen out is safer. Locate the stove in a protected area so that people do not walk by and accidentally knock it over. Establish a food preparation area away from the stove. Organize pots and pans in another area. If several helpers are in the kitchen, spreading out allows more space to move around.

◆ After selecting your meal, put away food that may become mixed up with ingredients for the current meal.

◆ Use food tarps to keep food and utensils off the ground, but be cautious about placing hot pots on the sheets of plastic. Keep lighters and pot grips handy for managing the stove.

◆ Provide a place away from the kitchen but nearby where hands can be washed. Make sure to have an adequate water container with some soap. Be sure to practice Leave No Trace principles for cleaning such as being at least 200 feet (60 meters) from water when using soap.

◆ Fuel should be stored at least 20 to 30 feet away (6 to 9 meters) from the kitchen. White gas is volatile, and fumes can travel along the ground and possibly ignite. Keeping unused fuel out of the cooking area prevents this from happening. A location away from the kitchen may also be a good place to store group gear such as water containers, shovels, and so on.

◆ When with a large group, establish areas where the group as a whole will store food and equipment, put up tents, cook meals, and gather for meetings. This arrangement eliminates confusion and keeps expedition members from cooking in someone else's tent site.

Activity 3: Cooking the Meal (45 Minutes)

For this first lesson on cooking, be sure to cook something that is familiar and has straightforward directions. Macaroni and cheese is an easy first meal, is nutritious, and is tasty to most people. If several instructors are working with smaller cooking groups within the large group, this lesson can be orchestrated among all the groups at the same time; otherwise it is assumed that you are cooking with one large group.

You have several options to approach the first cooking. The first option might be an abbreviated demonstration of mac and cheese preparation followed by an instruction for students to make their own. The second option is to provide students with a descriptive recipe for preparation. Make yourself available for consultation as students create the meal on their own. Assisting students in the successful preparation of their first meal promotes confidence and the willingness to experiment with future meals.

◆ Begin this meal by boiling a pot of water. With pasta, having significantly more water than pasta in the pot is essential. When cooking in the outdoors, a common mistake is to add too much into the pot, often resulting in boil over. Be aware of this problem and try to choose the appropriate size pots for your meals. A basic rule to remember when cooking outdoors is that it is easier to add than to take out. In other words, water and other ingredients can always be added throughout the cooking process. If too much of anything is added in the beginning, taking it out can be problematic.

◆ After the water is boiling, add the macaroni. When doing this in the backcountry have your partner steady the pot using the pot grips or remove the pot entirely from the stove while pouring the macaroni noodles into the boiling water. Spilled water could cause serious injury, a late dinner, or wasted food.

◆ Begin cutting up cheese to add to your macaroni. Having items like cheese divided into an allotment for meals is a good idea. The smaller the pieces are, the more easily they will melt into the hot noodles.

◆ Premix 1/2 cup (120 milliliters) of powdered milk and water and let it set for a few minutes. Tip: Adding powdered milk to boiling water creates lumps; premixing alleviates this problem.

◆ After the noodles are done you will need to drain the water from them. This task is always tricky in the backcountry; the common method is to use the lid as a strainer. A bandana along with the pot grips is an essential tool and will help in the process. Hold the pot firmly with the pot grips and use the bandana to apply pressure on the lid. Then, while maintaining the pressure, pour excess water into mugs for warm drinks.

◆ Now that the noodles are drained, add the milk and butter and slowly drop in pieces of cheese while mixing the noodles and cheese together. After it is well mixed and cheesy, bon appétit.

◆ The starchy water from the noodles tastes best while warm.

◆ Encourage creativity with this meal to spice up the dish. Spices, dried vegetables, meats, sunflower seeds, nuts, and so forth can enhance the taste and nutritional value of this meal.

Closure Activity

Cleanup (30 Minutes)

Close this lesson with the cleanup process after a meal. Demonstrating cleanup practices is critical to preventing misinterpretation. Leave No Trace principles play an important role in the kitchen cleanup process. Have students clean up their meal together based on the following information.

Cleaning Pots and Pans

◆ When cooking and eating with a group of people, everyone should be aware of **cross-contamination** issues. The reality of being outside for days on end is that we are probably not as clean as we might be in the front country, so working extra hard at cleanliness is important.

◆ Pots and pans used for cooking are generally considered to belong to the whole group. So avoid eating directly from them because to keep the expedition healthy we do not want to spread our germs. This stricture includes trying and tasting food with personal utensils while cooking.

◆ Try to cook appropriate amounts of food so that food is not left over; excess food must be carried out or stored and eaten later, both of which can be difficult.

◆ After the pot is empty of food, it can be scraped clean using a spatula or spoon and the food debris can be placed in a trash bag to be carried out.

◆ If the pot is truly clean at this point, it can be stored until the next use of the stove, or you can boil water in the pot both to sterilize it and to have a warm evening drink.

◆ Pots can also be dry cleaned. **Dry cleaning** uses **natural cleaners** from the forest such as pine straw or dry, dead grass. These fibers can be used in a dry pot to help scrub the pot clean, but all of the fibers must be carried out as trash. Because we usually boil water in our backcountry meals, sterilization of the pots is usually taken care of, but with a skillet you must remember to sterilize it before using it again. Water is not used in this process because the water would be tainted with food debris, and because natural cleaners were used the water cannot be consumed so it would have to be disposed of properly. Dry cleaning reduces the amount of food waste left in the backcountry and helps keep our campsites free of nuisance animals. Cleaning materials that are contaminated with food must be packed out.

Cleaning Personal Eating Containers

◆ Scrape them clean with a spoon. Ideally the scrapings are eaten instead of carried out. Again, be sure to cook appropriate amounts of food.

◆ After the container is clean of food debris, pour clean water into it and drink down any remaining food particles. Hot water can help this process, especially when containers are greasy.

◆ Ideally, personal bowls and spoons are not dry cleaned because we can scrape them clean with our eating utensils. Remember not to eat out of group cook sets.

Follow-Up Activity

Cooking Opportunities (90 Minutes)

Students should have the opportunity to do some cooking while you observe. Although many students are familiar with cooking, cooking with camp stoves and with ingredients that they may not be familiar with can be a challenge. Provide enough time in the schedule to allow some creativity with the meals. For example, have students plan a potluck meal after several days of cooking. This fun, group activity allows students to be creative and show off their new culinary skills. Take some time to organize who will bring what meals and try to emphasize cooking a pleasing meal for the group.

ASSESSMENT

- Check that students have the ability to set up a well-organized kitchen by observing them during the kitchen organization activity.
- Verify that students know how to use a stove properly and show the proper storage of fuel by observing them practice stove lighting in a small group with your supervision.
- Confirm that students can prepare a simple backcountry meal such as macaroni and cheese by observing them do so in the main activities.
- Assess whether students appreciate a well-prepared backcountry meal by observing them during the group potluck dinner.

TEACHING CONSIDERATIONS

- Try to plan this lesson when students are not starving or fatigued. A natural progression is to teach backcountry cooking when it is time to eat dinner, but be sure that you have your group's focus.
- For this first lesson on cooking, cook something that is familiar and has fairly straightforward directions.
- If cooking with several small groups during this activity, try to spread everyone out so that they can safely move around their kitchen areas. For learning purposes, have participants cook in smaller groups to provide opportunity for individual, hands-on experience.
- Incorporate this lesson early on in the curriculum and allow students to have some control over their food selection for the trip.
- When mixing dried milk, add water slowly to the powder mix and stir rather than add powder to water. This technique will reduce lumps.

▷ **Equipment Selection**

OVERVIEW

This lesson divides equipment into two primary categories: personal equipment and group equipment. Issues surrounding personal and group equipment will be discussed in a backpacking context. Students will be taught to evaluate all equipment using five important criteria: durability, weight, serviceability, altitude, and weather (DWSAW).

JUSTIFICATION

Proper selection of equipment for each trip is an essential skill and sometimes takes place months in advance of the trip. The participants' safety and enjoyment as well as good environmental stewardship hinge on the proper selection and use of equipment.

GOAL

To develop students' ability to assess and select equipment for backpacking trips.

OBJECTIVES

At the end of this lesson, students will be able to

- evaluate personal equipment selections based on durability, weight, serviceability, altitude, and weather (cognitive);
- distinguish between different equipment for varying climates (cognitive);
- plan and create a group equipment list for an expedition (cognitive); and
- value the need to assess and select appropriate equipment as part of the planning process (affective).

EQUIPMENT AND AREAS NEEDED

- An assortment of group equipment (figure BP5.1 on page 65)
- An assortment of personal equipment (figure BP5.2 on page 68)

RISK MANAGEMENT CONSIDERATIONS

- If a program or you are providing equipment, be sure to provide equipment that works and fits properly. This goes a long way toward ensuring the comfort of the students.
- Check to make sure that all group equipment is functional before issuing it to the students.
- Always examine the first aid kit for completeness before taking it into the field.

LESSON CONTENT

Introduction

A well-informed backpacker evaluates equipment using a convenient, comprehensive system known as DWSAW. This system ensures that backpackers will have a comfortable, environmentally sound trip. The following provides a brief explanation of DWSAW.

D (Durable)

Each piece of equipment must be a quality product that will not break during use on a multiple-day backpacking trip. When buying equipment, investigate thoroughly before purchasing and buy quality field-serviceable products. A product getting all the hype may not be field worthy. Any equipment taken into the backcountry should be reliable and easily repaired. Almost all equipment takes a beating on a multiday trip, so the user must know that it will work or be repairable in the field. Not having durable equipment leads to the potential of harming the environment when something goes wrong. For instance, how will you cook if your stove stops working? The obvious answer is by fire, but the impact of a fire goes far beyond that of a stove. Backpacks should have heavy duty zippers that can withstand being overstuffed and zipped closed. In addition, double-stitched seams and appropriately sized buckles for load-bearing parts of the pack should be the norm.

W (Weight)

Weight is a key factor in equipment selection when carrying everything on your back. Everything need not be lightweight, but you must consider everything that you are carrying with you. Many backpackers obsess about weight, but in the long run having the proper equipment is safer and more environmentally responsible. Modern outdoor equipment can be both durable and lightweight. New fabrics and design techniques have allowed substantial weight savings. Never rule out a durable high-quality product for something lighter but less durable and untested.

S (Serviceable)

Take serviceable equipment into the field. Repairs and ongoing maintenance should be simple to do, require minimal time, and call for only simple tools. Backpacking stoves provide a prime example of equipment that should be field serviceable. Stoves should need only one tool to service in the field and have few parts to work with.

A (Altitude)

Altitude is a key factor in equipment selection. Certain stoves won't work well at high altitudes. The location of the tree line might affect whether you want a tent or a tarp. Tarps won't stand up to high winds as well as a tent will.

W (Weather)

Weather determines the type of equipment as well; backpack weights for temperate climates tend to be much lighter than those used in the desert or for winter travel. In desert environments backpackers need to carry a lot of extra water, and in winter the need for extra bulky layers and calories can make packs much heavier.

Main Activities

When working with a group of people, dividing equipment into two categories, group equipment and personal equipment, allows an even weight distribution among expedition members, provides a system of organization, and prevents the idea of ownership over certain pieces of equipment that the whole group uses.

Activity 1: Group Equipment Assessment (45 Minutes)

Using the DWSAW system of assessment and selection, have students evaluate group gear.

◆ Lay out group equipment in a large space for students to access. Include additional, less functional equipment in the pile so that students can learn to distinguish appropriate from inappropriate equipment. An old canvas tent, a large hammer, and a large 5-gallon (20-liter) plastic water jug are examples of less-than-ideal items for backpacking.

◆ Divide students into small groups and ask them to create their own equipment lists (see figure BP5.1). Make sure that they explain and qualify each piece of equipment using DWSAW.

◆ After they complete their lists, have students discuss them as a large group. Use the following information to assist with the discussion.

Group Equipment

◆ Stoves—Stoves should be field serviceable and work at the altitude where you will be backpacking. See lesson 4 for more detail on fuels and types of stoves. The best stoves are those that fit your cooking style. Most do a decent job of boiling water at low altitudes, but if you like to make meals that include baking or any level of low-heat cooking, look for a stove that will simmer.

◆ Cook sets—Field cleaning can be hard on pots and pans, so be sure to get durable surfaces that can be scrubbed and sometimes scraped clean such as aluminum or

Group Equipment List

Shelter

☐ Tents or tarps depending on locale

☐ If tarps, cord and ground cloth

☐ Stakes, including an extra set

☐ Extra cord for repairs and windy days

Kitchen

☐ Stove for every three to four people

☐ Pots and lids

☐ Frying pans

☐ Spatula

☐ Rubber scraper

☐ Cooking spoon

☐ Slotted cooking spoon

☐ Lighters

☐ Fuel bottles

☐ Toilet paper

☐ Sealable containers

☐ Food sacks for individual food storage

☐ Collapsible water bladders or bags

☐ Water purification (iodine, chlorine, or water filters)

Other Items

☐ First aid kit

☐ Repair kit

☐ Soap

☐ Expedition ropes

☐ Collapsible or foldable shovel

☐ Field guide (flora and fauna)

☐ Shovel or spade

FIGURE BP5.1 This sample group equipment list should be adapted for the trip context.

other metals that can withstand harsh abrasives. Cookware with antistick coating can be useful, but when you burn something onto the cookware, what will happen to the coating when you scrape it with your spoon or sand? Size is important, depending on how many people will be in a cooking group, and having at least two pots per cook group is a good idea. For one to four people, one 1.5-liter pot and another 2.5- to 3-liter pot is a good idea. For a larger group of six to eight people, go with at least a 2-liter pot and a 4-liter pot (Curtis, 1998). Generally, small-group cooking is more efficient because small backpacking stoves boil water and cook food faster using smaller amounts of fuel.

◆ Water purification—Recent research suggests that most backcountry waters are actually quite safe for consumption and that contamination usually occurs from hand-to-mouth contamination. The most effective means of maintaining your gastrointestinal health in the backcountry is hand washing (Welch, 2004). Nevertheless, consider these methods of purification:

– Iodine has been heavily used as a water treatment for more than 20 years. Although iodine was originally considered a safe and effective means of water treatment, new research has begun to cast some doubt on its effectiveness. Iodine is highly temperature dependent, and the time for the chemical process to take effect increases significantly in cold weather. Recently, cryptosporidium cysts have shown resilience to iodine, making the chemical somewhat ineffective as regular water treatment. Iodine is still recommended for short-term emergency treatment of water. Topical iodine uses eight drops, and betadine uses four drops. Follow manufacturer's suggestions for crystals and tablets (Dietz, 1999). People with an iodine allergy, thyroid problems, or who are pregnant should avoid using iodine as a water treatment.

– Chlorine and chlorine derivatives like iodine have shown little effectiveness against cryptosporidium cysts. Two drops of regular soap-free chlorine beach will treat a quart (liter) of water, but like iodine, chlorine is not recommended for long-term use. Stabilized chlorine dioxide (no active chlorine) has shown promise of late, but it cannot be purchased in all 50 states. Stabilized chlorine dioxide works by releasing oxygen into the water and killing bacteria. It is effective against cryptosporidium, but the treatment time is almost 45 minutes in cold water. It does not work in water colder than 32 degrees Fahrenheit (0 degrees Celsius) or warmer than 100 degrees Fahrenheit (38 degrees Celsius).

– Water filters are probably the most effective means of water purification on the market. Some products use only a filter, whereas others also provide a chemical (like iodine or chlorine) to help purify the water. Many products are on the market. You should understand what size of particles the filter will remove and use the appropriate one for the bacteria and cysts in the area that you use most commonly.

– Boiling is the most effective means of purification against bacteria and cysts, which do not survive in water temperatures above 120 degrees Fahrenheit (50 degrees Celsius). But because of the amount of fuel consumed and the time required, boiling is not the most efficient method. Of course, boiling does not remove any chemical that may be contaminating the water.

◆ Shovel or spade—A shovel can be heavy, but be sure to choose the right one for the job. For instance, in some areas the soil is so rocky that a small spade will not do the trick. Additionally, having a proper shovel will encourage good Leave No Trace technique.

◆ Tents or tarps—Programmatically, tarps are an affordable solution for shelter, and they encourage quality workmanship and creativity. Some environments are not conducive to tarps and other forms of shelter. For instance, as mosquito-borne illnesses become more common, concern for student's health may outweigh the lower cost of tarps. In an area that has had reports of West Nile virus and where many mosquitoes are present, consider taking tents instead. Obviously, in severe weather and high winds, heavy-duty four-season tents are required.

◆ First aid kit—The following list itemizes suggested contents. Depending on the nature of your group and the area in which you are traveling, you may want to add items to this generic list.

  – 10 pairs of gloves (latex unless group members have known allergies to latex; if so take Nitrile or other synthetic)
  – Two ACE bandages
  – 10 assorted band-aids
  – Two packages of moleskin
  – Eight gauze pads, 4 inches (10 centimeters) square
  – One roll of cloth sports tape (coaches' tape)
  – One small tube of Neosporin
  – One small tube of hydrocortisone cream
  – 10 alcohol prep pads
  – Aspirin or Tylenol
  – Ibuprofen
  – Benadryl
  – Tums
  – Epinephrine
  – One small bottle of hand sanitizer
  – One package of powdered Gatorade
  – A lighter or waterproof matches
  – Pencil or pen and a pad of paper

◆ Water storage containers—Having a stash of water in camp for cooking and cleaning is helpful. Collapsible water bags are lightweight, easily compacted, and can store large quantities of water. Having a large storage container reduces the number of trips to water sources, which saves time and energy and reduces impact on fragile stream and lake banks.

◆ Expedition rope—A length of rope is often handy. It can be used for tarp setup, for hanging a bear bag, as a hand line in steep terrain, and as a clothesline on a sunny day. Many types of rope will work for an expedition line such as a throw rope used in whitewater rescue or a retired climbing rope in a 50- to 75-foot (15- to 25-meter) length.

◆ Repair kit—The repair kit should include at least a roll of duct tape. Other essentials might be an extra pack buckle, a stove repair kit, a speedy stitcher for serious repairs, a length of 3- to 5-millimeter cord, and a few safety pins.

Activity 2: Personal Equipment Assessment (45 Minutes)

Have students evaluate personal equipment using the DWSAW system of assessment and selection (see figure BP5.2).

◆ Backpack—The comfort of a pack and amount that it will carry are two decisive factors in pack selection. The new lightweight backpacks now on the market are

Personal Equipment List

Sleeping

- ☐ Sleeping bag (synthetic fill)
- ☐ Sleeping pad

Clothing and Other Equipment

- ☐ Rain jacket
- ☐ Rain pants
- ☐ Camp shoes (tennis shoes, sandals)
- ☐ Light hiking boots*
- ☐ Wool socks
- ☐ Wool or polypropylene underwear (top and bottom)
- ☐ Pile or synthetic sweater
- ☐ Underwear
- ☐ Lightweight wool or fleece gloves
- ☐ Stocking cap
- ☐ Hat with a brim
- ☐ Pile, down, or fleece jacket
- ☐ Nylon shorts
- ☐ Several synthetic T-shirts

* Boots are one of the most important pieces of personal equipment. You should have a medium-weight boot with semiflexible Vibram-type lug soles and a leather or leather-and-fabric upper.

Hydration

- ☐ Two 1-quart (1-liter) water bottles or
- ☐ One 1-quart (1-liter) water bottle and a hydration bladder (at least 70 ounces, or 2 liters)

Bathroom and Other Essentials

- ☐ Sunglasses
- ☐ Eye care (contact wearers)
- ☐ Eyeglasses
- ☐ Sunscreen
- ☐ Lip balm
- ☐ Comb
- ☐ Toothbrush
- ☐ Toothpaste
- ☐ Feminine hygiene products
- ☐ Nail clippers
- ☐ Small mirror
- ☐ Insect repellent
- ☐ Small towel
- ☐ Hand lotion
- ☐ Biodegradable soap
- ☐ Flashlight or headlamp
- ☐ Extra batteries
- ☐ Bandannas
- ☐ Pocket knife
- ☐ Lighter
- ☐ Watch with alarm
- ☐ Water bottles
- ☐ Camera
- ☐ Gaiters

Kitchen

- ☐ Bowl (plastic)
- ☐ Spoon
- ☐ Cup (possibly a thermal mug, just something to drink out of besides your water bottle)

Backpack

- ☐ Large backpack to carry all your gear while trekking. The pack should be strong and durable and have enough capacity to carry all your equipment and food (at least 4,500 cubic inches, or 75 liters). Internal frame preferred.

FIGURE BP5.2   This sample personal equipment list should be adapted for the trip context.

phenomenal for solo trips or with a group of friends who have all bought into the idea. If you are going on an expedition with a group of people, be sure to have a pack large enough to carry your fair share of the equipment.

- For most expeditions beyond four days, you will need a pack over 5,000 cubic inches (80 liters). Supplement the big pack by taking lightweight clothing and equipment and remember that you don't have to fill it up.

- Fit is critical when selecting a pack. Be sure that the pack fits your torso length and that the waist belt has extra cinch room to accommodate the slimmer you that may result after days on the trail. At a minimum, a good pack should have a well-padded hip belt with load adjustment straps and padded shoulder straps with load adjustment straps.

- Two common types of backpacks are available. Internal frame packs are the more commonly used packs on backpacking trips today. An internal frame pack allows more compact packing and tends to mold to your body more. It is an ideal pack for off-trail use and any kind of technical terrain. The design keeps the pack close to the body and allows the pack to move in a predictable fashion. An external frame pack has the frame outside the pack and tends to set the weight of the pack off the body. This design allows air to circulate behind the back to keep the hiker cooler. In recent years several companies have made internal–external hybrids, but they haven't gained popularity.

◆ Sleeping system—Sleeping bags and pads come in many varieties. Weather tends to dictate what works best. Mummy bags (sleeping bags with a hood) are the typical choice for backpackers because it is easier to keep warm in a bag that covers the head and provides a tighter fit. The designs vary widely, but typically mummy bags have a neck baffle, a baffle that runs the length of the zipper, and a hood that can be cinched down. A bag without a hood may work well in warm weather.

- The two standard types of fill, or insulation, are synthetic and down. Synthetic bags are ideally suited for a climate that gets lots of rain; they will dry relatively quickly and will continue to keep you warm, though not comfortable, while damp. A down bag, although light and incredibly warm, will not insulate after being saturated.

- The two distinct styles of sleeping pads are foam pads and inflatable pads, although some variation is found within each category. Foam pads have long been an easy choice for backpackers based on weight, durability, and cost. Foam pads vary in length and type of cover. Inflatable pads usually use some kind of foam or insulation inside the pad that also inflates with air. Several are self-inflatable. Typically, inflatable pads weigh more than the average foam pad but are generally more comfortable. If you choose an inflatable pad, be sure to have a repair kit for the occasional flat.

- Bivy sacks are a popular, lightweight addition among those who are sleeping under tarps or traveling ultralight. A bivy sack is typically made of a breathable, lightweight shell that basically covers the sleeper and the sleeping bag. The basic bivy has many variations, and although some offer a little more space than others, they typically aren't considered roomy.

◆ Clothing—Discussed in detail in lesson 6.

◆ Bowl, mug, and spoon—A bowl with a lid is especially useful for saving leftovers, and the lid keeps your bowl clean while it is in your pack.

◆ Hydration system—Hydration systems are far more efficient at keeping backpackers hydrated than water bottles are. Many backpacks now feature special pockets for hydration systems. If you are going to use a hydration system specifically for backpacking, be sure that the tube is long enough to extend from a loaded pack over your shoulders and to your mouth. A shutoff valve is also useful because the excess pressure on the water bladder from a loaded pack can sometimes cause it to leak.

◆ Bathroom and other essentials—Although this category is personal, students need to be taught to carry only the essentials. Overpacking in this area is easy. Perfumed shampoos, deodorants, makeup, and so on are not functional in the backcountry. Biodegradable soap, a toothbrush and toothpaste, a small brush or comb, bug repellent, sunscreen, and necessary hygiene products form the outdoor bathroom kit.

Closure Activity

Creating an Appropriate Personal Equipment List (45 Minutes)

Have students design their personal equipment lists for varying climates. Use DWSAW to evaluate the equipment that they place on their lists. Remember that there are no hard and fast rules and that in the end there is a lot to be said for being comfortable in the backcountry. This exercise forces students to think about their own equipment needs and look critically at each item. You could provide an example of a generic equipment list for comparison and class discussion.

Follow-Up Activity

Evaluating Equipment (10 Minutes to Present; Continued Throughout a Trip)

Students should use their journals for ongoing reviews of their equipment choices. Set up a system whereby students evaluate their equipment throughout the trip in their journals on an actual trip. Major questions should include the following:

◆ What do you have with you that you could have done without?
◆ What pieces of equipment are invaluable?
◆ What would you like to have with you that you didn't bring?
◆ What would you leave behind?

Through this evaluation process, students will learn what equipment to add and what they may want to leave behind next time. At the end of a trip have the students summarize items that they wanted during the trip, items that they could have left behind, and any other lessons about equipment. They can present these conclusions to their group for discussion.

ASSESSMENT

◆ Check that students can evaluate personal equipment selections based on durability, weight, serviceability, altitude, and weather by observing them throughout the course.
◆ Confirm that students can distinguish between different equipment needs for varying climates by reviewing the personal equipment lists for various climates that they developed in the closure activity.
◆ Verify that students can create a group equipment list for an expedition by reviewing the lists that they completed in the main activity.

◆ Assess whether students value the need to assess and select appropriate equipment as part of the planning process and evaluate their choices at the end of the trip by observing their performance.

TEACHING CONSIDERATIONS

◆ This lesson on equipment can be taught at any time. The best time may be weeks before a group expedition, not in route to the field.

◆ Be a role model with equipment and freely share personal choices with the students.

◆ Allow for different philosophies on equipment as long as they meet the risk management considerations of your course.

◆ Praise good equipment selection within your group to fine-tune the students' understanding.

UNIT 1, LESSON 6

▷ Clothing Systems

OVERVIEW

Staying comfortable in the backcountry is a formidable challenge for an ill-prepared backpacker. In this lesson students learn how to prepare adequate clothing lists for their expeditions, choose essential fabrics for their layering systems, and use the basic ideas of thermal regulation. The information in this lesson forms the foundational knowledge and builds the skills necessary to be safe and comfortable when participating in all outdoor pursuits.

JUSTIFICATION

Seldom can we count on the weather in any location to provide us with the necessary temperatures to stay comfortable throughout a multiday backcountry trip. Our clothing is critical to our well-being and to the safety of all group members. Clothing should be viewed as an investment in both comfort and safety.

GOAL

To develop students' ability to select a proper clothing system for a specific environment when backpacking.

OBJECTIVES

At the end of this lesson, students will be able to

◆ describe the properties of fabrics needed for different environments (cognitive),

◆ demonstrate an understanding of thermal regulation in backcountry environments (cognitive),

◆ distinguish between different fabrics and clothing equipment (cognitive),

◆ react to changing weather by altering and adapting a personal clothing system (psychomotor), and

◆ consistently select a functional clothing system while appreciating the characteristics of functional fabrics (affective).

EQUIPMENT AND AREAS NEEDED

- Lightweight, medium-weight, and heavyweight long underwear
- Liner, hiking, and expedition socks
- Ball cap, beanie, balaclava, neck gaiter
- Synthetic T-shirt
- Nylon shorts
- Nylon, soft-shell, or wool pants
- Fleece, wool, or soft-shell sweater
- Down or synthetic-fill jacket
- Waterproof jacket and pants
- Sleeping bag and pad
- Gloves, mittens, and liners
- Cotton T-shirt
- Sandals, hiking shoes, and hiking boots
- Water source or a bucket of water
- Pair of blue jeans and heavy cotton sweatshirt
- Personal clothing checklist (figure BP6.1)

RISK MANAGEMENT CONSIDERATIONS

- If you are teaching in the outdoors, be sure that the teaching area is clear of any hazards such as bees, dead tree limbs, and so on.
- Be aware of local weather patterns and be prepared for inclement weather.
- Have the students demonstrate their layering systems by laying out their clothes; this exercise ensures that they have the proper equipment before leaving on a trip.
- If heading out into the backcountry, have extra items available in case someone is missing an important item.

LESSON CONTENT

Introduction

Proper clothing selection before and during a backcountry outing provides proper thermoregulation and an enjoyable experience in the outdoors. **Thermoregulation**, or *thermal regulation,* is the process of maintaining a constant body temperature independent from the outside environment through layering of clothing, caloric intake, and activity. Demonstrating a proper clothing system while stressing the concepts of layering and specialized fabrics is extremely important. Use the **five Ws of clothing selection** (warm, wicking, weight, windproof, and waterproof) to begin conversations about appropriate clothing. Provide the concept of **CCORE** (convection, conduction, outdoors, radiation, and evaporation) to emphasize the importance of thermoregulation. Use the following information to prepare for the main activities.

The Five Ws

◆ **Warm**—The clothing is made of a material that can help keep you warm in a variety of environments and weather.

◆ **Wicking**—The clothing is able to move moisture away from your body to aid in maintaining warmth and dryness. Clothing that has these qualities is said to be **hydrophobic**, or fearing water, moving moisture away from the body so that it can dry off on the outer layer of the fabric.

◆ **Weight**—Some items do a great job of insulating, but they are extremely heavy. What clothing can you take that is both lightweight and warm?

◆ **Windproof**—To prevent convection, clothing must help prevent wind from blowing away heat produced by the body.

◆ **Waterproof**—Although many high-tech fabrics help us stay warm even when wet, once you are wet you always face an uphill battle to stay warm. A waterproof shell top and bottom are essential.

CCORE

◆ **Convection**—The transfer of heat from the body to the air that surrounds it is called convection. Air temperature combined with wind creates the ideal condition for the loss of body heat through convection. Prevent convective heat loss by adding layers consistent with the atmospheric conditions (a sweater for a cold, calm, sunny day; a sweater and a windproof jacket for the same day with wind).

◆ **Conduction**—The loss of body heat to a cooler surface like a rock or wet clothes is known as conduction. Minimize conduction of body heat by insulating between the body and the surface that is robbing the body of heat.

◆ **Outdoors**—In the context of CCORE, these principles and clothing systems are mostly used to regulate the body's temperature in the outdoors. In contrast, when we are inside in a climate-controlled environment we can wear fabrics like cotton that are comfortable in that environment.

◆ **Radiation**—Radiation is the passing of heat between two objects, like the warmth that passes from a campfire or the sun to the body. The body also loses heat through radiant heat loss. This loss is best prevented by providing insulating layers or using some kind of reflective layer that turns heat flow back to the body.

◆ **Evaporation**—The process in which body moisture during exertion is transformed into a vapor is called evaporation. This process requires energy and thus heat from the body. Wearing layers that wick (move moisture away from the skin) are key to minimizing evaporative heat loss. In warm weather, evaporation is the process by which the body cools itself.

Main Activities

Activity 1: Wet T-Shirts (15 Minutes)

The purpose of this activity is to introduce the idea of CCORE and the five Ws in evaluating clothing systems. Start by having the students imagine that they are in a rainstorm wearing a cotton T-shirt first and then a synthetic T-shirt. Discuss what each might feel like. Then do the following:

- Submerge a cotton T-shirt and a synthetic T-shirt into water and wring them out.
- Pass the T-shirts around to the participants and ask them which they would prefer to be wearing if they were wet.
- Explain convection, conduction, outdoor, radiation, and evaporation in terms of these two T-shirts.

Cotton T-shirts are invaluable for absorbing and holding moisture next to the body. When the body experiences cold temperatures, wearing a fabric that has these properties makes the process of staying warm extremely difficult. When wet, cotton conducts heat from the body to the shirt. Add wind to the equation, and convection significantly compounds the heat-loss problem. In addition, the insulating properties of wet cotton are nil, so the body is also losing heat through radiation. Evaluation with the five Ws reveals that cotton is not warm when wet, cannot wick moisture away from the skin, is very heavy once wet, and is neither windproof nor waterproof.

Wool and synthetic fabrics wick moisture away from the body and dissipate it on the outside of the fabric. The result is a fabric that is warm when wet, dries quickly, and is far more comfortable in heat-challenging environments. Because moisture moves to the outside of the fabric, convection helps dry the fabric quicker, and the conduction of heat from the inside aids in the process. Wool and synthetic fabrics hold in heat, allow less radiant heat loss, and reduce the effect of evaporation because the fabric continues to move moisture to the outside of the material. Synthetic and wool fabrics evaluate well with the five Ws: They are warm, wick moisture from the skin, are lightweight, and, depending on the weave and treatment, can be windproof and waterproof. Wool tends to weigh more than synthetic fabrics, especially when wet.

Activity 2: Introduction to Layering (25 Minutes)

Use this activity to teach the concept and importance of layering when choosing a clothing system.

- First, lay an entire clothing system in a pile for easy access. See figure BP6.1 for a three-season clothing list.
- Discuss a temperature baseline with the students. For example, a particular layering system may work well for temperatures down to 20 degrees Fahrenheit (−6 degrees Celsius).
- Have students select appropriate layers for a trip by designating a specific time of year. Concentrate on teaching principles rather than having a set list. Ideally, you would discuss the conditions that students will face on their first class trip.
- Start by laying down a sleeping pad and asking the participants to evaluate it using CCORE and the five Ws.
- Next is the sleeping bag, which lies on top of the sleeping pad. The sleeping system is the most important layer of the day, because the bag is the final place of comfort if everything else has gone wrong.
- Starting with thermal underwear, participants should build consecutive layers of clothing until they reach the outside waterproof and windproof shell, evaluating each layer in terms of CCORE and the five Ws.
- If clothing is not available, consider using figures BP6.2 and BP6.3 as an alternative activity to test students' ability to identify the components of each layer. Note that this activity includes additional clothing suitable for four-season use. Have

Personal Clothing List

Sleeping

- ☐ Sleeping bag (synthetic fill)
- ☐ Sleeping pad

Clothing and Other Equipment

- ☐ Rain jacket
- ☐ Rain pants
- ☐ Camp shoes (tennis shoes, sandals)
- ☐ Light hiking boots*
- ☐ Wool socks (at least two pair)
- ☐ Lightweight wool or polypropylene underwear (top and bottom)
- ☐ Medium-weight wool or polypropylene underwear (top and bottom)
- ☐ Nylon pants, like a stretch Cordura nylon or Schoeller fabric

- ☐ Nylon swimming or running shorts
- ☐ Fleece or soft shell synthetic sweater
- ☐ Fleece or soft shell synthetic pants
- ☐ Underwear
- ☐ Lightweight wool or fleece gloves
- ☐ Two stocking caps
- ☐ Hat with a brim
- ☐ Synthetic fill, down, or fleece jacket
- ☐ Nylon shorts
- ☐ Several synthetic T-shirts
- ☐ Gaiters

*Boots are one of the most important pieces of personal equipment. You should have a medium-weight boot with semiflexible Vibram-type lug soles and a leather or leather-and-fabric upper.

FIGURE BP6.1   A sample three-season clothing list.

the students attempt to fill in the blanks using figure BP6.3 first before referring to figure BP6.2 for the answers. Students should be able to not only identify each piece of clothing but also articulate the material makeup such as wool, cotton, and so on.

- Be sure to include in the pile a comfortable pair of blue jeans and a cotton sweatshirt. Of course, these items will not end up in the system. Use these items to discuss personal preferences and old habits to accentuate the functionality of a safe, comfortable outdoor clothing system. You can take this discussion further by emphasizing that improperly clothed backpackers may make decisions that have serious effects on the environment. For example, the properly dressed hiker will hike an additional 30 minutes rather than stop at an inappropriate campsite to warm up quicker.
- Discuss resources for finding information about a particular area and when this activity should occur in the process of planning a trip. The following are examples of where to search for this information: national park information pages, national forest service regional pages, Internet resources, and phone calls to local land managers.

Activity 3: Fitting Hiking Boots (10 Minutes)

Use the following tips to teach the skill of proper boot fitting using a lecture and demonstration method.

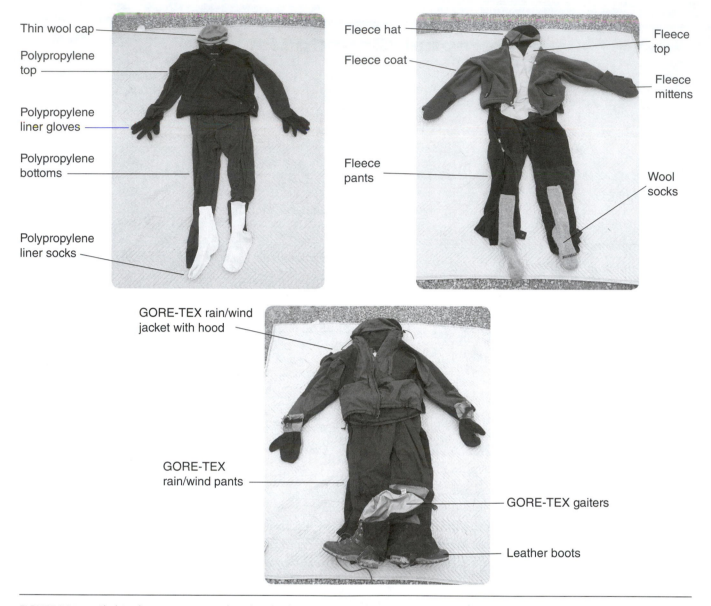

FIGURE BP6.2　Clothing layering sequence that identifies layers, items, and material makeup.

- ◆ The best approach is to go to a store and get fitted for a pair of boots. Mail ordering is handy, but the chances of getting a good fit, especially for your first pair, are low.

- ◆ A correct fit involves more than length and width. Those aspects of fit are important, of course, but you also need to evaluate the heel and toe boxes built into the boot. If the boot allows your heel to slip when on an incline, you will soon develop a blister. The same concern applies to the toe box—any side-to-side movement will cause a blister.

- ◆ Styles of boots range from all-leather hikers to nylon and hybrid combinations. The last is important in these boots; it is inside the sole of the boot and gives structure to the sole. The running-shoe-like boots are comfortable, but unless stated otherwise, they are usually made for someone who has a neutral foot position. A person with a neutral foot pattern hits dead center on the heel and rolls off the middle part of the foot when walking. People who overpronate strike on

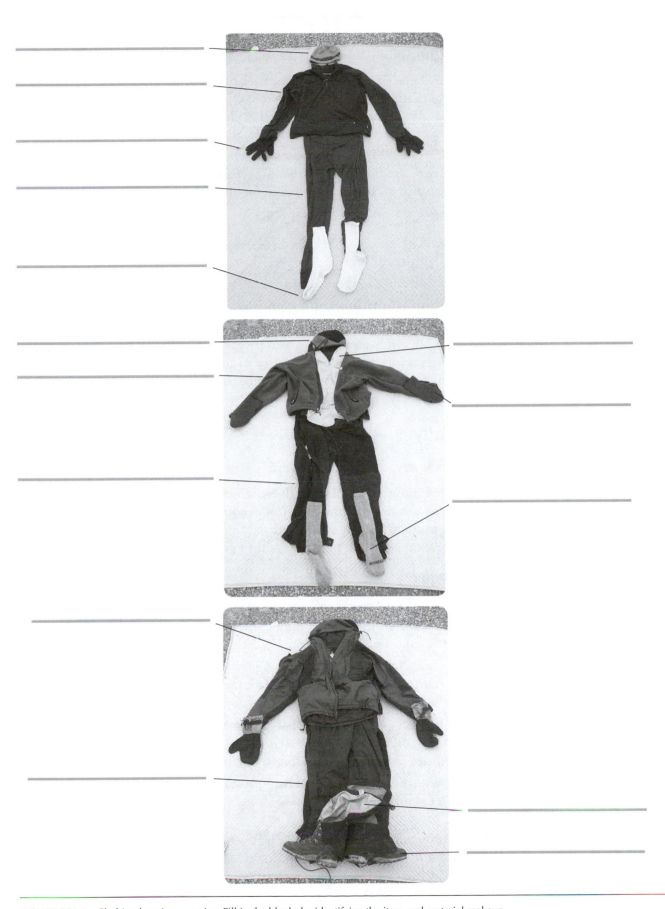

FIGURE BP6.3 Clothing layering exercise: Fill in the blanks by identifying the item and material makeup.

From M. Wagstaff and A. Attarian, 2009, *Technical skills for adventure programming: A curriculum guide* (Champaign, IL: Human Kinetics).

the outside of the heel and roll the foot to the big toe. These people need a boot with a firm last to give support to the movement of the foot.

- Socks and foot beds (orthotic inserts) play an important role in boot sizing as well. If you are planning to use a foot bed, be sure to size the boots with the foot bed. Several manufacturers are now selling do-it-yourself moldable foot beds. Similarly, with socks, be sure to size the boots with the socks that you plan to wear when backpacking.

- The time of the day when you size boots is also important. Ideally, you should size boots at the end of the day when your feet have had a chance to enlarge from a day of walking.

Closure Activity

Checking Layers (45 Minutes)

If beginning a trip or preplanning and if the participants have their clothing available, have them mimic your example of a proper layering system. Have the students spread out into a big circle so that they can display their layers and explain them. This activity offers an excellent opportunity to touch base with each participant and visually inspect his or her layers. At the beginning of a trip this activity is an important part of the risk management plan.

Follow-Up Activity

Testing Knowledge of Layering (60 Minutes)

Break the students into pairs and have them select a trip from a preselected list of destinations whose environmental conditions require various kinds of layering systems. Have them prepare a clothing list with explanations based on their destination and the time of year when they plan to travel there.

ASSESSMENT

- Check that students can describe the appropriate fabrics and the properties needed for different environments by observing them engage in the clothing assignment described in the follow-up activity.

- Verify that students understand thermal regulation in backcountry environments by observing them practice using an appropriate clothing system and make adjustments to maintain comfort while in the backcountry.

- Confirm that students can distinguish between different fabrics and clothing equipment by observing them sort through a clothing system and correctly identify the appropriate fabrics for the expedition as described in the closure activity.

- Check that students can react to changing weather conditions through altering and adapting a personal clothing system by observing them while on a backpacking trip.

- Verify that students can consistently select a functional clothing system while appreciating the characteristics of functional fabrics and demonstrating them to peers during outings.

TEACHING CONSIDERATIONS

◆ This lesson may be best taught in stages. First, explain the five Ws and the CCORE. Next, build a layering system to develop foundational knowledge. Students can then understand it conceptually and then move into hands-on experience to demonstrate their knowledge and their layering systems.

◆ Evaluate students throughout the course based on clothing selection, especially if you are teaching this course predominantly outside.

◆ Do not forget to discuss the base layer in detail. Novice backpackers often wear their favorite cotton underwear out of habit and fail to apply knowledge learned in this lesson.

◆ When teaching layering, add at least one extra layer that you might not normally take on the trip. This option gives the students a range in which to make a decision and allows someone who might be cold on the trip to have that extra layer.

◆ When researching weather in potential trip areas, be sure to find the historical highs and lows. Use these statistics to discuss an appropriate clothing system for the worst-case scenario.

UNIT 1, LESSON 7

▷ Pack Packing

OVERVIEW

Many diverse ideas surround the skill of packing and fitting a pack. In this lesson students learn the basic philosophy and principles of packing and fitting a well-balanced and comfortable backpack.

JUSTIFICATION

A correctly packed and fitted pack ensures a safer, more comfortable, and more enjoyable hike in the backcountry.

GOAL

To ensure that participants can pack and fit a pack so that it is comfortable and balanced for a day of backpacking.

OBJECTIVES

At the end of this lesson, students will be able to

◆ describe the areas of the pack where specific equipment might be packed (cognitive),

◆ demonstrate how to pack a backpack correctly and locate items within it (psychomotor),

◆ be able to fit and adjust a backpack to achieve a balanced and comfortable fit on oneself as well as others (psychomotor), and

◆ appreciate the comfort of a well-balanced pack and the ease of use by knowing where everything is located in the pack (affective).

EQUIPMENT AND AREAS NEEDED

- Internal frame backpack
- Sleeping bag
- Sleeping pad
- Stuff sacks
- Clothing, including footwear
- Cooking equipment
- Tent
- Pink flamingo (a crazy, funny object to accentuate the philosophy of carrying only the essentials and to help the students discover the flamingo-like items that they pack)

RISK MANAGEMENT CONSIDERATIONS

- A correctly loaded pack will help the student maintain balance while wearing the pack on difficult trails.
- Be wary of participants who may overload their packs. Weight is an issue. An excessively heavy pack may cause damage to the musculoskeletal system.
- Warn of skin abrasions that can occur with some types of material while the participant is stuffing her or his backpack.
- Be aware of outdoor conditions if teaching this topic outside.
- Check to make sure that each participant's pack is the correct fit for his or her body and that all straps and zippers are in working order.
- Warn students not to try lifting their full packs until you show them how to do it properly.
- Demonstrate a variety of methods for correctly getting a pack on the back.

LESSON CONTENT

Introduction

A well-packed pack should appear neat and contained. Generally, avoid having equipment and gear hanging or dangling off the sides or back of the pack. If something needs to be outside the pack, it should be durable and strapped securely. This lesson identifies appropriate equipment placement, weight distribution, and the concept of having a system of packing. The backpack is divided into four main compartments, identified as the lumbar, torso, shoulder, and brain. See figure BP7.1 for an example of a backpack with the four compartments identified.

Main Activities

Activity 1: Geography of a Backpack (30 Minutes)

This lecture and demonstration is designed to teach the specifics of packing a pack.

- Some items in the pack need to be kept dry. Which items need that treatment? An excellent example is the sleeping bag. This vital piece of equipment definitely needs some kind of waterproof encasement. Several companies now make

Important Terms

brain—The upper compartment, usually detachable from the main body of the pack. This is where you place things that you need to keep your own brain feeling good—extra hat, sunscreen, lip balm, any medications that you might need throughout the day, cup, bowl, spoon, toilet kit, and so on.

compression sack—A stuff sack that has several straps that can be used to compress the contents of the bag. The best ones compress the bulk vertically along the seams of the bag rather than horizontally.

external pockets—External pockets found on some packs that can hold miscellaneous equipment. Pockets are a perfect place for fuel bottles, which are ideally carried below and separate from food items. These pockets can also hold items that would go in the brain as well as additional layers and anything that you might need to access throughout the day.

lumbar—The very bottom part of the backpack. This part of the pack is directly connected to the hip belt.

shoulder—The upper section of the main compartment, closest to your shoulders. This part of your pack is reserved for items that you will probably use throughout the day, such as an extra layer, lunch, water, and perhaps a book or journal.

torso—The part of the pack where you carry most of the weight—tents, food, and other bulky or weighty items.

FIGURE BP7.1   The four main backpack compartments.

lightweight and durable waterproof stuff sacks, but a cheaper solution is a contractor's trash bag available from a building-supply store. These bags are more durable than everyday trash bags, at least 3 millimeters thick, and will stand up to lots of abuse. Lining your pack with a contractor's bag is an inexpensive way to keep the contents dry.

◆ Establish several piles of equipment and clothing and divide them according to function, when they will be used most, and their weight, size, and shape. (One pile might contain items used exclusively in camp, like a sleeping bag, camp clothes, tent, and cookware.)

◆ Starting with the lumbar, identify the items that best fit in each space. The lumbar area of an internal frame pack needs to be completely full. There should be no divots left in the pack because these spaces lead to poor weight distribution. If you are using the contractor bag method of waterproofing, be sure that it is in place before starting. The sleeping bag goes in immediately after the contractor's bag. Sleeping bags can be bulky, so use a compression sack to squeeze the bag into a smaller form. Use other items to fill in any voids left by the sleeping bag; ideally, you will not need these items during the day, such as layers that you wear in camp. Because the sleeping bag is the most important layer, place no liquid inside the waterproofing.

◆ The lumbar region should be packed tightly with most of the bulky items, including your sleeping bag, sleeping pad, clothes, and other items that must stay dry but take up a lot of space. This region of the pack is the base for the heavyweight items that you will pack in the torso region of your backpack.

◆ The torso area of your backpack is where most of the heavy items need to go. Food will be stored at this level, and possibly your water bladder as well. This is also a good place for pots and pans, cooking utensils, and tent. Many people like to waterproof their food separately depending on how it was packed. Obviously, a wet tent should be outside the waterproof layer that protects your sleeping bag and camp clothes.

◆ Because you will carry the bulk of the weight in the torso of your pack, you should consider a couple of points about the distribution of weight. Place the heaviest items in the center of the pack and toward the back so that the weight is over the hips of your body. Placing the weight too far from the lower back will pull the pack back and onto your shoulders, decreasing overall comfort. Centering the weight keeps the pack from putting excessive pressure on either side and spreads the load over the waist belt.

◆ The shoulder area will contain items that you need to access throughout the day. Some of these items are large and cannot fit into any of the external pockets. Lunch can live up there as well as rain gear and an extra layer. Other items for the top are the first aid kit, water filter, tent fly if the weather is threatening (to cover yourself for lunch or during a bad storm), and anything else that might be useful throughout the day.

◆ Most of the items placed in the shoulder area of the pack should not be heavy. To keep your pack balanced from top to bottom, these items should be relatively light.

◆ The brain of your pack holds items that are important to your health—medications, extra hat for warmth or sun protection, sunscreen, energy drink mix, camera, headlamp, batteries, bug net, toilet kit, and so on. Divide these items into small stuff sacks that are easy to identify. Don't forget to put rain gear in an accessible place—

accessible enough that if you were to throw your pack on the ground for a lightning drill, you could pull out your rain gear with ease while sitting on your pack.

♦ External pockets hold everything else that you might need during the day such as water bottles and field guides. External pockets are also a good place to store stoves and fuel so that they do not contaminate any food in the main compartment of your pack.

Activity 2: Packing the Pack (30 Minutes)

Now that students have basic packing information, have them pack their own packs. Packing a pack is a personal exercise in organization. Therefore, participants on group expeditions generally become comfortable carrying the same items each day.

♦ Divide your group into several smaller groups to facilitate the division of equipment. If you are using cook groups during your expedition, they provide a natural division method. Each group will have a full kitchen, a tent, fuel, and so on.

♦ Have students pack their packs one level at a time (first, the lumbar; second, the torso; and so on), sharing information with each other about where various items are best suited in the pack. If possible, include several levels of experience within each group to help generate conversation about packing techniques.

♦ Emphasize that creating a system is important. If students habitually put items in the same place each time, several advantages will surface. Packing becomes easy and speedy. Students can locate items at a moment's notice, or even in the dark!

♦ After packs are packed, have students partner up and critique each other's work. Challenge them to find voids that need to be filled. Judge the neatness and accessibility of critical items. Encourage them to discuss problems and issues.

Closure Activities

Activity 1: Lifting a Backpack (Eight Minutes)

Discuss and demonstrate how to lift a backpack to ensure the development of good habits. Using the correct technique to lift and lower a heavy backpack reduces injuries and wear and tear on the pack itself. Demonstrate the following three methods using students as models:

♦ Partner system—The simplest method for putting on a pack is to have a partner help the student lift and slip into the pack. Proper lifting techniques should be used. Students should be sure to lift the pack with the legs, not the back.

♦ Pairs or groups:
  – One or two group members lift the pack.
  – After the pack has been lifted to the correct height, the student simply slips into the pack.

♦ Solo:
  – In the solo method, the participant needs to make a bench with the leg on the harness side of the pack.
  – Then, while holding the haul loop, the student pulls the pack up to the top of the thigh, the bench.
  – At this point, the student simply slides one arm into the pack and moves it onto her or his back, sliding the other arm into the harness.

Activity 2: Fitting a Backpack (15 Minutes)

Fitting a pack is as easy as A, B, C, D.

Step A Begin by gently loosening all the straps on the harness of the backpack. In addition, the staves may need to be adjusted. The staves are found inside the pack and generally must be adjusted when the pack is not completely loaded. They should be in the proper place for the pack and located equally on both sides. Many packs have aluminum staves that are moldable to an individual's body shape. Some newer packs have molded back panels that are not adjustable, although they tend to be removable, so making sure that they are in the proper place is important. To mold aluminum staves, you must fit the pack empty and go through the following adjustments, by overtightening the tension and fitting the pack to your torso. Fasten the waist belt of the pack, and then tighten the waist belt of the pack until it is very snug. For parts of the pack, see figure BP7.1.

Step B The load adjustment straps are located on the backside of the waist belt and are attached to the main pack body. Pull these straps forward and slightly up. The pack should move into your lumbar region.

Step C Adjust the shoulder straps. Pull the shoulder straps downward to your waist so that the straps are snug on your shoulders but not tight. On many packs the shoulder straps can be moved up or down to gain the best position for the straps. The correct height of the shoulder straps allows for the D straps to be located several inches (centimeters) above the top of the shoulders.

Step D The upper load adjustment straps attach from the top of the shoulder straps to the main pack body under the brain. These straps pull the bulk of the weight over your waist belt. Pull these straps straight out in front of you at about the same height as your nose. The shoulder straps should feel slightly loose when the upper load straps are adjusted properly.

Follow-Up Activity

Making Adjustments (Time as Needed)

Give students time right before the hike begins to make adjustments. After hiking for some distance on the first day, take a break and provide another opportunity to make adjustments. Sometimes, students have to walk for a while with the weighted pack before determining the best adjustments.

◆ Allow participants to show off their well-packed and balanced backpacks to the group. Encourage students to name their packs, to give their packs identity, and to use those identities to explain the personalities of their packs. For instance, Bob, the original beast of burden, is a backpack that narrows as it reaches the top, so if dense and heavy items are packed high, the pack is unusually top heavy and unbalanced.

◆ Encourage students to help each other adjust their backpacks to the proper fit.

ASSESSMENT

◆ Check that students can describe areas of the pack where they might pack specific equipment through the partner critique described in the pack packing activity.

◆ Verify that students can pack a backpack correctly and be able to locate items within it by making note of days when they could have packed the pack differently and where they might have better placed those items.

◆ Confirm that students are able to fit and adjust a backpack to achieve a balanced and comfortable fit on themselves as well as others by observing them demonstrate a properly fitted pack and assist others with their fit.

◆ Assess whether students appreciate the comfort and ease of use of a well-balanced, organized pack by observing whether they improve their packing skills as a trip progresses.

TEACHING CONSIDERATIONS

◆ When teaching backpacking, you should follow a logical sequence of events for the participants. You would not want to teach packing a backpack before the students understand what gear they need to have.

◆ Be sure to use participants who have had previous experience backpacking during small-group breakouts. Participants are more likely to succeed when they hear varied ideas about where to pack things.

◆ Consider providing equipment so that all participants have the same experience with this lesson.

◆ Although this lesson used internal frame packs as the context for teaching packing and fitting, the same principles apply to external frame packs. Modern external frame packs are well padded, have the same features, and provide more opportunity to secure items outside the main compartment and to the frame.

UNIT 1, LESSON 8

▷ Health and Sanitation

OVERVIEW

Poor sanitation and hygiene practices can have a negative effect on the health of backpackers. This lesson provides introductory information on how to maintain health through appropriate sanitation and hygiene practices including hand washing, bathing, brushing teeth, sterilizing and cleaning dishes and cookware, treating water, and toileting.

JUSTIFICATION

Enjoyment is one of the main reasons that people backpack and spend time in the outdoors. If people do not follow appropriate sanitation principles, the effects could lead to illness, either while in the outdoors or shortly after returning. Proper hygiene while backpacking is vital to maintaining a healthy, happy group of participants. Many outdoor horror stories stemmed from inadequate sanitation or hygiene.

GOAL

To develop participants' ability to maintain optimal health by using appropriate sanitation and hygiene practices.

OBJECTIVES

At the end of this lesson, students will be able to

◆ explain how one person with poor hygiene practices can affect the health of the entire group (cognitive),

◆ describe the importance of hand washing in the backcountry (cognitive),

◆ describe appropriate toileting techniques in the backcountry (cognitive),

◆ demonstrate appropriate methods of disposing of waste such as dishwater and toothpaste (psychomotor),

◆ demonstrate how to sterilize dishes before cooking and how to clean dishes after cooking (psychomotor),

◆ appreciate the importance of bathing for health and social reasons (affective), and

◆ appreciate the need to treat water (affective).

EQUIPMENT AND AREAS NEEDED

◆ Lotion in squirt bottle

◆ Food coloring

◆ Bag of trail mix

◆ Liquid soap in a small plastic container

◆ Nailbrush

◆ Water

◆ Water bladder

◆ Washcloth or bandanna

◆ Large cooking pots

◆ Baking soda

◆ Salt

◆ Toothpaste

◆ Pots and pans

◆ Eating utensils

◆ Dishes

◆ Examples of strainers

◆ Chlorine—liquid drops or bleach

◆ Iodine—tablets, crystals, or liquid

◆ Water filters

◆ Ionization or ultraviolet light device

◆ Trowels

◆ Toilet paper

◆ Natural toilet paper (leaves, smooth sticks, or rocks)

RISK MANAGEMENT CONSIDERATIONS

◆ Be aware of the risk of burns from boiling water and hot pots and pans.

◆ Keep participants away from water spills and the resultant slippery surfaces.

◆ Chlorine and iodine can be toxic in large doses. More is not better.

◆ People with thyroid problems or shellfish allergies should consult a doctor before using iodine.

◆ Fluoride toothpaste should not be swallowed.

◆ If teaching in the outdoors, be sure to follow the recommended risk management practices listed in lesson 2.

LESSON CONTENT

Introduction

Beginning backpackers typically ask the following questions before beginning an outing:

◆ What are we going to eat?

◆ What are we going to drink?

◆ Where do we go to the bathroom?

◆ How do you keep from getting sick?

◆ How do you stand not taking a bath?

Although the lesson on food and nutrition (lesson 3, page 47) addresses the first question, this lesson addresses the other issues related to health and sanitation.

Health care professionals say that the single most important way to help prevent the spread of illness is washing your hands. The same principle holds true in the backcountry. Regular hand washing before cooking and eating and after using the bathroom is one of the best ways to avoid illness. Of course, hygiene is more than just washing your hands. Students should also understand how to treat water effectively to prevent waterborne illness. They should follow appropriate procedures when using the bathroom, minimize impact when brushing their teeth, and ensure that their cookware and dishes are clean and sanitized before eating off them. Bathing each day not only promotes good health but also can lift a person's spirits and remove offensive odor to make social encounters more pleasant.

Main Activities

Activity 1: The Shared Snack Bag (10 to 15 Minutes)

This activity serves two purposes. First, it illustrates how just one person with poor hygiene can affect the rest of the group. Second, it encourages participants to avoid sharing personal items to minimize the spread of disease throughout the group.

Important Terms

bacteria and protozoa—Single-cell organisms capable of causing disease (including giardia and cryptosporidium, which may have severe and relatively long-lasting effects).

viruses—Simple, smaller pathogens that usually cause milder and shorter bouts of illness.

This activity is best done in a classroom or at a trailhead where trash cans are available. You may want to choose something inexpensive for the trail mix, such as Cheerios.

◆ Ask the students how many times they wash their hands during a typical day. Tell them that in the backcountry, they should wash their hands as many times (if not more times) than they do at home.

◆ Take a little lotion that has had some food coloring mixed into it, squirt some into your hand and rub in onto both hands to represent germs.

◆ Pick up a bag of trail mix, open it, reach into the bag, and pull out a handful. Do not eat it!

◆ Pass the bag to one of the students. Ask the person to handle the bag as he or she normally would and to take a handful but not eat. Continue passing the bag around until the whole group has taken some.

◆ After passing the bag, ask the students to examine their hands and the trail mix in their hands. Many will see traces of dye on their hands and their food.

◆ Have all the students put their trail mix back in the bag and throw it away at the earliest possible time. The participants should not eat the food.

◆ To finish the activity, ask the students to brainstorm ways to maintain group and individual health.

Activity 2: Hand Washing (Five Minutes)

This lesson exposes students to how, where, and why they should wash their hands in the backcountry. The lesson also gives the students an opportunity to practice washing their hands.

◆ Set up a hand-washing station with soap, nailbrush, and water in an appropriate area. Explain to the students that to prevent contamination of the water source, to minimize the amount of foodlike smells around camp and areas where people congregate, and to promote privacy, hand washing and other hygiene activities should follow the **rule of 200** (rule of 60): People should move 200 feet (60 meters) from water sources, the camp site, and the trail before bathing, hand washing, brushing teeth, using the bathroom, and so on.

◆ Liquid soap in a small plastic container is usually more convenient and less messy than bar soap on backpacking trips. When selecting a soap to use, buy one that is both biodegradable (naturally breaks down) and phosphate-free (prevents algae blooms in water).

◆ Remind the students that hand washing should occur before handling food, before eating, and after using the bathroom. To demonstrate hand washing, start by putting a drop or two of soap in each participant's hand. Next, put a few splashes of water on each hand and ask the students to start scrubbing their hands. Remind them to clean between fingers, under and around rings, and under the nails. They should scrub for 10 to 30 seconds.

◆ If they notice that their nails are especially dirty, they should use a nailbrush to help remove dirt.

◆ Clean water should be used for rinsing off the hands. Water can be poured from a pot or water bottle, or a spout can be opened on a water bladder.

◆ Tell the participants that a convenient way to promote hand washing in camp is to set up a station by hanging a water bladder that has a spout on it. People can then wash their hands by themselves without having someone else pour water.

Activity 3: Bathing (30 Minutes)

In the backcountry there is no good reason not to bathe. Even when the temperature is extremely cold and water is somewhat scarce, participants can employ methods to promote cleanliness.

◆ Ask participants to come up with some important reasons why they should bathe in the backcountry. Most groups will come up with the primary three: to maintain health, to feel better, and to reduce odor. For women, feminine health is difficult to maintain without regular bathing.

◆ Ask participants how far away they should be from water sources, camp, and the trail when bathing. The answer should be 200 feet (60 meters). Describe the ways to bathe in the backcountry. Three common ones are the bird bath, the cooking pot bath, and the water bladder shower. On days when the schedule is tight, water is scarce, or the weather is extremely cold, participants should still take a bird bath and clean under the wings (armpits) and under the tail (between the legs).

◆ Although many people will be tempted to jump right into a water source and swim to get clean, bathing before swimming will help prevent water pollution from sunscreen, lotions, bug repellant, or other toiletry items. Remind people that they should not use soap directly in the water supply.

◆ This activity works well if someone can demonstrate the techniques to the group while wearing a swimsuit to protect privacy. If time allows, have participants practice taking a backcountry bath.

Bird Bath   You should have a washcloth (bandanna), soap, and water. Get the cloth wet and put a little soap on it. Clean the armpits and between the legs and then thoroughly rinse the cloth. Wipe the areas until you are free from soap, rinsing the cloth as many times as necessary. Although it adds more weight, and trash, if participants will be traveling in the desert and water will be scarce, they can pack baby wipes (alcohol-free) for bathing.

Cooking Pot Bath   Fill a couple of cooking pots with water. (If you have time and plenty of fuel, you can even heat the water a little on the stove). Pour some water on your body. Take some soap and scrub with a washcloth. Pour more water out of the cooking pot to rinse the soap off. For washing hair, having a partner pour the water is usually easier than doing it yourself.

Water Bladder Shower   Hang a water bladder from a branch (water can be heated by stove or sunlight). Remove your clothing and open the spigot on the bladder to get wet. Close the spigot. Use soap and a washcloth to wash your body. Open the spigot to rinse off the soap.

Activity 4: Tooth Brushing Broadcasting Contest (10 Minutes)

The primary difference between brushing teeth at home versus in the backcountry is what you do with the waste after brushing.

◆ No toothpaste—If you use no paste at all, there is no waste.

♦ Old-fashioned recipe (baking soda and salt)—Swallow the paste after brushing or use the same method as those using a fluoride toothpaste.

♦ Fluoride toothpaste—Fluoride toothpaste should never be swallowed for health reasons. Two methods of disposal are appropriate. For either method, use only a pea-sized amount of toothpaste. After brushing, get some extra water in your mouth. You may either dig a small hole and bury the paste or broadcast it widely by spraying it through pursed lips.

♦ The broadcasting practice follows the idea that the solution to pollution is dilution. By broadcasting, students are spreading out the waste, allowing nature to take care of it more quickly. Broadcasting also dilutes the smell, which decreases the chance of attracting wildlife.

  – Ask students to get a mouthful of plain water. Spread students widely throughout the area. Let them practice a few times before bringing the group back together. Inform the participants that you will be judging on three areas: length, width, and concentration. You can either give an overall winner or give four total awards, one for each category and one for overall dispersion.

  – Length: Mark the farthest point away from the line.

  – Width: Mark the starting and ending point from side to side.

  – Concentration: Note how fine the drops are; the finer, the better.

Activity 5: Dishes (10 to 15 Minutes)

At the beginning of every meal, all eating utensils, dishes, and pots and pans should be sterilized. As with every cooking activity, remind participants to be careful around stoves and to follow the instructions detailed in lesson 4.

♦ Bring a pot of water to a rolling boil. Submerge utensils and small dishes into the pot.

♦ Skillets or other pans can have boiling water poured into them and then be placed on the stove to come back to a full boil.

♦ Boiling the water and the dishes ensures that all the bacteria are killed before food preparation and eating.

After the meal, dishes should be cleaned. Ideally, all food is eaten and no traces of food remain. In that situation, the dishes are done when the food is consumed. They can be stored and then sterilized before the next meal. Although some people may want to use soap on their dishes, explain that in most cases this practice is not necessary because the dishes will be sterilized before the next meal. When dishes are extremely greasy, however, a small amount of soap may be used in the washing process. Soap may have a laxative effect, so be sure to rinse the dishes thoroughly.

Cleaning dishes may be more involved at times. If something sticks to a pan or if food remains, then dishes should be cleaned more thoroughly before storing. Use some soap, water, and a scrubber to clean the dishes before storing. Some backpackers choose to bring a scrub brush or sponge with a scrubber on one side. Others elect to use natural scrubbers such as leaves, pine needles, pinecones, sand, or baking soda to scrub their dishes. Place a catch basin below the dish being washed. Pour through a strainer to catch the food particles and then bag the particles. Strainers can be pieces of no-see-um mesh, a kitchen strainer, a bandanna, or knee-high panty hose. Rinse the dishes and scatter all the dishwater widely.

After discussing the basics of dish sterilization and cleaning, bring out some dirty dishes, pots, or pans so that students can practice cleaning dishes after a meal. Use the following list as a guideline to remind the participants of the steps.

1. Follow the rule of 200 (rule of 60).
2. Scrape the dishes to remove as much food as possible.
3. Bag all the scraped food so that it can be packed out with the other trash.
4. For stuck-on food, use some type of scrubber, soap, and water.
5. Strain to catch the food particles.
6. Bag the strained food so that it can be packed out.
7. Rinse the dishes.
8. Take the water from the catch basin and broadcast it widely using the rule of 200 (rule of 60).
9. Store pots, pans, and dishes.

Activity 6: Water Treatment (40 Minutes)

In a large group ask the students if water taken from natural sources should be treated. The answers may vary widely. Some people may believe that none is necessary. Explain that water may contain bacteria, protozoa, and viruses that may cause illness. Treating water helps eliminate those problems.

Break the students into small groups of about four or five and provide them with one purification method or piece of equipment along with background information about that method or equipment. Tell them to take a few minutes to educate themselves about proper technique. Each group will then teach the class about the positive and negatives of using their assigned method and demonstrate how to treat water using that method.

Chemical Sanitization—Chlorine   A variety of types of chlorine products can be used—tablets, liquid drops developed specifically for treating water, and bleach.

◆ Pros: Wide availability, inexpensive, easy to use.
◆ Cons: Chlorine does not always kill all giardia cysts; long waiting period after adding chlorine before drinking; chlorine changes the taste of water; large concentrated doses could be toxic.

Chemical Sanitization—Iodine   Iodine is commonly available in three forms—tablets, iodine crystals, and liquid (including tincture of iodine and povidone iodine available at drugstores).

◆ Pros: Wide availability; inexpensive; easy to use; iodine crystals and liquid are almost 100 percent effective in killing bacteria, protozoa, and viruses when used correctly.
◆ Cons: Long waiting period after adding iodine before drinking; changes the taste of water; large concentrated doses could be toxic. People with thyroid problems and shellfish allergies should consult a doctor before using iodine.

Water Filter   Water filters come in a variety of sizes, weights, filter speeds, and levels of protection. Most filters remove bacteria and protozoa. Some remove large viruses. If you are using a water filter, you should understand the pros and cons of the particular model. Each type operates a little differently and has unique maintenance requirements. When buying filters, compare the models carefully and ask a lot of questions of the sales associate to learn which model most closely meets your needs. If you are using a filter, carry maintenance supplies to keep the filter working properly.

◆ Pros: Convenient while on the trail; adds no chemical taste to water.

◆ Cons: May not remove all viruses; slow (one to three minutes per liter); expensive (filters and replacement cartridges); maintenance required.

Boiling Water is safe to drink when it reaches a full, rolling boil. No additional boiling time is necessary (although some sources recommend longer boiling times).

◆ Pros: Inexpensive (fuel is the only cost); 100 percent effective; adds no chemical taste to water.

◆ Cons: Takes time; uses fuel; inconvenient while on the trail.

Ionization and Ultraviolet Light The newest methods of water purification are small electronic devices that shine ultraviolet light or use a small electrical charge to sanitize water.

◆ Pros: 100 percent effective; adds no chemical taste to water.

◆ Cons: Expensive; requires batteries; device may break.

Activity 7: Toileting (20 Minutes)

Entire books have been written to discuss the complexities of using the bathroom in the woods, such as *How to Shit in the Woods* (Meyer, 1994). Using the terms *urinate* and *defecate* may seem strange to some instructors and participants; they may be more comfortable using terms like *#1* and *#2*, *big potty* and *little potty*, or *poop* and *pee*. When permanent restroom facilities are available, backpackers should always use them. Because facilities are often not available, appropriate toileting techniques should be taught to help participants feel more comfortable, to protect the environment, and to promote health.

Urination Urinating is a fairly simple and straightforward issue. Use the rule of 200 (rule of 60) and try not to urinate on foliage because the salt in the urine remains on the plants. Animals are attracted to the salt and may destroy the plants in the process of acquiring the salt that their bodies need. When possible, urinate on rocky or sandy ground, thereby creating a natural salt lick for the animals.

Women-specific note—Because women have shorter urethras, they should use special care to avoid urinary tract infections. Women should avoid dripping dry unless they feel comfortable enough and have time to wait until completely dry before pulling underwear and clothes back on. Several options are viable.

◆ Pantiliners
  – Pros: Sanitary; multiple pairs of underwear are unnecessary.
  – Cons: Must be changed each day, creating more trash to be packed out.

◆ Toilet paper
  – Pros: Sanitary; people feel more at home.
  – Cons: Creates more trash to be packed out.

◆ Cloth rag (bandanna)
  - Pros: Reusable.
  - Cons: Must be rinsed and washed regularly (at least every day); high visibility (it hangs off backpack).

Defecation The most common method of disposing of fecal waste is by digging a cathole. Be sure to use the rule of 200 (rule of 60).

◆ Give participants a trowel and ask them to practice digging a cathole. Explain that a cathole should be 6 to 8 inches (15 to 20 centimeters) deep, which is deep enough for the bacteria in the soil to break down the material efficiently. The hole should be about 4 inches (10 centimeters) in diameter.

◆ After using the bathroom, cover the waste and any natural toilet paper (leaves, smooth sticks, or rocks) with the dirt that was dug out of the hole during its construction. Disguise the cathole as much as possible with natural materials (fallen leaves).

◆ After students have constructed, filled in, and disguised the catholes, lead a discussion about disposing of toilet paper and other methods of disposing of human waste. Remind participants to wash their hands after toileting.

◆ If participants use toilet paper, they should bag it and pack it out. If participants use natural toilet paper (leaves, smooth sticks, or rocks), they may bury those with the waste. Any feminine hygiene products (tampons or napkins) must be bagged and packed out as trash.

Occasionally, backpackers use different techniques when visiting specific geographic areas or when group size and duration of the visit warrant a different technique than digging individual catholes. For example, latrines are constructed when a large group will be in an area for an extended period. A latrine is a long trench dug 6 inches (15 centimeters) deep. People start at one end and bury their waste as they use the facility. Land management agencies sometimes require all wastes to be packed out of an area because of specific limitations of the area. For more information on how to properly dispose of human waste, contact the local land management agency.

Closure Activity

Cathole Competition (20 Minutes)

Have the participants compete to become the cathole construction champion. Have a contest to dig the best cathole. Then have groups critique the quality of the holes and location. As a secondary activity, to relieve some of the tension and add humor, demonstrate some of the different bathroom positions—the hug-a-tree technique, the wall squat against a tree or rock, the free-standing squat, and so on.

Follow-Up Activity

LNT Research (Time as Needed)

Have students access the Leave No Trace Web site (www.lnt.org) and contact land managers in a variety of geographical locations—desert, alpine, river corridors, and so on—and find the specifics of toileting in those areas. Have students report that information to the group.

ASSESSMENT

◆ Confirm that students understand how one person with poor hygiene practices can affect the health of the entire group by observing their participation in and discussion of the shared-bag activity.

◆ Verify that students recognize the importance of hand washing in the backcountry by observing their participation in a discussion of the hand-washing activity.

◆ Check that students know appropriate toileting techniques in the backcountry by observing their participation in contests (best cathole) regarding toileting.

◆ Confirm that students understand appropriate methods of disposing of waste such as dishwater and toothpaste by observing their participation in group activities and contests.

◆ Verify that students know how to sterilize dishes before cooking and how to clean dishes after cooking by observing their participation in the dishwashing activity.

◆ Check that students appreciate the importance of bathing for health and social reasons by noting their participation in the bathing activity and their discussion of important health and social issues regarding bathing.

◆ Confirm that students appreciate the need to treat water by writing in their journals about the joys of backpacking and the disasters that result from consuming untreated water.

TEACHING CONSIDERATIONS

◆ Health and sanitation can quickly become a serious, heavy, boring topic. Use humor to keep the participants engaged and excited about the activity.

◆ This lesson can be a long one if taught all at once, so be sure to take appropriate breaks between the activities.

◆ If teaching these activities in the field, you may want to use teachable moments. For example, at the trailhead or during the first break, teach toileting techniques and hand washing. After arriving at camp, teach bathing. Right before the first meal, teach dish sterilization. Immediately after the first meal, teach dishwashing and tooth brushing.

UNIT 1, LESSON 9

▷ Basic Camping Skills

OVERVIEW

In this section students learn the basic knots for constructing and securing a shelter. Both tarp construction and tent setup are discussed. Basic knots covered in this lesson are common camp knots that serve multiple purposes and can be transferred to other adventure sports discussed in this book. Finally, campsite and shelter site selection are covered as well as general organization around the campsite, including hanging food bags.

JUSTIFICATION

Beginning backpackers should know how to construct a lightweight, stable shelter in the appropriate location and exercise the critical Leave No Trace skills of campsite selection and food protection.

GOAL

To develop students' understanding of basic camping skills such as knot tying, shelter construction, campsite selection, food bag hanging, and campsite organization.

OBJECTIVES

At the end of this lesson, students will be able to

- describe the key points of finding a Leave No Trace campsite (cognitive),
- distinguish between the different knots used for specific tasks in tarp and tent setup and bear bagging (cognitive),
- demonstrate the ability to set up secure tarps and tents and food bags (psychomotor), and
- exhibit pride in personal craftsmanship when constructing shelters and developing LNT campsites (affective).

EQUIPMENT AND AREAS NEEDED

- Tents
- Tarps
- Trekking poles, long sturdy sticks, or a flat, clear area with trees about 10 to 15 feet (3 to 5 meters) apart
- Twelve-foot (4-meter) lengths of parachute cords
- Expedition rope, 7 to 9 millimeters in diameter and 50 to 75 feet (15 to 25 meters) in length
- Stakes, 10 per tarp or an appropriate number for the tents
- Plenty of cord and scrap rope to practice knot tying
- An assortment of food bags (duffels, nylon stuff sacks)
- Carabiners

RISK MANAGEMENT CONSIDERATIONS

- Check the site for potential environmental hazards.
- Look for **deadfall**—large dead trees or limbs that could potentially fall on the shelter site during high winds. Avoid these sites for the shelters.
- Provide enough parachute cord and stakes for participants to secure their shelters during high winds and severe weather.
- When bear bagging, do not tie any type of heavy object to the end of the rope to throw over limbs or trees. The resulting pendulum is potentially fatal if someone is hit in the head or chest.

LESSON CONTENT

Introduction

Proper campsite selection sets up the trip for success by providing comfort to the group and offering adequate space to observe Leave No Trace practices that lessen damage to the environment. In this section, students learn basic knots used in setting up tents and tarps. Basic tarp setup is an essential skill. A tarp provides lightweight shelter and a true outdoor experience. Students become comfortable in the outdoors by sleeping in the open space provided by a tarp.

Main Activities

Activity 1: Campsite Selection (15 Minutes)

The process of selecting a campsite is best done when making your first camp. Using a place that you have visited before is helpful. This activity works well when students are on their first trip and must chose their first campsite. Allow enough time in the trip schedule for a systematic decision-making process.

When beginning the campsite selection process keep several key points in mind:

◆ The area must be large enough to accommodate the number of people that you have with you.

◆ A good Leave No Trace campsite is either a campsite that has already been used heavily or is in a place where the impact of a campsite will not be severe or noticed.

◆ In the tent or tarp area, there should be no danger of deadfall, also called widow makers. When selecting sleeping areas, look for fairly flat spots or locations where campers can position their heads slightly uphill.

◆ Establish separate areas for cooking, bear bagging, sleeping, and bathrooms.

◆ Is a water source within reasonable distance, or does the group have enough water packed to meet group needs?

◆ If the selected location is not a designated site, is it far enough from the trail that other hikers will be unaware of your presence?

◆ Is the campsite in an area free of animal trails and not blocking the wildlife's water source?

◆ Does the site consist of a **durable surface** to minimize impact?

Activity 2: Tarp Setup (45 Minutes)

Demonstrate how to set up a tarp. Tarp setup is a useful skill for backpackers. Tarps can be used not only as a sleeping shelter but also as a place to cook or meet. Tarp setup can be practiced before the first trip in small groups or conducted on the first trip.

◆ To set up a standard A-frame tarp, you first need to locate a couple of **trekking poles** or long, sturdy sticks that you can set vertically about 4 feet (1 meter) farther apart than the width of the tarp. Trees that are 10 to 15 feet (3 to 5 meters) apart can also be used. These trekking poles or sticks become the basis for constructing your shelter. Using trekking poles is an important skill to develop when trees or other natural poles are not available.

◆ Secure your tarp to the poles at either end of the ridgeline. The ridgeline is the center seam of the tarp, typically along the length and in the middle of the widest part of your tarp. To start, tie one of your 12-foot (4-meter) sections of parachute cord to the grommet of the tarp. The easiest knot to use here is a **girth hitch** (figure BP9.1). If you are using poles, girth hitch the middle of the 8-foot (2.5-meter) section to the grommet. On some tarps you may need to make a grommet or a chicken head by placing a smooth rock or wad of dead leaves in the tarp and tying a girth hitch or clove hitch around it (figure BP9.2).

◆ Determine the height at which you would like the ridgeline. The higher you pitch the tarp, the less surface area is covered. Pitched too low, the tarp will sag on the sides without enough height to maintain a taut pitch.

◆ After the cord is attached to the tarp, attach the parachute cord to the pole, using a square knot (figure BP9.3). Now run the two ends of the cord out at 45-degree angles and insert a stake in the ground at each angle. Tie a **taut line hitch** (figure BP9.4) around the stakes so that later you can adjust these tighter. Have them just snug for now. With trekking poles, this end of the tarp should stand by itself; with sticks another person may be needed. Do the same on the other side of the tarp.

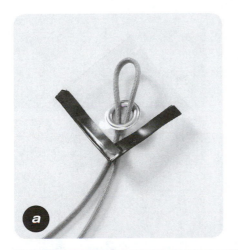 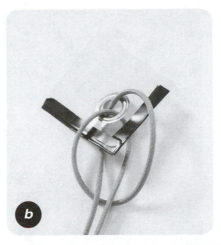 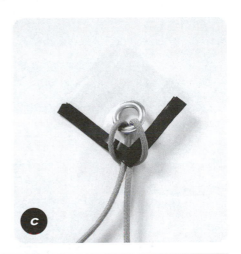

FIGURE BP9.1   Tying a girth hitch: *(a)* Place the bight through the grommet. *(b)* Pull both ends of the rope through the bight. *(c)* Pull for tension.

 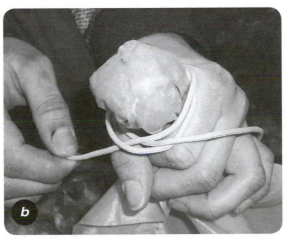

FIGURE BP9.2   Tying a chicken head using a clove hitch: *(a)* Place a wad of dead leaves in the top corner; *(b)* secure the clove hitch around the chicken head.

FIGURE BP9.3   Attaching tarp cord to a trekking pole with a square knot: *(a)* Tie an overhand; *(b)* tie a second overhand; *(c)* secure the knot. If tied correctly, it forms two bights with all ends exiting the knot symmetrically.

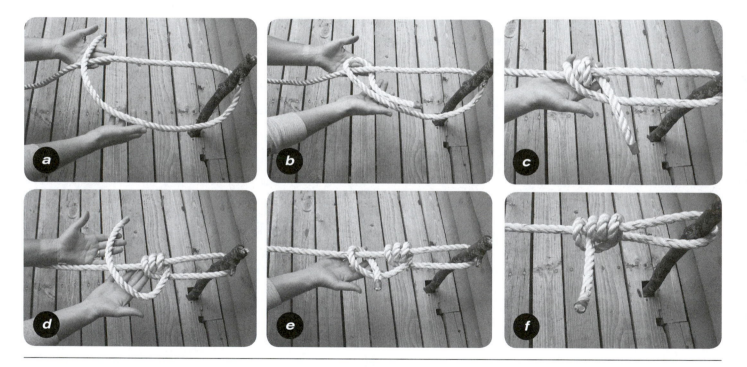

FIGURE BP9.4   Tying a taut line hitch: *(a)* Place the working end around a post. *(b)* Wrap the working end around the standing end. *(c)* Wrap the working end around the standing end a second time. *(d)* Wrap the working end around the standing end a third time. *(e)* Wrap the working end around the standing end a fourth time but on the opposite side. *(f)* Final result.

◆ Stake out the edges of the tarp. Attach the cords to the tarp using a girth hitch as described earlier. Place stakes in line with the angle made at the corner of the tarp. Tilt the head of the stakes away from the tarp when inserting them into the ground. An adjustable knot is needed to provide easy refinement of the setup. The ideal knot is the taut line hitch (figure BP9.4), which provides easy adjustment of the staked lines. Stake and hitch all four corners. For additional wind protection, more sections of the tarp may need to be secured as the corners were.

Activity 3: Tent Setup (20 Minutes)

Demonstrate and practice tent setup. Tents should be set up and checked before taking them into the field. Checking the tents for problems or missing parts before a trip is an excellent way to introduce tent setup.

- Tents are often easier to set up than tarps, but they provide a different experience when sleeping outdoors. Tents provide more protection from bugs and the elements than a tarp. On the other hand, tarps can be pitched in a variety of ways, making better use of irregularly shaped flat ground space. The choice of which type of shelter is better often comes down to personal preference. A person may use tarps in certain geographic areas and seasons and a tent at other times.

- Tents should be used in areas where snakes or insect-borne diseases are a threat.

- Get to know the tent that the expedition will be using before demonstrating setup. Although many tents have similar features, they set up differently.

- Most tent designs use a series of poles that follow seams of the main tent body.

- The poles are usually made of aluminum or fiberglass and should be handled with care. Poles should be assembled by affixing each sleeve to ensure that the housing is not damaged. Never flick a pole to put it together because this practice will damage the aluminum sleeves.

- Tents come in freestanding and nonfreestanding varieties. Nonfreestanding tents require stakes to make them erect. Freestanding tents do not, but stakes are needed to keep them from blowing away.

- Additional tiedown and stakeout points will be necessary in any area where high winds and severe weather are possible.

Activity 4: Bear Bagging (45 Minutes)

Demonstrate and practice bear bag hanging, also called food bag hanging. When the group reaches its first campsite, have the entire group gather around a potential site for a demonstration of how to hang a food bag. Have small groups hang their own bags and then take a group tour of all sites to critique each system (figure BP9.5).

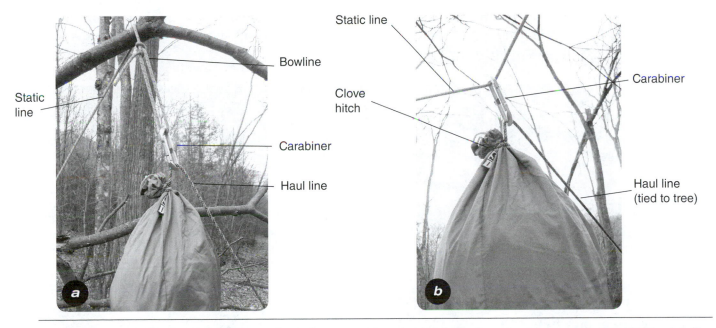

FIGURE BP9.5   Hanging a bear bag: (a) The static line is thrown over a branch. A bowline and carabiner are secured to the end of the static line. A haul line is clipped into the carabiner. (b) The static line is hung between two trees. The haul line is clipped into a carabiner that is attached to the static line.

◆ Bear bagging, or food bag hanging, is an essential skill to protect the expedition's food, not only from bears but also from other large animals and rodents.

◆ The ideal bear-bagging rope should be lightweight, strong enough to hold up to 40 pounds (18 kilograms), and be of sufficient diameter that it is easy to pull with bare hands. A 50- to 75-foot (15- to 25-meter) length of at least 7- to 9-millimeter rope is recommended. Old throw ropes from your river equipment make ideal ropes for this purpose. For more hanging options, carry two ropes.

◆ The bear bag site must be 100 yards (meters) or more from your campsite if you are in serious bear country. When selecting a tree, try to find a limb or series of trees that allow the bags to be 6 to 7 feet (2 to 3 meters) from the trunk of the tree while also hanging 6 to 7 feet (2 to 3 meters) below the limb. The bags should be 15 to 20 feet (5 to 6 meters) off the ground.

◆ One method to get the rope in the tree is to bundle the rope in one hand and then wrap the rope around the bundle into a big yarn ball (figure BP9.6). The ball should not be so big that you cannot throw it through or over a branch, but the ball should contain enough rope that as it unravels you can reach it from the ground. Success with this technique will often require several attempts, but with practice your proficiency will increase.

◆ Figure BP9.5 illustrates two methods of hanging a food bag. Each of these methods requires two ropes instead of a one-line system thrown over a branch. These two systems allow for greater flexibility in design options and alleviate damaging rope friction that tears into bark. Figure BP9.5*a* shows a rope thrown over a branch, connected to a carabiner with a **bowline** (figure BP9.7) to become the static line in the system. The second rope is attached to the nylon stuff sack using a clove hitch (figure BP9.8) and is threaded through the carabiner. The clove hitch works well because it tightens down on itself under tension. The second rope becomes the haul line. Figure BP9.5*b* demonstrates a similar system, but the static line is hung between two trees. This is convenient when large branches are not available. The haul line is threaded through a carabiner on the static line and connected to the food bag. If the food bag is a duffel bag with handles, a bowline can be used instead of a clove hitch.

FIGURE BP9.6   Create a rope bundle to make the rope easier to throw.

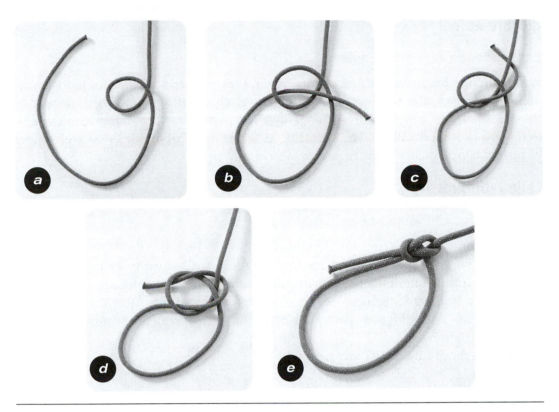

FIGURE BP9.7 Tying a bowline knot: *(a)* Form a loop. *(b)* Thread the working end through the loop. *(c)* Wrap the working end around the standing end. *(d)* Thread the working end back through the loop. *(e)* Pull to tighten.

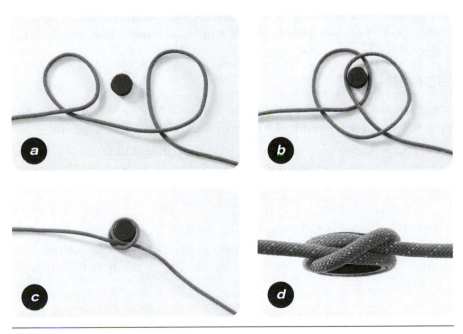

FIGURE BP9.8 Tying a clove hitch: *(a)* Form two loops, with the working ends over the standing ends. The loop on the right is made first. *(b)* Place the second loop over the first loop. *(c)* Pull both ends to tighten. *(d)* Final result.

Closure Activity

Scouting for a Site (30 Minutes)

When looking for an expedition campsite, send several scouting parties to locate an appropriate campsite for the rest of the group. Each scouting party needs to be able to return with the key selling points of their campsite. They in turn pitch their site to the group for a decision. The scouting parties should hit on all the key elements of proper campsite selection.

Follow-Up Activity

Knot Practice (30 Minutes)

An important skill discussed and demonstrated in this lesson is knot tying. Structure an activity so that students must practice their knots. Create a relay race by dividing the group into small teams. One member from each team must run from a starting line to a tying area to complete the knot that you call for. After the person has completed the knot, the next person in line runs to the tying area and ties another knot of your choice.

Knots covered thus far in this lesson:

◆ Square knot
◆ Bowline
◆ Taut line hitch
◆ Girth hitch
◆ Clove hitch

In addition, consider adding the trucker's hitch (figure BP9.9), which can be used in addition to the taut line hitch. The truckers' hitch is an excellent knot to know when tension must be placed and adjusted in the system. The knot is useful for stringing clotheslines, tarp lines, and so on.

ASSESSMENT

◆ Check that students can describe the key points of a Leave No Trace campsite by observing them describe and sell a campsite to the expedition group.
◆ Verify that students can distinguish between the different knots used for different tasks in tarp and tent setup and bear bagging by noting whether they use the most appropriate knots in the setups.
◆ Confirm that students have the ability to set up secure tarps and tents by examining their setups during practice and while on a trip.
◆ Check that students exhibit pride in personal craftsmanship when constructing shelters and developing LNT campsites by observing them as they practice and while on a trip.

TEACHING CONSIDERATIONS

◆ Provide enough equipment or rotate responsibilities so that everyone has a chance to set up a tarp or tent.
◆ Consider teaching only a few knots at a time so that students can gradually build a skill set that will enable them to construct quality shelters.

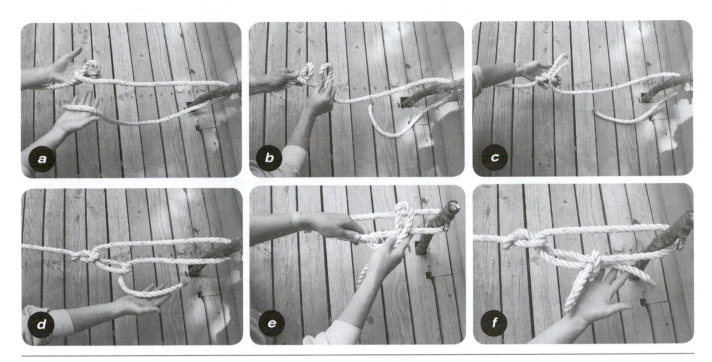

FIGURE BP9.9   Tying a trucker's hitch: *(a)* Wrap the working end around a post and form a loop in the standing end. *(b)* Create a bight in the standing end. *(c)* Thread the bight through the loop and tighten it to form a loop that slips. *(d)* Place the working end through the adjustable loop. *(e)* Pull the working end to the desired tension. *(f)* Finish with a quick-release overhand knot by wrapping a bight around the standing end and snugly against the slippery loop.

◆ Many systems work well for bear bagging. This lesson covers two basic methods. Consider expanding the student's food bag hanging skills by introducing and practicing additional systems and techniques. Several resources listed at the end of this unit, such as *Backcountry Classroom* (Drury, Bonney, Berman, & Wagstaff, 2005), provide this information. The same is true for tarp building. Challenge the students to be creative as they gain experience.

UNIT 1, LESSON 10

▷ Travel Techniques

OVERVIEW

The ability to cover significant distances while backpacking and enjoy the process depends not only on having a high fitness level before the start of the trip but also on using appropriate techniques while traveling. This lesson provides students with tips that will help them move more efficiently over varied terrain, such as energy conservation techniques, pack adjustments, and uphill and downhill hiking techniques. Specific group roles and techniques for backpacking in groups are provided. This lesson also discusses what to do when encountering others on the trail including other groups of backpackers, bikers, and horseback riders.

JUSTIFICATION

After a backpacking trip begins, participants need to know how to travel effectively over varied terrain so that they can meet the goals of the trip. Traveling on durable surfaces reduces environmental impact and helps backpackers "Leave No Trace." By using efficient travel techniques, backpackers can maintain appropriate levels of energy, comfort, and endurance necessary to cover the distance of planned hikes. Individual and group safety increases when backpackers employ proper travel techniques.

GOAL

To develop the participants' ability to use trail techniques that will increase their efficiency, safety, and group comfort.

OBJECTIVES

At the end of this lesson, students will be able to

- describe three techniques that will promote energy conservation (cognitive),
- explain what to do when encountering other groups on the trails (cognitive),
- demonstrate uphill hiking techniques (psychomotor),
- demonstrate how to descend hills (psychomotor),
- appreciate the use of trail assignments to organize the groups (affective), and
- value LNT principles related to traveling on durable surfaces (affective).

EQUIPMENT AND AREAS NEEDED

- Trivia game board (figure BP10.1, or draw your own on a dry erase board, a piece of paper, or a trash bag)
- Energy conservation trivia questions (figure BP10.2)
- Group travel technique scenario sheets for each small group (figure BP10.3)
- Eraser, dry erase marker, or pen
- Backpack
- Trekking poles

RISK MANAGEMENT CONSIDERATIONS

- If teaching in the outdoors, follow basic risk management considerations described in lesson 2.
- Be aware of heat index or chill factor in extreme weather.
- When the participants are climbing or descending hills, encourage them to use appropriate hiking techniques.
- Backpacks should be properly loaded and adjusted correctly.
- Before beginning a hike, be sure that hikers are wearing appropriate footwear.
- Hikes should progress at a pace appropriate for the whole group.
- Appropriate spacing is imperative, especially when using trekking poles.
- Be proactive in cases of distress caused by extreme weather or strenuous pacing of activities.

LESSON CONTENT

Introduction

One key to an enjoyable, pleasant backpacking experience is to be able to travel efficiently, comfortably, and safely to the intended destination. By understanding appropriate travel and trail techniques, participants minimize the amount of energy expended on the trail and arrive at camp with enough energy to set up their shelters, cook a satisfying, nutritious meal, and enjoy a pleasant evening of camaraderie before going to bed.

Main Activities

Activity 1: Energy Conservation Trivia (45 Minutes)

This activity covers the concepts of energy conservation including fitness, pace, breathing, rest breaks, and nutrition through a modified version of a famous trivia game show. Energy conservation is one of the most important elements in trail walking. When participants run low on energy, their performance suffers significantly.

Before beginning this activity either print a copy of the trivia board (figure BP10.1) or write the categories and point values on a dry erase board or trash bag. Then print the questions and answers (figure BP10.2). The game show host begins by dividing the participants into three or four small groups and asking each group to create a group name and write it on a poster board. The host then introduces each group, briefly explains the rules, and shares the categories with the participants.

- The group to the far left chooses the first category and point value.
- The host reads the question to the group. Only the host has a copy of the questions.
- Each group designates one person to answer the questions (groups should alternate who has this role).
- To try to answer a question, a team must be the first group to have its designated answerer raise her or his hand and be called on by the host.
- After a team is called on, the answerers from the other teams lower their hands. The answering team has three seconds to give the answer.
- If the team answers correctly, they receive the point value of the question and choose the next category and point value.
- If the team answers incorrectly, no points are deducted, but other teams have the opportunity to answer it correctly by raising their hands. (This process continues until a team answers correctly or all teams have answered incorrectly).
- In the event that no team gives the correct answer, the host shares the correct answer.
- The game ends when all the questions have been read and answered.
- A prize may be awarded to the winning team (or not).

If you are teaching this lesson in a classroom, write the category and point value matrix on a chalkboard or dry erase board. If you are teaching in the field, write the categories and points on a piece of paper or a white trash bag with a dry erase marker. As teams choose point values, erase or mark through the point value.

Energy Conservation Trivia Game Board

General energy conservation	Fitness	Pace	Breathing	Rest breaks	Hodgepodge
100	100	100	100	100	100
200	200	200	200	200	200
300	300	300	300	300	300
400	400	400	400	400	400
500	500	500	500	500	500

FIGURE BP10.1   Use this game board for the energy conservation trivia game.

From M. Wagstaff and A. Attarian, 2009, *Technical skills for adventure programming: A curriculum guide* (Champaign, IL: Human Kinetics).

Energy Conservation Trivia Questions and Answers

General Energy Conservation

100—What is energy conservation?

Answer—Expending as little energy as possible to arrive at a destination, employing practices such as physical fitness, appropriate pace, rhythmic breathing, rest breaks, nutrition, and water.

200—To what degree should energy conservation be practiced?

Answer—Depends on the purpose and goals of the trip (energy conservation may be less important if the primary goal is physical fitness).

300—How does energy conservation influence body temperature?

Answer—The temperature of the body does not change much, which minimizes perspiration and subsequent body temperature changes.

400—How do fast starts and long rests influence energy conservation?

Answer—They cause maximum fluctuation of heart rate and may contribute to greater energy use.

500—Describe three ways that energy conservation influences endurance.

Answer—(1) Less tired at the end of the day. (2) Able to go longer with fewer and shorter breaks. (3) Energy is available in the event of an emergency. (4) Chances of emotional outbursts because of exhaustion and frustration are minimized.

Fitness

100—How does physical fitness influence enjoyment during a backpacking trip?

Answer—Fatigue develops more slowly, allowing for greater enjoyment.

200—How does physical fitness influence interpersonal relationships during a trip?

Answer—If all participants are physically fit, frustration and conflict resulting from differences in pace and hike-length preferences are less likely to occur.

300—How does physical fitness influence participant health on a trip?

Answer—Those who are physically fit are less likely to become ill or be injured because of fatigue.

400—How does physical fitness influence emergency situations?

Answer—Those who are physically fit will be less fatigued and thus have clearer judgment, resulting in greater safety for all participants during an emergency.

500—How physically fit should the leader be?

Answer—At least as fit as the average participant in the group. The leader should aim to be as fit as the strongest person in the group.

Pace

100—What pace problem do most groups encounter?

Answer—Going too fast, leading to premature fatigue.

200—Describe how pace can influence conversation.

Answer—If carrying on a normal conversation while backpacking becomes difficult, the pace is too fast.

300—How can you determine whether the pace is appropriate for the group?

Answer—Throughout the day the group takes short, occasional breaks, and participants are not exhausted at the end of the day.

400—What is the group leader's goal related to pace?

Answer—Set and hike at a pace appropriate for the whole group, which is usually slower than the pace at which the leader would like to hike.

500—What two physiological functions should be coordinated to regulate the pace?

Answer—Heartbeat and breathing should determine the pace. Pace should not be established first and the heartbeat and breathing coordinated to match.

continued ▶

FIGURE BP10.2 Energy conservation trivia questions and answers for testing knowledge of energy conservation techniques.

Breathing

100—What type of breathing should backpackers employ to maximize energy conservation?

Answer—Rhythmic breathing.

200—What is rhythmic breathing?

Answer—Breathing at a steady controlled rate coordinated with the steps taken.

300—How should the length of your stride vary related to the slope of the terrain?

Answer—On flat ground take longer steps; on steeper ground (up or down) take shorter steps.

400—On flat ground, with a pack of average weight, what is an appropriate ratio of steps to breaths?

Answer—About three steps per breath.

500—On steeper terrain, at higher elevations, or with a heavy pack, how does the step-to-breathing ratio change?

Answer—As the going becomes more difficult, take more breaths in relationship to the number of steps. Extremely difficult conditions may require multiple breaths per step.

Rest Breaks

100—What is the purpose of rest breaks?

Answer—To prevent exhaustion.

200—How should you adjust if people find it difficult to make it to the next rest break?

Answer—Slow the pace or shorten the time between breaks.

300—How long should you hike between breaks?

Answer—Depending on fitness level, trip objectives, terrain, and weight of packs, rest breaks should occur every 20 to 60 minutes. In any case, stop before becoming tired.

400—How long should breaks be?

Answer—Breaks should be as short as possible. Aim for 5 minutes but take as long as necessary. (Five-minute breaks minimize the amount of lactic acid buildup in the muscles caused by activity).

500—List three factors that influence where to take a break.

Answer—(1) A reasonably comfortable yet durable site, (2) available water source, and (3) a place where the entire group can be on one side of the trail, out of the way of others who may be hiking.

Hodgepodge

100—Why is eating and drinking at breaks a good idea?

Answer—To replenish lost water and burned-up energy, to prevent fatigue, and to prevent crabbiness.

200—When does a break start?

Answer—When the last person in the group arrives at the location.

300—What information should the leader communicate to the group about and during breaks?

Answer—How long to hike between breaks, how long the break will be, and that backpackers should put on their packs when one minute of the break remains.

400—How does contouring influence energy conservation?

Answer—Contouring means avoiding elevation changes, a practice that helps conserve energy.

500—How does clothing relate to energy conservation?

Answer—Clothing is one way of regulating body heat. As the body heats up, layers of clothing should be removed; as the body cools, layers of clothes should be added. By adding and removing layers, the person does not have to work as hard to maintain constant body temperature.

FIGURE BP10.2   (continued)

Activity 2: Uphill Hiking (15 Minutes)

Special note: This activity is best taught on hilly terrain. When the terrain on which people are backpacking changes, unique challenges and solutions arise. This activity focuses on describing and demonstrating uphill hiking techniques, including body position, pack adjustment, switchbacks, and the rest step, and it offers participants an opportunity to practice those techniques.

◆ Ask the participants to describe some of the challenges that arise when hiking uphill. (Responses may include answers like shortness of breath, tired legs and calves, change in hiking pace, becoming tired.)

◆ Explain that besides basic energy conservation practices (see activity 1), some specific techniques have been discovered that help backpackers overcome some of those challenges.

Body Position

◆ When hiking uphill, participants should try to keep the torso in an upright position. This position maximizes balance and increases the chance of a quick recovery if the hiker loses footing. (Demonstrate and have participants practice without packs first and then with packs on.)

◆ Remind participants to take smaller steps than they would on flat ground to conserve energy.

◆ If an obstacle is too large to step over easily, hikers should go around it.

Pack Packing and Adjustment

◆ Before packing the backpack for the day, participants should review the route. If the hike is primarily uphill and includes steep inclines, they should pack heavier items a little lower than normal (toward the middle of the back).

◆ When ascending hills, backpackers may need to tighten the shoulder straps and pack stabilizer straps slightly to keep the backpack from pulling them backward. (Demonstrate and have students practice adjusting their packs.)

Switchbacks

◆ Trail builders use switchbacks on steeper slopes to help hikers conserve energy and to prevent soil erosion. **Switchbacks** are places where the trail creates a zigzag pattern along the side of a hill because the slope is too steep for the trail to go straight up or down it. Backpackers should always stay on the main trail and use the switchbacks rather than cut straight up or down a hill.

◆ The human body is most efficient at hiking up hills at an incline of less than 15 degrees. Even with switchbacks, a trail may be steeper than the optimal 15 degrees. When that happens, encourage students to walk in mini zigzags from one side of the trail to the other to decrease the elevation gain of each step. If backpackers use the mini switchback technique, they should avoid widening the trail by stepping onto the ground on the edges of the trail. (Demonstrate and have the participants practice.)

Rest Step

◆ The **rest step** is a technique designed to allow the muscles to rest while the skeletal structure supports the backpacker and the weight of the pack.

◆ To prevent calf muscle fatigue, keep the feet as flat as possible.

◆ Lift the back foot as little as possible and swing it forward.

◆ Straighten the leg and lock the knee. Let the bones, not the muscles, support the weight.

◆ Take shorter steps and lengthen the rest time between steps as altitude or steepness increases.

◆ Periodically the shoulders will need to rest from the weight of the pack. Slightly dip the shoulder on the same side of the body as the lead foot.

◆ Demonstrate and have the participants practice.

Activity 3: Downhill Hiking (15 Minutes)

Special note: This activity is best taught on hilly terrain. The activity focuses on describing and demonstrating downhill hiking techniques, including body position, equipment adjustment, using trekking poles, switchbacks, and side steps, and it offers participants an opportunity to practice those techniques.

◆ Ask the participants to describe some of the challenges that arise when hiking downhill. (Responses may include answers like knee strain, feeling off balance, shortness of breath, tired legs, hurting feet, change in hiking pace, becoming tired.)

◆ Explain that besides basic energy conservation practices (see activity 1), some specific techniques have been discovered that help backpackers overcome some of those challenges.

Body Position

◆ When hiking downhill, participants should try to bend their knees slightly the entire time. (Demonstrate and have participants practice without packs first and then with packs on.)

◆ Remind participants to take smaller steps than they would on flat ground to conserve energy and to help keep the body upright to prevent falling forward.

◆ If an obstacle is too large to easily step over, hikers should go around it.

Side Steps   Side steps can be used to reduce the strain on the knees when descending stair steps. Backpackers can turn the body perpendicular to the edge of the trail, bend the uphill knee, and place the hands on the thigh of the uphill leg for support and balance while lowering the downhill foot to the step below. (Demonstrate and have the participants practice.) Special note: This technique can also be used with trekking poles by planting the poles before stepping down and using the poles for support instead of the thigh of the uphill leg.

Equipment Adjustment

◆ Before packing the backpack for the day, participants should review the route. If the hike is primarily downhill and includes steep inclines, they should pack heavier items toward the bottom of the pack to help keep the body stable.

◆ When descending hills, backpackers may need to loosen the shoulder straps and pack stabilizer straps slightly to keep the backpack in a more upright position and to help prevent gravity from pushing them forward. (Demonstrate and have students practice adjusting their packs.)

◆ Because many people feel more friction on their feet when descending, students may need to try tying their boots differently. Because no single technique works best for everyone, the students will have to experiment.

◆ Many backpackers today use trekking poles. Using this piece of equipment significantly reduces the amount of strain that descending slopes puts on the knees.

Three primary techniques are employed for going downhill. Demonstrate each technique and have the participants practice.

1. When the slope is relatively smooth, use the poles normally, swinging them in a natural rhythm. Occasionally trails look similar to a flight of stairs. With each step or two there is a significant step down, sometimes 8 inches (20 centimeters) or more. When the trail has stair steps, the following two techniques may be used.

2. Plant poles beside you and step forward and down.

3. Plant poles in front of you and step forward and down.

Activity 4: Hiking in a Group (45 Minutes)

Backpacking with others poses some unique challenges. This activity lets students explore the concepts of role assignment, spacing, and pace, as well as concepts mentioned in other activities and lessons.

Before beginning this activity print the scenario (figure BP10.3). Divide the students into small groups of four or five. Give each group a copy of the scenario (but not the solutions, of course). Ask them to read the scenario and take about 10 minutes to brainstorm as many travel technique solutions as possible. Check on each group's progress and offer clarification where necessary. At the end of that period ask the groups to take five minutes to rate each of their solutions as a 1, 2, or 3 (1 being a completely nonviable alternative, 2 being an acceptable alternative, and 3 being an extremely viable alternative). After groups have completed the tasks, have them share their responses with the large group and continue the discussion. If students fail to generate all the useful techniques, discuss those with the group.

Activity 5: LNT Principles Related to Trail Techniques (20 Minutes)

This activity is a short introduction to two important LNT principles, "Travel and camp on durable surfaces" and "Be considerate of other visitors." For more information on LNT principles related to backpacking, see lesson 14 in this unit.

Travel and Camp on Durable Surfaces   Remind participants that established trails are considered the most appropriate durable surface to travel on when backpacking. Although travel off trails is sometimes necessary, backpackers should avoid hiking off trail whenever possible. Remind participants that widening the trail creates an impact for all who follow. Even when mud and puddles are on the trail, backpackers should stick to the middle of the trail to keep from harming additional vegetation and to prevent erosion problems.

Be Considerate of Other Visitors   People visit outdoor areas for a variety of reasons. Always treat other outdoor recreation participants with respect. Always be polite and say hello to people whom you meet on the trail.

◆ Other hikers and backpackers. When encountering other hikers and backpackers, good trail etiquette is to stop, step off the side of the trail, and let the group pass. If you are backpacking with a group and encounter another group, the group traveling downhill should step to the side.

◆ Mountain bikers. Mountain bikers should yield to backpackers. But when visibility is limited and the bikers are going fast, they may be unable to slow down. In those cases, step off the trail and let them pass. See the mountain biking unit for more information.

◆ Horseback riders. Horses can be high strung and may spook easily. When you see people riding horses, immediately step off the trail on the downhill side and then

Travel Technique Scenario

One of the participants has spent a lot of time backpacking (has through-hiked all the major trails in the United States) and goes trail running every morning when not backpacking. She is strong and fast, has a lot of endurance, and came to the area three days earlier to sightsee at the national parks. This person also employs many light-hiking techniques and carries a small, lightweight pack. Because this person has the most experience in the backcountry, she has been selected as the navigator and pacesetter for the group.

Another of the participants is a novice backpacker who is out of shape and has too much weight in his pack. The hiker flew into the Jackson airport at 8:00 p.m. the night before the trip on a flight originating in St. Louis.

The other three members of the group had some experience backpacking, were in good physical shape, and had spent the past month walking 3 to 5 miles (5 to 8 kilometers) per day with a weighted pack. They drove from Missouri to Wyoming and arrived in Jackson at noon the day before the trip was to begin. They spent the afternoon walking around the city of Jackson.

The group members completed their vehicle shuttle at 10:15 a.m. and hit the trail at 10:30 a.m. They started up the trail with great enthusiasm and high expectations. The navigator took off at her usual hiking pace. After hiking for 45 minutes and gaining 1,000 feet (300 meters) of elevation during the first .75 miles (1.2 kilometers), the leader stopped for lunch. Three of the group members were right behind her. After 15 minutes the last group member caught up to the first four, looking exhausted. They took an additional 15 minutes of break so that the last group member could eat some food.

When they took another break 45 minutes later, after climbing another 1,000 feet (300 meters) and covering another .75 miles (1.2 kilometers), they waited for 30 minutes before the last group member caught up. When they discussed taking only a 2-minute break so that their muscles wouldn't tense up before resuming the hike, the last group member said that he was going to rest for about 10 minutes and catch up. The initial group started hiking 2 minutes after the last group member arrived.

After 45 minutes, 1,000 feet (300 meters) of elevation gain, and .75 miles (1.2 kilometers), they took another break. After waiting for 1 hour and 15 minutes, the last group member arrived at the break spot. They still had to hike another .75 miles (1.2 kilometers) and gain 750 feet (225 meters) of elevation before they would reach the first viable camping spot on the trail. When the leader suggested heading out immediately, one member jumped up but the other three requested a group meeting to make some changes to their group hiking techniques.

_____

_____

_____

_____

_____

_____

_____

_____

continued ▶

FIGURE BP10.3 The travel technique scenario stimulates discussion of challenges and solutions when group hiking.

From M. Wagstaff and A. Attarian, 2009, *Technical skills for adventure programming: A curriculum guide* (Champaign, IL: Human Kinetics).

Possible Solutions

Although many solutions are feasible, any that involve splitting the group into groups of fewer than four is not recommended for safety reasons. If someone in a group of four participants is hurt, one person can provide care while the other two go for help. This approach prevents anyone from hiking alone.

1. Assign group roles.
   - Scout or navigator—determines appropriate route, navigates (understands trail signs and intersections, coordinates map and compass), creates path of least resistance (finds clear trails and best route around obstacles), stays slightly in front of the rest of the group, about 20 to 30 feet (6 to 10 meters).
   - Smoother—sets the pace and fine-tunes the scout's chosen route over obstacles.
   - Sweep—last person in the group, maintains relatively close proximity to the rest of the group, and does not let group members fall behind.
   - Logger—keeps track of start time, break time, and arrival at destination.
   - Leader—keeps track of the whole group, from front to back, moving throughout the group as needed; determines break times and starting times.

2. Use correct spacing.
   - Ideal spacing is about 10 feet (3 meters) between participants so that the group can stay together but not be on top of each other.
   - Maintaining enough distance between participants is important to prevent branches from flying back and hitting the next person in line.
   - Appropriate spacing allows slightly more flexibility in adjusting individual pace.
   - Sufficient spacing also allows enough room for maneuvering over, under, or around obstacles on the trail (downed trees, for example). If someone needs help, someone else is close by to lend a hand.

3. Hike at an appropriate pace.
   - Hike at the pace of the slowest person. Although faster people may not be comfortable and may not enjoy a slower pace, it is best for the morale, energy, and safety of the group. Accidents and altercations tend to happen when people are tired and stressed.

4. Employ appropriate uphill techniques (see activity 2).
   - Rest step
   - Pack adjustment
   - Body position
   - Switchbacks

5. Redistribute pack content among members.
   - Although most participants will want to carry their share of the weight, at times people should give up their ego and pride and receive the help that they need.

6. Reassign group roles.
   - Have the slowest person serve as the scout or pacesetter.

7. Play leapfrog.
   - Constantly rotate who is at the front of the group when going up steep or long hills. The whole group stops. The person in the back passes all group members and moves about 15 feet (5 meters) in front of the last person. The new back person passes all group members and moves about 15 feet in front of the last person. This continues until the group gets to the top of the hill. With this technique the slowest people (those who most need breaks) get several short breaks during the climb, but the group continues to make forward progress.

8. Play inchworm.
   - Like leapfrog, this approach involves a series of starts and stops, but no one changes position. The whole group stops about 15 or 20 feet (5 or 6 meters) apart. The person in the back moves up until he or she is directly behind the person ahead. The second-to-last person moves forward until he or she is right behind the next person. This process continues until the leader moves forward about 15 to 20 feet (5 or 6 meters) in front of the second person. At that point, the person in the back is signaled to start moving forward again.

9. Take more frequent but shorter breaks.

10. Encourage the slower people and engage them in conversation during the hikes.

FIGURE BP10.3 *(continued)*

stop moving. If the horse happens to shy away, it will go toward the uphill slope, rather than toward the downhill slope where it might lose footing and fall or slide down. As the horse and rider approach, say hello to the rider at a normal volume and engage the person in a short conversation. Hearing human voices will help keep the horses calm and help them understand that you really are human, even though your backpack has made your silhouette unrecognizable.

After ending this minilecture, give the students an oral pop quiz over the concepts. Call on different students to respond to each situation.

Closure Activity

Trail Roles (30 Minutes)

Ask the students to form small groups and assign each group a trail group role (introduced in the activity Hiking in a Group). Have the groups discuss their roles in more detail. Have each group explain the benefits of having a person in that role and the potential negative consequences of not having that role assigned.

Follow-Up Activity

Journal Exercise (Time as Needed)

Have the participants write in their journals about trail techniques. Ask them to address trail situations about which they feel comfortable and uncomfortable. Ask them to discuss the techniques that they have learned and how they think they will use them. When the students go backpacking ask them to try to use some of the new techniques and reflect on those techniques in their journals.

ASSESSMENT

- Check that students can describe three techniques that promote energy conservation by observing them work in small groups to create a list of at least three things that they can do to conserve energy while backpacking.

- Conduct a question-and-answer session in which you observe individual students' explanations of what to do when encountering other groups on the trails (backpackers going uphill, backpackers going downhill, a group of mountain bikers, and a group of horseback riders).

- Confirm that students can demonstrate uphill hiking techniques, including the rest step and one other thing that they can do to increase their efficiency while hiking.

- Check that students know how to descend hills effectively. Observe each student to see what techniques he or she uses to move more comfortably.

- Ensure that students appreciate the effectiveness of trail assignments in organizing groups by having them work in small groups, each assigned a different hiking group assignment. Each group explains the benefits of having a person in that role and the potential negative effects of not having that role.

- Verify that students value LNT principles related to traveling on durable surfaces by writing in journals about LNT principles.

TEACHING CONSIDERATIONS

◆ Although this entire lesson may be taught before a backpacking trip begins, specific hiking techniques, such as uphill and downhill techniques, may be best taught as teachable moments on the trail when first encountering hills.

◆ Consider letting the group struggle initially on a trip so that they experience inefficient hiking techniques. This experience creates a healthy readiness to try new techniques. This strategy works well when students come with experience and are set in their ways.

▷ Route Finding

OVERVIEW

Students learn in this lesson to maintain a map, identify map features and symbols, and interpret contour lines by identifying land features from map to land and land to map.

JUSTIFICATION

Land navigation using a contour map is one of the most difficult skills for backpackers to master. Even advanced backpackers may struggle. For this reason, students must have hands-on practice in the backcountry. Learning how to read a map and navigate difficult terrain increases confidence and adds an extra margin of trip safety. Knowledge of map reading also reduces impact on the land, promotes proper expedition planning, and reduces the likelihood of hiking extra, unneeded miles (kilometers).

GOAL

To develop the participants' ability to travel in the backcountry using a map.

OBJECTIVES

At the end of this lesson, students will be able to

◆ distinguish between different map features and symbols (cognitive),

◆ understand the different types of topographic maps and their basic orientation (cognitive),

◆ display the ability to fold and maintain a map to ensure its longevity (psychomotor),

◆ demonstrate the ability to create a route plan (psychomotor), and

◆ appreciate the ability to navigate confidently in the backcountry with or without trails (affective).

EQUIPMENT AND AREAS NEEDED

- Topographic maps for your area (ideally one for each student)
- A variety of topographic map types with different scales
- A location where you can see topographic land features and do some hiking
- Several packages of yarn with varying colors
- Journals and pencils

RISK MANAGEMENT CONSIDERATIONS

- If outdoors, check the teaching area for environmental hazards.
- Be prepared to do some hiking so that students can practice identifying land features on the map.

LESSON CONTENT

Introduction

- Maps are one of the most important tools used in backpacking. This lesson will teach navigation with maps and how to care for them properly. Many types of topographic maps are available today, and choosing the best map for a trip is important. Typically, maps that cover a larger area have less contour detail than maps that cover a smaller area.

- United States Geological Survey (USGS) topographic maps come in a variety of detail, but 1:24,000 maps offer the most detail. In recent years Trails Illustrated maps have gained popularity because they tend to include current trail locations. A Trails Illustrated map tends to have a much larger scale, in the range of 1:60,000 to 1:83,000. This scale does not provide great detail, but the maps include updated human-made features.

- More recently, custom maps have come on the scene. Several Internet sites, such as offroute.com and topozone.com, allow you to select an area and the contour interval and will then send you on waterproof paper a map of your trip location for a nominal fee. These custom maps are more expensive than USGS or Trails Illustrated maps, but they are a useful tool if you are crossing in and out of several standard maps. The USGS Web site (www.usgs.gov) allows you to download PDFs of topographic maps of any area in the United States.

Main Activities

Activity 1: Map Folding (10 Minutes)

Consider demonstrating map folding first and then assisting students as they fold their maps. Starting the navigation lesson with map folding promotes proper care and respect for this important backpacking tool.

Map folding is a useful art. Ultimately, maps can be folded in many ways that are helpful in land navigation, but they will wear out quickly if not cared for properly. The fold described here (figure BP11.1) allows the map to be stored in a zippered plastic bag. Keep in mind that the map type being described is a USGS topographical map.

◆ Begin by folding the map down the middle vertically with the printed side on the inside. Be sure that the edges line up before creasing the map.

◆ Now fold the map into fourths so that the printed side is visible.

◆ Fold the map in half horizontally.

◆ Fold the map into fourths horizontally so that the lower right corner of the map ends on top for easy identification.

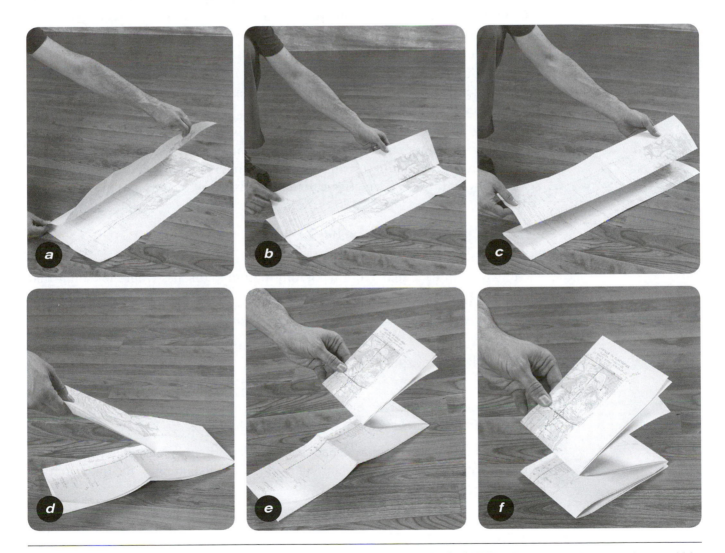

FIGURE BP11.1   Folding a map: *(a)* Fold the map in half, with information on the inside. *(b)* Begin folding the map vertically into fourths. *(c)* Fold the map so that the information in the bottom right corner is visible. *(d)* Fold it in half horizontally. *(e)* Fold it horizontally into fourths. *(f)* Final result.

Activity 2: General Map Information (10 Minutes)

Foster curiosity about maps and what they can tell us by asking questions about the following information, which will be useful when navigating in the backcountry.

◆ Identify various types of topographic maps, such as 1:24,000 USGS maps and Trails Illustrated maps, which are at a scale of about 1:80,000. This lesson refers to 1:24,000 maps as large-scale maps and maps above 1:65,000 as small-scale maps. The scale of 1:24,000 means that 1 inch on the map equals 24,000 inches, or 2,000 feet, on the land surface (1 centimeter on the map equals 24,000 centimeters, or 240 meters, on the land surface). So a scale of 1:65,000 means that 1 inch on the map equals 65,000 inches, or 5,417 feet on the land surface (1 centimeter on the map equals 65,000 centimeters, or 650 meters on the land surface).

◆ Notice the difference in detail between the two maps (the 1:24,000 map versus the 1:65,000 map). Large-scale maps provide more detail in terrain, whereas small-scale maps are more general. The small-scale maps may offer more detail about trails and consistently are more up to date.

◆ Information provided at the bottom of the map helps us understand more about the information presented on the map. The scale, the name of the quadrangle, and the distance scale are all found at the bottom. In the legend, we also find specifics about how the map portrays trails, roads, streams, rivers, and buildings.

◆ Next, have the students study the scale and calculate real-world distance from one point to another using a string or tic marks on a paper taken directly from the scale. They will need to practice calculating distance to complete the follow-up activity.

Activity 3: Map Symbols and Features (10 Minutes)

Divide students into small groups and have them identify as many symbols as possible in two minutes. Use the following information to discuss what they identified and other items that they did not find.

Symbols   Generally, the legend contains many symbols, usually identified as three types—point, line, and plane.

◆ Point symbols show places and buildings.

◆ Line symbols denote trails, roads, power lines, boundaries, and contours.

◆ Plane symbols usually use shading to identify some particular area on a map. For instance, forested areas are usually shaded in green.

Figure BP11.2 shows a sample legend that includes primary map symbols. Be sure to find some that are not represented on the map key at the bottom of the map such as

◆ buildings,

◆ bridges,

◆ BM (benchmarks), and

◆ map directions, like the true north symbol.

Features

◆ Water resources such as rivers, lakes, and springs are typically designated in blue. Forested areas tend to be designated in green, and open areas with low vegetation tend to be white in color.

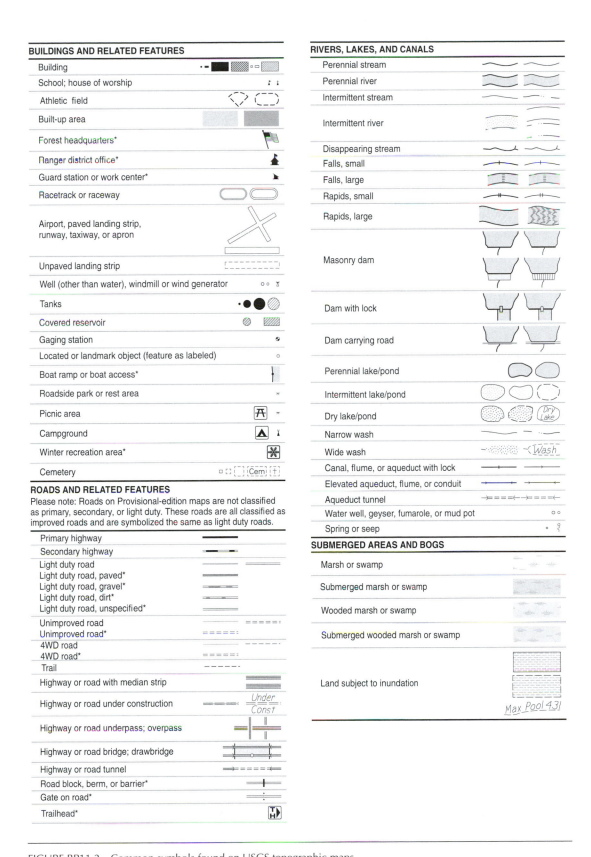

BUILDINGS AND RELATED FEATURES

Building	
School; house of worship	
Athletic field	
Built-up area	
Forest headquarters*	
Ranger district office*	
Guard station or work center*	
Racetrack or raceway	
Airport, paved landing strip, runway, taxiway, or apron	
Unpaved landing strip	
Well (other than water), windmill or wind generator	
Tanks	
Covered reservoir	
Gaging station	
Located or landmark object (feature as labeled)	
Boat ramp or boat access*	
Roadside park or rest area	
Picnic area	
Campground	
Winter recreation area*	
Cemetery	

ROADS AND RELATED FEATURES

Please note: Roads on Provisional-edition maps are not classified as primary, secondary, or light duty. These roads are all classified as improved roads and are symbolized the same as light duty roads.

Primary highway	
Secondary highway	
Light duty road Light duty road, paved* Light duty road, gravel* Light duty road, dirt* Light duty road, unspecified*	
Unimproved road Unimproved road*	
4WD road 4WD road*	
Trail	
Highway or road with median strip	
Highway or road under construction	Under Const
Highway or road underpass; overpass	
Highway or road bridge; drawbridge	
Highway or road tunnel	
Road block, berm, or barrier*	
Gate on road*	
Trailhead*	

RIVERS, LAKES, AND CANALS

Perennial stream	
Perennial river	
Intermittent stream	
Intermittent river	
Disappearing stream	
Falls, small	
Falls, large	
Rapids, small	
Rapids, large	
Masonry dam	
Dam with lock	
Dam carrying road	
Perennial lake/pond	
Intermittent lake/pond	
Dry lake/pond	Dry Lake
Narrow wash	
Wide wash	Wash
Canal, flume, or aqueduct with lock	
Elevated aqueduct, flume, or conduit	
Aqueduct tunnel	
Water well, geyser, fumarole, or mud pot	
Spring or seep	

SUBMERGED AREAS AND BOGS

Marsh or swamp	
Submerged marsh or swamp	
Wooded marsh or swamp	
Submerged wooded marsh or swamp	
Land subject to inundation	

Max Pool 431

FIGURE BP11.2   Common symbols found on USGS topographic maps.

From http://permanent.access.gpo.gov/websites/ergusgsgov/erg.usgs.gov/isb/pubs/booklets/symbols/index.html

◆ Contour lines delineate different elevations and show the shape and lay of the land. The closer the contour lines are to one another, the steeper the terrain is; the farther apart they are, the more moderate the terrain is. Contour lines are line symbols on the map and provide a wealth of information. On a 1:24,000 map, the contour interval is 40 feet. Thus, every contour line represents a 40-foot (12-meter) change in elevation. Contour lines are typically brown, and every fifth line is bold. With a 40-foot (12-meter) contour interval, every fifth line is a 200-foot (60-meter) change.

◆ Valleys are represented by contour lines in the shape of a V that always points up in elevation.

◆ Ridges are represented by Vs or sometimes Us that point to decreasing elevation.

◆ Summits are represented by small circles on the map.

◆ Depressions are also circles except that the contour lines have short, perpendicular lines that point toward the center.

◆ Students often have the most difficulty seeing the lay of the land on the map. Find a mountain or hill that is easily identifiable on the map. Talk about its features on the map. What is on the side that can't be seen? See figure BP 11.3 for an example of a topographic map with the features identified.

Activity 4: Mountain Ranges (40 Minutes)

Follow the map symbol and feature discussion by dividing the class into smaller groups to build mountain ranges. The following are the steps for building a mountain range:

◆ Break everyone into small groups of three or four.

◆ Have everyone collect sand or forest litter to build a mountain range. Ideally, the range should have multiple summits and drainages.

◆ Use yarn to add contour lines to the mountain ranges. Have students transfer the 3D image to paper by drawing it in their journals or on a piece of paper.

◆ Have students name their ranges. Check for accuracy through instructor or peer evaluation.

Closure Activity

Route Planning (30 Minutes)

Have students plan the backpacking route for the day by looking at it in terms of **macro** and **micro navigation**. The macro is the overview of the route, the big land features, and the general direction of travel for the day.

◆ In the macro picture, students should build in major backstops to aid in navigation throughout the day.

◆ **Backstops** are the major landmarks that backpackers use not only to judge where they are but also to form a boundary or sign that tells them to make a navigation change. For instance, Bennett Peak and the Alamosa River are the backstops for a popular hiking route in the southern San Juan Mountains. Therefore, the group would know not to descend into the Alamosa River valley or go beyond Bennett Peak.

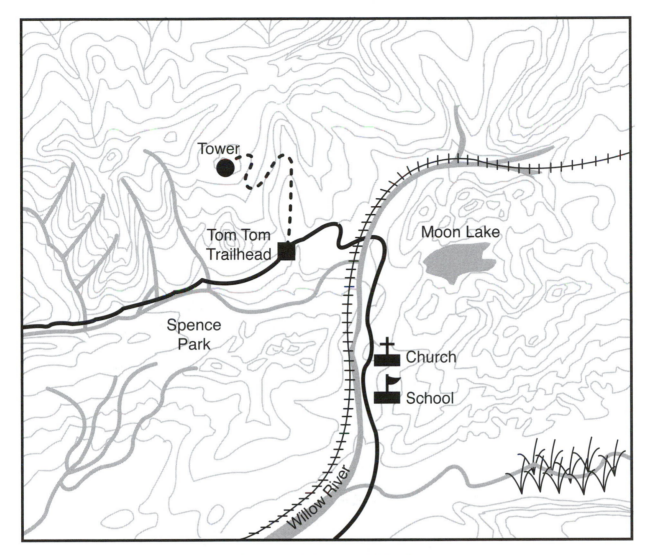

Contour interval 100 feet

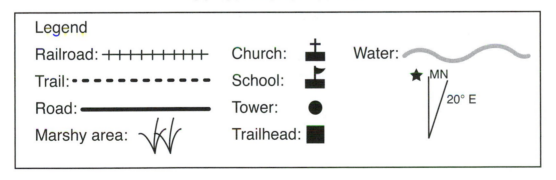

FIGURE BP11.3 Sample topographical map with features.

Reprinted, by permission, from C. Bunting, 2005, *Interdisciplinary teaching through outdoor education* (Champaign, IL: Human Kinetics), 113.

◆ Now have them look at the route in terms of micro navigation along the way. For example, identify specific land features that will be road signs for them. An example may be the junction of two streams or prominent cliffs on one side of a canyon. These **handrail** features should help the students identify where they are along the trail and provide confidence that they are on the correct route and heading.

Follow-Up Activity

Journaling Exercise (45 Minutes)

Have the students make a detailed route plan in their journals.

◆ Have them record the macro picture with total distance of the route, total elevation gain and loss, location where they are heading and the general direction of travel, and major landmarks along the way.

◆ They should then add micro navigation landmarks complete with elevation and distance remaining from that point.

ASSESSMENT

◆ Verify that students can distinguish between various map features and symbols through the activity Map Symbols and Features and during the first hike.

◆ Ensure that students understand the different types of topographic maps and their basic orientation by providing several different maps for the area where they will be traveling and by providing opportunities to use different maps.

◆ Confirm that students know how to fold and maintain a map to ensure its longevity by observing them during the activity Map Folding and throughout the trip.

◆ Check that students have the ability to create a route plan by creating a plan for the first scheduled trip in their journals.

◆ Help students develop the ability to navigate confidently in the backcountry with or without trails by providing opportunities for them to navigate through diverse terrain and travel on trail and off trail.

TEACHING CONSIDERATIONS

◆ Route finding using a map is best taught in the field. Symbols and features, as well as the contour activity, can be taught in the classroom, but to learn navigation with the map, students need field time.

◆ As an instructor, allow the students to make mistakes and have the opportunity to discover where they went wrong as long as they aren't putting themselves in danger.

◆ Student learning increases when all students have their own maps. Either ask students to buy certain topographic maps or provide the needed maps.

◆ Try not to teach too much information at one time. On the first day, map symbols may be enough information for hiking a trail. On the second day, work on contour lines and other elements to allow time for the students to see their importance.

UNIT 1, LESSON 12

▷ # Route Finding With a Map and Compass

OVERVIEW

Building on lesson 11, students learn in this lesson to identify compass parts using appropriate nomenclature and use a compass to orient a map. Students then learn to use the compass as an aid in navigating in combination with the map and land features.

JUSTIFICATION

The compass is an additional tool that backpackers can use in concert with a map to help decipher difficult navigational challenges, thus increasing safety and decreasing impact on the land. The compass is a simple, reliable tool that does not require batteries, unlike more modern navigational tools such as a Global Positioning System (GPS). Use of a compass is a basic, essential skill for any backpacker.

GOAL

To extend the participants' ability in route finding by adding the compass.

OBJECTIVES

At the end of this lesson, students will be able to

- identify compass features and their purpose (cognitive);
- display the ability to use a compass to determine direction of travel, true north, and the use of bearings (psychomotor);
- demonstrate the ability to navigate overland using topographic maps and a compass (psychomotor); and
- appreciate the ability to navigate confidently in the backcountry with or without trails while using a map and compass (affective).

EQUIPMENT AND AREAS NEEDED

- Several varieties of topographic maps
- Several varieties of compass
- P cord or string
- Length of rope
- Pencils

RISK MANAGEMENT CONSIDERATIONS

If teaching this lesson in the outdoors, pay attention to the considerations detailed in lesson 2.

LESSON CONTENT

Introduction

"When all else fails, trust your compass—it will keep you straight!" The first compass use in history was recorded by the Chinese in AD 1088. Around 1400 to 1500, Europeans began using marine compasses. Later people realized that they could substitute the compass for the sundial, and the portable field compass was born. It was not until the 1930s that the first inexpensive liquid-filled compass was available to the public. The Kjellstrom brothers of Sweden, avid participants in the sport of orienteering, were inspired to invent this compass, which led to the birth of the Silva Company.

Main Activities

Activity 1: Compass Nomenclature (20 Minutes)

Explain and identify the types and parts of a compass while giving students hands-on experience. A quiz allows for review and assessment.

Types of Compasses Backpackers use two primary types of compasses, the base-plate and the prismatic compass.

◆ The base-plate compass (figure BP12.1) is the most commonly used compass for teaching map and compass and backcountry travel. These inexpensive compasses use a revolutionary design that puts a fluid-filled compass on top of a protractor-type base, allowing the user to take a quick bearing from map to land.

◆ The prismatic compass with a base plate is a more serious tool for navigation and often provides more features than a standard base-plate compass does. The prismatic compass with a base plate has a sighting and mirror system that allows more accurate field bearings, and it generally has a set-and-forget **declination** adjustment and a clinometer, also known as an inclinometer. The clinometer is used to measure angles of slope, or the elevation of an object in relation to gravity (tilt meter).

Parts of a Compass

◆ Base plate—the flat, clear base of the compass that is marked with measurements and a direction-of-travel arrow.

◆ Scales in millimeters and inches—can be used for purposes such as calculating distance on a map.

◆ Direction-of-travel arrow—the arrow to follow when shooting a bearing.

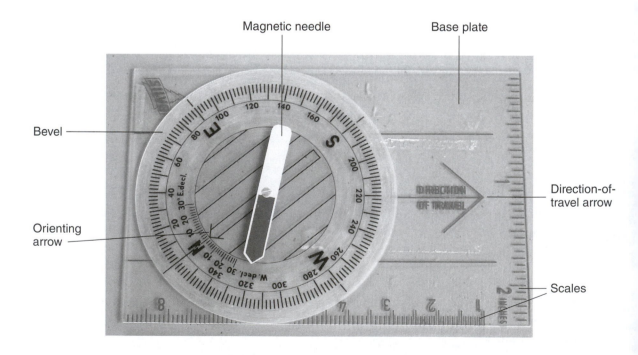

FIGURE BP12.1 Base-plate compass, a compass that backpackers often use.

Reprinted, by permission, from C. Bunting, 2005, *Interdisciplinary teaching through outdoor education* (Champaign, IL: Human Kinetics), 106.

◆ Bevel—round disc that marks direction (360 degrees including the cardinal directions north and south, east and west) and houses the orienting arrow and the magnetic needle.

◆ Orienting arrow—used to orient the compass to the north.

◆ Magnetic needle—the red end points north in the Northern Hemisphere.

◆ Sighting mirror—set-and-forget declination adjustments (not shown in figure BP12.1).

Quiz After discussing the compass parts, provide students with the image of a compass on a whiteboard or photocopied on individual sheets of paper. Test students' recall by having them identify and label the parts of the compass. The quiz and checking the answers should take about 10 minutes.

Activity 2: Orienting the Map (20 Minutes)

Demonstrate how to orient the map using the compass. Allow students to practice.

◆ The best time to orient your map is before leaving your known vicinity.

◆ If you are at a known location, use the land features, human-made features, and other information to find where you are on the map.

◆ Look for obvious land features, like a lake, that you can use to put the map into orientation. If a lake is in front of you and a peak behind you, and you know that you are between the two, turn the map so that you are looking at the lake with the peak behind you. You are now oriented.

◆ Check this orientation by using a compass.

- Align the base plate on the edge of a topographic map. Check to make sure that north on the map is at the top of the map by locating the compass rose.

- Turn the bevel of the compass to 0 degrees and turn the map, holding the compass firmly in place on the map until the red arrow is nested in the orienting arrow in the bevel.

- If the map was lined up with the land features correctly, only minor movement of the map should have occurred; otherwise reevaluate the location where you thought you were.

Activity 3: Teaching a Meaningful Declination Lesson (45 Minutes)

Use this hands-on activity and lecture to teach declination.

◆ Begin by finding the middle of a rope at least 100 feet (30 meters) long. The middle of the rope should be your north end, and the two ends will be your south.

◆ Identify one-half of the rope as the zero declination line. When on this line, your compass and map always point to true north.

◆ Compass angles are always measured in 360 degrees, so declination is the angle measured from true north as the starting point. True north to your current location is declination. True north is the **bight** (bend) in the middle of the rope and should remain in place. The half of the rope identified as zero declination should also remain constant. Have the group spread out on both sides of the zero declination line. Move the other half of the rope to each participant to demonstrate varying angles to true north from different points.

◆ Declination is the variation in angle from either side of this line, in other words, the difference in direction between true north and magnetic north. True north is the direction to the location of the geographic pole, an actual place. Magnetic north is a force, the direction in which the compass needle points. Because the Earth's magma core creates this force, the magnetic field varies over time. Maps indicate the correction declination at the bottom of the page, but be cautious about using maps that are more than 10 years old because the declination may be off considerably.

◆ The north arrow will always point toward this line, so if you are on the right side of it, the north arrow will point more west. This is called west declination. On the left side of the line, the compass arrow will always point more east, hence east declination (Curtis, 1998). The orienteering arrow of the compass has to be adjusted to point at true north, the physical location by which the maps are drawn. This adjustment, the process called declination, can be a confusing affair.

◆ For west declination, you are east of 0 degrees. For example, in Brevard, North Carolina, you will need to move the bevel 3 degrees west, so from 0 or 360, proper declination would be 357 degrees. For east declination, you are west of 0 degrees. In Alamosa, Colorado, for example, you would need to turn the bevel 9 degrees east. On a base-plate compass you will probably need to make this correction every time you go from a field bearing to a map bearing and vice versa. A prismatic compass with base plate may have a set-it-and-forget-it feature that makes the process smoother from time to time. See figure BP12.2 for a declination map of North America.

◆ For every degree of declination and 0.6 miles (1 kilometer), the error is about 60 feet (18 meters). In the San Luis Valley of Colorado, with a declination of 9 degrees east, the error would be over 1,000 feet in just 1 mile (190 meters in 1 kilometer).

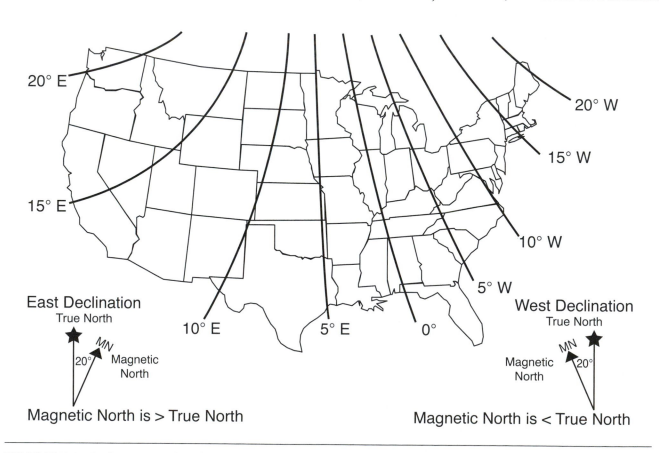

FIGURE BP12.2   Declination map of North America, used to demonstrate west and east declination.

Reprinted, by permission, from C. Bunting, 2005, *Interdisciplinary teaching through outdoor education* (Champaign, IL: Human Kinetics), 111.

◆ Fortunately, for human-powered travel we can generally work with only one declination setting for an entire trip.

Activity 4: Shooting a Bearing (One Hour)

Use this hands-on demonstration to teach how to shoot a bearing.

◆ Bearings are best used for confirmation of the current location.

◆ To take a field bearing, you should ideally have an identifiable landmark to take the bearing from. Using your compass, site your landmark and turn the bevel until the north arrow is inside the orienteering arrow. Your bearing is now the number at the line of the bottom of the direction-of-travel arrow on your base plate. Remember, to take this bearing to the map, you must account for declination.

◆ After adjusting for declination, and with the map oriented, line up the edge of your compass with the landmark and turn the compass until the orienting arrow is pointing to north on the map (parallel with the lines on the edge of the map). Your position will lie somewhere along the line created by the compass edge. Remember to use your landmarks and verify your position with the compass, not the other way around. Some variability in your compass bearings will always occur; be careful not to make it fit the map.

◆ For a map bearing, orient your map to magnetic north and then lay the side of your compass across the landmark that you are using. Turn the bevel until the north arrow is in the orienteering arrow. This is your bearing. Now, using that bearing, place your compass close to your chest and turn your body until the north arrow is again in the orienteering arrow. You should be looking at your landmark if it is in view.

Closure Activity

Orienteering Course (Three Hours)

First, prepare an orienteering course for practice. Allow two hours to develop the course and one hour to run the course. Hands-on practice is the best way to improve compass skills.

◆ Ideally, the course should have a variety of points in a mixture of terrain that will challenge the participants' ability to walk from point to point.

◆ Set points at the top of ridges and in the bottom of valleys and provide plenty of opportunity for them to travel without a trail.

◆ A course can be set up in a schoolyard or even in a gymnasium if necessary to start the learning of skills.

Follow-Up Activity

Practice on the Trail (Time as Needed)

◆ Provide opportunities for each student to be responsible for facilitating navigation for the day.

◆ On a backpacking trip, navigation should be part of everyone's daily duties, but being in charge of the process for the day is an excellent way for a student to demonstrate her or his skills.

◆ Set up the day of travel so that students note detailed navigational decisions in their journals for review at the end of the day.

ASSESSMENT

- Check that students can identify compass features and their purpose by testing their knowledge as described in activity 1.
- Confirm that students have the ability to use a compass to determine direction of travel, true north, and the use of bearings by providing an orienteering course so that they can demonstrate their skills.
- Confirm that students have the ability to navigate overland using topographic maps and compass by providing opportunities during an extended backpacking trip for them to travel off trail and demonstrate their skills.
- Help students appreciate the ability to navigate confidently in the backcountry with or without trails while using a map and compass by providing off-trail opportunities and setting them up for success during the trip.

TEACHING CONSIDERATIONS

- The students must have hands-on experience to become confident with a map and compass.
- Consider establishing small map and compass groups, having two people share a map, or having students buy individual maps to help with this process.
- Any student who does not have a map out is probably not learning to navigate. Encourage students to carry maps at all times.
- Regularly question students about where they are on the map, their direction of travel, and so forth during a trip. Watch for proper orientation of the map with land features and the compass during this process.

UNIT 1, LESSON 13

▷ Risk Management Plan

OVERVIEW

In this lesson, students learn the fundamental components of a risk management plan. Students apply knowledge by designing a risk management plan for their backpacking trip. They research an area and provide all the pertinent information necessary to deal with an emergency.

JUSTIFICATION

Students must understand the necessity of having thorough and accurate risk management plans for their trips. Having such plans allows everyone to respond appropriately and quickly to an emergency. A comprehensive risk management plan can save lives.

GOAL

To develop the students' understanding of a risk management plan and provide them with a thorough foundation for creating the plan.

OBJECTIVES

At the end of this lesson, students will be able to

◆ identify the major components of a risk management plan (cognitive),

◆ seek out the necessary information to complete the risk management plan (cognitive), and

◆ appreciate a well-developed risk management form and find comfort in a well-organized plan (affective).

EQUIPMENT AND AREAS NEEDED

◆ Computer with Internet access

◆ Phone with long-distance access if the trip is not local

RISK MANAGEMENT CONSIDERATIONS

◆ A well-developed and planned risk management plan will aid in smooth rescue in the event of an emergency. Ensure that students have the time to develop a satisfactory plan.

◆ Do not let students assume that they know where everything is just because the trip is local.

LESSON CONTENT

Introduction

Creating a risk management plan for backpacking trips is an essential skill. A thorough risk management plan can make rescue timelier and reduce guess work in the event of an emergency. Don't forget that planning prevents poor performance!

Main Activity

Creating a Risk Management Plan (One to Two Hours)

Students will design a standardized plan to use on their trip. Use the following information to discuss the components of a good plan. Then have the students divide into small groups and create a plan for their first trip. After they complete their plans, have them share information gathered and clarify any issues or problems.

A risk management plan should include numerous elements:

◆ Dates of the trip—trip starting and ending times

◆ The itinerary including directions to the trailhead and takeout, trip starting and ending times, and a daily schedule that includes route and campsites

◆ Topographic map clearly marked with intended route and campsites

◆ All logical evacuation points along the intended route

◆ Names and emergency contact info for each trip participant

◆ Participant medical information and medical insurance information

◆ Emergency numbers in the area where the trip is located, including sheriff, hospital, land management agencies, local rescue service

- A call list of people who can help at home
- Description of known contingency plans
- Emergency forms such as accident and incident reports

Note these additional guidelines to follow when creating a risk management plan:

- The plan should be duplicated and given to the key personnel in the front country. The trip instructors should keep a copy.
- All the information in the previous list should be included along with any additional information deemed necessary.
- Use as many resources as possible to obtain the proper information such as Internet resources, phone books, and phone calls to land management agencies and hospitals. Gathering this information can take some time, but the result is a clear and detailed plan. Printable maps from the Internet are a useful addition if the trip is to an unfamiliar area.
- Create or use written protocol to determine basic steps to take in an emergency.
- The plan should be specific and verifiable. Emergency phone numbers should be double checked.

If desired, you can print figure BP13.1 from the CD-ROM and use it as a risk management form template for this activity.

Closure Activity

Mock Scenario (45 Minutes)

Create a mock scenario of an accident before the first backpacking trip. For this exercise, pretend that the instructors are the ones who are injured and unable to assist. An exercise such as this will help the students determine whether all aspects of their plan are in place.

Follow-Up Activity

Assess the Plan (20 Minutes)

Assess the risk management plan near the end of the trip.

- Has the expedition stayed on the intended route?
- What changes should be made to the plan?
- What issues surfaced that should be included in the next plan?

ASSESSMENT

- Verify that students can identify the major components of a risk management plan by designing one for their trip.
- Check that students can find the information necessary to complete the risk management plan by observing them use the Internet, contact land management agencies, and locate other available information during the main activity.
- Confirm that students appreciate a well-developed risk management plan and find comfort in a well-organized plan by observing their participation in a mock emergency that tests the plan.

Risk Management Template

Trip: _____

Dates: _____

Group Members, Phone Numbers, Emergency Contact Info

1. _____

2. _____

3. _____

4. _____

5. _____

6. _____

Itinerary: ∧ Indicates Campsite

Day 1 _____

Day 2 _____

Day 3 _____

Day 4 _____

Day 5 _____

Day 6 _____

Day 7 _____

Day 8 _____

In the event of an emergency in which a student is being evacuated and you need outside assistance, please use the following call list.

Emergency Phone Numbers

Sheriff

_____

Your Agency's On Call Information

_____

Land Agency Dispatch

_____

In the event of an accident or incident in which you do not need outside assistance, please use the on-call list.

On Call

_____

_____

Land Agencies, Contacts, Phone Numbers

_____

_____

Emergency Contact Information

Emergency Contact 1:

Name: _____

Phone: _____

Emergency Contact 2:

Name: _____

Phone: _____

Emergency Contact 3:

Name: _____

Phone: _____

FIGURE BP13.1   Use this template as a risk management tool.

From M. Wagstaff and A. Attarian, 2009, *Technical skills for adventure programming: A curriculum guide* (Champaign, IL: Human Kinetics).

TEACHING CONSIDERATIONS

◆ Be sure to emphasize the importance of a thorough plan.

◆ Sometimes, emergency contact information is inaccurate, out of date, or otherwise deficient. Be sure to call critical numbers to check validity.

◆ Formats for emergency plans vary. For example, students could be challenged to design a form that encompasses the information. The material could be bound in a small, durable notebook suitable for packing or storing in a first aid kit.

UNIT 1, LESSON 14

▷ Leave No Trace Considerations

OVERVIEW

As outdoor leaders and educators, we have a responsibility to protect the outdoors from degradation and to leave it better than it was before our arrival whenever possible. During this lesson students will begin to explore the concept of outdoor ethics and learn to apply the principles of Leave No Trace (LNT) while backpacking.

JUSTIFICATION

Before the advent of mechanized equipment, before large numbers of people began flocking to the outdoors for solace, adventure, socializing, and therapy, there was little need to be concerned about people's impact on the backcountry. But as more people gained access to the outdoors, the natural landscape had less time to rejuvenate itself, and the animals, plants, and people visiting felt the results. To keep the natural environment natural, people had to change some of their habits. The LNT principles provide general guidelines and advice to help people make ethical outdoor decisions (Leave No Trace, Inc., n.d.).

GOAL

To develop participants' awareness of the LNT principles related to backpacking and to help them appreciate the ethical reasons behind the principles.

OBJECTIVES

At the end of this lesson, students will be able to

◆ explain the difference between ethical and nonethical outdoor behavior (cognitive),

◆ list and describe the seven LNT principles (cognitive),

◆ explain why waste should be disposed of properly (cognitive),

◆ describe how to minimize campfire impacts (cognitive),

◆ demonstrate the ability to walk on durable surfaces (psychomotor),

◆ empathize with other visitors (affective),

◆ appreciate the reasons behind leaving what you find (affective), and

◆ appreciate the importance of planning and preparation (affective).

EQUIPMENT AND AREAS NEEDED

- Paper (enough to make lists and draw sketches)
- Pens or pencils
- Picture of outdoor destination
- Zippered bags with different materials in each—gravel, dried grass, green grass, fallen leaves, graham crackers covered with green icing or mint Oreos with the top removed to represent moss
- Brown paper lunch bags (one for each participant)
- Chalk (one piece for each participant)
- Fire-building materials
- Student journals (ask them to bring their own)

RISK MANAGEMENT CONSIDERATIONS

- If teaching outdoors, follow basic recommendations listed in lesson 2.
- Campfires should be built only in safe, appropriate areas cleared of other combustible materials.
- Participants should wear gloves when handling food products because of allergy and sanitation issues.

LESSON CONTENT

Introduction

You may have heard the phrase "Take only pictures, leave only footprints." But the Leave No Trace (LNT) initiative encourages us to leave *nothing*, not even footprints! LNT is a not-for-profit agency designed to help people make ethical decisions and learn about protecting the environment through individual actions taken during visits to natural areas. Seven guiding principles help people have a **minimum-impact camping** experience (Leave No Trace, n.d.). During this lesson each of the following principles is examined in detail.

- Plan ahead and prepare
- Travel and camp on durable surfaces
- Dispose of waste properly
- Leave what you find
- Minimize campfire impacts
- Respect wildlife
- Be considerate of other visitors

Leave No Trace principles—Copyright: Leave No Trace Center for Outdoor Ethics. www.LNT.org

    LNT is not a set of rules, laws, or policies; it is a set of ethical principles. **Ethics** are closely related to values, morals, and principles. An ethical decision is one that was made because it was the right thing to do, not because of fear of punishment or the expectation of reward. Although many land management agencies have policies and regulations that require the observance of LNT principles, the spirit of LNT is that people will make the right choice because they want to.

Main Activities

Activity 1: Plan Ahead and Prepare (20 Minutes)

◆ Divide the students into small groups of about four people. Tell them that you are all going backpacking this weekend and that they need to create their gear and supply list. Tell them that you will check the lists in three minutes.

◆ At the end of three minutes show them a picture of an outdoor destination in a region different from the area that they planned for and change the season. Ask them whether they would change the items on their list. Discuss the importance of planning for a specific location and time of the year.

◆ Be sure to mention that part of planning and preparation is knowing the policies and procedures of the land management agency and recognizing that obtaining a permit might be necessary.

◆ Have the students come up with consequences for not being prepared. Then have them draw a picture or cartoon representing what could happen if a person or group was not prepared for a backpacking trip.

Activity 2: Travel and Camp on Durable Surfaces (10 Minutes)

Explain that a durable surface is one that can withstand a lot of walking, camping, and other activity and show little, if any, wear.

◆ Lay out zippered plastic bags with different types of materials in them, such as gravel, dried grass, green grass, fallen leaves, and graham crackers covered with green icing or mint Oreos with the top taken off to represent moss.

◆ Have the students arrange them in a line from most durable to least durable.

◆ Ask the students to get into a single-file line and step on each of the bags.

◆ After the students have stepped on the materials, examine the materials and ask the students whether their initial guesses were correct. Explain that because moss is the least durable surface, it is one of the worst places to walk and camp. Although moss is soft and would provide a comfortable sleeping surface, it would need a long time to recover to its original condition.

◆ Ask students to figure out other ways to have a soft bed.

◆ As a follow-up activity you can have them go outside and try to walk from one point to another by stepping on the most durable surfaces.

Special note: Students enjoy eating the squashed remains of the Oreo or graham cracker moss, so you may want to have some spoons and dishes available.

Activity 3: Dispose of Waste Properly (15 Minutes)

◆ Give the students one minute to write individual lists of different types of waste that would need to be disposed of during a backpacking trip.

◆ Have the students get into small groups and share their lists. Give them two minutes to come up with any other types of waste that would require disposal.

◆ Give the students two minutes to determine what should be done with each of the different types of waste.

◆ Have each small group share one type of waste and the appropriate methods for disposal with the entire group. If the students fail to mention certain types of waste, be sure to address those forms.

Sample list:

- Trash and recyclable materials (paper, plastic, metal, glass) should be put into garbage or recycling bags and packed out.
- Leftover food should be put into a garbage bag and packed out.
- Used toilet paper and feminine products should be put into a garbage bag and packed out if there are no bathroom facilities.
- Liquid human waste, bathwater, hand-washing water, toothpaste, and dishwater should be distributed at least 200 feet (60 meters) from trails, camp, and water sources. Wastewater should be broadcast—widely sprayed and scattered.
- Solid human waste should be buried in a cathole of appropriate diameter and depth at least 200 feet (60 meters) from trails, camp, and water sources. For certain activities in specific geographical areas, different methods may be employed.

Ask students why proper disposal of waste is important. Reasons include maintaining health of people, protecting wild animals, and keeping water sources nonpolluted.

Note: Because hygiene is discussed in lesson 8, spend less time on bathing, hand washing, brushing teeth, cleaning dishes, and using the bathroom in this lesson. Nevertheless, this activity will be a good review before the first trip.

Activity 4: Leave What You Find (10 to 15 Minutes)

- When people think of "Leave what you find," most think of natural items like wildflowers, rocks, or seashells that should be left where they are so that others will be able to see them when they visit the area. Others may think of leaving historical artifacts like arrowheads and pottery shards to help provide a historical record of the area. A third aspect of "Leave what you find" is one that people rarely think about: "Leave it as you found it." Before 1970 manipulating the environment to make a more comfortable camp was the norm. No one thought twice about a camper cutting pine boughs for a bed. Similarly, after pitching a tent, people often dug a trench around it to prevent flooding inside if it rained. To prove that they had passed that way, campers might carve their names into a tree or a rock. Today, these practices are not acceptable. Campers should take care to leave the natural environment as it was when they arrived, if not better.
- Ask participants to pull out their journals and writing instruments and in three minutes create a list of examples of actions taken by hikers, backpackers, or campers that they have seen or heard about that might violate the "Leave what you find" principle. They should include the examples that you share.
- Have the participants choose a partner and share their lists with each other.
- During the next five minutes, the pairs should come up with reasons why people did each of those things, describe why each of those behaviors is unnecessary, and provide suggestions for preventing those behaviors in the future.
- Go around the large group and have each pair share one behavior and the ideas and suggestions that they created. After all pairs have shared, ask whether anyone has another behavior that they would like to discuss.

As a rule, "Leave what you find" is a difficult principle for people to buy into, especially those who collect items. Students may also have questions about whether or not it is acceptable to eat foods growing in the wild. In those instances, talk about the following ideas:

◆ Abundance—is the item abundant in both the local area and other places?

◆ Resiliency—if taken, will it come back just as strong?

◆ Need—do you need it to provide additional minerals or vitamins that may be lacking in the foods that you packed?

◆ Portion gathered—take the minimum that you need so that others, including wildlife, will have what they need.

Activity 5: Minimize Campfire Impacts (One to Two Hours)

When people read this principle, they often assume that it means no fires. LNT principles do allow for the use of safe campfires that are constructed with appropriate materials, in appropriate locations, following the guidelines of the regulating land management agency. In this lesson, students learn how to decide whether to use a fire, where to build fires, and how to construct fires.

Deciding to Build   Fires are luxuries, not necessities, except in emergencies. If a group needs to signal for rescuers or to warm hypothermic patients, they should not hesitate to build a safe fire. In other cases, fires can be used for some cooking, and they provide a pleasant atmosphere.

Teach students to use the acronym FIRE when determining whether to build a fire.

◆ **F:** Fire regulations. Before deciding whether to build a fire, first check with the local land management agency to see whether fires are allowed in the area at that time. Some areas prohibit fires; others may establish temporary bans in the event of drought or other circumstances.

◆ **I:** Intimacy. Sitting around a campfire with others can be pleasurable. People enjoy singing songs and telling stories while watching the flames dance and the embers fade.

◆ **R:** Risk. Examine the safety consequences. Determine whether anything in the surrounding area can possibly catch on fire (dead vegetation or tents), how much rain has fallen recently, how windy it is, and whether the fire site will be able to contain the fire.

◆ **E:** Environment. Determine what the environmental effect of having a fire in that area would be. Adequate fuel should be on the ground relatively close to the site, the area should naturally replenish the fuel used in a short period, the fire should not leave any visual scars, and the group should be present at the fire long enough to see that the wood burns completely to ash. Fires should be built primarily in established fire sites.

Lead a guided discussion with the students about the choice to build a fire. Give the students the opportunity to ask questions and raise important questions.

Selecting a Fire Site   Fire site selection is just as important as campsite selection. Ask the students to brainstorm places that would be appropriate for a campsite. At a minimum, they should come up with the following answers. If they don't, provide the following list to them.

◆ In an existing fire ring. A **fire ring** is a circle of rock or metal built by humans inside of which a fire has been built.

◆ Out of direct wind.

◆ Away from flammable objects including vegetation (overhanging tree limbs, dead grass, dead leaves) and equipment (tents, clotheslines, and so on).

- Near water (if a natural body of water or hydrant is not nearby, water will have to be carried to the site).
- Away from rock faces or boulders that will scar.
- On a gravel or sand bar at the edge of a river or lake.

Ask the students whether an environmentally friendly and safe fire can be built in an area where no fire rings exist. Their answers may vary, but the correct answer is yes. Stress that using existing sites is always preferable but that there are ways to construct fire sites that will leave no visual impact.

Constructing a New Fire Site   Although some people carry a fire pan or small grill with them when they use other modes of transportation on a camping trip, backpackers find this impractical. A few other options exist, including mound fires and pit fires. Both require a significant amount of time and energy to build and dismantle.

Mound fires require digging up mineral soil—inorganic soil that is often sandy, usually 6 to 8 inches (15 to 20 centimeters) below the surface. Places to find mineral soil include stream beds or at the base of uprooted trees.

- Dig up enough soil to make a mound at least 3 inches (8 centimeters) thick and 18 to 24 inches (45 to 60 centimeters) in diameter. Building the mound on top of a tarp expedites cleanup of the site.
- After building the mound, start a small fire on top.
- When the wood burns completely to ash, wet the ashes to ensure that they are completely cool and then scatter the ashes widely. Return the mineral soil to its original location.

Another type of minimum-impact fire site is a pit fire. The campers must dig a hole in the ground to hold the fire according to the following instructions.

- Remove all the dead leaves, twigs, and organic material from a 4-foot (120-centimeter) diameter area and set it aside where it will not blow into the cleared area.
- Carefully cut out a circle 18 to 24 inches (45 to 60 centimeters) in diameter in the center of the cleared area. Try to keep the circle intact when removing it and setting it aside.
- Dig down approximately 8 inches (20 centimeters) to reach mineral soil. Line the sides of the pit with mineral soil to protect the surrounding area.
- Build a small fire inside the pit.
- After the fire burns completely, wet the ashes and scatter them.
- Refill the pit and replace the top circle. Camouflage the site by replacing the dead leaves and twigs.

Note: If campers are near a river or lake that has gravel bars, they can construct a pit fire by simply clearing the gravel from a 3- to 4-foot (90- to 120-centimeter) area close to the edge of the water, well below the high-water mark. The fire can then be built directly on the sand under the gravel. After wetting and dispersing the ashes, they simply replace the gravel.

Gathering Wood   After selecting or establishing an appropriate site, the next step in building a fire is to gather wood. Appropriate firewood follows the principle of the four Ds: dead, down, dry, and dinky.

◆ Dead and down—All firewood should come from branches and limbs that have fallen off trees and no longer have green leaves.

◆ Dry—Wet wood is difficult to burn and creates a lot of unpleasant smoke.

◆ Dinky—All wood gathered should be small enough to be broken with the hands. Larger pieces of wood may not burn completely. Different diameters and lengths of wood should be gathered, ranging from small twigs the size of toothpicks up to finger-size branches (diameter of the largest finger). The different sizes of materials are called tinder, kindling, and fuel.

– **Tinder** is usually small material that lights quickly like tiny twigs from evergreen trees, birch bark, dry evergreen needles, dried grass, lint, or paper. The fire builder lights the tinder first.

– **Kindling** includes small-diameter branches (smaller than 3/4 inch, or 2 centimeters) that burn from the heat of the tinder.

– **Fuel** is the larger pieces (finger size). Fuel pieces kept to finger size are more likely to burn up completely into fine, powdery ashes. After the fire is completely extinguished, the ashes can be broadcast to leave no trace.

Lighting the Fire   Before lighting the fire, double-check the area for flammable materials. People should be cautious of any flammable clothing that they might be wearing (especially nylon, polyester, and other synthetic materials).

◆ Participants with long hair should tie it back.

◆ Be sure that enough water is near the fire to put it out if necessary.

◆ Participants should be in an active lighting position, crouched so that they can quickly move away from the fire if necessary. They should use caution when lighting the tinder.

◆ The flame may need to be fanned a little to provide extra oxygen to get the flame to burn hotter and ignite the kindling (hats work well).

Adding the Fuel   After the kindling catches fire, slowly add fuel wood, one or two pieces at a time.

◆ As the fuel burns, add additional pieces of wood as necessary. Keep the fire small and under control.

◆ Stop adding wood about 30 minutes before retiring for the evening. If uncertain about whether the wood will burn completely before bed time, do not add any more.

◆ Never leave a fire unattended.

Extinguishing the Fire and Reclaiming the Site   Allow the fire to burn itself out completely. Make sure that the fire is extinguished before leaving the area or going to bed.

◆ When the wood has turned to ash, take some water and pour it over the ashes. Use a stick to stir the water and ashes so that the material cools. If necessary, add more water and stir again.

◆ After the ashes have cooled, use a trowel to disperse the ashes widely. Move away from the camp area and the edge of the water.

◆ After removing the ashes, return the area to its original condition. Refill pits and put mineral soil from mound fires back in the hole or stream from where it was gathered.

Note: If a fire site is already established, accepted practice is to remove the ashes. Doing so helps keep the site cleaner and the fire contained. If the fire ring contains any trash, remove it before building a fire and pack it out. Never put food scraps or trash in a fire, because they often will not burn completely and will attract wild animals to the site.

Activity 6: Respect Wildlife (20 Minutes)

This activity exposes the participants to ways of respectfully observing and interacting with wildlife. They will brainstorm potential wildlife encounters that might happen during a backpacking trip.

Quickly review key points related to respecting wildlife.

◆ Observe wildlife from a distance. Do not follow or approach them.

◆ Never feed animals. Feeding wildlife damages their health, alters natural behaviors, and exposes them to predators and other dangers.

◆ Protect wildlife and your food by storing rations and trash securely.

◆ Control pets at all times or leave them at home.

◆ Avoid wildlife during sensitive times: mating, nesting, raising young, or winter.

Ask the students to select a backpacking location (it could be one where your group is going) and list the types of wildlife that are common in the area. Have them brainstorm likely and potential interactions that may occur during the trip. Ask them to explain how they would act or react if they encountered an animal in a certain situation.

Activity 7: Be Considerate of Other Visitors (30 to 45 Minutes)

The golden rule states, "Do unto others as you would have them do unto you." Many people go backpacking and spend time in the backcountry to enjoy the peacefulness and solitude of the natural environment. Backpackers should remember that they are often not the only people in the outdoors, so they should behave in ways that allow others to feel alone and to enjoy the quiet. This activity reminds participants to act in ways that show consideration and respect for other people.

Several key concepts about respecting other visitors have already been discussed in lesson 10, Travel Techniques. Those principles include yielding to other users on the trail, stepping to the downhill side of the trail when encountering horses and other pack stock, and taking breaks off the trail.

Ask the participants to think of other concepts related to respecting other visitors that may arise on a backpacking trip.

◆ Divide the participants into small groups of three or four people.

◆ Have them share their thoughts about respecting others and come to a consensus about which idea they would like to share with the large group.

◆ After they have decided on a topic, give them 10 to 15 minutes to come up with a creative way to explain their topic, perhaps through a skit, role play, song, dance, poem, drawing, or other means.

◆ Ask each group to perform their concept for the large group.

◆ Lead a short discussion that addresses some of the comments and questions that may arise from the performances.

◆ Remind the group that we have all negatively affected the experiences of others but that we should strive not to do so. If we want peace and solitude, we should remember that others do too.

◆ Conclude by asking the students to write about this principle and the stories and experiences that they and other participants have had.

Leave No Trace principles—Copyright: Leave No Trace Center for Outdoor Ethics. www.LNT.org

Closure Activity

Ethical Dilemma (45 Minutes)

Describe the following scenario to the students and have them discuss what they would do in that situation.

One of the cars in your group has a flat tire on the way to the trailhead. You get the tire changed but arrive at the trailhead 2 hours late. Your group begins backpacking toward the planned campsite. When you get there, another group has already taken your customary site. You hike an additional 15 minutes to get to your contingency site, but a group is occupying that site as well. The sun is setting, and it will be dark in 45 minutes. You hike another 15 minutes and do not see any good options. Your two options are to camp right next to a stream in an area that tends to flash flood or in a fern grove where the ground is covered with moss. Darkness is 30 minutes away. What do you do and why?

◆ Follow this discussion with a conversation describing ethical behavior (behavior based on a specific set of moral values).

◆ Explain that in some situations you may not have any good option, and at that point, values dictate the decisions that are made.

◆ Remind the students that LNT does not require anyone to follow the principles; the principles are designed only to help people make environmentally sound decisions.

Follow-Up Activity

Learn More About the Center for Outdoor Ethics (Time as Needed)

◆ Have the students visit the LNT Web site (www.lnt.org) to learn more about LNT as a not-for-profit organization. Focus on the curriculum and the training process.

◆ Ask one group to learn about the different levels of training, including the requirements for workshops, trainer certificates, and master educator courses.

◆ Ask the second group to research LNT principles for diverse environments—ocean, desert, alpine, river corridors, and so on.

◆ When the groups come back together, have the students share the information they discovered.

ASSESSMENT

◆ Confirm that students can explain the difference between ethical and nonethical outdoor behavior by observing their participation in large-group discussion.

◆ Verify that students can list and describe the seven LNT principles in large-group discussion. Small groups discuss one of the LNT principles and then share basic information when reporting to the larger group.

- Check that students can explain why waste should be disposed of properly by observing their participation in large-group discussions.
- Confirm that students can describe how to minimize campfire impacts by listing ways to reduce fire-related incidents.
- Verify that students demonstrate the ability to walk on durable surfaces by observing them walk on a variety of surfaces.
- Ensure that students empathize with other visitors by having them write about things that others do that are disrespectful and about things that they themselves do that others might consider disrespectful.
- Confirm that students appreciate the reasons behind the principle "Leave what you find" by having them write about leaving an area as they found it, emphasizing why doing so might be difficult.
- Confirm that students appreciate the importance of planning and preparation by drawing a picture that represents the importance of planning and preparation.

TEACHING CONSIDERATIONS

- Many of these elements are embedded in other activities. Be sure to expand on the principles that have not been explained fully in other lessons.
- For more ideas and lesson plans visit the LNT Web site (www.lnt.org). Some excellent books with a variety of LNT activities in them are listed in the reference list (Reid, 2001; Leave No Trace, n.d.).
- Be sure to provide ample breaks between the activities.
- The fire lesson works best during a field experience so that participants can enjoy the fire that they have built. Do not have the students build fires unless sufficient time is available for the fire to burn completely.

UNIT 1, LESSON 15

▷ Inclusion and Accessibility

OVERVIEW

In this lesson students learn the importance of communication and trail and terrain assessment, and will be provided with an inclusion initiative. Inclusion is a complex topic; there are no formulas. Although many approaches can work, every person is different. Ultimately, inclusion is about communicating needs on both sides. Goals for both the participant and the instructors must be made clear from the beginning.

JUSTIFICATION

Understanding equipment, disabilities, and inclusion is a vital skill for today's outdoor leader.

GOALS

- To develop students' understanding of adaptive equipment.

◆ To foster respect for and understanding of the outdoor enthusiast who has a disability.

◆ To introduce problem-solving skills about adapting equipment and assisting an adventurer who has a disability.

OBJECTIVES

At the end of this lesson, students will be able to

◆ understand some of the issues surrounding an inclusive backpacking trip (cognitive);

◆ describe a trail section in terms of grade, cross slope, width, and surface (cognitive);

◆ determine what user groups would be likely to travel their section of trail based on its specifications (cognitive);

◆ demonstrate transfer techniques (psychomotor); and

◆ appreciate different levels of ability by understanding some of the challenges that someone who is less able might face (affective).

EQUIPMENT AND AREAS NEEDED

◆ Various pieces of adaptive equipment, ideally at least two wheelchairs, two pairs of crutches, blindfolds, and white canes (Keep in mind that wheelchair design varies greatly. A standard-issue hospital chair will not be effective on surfaces other than pavement.)

◆ A variety of surfaces at the location (pavement, gravel, grass, and so on); picnic tables and other items for transfer practice

◆ First aid kit

◆ Clinometers

◆ Tape measures

◆ Hiking equipment

◆ Pencil and paper

◆ Level and protractor (Without access to clinometers, use these to determine grade and cross slope in a rise–run format. Rise–run is most easily defined as elevation divided by distance multiplied by 100, which provides the percentage of slope. Most trails built to be accessible try to stay below 5 percent grade with short sections perhaps exceeding 5 percent but never more than 10 percent.)

RISK MANAGEMENT CONSIDERATIONS

◆ Check to make sure that all equipment is in working order. For example, tires must be properly inflated and seat cushions secured.

◆ Wheelchairs can easily tip, especially for first-time users, so use spotters on uneven surfaces and rough terrain. Spotters should walk almost directly behind the chair, with an additional spotter on the downhill side of steeper areas.

◆ Always examine the first aid kit for completeness before taking it into the field.

◆ Several manufacturers make wheelchairs specifically for challenging terrain. The chair must be somewhat lightweight, durable, and have the option of a 26-inch (66-centimeter) wheel so that standard mountain bike tires may be fitted. Typically, the casters (front wheels) should be closer to the rear wheels than normal, and the front tires on the casters should be larger as well. These chairs are expensive ($2,000 to $5,000) and typically have many custom features.

LESSON CONTENT

Introduction

People of all abilities can enjoy backpacking! A person who has a disability does not necessarily use a wheelchair. An important part of thinking about inclusion is first thinking about disabilities.

* A cognitive impairment will require different goals and equipment than a physical impairment will. For instance, a cognitive impairment may not affect the participant's physical abilities on the trip but may make communication more difficult. You may have to be clearer about risks and hazards along the way, because this person may not be able to recognize them. Similarly, if the person has a hearing or visual impairment, you may need an interpreter or a person to serve as a guide.

* A person who has **mobility impairment** may use a variety of equipment including trekking poles, walkers, forearm crutches, orthotics, and prosthetics.

Be sure to frame this lesson clearly. In no way does spending 30 minutes using a wheelchair make a student an expert on disabilities, nor does it give the person complete understanding of what it is like to have a disability. The overall goal is to give the students a glimpse of the challenges faced by a person who uses a wheelchair or other adaptive equipment. Students will have the opportunity to use several types of adaptive equipment, try out transfer techniques, and begin problem solving for inclusive programming.

Important Terms

cross slope—The difference in the height of a trail from one side to the other, measured with a clinometer. The severity of the slope is important for wheelchair use, because steeper cross slopes require far more energy and may be extremely difficult to navigate.

edge protection—Technically refers to having a 3-inch (8-centimeter) "curb" on the edge of a paved trail or boardwalk but can also refer to the difference in the surface of the trail and the surface of the areas near the trail. For people with visual impairments, a perceptible edge is critical. Above treeline and in off-trail conditions, a person with a visual impairment will need a guide to walk in front of him or her to warn of obstacles and describe terrain.

grade—Overall slope of a trail as measured with a clinometer, which determines the difference in height of various points on the trail.

maximum grade—The steepness of a trail over the distance of a single stride as measured with a clinometer in 24-inch (60-centimeter) sections. Sections of the trail may have a 0-degree grade, whereas others may have a grade of 5 degrees or more.

protruding objects—Anything that sticks out into the trail. Accessible trails require 80-inch (2-meter) clearance above the trail to prevent head injuries to people who have visual impairments.

slide board—A board, typically with a nonslip base and cut out handles, used in transfers from a wheelchair to a surface of similar height, such as a car seat. People place the board on each surface and then scoot across. Boards may be curved or straight and vary in size depending on the person's preference.

continued ▶

▶ **continued**

surface—Refers to the actual makeup of the surface that a person is traveling over. Generally, old logging roads are durable and well drained. Large rocks in the trail may require transferring around or over, because the chair may not have adequate clearance.

transfer—The act of assisting a person who uses a wheelchair from the chair to another surface or vice versa (figure BP15.1). Several techniques are used, and many people are capable of transferring themselves. Always ask what technique is preferred, and let the person know that you are happy to help when asked.

width—The standard requirement for wheelchairs is 28 to 36 inches (70 to 90 centimeters), with more, up to 48 inches (120 centimeters), required for turns. Hand bikes and off-road wheelchairs (such as the BT Trail by Lasher Sport) may require additional width. Twenty-eight inches (70 centimeters) is adequate for persons with other impairments as well.

FIGURE BP15.1   A student is transferred out of his wheelchair.

Main Activity

Inclusive Techniques (45 Minutes)

This activity concentrates on equipment, etiquette, and specific transfer techniques that may be valuable in an outdoor environment. Use the following information to discuss issues associated with facilitating an inclusive backpacking experience. The final stage of this activity involves practicing transfers.

Equipment   Introduce equipment to students. Describe who might use the equipment, what limitations they may have, and challenges of using the equipment.

◆ Cover basic etiquette. For example, wheelchairs are an extension of the person. Just as you would not walk up and touch someone's legs, you should not touch a wheelchair unless asked. Never move a person's adaptive equipment without being asked; canes, crutches, and wheelchairs should always be near the user.

◆ People with a disability will have their own prosthetics, walkers, wheelchair, crutches, canes, and so forth.

◆ Most people who use a chair have a basic repair kit with them. It should include screwdrivers, wrenches, tire tubes and patch kits, duct tape, and needle and thread. Generally, they will be skilled in changing a tire and making minor adjustments.

◆ Additionally, for any outdoor trip, you should have a length of rope (9 millimeters in diameter or larger), some tubular webbing, and possibly a sling that could work as a seat for a short distance over rough terrain.

◆ Familiarize yourself with the equipment used by the participant.

◆ What adaptations can be made that will make off-road travel easier? For example, knobby tires on the rear of the chair and balloon tires on the front will provide more traction and help prevent the person from sinking in sand, mud, and softer dirt.

◆ Will the equipment allow the participant to carry a backpack or some of her or his own gear?

Transfer Techniques   Understanding transfer techniques is critical to assisting a person who uses a wheelchair. Before beginning a transfer, take the following steps.

◆ With the participant, locate an appropriate area to transfer to and prepare the area for environmental conditions and time concerns. For instance, if the person will be on the ground for any length of time, he or she may need the seat cushion from the chair.

◆ Ask the participant about her or his preferred transfer method and ability to help. This is the most important step. Many participants may be capable of doing all transfers on their own. Others may need assistance only with specific movements. For instance, getting in and out of a car or moving to a bench from the chair could require no equipment or the addition of a lateral transfer or slide board. Getting in and out of a van, on the other hand, may require multiple steps.

◆ Ask if the person has any concerns or current painful areas to be avoided.

◆ Check that the chair is stable, that the brakes are locked, and that caster wheels and footrests are facing forward or otherwise out of the way. Remember that during the lift and initial moving, navigating around the chair is difficult.

◆ Be sure that everyone involved in the transfer understands the plan and steps involved.

One of the most commonly used transfer techniques is the two-person lift. This transfer does not require any assistance from the participant.

◆ To begin, support the participant while detaching the safety belt if present. One person should stand behind the participant.

◆ Have the participant cross his or her arms across the chest.

◆ Place your arms under the participant's upper arms and grasp his or her wrists.

◆ The second person places both hands under the patient's lower thighs and initiates and leads the lift at a prearranged count (1-2-3-lift).

◆ Be sure to practice good lifting technique by using your leg and arm muscles while bending your back as little as possible. Then gently lift the participant's torso and legs at the same time.

Modifications on this transfer include the side-by-side lift in which two people support the torso and legs by reaching behind and under the participant and grasping each other's forearms. Three people can also use this technique; the third person focuses specifically on the legs and terrain ahead. For more information on transfers, please refer to the resources at the end of the chapter.

After demonstrating one or more transfer techniques, allow the students to try different adaptive equipment and practice transfers. Be sure that students are able to try equipment on a variety of surfaces, including grass, gravel, mud, sand, or other soft ground.

Closure Activity

Inclusion: Test a Trail (Four Hours)

The goal of using clinometers in this activity is not so that students become dependent on them or expect to have to measure all trails before use, but so that they begin to understand general guidelines for what makes an accessible trail. The follow-up discussion should further help students to see that not all trails used by persons with disabilities are gravel, wide, and flat.

◆ Divide students in groups of three or four and provide each group with a set of materials. If you have only one clinometer, make sure that each group has a chance to use it after you provide general operating instructions.

◆ Have groups pick sections of trail that are roughly .25 miles (.4 kilometers) long and have each group develop a trail description for their section.

◆ Have students use the clinometer to check various locations for cross slope of no more than 5 percent and not over 10 percent for short sections (Zeller, Doyle, & Snodgrass 2006).

◆ When the overall gradient of the trail exceeds 5 percent, the slope becomes extremely difficult for mobility challenged people. Unless the trail is specifically designed for accessibility, you may need to provide rest every 50 feet (15 meters).

◆ Protruding objects need special attention. If the object reduces the overall width of the trail, a transfer may be necessary.

◆ Trail surface is a critical factor in deciding whether the trail can be used accessibly. Weather and cross slope are huge factors in determining whether a trail can be used.

After the students evaluate the trail using the preceding criteria, provide them the opportunity to maneuver the trail using a chair.

◆ Unless you are working with a trail designed specifically to be accessible, edge protection is likely to be negligible or absent, so sections of the trail may require additional spotting.

◆ Spotting is the process of safeguarding participants through particularly rough sections of trail by taking a position between the danger and the participant.

◆ If the participant is navigating the trail in a wheelchair, spotters should be on each side and behind in technical areas.

◆ For first-time chair users, as in this exercise, a spotter should always be positioned behind the chair, because sudden movements and balance shifts when crossing uneven terrain can cause a chair to tip backward suddenly.

Discuss the learning that took place and whether students' initial assumptions about the trail were correct.

Follow-Up Activity

Researching Current Trends (Two to Three Hours)

◆ Provide the students with an opportunity to learn what types of activities people with various disabilities are doing in the outdoors.

◆ Have students write a thorough report on inclusion and adventure-based activities. They could research individuals or the major players who are pushing the envelope in the outdoors in a specific adventure-based sport.

ASSESSMENT

◆ Check that students understand some of the issues surrounding an inclusive backpacking trip by their participation in the discussion of the information presented in the main activity.

◆ Verify that students can describe a trail section in terms of grade, cross slope, width, and surface by demonstrating the use of a clinometer to judge grade and cross slope, and accurately assess potentially accessible trails as described in the closure activity.

◆ Confirm that students can determine which user groups would be likely to travel their section of trail based on its specifications by trying various pieces of adaptive equipment.

◆ Check that students can demonstrate transfer techniques by practicing the techniques described in the main activity.

◆ Assess whether students appreciate different levels of ability by understanding some of the challenges that a person who has a disability might face.

TEACHING CONSIDERATIONS

◆ A brief experience that simulates having a disability in no way equates to the daily reality of having a disability. The goal of these exercises is to help students gain some understanding of what people with disabilities must deal with.

◆ To give students a real-life perspective, have a person who is active outdoors and has a disability speak to the group.

◆ Injuries may occur during this activity. Make sure that students who are using wheelchairs or other adaptive equipment have spotters in place, especially behind the chair. Remember, most people's first experience with a wheelchair is on smooth floors and pavement. The learning curve is steep!

GLOSSARY

backpacking—A leisure pursuit in which people carry in a pack on their backs a variety of equipment designed to carry out the basic functions of living outdoors.

backstops—Key land features like a ridge, river, or lake that act as stop signs in navigation. Typically, a backstop is a point where a navigation decision must be made.

bacteria and protozoa—Single-cell organisms capable of causing disease (including giardia and cryptosporidium, which may have severe and relatively long-lasting effects).

bight—A bend in the rope.

bowline—A strong knot that forms a loop that will not slip under force. A bowline is an excellent knot to anchor the rope to almost any object.

brain—The upper compartment of a backpack, usually detachable from the main body of the pack. The brain is where the backpacker places the things needed to keep his or her own brain feeling good, such as an extra hat, sunscreen, lip balm, medications that might be needed throughout the day, cup, bowl, spoon, and so on.

call list—A list of people who can help if an accident happens. If working with a program or school, this list may include supervisors and colleagues.

calories—Units of energy that people get from eating food.

CCORE—The acronym derived from the terms *convection, conduction, outdoors, radiation,* and *evaporation* further

Backpacking Skills Checklist

☐   1. Create a trip plan.

☐   2. Package trip food according to LNT principles.

☐   3. Set up a safe, functional kitchen area.

☐   4. Prepare a meal.

☐   5. Create a group equipment list.

☐   6. Create a personal equipment list.

☐   7. Properly pack a backpack.

☐   8. Dispose of waste properly.

☐   9. Sterilize dishes.

☐ 10. Set up a tarp.

☐ 11. Set up a tent.

☐ 12. Hang food.

☐ 13. Tie the following camp knots: (a) girth hitch, (b) taut line hitch, (c) bowline, (d) square knot, (e) trucker's hitch, and (f) clove hitch.

☐ 14. Demonstrate uphill hiking techniques.

☐ 15. Demonstrate descending techniques.

☐ 16. Identify topographic map features and symbols.

☐ 17. Identify the parts of a compass.

☐ 18. Fold a map properly.

☐ 19. Create a route plan.

☐ 20. Navigate using a compass and map (on and off trail).

☐ 21. Build a minimum-impact fire.

Use the backpacking skills checklist as an additional tool to assess skills learned throughout this unit.

From M. Wagstaff and A. Attarian, 2009, *Technical skills for adventure programming: A curriculum guide* (Champaign, IL: Human Kinetics).

delineates the importance of thermoregulation. People use these principles and clothing systems to regulate body temperature in the outdoors.

compression sack—A stuff sack that has several straps that can be used to compress the contents of the bag. The best ones compress the bulk vertically along the seams of the bag rather than horizontally.

conduction—The loss of body heat to a cooler surface like a rock or wet clothes. Minimize conduction of body heat by placing insulation between the body and the surface that is robbing the body of heat.

convection—The transfer of heat from the body to the air that surrounds the body. Cold air temperature combined with wind creates ideal conditions for the loss of body heat through convection. Prevent convective heat loss by adding layers consistent with the atmospheric conditions (for example, a sweater for a cold, calm, sunny day; a sweater and a windproof jacket for the same day with wind).

cross-contamination—The process in which food is contaminated by mixing with other foods or from hands that are soiled or have touched other food during cooking or eating. Being aware of this is important to the expedition's health as a whole. Make sure to thoroughly wash hands before cooking and be very conscious of food allergies of trip participants.

cross slope—The difference in the height of a trail from one side to the other, measured with a clinometer. Cross slope is especially important for wheelchair use, because steeper cross slopes require far more energy and may be extremely difficult to navigate.

deadfall—A large tree or limb of a large tree that is no longer alive and could potentially fall into the area where a tent or tarp might be set up. Also called a *widow maker*. Widow makers can cause serious injury or even death, so extreme caution should be exercised.

declination—The variation in angle from either side of the zero declination line; in other words, the difference in direction between true north and magnetic north. True north is the direction to the geographic pole location, an actual place. Magnetic north is a force, the direction in which the compass needle points. Because the Earth's magma core creates this force, the magnetic field varies over time.

dry cleaning—The process of using natural cleaners for cleaning pots and pans without adding water. Items like pine needles work well for cleaning when appropriate.

durable surface—A surface that can withstand a lot of walking, camping, and other activity and show little, if any, wear. Examples include rock, established campsites, established trails, gravel, and sand.

edge protection—Technically refers to having a 3-inch (8-centimeter) "curb" on the edge of a paved trail or boardwalk, but the term can also refer to the difference in the trail surface and the surface of the areas near the trail. For people with visual impairments, having a perceptible edge is critical. Above treeline and in off-trail conditions, a person with a visual impairment will need a guide to walk in front of him or her to warn of obstacles and describe terrain.

ethics—Set of moral principles that guide behavior.

evaporation—The process by which body moisture during exertion is transformed into a vapor. Evaporation requires energy and thus heat from the body. Wearing layers that wick (move moisture away from the skin) minimizes evaporative heat loss. In warm climates, evaporation is the process by which the body cools itself.

expedition behavior—"Good expedition behavior is an awareness of the relationships . . . which exist in the out-of-doors plus the motivation and character to be as concerned for others as one is for oneself" (Petzoldt, 1984, p. 168).

external pockets—Durable pockets on packs that can hold miscellaneous equipment. External pockets are a perfect place for fuel bottles, which are ideally carried below and separate from food items. These pockets can also hold items that would go in the brain as well as additional layers or other items that the person might need to access throughout the day.

fire ring—A circle of rock or metal built by humans inside of which a fire has been built.

fuel—Wood that burns for a long time in a campfire, usually 2 to 3 inches (5 to 8 centimeters) in diameter and able to be broken with bare hands.

girth hitch—A hitch used to attach to a grommet or pole that forms a loop fed back on itself.

grade—Overall slope of a trail, which is measured with a clinometer to determine the difference in height of various points on the trail.

handrail—Land features that act as handrails to keep a hiker on the route while navigating in the backcountry.

hydrophobic—In reference to clothing, a fabric that seeks to dissipate water from its surface. The fabric itself is water fearing.

kindling—Twigs and small branches used to build a fire. They burn from the heat of the tinder, or starting material.

Leave No Trace (LNT)—"[LNT] is first and foremost an attitude and an ethic. Leave No Trace is about respecting and caring for wildlands, doing your part to protect our limited resources and future recreation opportunities. Once this attitude is adopted and the outdoor ethic is sound, the specific skills and techniques become second nature" (Leave No Trace Center for Outdoor Ethics, n.d., Home, par. 2).

lumbar—The very bottom part of a backpack. On an internal frame pack, the lumbar is the bottom sans any divider separating the sleeping bag compartment. This part of the pack is directly connected to the hip belt.

macro navigation—The macro is the overview of the route and the big land features and major direction of travel in which the students are heading.

maximum grade—Measured with a clinometer in 24-inch (60-centimeter) sections, maximum grade is the steepness of a trail in a single stride. Sections of the trail may have a 0-degree grade, whereas others may have a steeper grade.

menu plan—A method of planning what food to bring on a trip by creating a menu for each meal and then determining all the ingredients for each meal.

micro navigation—Specific features on the map that will indicate where the hikers are along the route, like a stream crossing, junction, cliff, or other feature.

minimum-impact camping—A set of skills that campers use to leave as little trace of their experience as possible.

mobility impairment—A condition that limits physical ability, generally considered to include loss of use of a limb due to disease, amputation, paralysis, injury, or developmental conditions; or limitation of movement due to cardiovascular or other disease (Federal Highway Administration, 2007).

natural cleaners—Any natural item used to clean pots and pans, such as pine needles, grasses, sticks, sand, and so on.

nutrients—Substances that provide essential nourishment.

outdoors—Unlike a climate-controlled environment in which people can wear fabrics like cotton that are comfortable in that environment.

protruding objects—Anything that sticks out into the trail. Accessible trails require 80-inch (2-meter) clearance above the trail to prevent head injuries to people who have visual impairments.

radiation—The passing of heat between two objects, like the warmth that passes from a campfire or the sun to the body. The body also loses heat through radiant heat loss. This loss is best prevented by providing insulating layers or using some kind of reflective layer that turns heat flow back to the body.

rest step—A technique designed to allow the muscles to rest while the skeletal structure supports the backpacker and the weight of the pack.

rule of 200 (rule of 60)—Moving 200 feet (60 meters) from water sources, the campsite, and the trail before bathing, hand washing, brushing teeth, using the bathroom, and other activities that may pollute water or infringe on the privacy of others.

shoulder—The upper section of the main compartment, closest to the shoulders. This part of the pack is reserved for items that the backpacker will probably use throughout the day, including items like an extra layer, lunch, water, and perhaps a book or journal.

slide board—A board, typically with a nonslip base and cut out handles, used in transfers from a wheelchair to a surface of similar height, such as a car seat. People place the board on each surface and then scoot across. Boards may be curved or straight and vary in size depending on the person's preference.

surface—In reference to trails, refers to the actual makeup of the surface that a person is traveling over. Generally, old logging roads are durable and well drained. Large rocks in the trail may require transferring around or over, because the wheelchair may not have adequate clearance.

switchbacks—Places where the trail creates a zigzag pattern along the side of a hill because the slope is too steep for the trail to go straight up or down it.

taut line hitch—A handy camp knot because it is easily adjustable. Simply sliding the knot up or down the standing end of the rope tightens or loosens the line. The taut line works by applying friction when it is under tension.

thermoregulation—Maintaining a constant body temperature independent of the outside environment by layering clothing, taking in calories, and engaging in activity. Also called *thermal regulation*.

tinder—Small material that lights quickly and is lighted first when building a fire. Some examples of fire-starting materials are tiny twigs from evergreen trees, birch bark, dry evergreen needles, dried grasses, lint, and paper.

torso—The part of the pack in which most of the weight is carried, including the tent, food, and any other items of significant weight and bulk.

total food planning (TFP)—A bulk ration system in which participants select specific quantities of foods in appropriate balance without having specific meals in mind.

transfer—The act of assisting a person who uses a wheelchair to move from a chair to another surface or vice versa. Several techniques are used, and many people are capable of transferring themselves. Those who assist should always ask what technique is preferred and let the person know that they are happy to help when asked.

trekking poles—Two poles with handgrips that a hiker or backpacker uses to provide balance and transfer some of the weight off the legs, which helps protect the knee and ankle joints, especially while ascending and descending slopes. The height of most trekking poles can be adjusted to fit the user's height.

viruses—Simple, smaller pathogens that usually cause milder and shorter bouts of illness.

Five Ws of Clothing Selection:

- **warm**—Made of a material that can aid in keeping the wearer warm in a variety of environments and weather.

- **wicking**—Able to move moisture away from the body to promote warmth and dryness.

- **weight**—An important consideration for backpackers; ideally, clothing should be both lightweight and warm.

- **windproof**—To prevent convection, clothing must help prevent wind from blowing away heat produced by the body.

- **waterproof**—Although many high-tech fabrics help the wearer stay warm even when wet, after a person becomes wet, staying warm is always an uphill battle. A waterproof shell top and bottom are essential.

width—In considering a trail for a wheelchair, the standard requirement is 28 to 36 inches (70 to 90 centimeters) wide, with more, up to 48 inches (120 centimeters), required for turns. Hand bikes and off-road wheelchairs (such as the BT Trail by Lasher Sport) may require additional width. Twenty-eight inches (70 centimeters) is adequate for persons with other impairments as well.

REFERENCES AND RESOURCES

REFERENCES

Curtis, R. (1998). *The backpackers field manual.* New York: Three Rivers Press.

Dietz, T.E. (1999). *Water treatment methods.* Retrieved from the High Altitude Medicine Web site: www.high-altitude-medicine.com/water.html

Drury, J.K., Bonney, B.F., Berman, D., & Wagstaff, M.C. (2005). *The backcountry classroom: Lessons, tools, and activities for teaching outdoor leaders* (2nd ed.). Guilford, CT: Falcon Guide.

Federal Highway Administration. (2007). *Appendix B: Glossary—designing sidewalks and trails for access.* Retrieved from www.fhwa.dot.gov/environment/sidewalks/appb.htm

Gookin, J. (2003). *National Outdoor Leadership School instructors handbook.* Lander, WY: National Outdoor Leadership School.

Leave No Trace Center for Outdoor Ethics. (n.d.). *Leave No Trace.* Retrieved from the Leave No Trace Web site: www.lnt.org

Meyer, K. (1994). *How to shit in the woods* (2nd ed.). Berkeley, CA: Ten Speed Press.

Pearson, C. (Ed.) (2004). *The NOLS cookery* (5th ed.). Harrisburg, PA: Stackpole Books.

Petzoldt, P. (1984). *The new wilderness handbook.* New York: Norton.

Reid, S. (2001). *The Leave No Trace training cookbook: Training recipes for educators.* Boulder, CO: Leave No Trace.

Richard, S., Orr, D., & Lindholm, C. (1991). *NOLS cookery: Experience the art of outdoor cooking.* Harrisburg, PA: NOLS & Stackpole Books.

Welch, T.R. (2004). Evidence-based medicine in the wilderness: The safety of backcountry water. *Wilderness and Environmental Medicine, 15*(4), 235–237. Retrieved from the Wilderness Medical Society Web site: www.wemjournal.org/wmsonline/?request=get-document&issn=1080-6032&volume=015&issue=04&page=0235#TOC

Zeller, J., Doyle, R., & Snodgrass, K. (2006). *Accessibility guidebook for outdoor recreation and trails.* Retrieved from www.fs.fed.us/recreation/programs/accessibility/htmlpubs/htm06232801/index.htm

RESOURCES

Beneficial Designs. (2001). *The universal trail assessment process.* Retrieved from Beneficial Designs Web site: www.beneficialdesigns.com/trails/utap.html. Overview: Beneficial Designs works toward universal access through research, design, and education. They have developed a training protocol for trail assessment.

Drury, J., & Holmlund, E. (1997). *The camper's guide to outdoor pursuits: Finding safe, nature-friendly and comfortable passage through wild places.* Champaign, IL: Sagamore. Overview: This is an excellent text that provides an overview of basic outdoor living skills. It covers topics such as navigation, food rationing, equipment and clothing, trip planning, and emergency procedures.

Harvey, M. (1999). *The National Outdoor Leadership School's wilderness guide: The classic handbook* (rev. ed.). New York: Simon & Schuster. Overview: This book, a National Outdoor Book Award winner, includes information that backpackers need to know in a well-organized and easy-to-follow format.

Johnson, H. (2002). *Lightweight backpacking stoves notes.* Retrieved from the Howard Johnson Web site: www.kzpg.com/Backpacking/Stove/Stove_notes.htm. Overview: This useful Web site offers excellent information on lightweight backpacking stoves along with advantages and disadvantages. It has a fuel estimator and calculator as well.

Leave No Trace Center for Outdoor Ethics. (n.d.). *Teaching Leave No Trace.* Boulder, CO: Leave No Trace. Overview: This set of lesson plans provides additional resources for people working with young children, including background information, Quick Concepts, and Activity Plans for each of the seven principles. It also includes an additional list of LNT Resources in the appendix.

Macdonald, S. (2006). *Accessible trails.* Retrieved from the American Trails Web site: www.americantrails.org/resources/accessible/index.html. Overview: American Trails is an excellent resource for trails in the United States. The organization promotes the development of a variety of trails that support health and wellness.

National Center on Accessibility. (2003). *National trails surface study.* Retrieved from the National Center on Accessibility Web site: www.ncaonline.org. Overview: The NCA works with the National Forest Service to help promote accessible trails. The Web site is full of useful information and research on accessible trails.

National Center on Accessibility. (2003). *What is an accessible trail?* Retrieved from the National Center on Accessibility Web site: www.ncaonline.org. Overview: The NCA works with the National Forest Service to help promote accessible trails. The Web site is full of useful information and research on accessible trails.

Priest, S., & Gass, M.A. (1997). *Effective leadership in adventure programming.* Champaign, IL: Human Kinetics. Overview: Although this book would not serve students in an introductory backpacking course well, it is a useful resource for instructors.

Townsend, C. (1997). *The backpackers handbook.* Camden, ME: Ragged Mountain Press. Overview: A fine recreational backpacking guide useful for both beginning and advanced backpackers.

USGS Eastern Region Geography. (2004). *Topographic map symbols.* Retrieved from the USGS Mapping Information Web site: http://permanent.access.gpo.gov/websites/ergusgsgov/erg.usgs.gov/isb/pubs/booklets/symbols/index.html. Overview: The USGS Web site states, "As an unbiased, multi-disciplinary science organization that focuses on biology, geography, geology, geospatial information, and water, we are dedicated to the timely, relevant, and impartial study of the landscape, our natural resources, and the natural hazards that threaten us."

Rock Climbing

Shayne Galloway   ◆   **Aram Attarian**

UNIT 2, LESSON 1

▷ Introduction to Rock Climbing

OVERVIEW

Rock climbing is a diverse activity that appeals to a variety of people. Climbing has the potential to enhance your students' self-confidence and self-esteem, and teach them both teamwork and self-reliance. Climbing also encourages mental problem solving to work out the correct combination of moves. This lesson introduces students to the evolution and segmentation of climbing and provides a brief overview of the different types of climbing available to the aspiring climber.

JUSTIFICATION

Students benefit from understanding the context in which rock climbing evolved and the ways in which it is used.

GOAL

To develop students' understanding and appreciation of the history and evolution of the various types of rock climbing.

OBJECTIVES

At the end of this lesson, students will be able to

◆ distinguish between the different types of climbing (cognitive),

◆ identify when and where one might expect to encounter each type of climbing (cognitive), and

◆ appreciate the range and depth to which climbing has developed over time (affective).

EQUIPMENT AND AREAS NEEDED

◆ A chalkboard or dry erase board.

◆ Chalk or dry erase markers.

◆ Images or media that depict each type of climbing. Such images can be found in abundance on the Internet (www.rockclimbing.com) and in publications such as *Climbing Magazine* and *Rock and Ice*.

◆ Relevant quotes about why people climb. Some of these can be found in the following classics:
  – *Mount Analogue*, Rene Daumal (1986)
  – *The Ascent of the Riffleberg*, Samuel L. Clemens (1989)
  – *The Rope Broke*, Edward Whymper (1989)

◆ Feel free to select quotes that are meaningful to you and your students. The literature associated with rock climbing and mountaineering contains innumerable relevant passages.

RISK MANAGEMENT CONSIDERATIONS

- ◆ This lesson is normally part of the course introduction and frequently occurs indoors with no special risk management considerations.
- ◆ Should this discussion occur outdoors, check for environmental hazards specific to the teaching site and take appropriate precautions.

LESSON CONTENT

Introduction

"Demonstrate in the most stunning way of all that there is no limit to the effort humans can demand of themselves."

Walter Bonatti

Begin this lesson by drawing an outline of a mountain on the board (or ground). Have students randomly pick up one of the images depicting a type of climbing. Ask students to describe the type of climbing in the illustration and then have them place the image on the outline of the mountain where they might encounter this type of climbing. Discuss the reasons for their placements. Use this activity as the foundation for the remainder of the lesson.

Main Activities

This lesson is mainly lecture and allows for dialog with students regarding their exposure to and experience with the various types of climbing.

Activity 1: A Brief History of Climbing (10 Minutes)

Long (2004) equates climbing with the survival of Homo sapiens as a method of evading predators and enemies, as well as a means of procuring food.

- ◆ At some point, humans began to climb for reasons other than basic survival. Mountain summits were early goals.
- ◆ The first recorded mountain ascent was a climb of Mont Aiguille in the French Alps in 1492. Charles VIII ordered that the peak be climbed, and Antoine de Ville made the ascent using a combination of ladders and other artificial aids (Scott, 1974).
- ◆ After peaks accessible by glacier and snowfield were summited, European climbers began to attempt harder and more technically difficult routes on rock and ice.
- ◆ These attempts led to the development of rock- and ice-climbing techniques and equipment. In this fashion, rock climbing and its variations were largely developed in response to the desire to ascend a wide range of technically difficult routes.
- ◆ In the early 20th century, climbing expanded into regions with varied geology and cultures, and it evolved in adaptation to the seemingly innate need of human beings to get to the top.
- ◆ In Germany and Austria, areas with alpine rock, carabiners and pitons were developed to enable the development of high alpine rock routes.
- ◆ In England, climbers developed technical crag-climbing techniques on what were referred to as practice routes because of the lack of high peaks (Long, 2004).

◆ Early differences in climbing cultures led to the development of a generic climbing ethic that varied across the world.

◆ In continental Europe, the use of pitons and roped climbing was advocated and advanced, whereas in England their use was discouraged as being a less pure form of ascent.

◆ When climbing crossed to the United States in the 1920s, continental European climbing ethics were adopted, although later debates regarding the use of **bolts** and other forms of aid climbing reveal the influence of the British idea of a pure climbing ethic.

◆ Today, climbing ethics are as segmented as the types of climbing are.

Activity 2: Types of Climbing (35 to 40 Minutes)

Mountaineering *Mountaineering*, the collective term used to describe alpine activities, can include many types of climbing as well as expedition planning, backpacking, navigation, and other wilderness travel skills and knowledge. Mountaineering is also sometimes known as alpinism, particularly in Europe, and consists of two main types, rock climbing and snow climbing, depending on whether the route chosen is over rock or over snow and ice.

Free Climbing **Free climbing** consists of free solo climbing, "trad" climbing, multipitch climbing, top-rope climbing, and bouldering. Free climbing ethics stipulate that the climber places protection while ascending without climbing or resting on gear or permanently placing protection, although permanent protection can be placed on rappel.

Free Solo Climbing Free solo climbing is noted both as having the highest level of clean climbing ethic—no rope or equipment is used to protect the climber—and as being the most dangerous and foolhardy type of climbing. Although elite climbers continue to solo routes of amazing length and technical difficulty, the activity is not advisable and no credible climbing program or guide would use free solo climbing because of the obvious risks to participants.

Traditional Climbing Traditional, or trad, climbing arose from European alpine climbing and the use of pitons and roped climbing. Trad climbing involves a lead climber who places trad gear, or traditional protection, into rock features while ascending the route. Trad climbing requires that the climber be intimately familiar with the various types of protection required for the route and be able to set the piece while maintaining a hold on the rock. This type of lead climbing requires the mental and physical ability to climb above the climber-placed protection.

Multipitch Climbing Multipitch climbing is trad climbing with the addition of multiple pitches, or rope lengths. Typically, the leader ascends the route and establishes an **anchor**. After constructing the anchor, the leader then **belays** the second, who cleans the route by removing all the protection placed by the leader on that pitch. After both climbers have safely clipped in at the anchor, the second may take the lead or the original leader may continue.

Top-Rope Climbing   Top-rope climbing, the primary focus of this unit, is popular with organized groups and outdoor programs (see figure RC1.1). This form of climbing is how most people are introduced to climbing. Top-rope climbing requires that the anchor be established by a lead climber or by walking to the top of the climb by an alternative route. Typically, both ends of the rope are at the bottom of the climb. The climber is belayed to the top and then lowered back to the ground. Alternatively, the belayer may be situated at the top of the climb. In this case the climber finishes the climb and either assumes the role of the belayer or walks off the climb. In rare instances, the climber is lowered to the bottom of the climb only to climb back up. In all cases the climber is protected by an overhead belay.

Long (2004) has a number of suggestions for setting up top-rope rock climbs:

◆ Conduct a hazard evaluation of the site, paying particular attention to loose rock.

◆ The anchors should be extended over the edge to prevent rope drag and damage.

◆ Two independent strands of rope or webbing should extend over the cliff edge for redundancy.

◆ Avoid placing protection devices behind loose flakes, loose blocks, or other suspect features.

◆ Connect the climbing rope to the anchor with two opposite and opposed carabiners, one of which should be a locking carabiner.

◆ When possible, belay top-rope climbs from the ground because this method allows the belayer to watch and communicate with the climber more easily.

Bouldering   **Bouldering** is the newest manifestation of rock climbing to emerge as its own type. With bouldering, the climber is typically not far from the ground and is not using rope or other protection (see figure RC1.2). Attempts at these short and often difficult routes or problems are protected by a spotter, whose responsibility it is to "catch" or otherwise mitigate a fall, and a crash pad or large mattresslike pad placed beneath the climber to cushion a landing. Essentially, bouldering is soloing without the likely risk of death from a substantial fall. Typically, bouldering is a more high-impact sport that focuses on individual moves rather than the endurance required in traditional climbing.

FIGURE RC1.1   Top-rope rock climbing.

FIGURE RC1.2   Bouldering.

FIGURE RC1.3　Aid climbing.

Aid Climbing　Aid climbing includes the placement of artificial or permanent protection and the use of specialized equipment to aid in the ascent (see figure RC1.3). Aid climbing consists of using fixed and traditional gear placements to ascend routes that will not allow climbers to free climb. Big-wall climbing relies on aid-climbing techniques to cross seemingly featureless rock by placing gear and resting body weight on that gear.

Activity 3: Rating Rock Climbs (15 to 20 Minutes)

During the 1930s the Sierra Club developed a system to rate the difficulty of their climbing outings. That classification system is still in use today. The system includes six classes of climbing:

- 1st class—Hiking.
- 2nd class—Scrambling and boulder hopping. Hands are needed, but climbs generally involve little exposure or danger.
- 3rd class—Steep scrambling with exposure. An unroped fall on 3rd class terrain would likely be fatal.
- 4th class—Steeper scrambling on small holds. A rope is carried and may be used occasionally.
- 5th class—Steep rock climbing in which the rope is used to protect the climber. Further broken down by the **Yosemite Decimal System (YDS)**, developed by Don Wilson, Royal Robbins, and Chuck Wilts in 1956. The YDS begins with 5.0 (the easiest 5th class) to 5.15 (the hardest 5th class).
- 6th class—Aid climbing.

Closure Activity

What Excites You About Climbing? (20 Minutes)

This lesson concludes with the historical threads of climbing illustrated on the board and discussion of each type. Discuss the parameters of what the course at hand covers—not all climbing courses cover all types of climbing. Ask the students what aspects of climbing they are most excited about and allow time for questions.

Follow-Up Activity

What's Happening in the World of Climbing? (20 to 25 Minutes)

- Encourage students to explore the historical literature on climbing.
- This material is also included throughout the unit in discussions of the various aspects of climbing; it serves as foundation information for the remainder of the lessons.

ASSESSMENT

- Have students distinguish between the different types of climbing by completing a short paper that outlines their understanding of the different types of climbing.

- Have students identify when and where they might expect to encounter each type of climbing by describing the environments in which the various types of climbing occur.
- Check that students appreciate the range and depth to which climbing has developed over time by discussing the history of climbing past to present.

TEACHING CONSIDERATIONS

- This lesson is sometimes taught as a show and tell in conjunction with the types of equipment associated with each type of climbing. You can use an illustration of a mountain or draw a mountain shape on the board and discuss where and when each type of climbing occurs. With each type of climbing discussed, point out or pass around the types of gear specific to that type.
- Brief readings may be incorporated to illustrate the development of climbing over time (for example, Daumal, Clemens, Whymper, Long, or others).

UNIT 2, LESSON 2

▷ Introduction to Climbing Equipment

OVERVIEW

This lesson introduces the evolution and segmentation of climbing equipment. A brief overview of each type of climbing equipment is provided and illustrated.

JUSTIFICATION

Students benefit from understanding the different types of equipment used in rock climbing. Knowledge of the proper use of each piece of climbing equipment is critical to safe and enjoyable climbing. This foundational knowledge influences the remainder of the unit.

GOAL

To develop students' understanding and appreciation of the various types of equipment involved in rock climbing.

OBJECTIVES

At the end of this lesson, students will be able to

- describe the various types of climbing equipment and the development of each (cognitive),
- distinguish between the various applications for each type of climbing equipment (cognitive),
- determine the safe condition of each piece of equipment (cognitive),
- maintain the various types of climbing equipment (psychomotor), and
- appreciate the proper application and use of each piece of equipment (affective).

EQUIPMENT AND AREAS NEEDED

◆ This lesson requires that each piece of climbing equipment being presented be available for demonstration, for students to work with and explore.

◆ A potential list of equipment includes helmets, harnesses, dynamic and static rope, belay devices, webbing and presewn slings, locking and nonlocking carabiners, and mechanical (active) and nonmechanical (passive) placed protection.

RISK MANAGEMENT CONSIDERATIONS

◆ This lesson is normally part of the course introduction and frequently occurs indoors with no special risk management considerations.

◆ Should this discussion occur outdoors, check for environmental hazards specific to the teaching site and take appropriate precautions.

LESSON CONTENT

Introduction

Safe climbing involves understanding and skill in the use of equipment designed specifically for protecting rock climbers.

◆ Each piece of equipment is used as part of a dynamic range of systems.

◆ Becoming familiar with the design features and intended uses of each individual piece will add to the students' ability to use it, but to maximize their ability with climbing gear, they must spend time using the gear under actual climbing conditions.

Main Activity

You can teach this lesson in a variety of ways. For example, you can present climbing equipment while introducing the history and development of rock climbing in a hybridization of the first two lessons. You can also reinforce or add depth about a specific piece of equipment throughout the unit by adding new and applicable information as needed (teachable moments).

◆ Instructional setting and programmatic goals will contribute to how this material will be covered. For example, if this climbing class is a part of a program focused on family issues, then each piece of climbing equipment can assume a metaphoric role as well as its functional role (that is, the rope embodies the responsibility that we share for each other as family members). If taught independently, this lesson resembles show and tell.

◆ After you introduce and pass around each piece of equipment, students can practice using each item as you offer correction and explanation.

◆ Basic anchors may also be introduced to give students a sense of gear relationships in climbing systems. Be sure to identify weaknesses and red flags for each item of equipment.

Introduction of Climbing Equipment (30 Minutes)

A wide range of equipment is used during climbing. The basic safety system includes a harness, helmet, and shoes worn by the climber, and rope, webbing, and carabiners joined into some form of anchor and to which the climbers are attached.

Climbing Harness   The harness is used to attach the rope to the climber or belayer. Most harnesses used in climbing are worn around the waist, although other types may be seen occasionally, such as chest and full-body versions (figure RC2.1). Different types of climbing warrant particular features for harnesses. No matter what type of harness is used in your program, follow these safety considerations:

◆ Make sure that the harness leg loops fit properly and snug above the hips.

◆ You should check all buckles before allowing any climbing activity to proceed.

◆ Be sure to read the manufacturer's instructions for proper tie-in. The harness is constructed of nylon and is subject to wear and tear through normal use.

◆ Inspect each harness regularly for worn spots, tears, and damaged stitching.

◆ If a harness is damaged or worn, or has reached the manufacturer's recommendation for retirement, remove it from the climbing program and destroy it to prevent further use.

a   b   c

FIGURE RC2.1   Climbing harnesses: *(a)* waist harness, *(b)* chest harness, *(c)* full-body harness.

Helmet   Anyone participating in a climbing program must wear a helmet. The helmet is designed to protect the skull against impacts commonly caused by falling objects such as rocks or climbing equipment or by a falling climber striking his or her head (figure RC2.2).

Rope, Cord, and Webbing   Climbing ropes typically consist of a core of long twisted fibers and an outer sheath of woven colored fibers (figure RC2.3). The core provides most of the holding strength, and the sheath is a somewhat durable layer that protects the core. There are two classes of climbing rope: dynamic and static.

◆ **Dynamic ropes** have a certain amount of elasticity or stretch. This construction reduces the fall force loaded into the system in the event of a fall.

FIGURE RC2.2   Climbing helmet.

◆ Static ropes have limited stretch and high abrasion resistance, and are best suited for rappelling (or abseiling) because the limited stretch reduces bounce and makes descending easier. The standard length for a modern climbing rope is 50 to 60 meters (165 to 197 feet).

Cord (or cordelette) is the same as dynamic rope but with a smaller diameter (7 to 9 millimeters) and is used for the construction of anchors. Cord is not to be used as a climbing rope.

Webbing is nylon and other materials woven into flat tubular lengths (figure RC2.4). A versatile component of climbing equipment, webbing is often now made from exceptionally high-strength material. Webbing is usually tied or sewn into a loop and is then known as a **runner**, **sling**, or quick draw.

All rope and webbing should be used with care and closely inspected for worn sheaths and damaged core material before each use. Sand or other micro material can be ground into the fabric and cause damage that is not easily detected, so climbers must use care not to stand or walk on these items. Rope and webbing may be periodically washed in a soft detergent. See the manufacturer's recommendations for care.

Carabiners Carabiners are an important and versatile piece of equipment. Carabiners are aluminum loops or snap links with spring-loaded gates (openings) used to connect belayers to anchors, equipment to climbers, and so forth. Carabiners are manufactured in a variety of forms; the shape of the carabiner and the type of gate should be selected according to the use for which it is intended.

Carabiners are made with many different types of gates including locking and nonlocking, and straight gate or bent gate.

◆ Locking carabiners offer a method of preventing the gate from opening when in use and are ideal for building anchors and for attaching **belay devices** to the harness, or where an additional margin of safety is needed (figure RC2.5). Nonlocking carabiners do not have locking devices and are the standard for use in situations where a locking carabiner is not required.

◆ Straight-gate carabiners are the most commonly used (figure RC2.6*a*).

◆ Bent-gate carabiners are often used to clip the rope into placed protection (figure RC2.6*b*). Their shape makes clipping easier.

FIGURE RC2.3   Climbing rope.

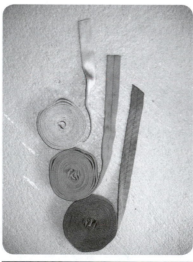

FIGURE RC2.4   Webbing.

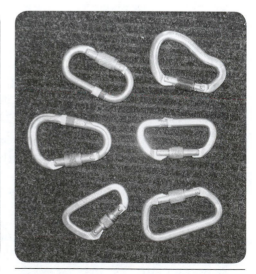

FIGURE RC2.5   Locking carabiners.

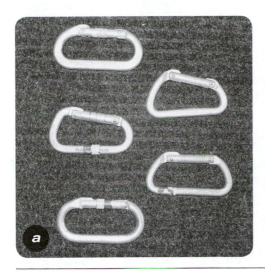 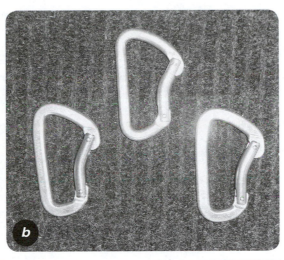

FIGURE RC2.6   Carabiners: *(a)* straight-gate and *(b)* bent-gate.

◆ Wire-gate carabiners are relatively thin, thus providing more room and a larger gate opening.

Carabiners should be periodically checked for dents, nicks, sticky gates, and damaged or nonfunctioning lock mechanisms on locking carabiners.

Belay and Rappel Devices   By adding friction to the belay system, mechanical belay and rappel devices allow careful control of the rope. Their main purpose is to allow locking of the rope with minimal effort. Many types of belay devices exist, and they may additionally be used as descenders.

◆ The Sticht plate, named for its designer, is the original belay device. It consists of a metal disk or plate with one or two oblong slots drilled through it. A bight of rope is pushed through one of the slots and attached to a locking carabiner (figure RC2.7), which in turn is attached to the harness of the belayer, who is then ready to belay. Sticht plates have become less popular because more modern designs provide smoother control over the rope and are less prone to jamming, especially when doubling as a **descender**.

◆ The slot-type belay device is a popular design that operates like a plate. The device is designed to facilitate slow, smooth feeding of the rope and has a large surface area to dissipate heat away from the rope (figure RC2.8).

◆ The figure-eight descender is most commonly used as a rappelling device, but it may be used as a belay device in the absence of more appropriate equipment. Its main advantage is efficient heat dissipation and ease of use with static rope (figure RC2.9).

◆ **Gri-gri**: The Gri-gri is a belay device that automatically locks the rope in the event of a fall (figure RC2.10). Gri-gris have become widely used in climbing gyms. They are simple to operate but offer hazards as well. The same downward motion that is used to brake a fall with a nonmechanical device (e.g., **ATC** or Reverso) will disengage the braking action of the Gri-gri, and this circumstance may serve as a point of momentary confusion for novice climbers. These devices should be introduced because students will encounter them in the field, but the discussion should occur only after students have mastered nonmechanical belay devices and techniques.

FIGURE RC2.7   Sticht plate.

FIGURE RC2.8   Slot-type belay device.

FIGURE RC2.9   Figure-eight descender.

FIGURE RC2.10   Gri-gri.

Protection Devices   Protection devices, collectively known as rock protection, or pro, provide the means to place temporary anchor points in the rock. These devices are categorized as either passive, such as hexcentrics and **stoppers** (figure RC2.11) or active, such as Friends and TCUs (figure RC2.12). Protection devices are discussed in more detail in lesson 6.

FIGURE RC2.11   Passive protection: stoppers, hexcentrics, and tri-cams.

FIGURE RC2.12   Active protection.

Climbing Shoes   Climbing shoes are specifically designed footwear for climbing. Designed to increase the grip of the foot on a climbing wall or rock face through greater friction, the shoe is covered with a sticky vulcanized rubber layer. The fit is snug.

Equipment Standards   Two major standards organizations certify the safety and reliability of climbing equipment: CEN (European Committee for Standardization) and UIAA (International Mountaineering and Climbing Federation). Equipment not tested by either of these groups or gear that has experienced conditions outside its design limits should not be used and should be discarded.

Tips for managing rock-climbing equipment:

- All rock-climbing equipment requires maintenance.
- How and when climbing equipment is used should be recorded in a logbook, especially rope and webbing.
- The adage is that if you take care of your gear, your gear will take care of you.
- Hardware or metal gear will collect dirt and grime over time. A light wash with a mild detergent is in order once a season, paying close attention to frayed wires or other wear and applying a dry lubricant to moving parts.
- Software or equipment made of fabric requires more care during use.
- Keeping ropes and webbing neatly coiled and stacked out from under foot will increase their lifespans and prevent unnecessary damage.
- Follow the manufacturer's recommendation for retiring equipment.

Closure Activity

Equipment Review (20 to 30 Minutes)

This lesson concludes with the students' manipulation of the gear.

- This lesson can flow into a discussion of basic anchors and other systems.
- You may also demonstrate the linkage of individual pieces into an anchor system and illustrate its strength by rappelling off it.
- Spend time with students going over the various ways of inspecting, storing, and maintaining gear.

Follow-Up Activity

Equipment and Its Use (Time as Needed)

The equipment presented in this lesson will be used throughout the unit. You can evaluate and correct student understanding of specific equipment as you identify knowledge and skill gaps.

Have students inspect a pile of used equipment and

- identify each item,
- explain the use of each item, and
- explain which items need to be retired and why.

ASSESSMENT

- Have students describe the various types of climbing equipment and the development of each by quizzing them on each item of equipment.
- Verify that students can distinguish between the various applications for each type of climbing equipment by observing them use equipment for its intended use.
- Have students determine the safe condition of each piece of equipment by closely observing and correcting them when gear is in use and improperly treated.

◆ Confirm that students can maintain the various types of climbing equipment by observing them inspect equipment during the follow-up activity.

◆ Check that students appreciate the proper application and use of each piece of equipment by observing them properly use equipment throughout the course.

TEACHING CONSIDERATIONS

◆ This lesson is sometimes taught in conjunction with the types of gear associated with each type of climbing.

◆ Incorporate simple stories of observing other students using gear inappropriately and how they were corrected on the rock. Consider assembling simple combinations of gear in the classroom, asking students to stand in as rocks or trees for anchor points. This activity foreshadows what they will be learning in the unit.

UNIT 2, LESSON 3

▷ Basic Climbing Knots

OVERVIEW

Knots are an important part of the climbing experience because they connect climbers and belayers to the rope and anchors. A climber doesn't need to know a large number of knots. Some suggest that knowing the bowline and figure-eight family of knots is enough to get most climbers through any climbing situation or application (Smith & Padgett, 1996). This lesson introduces basic climbing knots through a brief overview of each knot and illustrations.

JUSTIFICATION

Attention to detail when learning to tie knots and in their application is critical to the students' understanding of rock-climbing safety systems. Knot tying is a fundamental skill in safe rock climbing. Students must practice the skill to master it. It is also a perishable skill, so climbers must maintain the skill by using it. This basic knowledge will influence and be reinforced during the remainder of the unit.

GOAL

To develop students' understanding and appreciation of the various types of knots involved in rock climbing.

OBJECTIVES

At the end of this lesson, students will be able to

◆ describe the types of climbing knots and their application (cognitive),

◆ determine the condition and safety of each knot (cognitive),

◆ tie each knot appropriately and neatly (psychomotor),

◆ demonstrate the proper coiling of rope (psychomotor), and

◆ appreciate the importance of proper knot tying (affective).

EQUIPMENT AND AREAS NEEDED

◆ Four feet (1 meter) of cord or retired climbing rope for each student

◆ A 2-foot (60-centimeter) piece of 1-inch (25-millimeter) tubular webbing for each student

RISK MANAGEMENT CONSIDERATIONS

◆ This lesson is normally part of the course introduction and frequently occurs indoors with no special risk management considerations.

◆ Should this lesson occur outdoors, check for environmental hazards and take appropriate precautions.

LESSON CONTENT

Introduction

Simply put, "A knot not neat need not be tied." This maxim remains at the core of rock climbing. Skilled climbers have the ability to tie each knot and know when to use each one. A poorly tied knot or one applied inappropriately may become the weak link that causes the safety system to fail. In addition, knot tying is a perishable skill. Expertise in knot tying requires many hours of practice under varied conditions.

Important Terms

Figure RC3.1 shows some of the following rope concepts.

bight *(a)*—A bend in the rope where the ends of the rope exiting the bend do not cross.

loop *(b)*—A turn of the rope that crosses itself.

standing end *(c)*—The end of the rope that is not in use.

working end *(d)*—The end of the rope that is being used to tie the knot.

dressed knot—All parts of the knot are aligned, straightened, or bundled. A textbook perfect knot. An undressed knot may lose 50 percent of its strength (Smith & Padgett, 1996). Remember, a knot not neat need not be tied. Don't practice bad habits.

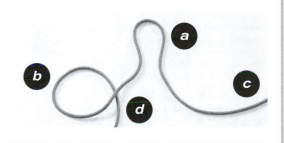

FIGURE RC3.1   Parts of a knot.

Main Activities

Activity 1: Tying Knots (One Hour)

To demonstrate knot tying, you must be able to tie the knot proficiently. A good method is to tie the knot for the students while discussing its proper usage. Students will have varied experience and ability with knot tying, and those already in possession of the skill can assist in the instruction. Encourage students to practice each knot until they have it memorized. After students can manage the basic knot, reinforce the importance of speed and efficiency through carefully selected activities. I use competitive games (that is, who can tie the fastest and best), as well as features of the climbing site. For example, select a spot where students can mount the base of a climb or a bouldering section and have them tie the knot one-handed while holding themselves on the rock, after which they may safely step down.

Overhand Knot Can be used as a backup knot to the figure-eight (figure RC3.2). It provides the foundation for the square knot.

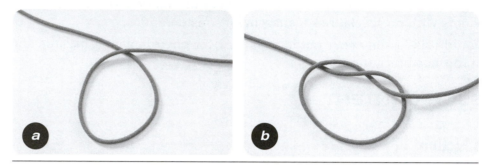

FIGURE RC3.2 Tying an overhand knot: *(a)* Create a loop. *(b)* Thread the working end through the loop.

Figure-Eight on a Bight Used to attach the climber or belayer to an anchor (figure RC3.3).

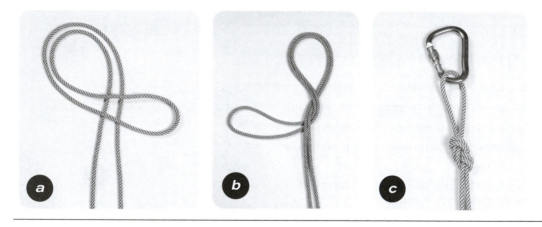

FIGURE RC3.3 Tying a figure-eight on a bight: *(a)* Tie a figure-eight knot in the rope, passing the working end through the point of attachment. Begin tracing the knot. *(b)* Continue tracing the original knot. *(c)* The knot is complete when the working end is parallel with the standing end and the knot is dressed and set.

Figure-Eight Follow-Through Used to attach the climbing rope to the harness (figure RC3.4).

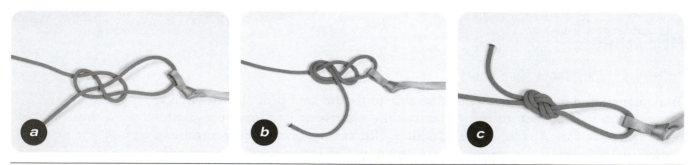

FIGURE RC3.4 Tying a figure-eight follow-through: *(a)* Pass the working end (bight) around the front of the standing end; *(b)* continue by passing the bight around the back of the standing end; and *(c)* finish by passing the bight through the loop, dressing, and setting the knot.

Double Fisherman's   A strong joining knot used to tie two ropes together (figure RC3.5).

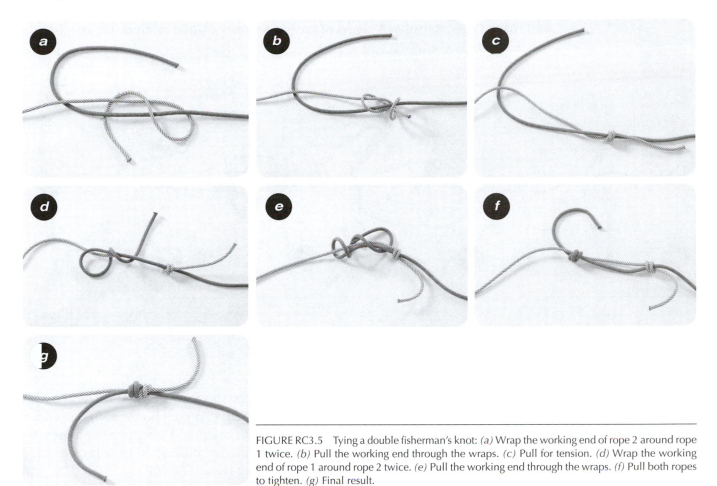

FIGURE RC3.5   Tying a double fisherman's knot: *(a)* Wrap the working end of rope 2 around rope 1 twice. *(b)* Pull the working end through the wraps. *(c)* Pull for tension. *(d)* Wrap the working end of rope 1 around rope 2 twice. *(e)* Pull the working end through the wraps. *(f)* Pull both ropes to tighten. *(g)* Final result.

Water Knot (or Ring Bend)   Used for tying webbing into loops or for joining ends of webbing (figure RC3.6).

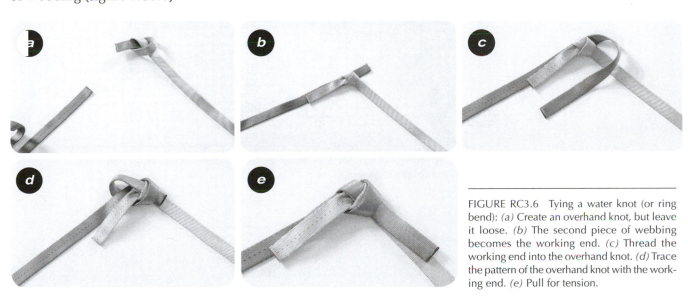

FIGURE RC3.6   Tying a water knot (or ring bend): *(a)* Create an overhand knot, but leave it loose. *(b)* The second piece of webbing becomes the working end. *(c)* Thread the working end into the overhand knot. *(d)* Trace the pattern of the overhand knot with the working end. *(e)* Pull for tension.

Prusik Knot   The Prusik knot was introduced by Austrian mountaineer Karl Prusik in 1931. This friction knot slides freely along the rope but grips the rope when loaded. The Prusik knot is used for belay escapes, climbing a fixed rope, and rescue applications. A series of girth hitches wrapped around the rope builds this knot (figure RC3.7).

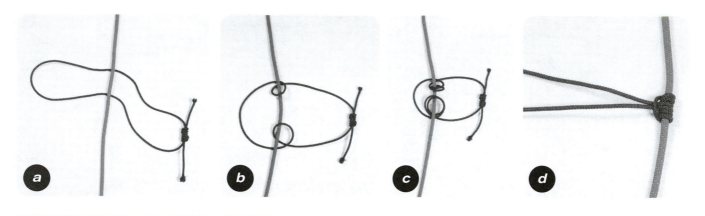

FIGURE RC3.7   Tying a Prusik knot: *(a)* Make a bight with the end of a sling. Lay this over or under the rope (the knotted end of the sling is the working end). *(b)* Move the working end over the rope and through the opposite bight. *(c)* Move the working end over the rope and through the opposite bight a second time. *(d)* Finish by dressing and setting the knot.

Munter Hitch   The Munter hitch was named for the Swiss mountain guide who invented it. Also known as the Italian friction hitch, this knot is commonly used for belaying. The hitch is a series of wraps using a rope or cord around a carabiner. Its main use is as a friction device for controlling the rate of descent in belay systems. The Munter hitch can also be used for rappelling (figure RC3.8).

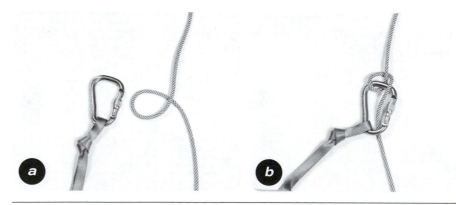

FIGURE RC3.8   Tying a Munter hitch: *(a)* Make a loop as shown and clip the carabiner into it; *(b)* hook the rope through the carabiner.

Munter Mule   The Munter mule (figure RC3.9) is a type of releasable hitch used in conjunction with the Munter hitch or belay device to tie off a weighted rope, allowing the belayer to free her or his hands.

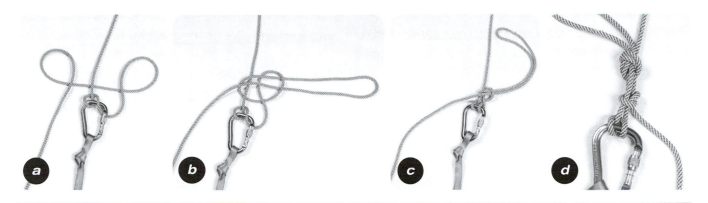

FIGURE RC3.9   Tying a Munter mule: *(a)* Create two loops in the working end of the rope. *(b)* Pass one loop through the other. *(c)* Loop the bight that is formed behind the standing end, and *(d)* finish with an overhand knot. Set and dress.

Activity 2: Coiling a Rope (10 Minutes)

Coiling a rope is a basic climbing skill that all climbers need to be familiar with. The two primary types of coils are the classic, or mountaineer's, coil and the butterfly coil.

◆ The mountaineer's coil can be carried over the shoulder or pack (figure RC3.10).

◆ The butterfly coil allows the climber to coil the rope faster, doesn't kink the rope, and can be attached to the climber's back if a pack is not worn (figure RC3.11).

FIGURE RC3.10   Mountaineer's coil.

FIGURE RC3.11   Butterfly coil.

Closure Activity

Random Knots (Time as Needed)

This lesson concludes by having the students tie the demonstrated knots. Randomly call out knots and assist students who need it.

◆ This lesson can flow into a discussion of basic anchors and other systems.

◆ You may also demonstrate the linkage of individual equipment with various knots into an anchor system and illustrate their function in the anchor.

◆ Challenge students by encouraging them to tie each knot with their eyes closed.

Follow-Up Activity

Knot Rodeo (30 Minutes or Longer)

These knots will be used throughout the unit. Consider using a game or contest for the fastest and best-tied knot among the students. Frequently, some students will master the knots and others will not. Have the more advanced students work with the knot novices in these activities.

◆ You can evaluate student understanding of specific knots as you identify knowledge or skill gaps.

◆ Always correct knots that are not neat.

ASSESSMENT

◆ Identify an application for a knot and have the students tie the appropriate knot. Check to make sure that students have tied the correct knot.

◆ Determine the condition and safety of each knot by checking the knot manually and visually before the student climbs or applies the knot.

◆ Check to see that students can tie each knot appropriately and neatly by having them compare and check their knots with one another. You can check the knots as well.

◆ Have students demonstrate the proper coiling of rope by observing them coil rope using either the mountaineer's coil or the butterfly coil.

◆ Assess whether students appreciate the importance of proper knot tying by asking them to explain the use of each knot.

◆ After a student states that the knot is tied, ask whether it is tied correctly and dressed. If the student cannot tie the knot or explain its proper use, deduct points. Students must retest to gain the remaining points.

TEACHING CONSIDERATIONS

◆ Encourage your students to visualize the finished knot and the steps required to tie it.

◆ Use the following sequence to teach knots:
  – With practice ropes in hand, have your students form a circle.
  – Have students place their practice ropes at their feet. All eyes should be focused on you.

- After you have the students' attention, go over the various terms associated with knots (bight, loop, working end, standing end, dressed, set).
- Next, as the students watch, tie the first knot on your list, step by step.
- After you tie the first knot, have students pick up their practice ropes and, with your oral explanation and continued demonstration, tie the knot.
- Repeat this sequence. During the second sequence walk around the circle and provide each student with feedback.
- Have students work at their own pace. Encourage students to help one another.
- Continue to walk around the circle, providing assistance as needed. After everyone has tied the knot correctly, move on to the next one.

UNIT 2, LESSON 4

▷ Belaying

OVERVIEW

The primary safety system in rock climbing is referred to as the belay. The word *belay* is a nautical term that means "to hold fast." In this lesson students learn how to belay and communicate effectively in a climbing environment.

JUSTIFICATION

Students benefit from understanding the various components of the belay system and the communication system associated with it. Students must understand the concepts and be able to perform the belay if they are to be safe while rock climbing. This ability and understanding constitutes the foundation for all rock-climbing applications.

GOAL

To develop students' understanding and appreciation of the belay system and their ability to implement the system.

OBJECTIVES

At the end of this lesson, students will be able to

- describe the various components of the belay system (cognitive),
- determine the condition and safety of the belay system (cognitive),
- set up a belay appropriately and neatly (psychomotor),
- demonstrate the belay (psychomotor), and
- appreciate the importance of proper belay technique (affective).

EQUIPMENT AND AREAS NEEDED

- This lesson requires that a "ground school" belay system be established for initial practice.
- Top-rope climbs should be established for belay practice after students grasp the basic concepts and mechanics of the belay and can communicate effectively.

Required materials include the following:

◆ One helmet and harness for each student

◆ One practice rope for each group of three students

◆ One locking carabiner for each student

◆ Three or four webbing or rope slings to construct belay anchors and sufficient climbing equipment for all students to belay and climb

RISK MANAGEMENT CONSIDERATIONS

◆ Belaying should be taught in two stages.

  – Primary belay instruction initially occurs in ground school, or on a horizontal plane. Introducing belaying at ground level allows students to make mistakes without the risk of ground fall. During ground school, check the area for trip hazards and dead overhead branches (widow makers). Require climbers to wear a helmet.

  – Secondary belay instruction occurs on the rock in protected situations with backup belayers and specific supervision.

◆ Staff and students must wear helmets and harnesses.

◆ The site should be clear of potential rockfall.

◆ Students and staff should be protected against falling from the site by being attached (clipped in) to an anchor. A useful guideline is that no one should ever be closer than one body length to the edge without being clipped in.

LESSON CONTENT

Introduction

The belay is critical to safe climbing. As in other areas of climbing, the belay has advanced from a basic body belay to the use of mechanical devices such as the ATC and Gri-gri. The basic principle, however, remains unchanged. The belayer offers some degree of friction to arrest the climber's fall and a mechanism for lowering the climber to a safe position on the ground.

Main Activities

To begin this lesson, draw an analogy between learning how to belay and learning how to fly an airplane. Before getting into an airplane, pilots attend ground school to learn about the various systems, rules, and skills of flying. Similarly, beginning climbers participate in ground school to learn the dynamics and communication system associated with belaying before getting on the rock.

Students should practice belaying in triads until the basic movements are committed to muscle memory.

General Tips

◆ Belay techniques vary in use by programs. Learn the technique used by your program and teach it as instructed.

◆ One method of belay is sufficient, so remember to model the use of a single method.

◆ The basic components of the belay system are anchor, friction, and position.
- The anchor can minimize the forces taken directly by the belayer and provide the belayer with more control. To prevent them from taking their job lightly, make novice belayers aware of the forces that may be exerted on them in the system.
- Every belay system requires friction, which is introduced into the system through the belay device. Friction allows the belayer control over a falling climber by holding fast.
- Position is the final factor to consider in the belay system. The belayer should face the anticipated direction of the force and stand in a position of braced balance.

Activity 1: Belay Circle (One Hour)

The belay circle exercise is a productive way of teaching the mechanics of the belay and commands.

◆ One complete climbing rope and belay device for each student are needed. A variety of belay devices may be used at one time.

◆ Place the students in a circle with harnesses on (helmets if conditions warrant) and with the belay device attached to the harness belay loop with one locking carabiner.

◆ Beginning with yourself, feed the rope through each belay device and feed slack into the system until each student has his or her belay device rigged properly for belay.

◆ For each method of belay that you are teaching, feed the entire length of rope through the student circle so that you can observe each student.

◆ The belay circle reveals any variation in student implementation of the belay technique.

◆ Belay commands can be incorporated into the belay circle with the students feeding and taking up slack, braking, and lowering through the rope length.

Activity 2: Ground School (One Hour)

A second and more traditional way to teach belaying is through ground school. Have students divide themselves into groups of three. In each group, have students identify one person as the belayer, one as the climber, and one as the backup belayer.

◆ The belayer clips into the anchor and tosses the rope to the climber, who has positioned herself or himself approximately 50 feet (15 meters) from the belayer.

◆ After the climber receives the rope, she or he ties in, initiates the belay contract, and begins "climbing" toward the belayer. Throughout this process, both the climber and the belayer use the appropriate commands, and the belayer concentrates on the dynamics of belaying (figure RC4.1).

◆ The backup belayer maintains contact with the rope to support the belayer and helps manage the rope.

◆ Continue this sequence until each student has the opportunity to practice in each position.

◆ Beginning belayers should have another student serve as a backup belayer, who stands ready with his or her hands on the rope a few feet (about a meter) down from the belayer's brake hand.

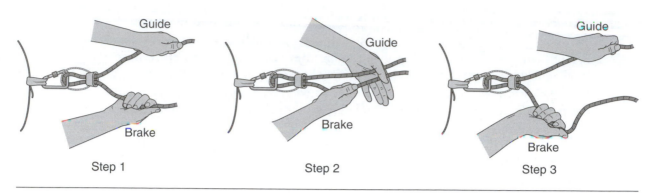

FIGURE RC4.1   The mechanics of belaying.

Activity 3: Belay Commands (One Hour or Longer)

Commands used in climbing have become standardized over time. Incorporate this communication system into all your belay activities, beginning with ground school.

Each command should be acknowledged with a response ("Please" and "Thank you" are excellent responses). Require students to use each other's names following each command. This method reduces confusion when multiple climber pairs are in a small area, as is frequently the case with climbing classes.

First, demonstrate the belay sequence, including both rope handling and belay signals.

- The belayer ties into the harness with a figure-eight follow-through.
- The belayer ties a figure-eight on a bight close to the harness and clips the loop into the anchor point with a locking carabiner.
- The climber ties into the harness with a figure-eight follow-through.

Next, demonstrate sequences of communication between climber and belayer.

Either the climber or the belayer can initiate the belay contract. In the sequence that follows, the climber initiates the contract:

- "On belay" (include belayer's or climber's name). Called by climber and belayer. Means "Are you ready to belay me?"
- "Up rope" (include belayer's name). Called by climber. Means "Take in all the slack rope."
- "That's me!" (include belayer's name). Called by climber. Means "That weight you feel on the end of the rope is me."
- "Climbing!" (include belayer's name). Called by climber. Means "I'm beginning to climb."
- "Climb on!" (include climber's name). Called by belayer. Means "I hear you. Go ahead and climb."

As the climber progresses upward, the belayer takes in the slack rope. During the climb, the climber may need slack, or may be moving faster than the belayer is taking in rope, or may need tension to feel more comfortable when making a difficult move.

- "Up rope!" (include belayer's name). Called by climber. Means "Take the slack out of the rope."
- "Slack!" (include belayer's name). Called by climber. Means "I need some extra rope to down climb," or the belayer is taking in the rope faster than the climber is climbing.

- "Climbing!" (include belayer's name). Called by climber after the belayer responds to "Up rope" or "Slack." Means "I am getting ready to climb again."
- "Climb on!" (include climber's name). Called by belayer. Means "I hear you. Start climbing."

Signal to use if the climber falls:

- "Falling!" (include belayer's name). Called by climber. Means "I'm falling! Make sure that you catch me!"

Signals to use after a falling climber is caught and is ready to start again:

- "Up rope!" (include belayer's name). Called by climber. Means "Take the slack out of the rope."
- "That's me!" (include belayer's name). Called by climber. Means "That weight you feel on the end of the rope is me."
- "Climbing!" (include belayer's name). Called by climber. Means "I'm beginning to climb."
- "Climb on!" (include belayer's name). Called by climber. Means "I hear you. Go ahead and climb."

Signals to use after the climber reaches the top of the climb:

- "Off belay" (include belayer's name). Called by climber. Means "I'm in a secure location and no longer need the belay."
- "Belay off" (include climber's name). Called by belayer. Means "Contract is terminated. I'm removing myself from the belay, but will remain attentive."

Other communication signals:

- "Rope!" (include climber's name). Called by those at the top of a climb. Means "Someone is throwing down a rope. Look up or take cover."
- "Clear!" (include climber's name). Called by those at the base of the climb. Means "It's safe to throw down a rope."
- "Rock!" Called loudly and repeatedly by anyone. Means "Look out for a falling rock or object."

Activity 4: Belaying on Rock (One Full Day)

Following a successful ground school experience, move to the climbing area.

- As in ground school, have students climb in triads (climber, belayer, backup belayer).
- Encourage students to be attentive, to work at their own pace, and to use all the skills they've recently learned.
- Watch the belays closely and correct any bad habits immediately.
- Always use a backup belayer until students are fully comfortable with belay skill.

Closure Activity

Mastering the Belay (Time as Needed)

This lesson concludes with the students' operation of belay systems on actual climbs. After they've mastered the belay, have each become certified by completing the belay checklist (figure RC4.2).

Belay Checklist

Climber's name: _____ Date: _____

The participant must successfully complete this checklist to become qualified to belay.

☐ 1. Have the climber put on his or her harness and demonstrate its proper use and application.

☐ 2. Have the participant tie into the harness using a figure-eight follow-through knot passed through the harness correctly (without assistance).

☐ 3. Have the participant demonstrate a proper belay setup. Hand the belay device, carabiner, and rope to the belayer as separate pieces. The belayer must demonstrate proper communication and belay technique (hands on rope at all times, no visible slack in rope).

☐ 4. Have the belayer catch an announced fall.

☐ 5. Have the belayer catch an unannounced fall.

☐ 6. Advise the participant that the belayer and climber are responsible for double checking each other.

☐ 7. If the participant passes, inform him or her of the rules and policies related to climbing in your program and invite the person to climb.

☐ 8. If the participant fails, invite him or her to come back after gaining more experience.

Completed by: _____ Date: _____

FIGURE RC4.2   Students complete this checklist to become certified after mastering the belay.

From M. Wagstaff and A. Attarian, 2009, *Technical skills for adventure programming: A curriculum guide* (Champaign, IL: Human Kinetics).

Follow-Up Activities

What's Wrong With This Picture? (30 Minutes)

This activity is an interactive way to reinforce newly acquired skills.

- Set up a belay system with you as the belayer.
- Be sure to include obvious and not so obvious mistakes that might include poor technique, poor mechanics, faulty communication, and careless attitude.
- Have students identify the problems.
- Alternatively, start the exercise by challenging students to identify the number of things wrong in the picture.

Consider using additional follow-up activities, such as these:

- Have students take a trust lean on their first climb to get a feel for the belay system.
- Have students take an announced and an unannounced fall during ground school and on one of the climbs that they do during the day.

ASSESSMENT

- Have students identify the various components of the belay system during the ground school activity.
- Have students determine the condition and safety of the belay system by discussing their findings during What's Wrong With This Picture? and by inspecting each belay before climbing.
- Observe students setting up a belay appropriately during ground school and subsequent climbing activities.
- Have students demonstrate the belay by successfully completing the belay checklist (figure RC4.2).
- Confirm that students appreciate the importance of proper belay technique by observing them catch an announced and an unannounced fall during the climbing portion of this lesson.

TEACHING CONSIDERATIONS

- Proper belay technique is critical to safe climbing. Modeling proper technique while belaying is critical for instructors—too often we unconsciously teach our bad habits to students.
- Belay technique is one area where fatigue and routine can lead you to demonstrate improper technique, so think twice when you begin to look for that comfy belay seat.
- You can teach all these skills on an indoor climbing wall. Indoor climbing walls provide a safe, controlled environment for teaching, reduce environmental impacts at natural climbing sites, and lessen conflicts with other climbers.

▷ **Basic Movement Over Rock**

OVERVIEW

"We climb with hands and heart, head and feet; these are primary—equipment is secondary. A climber holds life in his own hands; he must live by his own decisions. . . ."

Forrest Mountaineering catalog, 1975

This lesson introduces basic movement over rock. A brief overview of types of movement used in climbing is followed by student experimentation with movement over rock.

JUSTIFICATION

Students benefit from understanding the various types of movements found in rock climbing to become more efficient rock climbers.

GOAL

To develop students' understanding and appreciation of the various types of movements found in rock climbing.

OBJECTIVES

At the end of this lesson, students will be able to

- describe the types of movements used in climbing and relate them to particular situations found in rock climbing (cognitive),
- perform each basic type of movement (psychomotor), and
- appreciate the importance of mental and physical condition in rock climbing (affective).

EQUIPMENT AND AREAS NEEDED

This lesson can be implemented through a bouldering or top-roping session. Appropriate equipment should be available in either case. A potential list of equipment includes the following:

- One helmet for each student
- One harness for each student
- One dynamic and static rope for each group of three students
- One belay device for each pair of students
- Assorted webbing and presewn slings
- Eight to 10 locking and nonlocking carabiners

RISK MANAGEMENT CONSIDERATIONS

Note the following rock-climbing site management considerations:

- Students should wear helmets and harnesses.
- The site should be clear of potential for rockfall from above.
- Students and staff must be protected against falls from the site.

- Have communication and evacuation routes in place.
- If you are teaching the lesson in a bouldering session, set appropriate limits in terms of maximum climbable height. In any case, use spotters. Landing areas must be in reasonable condition to limit potential injury or padded with crash mats.

LESSON CONTENT

Introduction

Moving over rock entails the same types of movements that we've been making since birth—pulling, pushing, grabbing, stretching, and balancing. Humans are designed for climbing for several purposes—to escape predators, to gather food, and so forth. So moving over rock isn't about learning new ways to get from one place to another; it's about remembering the old. Rock climbing adds a vertical element that brings with it a sense of risk and thrill that can at times influence what we are able to do physically. For that reason, most climbers say that climbing is as much a mental effort as it is a physical one.

Main Activities

Activity 1: Watch and Learn (Time Varies)

Begin this lesson by having students climb. Watch how they move. Think about how you would attempt the same problems. Remember your breakthrough moments with particular movements and share them with students. A move may seem impossible or dangerous until someone accomplishes it or demystifies what is happening.

Demonstrate specific moves for particular problems. Traverse the climbing area close to the ground, shifting weight and moving up and down while describing the move. Break the movements down into hands, feet, and weight.

Hand Movements   Novice climbers seem to focus on gripping with their hands. Initially, they will overgrip and tire quickly. Male students are more inclined to try to pull themselves through a problem using upper-body strength. Some frequently taught types of hand movements include pinches, jams, pulls, hangs, and friction.

- Pinches are movements in which the climber grasps the hold between the fingers and thumb (figure RC5.1).
- Jams involve inserting the hand (or foot) into a crack or other feature and twisting or clenching it. These are some of the most secure movements (figure RC5.2).

FIGURE RC5.1   Pinch grip.

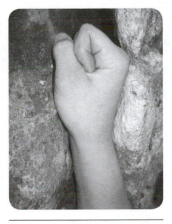

FIGURE RC5.2   Hand jam.

◆ Pulls involve upward and side-to-side motions. The former require a great deal of energy if used without support from the lower body.

◆ Hangs are often used in overhanging situations, often in combination with a jam.

◆ Friction may be used on sloping aspects and coarse rock by pressing downward with an open hand (or foot) flat on the rock. Many students feel insecure about relying on friction, but it can offer an extremely secure "hold."

Encourage students to use each type of hold and to notice the amount of energy required to maintain each. Hanging on bone is more efficient than hanging on muscle. Have students demonstrate this to themselves by hanging from bent arms (active muscle flexion) and from long straight arms (passive skeletal).

Foot Movements The feet are actually more useful to the beginning climber than the hands for several reasons.

◆ The feet are designed to be stood on, whereas the hands are not really designed to hold body weight.

◆ Feet and legs have greater endurance, and they can shift a greater amount of mass in control of the climber's center of gravity.

To emphasize this point, ask your students, "Can you do more pull-ups than you can deep knee bends?" Answer: No. You can do more deep knee bends. Use your legs!

Footwork for climbing involves using footholds consisting of edging, smearing, and jamming.

◆ Edging (figure RC5.3) is the use of the outside or inside edge of the foot.

◆ Smearing (figure RC5.4) is the used of the flat bottom of the foot.

◆ Jamming (figure RC5.5), as described earlier, involves the insertion of the foot into a crack or other feature and twisting it so that it creates a jam.

FIGURE RC5.3 Edging.

FIGURE RC5.4 Smearing.

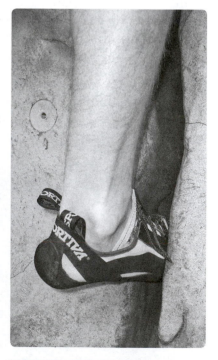

FIGURE RC5.5 Foot jamming.

Weight Shifts   Weight is critical in climbing, because shifting weight not only allows strained muscles to rest but also allows new holds to come into reach. The critical concept here is the climber's center of gravity. By shifting the center of gravity in or out (from the rock) or left or right, the climber makes available new options for advancing up the climb or simply finding a position of rest.

Other Considerations   As your students begin to climb, their attention will be focused on hand and foot placements and weight distribution. To make them more efficient climbers, remind them to take short reaches and small steps, keep their center of gravity over their feet, use their legs more than their arms (after all, you can do more deep knee bends than pull-ups!), and always look ahead for the next hand- or foothold—don't get tunnel vision! Most important, climbers must learn to breathe and stay in mental control.

◆ Some novice climbers often hold their breath through difficult moves or when stuck in a taxing spot. This works directly in opposition to the climber's goal and will result in a fall. Signs that this is happening include gasping sounds and a spasmlike movement of muscle that causes the arm or leg to move up and down rapidly like a sewing machine needle, an action that usually precedes a fall.

◆ Staying in mental control is also important. Feeling fear at being suspended only by a rope is normal. Climbers resort to many techniques (for example, meditation and visualization) to identify and harness those feelings to advance their climbing. The fear simply means that the climber is sane.

Special note: The types of movements that are available may be limited because of the type of rock where the climbing is being taught. For example, the sandstone of the Red River Gorge in Kentucky offers great friction for hand and foot options, but little in the way of the crack jamming climbing found in the deserts of Utah. Climbers who manage to climb on many different types of rock develop a great range of movement over rock.

Activity 2: Rock Climbing Skills Checklist (One-Half to One Full Day)

Have students complete the Climbing Techniques section of the skills checklist at the end of this unit (page 226) or develop and use your own. This activity encourages students to attempt a variety of climbs, which will require them to try a variety of techniques including stemming, lieback, face climbing, chimneying, and mantling.

◆ Stemming (figure RC5.6) involves pressing outward with hands and feet against two different faces, such as in a dihedral or a chimney. A dihedral looks like an open book with two walls meeting at an angle. A **chimney** is often a large crack or other feature that the entire body may fit into.

FIGURE RC5.6   Stemming.

◆ Liebacks involve pulling with the hands and pushing with the feet. The hands are gripping a long edge such as a fin of rock or a crack (figure RC5.7).

◆ When face climbing, the climber is usually facing a wall or face of rock and using the hands and feet to climb features on that face. Face climbing is much like climbing a ladder (figure RC5.8).

◆ Chimneying involves stemming techniques but may also include use of the shoulders, back, and hips in wider cracks (figure RC5.9).

◆ Mantling is a specific movement technique that uses downward hand and arm pressure to help the climber move the feet up to the level of the hands when there are no useful handholds above (figure RC5.10). This movement resembles the move that a gymnast makes to mount a pommel horse.

FIGURE RC5.7   Lieback.

FIGURE RC5.8   Face climbing.

FIGURE RC5.9   Chimneying.

FIGURE RC5.10   Mantling.

Climbing techniques are varied and may include endless combinations of the previously discussed techniques as well as others. Part of the interest and appeal of climbing is in developing a wide range of techniques that can be applied in different situations. Climbers should not be afraid to experiment!

Closure Activity

Climb On! (Time as Needed)

Conclude this lesson by having the students climb.

- ◆ Encourage the students to comment (as long as they do not distract the climber) on each other's moves, watch others climb, and visualize themselves making the same movements.
- ◆ Note that with the development of strength, conditioning, and experience, students will begin to climb with more confidence and begin to use a variety of techniques.

Follow-Up Activity

Climbing Competition (Time as Needed)

- ◆ Correct movements that seem to inhibit development (foot dragging or tapping) and provide encouragement throughout.
- ◆ Set up a climbing competition for your students either on an indoor climbing wall or outdoors on natural rock. Students score points for any attempted and completed climb. Additionally, award points for using various movement techniques. You can use the movement checklist (figure RC5.11) for ideas on movements to incorporate into a competition.

ASSESSMENT

- ◆ Describe the types of movements used in climbing and relate them to particular situations found in rock climbing by taking a tour of a natural climbing site. Have students identify climbs and the movements that they will use to complete the climb.
- ◆ Have students perform each climbing movement by completing a climbing skills checklist or by participating in a climbing competition.
- ◆ Check to see whether students appreciate the importance of mental and physical conditioning in rock climbing by observing them climb and improve their ability to overcome fears and attempt more difficult rock climbs.

TEACHING CONSIDERATIONS

- ◆ The ease with which instructors perform moves can be discouraging to students. Demystify the move by verbalizing each aspect of it.
- ◆ If you are teaching this lesson on roped climbs, make sure that the students feel comfortable with the anchor system.
- ◆ Practice falls or trust leans to reassure students that when they take risks with their movements the rope will hold.
- ◆ Encourage students to use a variety of techniques while they are climbing. You should be familiar with the climbing area and identify climbs where students can practice various techniques.
- ◆ Emphasize to your students that to be successful climbers they should take small steps and use short reaches, avoid using tunnel vision, maintain three points of contact, and keep the center of gravity over the feet (not hug the rock).

Movement Checklist

Instructions: The instructor of this course adds the names of the routes and assigns a point value to each based on the difficulty. More difficult routes should be given higher point values.

PART I	
Climb	**Score**
Route name (point value)	
Route name (point value)	
Route name (point value)	
Route name (point value)	
Route name (point value)	
Route name (point value)	
Route name (point value)	
Route name (point value)	
	Total I _____

PART II	
Bonus points (2 pts. per technique, awarded once per climb, must be called by the climber)	
1. Lieback	
2. Stem	
3. Foot jam	
4. Pinch grip	
5. Smear	
	Total II _____

PART III		
Penalties	**Number of times**	**Total**
1. Stepped on rope (5 pts.)		
2. Did not wear helmet (5 pts.)		
3. Did not communicate (5 pts.)		
4. Coiled rope poorly (5 pts.)		
5. Used improper belay technique (5 pts.)		
6. Committed any unsafe act (5 pts.)		
7. Used poor technique (5 pts.)		
		Total III _____

Rules

1. Each climb can be attempted only once.
2. The climber must exhibit good technique on all climbs.
3. An attempt earns half the point total of a completed climb.

Total I _____ + total II _____ – total III _____ = score _____

FIGURE RC5.11   A sample checklist for keeping score during the climbing competition.

▷ Top-Rope Anchors I (Natural Anchors)

OVERVIEW

"Some of the very best protection is already in place, just waiting for you. It's natural protection: trees and bushes, horns and flakes, chockstones, boulders, and other natural features. . . . Only the simplest tools—runners and carabiners—are needed to take advantage of these gifts from Mother Nature."

Graydon, 1992

This lesson introduces top-rope anchors using natural features. A brief overview of climbing anchors is followed by student construction and evaluation of climbing anchors.

JUSTIFICATION

Anchors using natural features are among the least gear intensive and most commonly used in rock climbing. The ability to take advantage of natural features reduces reliance on equipment and increases the available options students have for constructing safe, reliable climbing anchors.

GOAL

To develop students' understanding and appreciation for the safe construction of top-rope anchors using natural features for protection.

OBJECTIVES

At the end of this lesson, students will be able to

- describe the types of natural features that may be used for building safe anchors (cognitive),
- determine the condition and integrity of each anchor (cognitive),
- construct appropriate and neat top-rope anchors using natural features (psycho-motor), and
- appreciate the importance of proper anchor building (affective).

EQUIPMENT AND AREAS NEEDED

Each student should have the following:

- Various lengths (4 to 20 feet, or 1 to 6 meters) of 7-millimeter accessory cord
- Several 2- and 4-foot (60- and 120-centimeter) lengths of 1-inch (25-millimeter) tubular webbing or presewn runners
- A climbing rope
- Several oval nonlocking and locking carabiners

RISK MANAGEMENT CONSIDERATIONS

Before constructing any natural anchor, the climber (and then you) should examine each feature for reliability. For example, the student should be sure that trees are alive and healthy, and they should be tied off close to the ground. Chockstones, flakes, and horns should be tested by striking them with the heel of the hand and checked for hairline fractures that may suggest weakness.

- Primary instruction in top-rope anchors occurs at ground level with no risk of a fall.
- Secondary anchor instruction occurs on the rock in protected situations.
- Staff and students should wear helmets and harnesses.
- The site should be clear of potential rockfall.
- Students and staff should be protected against falls from the site.
- Communication and evacuation routes must be in place.
- Climbing equipment should be protected against abrasion across rock edges. Offer this reminder to students: Take care of your gear and it will take care of you.

LESSON CONTENT

Introduction

Climbing anchors are critical to the safety and enjoyment of the activity and constitute the foundation that protects climbers and belayers. This lesson focuses on anchors that use natural features (rock features, trees, or anything that the natural environment provides) to protect the climbing team.

Main Activity

Building a Natural Anchor (One Hour, or More if Needed)

Instruction about climbing anchors involves a lot of hands-on practice. Rather than focus on the intricacies of each type of anchor that might be built and safely used, the lesson uses a systems approach. A climbing anchor is part of a system that can be applied to most climbable rock—the various pieces and configuration of the system will vary depending on the site and the skill of the builder. After all the component parts of the system are in place, the system should be ready to use.

- Anchor systems consist of a combination of natural protection (appropriately sized rock formations and trees located near the top of a climb), 7-millimeter by 16-foot (5-meter) cordelette, webbing, and carabiners.
- A good test for students to apply about whether an anchor is correctly constructed is the question "What's wrong with it?" The rationale is simple: Students will need to evaluate climbing systems for safety after they are climbing on their own; therefore, the most important outcome is this self-evaluative function. When the answer is "Nothing," then the anchor system should be safe to use. Students struggle with this question because it places the responsibility on them for positive safety statements.
- To test anchors built at ground level, the instructor weights the anchor only after the student has evaluated it as being safe. Some care should be used here because the initial anchors that students build often fail when weighted, but seeing the anchor fail reinforces for students the importance of correct anchor building.

Students should follow these guidelines when constructing natural anchors:

◆ Trees need to be at least 6 inches (15 centimeters) in diameter, alive, well rooted, and not on the cliff edge (figure RC6.1).

◆ Construct climbing anchors using rock features such as boulders, horns, or chicken heads—features that protrude from the rock face and make good natural anchors, handholds, or footholds.

◆ Use the hug test: Any boulder that you can get your arms around is too small to use as an anchor (Powers & Cheek, 2000).

◆ Boulders used for anchors should be secured to the surrounding environment and should not move when tested (figure RC6.2). Rule out any boulder that appears ready to be tipped over the edge.

◆ Horns and chicken heads should be evaluated for their ability to hold the anchor. Webbing should not slip when slack, and the integrity of the feature should be closely inspected. A variety of techniques can be used to utilize horns and chicken heads as anchors (figure RC6.3).

◆ Boulders and other rock features are tied off in the same manner as trees.

◆ Caution should be used regarding any sharp edges or constrictions that could damage or hinder the anchor. Rope bags and pieces of used carpet are useful to pad suspect edges.

◆ Cordelette or webbing extensions are used to locate the master point at the top of the climb.

FIGURE RC6.1   Tree used as a top-rope anchor. A cordelette is passed around a tree and tied off with a figure-eight on a bight to create the master point.

FIGURE RC6.2   Boulder used for a top-rope anchor. A webbing loop is passed around the boulder and tied off with an overhand knot to create the master point.

FIGURE RC6.3   Horn used for a top-rope anchor. A web runner is threaded through the horn and tied off with an overhand knot to create the master point.

Closure Activity

Building Anchors Using Natural Features (Time as Needed)

This lesson concludes by having the students build multiple anchors using natural features.

◆ This lesson can flow into a discussion of more complex anchors and other systems.

◆ Students should have some grasp of anchor weaknesses to look for and solutions that can improve anchor safety. One activity to assess anchors is a round-robin assessment in which each student or pair of students constructs an anchor using natural features. Other students then critique the anchor. Students continue building and critiquing anchors until everyone has had a chance to build and critique several anchors.

Follow-Up Activity

Natural Anchor Assessment (Time as Needed)

Find a new climbing area or site and have students conduct a natural anchor assessment. After students have identified potential anchors, have the rest of the group critique each selection.

◆ For a different approach have students identify potential natural anchors by identifying rock features only or vegetation features only.

◆ Follow each assessment with a peer critique.

◆ As a final follow-up activity, identify at least three safe and three unsafe natural anchors. Have your students describe the anchor as safe or dangerous and explain why. Follow up with a short discussion.

ASSESSMENT

◆ Have students describe the types of natural features that may be used for building safe anchors by pointing these out during a climbing site tour before climbing or during the follow-up activity.

◆ Evaluate how well students determine the condition and safety of each anchor by testing and inspecting the anchors during the round-robin assessment and before climbing.

◆ Check that students can construct appropriate and neat top-rope anchors using natural features by observing them as they construct anchors before climbing or during the follow-up activity.

◆ Be sure that students appreciate the importance of proper anchor building by observing them as they progress in skill development and knowledge throughout this unit.

TEACHING CONSIDERATIONS

◆ Move among student pairs to provide feedback on progress.

◆ After an anchor is suitable (and in a protected ground position), have a student clip in to the anchor and weight it to observe the effect on the anchor.

▷ Top-Rope Anchors II (Artificial Anchors)

OVERVIEW

This lesson introduces top-rope anchors using artificial, or placed, protection. Initially, climbers usually seek natural features to construct top-rope anchors. In the absence of natural features, climbers use artificial, or placed, protection to construct anchors. Artificial anchors include both active and passive camming or wedging devices, some of which are explored in this lesson. A brief overview of climbing anchors is followed by having students construct and evaluate these anchors.

JUSTIFICATION

Students benefit from understanding top-rope anchors that use placed protection. Placing artificial protection remains critical to attempting climbs where no natural or fixed protection exists. Artificial protection is also often required to back up fixed protection. Knowledge, skill, and ability in the construction of top-rope anchors using placed (or artificial) protection opens a vast range of climbing opportunities to the climber.

GOAL

To develop students' understanding and appreciation of the safe construction of top-rope anchors using placed protection.

OBJECTIVES

At the end of this lesson, students will be able to

- describe the types of placed protection that may be used for anchor construction (cognitive),
- determine the condition and safety of each anchor (cognitive),
- place individual pieces of protection appropriately and securely (psychomotor),
- construct top-rope anchors using placed protection (psychomotor), and
- appreciate the importance of proper anchor building (affective).

EQUIPMENT AND AREAS NEEDED

- A demonstration of anchors using placed protection from the ground requires the preparation of an anchor station in advance.
- One climbing rope for each pair of students.
- The following items for each student:
  - One 16- to 20-foot (5- to 6-meter) length of 7-millimeter accessory cord
  - Three 2-foot (60-centimeter) and three 4-foot (120-centimeter) lengths of 1-inch (25-millimeter) tubular webbing or presewn runners
  - Eight to 10 assorted nonlocking and locking carabiners
  - Three nut tools
  - Assorted artificial protection (placed protection) to provide students a wide selection from which to choose when building anchors

RISK MANAGEMENT CONSIDERATIONS

- ◆ Primary instruction in top-rope anchors occurs at ground level with no risk of a fall.
- ◆ Secondary anchor instruction occurs on the rock in protected situations.
- ◆ Staff and students must wear helmets and harnesses.
- ◆ The site should be clear of potential rockfall.
- ◆ Students and staff must be protected against fall from the site.
- ◆ Communication and evacuation routes must be in place.
- ◆ Climbing equipment must be protected against abrasion across rock edges. Offer this reminder to students: Take care of your gear and it will take care of you.

LESSON CONTENT

Introduction

"The strength and security of an anchor are not the same thing. Strength is the ability of an anchor to hold a fall. Security is its ability to stay put until the fall comes. Both should be considered in placing nuts."

Great Pacific Iron Works, 1974

Climbing anchors are critical to the safety and enjoyment of the activity and constitute the primary safety system that protects climbers and belayers. This lesson focuses on anchors that use placed protection to protect the climbing team.

- ◆ This type of anchor places maximum responsibility on the student to ensure proper construction and is the most complex to build.
- ◆ Conversely, the student has a great deal of freedom in the design and implementation of placed protection as long as placements are efficient and effective and systems principles are applied.

Main Activity

The Art of Placing Artificial Anchors (Time Varies)

Artificial protection comes in many forms, but all operate on principles of friction and constriction. To develop cognitive and muscle memory for efficient and effective use of both active and passive protection, students must spend time with each form. In traditional (trad) climbing, in which climbers most often use placed protection anchors, they must construct the anchor before fatigue sets in.

Both active and passive artificial protection, or pro, is manufactured in a variety of sizes and configurations so that it can be placed in cracks of varying size, shape, and depth. Some of the more common types are described in the following sections.

Artificial Chockstones (Chocks)   These wedge or uniquely shaped devices are examples of passive cams, which are relatively easy to place by either wedging against the narrow portion of a crack or by camming, that is, by slightly rotating the device within a crack. **Chocks** (or **chockstones**) are also designed not to damage the rock when removed. Some common types include stoppers (figure RC7.1) and hexcentrics (figure RC7.2).

Cams   A **cam** (also known as a spring-loaded camming device, or **SLCD**) features a spring-loaded wedging unit that has two sliding cams working in opposition. The unit operates by engaging a trigger mechanism, which controls the position and width of the cams. SLCDs can be used in a variety of crack sizes, including flared, tapered, and shallow cracks (see figure RC7.3).

FIGURE RC7.1   Stopper in use.

FIGURE RC7.2   Hexcentric in use.

FIGURE RC7.3   SLCD in use.

Placing Protection   Allow students time to place artificial protection in single placements first and then in the combinations that will allow for later anchor building. You can move among the students at their ground stations and provide feedback on placements.

- After students display some proficiency for placement, they can build initial anchors.
- Ideally, when constructing an anchor using artificial protection, an equalized anchor (figure RC7.4) or preequalized anchor (figure RC7.5) should be constructed by using webbing or a cordelette.
- The cordelette is clipped into each of the carabiners. The cordelette can then be gathered by pulling down the segments between the carabiners to a central gathered loop and tied off in the desired direction of pull.
- Protection should be placed so that the cordelette between them will have no more than a 90-degree angle and preferably much less (figure RC7.6).
- After the overhand knot is tied, two carabiners can be clipped opposite and opposed (called the master point), and the rope can be slung for climbing.
- Considerations for placing protection anchors include the direction of pull, edge, and rope management. The anchor must be built so that it points directly down the fall line, or direction of pull.
- Having several nut tools handy is useful because students' zeal for safe placements can lead to stuck placements.

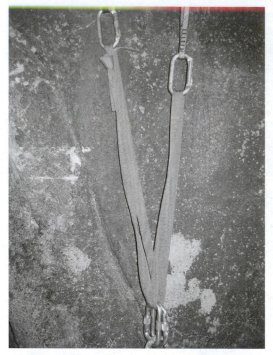

FIGURE RC7.4   Equalized anchor.

FIGURE RC7.5   Preequalized anchor.

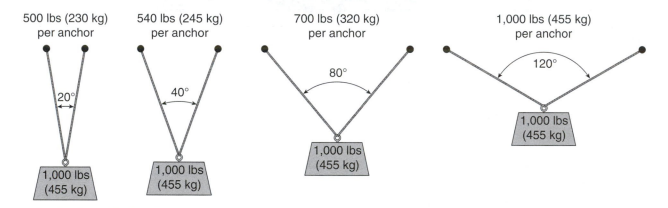

FIGURE RC7.6   The lower the angle, the less weight each anchor has to hold.

ERNEST Principles   Ultimately, students should be able to apply ERNEST principles to anchor construction and determine its safety accordingly. ERNEST is an acronym that stands for equalized, redundant, nonextending, solid and simple, and timely. You can demonstrate these principles during the construction of an anchor.

◆ *Equalized* indicates that the central anchor point, or master point, is placed in such a way that the weight of the climber is distributed evenly among the anchor placements.

◆ *Redundant* means that more than one anchor placement is being used and that they are equally capable of holding a fall.

◆ *Nonextending* implies that should one anchor placement fail, then the remaining anchor points will not be shock loaded. Minimization of shock loading is accomplished by tying an overhand knot just above the carabiners used for the central anchor point.

◆ *Solid and simple* means that the features selected and their webbing attachments are capable of holding a fall and are easily checked for completion.

◆ *Timely* means that the anchor is kept as simple as possible to avoid confusion, tangled webbing, or twisted ropes. Students must take their time to check anchors and parts of the system.

Closure Activity

Anchor Placement With a Peer (Time as Needed)

Have students pair up and distribute equipment equally. Instruct them to construct anchors using the information and equipment provided. Have them focus on rock integrity, direction of pull, and other dynamics associated with anchor construction. Evaluate each pair's progress and provide feedback.

◆ This lesson can lead into a discussion of more complex anchors and other systems.

◆ Following this activity, students should have an idea of anchor weaknesses to look for and begin to take responsibility for anchor safety.

Follow-Up Activity

Artificial Anchor Assessment (Time as Needed)

These anchors will be used throughout the unit. You can evaluate student understanding of top-rope anchors and correct it as you identify knowledge and skill gaps. Have your students do a round-robin assessment.

◆ Working in pairs, students construct a set of anchors using artificial protection.

◆ After all pairs have constructed their anchors, students critique the anchor setups for ERNEST.

◆ This process continues until each pair's anchors have been critiqued.

◆ Always correct anchors that are not neat, clean, and ERNEST.

Create anchor challenges with your students by introducing them to various climbing environments. Each new environment should possess challenging new anchor problems. This process will help them review and apply previous lessons, stimulate them to ask questions, and require them to evaluate new settings.

ASSESSMENT

◆ Have students describe the types of placed protection that can be used for anchor construction, both orally and in written assessments.

◆ Have students determine the condition and safety of each anchor through testing and inspection by you and their peers during the round-robin assessment and before climbing.

◆ Check to see that students place individual pieces of protection appropriately and securely by observing them during the round-robin assessment and before climbing.

◆ Have students construct top-rope anchors using placed protection by providing them with various types of artificial protection and asking them to construct an anchor.

◆ Be sure that students appreciate the importance of proper anchor building by observing them construct complex anchors and apply them to various climbing situations.

◆ Have students determine the condition and safety of each anchor by inspecting each for ERNEST before climbing.

TEACHING CONSIDERATIONS

◆ This lesson consists of a demonstration of anchor system construction followed by student practice and application.

◆ Move among student pairs and provide feedback on progress.

◆ After an anchor is suitable (and in a protected position) have the student clip into the anchor and weight it to observe the effect on the anchor.

UNIT 2, LESSON 8

▷ # Top-Rope Anchors III (Fixed or Permanent Anchors)

OVERVIEW

Fixed, or permanent, anchors are protection devices that are drilled or hammered into the rock to provide anchors where no other opportunities exist. The fixed anchors remain in place for subsequent climbers to use. This lesson introduces top-rope anchors using bolts, pitons, and other hardware including shuts and chains. A brief overview of climbing anchors is followed by having students construct and evaluate climbing anchors.

JUSTIFICATION

Students benefit from understanding fixed top-rope anchors because of their prevalence in rock climbing today. Although these fixed anchors provide access to otherwise unprotectable routes, they present certain risks. Students will benefit from developing knowledge and skill in the inspection and proper use of these types of anchors.

GOAL

To develop students' understanding and appreciation for the safe construction of top-rope anchors using fixed protection devices (bolts, shuts, and chains).

OBJECTIVES

At the end of this lesson, students will be able to

◆ describe the various types of fixed anchors available (cognitive),

◆ determine the condition and safety of each type of anchor (cognitive),

◆ construct top-rope anchors using fixed anchors (psychomotor), and

◆ appreciate the importance of proper anchor building (affective).

EQUIPMENT AND AREAS NEEDED

- A demonstration of fixed anchors from the ground requires the preparation or identification of an anchor station in advance.
- One climbing rope for each pair of students.
- This lesson requires that each student have the following:
    - One 16- to 20-foot (5- to 6-meter) length of 7-millimeter accessory cord
    - Three 2-foot (60-centimeter) and three 4-foot (120-centimeter) lengths of 1-inch (25-millimeter) tubular webbing or presewn runners
    - Eight to 10 assorted nonlocking and locking carabiners

RISK MANAGEMENT CONSIDERATIONS

- Primary instruction in top-rope anchors occurs at ground level with no risk of a fall.
- Secondary anchor instruction occurs on the rock in protected situations.
- Both staff and students will wear helmets and harnesses.
- The site should be clear of potential rockfall.
- Students and staff must be protected against fall from the site.
- Communication and evacuation routes must be in place.
- Climbing equipment must be protected against abrasion across rock edges. Offer this reminder to students: Take care of your gear and it will take care of you.

LESSON CONTENT

Introduction

Establishing anchors using fixed anchor points opens the way to many challenging rock-climbing routes. Proper use of these climbing anchors is critical to the safety and enjoyment of the activity. Climbing anchors constitute the primary safety system that protects climbers and belayers. This lesson focuses on anchors that use fixed protection devices including bolts, pitons, shuts, and chains to protect the climbing team.

Main Activity

Overview of Fixed Anchors (45 to 60 Minutes)

- Make sure that you have examples of each anchor type on hand for students to see and distinguish from one another.
- When working with fixed anchors, students should use the ERNEST principles for anchor construction (see lesson 7, page 194).
- Anchors that use bolts, pitons, shuts, and chains are among the simplest anchors to construct.
- For safety reasons, always use bolts, pitons, and shuts in pairs, because a single anchor point is considered unsafe (no backup is in place if the anchor fails).

Bolts   Bolt anchors are permanent anchors that require drilling to place. A bolt anchor is usually composed of three parts: the bolt, or securing device, the sleeve, and the hanger (figure RC8.1). Bolts should be at least 3/8 inch (.95 centimeters) in diameter and placed into good-quality rock.

Bolts can be inspected to determine their integrity by remembering the acronym BLAHS:

◆ Bolt—Inspect the bolt or cap screw. Is weight placed on the threads? Check the hanger; it should not be hanging on the threads. Grab the bolt hanger and attempt to move the bolt. If the bolt moves in its hole, do not use it. Make sure that the bolt head is not deformed. Never hammer the bolt head or hanger after the bolt has been placed because the impact may compromise the ability of the bolt to hold a fall or force.

◆ Loose—Check to see whether the entire placement is loose or secure by clipping a carabiner into the hanger and torquing the bolt around in all directions. Try an outward pull to see whether the bolt is secure. It is acceptable for the hanger to be loose, but not too loose. In any case, the bolt should not move.

◆ Angle—This condition will be more difficult to determine. By viewing the bolt head and any part of the exposed bolt shaft under the hanger, you may be able to assess the angle. The load should be 90 degrees to the bolt shaft.

◆ Hangers—Examine the hanger. Look for hairline cracks by focusing on the area around the bolt and carabiner hole. If the bolt or hanger appears to be damaged in any way, seek another anchor.

◆ Surfaces—Is the rock surface around the bolt crack free? Was the bolt placed in a loose flake, detached block, or other questionable location?

Pitons   A piton (or pin) is a sharply pointed piece of metal that is driven into a crack or seam in the rock with a hammer. A piton consists of a eye and a blade, which acts as an anchor (figure RC8.2).

Before clipping any fixed pin consider the following:

◆ Always visually and manually inspect the pin before clipping into it. Check the eye for cracks. Is it broken or badly rusted? Is the pin overdriven? Is the pin loose enough to remove by hand? Is it bent?

FIGURE RC8.1   Bolt.

◆ Loose or marginal pins can be checked by attaching a sling and giving a few good jerks (make sure that you're clipped in when you do this).

◆ Ideally, the pin should be fixed perpendicular to the direction of pull.

◆ When possible, back up all suspect pins by incorporating an additional anchor.

Shuts   Shuts were originally manufactured for quick (temporary) chain repair applications. These *cold* shuts available in hardware stores have been found to be dangerous and are not recommended for use in climbing. Some shuts, however, have

FIGURE RC8.2   Piton.

been manufactured specifically for climbing (figure RC8.3). A climber should be able to distinguish between the two.

Chains Chains are often attached to bolts for the purpose of lowering the climber to the ground or rappelling.

◆ Some of the most questionable anchors are chains attached to bolts with spacer washers, because the bolt sticks farther out of the hole. This configuration increases the bending forces on the bolt 10 fold.

◆ Examine the quality of the chain. Even new ones may be suspect. To determine whether a chain is in good condition, inspect each link for cracks and excessive rust. If attached with a bolt and hanger, follow the BLAHS approach described earlier. When in doubt, use other anchoring methods.

◆ Some manufacturers make chains with hangers permanently attached, which is a good idea, as long as the chain is high quality and ASTM tested and certified (figure RC8.4).

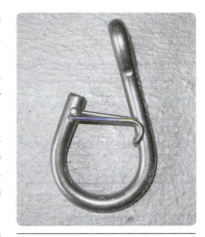

FIGURE RC8.3 Shut designed for climbing.

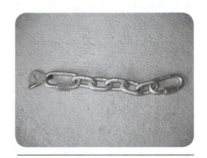

FIGURE RC8.4 Chain configured as a climbing anchor.

Closure Activity

Fixed Anchor Review (Two to Three Hours)

This activity is designed to reinforce the material presented in this lesson. The activity also allows for the introduction of new information, thus giving students a better understanding of fixed anchors.

◆ Assign each pair of students a type of fixed anchor to investigate. Each pair should conduct a literature review on their assigned anchor type. A good place to start is the American Safe Climbing Association Web site (www.safeclimbing.org).

◆ Have students report on the pros and cons of the anchors that they investigated.

◆ Students should have some grasp of anchor weaknesses to look for and begin to evaluate anchor safety.

◆ This lesson concludes by having the students build multiple anchors using bolts, shuts, and chains. This session can flow into a discussion of more complex anchors and other systems.

Follow-Up Activity

Fixed Anchor Inventory (One to Two Hours)

◆ Conduct a fixed anchor inventory at a natural climbing area. In the process identify the types and condition of fixed anchors.

◆ Make recommendations on how to address potentially dangerous or suspect anchors.

ASSESSMENT

- Have students describe the various types of fixed anchors available as they conduct an inventory of fixed anchors during a tour of a natural climbing area before climbing.

- Have students determine the condition and safety of each type of anchor by inspecting a sample of fixed anchors at a local climbing area before climbing.

- Observe students construct top-rope anchors using fixed protection devices when setting up a top-rope rock climb. Check to make sure that students are following the ERNEST principle.

- Check to see whether students appreciate the importance of proper anchor building by asking them to describe their feelings after constructing and using the anchor.

TEACHING CONSIDERATIONS

- This lesson consists of a demonstration of anchor system construction followed by student practice and application. Move among student pairs to provide feedback on progress.

- After an anchor is suitable (and in a protected position), have the student clip into the anchor and weight it to observe the effect on the anchor.

- Each of these anchors can be set up on indoor climbing walls, which offer a relatively safe, controlled environment for teaching. Skills learned indoors can be applied outdoors.

UNIT 2, LESSON 9

▷ Rappelling

OVERVIEW

After a rock climb is completed, it is really only half over. The climber has three choices for the descent: hike to the base of the cliff, be lowered, or rappel. Rappelling is a basic climbing skill that requires the climber to slide down the rope in a controlled manner. In most climbing environments, the rope is doubled through the anchor, allowing the climber to retrieve the rope by pulling on one end. This attribute accounts for the name *rappel*, a French word meaning "to recall" (Robbins, 1982). This lesson introduces students to the fundamental skills and techniques associated with rappelling. A brief overview of rappelling technique is followed by having students set up a supervised rappel and then rappel.

JUSTIFICATION

Students benefit from understanding rappel systems and techniques. The rappel remains critical for the safe descent from many climbs. Having the knowledge, skill, and ability to establish and use a rappel system is fundamental to rock climbing.

GOAL

To develop students' understanding and appreciation for safe rappelling.

OBJECTIVES

At the end of this lesson, students will be able to

◆ determine the condition and safety of the rappel setup (cognitive),

◆ demonstrate a rappel (psychomotor),

◆ demonstrate a leg wrap (psychomotor), and

◆ appreciate the importance of proper rappelling (affective).

EQUIPMENT AND AREAS NEEDED

◆ A demonstration of rappelling on the ground requires the preparation of a rappel station in advance.

◆ This lesson requires that the following items are available on site:

  – Various lengths (4 to 20 feet, or 1 to 6 meters) of 7-millimeter accessory cord and 1-inch (25-millimeter) tubular webbing tied in 2- and 4-foot (60- to 120-centimeter) lengths or presewn runners for constructing anchors

  – Ten locking carabiners

  – Two figure-eight descenders

  – Two pairs of leather gloves

  – Two static ropes for rappelling

  – One dynamic rope for belaying

  – One dynamic rope for rescue purposes

RISK MANAGEMENT CONSIDERATIONS

◆ Primary instruction for rappelling occurs at ground level with no risk of a fall.

◆ Secondary rappel instruction occurs on the rock in protected situations.

◆ Students should always be protected with a top-rope belay.

◆ You should demonstrate the rappel and leg wrap. Students should practice both.

◆ The rappeller should wear a glove on the brake hand.

◆ Both staff and students must wear helmets and harnesses.

◆ The site should be clear of potential rockfall.

◆ Students and staff must be protected against a fall from the site.

◆ Communication and evacuation routes must be in place.

LESSON CONTENT

Introduction

Safe return to the base of the climb is a vital part of climbing. Rappelling offers the climber the option of a safe descent from the top of a climb or an escape from hazardous or unclimbable terrain. Many people consider rappelling an exciting adventure in its own right.

Main Activity

The Rappel (One Hour or Longer)

Rappelling can be introduced during ground school or directly through a short rappel.

Preparation

♦ Anchors for rappelling are constructed using natural, artificial, or permanent anchors.

♦ A rappel station should be set up with two independent anchor systems: one for the rappel rope and the other for the belay. Never use the same anchor for both the belay and rappel.

♦ Students rappel using a figure-eight descender. Use other methods if time permits.

♦ Consider rappelling on a double rope instead of a single rope, because a double-rope rappel provides the novice with more friction and thus more control and peace of mind.

♦ Arrange a progression of rappels from low-angled slopes to hanging free rappels.

Emphasize to students the following key points:

♦ Always maintain the brake hand.

♦ Tie up hair and tuck in any loose clothing.

♦ Remove any jewelry.

♦ Be sure that fingers, hair, beard, or the helmet chinstrap do not become caught in the descender.

Demonstration and Practice   As the instructor, you will need to demonstrate the rappel. Show how to control and stop the descent by placing the brake hand in the brake position and demonstrate the leg wrap. This demonstration will give your students an opportunity to see what it takes to rappel.

♦ Demonstrate with your feet flat against the rock, legs slightly apart, and body in an L position. Look down the rope and move slowly.

♦ Emphasize holding on with the brake hand. Wear a glove on the brake hand (optional).

♦ Stay in control of your speed and don't bounce.

♦ Keep your hands and fingers well away from the belay device.

♦ Explain a leg wrap (see below) and have the students practice the technique. This important self-rescue technique allows the rappeller to free both hands to deal with a descender jam or other problem.

Leg Wrap   To demonstrate a leg wrap, ask a student to rappel a quarter- to halfway down the rock. Have the rappeller stop. Still grasping the rope, have the rappeller place the brake hand in the lower part of the back. This is referred to as the brake position. From the brake position, the rappeller is ready to execute the leg wrap.

The rappeller begins the leg wrap by kicking the leg back on the brake-hand side to grab the rope with the foot and bring it forward between the legs. After the rope has been secured with the kicking motion and brought forward, the guide hand (the hand opposite the brake hand) grabs the rope and secures or wraps it around the upper thigh of the leg. The brake hand maintains contact with the rope throughout this maneuver.

The rappeller performs this action two more times until there are at least three wraps around the leg on the rappeller's brake-hand side. When the leg wrap is secure, the rappeller can let go with the brake hand.

Communication   The rappeller and belayer use the following sequence to communicate actions:

◆ "On belay" (include belayer's or climber's name). Called by belayer and rappeller.

◆ "On rappel!" Called by rappeller to the base of the rock to warn people below that a rappel is about to begin.

◆ "Off belay." Called by rappeller when safely on the ground.

◆ "Off rappel, up rope." Called by rappeller when clear of all ropes. Belayer pulls up the belay rope and readies it for the next rappeller.

Closure Activity

On Rappel! (Time as Needed)

Conclude this lesson by having students do a rappel and initiate a self-rescue incorporating a leg wrap.

◆ Set up a short rappel (less than 50 feet, or 15 meters, in length). Your role is to coach each student as he or she rappels.

◆ Get each student ready for the rappel by making sure that he or she is attached to the rappel rope correctly and is on belay. Enforce use of the communication system introduced earlier in this lesson.

◆ When the student is ready, have him or her move to the edge of the cliff. For many, getting over the edge is the most demanding part of the rappel. Coach (not coax!) the rappeller over the edge.

◆ After the rappeller is over the edge, encourage him or her to maintain good position and technique. Encourage the belayer to take his or her time.

◆ When the rappeller is approximately a quarter of the way to halfway down the rappel, have him or her stop and execute a leg wrap. Make sure that the student can demonstrate this skill. Coach as needed.

◆ After the rappeller has successfully completed the leg wrap, have him or her reverse the technique and rappel to the ground, where he or she calls, "Off belay" and then, when clear of all ropes, "Off rappel."

Follow-Up Activity

High-Impact Rappel (Time as Needed)

After students have become comfortable rappelling, provide them an opportunity to perform a high-impact rappel. A high-impact rappel is typically 150 to 200 feet (45 to 60 meters) in length, may incorporate an overhang, and gives the student a high sense of exposure.

ASSESSMENT

◆ Have students determine the condition and safety of the rappel setup by evaluating each rappel anchor as it is constructed. Continuously evaluate and correct student skills for proper technique and attention to detail.

◆ Observe each student do at least one rappel under your supervision.

◆ Require each student to demonstrate a leg wrap during her or his first rappel.

◆ Check to see that students appreciate the importance of proper rappelling by observing them during a high-impact rappel and discussing the experience.

TEACHING CONSIDERATIONS

For some, rappelling can be an anxiety-filled experience. Adjust the tone and safety considerations so that those less than excited about rappelling can enjoy it.

UNIT 2, LESSON 10

▷ Rappel Rescue

OVERVIEW

Rappelling is a basic climbing skill taught in almost all introductory climbing programs. When introduced correctly, rappelling can be an exciting addition to any climbing program. But like any climbing activity, if not supervised properly rappelling can lead to a variety of problems. This lesson introduces a number of options that both the instructor and student can initiate to conduct a rappel rescue.

JUSTIFICATION

Students benefit from understanding rappel rescue techniques to facilitate self-rescue and enhance self-reliance, a hallmark of a good climber. Knowledge, skill, and ability in this area will facilitate an enjoyable and safe rappelling experience.

GOAL

To develop students' understanding and appreciation of rappel rescue.

OBJECTIVES

At the end of this lesson, students will be able to

◆ describe rappel rescue self-rescue techniques (cognitive),

◆ describe the various components of a releasable rappel system (cognitive),

◆ demonstrate the ability to execute a rappel rescue using one or more techniques (psychomotor), and

◆ execute a releasable rappel (psychomotor).

EQUIPMENT AND AREAS NEEDED

◆ A series of accident reports from *Accidents in North American Mountaineering* (available from the American Alpine Club [www.americanalpineclub.org], Golden, Colorado, or other sources with a focus on rappelling)

- Two rappel ropes, preferably static ropes
- Two climbing ropes
- One 16-foot (5-meter) cordelette
- One 2-inch (5-centimeter) web sling
- Six locking carabiners
- One pear-shaped carabiner

RISK MANAGEMENT CONSIDERATIONS

Introduce the following techniques in ground school. Through this approach, students can learn the various skills associated with this technique in a safe environment, move freely between sites to inspect and critique one another's work, and receive your feedback. If you teach rappel rescue systems on site, rock-climbing site management considerations come into play:

- Staff and students must wear helmets and harnesses.
- The site must be clear of potential for rockfall from above.
- Students and staff must be protected against falls from the site.
- Communication and evacuation routes must be in place.

LESSON CONTENT

Introduction

Rappelling is an equipment-intensive activity that requires the climber to be certain that the harness is buckled properly and in good condition, that the anchors are properly constructed, and that the rappel device is attached correctly to the rope and harness. In addition, the climber must use good technique and be aware of the environment.

Main Activities

Activity 1: Rappel Rescue Techniques (45 Minutes or Longer)

One potential problem with rappelling is that the climber may get her or his hair or other objects (especially articles of clothing) stuck in the descending device. When this happens the student finds herself or himself in an uncomfortable and possibly painful situation that needs to be addressed immediately.

The following sequence of techniques was created to help climbing instructors assist a rappeller in distress (North Carolina Outward Bound, 1993):

- Encourage the student to execute a leg wrap (see lesson 9, page 202).
- If the student can't do a leg wrap, pull up on the belay rope. This initial step may reduce the load on the rappel rope enough so that the rappeller can remove whatever is caught in the descending device.
- If pulling up on the belay rope doesn't work, tie a foot loop in the end of a rescue rope and lower it to the rappeller. Have the rappeller place one foot in it and stand up. This action may reduce the load on the rappel rope enough so that the rappeller can remove whatever is caught in the descending device.
- As a last resort, lower rappel ropes.

Always have an extra rope (rescue) available at the rappel site so that you can use these techniques as needed.

Activity 2: Rappel Lowering System (45 to 60 Minutes)

The American Mountain Guides Association (1996) popularized the rappel lowering system. When you execute this technique properly, you can lower the entire rappel system, rappeller included, to the ground efficiently and effectively.

Demonstrate the rappel lowering system (see figure RC10.1). If sufficient time is available, have students practice constructing this system. To execute this system, follow these steps:

◆ Build a belay anchor and establish a belay (Munter hitch belay, Gri-gri, and so on).

◆ Build a rappel anchor.

◆ Build a releasable anchor with a separate rope that runs through a pear-shaped locking carabiner using a Munter hitch.

◆ Block the Munter hitch with a mule knot.

◆ Back up the mule knot by tying an overhand knot with the tail of the mule knot.

◆ Attach the main rappel ropes and the releasable rappel rope together using figure-eight knots and reversed and opposed carabiners.

◆ Back up the rappel ropes by clipping a sling into the figure-eight knot. Then clip the sling (with some slack) into the anchor master point.

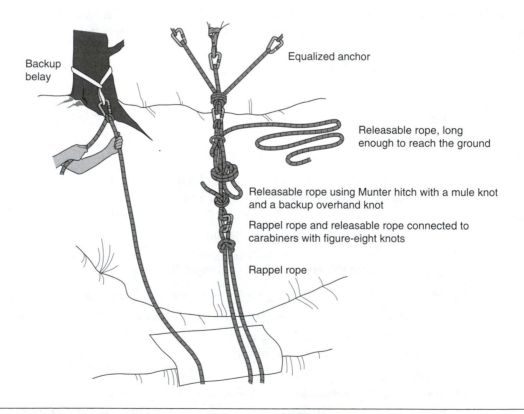

FIGURE RC10.1   Rappel rescue.

American Mountain Guides Association 1996.

Closure Activity

Rappel Accident Analysis (30 Minutes)

◆ Divide students into small groups of two to four. Give each group a rappel accident description from *Accidents in North American Mountaineering* by the American Alpine Club with the analysis portion of the report removed.

◆ Have them read the report, discuss among themselves the factors that contributed to the incident, and suggest practices that they would implement to prevent the incident from happening to them.

◆ Close this activity by having each group report their findings to the larger group.

Follow-Up Activity

None.

ASSESSMENT

◆ Randomly select students throughout this lesson and have them recite the list of rappel self-rescue techniques.

◆ Have students describe the various components of a releasable rappel system by diagramming the system in their notebooks.

◆ Haves students demonstrate the ability to execute a rappel rescue using one or more techniques during the simulation activity.

◆ Check that students can execute a releasable rappel by observing them use the system in ground school and at the rappel site.

TEACHING CONSIDERATIONS

◆ Practice the various components (knots, techniques) for each of the activities listed. As the instructor, you should be familiar with each of these and be able to troubleshoot when the need arises.

◆ Demonstration by an instructor helps students visually see what is expected of them.

◆ Before you and your students implement these techniques, introduce them in a ground school. This approach allows students to make mistakes and correct them before committing themselves to the vertical world.

◆ Get students in the habit of checking all systems before committing to them. Set the tone early on in your program that even simple mistakes or overlooked safety practices have the potential to become serious accidents.

UNIT 2, LESSON 11

▷ Top-Rope Site Management

OVERVIEW

Top-rope climbing (or top roping) is a type of climbing common in schools and outdoor programs in which the rope runs from the belayer positioned at the base of the climb through an anchor point at the top of the climb and back down to the climber. This configuration creates a relatively safe and efficient system for belaying, climbing, and communicating. Top-rope climbing allows climbers to attempt difficult rock climbs and is commonly employed on indoor climbing walls. This lesson introduces top-rope site management considerations.

JUSTIFICATION

The knowledge, skill, and ability to manage the inherent risks involved in rock climbing is vital to safe and enjoyable participation in the activity. Students benefit from this lesson by learning to implement safe top-rope management principles to enhance their climbing experiences.

GOAL

To develop students' understanding and appreciation for safe top-rope site management.

OBJECTIVES

At the end of this lesson, students will be able to

- describe the basic principles of safe top-rope site management (cognitive),
- implement measures to manage risks (cognitive),
- conduct safe top-rope site management (psychomotor), and
- appreciate safe top-rope site management (affective).

EQUIPMENT AND AREAS NEEDED

- This lesson should be taught at a climbing site with established climbs.
- Equipment necessary to set up a variety of climbs and a rappel is required. A potential list of equipment includes the following:
  - One harness for each student
  - Dynamic and static rope
  - One belay device for each pair of students
  - Assorted webbing and presewn slings
  - Eight to 10 locking and nonlocking carabiners

RISK MANAGEMENT CONSIDERATIONS

This lesson occurs with top-rope climbs established to allow a tour of the site.

- Enforce appropriate edge behavior—students and staff should be clipped in when they are closer than one body length to the edge.
- Staff and students must wear helmets and harnesses.
- The site should be clear of potential for rockfall from above.
- Communication and evacuation routes must be in place.

LESSON CONTENT

Introduction

Site management is critical to safe climbing. The development of program climbing has reinforced site safety. Ideally, effective site management protects everyone in a climbing location from mishaps.

Main Activity

Rock Climbing Safety: The Basics (30 to 45 Minutes)

Safety is an attitude rather than a particular set of actions. Accidents can arise from unsafe site conditions, unsafe actions, and errors in judgment. The Williamson–Meyer matrix (table RC11.1) lists several potential causes in each area (Gookin, 2003).

◆ Identify and address potentially unsafe conditions before students arrive on site.

◆ Establish boundaries for any potential source of risk (for example, a cliff edge) using pieces of webbing or cord tied to block access to the hazard. Far more effective is establishing a tone of safety in the class itself.

◆ Train students to look after one another in all aspects of the experience. Harness, knot, and helmet safety checks performed by students under your supervision build this environment, as does the metaphor offered to the belay pair—having shared responsibility for each other's well-being.

◆ Walk your students around the site, point out the various unsafe conditions, and discuss the ways in which they have been addressed.

◆ Elicit active student participation in this process. When viewing from areas where falls are possible, always have students clip into a fixed line. Unless clipped in, no staff or student may be closer than one body length from the cliff edge.

◆ Potential unsafe acts may be more troubling to mediate, particularly if the maturity level of the student group is low or if behavioral issues are present within the group.

◆ Establish ground rules for acceptable behavior at climbing sites, which can be extensions of existing program ground rules. Examples can include the following: No bouldering above shoulder height, wearing a helmet at all times, no throwing of objects, and establishing a "student box" where students are to remain unless otherwise directed.

◆ Leadership in site management situations can be directive and autocratic. Do your best to demystify why your concerns are present and recruit everyone in the course to assist in safety. This approach engenders a sense of teamwork and shared responsibility.

TABLE RC11.1 Principal Causes of Accidents in Outdoor Pursuits

Potentially unsafe conditions	Potentially unsafe acts	Potential errors in judgment
Falling rocks or objects	Poorly placed protection	Desire to please others
Weather	Poor instruction	Trying to adhere to a schedule
Swift or cold water	Poor supervision	Misperception
Inadequate area security	Improper procedure	Disregarding instinct
Equipment or clothing	Unsafe speed	Fatigue
Animals or plants	Not satiated or hydrated	Distraction
Physical or psychological profile	Poor position	Miscommunication
	Unauthorized or improper procedure	

Adapted, by permission, from J. Gookin, 2006, *Wilderness educator notebook* (Lander, WY: National Outdoor Leadership School).

◆ Check all climbing equipment at the beginning of each climbing day.

◆ Use only approved climbing areas.

◆ Technically competent staff must supervise all climbing. An appropriate instructor-to-student ratio is 1:6.

◆ Establish and follow lightning protocol.

◆ Use sites suitable for the skill level of the students.

◆ Establish an emergency action plan that includes first aid and evacuation equipment required by the site.

Closure Activity

Accident Reviews (Time as Needed)

To help review and reinforce some of the important points of this lesson, make available to your students copies of *Accidents in North American Mountaineering*. Have students read through a few of the accidents outlined in the document and have them identify

◆ unsafe site conditions,

◆ unsafe actions, and

◆ errors in judgment that may have contributed to the accident.

Follow-Up Activity

Climbing Site Risk Management Assessment (Time as Needed)

◆ Identify and correct any and all safety concerns. Remember to engender shared responsibility.

◆ For example, have students do a site assessment when you arrive at your climbing site or enter a new climbing area. Alternatively, have them observe another climbing group and discuss among themselves any risk management issues that they discover. Have students call out one another if they see any unsafe practices.

ASSESSMENT

◆ Have students describe the basic principles of safe top-rope site management by sharing their findings from their review of *Accidents in North American Mountaineering*.

◆ Observe students implement measures to manage risks while setting up a site for a day of climbing.

◆ Have students conduct safe top-rope site management by soliciting feedback through peer and instructor observation. Provide feedback on any unsafe practices.

◆ Check that students appreciate safe top-rope site management by observing them as they develop skill and knowledge throughout this unit.

TEACHING CONSIDERATIONS

◆ This lesson offers many teachable moments. Be prepared to identify and discuss site safety considerations with each new activity in each lesson.

- Take advantage of opportunities to reinforce the importance of safety. Use stories of events or near misses that you are aware of to reinforce the importance of risk management.

- Ask students to imagine what might happen in a given situation. Introduce the concept of a "premortem"—a postmortem done in advance. Use a focusing question—What can go wrong in this situation, and have I double-checked it?—so that students can begin to assess the risks in a situation before they get into it.

- Risk management is a dynamic process and should be reinforced throughout the course.

▷ Belay Escape

OVERVIEW

A belay escape is the initial step that a climber turns to if something goes wrong while belaying her or his partner. The belay escape allows the climber to remove her- or himself from the belay to assist the partner or initiate a rescue. In addition, the various components of the belay escape are excellent tools in their own right that the climber should have in the toolbox for emergencies or other situations.

JUSTIFICATION

The belay escape is an essential tool for partner and self-rescue that all climbers serious about pursuing this activity should know. Successful execution of a belay escape can enhance the mechanical reasoning ability and self-confidence of your students and provide them with a diverse set of applicable skills.

GOAL

To develop students' understanding and appreciation for the safe construction and execution of a belay escape.

OBJECTIVES

At the end of this lesson, students will be able to
- determine the safety of a belay escape (cognitive),
- describe the various steps to an efficient belay escape (cognitive),
- demonstrate a belay escape (psychomotor), and
- appreciate the importance of a properly executed belay escape (affective).

EQUIPMENT AND AREAS NEEDED

- One notebook and a pen or pencil for each student
- The following equipment for each student pair:
  - One 16-foot (5-meter) cordelette
  - Three to six sections of 1-inch (25-millimeter) tubular webbing tied in 2- and 4-foot (60- and 120-centimeter) lengths or presewn runners

- One 70- to 80-foot (20- to 25-meter) climbing rope
- Four nonlocking carabiners
- Four locking carabiners
- One pear-shaped carabiner (HMS carabiner)
- One belay device

RISK MANAGEMENT CONSIDERATIONS

Introduce the following techniques through ground school. Through this approach, students can learn the various skills associated with this technique in a safe, controlled environment, move freely between sites to inspect and critique one another's work, and receive your feedback. When taught on site, rock-climbing site management considerations are present:

- ◆ Staff and students must wear helmets and harnesses.
- ◆ The site must be clear of potential for rockfall from above.
- ◆ Students and staff must be protected against falls from the site.
- ◆ Communication and evacuation routes must be in place.

LESSON CONTENT

Introduction

The belay escape involves a series of steps that must be executed efficiently and properly (figure RC12.1). Students must use previously introduced skills, techniques, and knots in the belay escape, so this activity refines those skills and applies them in a new situation.

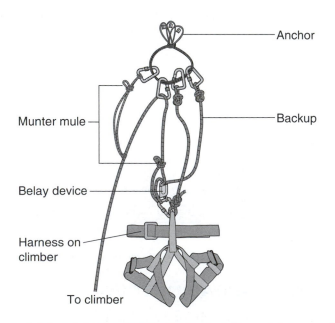

FIGURE RC12.1   All of the components of a successful belay escape are shown. The belayer has been removed from the diagram for clarity.

Adapted, by permission, from NCOBS, 1984, *Instructor field manual* (North Carolina Outward Bound School).

Main Activity

Practicing the Belay Escape (One Hour or Longer)

To demonstrate the belay escape in ground school use the following sequence:

- Construct a belay anchor and clip yourself in.
- Toss the rope to one of your students who has volunteered to be your climber. Have the student tie into the rope.
- Begin the belay contract.
- Have the student climb toward you several feet (a meter or two).
- Have the student simulate a fall by loading the rope.

  After the student's weight is on the rope, begin the belay escape sequence:

- Lock and block the belay device with a mule hitch. Placing the knot allows the belayer to work with both hands.
- Using a cordelette, attach a three-wrap Prusik (or other friction hitch) to the rope.
- Attach the Prusik to the belay anchor with a Munter mule or other releasable hitch.
- Tie a figure-eight on a bight on the rope that is on the belayer's side of the belay device and clip this knot to the anchor as a backup.
- Unblock the belay device and transfer the load onto the Prusik–cordelette combination.
- Escape the belay.

Closure Activity

Belay Escape Competition (Two to Three Hours)

After students have had the opportunity to practice the belay escape, have them participate in a belay escape contest. The objective of this contest is to escape the belay while allowing the weight to drop as short a distance as possible.

Contest sequence:

- Anchor the belayer and attach a weight, perhaps a burlap bag filled with sand weighing 125 to 150 pounds (60 to 70 kilograms) or something similar, on a top rope. The weight starts at a specified distance from the floor (for example, 4 feet, or 1 meter).
- Time the climber's effort to escape the belay. Timing begins as soon as the climber is on belay, the weight is in position, and you give the signal to start. Timing ends when the rope is secured in baseline to the ground anchor and the climber is free from the anchor and rope system.
- Measure the distance that the weight drops during the belay escape at the end of the event. This figure is used in calculating the overall time awarded to the climber.
- The student who most quickly completes the escape (including any added penalties) is declared the winner.

Contest rules:

◆ The climber must belay using an approved belay device (tube style or Sticht plate).

◆ Climbers will be required to escape the belay using equipment that you provide them.

◆ Assess the following time penalties for the distance that the weight drops: 0–1 foot (0–30 centimeters): 0:00 (no penalty), 1–2 feet (30–60 centimeters): 0:30, 2–3 feet (60–90 centimeters): 1:00, 3–4 feet (90–120 centimeters): 1:30, hits the floor: 5:00.

◆ A maximum time of 15:00 is allowed to complete the belay escape.

◆ Practices that you judge unsafe will incur time penalties in increments of 15 seconds.

Follow-Up Activity

Real-World Belay Escape (Two to Three Hours)

◆ Have students execute a belay escape at a natural climbing site.

◆ During the activity have students identify potential situations in a top-rope climbing environment that might warrant a belay escape.

ASSESSMENT

◆ Have students determine the safety of a belay escape by observing the belay in use. You can observe as well and provide feedback as needed.

◆ Have students describe the various steps to an efficient belay escape by requiring each student to verbalize each step before executing it during ground school training.

◆ Observe students perform belay escapes during ground school and while participating in the belay escape contest.

◆ Check that students appreciate the importance of a properly executed belay escape by observing their performance during the contest and soliciting their feedback on their performance.

TEACHING CONSIDERATIONS

◆ Make sure that students have mastered the prerequisite knowledge and skills before beginning this lesson.

◆ Introduce the belay escape in a step-by-step manner.

◆ Have students write these steps in their notebooks.

UNIT 2, LESSON 13

▷ Hauling and Lowering Systems

OVERVIEW

This lesson introduces basic hauling and lowering systems. A brief overview of these systems is followed by having students construct and evaluate each.

JUSTIFICATION

Students benefit from understanding simple hauling and lowering systems to facilitate more advanced climbing opportunities and to apply to partner rescue and self-rescue situations. These systems aid in rescue situations and are useful for managing the large amount of equipment needed at times in rock climbing. Knowledge, skill, and ability in these advanced areas will facilitate an enjoyable and safe rock-climbing experience.

GOAL

To develop students' understanding and appreciation of the safe construction of hauling and lowering systems.

OBJECTIVES

At the end of this lesson, students will be able to

◆ determine the condition and safety of a hauling or lowering system (cognitive),

◆ construct a hauling system (psychomotor),

◆ construct a lowering system (psychomotor), and

◆ appreciate the importance of a properly constructed hauling or lowering system (affective).

EQUIPMENT AND AREAS NEEDED

◆ A demonstration of hauling and lowering systems from the ground requires the preparation of anchor stations in advance.

◆ One notebook and pencil or pen for each student

◆ The following equipment is needed for each pair of students:

- Various lengths (4 to 20 feet, or 1 to 6 meters) of 7-millimeter accessory cord
- Three to six sections of 1-inch (25-millimeter) tubular webbing tied in 2- and 4-foot (60- and 120-centimeter) lengths or presewn runners
- One climbing rope
- Six nonlocking carabiners
- Six locking carabiners
- One pair of Prusik loops (ascenders)
- Two pulleys
- One belay device

RISK MANAGEMENT CONSIDERATIONS

Introduce the following techniques through ground school. With this approach, students can learn the various skills associated with this technique in a safe, controlled environment, move freely between sites to inspect and critique one another's work, and receive your feedback.

Because hauling and lowering systems are taught on site, rock-climbing site management considerations are present:

◆ Staff and students must wear helmets and harnesses.

◆ The site must be clear of potential for rockfall from above.

◆ Students and staff must be protected against falls from the site.

◆ Communication and evacuation routes must be in place.

◆ After students have mastered the appropriate skills, have them build and then use their newfound skills at the climbing site.

LESSON CONTENT

Introduction

Hauling and lowering systems are used in climbing environments to aid in partner rescue and self-rescue situations or to assist a climber over difficult terrain. Each system can be built directly from an ERNEST anchor (see lesson 7, page 194) or from single points of protection, depending on the weight and availability of protection points.

◆ Build hauling and lowering systems on anchors other than the ones supporting climbers.

◆ Should it be necessary to clip both a hauling or lowering system and a climber into the same anchor, back up the system so that if the anchor fails the force does not directly hit the climber's anchor.

◆ When practicing these techniques at a natural climbing site, all climbers should be on belay with separate anchors.

Main Activities

Activity 1: Hauling (One Hour or Longer)

Begin this lesson in ground school. From a position where students can observe, construct and clip into an anchor to demonstrate a haul (figure RC13.1). A simple haul, sometimes called a Z-drag because of the configuration that the rope takes, provides a 3:1 mechanical advantage. In other words, for every 3 feet (meters) pulled by the belayer or rescuer, the climber moves 1 foot (meter).

◆ Students should practice building the hauling system on several anchors with different construction possibilities.

◆ Hauling is difficult to perform when working alone. The climber should assist whenever possible.

◆ Encourage neat rope management and efficient hauling actions. Encourage students to experiment with haul systems using different gear sets (pulleys, carabiners, Munter hitch, or belay devices).

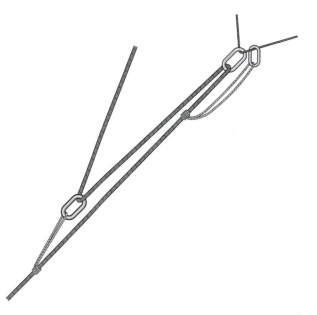

FIGURE RC13.1   Haul setup.

Adapted, by permission, from NCOBS, 1984, *Instructor field manual* (North Carolina Outward Bound School).

Activity 2: Lowering (One Hour or Longer)

Lowering systems can be constructed by using belay devices set up on a lower anchor point (or the climber's harness if the weight and time to be spent lowering is not too great) and feeding the rope through the device so that the climber can easily apply the brake.

◆ The Gri-gri and Munter hitch are ideally suited for this purpose.

◆ Should lowering need to be halted midway, a Munter mule or other releasable hitch can be used to tie off the belay system and free the climber for other tasks.

Closure Activity

Pick-a-System Review (One to Two Hours)

◆ Write "Haul" on a number of slips of paper and write "Lower" on an equal number of slips of paper. Place them in a bag.

◆ Have students in pairs reach into the bag and pull out a piece of paper.

◆ The pair of students then demonstrate the chosen skill.

◆ Evaluate each pair.

◆ Always correct systems that are not neat, clean, and efficient.

Follow-Up Activity

Practice What You Preach (Time as Needed)

These systems will be used periodically throughout the unit. After students have mastered these techniques in ground school, move on to the rock. To ensure that students have gained the basic knowledge, skills, and ability in this area, ask them to do the following:

◆ Assemble a haul system.

◆ Raise a fellow student.

◆ Lower that student.

◆ Rappel to the ground.

ASSESSMENT

◆ Ask students to describe the types of basic hauling and lowering systems by illustrating these systems in their notebooks.

◆ Have students determine the condition and safety of hauling and lowering systems by inspecting each system before using it. Students should do their inspections under your watchful eye.

◆ Check that students can construct hauling and lowering systems appropriately and neatly by observing them go through each of the steps illustrated earlier.

◆ Check that students appreciate the importance of a properly constructed hauling or lowering system by observing their reaction to each constructed system.

TEACHING CONSIDERATIONS

◆ This lesson consists of a demonstration of hauling and lowering systems construction followed by student practice and application.

◆ You can move among student pairs to provide feedback on progress.

◆ After the system is suitable (and in a protected position), have a student clip into the hauling system (as the weight) and have another student haul the first student, switch the system over, and then lower the student the short distance to the ground.

▷ **Leave No Trace Considerations**

OVERVIEW

Over time, rock climbing has gained a reputation for having a significant negative impact on the environments in which it occurs. Leave No Trace principles can help climbers minimize the impacts inherent to this activity and provide a baseline ethic for appropriate behavior for any user of outdoor settings for recreational purposes. This lesson introduces students to Leave No Trace (LNT) for rock climbing.

JUSTIFICATION

Students benefit from understanding Leave No Trace principles for rock climbing. Future access to climbing areas depends on the behavior of each climber who visits. Appropriate knowledge, skill, and the ability to implement Leave No Trace principles will help each student have a share in that future.

GOAL

To develop students' understanding, appreciation, and practice of Leave No Trace principles for rock climbing.

OBJECTIVES

At the end of this lesson, students will be able to

◆ describe Leave No Trace principles for rock climbing (cognitive),

◆ implement appropriate Leave No Trace principles for rock climbing (psychomotor), and

◆ appreciate the effect of Leave No Trace on the climbing community and the environment (affective).

EQUIPMENT AND AREAS NEEDED

Each student needs the following items:

◆ Helmet

◆ Small trash bag

◆ Notebook and pen

RISK MANAGEMENT CONSIDERATIONS

◆ Staff and students must wear helmets.

◆ The site must be clear of potential for rockfall from above.

◆ Students and staff must be protected against falls from the site.

◆ Communication and evacuation routes must be in place.

LESSON CONTENT

Introduction (One Hour)

Climbing, like any other outdoor recreation activity, has the potential to affect ecological, social, and cultural resources. Realizing this, the climbing community has become proactive and has introduced a variety of practices to limit the impacts associated with climbing activity. To help in this process, the Leave No Trace Center for Outdoor Ethics (www.lnt.org) developed a series of principles to aid climbers in protecting climbing areas from resource damage and possible closures. These principles make up most of this lesson.

- Leave No Trace rock climbing can be taught as a stand-alone lesson or taught and reinforced throughout the unit.
- Teachable moments may also provide an outlet for this information.
- Establish ground rules and maintain them until students are self-policing and reinforcing LNT practices.
- Teach LNT as a part of climbing. It is as much a part of climbing as the rope, harness, and helmet.

Main Activity

LNT Practices for Rock Climbing (45 Minutes to One Hour)

Grassroots climbing organizations and special interest groups have formed nationwide to help land managers maintain local crags and trails (see www.accessfund.org for more information). Include the following Leave No Trace guidelines in course ground rules and reinforce them along the way. Additional resources are available at www.lnt.org.

Plan Ahead and Prepare
- Research climbing routes, their difficulty, and the kinds of protection needed.
- Check with land managers for advice and regulations specific to the area, especially wildlife enclosures. Local climbers, climbing shops, and guide services or climbing schools can also provide essential information.
- Take into consideration the level of impact that an area can withstand. Are any environmental considerations present in the area? Are certain areas so sensitive that you should avoid them?
- As leader, are you aware of current access issues?
- Is your group a manageable size?
- Can you reduce overcrowding by communicating with other climbing groups?
- Can you time your visits to avoid popular climbing areas during weekends and holidays?
- Do any preliminary skills teaching before leaving for the climbing site. This approach will reduce the amount of time that you spend at the climbing area.

Travel and Camp on Durable Surfaces   Wherever you climb, try to unload your gear and take breaks on large, flat rocks or other durable ground to avoid damaging vegetation.

Dispose of Waste Properly

◆ Popular crags often have outhouses nearby. When you are beyond access to outhouses, urinate on bare ground away from vegetation, climbing routes, and trails.

◆ Dispose of solid human waste in a cathole at least 200 feet (60 meters) away from trails, the bases of climbs, water sources, or campsites. Alternatively, use a Wag Bag, a biodegradable double-bag toilet system made from puncture-resistant material.

Leave What You Find

◆ Do not chip holds, drill pockets, or glue holds onto the rock.

◆ Cleaning loose or friable rock from faces is sometimes necessary for safety on new routes, but avoid changing the rock to make the route easier or more comfortable.

◆ Leave unique artifacts and features in place.

◆ Minimize trampling vegetation at the base of climbs and do not remove vegetation from the rock.

◆ Vertical walls represent unique biological communities. Some plant and lichen species living in cracks and on cliff faces may be rare, so if possible, don't disturb them. Instead, climb around or avoid them.

◆ Use removable protection and natural anchors wherever practical.

◆ Bolts and pitons permanently change the rock. Placing them is a serious endeavor. Think before you drill or hammer.

◆ The Wilderness Act prohibits use of motorized drills in designated wilderness areas and wilderness study areas.

◆ If you are contemplating developing new climbing routes, consider whether the local ecology can withstand the increased traffic that a set of new routes will create.

◆ Use anchors where provided, rather than trees.

◆ To lessen the visibility of sport climbs, use discreet anchors at the top of climbs.

◆ If you use chalk, choose a color that blends in well with the rock.

◆ Do not attempt new routes near archeological or historical sites.

Minimize Campfire Impacts

Fire rings and pits at the base of any crag are unacceptable. Fires built in alpine areas will leave scars for decades.

Respect Wildlife

◆ Avoid raptor nesting sites on or near the crags in the spring and early summer. To identify places to avoid, watch the birds as they circle and land near their nests. If you encounter nests on a climb, don't touch them. Human contact may cause the adults to abandon the nest and its eggs or young.

◆ Adhere to seasonal closures; you can always find another place to climb. For more information on seasonal wildlife restrictions check the Access Fund Web site (accessfund.org).

Be Considerate of Other Visitors

◆ Colorful slings are easily seen from the ground and may bother hikers and other recreationists. To prevent visual impacts, use natural-colored slings and apply paint to bolt hangers to disguise them better.

◆ Maintain a low profile by removing your climbing equipment at the end of each day.

◆ Protect access through courtesy. Excessive noise can have a negative effect on the recreation experience of others and on wildlife.

◆ Establish geographical boundaries for your activities to help keep control of your group.

◆ Park in designated areas or off the road away from gates and driveways. Always respect the privacy of local landowners. Carpool when practical.

Leave No Trace principles—Copyright: Leave No Trace Center for Outdoor Ethics. www.LNT.org.

Closure Activity

Climbing Site Evaluation (Two to Three Hours)

◆ Have students conduct a site assessment of your local climbing areas to determine climbing-related impacts. Have them record this information in their journals for comparison later.

◆ Have your class interview a local land manager to get a management perspective on the potential impacts of rock-climbing activity.

Follow-Up Activity

Giving Something Back to the Environment (Time as Needed)

Get your class involved in a service project at a local crag. For example, participate in or organize an Adopt-a-Crag event in your local area (for more information on Adopt-a-Crag, contact the Access Fund, Boulder, Colorado, accessfund.org).

ASSESSMENT

◆ Have students describe the Leave No Trace principles for rock climbing by listing them in their journals.

◆ Check that students implement appropriate Leave No Trace principles for rock climbing by observing them use these principles while climbing.

◆ Have students gain appreciation for the effect of Leave No Trace on the climbing community and the environment by participating in a service project at a local climbing area (affective).

TEACHING CONSIDERATIONS

◆ This lesson can be supported through many teachable moments when you can point out and correct non-LNT behaviors and evidence of past non-LNT behavior.

◆ Lead by example here—clean the climbing site when you arrive and again when departing.

◆ Use LNT as an educational tool, not as an opportunity to shame others into these behaviors. Embarrassing your students will only backfire.

UNIT 2, LESSON 15

▷ Inclusion and Accessibility

OVERVIEW

Rock-climbing activities can provide people with disabilities the opportunity to experience challenge and personal growth in a natural setting, within a given community. Like many other adventure activities, rock climbing can be specifically tailored to accommodate a person's physical and mental abilities. This lesson introduces inclusion and accessibility in rock climbing.

JUSTIFICATION

Students benefit from gaining appreciation for the range of people who can enjoy rock climbing as a form of recreation and personal development.

GOAL

To develop students' understanding and appreciation for the range of human capability in rock climbing.

OBJECTIVES

At the end of this lesson, students will be able to

◆ describe the senses required to participate in rock climbing (cognitive) and
◆ appreciate the benefits of providing access to people with different physical abilities and limitations (affective).

EQUIPMENT AND AREAS NEEDED

◆ Complete top-rope setups adequate for all climbers
◆ Blindfolds (bandannas work well for this) and earplugs for each climber

RISK MANAGEMENT CONSIDERATIONS

◆ Risk management procedures should be in place as required for top-rope climbing.
◆ Because climbers will be barred from normal use of their eyes and ears, select routes of moderate difficulty that are free of ledges and other protrusions that a sighted climber would be able to avoid in the event of a fall.
◆ For the hearing impairment activity, teach climbing commands that use short, sharp pulls on the rope for communication between climber and belayer.

LESSON CONTENT

Introduction

Some assume that rock climbing as an activity is precluded by physical limitations, such as being sight or hearing impaired. With the proper precautions, however, rock climbing can be made accessible to people with disabilities.

This lesson explores the limitations and advantages experienced by people with different abilities to sense and perceive the world while rock climbing. The following activities provide sighted and hearing students with direct access to the rock-climbing experience of people without those senses. All students can benefit from the focus required to use different senses when exploring the rock-climbing environment.

Main Activities

Activity 1: Blindfolded Climbing (Two Hours or Longer)

This excellent activity challenges students who feel as though they need a more challenging rock-climbing experience. Rock climbing is inherently a tactile experience. The climber must explore the rock and its features with the hands to secure the best holds, which are often not visible from the climber's stance. Blindfolding the climber forces her or him to use the sense of touch rather than sight to accomplish the climb.

◆ Provide each climber with a blindfold; make sure that the blindfold is tied securely and that the ends are safe from becoming entangled in any climbing equipment. The climber can proceed to ascend without use of the eyes.

◆ Advice or direction from below is optional, depending on the goals of the particular course or the needs of the climber.

◆ The student will be able to take advantage of almost any move available to a sighted climber, although direction from below regarding overhangs or simple dynamic moves is beneficial.

◆ The belayer can measure the tension on the rope as an indication of the amount of slack in the rope. An active but gentle belay can maintain the proper amount of tension in the belay system.

Activity 2: Nonverbal Climbing (Two Hours or Longer)

Rock climbing involves effective communication and teamwork. In this activity, the climber and belayer create a nonverbal communication system. They do this by creating a rope signal system that incorporates a series of tugs on the rope, such as the following example:

◆ On belay = three sharp, short pulls on the rope

◆ Off belay = three long pulls on the rope

◆ That's me = one sharp, short pull

Any student who has difficulty on a top-rope rock climb can be assisted by incorporating a belayer-assisted hauling system (BAHS) (figure RC15.1). Setup of this system begins by attaching the top rope directly to the top-rope anchor. From this point the rope drops directly to the climber. Clip the rope to two locking carabiners attached to the student's belay–rappel loop. The rope leaves the belay–rappel loop and runs back up to the top-rope anchor. Here another bight is attached to an additional carabiner clipped into the top-rope anchor. The bight leaves the top-rope anchor and is attached to the belayer with the belay device. By pulling forcefully on the rope, the belayer can help the climber progress upward. (The BAHS is a modification of the 3:1 haul system described in lesson 13.)

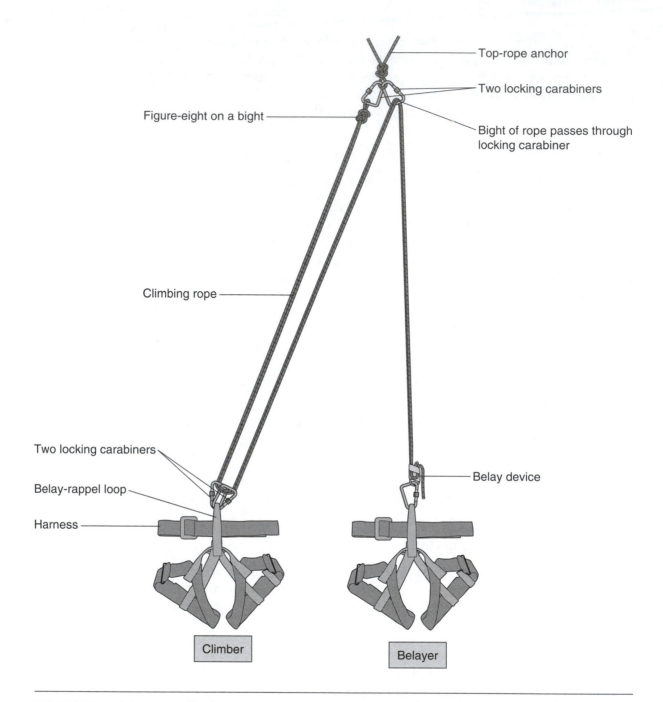

FIGURE RC15.1 Belayer-assisted hauling system (BAHS).

The climber and belayer may use hand signals as well. For example, the climber, noticing a larger than desired amount of slack in the rope, may signal this with an upward pull on the rope. The climber may appreciate the lack of distracting noise.

Although the necessary communication between climber and belayer can take many specific forms, the vital requirement is that both members of the team understand the code that they are using. Work with your students so that they develop a set of signals thorough enough to cover all parts of the belay contract. They should practice this code on the ground to ensure that it is embedded.

Closure Activity

How Do You Feel? (20 to 30 Minutes)

◆ Frontload this experience by asking students to discuss their feelings, thoughts, and attitudes regarding their climbing experience. What did they learn about themselves?

◆ Students should reflect on the different experiences they had during these activities. What aspect was more difficult? What was gained by the restriction of one sense?

Follow-Up Activity

Sensory Awareness (Time as Needed)

Develop students' use of their senses and communication ability by incorporating this aspect into any class or to provide more demanding climbing experiences, especially for students looking for more challenge.

ASSESSMENT

◆ Have students describe the senses required to participate in rock climbing by reflecting on the difference that the restriction of one sense had on their overall climbing experience during each of the climbing activities presented.

◆ Check that students appreciate the benefits of providing access to people with different physical abilities and limitations by facilitating a discussion about the topic and the development of advanced tactile and communication techniques.

TEACHING CONSIDERATIONS

From a social perspective, tact is required when introducing these activities, whether or not students with hearing or sight impairments are present in the course. This lesson is not about what it's like to "be blind or deaf"; rather, it is best framed as an opportunity to focus on different abilities and skill sets and to have the experience of others while rock climbing.

Rock Climbing Skills Checklist

Listed below are the climbing skills covered in this unit. It is your responsibility to practice and master these skills. This checklist will be used to assess your progress. Skills should be reviewed and okayed by a partner and checked off in the peer review column. Once you feel that you've mastered any skill, you may demonstrate it for the instructor for a final checkmark. The entire sheet must be completed before the end of the semester to receive full credit for your skill grade. *All skills must be initialed and dated by the instructor to be valid.*

Skill	Peer review	Needs improvement	Acceptable
KNOTS			
Overhand			
Figure-eight follow-through			
Figure-eight on a bight			
Munter hitch			
Munter mule			
Water knot			
Double fisherman's			
Prusik knot			
COILING A ROPE			
Mountaineer's coil			
Butterfly coil			
ANCHORS			
Natural anchors (horn, boulder, tree)			
Artificial anchors (stoppers, hexcentrics, SLCD)			
Equalized			
Preequalized			
CLIMBING TECHNIQUES			
Stemming			
Lieback			
Face climbing			
Chimneying			
Mantling			
BELAYS			
Belay with device			
Munter hitch belay			
Belay escape			
RAPPELLING			
With a figure-eight			
With a belay device			
Rappel lowering system			
OTHER SKILLS			
Z-drag			

Use the rock climbing skills checklist as an additional tool to assess skills learned throughout this unit.

From M. Wagstaff and A. Attarian, 2009, *Technical skills for adventure programming: A curriculum guide* (Champaign, IL: Human Kinetics).

anchor—An arrangement of one or (usually) more pieces of gear set up to support the weight of a belay or top rope.

ATC—A type of belay device manufactured by Black Diamond Equipment.

belay devices—Mechanical devices used to create friction when belaying by putting bends in the rope.

belays—Protects a climber from falling using a rope, friction, and an anchor. Means "to hold fast."

bight—A bend in the rope where the ends of the rope exiting the bend do not cross.

bolts—Protection permanently installed in a hole drilled into the rock, to which a metal hanger is attached, having a hole for a carabiner or ring.

bouldering—Climbing on large boulders, close to the ground. Protection takes the form of crash pads and spotting instead of belay ropes.

cam—A type of artificial protection consisting of three or four cams mounted on a common axle or two adjacent axles, so that pulling on the axle forces the cams to spread farther apart. The cam is used by pulling on the trigger (a small handle) so that the cams move together, inserting the device into a crack in the rock, and then releasing the trigger to allow the cams to expand. At this point the climbing rope can be attached to a sling and carabiner at the end of the stem. A spring-loaded device used as protection.

chimney—A rock cleft with vertical sides mostly parallel and large enough that the climber can fit his or her body into it.

chocks, or chockstones—A generic term for an artificial chockstone, any of many designs of passive protection that rely on wedging in a constriction for security: hexes, stoppers, tricams, and so on.

descender—A device for controlled descent on a rope.

dressed knot—All parts of the knot are aligned, straightened, or bundled. A textbook perfect knot.

dynamic ropes—Climbing ropes designed to stretch and absorb the force of a falling climber.

free climbing—Climbing using the hands and feet for upward progress. Climbing equipment is used only to provide protection in the case of a fall.

Gri-gri—An autolocking belay device manufactured by Petzl.

loop—A turn of the rope that crosses itself.

runner—Another term for sling.

SLCD—Spring-loaded camming device (*see* cam).

sling—Webbing sewn or tied into a loop using a water knot.

standing end—The end of the rope that is not in use.

stoppers—Wedge-shaped nuts.

webbing—Tubular and flat nylon strip, mainly used to make runners and slings.

working end—The end of the rope that is being used to tie the knot.

Yosemite Decimal System (YDS)—A numerical system for rating the difficulty of individual class 5 moves on a scale from 5.0 to 5.15; routes above 5.10 are further broken down into subratings, a through d (for example, 5.12a). The scale runs from 5.0 to 5.15.

REFERENCES AND RESOURCES

REFERENCES

American Mountain Guides Association. (1996, June). Rappel rescue. *AMGA Mountain Bulletin*, Boulder, CO: Author.

Clemens, S. (1989). The ascent of the Riffleberg. In D. Ruther & J. Thorn (Eds.), *The armchair mountaineer*. Birmingham, AL: Menasha Ridge Press.

Daumal, R. (1986). *Mount Analogue: A novel of symbolically authentic non-Euclidean adventures in mountain climbing*. Boston: Shambhala.

Gookin, J. (2003). *National Outdoor Leadership School instructors handbook*. Lander, WY: National Outdoor Leadership School.

Long, J. (2004). *How to rock climb* (4th ed.). Helena, MT: Chockstone Press.

North Carolina Outward Bound. (1993). *The instructor's handbook—North Carolina Outward Bound School*. Asheville, NC: Author.

Powers, P., & Cheek, M. (2000). *NOLS climbing instructor notebook*. Lander, WY: National Outdoor Leadership School.

Robbins, R. (1982). *Basic rockcraft*. Glendale, CA: La Siesta Press.

Scott, D. (1974). *Big wall climbing: Development, techniques, and aids*. New York: Oxford University Press.

Smith, B., & Padgett, A. (1996). *On rope*. Huntsville, AL: National Speleological Society.

Whymper, E. (1989). The rope broke. In D. Ruther & J. Thorn (Eds.), *The armchair mountaineer*. Birmingham, AL: Menasha Ridge Press.

RESOURCES

Access Fund. (1995). Retrieved from Access Fund Web site: www.accessfund.org. Overview: The Access Fund is a national, nonprofit organization dedicated to keeping climbing areas open and to conserving the climbing environment. Check the Web site for resources on programs, stewardship, and conservation.

American Alpine Club. (1949–2006). *Accidents in North American mountaineering*. Golden, CO: North American Alpine Club. Overview: The Safety Committee of the American Alpine Club compiles rock climbing and mountaineering accidents each year and presents them in *Accidents in North American Mountaineering*. The accidents reported are effective training tools as well as concrete evidence of the dangers inherent in mountaineering.

Costantino, M. (2007). *The knot handbook*. New York: Sterling. Overview: A complete handbook on tying knots. Everything is shown in close-up, color, how-to photographs, along with information on types of rope, rope making, maintenance, and terminology.

Cox, S.M. (2003). *Mountaineering: The freedom of the hills*. Seattle, WA: The Mountaineers Books. Overview: Known as the climber's bible, this text should be in every climber's library.

Fasulo, D. (1996). *Self-rescue*. Guilford, CT: Globe Poquot Press. Overview: Covers all aspects of rescuing a fallen climber, from freeing oneself from a harness to ascending or descending the rope to hauling the victim to safety. Excellent resource for climber rescue and self-rescue.

Lewis, S.P., & Cauthorn, D. (2000). *Climbing: From gym to crag*. Seattle, WA: The Mountaineers Books. Overview: Assists indoor climbers in safely making the transition from a controlled climbing environment, which requires few technical skills and presents no objective dangers, to the outdoor environment, where the risks and rewards require a set of basic skills and awareness.

Long, S. (2007). *The climbing handbook: The complete guide to safe and exciting rock climbing*. Richmond Hill, ON: Firefly Books. Overview: Written for beginners to introduce advanced techniques and tactics. Includes photographs and easy-to-understand diagrams. Combines step-by-step exercises with practice programs that will allow climbers to pursue the sport safely.

Luebben, C. (2004). *Rock climbing: Mastering basic skills*. Seattle, WA: The Mountaineers Books. Overview: Comprehensive instruction in top rope, sport, traditional climbing, and bouldering. An excellent resource.

Raleigh, D., & Clelland, M. (1998). *Knots and ropes for climbers*. Mechanicsburg, PA: Stackpole Books. Overview: A useful book for learning knots and their uses. Great illustrations and highly recommended.

Caving

David Goodman

UNIT 3, LESSON 1

▷ **Introduction to Caving**

OVERVIEW

This unit begins with a discussion of the history of caving and its evolution as a recreational activity. Basic terminology is covered to help students gain an understanding of the activity. In this unit the emphasis is on caving in **wild caves** rather than in **commercial caves**. Discussion in this first lesson revolves around distinguishing between the two experiences. Finally, this lesson introduces professional organizations and organized caving groups (grottos) to provide an overview of resources and opportunities for involvement in the sport.

JUSTIFICATION

Understanding and appreciating the history of caving and its evolution as a recreational pursuit helps students gain respect and passion for the activity. The information in this lesson also provides information about becoming a **caver** through safe, responsible means. Learning about caving organizations can be useful because those groups provide opportunities to engage in the activity in a safe, ethical manner.

GOAL

To develop students' understanding, appreciation, respect, and passion for caves and caving.

OBJECTIVES

At the end of this lesson, students will be able to

◆ understand the history of caving (cognitive),

◆ explain the evolution of caving as a recreational activity (cognitive),

◆ identify professional organizations and clubs associated with this adventure activity (cognitive), and

◆ demonstrate an appreciation for caving as an adventure activity (affective).

EQUIPMENT AND AREAS NEEDED

◆ Presentation (slides or Internet photos) that depicts people caving

◆ Overhead projector and screen

◆ Computers with Internet access

◆ History trivia and terminology cards

RISK MANAGEMENT CONSIDERATIONS

Some students may immediately express fear of being underground in tight, confined spaces. This first lesson is an appropriate time to dispel those fears by clearly explaining the activity of caving and noting that people of all abilities face challenges at many levels.

All of unit 3 is based on National Speleological Society's, 2003, *A guide to responsible caving.*

LESSON CONTENT

Introduction (10 Minutes)

"Caving—the last great frontier on earth." Begin this lesson by polling the group for caving experience. Have students share their experience. Then show slides or photos to help students visualize the activity. Searching the Internet for **show cave** or commercial cave Web sites will supply adequate examples. Also check the **National Speleological Society** (NSS) Web site (www.caves.org) for photographs.

This introductory lesson is an appropriate time to talk about fears. You can dispel fears by discussing challenge by choice (see page 24). First-time cavers, also known as **spelunkers** in some circles, typically fear the thought of becoming stuck in tight passes or becoming hopelessly lost in a vast, dark maze. Some may have misperceptions regarding cave life such as bats. Explain that caves offer a variety of challenges for people of all levels of experience and ability.

Main Activity

History and Terminology Overview (45 Minutes)

◆ Print the caving cards (figure CV1.1) from the CD-ROM and hand them out to the class. Some students may end up with more than one card.

◆ Have students take turns reading the cards. Discuss each item as necessary. Start with history cards first and then move to the terminology cards.

◆ Follow the discussion with visual examples of people caving.

Closure Activity

Exploring the NSS Web Site (30 Minutes)

◆ Have students use a computer to explore and navigate the NSS Web site. They should write down points of interest and find the **grotto** in their area.

◆ Have students report back to the group with their findings. The students can create a list of resources such as books, films, vendors for caving gear, caving information, local grotto contacts, and so on.

◆ An activity that will enhance this lesson but require an additional time commitment is to visit a local grotto to further the students' understanding of the NSS and the member-based grottos.

Follow-Up Activity

Commercial Versus Wild Caves (One Hour)

◆ To ensure that students can distinguish between a wild cave experience and a commercial cave experience, have them research popular commercial caves open to the public.

◆ Have them report their findings, specifically addressing access issues, recommended dress, tour description, and so forth.

◆ After the group discusses the findings, facilitate a discussion on the differences between wild caving and commercial caving. Use this discussion as a way to introduce the rest of the content in this unit.

◆ To further the students' understanding of the differences between show caves and wild caves, organize a class trip to a show cave if time and resources permit.

Caving History and Terminology Cards

History Card 1

"Under the earth's crust there exists such an enormously great world, in absolute darkness, that we can with some justice speak of a new continent." Alfred Bogli, Swiss speleogist.

Terminology Card 1

Cave—a natural void beneath the surface usually made up of several rooms and passages. Caves are located on all seven continents.

History Card 2

Serious cave explorers realized the need for an organization to advance cave exploration. The National Speleological Society began in 1941 in the United States.

Terminology Card 2

Caver—a person who explores caves in a safe and respectful manner.

History Card 3

The National Speleological Society currently consists of over 12,000 members and 200 grottos.

Terminology Card 3

National Speleological Society (NSS)—an organization devoted to the study, exploration, and preservation of caves.

History Card 4

In 1925 Floyd Collins became trapped in Sand Cave (Kentucky) as he was digging out a sinkhole to start a show cave. This story brought caving to the attention of the public and made international headlines. Floyd's brother offered $500 to anyone who would rescue him. Locals, journalists, hot dog vendors, and sightseers gathered outside the cave to await his rescue. Collins died after numerous days of entrapment that resulted when a rock pinned his leg. Musicals and plays have since been written to depict this tragic, colorful event.

Terminology Card 4

Grotto—a group of local cavers who have organized themselves as a general interest group. A grotto may join the NSS and become recognized as a local chapter. Grottos set their own standards for membership and caving protocol. A grotto is also a small room or chamber opening off a larger one.

History Card 5

The cave wars of central Kentucky became famous because of the competition between commercial caves. Smaller local show caves attempted to compete with Mammoth Cave. Fights broke out, and fierce competition ensued to bring in business.

Terminology Card 5

Show cave (or commercial cave)—a cave open to the public, usually with modifications such as electrical lighting and developed trails.

continued ▶

FIGURE CV1.1   Hand out cards to students to help them learn about the history and terminology of caving.

From M. Wagstaff and A. Attarian, 2009, *Technical skills for adventure programming: A curriculum guide* (Champaign, IL: Human Kinetics).

History Card 6

Mammoth Cave in Kentucky is the largest known cave in the world. The cave contains 350 miles (550 kilometers) of known passages with potential for more to be explored.

Terminology Card 6

Spelunker—the noncaver's term for a caver. This term fell out of favor with the caving community when the media began to use it to describe all people who go into a cave. Cavers consider themselves experienced people with training and technical knowledge. Spelunkers tend to be stereotyped as novice cavers with little experience and knowledge. A humorous saying among cavers is "Cavers rescue spelunkers."

History Card 7

The VPI (Virginia Polytechnic Institute) Grotto, located in Blacksburg, Virginia, was the first college student group of the NSS.

Terminology Card 7

Wild cave—an undeveloped cave in its natural state, in contrast to a show, or commercial, cave where lighting and paths have been added. Many grottos, university outdoor clubs, and organized groups seek out and explore wild caves.

History Card 8

Caves have been used throughout time. Ancient humans used them as shelters. Native Americans used caves for ceremonial purposes. Caves are used for the storage of foods and goods; they were once proposed as nuclear fallout shelters. Caves serve as meeting places such as churches and recreation halls, as places to escape the summer heat and winter cold, as hiding places (Underground Railroad), and even as taverns.

Terminology Card 8

Caving conventions—regional and national gatherings where cavers socialize, share information, engage in competitions, and view new gear on the market.

FIGURE CV1.1   *(continued)*

From M. Wagstaff and A. Attarian, 2009, *Technical skills for adventure programming: A curriculum guide* (Champaign, IL: Human Kinetics).

ASSESSMENT

- Check students' understanding of the history of caving by noting their participation in the discussion of information provided in the main activity.
- Have students explain the evolution of caving as a recreational activity through discussion and guided questioning throughout the lesson.
- Have students identify professional organizations and clubs associated with the sport by researching caving organizations.
- Have students demonstrate an appreciation for caving as an adventure sport by researching resources and learning basic history and terminology.

TEACHING CONSIDERATIONS

- The closure activity can be done as a group in a computer lab or as homework.
- Have a member from a local grotto visit the class and share information to enhance the follow-up activity.

▷ **Cave Life and Cave Geology**

OVERVIEW

Students learn in this lesson how several types of caves are formed and how to identify various cave formations. Students are exposed to the categories of cave life, their habitats, and examples in each category.

JUSTIFICATION

By understanding how caves are formed, students will be able to explain the process to others when they are in a leadership position. By gaining geological and environmental knowledge, they develop a deeper appreciation for this unique, fragile environment. A base knowledge of geology enhances the understanding of caves and their complexities. An understanding of cave life enhances knowledge and dispels false perceptions.

GOALS

- To develop students' ability to identify and explain cave formations and how caves are formed.
- To develop students' ability to identify and explain various forms of cave life.

OBJECTIVES

At the end of this lesson, students will be able to

- describe different types of caves (cognitive),
- explain different classifications of cave life (cognitive),
- identify common cave formations (psychomotor), and
- appreciate that the cave ecosystem is a unique, fragile environment (affective).

EQUIPMENT AND AREAS NEEDED

For main activity 1, Layers of the Earth:

- Modeling clay in a variety of colors
- Dental floss
- A geology map

For main activity 2, Solution Caves:

- Salt blocks approximately 4 inches by 6 inches (10 centimeters by 15 centimeters) (any size works)
- Large rubber bands
- Container for water
- Piece of cord
- Scissors

- Towels
- Sink or large plastic tub
- Handful of rocks to prop up salt blocks in tub or sink to avoid dissolving the bottom of the salt block

For main activity 3, Sinkhole in a Cup:

- Bag of sugar
- Bag of sand (different colored sand can be used in clear cups)
- Piece of construction paper
- Styrofoam cups or clear plastic cups
- Water
- Small toy houses or vehicles for extra visual effect

For various activities:

- Pictures of caves and examples of cave life
- Scissors
- Glue stick

RISK MANAGEMENT CONSIDERATIONS

- Caution students about rubbing their eyes when handling salt or sand.
- Use safety scissors when working with younger populations.

LESSON CONTENT

Introduction (10 Minutes)

This lesson presents important geological and environmental information supported by activities from a national program titled Project Underground (Zokaites, 2006). The logical place to begin is with information and activities that demonstrate how caves are formed. The lesson then delves into basic **cave formations**. Finally, students learn about various types and categories of cave life.

Provide basic introduction to the formation of caves, cave formations, and cave life that resides in different sections of the cave using the Important Terms sidebar.

Important Terms

bedding plane—The surface or boundary that divides two adjacent beds of sedimentary rock like limestone.

calcite—The most common cave mineral, a crystalline form of calcium carbonate.

carbonic acid ($CaCO_3$)—A weak acid made from carbon dioxide and rain or soil water that slowly dissolves limestone to form caves.

cave—A natural void beneath the surface usually made up of several rooms and passages. Caves are located on all seven continents.

column—A speleothem formed when a stalactite and a stalagmite have reached and grown together; also called a pillar.

continued ▶

domepit—A large dome-shaped cavity above a room or a passage created by solution, not breakdown. A domepit is often close to the surface because of water flow.

drapery—A thin curtain-shaped speleothem caused by a consistent stream of dripping water going down the same path like melted wax from a candle.

flowstone—Calcite deposits that have accumulated from water slowly flowing along a cave floor or wall.

groundwater—Water that infiltrates the soil and is stored in slowly flowing reservoirs (aquifers); used loosely to refer to any water beneath the land surface.

ice caves—Formed by melting water that runs underneath glaciers.

karst—Landscape characterized by exposed limestone, thin soil layers, sinking streams, sinkholes, underground drainage, and the abundance of caves.

lava caves—Formed when cooling lava forms a rock roof while lava below continues to flow through a tube. When the lava cools, a hollow tube remains.

limestone—A gray blue sedimentary rock deposited in sea basins and composed of calcium carbonate, $CaCO_3$. Most caves are formed by the dissolution of limestone by acidic water.

rimstone dam—A wall-shaped calcite deposit that impounds, or formerly impounded, a pool of water.

sandstone caves—Located at the base of cliffs carved out by water or wind over time. These caves are typically shallow.

sea caves—Formed by ocean waves that erode rock at the base of cliffs.

sinkholes—Depressions apparent in the ground caused by dissolution of the underlying rock or by the collapse of the roof of an underlying cavern. Sinkholes may be steep-sided or shallow depressions.

soda straw—A thin, hollow stalactite that resembles a sipping straw. The growth at the tip is caused by water flowing down the inside of the straw. All stalactites begin this way.

solution caves—Usually formed in limestone (although sometimes in gypsum or dolomite), these are the most common type. Groundwater dissolves or erodes the soluble rock by flowing through cracks, faults, joints, and bedding planes to form caves.

stalactite—A cylindrical or conical speleothem that hangs from a ceiling or ledge.

stalagmite—A cylindrical or conical speleothem that rises from a floor or ledge.

troglobites—Animals that are fully adapted to life in total darkness and can live only underground. Most troglobites ("cave dwellers") exhibit various degrees of depigmentation and loss of eyes over many generations of evolution. These animals are usually smaller and have adapted larger antennae. Examples include albino cave fish, isopods, amphipods, and albino crawfish.

troglophiles—Animals that may live underground but may also be found on the surface. Troglophiles ("cave lovers") can live either in or out of caves but move significantly up the food chain in caves. Many species of troglophiles mutate over time to become troglobites. Examples include segmented worms, snails, copepods, spiders, mites, millipedes, and cave crickets.

trogloxenes—Animals, such as bats, that visit caves for part of their activity but do not use the cave as their food source. Trogloxenes ("cave guests") cannot complete their life cycle in caves; these animals live or hibernate in caves but regularly leave caves as well. Examples include crickets, bats, pack rats, flies, cave salamanders, and gnats.

Main Activities

Activity 1: Layers of the Earth (20 Minutes)

This activity helps students visualize how layers of rock underground are not in neat layers as well as how they can be exposed on the surface of the ground. Students will be able to visualize in a three-dimensional format how layers are structured. Layers are intertwined, twisted, uplifted, exposed, and so forth. Exposed limestone is the key feature of karst topography. Caves are found in karst regions throughout the world.

◆ Consider dividing the class into small groups.

◆ Flatten different colors of modeling clay like pancakes.

◆ Stack layers of clay on top of each other. The layers will be visible in the array of colors.

◆ Have students use their hands to push the ends together to form a hump or ridge in the center.

◆ Take the dental floss and cut a cross-section to see the different layers and thicknesses of each layer.

◆ Place the two cut sections back together in any form; for example, students could stack them or fold them.

◆ Students can stretch, compress, twist, push side to side, or fold over to simulate geological movement. Then have students cut both horizontally (to expose the horizontal plane) and vertically (to expose a clear view of a cross-section) to see how layers shift.

◆ You should have a multicolored geological representation of multicolored layers as a visual aid to assist in the interpretation of this activity.

Activity 2: Solution Caves (Two Hours)

Discuss different types of caves found in the world. Use the following information to support the discussion.

See the Important Terms sidebar on page 236 for definitions of the following types of caves:

◆ Solution caves

◆ Sandstone caves

◆ Sea caves

◆ Lava caves

◆ Ice caves

Next, show how solution caves are formed.

◆ Consider dividing the class into small groups.

◆ Prop up one salt block on its long side with a handful of rocks inside a sink or tub.

◆ Place two salt blocks side by side (by the long side) and secure them together with a large rubber band.

◆ Place these two salt blocks on top of the elevated block already in the sink or tub. Fill a container with water and have a string running from the container between the salt blocks. The string will act as a constant water source that feeds water between two layers of "limestone." The water will dissolve the salt and leave a cavity in the blocks.

- This process may take several hours but can be sped up by increasing the water flow. After several hours, have students remove the rubber bands and observe how the inside has dissolved to form a cave. Students can engage in other activities while this process works.

- Explain that limestone is a porous rock and that water forms the vast majority of caves in limestone in the world.

- For extra visual effect, have students add a little food coloring to the water.

Activity 3: Sinkhole in a Cup (20 Minutes)

First, review and discuss information related to karst topography.

- Explain that limestone caves are the most common type of cave.

- Sinkholes are important phenomena to understand because their presence signifies the possibility of caves in the area.

- This activity helps students understand that sinkholes are formed by the collapse of surface soils because a void was created beneath the surface. The activity demonstrates that the void is created by changes in water level, direction of flow, and the amount of flow.

- Problems occur when urban development (housing subdivisions, construction) changes the water table, causing sinkholes that swallow up roads and buildings.

Next, carry out the activity.

- Consider dividing the class into small groups.

- Have students roll the construction paper into a cylinder shape and place it vertically in a cup. One end will be touching the bottom, and the other should be above the rim of the cup.

- Pour sugar down the cylinder of paper but not to the rim of the cup. Now place the sand in the cup around the outside of the paper. The cup should be filled equally with sugar and sand.

- Remove the paper from the cup. Try not to disturb the sugar placement in the sand.

- Cover the whole area in the cup with a little more sand so that the sugar is no longer visible.

- Fill the cup about halfway with water so that it saturates the sand.

- Have a student poke a hole in the bottom of the cup with a finger. Let the water drain out. A simple sinkhole can be observed.

- Students can place small toy houses or cars in the cups, or groups can exchange cups and randomly place these houses or cars on the surface of another's cup (to increase randomness) to facilitate a discussion on the capricious nature of sinkholes (they will form regardless of who has property on the land). From this activity, students see how groundwater displacement can affect surface areas.

Adapted, by permission, from Project Underground, *Project Underground: A natural resource guide*, 3rd ed., edited by C. Zokaites (Radford, VA). © Project Underground, Inc.

Activity 4: Speleothems (10 Minutes)

Reunite the class and describe the various cave formations (figure CV2.1), or **speleothems**—secondary mineral deposits such as stalactites and stalagmites—that form in a cave. Use pictures and illustrations as visual aids. Books and the NSS Web site (www.caves.org) provide excellent examples of cave formations. Also consider visiting the Web sites of commercial caves such as Carlsbad Caverns at www.nps.gov/cave/photosmultimedia/index.htm or the Cave Formation Web site at www.scsc.k12.ar.us/ChadickD/cave_formations.htm to view formation examples.

See the Important Terms sidebar on pages 235 to 236 for definitions of the following cave formations:

- Column
- Drapery
- Flowstone
- Rimstone dam
- Soda straw
- Stalactite
- Stalagmite

Instructor note: This list includes only the most common and basic types of formations in limestone caves. Students who desire a more advanced lesson can research additional formations that are more complex.

Activity 5: Introduction to Cave Life (15 Minutes)

Keep the class in one large group for a lecture that introduces the categories and types of cave life. Have pictures or illustrations ready to use as visual aids during this lecture. The NSS Web site features examples of cave life.

FIGURE CV2.1   Cave formations: (a) soda straw stalactites, (b) draperies, (c) stalactites, (d) breakdown, (e) stalagmites, (f) column, (g) rimstone, and (h) flowstone.

Courtesy of Indiana Geological Survey.

See the Important Terms sidebar on page 230 for definitions of the following types of cave life:

* Troglobites ("cave dwellers")
* Troglophiles ("cave lovers")
* Trogloxenes ("cave guests")

Closure Activities

Activity 1: Cave Trivia Quiz (30 Minutes)

This activity covers basic layers, cave types, and cave formations. This activity is an effective, fun way to review.

* Divide the class into groups.
* Hold up pictures or slides, or just pose questions. The first group to answer correctly scores points. You can decide on appropriate prizes for the winning team.

Activity 2: Hello, Who's There? (30 Minutes)

* Divide the class in half.
* Give half the class strips of paper with various cave-life illustrations and names.
* Pass out clues that describe each of the animals to the other half.
* Have students work together to match the description with its owner and note to which category of cave life the animal belongs (troglophile, trogloxene, troglobite).
* Discuss correct answers as a class. Provide guidance and correct misunderstandings where appropriate.

Adapted, by permission, from Project Underground, *Project Underground: A natural resource guide,* 3rd ed., edited by C. Zokaites (Radford, VA). © Project Underground, Inc.

Follow-Up Activities

Activity 1: Cave Formations (20 Minutes)

* Write the names of cave formations on a chalkboard or whiteboard.
* Have each student draw a picture of a cave and label each of the formations with a brief explanation of how they are formed and how they are interrelated.
* Collect the drawings for review. You then write feedback, correct misunderstandings, and return the drawings to the students.

Activity 2: Cave Life (30 Minutes)

* Send students home with knowledge of the three categories of cave life.
* Have each student come up with a creative phrase to associate with a specific term that will help him or her remember the different types of cave life and which animals belong in each. For example, troglobites can't see who they bite.

Activity 3: Cave Visit (Time as Needed)

* Take students to a cave.
* Have students review and identify formations that they see and any cave life that they encounter.

ASSESSMENT

◆ Have students describe different types of caves and cave formations by engaging them in group discussion and a trivia quiz activity.

◆ Have students describe and explain different classifications of cave life by creative word association and participation in the cave life game.

◆ Have students describe and explain different types of cave formations by illustrating, labeling, and explaining each formation.

TEACHING CONSIDERATIONS

◆ Because of the volume of information in this lesson, consider creating minilessons according to time availability.

◆ Because of the time commitment required for cave trips, set aside one class period to visit a cave site.

UNIT 3, LESSON 3

▷ Caving Equipment

OVERVIEW

This lesson introduces the novice caver to the personal equipment appropriate for caving. The lesson covers equipment selection, use, and care. Emphasis is placed on proper dress to ensure a safe, enjoyable trip.

JUSTIFICATION

Developing knowledge of proper personal caving equipment and its use is vital for safe caving practices and good environmental stewardship. Using this knowledge will provide students the opportunity to enhance their pride and self-reliance. Students will be more comfortable and enjoy the caving experience more if personally prepared.

GOAL

To develop the students' understanding of caving equipment, appropriate selection for different activities, and proper use.

OBJECTIVES

At the end of this lesson, students will be able to

◆ identify different types of caving equipment (cognitive);

◆ select appropriate equipment for their specific caving trip (cognitive);

◆ practice proper equipment selection, use, and care (psychomotor); and

◆ demonstrate pride in proper identification of gear, selection of equipment, and use of hardware (affective).

EQUIPMENT AND AREAS NEEDED

- Headlamps (electric and carbide)
- Various types and brands of helmets
- Appropriate attire for caving
- Gloves
- Knee and elbow pads
- Appropriate footwear
- Cave packs
- Carbide
- Batteries
- Watertight containers

RISK MANAGEMENT CONSIDERATIONS

- Carbide is flammable when combined with water; handle with caution.
- Emphasize proper care and handling of equipment.
- Batteries tend to corrode in cave environments. Caution students to handle older batteries with care and avoid contact with eyes.
- Remove batteries from headlamps when storing equipment and clean headlamps after use to maximize their use over time.

LESSON CONTENT

Introduction (10 Minutes)

Basic concepts of equipment selection and use begin with

- obtaining information about caves to be visited and
- having appropriate equipment for specific cave environments.

Review the importance of understanding the environment of the specific cave being visited and choosing equipment and clothing accordingly. Cave environments are of two distinct types—wet and dry—although some caves manifest a combination of both. The attire and equipment vary depending on the type of cave as well as personal preference. Always research the cave environment to be visited and plan accordingly based on the information given about appropriate cave attire. Plan to avoid hypothermia; staying warm is easier than getting warm.

Main Activity

Dress for Success (30 Minutes)

To begin this lesson, keep the class in one group for an interactive discussion. Pass around equipment for students to handle and see as it is being discussed. Use the following information to facilitate orientation to caving equipment.

Clothing

- Appropriate footwear for caving includes close-toed, ankle-supporting shoes with good traction (preferably high-ankle-supporting, lug-soled boots). Cavers should wear a wicking base layer of socks and a warm exterior layer, such as wool or a synthetic blend. Neoprene socks or booties are recommended for wet caves.

◆ Knee pads come in various shapes, widths, and lengths. Knee pads should be chosen based on personal preference and can be worn either outside the clothes or underneath the outer layer; if placed underneath, however, they remain cleaner and are less likely to be snagged while crawling. When buying pads, choose pads specifically designed for caving, which form to the leg and bend when crawling. The commercial pads used for athletic sports (especially the hard shell pads) tend to become snagged, damage formations, and do not adequately protect the knee.

◆ The bottom base layer (waist down) should be a base wicking layer, usually a synthetic fabric. This layer can be doubled up for extra warmth depending on location and personal preference. The bottom can be finished with heavyweight denim jeans or a heavy nylon caving coverall. Jeans or coveralls are preferred because they are durable and affordable. Clothing takes a beating in a cave!

◆ The top base layer (waist up) should be a base wicking layer, usually a synthetic fabric. This layer can be doubled up for extra warmth depending on location and personal preference. The top can be finished with a long-sleeved button-up shirt or lightweight fleece if coveralls are not worn. The idea is to be able to remove layers easily if one becomes overheated.

◆ Caving coveralls can be custom made or bought off the shelf. They are typically made with a heavy, durable nylon that withstands the rigors of long-term caving. Occasional cavers will find that regular work coveralls are acceptable. Commercial caving coveralls—designed with pit vents, map pockets, pad inserts, hoods, and other custom design features—can run up to hundreds of dollars.

◆ Elbow pads come in various shapes, widths, and lengths. Elbow pads should be chosen based on personal preference and can be worn either outside the clothes or underneath the outer layer; if placed underneath, however, they remain cleaner and are less likely to be snagged while crawling.

◆ If one chooses to wear gloves, durable gardening gloves are preferred. Gloves should have a snug fit and a durable surface on the palm. For wet caves, some cavers buy rubberized gloves that extend up the forearm.

◆ Many types and brands of adequate caving helmets are available; cavers can choose based on personal preference. Wearing a warm hat underneath the helmet will yield added warmth. Knit or wool hats fit easily under the straps in most helmets. The minimum standard for a caving helmet is a chinstrap; a high-density, impact-absorbing liner; and a reliable mounting system for the primary light source. Note: A convenient way to carry a wool or synthetic hat is to stuff it under the suspension system of the helmet for storage until needed.

◆ Extra layers including a hat and gloves for warmth.

Light Sources

◆ The two types of headlamps are electric and carbide. The caving community is still debating about the best light source for caving. Cavers can choose based on personal preference. Each type has pros and cons related to cost, weight, and duration of light source.

 – Electric lamp—*Strengths*: easy to repair, batteries more readily available than carbide, less weight on helmet, no open flame, and fewer problems in wet caves. *Weaknesses*: nonheat source, must carry the weight of backup batteries, must dispose of dead batteries (if batteries are not rechargeable). Electric lights vary in cost and quality. Cavers can spend as little as $30 for a reasonable headlamp and up to hundreds of dollars for specialized lights.

- **Carbide lamp**—a lamp that produces light by burning acetylene gas resulting from a mixture of carbide and water. Carbide is the shortened term for the rocklike chemical calcium carbide, or CaC_2. *Strengths*: longer duration of light, alternative heat source, extremely bright. *Weaknesses*: danger of open flame during rope work; potential of soot damage to the cave; many working parts; problem of disposing of spent carbide (carbide left over after use), which is poisonous and defaces the cave if emptied inside; heavier on helmet; difficult to use in wet caves.

◆ Carry three sources of light. The second source of light should be as good and reliable as the primary source. The third source could be a candle or miniheadlamp. Carry extra batteries or carbide.

Additional Equipment

◆ Cave packs should be versatile (worn over the shoulder, around the waist, like a book bag), simple (no unnecessary pockets, straps, or loops), large enough to carry what is needed but compact enough to be dragged or pushed through a crawlway, durable, and with closure by some type of flap with a drawstring (zippers can become immobilized by mud). Consider lining packs with heavy plastic bags, especially in wet caves. Many commercial caving packs have drain holes. Dry bags may be appropriate in some situations.

◆ Hard-shelled, watertight containers are optimal for carrying needed supplies (carbide, batteries, camera, food, and so on).

◆ Wet suits are commonly used in wet caves. Although they can be used as an outer layer, they are easily torn and damaged. Depending on the cave, coveralls may be needed to protect the neoprene. Under extreme conditions or for long periods, cavers wear multiple layers of neoprene. In ice caves, cavers wear fleece suits and thick insulation layers.

◆ In warm regions, such as caves in southern climates, some cavers wear durable Cordura shorts.

◆ To collect urine, use a nalgene pee bottle.

◆ Bring enough food and water to meet personal needs based on the length and type of trip.

◆ Plastic bags are versatile items that can be used to create an emergency shelter or to pack dirty gear in.

◆ A camera is great for documenting the experience.

Personal equipment should be cleaned after each trip with water and properly stored after drying. Emphasize that when mud dries, it crystallizes and damages the integrity of the cloth over time. First aid kits should be opened and dried also. In some cave environments, the humidity infiltrates everything, even items in waterproof containers. Batteries should always be removed after use to prevent corrosion of contact surfaces.

Leave valuables in the vehicles or in a safe place outside the cave. Money and car keys are of little use in the cave!

Closure Activities

Activity 1: Appropriate Cave Attire (10 Minutes)

- Divide the class into three groups. Designate a different cave environment for each group (wet, dry, mixture).
- Have students design an appropriate caving outfit and a comprehensive equipment list for their respective environments.
- Have each group report their results to the larger group.

Activity 2: A Heated Debate (15 Minutes)

- Divide the class into two groups and facilitate a debate of carbide versus electric lighting sources.
- Facilitate a discussion after the debate to clarify issues and misunderstandings.

Follow-Up Activity

Fashion Show (10 Minutes)

- When students gather for a trip, have them present a brief fashion show to demonstrate clothing and equipment choices.
- Show the group what you have in your pack to identify equipment to take and how to pack it. Have the students identify each piece of equipment.

ASSESSMENT

- Have students identify different types of caving equipment through discussion in the main activity section and through the follow-up activity.
- Check that students select appropriate equipment for their specific caving trip through the closure activity as well as the fashion show follow-up activity.
- Check that students practice proper equipment selection, use, and care in a cave setting through observation during the group's first trip. Be sure to allow plenty of time after the first trip for cleaning and maintenance.
- Assess whether students demonstrate pride in proper identification of gear, selection of equipment, and use of hardware through observation and students' self-report.

TEACHING CONSIDERATIONS

- Have extra clothing for the fashion show because novice cavers may not have synthetic fabrics, coveralls, or wet suits.
- Have a general price guide and a list of outfitters handy to share with students who may want to know how much certain items costs and where they can be purchased.

▷ **Movement Through Caves**

OVERVIEW

This lesson covers how to maneuver safely and efficiently through a cave using basic techniques. The lesson emphasizes specific techniques such as crawling, stooping, rolling, squeezing through tight passages, and negotiating slopes. Suggestions for practicing basic movements before going into the first cave are offered as well. These may be particularly appropriate for groups with lower levels of ability.

JUSTIFICATION

Proper energy conservation techniques are useful to those leading or participating in a caving experience. Group leaders must understand techniques and maneuvers appropriate for those of all skill levels so that they can guide their participants in a successful, safe experience. Improper technique leads to injuries and extremely difficult evacuations. Proper movement also helps maintain the integrity of the environment.

GOAL

To develop students' ability to use proper techniques to move efficiently and safely through a cave.

OBJECTIVES

At the end of this lesson, students will be able to

- understand various techniques and skills for maneuvering in a cave (cognitive),
- practice the appropriate technique for a specific application (psychomotor), and
- feel confident moving through caves while using various techniques (affective).

EQUIPMENT AND AREAS NEEDED

- Seven or eight chairs of various heights and widths
- Five or six tables of various heights and widths
- Other objects that can be used in an obstacle course such as boxes, pipes, uneven areas, slopes, and so on

RISK MANAGEMENT CONSIDERATIONS

- Because students will be crawling and climbing, check the instructional area for sharp objects and unstable chairs or tables. Spotting may be necessary.
- Make students aware that muscle strains and sprains may occur when they practice movements.

LESSON CONTENT

Introduction (20 Minutes)

The basic concepts to remember in movement through caves are to use controlled movements and a steady pace and to assist one another through spotting when necessary.

While reviewing basic concepts, demonstrate uncontrolled movement and an erratic pace, such as

- walking and not looking ahead,
- fast-paced walking,
- walking quickly over a log or balance beam, and
- walking close together in a group so as to hinder movement.

Facilitate a class discussion on the safety concerns of each improper way of movement.

Provide basic information about and a demonstration of the task of spotting.

- Encourage students to spot one another when necessary.
- Spotters should have a solid stance with feet spread apart to ensure balance when breaking a fall.
- Spotters should raise their hands and be ready at all times when spotting is required.
- Spotters should keep their eyes and attention on the climber at all times.
- Spotters should constantly communicate with the climber.
- Climbers should feel comfortable asking for a spot when needed.
- Climbers must communicate with spotters and begin climbing only when spotters are prepared.
- To ensure consistency, consider teaching a command system like the following:
  - Climber: "Ready."
  - Spotter: "Ready."
  - Climber: "Climbing."
  - Spotter: "Climb."

Main Activity

Basic Movement (30 Minutes)

Begin this activity with some basic reminders:

- Avoid touching formations unless doing so is the only way to avoid a fall. Touching formations can cause irreversible or long-term damage.
- Stretch before entering the cave or start slowly to allow the body to warm up.
- Use three points of contact—typically two feet and one hand. Using this method will ensure secure contact that will prevent a big spill. Three points of contact can also mean using your feet and butt to slide down a wet or muddy area. In some areas of a cave you may want to use four points of contact—both hands and both feet.

Next, describe and demonstrate the following techniques.

Crawling on Hands and Knees   Conserve energy and crawl at a comfortable pace. Use arms and legs together rather than just pull yourself forward with arms only. Allow enough space so that you can't grab the feet of the person in front of you. Instead of pushing the person in front to move faster, the follower should slow down. Some folks will become anxious when crawling because people crawling in front of and behind them create a closed-in feeling. A leader can address potential problems before the group enters a crawlway. The leader can have hesitant cavers follow directly behind him or her so that they can be coached and monitored. Knowing the names of the person in front and the person behind fosters quick and efficient communication.

Crawling on the Belly   The other common crawl is the belly crawl. This technique allows cavers to negotiate narrow passages. Keep the arms out in front of the head to prevent them from becoming pinned at the sides. This technique makes the caver smaller.

Stooping   Moving with this method tends to make backs sore! The bear walk (four points of contact—both hands and feet) is a common technique. People may run into formations because looking up is difficult. People tend to rush because of discomfort and may trip and fall. The duck walk, crouching down and shuffling on both feet, is another common technique, although it can be tough on the knees.

Rolling   This technique is not widely accepted except in well-known, safe areas. The caver lies on the cave floor, stretched out, and rolls (like a rolling pin) through a passageway. The technique is useful when the ceiling and floor are so close together that the caver cannot stand and does not want to crawl on hands and knees for a long distance.

Rolling can be an effective way to cover long distances under the right conditions. It takes less energy than crawling does. But rolling offers little control, and a caver may roll over sharp objects or cave life or into formations.

Steep Slopes   The caver should maintain three or four points of contact, sitting on the butt if necessary and keeping the feet forward. The idea is to create as much friction as possible by maximizing surface area contact. Maintain adequate spacing between cavers. Provide spotters if needed.

Chimney   When walls are close together and the caver must accomplish a vertical or horizontal climb, several techniques are useful. The basic concept is to wedge the body between the walls. The caver essentially makes the body as wide as possible and creates opposing forces on each wall to move slowly horizontally or vertically.

Movement With a Pack or Equipment   Keep control of your gear. Don't throw it because gear may fall into cracks and out of reach. Gear can be passed by the group in a chain format and organized in a designated place. Passing gear though a passageway is easier than dragging or pushing it. Cave packs can be pushed ahead by someone crawling in a tight passageway.

The ball-and-chain technique requires the caver to loop the pack strap around an ankle and drag it while crawling. Do not tie the strap because if the pack snags, the caver will be stuck.

Closure Activity

Obstacle Course (20 Minutes)

Have students maneuver their way through an obstacle course using the movements that they have just learned. For more fun, divide the group in half and turn the activity into a race. The time required for this activity will vary depending on group size and the length of obstacle course.

◆ Build the course out of simple props. Use chairs for crawlways. Place tables on their sides and push them together for a side squeeze. Make formations from rolled-up paper or spray foam. Attach them with Velcro or tape under a tabletop to simulate a crawl with obstacles to go around.

◆ Also attempt to simulate simple climbing problems. Spotting may be necessary.

◆ To spice it up, turn out the lights and use helmets and headlamps so that the obstacle course has the feel of a real cave.

This activity is particularly helpful when you are attempting to size up the physical ability of the group. This information can help you choose a cave for their first trip.

Follow-Up Activity

Practicing Movement (One to Two Minutes per Student)

Take students on a caving trip to practice their new skills and gain confidence. While caving, allow each student an opportunity to describe an appropriate maneuver for that area of the cave.

Be sure to debrief the group after the trip ends. This discussion is an excellent time for students to reflect on challenging parts of the cave and the techniques required to meet the challenges.

ASSESSMENT

◆ Check that students understand various techniques and skills for maneuvering in a cave by having them assess appropriate techniques during their first trip as described in the follow-up activity.

◆ Assess whether students practice appropriate techniques in a variety of applications by observing them during practice and on their first trip.

◆ Assess whether students feel confident moving through caves while using various techniques through observation and student self-reporting after a trip.

TEACHING CONSIDERATIONS

◆ Have the class assemble their own obstacle course. They can change and adapt the course to challenge themselves at all levels.

◆ Ensure that all students are able to participate (because of various personal size constraints, that is, height and weight).

◆ In more difficult situations such as steep slopes or climbs, consider establishing a hand line. After beginners become more comfortable and confident, you can eliminate hand lines.

▷ Anchor Systems and Equipment

OVERVIEW

In wild caves, cavers often face difficult terrain that requires hand lines, technical ascending, and technical descending. This lesson covers basic anchor systems used in caving. See also the discussions in the rock-climbing and mountaineering units. This lesson focuses on tensionless systems using natural anchors. Students discuss the challenges of building anchors in caves and practice building two main anchor systems, high-strength tie-off and webbing wraps.

JUSTIFICATION

Basic anchor systems are used in a variety of outdoor activities, including caving. Learning proper anchor systems is imperative to safe vertical caving and traversing technical terrain. Careful attention to anchor building also protects the environment. Knowledge and application of safe anchors enhances the student's self-reliance, pride, and craftsmanship.

GOAL

To develop students' ability to build and apply high-strength tie-offs and webbing-wrap anchor systems using appropriate gear.

OBJECTIVES

At the end of this lesson, students will be able to

- understand the strengths and limitations for each anchor system (cognitive),
- distinguish the appropriate anchor system to use in a specific context (cognitive),
- demonstrate the ability to build anchor systems using natural features (psychomotor), and
- take pride in building safe, efficient anchor systems (affective).

EQUIPMENT AND AREAS NEEDED

- Various lengths of static rope and nylon webbing
- Locking carabiners
- Diagrams of anchors
- Padding (old carpet, scrap cloth, old towels)

RISK MANAGEMENT CONSIDERATIONS

- Faulty anchor systems can lead to falls, possibly resulting in serious injury or death. Carefully inspect all anchors before use.
- If the outdoor program or agency that you are caving with has local operating procedures, be sure to exercise the approved protocol when building technical systems such as anchors.

LESSON CONTENT

Introduction (10 Minutes)

Introduce the basic concepts of building adequate anchors for ascending or descending in a cave.

◆ A good anchor should be relatively easy to assemble and disassemble.

◆ A good anchor system should be able to service the load for which it is intended safely and effectively while maintaining the integrity of the cave.

Explain that in this lesson you will discuss two commonly used systems to build natural anchors—high-strength tie-offs and webbing wraps—and have the students practice using them. Many natural features outside and inside the cave can supply an anchor point. Bolts may be available in popular, heavily used caves.

Review unit 2 (Rock Climbing) for basic anchor information. The techniques described in that unit apply here as well.

Main Activity

Building Anchors (30 Minutes)

Two common natural anchor systems used for vertical caving are high-strength tie-offs (tensionless hitches) and webbing wraps.

When teaching either anchor system, carefully describe and demonstrate as students observe. During this explanation, remind students to use as many natural formations as possible before they consider bolting. If all natural resources are exhausted, bolting is acceptable. Two natural features other than columns and stalagmites may serve as anchors:

◆ A **breakdown** is a large pile of rocks or boulders that have fallen from the cave walls or ceiling during some point in its geological history.

◆ A **chockstone** is a rock wedged in a crack, around which a rope can be run to create an anchor point.

Using Formations as Anchors   Formations are fragile and can be permanently scarred. Use them only if no other options exist.

◆ Create an anchor that will not damage the formation.

◆ If the formation is questionable, look for another one. Use the strongest formation available.

◆ Search for fractures and cracks in the formation that might compromise anchor strength. Certain types of formations can be brittle and weak.

◆ Observe the shape of the formation and determine whether the rope will slide off. Also check for sharp edges.

◆ After the anchor is built, pull in the direction of the intended load because the rope may slip unexpectedly (Smith & Padgett, 1996).

High-Tension Tie-Off   This anchor is also known as a tensionless hitch. The high-tension tie-off is an excellent option when the application allows the rope to be directly rigged to the anchor.

- The high-tension tie-off is one of the strongest possible anchors because tension (force) is not applied to a knot; knots weaken the strength of a rope.

- This type of anchor can be untied under tension, allowing disabled climbers to be lowered.

- Ideally, this anchor should be wrapped only twice to reduce torque on the anchor (figure CV5.1). However, additional wraps may be added if friction is not adequate, as seen in the figure.

- Use a carabiner to finish off the anchor to reduce potential nylon-on-nylon friction.

- No deviation should be present in the main line as it comes off the anchor; it should be in a straight line.

- Consider padding the anchor to reduce damage or wear on the rope (Smith & Padgett, 1996).

Webbing Wrap Webbing may be used when the rope cannot be connected directly to the anchor or if the anchor must be left in the case of a rappel.

- One-inch (25-millimeter) tubular webbing is an effective anchor material.

- When wrapping, place the water knot (ring bend) at the point of least tension and in a visible position. This placement ensures that little or no tension is placed on the knot. Water knot information can be found in the rock-climbing unit (page 169).

- When referring to wrapped anchors, *wrap* refers to how many times the webbing is wrapped around the anchor, and *pull* refers to how many coils are pulled to be placed in the carabiner.

Common configurations:

- Wrap 2, pull 1 (figure CV5.2)
- Wrap 3, pull 2 (figure CV5.3)

FIGURE CV5.1 High-tension tie-off with a single line.

FIGURE CV5.2 Wrap 2, pull 1 webbing anchor.

FIGURE CV5.3 Wrap 3, pull 2 webbing anchor.

Approximate strength:

- 1-inch (25-millimeter) webbing, approximate breaking strength = 4,000 pounds of force (lbf), or 20 kilonewtons (kN).
- Wrap 2, pull 1, breaking strength = 8,000 lbf (40 kN); it doubles in strength!
- Wrap 3, pull 2, breaking strength = 17,000 lbf (77 kN).
- Keep the angle of the webbing at the carabiner less than 30 degrees to maintain full breaking strength (figure CV5.3) (Smith & Padgett, 1996).

Closure Activity

Anchor Practice (30 Minutes)

Have small groups of students build anchor systems using the high-strength tie-off and the webbing wraps.

- Practice on trees, boulders, and other natural features if available. If natural features are not available, simulate anchors with items such as the backs of chairs, trashcans, and so forth.
- Have students circulate and study the anchor systems that other groups have built. Each student should write a critique of each observed anchor system.

Follow-Up Activity

Anchor Identification (Time as Needed)

During the students' first caving trip, identify and critique potential anchors as a group. If feasible and environmentally sound, have students build anchors using natural cave features or natural features at the entrance to the cave.

ASSESSMENT

- Check that students understand the strengths and limitations of each anchor system by having them take notes during the demonstration and build the anchor immediately afterward.
- Assess whether students can select the appropriate anchor system to use in a specific context by observing groups as they build various anchor systems.
- Check that students have the ability to build anchor systems using natural features by observing groups build anchors in a cave setting.
- Evaluate whether students take pride in building safe, efficient anchor systems by observing them during anchor construction and hearing student self-reports.

TEACHING CONSIDERATIONS

- Students with limited background in caving or climbing may not retain all anchor information and skills in one session. Consider breaking instruction into several class meetings as necessary, based on class experience.
- Consider using one class period to visit a vertical cave to practice setting up various anchor systems.
- Remind students that a simple bowline is an excellent option for rigging a hand line. Have students practice rigging hand lines. Information about the bowline can be found in the backpacking unit (page 101).
- Have experienced students serve as peer teachers in the group exercises.

▷ Rappelling

OVERVIEW

As cavers develop their skills, exploring vertical caves adds an exciting dimension to the sport. In this lesson students learn and apply safe descending (rappelling) techniques. The lesson introduces specific equipment used in a caving context such as rappelling devices and static ropes. This lesson builds on the rappelling information included in unit 2. Rappelling into a vertical cave, however, is considered an intermediate skill. You must have background knowledge and experience to deal with complex issues if a student becomes disabled. Also, ascending may be the only way back out. You must have advanced technical knowledge and skills to assist disabled cavers when vertical caving.

JUSTIFICATION

The knowledge and ability to descend safely into caves increases the enjoyment of caving and provides the necessary tools to manage the risks associated with vertical caving. Equipment for caving varies slightly from traditional rock-climbing gear used to rappel. Knowledge of the appropriate equipment and techniques helps cavers better manage the objective risks.

GOAL

To develop students' ability to use rappelling gear and associated equipment to descend safely into a vertical cave.

OBJECTIVES

At the end of this lesson, students will be able to

- identify appropriate descending equipment for caving (cognitive),
- understand a basic rappelling system (cognitive),
- demonstrate the ability to use appropriate equipment by safely executing a practice descent (psychomotor), and
- demonstrate a sense of confidence in self as well as instill confidence in group members (affective).

EQUIPMENT AND AREAS NEEDED

- Various lengths and diameters of static rope
- Steel and aluminum brake racks (also known as rappel racks)
- Various types of figure-eights
- A bobbin device
- Edge pads

RISK MANAGEMENT CONSIDERATIONS

◆ Check the outdoor instructional area for environmental hazards.

◆ Ensure that all anchors are appropriate.

◆ Manage falls and incidents by exercising proper protocol such as rappel commands, safety checks, and backup systems.

◆ Carefully manage students' use of rappel devices so that items like clothing, hair, and helmet straps do not become caught in the system.

◆ When training novices, create a backup lowering system or back up the belay in case someone descending becomes disabled or otherwise unable to continue.

LESSON CONTENT

Introduction (Three Minutes)

Rappelling deep into a wild cave will make the adrenaline pump. As cavers gain experience and attempt advanced caves, single rappels can cover hundreds of feet (100 meters or more), and some rappels can extend over 1,000 feet (300 meters).

Cavers use rappelling techniques and equipment different than people who rappel above ground, such as rock climbers. The sheer weight of the rope and the amount of friction (heat) generated dictate that cavers do things differently. Short rappels into caves, however, do not require specialized equipment, and traditional rock-climbing gear such as figure-eights can be used.

Main Activities

Activity 1: Rappelling Equipment (30 Minutes)

First, familiarize students with basic descending equipment used in a caving context. Review and discuss the gear listed here. Consider loading a figure-eight and rappel rack for demonstration purposes for this activity.

Figure-Eight Descender   A **figure-eight descender** is a **fixed friction device** used for rappelling and, in some cases, for lowering. The device is in the general shape of an eight. The large ring creates friction on the rope, and the smaller ring attaches to a seat harness. Note these additional tips:

◆ Figure-eights are generally good for descents of less than 150 feet (45 meters). The rappeller can maintain reasonable control at this height in a free-rappel situation.

◆ Figure-eights designed with ears, known as rescue eights, are preferable. Eights with ears are not as likely to lock off (girth hitch) by accident.

◆ Steel eights are heavier than aluminum eights and do not wear as quickly.

◆ The design of the eight causes ropes to twist. Twisting can create awkward and troublesome kinks in the rope that may be difficult for beginners to manage.

◆ A variety of methods can be used to rig an eight for extra friction or to lock off an eight.

Bobbin A **bobbin** is a fixed descending device of European origin that uses two fixed friction wheels (capstans) made of aluminum. The rappel rope is snaked through the device (see figure CV6.1). Note these additional tips about the bobbin:

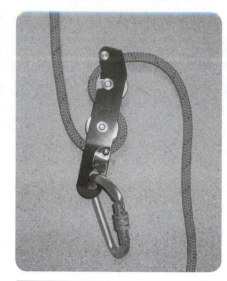

FIGURE CV6.1 Bobbin.

- Typically for personal use in the United States
- Common rappel device used in other countries, popular in Europe
- Good for drops shorter than 150 feet (45 meters)
- Strong, light, and relatively small
- Designed with two fixed pulleys within an aluminum frame
- Can be threaded with rappelling rope while attached to the harness
- Connects to the harness with a carabiner
- Can be rigged to produce additional friction using a variety of methods—additional carabiner, Munter hitch, and so on
- Can be locked off easily
- Instructions included on the frame of most commercially made bobbins

Brake Bar Rack, or Rappel Rack A **brake bar rack**, or rappel rack, is a **variable friction device** consisting of a U-shaped metal bar to which are attached several metal bars that create friction on the rope. Rappel racks come in a variety of designs based on intended use. Note these additional tips about the rappel rack:

- The term **brake** is sometimes used as slang for brake bar rack, particularly in North America.
- The brake bar rack is ideal for short or long rappels, especially anything over 150 feet (45 meters).
- The rappeller can vary the amount of friction when threading the rope by changing the distance between the bars, changing the number of bars threaded, or changing the tension on the rope with the **brake hand**.
- To set up a new rack, assembly may be required. If assembled incorrectly, death or injury can occur. Bars can be replaced as needed. Typically the top bars wear first.
- Racks can be made of aluminum or steel.
- Miniracks, which typically have five bars, are used for shorter rappels and light weight.
- Long racks have extra bars and a longer frame, and are used for rappels over 1,000 feet (300 meters).
- Racks come left-handed or right-handed.
- Eyelets come in different angles and designs. The design dictates the orientation of the rack when it is connected to the harness.
- Bars can be constructed in different shapes made of aluminum or steel—squares, tubular, solid, or U-shaped.

- Racks come in various designs to reduce or create more friction.
- Be careful not to load the rack backward; the rope will come undone after the rappel is underway!
- Even brake bar racks become hot. The rappeller must use proper descending technique and constantly monitor heat buildup.

Rappel Glove   A **rappel glove** is a leather-palmed glove used while rappelling to prevent rope burn. Typically lightweight and tight fitting, its design is different from a work glove.

Static Rope (Low Stretch)   A **static rope** is a type of rope designed to be used in applications such as rescue, rappelling, and ascending where high-stretch, or dynamic, rope would be a disadvantage and where no falls, or very short falls, are expected before the rope catches the person. Note these tips about static ropes:

- Diameter—Cavers use ropes with a diameter ranging from 10 up to 12 millimeters. Ropes with larger diameters create more friction.
- Coiling—When in the cave, many cavers use the caver's coil (see figure CV6.2). When storing the rope, most coils work. Stiff, dirty caving ropes can also be daisy chained to make them more manageable.
- Washing—Keep ropes as clean as possible.

FIGURE CV6.2   Caver's coil.

Edge Pad   An edge pad is a commercial or homemade pad used to protect the rappel rope from sharp edges.

Activity 2: Ground School (45 Minutes)

Prepare the site by creating anchors on trees with rappelling ropes attached (preferably on a hillside) to simulate rappelling into a cave. Create enough stations so that you can divide the class into small practice groups.

- First demonstrate the attachment, loading, and use of a rescue eight and then a brake bar rack.
- After the demonstration, send small groups to practice attaching the friction device to the harness and loading the rope.
- Have students build their own stations (anchors, attaching the rappel rope, and so on) using skills learned in previous lessons.
- Use the following information to supplement the demonstration.

Rescue Eight   Loading a rescue eight (figure CV6.3):

- The rescue eight must be threaded before attaching it to the harness.
- A left- or right-handed thread can be arranged.

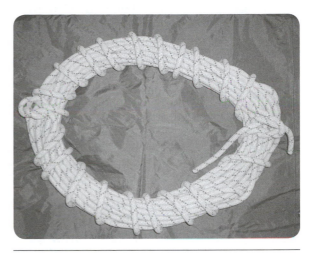

FIGURE CV6.3   Loaded rescue eight (threaded for right-hand use).

◆ A bight of rope is first threaded through the large eye and then placed around the smaller eye.

Using a rescue eight:

◆ The brake, or braking, hand is the hand that allows the rope to slide through it before it enters the rappel or friction device. Gripping the rope or pressing it against the thigh can add substantial friction to this system.

◆ The rappeller must be careful not to allow the brake hand to become too close to the device because the hand could become entangled in the device.

◆ The control (guide) hand can hang free or work in combination with the brake hand behind the back.

◆ Novice rappellers tend to form a death grip with the control hand by holding on to the rope above the threaded device. They should avoid doing this.

Brake Bar Rack Loading a brake bar rack:

◆ Notice the differences between the threaded racks in figure CV6.4. Use the following criteria to compare them.

◆ Load at least five bars (never use fewer than four bars on a standard six-bar rack).

◆ If the rappeller begins a descent and has difficulty making progress because of excessive friction, he or she can drop a bar (but must not use fewer than four).

◆ Spread bars to reduce friction.

◆ For a standard rack, always orient the rope over the top of the first bar.

◆ Most of the friction is on the first three bars.

◆ Use the control hand to space out the bars as needed while leaving the brake hand in place.

◆ Be cautious of the placement of the control hand so that the fingers do not become jammed. Fingers will break!

◆ If the rope is wet (as may occur when rappelling down a waterfall), less friction will be created. Use all bars to begin with.

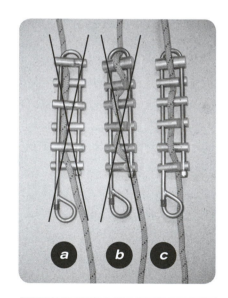

FIGURE CV6.4 Threaded racks: *(a)* incorrect, *(b)* not optimal, *(c)* correct.

Activity 3: Demonstration and Practice (45 Minutes)

The next phase of ground school requires you to demonstrate a basic safety check before rappelling and then demonstrate lock-off procedures. You can also use this part of the process to refine students' rappelling technique. After the demonstration is complete, send students back to their stations to practice. Use the following to supplement the demonstration.

Safety   Review safety protocol and complete the safety systems check:

◆ Check the anchor. Is it rigged correctly and ready for use?

◆ Check the rope. Has it been properly attached to the anchor? Was it properly uncoiled and lowered into the cave?

◆ Perform a harness check. Has the harness been properly put on and secured? Are buckles secure (doubled back in some cases)?

◆ Check the rappel device. Has it been properly secured to the harness? Has the device been properly threaded?

◆ Check the helmet. Is it secure and fitted properly?

◆ Check the rappeller's readiness. Are all loose objects, hair, pack straps, and so forth free of the rappel device? Does the rappeller have all necessary gear for the trip? Is the rappeller balanced and in position to rappel?

◆ Double-check the backup system. This procedure will vary depending on the system.

- If providing a backup belay, is the backup anchor secure? Is the belayer ready? Is the system attached properly?

- If providing a backup lowering system, is the lowering system ready and functional?

- If the rappeller is required to ascend out as the backup, is she or he prepared to do so?

Lock-Off Procedures   Rappellers must be prepared to stop any time during the rappel to deal with unforeseen issues. Students must have the ability to stop the action, lock off, and deal with issues or problems. A lock-off allows both hands to be free from the system. For example, if an object becomes caught in the rappel device, the rappeller must be able to self-rescue. If the rappeller needs to take a break, take a photo, or readjust gear, he or she may need to lock off.

Lock-off tips for the figure-eight:

◆ Leg wrap—using the brake hand to bring the rope around the waist and create multiple wraps around the thigh of the closer leg

◆ Figure CV6.5 shows the process to lock off a figure-eight. To finish the lock-off, pull firmly with the brake hand so that the rope is completely trapped under the load line. This wrap can be repeated as necessary.

Lock-off procedures for a rack—be aware that there are a variety of techniques for locking off. Only the half hitch lock-off is presented here:

◆ The half hitch lock-off, a standard technique, is easy, quick, and efficient (figure CV6.6).

◆ Use the brake hand to wrap the rope between the main rope and the top bar. Then tie off on the short side of the frame (short leg) with two half hitches.

◆ When removing to continue, use caution and be prepared to move again.

FIGURE CV6.5   Figure-eight in the process of being locked off.

Note these additional tips for descending:

◆ When stopping, make sure that the device is not too hot.

◆ The rate of descent should be constant and smooth. Avoid bouncing, which causes shock to the anchor and rubbing (abrasion).

◆ The slower the rappel is, the less the heat builds up.

◆ On extremely long rappels, over 1,000 feet (300 meters), use water to cool the rack.

Closure Activities

Activity 1: Friction Devices (15 Minutes)

Supply additional friction devices such as U-shaped racks, miniracks, J-bars, and so on. If you do not have the device, photos or illustrations will provide awareness. Use these examples to discuss further the advantages and disadvantages of rappel devices.

Activity 2: Rebuilding Racks (15 Minutes)

Place students in small groups. Provide each group with a rappel rack that has been dismantled. Have students rebuild the rack and thread it with a rope. This exercise will heighten the students' awareness of rack design, use, and safety.

Follow-Up Activity

Vertical Caving (One to Five Hours)

Take students to a vertical cave and have them rappel using a device of their choice. Back up the rappels with a top-rope belay system for safety. Before they rappel, have students explain why they chose their device and the mechanics involved.

As an option, use a climbing wall or climbing tower in your area to practice rappelling before attempting the first cave.

ASSESSMENT

◆ Check that students can identify appropriate descending equipment for caving through class discussion and equipment demonstrations.

◆ Assess whether students understand a basic rappelling system through ground school practice that includes building rappel stations and simulating the descending process.

◆ Check that students can use appropriate equipment to make a safe, successful descent on a practice wall or in a beginner's vertical cave.

◆ Evaluate whether students demonstrate a sense of confidence in self and instill confidence in group members by observing them practice basic descending skills through a progression of activities.

FIGURE CV6.6   Half hitch lock-off (short leg tied off with two half hitches).

TEACHING CONSIDERATIONS

◆ Practicing rappelling technique on a climbing wall, rappelling tower, or any above-ground site is recommended. Depending on their ability, students may need to refine their skills in a more controlled environment.

◆ Consider simulating a self-rescue or a lower during the practice activities. Also consider having students practice with heavy packs to experience rappelling with gear.

◆ Starting a rappel can be tricky, depending on the situation. For example, a rock face that creates a sharp overhang into a **free rappel** requires more advanced techniques and confidence. A good demonstration and practice may be needed to prepare students properly.

◆ For a vivid demonstration of how heat affects the integrity of a nylon rope, heat up a metal object (such as an old carabiner) with a propane torch. Then clip a scrap piece of rope into the carabiner. Monitor this exercise carefully for safety because it is easy to be burned. Pliers, thick leather gloves, water, and an area free of debris are recommended.

UNIT 3, LESSON 7

▷ **Ascending**

OVERVIEW

As cavers develop greater skill, exploring vertical caves adds an exciting dimension to the activity. In this lesson students learn and apply basic ascending techniques. Equipment options such as froggers and rope walkers are introduced. The lesson only introduces basic concepts and skills and does not cover the vast body of knowledge associated with ascending. As stated in lesson 6 (rappelling), you must have background knowledge and experience if you choose to engage students in this activity. If serious problems arise, you must be equipped to build rescue systems (hauling and lowering systems) to assist disabled ascenders. This unit does not include comprehensive rescue information.

JUSTIFICATION

The knowledge and ability to descend safely into caves increases the enjoyment of caving and provides the necessary tools to manage the risks associated with vertical caving. In many cases, if cavers descend (rappel) into a cave, they must ascend back out. If you do not intend to provide an ascending experience in a cave, you can use this lesson to introduce the concept and technical aspects of ascending to raise the student's awareness of the complexities and diversity of caving. Knowledge of basic equipment, technique, and safety allows the intermediate caver to tackle less difficult ascents with proper instructional support.

GOAL

To develop students' knowledge and ability to use ascending gear and assist others with the process.

OBJECTIVES

At the end of this lesson, students will be able to

- recognize common equipment for ascending out of a cave (cognitive),
- understand the ascending process using at least one system (cognitive),
- demonstrate the ability to use appropriate equipment to make a safe and successful practice ascent (psychomotor), and
- demonstrate a sense of confidence in self as well as instill confidence in group members (affective).

EQUIPMENT AND AREAS NEEDED

- Various lengths of static rope
- Frog systems
- Rope-walking systems
- Helmets
- Harnesses
- Anchor materials (webbing, carabiners, pulley, and rappel rack)
- An area where top-rope anchor systems can be built, such as the rafters in a gymnasium, belay cables on a ropes course, or large tree branches

RISK MANAGEMENT CONSIDERATIONS

- Check the outdoor instructional area for environmental hazards.
- Ensure that all anchors are appropriate.
- Manage falls and incidents by exercising proper protocol such as climbing commands, safety checks, and backup systems.
- Inspect equipment and ensure that everything is in proper working order.
- Monitor students who are ascending for potential problems. Use radios to communicate more effectively whenever rappelling or ascending with a group. Have knowledgeable cavers (other instructors or advanced students) stationed at the top and bottom while students ascend.
- Be aware of potential rockfall.

LESSON CONTENT

Introduction (10 Minutes)

Briefly introduce types of ascending systems. Students will discover that ascending requires significant effort. The ascending system chosen dictates the amount of physical energy needed, the difficulty, and the time required to accomplish an ascent. Cavers have several options available: classic three-knot **Prusiks**, Texas system, Mitchell system, inchworm, **frog system**, or bungee systems. *On Rope* by Smith and Padgett (1996) offers excellent explanations and comparisons of these systems.

The system of choice should be versatile, easy to use, compact, lightweight, and familiar to the user. Cavers must practice and become competent with the system that they choose.

Main Activity

Ascending (30 Minutes)

Demonstrate and discuss the use of an ascending system. First, you must find an appropriate site to rig an ascending practice station. Find an appropriate anchor at least 12 feet (4 meters) off the ground. Attach a pulley to the anchor above. Rig a rope through the pulley and down to a rappel rack that is attached to a ground anchor. The rack is present to control the speed of the rope.

This system allows for an ascender to climb a significant distance while staying close to the ground. The rope is simply fed through the rack as the climber ascends the rope. See figure CV7.1 for an example of a practice ascending station.

FIGURE CV7.1   Challenge course belay cables make an excellent practice ascending station.

This lesson does not detail procedures for specific systems. You must choose and teach the appropriate system based on personal experience and knowledge.

Sit–Stand Method Systems   Sit–stand methods (Prusiks, Texas system, frogger, and inchworm) make up one system of ascending. This method requires a deep-knee-bend motion. The frogger may be the most well known sit–stand system and most widely used system in the world (Smith & Padgett, 1996). See figure CV7.2 for an example of a frogger system.

FIGURE CV7.2   Frogger system—a sit–stand assending method.

Rope-Walking Systems Rope-walking systems make up a second category of ascending systems (Mitchell system, single and double bungee systems). The motion used is similar to walking up stairs. See figure CV7.3 for an example of a rope-walking system.

Safety Checks Like those who descend, ascenders must complete a safety check system before climbing.

FIGURE CV7.3   A rope-walking system at a practice station.

◆ Take clothing layers off before the climb if necessary—ascenders will become hot!

◆ Make sure that headlamps are working at full capacity.

◆ Remove all slack from the rope before climbing.

◆ Use commands. After taking position (directly underneath the anchor to avoid excessive swinging or a pendulum), use the command "Climbing."

◆ Be aware of rockfall if the rope shifts.

◆ Having someone weight the rope below the ascender to take out slack makes it much easier to get started. In some situations, the last person can weight the end of the rope by connecting a pack with extra gear to take the slack out.

◆ Ascend at a steady, comfortable pace. The most important point is to relax and find your personal rhythm.

◆ Shorter steps can conserve energy during a sustained climb. Efficient climbers tend to step between 8 and 14 inches (20 and 35 centimeters) at a time (Smith & Padgett, 1996).

◆ Take breaks when necessary but for only a short time (one minute or less). The goal is to climb without stopping because of the inherent dangers of hanging for long periods (impaired circulation and exposure to the elements). In addition, others waiting their turn to ascend may become uncomfortable.

◆ Use an elbow or shoulder to push away from the rock if you are experiencing difficulty. Pushing away from the rock allows the equipment to slide more easily up the rope without obstruction from the rock. Another option is to orient your back toward the rock face.

Closure Activity

Practice Stations (10 Minutes per Student)

At this point, facilitate student skill development by using ascending practice stations. Have students take turns ascending and belaying. Practice all phases of the process—attachment of the system to the climber, attachment of the system to the rope, safety check system, and commands.

Follow-Up Activity

Lowering a System (10 Minutes per Student)

Create a scenario so that a climber cannot continue to ascend. Practice problem-solving skills to remedy the situation. This exercise might include descending or lowering the whole system. The issue is that the frogger and rope walker cannot be reversed to descend. Prusiks will have to be rigged above the ascending system so that the climber can unweight the system to unrig and transfer to a rappelling system.

This complicated process requires additional knowledge and skills. Instructors with the proper background can cover this information. Minimally, the group should simulate lowering the entire system. This activity impresses on students how serious this situation can be. They must be trained, well practiced, and take ascending seriously.

ASSESSMENT

- Check that students can recognize common equipment for ascending out of a cave by discussing and practicing ascending in a simulated situation as described in the main activity.
- Confirm that students understand the ascending process through demonstrating and discussing at least one system described in the main activity.
- Assess whether students can use appropriate equipment and safely make a successful practice ascent through simulated practice.
- Evaluate whether students have a sense of confidence in self as well as instill confidence in group members by practicing and solving potential problems.

TEACHING CONSIDERATIONS

- During the closure activity, set up multiple stations with various systems to save time, if possible.
- Stress the importance of safety and systems checks even when practicing. Injury could result from practice using the simulated ascending station.
- If possible, let students experiment with various systems to allow them to compare and contrast systems. Minimally, let them try one sit–stand system and one rope-walking system.
- With more advanced students, you can cover techniques for maneuvering around overhangs and other difficult situations.

UNIT 3, LESSON 8

▷ Caving Safety

OVERVIEW

This lesson familiarizes students with caving safety protocols, safe caving techniques, and equipment to aid in safe caving. This topic includes learning how to navigate in a cave using a cave map. In addition, the lesson covers basic items such as preparing properly before caving, conduct while in the cave, and the contents of a cave leader's pack.

JUSTIFICATION

Students should be able to feel confident in their knowledge of safe caving protocols so that they can travel safely as a group. Cave rescues are extremely difficult, time consuming, and expensive. Rescuers are put at risk when executing a rescue. Moreover, protecting the cave environment becomes second priority when a full rescue operation is under way. Understanding caving protocol and attending to safety reduce the chances that a serious incident will occur.

GOAL

To familiarize students with safe caving protocols, techniques, and equipment.

OBJECTIVES

At the end of this lesson, students will be able to

- know appropriate safe caving protocols and techniques (cognitive),
- demonstrate safe caving practices (psychomotor), and
- value the need to be attentive and follow strict caving protocol when traveling as a group (affective).

EQUIPMENT AND AREAS NEEDED

- Cave maps
- Flagging tape
- Marker (to number flagging tape)
- Rescue litter and appropriate materials (straps and padding)

RISK MANAGEMENT CONSIDERATIONS

When practicing a litter carry, be careful and maintain good group communication. This exercise is physically demanding. Strained backs, twisted ankles, twisted knees, strained shoulders, and other injuries are possible. Be sure to secure the victim to prevent dropping.

LESSON CONTENT

Introduction (15 Minutes)

The basic concept of safe caving is to be prepared and adequately equipped. Discuss the importance of these points. Facilitate a class discussion about emergencies that might occur on a caving trip. Brainstorm how a trip leader should handle (or could have avoided) the problems in the following scenarios.

Scenario 1

A group encounters a 35-foot (10-meter) mud slide. A traditional practice is to pour water on the slide to make it a slick ride to the bottom. After the group does this, however, a group member hits the bottom at full speed, severely twists his ankle, and is then unable to walk. The group is only 30 minutes into the trip.

Scenario 2

A group encounters a 20-foot (6-meter) down climb called a corkscrew. The leader does not rig a hand line. His grotto's unspoken ethic is that if people choose to attempt the climb, they must be able to do it on their own. Unfortunately, a participant falls and breaks her arm.

Scenario 3

A group comes to a room that forces them to choose from among three routes. The group cannot reach a consensus. They decide to split into three smaller groups so that each can explore one of the routes. They agree to meet back in the main room in one hour. After two groups return on time, they wait an additional hour. The third group still does not appear.

Scenario 4

A group was scheduled to complete their caving trip by 2:00 p.m. At 4:00 p.m., the group's emergency contacts on the outside have not heard from them.

Scenario 5

A well-prepared group is ready to start their caving trip. As they are about to enter the cave, the leader of a youth group approaches and explains that he has 10 boys and girls who would like to go caving but have never tried it before. The children are wearing T-shirts and carrying handheld flashlights. The youth leader asks if he and his group can tag along with the experienced cavers.

Main Activities

Activity 1: Techniques and Protocol for Safe Travel (15 Minutes)

Review the following information in the form of a discussion. Pose the primary questions listed here and discuss the rationale for each issue. This activity gives students the basic tools they need to travel safely in a wild cave.

Before Entering the Cave

- Establish a reliable outside contact. Establish time in and time out.
- The contact must be available, know how to assist if problems occur, and know where the cave is. The contact should know how many are in the group and in some cases should have a list of group members.
- Establish an emergency procedure plan that includes a call list.
- Leaders should pack their packs together before entering the cave so that everyone knows the location of vital gear.
- Have the group stretch and warm up.
- Make sure that dry, warm clothes are accessible for the return trip.
- Make sure to obtain proper permission to use the cave. When applicable, sign the log book or registry. Registries can be found in waterproof containers, plastic bags, PVC pipes, or other protective containers in the entrance room of a cave. Alternatively, the log book or registry may be located in a location convenient for the **landowner** outside the cave. Cavers must gain permission from the local landowner before entering a cave.
- Make one last gear check. Fixing a headlamp is easier above ground.

Establishing Movement Protocol

◆ Group size—A group should include no fewer than four members for emergency purposes. If an injury occurs, one can stay to monitor the victim and two can go for help. Group size depends on the nature and difficulty of the cave. Larger groups take longer to move and can create more environmental damage. A group size of 12 to 14 is acceptable for **program trips**.

◆ Lead and sweep roles—When traveling as a group, designate a lead and a sweep. The lead sets the pace and focuses on route finding. The lead must manage the group by keeping it together. The sweep is always last and ensures that no group member is left behind. If necessary, the sweep can slow the group down by passing a message up the line to the lead.

◆ Roles that members play when assisting each other—Groups usually travel in a follow-the-leader pattern. Each person is responsible for the person traveling in front of and the person behind her or him. People should assist and spot as needed. The lead can orally pass information and warnings down the line to the sweep.

◆ Letting eyes adjust after entering—After first entering the cave, find a place large enough for the group to gather and sit if possible. Turn all lights out and address any issues or conduct a miniorientation to the cave. When lights are turned back on, eyes are adjusted and cavers are ready to go.

◆ How to keep up with group members—The lead and sweep play important roles in this task. When encountering difficult terrain, the lead must wait for other group members and be patient. The group can use a count-off system starting at the front, moving to the back, and then moving back to the front. Splitting up is OK, but the group must maintain the group minimum and have a plan—a timeframe and a course of action.

◆ What to do if someone becomes separated or lost—The person in this situation should sit down, stay put, conserve light sources, and call out occasionally. Calling out too much can be confusing. Voices travel, echo, and can become misleading. The lost member should put on the extra clothing layers packed in his or her bag. By staying put, the person is much more likely to be found because the group can simply retrace their steps to find him or her. In extreme cases when search parties are organized, the chances of being found are much greater if lost people do not move around.

Rigging Hand Lines

◆ Hand lines are typically used as a self-assist system that allows group members to navigate difficult, steep terrain. Basic anchoring principles apply when setting up a hand line.

◆ The ethics and practice of rigging hand lines vary in the caving community. Many purists like to move through caves without the assistance of a hand line. This approach provides a more challenging trip. Setting up hand lines also slows down the trip, which can dramatically affect group progress. But institutions that guide and are responsible for clients may set up hand lines as a risk management practice.

◆ As a rule hand lines should be constructed

    – when agency protocol mandates the practice at a particular location,

    – when potential for serious injury exists, or

    – when leaders choose to use them because of the group's ability level, experience level, comfort level, or energy level.

Turning Back

◆ How do you know when your group should turn back? Decide before you go what the plan will be. Establish the goal up front.

◆ Watch for mental and physical fatigue within the group.

◆ If you become disoriented, return to the last known location.

◆ Remember the timeframe established with the contact. A group that discovers a new passage can get virgin passage fever and lose track of time.

◆ Know how much light source time is left. Carry two to three times the amount of light time needed.

Dealing With Injuries

◆ Assess the severity of the injury. Determine whether to self-evacuate or whether outside help is needed.

◆ Stabilization is critical with any injury to prevent further complications such as hypothermia. Hypothermia can mask many problems and create others.

◆ Keep the remainder of the group safe.

Getting Stuck

◆ Do not panic. Relax and control breathing.

◆ People who believe themselves to be stuck can panic. Remember that if you can make even small movements toward progress, you are not truly stuck.

◆ Extra layers of clothing can be removed for snug passageways.

◆ If the caver is contemplating taking the helmet off to fit through a passage, she or he should reevaluate!

◆ If truly stuck, consider applying a lubricant such as mud or water. Too much water, however, could cause hypothermia! Also, try peeling off clothing.

◆ If stuck, have people on both ends to push and pull and search for spaces to create movement.

Activity 2: Cave Navigation (30 Minutes)

Navigating in a cave can be difficult and intimidating for novice cavers. Even experienced cavers can become extremely disoriented if proper precautions are not taken. Being able to interpret a cave map and establish a marked route are two important skills. In this activity, discuss cave maps and practice interpreting a cave map. Also, discuss techniques for establishing routes.

Cave Maps

◆ Maps are typically created in two planes—a profile view (cross-section) and a plan view from overhead (bird's eye view looking down).

◆ Maps range from those that are extremely detailed to basic line maps (figure CV8.1).

◆ Maps are created by conducting surveys. Data are collected with a measuring tape or sight lasers.

◆ Typically, cave maps have symbols but not legends (see figure CV8.2).

◆ Cave maps can be confusing, so cavers should practice to gain proficiency. Confusion occurs because multiple levels are stacked on top of one another and passages are intertwined (three-dimensional) using a one-dimensional diagram.

◆ Cavers should constantly stop and orient themselves with the map.

Adventure Cave
Karst County, VA

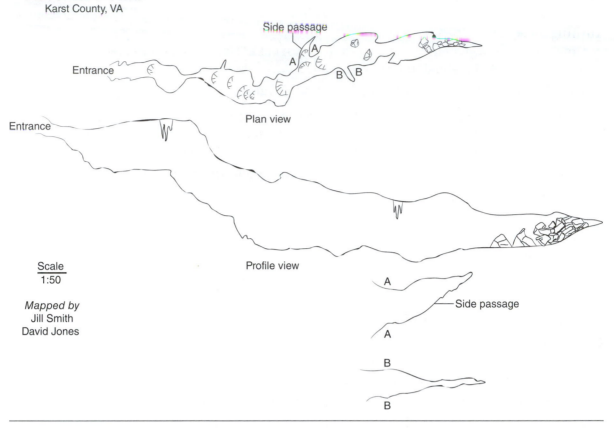

Side passage

Entrance

Plan view

Entrance

Profile view

Scale
1:50

Mapped by
Jill Smith
David Jones

A

A

Side passage

B

B

FIGURE CV8.1   This sample cave map demonstrates an overhead (or plan) and profile view.

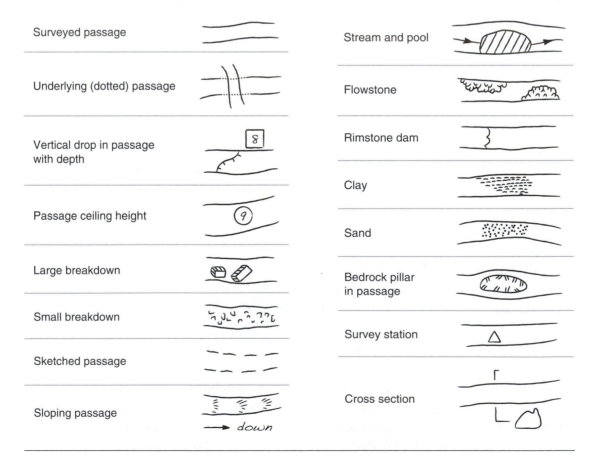

Surveyed passage			Stream and pool	
Underlying (dotted) passage			Flowstone	
Vertical drop in passage with depth			Rimstone dam	
Passage ceiling height			Clay	
Large breakdown			Sand	
Small breakdown			Bedrock pillar in passage	
Sketched passage			Survey station	
Sloping passage			Cross section	

down

FIGURE CV8.2   Common symbols found on cave maps.

Adapted from "Common cave map symbols in the 1976 NSS standard map symbols," *The NSS Bulletin,* April, 41(2): 35-48.

Establishing Routes

◆ Cavers establish or mark routes when they are exploring new caves.

◆ Plastic flagging tape is the most common environmentally sound way to mark a route. As the group moves through the cave, they strategically place pieces of tape that they can see when they backtrack. Each piece of tape is sequentially numbered to avoid confusion. The group should collect the tape on the way back out.

◆ Only advanced cavers should use this technique. Beginner and intermediate cavers should go into caves only with a knowledgeable person. Therefore, novices do not practice marking or flagging.

Activity 3: Safety Equipment (20 Minutes)

This activity focuses on a discussion of basic safety equipment to ensure that a group is adequately equipped and prepared. Take the contents of a cave leader's pack and spread the contents on the floor. Ask each group member to grab a piece of equipment. Go around the circle and have each student introduce the item with your support. Discuss the items as they are shared.

Typical contents in a cave leader's pack:

◆ The leader's personal gear including extra light sources

◆ Extra food and water for the group

◆ Spare parts to repair group gear, especially light sources

◆ Spare batteries or carbide

◆ Duct tape

◆ First aid kit

◆ Emergency blanket

◆ Emergency heat source (candle or carbide lamp, and lighter or matches)

◆ Hand line (at least 25 feet, or 8 meters, long)

◆ Large trash bags (to make heat tents or seats, to carry trash, and so on)

◆ Knife

◆ Carabiners

◆ Small cord (to repair shoestrings and for other purposes)

◆ Pen and paper in waterproof container

◆ Human waste disposal system

◆ Watch

Additional safety equipment to consider:

◆ Rescue litter or backboard (figure CV8.3)—Portable or collapsible litters are on the market. These can be stored in shuttle vehicles and easily packed into a cave in an emergency.

◆ Cable ladders (figure CV8.4)—In situations where hand lines are not practical, cable ladders are useful. Cavers are put on belay when using ladders. Cable ladders are an alternative to rappelling and ascending vertical, free-hanging terrain.

◆ Guidebook—Guidebooks are difficult or impossible to find. Local grottos are the best source for cave information.

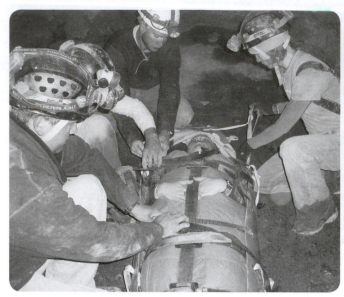

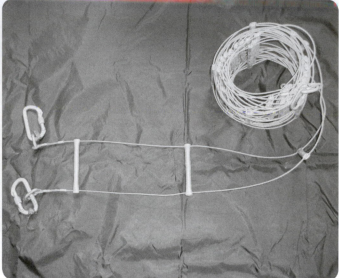

FIGURE CV8.3   Cavers practicing an evacuation with a rescue litter.

FIGURE CV8.4   A 30-foot (9-meter) cable ladder that is easily transported in a cave pack.

Closure Activity

Create a Safety Speech (20 Minutes)

Break the class into groups and challenge them to develop a safety speech for a group of novices who are going caving. This exercise requires the synthesis of all lecture and discussion information given during the main activities. Have one group volunteer to present their safety speech. After the presentation, have the other groups offer a critique.

Follow-Up Activities

Activity 1: Mock Evacuation (One Hour)

Have students conduct a short mock evacuation using a group member. An appropriate litter will be needed, and you must monitor group safety. Lifting and carrying heavy weight in a cave is dangerous. The activity must not cause damage to the cave. This exercise deepens student appreciation for practicing appropriate caving safety protocol.

Activity 2: Route-Finding Exercise (30 Minutes)

Divide the class into smaller groups. Provide a cave map and challenge the groups to find a route through the cave. Have each group outline their route and describe challenges, obstacles, and cave features along the way. Bring the groups together to share their findings as a larger group.

ASSESSMENT

♦ Evaluate whether students understand and can describe appropriate safe caving protocols through class discussions and guided questions. Evaluation can also be done through the safety speech closure activity.

♦ Check that students demonstrate safe caving practices by observing class travel during their first trip.

◆ Assess whether students value the need to be attentive and follow strict caving protocol when traveling as a group by observing class behavior when caving.

TEACHING CONSIDERATIONS

◆ Given the complexity of cave mapping, find a simple, straightforward map for the follow-up activity.

◆ Consider dividing this lesson into smaller lessons based on time constraints and the ability of the students.

◆ The mock evacuation activity is a powerful learning tool. You must judge whether your group is capable of executing this exercise. The cave used for this exercise should be conducive to practice.

UNIT 3, LESSON 9

▷ Caving Ethics

OVERVIEW

Students gain in this lesson an understanding of ethical practices associated with caving. Ethical behavior relates to a variety of topics such as access issues, safety protocol, environmental stewardship, and expedition behavior. Ethical codes associated with professional organizations are visited as part of this lesson. Also, environmental ethics in the context of Leave No Trace are discussed.

JUSTIFICATION

Practicing ethical caving behavior results in a number of benefits. Healthy relationships with landowners ensure access. Respecting other users promotes more enjoyable experiences. Following safety protocol reduces the number of accidents and costly, dangerous rescues. Caves are unique, fragile environments that can be damaged forever from a simple touch or misplaced breath. Because cave environments cannot recover from user impact, cavers must learn to minimize their impact. This understanding will lead to respect for the environment and the knowledge to teach others.

GOAL

To develop students' understanding of ethical principles regarding caving and to put those principles into practice.

OBJECTIVES

At the end of this lesson, students will be able to

◆ understand basic ethical principles associated with caving (cognitive),

◆ practice ethical behavior in a cave environment (psychomotor), and

◆ value the need to practice ethical behavior and consistently model this behavior when caving (affective).

EQUIPMENT AND AREAS NEEDED

- ◆ Trash bags
- ◆ Old reliable water bottle
- ◆ Flagging tape and marker
- ◆ Resealable plastic bags
- ◆ Snack foods
- ◆ Commercial and homemade solid waste disposal systems

RISK MANAGEMENT CONSIDERATIONS

- ◆ Choke hazards with snack foods
- ◆ Potential food allergies
- ◆ Inappropriate horseplay with plastic bags
- ◆ Consumption of "old reliable water bottle" contents (aka urine) in a dark cave

LESSON CONTENT

Introduction (30 Minutes)

The caver's motto: "Take nothing but pictures, leave nothing but footprints, kill nothing but time" (Jones, 2003).

Introduce students to caving ethics and have them review established principles. Copies of ethical guidelines are easily found on organizational Web sites, both national and international:

- ◆ In the United States, the National Speleological Society (NSS) has a PDF file download titled *A Guide to Responsible Caving* available under their list of brochures at www.caves.org/brochure.
- ◆ The New Zealand Speleological Society posts their code of ethics at http://caves.org.nz/pmwiki/pmwiki.php/NZSS/Ethics.
- ◆ The Australian Speleological Federation's code of ethics can be found at www.caves.org.au/s_code_of_ethics.htm.
- ◆ The National Caving Association of England, Scotland and Wales provides Web site links to their minimum impact caving code and code of ethics at http://web.ukonline.co.uk/nca/.

Use these formal guidelines to facilitate discussion during the main activity. These principles will provide a basic foundation to enhance the students' discussion and understanding of the Leave No Trace (LNT) principles discussed in the following sections.

Main Activity

Caving Ethics and LNT Principles (45 Minutes)

Begin by giving the students various snack foods. Let them munch on the snacks as you begin the activity. Do not tell them what you are doing until you reach principle number 3 in the discussion. Their inevitable spilling of small pieces of the snacks will illustrate the environmental impact of eating crumbly food in the cave environment. While students are snacking, explain that the group will address each of the seven LNT principles. Encourage them to apply information gleaned from the introductory activity into the discussion.

Plan Ahead and Prepare
- Know the regulations and special concerns for the cave that you will visit. Refer to state law and regulations and federal law; both protect caves.
- Gain permission and be aware of the landowner's wishes. Obtain appropriate permits when caving on public land. Basic concepts in landowner relations include the following:
    - The landowner controls access to the land; it is not public property.
    - Always be polite and respectful regardless of the situation or the landowner's attitude.
    - Abide by the landowner's rules and regulations for use.
- Prepare for extreme weather, hazards, and emergencies. For example, lightning strikes can run deep underground following paths of least resistance. In addition, groups have occasionally been trapped in caves because the exit became blocked by large amounts of snow and ice that fell while the group caved. Wet cavers that have a significant hike back to their vehicles in cold weather must be prepared.
- Cave in small groups. Split larger parties into smaller groups based on the nature of the cave. Typically, groups of 12 to 14 or smaller are appropriate.
- Repackage food to minimize waste and pick food appropriate for the cave environment. Food that does not crumble is best.
- Use a map and flagging tape to eliminate the use of marking paint or rock cairns. Beginner and intermediate cavers typically do not need to flag or mark as explained in the lesson about safety considerations.

Travel and Camp on Durable Surfaces
- If an obvious, well-used path exists, stay on it. Avoid creating additional trails if possible.
- Use established expedition camping and eating areas. Some caves are conducive to overnight or multiday caving. Attempt to concentrate activities like eating and camping in designated or well-used areas.
- Avoid camping or concentrating activities in pristine areas. One of the great thrills of visiting wild caves is experiencing a pristine environment with little or no visible human impact.
- Follow protocols specific to each cave; for example, in some areas of certain caves, cavers are not allowed to wear boots and must cave barefoot to avoid soiling pristine formations and areas.

Dispose of Waste Properly
- Pack it in, pack it out. Inspect all areas visited for trash or spilled foods. Pack out all trash, leftover food, and litter. Cavers may encounter excessive cave mold, sometimes in significant amounts when leftover food and litter is left in the cave. Items such as food do not decompose as they do on the surface. Food and litter can remain for long periods, contributing to mold production.

◆ Deposit solid human waste in an appropriate container to be carried out. A home-made toilet consisting of a 5-gallon (20-liter) plastic bucket lined with a plastic bag and equipped with a tight-fitting lid works well. Commercial chemical waste disposal systems also work well.

◆ At this point in the discussion, have students look at the surrounding area, pick up all crumbs, and place them in a clear plastic bag. Then pass the bag around the group to emphasize the quantity of food that a group can deposit on the ground when eating.

Leave What You Find

◆ Preserve the past: Examine, but do not touch, cultural or historic structures and artifacts.

◆ Leave cave formations and natural objects as you find them.

◆ Do not touch formations unless absolutely necessary for safety. While observing formations and natural features, avoid breathing directly on the objects. Even the human breath can contaminate and affect fragile formations.

Minimize Campfire Impacts   Campfires are not appropriate in the cave environment because of lack of ventilation and risk of smoke inhalation to humans and cave life. Fires cause significant damage.

Respect Wildlife

◆ Observe wildlife from a distance. Do not follow or approach.

◆ Never feed animals. Feeding wildlife damages their health, alters natural behaviors, and exposes them to predators and other dangers.

◆ Protect wildlife and your food by storing rations and trash securely.

◆ Avoid wildlife during sensitive times—when they are mating, nesting, raising young, or during hibernation periods or winter.

◆ Understand how to coexist with cave life, especially bats (see the sidebar).

Bat Tips

◆ If bats are disturbed during hibernation and are awoken, they may die because they will exhaust the energy they need to survive the winter.

◆ Do not shine lights directly on bats. Direct light off to the side while observing.

◆ Do not touch or move bats—fallen bats should not be rehung!

◆ Bats can bite, and some (less than 1 percent) carry rabies.

◆ Bats have excellent sight and hearing. They use echolocation to navigate dark caves.

◆ On average, bats consume 600 insects per hour.

◆ Bats range widely in size. Some are the size of a bumblebee, and others have a 6-foot (1.8-meter) wingspan.

◆ For more information on bats, visit Bat Conservation International (BCI) at www.batcon.org.

Be Considerate of Other Visitors

◆ Respect other visitors and protect the quality of their experience. Keep voices down— no yelling, singing, and so on. Novice groups tend to want to experience the dynamic acoustics found in many caves. Loud noise affects wildlife and other users.

◆ Be courteous. Yield to other users of the cave. Maintain appropriate distance between groups.

◆ If you encounter another group, communicate and work out a plan to move and eat in different areas.

◆ Avoid visiting caves during times of peak use.

Leave No Trace principles—Copyright: Leave No Trace Center for Outdoor Ethics. www.LNT.org.

Closure Activity

Landowner Relations (45 Minutes)

Divide the class into small groups. Hand out scenario cards (figure CV9.1) for the groups to use to develop a skit that illustrates relations with landowners. Students can use whatever costumes or props are available. Upon completion of the skits, the class will reunite and discuss what they observed in each skit, identify evidence of positive or negative landowner relations, and offer suggestions for improvement.

Follow-Up Activity

Identifying Poor LNT Practices (Time as Needed)

During a caving trip, have students identify remnants of negative LNT practices (for example, carbide waste, litter, cave mold). Discuss the impacts encountered to raise awareness.

ASSESSMENT

◆ Evaluate whether students understand basic ethical principles associated with caving by reviewing codes developed by professional associations and discussing ethical principles in an LNT context.

◆ Check that students practice ethical behavior in a cave environment during the group's first caving trip.

◆ Assess whether students value the need to practice ethical behavior and consistently model this behavior when caving by observing their practices when visiting caves.

TEACHING CONSIDERATIONS

◆ Set aside one to five hours for a class caving trip.

◆ Because of time constraints and the quantity of lecture material, you may want to break the lesson into two class sessions.

◆ Ask students who are already familiar with LNT principles and practices to help you explain and give feedback to novices.

Landowner Relations Scenario Cards

Scenario 1

The group leader calls and speaks to a member of the family. This person welcomes the group over the phone a week before the trip. Upon arrival another member of the family comes out to meet the group and wonders why the group is in their front yard.

Scenario 2

A group has a longstanding relationship with a landowner. They come and go as they wish. One day, after coming out of the cave, the group encounters a family member with a police officer. Trespassing charges are pressed. The group learns that the original landowner passed away two weeks earlier.

Scenario 3

A group comes out of a cave extremely wet, muddy, cold, and hungry. Their cars are parked in an open field adjacent to the landowner's house. Group members ask the group leader, "Where do we change?" Family members are approaching to ask about the experience and to visit a bit.

Scenario 4

One group member goes ahead to rig the entrance for a rappel. The rigger forgets a piece of gear and heads back to the cars. On the way back, in a hurry, the rigger forgets to close some of the gates. The rest of the group proceeds to the cave entrance. They pass through several gates, noting that some are open and some are closed. They observe livestock in various fields. When leaving the cave, they encounter an enraged, intoxicated farmer carrying a firearm and screaming, "You let my cows out. Why did you leave the damn gate open?"

FIGURE CV9.1   Scenario cards for the landowner relations activity.

From M. Wagstaff and A. Attarian, 2009, *Technical skills for adventure programming: A curriculum guide* (Champaign IL: Human Kinetics).

Caving Skills Checklist

☐ 1. Identify common cave formations.

☐ 2. Properly pack a cave leader's pack.

☐ 3. Clean and maintain a caving headlamp after use.

☐ 4. Construct a high-strength tie-off anchor system.

☐ 5. Build a wrap 2, pull 1 webbing wrap anchor system.

☐ 6. Build a wrap 3, pull 2 webbing wrap anchor system.

☐ 7. Construct a handline using a natural anchor.

☐ 8. Load and descend using a rappel rack device.

☐ 9. Load and descend using a figure-eight device.

☐ 10. Load and descend using a bobbin device.

☐ 11. Implement an ascending system using one of the sit–stand methods.

☐ 12. Implement an ascending system using one of the rope-walking systems.

☐ 13. Coil a rope using a caver's coil.

☐ 14. Navigate through a cave using a cave map.

☐ 15. Execute a mock cave evacuation using a litter.

Use the caving skills checklist as an additional tool to assess skills learned throughout this unit.

From M. Wagstaff and A. Attarian, 2009, *Technical skills for adventure programming: A curriculum guide* (Champaign IL: Human Kinetics).

GLOSSARY

bedding plane—The surface or boundary that divides two adjacent beds of sedimentary rock such as limestone.

bobbin—A descending device of European origin using two fixed friction wheels (capstans) made of aluminum. The rappel rope is snaked through the device. For personal use.

brake—To stop. Also a slang term for brake bar rack.

brake bar rack—A descending device consisting of a U-shaped metal bar to which are attached several metal bars that create friction on the rope. Some racks are restricted to use for personal rappelling, whereas others may also be used for rescue lowering. Also called a *rappel rack*.

brake hand—The hand that allows the rope to slide through it before it enters the rappel or friction device. Gripping the rope or pressing it against the thigh can add substantial friction to the system.

breakdown—Large piles of rocks or boulders that have fallen from the cave walls or ceiling during some point in its geological history.

calcite—The most common cave mineral, a crystalline form of calcium carbonate.

carbide lamp—A lamp that produces light by burning acetylene gas resulting from a mixture of carbide and water. Carbide is the shortened term for the rocklike chemical calcium carbide, CaC_2.

carbonic acid ($CaCO_3$)—A weak acid made from carbon dioxide and rain or soil water that slowly dissolves limestone to form caves.

cave formations—*See* speleothems.

caver—A person who explores caves in a safe and respectful manner.

caves—Natural void beneath the surface usually made up of several rooms and passages. Caves are located on all seven continents.

chockstone—Rock wedged in a crack, around which a rope can be run to create an anchor point.

column—A speleothem formed when a stalactite and a stalagmite have reached and grown together; also called a pillar.

commercial cave—*See* show cave.

domepit—A large dome-shaped cavity above a room or a passage created by solution, not breakdown. A domepit is often close to the surface because of water flow.

drapery—A thin curtain-shaped speleothem caused by a consistent stream of dripping water going down the same path like melted wax from a candle.

figure-eight descender—A device used for rappelling and, in some cases, for lowering. The device is in the general shape of an eight. The large ring creates friction on the rope, and the smaller ring attaches to a seat harness.

fixed friction device—A device that provides the same amount of friction from the top to the bottom of the rappel.

flowstone—Calcite deposits that have accumulated from water slowly flowing along a cave floor or wall.

free rappel—The term used when a rappeller hangs free without contacting a surface such as a rock face or cave wall. The rappeller literally hangs free, suspended in the harness while descending.

frog system—A sit–stand rope climbing system of European origin.

grotto—A group of local cavers who have organized themselves as a general interest group. A grotto may join the NSS and become recognized as a local chapter. Grottos set their own standards for membership and caving protocol. A grotto is also a small room or chamber opening off a larger one.

groundwater—Water that infiltrates the soil and is stored in slowly flowing reservoirs (aquifers); used loosely to refer to any water beneath the land surface.

ice caves—Formed by melting water that runs underneath glaciers.

karst—Landscape characterized by exposed limestone, thin soil layers, sinking streams, sinkholes, underground drainage, and an abundance of caves.

landowner—One who owns the property on which the specified cave entrance is located.

lava caves—Formed when cooling lava forms a rock roof while lava below continues to flow through a tube. When the lava cools, a hollow tube remains.

limestone—A gray blue sedimentary rock deposited in sea basins and composed of calcium carbonate, $CaCO_3$. Most caves are formed by the dissolution of limestone by acidic water.

National Speleological Society—An organization devoted to the study, exploration, and preservation of caves.

program trips—Institutional or commercial trips sponsored by an agency such as a school, university, parks department, or commercial cave operation. Trained leaders manage the group and follow agency protocol.

Prusiks—A type of friction hitch used in ascending and belaying.

rappel glove—A leather-palmed glove used while rappelling to prevent rope burn.

rimstone dam—A wall-shaped calcite deposit that impounds, or formerly impounded, a pool of water.

rope-walking systems—Any rope-climbing system that allows a climber to ascend a rope using a motion similar to walking up stairs.

sandstone caves—Located at the base of cliffs carved out by water or wind over time. These caves are typically shallow.

sea caves—Formed by ocean waves that erode rock at the base of cliffs.

show cave—A cave open to the public, usually with modifications such as electrical lighting and developed trails. Also known as a *commercial cave*.

sinkholes—Depressions apparent in the ground caused by solution of the underlying rock or by the collapse of the roof of an underlying cavern. Sinkholes may be steep-sided or shallow depressions.

soda straw—A thin, hollow stalactite that resembles a sipping straw. The growth at the tip is caused by water flowing down the inside of the straw. All stalactites begin this way.

solution caves—Usually formed in limestone (although sometimes in gypsum or dolomite), these are the most common type. Groundwater dissolves or erodes the soluble rock by flowing through cracks, faults, joints, and bedding planes to form caves.

speleothems—Secondary mineral deposits, such as a stalactite or stalagmite, that form in a cave.

spelunkers—The noncaver's term for cavers. This term fell out of favor with the caving community when the media used it to describe all people who go into a cave. Cavers consider themselves experienced people with training and technical knowledge. Spelunkers tend to be stereotyped as novice cavers with little experience and knowledge. A humorous saying among cavers is "Cavers rescue spelunkers."

stalactite—A cylindrical or conical speleothem that hangs from a ceiling or ledge.

stalagmite—A cylindrical or conical speleothem that rises from a floor or ledge.

static rope—A type of rope designed to be used in applications such as rescue, rappelling, and ascending where high-stretch, or dynamic, rope would be a disadvantage and where no falls, or very short falls, are expected before the rope catches the person.

troglobites—Animals that can only complete their life cycles underground ("cave dwellers"). Most troglobites exhibit various degrees of depigmentation and loss of eyes over many generations of evolution. These animals are usually smaller and have adapted larger antennae. Examples include albino cave fish, isopods, amphipods, and albino crawfish.

troglophiles—Animals that can live either in or out of the cave but move significantly up the food chain in caves ("cave lovers"). Many species of troglophiles mutate over time to become troglobites. Examples include segmented worms, snails, copepods, spiders, mites, millipedes, and cave crickets.

trogloxenes—Animals that cannot complete their life cycle in the cave; these animals live or hibernate in caves but regularly leave caves as well ("cave guests"). Examples include crickets, bats, pack rats, flies, cave salamanders, and gnats.

variable friction device—A friction device designed so that the rappeller is able to vary the amount of friction (more or less) while descending.

wild caves—An undeveloped cave in its natural state, in contrast to a show, or commercial cave, where lighting and paths have been added.

REFERENCES AND RESOURCES

REFERENCES

Jones, C. (2003). *A guide to responsible caving* (3rd ed.). Huntsville, AL: National Speleological Society.

Smith, B., & Padgett, A. (1996). *On rope: North American vertical rope techniques* (new rev. ed.). Huntsville, AL: National Speleological Society.

Zokaites, C. (Ed.). (2006). *Project underground: A natural resource education guide* (3rd ed.). Richmond, VA: Richmond Area Speleological Society.

RESOURCES

Boga, S. (1997). *Caving.* Mechanicsburg, PA: Stackpole Books. Overview: This user-friendly book discusses cave geology as well as caving practice, technique, and equipment.

Burger, P. (2006). *Cave exploring: The definitive guide to caving technique, safety, gear, and trip leadership.* Guilford, CT: Falcon Guide. Overview: A basic overview of caving as an adventure activity.

Hill, C., & Forti, P. (1997). *Cave minerals of the world* (2nd ed.). Hunstville, AL: National Speleological Society. Overview: A scientific explanation of every known mineral that a person would encounter in a cave.

Judson, D. (1995). *Caving practice and equipment.* Birmingham, AL: Menasha Ridge Press. Overview: A British approach to various aspects of caving, including equipment and techniques.

Leave No Trace (n.d.). Retrieved from www.lnt.org. Overview: A comprehensive site that includes information on LNT principles; practices; merchandise; teaching tools; and a list of programs, trainers, events, and partnerships.

Marbach, G., & Tourte, B. (2002). *Alpine caving techniques: A complete guide to safe and efficient caving* (English ed.). Allschwil, Switzerland: Speleo Projects, Caving Publications International. Overview. This book has excellent illustrations of systems and an outstanding overview of ascending and descending techniques. Keep in mind this is a French technique book and some of the terms may be different.

McClurg, D. (1996). *Adventure of caving.* Carlsbad, NM: D&J Press. Overview: This book offers a comprehensive overview of cave conservation, safety, hazards, equipment, knots, anchors, rigging, maneuvering, rappelling, and ascending.

Moore, G. (1997). *Speleology: Caves and the cave environment.* St. Louis: Cave Books. Overview: A comprehensive look at how caves are formed, speleothems, and cave life.

National Speleological Society. Retrieved from www.caves.org. Overview: An international source for overall caving information.

Rea, G. (Ed.). (1992). *Caving basics: A comprehensive guide for beginning cavers* (3rd ed.). Huntsville, AL: National Speleological Society. Overview: This book explains how to choose appropriate equipment for various cave environments and provides information about safe caving techniques, landowner relations, and cave geology.

Vines, T., & Hudson, S. (1999). *High angle rescue techniques* (2nd ed.). St. Louis: Mosby. Overview: Includes fully illustrated step-by-step skills for rescue work, and objectives and evaluations to provide a focus for learning new skills and clarifying existing skills in rope rescue.

Mountain Biking

Josh Whitmore

▷ **Introduction to Mountain Biking**

OVERVIEW

This lesson introduces the sport of mountain biking. It covers the history and development of the sport including some of the pioneers of mountain biking. The lesson also explores some of the current uses of mountain bikes and the role that they play in outdoor programs.

JUSTIFICATION

An exploration of the history of mountain biking can promote students' development as educated mountain bikers. Through the study of mountain biking, students learn that current techniques and practices have evolved over the past 30 years and that those approaches are likely to provide an enjoyable backcountry experience.

GOAL

To develop students' understanding of the history of mountain biking.

OBJECTIVES

At the end of this lesson, students will be able to

* identify the key historical figures responsible for the development of mountain biking (cognitive) and
* appreciate the history of mountain biking and how it contributes to the activity (affective).

EQUIPMENT AND AREAS NEEDED

None

RISK MANAGEMENT CONSIDERATIONS

* This lesson is normally part of the course introduction and frequently occurs indoors with no special risk management considerations.
* Should this discussion occur outdoors, check for environmental hazards specific to the teaching site and take appropriate precautions.

LESSON CONTENT

Introduction

By learning about the history of mountain biking, students can better understand the sport.

* This unit focuses on mountain biking in a group setting. Lessons in this unit were developed in a summer camp setting in which mountain biking was a program activity. In this setting, basic lessons were taught on camp property.

◆ Overall, the lessons contained herein are designed to be an example of a skills progression for the sport and to provide some examples and motivation for the knowledge and creativity of mountain bike instructors.

◆ The lessons in this unit include a wide range of topics. Naturally, some lessons are designed to help students learn the actual skill of riding a mountain bike, but other lessons concern mountain bike impact and etiquette, risk management techniques for instructors, bicycle maintenance, and games to play with groups.

Main Activity

History of Mountain Biking (30 Minutes)

The primary activity for this lesson is to deliver information to your students that you feel is relevant to your program. Students can play a significant role in the delivery of this information. For example, you can provide them with the following material printed on a series of notecards and charge them to create a short presentation based on the information.

◆ Bicycles have been ridden off-road since they were invented. The history of how the modern sport of mountain biking began is debatable, but most likely it began in the United States in the 1970s. Several groups of riders in different areas of the country can make legitimate claims to playing a part in the birth of the sport. Riders in Crested Butte, Colorado, and Cupertino, California, tinkered with bikes and adapted them to the rigors of off-road riding. Other riders around the country were riding their bikes on trails and fire roads much as their friends did with motorcycles (Warland, 2003).

◆ The Mountain Bike Hall of Fame recognized a group of riders in Marin County, California, as having played a central role in the birth of the sport as we know it today. These riders began racing down Mount Tamalpais (Mt. Tam) on old 1930s and 1940s Schwinn bicycles retrofitted with better brakes and fat tires. This group included Joe Breeze, Otis Guy, Gary Fisher, and Keith Bontrager, among others (Warland, 2003).

◆ Joe Breeze was the first to build a bicycle made purposely for the demands of off-road riding. He produced his first mountain bike in 1977. Tom Ritchey built the first regularly available mountain bike frame, which was accessorized by Gary Fisher and Charlie Kelly and sold by their company, which they called Mountain-Bikes. The name was later changed to Gary Fisher Bicycle Company (Warland, 2003).

◆ The first two mass-produced mountain bikes—the Specialized Stumpjumper and Univega Alpina Pro—were sold in 1982 (Warland, 2003).

◆ Since the first production of mountain bikes, the sport has continued to grow. Increasing numbers of people are visiting the backcountry on bicycle. Indeed, bicycling is a great way to travel and experience nature.

◆ Mountain bikers can move quietly and efficiently in the backcountry, so they can see a lot of terrain during a day trip.

◆ As the popularity of the mountain bike has grown, the demand for its inclusion in educationally based adventure programs has also increased (Kelly & Warnick, 1999).

◆ Summer camps, outdoor education programs, guide services, and other organizations around the world are using the mountain bike as a tool to reach program goals. As the percentage of programs that use mountain bikes grows, the need for experienced and knowledgeable mountain bike trip leaders also increases.

◆ This unit is designed as a reference for those trip leaders. It is intended to supplement the knowledge of experienced mountain bike trip leaders and to introduce them to the teaching of mountain biking for groups.

Closure Activity

What Is Your Cycling History? (10 Minutes or Longer)

Get a feel for the level of bicycle experience in your group.

◆ Have people ridden mountain bikes before? If so, on what kind of terrain?

◆ Have they ridden other types of bikes?

◆ What do participants hope to get out of the class?

◆ Discuss their expectations and your expectations as the instructor.

◆ Create a trivia quiz based on the information provided as a way to review the history of mountain biking.

Follow-Up Activity

Research on the History and Development of Mountain Biking (Time as Needed)

Create an opportunity for students to research additional text and materials on the history and development of mountain biking. A trip to the library or time on the Internet can yield a wealth of information on the subject. Viable topics of inquiry include the following:

◆ The advancement of technology throughout mountain bike history, such as the development of shock absorbers and disc brakes

◆ Mountain bike destinations and guidebooks

◆ The history of mountain bike racing

◆ The debate over mountain bike access to public lands

◆ Trail building and maintenance techniques

Create a trivia quiz based on the information provided as a way to review the history of mountain biking (figure MB1.1).

ASSESSMENT

◆ Evaluate whether students can identify the key people responsible for the development of mountain biking by having them verbally identify three major figures and their contributions to the development of the sport.

◆ Check that students appreciate the history of mountain biking and how it contributes to the activity by asking them to address this concept in small-group discussions.

Multiple Choice

1. Groups from which of the following areas can lay claim to the birth of the sport of mountain biking?
   a. Crested Butte, Colorado
   b. Cupertino, California
   c. Marin County, California
   d. all of the above
2. The first "mountain biking" on the slopes of Mount Tamalpais (Mt. Tam) was done on
   a. custom, purpose-built bicycles
   b. 1930s and 1940s Schwinn bicycles retrofitted with better brakes and fat tires
   c. the Specialized Stumpjumper
   d. the Univega Alpina Pro
3. When was the first bicycle purposely made for the demands of off-road riding produced?
   a. 1953
   b. 1966
   c. 1977
   d. 1982

Short Answer

(Answers are not in the unit text, but they are readily available through student independent research.)

4. Who was the winner of the first official mountain bike world championship race that took place in 1990 in Durango, Colorado?
5. What are some popular mountain bike destinations in North America?
6. What was the name of the first mass-produced shock absorber for mountain bikes?
7. Are mountain bikes allowed in designated wilderness areas? Why or why not?

Answers on following page ▶

FIGURE MB1.1   Sample quiz for the follow-up activity.

TEACHING CONSIDERATIONS

- The amount of time that you spend on this lesson depends on the effort that you choose to devote to the history and evolution of mountain biking.
- Consider placing text materials on reserve for students to research before and after initial mountain biking introductions.
- Slide or PowerPoint presentations depicting historical characteristics can add to student development and appreciation for mountain biking.
- The progression presented herein reflects the learning of skills in a controlled setting such as a grassy field before tackling challenging terrain on trails.
- The primary group that these lessons were designed for is 11- to 16-year-olds who have no experience with mountain biking. A group size of 6 to 12 students with 1 or 2 instructors is a standard student-to-instructor ratio.
- Although these lessons were designed with this population in mind, the entire unit can be adapted to suit any age, group size, or experience level.

Answers

1. d. all of the above
2. b. 1930s and 1940s Schwinn bicycles retrofitted with better brakes and fat tires
3. c. 1977
4. Ned Overend
5. Moab, Utah; Durango, Colorado; Snowshoe, West Virginia; Mammoth, California; Whistler, British Colombia, Canada; Western, North Carolina
6. Rock Shock
7. No, wilderness area management guidelines dictate nonmechanized forms of transportation and technology to maintain the primitive nature of the area. This has been interpreted by land managers to exclude the use of mountain bikes within wilderness area boundaries.

FIGURE MB1.1   *(continued)*

UNIT 4, LESSON 2

▷ Bicycle Sizing and Basic Operation

OVERVIEW

Bicycle fit, like the fit of a shoe, is critical for the user's comfort. Fit is also the basis for rider safety. In this lesson, students learn how to choose the right size of bike and customize the fit to their dimensions. This lesson also serves as the first step in teaching students how to operate the controls of the bicycle, including brakes and shifters.

JUSTIFICATION

People with little mountain bike experience usually begin the sport on a borrowed or rented bike. By understanding how to fit a bike, people will end up on the correct bike and will develop more quickly because they can attain fit consistency from one bike to the next. New riders, especially young new riders, often need instruction in the basic operation of brakes and shifters. This knowledge is necessary for rider safety and contributes to comfort on the bike.

GOALS

◆ To teach students how to choose the correct size of bicycle and fit themselves to it.
◆ To develop participants' ability to use the brakes and shifters of a mountain bike properly.

OBJECTIVES

At the end of this lesson, students will be able to

◆ describe how manufacturers size mountain bikes (cognitive);
◆ understand the principles of mountain bike gearing, gear selection, and braking (cognitive);

◆ demonstrate the ability to choose the correct size of bicycle and set the correct seat height (psychomotor);

◆ consistently choose the correct gear for the terrain and use brakes safely (psychomotor); and

◆ find confidence in knowing how to size a bike and operate its controls correctly (affective).

EQUIPMENT AND AREAS NEEDED

◆ Several bikes of different sizes to demonstrate how bikes are sized

◆ A bicycle **work stand** (a device that holds the bike off the ground and allows pedaling and shifting) to demonstrate proper usage of gears

◆ A large grassy field, if possible

RISK MANAGEMENT CONSIDERATIONS

◆ During these activities, students will be focused on themselves and their bicycles. Check the practice riding area for potential hazards such as low-hanging branches, hidden holes, and other environmental hazards that may catch them off guard.

◆ Have students move in a designated direction, clockwise or counterclockwise, to reduce the possibility of collisions between riders. Warn participants to look out for each other and pay attention to where they are going.

◆ Care must be taken with younger students who may have never ridden a mountain bike before. They may be good riders, but some have likely never used hand brakes. When going downhill for the first time, some riders grip the bars tightly and have a hard time letting go to grab the brakes.

◆ For beginner riders, you should try to instill a sense of conservatism and control when riding. Communicate that the best riders never ride recklessly or push beyond the edge of their ability level. Emphasize that riders with the most style always ride smoothly and in control.

◆ As with all mountain bike activities, include a pretrip talk before each day's activities. Make sure that all students have a properly fitted helmet that they wear correctly anytime that they are on the bike. Conduct a safety check on every bicycle before each ride.

LESSON CONTENT

Introduction (Five Minutes)

A mountain bike should feel like an extension of the body. With enough practice, riding a mountain bike through rough terrain should feel as easy as walking. The first step is for the student to choose the right size bike and properly fit it to her- or himself. Walking in the wrong size shoes is not comfortable and can be difficult. The same applies to a bicycle. After the participant has the right bike, she or he must understand some basic operations, such as shifting and braking. A firm grasp of these concepts will aid the rider in confidence and development.

Main Activities

Activity 1: Bike Fit (15 to 30 Minutes)

Adult mountain bikes usually come in five frame sizes, all with 26-inch (66-centimeter) wheels. Generally, they are measured from the center of the **bottom bracket** (A in figure MB2.1) to the center or top of the **top tube** (B in figure MB2.1).

FIGURE MB2.1   Bottom bracket and top tube.

Frame Size Measurement

◆ Proportionally, as the bike becomes taller it also becomes longer (as A becomes taller, B becomes longer).

◆ Youth mountain bikes are available in 24-inch (61-centimeter) and 20-inch (51-centimeter) wheel sizes and generally do not come in different frame sizes.

◆ As a child grows, he or she may go from a 20-inch (51-centimeter) wheel bike to a 24-inch (61-centimeter) wheel bike to the smallest frame size of the adult bikes.

Bike Size

◆ Pick a bike proportionate to the participant's height. A shorter person will ride a smaller bike.

◆ Have the student stand over the top tube, between the seat and the handlebars, with both feet flat on the ground.

◆ The clearance between the top tube and the crotch of the student should be a minimum of 1 to 2 inches (2.5 to 5 centimeters).

◆ Ideally, the clearance should be 2 to 3 inches (5 to 7.5 centimeters). An easy way to determine clearance is to have the student stand over the bike and put one hand on the handlebars and one on the seat. Then have the student pick up the bike as high as possible (figure MB2.2). Look for clearance between the tires and the ground. If the clearance is less than 2 inches (5 centimeters), the participant needs a smaller bike. If the clearance is greater than 4 to 5 inches (10 to 12.5 centimeters), the participant may be more comfortable on a larger bike.

◆ When sitting on the seat with hands on the handlebars, the student should not appear to be stretching to reach the handlebars, nor should the handlebars appear to be too far up under the student.

FIGURE MB2.2   Standover height.

Seat Height   Generally, the seat should be high enough to give the knee a slight bend when the foot is at the six o'clock (bottom) position in the pedal stroke. This seat height allows the leg to be in the position of the greatest power output for the down stroke. The following procedure is a fast and generally effective way to set seat height (figure MB2.3).

◆ Have the participant sit on the seat while you hold the bike up. When pedaling, the ball of the foot is usually directly over the pedal axle.

◆ Have the student slide the foot forward on the pedal until the heel is directly over the pedal axle (figure MB2.3*a*).

◆ Have the student pedal backward. With the heel on the pedal, the legs should extend all the way to the bottom of each pedal stroke. The knee should not bend and the hips should not rock on the seat to maintain foot contact on the pedal.

◆ Move the seat until proper extension occurs. When the student moves the foot back to the normal spot, the knee should receive the proper amount of bend during the pedal stroke (figure MB2.3*b*).

Bike fitting can be a time-consuming and chaotic activity. If working with a big group, demonstrate finding the correct size of bike and setting the seat height with the method explained earlier. Then have participants work in pairs to find a bicycle that fits and to set each other's seat height. Monitor the group and help when necessary.

FIGURE MB2.3   Knee bends: *(a)* the heel is directly over the pedal axle; *(b)* move the seat until proper extension occurs.

Activity 2: Brake Operation (30 to 45 Minutes)

Almost all mountain bikes in the United States are set up so that the right hand operates the rear brake and the left hand operates the front brake.

◆ A quick way to remember is to say, "Right, rear."

◆ The front brake produces about 70 to 80 percent of the braking power. The rider must take care, however, not to engage the front brake too firmly. Doing so could cause the front wheel to lock up, possibly resulting in the rider being thrown over the handlebars. This occurrence is known as an **endo**.

◆ Have students practice using their brakes, preferably on a flat, grassy surface. Have them stop by using just the rear brake and then by using just the front brake. They will begin to feel the difference between the two and will notice that the front brake is more powerful.

◆ Riders can slow the bike most effectively by using both brakes at the same time. They should avoid locking up the wheel or skidding. This action not only damages the trail but also compromises control because the wheels do not remain in motion. The concept is similar to the antilock brake system found in modern automobiles.

Activity 3: Gearing (30 to 45 Minutes)

Most mountain bikes have 24 or 27 possible gear combinations. This number of combinations results from having three **chainrings** in the front and eight or nine **cogs** in the rear. The front and rear **derailleurs** move the chain from one chainring to another or from one cog to another. As with the brakes, the right hand operates the shifter that controls the rear derailleur and the left hand operates the shifter that controls the front derailleur.

◆ The front chainrings set the range of gearing. This system is similar to that in a four-wheel drive truck that has four-wheel high and four-wheel low settings. The smallest chainring is used when going slowly or uphill. The middle chainring is used on relatively flat ground. The large chainring is used when going fast or downhill.

◆ After shifting the front derailleur to match the general terrain or speed, the rider fine-tunes the gearing with the rear shifter.

◆ Notice that as the chain moves closer to the centerline of the bike, in both the front and the rear, pedaling becomes easier.

◆ A rule of thumb is to shift before necessary. For instance, when approaching a steep uphill, the rider should shift into an easier gear before reaching the hill.

Two gear combinations, sometimes called **cross-chaining**, should be avoided (figure MB2.4).

◆ The first combination to avoid is having the chain on the smallest chainring in the front and the smallest cog in the rear. This gear combination is known as small and small (figure MB2.4a). Notice how this combination puts unneeded stress on

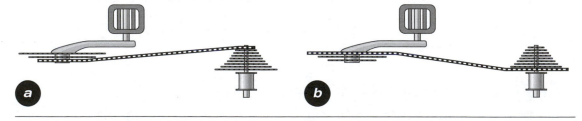

FIGURE MB2.4   Avoid these cross-chaining gear combinations: *(a)* smallest chainring to smallest cog; *(b)* biggest chainring to biggest cog.

the chain by moving it all the way toward the centerline of the bike in the front and far from the centerline in the rear. The chain must bend severely to line up for this gear combination.

◆ The other gear combination to avoid is the opposite of the first. In this combination the chain is on the biggest chainring in the front and the biggest cog in the rear. This gear combination is known as big and big (figure MB2.4b).

Teach braking before shifting. Being comfortable with the brakes is important for rider safety.

◆ A well-prepared instructor will ensure that all bikes are in the easiest (slowest) gear combination before the lesson begins.

◆ The best way to explain how to use the shifting systems is to demonstrate with a bike propped up on a work stand. A work stand holds the bike off the ground and allows you to turn the pedals with one hand and shift with the other.

◆ Demonstrate choosing the correct front chainring to match the terrain and then fine-tuning with the rear shifter.

◆ For practice time, stand in the center of a grassy area and have participants ride by. Call out various gear combinations as they approach. Include the easiest gear, or "granny gear," and the hardest gear. Watch to see that students are in the proper gears.

Closure Activity

Let's Ride! (20 Minutes to Two Hours)

After students show basic proficiency with these skills, it's time to go for a ride. Gravel roads or wide, smooth bike paths are good to start with.

◆ Pick a route that is not too strenuous but has some uphill and downhill sections. Monitor students on the ride and give feedback on gearing selection and braking use.

◆ Use terrain on the ride to demonstrate use of gears and brakes. For example, stop before a steep uphill to allow each student the chance to practice shifting into an easier gear before reaching the steep part of the hill. Stop on a steep downhill to coach proper brake usage.

Follow-Up Activity

Keep Practicing (20 Minutes to Three Hours)

The best follow-up activity is continued practice with these skills on subsequent rides.

◆ To help students learn what gear to be in for different terrain, call out gear combinations, such as "easiest gear" or "middle chainring" as needed while you are leading the group. Have the students pass the information back through the line, calling out the same information that you gave the first rider.

◆ Be sure to give frequent, specific, and appropriate feedback to each student on individual performance.

ASSESSMENT

◆ Check that students understand how manufacturers size bikes, know how to choose the correct size of bicycle, and can set the correct seat height by allowing them to fit themselves and help others do the same (your observation).

◆ Assess whether students understand the principles of mountain bike gearing, gear selection, and braking by observing their operation of the bicycle during drills before a ride as well as on the trail.

◆ Evaluate whether students consistently choose the correct gear for the terrain and use brakes safely by observing them operate the bicycle during drills before a ride as well as on the trail.

◆ Assess whether students found confidence in knowing how to size a bike and operate its controls correctly by observing them go through a progression of comfort and confidence while riding.

TEACHING CONSIDERATIONS

◆ Although this lesson is primarily designed for young beginner riders in a group setting, the principles covered are important for all age groups and ability levels.

◆ Depending on the age and experience of your students, this lesson can range from a 10-minute reminder for experienced riders designed to help assess their knowledge to a full 2-hour activity designed to introduce first-time mountain bikers to the bike and the sport.

UNIT 4, LESSON 3

▷ Group Games

OVERVIEW

This lesson outlines several games that a group of mountain bikers can play. Some are adaptations of group initiatives that you've probably played before. Some come directly from the sport of mountain biking itself. These activities were developed in a summer camp setting in which the groups were large, time was short, and access to mountain bike trails was limited. These games can serve as stand-alone activities or as follow-up activities to other lessons in this unit.

JUSTIFICATION

Mountain bike group games help students improve their riding skills in a fun setting while promoting group unity and team building. In this way, mountain biking, like other activities, can serve as a medium to help achieve program goals such as enhancing pride, craftsmanship, self-confidence, teamwork, and communication.

GOAL

To develop students' mountain biking skills while promoting group unity and teamwork.

OBJECTIVES

At the end of this lesson, students will be able to

- know each other's names (cognitive),
- demonstrate effective communication within a group (cognitive),
- show improvement in riding skills, especially fine-motor skills and balance (psychomotor), and
- achieve a greater sense of the importance of teamwork (affective).

EQUIPMENT AND AREAS NEEDED

- Twelve pieces of cord or string 25 feet (7.5 meters) long
- Twenty tent stakes
- Buzzer and bell (verbal sound effects can be substituted)
- Flagging tape
- Large grassy area, if possible

RISK MANAGEMENT CONSIDERATIONS

- During these activities, students will be focused on themselves and their bicycles. Check the practice riding area for potential hazards such as low-hanging branches, hidden holes, and other environmental hazards that may catch them off guard.
- As with all mountain bike activities, include a pretrip talk before each day's activities. Make sure that all students have a properly fitted helmet that they wear correctly anytime that they are on the bike. Conduct a safety check on every bicycle before each ride.

LESSON CONTENT

Introduction (15 Minutes)

"It is the sin of the soul to force young people into opinions—indoctrination is of the devil—but it is culpable neglect not to impel young people into experiences."

Kurt Hahn

Lead the class through an icebreaker known as the bicycle name game.

- Have all participants introduce themselves by name and identify themselves with a bicycle part. For example, a student can say, "Hi, my name is Fred, and I am the handlebars."
- After all students have introduced themselves, have the group construct a bicycle out of their bodies, using the parts that they claimed to be. Fred might stand with his arms out straight, and someone else might ball up between his feet as the front wheel.
- A variation has students draw their parts on paper, cut them out, and assemble the pieces of paper into a bicycle.
- For a group that already knows one another, have students pick a bicycle part that they identify with. For instance, Fred might be the handlebars because he likes to be in charge and steer things. This activity can lead to a discussion of the strengths that each person can bring to the group.

Main Activities

Activity 1: Entrapment (10 Minutes)

This fun activity helps students work on fine-motor skills and balance on the bike. It works well with big groups and can be an effective way to work on riding skills without going for a ride on trails.

◆ Create boundaries using rope to make a circle that is 30 to 40 feet (10 to 12 meters) in diameter. Keep the circle small enough to prevent riders from generating much speed. Make the circle smaller as people are eliminated.

◆ Everyone rides in a circular motion outside the circle until you signal the start of the game. Then everyone enters the circle, and the game is on.

◆ The object is to ride around and eliminate other riders from the game using the following rules:

– If your foot touches the ground, it is considered a **dab** and you are out.

– If you ride out of bounds, you are out.

– If you run into another rider or touch another rider in any way, then you (the offending rider) are out.

◆ The last person in the circle wins.

◆ This game is meant to be a low-speed game that works on riders' balance. Stress the importance of grace and balance rather than the battering-ram style of competition.

Activity 2: The Maze (30 Minutes)

This activity simultaneously works on two goals. First, it helps students develop balance and maneuverability on the bike. Second, the group initiative nature of the activity can be framed and debriefed to accomplish common group goals such as effective communication, teamwork, and leadership.

Setup

◆ Use the 12 pieces of rope or string that are 25 feet (7.5 meters) long to create a square grid system that is five cells wide and five cells long. Each cell is 5 feet (1.5 meters) square.

◆ Use the tent stakes to fix each end of the string. Make sure that the tent stakes do not stick out of the ground and create a hazard for falling riders.

◆ Predetermine a path through the maze. The path should start on one side of the maze and exit on the opposite side. In between, the route can go forward, sideways, or backward (no diagonal moves and not to a previously used square). You should keep the route secret from the students.

◆ The object of the game is to discover and ride the correct path through the maze.

Procedure

◆ Students go one at a time and must ride their bikes through the maze. If a rider's foot touches the ground within the maze, she or he must exit the maze and go to the back of the line.

◆ The first person must choose an entry square. If the rider gets it wrong, she or he gets the buzzer and must exit the maze. If the rider gets it right, she or he gets the bell and can choose another square.

- Each rider then makes her or his way through the maze, making decisions based on previous riders' experiences.
- The group must work together to memorize what squares were buzzers and figure out the route through the maze. Some tight maneuvering will be necessary to negotiate the route.
- After the group determines the route through the maze, the entire group must ride the route successfully.

Activity 3: Trials Competition (10 to 60 Minutes)

A scaled-down version of this competition can be extremely fun and an excellent way for students to refine technical handling skills. This activity does not require going to the trails to ride; it can be set up anywhere.

Trials competition is an international sport. We've all seen those crazy people on television doing unbelievable stunts—hopping over boulders, cars, and log piles. Those riders do not really appear to pedal their bikes anywhere; it seems as though they just leap from one place to another.

The competition is interesting. Officials create a section, and competitors take turns riding (or leaping) through the section without putting their feet down. Every time a foot touches the ground, an occurrence called a dab, the competitor gets a point. The person with the least number of points at the end of the day wins.

Setup

- Use flagging tape or rope to mark off a section of trail or any other place where a bicycle can reasonably be ridden. Find a place that is technically demanding and requires precise maneuvering to negotiate successfully. An area of trees where tight turns are necessary to maneuver can work well. The section may have logs, rocks, or other obstacles that must negotiated.
- Sections can be any length, but make it 20 to 30 feet (6 to 9 meters) long to make it interesting.
- Put one piece of tape on the right and one on the left. Each rider must stay between the tapes. Where the two pieces of tape start is the entrance, and where the pieces of tape end is the exit.
- The object of the game is to ride through the section without putting the feet down.
- Competitors cannot practice or ride the section before the competition.

Procedure

- Appoint someone as the judge to keep score or do this yourself.
- Riders take turns riding through each section. Their score starts when they enter the section and ends when they exit the section.
- Each rider tries to make it through the section by pedaling, jumping, hopping, or using any other technique to negotiate the section without touching the ground with the feet.
- Each time the rider's foot touches the ground, it is considered a dab, and the rider receives 1 point. Hands can also dab. For instance, an outstretched hand to a tree counts as a dab and receives 1 point.
- A rider can receive a maximum of 5 points for each section. After reaching 5 points, the rider must leave the section. Riders automatically receive 5 points if they touch both feet to the ground at the same time or run over the flagging tape and go out of bounds.

- If the rider makes it all the way through the section without putting down a foot, he or she has "cleaned" the section and receives 0 points.
- Each rider completes each section. The rider with the lowest score at the end wins.

Closure Activity

Slow Race (10 Minutes)

This classic activity works on balance and agility and can be done anywhere.

- Create start and finish lines.
- Riders must travel in a straight line from start to finish.
- If a rider's foot touches the ground, that person is out.
- The last person to the finish line wins.

Follow-Up Activity

What Was My Role? (30 Minutes or Longer)

As a debriefing tool, have each student pick a bicycle part that most represents his or her role in the previous activity and have the student describe why. For example, Isabel might pick a tire because she felt as though she provided the traction where the rubber meets the road to make the solution work.

ASSESSMENT

- Check that students know each other's names by quizzing them on others' names and offering an incentive like being able to go first or last.
- Evaluate whether students demonstrate effective communication within a group by observing group communication patterns when problem solving in activities.
- Assess whether students show improvement in riding skills, especially fine-motor skills and balance, by running a slow race at the beginning and end of the day or by leaving the trials competition sections set up to revisit on future rides.
- Evaluate whether participants achieve a greater sense of the importance of teamwork by observing group interaction during group games and tasks.

TEACHING CONSIDERATIONS

These activities are some ways in which mountain bikes can be used in group games. The activities work well with groups of 6 to 12 people. With a little creativity, a number of common group initiative games can be adapted to mountain bikes and can accommodate groups of various sizes. These activities are an excellent way to provide practice in skills when you do not have access to trails. Use them to assess students' skill level before riding through difficult terrain.

▷ Basic Safety Tips

OVERVIEW

This lesson outlines the basic safety issues and practices that you, as a mountain bike instructor, should be concerned with. The lesson includes several activities that can help a group of novice mountain bikers develop their awareness of safety and injury prevention. It also includes principles and practices that should become a part of the psyche of any mountain bike instructor.

JUSTIFICATION

Inherently, mountain biking has the potential to exhibit more objective risk than most other activities found in this book. Belays or throw ropes cannot catch a student when things go wrong. A mountain bike can rapidly reach extreme speeds. Add to the mix inexperienced riders and challenging terrain, and a potent recipe for disaster is present.

A complicating factor is that most novices who crash on a mountain bike remark that they were doing fine and were totally comfortable until something unforeseen caused them to crash. In fact, their inexperience blinded them to potential hazards. The mountain bike instructor must make students aware of these hazards and help them develop a sense of conservatism when riding in a group setting.

GOAL

To develop both the students' and the instructor's awareness of risk management in mountain biking.

OBJECTIVES

At the end of this lesson, students and instructors will be able to

- understand the proper safety equipment needed for mountain biking (cognitive);
- perform a daily safety check on their bicycles (psychomotor);
- manage the risk involved in tricky terrain, including scouting, spotting, and dismounting for particular sections (psychomotor);
- appreciate the skill of a conservative, always-in-control rider (affective); and
- adopt a sense of safety in a group setting (affective).

EQUIPMENT AND AREAS NEEDED

Three or four gym mats for roll practice

RISK MANAGEMENT CONSIDERATIONS

◆ Include a pretrip talk (outlined in the following section) before each day's activities.

◆ Make sure that all students have a properly fitted helmet that they wear correctly anytime that they are on the bike.

◆ Conduct a safety check (outlined in the following section) on every bicycle before each ride.

LESSON CONTENT

Introduction (Five to Seven Minutes)

As with all activities, instructors are obligated to inform their students of the risks inherent in mountain biking. The pretrip talk should become a regular part of every mountain bike experience that you instruct. You should also review the points in the pretrip talk before each subsequent ride with a group. Discuss the following points:

◆ Know common types of injuries: The most common injuries in mountain biking are scrapes and bruises, but the possibility does exist for more serious injury and even death. High-speed impact most often causes the more serious injuries such as broken bones or head injuries.

◆ Stay in control: The best way to avoid all injuries is to stay in control at all times. Never ride above your ability level and always ride slow enough to stop within sight distance.

◆ Wear a helmet: Always wear a helmet that is properly fitted and buckled anytime that you are on the bike.

◆ Avoid the endo: Serious injuries can occur as a result of being thrown over the handlebars. Take precautions to keep your weight back when riding downhill and be careful with that front brake.

Main Activities

Activity 1: Daily Safety Check (10 Minutes)

Conducting a basic safety check of the bicycle before the ride begins will prevent most incidents that arise from bicycle malfunction. The daily safety check (figure MB4.1) ensures that the bicycle has been properly assembled after transport and is in safe working condition. Check the following:

◆ Tire pressure: Squeeze each tire to see that it is properly inflated. Check with a tire pressure gauge if necessary.

◆ Quick releases: These devices hold the wheels to the bike and should be checked by making sure that they are tight.

◆ Brakes:
  – Many brake systems have a cable-release mechanism that allows the wheel to be easily removed for transport. Make sure that these have been reconnected.
  – Squeeze the brakes once to check for damaged or broken cables.
  – Pick up the bike a few inches (centimeters) and spin each wheel. Check to make sure that the brake pads are not rubbing the tire at any point in the revolution.

Daily Safety Check

Each day before riding, perform a basic safety check of your bicycle to ensure that it is in safe working condition.

- ☐ Tire pressure: Squeeze each tire to see that it is properly inflated. Check with a tire pressure gauge if necessary.

- ☐ Quick releases: These devices hold the wheels to the bike. Check to make sure that they are tight.

- ☐ Brake cable release mechanism: Make sure that it is connected.

- ☐ Brake cables: Squeeze the brakes once to check for damaged or broken cables.

- ☐ Brake pads: Pick up the bike a few inches (centimeters) and spin each wheel. Check to make sure that the brake pads are not rubbing the tire at any point in the revolution.

- ☐ Bounce test: Pick up the bike a few inches (centimeters) and drop it. Check any loose rattling parts.

- ☐ Twist test: Hold the front wheel between your legs and twist the handlebars; they should remain tight.

- ☐ Quick visual test: Give the bike a quick look over to check for any obviously loose or broken parts.

FIGURE MB4.1   Perform these daily safety checks to ensure that bicycles are properly assembled.

- ◆ Bounce test: Lift the bike a few inches (centimeters) off the ground and drop it, listening for any loose rattling parts. The bike should sound solid. Any rattling could indicate loose bearings or other parts somewhere on the bike.

- ◆ Twist test: Hold the front wheel between your legs and give the handlebars a twist. They should remain tight.

- ◆ Quick visual test: Give the bike a quick look over to check for any obviously loose or broken parts.

Activity 2: Introduction to Safety Equipment (10 to 15 Minutes)

As an instructor, you must outfit your students and yourself with the proper safety equipment to manage risk. The following is a list of required safety equipment and their purposes.

- ◆ Helmet: The use of helmets is standard for all organized programs. Proper fit is essential. Ensure that students wear their helmets correctly. A helmet that comes off is no help.

- ◆ Gloves: The first thing to hit the ground is usually a person's outstretched hands. A simple pair of riding gloves will prevent scrapes and cuts to palms, a place that causes a lot of pain and heals slowly.

- ◆ Protective eyewear: Glasses prevent objects such as branches or debris from the trail such as dirt or pebbles from hitting riders in the eyes. Well-ventilated, wraparound-style sunglasses work well. Wearing glasses is recommended except in conditions when glasses can limit visibility such as rain, fog, or low-light conditions such as dusk.

◆ First aid kit: Most people don't carry a first aid kit on their personal mountain bike rides. As an instructor, you should carry some basics. A small kit that contains items that are hard to improvise will be necessary to take along on the ride. A more complete kit can be kept in the vehicle. Take-along items include the following:
  – Gloves.
  – Microshield or other small pocket mask.
  – Tape—1.5-inch (4-centimeter) athletic tape is best.
  – Injectable epinephrine, most commonly for anaphylaxis resulting from bee stings, is advisable in backcountry settings where definitive medical care is over an hour away. Whether you should administer epinephrine depends on your medical certification and program guidelines.
  – Gauze to help stop bleeding in cuts and abrasions.

◆ Small tool kit: Small malfunctions with bicycles can become hazardous if not fixed.
  – At the minimum, you should carry the tools that will allow you to fix a flat tire or broken chain.
  – A small assortment of Allen wrenches or a bicycle-oriented multitool are usually sufficient for other field repairs.

Activity 3: Judo Roll (20 to 30 Minutes)

The object of the judo roll activity is to teach people how to crash. The best riders in the world crash, but they crash with skill. When things go wrong, a controlled crash will minimize injuries.

The best time to initiate this activity is after the initial instruction on sizing, basic operation, daily safety check, and before the first trail ride. This is a nonbicycle activity. Young teenage riders tend to do well with this activity.

◆ Set up the gym mats on a flat surface.

◆ Make sure that students are wearing helmets.

◆ Explain that a well-executed roll upon hitting the ground will spread out the impact and prevent injury.

◆ Have students start with a simple slow-motion somersault. They bend over and put their heads on the ground. Then they pitch over, rolling on their backs.

◆ They should practice this somersault with a bit more speed.

◆ Now, have them practice it at angles. Instead of rolling straight over, they can roll to the side, or fall to the side and roll. The idea is to mimic as many ways of falling as possible and then roll out of them. Train the body to roll instinctively when it meets the ground.

Closure Activity

Risk Assessment (10 to 30 Minutes)

After a ride, have students conduct a risk debriefing about the hazards encountered during the day. Here are some examples of questions to include:

◆ What was the most dangerous part of the trail today? What do think would have happened if someone had crashed there? What did we do to manage that risk?

◆ Did we have any crashes today? What caused them?

◆ Were you scared at any point today? Why?

Instructor Risk Management Toolbox

A good mountain bike instructor can quickly recognize a potential risk, accurately assess the skill level of the group, and apply the correct technique to manage the risk safely. The following is a list of management techniques that range from least to greatest intervention.

- Ride in front and reduce speed for tricky sections, preventing those behind from going excessively fast.
- Provide oral warnings while riding. Simple cues like "Watch your head" or "Slow down for this section" can alert riders to potential hazards.
- Stop the whole group before a tricky section and have them ride one at a time. You then have a chance to evaluate and coach each rider.
- Scout the section. Leave bikes behind and walk the section talking about hazards and proper technique needed to negotiate tricky segments.
- Spotting can be effective for mountain biking. As with spotting for rock climbing, the proper spotting stance is one foot in front of the other with hands up. The idea is not to catch the rider but to prevent her or him from falling a great distance (such as at a steep drop-off to the side of the trail) or hitting a hazardous object (such as sharp rocks, stumps, or roots). Good spotting cannot absorb all the impact of a falling rider, but it can help guide the rider to a safer landing. Use caution when spotting because the bicycle can become a hazard to the spotter.
- Dismount for some sections. Sometimes, the risk of riding is too great for the skill level of the group. If in doubt, it's always better to walk. As an instructor, you must serve as a role model in making these decisions and then stick to them.

- Was there ever a point that you felt as if you were about to crash? What caused this? How did you prevent yourself from crashing?

Follow-Up Activity

Safety Team (Time as Needed)

- On a subsequent trail ride, appoint a student or pair of students to be the safety team. Their job, with your careful supervision, is to make the risk management decisions for the group.
- For each hazard, they must choose one of the techniques from the risk management toolbox.

ASSESSMENT

- Check that students conduct a daily safety check on their bicycles by observing this ritual and making it part of every ride.
- See that students understand the safety equipment needed for mountain biking by having them debrief the risk management issues and practices initiated during the day.
- Check that students manage the risk involved in tricky terrain, including scouting, spotting, and dismounting for dangerous sections, by observing them to assess whether they perform these techniques and by having students lead the group in risk management as described in the follow-up activity.

◆ Evaluate whether students appreciate the skill of a conservative, always-in-control rider by observing their conduct and attitude on every ride.

◆ Assess whether students adopt a sense of safety in a group setting by participating in the daily risk debriefing and whether they make appropriate safety calls for themselves.

TEACHING CONSIDERATIONS

◆ Risk management is not just a couple of topics to present and then forget about.

◆ Risk management should be prominent in all activities and at all times on a ride.

◆ Consistency and role modeling are key to making risk management part of the culture of your group.

UNIT 4, LESSON 5

▷ Riding Techniques

OVERVIEW

Going beyond the basic operation of a bicycle, this lesson focuses on specific techniques that riders commonly use while mountain biking. These skills include starts and dismounts on tricky terrain, riding over logs or other obstacles, downhill and uphill techniques, and cornering.

JUSTIFICATION

This lesson contains the bulk of information about mountain bike riding techniques. Skills presented here are what separate mountain biking from other forms of cycling. Specific instruction and concentration on an appropriate progression of these techniques speeds the development and confidence of the rider, which in turn makes a more competent and safe rider. For beginner riders, this lesson provides proper instruction in technique so that they learn the right way the first time and avoid learning bad habits or improper technique that they must later unlearn to progress.

GOAL

To develop students' ability to negotiate typical mountain bike terrain with proper technique.

OBJECTIVES

At the end of this lesson, students will be able to

◆ use the appropriate riding technique for a specific context (cognitive),

◆ understand the biomechanics and physics involved with bicycle and body movement over varied terrain (cognitive),

◆ demonstrate proper riding technique on typical mountain bike terrain (psychomotor), and

◆ achieve pride and confidence in properly executed riding techniques (affective).

EQUIPMENT AND AREAS NEEDED

◆ Sections of logs 3 to 4 feet (90 to 120 centimeters) long, ranging from 3 to 4 inches (8 to 10 centimeters) in diameter to 10 to 12 inches (25 to 30 centimeters) in diameter

◆ Stakes or wedge materials to prevent the log sections from rolling

◆ Large grassy field for log practice

◆ 10 feet (3 meters) of rope

RISK MANAGEMENT CONSIDERATIONS

◆ During these activities, students will be focused on themselves and their bicycles. Check the practice riding area for potential hazards such as hidden holes, low-hanging branches, and other environmental hazards that may catch them off guard.

◆ Have students move in a designated direction, clockwise or counterclockwise, to reduce the possibility of collisions between riders. Warn participants to look out for each other and to pay attention to where they are going.

◆ Ensure that students follow a designated progression. That is, they should attempt small logs before big logs or moderate hills before steep hills. Students must master each level before progressing to the next one. Don't let them skip steps.

◆ Much of this lesson will occur on the trail when ideal teaching locations are encountered. You must have knowledge of the trail and awareness of the difficulty and danger of technical sections of that trail.

◆ The difficulty of the trail should never exceed the skill level of students. Consider making certain sections mandatory dismounts until students demonstrate appropriate skill level. Another option is to scout the upcoming section, much as you would scout a rapid on the river. Examine the hazards and discuss proper line and technique.

◆ As with all mountain bike activities, include a pretrip talk before each day's activities. Make sure that all students have a properly fitted helmet that they wear correctly anytime that they are on the bike. Conduct a safety check on every bicycle before each ride.

LESSON CONTENT

Introduction

When you were very young, you learned how to walk. Today, you can walk over virtually any terrain with comfort. Your body learned how to balance with fine-motor skills to keep you upright. Learning how to ride a mountain bike resembles that process. At first, riding feels strange and awkward, but with practice and consistency, it can become as natural as walking. The way to speed this progression is to work deliberately on skills and work in a progression. Let the mastery of one skill lead to more advanced skills, a building process. Soon your body will react naturally and be able to achieve a synergy of bicycle, body, and terrain.

Main Activities

This lesson encompasses a large range of skills from beginner-oriented techniques to those suited to more expert riders. You can present these skills in a variety of ways to match the size and experience level of your group.

◆ Some skills such as riding over logs and obstacles are best presented to students in a practice setting before they encounter them on the trail.

◆ A large grassy field works well for this purpose because it allows practice in a controlled setting.

◆ Other skills are best taught when the opportunity arises on the trail. In any case, for each of these topics provide an explanation of the skill, a well-modeled demonstration, and lots of time to practice while giving direct feedback on performance.

Activity 1: Starts and Dismounts (10 Minutes)

Getting started on a bicycle and eventually coming to a stop are basic skills that we should not take for granted. Mountain biking involves starting and stopping in difficult terrain where attention to technique is critical to success.

Beginning Riders   These are the basic techniques for beginner riders and can be taught in conjunction with the basic operation lesson.

◆ Starting:
- Straddle the bike.
- Place one foot on the pedal in the two o'clock position, ready to initiate the **power stroke**.
- With both hands on the handlebars, push with the foot that is still on the ground.
- After the push, pedal forward with the foot that is already on its pedal. This technique should provide enough momentum to get going.
- Position the other foot on its pedal as soon as possible.

◆ Basic dismount:
- Apply the brakes.
- Disengage one foot from the pedal in the up, or twelve o'clock, position.
- As you stop, rise from the seat and place that foot on the ground for stability.

Intermediate Riders   The following techniques work well on steep inclines where producing sufficient momentum with the basic standing start is difficult or when you want to stop on a steep downhill.

◆ Tree start:
- Straddling the bike with one hand on the handlebars, hold the brake. Place the other hand on a nearby tree.
- Use the tree for balance and situate both feet on the pedals. Have one pedal at the two o'clock position ready to apply the power stroke.
- With one motion, push from the tree and pedal forward to gain enough momentum to get started.

◆ Tree stop:
- Pick a tree near the trail that you can easily reach with one hand.
- Slow down and come almost to a stop beside the tree.
- Reach out and grab the tree to maintain balance.

- Hang on to the tree with your feet on the pedals while you rest or wait for others. Alternatively, you can disengage your feet from the pedals and get off the bike.

Advanced Riders   These techniques are most commonly used by racers to dismount and remount the bike quickly, leap over obstacles, or run up sections of trail that are too steep to ride.

◆ Flying start:
  - Pushing with both hands on the handlebars, take three or four running steps next to the bike.
  - In one fluid motion, leap onto the seat and throw the leg closer to the bike around the back and over the seat. Done properly, you should land with the seat hitting you on the inner thigh.
  - Slide the rest of the way onto the seat and engage both feet on the pedals at the same time.
◆ Running dismount:
  - Apply the brakes but don't come to a complete stop.
  - Disengage one foot in the up position.
  - Swing that leg around behind the bike and then between the other leg and the bike while the bike is still moving.
  - In one motion, disengage the foot that is still on its pedal and step to the ground with the other foot, the first foot you disengaged.
  - Done properly, you should hit the ground running, ready to leap quickly over unrideable objects.

Activity 2: Riding Over Obstacles (One Hour)

To teach these skills effectively, set up practice logs in a large grassy field where consequences of a fall are minimal. Develop students' skill thoroughly in this controlled setting before venturing onto the trail to practice.

Beginning Riders   Use small logs, no larger than 4 inches (10 centimeters) high.

◆ One option is to run over the log without lifting the front wheel. The best way to do this is to be in a standing position on the bike and use the arms and legs as shock absorbers to soak up the impact. Have students see how large a log they can clear with this technique.
  - Before reaching the log, gain enough momentum to carry yourself easily across the obstacle while coasting.
  - Coast in the standing position with the arms and legs slightly bent.
  - Ride over the log, absorbing the impact with arms and legs.
◆ Another option for riding over small logs is to lift the front wheel over the log and let the rear wheel roll over the log. Practice the wheel lift first by placing a rope on the ground to stand in as the log.
  - Approach the rope coasting in the seated position.
  - Bend the arms to move the upper body closer to the handlebars.
  - Thrust the body upward and pull up on the handlebars to lift the front wheel off the ground.
  - You can increase the amount of wheel lift by using a strong pedal stroke in conjunction with the arm lift.
  - Use the rope as a timing cue and try to clear it with the front tire.

✦ When students are proficient with the wheel lift and can properly time the crossing of the rope, have them move on to the small practice logs.

✦ After the front tire has cleared the log and landed back on the ground, the rider should stand up to allow the legs to absorb the impact of the rear wheel crossing the log.

Intermediate Riders   Use medium logs, 4 to 10 inches (10 to 25 centimeters) high. Logs of this height require a front wheel lift. After the front wheel is over, the next consideration is whether the chainrings will hit the log.

✦ If not, allow the rear wheel to roll over the log, keeping your weight far enough back to avoid being thrown over the front of the handlebars (the endo).

✦ If the chainrings are going to hit the log, use the **chainring method of log crossing**.

– Lift the front wheel only to the top of the log.

– Roll forward until the chainrings hit the log. Time your pedal stroke so that the bottom of one of the pedals (with your foot on top) ends up on top of the log.

– Pedal forward (step down) using the chainrings to pull the bike over the log. Be careful not to damage the chainrings.

– After the rear wheel is on top of the log, pedal forward and keep weight back to avoid the endo.

Advanced Riders   Advanced riders should cross logs using the **lunge method of log crossing** (for logs over 10 inches, or 25 centimeters, high) or by bunny hopping (can be used on any size log).

The lunge method can be used on any log high enough to hit the chainrings when crossing. The chainring method (described in previous section) can be used to get over these logs, but the method is generally slow and can cause damage to the chainrings. The lunge method, when done properly, allows riders to clear such logs quickly without hitting their chainrings. Allow plenty of time for practice because this method is difficult to master.

✦ Lift the front wheel to the top of the log.

✦ The moment that the front wheel touches the top of the log, initiate a lunge, throwing the bike forward and lifting with the feet, placing the rear tire on top of the log. Your torso will remain temporarily stationary over the log as you execute the lunge.

✦ Done properly, the front tire will touch the top of the log and then roll forward to the ground as the rear tire is lifted to the top of the log.

✦ Roll forward and keep your weight back, being careful not to be thrown over the handlebars when the front wheel hits the ground.

The **bunny hop** can be effective to clear objects such as logs, roots, rocks, puddles, and ditches. A lot of speed is required to execute the move successfully, and therefore the bunny hop is the fastest way to clear obstacles. Mastery of bunny hopping takes a lot of practice and can be harsh on bikes, especially wheels. Because of the speed involved, hopping can be dangerous. Be sure that students are ready before introducing this skill.

◆ Locate the object to be cleared. Timing is critical. When first practicing, pick an imaginary spot on the ground. Practice hopping this spot until you have the timing down.

◆ Gain enough speed to carry you over the object. The approach is faster than it would be if you were going to cross the object using another method, such as the lunge.

◆ Here, you use either of two methods, depending on the task. One is for distance, to clear a puddle or a ditch, for example. The other technique is for height, to use in clearing a log.

◆ To clear for distance, follow these steps:
 – Crouch down close to the bike.
 – Spring upward, pulling equally with the hands and feet. The wheels will come off the ground at the same time, achieving the same height.
 – Pull the bike up as far underneath you as possible by bending your knees and elbows.
 – Both wheels should return to the ground at the same time.

◆ To clear for height, follow these steps:
 – Crouch down close to the bike.
 – Spring upward, pulling first with the hands and then with the feet. The front tire should come off the ground first, closely followed by the rear.
 – When the front tire is directly over the object, push forward on the handlebars and lift with the feet, bringing the bike as far up underneath you as possible to clear the object. The motion is like a quick version of the lunge method although the bike does not touch the object.
 – Lightly set the bike back down to the ground.

Activity 3: Descending (20 Minutes)

Teach going downhill in a controlled setting such as a grassy incline or a smooth section of trail that has minimal consequences if a fall occurs. Present the skills and have students demonstrate them in this setting before progressing on to more challenging terrain.

Standing Up
◆ Stand up to allow for more shock absorption through the arms and legs.
◆ Keep the knees and elbows slightly bent to allow shock absorption.
◆ Keep the pedals level to the ground, at three o'clock and nine o'clock for greater clearance and better weight distribution.

Weight Distribution
◆ Shift weight back to maintain the center of gravity between the wheels. The steeper the slope is, the farther back you must shift your weight to prevent the endo.
◆ On slight grades squeeze the seat between your thighs for added stability.
◆ On steeper grades you must move your weight farther back. Spread your legs slightly to allow the seat to pass between them. Push with your arms to get your weight as far behind the seat as possible. In extreme downhill situations, your bottom may occasionally rub the rear tire.

Braking: Front Versus Rear

◆ The front brake provides 70 to 80 percent of the stopping power, but you must take care not to press the front brake too firmly. Doing so could throw you over the handlebars.

◆ Use both brakes at the same time, always being careful not to apply the front brake too firmly.

◆ Shift your weight farther back when braking because momentum will tend to throw you forward.

◆ Never skid your tires. By not locking your wheels, you maintain more control and minimize damage to the trail.

Activity 4: Techniques for Better Climbing (15 Minutes)

Going uphill can be one of the hardest things to do on a bicycle. A few simple techniques will make the task easier on the bike and the body.

Gearing

◆ Shift before the hill. Shifting under load can be difficult and harmful to the bike. If shifting on the hill under load, just before shifting give the pedals a quick, hard revolution to gain momentum. While shifting, pedal softly to allow the shift to happen smoothly without being under load. Practice timing to achieve a quick, efficient shift.

◆ Select an appropriate gear. Choosing a gear that is too high will cause you to bog down. Choosing a gear that is too low will cause you to spin out and lose momentum.

Weight Distribution

◆ Lean forward or slide forward on the saddle to maintain the center of gravity between the wheels. The steeper the grade is, the farther forward you have to shift.

◆ Seek that happy medium between shifting weight too far forward and losing traction, and not shifting weight forward enough and having the front wheel lift off the ground.

Momentum

◆ Keep enough momentum to balance and roll over obstacles.

◆ On steep technical slopes, going faster will help you roll over the bumps. Rest where the trail is smooth and does not require much momentum to negotiate.

Standing Versus Sitting

◆ Sitting is more efficient, but standing is occasionally necessary to power over short hills.

◆ Standing is also necessary when large obstacles, such as steps or ledges, are on the trail.

◆ Otherwise, stay seated to conserve energy and maintain traction.

Activity 5: Cornering (15 Minutes)

◆ Do the majority of the braking before the turn. Heavy braking in the turn can cause loss of control and prevent you from executing an efficient, smooth turn.

- If you need to brake in the turn, feather the brakes lightly with smooth transitions on and off the brake. Avoid sudden jerky or aggressive braking, which will cause the wheels to lose traction.
- Lean the bike into the turn.
    - The higher your speed, the more you have to lean to maneuver through the turn.
    - In bad traction situations—loose, sandy, or wet—try to keep the bike more upright to prevent the wheels from losing traction and washing out. Lean your upper body deep into the turn, keep the bike more upright, and hang out the inside foot for added stability.
    - Put the outside pedal down, in the six o'clock position, for greater clearance and stability.

Closure Activity

Let's Ride (20 Minutes to Three Hours)

- The best way to solidify the skills learned in this lesson is to ride, ride, ride. Pick trails that appropriately use and challenge the skills that your group is developing.
- Rather than blast through the ride, stop at each section on the trail that puts these skills to use.
- Monitor each student through the section and provide feedback on the performance of each.
- Deliberate reinforcement of the skills that the students have learned will enhance their ability to apply them to differing settings.

Follow-Up Activity

Using the Skills in Different Ways (Five Minutes to Two Hours)

- For weight distribution, discuss the principles outlined earlier and have students try shifting their weight forward and back on a steep climb to see how doing so affects traction and steering.
- A further progression of skills is to have students practice ascending a step in the trail (usually logs or timbers placed horizontal to the direction of the trail to prevent erosion).
- The technique that riders should use is similar to that used to cross a log, but they need much more momentum because of the slope.
- In teaching settings such as a summer camp in which you have ample time with students, you can have them undertake follow-up projects that may include writing in a journal, drawing specific riding techniques, or creating a video that models each skill to the best of their ability.

ASSESSMENT

- Check that students can select the appropriate riding technique to use in a specific context by asking them to describe the proper technique before attempting an obstacle or section of trail.

- Assess whether students understand the biomechanics and physics involved with the bicycle and body movement over varied terrain by asking them specific questions such as "If you hit that rock in that direction, which way will the momentum make your body move?"
- Have students demonstrate proper riding technique on typical mountain bike terrain by observing them ride both in practice settings and along the trail.
- Assess whether students achieve pride and confidence in properly executed riding techniques by observing their attitude and monitoring their drive to improve.

TEACHING CONSIDERATIONS

- A common mistake among riders is to go too fast for their ability level. Excessive speed leads to reckless riding and many accidents. From the beginning you must instill a sense of conservatism and control.
- Remember that these skills represent a progression. Always start with the basic skills before moving on to advanced skills.
- Realize that a rider will not progress through all these skills in one day. Riders will require many rides, possibly even years, to become proficient with all skills presented in this lesson.
- The key is to match your teaching to the skill level of your students. In fact, presenting skills that fall somewhat short of your students' current ability reinforces those skills and helps you assess what they need.
- On the other hand, overestimating the skill level of your students can have dire consequences.

UNIT 4, LESSON 6

▷ Leave No Trace Considerations

OVERVIEW

This lesson outlines the recommendations for mountain biking suggested by the Leave No Trace Center for Outdoor Ethics. Many LNT principles are consistent across all activities and settings, but this lesson focuses on specific practices and considerations for mountain bike day trips.

JUSTIFICATION

Access to public lands for mountain bikes is a sensitive subject. In some areas, conflicts have occurred between mountain bikers and other user groups such as horseback riders and hikers (Cessford, 2002). The average person who is not a mountain biker would characterize the sport as extreme and damaging to the environment (Cessford, 2002). Research has shown, however, that mountain biking is in fact less damaging to trail systems than horse use and causes no greater impact than human foot traffic when the appropriate riding techniques are followed (Wilson & Seney, 1994; Thurston & Reader, 2001). With proper knowledge and practice of LNT principles, mountain bikers can minimize their impact and improve or maintain relationships with other user groups, thus improving their overall image. To maintain access to public lands, mountain bikers must assume a high degree of responsibility on this topic.

GOAL

To improve students' understanding and practice of LNT principles of mountain biking.

OBJECTIVES

At the end of this lesson, students will be able to

◆ describe LNT practices for mountain biking (cognitive),

◆ assess specific situations based on LNT ethics and critique practices (cognitive),

◆ demonstrate specific LNT practices while riding (psychomotor), and

◆ develop a personal ethic regarding the impacts associated with mountain biking (affective).

EQUIPMENT AND AREAS NEEDED

◆ Note cards

◆ Pen or marker

◆ Leave No Trace materials including plastic cards that list the seven LNT principles or the mountain biking edition of the LNT pamphlet (2001), available for purchase at www.lnt.org

RISK MANAGEMENT CONSIDERATIONS

The greatest potential for risk in this activity is an emotional one. Your students may closely identify with authors of the quotations in the activity. Close friends or members of their families may also hold attitudes similar to those expressed in the quotations. Care should be taken to avoid any negative connotation with the attitudes expressed in the quotations. Include a briefing before any role-play or skit activity to communicate the expectation not to portray people in a negative manner.

LESSON CONTENT

Introduction

The seven LNT principles should serve as the foundation for personal practices when participating in any outdoor recreation activity. This section outlines the seven principles and their application to mountain bike day trips.

Main Activities

Activity 1: Leave No Trace Principles (One Hour)

The following information can be conveyed through a lecture format, through teachable moments along the trail, or by other creative means such as flashcards or games.

Plan Ahead and Prepare Riders can avoid causing impacts through adequate preparation. Be informed.

◆ Know the area in which you will be riding and the conditions that you are likely to encounter.

◆ Ride only on open trails. Find out which trails are open to mountain bikes and whether any are seasonally or temporarily closed to bikes.

◆ Don't count on a signpost at the trail to give you information. Carry a map if riding in unfamiliar territory.

◆ Plan for the worst-case scenario. Mountain biking is a unique backcountry activity because a rider can travel a great distance in a short time. In 30 minutes, a rider can be several miles (kilometers) from a trailhead and definitive medical care. Some preparation is required in case the worst happens to you.
  – Wear a helmet.
  – Carry some food. If you'll be out longer than 90 minutes, your body will need a little fuel.
  – Carry tools, tube, pump, and patch kit. Be prepared for flats or other mechanical failures. A breakdown could result in a long walk out.
  – Take adequate clothing. Be prepared for the weather and environment that you will encounter. Does your route take you to a higher elevation that is likely to be more exposed and cooler? Are you expecting rain, which may require you to add additional layers to maintain warmth?

Travel and Camp on Durable Surfaces For mountain bike travel, durable surfaces are trails, dirt roads, and pavement. Never travel off trail on a mountain bike.

◆ Don't widen trails. Stay in the center of even the narrowest single track. Ride over obstacles, not around them. If the obstacle is not appropriate to ride over, dismount and walk over it. In worst-case scenarios, trails are widened as riders continually seek a fresh smooth line around difficult sections. Be sensitive to stay off the downhill edge of trails. This edge of the trail is more prone to breaking away, creating a potential path for rainwater runoff erosion.

◆ Don't alter the trail or create new ones. Ride the mountain; don't make the mountain rideable by altering obstacles or sections of trail.

◆ Avoid skidding. You maintain more control over your bicycle when the wheels are still turning. Skidding creates ruts and other damage that speeds erosion and can leave marks on slickrock.

◆ Avoid riding when trails are muddy.
  – When the trail is soft, mountain bikes can gouge the trail and hasten erosion.
  – In places of perpetual mud or when encountering isolated muddy sections, ride slowly through the middle of the mud hole to avoid making the spot wider.

◆ Avoid riding through water crossings if
  – muddy sections at the entrance or exit could contribute to stream bank erosion or
  – the water is deeper than your **hubs** or bottom bracket. Submersion of these parts may not only damage the bike but also release harmful chemicals or lubricants into the water body.

If you plan to camp on your mountain bike trip, follow the appropriate guidelines for using durable surfaces.

Dispose of Waste Properly   Pack it in, pack it out. Remove all items that you brought with you.

◆ Punctured tubes, foil backing to patches, and energy gel wrappers are common items of trash related to mountain biking found on trails.

◆ Food-related scraps such as apple cores, banana peels, and crumbs are also items that riders should pack out. This also helps keep animals safe by preventing their dependence on scraps or handouts as a food source.

◆ Follow the recommended human waste disposal methods for your area. Be aware that solid and liquid human waste can pollute water sources, affect flora and fauna of the area, and create social impacts for other visitors.

Leave What You Find   Because mountain bikes can travel great distances, the potential to transport nonnative plants that stick to bikes or clothing is high. Such transportation can hasten the spread and proliferation of these species.

◆ Learn what concerns exist for exotic species in your area and how to identify the aberrant plants.

◆ Check clothes and bikes before and after each ride for plant seeds.

◆ Wash bikes after traveling in areas where exotic species are known to be present.

Minimize Campfire Impacts   If you plan to camp on your mountain bike trip, follow the appropriate guidelines for campfire use in your area.

Respect Wildlife   Mountain bikers travel more quietly and quickly than other trail users, so they have the potential to surprise wildlife. On the other hand, they follow more predictable travel patterns and directions than hikers do. Like all backcountry travel, mountain bikers should keep the following points in mind:

◆ Don't follow or approach animals. Keep your distance from animals and let them depart the area in their own time. Avoid spooking or pursuing animals, and never feed them.

◆ Stick to the trail. Predictable travel patterns are less obtrusive to wildlife as they become habituated to human travel on the trails. When you stick to these patterns (staying on trail), wildlife are less likely to perceive you as a threat.

◆ Avoid sensitive times for wildlife. Animals that are mating, nesting, or raising young are more susceptible to human activity. Many areas are closed to human use during certain times of the year for this reason. Check with your local management agency to understand these closures or concerns.

Be Considerate of Other Visitors   Social interactions are another important category of impacts to consider. The nature of mountain biking can create negative interactions with other user groups, even among other riders. A few simple guidelines can help:

◆ Yield to hikers and horses. Slow down and orally acknowledge your presence. For horses, stop completely and dismount your bicycle. Ask stock users what they would prefer you to do. Some will want you to remain still as they pass; others will instruct you to pass as they remain stationary. Most will prefer that you maintain oral contact with them and step to the downhill side of the trail so that the animals do not feel threatened by your being above them.

◆ Don't race on recreational trails. Always maintain a speed that will allow you to stop within your sight distance. Fast riding on popular recreation trails at busy times is dangerous to both mountain bikers and other users.

◆ When descending, yield to climbing cyclists. Getting started again is much more difficult when riding uphill.

◆ Travel in small groups. Try to ride in groups of no larger than five to avoid kicking up large amounts of dust, creating lots of noise, and making other users feel crowded.

Leave No Trace principles—Copyright: Leave No Trace Center for Outdoor Ethics. www.LNT.org.

Activity 2: Addressing a Bad Reputation (30 to 45 Minutes)

The goal of this activity is to paint a picture of the negative reputation that mountain biking has received from some people. Figure MB6.1 presents quotation cards that reflect the attitudes and opinions of various people about mountain biking. These quotations create a starting point for discussing the nature and type of impact that mountain bikes have and the need to be sensitive to impacts on the land and other visitors.

◆ Photocopy the cards or print them from the CD-ROM and hand one card to each student or small group.

◆ Have a student read a quotation aloud and make up a story that leads to the quotation or a potential reason for the speaker's attitude.

◆ The story can be presented to the group as a skit, a creative journal entry, or as an oral description.

Closure Activity

Overcoming a Bad Reputation (30 Minutes)

Have students revisit the quotations from the previous section. For each quotation, have students

◆ address how they would interact with each of those people if they met them on the trail and

◆ identify LNT practices that could be implemented to prevent the attitudes represented in the quotations.

Follow-Up Activity

Be Aware, Get Involved (5 to 10 Minutes)

On the trail, take advantage of teachable moments to emphasize LNT practices.

◆ Spending some time to look at the physical impacts on trails in your area is an excellent way to understand what mountain bikers can do to tread lightly. For instance, trailwide mud holes where riders are widening the trail by riding around the mud or downhill sections where riders commonly skid their wheels are easily identifiable examples of places where better practice could prevent impact.

◆ Enforcing practices and creating discussion around specific examples on the trail reinforce information and promote a personal ethic in your students.

Bad Rep Quotation Cards

Card 1

"Mountain bikes cause more trail impacts than horses and hikers combined!" (Average person, non-mountain biker).

Card 2

"Mountain bikes should be banned from these lands. There is a lot of horse use here and a lot of these trails have steep drop-offs on one side. An accident is just waiting to happen when one of those crazy idiots comes barreling around the corner all out of control and spooks a horse" (Sixty-three-year-old horseback rider who has been riding on this land since he was a child).

Card 3

"Well, of course mountain bikes tear up trails. You can hardly go for a hike anymore without having to tromp through the mud that those things create. All the tiny little foot paths around here have gotten a lot bigger and wider since the mountain bikers found them" (Thirty-two-year-old hiker, member of the local volunteer trail crew that helps maintain trails in the area).

Card 4

"I had to ban mountain biking from my property because I was afraid of getting sued. It's an extreme sport filled with people who take big risks with their safety. Chances are that someone would end up seriously hurt on my property and they would look to me as the owner for responsibility. 'Why didn't you make the trails safer?' they would ask. I decided it was best to just ban the activity and not take the risk" (Owner of a large tract of land that contains an extensive trail system, now only open to foot traffic).

Card 5

"I come to this area to get away from civilization and mechanized things. There is nothing more primitive and peaceful than to walk through the wilderness. Mountain bikes are a lot of technology, a lot of civilization that can pierce deep into the wilderness. To me there is no difference between a mountain bike and a motorcycle in the backcountry. They ruin the primitive nature of this area" (Dedicated wilderness advocate).

Card 6

"I've noticed a decline in the amount of big trout in this stream since the area became popular for mountain biking. The trails go right through the creek. Every time someone rides through the water, it kicks up a bunch of silt which floats downstream. Fish don't like that silt" (Fly fisherman who has been fishing here for 23 years).

Card 7

"Sure, we get lots of emergency calls from mountain bikers. They can get deep in the backcountry pretty quick. Most of the time they've gotten lost or hurt way out there and with the increased use of cell phones, they end up calling 911. We get the call here at the rescue squad and go out to help them. Mountain bike rescues are a little more involved than most since they are typically farther away from trailheads than hikers and often involve high-speed crashes with bigger trauma. People just don't get hurt like that hiking" (Member of a county rescue squad that is located near U.S. Forest Service land, when asked about the types of rescues that they do in the backcountry).

FIGURE MB6.1   Quotations that reflect the attitudes and opinions different people have about mountain biking.

From M. Wagstaff and A. Attarian, 2009, *Technical skills for adventure programming: A curriculum guide* (Champaign IL: Human Kinetics).

Another way for your students to become more intimate with impacts is for them to volunteer on a trail maintenance or trail-building project.

◆ Check with your local land management agency to ask whether any pending projects could use your group's assistance.

◆ Many regions have mountain bike clubs that are active in maintaining trails. They often sponsor trail days for the local community to become involved.

◆ The International Mountain Bicycling Association (www.imba.com) is a great resource for trail maintenance information and volunteer projects.

ASSESSMENT

◆ Have students describe the LNT practices for mountain biking by participating in the closure activity with quotations or on the trail through quick oral quizzes. For example, stop at a narrow point along the trail and ask students to describe what they would do if they met a group of horses in that spot.

◆ Have students assess specific situations based on LNT principles by allowing them to make choices on the trail and then providing feedback on their decisions afterward.

◆ Check that students demonstrate specific LNT practices while riding by observing their actions while on the trail.

◆ Evaluate whether students develop a personal ethic regarding the impacts associated with mountain biking by putting them in real situations where they must make decisions about practices and interact with other user groups.

TEACHING CONSIDERATIONS

More than just a topic briefly covered with students, LNT principles should saturate all your lessons, instruction, and riding time. Rather than give a long lecture, consider introducing pieces at intervals as they become salient. Too much talking before riding leads to impatient students. LNT practices can serve as good topics for breaks during rides.

UNIT 4, LESSON 7

▷ Maintenance and Repair

OVERVIEW

This lesson focuses on routine maintenance and the repairs that riders are most likely to have to perform along the trail. A professional mechanic at your local bicycle dealer should handle more complicated repairs.

JUSTIFICATION

Bicycle malfunctions occur on many rides. Being able to resolve these issues quickly can prevent a long walk out of the backcountry. Something as simple as a torn tire can ruin the ride for the entire group. Mechanical issues could also present a safety concern if a bicycle is not functioning properly. For many, part of the joy of mountain biking is tinkering with its parts. Care and maintenance of the bicycle should be part of any mountain bike program.

GOAL

To develop students' ability to maintain the bicycle and fix common problems that they may encounter on a ride.

OBJECTIVES

At the end of this lesson, students will be able to

◆ understand how to clean and lubricate a bicycle (cognitive),

◆ fix a flat tire and repair a broken chain (psychomotor), and

◆ achieve confidence in being self-sufficient in making repairs (affective).

EQUIPMENT AND AREAS NEEDED

◆ For bike cleaning: hose, buckets, lots of rags, brushes of different sizes and shapes, a few sponges, dishwashing soap, and citrus degreaser

◆ Chain lube

◆ For fixing a flat: tubes, tire levers, tube patches, a floor pump or compressor for teaching, and a small hand pump for emergency inflation on the trail

◆ For repairing a broken chain: several chain tools and a small length of chain for each student

◆ Bicycle work stand for demonstration

RISK MANAGEMENT CONSIDERATIONS

◆ If working on a bike along the trail, be careful of other riders who may not be expecting to encounter people stopped in the middle of the trail. Move yourself and the bike to a safe location that is out of the path of other riders.

◆ When working with an air compressor to inflate tires, make sure that the tire is properly seated on the rim and do not overinflate. Some air compressors can quickly force a lot of air into the tire, causing the tire to burst unexpectedly.

LESSON CONTENT

Introduction (10 Minutes)

A quick skit can be a fun way to communicate the need to be ready for unforeseen repairs. The following scenario might seem funny to some, but acting it out can drive home the need to be prepared for repairs.

A person goes on a solo mountain bike ride. He rides for a long time into the backcountry. Suddenly, he gets a flat tire and realizes that he does not have the items necessary to fix the flat, nor does he know how. With no one else in sight he starts walking back to the trailhead. Hours later, thirsty, hungry, and tired, he is still walking. He finally reaches the trailhead after dark.

Main Activities

Activity 1: Cleaning and Lubing (20 Minutes)

Get students in the habit of keeping their bikes clean. A clean bicycle operates better and resists wear longer. The more dirt and grime that builds up, the harder it will be to clean it off. The best time to clean the bike is just after a ride before the dirt and mud dry into an impossible cement.

Cleaning

◆ Hose off big chunks of mud. Be careful not to direct a forceful stream of water at any of the bearings (hubs, **headset**, bottom bracket). Doing so could wash the grease out of the bearings and force in dirt and grime. Squirt mud off the chain, but try not to wash off too much of the chain lube.

◆ Use brushes and sponges with soapy water on the entire bike. Make contact with every surface of the bicycle.

◆ Use a diluted solution of citrus degreaser for the stubborn parts, such as rims covered in black brake residue or chainrings covered in black grease.

◆ Rinse off soap and degreaser with a light shower of water.

◆ Use rags to dry the bike and restore a shine.

Lubing

◆ After every cleaning, especially if you used a degreaser, you must relube the chain.

◆ Use products specifically designed for the purpose such as a light chain oil or dry wax lube.

◆ If riding mostly on dry trails after which cleaning is not necessary, lube the chain before it becomes dry or shiny looking.

◆ Avoid overlubing, which can be more of a mess than a benefit.
  – Hold lube over the chain in one spot.
  – Pedal backward with the other hand, evenly distributing the lube on the chain.
  – Continue pedaling backward for 20 to 30 seconds to work the lube into the interior parts of the chain.
  – Hold a rag on the chain while pedaling backward to wipe off any excess lube. Lube on the outside surfaces of the chain does little for performance. The inside surfaces are what count.

Activity 2: Fixing a Flat Tire (45 Minutes)

Have students practice this skill by having everyone take a wheel off her or his bike, deflate the tire by hand, disassemble the tire and tube from the rim, and put it all back together. Give a complete demonstration beforehand and coach students while they're practicing. After everyone is done, give some tips on how to deal with special situations such as a torn tire or multiple flats.

◆ Remove the wheel. On bikes with rim brakes, unhook the brake cable to allow the wheel to pass through the brake pads. If the flat is in the rear, shift the rear derailleur into the smallest cog. Doing this will allow greater clearance and serve as a reference for putting the wheel back on the bike. Pull the quick-release lever and remove the wheel.

◆ Remove the tire from the rim. Use the tire levers to pry one side off at a time. Always use plastic tire levers. Items such as a flat-head screwdriver will puncture the tube.

◆ Inspect the tire and rim. Look at the inside of the rim to make sure that the rim tape is intact and covering all sharp metal edges. Run your fingers along the inside of the tire to check for thorns or punctures protruding through the tire. At the same time, inspect the outside of the tire for any blowouts. Figuring out the cause of the flat can prevent the same thing from happening again.

◆ Inflate the new tube just enough to give it shape. Reinstall just one side of the tire on the rim. Position the tube inside the tire and then install the other side on the rim using the tire levers and being careful not to puncture the tube.

◆ Inflate to 5 to 10 pounds per square inch (35 to 70 kilopascals) and check to make sure that the tire bead is seated evenly on the rim. Manipulate by hand if necessary. Continue to inflate. Estimating tire pressure without a gauge can be difficult. Squeeze the other tire with your hand and try to match its firmness.

◆ Put the wheel back on the bike. Insert the axle in the dropouts in the frame. Make sure that the wheel is completely inserted or is all the way up in the dropouts. The tire should be centered in the frame. On the rear wheel, align the chain on the smallest cog as you insert the wheel into the frame. Close the quick-release lever. You achieve the proper tightness of the quick release when the lever meets resistance halfway through its motion. Closing it all the way should be fairly difficult. You can make adjustments with the nut that makes up the other side of the quick release until you achieve proper tension.

◆ Reconnect the brake cable. Pick up the bike a few inches (centimeters) and spin the wheel. Check to make sure that the tire is not rubbing the brake pads or the frame. Readjust the wheel in the dropouts as necessary.

Special Situations

◆ Sometimes a flat is caused by a hole or tear in the tire. When this occurs you will have to create a **tire boot** to prevent the tube from protruding through the hole. You can make a tire boot from plastic soda bottles, energy bar wrappers, paper currency, or other items.

◆ In extreme cases when you have no spare tube or multiple flats occur, find the hole in the tube, cut or tear the tube completely in half, and make it one long straight piece. Take the two ends and tie them together using a square knot to make a circle again. Stretch the tube on to the rim and inflate as normal. The ride is a little bumpy, but the tube will hold air quite well.

Activity 3: Broken Chains (30 Minutes)

An old chain broken into many pieces serves well as practice for students. Give a small piece to each student and let students practice pushing the pins in and out. It is best not to have students practice on the chains on their bicycles, because frequent removal of chains can damage or weaken the connections. The basic operation of a chain tool is explained in the directions that come with it. Here are some tips that can make the process easier.

- When a chain breaks while riding, removing a link to join the chain back together is usually necessary. Take out the link or links necessary to have undamaged male and female ends ready to be joined.

- Never, when pushing out a pin, push it all the way out. Pins are nearly impossible to put back into the hole when they come all the way out. Instead, push the pin with the tool, as the manufacturer directs, until it is most of the way out but is still attached to the side plate. Practice to get the feel of how far to push the pin.

- Put the new ends back together by hand. Use the tool to push the pin back in, making sure that the pin, tool, and side plate holes are all aligned.

- After pushing the pin all the way in, you will often find that the link is stiff (difficult to rotate). Many chain tools have a second feature to allow you to push the side plates apart a bit to allow smooth rotation of the link. Follow the directions for the specific tool. You can also fix a stiff link by holding the chain on either side of the link and bending it back and forth from side to side, in the way opposite that a chain is supposed to bend. This action will have the effect of loosening the link.

Closure Activity

Maintenance Relay Race (45 Minutes)

A bicycle maintenance relay race is a fun way to solidify newly acquired skills. Stations can include removal and reinstallation of a tire and tube from a rim, breaking and rejoining a section of chain, and removal and reinstallation of both wheels of a bicycle from the frame. The race can be an individual skills rodeo or a timed team relay race.

Follow-Up Activity

Self-Contained and Self-Reliant (Time as Needed)

- If one of these problems arises on the trail, allow the student to fix the problem for himself or herself. If not practiced from time to time, these skills are often lost, so include these skills in subsequent programs with students.

- As a follow-up activity, have students perform the original skit in the introduction again. At the point where the rider with the flat begins to walk, a group of your students arrives on the scene and helps fix the flat. With some creativity, this skit can serve to reinforce the skills learned and build some pride in having the knowledge to help others.

ASSESSMENT

- Check that students understand how to clean and lube a bicycle by observing them clean and lube their bicycles after every ride.

- Evaluate whether students are able to fix a flat tire and a broken chain by observing their participation in the relay race activities.

- Assess whether students have achieved confidence in being self-sufficient in repairs by observing them fix their own problems on the trail.

TEACHING CONSIDERATIONS

◆ With so much to teach before a ride, instructors often ignore maintenance. Teachable moments along the trail offer good opportunities to introduce these topics. You may not have enough supplies for all to practice, but a quality demonstration can be completed and revisited later.

◆ Maintenance and repair are great rainy day activities when trail riding is washed out.

Mountain Biking Skills Checklist

The following mountain biking skills will be introduced during this unit. You are responsible for learning these skills. Periodically review this checklist to assess your knowledge and ability to perform these skills. When you are comfortable with a skill, have the instructor assess your ability to perform it.

All skills need to be initialed and dated by the instructor to be valid. Add skills as needed.

General Mountain Biking Skills

☐ Properly size a bicycle

☐ Properly fit a helmet

☐ Conduct the eight-point daily safety check

Maintenance Skills

☐ Clean and lubricate a bicycle

☐ Fix a flat tire

☐ Repair a broken chain

Riding Fundamentals: Beginner

Starting and stopping:

☐ Demonstrate a basic start

☐ Demonstrate a basic dismount

Riding over obstacles:

☐ Wheel lift

Riding Fundamentals: Intermediate

Starting and stopping:

☐ Demonstrate a tree start

☐ Demonstrate a tree stop

Riding over obstacles:

☐ Chainring method

Riding Fundamentals: Advanced

Starting and stopping:

☐ Demonstrate a flying start

☐ Demonstrate a running dismount

Riding over obstacles:

☐ Lunge method

☐ Bunny hop

Other

☐ Descend

☐ Climb

☐ Cornering

Use the mountain biking skills checklist as an additional tool to assess skills learned throughout this unit.

From M. Wagstaff and A. Attarian, 2009, *Technical skills for adventure programming: A curriculum guide* (Champaign IL: Human Kinetics).

bottom bracket—Located in the center of the front chainrings, these are the bearings that allow the crankarms to turn.

bunny hop—A technique used by advanced riders in which both tires leave the ground at the same time to clear obstacles in the trail.

chainring method of log crossing—Method of crossing logs by using the front chainrings to grip and pull up and over the log.

chainrings—Gears located in the front of the bike near the pedals.

cogs—Individual gears located in the back of the bike on the rear wheel.

cross-chaining—Shifting into the smallest cog in the rear and the smallest chainring in the front, or the opposite of this, shifting into the largest cog and the largest chainring. Either combination causes the chain to bend abnormally, potentially damaging it.

dab—A touch of a foot to the ground. The term is most commonly used in trials competitions.

derailleurs—Devices on a bicycle that physically push the chain from one cog to another or from one chainring to another. This action changes the gear ratio, making the bicycle easier or harder to pedal.

endo—An endo occurs when a rider is thrown over the front of the handlebars.

headset—Not the earphones that you may be thinking of. The headset on a bicycle contains the bearings in the front of the frame that allow the handlebars and front wheel to turn.

hubs—The center part of bicycle wheels where the bearings and axle are located.

lunge method of log crossing—An advanced technique for log crossing in which the rider uses momentum and body weight to cross a tall log. In this technique only the tires of the bicycle touch the log.

power stroke—The portion of the circular motion of the pedals that creates the most power. Leg muscles can generate the most power when pushing down the front of the pedal stroke, from about the two o'clock position to the five o'clock position.

tire boot—An item placed on the inside of a tire between the tire and the tube to prevent the tube from protruding from a hole or tear in the tire. A tire boot can be made out of soda bottle plastic, foil wrappers from energy bars, dollar bills, or other items.

top tube—The horizontal part of the frame that goes from underneath the seat to the handlebars.

work stand—A device that holds the bike off the ground, usually by the seat post. Use of the work stand allows you to turn the pedals with one hand and shift with the other.

REFERENCES AND RESOURCES

REFERENCES

Cessford, G.R. (2002, February). Perception and reality of conflict: Walkers and mountain bikes on the Queen Charlotte Track in New Zealand. In A. Arnberger, C. Brandenburg, & A. Muhar (Eds.), *Monitoring and management of visitor flows in recreational and protected areas*. Conference proceedings of the Institute for Landscape Architecture and Landscape Management, Bodenkultur University, Vienna, Austria.

Kelly, J.R., & Warnick, R.B. (1999). *Recreation trends and markets: The 21st century*. Champaign, IL: Sagamore.

Leave No Trace Center for Outdoor Ethics. (2001). *Mountain biking* [Brochure]. Boulder, CO: Leave No Trace.

Thurston, E., & Reader, R.J. (2001). Impacts of experimentally applied mountain biking and hiking on vegetation and soil of a deciduous forest. *Environmental Management, 27*(3): 397–409.

Warland, S. (2003). *The mountain bike book*. St. Paul, MN: MBI.

Wilson, J.P., & Seney, J.P. (1994). Erosional impacts of hikers, horses, motorcycles and off-road bicycles on mountain trails in Montana. *Mountain Research and Development, 47*(1): 77–88.

RESOURCES

International Mountain Bicycling Association. (2006). Retrieved from www.imba.com. Overview: IMBA has a comprehensive Web site for mountain bike advocacy, impact, and access. It includes the IMBA rules of the trail, a code of conduct for mountain bikers. The Web site has many resources, such as links to scientific research on mountain bike impact and proper trail-building techniques.

Lopes, B., & McCormack, L. (2005). *Mastering mountain bike skills*. Champaign, IL: Human Kinetics. Overview: A fairly recent and comprehensive look at mountain biking skills.

Nealy, W. (1992). *Mountain bike, a manual of beginning to advanced technique*. Birmingham, AL: Menasha Ridge Press. Overview: Along with all of William Nealy's books, this is an illustrated depiction of the sport that contains some good tips and provides lots of laughs.

Overend, N., Hewitt, B., & Pavelka, E. (1999). *Mountain bike like a champion*. Emmaus, PA: Rodale Press. Overview: This book is geared a little more toward mountain bike racing and training but contains a fair amount of useful reference information for teaching mountain biking.

Sprung, G. (2004). Natural resource impacts of mountain biking. Retrieved from www.imba.com/resources/science/impact_summary.html. Overview: This article on the International Mountain Bicycling Association Web site gives a good summary and overview of research on mountain bike impact.

Tread Lightly. (2005). Retrieved from www.treadlightly.org. Overview: Very similar to Leave No Trace, this Web site offers minimum-impact tips for many outdoor activities. The site has a strong focus on motorized travel but has a page dedicated to mountain bikes.

Zinn, L. (2001). *Zinn and the art of mountain bike maintenance* (3rd ed.). Boulder, CO: Velo Press. Overview: A comprehensive guide to the maintenance and repair of mountain bikes.

Water-Based Units

The world of paddle sports provides a dynamic mode of travel to experience our earth's water resources. We can explore our oceans, rivers, lakes, and wetlands by human-powered craft. Part II covers sea kayaking, whitewater kayaking, canoeing, and rafting as activities that outdoor leaders facilitate. These activities allow people to experience many environments that are accessible only by water. Besides experiencing unique environments, participants gain many other benefits. The physical and mental challenge of navigating open or moving water constitutes a healthy recreational activity. Boating challenges the body and mind in many ways. Proper paddling technique promotes a total-body workout. Getting outside and spending time on the water promotes the movement that our obese society discourages. The concentration and focus needed to navigate rapids or ocean currents exercises the mind and promotes living in the moment, thereby reducing daily stress. Paddling also constitutes a popular social activity for friends or family. Great personal satisfaction occurs as novice boaters master their craft, allowing them to advance to more difficult challenges.

The authors of these units provide you with information and tools to teach paddle sports. Proper instruction promotes safety, enjoyment, and environmental stewardship. Participants who discover the joy of paddling are able to make it a lifetime activity. Each author takes a personal approach to teaching his or her topic. The lessons offered reflect years of teaching experience and practice. We want to bring your attention to several specific topics and issues as you plan your water-based lessons.

Inclusion

In unit 7, lesson 10, author Laurie Gullion provides a water-based inclusion lesson. Laurie has significant experience in this area and does an excellent job of providing ideas and adaptations to make canoeing accessible. Her concepts and ideas can easily be transferred to the other water-based activities. Her four basic concepts to create accessible canoeing programs apply as well to kayaking and rafting. Laurie provides advice for paddling with visual impairments, hearing impairments, lower- and upper-limb impairments, and trunk impairments. The tips and ideas that she provides in each of these categories apply to other paddle sports.

Leave No Trace

As most of you know, Leave No Trace considerations for the various water-based activities are the same. But some differences do exist depending on the environment and length of trip. To avoid redundancy, each author took a different approach.

- In unit 5, Sea Kayaking, the LNT information focuses on saltwater and large open-water environments.
- Unit 6, Whitewater Kayaking, approaches LNT from a land management perspective.
- Unit 7, Canoeing, provides several activity-based lessons to teach the topic.
- Unit 8, Rafting, discusses camping practices in the river environment.

Rescue Techniques and Safety Information

Rescue techniques and safety information is another topic that includes many commonalities among the different paddle sports. Generic rescue and safety information is sprinkled throughout the units, yet each author discusses rescue information specific to the particular topic. To assist you in sorting out rescue information, use the following as a quick reference guide:

- In unit 5, Sea Kayaking, lesson 5 addresses T-rescues with a kayak, the bow rescue, and techniques specific to sea kayaking. Lesson 12 addresses a risk management decision-making model that can be applied to the other paddle sports.
- In unit 6, Whitewater Kayaking, lesson 10 discusses self-rescues and assisted rescues in the event of flips, swims, and pins. Lesson 7 describes teaching the kayak roll. Lesson 9 introduces the rescue curve as a framework for safety and risk management.
- In unit 7, Canoeing, lesson 7 addresses T-rescues with canoes, self-rescues, and a tow rescue. Lesson 8 discusses mechanical rescues for pinned boats. Lesson 9 focuses on managing groups.
- In unit 8, Rafting, lesson 3 discusses pre-planning information, safety briefings, and signaling. Lesson 8 covers throw-bag use and capsized rafts. Lesson 9 describes foot entrapment rescue, rescue from hydraulics, and recovering a pinned raft.

Connecting Units

Throughout this and other parts of this book, you'll find that the authors refer to other units within their lessons if a topic is found elsewhere. For example, the parts of a single-blade paddle are covered in unit 7 and not revisited in the paddle lesson of unit 8.

A final note worth mentioning relates to stretching and warm-ups. Before students participate in any physical activity, make sure that they warm up sufficiently. You may choose to perform traditional stretching or simply have your students engage in the activity at a very slow pace initially. All units mention stretching and warm-ups, but unit 6 devotes an entire lesson to stretching (lesson 3). Upper-body injuries are prevalent in paddle sports, as emphasized in Bruce Martin's comprehensive lesson on stretching.

Sea Kayaking

Tommy Holden

▷ Introduction to Sea Kayaking

OVERVIEW

Knowledge of the sport of sea kayaking is essential to appreciate and respect both coastal and inner-coastal kayaking. Students learn in this lesson the history and progression of the sport and the many variations of sea kayaking seen today. Note that although most of the information in this section applies to both coastal and inner-coastal environments, certain lessons naturally lend themselves to specific coastal environments.

JUSTIFICATION

Knowledge of the history, progression, and various forms of sea kayaking provides students with a foundation and basis from which their interest in the sport may progress. This lesson helps explain the increase in the popularity of sea kayaking in recent years.

GOAL

To give students a clear understanding of the history, progression, and many variations of the sport of sea kayaking.

OBJECTIVES

At the end of this lesson, students will be able to

- describe the history of sea kayaking (cognitive) and
- appreciate and respect the sport of sea kayaking (affective).

EQUIPMENT AND AREAS NEEDED

- One or more sea kayaks (provide a variety of types if possible)
- One paddle
- One personal flotation device (PFD)
- One spray skirt

RISK MANAGEMENT CONSIDERATIONS

- If you conduct this lesson outside, check the outdoor teaching area for environmental hazards such as fishhooks, broken glass, bees' nests, extended sun exposure, and so on, and take appropriate precautions.
- Ensure that participants have appropriate clothing for the setting and adequate water, sunscreen, and shade.

LESSON CONTENT

Introduction

To gain better understanding of sea kayaking and become more proficient at it, students should learn about the history of the sport. The main activity explores the first kayaking cultures and the transition from subsistence use to recreational use of sea kayaks. This lesson also includes a trivia quiz activity to reinforce historical knowledge.

Main Activity

History and Progression of Sea Kayaking (30 Minutes)

The main activity of this lesson is to give the following information to the students. This can be a lecture-style lesson. Deliver from the following what you think is pertinent to your program. As an alternative to a lecture-style presentation, you can design a more experientially based lesson. Create note cards using the information that follows. Then pass out the cards to students and challenge them to develop a one-minute presentation based on the material and present it to the rest of the class.

Early Kayaks: Aleut and Inuit People

◆ Although the sport of sea kayaking is relatively new in the adventure recreation arena, humans have used sea kayaks for more than 3,000 years (Loots, 2000). The first designers of seagoing kayaks (meaning "hunter's boat") were the Aleut people (of southwest Alaska and the Aleutian Islands in the Bering Sea) and the Inuit people (from North America and Greenland). They used kayaks to hunt whales and seals to provide food and clothing for themselves.

◆ The first sea kayaks were made from whalebone, wood, and sealskin and provided some protection from the frigid waters (Loots, 2000). Many kayaks used a narrow bow to slice through waves and pack ice and an upswept bow to keep the boat dry in rough conditions.

◆ The hunter (paddler) wore a one-piece sealskin tuilik, which was an earlier version of today's spray skirt. The tuilik covered the hunter's head, torso, and arms and attached to the rim of the cockpit. It provided warmth and waterproofness for the hunter.

◆ The hunter had to be proficient in the kayak roll. Certain death would occur if the hunter exited the kayak and became exposed to the frigid waters. The hunters were proficient in over 40 different types of kayak rolls (on both sides) including rolls using only their hands, rolls using only their throwing sticks, and rolls with their arms tied together (simulating their arms becoming entangled in the rope used to catch seals or whales). Today, competitions exist in traditional Greenland-style kayak rolling in which competitors perform the styles of rolls used by the Aleut and Inuit.

Recreational Kayaks

◆ Sea kayaks were first introduced for recreational use in the early 1930s.

◆ The early **recreational kayaks** were made of wood and canvas (Loots, 2000). Composite materials, such as fiberglass, were introduced in the 1950s. Other composites, such as Kevlar and carbon fiber, were introduced in the 1970s and 1980s.

◆ In the late 1980s, the introduction of rotomolded plastics allowed manufacturers to mass-produce sea kayaks and lower the price to consumers (Loots, 2000).

Current Kayaks

- Sea kayaking has many similarities to the sport of whitewater kayaking. Equipment such as paddles, PFDs, spray skirts, and even boat design share many characteristics.

- Sea kayaking differs from whitewater kayaking in a variety of ways, but the main differences lie in the safety equipment used in sea kayaking (VHF, EPIRB, flares, and so forth) and tide and weather prediction associated with the sport (Loots, 2000).

- The modern sea kayak has a closed deck and large waterproof storage compartments (dry hatches). The kayak is designed to travel long distances with little effort and can carry camping gear, food, and water for multiday trips.

- Today's sea kayaks are not relegated to use as oceangoing vessels; they are increasingly being used on lakes, rivers, and other inland bodies of water (Loots, 2000).

Rules of the Road

- The sport of sea kayaking is driven by a massive body of nautical know-how that is supported by a system of rules pertaining to nautical rules of the road and safety regulations (Loots, 2000, pp. 8–11).

- Sea kayakers abide by rules and regulations that pertain to all vessels that travel on coastal, inner-coastal, and open waters.

- Governmental agencies such as the United States Coast Guard and the **National Oceanic and Atmospheric Administration (NOAA)** provide information and guidelines for boating safety and regulations that sea kayakers should be familiar with in their area of recreational kayaking.

Popularity

- Outdoor recreational sports continue to be a big business in the United States. According to the state of the industry report conducted by the Outdoor Industry Association (OIA), "Outdoor recreational sports added $730 billion last year to the U.S. economy, supported 6.5 million jobs and contributed $88 billion to federal and state tax revenue" (Malhotra, 2006).

- According to a participation study conducted by the OIA, "about 12.6 million have taken up kayaking (recreational, sea, and whitewater) since 2005" (Malhotra, 2006).

- Kayaking became popular in the mid-1980s with the advent of the mass-produced plastic kayak. Various sea kayaking festivals and the start of *Sea Kayaker* magazine in the mid-1980s increased the visibility of the sport. "The market has skyrocketed from 1998 to 2002 due to its appeal as low-impact outdoor recreational activity" (Malhotra, 2006).

- One of the most popular recent areas of interest has been in the fishing kayak sector.

- As manufacturers continue to improve plastics, making them more durable and lighter in weight, the sport of sea kayaking continues to grow.

Closure Activities

Activity 1: Student Goals and Expectations (5 to 10 Minutes)

Ask students if they have ever been kayaking (whitewater or sea kayaking). Ask what they hope to get out of the class. Why are they here? What type of kayaking do they plan to do in the future? Discuss their expectations of the class and your expectations as an instructor.

Activity 2: Trivia Quiz (15 Minutes)

Design and play a trivia quiz based on historical and current information presented to your group related to the sport of sea kayaking. This activity provides an excellent review of the information shared in the main activity section. Questions may include the following:

- How long have sea kayaks been around?
- What group of people first used sea kayaks?
- What were sea kayaks originally designed for?
- What was the original spray skirt called?
- What was the tuilik made out of?
- What were the first sea kayaks made out of?
- Name important original sea kayak designs and their purposes.
- List several different materials used to make sea kayaks today.
- List several differences between sea kayaking and whitewater kayaking.
- Where may sea kayaks be used?
- Name one governmental agency that provides information and guidelines for boating safety and regulations that sea kayakers should be familiar with.

Follow-Up Activities

Activity 1: Story Time (45 Minutes)

An important follow-up activity can occur throughout the class by referring to the history of sea kayaking in the lessons that deal with equipment use, boat design, navigation skills, and other topics.

Have students obtain guidebooks and information regarding popular sea kayaking trips in the library and share their findings with the rest of the students each night as an evening activity if the group takes an expedition-style trip. Alternatively, students can present their findings at the end of a class session.

Activity 2: Trivia Game (30 Minutes)

One way that students may learn new information about sea kayaking is to create a trivia game using note cards. Because the information is new to the students, they should create multiple-choice questions that will allow fellow students to figure out the correct answer. You can play with teams or individuals. Keep score with your whiteboard or in the sand.

- Keeping the note cards in place in windy conditions can be difficult. One trick is to use a hole punch to put a hole in the top of each note card and use golf tees to hold the note cards in place in the ground.
- Because students don't have buzzers, be creative by having them make their favorite barnyard animal sound.
- Prizes for the winners can be food treats or one night free of dish duty. Again, creativity works well!

ASSESSMENT

- ◆ Check that students can describe the history of sea kayaking by administering a written or oral exam or by assessing their knowledge during the closure trivia quiz.
- ◆ Evaluate whether students appreciate and respect the sport of sea kayaking by observing them as they progress in skill development and knowledge.

TEACHING CONSIDERATIONS

- ◆ Because this is a lecture-style lesson, keeping students' attention is sometimes difficult. Any activity in which they can get their hands on boats and gear keeps them engaged.
- ◆ Exciting stories that incorporate the history of sea kayaking will obviously keep the students' attention. Refer to your library of books for descriptions and stories related to the history of sea kayaking and lessons that can be learned from others' adventures. An interesting and exciting book is *Sea Kayaker's Deep Trouble: True Stories and Their Lessons from Sea Kayaker Magazine* (Broze & Gronseth, 1997), which includes 20 real-life harrowing tales of various sea kayakers' adventures. This gripping book may hook students on the sport of sea kayaking.

UNIT 5, LESSON 2

▷ Equipment and Use

OVERVIEW

Students learn in this lesson about the essential equipment used for sea kayaking, optional equipment, and the intended use of the equipment. Much of the equipment discussed in this lesson relates to other water-based sports. Therefore, specific mention is made when equipment applies only to sea kayaking. Sea kayaking safety equipment is described in lesson 11. Refer to unit 1, lesson 6 for proper layering of clothes for sea kayaking and other water-based activities.

JUSTIFICATION

Knowledge of sea kayaking equipment and its use is essential for a person to become proficient in the sport of sea kayaking. The ability to select and use appropriate equipment maximizes safety. In addition, familiarity with equipment increases self-reliance and fosters responsibility.

GOAL

To develop students' knowledge of basic equipment used for sea kayaking.

OBJECTIVES

At the end of this lesson, students will be able to

- ◆ identify sea kayaking equipment (cognitive) and
- ◆ appreciate the differences in equipment choices based on design and material makeup (affective).

EQUIPMENT AND AREAS NEEDED

◆ Sea kayaks (one per person)

◆ Spray skirts (one per person)

◆ Paddles (one per person)

◆ PFDs (one per person)

RISK MANAGEMENT CONSIDERATIONS

◆ See lesson 1 for details on general risk management considerations.

◆ Ensure that boats are transported correctly to avoid injuries caused by improper lifting or carrying.

LESSON CONTENT

Introduction

Like many outdoor adventure sports, sea kayaking can be gear intensive. Sea kayakers must wade through many equipment options on the market to find the gear appropriate for their needs. Even deciding on the minimal equipment needed to start sea kayaking (sea kayak, spray skirt, paddle, and PFD) can be a daunting task.

Main Activity

Equipment Overview and Use (35 to 40 Minutes)

Go through all the gear at hand (sea kayak, spray skirt, paddle, and PFD) and explain the importance of each item. Engage students in dialogue regarding the options available on the market. Be sure to stress the function of each item and how its use relates to safety, comfort, and enjoyment. Refer to lesson 1 about the history of the sport to incorporate the evolution of sea kayaking equipment.

Personal Flotation Device   Your personal flotation device (PFD) is an essential piece of paddling gear. You should always wear it when sea kayaking. For that reason it should fit well. A well-fitted PFD is comfortable to wear all day long.

◆ The PFD should not constrict, chafe, or hinder any movement.

◆ It should be adjustable enough to fit over layers of clothing yet fit snugly on those days when the air and water are warm enough for just a swimsuit.

◆ Many newer PFDs designed for sea kayaking have reflective taping for visibility, large pockets to accommodate VHF radios or communication devices, attachments for strobe lights (usually on the rear of the PFD), higher cut backs to accommodate the backband in the cockpit, integrated harness systems for towing, and attachment points for hydration systems (water bladders). Prices for sea kayaking PFDs range from $55 to $185.

There are five types of PFDs.

◆ Type I PFDs are good for open, rough, remote water. This type floats the best, turns most unconscious wearers face up, and is highly visible, but bulky.

◆ Type II PFDs are appropriate for calm water, turn some unconscious wearers face up, are less bulky than type I devices, but are not appropriate for long hours in rough water.

◆ A type III Coast Guard approved PFD is the best choice for both coastal and inner-coastal sea kayaking because it allows maximum arm movement and comfort when sea kayaking and has adequate flotation. It is designed for general boating activity. A type III PFD is good for conscious users.

◆ Type IV flotation devices are throwable items such as cushions, rings, and buoys.

◆ Type V PFDs are special-use devices that have specific applications and instructions. The performance of the type V is equal to types I, II, and III only if used according to instructions.

Sea Kayak Sea kayaks today have come a long way since the early kayaks used by the Aleut and Inuit people. Before attempting to understand hull materials and sea kayak designs, students should become familiar with the parts of a sea kayak as shown in figure SK2.1.

Students should be able to identify the following basic parts of the sea kayak: bow, stern, **access hatches**, **bulkheads**, cockpit, cockpit combing, foot rests or pegs, thigh braces, toggles or handles, dry storage compartments, bungee cords, deck, **deck rigging**, **skeg** or **rudder** (and associated steering rigging), waterline, and freeboard.

Sea kayaks are made out of three basic materials: rotomolded plastic, fiberglass, or Kevlar.

◆ Rotomolded plastic is the most inexpensive of the three materials. Plastic is durable but difficult to repair. It is heavier than the other materials and has a shorter lifespan. Plastic boats are great for paddling around oyster shells and coral, or any place that can scrape or cut the boat. Paddlers don't have to baby them as much as they do fiberglass and Kevlar boats. A disadvantage of plastic boats is that they tend to flex more when paddling and are therefore not as efficient in energy transfer. The other disadvantage is that the sun breaks down the properties of the plastic, reducing the lifespan of the boats compared with fiberglass and Kevlar boats. A typical kayak (16 to 17 feet [4.9 to 5.2 meters] in length) costs around $1,300 in rotomolded plastic.

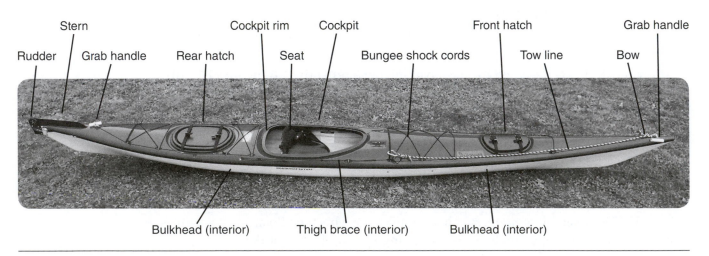

FIGURE SK2.1 Parts of a sea kayak.

◆ Fiberglass and Kevlar boats are strong, lightweight, fast, stiff (allowing great energy transfer), and long lived, but they are expensive. Both materials are relatively easy to repair, but they are easily damaged and must be carefully paddled and handled around oyster beds and dead coral. A typical **touring kayak** in fiberglass can cost between $2,200 and $3,500, while one made of Kevlar can cost between $3,000 and $4,500.

Modern sea kayaks are produced in many different designs. The design and shape greatly affect how the kayak performs. The shape of the cross-section of the kayak below the waterline has a direct effect on its stability.

◆ Initial stability is the stability of the kayak when it is floating flat on its bottom. Secondary stability is the stability of the kayak when it is leaning on its side. A flat-bottom kayak has great initial stability on flat water, but it does not handle as well in rough conditions and is extremely unstable when placed on its side.

◆ A round-bottom shape has low initial stability and poor tracking, but its secondary stability is high. This greater secondary stability allows the sea kayaker to lean the kayak and to roll with and handle waves.

◆ Rocker is the rise in the ends of the sea kayak along the keel line. As rocker increases, the sea kayak turns easier, but this increase in maneuverability decreases its tracking, or its ability to travel in a straight line. To combat the decrease in tracking ability, kayaks can be outfitted with either retractable skegs or rudders.

A debate continues about which is better, a skeg or a rudder. Both have pros and cons. Emphasize to students that neither can take the place of well-refined strokes.

◆ A retractable skeg offers the sea kayaker a clean stern (no cables), an important advantage in the event of a capsize in rough water because the sea kayaker won't be entangled in or cut by the rudder or rudder cables.

◆ The skeg allows the sea kayaker to keep the feet stationary against the foot braces while paddling (no steering required). This setup allows better energy transfer from the sea kayaker to the boat and better stability.

◆ The skeg also allows the sea kayaker to dial in the direction or heading by adjusting the deployment of the skeg.

◆ One drawback to the skeg is that the skeg box takes up storage space in the stern hatch, which can be critical on extended paddling trips. The rudder, however, allows the sea kayaker to actually steer the boat and is easy to operate.

◆ If a sea kayaker uses the rudder when learning how to sea kayak, it can become a crutch to replace inadequate stroke technique.

◆ Another disadvantage of the rudder is that it comprises many moving parts that tend to fail, or break, when they are stressed, usually when the sea kayaker needs them the most. This is another reason not to rely on the rudder system.

◆ Both systems are delicate and can break if the sea kayak is paddled into shallow water while they are deployed. Emphasize to students that if their paddles touch the bottom where they are paddling, they should retract the skegs or rudders.

◆ It is important to mention that when using a rudder or skeg, the purpose is to prevent the sea kayak from turning up into the wind, or **weather cock**, by providing resistance to the stern of the boat (which typically gets blown downwind, causing the bow to turn up into the wind if the paddler does not use the rudder or skeg).

Paddles

A vast number of sea kayak paddles are available. They are made out of everything from wood to space-age synthetic fibers and resins. A paddle should be as durable and as comfortable as the boat.

Explain the following parts of the sea kayak paddle: blade, blade tip, **paddle shaft**, **drip ring**, **ferrule**, power face (the surface of the blade that grabs the water when the paddle is oriented for a forward stroke), and nonpower or back face of the blade (the backside of the blade when oriented for a forward stroke), as shown in figure SK2.2.

Paddle width:

◆ Most paddles have blade widths of 4 to 6 inches (10 to 15 centimeters). A wider blade grabs more water and puts more power into the stroke. It also provides more surface area for braces.

◆ A narrow blade is usually light, has more flex, and reduces paddle fatigue.

Paddle length:

◆ Selecting a paddle of the appropriate length is an important consideration for sea kayaking, yet there is no exact formula or calculation.

◆ Paddles generally come in lengths between 210 and 240 centimeters. To choose a length, place the paddle upright with one end on the ground by your feet. Reach with your arm up the length of the paddle. An appropriate length would be somewhere between a length that allows your fingers to curve over the top of

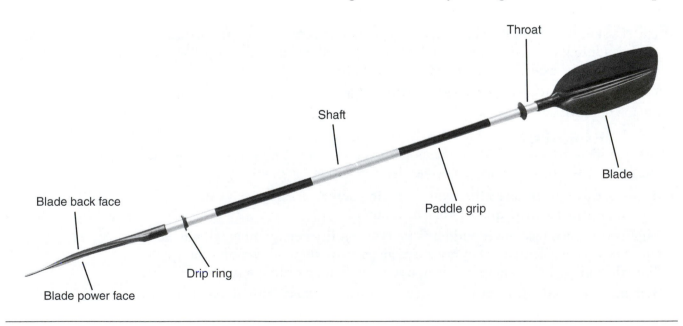

FIGURE SK2.2 Parts of a sea kayak paddle.

the blade tip and a length that is 6 inches (15 centimeters) from your extended fingertips (see figure SK2.3).

◆ A slightly longer shaft provides more leverage, whereas a shorter shaft can increase stroke rate and is less cumbersome to swing. A wider or longer boat might require a longer paddle.

 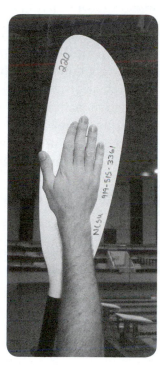 

FIGURE SK2.3 Quick method for fitting a paddle.

Paddle weight:

◆ Weight is another consideration. You will be lifting that paddle all day.

◆ Fiberglass paddles ($200) are considerably lighter than plastic or aluminum paddles ($70).

◆ Carbon fiber paddles are the lightest paddles but also the most expensive ($350 to $500).

Paddle design:

◆ Some paddles come with bent shafts, a more ergonomic design but one that takes some getting used to.

◆ Using the ferrule in the middle of the paddle shaft, two-piece paddles can be set up as feathered (blades offset) or nonfeathered (blades in line) depending on water and wind conditions. Newer paddles can be feathered for left- or right-hand-control sea kayakers. Some programs opt for one-piece paddles, because they require less maintenance. In addition, the ferrule is less likely to seize up from exposure to saltwater.

General tips:

◆ A suggestion for the beginning sea kayaker is to select a paddle that is moderately expensive and durable. Then as your skill level and interest in the sport increase, invest in a state-of-the-art synthetic or wooden paddle. You will really notice the difference.

◆ Remember that you should always have a spare paddle with you on any trip.

Spray Skirt The spray skirt is the modern version of the Inuit's sealskin tuilik. The spray skirt keeps water from coming in the cockpit and helps keep the sea kayaker warm and dry. Spray skirts generally cost between $15 and $85.

Many different materials are used for spray skirts including nylon, waterproof breathable fabrics, and neoprene. Spray skirts should be worn underneath the PFD to keep water out of the cockpit in case of capsize, as seen in figure SK2.4.

Closure Activity

Equipment Identification Game (10 Minutes)

Have students identify sea kayaking equipment and parts described in this lesson by playing an equipment identification game.

◆ Make two sets of index cards, each labeled with an equipment part.

◆ Divide students into two teams. Each team has its own pile of equipment.

◆ The goal is to identify equipment parts by placing the correct card on the corresponding equipment part. See how many parts each team can identify correctly.

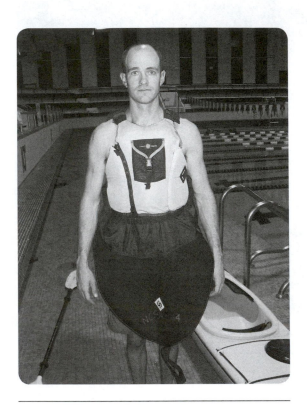

FIGURE SK2.4   Spray skirt worn under the PFD.

Follow-Up Activity

Equipment Review (5 to 10 Minutes)

The follow-up activity takes place at the beginning of the next two lessons when you review the topic of sea kayaking equipment by asking your students guided questions. In the following lessons, each student will have a boat. Have the student describe to other students what he or she liked and disliked about the boat design and other equipment used.

ASSESSMENT

◆ Evaluate whether students can identify sea kayaking equipment by engaging them in an identification activity as described in the closing activity.

◆ Assess whether students appreciate the differences in equipment design and materials by engaging them in a discussion of their preferences after they have had the opportunity to try different types of equipment.

TEACHING CONSIDERATIONS

- This lesson may take place inside or outside, poolside or shoreline. Make sure that the students can hear you and arrange them so that their backs are facing any potential distractions (boat traffic, onlookers, or wildlife).
- Prepare for the lesson by laying out the equipment to follow the progression of the lesson. Sort sizes of PFDs, spray skirts, and paddles to make it easier for students to find sized equipment of the appropriate size.
- Provide a variety of spray skirts, boats, and PFDs to accentuate the differences in design and function. Students develop a better appreciation for equipment differences and design if a variety of equipment is available.

UNIT 5, LESSON 3

▷ Transporting and Carries

OVERVIEW

This lesson focuses on the issues and techniques related to transporting and carrying sea kayaks. It introduces students to transporting sea kayaks on a boat trailer, carrying sea kayaks properly, both loaded and unloaded, and lifting the boats in a way that avoids damaging boats or injuring students. This lesson does not address vehicle-top carries. Refer to lesson 3 in unit 7 for details regarding vehicle-top carries.

JUSTIFICATION

Traveling to and from your paddling destination on public roads is always the most dangerous part of your trip. Properly securing the sea kayaks to a trailer is extremely important. The responsibility of the secured boats ultimately rests with the driver. In addition, students must learn how to load and unload boats and carry them properly to avoid injury to themselves and damage to the boats.

GOAL

To develop participants' ability to transport and carry a sea kayak efficiently.

OBJECTIVES

At the end of this lesson, students will be able to

- recognize unsafe body positions that may cause injury (cognitive),
- demonstrate how to lift a sea kayak on and off a boat trailer (psychomotor),
- secure the sea kayaks to the boat trailer using cam straps (psychomotor),
- use a hand carry to transport a loaded sea kayak and an unloaded sea kayak (psychomotor),
- use a sea kayak sling to transport a loaded sea kayak (psychomotor),
- gain a measure of self-reliance and craftsmanship by being able to secure sea kayaks to a trailer correctly and carry sea kayaks properly (affective).

EQUIPMENT AND AREAS NEEDED

- 12-foot (4-meter) cam straps (two for each two boats)
- Two 10-foot (3-meter) sections of 2-inch (5-centimeter) webbing (two per boat) (sea kayak slings)
- Boat trailer
- Sea kayaks (one per person)

RISK MANAGEMENT CONSIDERATIONS

- See lesson 1 for details about general risk management considerations.
- Make sure that the space around the trailer is sufficient to accommodate students and boats being lifted on and off the trailer.
- Taller students should be positioned where they can get the boats higher up on the trailer and to ensure proper backup spotting technique.
- Make sure that students realize the potential for back injury when lifting and carrying boats.
- Caution students about having greasy hands from sunscreen application when lifting and carrying boats.

LESSON CONTENT

Introduction

Emphasize to students that they must do a fair amount of work before they can paddle a sea kayak (unload the kayaks and carry them and the equipment to the waterfront). Typically, some students stand around and watch others do the necessary work of unloading and loading the boats and carrying the equipment. Make sure that students understand that everyone must participate in the activities. Statements such as "Many hands make light work," "Proper care of the sea kayak helps ensure the sea kayaker's safety and financial investment," and "Knowing how to carry, load, and unload the boat will allow novice paddlers to enjoy the sport long after this class" will help students buy into the activities.

Main Activities

Activity 1: Unloading the Trailer (10 Minutes)

Gather the students so that they can clearly see what you are demonstrating. Identify the parts of the trailer, notably the **boat trailer crossbar** (what the sea kayak rests on) and the **boat trailer post** (the main part of the trailer that all the crossbars attach to).

- Next identify the parts of the **cam strap** (webbing and buckle). Ask the students to make a mental picture of how the boats are attached to the trailer (noting the path of the strap around the crossbar and post and how the end of the strap is secured to prevent it from flapping in the wind) because they will soon be securing the kayaks with this method.
- Next, demonstrate how to release the buckle and strap. Have one student press against the center of the boat to keep it from falling off the trailer after you release the straps.

- Have the students work in groups of three, one at each end of the kayak releasing the straps and one holding the kayak in place until ready to unload.

- When the students are taking the boat off the crossbar, have them decide which way they will roll the boat before they lift it off the trailer.

- Make sure that the trailer is unloaded from the lowest crossbar to the top. This method will allow easier access to the cam straps and boats. Students should not release the cam straps on the boats above until the tier below it is clear of boats (to prevent boats from falling on students).

- One trick to unloading boats on higher tiers for students who have trouble reaching the boats is to have one student grab an end of the boat and pull down on it just enough to counteract its weight while another student guides the opposite end of the boat down to a lower crossbar. With the boat now at a slant, they follow the same procedure in reverse until the entire boat is down on the lower crossbar, where taking it off the trailer is easier.

Activity 2: Carrying Empty Sea Kayaks (10 Minutes)

With most of the boats now around the trailer, enlist a volunteer to help carry a boat to the edge of the water. This is a good time to review the parts of the sea kayak. Simply point to parts of the boat without saying anything to see whether students can remember the names of the parts. Have them call out the names. See how fast you can point to the parts and receive the correct response.

- Demonstrate how to carry an unloaded boat properly. One person must be on each end of the boat with one hand on the **handle**, or toggle, and the other hand cradling the boat. Some may find it more comfortable to carry the boat by positioning themselves on opposite sides of the sea kayak.

- Emphasize that hands tend to be slippery when wet or coated with sunscreen, so each person must always have both hands on the boat.

- Generally, two people can comfortably carry an unloaded boat. Demonstrate the proper lifting technique by keeping your back straight and bending your legs (in a squatting position). Emphasize lifting with the legs, not the back.

- Walk the boat down to the edge of the water. Mention to students that they must be aware of the surface on which they place the boats. They must be sure to avoid jagged edges that could damage the hull. If you are working around oyster shells, coral, or other sharp ground, find padding to place under the boats. Detritus, washed-up seaweed, or anything from the **rack line** will work fine.

Activity 3: Carrying a Loaded Boat (10 Minutes)

With the remaining boats around the trailer, you can pretend that one boat is loaded for this demonstration.

- Emphasize that the weight of the gear carried in the boat can severely damage the hull if the boat is not carried properly. Suggest that students load heavier items, such as water, at the edge of the water before departing from shore. Carrying the boat with heavier items loaded is OK; doing so will just require more hands to help.

- A minimum of four people are required to carry a loaded boat, one at each end of the boat and one on each side of the cockpit. The people on the cockpit count off the lifting because the curvature of the hull (rocker) will result in their carrying most of the weight. Again, emphasize lifting with the legs, not the back.

Activity 4: Using the Sea Kayak Sling (10 Minutes)

The **sea kayak sling** provides more comfort for the carriers and more support for the boat when carrying it. Demonstrate the following and let students practice.

- To use the two sea kayak slings (two per boat), slide the 2-inch (5-centimeter) webbing under the bulkheads (the most rigid part of the boat) and have two people on each side of the boat grab the ends of the webbing. Each of these four people, two for each sling, places an end over one shoulder (the shoulder closer to the boat) and holds the end of the webbing tightly. Now you have four people carrying the boat, two on each sling at the bulkheads (figure SK3.1).

- The sling is helpful because it distributes the weight of the boat and is adjustable to allow easier walking with a heavy boat. The people using the slings call out when to lift the boat when using an additional two people, one at each end, for a total of six carriers. Again, remind them to lift with the legs.

Activity 5: Loading the Trailer (10 Minutes)

The trailer should be loaded from the top down. Each tier of boats must be secure before the tier below it is loaded. Usually only one boat is loaded on each side of the top tier.

- Boats should be placed upside down (cockpit facing down) so that they don't collect water if it rains.

- When loading the top tier, make sure that the cam strap wraps around the post and that both the end of the webbing and buckle drape over the boat. Place the buckle about one hand span (6 to 8 inches, or 15 to 20 centimeters) from the crossbar. Wrap the end of the webbing around the crossbar once to create friction and then thread the webbing up through the buckle. Pull down on the webbing but do not overtighten.

FIGURE SK3.1 Using a sea kayak sling to carry the kayak with four people.

- If you have glass sea kayaks, make sure that the metal buckle is not against the glass. Overtightened straps can crack glass boats and separate bulkheads from plastic hulls. Also, plastic boats will tend to warp if they are left in the sun with overtightened straps. Make sure that you have adequate padding for glass boats.

- To keep the end of the strap from flapping in the wind and becoming frayed, tuck away the excess or finish it off by placing a bight through an overhand knot.

- For tiers with two boats, try to pair up boats with similar hulls. They will cradle each other when they are loaded.

- Place the boats at 45-degree angles with cockpits facing down and bows facing forward (it's bad luck to pull a trailer with sterns pointing forward!). Wrap the cam strap around the post and drape it over both boats.

◆ Have one person press against the middle of the boats to keep them from sliding off the crossbars. Pull the buckle end of the strap one hand span from the crossbar and thread the free end of the strap over the first boat, around the crossbar, and then over the second boat (see figure SK3.2).

◆ Finish tightening the straps the same as securing the single kayak. Test all the boats with a tug before departure.

◆ For long trips, tie bow and stern lines (also called *painters*) around the posts of the trailer for added security.

Closure Activity

Debriefing Transporting and Carries (5 Minutes)

FIGURE SK3.2   A loaded trailer using cam straps to secure the kayaks.

Debrief unloading, loading, and carries by asking the students whether any tricks or techniques were helpful. Point out that unloading, loading, and carries will become easier and faster through practice. Provide positive reinforcement. Make sure to discuss the issues of teamwork and good communication. Poor communication and lack of teamwork are the major causes of accidents when loading, unloading, and carrying watercraft.

Follow-Up Activity

Transporting and Carry Review (5 to 10 Minutes)

The follow-up activity takes place at the beginning and end of each lesson as students continue to practice loading, unloading, and carries. Have individual students volunteer to oversee the process in a leadership position. Having one person call the shots in a large group helps manage the risks and allows individuals to exercise their knowledge and skill. For loading a kayak on a vehicle top, refer to lesson 3 in unit 7.

ASSESSMENT

◆ Check that students recognize unsafe body positions that can cause injury by observing them carry and lift sea kayaks with proper body position.

◆ Verify that students can properly lift a sea kayak on and off a boat trailer by observing them load and unload the boat trailer during the main activities.

◆ Confirm that students can properly secure the sea kayaks to the boat trailer using cam straps by observing them and testing the kayaks with a tug to make sure that they are securely attached to the trailer.

◆ Make sure that students can use a hand carry to transport a loaded kayak and an unloaded kayak by observing them carry kayaks to and from the water.

◆ Check that students can use a sea kayak sling to transport a loaded sea kayak by observing them carry a loaded sea kayak with four people and two sea kayak slings.

◆ Assess whether students' self-reliance and craftsmanship have improved by observing them take a greater role in loading and unloading the trailer correctly and carrying the boats properly without your direction.

TEACHING CONSIDERATIONS

◆ Make sure that the ground is level when students first learn to load, unload, and carry the boats so that they avoid slipping or twisting their ankles.

◆ Pair up students of similar height to make loading and unloading easier.

◆ Naturally, some students will tend to stand around and watch while the more energetic students jump in to complete the tasks. Encourage students who feel shy about jumping in by pairing them up with students who are more energetic.

◆ When demonstrating the correct method for securing the boats on the trailer, make sure that all students can see the correct path of the cam strap. Boats can obstruct the students' view of the your demonstration.

◆ Solo carries of sea kayaks are possible, although this method is not advised if students are present to help. You can easily pull a muscle in your lower back when carrying a sea kayak solo. The typical way to carry the sea kayak solo is to squat next to the cockpit and roll the kayak up on to your knee. Next, slide your shoulder in the cockpit and rest the combing on your shoulder. This is the midpoint of the kayak, and the boat is easier to balance at this point. Advise students to carry a sea kayak solo only if no one is around to help carry it.

UNIT 5, LESSON 4

▷ Getting Comfortable With the Sea Kayak

OVERVIEW

This lesson is designed to assess the comfort levels of students in deep water and in the sea kayak. From a risk management perspective, you should see that students can exercise these two important skills: Students must be able to wet exit a sea kayak comfortably and demonstrate the minimal swimming skills of swimming 100 yards (meters) and treading water for five minutes. Professionally run sea kayaking programs have written requirements and guidelines in place before students can enroll in a class. The sea kayaker assessment procedures in this lesson reflect common practices used by various outfitters and organizations.

JUSTIFICATION

To ensure everyone's safety, make sure that class participants can swim and feel comfortable entering and exiting a sea kayak in deep water.

GOAL

To make sure that participants can comfortably swim approximately 100 yards (meters), tread water for five minutes, comfortably perform a wet exit and deep-water reentry, and to make sure that they are properly fitted in a sea kayak.

OBJECTIVES

At the end of this lesson, students will be able to

- describe the proper fit of a sea kayak (cognitive),
- describe the HELP position (cognitive),
- execute a wet exit (psychomotor),
- complete a deep-water reentry (psychomotor),
- enter and exit a sea kayak from land (psychomotor),
- comfortably swim 100 yards (meters) (psychomotor),
- tread water for five minutes (psychomotor), and
- take pride in becoming more proficient and confident at the sport of sea kayaking (affective).

EQUIPMENT AND AREAS NEEDED

- Sea kayaks (one per person)
- Paddles (one per person)
- PFDs (one per person)
- Spray skirts (one per person)

RISK MANAGEMENT CONSIDERATIONS

- See lesson 1 for details on general risk management considerations.
- Make sure that the wet exit practice area is deep enough that students will not hit the bottom when flipping over (3 to 4 feet, or 90 to 120 centimeters, deep).
- If practicing in a pool, make sure that you have enough room that you don't intrude on other pool users.
- Constantly conduct head counts when students are swimming and treading water, or set up a buddy system and monitor carefully.
- Have PFDs ready for anyone who might need assistance swimming or treading water.
- Wear PFDs when practicing wet exits and deep-water reentries.
- Have a safety system in place when conducting swim tests.

LESSON CONTENT

Introduction

Set the tone of this lesson with enthusiastic statements such as "Today we get to play with the boats and get really wet!" and "Today we will review parts of equipment used in sea kayaking, take a water comfort test, and practice wet exits, deep water reentries, and getting in and out of the boat." Students are generally excited about flipping kayaks and learning new skills that allow them to play in the water.

Main Activities

Activity 1: Swim Test (45 to 60 Minutes)

The first part of the water comfort test is to have everyone swim 100 yards (meters). Emphasize to students that the test is not a race. They can swim the 100 yards (meters) in any way they choose (backstroke, crawl, or dog paddle) and at any speed. The important criterion is being able to stay above water comfortably for the 100 yards (meters).

◆ After the students have finished the swim, allow them to rest and catch their breath.

◆ After they have rested, have them tread water for five minutes.

◆ If any students cannot swim the 100 yards (meters) or tread water for five minutes, discretely encourage them to enroll in basic swim classes. Ultimately, the decision to allow them to take the class is up to you, but be aware that one student can put the whole class in danger. Not being able to pass the minimum water comfort test should be a red flag.

FIGURE SK4.1   The heat escape lessening position (HELP).

Reprinted, by permission, from American Canoe Association, 2008, *Outdoor adventures: Canoeing* (Champaign, IL: Human Kinetics), 122.

Activity 2: Introduction to HELP (Five Minutes)

Describe the heat escape lessening position (**HELP**). Someone who is caught in the water and can't get out until help arrives can reduce the loss of heat by maintaining the HELP position as shown in figure SK4.1. The person can reduce heat loss by keeping the extremities and limbs close to the torso, thus trapping body heat and keeping water from taking heat away from the skin. Note that the man in figure SK4.1 is demonstrating a more relaxed position with his legs extended. If possible, maximize heat retention by pulling your knees up to your chest and hold them there by locking your arms around them.

Have at least one student demonstrate. Then allow students to practice before moving to the next topic. Make sure that lifejackets are available for this exercise.

Activity 3: Fitting and Entering a Kayak (30 to 45 Minutes)

Demonstrate the proper body position while sitting next to the boat (not in the boat) so that the students will get a visual indication of what the body should look like while in the boat (see figure SK4.2). Emphasize that the more points

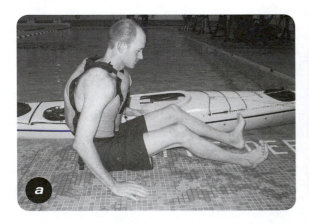

FIGURE SK4.2   First *(a)* demonstrate proper body position outside the boat, then *(b)* demonstrate proper body position inside the boat.

of contact the body has with the boat, the better stability, boat control, and energy transfer they will have.

Fitting the Kayak   Emphasize these points to achieve a good fit in the kayak:

- ◆ The balls of the feet are on the foot braces, and the ankles have a 90-degree bend.
- ◆ Thighs are securely intact with the thigh braces.
- ◆ Legs are slightly bent, not straight out.
- ◆ The back band is snug against the lower back, and the torso is slightly forward.

Spend time with each student to make sure that all have a good fit in the boat. Students are often so eager to get in the water that they rush through boat fitting and end up prematurely fatigued. Finally, have participants properly fit and secure their spray skirts and PFDs.

Getting In and Out   Several options are available for first entering the boat. The most stable way to enter the kayak is to have someone stabilize it as the person enters. A key concept to remember is to keep the center of gravity low. If someone stabilizes the boat, make sure that the person holds the boat in a way (behind the cockpit) that does not hinder the student who is entering the boat. Stabilizing the boat by holding the bow or stern is not as effective as holding on at the cockpit because the holder cannot gain as much leverage.

One method of entering the boat is to get the rear end in the cockpit first (thus lowering the center of gravity).

- ◆ When entering the cockpit, the person must remember to keep the head low and lean toward land, using the land to help stabilize the boat.
- ◆ The person should have the legs on either side of the cockpit acting as outriggers. The legs help balance and stabilize the person.
- ◆ The person slides the legs into the cockpit one at a time. Figure SK4.3 shows the progression. Notice that the progression in the figure also works when no one is stabilizing the boat.

Some students may have difficulty entering the boat using the previously described method. Another method that works well for students with longer legs starts with sliding the feet in the cockpit first as the person sits on the back edge of the cockpit. This method requires more balance because the center of gravity is higher. Figure SK4.4 shows the progression using a paddle as an outrigger for added stability.

FIGURE SK4.3   Getting into a kayak: *(a)* Start from the rear—stay low and lean toward land; *(b)* slide the legs in one at a time; *(c)* keep one leg out as an outrigger for balance; *(d)* get into position and release from land.

◆ To enter the kayak, park the boat parallel to shore.

◆ Place the blade of the paddle behind the cockpit.

◆ Place the paddle perpendicular to the boat, acting as an outrigger.

◆ Grasp the blade and shaft of the paddle to the cockpit, with the combing behind you for added support, and lean toward the outrigging paddle to provide stability (figure SK4.4).

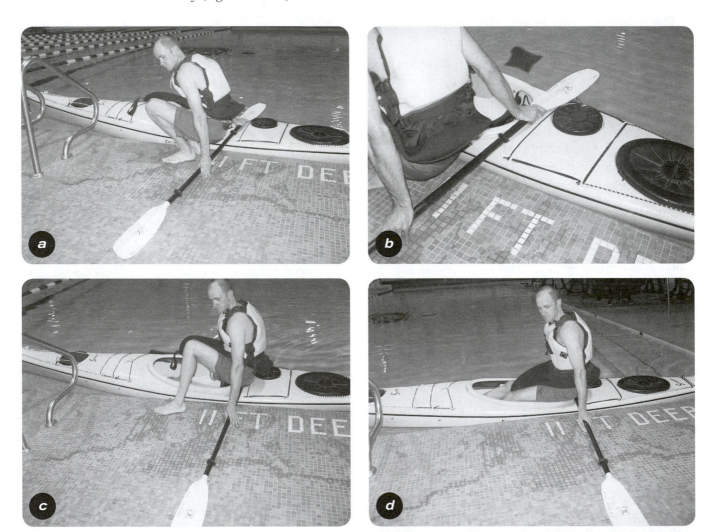

FIGURE SK4.4   Getting into a kayak using a paddle for stability.

To get out of the kayak, students can use either method in reverse, depending on their comfort level.

Activity 4: The Wet Exit (40 Minutes)

The **wet exit** is a basic skill that every kayaker should be familiar with. Being upside down in a kayak can be unnerving. The wet exit allows the kayaker to remove herself or himself from the kayak after it capsizes. At most, the wet exit takes only a few seconds, but this can be a daunting task for beginners. Let students know that it is OK to be anxious about the wet exit.

To help students be more comfortable, demonstrate the following sequence of the wet exit on dry land. First, place yourself in the cockpit and demonstrate how to attach the spray skirt to the cockpit, starting from the back of the cockpit above the back band and working your way toward the front of the cockpit (figure SK4.5).

◆ You can use your elbows and forearms to keep the spray skirt in place.

◆ The area of the spray skirt with the grab loop (or pull handle) should be the last part of the spray skirt affixed to the combing. Make sure that the grab loop is exposed, as shown in figure SK4.5.

◆ If the spray skirt is hard to get on, you may need someone to help pull it on, or you can wet it so that it stretches easier.

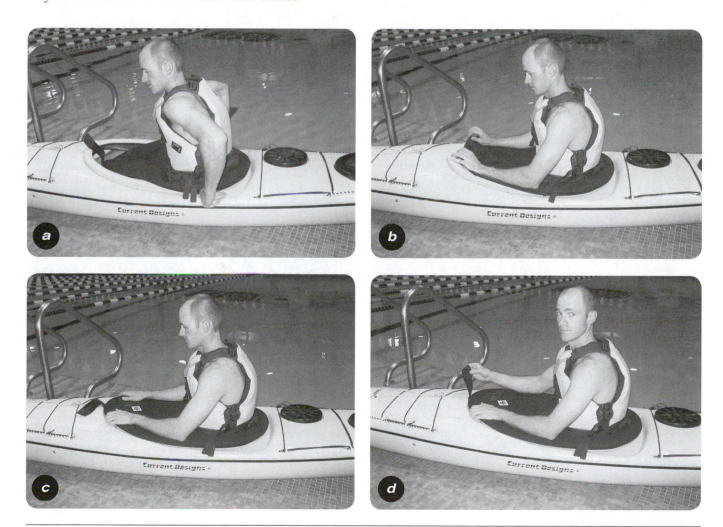

FIGURE SK4.5   When attaching a spray skirt to a kayak, make sure the grab loop remains exposed.

Next, describe the following wet-exit progression on land in front of the students (figure SK4.6).

- Once overturned, bend forward, placing your head toward the deck of the boat (this will lessen the amount of water that goes up your nose!).
- Pull the spray skirt grab loop up and away from you.
- Place your hands by your hips on the cockpit combing and bend forward.
- Finally, push down at your hips at the cockpit combing so that your rear end exits the boat first. Note that the flotation of your PFD will aid in you getting out of the boat.

After you have completed a dry run on land, demonstrate the sequence in the water. Involve the students by asking them to count how long it takes you to perform the wet exit. This activity tends to relieve some of the anxiety for students who are afraid of the wet exit.

- After you are in the boat, review how to put the spray skirt on the cockpit, emphasizing the exposed grab loop.

FIGURE SK4.6   Performing the wet exit progression on land first before demonstrating an actual wet exit on the water.

◆ Introduce the challenge of tapping on the bottom of the boat when upside down and running both hands along the bottom of the hull. Explain that the tapping attracts the attention of others and that this exercise will lead to rescue skills covered in future lessons. This challenge also helps you determine the students' comfort level.

◆ Have the students count for you as you demonstrate the wet exit.

◆ After you surface, demonstrate how to let others know that you are OK by tapping your head.

Activity 5: Unassisted Deep-Water Reentry (30 Minutes)

After you have demonstrated the wet exit, demonstrate the **deep-water reentry** (figure SK4.7) because you are already in the water.

◆ Reach with your dominant hand to the opposite side of the cockpit combing of the sea kayak.

◆ With a strong scissors kick, pull yourself out of the water and rotate your body to get your rear end in the sea kayak first. This lowers your center of gravity, making the boat more stable.

◆ After your rear end is in the boat, choose your preferred method for entering the boat as mentioned previously.

◆ A sea kayak filled with water is much harder to balance and provides a great opportunity for students to become more accustomed to the boat and more comfortable with getting in and out.

Another option for deep-water reentry for students with longer legs is to climb on the back deck of the sea kayak (figure SK4.8). This method is much more difficult and requires greater balance. Key points include the following:

◆ Keep your head low as you back your legs into the cockpit, and keep your arms out perpendicular to the sea kayak to help you maintain balance.

◆ Slide backward into the cockpit as you continue to face the stern of the boat.

◆ After your rear end is over the seat, quickly turn around to face the bow of the boat.

◆ This activity gives students another excellent opportunity to become familiar with the sea kayak and more confident with getting in and out of it.

Activity 6: Student Practice (45 Minutes)

After you have finished demonstrating the wet exit and deep-water reentry, have students practice by pairing up.

◆ Have one student in the boat and the other student in waist-deep water acting as a spotter.

◆ Start students off by having them wet exit the boat without the spray skirt attached. Then have them wet exit with it attached.

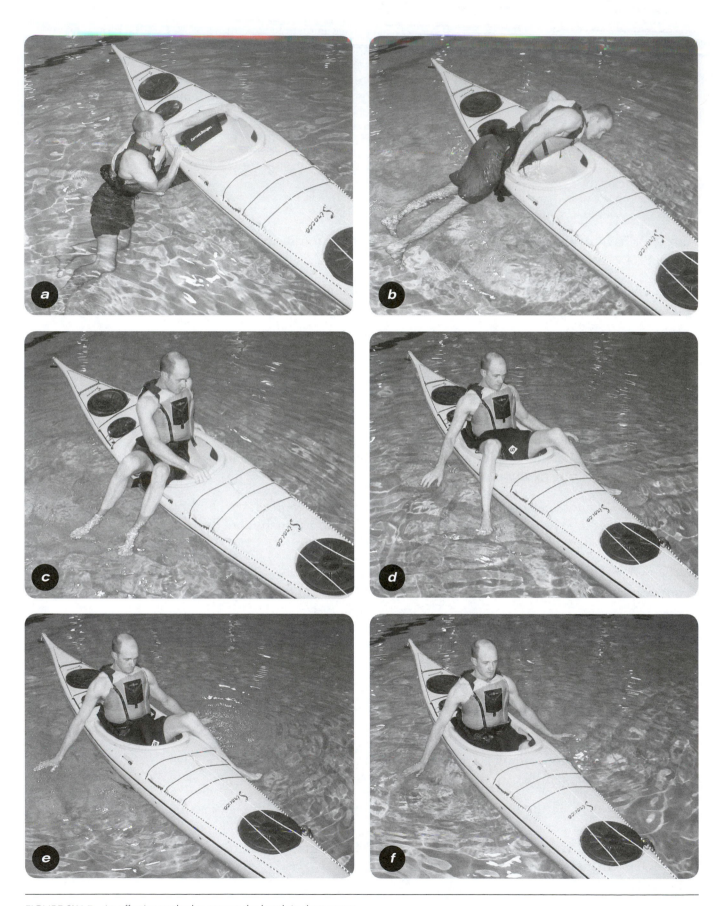

FIGURE SK4.7 An effective method to reenter the kayak in deep water.

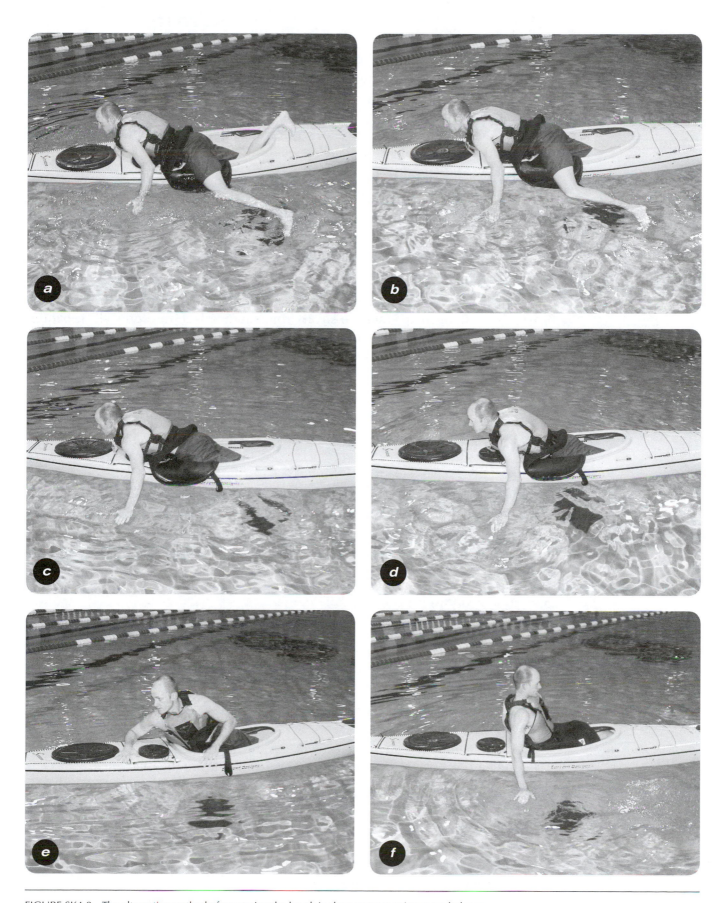

FIGURE SK4.8   The alternative method of reentering the kayak in deep water requires more balance.

- A suggestion that can help students prevent water from running up their noses (if nose plugs are not available) is to have them pick a current favorite song and hum it through the nose (this forces air out of the nose, keeping the water out).
- Next, have them practice the wet exit again. This time have them bang on the bottom of the boat after it is overturned and before they wet exit. As they become more comfortable with the wet exit, see how long they can bang on the boat before wet exiting (see whether they can bang out the rhythm of their favorite song and have other students guess what it is!).
- After each wet exit, have them practice the deep-water reentry.

Closure Activity

Wet-Exit Relay Race (15 Minutes)

Have the students continue to practice exiting and reentering the boat. One way to practice these skills is to divide the class into two teams and have a relay race in which students must enter the kayak from shore, attach the spray skirt, paddle out and wet exit, reenter the boat in deep water, paddle back to shore, and switch kayakers. This activity promotes coaching by other students in the class.

After the relay race is over, have the losing team return the equipment, making sure to hang up PFDs and spray skirts, and drain water out of the boats so that the equipment will dry.

Follow-Up Activity

Wet Exit and Deep-Water Reentry Debrief (5 to 10 Minutes)

Debrief the wet exit and deep-water reentry. Ask the students whether they have any suggestions for practicing (for example, what worked well? what gave you trouble?). Encourage students on their progressions and provide positive reinforcement. The other part of this follow-up activity is to review attaching the spray skirt and the sequence of the wet exit at the beginning of the next lesson.

ASSESSMENT

- Check that students can describe the proper fit of a sea kayak by observing them assist each other fitting the sea kayaks and by asking them to describe the proper fit of a sea kayak on a written final exam at the end of the class.
- Verify that students can describe the HELP position by asking them to describe, during a debriefing or on a written test, how to reduce heat loss if they are in the water for an extended period.
- Check that students can execute a wet exit during the main activities part of this lesson and by observing them perform wet exits during the relay race.
- Check that students can complete a deep-water reentry during the main activities part of this lesson and by observing them perform a deep-water reentry during the relay race.
- Evaluate whether students can enter and exit a sea kayak from land during the main activities part of this lesson and by observing them get in and out of the sea kayak from land during the relay race.
- Verify that students can comfortably swim 100 yards (meters) by completing a formal swim test.

- Verify that students can tread water for five minutes during the formal testing described in the main activities section of this lesson.
- Assess whether students take pride in becoming more proficient and confident at sea kayaking by observing them practice and master skills through additional activities such as the relay race.

TEACHING CONSIDERATIONS

- If students cannot complete the swim test, tread test, wet exit, or deep-water reentry, strongly suggest that they take a class other than sea kayaking. The safety of the entire group is involved. If all students can pass these basic skills, you are free to focus on the skills more central to sea kayaking.
- Wet exits can be daunting to beginning sea kayakers. Make sure to encourage and be patient with students hesitant to try the wet exit. Nose plugs and even goggles or a mask are recommended when practicing wet exits for the first time.
- Have students who catch on quickly help those who are struggling with these skills.

UNIT 5, LESSON 5

▷ Rescues

OVERVIEW

In this lesson students learn self-rescue skills and assisted-rescue skills that are useful for the sport of sea kayaking. Specifically, the lesson covers paddle float rescues, boat-over-boat rescues (T-rescues), Eskimo bow rescue, towing, and using slings for assisted reentry.

JUSTIFICATION

Sea kayakers should become proficient in both self-rescue and assisted-rescue techniques. Sea kayaking takes place in dynamic environments. Conditions change rapidly; therefore, a proficient sea kayaker must be prepared for a variety of conditions and environments.

GOAL

To develop students' ability to execute proper self-rescue and assisted-rescue techniques.

OBJECTIVES

At the end of this lesson, students will be able to

- understand when to use different types of rescues (cognitive),
- execute a paddle float rescue (psychomotor),
- demonstrate a boat-over-boat rescue (psychomotor),
- demonstrate an Eskimo bow rescue (psychomotor),

◆ demonstrate how to tow another sea kayaker (psychomotor),

◆ demonstrate using a sling for an assisted deep-water reentry (psychomotor), and

◆ take pride in becoming a more self-reliant and competent sea kayaker (affective).

EQUIPMENT AND AREAS NEEDED

◆ Four sea kayaks

◆ Four paddles

◆ Four paddle floats

◆ Four spray skirts

◆ PFDs (one per person)

◆ Masks or goggles (optional) (one per person)

◆ Four bilge pumps

◆ Two 12-foot (4-meter) pieces of rope or webbing tied into a sling

◆ Two tow systems with quick release

RISK MANAGEMENT CONSIDERATIONS

◆ See lesson 1 for details about general risk management considerations.

◆ Make sure that the rescue practice area is deep enough that students won't hit their heads when flipping over (3 to 4 feet, or 90 to 120 centimeters, deep).

◆ If practicing in a pool, make sure that you have enough room that you don't intrude on other pool users.

◆ Perform a head count constantly when students are practicing rescues.

◆ Have students work in pairs and use the buddy system to keep a count of everyone in the class.

◆ Have students wear PFDs when practicing rescues.

◆ When practicing rescues in a natural environment, make sure that the class is far away from potential hazards such as boat traffic and channels.

LESSON CONTENT

Introduction

Basic rescue skills are a must for sea kayaking! Most sea kayakers don't go out looking for trouble, but every once in a while, trouble finds them. When they least expect it, that's when they should expect it! Sea kayakers can't practice rescue skills too much. Have students review wet-exit skills and deep-water reentry skills from the last lesson before moving into the main activities.

Main Activities

You should demonstrate self-rescues and assisted rescues and have students practice the techniques until they develop a comfortable level of proficiency.

Activity 1: Self-Rescue (30 Minutes)

A sea kayaker paddling without a partner in rough conditions who needs to reenter the boat will find a **paddle float** rescue extremely helpful. A person must practice the paddle float rescue many times to increase the chances of achieving a fast and safe rescue. The paddle float rescue takes a good bit of time, even when done proficiently. As conditions worsen, the rescue becomes more difficult.

Demonstrate the progression of the paddle float rescue on land first and then in the water. Make sure that students are able to see and hear you as you talk about the progression. It is easy to find yourself facing away from the students with this demonstration, so make sure to plan the layout of the classroom ahead of time.

◆ After you have exited from the boat, make sure that you quickly toss any loose objects back into the cockpit or secure them to the bungee cords on the deck.

◆ Position yourself on the downwind side of the sea kayak because the boat will move much faster across the water than you or your paddle will.

◆ Hold on to the boat or place one leg in the cockpit to free up your hands. (Note: Make sure that you lean back and allow your PFD to float you. If you don't lean back and remain vertical with your leg in the cockpit, the boat will tend to turn over, allowing more water in the cockpit.)

◆ Next, inflate the float and secure it to the paddle blade with the keeper strap on the float. Figure SK5.1 shows the initial steps of the paddle float rescue.

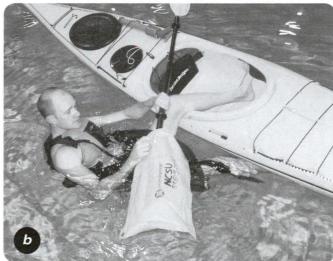

FIGURE SK5.1   Initial set of steps for paddle float self-rescue technique: *(a)* partially inflate the float; *(b)* place the float on the paddle with a keeper strap; *(c)* fully inflate the float.

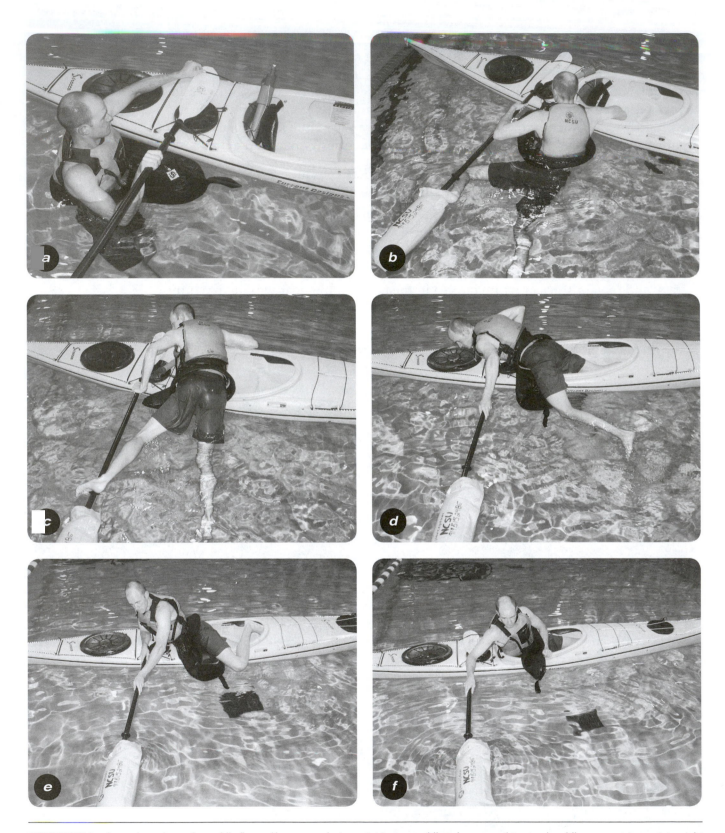

FIGURE SK5.2   Second set of steps for paddle float self-rescue technique: *(a)* Secure paddle to bungees; *(b)* extend paddle as an outrigger; *(c)* weight the paddle with the foot; *(d)* stay low; *(e)* work your way into the cockpit; *(f)* use the paddle as a stabilizer until situated.

◆ After you inflate the float, secure the blade opposite the float to the deck behind the cockpit under the bungee cords.

◆ Make sure to keep the paddle perpendicular to the boat so that it acts as an outrigger and stabilizes the boat.

◆ Place one foot, or both feet, on the shaft of the paddle and work your way to the stern of the boat (figure SK5.2).

◆ Make sure to keep weight on the float, keep it perpendicular to the boat, and keep your head low to lower your center of gravity and increase your stability.

◆ After you are back in the cockpit, put your spray skirt over the combing and pump the remaining water out of the cockpit (figure SK5.3). Disassemble the paddle float only after securing the spray skirt on the cockpit combing.

FIGURE SK5.3   Final set of steps for paddle float self-rescue technique: *(a)* place the spray skirt on partially and pump water out of the cockpit; *(b)* secure the spray skirt and disassemble the paddle float.

Activity 2: Assisted Rescue—Boat Over Boat (30 Minutes)

If you have a contained classroom without other distractions, you can walk through the boat-over-boat rescue, or T-rescue, in the water with a volunteer student in the other boat to rescue you (figure SK5.4). Otherwise, do a dry run on land first and then get in the water and walk students through the progression.

◆ Flip the sea kayak and perform a wet exit.

◆ After you are in the water, signal to the rescuer that you are OK by tapping the top of your head.

◆ Next, gather your belongings and swim them over to the rescuer (paddle and other miscellaneous items floating around).

◆ Next, swim the bow of your boat over to the rescuer and keep your boat perpendicular to the rescuer's boat (forming the letter T). Having the boats perpendicular stabilizes both boats during the rescue.

◆ The rescuer grabs the bow of your sea kayak, not the stern, for two reasons:
  – The bow has no skeg or rudder to contend with.
  – Because of the shape of the deck, after the bow is lifted slightly out of the water, the water drains quickly, making the cockpit almost completely dry.

- Next, swim to the stern of your boat. On the rescuer's count, you push down on the stern and toward the rescuer, breaking the seal of air on the cockpit.

- The rescuer pulls up on the bow, just enough to empty the cockpit of water. The rescuer does not need to drag your boat across the deck of her or his boat if the bow of your boat is lifted out of the water first, contrary to past methods of sea kayak T-rescues.

- The rescuer then parallel parks your boat so that the boats are stern to bow (facing opposite directions). This positioning allows the rescuer to remain out of the way of the cockpit and rear deck so that you can more easily reenter the sea kayak using the deep-water reentry techniques mentioned in the previous lesson.

- The rescuer should keep your boat stabilized until you have securely attached your spray skirt and are comfortable enough to paddle on your own again. Note: If water fills the cockpit while you are reentering the sea kayak, the rescuer may assist bilging the cockpit to speed up the rescue.

- Another helpful hint is to attach the spray skirt around the combing and place the **bilge pump** down the tunnel of the spray skirt, allowing the spray skirt to shed water coming over the deck.

(continued)

FIGURE SK5.4 Boat-over-boat assisted rescue, also known as the T-rescue: *(a)* The rescuer grabs the bow; *(b)* together they lift the boat and empty the water; *(c)* then they roll the empty boat over.

FIGURE SK5.4   *(d)* The swimmer and rescuer bring the boats together. As the rescuer stabilizes the boat, *(e)* the swimmer climbs in using deep-water reentry techniques. *(continued)*

Activity 3: Assisted Rescue—Eskimo Bow (30 Minutes)

The Eskimo bow rescue (figure SK5.5) is a fast and easy way to remain in the sea kayak if it flips over, although it is a more advanced assisted rescue. To execute this rescue successfully, the sea kayaker needs to have a reliable paddling partner who pays attention to his or her whereabouts, be able to hold his or her breath for a few seconds, and be able to remain calm under water until help arrives. As with any rescue, sea kayakers should practice the Eskimo bow rescue in a safe environment until it becomes second nature.

◆ When you realize that you are going to flip over, grab a big gulp of air.

◆ After you flip over, bang on the bottom of the sea kayak and run your hands back and forth toward the bow and stern of the boat. Banging your hands on the hull will, you hope, get your partner's attention. Running your hands back and forth will lessen the chances of a finger or hand being crushed by the rescue boat as it approaches and increase your chances of a faster "find" of the rescue boat.

◆ After you "find" your rescue boat, simply right yourself by pushing on the bow. You need to execute a good hip snap, which requires you to remain loose at your waist. Lift a knee to intiate a powerful hip snap, and then swivel (or snap) your hips independently from your upper body. The upper body should remain motionless underwater during the hip snap. As the kayak rolls upright, the upper body and head emerge last. Keeping your head down and rolling the kayak up with your hips makes this rescue easier to execute.

FIGURE SK5.5 Eskimo bow rescue: *(a)* Roll upside down and move the arms up and down the hull; *(b)* the rescuer presents the bow; *(c)* execute a hip snap to right the boat; *(d)* stabilize the boat before letting go.

◆ The less experienced sea kayaker should be in front of the more proficient sea kayaker when traveling together. This positioning will allow a faster rescue because the more experienced sea kayaker can paddle up to the overturned boat instead of having to turn around to rescue the capsized boat.

Activity 4: Assisted Rescue—Sling Reentry (30 Minutes)

The sling reentry is helpful for someone who is too tired to reenter the boat in deep water.

- The rescuer ties a 12-foot (4-meter) section of polypropylene rope or webbing into a sling.
- With the rescuer's boat and the swimmer's boat side by side facing opposite directions, the rescuer wraps the sling around the cockpit combing of her or his boat and drapes it over the cockpit of the swimmer's boat until it reaches the water.
- The swimmer uses the sling as a step to reenter the sea kayak.
- One potential hazard with this method is that the sling may become unattached from the rescuer's combing and tighten around her or his waist, potentially injuring the rescuer or capsizing the kayak.
- Another variation of using the sling is to slide the swimmer's paddle through the sling, place the paddle in the water under the two boats, and drape the sling over the swimmer's cockpit and into the water. The swimmer uses the sling as a step just as in the first application of the sling. This method causes fatigue to the shaft of the paddle.

Activity 5: Assisted Rescue—Towing (30 Minutes)

Towing can be an effective way to assist a fatigued or injured sea kayaker. The tower should always use a system that can be released quickly if necessary. If the sea kayaker being towed is able to stabilize his or her sea kayak without help, then a single boat tow is possible; single boat tows, however, quickly tire out the tower.

- The towline is typically attached to the rescuer's PFD quick-release system.
- The towline should always be attached to the disabled boat's bow handle. Assisted tows work better over long distances when two boats tow the disabled boat in single-file formation.
- If the sea kayaker being towed is injured and cannot keep the boat stable, a third boat is required to help stabilize the boat by rafting up beside it. In this situation, two boats at a minimum are required to tow, again towing in single-file formation.

Closure Activity

Practice and Review (20 Minutes)

Have the students continue to practice self-rescues and assisted rescues. Check in with each student to make sure that all students understand the rescues and feel comfortable with the progression. This is a great opportunity to have students time their efforts and strive to reduce the time and energy to execute the rescues described in this lesson.

- After all students feel comfortable, have them return the equipment, making sure to hang up PFDs and spray skirts and to drain water out of the boats so that the equipment will dry.
- Debrief the rescues and ask the students whether they have any suggestions for practicing (for example, what worked well? what gave you trouble?).
- Encourage students on their progressions and provide positive reinforcement.

Follow-Up Activity

All-In Drill (10 to 15 Minutes)

After you think that students are comfortable in the sea kayaks and fairly competent with rescues, pick a time during your sea kayaking cruise to practice an all-in drill. The object of the all-in drill is to see how students react to a suddenly chaotic situation.

Pick a protected area (free from boat traffic and out of a channel) and ask one student to flip over his or her boat (unannounced, although you warned the group earlier in the trip that they would practice unannounced drills).

The victim also flips over a few others by acting as if he or she is having trouble getting back in the boat. This situation will involve multiple students in the exercise. Make sure that at least one instructor stays in a boat for safety purposes.

ASSESSMENT

- Check that students understand when to use a particular skill by discussing their experience after practicing the various skills.

- Verify that students can execute a paddle float rescue by observing them practice the rescue during the main activities and closing activities of the lesson.

- Confirm that students can perform a boat-over-boat rescue by observing them practice the rescue during the main activities, closure activity, and the all-in drill.

- Make sure that students can execute an Eskimo bow rescue by observing them practice the rescue during the main activities and closure activity.

- Check that students can tow another sea kayaker by observing them practice the rescue during the expedition phase of the course.

- Verify that students can use a sling for an assisted deep-water reentry by observing them practice the rescue during the main activities, closure activity, and the all-in drill.

- Assess whether students take pride in becoming self-reliant and competent sea kayakers by continuously practicing various rescue skills.

TEACHING CONSIDERATIONS

- Practice the rescues in a completely protected environment, preferably in a pool. After the students become comfortable with the rescues, practice the rescues in the outdoor environment.

- Everyone in the group should practice rescues, including instructors. You should lead by example, showing that a sea kayaker can never practice rescues enough. The more realistic you can make the conditions, the better students will learn the techniques. Most rescues don't take place in calm, clear, warm water, like that in a swimming pool.

- Encourage the use of goggles or masks for more advanced rescues such as the Eskimo bow rescue. Many students have a hard time visualizing body movement and body position under water. Goggles or masks help give a visual reference for body movement underwater.

- Encourage students to keep their heads low when reentering the sea kayak with any rescue. A common mistake is to allow the head to remain high above the water, raising the center of gravity and reducing the stability of the sea kayak. Lowering the head greatly increases stability, making reentry much easier.

▷ The Sea Kayak Roll

OVERVIEW

This lesson refers to the more detailed instruction of the kayak roll described in unit 6, lesson 7. Although there are many sea kayak rolls, the basic C-to-C roll is perfectly adequate. The sea kayak roll is not an essential self-rescue technique for beginning sea kayakers, and some students may be unable to master the roll in one class session. Emphasize practicing the roll to allow students to become more comfortable with bracing and wet exits. The more time that students spend in the kayak, both right side up and upside down, the more comfortable they will become and the more confidence they will gain.

JUSTIFICATION

The sea kayak roll, although it is an advanced skill, is a useful self-rescue technique for sea kayaking. By simply practicing the roll, students become more proficient with bracing and wet exiting. Therefore, they develop greater confidence as they continue to sea kayak.

GOAL

To advance students' understanding of the mechanics of rolling a kayak and increase their confidence and comfort with the sea kayak.

OBJECTIVES

At the end of this lesson, students will be able to

- describe the appropriate progression of a kayak roll (cognitive),
- demonstrate the mechanics of a sea kayak roll (psychomotor), and
- feel more confident and comfortable in a kayak (affective).

EQUIPMENT AND AREAS NEEDED

- Two sea kayaks
- Two paddles
- Two spray skirts
- PFDs (one per person)
- Two paddle floats

RISK MANAGEMENT CONSIDERATIONS

- One of the primary barriers to performance of the kayak roll is emotional anxiety, especially for students who are fearful of being trapped upside down in a kayak. Be especially attuned to the emotions of students during this lesson.
- Make sure that the site is free of rocks close to the water surface so that students do not hit them while practicing the roll. Before the practice session, reemphasize the importance of tucking.

- Shoulder injuries can occur because of using poor technique while performing the kayak roll. Introduce the concept of the paddler's box and the need to exercise care in performing the technique to avoid shoulder dislocations or muscle tears. See unit 6, lesson 4 for an explanation of the paddler's box.

- Recommend use of nose plugs for a more enjoyable learning experience.

- Be cautious of uncontrolled and wild paddle movements when teaching students the roll. Stay on guard as students are sweeping their paddles from the setup to the 90-degree position when learning the roll. They should keep the forearms up and in front of the face.

- If information or terms are not clearly related to risk management issues listed here, see unit 6, lesson 7, for more information.

- See lesson 1 for details about general risk management considerations.

LESSON CONTENT

Introduction

The roll is an important self-rescue technique that sea kayakers must learn as they progress to more challenging environments. To teach this skill and develop students' proficiency, a supportive learning environment is essential. For many, the roll is a complex physical task that takes effort and practice to master. Students can become discouraged if the roll proves difficult to learn.

Main Activity

The Sea Kayak Roll (One Hour)

- Refer to the whitewater kayaking unit, lesson 7, for step-by-step techniques to teach a kayak roll.

- Besides having students perform the whitewater kayaking roll activities, you may want to have them practice the Eskimo bow rescue as described in lesson 5. This rescue allows students to practice the hip snap, a key element in a successful kayak roll, and holding their breath upside down in the kayak.

- Another helpful aid to allow participants to practice the brace and hip snap is to attach a paddle float on the end of the paddle blade to act as an outrigger as described in lesson 5. The paddle float stabilizes the paddle and allows students to build confidence and comfort as they practice the kayak roll.

- Consider showing an instructional video or DVD (Whiting & Emerick, 2005) about the kayak roll. You can show the video before or after the initial pool session. This teaching technique will be helpful for students with specific learning styles.

Closure Activity

Combat Rolls (30 Minutes)

Ideally, you should have students practice their rolls under realistic conditions. When students can execute a consistent roll in a swimming pool or on flat, calm water, have them test their skills in more adverse conditions.

- Have them attempt the roll in cold water or in small waves. Practicing their "combat" rolls builds confidence and skill.

◆ Also consider having students practice with a sea kayak fully loaded with camping gear. Many times, students will find it more challenging to roll a fully loaded boat. Again, this activity will build confidence and prepare them for realistic conditions.

Follow-Up Activity

Practice, Practice, Practice! (Time as Needed)

Students who are having difficulty learning to roll should be given additional time to practice. One-on-one practice is beneficial for students who are having trouble mastering the skill. Schedule additional roll practice sessions and solicit the assistance of students who have mastered the roll.

ASSESSMENT

◆ Check that students can describe the appropriate progression of a kayak roll by having them assist and coach one another during the learning process.

◆ Confirm that students can demonstrate the mechanics of a kayak roll by having them execute the fundamental moves as they practice.

◆ Assess whether students feel more confident and comfortable in a kayak by observing them as they practice rolling under more realistic and challenging situations as described in the closure activity.

TEACHING CONSIDERATIONS

◆ Although many students find this skill difficult to master, it is one of the skills that students most want to learn. Be patient with students and offer lots of positive reinforcement.

◆ Be sure to tell students that mastering the kayak roll in one lesson is difficult. Even if the students do not master the skill, they gain confidence in their ability to wet exit and brace, and they feel more comfortable and confident in the kayak.

◆ Do everything possible to fit students in their boats properly. Learning to roll is much easier if the boat fits properly. Consider duct taping pads in key areas to ensure a tighter fit.

UNIT 5, LESSON 7

▷ Basic Strokes

OVERVIEW

In this lesson participants learn the basic strokes associated with sea kayaking. Participants also learn the fundamental parts of strokes, correct body movement, and correct paddle placement to produce the most efficient and effective strokes. The lesson addresses forward and reverse strokes, sweep strokes, draws, and sculling draws. Bracing is addressed in the whitewater kayaking unit, lesson 4. The lesson also emphasizes proper stretching before engaging in sea kayaking.

JUSTIFICATION

Knowledge and performance of basic strokes form an important building block to mastering the sport of sea kayaking. Students become more confident and more self-reliant as their paddling skills develop. In challenging water and weather, mastery of basic strokes becomes essential. Proper paddling technique and stretching also improves physical fitness and reduces the chance of injury.

GOAL

To develop students' ability to control the sea kayak by understanding the mechanics of basic strokes associated with sea kayaking.

OBJECTIVES

At the end of this lesson, students will be able to

- understand the body movement involved in the correct execution of basic strokes (cognitive),
- demonstrate the forward and reverse strokes (psychomotor),
- execute the forward and reverse sweeps (psychomotor),
- demonstrate a draw and a sculling draw (psychomotor),
- increase self-reliance and confidence by becoming proficient in the execution of basic strokes (affective), and
- increase awareness of personal safety by avoiding injury associated with improper technique (affective).

EQUIPMENT AND AREAS NEEDED

- Sea kayaks (one per student)
- Paddles (one per student)
- Spray skirts (one per student)
- One large beach ball (3 feet, or 1 meter, in diameter)
- Sponges (one per student)

RISK MANAGEMENT CONSIDERATIONS

- See lesson 1 for details about general risk management considerations.
- Find a protected area where students can see clearly defined boundaries when practicing strokes (lake, pond, lagoon). Using a well-defined venue will keep the class together as students practice the strokes.
- Make sure to have at least one instructor for each six students. Many prominent adventure recreation organizations use this instructor-to-student ratio.
- Boat traffic, especially jet skis and other personal watercraft, will be the most dangerous hazard when practicing strokes.
- Carefully observe students' paddling technique so that you can help them avoid shoulder injuries.

LESSON CONTENT

Introduction

People usually find that making a sea kayak go where they want it to go can be difficult and frustrating. The sea kayak is made to go straight and fast. Turning it is difficult, and many factors can cause the kayak to deviate from its intended course. Ask students to brainstorm factors that make the kayak deviate. Answers should include wind, current, waves, paddling ability, boat design, and leaning the boat. By learning the basic strokes, students will increase their enjoyment and sense of control for this lifetime sport.

Main Activities

The main activities consist of describing, demonstrating, and practicing the essential strokes. Before they do the first activity, have students form a circle and spend 5 to 10 minutes stretching. Have each student pick a favorite stretch and lead the rest of the students in the stretch circle. Emphasize that although many people assume that sea kayaking is an upper-body sport, it utilizes many lower-body muscle groups. Make sure that stretches address the calves, hamstrings, torso, forearms, hip flexors, neck, and shoulders.

Set aside 5 to 10 minutes each day for students to stretch before they paddle. Emphasize the importance of adequately stretching before any aerobic activity.

Activity 1: Paddle Grip (30 Minutes)

First, review the proper way to size the paddle by referring to lesson 2. When everyone has a paddle, discuss the proper way to hold it.

- With the class spread out facing you on dry land, have everyone hold a paddle as if they were in the boat ready to paddle.
- The dominant hand is called the control hand. The knuckles on the dominant hand line up with the top of the blade on the control hand side of the paddle.
- Make sure that the shorter part of the blade is down, the longer part of the blade is on top, and the power face (the concave part of the blade) is facing the sea kayaker.
- The other hand, called the nondominant hand, rests loosely on the shaft. Make sure that the students' hands are spread slightly wider than shoulder-width apart.
- Emphasize to students that if they hold the paddle too tightly, employing the death grip technique, they will soon develop hot spots that will turn into blisters. They should hold the shaft lightly in their fingers.

If you use two-piece paddles with ferrules, call their attention to the ferrule on the shaft and allow them to offset the blades or keep them nonoffset. Emphasize they should practice strokes with the blades in both positions, offset and nonoffset.

- Offset blades (feathered blades) work well when paddling into the wind because the top blade (the blade out of the water) slices through the air, reducing resistance.
- Nonoffset blades work well when paddling with the wind because the top blade acts as a sail, catching the wind.

♦ When using the paddle in the offset position, the control hand must rotate toward the sea kayaker (make the analogy of revving up your motorcycle) to put the opposite blade in position for the catch phase.

♦ Have students practice this motion a few times because catching on can be somewhat difficult at first.

Activity 2: Stroke Phases (10 Minutes)

Every stroke has three phases:

♦ The first is the catch phase (C), during which the blade enters the water.

♦ The second is the power phase (P), during which the blade propels the boat. Note that in unit 6, Whitewater Kayaking, the power phase is referred to as the *propulsion phase*. Both terms mean the same thing and are acceptable.

♦ The third is the recovery phase (R), during which the blade exits the water.

Every stroke includes these three phases, as students will see with the various basic strokes.

Activity 3: Forward and Reverse Stroke (50 Minutes)

On dry land, either on the ground or on a picnic table, pretend that you are in the cockpit of the sea kayak. Have students gather around you as you review the points of contact with the boat and the importance of maintaining a tight fit in the cockpit. Then demonstrate the forward stroke and the reverse stroke, as detailed here.

Forward Stroke   Demonstrate the forward stroke using the offset blades. Talk participants through the complete motion, emphasizing the following points.

♦ Horizontal shaft angle is better for long-distance touring because it creates less wind resistance, provides better stability, and prevents fatigue because the paddler doesn't have to raise the paddle as far off the water.

♦ Emphasize that participants should keep the arms extended (not locked out) as they progress through the stroke.

♦ Students should rotate the torso, which is much stronger than even the burliest biceps. Refer to torso rotation in unit 6, lesson 4, and unit 7, lesson 4, for details. One major problem that new sea kayakers start to develop is relying too much on their biceps in the forward stroke. Make sure that participants understand that the biceps will fatigue much faster than the torso will.

♦ To demonstrate the proper forward stroke, inflate the beach ball and place it between your chest and paddle shaft (figure SK7.1).

♦ Go through the motions of the forward stroke, concentrating on the points mentioned. Do this several times with the beach ball so that students will have a visual of a good forward stroke (figure SK7.2).

FIGURE SK7.1   Place a beach ball to promote the proper technique for forward stroke.

FIGURE SK7.2   Forward stroke motion sequence with beach ball.

- One way to make sure that students maintain a good horizontal shaft angle is to tell them that their hands should not go higher than their eyes. This pointer gives them a good visual reference point.
- Keeping a good horizontal shaft angle also prevents overextension and reduces the possibility of shoulder injuries (figure SK7.3).

FIGURE SK7.3   Forward stroke sequence.

Reverse Stroke   The reverse stroke is just the opposite of the forward. Paddlers should use it when they need to back up or stop (when heading toward something or someone). Again, emphasize torso rotation (figure SK7.4).

FIGURE SK7.4   Reverse stroke.

Stroke Practice   Have students sit on the ground and practice their forward strokes as if they were in their own sea kayaks. Provide individual feedback as you make sure that everyone is demonstrating proper technique.

◆ Have students enter their boats. After all participants are securely in their boats with spray skirts and PFDs on, paddle to a protected location to practice the forward stroke on water. Again, provide each person with individual feedback.

◆ A helpful drill is to have everyone raft up and face you. Tell the students that you will paddle toward them three times and that you want to receive their critique of each stroke.

◆ After the first pass, make sure that they point out excessive use of the biceps, vertical shaft position, and slouched posture. The second pass should be better, and the third pass should be perfect. This visual comparison helps participants understand what a proper forward stroke looks like.

◆ The forward stroke is the foundation for all other strokes. Make sure that students are solid on the forward stroke before progressing to the sweeps.

Activity 4: Forward and Reverse Sweeps (40 Minutes)

With everyone rafted up, discuss the difficulties of turning a 16-foot (5-meter) sea kayak. Introduce turning and correction strokes, the forward and reverse sweeps.

Forward Sweep
◆ Demonstrate the forward sweep by placing the blade 3 to 4 feet (90 to 120 centimeters) from the boat and executing a turn.

◆ Next, exaggerate the sweeps, making big arcs with an extended blade. Fix your eyes on the blade as it makes the arc, a technique that emphasizes good torso rotation.

◆ Make note that the farther the blade is from the pivot point of the boat (the seat of the kayak), the more effective the sweep is. Basic physics says that an increased lever arm produces greater force.

◆ Next, demonstrate proper forward sweeps (figure SK7.5), emphasizing a horizontal shaft angle, good torso rotation, and making a big arc with the paddle blade beside the sea kayak.

◆ The forward sweep is a useful stroke because it allows the sea kayaker to correct the direction of the sea kayak without losing momentum or slowing down.

◆ As students become more comfortable with the forward sweep, they can use it in conjunction with forward strokes to keep the sea kayak going straight while maintaining speed.

FIGURE SK7.5   Forward sweep: *(a)* Place the blade toward the bow for the catch; *(b)* arc the blade out, moving toward the stern; *(c)* finish with the blade at the stern—the torso has rotated.

Reverse Sweep

◆ Demonstrate the reverse sweep by placing the blade at the stern of the sea kayak and emphasizing good torso rotation.

◆ A good visual is to compare your wound-up torso (with the blade at the back of the boat) with a loaded mousetrap. Point out to students that the reverse sweep is one of the strongest strokes because its power relies completely on the torso.

◆ Next, arc the blade toward the bow of the boat (figure SK7.6).

FIGURE SK7.6   Reverse sweep: *(a)* Place the blade at the stern, and *(b)* arc the blade toward the bow.

◆ The reverse sweep should be used to turn the boat only when maintaining momentum is not important. The reverse sweep slows the sea kayak tremendously, but it sets up the sea kayaker for a low brace nicely, and this combination of strokes is useful in rough water.

Activity 5: Student Practice and Boat Leans (30 Minutes)

◆ Have students pair up and practice turning their boats 360 degrees.

◆ After they practice, provide feedback and have them raft up again. Introduce completing the sweeps in conjunction with boat leans.

◆ The boat lean is effective because it reduces the surface area of the boat in contact with the water. Ask students to think of trying to turn a banana on a table versus turning a hot dog on a table. The one with less surface area on the table, the banana, will turn easier because it has less resistance. They can think of the upright sea kayak as the hot dog and the leaned sea kayak as the banana.

◆ Again, have students pair up and practice sweeps with boat leans. Keep an eye on students because many of them will capsize when they practice leaning the boat. Of course, capsizing will allow them to practice their wet exits in a realistic environment.

Activity 6: Draws and Sculling Draws (40 Minutes)

Have students raft up again and show them the draw and sculling draw strokes. Emphasize that both can be unstable strokes, but they can allow sea kayakers to raft up, or parallel park, much faster.

Draw Stroke

◆ Emphasize torso rotation. The sea kayaker's chest is turned to face the paddle, which is placed in the water at the sea kayaker's hip.

◆ The catch phase of the stroke starts with the paddle extended from the boat and maintaining a vertical shaft angle (figure SK7.7).

◆ The power phase of the stroke occurs when the sea kayaker brings the blade to himself or herself, again keeping the shaft vertical and torso rotated (figure SK7.8).

FIGURE SK7.7   Catch phase of the draw stroke.

FIGURE SK7.8   Power phase of the draw stroke.

The recovery phase of the draw includes two options.

◆ One option is simply to pull the blade out of the water after it reaches the sea kayak.

◆ The other option, called the in-water recovery, is preferable because the sea kayak is more stable with the blade in the water. To execute the in-water recovery, the sea kayaker turns the blade perpendicular to the boat after it has reached the hull and slides it back away from the boat to set up for another catch phase of the stroke. Figure SK7.9 shows the path of the blade as it would look submerged in the water. Hands and shaft angle stay in the same position for the recovery as they do in the catch and power phases of the stroke.

FIGURE SK7.9   In-water recovery of the draw stroke: *(a)* Rotate the shaft so that the back face of the blade is forward; *(b)* slice the blade away from the hull in a vertical position; *(c)* position the blade for the next catch phase.

Sculling Draw   The sculling draw is similar to the regular draw in that it moves the sea kayak from side to side. The sculling draw, however, also allows the sea kayaker to move and turn the bow or stern of the boat at the same time.

◆ To execute the sculling draw, maintain a vertical shaft angle and good torso rotation.

◆ The main difference between the draw and the sculling draw is that in a sculling draw the blade continues a figure-eight pattern to move the boat. The sculling draw constantly moves, braces, and draws all at the same time. Figure SK7.10

FIGURE SK7.10   Sculling draw.

demonstrates the figure-eight pattern that the blade makes in the water as the boat slips toward the blade.

◆ The sculling draw is in essence a draw combined with a high brace. It can be very stable and effective with practice. Have students practice both types of draws in pairs. Then have them practice rafting up with the newly learned draws.

Closure Activity

Stinky Fish (30 to 60 Minutes)

Have students continue to practice the varying strokes by playing a game called Stinky Fish. Before the lesson, cut various fish profiles out of sponges. The more creative and elaborate the fish are, the more entertaining the game will be.

◆ Everyone starts the game with a fish placed on her or his spray skirt or in the cockpit (if they don't have spray skirts on). The object of the game is to end up with the fewest stinky fish in the boat.

◆ The only way to get rid of the stinky fish is to throw it into the cockpit or on the spray skirt of another sea kayaker. If the stinky fish doesn't land on the spray skirt or in the cockpit, then the person has to retrieve the fish, plus the fish of the person who was the target.

◆ You can time the game to fit the schedule for the day.

◆ Emphasize boat control. Make sure that students are aware of their paddles. Some participants really get into the game, and you don't want anyone to catch a blade of a paddle in the face.

Follow-Up Activities

Activity 1: Torso Rotation Stretch (Five Minutes)

Do this follow-up activity or a slight variation of it each day before departing. This activity is a stretch that emphasizes good torso rotation.

◆ Form a circle with everyone in the class (instructors included), making sure that everyone is comfortably standing in a tight circle. Participants' shoulders should not be touching, but they should be close.

◆ The goal is to pass a sea kayak paddle from person to person, in a complete circle. When passing the sea kayak paddle around the circle, participants' feet should stay fixed in the same stance.

◆ The first person holds the paddle vertically and rotates his or her torso in a counterclockwise motion (to the left) to try to face the person on the right. Remember, this stretch emphasizes torso rotation, so the counterclockwise rotation will be difficult.

◆ The person to the immediate right rotates her or his torso clockwise to receive the handoff of the paddle. The participant now holding the paddle has to rotate the torso counterclockwise to pass the paddle off to the next person, who rotates clockwise. This sequence continues until the paddle makes a complete circle.

◆ Variations of this stretch are endless. Participants can go in opposite directions, make numerous trips around the circle, and so on. The important point is that everyone must concentrate on good torso rotation.

Activity 2: Videotaped Practice (45 Minutes)

Videotape stroke practice and several activities. Have students critique themselves and one another for proper stroke technique. This is an excellent method of helping students understand proper torso rotation and stroke execution.

ASSESSMENT

◆ Confirm that students can demonstrate the forward and reverse strokes by observing them practice in the main lesson and during the game in the closing activity.

◆ Verify that students can demonstrate the forward and reverse sweeps by observing them practice in the main lesson and during the game in the closing activity.

◆ Check that students can demonstrate a draw and a sculling draw by observing them practice in the main lesson and during the game in the closing activity.

◆ Confirm that students can describe the key parts of any stroke by having them take a written exam at the end of the class.

◆ Check whether students understand the body movement involved in the correct execution of basic strokes by asking them to lead stretches pertaining to the correct stroke techniques and by asking them to critique their videotaped performance.

◆ Assess whether students have increased their self-reliance and ability to sea kayak safely by becoming proficient in the execution of basic strokes by observing them practice throughout the class.

TEACHING CONSIDERATIONS

◆ If you are having students practice strokes on the water, make sure that you are on the **leeward side** of the shore. Have students raft up as much as possible while giving instruction. Make sure that they all face the same direction as you talk to them and that they are not facing any distractions.

◆ If even one boat is not rafted up to the others, that boat will distract the group as it is blown away from the others or as the student tries to stay facing in the same direction.

◆ Stroke refinement is an ongoing process. Let students know that they will receive pointers from you throughout the course and that they should not expect to master the skills in one lesson.

◆ Try to avoid rudder or skeg use during this lesson. Rudders and skegs are mechanical devices that tend to fail when the paddler needs them most. Promote correct paddle strokes instead of reliance on the rudders or skegs.

◆ Make sure that students are aware of other sea kayaks and paddles when playing the game Stinky Fish. Injuries can occur when students lose control of their boats and ram into other sea kayakers or hit another sea kayaker with a paddle blade.

UNIT 5, LESSON 8

▷ Navigation

OVERVIEW

Students learn in this lesson the basics of chart use for sea kayaking. Emphasis is placed on reading and interpreting information on charts. Also, tricks and tips used for sea kayak navigation will be discussed. The lesson will not address GPS and compass use; you should refer to lesson 12 in unit 1 to incorporate compass use while sea kayaking. Although the general principles of compass use are the same for backpacking and sea kayaking, refer to the teaching considerations section of this lesson for specific tips related to sea kayaking.

JUSTIFICATION

Navigation is a critical part of sea kayaking. Understanding the basics of chart use is a required skill for any sea kayaker. Being able to navigate enhances enjoyment and is a critical safety skill.

GOAL

To advance students' understanding of the difference between a chart and a map and to develop their navigational skills.

OBJECTIVES

At the end of this lesson, students will be able to

◆ describe the features of a chart (cognitive),
◆ distinguish between a chart and a map (cognitive),
◆ demonstrate the ability to navigate using a chart (psychomotor), and
◆ take pride in developing and improving navigational skills associated with sea kayaking (affective).

EQUIPMENT AND AREAS NEEDED

◆ Charts (one per person)
◆ One whiteboard
◆ Assorted colored markers

RISK MANAGEMENT CONSIDERATIONS

See lesson 1 for details about general risk management considerations.

LESSON CONTENT

Introduction (Five Minutes)

Pass out a **chart** to each person and ask the students to inspect them. Ask them to pick one feature on the chart. As you go around the circle, list those items on the whiteboard.

When first looking at a chart, students can be overwhelmed by the complexity of numbers and colors. Many students experience information overload and become confused. This exercise allows students to inspect a chart, try to figure out what the symbols and information represent, and feel more comfortable by learning that they are not alone in thinking that the chart contains a lot of bizarre information. You will address all the features that you write on the whiteboard in the main activity section of the lesson.

Main Activity

Chart Interpretation (15 to 20 Minutes)

A chart focuses on water features, whereas a map focuses on land features. With a chart, a few land features might be displayed (towers, lighthouses, church steeples, roads), but most of the information concerns water features (figure SK8.1).

On the other side of the whiteboard, write the five Ds of chart use (described in the following list). They provide an easy way to teach and learn the basics of chart use. For general information regarding map interpretation, refer to the backpacking unit, lesson 11.

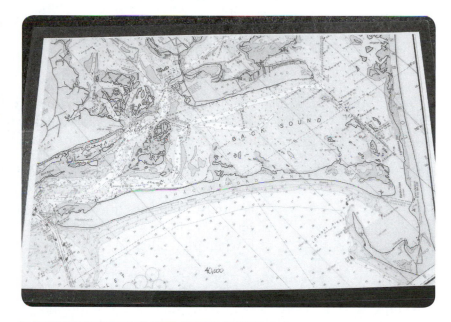

FIGURE SK8.1 Sample chart.

- Description: key features, latitude and longitude, date, adjoining charts.

- Direction: in relation to true north (top of chart).

- Distance: chart scale (for example, 1:40,000 or 1:80,000), distance indicator in nautical miles (1 nautical mile = 6,076 feet, or 1,852 meters).

- Designation: place names.

- Details: Chart symbols, mean low water (numbers on the chart indicate mean low water depth, or average depth of the water at low tide).

Ask students what the various colors on the charts mean. Although these colors are the same as those used on maps, charts include less description of land features and more description pertaining to water (depth, inlets, marshes, and so on).

- Black: manmade features
- Blue: water (white: shallow water)
- Brown: topographic features and landforms
- Green: forested areas or marsh areas

After discussing the preceding information, go over the items that the students identified during the introduction activity. Have them claim their features and identify them by using the five Ds. Debrief the discussion by giving an accurate and detailed explanation of the information given by the chart.

Closure Activity

Mariner's Saying (Five Minutes)

A major challenge of navigating is transferring information from the chart to the surroundings. One way to help students with navigating the water is to encourage then to use and remember the mariner's saying:

◆ "Blue, blue, come on through"—the water is deep enough to get your boat through. Dark blue water is usually the deepest water.

◆ "Green, green, nice and clean"—the water is deep enough to get your boat through.

◆ "White, white, you just might"—the depth is questionable. You might make it through or you might run aground.

◆ "Brown, brown, run aground"—the water is very shallow. You will run aground.

Follow-Up Activity

Navigation Practice (Five Minutes)

A navigational trick useful when sea kayaking is the hand span method. This method allows a person to make a quick estimate of how far it is from one point to another.

◆ Take the scale of the chart (say, 1:40,000) and move the decimal place to the left four places (with 40,000, move the decimal to read 4.0000).

◆ This number indicates the distance in miles from the thumb to the index finger when the two fingers are spread out in the L position, or the position that a person uses when pretending to hold a gun (see figure SK8.2). (For kilometers, multiply the number by 1.6.)

Review this method by asking the students to name the distance indicated by the thumb and index finger if the scale was 1:80,000. The answer would be 8 miles (for kilometers, the answer would be 8 multiplied by 1.6, or 12.8).

Have the students practice figuring out how far it is between two points on the charts. This method is useful when trying to navigate on the water with the chart on the deck of the boat.

ASSESSMENT

◆ Verify that students can describe the features of a chart by observing them discuss intended route options for the day.

FIGURE SK8.2   The hand span method of estimating distance on a chart.

◆ Check that students can distinguish a chart from a map by questioning them during informal discussion during the main activity and the closure activity or through a formal quiz.

◆ Check that students can navigate by using a chart by observing them navigate during each day's paddle.

◆ Assess whether students take pride in developing and improving their navigational skills by observing them make correct decisions when route finding and become more self-reliant in their navigational decision making.

TEACHING CONSIDERATIONS

◆ Using a chart and transferring information from the chart to the natural environment is a difficult task for many students. Make sure that you provide ample review of chart use throughout the sea kayaking trips.

◆ All participants should review the intended route before departing each morning. Make sure that you place the chart where everyone can see it easily. Use a pointer (blade of grass, twig, or other item) to point out hazards, the intended route, landings, possible lunch spots, and so forth, instead of your finger. Pointing to small details on the chart is much easier with a pointer. When you use your finger, your hand obstructs views of the chart, so the longer the pointer, the more of the chart everyone can see.

◆ Before departing, make sure that everyone can point to a land feature toward which they are heading. Many students say that they understand where they are going, but in fact they are far off the intended route. Having them confirm their course allows you to offer immediate feedback, which can help them improve their navigation ability.

◆ Encourage students to look constantly at their surroundings and try to figure out where they are on the chart. Have the students pod up (or raft up, by maneuvering all the sea kayaks side by side and holding on to each other's boats) on the water frequently and ask them to point out features and landmarks that indicate where they are on the chart. Practice helps the students become more proficient with navigation.

◆ A way to have enough weather worthy charts for everyone in the class is to make a color copy of the paddling destination from the original chart. Most copy stores can make an 8.5-inch-by-17-inch (21.6-centimeter-by-43.2-centimeter) copy of the relevant section of the chart. This small chart fits perfectly under most deck bungees of sea kayaks. Make sure that you laminate the chart and allow for about a half-inch (1-centimeter) border of laminate around the edges of the chart. When cutting the lamination, round off the corners. Sharp corners tend to delaminate easier than rounded corners do, causing the chart to become waterlogged.

◆ Another trick is to make sure that all pertinent information (campsites, water resupplies, and so on) is clearly labeled on the original chart before running copies so that the students' copies of the chart will have enough information for them to make correct decisions when route finding. Also, write the scale of the chart somewhere on the small chart where it is easily visible.

◆ A useful trick for using compasses and sea kayaks is to girth hitch the lanyard on the deck bungee in front of the cockpit. Slide the chart under the deck bungee in front of the cockpit and always have both the compass and chart visible (that is, don't place items such as bilge pumps, hats, or water bottles on top of the chart). The bow of the sea kayak will become an extension of the direction-of-travel arrow on the compass, so make sure that the compass is always oriented correctly.

> When crossing large bodies of water where you lose sight of land, take a map or chart bearing just as you would when backpacking. Follow the heading. Depending on the wind, waves, and tides, you might need to make an adjustment when taking your chart or field bearing to reach the intended destination. The adjustment would compensate for the wind, waves, or tide. For instance, you might need to aim more into the wind or against the tide to prevent your group from being blown downwind or carried past your intended destination.

UNIT 5, LESSON 9

▷ Preparing to Paddle

OVERVIEW

This lesson emphasizes the importance of expedition behavior, boat packing, and preparing to launch. Instruction on paddle signals, whistle use, and general information on leadership and self-responsibility is stressed. You should address the diverse skills covered in this lesson before launching on the first trip. If you are giving this lesson at the put-in site, be sure that you have enough room to spread out gear and hold class without interfering with other users of the area.

JUSTIFICATION

Knowing that help is not just a phone call away will help students appreciate that their decisions and behaviors can have significant ramifications. Students should understand how to pack the sea kayak so that it will travel efficiently and be more stable. Excessive weight can greatly affect the performance of the boat and the enjoyment of the trip. On extended trips, boat space becomes a premium, so students need to learn how to use every square inch (centimeter) of the kayak for storing food, water, and gear.

GOAL

To develop participants' awareness of the importance of expedition behavior, including paddle signals, whistle use, and boat packing.

OBJECTIVES

At the end of this lesson, students will be able to

- describe proper expedition behavior (cognitive),
- demonstrate the proper way to pack a sea kayak (psychomotor),
- use appropriate paddle signals (psychomotor),
- execute proper whistle signals (psychomotor),

◆ feel more self-reliant by knowing how to use paddle and whistle signals to manage the group on the water (affective), and

◆ take pride and become more vested in the group by practicing appropriate expedition behavior (affective).

EQUIPMENT AND AREAS NEEDED

◆ One paddle

◆ One whistle

◆ Whiteboard

◆ Multicolored markers

◆ One sea kayak

◆ Your gear for the trip

RISK MANAGEMENT CONSIDERATIONS

See lesson 1 for details about general risk management considerations.

LESSON CONTENT

Introduction

Energetically introduce to students the idea that although packing a sea kayak can be a daunting task, a little forethought and practice can make packing as easy as learning the ABCs. Also emphasize that when paddling their sea kayaks, students should think of wanting to travel in style, meaning that the boats should be sleek and well packed, without equipment randomly attached to the decks, bungees, and other parts of the boats where they might easily fall off.

Review and briefly describe the predeparture schedule of events, packing the sea kayak, expedition behavior, paddle signals, and whistle use.

Main Activities

Activity 1: ABCs of Packing (30 Minutes)

Start the lesson by gathering all the gear that will be packed into your boat. Place gear alongside the boat, but as if it were packed in the boat. Students should be in a semicircle facing the boat.

With the whiteboard and facing the students, write the letters A, B, and C. Tell the students that packing their sea kayaks is as easy as learning the ABCs. Packing just takes time, patience, and practice. By each letter on the whiteboard fill in the appropriate word and describe the following, using the gear and sea kayak in front of you for demonstration.

◆ A for accessibility—When you pack your boat you should think about how accessible certain items need to be.

- For instance, you don't need to have your tent in the day hatch or your sleeping pad in the cockpit. You won't need those items until you get to camp, so you can place them at the ends of the boat.

- Items such as a water bottle, rain jacket, sunscreen, first aid kit, and so on should be easily accessible.

- First aid items and rescue equipment should be placed in the most easily accessible areas, perhaps bungeed on the rear deck or tucked behind the backrest in the cockpit.

◆ B for balance—The sea kayak should be evenly balanced both side to side and bow to stern.

- Place heavier items as close to the center of the boat as possible. Food and water typically weigh the most, so they should be close to the cockpit.
- On extended trips in a marine environment, sea kayakers commonly have many gallons (liters) of water in the cockpit acting as leg support and back support. Water containers fit nicely into the front of the cockpit (in front of the foot braces) and are therefore easy to get to when you need to refill your water bottle when paddling.
- Lighter items, such as sleeping pads and tents, fill the voids at the ends of the sea kayak and are large enough to be easy to retrieve from the ends of the boat.

◆ C for compactness—When every bit of space counts in the sea kayak, making things as compact as they can be is important.

- You should "burp" dry bags by squeezing all the air out of them before closing them up so that they will fit in the smallest space possible.
- Nylon dry bags tend to work best for keeping soft goods (sleeping bags and clothes) dry, and they slide in and out of the hatches easier than rubber dry bags do. Nylon bags are more pliable and easier to seal in colder weather.
- Clear rubber dry bags work well for storing food because you can see what food items are in each bag. Numbering and labeling all dry bags aids in identification. Food dry bags are usually prepacked according to meals (for example, dry bag number 4 contains breakfast for day 2).
- When dividing group gear, make a number of piles that corresponds to the number of students you have.
- When students start to pack food bags, allow them to remove the contents of the bags if doing so will allow them to pack the contents more efficiently. Just make sure that they make mental notes of what they are taking out of the bags and placing elsewhere in their boats. For instance, canned food doesn't need to stay dry in a dry bag, so those items can be packed in voids in the sea kayak. As the trip progresses, however, the cans may become lost in the kayak. Make sure that students know and remember what items of group gear they have.
- Make sure that bulky items that don't need to stay dry are not placed in the dry bags (bowls, sunscreen, canned food, insect repellent, and so forth). Those items fit well at the far ends of the sea kayak, but students must be sure that they have a way to get them out.
- An item stuck at the very end of the boat can be fished out with a tent pole.

Go around and help participants pack their boats. Demonstrate how to pack difficult items one on one. After all participants have finished packing their boats, make sure that you haven't left anything behind. Walk the boats down to the water, reminding folks how to carry loaded boats.

Activity 2: Expedition Behavior (20 Minutes)

After loading boats, have everyone (including you) sit in a circle. Pass the whiteboard around and ask students to write down one thing that they think might ruin or sabotage the trip. Frame this activity as "anything goes," meaning that students are free to suggest anything that they believe will sabotage the trip. After everyone has had a chance to write something, debrief the activity by reading the list aloud and asking what the items mean. Initiate discussion by asking guided questions.

- Consider including topics such as drug use, exclusive relationships, horseplay, and not taking care of oneself as items that may sabotage the trip. The idea of this exercise is to call attention to expedition behavior.

- Emphasize that after the group leaves on the expedition, getting help or evacuating someone is a major ordeal. Having everyone see the list of items that can sabotage the trip lets them know what they should or should not do (expectations) and, more important, allows them to call out others if they have not bought into the unified front, or the expectations of the entire group.

- At this point, you can facilitate a full-value contract discussion to set appropriate group norms. In other words, the students contract how they will behave during the trip based on trip goals and personal goals.

Activity 3: Signaling and Safety (10 Minutes)

After the expedition behavior activity, have everyone get suited up for the paddle (PFDs, spray skirts, sunscreen, and so on) and circle up one last time. Review the paddle signals before departure. Information on paddle signals can be found in unit 8, lesson 3.

Review whistle signals.

- One blast gets everyone's attention.

- Three short blasts means that someone needs immediate help.

- Make sure to emphasize that whistles are difficult to hear in windy conditions, especially by those upwind of the whistle blow. Therefore, participants should stay close enough together when paddling that they can converse without yelling.

- If a student cannot hear the person paddling next to her or him unless that person yells, the paddlers are too far apart.

- Decide what the group members will do when they hear the whistle. Typically, when one whistle blow is heard, everyone paddles up to the lead sea kayaker, pods up, and waits for further instruction. If three short blasts are heard, everyone converges to the whistle blows.

Closure Activity

Speed Review (Five Minutes)

Have all students get in their boats and convene just offshore until everyone is ready to paddle away. Quickly review paddle signals and whistle signals by means of a speed review, which is a fun and fast way to review the signals. You lead the exercise the first time, but after that, a different student leads the activity each day before paddling.

- Have the students form a semicircle on the water in their sea kayaks so that everyone is facing the center of the semicircle.

- One person paddles to the center of the semicircle.

- The person in the center of the semicircle performs the paddle signals and whistle signals as fast as he or she can.

- After the person performs each signal, the group names or describes what the signal means.

Follow-Up Activities

Activity 1: Daily Review (Five Minutes)

Review the signals and observe or help students pack each day until they are proficient enough to do it on their own.

Activity 2: Daily Packing Practice (15 Minutes)

You have two ways of giving students opportunities to practice boat packing: a packing race and a packing battle.

Boat Packing Race The first option is to have a race each morning of the trip to see who can have her or his boat packed correctly first. The winner may be relieved of a group chore or receive some type of food treat.

Boat Packing Battle Another option is to break the group into two teams and divide group gear into two equal piles. The object of the game is to be the first group to pack all the gear correctly into the sea kayaks.

◆ You are the judge of the game and must go through the boats to evaluate the packing based on the ABCs of packing.

◆ Have all the students follow the evaluation so that they can see where items might fit well in the boat and where they may not fit so well.

◆ A boat receives a perfect score if all the ABCs are addressed correctly.

◆ Deduct points for loose items, dry bags not fully closed, inaccessible safety equipment, and so on. You have complete discretion in the judging.

◆ The team with the most points wins the boat packing battle and receives the agreed-upon prize.

ASSESSMENT

◆ Assess whether students can describe proper expedition behavior by conducting an expedition behavior briefing before the group's first launch and having students create a full-value contract.

◆ Check that students can demonstrate the proper way to pack a sea kayak by observing them throughout the trip and evaluating the boat packing battle game.

◆ Verify that students understand paddle signals by reviewing quickly before departing and observing participants on the water during the speed review.

◆ Check that students understand whistle signals by reviewing quickly before departing and observing participants on the water during the speed review.

◆ Assess whether students feel more self-reliant through knowing how to use paddle and whistle signals to manage the group on the water by observing their confidence and involvement in group management on the water.

◆ Assess whether students take pride and become more vested in the group by having them debrief their successes and shortcomings throughout the trip.

TEACHING CONSIDERATIONS

◆ This lesson is often the last one before departing, so students are usually eager to get on the water. They tend to miss important information because they are distracted. Make sure that you keep a tight rein on the group and have everyone's attention. Review and ask guided questions to allow the information to sink in better.

◆ When demonstrating boat packing, place gear so that the students can easily see it. Position yourself on the opposite side of the boat so that you are facing the students.

▷ Tides and Crossings

OVERVIEW

A coastal sea kayaker needs to know about tides, tidal currents, and channel crossings. Students learn in this lesson how to predict when the tides will be strongest, when to cross a channel according to tide charts, and how to maneuver a kayak safely across a channel in a fast current. Emphasis is placed on decision making in relation to predicting tides and currents.

JUSTIFICATION

Tides and crossings are an important part of coastal sea kayaking. Just as sea kayakers should be proficient with the wet exit, they should be able to predict tides and understand the movement of water in a marine environment. Ultimately, the student should leave this lesson with knowledge that will aid in deciding when and where to paddle across a channel in relation to the tidal changes.

GOAL

To develop participants' ability to identify the safest times to paddle across channels and to predict tidal changes.

OBJECTIVES

At the end of this lesson, students will be able to

◆ describe the rule of 12ths (identify raging and slack tides) (cognitive),
◆ demonstrate the ability to predict the appropriate window of opportunity for crossing a channel (cognitive),
◆ identify potential hazards involved with crossing a channel (cognitive),
◆ ferry the sea kayak across a channel (psychomotor), and
◆ take pride in becoming self-reliant by being able to make correct decisions about crossing channels and predicting tides (affective).

EQUIPMENT AND AREAS NEEDED

◆ One large, yellow, soft bouncy ball (to represent the sun)
◆ One medium-sized soft bouncy earth or equivalent
◆ One golf ball half colored black with marker (to represent a full moon and a new moon)
◆ One section of rope (6 feet, or 2 meters, in length)
◆ 12 shells, sticks, or people (anything close by that will demonstrate the rule of 12ths)

RISK MANAGEMENT CONSIDERATIONS

- See lesson 1 for details about general risk management considerations.

- If you decide to practice ferries, attempt them first on an incoming slack tide. Then, as participants become more proficient, they may attempt the ferries on an incoming raging tide.

- Be aware of boat traffic, especially jet skis and other personal watercraft, when practicing ferries.

- At least one instructor safety boat should be in position for rescue downcurrent of participants who are practicing ferries.

- Participants are not required to be able to roll when practicing ferries, but they should be comfortable with wet exiting and be proficient at assisted and self-rescues.

LESSON CONTENT

Introduction (5 to 10 Minutes)

Understanding **tides** and currents will keep you and your group from taking unnecessary risks.

- With students in a semicircle facing the props (sun, moon, earth, and rope), start the activity by holding up each item and asking the students to identify it.

- Ask the students, "Which body (item) rotates around which?" The earth rotates around the sun, and the moon around the earth. Then ask the guided question, "What do these objects have to do with sea kayaking?" You hope that someone will respond by stating that the rotation of the bodies has a gravitational effect on the tides. This exchange will lead into the discussion of tides.

- You now emphasize how important it is to understand how tides work, that tides can be a hazard, and that every sea kayaker should be able to predict tides and currents.

Main Activities

Activity 1: Predicting Tides and Currents (25 to 30 Minutes)

Tides can be complicated and difficult to understand. Understanding how tides work and how to read tidal currents is a necessary skill for any sea kayaker. The following information will help participants become more comfortable in predicting tides and making crossings in tidal currents. Ask the participants as many guided and directed questions as possible. Address the following points:

Tides
- Tides are the alternate and regular rise and fall of sea level in oceans and other large bodies of water.

- Tides originate from the bulge of water that occurs because of the moon's pull on the earth. The bulge follows the moon, which explains the variation of the daily and monthly tides.

◆ Mimic figures SK10.1 and SK10.2 with the earth, sun, and moon props and colored rope (indicating the water of high and low tides) to describe the effect of the gravitational pull during spring and neap tides.

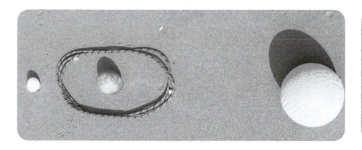

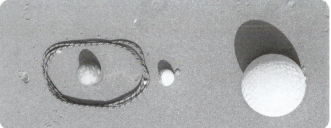

FIGURE SK10.1   Effect of the gravitational pull on spring tides.

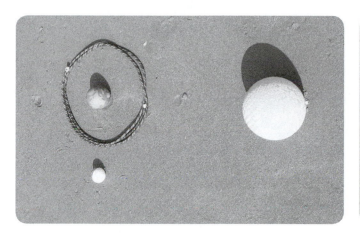

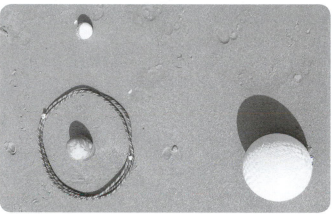

FIGURE SK10.2   Effect of the gravitational pull on neap tides.

High Tides and Low Tides

◆ Two high tides and two low tides occur each day, and about 6.25 hours pass between high and low water. A rising tide is said to be **flooding**, and a receding tide is said to be **ebbing**.

◆ The tides occur about 50 minutes later each day. So if a tide is high at 8:00 a.m. on Monday, high tide will occur at approximately 8:50 a.m. on Tuesday.

◆ Again, mimic figure SK10.1 when describing how many tides occur daily. The sections of rope that are closest to the earth in figure SK10.1 indicate the two low tides (one on each side of the earth), and the sections of rope that are farthest from the earth in figure SK10.1 indicate the two high tides (one on each side of the earth).

Spring Tides and Neap Tides

◆ **Spring tides** are higher high tides and lower low tides than usual, and they occur during the new moon and the full moon (twice each month).

◆ **Neap tides** show the least difference between high and low tides, and they occur during the first quarter and last quarter of the moon.

Tide Tables

◆ Tides are predicted for areas annually (actually, tides can be predicted indefinitely since they are cyclical).

◆ Adjustments are given for places other than the location on which the table is based. The adjustment varies with the distance from that location.

Rule of 12ths   Tides flow at different speeds depending on the quarter of the tide cycle. You can follow the rule of 12ths to predict the **slack tide** and **raging tide** (see table SK10.1). Water moves slowest during a slack tide and fastest during a raging tide.

TABLE SK10.1   Rule of 12ths

Hour of day	Amount that tide rises	Speed of tide
6 a.m.–7 a.m.	1/12 of its total	Slowest (slack tide)
7 a.m–8 a.m.	2/12 of its total	
8 a.m.–9 a.m.	3/12 of its total	Fastest (raging tide)
9 a.m.–10 a.m.	3/12 of its total	Fastest (raging tide)
10 a.m.–11 a.m.	2/12 of its total	
11 a.m.–12 p.m.	1/12 of its total	Slowest (slack tide)

Example: Low tide occurs at 6:00 a.m.

The flow is fastest during the middle two hours (when the tide rises 3/12 of its total each hour); this is the raging tide. The flow is slowest during the first and last hour of the tide (when the tide rises 1/12 of its total each hour); this is the slack tide.

The best way to demonstrate the rule of 12ths is to use props such as shells, people, or any objects that you can easily move. You must have 12 objects to follow the rule of 12ths. Refer to figure SK10.3,

FIGURE SK10.3   Rule of 12ths.

which demonstrates the rule of 12ths described here. Writing in wet sand (demonstrate at low tide) is better than writing in dry sand because the writing can be more detailed and is more visible.

- To demonstrate this, have one object in the first hour of tide change, two objects in the second hour of tide change, three objects in the third hour of tide change, and so on.
- Emphasize that the first and last hour of tide change are the slack tide and the most opportune time to cross a channel (incoming slack tide is best).
- Emphasize that the third and fourth hours of tide change are the raging tide (when half of all the water is moving), which is the most dangerous time to cross.

Activity 2: Ferrying (30 Minutes)

How do you cross a channel on a raging tide? A raging tide can help you if the current is going in the direction that you want to go, but if you have to go against the tide, crossing can be problematic. Some currents can move faster than 6 miles (10 kilometers) per hour, and most sea kayaks travel 3 to 4 miles (5 to 6.5 kilometers) per hour at best. So let physics work for you, not your muscles.

To cross a channel against the current, practice ferrying across (figure SK10.4). To **ferry** is to cross the current without losing ground or being swept downcurrent.

- Set your ferry angle according to how fast the current is moving.
- Point your bow upcurrent until you are in the current.
- Your ferry angle should not be larger than 30 degrees.
- The faster the current is, the smaller your ferry angle should be.
- If you start being swept downcurrent, lessen the angle.
- If you are not moving, widen, or increase, your ferry angle.

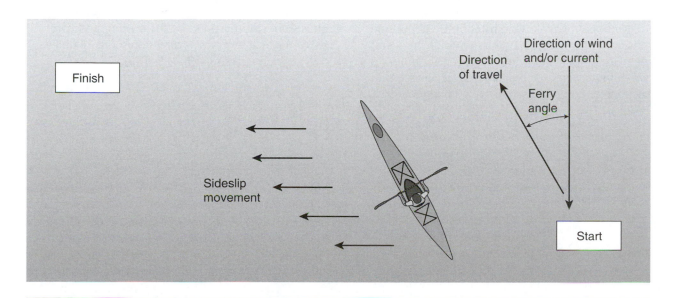

FIGURE SK10.4 Ferry angle for crossing a channel against the current.

Closure Activity

Story Time (10 Minutes)

To increase the participants' interest in tides and currents, share a few or all of the interesting facts about tides and currents by writing down each of the following facts on individual index cards (figure SK10.5). Randomly distribute the index cards to students and have them read the facts aloud to the other students.

Card 1

"The greatest tides occur in the Bay of Fundy, Nova Scotia, where there is an extreme range of 57 feet (17 meters) between high and low tides" (Hendrickson, 1984, p. 135).

Card 2

"The strongest current is in British Columbia's Nokwakto Rapids, which travels at up to 18.4 mph (29.6 kilometers per hour)" (Hendrickson, 1984, p. 135).

Card 3

"Tidal friction slows the earth's rotation and makes the days longer. This occurs when the tidal bulge scrapes shallow sea floors in traveling about earth, the frictional heat slowing rotation by about one second every 100,000 years—which may not seem like much but comes to over six hours in two billion years, or the difference between an 18-hour day and a 24-hour day" (Hendrickson, 1984, p. 135).

Card 4

"We are all heavier at low tide. Because of the saltwater content of our bodies, we each lose a fraction of a pound in weight with each rise of the tide, only to gain it back again when the tide recedes" (Hendrickson, 1984, p. 135).

Card 5

"Monthly tidal rhythms, averaging about 29.5 days, are reflected in the reproductive cycles of many plants and animals, including the menses of human females" (Hendrickson, 1984, p. 135).

Card 6

"Aristotle is said to have drowned himself because he could not explain the current in a channel of water off the island of Euboea in the Aegean. Scientists are still mystified by the current and can't explain why it reverses its direction some 14 times a day" (Hendrickson, 1984, p. 135).

FIGURE SK10.5   Facts about tides and currents.

From M. Wagstaff and A. Attarian, 2009, *Technical skills for adventure programming: A curriculum guide* (Champaign, IL: Human Kinetics). Based on R. Hendrickson, 1984, *The ocean almanac* (New York: Broadway Books), 135.

Follow-Up Activity

Ferry Practice (10 Minutes Without Practicing Ferries, 90 Minutes With Ferries)

To make sure that the participants are ready to lead the group in crossing a channel and predicting the tides, ask the following questions.

> Q: If you needed to cross a channel and the reported low tide was at 8 a.m. and the high tide was at 2 p.m., what would be the best window of opportunity to cross? Answer by giving the time frame and state what that time frame is called.

> A: The best time would be on an incoming slack tide (from 8 to 9 a.m. and from 1 to 2 p.m.). That way, if you flip you will be swept back inshore. The other period that would be OK is from 7 to 8 a.m. and from 2 to 3 p.m., again a slack tide but an outgoing slack tide. Remember the rule of 12ths. The raging tide will occur when the most water is moving through the channel, which would cause a rescue to be more difficult. The raging tides are in the third and fourth hours of the tides, so raging tide would be from 10 to 12 a.m., not when you would want to cross.

> Q: What hazards should you look for when crossing a channel?

> A: Boat traffic (use a pod formation, ideally a close diamond shape, and try to avoid a single-file formation), wind and weather, current, and waves (sea state).

ASSESSMENT

- ◆ Confirm that students can describe the rule of 12ths (identify raging and slack tides) by having them correctly answer the question in the follow-up activity.
- ◆ Verify that students can predict the window of opportunity for crossing a channel by having them correctly answer the question in the follow-up activity and by reviewing each morning when discussing the plan for the day.
- ◆ Check that students can identify potential hazards involved with crossing a channel by having them answer the follow-up activity correctly and by setting up the ferrying drill.
- ◆ Confirm that students can ferry the sea kayak across a channel by observing them during the ferrying drill.
- ◆ Assess whether students take pride in becoming self-reliant by being able to make correct decisions about crossing channels and predicting tides by observing them throughout the course and by handing over more responsibility to them.

TEACHING CONSIDERATIONS

Consider having students perform their first crossing during a slack incoming tide. As they become more proficient with their paddling strokes, cross a channel at a raging incoming tide. Be prepared to cross a channel at either a raging tide or a slack tide and use it as a teachable moment during the progression of the course.

▷ Safety Equipment

OVERVIEW

This lesson provides an overview of the basic safety equipment that sea kayakers should take on an outing. The equipment discussed reflects the items needed to deal with most situations. Optional safety equipment is also presented as a way to inform students of other available resources. Sea kayakers must know how to use this equipment and ensure that it is United States Coast Guard approved. The knowledge and skills discussed in this lesson are critical to overall trip safety.

JUSTIFICATION

All sea kayakers must take responsibility for themselves when participating in the sport, whether they are paddling for the day or on an overnight trip. Although kayakers may have sound judgment in their decision making, they must be prepared for unexpected situations. Taking the appropriate safety precautions, such as carrying the essential safety equipment, will better prepare them to confront difficult situations.

GOAL

To develop participants' awareness of safety equipment needed for sea kayaking and their knowledge of how to use the equipment should the situation arise.

OBJECTIVES

At the end of this lesson, students will be able to

+ identify safety equipment needed for sea kayaking (cognitive),
+ demonstrate how to use each piece of safety equipment needed for sea kayaking (psychomotor),
+ appreciate the importance of safety equipment and the ability to use these resources in difficult situations (affective), and
+ feel more self-reliant and take pride in being able to use the group safety equipment (affective).

EQUIPMENT AND AREAS NEEDED

+ One EPIRB (if available)
+ One VHF radio
+ One cell phone or satellite phone with waterproof container
+ One waterproof container with flares
+ One air horn (or comparable)
+ One whistle and signaling mirror per PFD
+ One strobe light per person
+ One tow system
+ One paddle float

- One trauma first aid kit
- One repair kit
- One bilge pump
- One pair of binoculars
- One sea anchor

RISK MANAGEMENT CONSIDERATIONS

See lesson 1 for details on general risk management considerations.

LESSON CONTENT

Introduction

Plan for the worst and hope for the best. The wonderful thing about sea kayaking is that it is an extremely dynamic sport, much like mountaineering, and participants must contend with many factors. These include the following:

- Subjective hazards, or hazards within human control (inadequately equipped group, a group not paying attention, a group spread too far apart)
- Objective hazards, or hazards outside of human control (environment, weather, wind, tides, waves), which require constant decision making and group management

Proper planning and exercise of sound judgment do not guarantee an incident-free trip. Sea kayaking is an exciting sport that takes place in an ever-changing environment. Planning for the moment is not enough; sea kayakers must plan and prepare for the unexpected. When conditions deteriorate, they must be able to respond confidently and proficiently with the appropriate safety equipment.

Main Activity

Safety Equipment Identification and Use (30 to 40 Minutes)

Pass out safety equipment so that each student has one piece. Ask them to take a few minutes to look at the equipment. Tell them that they will introduce the equipment to the group and describe what they think its purpose is. You should follow up each introduction by ensuring that students have an accurate understanding of the following items:

EPIRB   EPIRB stands for emergency position indicating radio beacon. This signaling device sends a one-way signal to the Coast Guard. EPIRBs use satellites to relay signal transmissions; therefore, their communication range is much longer than that of radios or phones. The only confirmation that the signal is being received is when help arrives.

EPIRBs are expensive and are not usually used for recreational paddling. This optional piece of equipment is not required for inshore sea kayaking, but it should be considered if the group might paddle offshore or in the ocean.

VHF Radio   A VHF **(very high frequency) radio** is a must for anyone who spends time on the water. The VHF radio is much like a cell phone in that it provides two-way communication; however, the range is usually line of sight, which is much shorter than the range of cell phones. Handheld VHF radios are generally waterproof and provide direct communication to the Coast Guard (channel 16) and other boaters on the water. VHF radios also receive weather forecasts (channels 1–10). Spare batteries should be carried with the VHF radio. The radio should be easily accessible. A PFD pocket is a good place to carry it.

Strict protocols must be observed when transmitting on a VHF radio, and the radio can be used only on the water. Check with the Coast Guard for current regulations.

Cell or Satellite Phone in Waterproof Container   Satellite phones are more expensive than cell phones, but, of course, cell phone coverage can be spotty. Many paddling destinations can now receive cell phone signals up to 5 miles (8 kilometers) offshore. For those paddling in remote locations, a satellite phone is the ideal two-way communication device. The satellite phone generally transmits a phone call from anywhere in the world, using satellites to relay the signal. Cell phones use towers on the ground to relay signals. Spare batteries should be taken with either communication device and stored in a tested waterproof container.

Flares in Waterproof Container   Handheld **flares** are the best overall signaling device. Many flares are available: meteor flares, parachute flares, handheld flares, and smoke flares. Determine what your program's needs are and familiarize yourself with the appropriate flares. Have at least three sets consisting of three flares per group. Nalgene bottles work well as waterproof storage containers.

Air Horn   An air horn is another useful signaling device. Although an air horn is bulky and the canisters are susceptible to rust in a marine environment, a horn is much louder than a whistle. The most important use of an air horn is to warn approaching boats of the group's whereabouts. Make sure to test the horn before departing. Although they are not as loud, plastic blaster horns, which do not require Freon as typical air horns do, are effective as a backup.

Whistle and Signaling Mirror   A good practice is to have a whistle and signaling mirror attached to each PFD. Make sure that students know your system of whistle and signal mirror use.

Strobe Light   You should include one **strobe light** per person. A strobe light is worn on the PFD or placed on the sea kayak to identify the sea kayaker's position. Strobe lights are ideal when sea kayaking at dusk, at dawn, or in low-visibility conditions.

Tow System   One tow system should be available for every three students. Tow systems should be stored on the deck of the boat or attached to the sea kayaker. Many tow systems on the market are integrated into a PFD harness. Many come with bungee cords to absorb the shock of towing a sea kayaker. Various lengths of towline can be used. If a sea kayaker needs assistance but still has control of the boat, a longer towline should be used. If a sea kayaker is injured and the rescuer needs to keep the boats close, a shorter towline should be used. Towing should be practiced in calm water first and then in rougher water.

Paddle Float   Paddle floats should be carried on every other boat, securely stored on the deck for easy access.

Trauma First Aid Kit   Make sure that students know what you carry in your trauma first aid kit or major medical first aid kit. Showing students what is in the kit promotes their self-reliance in taking care of personal needs.

Repair Kit Mechanical devices break, especially when exposed to marine conditions. Prepare an adequate boat repair kit for your paddling destination. Minimum requirements include AquaSeal (a durable waterproof glue), Ding Stick (a quick-hardening adhesive used to repair holes in boats), zip ties, extra nuts and bolts, Phillips head and flat-head screwdrivers, adjustable wrench, bungee, extra cables, no-see-um netting (to repair torn no-see-um netting on tents), and, of course, duct tape!

Bilge Pump Each boat should have a bilge pump on the deck for quick access to bail out water in the cockpit or hatches of a boat.

Binoculars Binoculars allow you to assess potential crossings, routes, campsites, sea state (condition of the water), other boaters, and wildlife from a safe distance.

Sea Anchor A **sea anchor**, sometimes referred to as a drift sock, is a piece of nylon in the shape of a pyramid. When filled with water as it is submerged, a sea anchor expands and provides resistance to reduce the drift of a boat or group in windy conditions. The sea anchor can also be used for surf landing. For this application, the kayaker attaches the sea anchor to the stern. The kayaker faces away from shore, allowing him or her to see approaching waves. The water from the waves fills the anchor and pulls the sea kayaker backward toward shore. If an approaching wave starts to break, the sea kayaker can paddle directly into the wave (the most stable position) and punch the bow through the breaker.

Closure Activities

Activity 1: Equipment Review and Questions (5 to 10 Minutes)

Ask students whether they have any questions about the equipment. Divide up the equipment among the students. Make sure that they know what equipment they are carrying and how to use it, as described in the main activity section of this lesson. Note: You (with other instructors if you are not the only instructor) should carry at least one of each of the following items: trauma first aid kit, cell phone, VHF radio, EPIRB, flares, air horn, and tow system.

Make sure that students know that the equipment must be easily accessible (that is, stored securely on the deck or behind the seat). Try to avoid storing items in a dry hatch. In rough conditions, sea kayakers must have easy access to the safety equipment.

Activity 2: Safety Equipment Relay Game (20 Minutes)

The safety equipment relay is a game that reinforces students' new knowledge of the safety equipment.

- Divide the group into two teams.
- Place the safety equipment used for the group in the rear hatch of one sea kayak. One team stands a predetermined distance away from the boat.
- The object of the game is for one person on the team to run to the sea kayak, grab a piece of safety equipment out of the rear hatch, and describe to you and the other team what it does and what it is used for.

- If the student correctly describes the equipment, she or he places the equipment in the front hatch of the boat and runs back to the starting line. The next person on the team continues the game, repeating the process of running to the rear hatch to grab a new piece of equipment, describe its use, and place it in the front hatch.

- If the student fails to describe the equipment correctly, she or he must place the gear back in the rear hatch, leaving it for a teammate to identify correctly.

- The goal is to describe all the safety equipment correctly in the shortest time. The team with the shortest relay time wins the game.

Follow-Up Activity

Safety Equipment Practice (One Hour)

Allow students to practice with certain safety equipment.

- Students should test the towing systems brought on the trip. Have students practice towing abled and disabled sea kayakers.

- Stage a mock radio conversation with the Coast Guard.

- Have students practice proper procedure by creating a rescue scenario.

- Have students practice using the paddle floats under challenging conditions as they gain experience.

ASSESSMENT

- Check that students can identify safety equipment needed for sea kayaking by observing them during the main activity part of the lesson and the safety equipment relay race.

- Verify that students can demonstrate how to use each piece of safety equipment needed for sea kayaking during the safety equipment relay race in the closure activities.

- Assess whether students appreciate the importance of safety equipment and being able to use these resources in difficult situations by observing them in a series of practice activities during the course of the trip and staged scenarios.

- Evaluate whether students feel more self-reliant and take pride in being able to use the group safety equipment by observing them practice using the equipment during staged scenarios and the safety equipment relay race.

TEACHING CONSIDERATIONS

- Although you can present this lesson at any time, try to work it in close to the start of an expedition, perhaps when going over group gear, so that students will have more opportunity to use safety equipment such as tow systems and VHF radios. Many instructors believe that the lesson works better when presented after lesson 2 (Equipment and Use). Be aware, however, that at that point in the progression many students really want to get into the sea kayaks. Their attention span may be extremely short at that point. Waiting until the students have some experience in the sea kayaks will give them a better opportunity to comprehend and appreciate the use of safety equipment.

◆ With a group of inexperienced sea kayakers, consider assigning individual pieces of equipment beforehand when conducting the main activity in this lesson. That approach prevents students from floundering around with confusing guesses and enables them to provide accurate, meaningful information to the group. The research process promotes knowledge development before the lesson.

◆ Some students will naturally want to play with the equipment (blow the air horn, sound whistles, play with the signaling mirrors, play with the VHF radio). Make sure that students know that the safety equipment is expensive and that they should use items such as whistles, horns, mirrors, and flares only in real emergencies. No crying wolf. The Coast Guard can levy fines.

UNIT 5, LESSON 12

▷ Safety Considerations

OVERVIEW

This lesson emphasizes safety considerations not addressed in other lessons within the sea kayaking unit. The lesson discusses an evaluation tool developed by the National Outdoor Leadership School (NOLS) called the seamanship triangle. The seamanship triangle is used to address subjective hazards, or hazards within human control (a group of sea kayakers inadequately equipped, fatigued, or unenthusiastic), and objective hazards, or hazards outside human control (environment, weather, wind, tides, waves), in a decision-making context. Students are empowered to assess the situation so that they can take appropriate action during a trip.

This lesson serves only as an introduction to this important topic. You should seek other information (see the resources section of this unit) and provide additional lessons if you need to offer more detail and content to prepare the group properly.

JUSTIFICATION

The sport of sea kayaking is a potentially dangerous activity because of its dynamic nature. The sea kayaker must constantly assess current and potential conditions when paddling with a group. Events can go from bad to worse in a matter of moments. Safety considerations when sea kayaking cannot be overstated.

GOAL

To develop students' ability to identify potential hazards and exercise proper safety protocol based on sound judgment and decision making.

OBJECTIVES

At the end of this lesson, students will be able to

◆ describe and identify potential subjective and objective hazards when sea kayaking (cognitive),

◆ demonstrate correct group travel in a pod formation (psychomotor), and

◆ feel more self-reliant, confident, and competent in the sport of sea kayaking by identifying potential hazards involved with the sport (affective).

EQUIPMENT AND AREAS NEEDED

- 1-quart (1-liter) water bottle
- Whiteboard
- Colored overhead markers

RISK MANAGEMENT CONSIDERATIONS

- See lesson 1 for details about general risk management considerations.
- Boat traffic, especially jet skis and other personal watercraft, always pose a potential hazard. Make sure to pick an appropriate route each day to limit exposure to these hazards.

LESSON CONTENT

Introduction

The sport of sea kayaking is fun and exciting. The sport always keeps its participants on their toes because of the constantly changing environment. Knowing how to make good decisions and how to identify potential hazards are important parts of sea kayaking.

Main Activities

Activity 1: Seamanship Triangle (30 Minutes)

Draw a large triangle on the whiteboard or in the sand. Let students know that the triangle is a decision-making tool that the group will use each day to assess current conditions. The tool will help the group determine whether to follow the intended route or institute a change of plans. The tool, called the seamanship triangle, was developed by National Outdoor Leadership School (NOLS) instructors to facilitate decision making in dynamic environments such as sea kayaking and mountaineering.

The seamanship triangle comprises four parts and encompasses various safety considerations for sea kayaking, as shown in figure SK12.1. Introduce each of the four components of the triangle to students by asking guided questions such as the following:

- What are the sea conditions?
- What is the weather doing?
- What hazards should we be aware of when launching our boats?
- How do folks feel?

Guided questions will facilitate a discussion that addresses the four parts of the triangle.

- Sea conditions—waves (height, length, steepness, breaking, rate of change), tides (incoming or outgoing, raging or slack), currents, sea state (condition of the water), and water temperature (ice).
- Weather conditions—wind (direction, force, **fetch,** duration), air temperature, fog or precipitation, cloud (type, progression), local patterns, barometer changes, and weather report (on VHF radio).

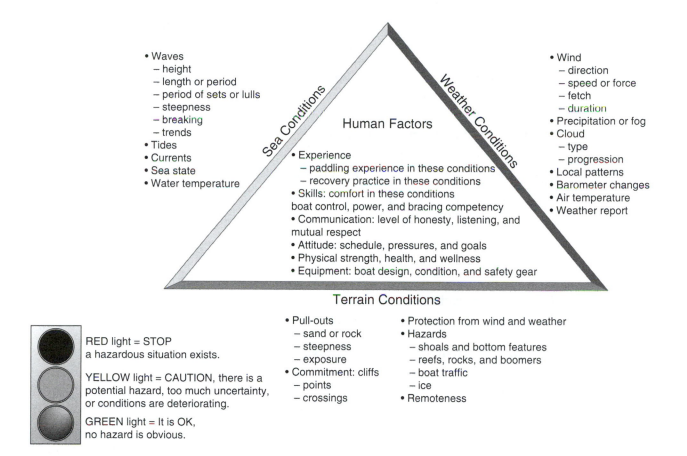

Sea Conditions

- Waves
  - height
  - length or period
  - period of sets or lulls
  - steepness
  - breaking
  - trends
- Tides
- Currents
- Sea state
- Water temperature

Weather Conditions

- Wind
  - direction
  - speed or force
  - fetch
  - duration
- Precipitation or fog
- Cloud
  - type
  - progression
- Local patterns
- Barometer changes
- Air temperature
- Weather report

Human Factors

- Experience
  - paddling experience in these conditions
  - recovery practice in these conditions
- Skills: comfort in these conditions boat control, power, and bracing competency
- Communication: level of honesty, listening, and mutual respect
- Attitude: schedule, pressures, and goals
- Physical strength, health, and wellness
- Equipment: boat design, condition, and safety gear

Terrain Conditions

- Pull-outs
  - sand or rock
  - steepness
  - exposure
- Commitment: cliffs
  - points
  - crossings
- Protection from wind and weather
- Hazards
  - shoals and bottom features
  - reefs, rocks, and boomers
  - boat traffic
  - ice
- Remoteness

RED light = STOP a hazardous situation exists.

YELLOW light = CAUTION, there is a potential hazard, too much uncertainty, or conditions are deteriorating.

GREEN light = It is OK, no hazard is obvious.

FIGURE SK12.1 The seamanship triangle is a safety tool used to facilitate sound decision making.

Thanks to Jill Fredston, Doug Fesler, and Roger Schumann for helping with this project. Used with permission. From the NOLS Sea Kayak Instructor Notebook. Copyright retained by the National Outdoor Leadership School.

- ◆ Terrain conditions—pull-outs (sand or rock, steepness, exposure); points, crossings, cliffs; protection from wind and weather; hazards (shoals and bottom features; reefs, rocks, and boomers; boat traffic; ice); remoteness.

- ◆ Human factors—experience (paddling, recovery); skills (boat control, power, bracing); communication (level of honesty, listening, mutual respect); attitude (schedule, pressures, goals); physical strength (health, seasickness); equipment (boat design and condition, safety gear).

When analyzing the four components of the triangle, the group determines which stoplight color to assign to each component based on their observations of the conditions. Red would mean stop, yellow would mean caution, and green would mean go. The colors reflect the severity of the condition. Consider this example:

- ◆ If the sea condition is favorable and does not pose any threat, it receives a green light, meaning that the group is "on go" with the plan for the day.

- ◆ If the sea condition is dangerous, a red light is assigned to it, meaning that the group is "on stop" with the plan for the day.

- ◆ If mixed feelings are present among the group members about the sea condition, it gets a yellow light, indicating that caution should be taken with the planned activities.

The group then totals up the colors of the lights to determine whether they will continue with the planned activities.

- When two or more red lights appear in the triangle, the plan for paddling that day should be altered. Paddling is not advised.
- If one red light and three yellow lights are present, the group should strongly consider not paddling as planned.
- Remember that a good approach is to err on the conservative side. Obviously, if four green lights appear, the plan is on go.
- Although there is no set pattern to follow, it is ultimately up to you to decide what is safest for the group given the prevailing conditions.

The seamanship triangle allows the group to talk through decisions and ultimately practice good decision making. You are a key player in this equation because you can have a major role in the facilitation process, thus promoting good decision making, a true skill in sea kayaking.

Activity 2: Pod Travel (10 Minutes)

Although no single formation is always the best for group travel, some formations work better than others. A good all-purpose formation is a diamond shape, which gives the group members enough space to paddle comfortably but also allows them to stick close together. If a paddler has to yell to the person beside him or her when carrying on a conversation, then the group is spread out too far.

- Typically, a group has a lead sea kayaker (the sea kayaker in front of the diamond) who sets the pace, two flank sea kayakers (sea kayakers on either side of the diamond), and a sweep (the last sea kayaker).
- The sea kayakers with the most paddling experience should be on the flanks and the sweep until students become more comfortable and proficient with sea kayaking. The flank and sweep sea kayakers are in the best position to initiate a rescue because they don't have to turn around to rescue someone; they can simply paddle to the person in trouble.
- When teaching the diamond shape formation, practice first on land by spacing out participants with their paddles in hand. This dry land exercise gives them a good visual for a tight formation. Keeping a group close enough together is one of the biggest challenges with sea kayaking in a group.
- After practicing the formation on dry land, the group should continue to practice the formation as they paddle. Set a high standard for the group from the beginning by calling them out if they begin to spread out too far, beyond talking distance from each other.
- Front loading this lesson and emphasizing the importance of staying close together are critical instructional steps. Rescues, dealing with injuries, lunch, and communication in general all work better with a close formation.

Closure Activity

Seamanship Triangle Debriefing (10 Minutes)

Debrief the seamanship triangle by allowing students to ask questions. Then have them decide what the triangle tells them about the plan for that day. Also, let students know that they will be using the seamanship triangle each day before they leave on their intended sea kayaking route. If you are practicing in the classroom, come up with various scenarios to practice the seamanship triangle, such as adverse weather, heavy boat traffic, and a lethargic group.

Follow-Up Activity

Seamanship Triangle Use (15 Minutes)

Follow-up activities occur each morning before departure. Students will be responsible for using the seamanship triangle to determine whether to proceed with the intended route.

ASSESSMENT

◆ Check that students can demonstrate correct group travel in a pod formation by observing them during each day's travel.

◆ Verify that students can describe and identify potential subjective and objective hazards when sea kayaking by addressing the seamanship triangle before each day's paddle and by assessing students' knowledge with a written exam.

◆ Assess whether students feel more self-reliant, confident, and competent in the sport of sea kayaking by knowing how to identify potential hazards involved with the sport by observing them during the evaluation of the seamanship triangle before each day's paddle.

TEACHING CONSIDERATIONS

◆ An alternative way to teach the seamanship triangle is to draw a big triangle in the sand. Have students stand at each point of the triangle and in the middle of the triangle. Have the students act out the different parts of the seamanship triangle: sea conditions, weather conditions, terrain conditions, and human factors. Facilitate the decision-making process and have students make the appropriate decisions. This activity can be entertaining and engaging.

◆ Students tend to be overzealous and can be caught up in the goal of getting to the destination. Because they are new to sea kayaking, they are truly unaware of the natural consequences involved. As an instructor and as a person who knows much more about the consequences associated with sea kayaking, you must make sure that students carefully craft an informed decision. Emphasize making conservative calls as opposed to making decisions to go for the goal.

UNIT 5, LESSON 13

▷ Leave No Trace Considerations

OVERVIEW

This lesson addresses Leave No Trace principles pertaining to sea kayaking. The seven principles are discussed in this lesson only as they relate to sea kayaking. When traveling in marine environments or around large open bodies of water, sea kayakers need specific knowledge and skills to protect the environment.

JUSTIFICATION

As sea kayaking becomes more popular, sea kayakers must follow through on their ethical and moral responsibility to take care of the natural environment. Leave No Trace principles provide a good foundation, but specific Leave No Trace practices are associated with freshwater and saltwater environments. Without this knowledge, sea kayakers have the potential to harm fragile ecosystems and negatively affect the experience of others.

GOAL

To educate students about Leave No Trace practices specific to sea kayaking.

OBJECTIVES

At the end of this lesson, students will be able to

◆ understand the seven principles of Leave No Trace as they pertain to sea kayaking (cognitive),

◆ demonstrate Leave No Trace practices (psychomotor), and

◆ take pride in knowing that they are leaving the natural environment better than when they found it (affective).

EQUIPMENT AND AREAS NEEDED

◆ One commercial human waste disposal system (e.g., Wag Bag)

◆ One trowel

◆ One lighter

◆ One roll of toilet paper

◆ One water bottle full of water

◆ One large shell

◆ One piece of white cardboard laminated with heavy laminate

◆ Several colored overhead projector markers (easier to clean off the laminate surface than other markers)

RISK MANAGEMENT CONSIDERATIONS

◆ See lesson 1 for details about general risk management considerations.

◆ Emphasize the need to wash hands thoroughly to maintain proper sanitation.

LESSON CONTENT

Introduction

Spark students' interest in Leave No Trace ethics by asking them the following questions: "What does Leave No Trace mean?" "What does 'take only pictures, leave only footprints' mean?" "What does minimum-impact camping mean?"

Address these questions and include information about Leave No Trace that was included in the introductory chapters of this manual.

Main Activity

Applying the Seven Principles (30 to 40 Minutes)

Write the seven principles of Leave No Trace on the whiteboard with colored markers. Go over the seven principles with students by asking guided questions such as "What do we mean by plan and prepare?" and "What are durable surfaces?" Continue the dialog, making sure that the following points are made for each principle. Include the following information using the materials and supplies listed.

Plan Ahead and Prepare

- Make sure that permits are in place and that you have checked and rechecked the weather.

- Confirm that the food you have planned is durable enough to withstand the length of time that you plan to be out on expedition and is durable enough to stand up to the dampness and temperature of the trip. For example, you should eat fresh vegetables at the beginning of the trip and save dried and canned food for the end of the trip.

Travel and Camp on Durable Surfaces

- Water is the most durable surface to travel on because you don't leave footprints or damage the surface when you travel on it, as you might if you were hiking on land.

- When camping in a marine environment, make sure to place your tent above the rack line (the highest high-tide line, usually indicated by a line of seaweed).

- Stay off dunes, and stay away from sea oats because they anchor the sand that makes up the dunes. Camp in designated areas. Check with the local governing agency about camping regulations.

Dispose of Waste Properly

- Pack out all trash, even apple cores and orange peels. Animals pick them up before they decompose.

- Proper hand washing is a must after disposing of trash or using the bathroom.

- Several options are available for disposing of human waste.
  - First, display the Wag Bag and describe how it is used. Mention that it is the preferred method because it leaves nothing behind; you pack everything out. Other similar methods are available (the Groover, ammo can, and so on).
  - The second option is to find a big seashell and poop in it. After you are done, throw the shell as far out into the ocean side of the water as possible (some call this the shell put). The current will break down the fecal matter. Throwing fecal matter into water that does not ebb and flow is not advised.
  - The third option is to do the "aqua poop," which requires the participant to walk knee deep into the surf and time the wave action so that the fecal matter is washed out to sea, not onto the shore. No toilet paper is used with this method. Water and the left hand are used for cleansing. This method is advised only where wave action will break down the fecal matter, not in still or calm water.
  - The fourth option is to dig a cathole 6 inches (15 centimeters) deep between the dunes. Pack out toilet paper. Urinate below the waterline, especially in a marine environment. Urinating above the high-tide line in the sand will leave a distinct odor that will become more intense as the sun warms the sand.

Leave What You Find   Check with the local governing agency about its policies. Some agencies allow visitors to take up to 1 gallon (4 liters) of seashells per day. Otherwise, take only pictures.

Minimize Campfire Impacts

◆ If building a campfire, build it on a firepan or below the high-tide line. The tide will wash the ashes out to sea.

◆ Broadcast all the ashes out into the water the next day. Scoop the sand up with a paddle and fling it out into the water.

Respect Wildlife

◆ Don't harass pesky critters such as raccoons.

◆ Make sure that all food and water is packed away in boat hatches to avoid confrontations with animals that want your food.

◆ Observe nesting bird restrictions.

◆ Be able to identify wildlife that is site specific to your paddling area (be sure not to step on live coral).

Be Considerate of Other Visitors

◆ Avoid cell phone use and other distracting acts that take away from the solitude and the natural environment of the outdoors.

◆ Try not to spread equipment so widely that it resembles a yard sale or infringes on others' use of the space.

◆ Stay relatively close together so that other visitors have plenty of room.

Leave No Trace principles—Copyright: Leave No Trace Center for Outdoor Ethics. www.LNT.org.

Closure Activities

Activity 1: LNT Questions (Five Minutes)

Ask whether students have any questions. Make sure that everyone knows where the bathroom supplies are (toilet paper, Wag Bag, and so on) and where the designated bathroom area is if your program uses a community toilet. Also, make sure that no one has left personal food in dry bags or tents and suggest that students bring their personal food to the kitchen area.

Activity 2: LNT Game (15 to 20 Minutes)

You can make this game as long and as detailed as time allows. The premise is to take note cards, create seven categories based on the seven principles, and under each category have a series of answers related to the category. Each card is worth a certain number of points that are written on one side of the note card. The answers are on the opposite side of the card. Students earn the points if they answer the card with the correct question. You can play with teams or individuals. The team or person with the most points at the end of the game wins. Keep score on your whiteboard or in the sand.

◆ Keeping the note cards in place in windy conditions can be difficult. One trick is to use a hole punch to put a hole in the top of each note card and use golf tees to hold the note cards in place in the ground.

◆ Because students don't have buzzers, be creative by having them make their favorite barnyard animal sound.

◆ Prizes for the winners can be food treats or one night free of dish duty. Again, creativity works well!

Follow-Up Activity

LNT Daily Quiz (Five Minutes per Day)

The follow-up activity is to check in with participants as the trip progresses and make sure that they are following the Leave No Trace principles. Each day you can ask students a Leave No Trace question and reward the first correct answer with a food treat or a free chore card, which can be redeemed anytime during the trip. The free chore card excuses the participant from participating in a group chore.

ASSESSMENT

◆ Verify that students understand the seven principles of Leave No Trace as they pertain to sea kayaking by testing their knowledge through an LNT game.

◆ Check that students can demonstrate Leave No Trace practices by observing behaviors throughout the expedition.

◆ Assess whether students take pride in knowing that they are leaving the natural environment better than when they found it while becoming more self-reliant by observing their behavior for consistency.

TEACHING CONSIDERATIONS

◆ Teach this lesson either before a trip or as soon as the class reaches camp the first day and before people get too busy setting up camp.

◆ Conduct the lesson near the shore by the rack line to allow students to have a better visual about the points made in the lesson.

◆ Some students find it difficult to talk about human waste and go to the bathroom in the backcountry. Try to bring a relaxed feel to the lesson by acting silly, mentioning common names for the bathroom, and helping students talk about their fears. Also make sure that the bathroom area is secluded enough to allow modest students to feel comfortable.

◆ Arrange the classroom so that students are not distracted by other visitors in the area, boat traffic, or the sun shining in their eyes.

GLOSSARY

access hatches—Hatches on a sea kayak that give access to storage compartments, typically designated as dry hatches formed by the bulkheads and waterproof seals.

bilge pump—A long slender tubular device used to pump water from the bottom of a boat.

boat trailer crossbar—The horizontal bar on a trailer where the boat rests.

boat trailer post—The vertical bar on a trailer that the crossbar attaches to.

bulkheads—The foam or fiberglass walls in a sea kayak that provide rigidity and waterproof storage and flotation at both ends of the boat.

cam strap—A piece of webbing attached to a camming buckle that allows the strap to be tightened down without use of a knot. The cam strap is used to secure boats to a boat trailer or roof top carrier.

chart—A navigational aid that describes water features, including water depth, navigational buoys, shorelines, and so on.

deck rigging—Bungee cords and rope secured to the deck of a sea kayak that are used for rescue or to secure items to the deck when paddling.

deep-water reentry—A self-rescue technique that a person uses to reenter the sea kayak by using a strong scissor kick to project himself or herself out of the water and into the boat.

Sea Kayaking Skills Checklist

☐   1. Describe the history of sea kayaking.

☐   2. Identify and describe the use of basic sea kayaking equipment.

☐   3. Identify and describe boat designs and materials.

☐   4. Demonstrate how to lift a sea kayak on and off a boat trailer.

☐   5. Properly secure the sea kayaks to the boat trailer using cam straps.

☐   6. Demonstrate the use of a hand carry to transport a loaded sea kayak and an unloaded sea kayak.

☐   7. Demonstrate the use of a sea kayak sling to transport a loaded sea kayak.

☐   8. Demonstrate and describe the proper fit of a sea kayak.

☐   9. Demonstrate the HELP position.

☐ 10. Execute a wet exit.

☐ 11. Complete a deep-water reentry.

☐ 12. Enter and exit a sea kayak from land.

☐ 13. Execute a paddle float rescue.

☐ 14. Execute a boat-over-boat rescue.

☐ 15. Execute an Eskimo bow rescue.

☐ 16. Demonstrate how to tow another sea kayaker.

☐ 17. Demonstrate how to use a sling for an assisted deep-water reentry.

☐ 18. Demonstrate the progression and mechanics of a sea kayak roll.

☐ 19. Execute the forward and reverse strokes.

☐ 20. Execute the forward and reverse sweeps.

☐ 21. Execute a draw and a sculling draw.

☐ 22. Describe the features of a chart.

☐ 23. Distinguish between a chart and a map.

☐ 24. Demonstrate the ability to navigate using a chart.

☐ 25. Demonstrate and describe the proper way to pack a sea kayak.

☐ 26. Demonstrate appropriate paddle signals.

☐ 27. Demonstrate proper whistle signals.

☐ 28. Describe the rule of 12ths (identify raging and slack tides).

☐ 29. Demonstrate the ability to predict the appropriate window of opportunity for crossing a channel.

☐ 30. Identify potential hazards involved with crossing a channel.

☐ 31. Ferry a sea kayak across a channel.

☐ 32. Identify and demonstrate the use of safety equipment needed for sea kayaking.

☐ 33. Identify and describe potential subjective and objective hazards when sea kayaking.

☐ 34. Demonstrate correct group travel in a pod formation.

☐ 35. Describe and demonstrate the seven principles of Leave No Trace as they pertain to sea kayaking.

Use the sea kayaking skills checklist as an additional tool to assess skills learned throughout this unit.

From M. Wagstaff and A. Attarian, 2009, *Technical skills for adventure programming: A curriculum guide* (Champaign, IL: Human Kinetics).

drip ring—A rubber gasket attached to the shaft of the sea kayak paddle that prevents water from running down the shaft of the paddle and dripping into the cockpit of the boat.

ebbing—A receding tide.

EPIRB—Emergency position indicating radio beacon. An electronic safety device used to transmit a signal to satellites that then transmit to the Coast Guard in an emergency.

ferrule—The attachment point where two-piece paddles are locked into place. The ferrule can be feathered in specific degree increments to allow the blades of the paddle to be offset.

ferry—To cross the current without losing ground or being swept downcurrent.

fetch—The unobstructed distance across a body of water over which the wind blows.

flares—A pyrotechnic rescue device used to signal for help in an emergency.

flooding—A rising tide.

handle—The plastic piece attached to either end of the sea kayak used to carry or move the boat. Sometimes called a *toggle*.

HELP—Heat escape lessening position. The body position used to reduce heat loss in water immersion. The person balls up by tucking the legs next to the chest and wrapping the arms around the knees.

leeward side—The side of an island protected from the wind.

National Oceanic and Atmospheric Administration (NOAA)—A federal agency that focuses on oceans and the atmosphere. NOAA provides charts and weather forecasts. The weather forecasts are available on VHF radios.

neap tides—Tides that show the least difference between high and low tides and occur during the first and last quarter of the moon.

paddle float—A flotation device, either inflatable or Styrofoam, that slides on one end of the paddle to assist reentry into the sea kayak during a self-rescue. With the paddle float secured to the paddle, the paddle becomes an outrigger to stabilize the kayak upon reentry.

paddle shaft—The part of the paddle that the sea kayaker holds. The blades attach to the paddle shaft.

rack line—The line of detritus (dead seaweed) that marks the highest high tide.

raging tide—Occurs when the current of the changing tide is the fastest, during the third and fourth hours of the changing tide.

recreational kayaks—Kayaks used for inshore paddling, usually 15 feet (4.5 meters) in length or less and very stable.

rudder—A steering device 16 to 20 inches (40 to 50 centimeters) in length used on the stern of a sea kayak. When deployed into the water, the rudder can be controlled (turned) by foot pedals in the cockpit.

sea anchor—A piece of nylon fabric that resembles a parachute and is deployed into the water to slow the drift of a sea kayak. Also used when landing in a rough surf zone by being deployed from the stern of the boat as the bow faces into the breaking waves. Sometimes called a *drift sock*.

sea kayak sling—A certain length of 2-inch (5-centimeter) webbing used to cradle the sea kayak when carrying or moving the boat.

skeg—A piece of plastic or aluminum deployed at the stern of a sea kayak used to improve the tracking ability of the sea kayak by providing resistance to the stern of the boat.

slack tide—Occurs when the current of the changing tide is the slowest, during the first and last hours of the changing tide.

spring tides—Tides that are higher high tides and lower low tides than usual and occur during a new moon and a full moon (twice each month).

strobe light—A battery-operated signaling device usually attached to the sea kayaker or sea kayak to indicate the position of a sea kayaker who needs assistance or to alert other boaters of the location of the sea kayak.

tides—The alternate and regular rise and fall of sea level in oceans and other large bodies of water.

touring kayak—A kayak used for both inland and offshore kayaking, typically 16 feet (5 meters) in length or longer and having a narrow beam of 20 to 23 inches (50 to 58 centimeters).

VHF (very high frequency) radio—A communication device used to observe weather reports issued by NOAA and to communicate with other boaters and the Coast Guard.

weather cock—Occurs when a sea kayak turns into the wind because the stern is being blown downwind.

wet exit—A rescue technique used to exit a capsized sea kayak. The sea kayaker removes himself or herself from the overturned sea kayak by pulling the grab loop of the spray skirt and exiting the boat.

REFERENCES AND RESOURCES

REFERENCES

Broze, M., & Gronseth, G. (1997). *Sea kayaker's deep trouble: True stories and their lessons from Sea Kayaker magazine*. Camden, ME: McGraw Hill.

Hendrickson, R. (1984). *The ocean almanac*. New York: Broadway Books.

Loots, J. (2000). *Sea kayaking: The essential guide to equipment and techniques.* London: New Holland Publishers.

Malhotra, H. (2006, September 18). Kayak industry seeks ways to boost outdoor recreation. *The Epoch Times*, Washington, DC. Retrieved from www.theepochtimes.com/news/6-9-18/45900.html

RESOURCES

American Canoe Association (ACA) is a nationwide, nonprofit organization that promotes the sport of paddling through education and stewardship of various paddling locations, programs, and events. Contact information:

> American Canoe Association
> 1340 Central Park Blvd., Suite 210
> Fredericksburg, VA 22401
> 540-907-4460
> www.americancanoe.org/index.lasso

The Trade Association of Paddlesports (TAPS) is a nonprofit organization that promotes the commerce of paddle sports in an ethical and professional manner. TAPS represents manufacturers, retailers, outfitters, instructional centers, and publications throughout the paddle sports industry. Contact information:

> TAPS
> P.O. Box 243
> Milner, BC
> Canada, V0X-1T0
> 800-755-5228
> www.gopaddle.org

American Canoe Association. (1996). *Introduction to paddling: Canoeing basics for lakes and rivers.* Birmingham, AL: Menasha Ridge Press. Overview: Although this is primarily a canoeing book, it contains good information on basic concepts of paddling, boat movement, and basic equipment that easily carries over into sea kayaking.

American Canoe Association. (n.d.). *Kayak instruction.* Retrieved from www.acanet.org/instruction/kayak_instruction.lasso. Overview: A comprehensive description of sea kayaking instruction and a good reference for instructors of both inland and coastal kayaking. Each easy-to-follow lesson is detailed with teaching goals, objectives, a timeline, and safety considerations.

Ballantine, T. (1991). *Tideland treasure.* Columbia: University of South Carolina. Overview: A comprehensive and easy-to-read description of marine life, coastal ecology, and coastal environment in the southeast coastal area of the United States.

Conlan, T. (1998). *NOLS sea kayaking instructor handbook.* Lander, WY: National Outdoor Leadership School. Overview: This comprehensive instructor handbook for sea kayaking includes diagrams, risk management issues, and group management for open water. The diagrams are easy to follow. The basic to advanced concepts are well explained, and the emphasis is on group management and group instruction.

Gullion, L. (1987). *Canoeing and kayaking instruction manual.* Newington, VA: American Canoe Association. Overview: This comprehensive guide to both canoeing and kayaking contains good information on basic concepts of paddling, boat movement, and basic equipment. This book includes detailed diagrams and easy-to-follow instructions.

Hutchinson, D. (2002). *The complete book of sea kayaking* (4th ed.). London: A&C Black. Overview: Many consider this book the bible of sea kayaking. Derek Hutchinson gained fame back in the 1970s when he crossed the North Sea in his sea kayak. The book includes many advanced techniques as well as basic skills. This comprehensive book is sometimes hard for the beginner sea kayaker to follow.

Rounds, J. (2003). *Basic canoeing: All the skills and tools you need to get started.* Mechanicsburg, PA: Stackpole Books. Overview: Although this book focuses on canoeing, it offers good information on basic concepts of paddling, boat movement, and equipment that transfers readily to sea kayaking.

Sloane, E. (1952). *Eric Sloane's weather book.* New York: Hawthorn/Dutton. Overview: This classic book on weather concepts is a must for sea kayakers as well as other outdoor enthusiasts. The diagrams and illustrations in the book are easy to follow, and basic concepts of weather patterns are explained well. The book lists many interesting sayings related to the weather.

Whiting, K. (Producer), & Emerick, C. (Eds). (2005). *The ultimate guide to sea kayaking: With Ken Whiting and Alex Matthews* [DVD]. Beachburg, ON: Heliconia Press. Overview: This instructional video in DVD format is informative and entertaining. Navigating between the different topics and skills covered is easy. Skills covered in the video range from basic equipment, transporting, and strokes to advanced topics such as rolling, advanced strokes, and sea kayaking locations.

Whitewater Kayaking

Bruce Martin

▷ **Introduction to Whitewater Kayaking**

OVERVIEW

This lesson introduces students to the history and evolution of the sport of white-water kayaking, various styles of whitewater kayaking, and opportunities for growth in the sport. In addition, the lesson covers instructor and student expectations and provides an overview of what will be taught in the unit. The lesson also provides an opportunity for students to get to know one another through name games and introductory activities.

JUSTIFICATION

This lesson is important for three primary reasons. First, introducing students to the nature of whitewater kayaking and to what participation in the unit entails is essential to adherence to the principles of **challenge by choice**. Students must be aware of the challenges and risks associated with the sport and other water-based activities if they are to choose to accept those challenges and risks.

Second, the lesson allows students and instructors to calibrate expectations of the unit. You can modify the unit to some extent to meet individual student expectations, and students can get a sense of what you will expect of them.

Third, introducing students to the history and evolution of the sport of whitewater kayaking will give them a greater appreciation of the sport and a sense of the range of opportunities available to them in the sport.

GOALS

♦ To make students aware of what participation in the unit entails and, subsequently, to allow them to make conscious choices about whether to participate in the unit.

♦ To introduce students to the nature of the sport of whitewater kayaking.

♦ To begin to develop a sense of community among students.

OBJECTIVES

At the end of this lesson, students will be able to

♦ describe basic challenges and risks associated with the sport of whitewater kayaking (cognitive),

♦ understand basic expectations of participation in the class (cognitive),

♦ identify key developments in the evolution of the sport of whitewater kayaking (cognitive),

♦ distinguish between different styles of whitewater kayaking (cognitive),

♦ take pride in embracing a new challenge (affective), and

♦ feel a sense of community to enhance the group learning experience (affective).

EQUIPMENT AND AREAS NEEDED

◆ Whitewater kayaking instructional videos (see resource list at the end of the unit)

◆ Whitewater kayaking skills and knowledge checklists (page 486) (one per student)

◆ Waiver forms (one per student)

◆ Health history forms (one per student)

◆ Unit policies and expectations statement (one per student)

◆ Chalkboard, dry erase board, or flip chart

◆ Chalk or markers

RISK MANAGEMENT CONSIDERATIONS

Students may enter the class with a certain amount of apprehension about the sport. This introductory lesson is your first opportunity to make students aware of the challenges and risks associated with the sport. Although accomplishing this is important, be sensitive to student apprehensions. Avoid heightening the anxieties of already anxious students.

LESSON CONTENT

Introduction (10 Minutes)

Show video of whitewater kayaking to give students a taste of the sport. Two good selections are *Give Us a River* and *Jackson Kayak 2006 Promo Video*. *Give Us a River* is a good choice because it shows footage of both contemporary whitewater kayaking and whitewater paddling in the 1960s and 1970s. The video helps to illustrate the heritage of the sport. *Jackson Kayak 2006 Promo Video* provides excellent footage of world champion kayaker Eric Jackson and Team Jackson Kayak performing a wide range of play-boating and river-running techniques on the Nile and Zambezi rivers in Africa. A soundtrack that captures the flavor of the region accompanies the well-made video. Both videos will rouse the excitement of students and give them something to aspire to in the sport.

An alternative introductory activity is to administer the whitewater kayaking skills checklist at the end of this unit (page 486) to students at the start of the class. This self-evaluation serves two purposes. First, it provides an initial introduction to the various skills that students will learn in the course. Second, it provides you a tool for preassessing student abilities.

Important Terms

challenge by choice—A philosophy used to empower students as a part of the educational process. This philosophy enables students to determine the level of challenge that they will accept as a part of an educational activity. This framework is especially important in outdoor adventure activities such as whitewater kayaking in which the perceived risks in the environment may be high and the emotional safety of students is a concern. Challenge by choice also gives students a sense of freedom in the experience, which can lead to greater levels of personal motivation to participate in the activity for the sake of confronting fears and developing greater proficiency in the sport.

Main Activities

Activity 1: Introductions and Expectations (15 to 20 Minutes)

An excellent way to introduce students to one another is to have them conduct peer interviews.

◆ Ask students to pair up with someone in the class whom they do not know.

◆ Give the students five minutes to get to know one another: name, hometown, paddling history, and a statement of expectations of the unit. Have students take notes because each student must introduce his or her partner to the class.

◆ Record the students' expectations of the unit by writing them down as students volunteer them (you will need a record of expectations for the follow-up activity).

Activity 2: Unit Overview (10 Minutes)

The following are two primary points of emphasis in giving the unit overview.

◆ First, articulate how the unit will meet each of the students' expectations. For instance, in the student introductions, students may express excitement about the opportunity to learn the kayak roll. Play on that excitement when introducing that part of the unit.

◆ Second, clearly articulate policies and expectations, especially those pertaining to safety and risk management. Distribute a written statement of policies and expectations at the beginning of the unit overview.

Activity 3: Acknowledgment of Risks and Assumption of Liability (15 Minutes)

This activity focuses on introducing students to risks associated with whitewater kayaking. The purpose is to make sure that students are aware of these risks so that they can make a conscious decision about whether to accept the risks and participate in the unit.

◆ Ask students to identify risks associated with whitewater kayaking.

◆ As students identify risks, note them on the chalkboard.

◆ After students compile a comprehensive list of risks, either have them complete administrative paperwork or review their completed paperwork such as health history forms and agreement-to-participate forms. It is important that all administrative functions be completed before beginning activities. Also, students must be fully informed of the risks and associated hazards from a risk-management standpoint, and this can be accomplished by completing or reviewing forms.

Activity 4: History of Whitewater Kayaking (20 Minutes)

Give a brief lecture that introduces students to the history and evolution of the sport. Start the lecture with the quote from Charlie Walbridge: "If you were a whitewater kayaker in the 1960s, you were a boat builder." This quote emphasizes the relative newness of the sport of whitewater kayaking. Key points include the following:

◆ Contextualize the development of whitewater kayaking within the broader development of kayaking, which dates back to prehistoric times in Arctic regions (see unit 5 for an overview of the history of sea kayaking).

◆ Discuss the role of rivers as highways throughout history and the roles of canoes, bateaus, dories, and other craft as historic modes of travel in the United States and around the world. Examples of resources that provide information on the history of river travel and exploration in North America include *The Exploration of the Colorado River and Its Canyons* by John Wesley Powell and *Making the Voyageur World: Travelers and Traders in the North American Fur Trade* by Carolyn Podruchny.

◆ Focus on important trends during the past four decades, including participation trends, evolution of the whitewater kayaking industry (manufacturers, retailers, guide services, and outfitters), evolution of whitewater kayak design and construction, and the development of various styles of whitewater kayaking. *The River Chasers: A History of American Whitewater Paddling* by Susan Taft is an excellent source of information on the history of kayaking during the past several decades.

Closure Activity

Student Roundup (Five Minutes)

Answer any lingering questions or concerns that students have about participating in the class. Have the group form a circle with their hands in the middle for a closing "Whoop."

Follow-Up Activity

Review of Student Expectations (20 to 30 Minutes)

At the end of the unit, gather the group in a circle, ask them to sit, and revisit student expectations.

◆ First, have the students close their eyes. Recount what happened during the unit for the students, giving a narrative that describes key moments and highlights during the unit. After you finish, have students open their eyes.

◆ Next, give students a moment to reflect on their initial expectations of the unit. Showing students their initial expectations in writing is helpful. Before this exercise, prepare a flip chart that notes the record of expectations from the introductory exercise. Then ask the group to review it.

◆ After the group has reflected on their initial expectations for a moment, ask the following questions. Were your expectations of this unit fulfilled? Did your expectations change during the unit? If so, how? Did the unit exceed your expectations? If so, how? If you were to seek future instruction in whitewater kayaking to develop your knowledge and skills in the sport further, where would you want to go from here?

ASSESSMENT

◆ Check that students can describe basic challenges and risks associated with whitewater kayaking by eliciting a list of these challenges and risks from the students and noting them on a flip chart, dry erase board, or chalkboard.

◆ Verify that students understand basic expectations of participation in the class by signing a policies and expectations statement that acknowledges their commitment to adhere to these policies and expectations.

- Assess whether students can identify key developments in the evolution of the sport of whitewater kayaking through open discussion while reviewing kayaking history.
- Check that students can distinguish between different styles of whitewater kayaking by observing kayaking videos and discussing those differences.
- Assess whether students take pride in embracing a new challenge by recording their expectations and hopes during the introductory activity.
- Evaluate whether students feel a sense of community to enhance the group learning experience through introductory activities.

TEACHING CONSIDERATIONS

- This lesson is best presented in the form of a pretrip meeting. The lesson on clothing and equipment should follow to give students an opportunity to gather personal clothing and equipment not provided as a part of the unit before getting on the water. An appropriate interval should pass between these two lessons and getting on the water.
- An alternative approach to introducing the history and evolution of whitewater kayaking is to write out whitewater kayaking history and facts on a series of note cards. Pass out the note cards and have students present their facts as discussed in other water-based units. This method facilitates a more experiential process when covering background information.

UNIT 6, LESSON 2

▷ **Introduction to Equipment and Use**

OVERVIEW

This lesson introduces students to equipment and clothing required for whitewater kayaking. Students learn nomenclature of the boat, paddle, and other equipment used in whitewater kayaking, and the purpose of these pieces of equipment. Students are also introduced to different types of kayaks used for different styles of kayaking.

JUSTIFICATION

Knowing the equipment needed for whitewater kayaking and being able to identify equipment and corresponding parts by name is one of the first steps to becoming a fully outfitted and competent kayaker.

GOAL

To develop students' knowledge of names, design features, and purposes of kayaking equipment and parts.

OBJECTIVES

At the end of this lesson, students will be able to

- identify the five essentials of whitewater kayaking (cognitive);

- identify safety equipment that is essential to whitewater kayaking (cognitive);
- understand the importance of additional clothing and equipment that can be used in whitewater kayaking (cognitive);
- identify the parts of a kayak, along with the function of those parts (cognitive);
- distinguish between various whitewater kayak designs and the style of kayaking for which each design is intended (cognitive);
- adjust kayaks, personal flotation devices, and other equipment to fit (psychomotor); and
- appreciate the role of good equipment in ensuring a safe and enjoyable kayaking experience (affective).

EQUIPMENT AND AREAS NEEDED

- Kayak (If available, include a variety of types of kayaks to demonstrate various hull designs—for example, creek boat, squirt boat, rodeo kayak, downriver kayak, and slalom kayak. Photos will suffice in the absence of actual boats. A quick and easy way to obtain boat design photos is to download information from manufacturer's Web sites such as Dagger, Wave Sport, Jackson Kayaks, and others.)
- Paddle
- Helmet
- Spray skirt
- Personal flotation device (PFD)
- Clothing for cold weather: spray jacket and pants, fleece tops and bottoms, wet suit, dry suit, hat, pogies, neoprene booties
- Clothing for warm weather: swim suit, shorts, shirt, sandals or booties
- Rescue equipment: throw rope, pulleys, slings, carabiners, whistle, river knife
- First aid kit
- Duct tape
- Car top carrier (rack system)
- Equipment checklist

RISK MANAGEMENT CONSIDERATIONS

Be aware of environmental conditions and make appropriate accommodations to minimize risks.

LESSON CONTENT

Introduction

Open the lesson by explaining to students that equipment used in whitewater kayaking falls into three basic categories (see figure WK2.1 on page 423):

- The five essentials (kayak, paddle, personal flotation device [PFD], helmet, and spray skirt)
- Safety and rescue equipment (first aid kit, throw rope, carabiners, pulleys, slings, and rescue PFDs as an alternative to regular PFDs)
- Personal clothing and equipment (swimsuit, shorts, shirt, sandals or booties, spray jacket and pants, fleece tops and bottoms, wet suit, dry suit, hat, and so on)

Important Terms

back band, or back brace—The final point of contact with the kayak. The back brace provides lumbar support, which helps the paddler maintain good posture while sitting in the kayak. Good posture lends itself to good paddling technique.

bow—The front of the boat.

bulkheads—An alternative to foot pegs. Bulkheads are more common than foot pegs in contemporary kayaks.

chine—The sides of the boat between the deck and the hull. Displacement hull kayaks typically have soft, or rounded, chine. Planing hull kayaks typically have harder, or straight, chine. The softer the chine, the more stable the boat is when on edge. The harder the chine, the less stable the boat is when on edge.

cockpit—The open area in the center of the kayak where the kayaker sits.

cockpit combing—The lip around the cockpit to which the spray skirt is attached.

deck—The top of the boat.

displacement hull—Kayak hull that is rounded.

drain plug—A plug in the stern of the kayak that can be unscrewed to drain water from the boat. The drain plug must be screwed in at the start of each paddling experience.

foot pegs—Another primary point of contact with the kayak. Foot pegs are adjustable to accommodate different leg lengths among paddlers.

grab loop—Loops at either end of the boat used primarily for carrying the boat but also for assisted rescues when on the river.

hip pads—Another point of contact with the kayak. Hip padding helps ensure that the hips fit snugly, preventing the paddler from shifting around in the seat of the kayak, thus making it easier to tilt, edge, or lean the boat.

hull—The bottom of the boat. There are two types of hulls on whitewater kayaks: planing hulls and displacement hulls. Planing hulls are flat. Displacement hulls are rounded. Planing hulls have supplanted displacement hulls in recent years as the standard hull design for whitewater kayaks. This shift has occurred because planing hulls allow greater maneuverability and greater stability in the kayak, two key assets in whitewater kayaking. Planing hulls are also ideal for surfing. Displacement hulls are still the norm in sea kayaking because of their efficiency in tracking through open water.

planing hull—Kayak hull that is flat.

rescue loop—Point to which carabiners and ropes can be attached to the boat for rescue purposes.

rocker—The curvature of the hull from bow to stern. The more pronounced the rocker is, the more maneuverable the kayak is. Pronounced rockers are common on whitewater kayaks. Compared with whitewater kayaks, sea kayaks have little to no rocker.

seat—One of five primary points of contact with the kayak.

stern—The back of the boat.

thigh brace—Yet another point of contact with the kayak, the point at which the thighs contact the boat. Thigh braces are used to help tilt, edge, or lean the kayak. They also help the kayaker remain in the kayak when it is upside down.

wall—The foam wall along the centerline of the kayak. The wall gives structural integrity to the kayak.

Main Activities

Activity 1: Introduction to the Five Essentials (Five Minutes)

Introduce this activity by asking students to identify the five essentials. Have a student demonstrate the process of getting geared up as the items are identified (for example, proper PFD fit and use of straps when the PFD is introduced). Use the following information to guide the discussion.

Kayak   Whitewater kayaks come in all shapes and sizes, depending on the intended use. Whitewater kayaks can be as short as 6 feet (1.8 meters) or as long as 12 feet (3.6 meters) in length. Longer, higher-volume boats tend to be used for general river running, especially for multiday trips when gear is carried. Creek boats tend to be short, high-volume boats with turned up bows designed to navigate steep, narrow creeks. Playboats, also known as freestyle or rodeo boats, are typically short, low-volume boats designed to execute tricks or gymnastic-type maneuvers. Squirt boats are usually lightweight composite boats that are longer and flatter than the average playboat. Squirt boats are designed to execute specialized maneuvers on top and under water. Slalom boats, or racing kayaks, are built based on required dimensions. In summary, whitewater kayaks are designed to be highly maneuverable in order to navigate the challenging environment of whitewater rivers.

Paddle   See unit 5, lesson 2 (page 338), for a general description of kayak paddles as well as the anatomy of a kayak paddle. Note, however, the important distinctions between sea kayak paddles and whitewater kayak paddles.

◆ Whitewater kayak paddles typically range in length from 192 to 200 centimeters, whereas sea kayak paddles typically range in length from 210 to 240 centimeters. Sea kayaks are typically much longer than whitewater kayaks; consequently, sea kayakers need longer paddles to provide sufficient reach and leverage in maneuvering the kayak. On the other hand, whitewater kayaking requires agility, an attribute promoted by the use of shorter, less cumbersome paddles.

◆ The blades of whitewater kayak paddles are typically wider than those of sea kayak paddles, providing more surface area with which to catch water during strokes. Wider blades are important in whitewater kayaking because they allow more powerful strokes and more effective bracing.

◆ Sea kayak paddles typically come in two pieces, whereas whitewater kayak paddles typically come in one piece. The advantage to sea kayakers is that the degree to which the blades are offset can be adjusted for different conditions, from no offset to 90 degrees. The degree of offset for whitewater kayak paddles typically ranges from 30 to 45 degrees. The advantage of a lower offset is the reduction in work for the wrist. The repetitive motion of rotating the paddle shaft to account for the offset of the blades can lead to tendinitis. The advantage of a higher offset is that as one blade pulls through the water, the other slices more efficiently through air or water.

◆ Whitewater kayak paddles do not have drip rings, which are typically found on sea kayaking paddles.

◆ When selecting a whitewater kayaking paddle, kayakers shorter than 5 feet, 8 inches (173 centimeters) in height should choose a paddle that is 192 to 196 centimeters in length, whereas kayakers who are taller than 5 feet, 8 inches (173 centimeters) in height should choose a paddle that is 196 to 200 centimeters in length. If a person can stand a paddle next to her or him and wrap the fingertips around the tip of the paddle blade without fully extending the arm (keeping a crook in the elbow), the person has found a paddle that should be a good fit.

Personal Flotation Device See unit 5, lesson 2 (page 335), for a general description of personal flotation devices (PFDs). A U.S. Coast Guard approved type III PFD is recommended for whitewater kayaking. A **rescue PFD** is an alternative for those who are trained in river rescue techniques. Those not trained to use rescue PFDs should not wear them.

Spray Skirt **Spray skirts** are used to seal the cockpit of the kayak and keep water out of the boat.

◆ Spray skirts for whitewater kayaks are typically made from neoprene.

◆ To enhance durability, many are reinforced with Kevlar or rubber along the area that wraps around the cockpit combing.

◆ Spray skirts have a nylon grab loop that serves as an ejection cord. Make sure that this loop is always accessible when the spray skirt is attached to the kayak; the loop must not be tucked underneath the skirt and inside the boat. If it is, the kayaker may struggle to make a wet exit.

◆ The skirt should fit snugly around the waist and be cut to fit the cockpit opening.

Helmet A helmet is one of the more important items used in whitewater kayaking. It protects the head from injury in case of a capsize in moving water and whitewater environments.

◆ Helmets should be worn at all times when whitewater kayaking.

◆ Helmets are made from plastics and composite materials, such as Kevlar and fiberglass.

◆ The inside of the helmet should be padded with foam.

◆ The kayaker should choose a helmet that provides good coverage to the forehead, temples, and ears.

◆ The kayaker should choose a helmet that fits snugly on the head. The helmet should not move around on the head, especially when underwater. The chin strap must be clipped on and snug to keep the helmet on the head.

◆ The structural integrity of a helmet can be checked by squeezing the sides of the helmet. A sturdy helmet will not give much when given a firm squeeze.

Activity 2: Kayak Anatomy (15 Minutes)

After you present the five essentials, introduce the parts of a kayak through a game of Name That Part (see figure WK2.2). Following are two good variations of this game.

◆ Give the students 60 seconds to explore the kayak. Each student must identify at least one part of the kayak (maybe two or three parts of the kayak with smaller groups). The students must give a name to the part and describe its function. The creativity of students can add a little fun to this exercise.

◆ Provide students with labels for each part of the kayak, along with an adhesive. Students must label the parts of the kayak. You can review the labels and describe the characteristics of each part of the kayak.

Equipment Checklist

Individual Equipment (One per Participant)

The Five Essentials

- ☐ Kayak
- ☐ Paddle

- ☐ Helmet
- ☐ PFD

- ☐ Spray skirt

Personal Clothing and Equipment

Clothing for warm weather

- ☐ Bathing suit
- ☐ Shorts

- ☐ Shirt
- ☐ Sandals or booties

Clothing for cold weather

- ☐ Spray jacket and pants
- ☐ Fleece tops and bottoms

- ☐ Wet suit or dry suit
- ☐ Hat

- ☐ Pogies or neoprene gloves
- ☐ Neoprene booties

Additional personal clothing and equipment

- ☐ Sunglasses with keeper strap
- ☐ Sunscreen

- ☐ Water bottles
- ☐ Change of clothes

Safety and Rescue Equipment

- ☐ Throw rope (one per instructor)
- ☐ Pulleys
- ☐ Slings
- ☐ Carabiners

- ☐ Whistle (attached to each PFD)
- ☐ River knife (one per instructor)
- ☐ First aid kit

FIGURE WK2.1   Checklist of whitewater kayaking equipment, separated by category. Refer to this checklist often throughout this unit.

From M. Wagstaff and A. Attarian, 2009, *Technical skills for adventure programming: A curriculum guide* (Champaign, IL: Human Kinetics).

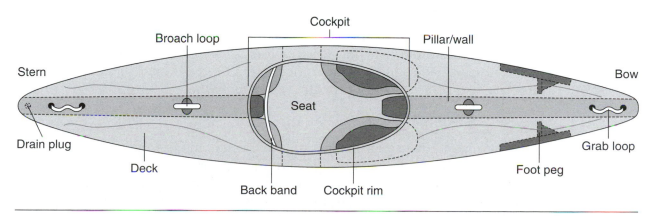

FIGURE WK2.2   Kayak anatomy.

Activity 3: Personal Clothing and Equipment (10 Minutes)

◆ Introduce personal clothing and equipment by showing your own gear to students. Pass articles around the group, allowing students to explore the features of your clothing and equipment.

◆ Discuss the concept of layering as you introduce clothing. Discuss when it is appropriate to wear cotton and when it is not. Discuss the value of alternative fabrics such as wool, fleece, neoprene, nylon, and Gore-Tex in river environments.

◆ See unit 1, lesson 6, for a general overview of clothing systems and the concept of layering.

◆ Have students refer to figure WK2.1 for a complete checklist of equipment and clothing.

Closure Activity

Whitewater Whiz, Round 1 (20 Minutes)

Quiz students on equipment and clothing needed for whitewater kayaking through a game of Whitewater Whiz. To play the game, follow these steps:

◆ Divide the class into pairs. Students remain in these pairs for subsequent rounds of the game as well as for other class activities.

◆ Lay equipment out in front of the group and point to different pieces of equipment and equipment parts.

◆ Students must raise their hands to volunteer an answer. Call on the first pair to raise a hand. If a pair gives an incorrect answer, move through the group in order of hands raised until you hear the correct answer. Students must not only give the name of the equipment or equipment part but also describe its function. You can give partial credit if the pair provides the name but not the function. In such cases, allow other groups the opportunity to gain the remainder of the credit by describing the function.

◆ Award points for correct answers. Keep a running tally of points earned so that students can add to their point totals in subsequent rounds of the game. Crown the winning students as Whitewater Whizzes at the end of the unit.

Follow-Up Activity

Equipment Stampede (15 Minutes)

Allow students to select spray skirts, PFDs, helmets, paddles, and kayaks to use during the unit. Allow them time to become adjusted to the equipment, particularly to their kayaks (adjusting bulkheads, foot pegs, hip pads, and so forth). You can circulate among the students, providing assistance where needed.

ASSESSMENT

◆ Check that students can identify the five essentials of whitewater kayaking, nomenclature of kayak and paddle parts, and general safety equipment by quizzing them using the closure activity. You could also administer a written exam to assess students' knowledge of kayaking equipment and parts. Matching labels with parts of the kayak and paddle is yet another assessment tool.

◆ Verify that students can identify safety equipment essential to whitewater kayaking by engaging them in a game of Whitewater Whiz.

◆ Assess whether students understand the importance of additional clothing and equipment that can be used in whitewater kayaking by observing what they bring when on the river.

◆ Check that students can identify the parts of a kayak and the function of those parts by engaging them in a game of Whitewater Whiz.

◆ Evaluate whether students can distinguish between various whitewater kayak designs and the style of kayaking for which each design is intended by describing a style of kayaking and asking them to identify the type of boat appropriate for that style. Students must explain why one kayak design is more appropriate than others for the style of kayaking.

◆ Check that students can adjust kayaks, personal flotation devices, and other equipment to fit during the follow-up activities.

◆ Assess whether students appreciate the role of good equipment in ensuring a safe and enjoyable kayaking experience through discussion and observation as they use different pieces of equipment on the river.

TEACHING CONSIDERATIONS

◆ This lesson provides a good opportunity to discuss weather-related hazards associated with whitewater kayaking, specifically the risk of hypothermia. An alternative introduction might involve showing the film *Cold, Wet, and Alive*, found in the resources section of this unit, to illustrate the importance of being properly dressed and equipped for a kayaking experience. The film illustrates the importance of preparing for changes in the weather.

◆ Pack additional clothing in case students arrive unprepared for the river. Include several pairs of river booties or aqua socks in a range of sizes for students who arrive in inappropriate footwear (for example, sneakers that do not fit into the kayak).

◆ This lesson contains a lot of information, especially about the parts of the kayak and kayak design. You can either limit the amount of information that you cover about the boat or limit your expectations when it comes to student retention of the information. Emphasize key information: the five essentials and safety equipment. Continually revisit the names of equipment and equipment parts throughout the unit.

◆ If you use personal clothing and equipment for demonstration purposes, make sure that it is clean and in good shape.

◆ One of the biggest challenges to beginner kayakers can be the task of attaching the spray skirt to the cockpit combing. When teaching this skill, inform students that wetting the spray skirt increases the elasticity of the spray skirt material, which makes wrapping the skirt around the cockpit combing easier.

UNIT 6, LESSON 3

▷ Stretching

OVERVIEW

Knowledge and skills related to stretching are essential to ensuring personal comfort and safety in whitewater kayaking and other water-based sports. Students learn general stretching techniques as well as stretches specific to whitewater kayaking.

JUSTIFICATION

Stretching is an essential part of overall conditioning for whitewater kayaking. It contributes to peak performance in kayaking by contributing to the kayaker's range of motion in performing kayaking techniques. More important, stretching contributes to safety by helping to minimize the risk of joint and muscle injuries during kayaking. Someone starting cold in kayaking is more prone to muscle and joint injuries than someone who has taken the time to warm up and stretch.

GOAL

To develop students' ability to prepare for paddling through proper stretching technique.

OBJECTIVES

At the end of this lesson, students will be able to

- identify specific muscle groups used in whitewater kayaking (cognitive),
- describe the physiological benefits of stretching to performance in whitewater kayaking (cognitive),
- describe the importance of stretching to the prevention of specific muscle and joint injuries (cognitive),
- demonstrate general stretching techniques as well as techniques that are specific to whitewater kayaking (psychomotor), and
- demonstrate a commitment to ensuring safety and enhancing performance through consistent stretching (affective).

EQUIPMENT AND AREAS NEEDED

Kayak paddle (one per student to assist in performing particular stretches)

RISK MANAGEMENT CONSIDERATIONS

- Improper stretching (such as bouncing or overstretching) can lead to injury, so be sure that students use proper technique during stretching exercises. They should start slow and not push the body to the point of pain. Make stretching a progressive activity and control the pace of the group.
- Stretching requirements vary depending on many factors such as age, physical condition, prior injuries, and so on. Be sure to meet the specific needs of each individual. Also, consider leading simple warm-ups before stretching.

LESSON CONTENT

Introduction

Whitewater kayaking requires full range of motion from the body for peak performance. Stretching contributes to flexibility, which helps to maximize the range of motion in whitewater kayaking. Stretching also helps to minimize risk of joint and muscle injury to the kayaker. Common injuries that kayakers work to avoid through stretching include shoulder dislocations, tendinitis (especially in the wrist and elbow), and pulled muscles.

Main Activities

Activity 1: Warm-Ups (10 to 20 Minutes)

You can incorporate warm-ups to stretching into the lesson in several ways.

◆ One approach is to have students enter their kayaks and paddle around for a while before they perform stretching exercises.

◆ Another approach is to have the students engage in a physically active sing-along such as the Hokey Pokey before stretching.

Appraise your students and choose an approach that seems best suited to them. Some students might not have the lightheartedness to enjoy something as silly as the Hokey Pokey. Alternate between on-land and on-water approaches during the course.

Activity 2: Stretching (10 to 20 Minutes)

Describe and demonstrate stretches, and have students join in. Where appropriate, describe fundamental movements in kayaking and perform stretches that simulate those movements. For example, torso rotation is a key element of almost every paddling technique and kayaking maneuver. Incorporate stretches that involve torso rotation into the stretching routine. Stretching should focus on the following areas of the body: the neck, arms, and shoulders; the torso; and the lower back and legs. Introduce stretches in a sequence from the neck to the calves. Figure WK3.1 shows various muscles referenced throughout this lesson.

The Neck (Trapezius)   Stretching the neck is important because it is used in performing a variety of maneuvers, especially bracing and rolling maneuvers.

◆ Stretch 1. Drop the head forward (figure WK3.2*a*).

◆ Stretch 2. Drop the head back (figure WK3.2*b*).

◆ Stretch 3. Turn the head from side to side (figure WK3.2*c*).

◆ Stretch 4. Tilt the head from side to side (figure WK3.2*d*).

Shoulders (Deltoids)   Shoulder injuries are one of the most common injuries in whitewater kayaking; consequently, you should emphasize the shoulders during stretching exercises to minimize the risk of shoulder injury.

◆ Stretch 5. Extend the arms and slowly rotate them in one direction for approximately 30 seconds. Change direction and slowly rotate the arms for another 30 seconds (figure WK3.3*a*).

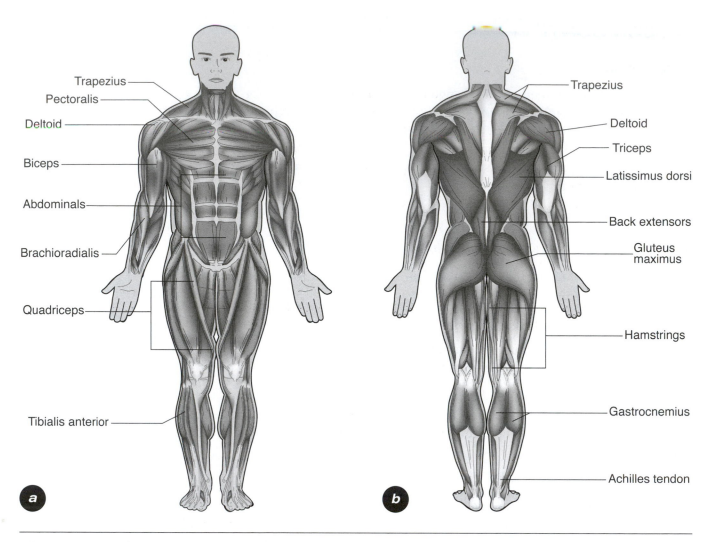

FIGURE WK3.1 Muscle groups: (a) front view; (b) rear view.

Reprinted, by permission, from C. Corbin, G. Le Masurier, and D. Lambdin, 2007, *Fitness for life: Middle school* (Champaign, IL: Human Kinetics), 90.

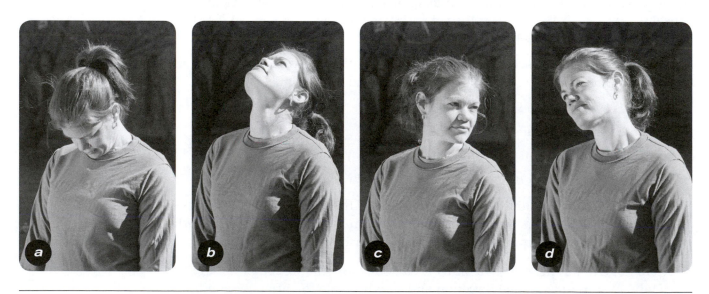

FIGURE WK3.2 Neck stretches: (a) stretch 1, (b) stretch 2, (c) stretch 3, and (d) stretch 4. See descriptions in the text.

FIGURE WK3.3   Shoulder stretches: *(a)* stretch 5, and *(b)* stretch 6. See descriptions in the text.

◆ Stretch 6. Reach the arm across the chest and hold it above the elbow with the opposite hand. Hold for approximately 15 seconds (figure WK3.3*b*). Repeat with the other arm.

Arms (Triceps, Biceps, Forearms, and Wrists)   Stretching the arms and wrists can help to minimize the risk of repetitive movement injuries such as tendinitis in the wrists and elbows as well as muscle injuries.

◆ Stretch 7. Holding the paddle, reach one hand behind the head with the elbow pointed up. Reach the other hand behind the back, grabbing the paddle shaft. Relax the upper arm and hold for 15 to 20 seconds. Repeat with the opposite arm. This particular stretch focuses on the triceps (figure WK3.4*a*).

◆ Stretch 8. Kneel with the palms flat on the ground and the fingers pointed toward the knees. Lean gently back. Hold for approximately 20 seconds. This stretch focuses on the forearms and wrists (figure WK3.4*b*).

◆ Stretch 9. Extend one arm to the side with the elbow bent at a 90-degree angle, the forearm pointed up, and the palm of the hand pointed forward. Hold for 15 seconds. Rotate the arm slowly forward until the forearm is pointed down and the palm is facing backward. Hold for 15 seconds. Repeat with the opposite arm. This stretch focuses on the biceps and the shoulders (figure WK3.4*c*).

Torso   The torso includes the following muscle groups: the chest, the abdominal muscles, the upper back, and the latissimus dorsi (lats). Stretching these various

FIGURE WK3.4   Arm stretches: (a) stretch 7, (b) stretch 8, and (c) stretch 9. See descriptions in the text.

muscles increases flexibility in the torso and helps prevent strained or pulled muscles. Torso rotation is a key element of nearly every paddling technique.

◆ Stretch 10. Rotate the torso from side to side with the feet planted. This stretch can also be performed while sitting in a kayak by gripping the sides of the kayak as a way to extend the stretch. Hold for 15 to 20 seconds. Repeat in the opposite direction. This stretch focuses primarily on the upper back (figure WK3.5a).

◆ Stretch 11. While standing with the feet apart, lean to one side. Hold the calf with one hand for support. Extend the opposite arm over the head in the direction of the lean. Hold for 15 to 20 seconds. Repeat in the opposite direction. This stretch focuses primarily on the lats. It emulates the body movement used to perform the C-to-C, an element of the kayak roll. The student can also perform this stretch while holding the kayak paddle overhead with a wide grip and leaning from side to side (figure WK3.5b).

◆ Stretch 12. Grip the paddle shaft near the throat of the paddle so that the arms are straight. Lift the arms up, over, and behind the head. Hold for 15 to 20 seconds. This stretch focuses on the chest (figure WK3.5c).

Lower Back and Legs   Paddling is often thought of as primarily an upper-body workout, but it also involves the lower back and legs. Muscle groups in this area of the body include the lower back, the gluteal muscles (buttocks), the hamstrings, the calves, the abductors (hips), the adductors, and the quadriceps. These muscle groups come into play when leaning or tilting the kayak and when performing kayak rolls. Also, the lower back is one of the muscle groups most susceptible to injury, especially when lifting boats.

FIGURE WK3.5   Torso stretches: *(a)* stretch 10, *(b)* stretch 11, and *(c)* stretch 12. See descriptions in the text.

◆ Stretch 13. Spread the legs until a gentle pull is felt along the adductors (the inner thigh). Lean forward and grab the calves or ankles. Hold for 15 to 20 seconds. This stretch focuses on the lower back, the hamstrings, the adductors, and the calves (figure WK3.6*a*).

◆ Stretch 14. Lie on the back with the legs straightened out. Grasp one knee and pull it to the chest. Hold for 20 to 30 seconds. Repeat on the opposite leg. This stretch focuses on the buttocks (figure WK3.6*b*).

◆ Stretch 15. Using the paddle for support, stand on one foot while bending the other leg behind the body and grasping the foot in the hand. Hold for 15 to 20 seconds. Repeat on the opposite leg. This stretch focuses on the quadriceps (figure WK3.6*c*).

FIGURE WK3.6   Lower back and leg stretches: *(a)* stretch 13, *(b)* stretch 14, and *(c)* stretch 15. See descriptions in the text.

Closure Activity

Whitewater Whiz, Round 2 (20 Minutes)

See lesson 2 (page 424) for a description of this activity. In this round of Whitewater Whiz, you (or an assistant) demonstrate a particular stretch.

◆ Working in previously established pairs, students must identify the muscle group or groups for which the stretch is intended. Students must raise hands to volunteer an answer.

◆ You can award additional points to students who identify paddling techniques and kayak maneuvers that rely on the muscle groups that they identify.

◆ Add points to the running tally of points.

Follow-Up Activity

Cool-Down Exercise and Stretch (Time as Needed)

Lead a cool-down exercise and stretch at the end of each day. The cool-down can involve a mild paddle through a stretch of flatwater at the end of a run. Then conduct an end-of-the-day stretch using the stretching routine described in main activity 2. This activity will help to minimize muscle soreness among students who are out of shape or who have used muscles that they are not accustomed to using. Begin this follow-up exercise by asking, "How many of you used muscles today that you never knew you had?" Several students will likely answer in the affirmative. Some students might even beat you to the punch.

On multiday courses, you will have several opportunities to engage in stretching. Help students internalize the information delivered in this lesson by giving them the opportunity to lead subsequent stretching sessions. Students can lead stretching routines individually or in pairs. Also encourage students to warm up and stretch individually after long periods of downtime between activities.

ASSESSMENT

◆ Verify that students can identify specific muscle groups used in whitewater kayaking and appropriate stretching techniques for those muscle groups by identifying and demonstrating appropriate stretches for particular muscle groups on your request.

◆ Check that students can describe the importance of stretching to the prevention of specific muscle and joint injuries through discussion or on a written exam.

◆ Ensure that students can demonstrate both general stretching techniques and techniques specific to whitewater kayaking during group stretching exercises as described in the main activities and in the closure activity.

◆ Assess whether students demonstrate a commitment to ensuring safety and enhancing performance through consistent stretching by observing them later in the course to see whether they initiate stretching activities without your incentive.

TEACHING CONSIDERATIONS

◆ Timing is a key factor. You should normally introduce stretching before students engage in physically strenuous activity. Avoid introducing stretching before a period of inactivity, especially when air temperatures are cool. Cold weather requires greater attention to keeping muscles and joints warmed up and stretched.

◆ Incorporate the paddle as a prop in the lesson. Students can hold on to the paddle during certain stretches as a way to simulate particular paddling techniques during the stretching lesson. This approach is particularly useful when introducing stretches specific to whitewater kayaking.

◆ To attain an effective group formation, gather the students in a large circle with enough space between them so that their paddles do not touch.

◆ The list of stretches in this lesson does not include all appropriate stretches. You can expand this lesson to include additional stretches.

◆ Allow students to contribute stretches as a way to engage them in the stretching exercises, but be sure that they are modeling correct stretching techniques. Do not hesitate to correct improper technique. Start each session with a precautionary note about things to avoid in stretching (see risk management considerations).

UNIT 6, LESSON 4

▷ Strokes

OVERVIEW

This lesson builds on unit 5, lesson 7, which covered the forward stroke, the reverse stroke, sweeps, the draw, and the sculling draw. This lesson introduces students to bracing strokes and bow and stern draws. Students learn the most efficient way to perform each stroke using proper body movement and paddle placement. The concept of the paddler's box is introduced as a framework for encouraging effective, efficient paddling technique and as a framework for minimizing the risk of injury caused by using improper technique.

JUSTIFICATION

The strokes introduced in this lesson are foundational to a variety of maneuvers and techniques in whitewater kayaking, including ferries, peel-outs, eddy turns, surfing, and kayak rolling, among others. Mastering these strokes is essential to progressing in the course and in the sport. In addition, the development of proper technique in each of these strokes contributes to peak performance in the kayak and minimizes the risk of injury caused by using improper paddling technique.

GOAL

To develop students' ability to use bow and stern draws as corrective and turning strokes in maneuvering the kayak and to use the bracing stroke to prevent capsize.

OBJECTIVES

At the end of this lesson, students will be able to

◆ understand and apply efficient stroke mechanics, the three phases of each stroke, and the concept of the paddler's box (cognitive);

◆ demonstrate proficiency in executing the bow draw, stern draw, high brace, and low brace (psychomotor);

◆ demonstrate an appreciation of efficient paddling technique in minimizing the risk of injury (affective); and

◆ demonstrate increased confidence as a kayaker by using bracing strokes to stay upright in the kayak (affective).

EQUIPMENT AND AREAS NEEDED

◆ The five essentials: kayak, paddle, helmet, spray skirt, PFD

◆ Appropriate clothing (see figure WK2.1 from lesson 2)

◆ Standard rescue equipment (see figure WK2.1 from lesson 2)

RISK MANAGEMENT CONSIDERATIONS

◆ Be sure that students are dressed for the weather, especially when practicing bracing strokes. Check with students after swims to make sure that they are staying warm.

◆ Establish boundaries for the practice area to ensure that the group stays together and close to you and other instructors.

◆ Use a buddy system when practicing bracing strokes. When practicing braces, each student should have a spotter to provide a rescue or to call for help in case of capsize.

◆ Emphasize the development of proper paddling technique as a means to minimize the risk of joint and muscle injuries, particularly when teaching the high brace. In particular, emphasize caution concerning shoulder injuries.

◆ Be sure that students remain well hydrated and protected from the sun (sunscreen) during these activities.

LESSON CONTENT

Introduction

There are three basic categories of strokes in whitewater kayaking: power strokes, turning or corrective strokes, and bracing strokes.

◆ Power strokes are intended to generate momentum to propel the kayak from point A to point B. There are two basic types of power strokes: forward and backward.

◆ Turning or corrective strokes are intended either to turn or to help maintain the current direction of the kayak. The two basic types of turning or corrective strokes are sweeps (forward and backward) and draws (bow and stern).

◆ Bracing strokes are intended to help keep the kayak upright. The two basic types of bracing strokes are high braces and low braces.

Variations of these strokes do not neatly fit into these three categories (for example, the a-beam draw). Nonetheless, these categories provide a good framework for the introduction of kayak strokes. Unit 5, lesson 7, covers power strokes, sweep strokes, and draw strokes (also known as a-beam draws). This lesson covers bow and stern draws and leans and braces. This lesson also introduces the concept of the paddler's box.

Main Activities

Activity 1: The Paddler's Box (10 Minutes)

The **paddler's box** is an imaginary box within which the paddler should keep the hands and arms when performing nearly all kayak strokes (figure WK4.1). Outline the parameters of the paddler's box by using your paddle to trace the sides of the box. Extend the paddle shaft away from the waist on an even plane, raise the paddle shaft to shoulder height, bring the paddle to the chest parallel to the collarbones, and drop the paddle shaft to the waist. Note that the paddler's box rotates as the torso rotates. Rotating the torso from side to side will help to illustrate the movement of the box as the torso moves.

Keeping the hands and arms inside the paddler's box when performing strokes minimizes the risk of injury caused by hyperextension of the shoulders. Keeping the hands and arms inside the paddler's box also typically helps to maximize the mechanical efficiency of strokes.

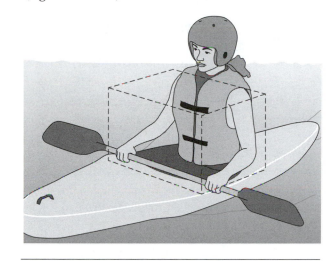

FIGURE WK4.1 The paddler's box.

Activity 2: Bow Draw (30 to 45 Minutes)

The bow draw is a turning stroke. On flatwater, the paddler uses it to spin the kayak. On whitewater, the paddler uses it to perform eddy turns and peel-outs.

Catch Phase When demonstrating the catch phase of the stroke, emphasize paddle shaft angle, blade orientation, and staying within the paddler's box.

◆ Enter the blade of the paddle 45 degrees away from the bow of the kayak.

◆ The wrists should be cocked back, and the power face of the paddle should be pointed forward toward the bow of the kayak.

◆ The forward arm should be bent at the elbow.

◆ The backward arm should be bent with the elbow pointed forward and the hand next to the shoulder.

◆ The paddle shaft angle relative to the surface of the water should be approximately 45 degrees (a moderate paddle shaft angle).

Propulsion Phase When demonstrating the propulsion phase of the stroke, emphasize torso rotation and keeping the forward arm in a static position. Note that in unit 5, the propulsion phase is referred to as the *power phase*. Both terms mean the same thing and are acceptable.

◆ The paddler should use torso rotation to execute the propulsion phase of the bow draw.

◆ A common mistake in executing the bow draw is to use the forward arm to push the blade of the paddle toward the bow. Instead, the forward arm should remain in a static position while torso rotation is used to execute the stroke.

Recovery Phase Exit the paddle blade from the water before it hits the bow of the boat and repeat the stroke. Figure WK4.2 shows an example of a bow draw.

FIGURE WK4.2   Bow draw.

FIGURE WK4.3   Stern draw.

Activity 3: Stern Draw (20 to 30 Minutes)

The stern draw is used both as a turning stroke and as a corrective stroke. On flatwater, the paddler uses it to spin the kayak. On whitewater, the paddler normally uses it to maintain or correct the angle of the kayak when surfing or performing ferries.

Catch Phase   When demonstrating the catch phase of the stroke, emphasize paddle shaft angle and staying within the paddler's box.

- Enter the blade of the paddle 45 degrees away from the stern of the kayak.
- At the start of the stroke, the back arm should be straight and the forward arm should be bent at the elbow with the hand just in front of the opposite shoulder.
- The paddle shaft angle should be approximately 45 degrees relative to the surface of the water (a moderate paddle shaft angle).

Propulsion Phase   The stern draw is essentially the tail end of a forward sweep. The propulsion phase of the stern draw involves the following steps:

- Rotate the torso in the direction of the draw.
- Bend and pull the back elbow across the back deck of the boat.
- Straighten the front arm while keeping the front hand at shoulder height.

Recovery Phase   Exit the paddle blade from the water before it hits the stern of the boat and repeat the stroke. Figure WK4.3 shows an example of a stern draw.

Activity 4: Leans and Braces (60 to 90 Minutes)

The brace is used to prevent capsize should the kayaker lose his or her balance while on the water. Paddlers use the brace spontaneously when they unexpectedly lose their balance in the kayak. They also often anticipate the need for the high brace when performing kayak maneuvers that require leaning the kayak on its edge and are prepared to use the brace to prevent capsize should the kayak lean too far. Examples of such maneuvers include side surfing, peel-outs, and eddy turns.

Boat Leans The best way to explain the mechanics of the brace is to describe boat lean at the same time. There are three levels of boat lean. The mechanics of boat lean are the same in whitewater kayaking and sea kayaking (see unit 5, lesson 7). The explanation of boat leaning that follows provides you with an additional way to explain this important skill. Students learn in different ways. By having alternative ways to teach boat lean, you will be more effective when a different approach is needed for a particular student.

◆ A level-1 lean is a mild lean that entails shifting body weight to one butt cheek to rotate the kayak slightly onto its edge.

◆ A level-2 lean is a moderate boat lean that entails shifting body weight to one butt cheek while lifting the opposite knee to rotate the kayak farther onto its edge.

◆ A level-3 lean is an extreme boat lean that incorporates the entire body (feet, legs, hips, torso, and head) into rotating the kayak onto its edge. The idea in a level-3 lean is to find the tipping point of the kayak and remain balanced on that point.

When teaching boat leans, emphasize the need to keep the torso perpendicular to the water when leaning the boat. Beginner kayakers often try to lean the boat by moving their bodies out over the edge of the boat rather than rotating the boat up onto its edge. Boat leans, whether in a sea kayak or a whitewater kayak, are commonly called J-leans (see figure WK4.4), because the configuration that the body and boat create when performing the technique resembles a J.

Other expressions commonly used to describe boat leans include edging the kayak and tilting the kayak. This unit uses leaning, edging, and tilting interchangeably to describe boat leans.

To bring the boat down off its edge, execute a **hip snap** (see unit 5, lesson 5, for a description of the hip snap.)

FIGURE WK4.4   The J-lean technique is used in both whitewater and sea kayaks.

High Brace   To perform the high brace, move the paddle into the high-brace ready position.

◆ The paddle shaft should be close to the chest and parallel to the collarbones.

◆ The power face of the paddle blade should be pointed toward the water, and the knuckles should be pointed toward the sky in the ready position.

The catch, propulsion, and recovery phases of the high brace occur almost simultaneously.

◆ To initiate catch and propulsion phases of the stroke, simply smack the blade of the paddle against the surface of the water.

◆ To initiate the recovery phase of the stroke, feather the blade of the paddle toward the surface and quickly slice it from the water to prepare for a second brace if needed.

Emphasize keeping hands and arms inside the paddler's box when performing the high brace to minimize the risk of shoulder dislocation or hyperextension. Figure WK4.5 shows an example of a high brace.

FIGURE WK4.5   High brace ready position. Note the power face on the paddler's right facing the water.

Low Brace   To perform the low brace, move the paddle into the low-brace ready position.

◆ The paddle shaft should be close to the waist and horizontal to the surface of the water. The back face of the paddle blade should be pointed toward the water.

◆ Knuckles should be pointed toward the surface of the water as well.

The catch, propulsion, and recovery phases of the low brace occur almost simultaneously.

◆ To initiate catch and propulsion phases of the stroke, smack the blade of the paddle against the surface of the water.

◆ To initiate the recovery phase of the stroke, feather the blade of the paddle toward the surface and quickly slice it from the water to prepare for a second brace if needed. Figure WK4.6 shows an example of a low brace.

FIGURE WK4.6   Low brace ready position. Note the back face on the paddler's left facing the water.

Alternating Between Low and High Braces   Kayakers often alternate between low and high braces when side surfing a kayak. This method helps to minimize fatigue. One type of brace can also often serve as a backup to the other.

Sculling Braces   A sculling brace can be used with both high and low braces to remain continually on edge in the kayak.

To perform a sculling brace, scull the blade of the paddle backward and forward across the surface of the water, lifting the leading edge of the blade to keep the blade from sinking. This technique is especially useful when side surfing.

Tips for Teaching Leans and Braces

- Encourage students to rock their kayaks from side to side, shifting their hips as though grooving on a dance floor, to get comfortable with the idea of edging their kayaks.
- Encourage students to start slowly. They should start with level-1 leans and gradually progress to level-3 leans.
- Stress the importance of having the paddle in the high- or low-brace ready position before initiating the lean.
- Stress the simultaneity of the hip snap and brace in executing a successful brace by saying, "Hip snap, paddle smack!"

Closure Activity

Human Slalom (20 Minutes)

Playing a game of Human Slalom can help students develop greater boat control by practicing the various strokes that they have learned during a flatwater program.

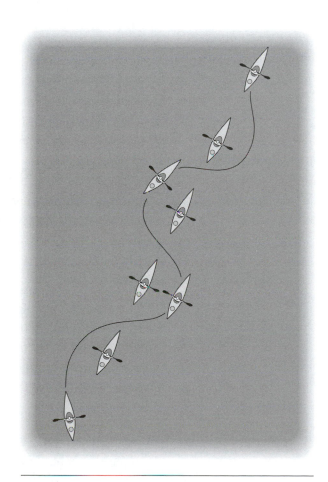

- Pick a destination in the distance.
- Assign each group member a number, starting with 1.
- Student 1 paddles a few kayak lengths toward the destination and stops to become a slalom gate.
- Student 2 paddles one or two kayak lengths past student 1 and stops to become a slalom gate.
- Student 3 paddles between students 1 and 2, stopping one or two kayak lengths ahead of student 2 to become the third gate in the line to form a human slalom course (figure WK4.7).
- Each subsequent kayaker must weave his or her way through the gates to reach the front of the line, at which point he or she becomes a slalom gate in the course.
- After everyone passes by student 1, he or she again becomes a racer and must weave through each of the gates to reach the front of the line.

FIGURE WK4.7   Human slalom course.

◆ The activity ends when the group reaches the destination. This activity provides an opportunity to practice various power and turning strokes to develop greater boat control skills.

Follow-Up Activity

Video Analysis (45 Minutes)

Make a video recording of students performing each of the strokes taught during the lesson. Students can use the critique as a basis for refining their technique as the course progresses. As students begin to appreciate the value of video critique for analyzing their technique, you can include them in the process by allowing opportunities for self and peer critiques. Attempting to diagnose problems in one's own technique and the technique of others can help develop greater understanding of the mechanics and performance of each stroke.

ASSESSMENT

◆ Confirm that students can perform efficient stroke mechanics, know the three phases of the stroke, and understand the concept of the paddler's box by observing their performance of each stroke. Students' performance of each stroke will be documented by video recording in the follow-up activity.

◆ Confirm that students can demonstrate proficiency in executing the bow draw, stern draw, and high and low braces by observing them practice the techniques as a part of each lesson activity. Students' performance of each stroke will be documented by video recording in the follow-up activity.

◆ Check that students appreciate the role of efficient paddling technique in minimizing the risk of injury through persistence in mastering technique and by describing potential consequences of poor technique.

◆ Assess whether students demonstrate increased confidence as kayakers through making a commitment to achieving proficient level-2 and level-3 leans.

TEACHING CONSIDERATIONS

◆ The ideal site for teaching strokes is a pond or small lake that has good water quality. A site with a staging area that has a relatively durable surface (sandy, grassy, or rocky beaches or banks rather than muddy, slippery ones) is desirable. A good staging area reduces the amount of mud and grime that ends up in kayaks throughout the day, reduces soil erosion and consequent water turbidity, aids in group management throughout the day, and makes for a more pleasant instructional experience in general. The lake or pond should be fairly protected from wind. High wind can wreak havoc on open water when it comes to group management during practice sessions.

◆ Review the elements of each stroke after the learning activity. Explain that each stroke is foundational to techniques and maneuvers that will be taught in subsequent lessons in the course. This discussion will help students see the relevance of what might otherwise seem a boring flatwater program.

◆ You can teach the concept of the paddler's box on land as well as on water. Teaching the paddler's box on land can be a good follow-up activity to stretching because the group is already gathered in a large circle with paddles in hand.

- Unit 5, lesson 7, on basic strokes introduced the draw, also known as the a-beam draw. The a-beam draw serves as a starting point in teaching draws, so include a lesson on a-beam draws before teaching the bow and stern draws.

- You may want to give students the opportunity to practice the Eskimo bow rescue (see unit 5, lesson 5) immediately before you teach leans and braces. This activity will give students the confidence to remain in their kayaks and await rescue rather than immediately perform a wet exit should they capsize during practice exercises. If students are proficient with the Eskimo bow rescue, you can teach the lesson more efficiently because you will not have to spend as much time recovering swimmers.

- Despite practicing the Eskimo bow rescue before teaching braces, some students will inevitably capsize and swim while practicing the brace. To lessen the stigma of swimming, form a swim team. The first student to swim becomes the captain of the swim team. Each subsequent swimmer becomes a member of the swim team. The initial captain of the swim team is displaced by whoever has the most swims at the end of the day. This approach is a fun way to develop camaraderie among members of the group. The swim team can continue to grow as swims occur later in the course (for example, while practicing eddy turns and peel-outs).

UNIT 6, LESSON 5

▷ River Reading

OVERVIEW

"All drains lead to the sea. . . ."

From *Finding Nemo*

"When in doubt, let your friends try it out."

Source unknown

In this lesson, students learn to read the river. River reading involves the ability to identify river features and the physical dynamics that create these features. Students develop the ability to choose navigable routes down the river, especially through whitewater rapids, based on their knowledge of river features and river dynamics. Most important, students learn to distinguish between friendly and unfriendly features on the river so that they can avoid river hazards. In addition, students learn to categorize rapids according to their level of difficulty using the International Scale of River Difficulty.

JUSTIFICATION

Recognizing river features, selecting navigable routes through rapids, and matching one's ability to the difficulty of the whitewater are essential to successful, enjoyable whitewater kayaking and, more important, to ensuring one's safety on the river.

GOAL

To develop students' knowledge of river features, river dynamics, and the river classification system and to develop their ability to select navigable routes through whitewater rapids.

OBJECTIVES

At the end of this lesson, students will be able to

◆ understand and identify river features and river dynamics (cognitive),

◆ read and interpret a whitewater rapid (psychomotor), and

◆ appreciate the role of river reading in safe and successful navigation through whitewater (affective).

EQUIPMENT AND AREAS NEEDED

◆ Dry erase board to diagram river features

◆ Markers

◆ Physical examples or illustrations of river features and dynamics described in the terminology list (pages 446 to 448)

◆ Whitewater kayaking equipment checklist (figure WK2.1 in lesson 2)

RISK MANAGEMENT CONSIDERATIONS

◆ Require students to wear helmets and PFDs as they engage in the scouting exercise. These items provide added protection in case of slips and falls when moving along the shoreline.

◆ Caution students about hazardous flora and fauna (poison ivy, snakes, bees, and so forth) before the scouting exercise.

◆ Students should always wear proper footgear, even when in the kayak. Double-check students before the scouting exercise to be sure that they are wearing proper footgear as they walk along the shoreline.

◆ Carry a throw rope and a paddle to use as reaching devices in case someone falls into the river.

LESSON CONTENT

Introduction

One of the most exciting aspects of kayaking is exploring new terrain. To explore new terrain, paddlers must be able to read the river. Paddlers should always be sure of their route before attempting to navigate their boats down a river, especially on unfamiliar rivers. Sometimes routes are simple and require little interpretation in choosing them. Other routes are complex and require a good bit of interpretation to choose them successfully.

In this latter instance, kayakers should scout the river ahead and be sure of the route before paddling downstream. In many instances, this can be done from the kayak while paddling. This method is called reading and running, or boat scouting the river. In some instances, the kayaker can do this by remaining stationary in the kayak above a rapid while interpreting what she or he sees ahead. In other instances, the kayaker may have to pull ashore to scout a rapid. To read or scout a river accurately, paddlers need a thorough understanding of river features and river dynamics.

Main Activities

Activity 1: Basic Concepts (5 to 10 Minutes)

Deliver a brief lecture on the water cycle, watersheds, topography, river gradient, drop pool versus continuous flow, cubic feet per second (CFS), and so on. The U.S Geological Survey Web site and the U.S. Environmental Protection Agency Web site provide a wealth of information on this topic. See the terminology list on pages 446 to 448 for explanation of concepts.

Activity 2: River Features (20 to 30 Minutes)

At the approach of a class II rapid, divide the class into small groups and ask each group to identify a river feature. Give the students a few minutes to explore the river to identify a river feature, give a name to the feature, and identify the nature of the feature. Gather the group for a review of features. Use figure WK5.1 as a visual reference for the various river features. Figure WK5.2 shows the same river, but without labels on the features. Photocopy or print the blank template and challenge the students to fill in the blanks by identifying river features as you discuss them.

Activity 3: Scouting (20 to 30 Minutes)

Assign the same small groups the task of choosing a navigable route through the rapid. Give the students 5 to 10 minutes to choose a route and have them report to the larger group. Look for similarities and variations in each of the plans. Challenge the large group to come up with a unified plan. Critique the plan, using the critique as an opportunity to discuss proper scouting technique.

Activity 4: River Classification (10 to 15 Minutes)

Using a lecture format, present the **river classification** system. Emphasize matching level of challenge with level of ability. Encourage students to make a slow progression so that they can develop and refine their kayaking skills as they move from one level of difficulty to the next. River difficulty is rated on a scale from class I to class VI, with I being the easiest and VI being the most extreme. See figure WK5.6 on page 449, American Whitewater's International Scale of River Difficulty, for a description of the characteristics of each classification.

River classification is not exact. Factors that can influence classification include river volume and cold weather. High water typically increases the power of the river and consequently the level of difficulty; cold air and water temperatures increase the risk of hypothermia and consequently the rating of the river. In other words, the classification of a particular rapid can vary based on conditions that influence the character of the rapid and the level of risk involved in running the rapid. Also, a certain degree of subjectivity is present in the rating of rapids.

Closure Activity

Route Selection Test (20 to 30 Minutes)

Allow students to run the class II rapid by following the route that they selected during the scouting exercise. Set safety points along the rapid. Have the students paddle through the rapid one at a time. Critique the first few kayakers who run the rapid to refine the route.

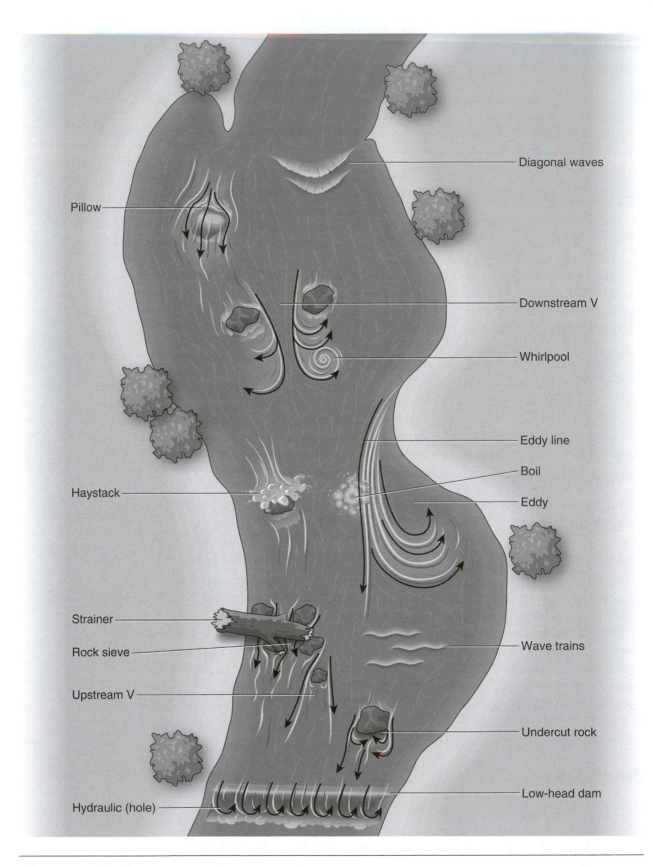

Pillow

Haystack

Strainer

Rock sieve

Upstream V

Hydraulic (hole)

Diagonal waves

Downstream V

Whirlpool

Eddy line

Boil

Eddy

Wave trains

Undercut rock

Low-head dam

FIGURE WK5.1   River features.

FIGURE WK5.2   River features template.

From M. Wagstaff and A. Attarian, 2009, *Technical skills for adventure programming: A curriculum guide* (Champaign, IL: Human Kinetics).

Important Terms

The terms and explanations that follow are provided initially as a quick reference to critical terms that instructors might need when teaching a river-reading lesson for any whitewater sport. Review the following terms to enhance your ability to teach this lesson.

boils—Caused by water welling up to the surface, creating what appears to be a boiling effect in the river. They are often found along eddy lines in high-volume rivers, such as the Colorado River. They are also a feature of hydraulics.

bridge abutments—Another common obstacle on rivers. They should be treated like any other rock or obstruction that you encounter on the river, something to go around.

continuous flow—Characterizes a river whose rapids flow continuously from one into the next with little or no break between them. Continuous flow rapids are typically found on rivers with steeper gradients (more than 100 feet per mile, or 20 meters per kilometer).

cubic feet per second (CFS)—Refers to the volume and the rate of flow of water in the river. (The measure used in most countries is cubic meters per second.) One cubic foot of water is approximately 7.5 gallons of water (1 cubic meter of water is exactly 1,000 liters). To say that a river is flowing at 2,200 CFS (62 cubic meters per second) is to say that 2,200 cubic feet (62 cubic meters) of water is flowing past a particular point in the river each second. CFS is sometimes referred to in terms of river level. River level is often measured in terms of feet or meters on a river gauge. The advantage of measuring river levels by CFS is that CFS provides a true measure of the volume and rate of flow of water in a river. Traditional river gauges measure river level with arbitrary measuring sticks that are not universal to all points along a river. A gauge at one point along a river might read 3 feet (.9 meters), whereas a gauge at another point on the same river might read 15 feet (4.5 meters). Also, zero is an arbitrary point that does not mean that the river contains no water. Indeed, some gauges measure river level in negative terms. The CFS system is a more efficient model for measuring river volume and flow.

downstream V, or tongue—Created by water being diverted into a channel by obstructions (rocks, canyon walls) on either side of the V. A downstream V has the appearance of a ramp or tongue of water with the vertex, or tip, of the V pointed downstream. Tongues represent the deepest and typically the safest route through a rapid. See figure WK5.3a.

drop pool—Characterizes a river whose rapids are separated by pools of water. Drop pool rapids are typically found on rivers with minor to moderate river gradients (a gradient of 5 to 50 feet per mile, or 1 to 10 meters per kilometer).

eddy—A calm spot on the river created when an obstruction (rocks, shorelines, logs, or other obstacles) diverts the flow of the river around it. As the current flows around the obstruction, it accelerates downstream, leaving a depression behind the obstruction. To fill in this depression, current begins to flow upstream toward the obstruction, creating a safe zone in the river. Eddies are a good place to stop, recoup, and scout what lies ahead.

eddy line—The divide between current that is flowing upstream in an eddy and current that is moving downstream around the obstruction that is creating the eddy.

horizon line—On a river, the line where the surface of the water meets the sky from the perspective of the paddler. Horizon lines are created when the river suddenly drops over ledges or falls or disappears around bends. Sometimes horizon lines are difficult to see. Indications of a horizon line include seeing the tops of trees and bushes but not the bottoms, splashes of water on what appears to be a calm surface, and so on.

hydraulics, or holes—A horizontal whirlpool created by water dropping over a ledge and being recirculated at the base of the ledge (figure WK5.4). After dropping over the ledge, the current dives toward the river bottom to continue its downstream flow. Just downstream of the ledge, or falls, a hole, or depression, appears between where the current is and where the water level should be. As current begins to boil or well up to the surface just downstream of the falls, some of it begins to flow downstream and some of it begins to flow upstream to fill in the hole. This upstream flow creates a backwash, or circular flow of water, that gives this river feature the appearance of a horizontal whirlpool. The point at which water boils to the surface in the hydraulic is referred to as the boil line.

Some hydraulics are considered to be user friendly, and some are not. Hydraulics can hold debris, boats, and people, recirculating them in their whirlpool motion. Keeper hydraulics, sometimes called terminal hydraulics, can be difficult and sometimes impossible to escape. Being able to distinguish between friendly and unfriendly hydraulics is essential in whitewater kayaking.

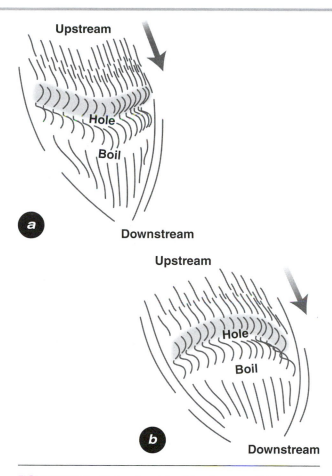

FIGURE WK5.3 Hydraulics: (a) unfriendly versus (b) friendly.

Reprinted, by permission, from American Canoe Association, 2008, *Canoeing: Outdoor adventures* (Champaign, IL: Human Kinetics), 103.

– Two key factors that help to distinguish between the two are (1) the shape of the hydraulic relative to the direction that the current is flowing and (2) the strength of the hydraulic.

– Pay attention to whether the hydraulic is smiling or frowning when looking up at it from downstream. Frowns are expressions of disap-

pointment, because the hydraulic knows that it cannot keep you. Smiles are deviant grins, because the hydraulic knows that it will keep you. To determine the general strength of the hydraulic, gauge the distance of the boil line from the ledge creating the hydraulic. The farther away the boil line is from the ledge, the stronger the hydraulic is. Lesson 8 will further address the distinction between friendly and unfriendly hydraulics. Figure WK5.3 shows the two types of hydraulics.

– Should you find yourself in a hydraulic, the best way to exit is to paddle or swim to one of the corners of the hydraulic and use the downstream current to extricate yourself from it. This method is easier when the corners of the hydraulic point downstream. When the corners point upstream, paddling or swimming against the flow of the current to reach them becomes nearly impossible. If you are caught surfing in a hydraulic and cannot reach its corners, attempt to turn the bow of your kayak upstream and perform an ender to use the force of the current to thrust your kayak out of the hydraulic and beyond the boil line. If you are caught swimming in a hydraulic and cannot reach its corners, attempt to go deep in the hydraulic and swim with the downstream current beneath the froth to get beyond the boil line and the grasp of the hydraulic. The rafting unit provides specific rescue information for a swimmer caught in a hydraulic (unit 8, lesson 9).

log jams—Obstacles to be avoided on the river. Log jams are created when trees fall into the river and collect all sorts of debris and flotsam on their upstream sides. These features pose the same risk as undercut rocks and strainers. If you find yourself underneath one, rescue is extremely difficult if not impossible.

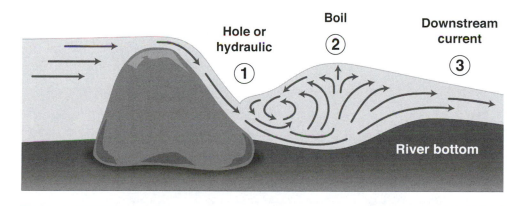

FIGURE WK5.4 Anatomy of a hydraulic.

Reprinted, by permission, from American Canoe Association, 2008, *Canoeing: Outdoor adventures* (Champaign, IL: Human Kinetics), 102.

continued ▶

low-head dams—Human-made contraptions found on most rivers in the United States. Many of these dams were created to divert water into canals, irrigation ditches, and hydropower plants. Water flows over the tops of these dams, typically creating keeper hydraulics at the base of the dams. These dangerous river features must always be avoided by conducting a portage.

pillows—Formed by the current being forced over the top of a stationary obstacle such as a rock. From upstream they look like glassy mounds of water that have a small horizon line on the downstream side of the obstacle. They should be scouted before traveling over them, or they should be avoided.

river gradient—Refers to the average rate of descent of a river over a particular distance. For instance, the New River in West Virginia descends 750 feet (230 meters) over 50 miles (80 kilometers) from Bluestone Dam to Gauley Bridge. The average gradient of the river between these two points is 15 feet per mile (2.9 meters per kilometer) (U.S. National Park Service [NPS], n.d., "Geology Fieldnotes").

rock sieves and strainers—Jumbled piles of rocks or downed trees that act like strainers when debris, boats, and people become caught in them. They are considered as dangerous as undercut rocks.

undercut rocks—A rock that is settled on an uneven kilter in the river. The upstream side is hollow underneath and can trap debris, boats, and people that are washed beneath them. Undercut rocks are one of the most dangerous features that you will encounter on a river. You should always avoid them. Never allow yourself to be caught on the upstream side of an undercut rock. If you do, your boat will likely be pushed beneath the rock. Often, undercut rocks have only a mild slope. Even so, they can be veritable caverns in which both boat and body can be lost.

upstream V—Unlike a downstream V, signifies that an obstruction is just beneath the surface of the water. The current is being diverted to either side of the obstruction, creating the V shape. The paddler should avoid these points in the river. See figure WK5.3*b*.

waterfall—A point in the river where water drops or falls over a ledge. Waterfalls can range from only a few feet (a meter) in height to showering cascades that drop from hundreds of feet (meters) above.

watershed—Sometimes referred to as a drainage basin, a region in which all precipitation and groundwater drains into one river course as it progresses toward sea level. Watersheds are separated by geographical divides, such as continental divides. John Wesley Powell referred to watersheds as "bounded hydrologic systems, within which all living things are inextricably linked by their common watercourse . . ." (as cited in U.S. Environmental Protection Agency [EPA], n.d., "What Is a Watershed?").

waves—Created in rivers where a change occurs in the velocity or speed of the current. These changes result from a number of factors: water being constricted within a narrow channel in the river; changes in river gradient that cause the current to flow more rapidly downstream; and irregularities created by rocks, ledges, and other obstructions along the river bottom. Unlike ocean waves, which are typically generated by wind and represent the transfer of energy through the water, waves in a river stand relatively still, and the energy is contained in the flow of water. A wave consists of a peak (or crest), a trough, a face, and shoulders on either side. Figure WK5.5 shows the anatomy of a wave.

– **diagonal waves**—Waves that are diagonal to the flow of the current.

– **haystacks**—Waves that surge upward into an unstable mass of whitewater.

– **wave trains**—A series of standing waves with short intervals between them. Waves are separated by troughs.

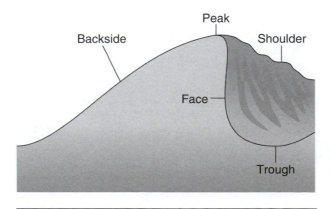

FIGURE WK5.5   Anatomy of a wave.

American Whitewater's
International Scale of River Difficulty

Class I Rapids

Fast-moving water with riffles and small waves. Few obstructions, all obvious and easily missed with little training. Risk to swimmers is slight; self-rescue is easy.

Class II Rapids: Novice

Straightforward rapids with wide, clear channels that are evident without scouting. Occasional maneuvering may be required, but rocks and medium-sized waves are easily missed by trained paddlers. Swimmers are seldom injured and group assistance, while helpful, is seldom needed. Rapids that are at the upper end of this difficulty range are designated class II+.

Class III: Intermediate

Rapids with moderate, irregular waves that may be difficult to avoid and that can swamp an open canoe. Complex maneuvers in fast current and good boat control in tight passages or around ledges are often required; large waves or strainers may be present but are easily avoided. Strong eddies and powerful current effects can be found, particularly on large-volume rivers. Scouting is advisable for inexperienced parties. Injuries while swimming are rare; self-rescue is usually easy but group assistance may be required to avoid long swims. Rapids that are at the lower or upper end of this difficulty range are designated class III– or class III+, respectively.

Class IV: Advanced

Intense, powerful, but predictable rapids requiring precise boat handling in turbulent water. Depending on the character of the river, it may feature large, unavoidable waves and holes or constricted passages demanding fast maneuvers under pressure. A fast, reliable eddy turn may be needed to initiate maneuvers, scout rapids, or rest. Rapids may require "must" moves above dangerous hazards. Scouting may be necessary the first time down. Risk of injury to swimmers is moderate to high, and water conditions may make self-rescue difficult. Group assistance for rescue is often essential but requires practiced skills. A strong Eskimo roll is highly recommended. Rapids that are at the lower or upper end of this difficulty range are designated class IV– or class IV+, respectively.

Class V: Expert

Extremely long, obstructed, or very violent rapids that expose a paddler to added risk. Drops may contain large, unavoidable waves and holes or steep, congested chutes with complex, demanding routes. Rapids may continue for long distances between pools, demanding a high level of fitness. What eddies exist may be small, turbulent, or difficult to reach. At the high end of the scale, several of these factors may be combined. Scouting is recommended but may be difficult. Swims are dangerous, and rescue is often difficult even for experts. A very reliable Eskimo roll, proper equipment, extensive experience, and practiced rescue skills are essential. Because of the large range of difficulty that exists beyond class IV, class V is an open-ended, multiple-level scale designated by class 5.0, 5.1, 5.2, and so on. Each of these levels is an order of magnitude more difficult than the last. For example, increasing difficulty from class 5.0 to class 5.1 is a similar order of magnitude as increasing from class IV to class 5.0.

Class VI: Extreme and Exploratory Rapids

These runs have almost never been attempted and often exemplify the extremes of difficulty, unpredictability, and danger. The consequences of errors are very severe and rescue may be impossible. For teams of experts only, at favorable water levels, after close personal inspection and taking all precautions. After a class VI rapids has been run many times, its rating may be changed to an appropriate class 5.x rating.

FIGURE WK5.6   American Whitewater's International Scale of River Difficulty describes the characteristics of each classification of rapid.

After everyone has run the rapid, debrief the activity. Ask questions such as the following: Was the original plan a good one? What did you decide to do differently after seeing the first few kayakers run the rapid? What surprised you about the rapid? What did you learn that you can apply to the next rapid?

Follow-Up Activity

Whitewater Whiz, Round 3 (20 Minutes)

Quiz the students on the names of river features and the nature of river dynamics through another round of Whitewater Whiz. See lesson 2 for the activity description. You can point either to actual river features or to illustrations of river features. Students must not only be able to identify the feature but also be able to describe the dynamics of the feature and the significance of the feature to kayaking.

Note: Information on hazardous river features will be revisited in lesson 9 on kayak safety considerations.

ASSESSMENT

◆ Verify that students can understand and identify river features and river dynamics through an oral quiz in the follow-up activity at the end of the lesson and through a written quiz at the end of the unit.

◆ Confirm that students can read and interpret a whitewater rapid through the scouting exercise and through a written quiz at the end of the unit.

◆ Assess whether students appreciate the role of river reading in safe and successful navigation through whitewater based on their engagement in the scouting exercise and their interest in refining route selection during the closure activity.

TEACHING CONSIDERATIONS

◆ This lesson could be taught in conjunction with lesson 9 on kayak safety. Although this lesson focuses on identifying various river features and understanding river dynamics to improve route selection and navigation, being able to identify hazardous features is important in knowing where not to go.

◆ You must find an appropriate site for this lesson. The site should include a class II rapid that contains a variety of different river features. The rapid should have some complexity to add challenge in choosing a route. The site should also include a good staging area, such as a large rock at the top of the rapid. Trail access along the riverbank is also helpful in allowing students to explore the rapid from top to bottom.

UNIT 6, LESSON 6

▷ Basic River Maneuvers

OVERVIEW

Being able to maneuver kayaks in whitewater is an essential skill. This lesson discusses basic maneuvers such as eddy turns, peel-outs, and ferries. Information such as proper strokes to execute maneuvers, boat angles, and boat lean will be covered.

JUSTIFICATION

Learning basic whitewater maneuvers is essential to maintaining control of any craft on the river, to navigating successfully down the river, and to remaining safe on the river. In addition, executing appropriate maneuvers increases the overall fun and enjoyment of the paddling experience.

GOAL

To develop students' ability to perform basic starting, stopping, traversing, and side-slipping maneuvers on the river.

OBJECTIVES

At the end of this lesson, students will be able to

* demonstrate an understanding of how to perform ferries, peel-outs, and eddy turns (cognitive);
* execute basic maneuvers as well as proper paddling technique (psychomotor);
* determine when different maneuvers are required at different points along the river (psychomotor); and
* appreciate the precision required to perform basic kayak maneuvers successfully (affective).

EQUIPMENT AND AREAS NEEDED

* The five essentials: kayak, paddle, helmet, spray skirt, PFD
* Appropriate clothing (see figure WK2.1 from lesson 2)
* Standard rescue equipment carried on a river trip (see figure WK2.1 from lesson 2)

RISK MANAGEMENT CONSIDERATIONS

* The site should be conducive to teaching basic maneuvers to first-time kayakers. Start in a moving-water context that includes well-defined eddies and gentle current.
* Be prepared for capsizes. An instructor should be in a kayak just downstream of the site in case Eskimo bow rescues are needed. Be sure that the channel is deep enough that kayakers do not hit rocks or other obstructions in case of capsize. Students can operate in pairs to provide immediate assistance to one another. Plenty of recovery time should be available below the rapid.
* Be sure that students remain well hydrated during activities.

LESSON CONTENT

Introduction

This lesson focuses on basic maneuvers needed to navigate a kayak successfully down a river. These maneuvers are based on all the paddling skills and knowledge of the river that students have developed to this point.

* Students will use many of the strokes, leans, and other elements of kayaking that they have learned thus far to maneuver the kayak successfully on the river.
* Knowledge of river features and the ability to read the river are also related to maneuvering the kayak successfully downriver. Knowing how to read the river is essential to making good decisions about which maneuvers to use at different points in the journey downstream.

Main Activities

Activity 1: Ferries (45 Minutes)

Ferries are used to maneuver the boat laterally across the current, usually from eddy to eddy or onto a wave to surf. The two types of ferries are upstream ferries and downstream ferries.

- To perform an upstream ferry, the paddler points the bow of the boat upstream and toward the direction of travel, using forward strokes to generate momentum.

- To perform a downstream ferry, the paddler points the stern of the boat upstream and toward the direction of travel, using reverse strokes to generate momentum. Current helps to push the kayak laterally across the current by applying pressure against the upstream side of the boat and creating a vacuum on the downstream side of the boat. This vacuum pulls the kayak across the current in much the same way that the vacuum created on the leeward side of a sail pulls a sailboat across the water.

Describe and demonstrate the mechanics of the ferry using the acronym PAST.

- P is for the position of the boat in the eddy relative to the eddy line and the top of the eddy. The boat should be positioned several feet (meters) downstream from the top of the eddy and several feet (meters) away from the eddy line.

- A is for the angle of the boat relative to the eddy line. In an upstream ferry the bow of the boat should be pointed upstream at an angle of approximately 45 degrees to the eddy line. In a downstream ferry the stern of the boat should be pointed upstream at an angle of approximately 45 degrees to the eddy line. The angle of the boat depends on the strength of the current. The stronger the current is, the sharper the angle should be; the weaker the current is, the wider the angle should be.

- S is for the speed needed to cross the eddy line. Paddle strokes create speed. Forward strokes are used for upstream ferries; reverse strokes are used for downstream ferries.

- T is for tilt. A level-2 lean (or J-lean) away from the oncoming current is needed to avoid capsizing the boat. See lesson 4 for a description of boat leaning. Tilting the upstream edge of the boat away from the oncoming current allows current to slip beneath the boat rather than grab and submerge the upstream edge of the boat.

Describe and demonstrate the strokes used during each phase of the upstream ferry: forward power strokes to gain speed; stationary stern draw to maintain angle while traversing the current, with a mix of corrector strokes if needed; and forward power stroke to stay in the new eddy.

Have students practice the ferry maneuver. Refer to the pertinent video clip from *The River Runner's Edge* or *EJ's River Running Basics* as a resource to assist students in learning the ferry. Figure WK6.1 shows an example of ferrying.

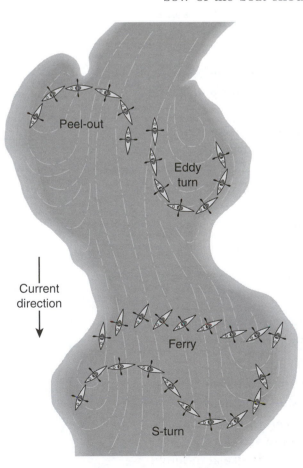

FIGURE WK6.1   Basic maneuvers: ferry, peel-out, and eddy turn.

Activity 2: Peel-Outs (45 Minutes, Taught in Conjunction With Eddy Turns)

A **peel-out** is a starting maneuver in which the kayak moves from the eddy into the current. The peel-out is the most efficient way to exit an eddy. The alternative is to paddle against the current in the eddy to exit the bottom of the eddy. In using the peel-out, the paddler takes advantage of the current in the eddy by paddling with the current and exiting at the top of the eddy.

Describe and demonstrate the peel-out using the acronym PASST. Emphasize the additional S in pronouncing this acronym to distinguish between the acronyms PAST and PASST.

◆ P is for position in the eddy.

◆ A is for angle relative to the eddy line.

◆ S is for speed.

◆ S is for sweep. The paddler uses a forward sweep stroke to initiate the turn just before crossing the eddy line. The timing of the sweep is important. If the stroke is performed too soon, the boat will spin on the eddy line and remain in the eddy. If the stroke is performed too late, it is difficult to perform a level-2 lean (or tilt) while trying to perform a forward sweep. The sweep compromises the tilt and vice versa.

◆ T is for tilt.

Describe and demonstrate strokes used during each phase of the maneuver: forward power strokes to gain speed in the eddy, a forward sweep to initiate the turn, a high-brace ready position in case you lose your balance, and a forward power stroke to develop downstream momentum.

Have students practice peel-outs. Refer to the pertinent video clip from *The River Runner's Edge* or *EJ's River Running Basics* for a demonstration of this maneuver. Figure WK6.1 shows an example of a peel-out.

Activity 3: Eddy Turns (45 Minutes, Taught in Conjunction With Peel-Outs)

An **eddy turn** is a stopping maneuver in which the kayak moves from the downstream current into an eddy. Kayakers should be able to make a controlled stop on the river, much as a skier does on a slope. Performing an eddy turn is the most efficient way to enter an eddy. The maneuver involves the same mechanics and paddling techniques used in performing a peel-out. The difference is that the paddler is moving from the current into an eddy. Unlike the peel-out, the eddy turn requires the kayaker to anticipate the maneuver while on the go. Quick execution of all parts of the maneuver is required. Otherwise, the kayaker is likely to float past the desired stopping point.

Describe and demonstrate the eddy turn using the acronym PASST.

◆ P is for position of the boat in the current relative to the eddy. Again, the paddler must anticipate the maneuver far in advance and position the boat so that she or he can enter the eddy with momentum at an angle of approximately 45 degrees.

◆ A is for angle of the boat relative to the eddy line. The more powerful the current is, the sharper the angle should be; the weaker the current is, the wider the angle should be.

◆ S is for speed.

◆ S is for sweep.

◆ T is for tilt.

Describe and demonstrate strokes used during each phase of the maneuver: forward power strokes to gain speed in moving toward the eddy, a forward sweep to initiate the turn, a high-brace ready position in case you lose your balance while making the turn, and a forward power stroke to stay in the eddy.

Have students practice eddy turns. Refer to the pertinent video clip from *The River Runner's Edge* or *EJ's River Running Basics* for a demonstration of the eddy turn. Figure WK6.1 shows an example of an eddy turn.

Closure Activity

Ride the Conveyor Belt (30 Minutes)

Create a practice course where the group as a whole, or in pods, can practice peel-outs, eddy turns, and ferries in succession. The nature of your practice course will depend on the river features available to you. An ideal setting for this activity would be a spot on the river where large, well-defined eddies are present on either side of a slower moving current.

◆ First, have students practice C-turns by peeling out of and eddying into the same eddy. C-turns are shown in unit 7, lesson 5 (page 525).

◆ Second, have students practice S-turns by peeling out of one eddy and eddying into another eddy on the opposite side. Students can perform a figure-eight by ferrying back to the original eddy to practice the S-turn again. Figure WK6.1 shows an example of an S-turn.

During the closure activity, make a video recording of students performing kayak maneuvers. At the end of the day, use the video to analyze student technique. First, allow students to perform a self-critique. Next, allow for peer critiques, assigning partners the task of critiquing each others' technique. Finally, you should critique student performance. This activity is especially valuable if students will have time within the context of the class to continue practicing their kayak skills and maneuvers. Before the peer critiques, encourage partners to keep it positive and constructive by focusing on what the other person needs to do to perform skills and maneuvers correctly as opposed to focusing on what the other person is doing wrong.

Follow-Up Activity

Eddy Hops (Time as Needed)

As the group paddles downstream, have them practice the various maneuvers as opportunity allows. They can eddy hop their way downstream. They catch an eddy, peel out, catch another eddy, peel out, catch another eddy, ferry to another eddy, and so on. A game of follow the leader works well in this situation.

ASSESSMENT

◆ Verify that students understand how to perform ferries, peel-outs, and eddy turns by having them state the acronyms PAST and PASST and indicate what each letter in the acronyms signifies.

◆ Assess whether students can execute basic maneuvers and proper paddling technique through the video analysis in the closure activity.

◆ Confirm that students can determine when different maneuvers are required at different points along the river by allowing them to lead particular stretches of the river during the follow-up activity. If you are uncomfortable with allowing students to take the lead position, assess this ability during a scouting exercise by having them state the maneuvers that they would use to navigate through the particular rapid or section of river.

◆ Assess whether students appreciate the precision required to perform basic kayak maneuvers by observing their efforts to refine and master the techniques during practice sessions. You can also assess this aspect through students' self-critiques during the video analysis in the closure activity.

TEACHING CONSIDERATIONS

◆ Students are likely to capsize and swim while practicing maneuvers. One way to lessen the stigma of messing up is to form a swim team. The first student to swim becomes the captain of the swim team. Each subsequent swimmer becomes a member. The initial captain of the swim team is displaced by whoever has the most swims at the end of the day. This approach is a fun way to develop camaraderie among members of the group.

◆ In the follow-up activity, catch eddies that are large enough to hold your entire group. Corral all students into the eddy before proceeding to the next. Larger groups can be divided into pods of four to five students, with each pod under the supervision of an instructor. The pods should stay in fairly close range but can navigate independently of one another as they move downstream.

◆ A useful and fun exercise is to have students carve miniature kayakers out of closed cell foam. You and the students can use these miniature kayakers to demonstrate particular kayak maneuvers throughout the course. These demonstrations can be done using miniature rapids along the shoreline or diagrams of rapids drawn in the sand along the riverbank.

UNIT 6, LESSON 7

▷ The Kayak Roll

OVERVIEW

In this lesson, students learn how to perform a kayak roll. The lesson builds on skills learned in earlier lessons—the wet exit, the T-rescue (or Eskimo bow rescue), and high braces. The kayak roll involves elements of all these skills. The development of the kayak roll represents a culmination in the progression of the development of this series of skills.

JUSTIFICATION

The kayak roll can be viewed as a threshold to the sport. Without an effective roll, a kayaker is unlikely to progress very far in the sport. The kayak roll has two specific purposes.

◆ Performing a kayak roll is much more efficient than performing a wet exit or a T-rescue in the event of capsize.

◆ Performing a kayak roll is essential to minimizing risks and ensuring personal safety when paddling in whitewater, especially when the air and water are cold.

Having an effective kayak roll will give the student the ability and the confidence needed to engage fully in the sport of whitewater kayaking.

GOAL

To develop students' ability to perform a kayak roll in both flatwater and whitewater contexts and, in doing so, to give them the confidence needed to engage fully in the sport.

OBJECTIVES

At the end of this lesson, students will be able to

◆ describe the steps involved in performing a kayak roll (cognitive),

◆ identify common elements of the kayak (cognitive),

◆ perform the kayak roll with the assistance of an instructor or peer as described in the main or closure activity (psychomotor), and

◆ develop a greater sense of confidence in their potential for growth in the sport of whitewater kayaking (affective).

EQUIPMENT AND AREAS NEEDED

◆ Whitewater kayaking instructional videos (see resource list at the end of the unit)

◆ The five essentials (kayak, paddle, spray skirt, helmet, PFD)

◆ See lesson 2 for additional equipment

RISK MANAGEMENT CONSIDERATIONS

◆ One of the primary barriers to performance of the kayak roll is emotional anxiety, especially for students who are fearful of being trapped upside-down in a kayak. Be especially attuned to the emotions of students during this lesson.

◆ Make sure that the site is free of rocks close to the surface so that students do not hit rocks while practicing the roll. Before the practice session, reemphasize the importance of tucking.

◆ Shoulder injuries can occur because of poor technique while performing the kayak roll. Revisit the concept of the paddler's box and the need to exercise care in performing paddling techniques to avoid shoulder dislocations or muscle tears.

◆ Recommend the use of nose plugs for a more enjoyable learning experience.

◆ Be cautious of uncontrolled and wild paddle movements when teaching students the roll. Stay on guard as students are sweeping their paddles from the setup to the 90-degree position when learning the roll. Keep your forearms up and in front of your face.

LESSON CONTENT

Introduction (10 Minutes)

To progress in the sport of whitewater kayaking, students must learn the kayak roll. Indeed, the kayak roll can be viewed as one of the thresholds to the sport. The two basic styles of kayak rolling are the C-to-C roll and the sweep roll. Each style of rolling has advantages and disadvantages. Both styles are worth learning. The kayaker who knows how to perform both styles is more versatile.

Two videos that are useful when teaching the sweep roll are *The Kayak Roll* and *EJ's Rolling and Bracing*. If you do not have access to instructional videos, introduce the lesson by personally demonstrating the different styles of kayak rolling to your students.

Main Activity

The Kayak Roll (One Hour)

You should use a whole–part–whole approach (Gullion, 1987) to explain and demonstrate the **kayak roll**. First, demonstrate the roll several times. Second, explain the elements of the roll. Finally, synthesize the explanation of the roll with another demonstration.

The kayak roll is used to maneuver the kayak from an upside-down position to an upright position without assistance. The two basic types of kayak rolls are the C-to-C roll and the sweep roll.

C-to-C Roll   A **C-to-C roll** is the body motion used to roll the kayak from an upside-down position to an upright position. The body and boat move from one C configuration to another as the boat rotates on the axis of its centerline from an upside-down position to an upright position. Three basic steps are involved in performing the C-to-C roll (figure WK7.1):

1. Get into the setup position—leaning forward with the paddle parallel to boat and the power face up.
2. Reorient the paddle and body from the setup position to the first C position.
3. Initiate the roll by performing the hip snap and using the blade of the paddle as a point of leverage against the surface of the water.

In explaining the C-to-C roll, first point to the elements of the maneuver that students have already developed. For example, students already know how to get into the setup position because they have learned and practiced that skill to perform wet exits and Eskimo rescues. They already know how to perform a hip snap and a C-to-C because they have learned and practiced those skills to perform bracing maneuvers and the Eskimo rescue found in unit 5, lesson 5. Students also already know how to use their paddles as a point of leverage against the surface of the water because they have developed that skill to perform the high brace. Emphasize that the only new skill that students must learn to accomplish the roll is to reorient the paddle and body from the setup position to the first C position.

Tips for success in performing the C-to-C:

◆ To roll the kayak, rely primarily on body movement rather than the arms and paddle. Imagine the boat rotating around an axis that runs along the centerline of the boat. The objective is to use the body—knees, hips, torso, and head—to rotate the boat 180 degrees around the axis from an upside-down position to an upright position. Use the leading knee to apply pressure against the thigh brace to help roll the boat into the upright position. Drop the opposite knee. Use a hip snap to help initiate the rotation of the kayak around the centerline. Move the torso and the head from the first C to the second C to assist in the rotation of the kayak from the upside-down position to the upright position.

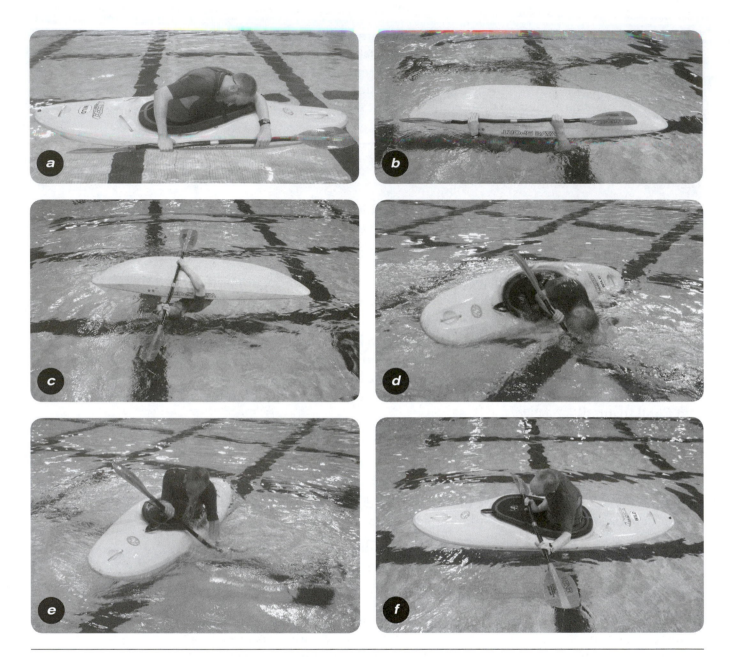

FIGURE WK7.1 C-to-C roll sequence: *(a)* Setup position; *(b)* roll over, maintaining the setup position; *(c)* initiate the first C position; *(d)* initiate the hip snap, keeping the head down; *(e)* ensure that the body is centered over the kayak by pulling the paddle forward; *(f)* finish in the final C position. Note that the point of view shifts—from being on the paddler's right to being on his left—between *(a)* and *(b)* to better show the steps.

◆ Avoid lifting the head and going for air when performing the C-to-C. Although it may seem counterintuitive, allow the head to be the last part of the body to exit the water by performing a "head dink" as you perform the C-to-C. The quotation by Ray in the movie *Jerry Maguire* is relevant here: "Jerry, did you know the human head weighs 8 pounds (3.5 kilograms)?" The weight of the head counteracts the roll.

◆ Be sure to recenter your body over the kayak as you complete the roll. Do this by pulling your blade in toward the boat as though you are preparing to take a stroke or perform a brace.

Sweep Roll   The sweep roll is another common way of performing the kayak roll. This technique can be a useful alternative for those who lack the flexibility to perform a C-to-C roll. The disadvantage is that the sweep roll can expose the kayaker's face to hazards underwater. With the sweep roll, the hip snap occurs as the kayaker executes the sweep. Three basic steps are involved in performing the sweep roll (figure WK7.2):

1. Setup position
2. Sweep
3. Recovery

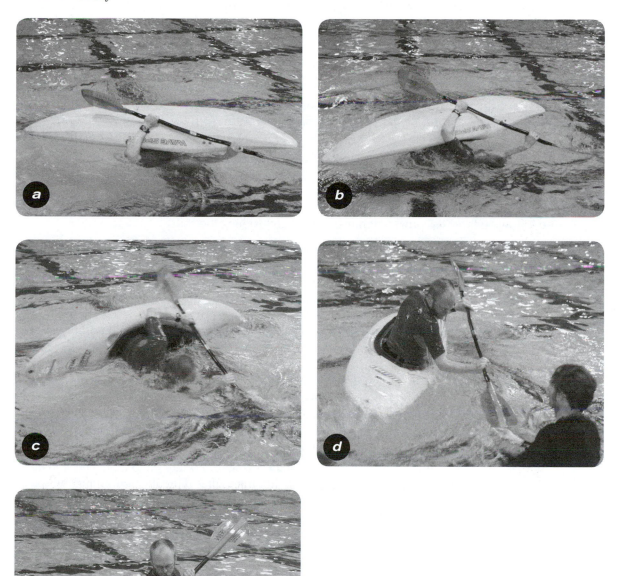

FIGURE WK7.2   Sweep roll sequence: *(a)* Start upright in the setup position, and roll over while maintaining the setup position; *(b)* initiate a sweep with the paddle; *(c)* sweep the paddle from bow to stern; *(d)* initiate the hip snap as soon as the sweep begins; use torso rotation to sweep the paddle; *(e)* recover by centering the body weight over the kayak, and finish by looking down at the paddle.

The setup position mirrors the setup for the C-to-C. The sweep involves sweeping the blade of the paddle across the surface of the water starting at the bow to approximately 45 degrees from the stern of the kayak. After completing the sweep, the kayaker should be looking down the paddle shaft toward the stern of the boat. The elbows should be tucked close to the torso to minimize the risk of shoulder injury.

Tips for success in performing the sweep roll (in addition to the tips for success in performing the C-to-C):

◆ In performing the sweep, keep the blade angle in a neutral position (flat against the surface of the water). Angling the blade against the surface of the water creates resistance that can impede the success of the roll.

◆ The success of the sweep roll relies largely on torso rotation during the sweep. Be sure that the arms remain relatively stationary during the sweep; use torso rotation to sweep the paddle blade across the surface of the water.

◆ Grip the paddle shaft relatively loosely while performing the sweep to help keep the blade from diving toward the bottom of the pool, lake, or river.

Teaching the Roll

The following four-step progression is useful when teaching the roll:

1. Instruct the student to get into the setup position before capsizing. Stand beside and just behind the student on the side of the boat opposite the paddle. Instruct the student to capsize by rolling toward you. Support the student by grabbing the back of the PFD or the torso before she or he completely capsizes. Allow the student to sweep the paddle into position and to initiate the roll. Coaching tip: Gradually allow the student to go lower and lower into the water until she or he is comfortable with going totally under.

2. Repeat step 1 but rather than catch the student, allow the student to capsize on his or her own. Instruct the student to allow you to help by guiding the paddle from the setup position to the 90-degree position. After the paddle is in the 90-degree position, support the tip of the blade and bang the bottom of the boat as a cue for the student to initiate the roll. Coaching tip: Provide a minimal level of support so that the student does not learn to rely on the blade to perform the roll.

3. Repeat steps 1 and 2, only this time allow the kayaker to orient the paddle and initiate the roll without assistance. Coaching tip: If the student has difficulty performing the roll because of an inadequate hip snap or a tendency to lift the head from the water, take a step back and have the students work on more fundamental techniques before progressing with the roll.

4. Instruct the student to get into the setup position and roll in the direction toward which he or she is set up. Allow the student to orient the paddle and initiate the roll without assistance. Coaching tip: Students often become confused about how to orient the paddle from the setup to the 90-degree position when changing the direction of the roll. If this is the case, instruct the student to capsize in the direction toward which he or she is set up so that you can guide the paddle from the setup to the 90-degree position. After the paddle is in position, bang on the bottom of the boat as a cue to the student to initiate the roll. After the student has developed a sense of how to orient the paddle, allow him or her to orient the paddle and initiate the roll without assistance.

Closure Activity

Roll Practice (Time as Needed)

Have students pair up for a roll practice session. One student serves as spotter while his or her partner practices the roll. If students are unable to perform the roll, instruct them to serve as surrogate coaches to one another. Articulate the process by which you instruct kayak rolling. Teach each of the students how to serve in the instructor's role. Students can be an invaluable resource to one another in learning how to perform this maneuver.

Follow-Up Activity

Combat Roll (Time as Needed)

A **combat roll** is a roll performed in a moving-water or whitewater context. Participants can prepare for the combat roll in calm water by using the following two techniques:

- Gain forward momentum in the boat using a forward power stroke and capsize the boat without getting into the setup position. After capsizing, immediately get into the setup position and initiate a roll.
- A partner can push or pull the capsized boat through the water as the student attempts the roll.

These techniques can help to simulate the turbulence that kayakers feel when performing a combat roll. Water turbulence makes the combat roll more challenging than a calm water roll.

Another excellent follow-up activity to the initial lesson on kayak rolling is the application of the skill in a moving-water or whitewater setting. Establish a safe site on the river for practicing combat rolls. Allow students an opportunity to test their ability in that setting.

Encourage students who successfully perform the roll to attempt a hand roll, that is, to roll the kayak using only the hands, not the blade of a kayak paddle, as a point of leverage against the surface of the water. You should be able to perform the hand roll to demonstrate proper technique if you include it as a follow-up activity.

ASSESSMENT

- Check that students can describe the steps involved in performing a kayak roll by articulating the progression to you or a peer partner during each phase of the instructional process. For example, before capsizing, students should describe the steps involved in performing the kayak roll.
- Check that students can identify common elements of the roll by connecting the sequence to previously learned skills such as the wet exit, the Eskimo rescue, and the high brace through a written assessment or discussion.
- Confirm that students can perform the kayak roll with your assistance or the assistance of a peer as described in the main or closure activity.
- Assess whether students develop a greater sense of confidence in their potential for growth in the sport of whitewater kayaking through their ability to perform the kayak roll during combat roll practice.

TEACHING CONSIDERATIONS

◆ Revisit the principles of challenge by choice before this lesson. Students who are uncomfortable attempting to perform the kayak roll should not be judged or graded negatively if they decide to opt out. Instead, encourage them to work on other skills that are fundamental elements of the roll, such as the hip snap or the Eskimo rescue. They can also provide support to students who are attempting to learn the roll by spotting, cheerleading, and so forth.

◆ When possible, teach the roll in a pool. Students are more likely to feel comfortable in a controlled setting than they would in natural settings such as lakes and rivers. Conduct follow-up activities in natural flatwater and whitewater contexts.

◆ A snug fit in the boat is required to perform a successful roll. Boats must be properly outfitted with back bands, hip padding, and padding for knees and thighs. Bulkheads or foot pegs must be properly adjusted.

◆ Practice sessions should last no longer than 20 or 30 minutes. Practice becomes self-defeating when students reach a point of exhaustion or fatigue in attempting to perform the roll. Encourage students to end their practice sessions on a high note—after successfully performing a roll.

◆ If students are having trouble with their hip snaps, consider using a PFD or the side of the pool to replace the paddle. For some students, manipulating the paddle gets in the way of focusing on a good hip snap. Rolling up by holding on to a rolled up PFD can increase a student's confidence and help solidify the step-by-step progression when learning the roll.

◆ To increase the students' bag of tricks for avoiding wet exits, consider teaching the paddle extension roll. Although this technique is inefficient in a whitewater context, it can be a helpful alternative when the paddler is exhausted but does not want to resort to swimming. The paddle extension involves extending the entire length of the paddle perpendicular to the boat while upside down. The full length of the paddle provides a significant amount of leverage if the student can keep the paddle on the surface or close to the surface. Be careful not to promote reliance on this technique. In some cases, this technique is an excellent alternative roll for people with specific mobility problems.

UNIT 6, LESSON 8

▷ Play Boating

OVERVIEW

"Sometimes you surf the hole, and sometimes the hole surfs you."

Source unknown

This lesson introduces students to basic play-boating techniques in whitewater kayaking, including front surfing, back surfing, spins, and side surfing. Although more advanced techniques exist, teaching those skills is beyond the scope of this unit. Students can seek additional instruction in kayak play techniques in intermediate-level whitewater kayaking courses.

JUSTIFICATION

Kayakers should learn play techniques for three key reasons.

◆ Kayakers enjoy paddling for a variety of reasons: the simple thrill of paddling downriver through whitewater, the aesthetic beauty of the river, the physical exertion that the sport requires, and others. Play boating provides a great source of satisfaction for many paddlers.

◆ Developing the ability to perform various play techniques dramatically increases kayakers' performance, which can lead to greater satisfaction with the sport.

◆ More important, learning to perform play techniques can provide kayakers with a bag of tricks that can be useful in handling misadventures on the river (for example, becoming unintentionally surfed in a hole, developing a bombproof roll for those inevitable capsizes).

GOAL

To develop students' knowledge and skills of basic play techniques in whitewater kayaking.

OBJECTIVES

At the end of this lesson, students will be able to

◆ understand the dynamics of surfing waves and hydraulics in river (cognitive),

◆ distinguish between friendly versus unfriendly river features (psychomotor),

◆ perform each of the play techniques as well as proper paddling (psychomotor), and

◆ demonstrate a sense of camaraderie and community spirit through play-boating exercises (affective).

EQUIPMENT AND AREAS NEEDED

◆ Play boat (rodeo kayak). Although any boat can be used to perform various play techniques, some kayaks are designed specifically for play boating. Introduce students to the various types of kayaks as well as the different types of kayaking. Focus on the advantages of a play boat during this lesson.

◆ See lesson 2 for additional equipment.

◆ Instructional videos illustrating various play techniques. *EJ's Play Boating Basics* and *The River Runner's Edge* are good choices.

RISK MANAGEMENT CONSIDERATIONS

◆ Be prepared for capsizes. You should set safety points in boats or on land below play sites and ensure that ample room is available below the sites for recovery. Have students pair up to provide immediate assistance in case of capsizes.

◆ Make sure that the site is free of rocks close to the surface so that students do not hit rocks in case of capsizes. Nonetheless, reemphasize the importance of tucking (leaning forward toward the deck of the boat) in case of capsize.

♦ Shoulder injuries commonly occur as a result of poor paddling technique. Remind students of the concept of the paddler's box and good technique before practicing play techniques, especially side surfing and spinning.

♦ Recommend use of nose plugs and ear plugs for a more enjoyable learning experience.

♦ Take plenty of breaks and be sure that students remain hydrated during physical activity.

LESSON CONTENT

Introduction

Ask your students whether they have ever imagined surfing on a river. Discuss the similarities and differences between surfing in the ocean and surfing on a river. Then state that surfing is not just for the ocean anymore. One of the primary sources of pleasure for many kayakers is play boating, which involves taking advantage of waves, hydraulics, and other river features to perform surfing and other acrobatic techniques in a kayak. This lesson helps students develop a solid foundation for developing play-boating skills.

Main Activities

Activity 1: Wave Surfing (45 to 60 Minutes per Technique)

Three different wave-surfing techniques will be covered in this activity—**front surfing**, back surfing, and spins.

A kayaker performs **wave surfing** by paddling a kayak onto the face of a wave and remaining there. Friction and gravity counteract one another to keep the kayaker on the face of the wave.

Waves can be entered from eddies or by drifting onto them from upstream, but in teaching beginner kayakers how to wave surf, the best method is to teach them to enter the wave from an eddy. Initially, the goal is to get onto the wave and to stay on it in the front-surfing position. After students have accomplished this, you can progress them to more advanced wave-surfing techniques such as back surfing and spins.

Front Surfing   Setting up to get onto the wave to front surf (figure WK8.1) is much like setting up to perform an upstream ferry. Review the acronym PAST—position, angle, speed, and tilt. The kayaker uses the same technique until the kayak crosses the eddy line.

♦ The kayak should cross the eddy line just upstream of the crest of the wave. After the kayak crosses the eddy line, point the bow of the boat upstream and keep the angle of the boat in line with the direction of the flow.

♦ If the oncoming current begins to bury the bow of the boat, lean backward in the kayak to keep the bow up.

♦ If the boat drifts up onto the crest of the wave, lean toward the bow and paddle forward to bring the kayak back down into the trough of the wave.

♦ If the kayak veers or the current pushes it in one direction or the other, use forward corrective strokes (sweeps and draws) to correct the angle of the kayak. On powerful waves, use pry strokes (the initial part of the reverse sweep) to correct

FIGURE WK8.1   Front surfing a wave.

the angle of the kayak. In milder current, pry strokes will drag the kayak off the wave. Forward power strokes can help correct the angle of the kayak and keep it on the face of the wave.

◆ Practice carving the face of the wave by alternating the direction of the boat back and forth across the face of the wave. Always tilt, or edge, the kayak in the direction of travel (away from the oncoming current). The goal is to stay in the trough of the wave, between the shoulders of the wave, traversing back and forth beneath the peak of the wave. The more aggressive the edging is, the more aggressive the surf is.

Back Surfing   To back surf a wave, the kayaker must first spin the kayak 180 degrees from the front surf position to a back surf position. In **back surfing**, the stern of the boat points upstream. To spin the kayak, the kayaker allows the boat to rise to the peak of the wave, releases the hull of the kayak from the wave by pivoting the kayak in the direction of the spin while slightly dropping the edge of the bow into the current, executes a reverse sweep, and leans toward the bow of the kayak. The kayak should now be surfing backward on the wave. Keeping the kayak relatively level during the spin is important. To avoid being dragged off the wave, the kayaker must not lean the kayak downstream during the spin.

◆ Back surfing involves the same principles as front surfing, only in reverse. To control the angle of the kayak, use reverse corrective strokes (bow draws and reverse sweeps). A reverse power stroke can also be used to stay on the face of the wave.

◆ Practice carving the kayak back and forth across the face of the wave to develop greater control of the kayak.

Spinning   After students have mastered front surfing and back surfing, you can progress them to spinning. **Spinning** is performed by turning the kayak 360 degrees on the face of the wave.

- See the earlier section on back surfing for tips about spinning from a front surf to back surf position.

- To spin from a back to a front surf position, allow the kayak to rise to the peak of the wave, pivot the stern of the kayak in the direction of the spin while dropping the edge of the stern slightly into the current, execute a forward sweep, and lean toward the stern of the kayak. A few forward power strokes may be needed to stay on the face of the wave.

- Combine the forward-to-backward and backward-to-forward spins for a complete 360-degree spin.

- Practice performing continuous 360-degree spins, alternating the direction of the spin from time to time.

Activity 2: Hole Surfing (One to Two Hours)

Hole surfing is performed when the kayaker enters a hydraulic and keeps the kayak perpendicular to the direction of flow. Gravity holds the kayak in the hole, aided by the circular flow of the water. The kayaker can then perform a number of play techniques in the hydraulic. This lesson focuses on side surfing and spins.

Choosing the Right Hole Being able to distinguish between friendly and unfriendly hydraulics is essential to having a safe, enjoyable hole-surfing experience. Whether a hydraulic is friendly or not depends on the ease with which the kayaker can exit it.

- Choose a hydraulic that has at least one corner pointing downstream. The best way to exit the hydraulic is from one of its corners. Paddling downstream toward the corners of the hydraulic is much easier than paddling upstream.

- Choose a hydraulic whose boil line is no farther than one-third the length of your kayak from the ledge. Such hydraulics typically allow the kayaker to flush out of the hole after flipping.

- As a beginner or intermediate paddler, be careful about judging the strength of a hole based on the experiences of others. Experienced paddlers may make the hole look easy to get out of. Ask experienced paddlers whom you trust about the hole before jumping in yourself.

- Never enter into a hydraulic at the base of a low-head dam. See lesson 5 for additional details on this topic.

Entering the Hydraulic Hydraulics can be entered at their corners from adjacent eddies, by paddling up through the backwash of the hydraulic and into the froth or by drifting into them from upstream.

- For beginner kayakers learning how to side surf, the easiest way to enter the hydraulic is from an eddy.

- After entering the hydraulic, turn the boat sideways to the current. This is called side surfing.

Staying Upright in the Hydraulic Tilt the kayak into a level-2 or level-3 lean away from the oncoming current. The degree of the lean depends on how deep the hole is as well as how strong the current is. Finding the optimal lean is important in ensuring a smooth ride in the hole.

◆ Use a high brace for support on the downstream side of the kayak. Do not dip the paddle upstream of the kayak—unless you want to capsize. To minimize the risk of hyperextension of the shoulders, be careful not to overextend the arms and shoulders in executing the brace.

◆ To move the kayak forward in the hydraulic, use a combination high brace, forward sweep stroke. To move backward in the hydraulic, use a combination low brace, reverse sweep stroke.

◆ The technique used in spinning in a hole is nearly identical to the technique used in spinning on a wave (see earlier description for an explanation of the technique). To spin the kayak in the hole, move the kayak to the corner of the hole and allow the current to drag the bow of the boat downstream so that the kayak is in a back surf position. Then execute a forward sweep to swing the bow of the boat around and complete the turn.

◆ To exit the hole, move to the corner of the hole and use the current to pull out of the hole.

Closure Activities

Activity 1: Whitewater Rodeo (30 Minutes)

Simulate a whitewater rodeo competition. Assemble a panel of two or three judges from among the students and instructors. Create a points system that awards points based on such factors as length of time in the hole or on the wave, number of tricks performed while in the hole or on the wave, and style.

Activity 2: Play Time (10 Minutes)

After learning and practicing play techniques at the teaching site, an instructor can lead the group off by strutting his or her stuff on a wave or in a hydraulic for a short period and then paddling a short distance downstream to corral oncoming kayakers into an eddy. Each student should have a chance to play on the wave or in the hydraulic before heading downstream. The instructor serving in the sweep position should immediately follow the last student to the rallying point downstream.

Follow-Up Activities

Activity 1: Stop and Play (as Time Allows)

Have students identify potential play sites as the group continues down river. Stop to play at these sites as time allows. Help students identify characteristics of different sites so that they learn what makes a good site and what makes a bad one.

Activity 2: Video Critique (30 Minutes)

During the rodeo competition, make a video recording of students performing play techniques. At the end of the day, use the video to analyze student technique. First, have students perform a self-critique. Next, allow for peer critiques. Assign partners the task of critiquing each others' technique. Finally, you should critique student performance. Remind partners to keep it positive and constructive by focusing on what the other person needs to do to perform skills and maneuvers correctly as opposed to focusing on what the other person is doing wrong.

ASSESSMENT

- Assess students' understanding of the dynamics of surfing waves and hydraulics in river settings by observing them critique the videotaped practice sessions.

- Confirm that students can distinguish between friendly and unfriendly river features by describing feature characteristics.

- Assess whether students can perform each of the play techniques as well as proper paddling technique by observing them compete in a class-run rodeo competition.

- Evaluate whether students demonstrate a sense of camaraderie and community spirit in the play-boating exercises by cheering one another on during the practice sessions and during the rodeo competition.

TEACHING CONSIDERATIONS

- The ideal wave for teaching beginner kayakers how to front surf is approximately 2 to 4 feet (60 to 120 centimeters) high. The ideal hydraulic is one whose corners point downstream and is just large enough to hold a kayak but small enough to allow for a calm ride and easy exit. The wave or hydraulic should be adjacent to a large eddy with a well-defined eddy line. Plenty of recovery space should be available below the wave or hydraulic (distance between the wave or hydraulic and any obstructions or rapids). Ideally, you should have a place to stand or position your kayak next to the wave or hydraulic for teaching and coaching. That way you can help students develop an understanding of boat angles and leans as they learn to surf. A big rock on which the class can gather to observe is another useful feature.

- In locations where you can safely stand upstream of the wave, a way to help students maintain the proper boat angle in learning to front surf is to run a rope through the grab loop on the bow of the kayak. You hold on to both ends of the rope to keep the boat on the wave, angled in the direction of the water flow. When the student is ready to exit the wave, or if the student capsizes, you can let go of one end of the rope to allow the rope to pass through the grab loop, freeing the kayak to drift off the wave. Note: The rope must be free of knots so that it can slide completely out of the grab loop, freeing the kayak. Be careful not to put the student in a situation where she or he can become entangled in the rope.

- You should not expect students in an introductory whitewater kayaking course to perform most of these play techniques successfully. Given adequate time and practice, however, students may begin to develop competency in front surfing, side surfing, and spins. Other more advanced techniques may be beyond their reach within the context of the course. In this case, you can simply explain and demonstrate more advanced techniques to show students what awaits them if they continue to pursue the sport. You can do this as one of the final lessons in the class after students have already developed the fundamental skills on which these techniques build.

▷ Kayak Safety Considerations

OVERVIEW

"There are old paddlers and bold paddlers, but there are few old, bold paddlers."

Source unknown

Safety considerations specific to whitewater kayaking are the topic of this lesson. The rescue curve (Kauffman & Carlson, 1992) is introduced as a framework for thinking about safety and risk management in whitewater kayaking. This lesson focuses on accident prevention. Self-rescues and assisted rescues will be addressed in lesson 10.

JUSTIFICATION

Whitewater kayaking is an inherently risky sport. Although risk is integral to adventure and should be embraced to a degree because of the rewards that it can yield, every precaution should be taken to avoid accidents and injuries and to minimize the consequences of an accident should one occur.

GOALS

- ◆ To develop students' ability to recognize objective and subjective risks associated with whitewater kayaking.
- ◆ To develop students' ability to balance risk and competency to create an optimal kayaking experience.

OBJECTIVES

At the end of this lesson, students will be able to

- ◆ understand the value of the rescue curve as a framework for managing risks and ensuring safety in whitewater paddling (cognitive),
- ◆ distinguish between subjective risks and objective risks in whitewater kayaking (cognitive),
- ◆ develop the ability to account for general safety considerations in whitewater kayaking (cognitive), and
- ◆ demonstrate appreciation for safety considerations in whitewater kayaking (affective).

EQUIPMENT AND AREAS NEEDED

Cold, Wet, and Alive video (Nichols, 1989; see resources list at the end of this unit)

RISK MANAGEMENT CONSIDERATIONS

Be aware of environmental conditions and make appropriate accommodations to minimize risks.

LESSON CONTENT

Introduction

The **rescue curve** (Kauffman & Carlson, 1992; Martin, Cashel, Wagstaff, & Breunig, 2006) serves as an effective framework for thinking about safety and risk management in whitewater kayaking (see figure WK9.1).

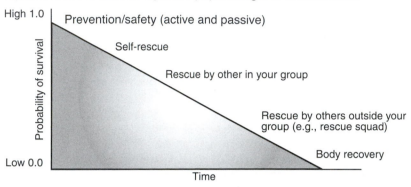

A person's line of defense against injury, damage, or loss includes:

FIGURE WK9.1   Rescue curve.

Adapted, by permission, from R. Kauffman and G. Carlson, 1992, "The rescue curve: A race against time," *American Canoeist* (March): 10–13.

The concept of the rescue curve posits that four steps can intervene between participating in an outdoor adventure activity and winding up dead as a result of an accident during the activity:

1. Accident prevention
2. Self-rescue
3. Rescue from within the group
4. Rescue from an outside party

As the amount of time in responding to an incident increases, the victim's chances of survival decrease. Effective accident prevention and rescue techniques are essential to minimizing the possibility that an accident will occur and to minimizing the consequences of an accident should one occur during an adventure activity.

Important Terms

objective risks—Risks that arise from the natural environment (for example, extreme weather; high water; animals; level of challenge presented by the river; and specific river hazards such as strainers, undercut rocks, and keeper hydraulics).

subjective risks—Risks that arise from people and can be controlled by people (for example, ability level relative to the level of challenge presented by the river, horseplay, alcohol or drug use, and knowledge of and preparedness for weather).

Main Activities

Activity 1: Misadventures in Whitewater Kayaking (20 to 30 Minutes)

Show the video *Cold, Wet, and Alive* to introduce this lesson. After the video ends, engage students in a critical analysis of the video by asking students to identify the circumstances and events that led to the misadventure portrayed in the video. Help the students to determine how the situation could have been avoided. If you do not have access to this video, share similar examples of whitewater misadventures orally with students as a basis for critical analysis and discussion.

To synthesize the discussion, use the rescue curve as a framework for analyzing the story depicted in the film or in your vignette.

Activity 2: General Safety Considerations (30 Minutes)

This part of the lesson focuses on general safety considerations that can help prevent incidents and accidents from occurring. You can present safety considerations all at once in a lecture format as a part of a safety briefing at the beginning of the day, or you can present them as opportunity allows during your course.

The safety code of American Whitewater (www.americanwhitewater.org/content/Wiki/safety:start#safety_code_of_american_whitewater) is an excellent resource for outlining safety considerations for whitewater kayaking. Many of the safety considerations outlined in this code are found elsewhere throughout this unit. Introduce the following additional considerations to your students.

Developing a Trip Plan Kayakers who plan to go on an outing should develop a trip plan that details the trip itinerary, logistical considerations, contingency plans, and emergency management plans. They should leave the trip plan with a responsible party who can initiate a search and rescue should they fail to return from their trip. Contingency plans should be developed to address various what-ifs that might arise during the trip. For example, what if the river level is too high? What if night falls before the trip is complete?

Emergency management plans should be developed to address possible rescue scenarios that might arise when on the river. How will medical emergencies, drowning, and other incidents be handled should they occur? What is the easiest route of evacuation should one be needed? Where is the nearest full-service hospital or emergency care center? What are the telephone numbers of local rescue personnel?

Planning ahead and preparing are essential to minimizing risks and ensuring safety in whitewater kayaking.

Group Size and Organization Groups should include a minimum of three people and two crafts. As noted earlier, paddling in a group enhances the probability of survival should self-rescue fail. Groups should stick together, paddling as a team, when on the river. Partners can easily lose sight of one another on the river, which can increase response time in case of an emergency.

- One person should serve as lead and another as sweep. Everyone else remains between the two.

- Group members should be familiar with universal river signals to ensure effective communication among group members when voices cannot be heard on the river (see the rafting unit, lesson 3).

- Group members should be willing to speak with anyone who engages in dangerous actions on the river.

Individual and Group Ability Level Matching the level of river difficulty with the ability of individual group members and the group as a whole is essential to ensuring safety on the river. The safety code of American Whitewater indicates that each paddler is responsible for deciding whether he or she is up for the challenge ahead. Paddlers should stay within their ability level to avoid misadventure. Unfortunately, not everyone has the good judgment to make that determination. Consequently, the group is responsible for ensuring that all group members are prepared for the level of challenge ahead. The level of challenge should match the ability level of the least skilled member of the group. Group members must not pressure paddling partners to attempt rivers that exceed their skill level.

Proper Outfitting and Maintenance of the Kayak   Properly outfitting and maintaining the kayak is essential to kayak safety. This consideration is covered in lesson 2. Kayakers must make sure that equipment functions reliably and is in good condition before each paddling excursion.

Rescue Equipment   Kayakers should carry proper rescue equipment and know how to use it. This equipment is covered in lesson 2. In covering this point, you should discuss the limitations of an introductory kayaking course and point to opportunities for further training and development (particularly in river rescue and wilderness medicine) outside the context of the course.

River Conditions   Kayakers should be familiar with the character of the river that they intend to run as well as current river conditions. Information can be gained through guidebooks, maps, the USGS Web site, and local knowledge. Paddlers should establish no-go criteria for running the river in marginal river conditions (for example, the trip is a no-go if the flow exceeds 5,000 cubic feet, or 140 cubic meters, per second).

Weather   Cold weather is a primary safety consideration. The film *Cold, Wet, and Alive* highlights this consideration. The film provides an excellent introduction to hypothermia and the value of proper equipment in minimizing the risk of hypothermia. Kayakers should use wet suits, dry suits, and other insulating materials when the combined air and water temperature is less than 110 degrees Fahrenheit (43 degrees Celsius). Paddlers should establish no-go criteria for running the river in marginal weather (for example, the trip is a no-go if the combined air and water temperature is below 100 degrees Fahrenheit, or 38 degrees Celsius). Other weather conditions that should be considered include severe storms, extreme heat, and fog.

Specific River Features   Common river features that represent threats to safety include rock sieves and strainers, undercut rocks, low-head dams, **keeper hydraulics**, and log jams. These features are covered in lesson 5.

Hazardous Flora and Fauna   Although hazardous flora and fauna vary by geographical region, kayakers should identify them as a safety consideration. Copperhead snakes are a common hazard on rivers in the East. Grizzly and brown bears are a common hazard in the Northwest, Canada, and Alaska. Poison ivy, oak, and sumac are common hazards throughout the United States. Paddlers should become familiar with hazardous flora and fauna unique to their area and work to avoid them.

Other Watercraft   Other watercraft often present hazards to kayakers. On busy rivers such as the Youghiogheny in Maryland and western Pennsylvania, rafts can be a hazard to whitewater kayakers, especially to beginners and novices. A kayaker can become pinned underneath a raft. Kayakers should be careful to steer clear of rafts when paddling in whitewater.

Closure Activity

Whitewater Whiz, Round 4 (10 Minutes)

Quiz the students on kayak safety considerations through another round of Whitewater Whiz. See lesson 2 for a description of the activity. Examples of questions for this round of Whitewater Whiz include the following:

◆ What is the minimum number for any group of paddlers? Answer: Three people and two craft.

◆ What is the combined air and water temperature below which kayakers should wear protective clothing when whitewater kayaking? Answer: 110 degrees Fahrenheit (43 degrees Celsius).

◆ What is the name and Web address of the government agency that provides information about river flows? Answer: U.S. Geological Survey at http://water. usgs.gov.

Follow-Up Activity

Trip Planning Exercise (Time as Needed)

Assign students to work in pairs to develop a trip plan for a two-day kayaking trip. The trip plan must include the following elements: trip goals and objectives, equipment list, trip itinerary and time control plan, river description (including maps), contingency plan, and emergency management plan. Students should submit the trip plan to you in written format.

ASSESSMENT

◆ Confirm that students understand the value of the rescue curve as a framework for managing risks and ensuring safety in whitewater kayaking through their critical analysis of the story depicted in the film *Cold, Wet, and Alive* or other examples of whitewater misadventures. You can also assess students on this topic through the Whitewater Whiz exercise.

◆ Confirm that students can distinguish between subjective dangers and objective dangers in whitewater kayaking by observing them during trips when scouting and by written examination.

◆ Check that students can account for general safety considerations in whitewater kayaking through the follow-up activity in which they must prepare a trip plan for a two-day kayaking trip.

◆ Assess whether students appreciate safety considerations in whitewater kayaking by observing their adherence to the safety protocols that you established during the class.

TEACHING CONSIDERATIONS

◆ Elements of this lesson can be taught in conjunction with lesson 5 (River Reading). Understanding the nature of objective dangers such as strainers and keeper hydraulics is integral to successful route selection and navigation on the river.

◆ In this lesson, emphasize the importance of developing whitewater kayaking skills through a gradual progression. Caution students against jumping immediately from introductory-level whitewater to advanced whitewater. Also, caution them against such pitfalls as peer pressure and pleasing others as motivations in choosing the level of challenge that they are willing to accept in the sport.

▷ Rescues

OVERVIEW

"People first, equipment second."

Source unknown

Lesson 9 (Kayak Safety Considerations) introduced the concept of the rescue curve (Kauffman & Carlson, 1992) as a framework for considering safety and risk management in whitewater kayaking. That lesson focused on step 1 in the rescue curve: accident prevention. This lesson focuses on steps 2, 3, and 4 in the rescue curve: self-rescue and assisted rescue from both within and outside the group. Specifically, the lesson addresses how to perform self-rescues and assisted rescues in the event of flips, swims, and pins in whitewater kayaking.

JUSTIFICATION

Learning rescue techniques is essential to minimizing the risk of injury or death resulting from an accident in an adventure activity. Returning home at the end of the day with more boats and paddles than paddlers isn't good.

GOAL

To develop students' ability to perform a self-rescue and to provide assistance to others should a rescue situation arise while on the river.

OBJECTIVES

At the end of this lesson, students will be able to

- identify opportunities for advanced training in river rescue and wilderness first aid outside the course (cognitive);
- identify equipment essential to performing rescues in whitewater kayaking (cognitive);
- demonstrate basic river rescue techniques, including boat and swimmer tows, boat plows, rope throws, tag lines, and snag lines (psychomotor);
- demonstrate a concern for the safety of fellow students (affective); and
- demonstrate interdependence in performing basic assisted-rescue techniques (affective).

EQUIPMENT AND AREAS NEEDED

- The five essentials (kayak, paddle, spray skirt, helmet, PFD)
- First aid kit
- Whistle
- River knife
- Throw rope
- Carabiners

- ◆ Pulleys
- ◆ Web slings
- ◆ Prusik loops
- ◆ Towline
- ◆ See lesson 2 for additional equipment

RISK MANAGEMENT CONSIDERATIONS

- ◆ Pay attention to emotional safety. Be sensitive to student apprehensions about risks associated with whitewater kayaking. This lesson can heighten the anxieties of already anxious students. On the other hand, you can and should use this lesson to temper the enthusiasm of students who exhibit little respect for the risks associated with whitewater kayaking.

- ◆ Select a relatively benign site for this lesson. You should be familiar with all features of the rapid, including the river bottom, to avoid placing students at undue risk when practicing rescue techniques. Be careful that a mock rescue does not turn into the real thing.

- ◆ Require students to wear helmets and PFDs as they engage in practicing rescue techniques. Besides keeping students prepared to enter the river at any time during rescue scenarios, helmets and PFDs provide added protection to anyone who slips and falls while moving along the shoreline or falls into the river.

- ◆ See lesson 9 for additional risk management considerations.

LESSON CONTENT

Introduction

Emphasize the importance of being prepared to assist both self and others in rescue situations. This idea entails developing the basic skills necessary to perform self-rescues and assisted rescues. Being prepared means possessing the equipment necessary to perform rescues. Being prepared also entails positioning one's team to help one another in case of flips, swims, or pins while on the river. Safety points should be set in eddies, along the shore, or at the bottom of rapids. Team members should position themselves within reach of swimmers or potential pinning positions when running challenging or difficult drops. Throw ropes and other rescue gear should be easily accessible and ready to use when traveling downriver. Being prepared to assist entails paddling and working as a team to ensure each other's safety while on the river.

The film *Heads Up* is a 20-minute video that provides an excellent illustration of the concepts of self-rescue and assisted rescue as they apply to whitewater kayaking, canoeing, and rafting. The film relies on the concept of the rescue curve to illustrate rescue procedures and techniques.

Main Activities

This lesson introduces rescue techniques that are unique to whitewater kayaking and decked canoeing. General information on rescues, such as whitewater swimming, use of throw ropes to assist swimmers, and rope-pulling systems are addressed in other water-based units. Please see the overview to part II (pages 327 to 328) for more information on where to find specific rescue information and skills. Incorporate that information into whitewater kayaking lessons on rescues.

Activity 1: Flips (Time as Needed)

Some paddlers assert that things have gone wrong when a flip occurs. Discuss, demonstrate, and practice the following three options as needed depending on the students' progress in skill development.

- Bracing—The first form of self-rescue in whitewater kayaking is the bracing stroke, which the paddler uses to avoid the flip. Bracing strokes are addressed in lesson 4.
- The kayak roll—When the brace fails and the kayaker flips upside down, he or she uses the second form of self-rescue, the kayak roll. Lesson 7 addresses this skill in detail.
- The Eskimo rescue—When the kayak roll fails, the kayaker can rely on team members to provide an assisted rescue, the Eskimo bow rescue. This skill is covered in unit 5, lesson 5.

Activity 2: Swims (One Hour)

When the brace, kayak roll, and Eskimo bow rescue all fail, the paddler is left with the inevitability of swimming. See lessons in the rafting and canoeing units about passive and aggressive whitewater swimming and use of throw ropes. Teach the following topics using explanation, demonstration, and practice.

Towing Swimmers   Often, towing fatigued swimmers is easier than retrieving them with a throw rope.

- Approach the swimmer with caution; be sure that the swimmer is behaving rationally before paddling within reach.
- Invite the swimmer either to grab your stern grab loop or to pull his or her torso onto the back deck of your kayak while holding on to the cockpit combing.
- Instruct the swimmer to kick his or her feet to assist with propulsion of the boat.
- If a panicked swimmer attaches himself or herself to you, flip your kayak and perform a kayak roll. This method is a sure way to get the swimmer off you.

Towing Boats   An important piece of safety equipment is a **towline**, which is used to retrieve a swimmer's kayak. Towlines can be carried in several ways where they are easily accessible for use.

- First, they can be mounted on the back deck of the kayak by attaching one end to the stern grab loop and the other to a cleat positioned just behind the cockpit. Several towing systems on the market are built into the kayak. This system is typically designed with a jam cleat, shock cord, or some other device that is attached directly behind the cockpit to the kayak deck. A rescue line can be attached to the system a number of ways, depending on the setup. For example, the tow line is tied to the rescuer's stern grab loop. This allows the tow line to be removed from the jam cleat, threaded through the grab loop of the swimmer's boat, and reattached to the jam cleat. The rescuer is then ready to tow.
- Second, they can be stowed in the cockpit or around the waist with a carabiner attached to one end of the towline.
- Third, many rescue PFDs come equipped with harness systems and tethers built in.

When towing a kayak, flip the kayak into the upright position for easier maneuvering. Be careful to avoid entanglement in the towline. Also, avoid creating a fixed attachment to the boat that you are towing.

◆ When using the mounted system, run the towline through the bow grab loop of the boat that you are towing and reattach the working end to the cleat. This method allows an easy escape by simply removing the working end of the rope from the cleat and allowing it to slide out of the grab loop. PFD harness systems typically come equipped with quick-release devices that allow easy escape from the tether (figure WK10.1).

◆ When using the handheld system, be sure not to wrap the rope around your hands, arms, or torso. Use slip knots that are easy to untie if you attach the towline to your boat.

FIGURE WK10.1   Rescue PFD harness and tether tow system.

Towing Boats and Swimmers   Often, you can retrieve the kayak and the swimmer simultaneously. When this opportunity presents itself, instruct the swimmer to grab the stern grab loop of your kayak with one hand and the bow or stern grab loop of her or his kayak with the other. The swimmer's kayak should be in the upright position, and the swimmer should kick to help with propulsion.

Boat Plows   An alternative to the **boat tow** is the **boat plow**. The boat plow involves pushing the empty boat from the current into an eddy or to shore. Tip the kayak into an upright position. Align the kayak so that it is parallel with the flow of the current. Target the pivot point of the empty boat with your bow as you push the boat to shore with your kayak. Approaching the empty boat from upstream is easier. Maintain the angle of the empty boat by pushing to either side of the pivot point.

Activity 3: Pins and Broaches (One Hour)

The two general types of pins in whitewater kayaking are vertical pins and horizontal pins.

◆ **Vertical pins** occur when the bow of a kayak becomes trapped in a crevice as it drops over a ledge or waterfall.

◆ **Horizontal pins (or broaches)** occur when a kayak broaches sideways against rocks, strainers, or other obstructions in the river. In a horizontal pin, the force of the current applies hundreds of pounds (kilograms) of pressure against the kayak, trapping it against the obstruction.

Preventing the Pin or Broach   Preventing a pin or broach from occurring to begin with is the best approach. This sometimes entails a tradeoff of consequences. For instance, you may accept the consequences of a swim as opposed to a pin. You can do several things to prevent pins and broaches.

◆ When hitting a rock is inevitable, get affectionate with the rock! Lean into the rock rather than away from it, as beginner kayakers typically do. By leaning in, you allow water to flow underneath the kayak rather than grab the edge of the kayak and cause a flip. Leaning into the rock allows you to attempt to push yourself and the kayak in one direction or the other around the rock.

◆ Swimming is preferable to becoming trapped in a pinned or broached kayak. When the kayak begins to stick to the rock, it is time to exit, whether the boat is upright or upside down. If you feel your kayak begin to stick to a rock, exit and climb onto the rock or swim to safety before you become trapped in the kayak. Contemporary kayak cockpit design allows an easy exit. Even so, snug outfitting and the pressure of the current against the hull can make exiting the kayak difficult. If you become trapped in your kayak, there is little that you can do to initiate your own rescue.

◆ Vertical pins are most likely to occur when running drops of 3 feet (1 meter) or more. To avoid vertical pins, keep the bow of the kayak from going deep when paddling over waterfalls and steep drops. Keep the bow up by thrusting it forward with a strong forward power stroke and lifting the thighs when paddling over the lip of the drop. This advanced kayaking technique is called **boofing**. When boofing, be careful to avoid flat landings. Improper boofing technique can result in spinal injury caused by spinal compaction. Creek boats, which are high volume and bulbous in shape, are especially designed for buoyancy to avoid vertical pins.

Overcoming the Pin or Broach   Following are a series of considerations and actions that you should take if you encounter a pinned or broached kayak.

First, stabilize the situation. If a kayaker becomes trapped in a kayak, the first priority for other team members is to ensure that the pinned kayaker remains heads up in the river. Team members should immediately work to stabilize the situation by providing physical support to help the victim keep his or her head above the water. This can be done by physically holding the victim above water if he or she is within reach. It can also be done by extending a stabilization or tag line for the victim to hold on to until the situation can be resolved (figure WK10.2). See lesson 9 in the rafting unit for more detail on the use of tag lines, specifically in rescuing victims of foot entrapment. The principles in using tag lines to support foot-entrapped victims are the same as those for using tag lines to support pinned or broached kayakers trapped in their boats.

Second, free the victim. After the pinned kayaker has a firm grip on the tag line or is within the grip of a rescuer, begin to work to free the kayaker from the entrapment.

◆ The first rule when trying to free the kayaker from a pinned position is not to make the situation any worse. Do not compromise stabilization when trying to free a pinned kayaker.

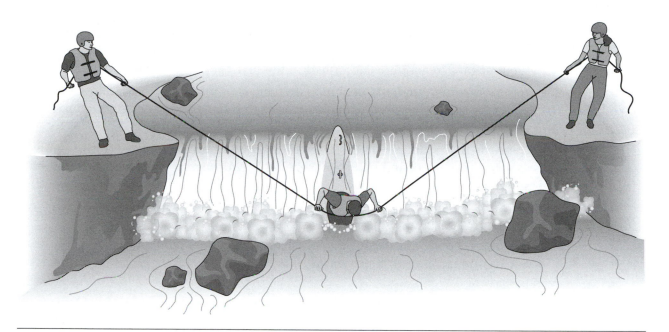

FIGURE WK10.2   Using a tag line to stabilize a pinned kayaker.

◆ When supporting an entrapped kayaker with a tag line, a separate rescue rope should be used to attempt to free the kayaker and boat from the pinned position. This separate rescue rope is called a snag line.

A rope pull is another potential technique for freeing a pinned kayaker. The technique depends on the nature of the pin. Rope pulls are addressed in the rafting and canoeing units; see those units for information.

Closure Activity

Rescue Skills Practice Session (30 to 60 Minutes)

Give students the opportunity to practice various assisted-rescue techniques in a whitewater context. Start with Eskimo rescues and then progress to other skills. Give students the opportunity to develop their expertise as both rescuers and victims.

Follow-Up Activity

Identification of Rescue Training Opportunities (One Hour)

Give students a homework assignment to research formal rescue training opportunities and certifications through organizations and associations. Have students identify levels of training, sponsoring agencies, time commitment, price, locations, curriculum, and benefits. Have students contrast and compare their findings as a group.

ASSESSMENT

◆ Check that students can identify opportunities for advanced training in swift water and river rescue and wilderness first aid through doing the research assignment as described in the follow-up activity.

◆ Confirm that students can identify and use equipment essential to performing rescues in whitewater kayaking by observing them use the equipment during rescue practice exercises.

- Verify that students can perform basic river rescue techniques, including boat and swimmer tows, boat plows, rope throws, tag lines, and snag lines, by observing them engage in activities described in the main activities section.
- Assess whether students demonstrate concern for the safety of fellow students by observing their attention to ensuring each other's safety during practice exercises.
- Confirm that students can demonstrate interdependence in performing basic assisted-rescue techniques by observing them work in teams during practice sessions.

TEACHING CONSIDERATIONS

- Students should develop competency and a high level of teamwork in performing basic rescue techniques on dry land before practicing those techniques on the river.
- The site should include a good staging area, such as a large rock at the top of the rapid. Trail access along both riverbanks is also helpful in allowing students to move without having to scramble and bushwhack along the shoreline. The presence of trails will also help minimize environmental impacts.
- Elements of a variety of other lessons are foundational to this lesson, including the brace, the kayak roll, the Eskimo rescue, river features, and river dynamics. Students should be made aware of the connections between the various lessons.
- The extent to which rescue skills can be addressed in an introduction to whitewater kayaking class is fairly limited. Although an introduction to whitewater kayaking class offers an opportunity to give students initial exposure to those skills, you should strongly encourage students to seek additional training by participating in swift water and advanced river rescue classes.

UNIT 6, LESSON 11

▷ Leave No Trace Considerations

OVERVIEW

In this lesson students are introduced to the river conservation movement in the United States and to principles and practices of Leave No Trace as they apply to the sport of whitewater kayaking. The lesson emphasizes the role of governmental agencies in managing and protecting rivers, specific rules and regulations that govern recreational and educational use of rivers, interactions with landowners adjacent to waterways, interactions with other users of the resource, and specific environmental impacts along river corridors.

JUSTIFICATION

One of the primary goals of instructors of outdoor adventure activities is to teach students to become stewards of the natural environment. Therefore, you should teach the principles and practices of Leave No Trace as an integral aspect of a whitewater kayaking class. In particular, you should make your students aware of the potential environmental and social impacts of whitewater kayaking and what they can do to minimize those impacts. This lesson also provides an opportunity to encourage student involvement in general efforts to protect and preserve river systems around the nation and throughout the world.

GOAL

To introduce students to the river conservation movement in the United States and to the principles and practices of Leave No Trace as they apply within the sport of whitewater kayaking.

OBJECTIVES

At the end of this lesson, students will be able to

- demonstrate an awareness of the role of governmental agencies in managing and protecting the nation's waterways as well as the rules and regulations under which those waterways are managed (cognitive),
- describe common social impacts resulting from whitewater kayaking (cognitive),
- identify opportunities to become involved in the river conservation movement (cognitive),
- demonstrate good judgment in environmental decision making through their interactions with the environment and other users of the environment (psychomotor), and
- exercise care for the natural environment as well as consideration for other users of the environment (affective).

EQUIPMENT AND AREAS NEEDED

Visual aids and environmental examples that illustrate the principles and practices of Leave No Trace

RISK MANAGEMENT CONSIDERATIONS

- When picking up others' trash, be careful of sharp objects (such as glass and metal) and potentially contaminated materials such as toilet paper.
- Help students identify appropriate ways to confront others who are causing negative impacts and to recognize when confrontation is not safe or appropriate (that is, when to call law enforcement instead).

LESSON CONTENT

Introduction

- The American Canoe Association (founded in 1880), American Whitewater (founded in 1954), and American Rivers (founded in 1973) are three prominent organizations in the United States dedicated to river conservation and stewardship. These organizations are committed to restoring and protecting America's rivers and waterways for the sake of sustaining both healthy water resources and quality recreational use of those resources. Our waterways are the lifeblood of our sport. Invite your students to join the movement to protect them.

- Students have surely heard the quote, "Take only pictures, leave only footprints." Paddlers leave only a small wake that will soon dissipate. Consequently, paddling can be one of the most environmentally friendly modes of travel.
- Briefly review the principles and practices of Leave No Trace to frame the discussion (see appendix A).
- Activities focus on three primary concerns specific to whitewater kayaking: the role of governmental agencies in managing and protecting our nation's waterways (including rules and regulations that govern recreational use of those waterways), interactions with other users of river environments, and environmental impacts specific to whitewater kayaking.

Important Terms

asymmetrical conflict—A situation in which one party perceives conflict to exist while another party does not. For example, encounters between jet skiers and paddlers often create aggravation and tension among paddlers but not among jet skiers. Asymmetrical conflict occurs when perceptions of conflict are one-sided (Vaske, Dyar, & Timmons, 2004; Vaske, Donnelly, Whittmann, & Laidlaw, 1995).

Main Activities

Activity 1: Plan Ahead and Prepare (45 Minutes)

This activity relates to the Leave No Trace principle "Plan ahead and prepare." Involve students in the task of planning a river trip to a federally protected stretch of river. Choose a popular stretch of river that will capture the imagination of your students, such as the Colorado River in the Grand Canyon. Working in pairs, students must discover what the group must do to obtain permission to run the river. Students must also find all applicable rules and regulations that affect recreational use of the river. Students then report their findings to the class. Use these reports as an opportunity to discuss the following points:

- Introduce governmental agencies responsible for managing the nation's rivers, including the Bureau of Reclamation, the Army Corps of Engineers, the National Park Service, the National Forest Service, state departments of natural resources, municipal parks, and so on.
- Introduce various river designations under which rivers are managed and protected: wild and scenic rivers, national rivers, national recreation areas, American heritage rivers, Nationwide Rivers Inventory, state scenic river systems, greenways and water trails, and so on. Help students distinguish between different agencies and different river designations by offering examples, two of which are the Maryland Department of Natural Resources' Greenways and Water Trails program (see www.dnr.state.md.us/greenways/commission.html for information) and the Chattooga River in North Carolina, South Carolina, and Georgia. The Chattooga is designated as a wild and scenic river and falls within the jurisdiction of the National Forest Service (see www.fs.fed.us/r8/fms/forest/recreation/chattooga.shtml for information).

◆ Discuss differences in permitting across governmental agencies and across tiers of government, and differences in rules and regulations from agency to agency and river to river.

◆ Discuss the value of effective resource management as a tool for mitigating conflicts among multiple users of the resource.

◆ Discuss water rights issues in the western United States, river access on private property, and landowner relations.

Activity 2: Be Considerate of Others (45 Minutes)

This lesson relates to the Leave No Trace principle "Be considerate of others." Introduce this activity by stating the golden rule: "Do unto others as you would have them do unto you." Introduce a series of scenarios to the group and ask them how they would like to be treated in each scenario.

Scenario 1   You have taken the weekend off to go fishing with a couple of your friends. You have traveled a good distance to get to your favorite fishing spot. This spot happens to be along a river that is popular among canoeists, rafters, and kayakers. Literally hundreds of paddlers travel down the river each day.

Request that students brainstorm all the negative ways in which paddlers on the river might affect the anglers. Next, ask students how they would want to be treated if they were the anglers?

Scenario 2   You and some friends are paddling down the river in kayaks when an angry landowner approaches you along the shore and yells at you to get off his river. What do you do?

Give your students time to discuss the situation as a group. Help them to formulate various options. Use this discussion as an opportunity to discuss water rights issues, instances of river access disputes among landowners and paddlers around the country, and proper ways to respond in such situations. The issue of water rights and river access is more prevalent in the western United States than it is in the East; nevertheless, heated disputes occur about this issue in the East as well.

Scenario 3   You are approaching a rapid from upstream when you suddenly see a kayaker surfing what appears to be a perfect wave in the middle of the rapid. You hesitate for a moment, giving the kayaker time to exit the wave, but the kayaker continues to surf without any regard for oncoming traffic. The rapid is narrow, and the space to maneuver around the kayaker is limited. Moreover, the kayaker is surfing in the part of the rapid that is the most fun to run. What do you do? Who has the right-of-way?

Give students a few minutes to discuss this scenario. Use this scenario as an introduction into a general discussion of river etiquette. Discuss the principle of asymmetrical conflict to evaluate the potential for conflict among users of different kinds of watercraft, such as rafts, jet skis, and kayakers. See Whiting and Varett's *The Ultimate Guide to Whitewater Kayaking* for a discussion of river etiquette.

Activity 3: Travel and Camp on Durable Surfaces (Time as Needed)

This activity relates to the Leave No Trace principle "Travel and camp on durable surfaces." Take advantage of a teachable moment to introduce students to potential environmental impacts resulting from whitewater kayaking, such as destruction of vegetation, soil compaction, bank erosion, and water turbidity. Such moments typically present themselves at put ins, take-outs, lunch stops, and portages. When the class encounters a well-worn location, point it out and discuss ways to mitigate further damage to the area. Mitigation might include proper trail maintenance, construction of steps at take-outs or put-ins, consolidating impact by walking through a sloppy trail rather than around it, and so forth.

Leave No Trace principles—Copyright: Leave No Trace Center for Outdoor Ethics. www.LNT.org.

Closure Activity

Shrinking My Footprint (30 Minutes)

Ask students to identify ways in which they have caused negative impacts on river environments or the experiences of others in the past as well as during the course (excessive noise around other users, trampling vegetation, and so on). Encourage them to resolve to avoid causing future impacts. You can facilitate this activity as a group discussion or through student journaling.

Follow-Up Activities

Activity 1: Identifying and Mitigating Local Resource Impacts (Time as Needed)

Have students identify negative impacts during the remainder of the trip and work to mitigate those impacts when possible (littering, campfire impacts along a river, and so forth).

Activity 2: Getting Involved (One Hour)

Assign students the task of exploring the Web sites of the American Canoe Association, American Whitewater, and American Rivers to introduce them to strategies for becoming involved in the river conservation movement. Design a take-home quiz that requires students to navigate through each of the sites to find specific information. Besides helping students identify opportunities to become engaged in the river conservation movement, this exercise can be used to help students identify opportunities for further training and development in the sport of whitewater kayaking. Students must submit the quiz to you before the end of the unit.

ASSESSMENT

- Check that students demonstrate awareness of the role of governmental agencies in managing and protecting the nation's waterways as well as the rules and regulations under which those waterways are managed through completion of main activity 1.

- Verify that students can describe common social impacts resulting from whitewater kayaking through a discussion of the scenarios in main activity 2.

- Confirm that students can identify ways to become involved in the river conservation movement through the take-home quiz described in follow-up activity 2.

- Assess whether students demonstrate good judgment in environmental decision making by observing their interactions with the environment during the unit.

- Evaluate whether students exercise care for the natural environment and consideration for other users by observing their actions during the unit.

TEACHING CONSIDERATIONS

The principles and practices of Leave No Trace represent a broad environmental ethic that every outdoor adventure instructor should attempt to teach to students. Like safety, this ethic should be integral to every lesson taught in whitewater kayaking or any other outdoor adventure pursuit. This lesson focuses on three activities that you can teach at different times throughout the unit. These activities address some of the primary concerns of Leave No Trace as they apply to whitewater kayaking. You could identify other concerns and address them using similar teaching techniques and lesson activities.

GLOSSARY

asymmetrical conflict—A situation in which one party perceives conflict to exist while another party does not.

back band, or back brace—Provides lumbar support, which helps the paddler maintain good posture while sitting in the kayak.

back surfing—Front surfing in reverse. In back surfing, the stern of the boat is pointed upstream.

boat plow—Involves pushing the empty boat from the current into an eddy or to shore; an alternative to the boat tow.

boat tow—Involves towing a swimmer or his or her boat from the current into an eddy or to shore.

boils—Caused by water welling up to the surface, creating what appears to be a boiling effect in the river. They are often found along eddy lines in high-volume rivers, such as the Colorado River. They are also a feature of hydraulics.

boofing—An advanced kayaking technique used to avoid vertical pins when paddling over waterfalls and steep drops.

bow—The front of the boat.

bridge abutments—A common obstacle on rivers. They should be treated like any other rock or obstruction that you encounter on the river, something to go around.

bulkheads—An alternative to foot pegs; more common than foot pegs in contemporary kayaks.

challenge by choice—A philosophy used to empower students by allowing them to determine the level of challenge that they will accept as a part of an educational activity.

chine—The sides of the boat between the deck and the hull.

cockpit—The open area in the center of the kayak where the kayaker sits.

cockpit combing—The lip around the cockpit to which the spray skirt is attached.

combat roll—A kayak roll performed in a whitewater context.

continuous flow—Characterizes a river whose rapids flow continuously from one to another with little or no break between. Continuous flow rapids are typically found on rivers with steeper gradients (more than 100 feet per mile, or 20 meters per kilometer).

C-to-C roll—The body motion used in rolling the kayak from an upside-down position to an upright position. The body and boat move from one C configuration to another as the boat rotates on the axis of its centerline from an upside-down to an upright position.

cubic feet per second (CFS)—Refers to the volume and rate of flow of water in the river. (The measure used in most countries is cubic meters per second.) One cubic foot of water is approximately 7.5 gallons of water (1 cubic meter of water is exactly 1,000 liters). River level is often measured in terms of feet or meters on a river gauge. The advantage of measuring river levels in terms of CFS is that CFS provides a true measure of the volume and rate of flow of water in a river whereas river gauges do not.

deck—The top of the boat.

diagonal waves—Waves that are diagonal to the flow of the current.

displacement hull—Kayak hull that is rounded.

downstream V, or tongue—Created by water being diverted into a channel by obstructions (rocks, canyon walls) on either side of the V. A downstream V has the appearance of a ramp or tongue of water with the vertex, or tip, of the V pointed downstream. Tongues represent the deepest and typically safest route through a rapid.

drain plug—A plug in the stern of the kayak that can be unscrewed to drain water from the boat. The drain plug must be screwed in at the start of each paddling experience.

drop pool—Characterizes a river whose rapids are separated by pools of water. Drop pool rapids are typically found on rivers with minor to moderate river gradients (a gradient of 5 to 50 feet per mile, or 1 to 10 meters per kilometer).

eddy—A calm area in whitewater and moving water found behind obstructions in the river (rocks, shorelines, logs, and other obstacles).

Whitewater Kayaking
Skills and Knowledge Checklists

Skills Checklist

Note: Wet exits and Eskimo rescues are covered in unit 5, Sea Kayaking, but are included among the skills necessary for whitewater kayaking.

- ☐ Bow draw
- ☐ Stern draw
- ☐ Forward sweep
- ☐ Reverse sweep
- ☐ High brace
- ☐ Low brace
- ☐ Sculling braces
- ☐ J-lean
- ☐ Ferry

- ☐ Eddy turn
- ☐ Peel-out
- ☐ Wet exit
- ☐ Eskimo rescue
- ☐ Kayak roll (both sweep roll and C-to-C roll)
- ☐ Wave surfing (front surfing, back surfing, and spinning)
- ☐ Hole surfing (side surfing and spinning)
- ☐ Basic self-rescue (passive and aggressive whitewater swimming)
- ☐ Basic rescue (towing a swimmer, towing a boat, and retrieving a swimmer using a throw rope)

Knowledge Checklist

- ☐ The five essentials
- ☐ Kayak anatomy

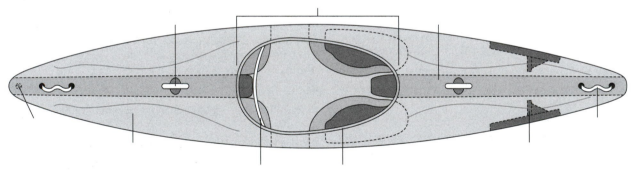

- ☐ Watershed
- ☐ River gradient
- ☐ Drop pool
- ☐ Continuous flow
- ☐ Cubic feet (meters) per second
- ☐ Horizon line
- ☐ Eddy
- ☐ Eddy line

- ☐ Downstream V (or tongue)
- ☐ Upstream V
- ☐ Wave
- ☐ Wave train
- ☐ Waterfall
- ☐ Hydraulic (or hole)
- ☐ Pillows

- ☐ Undercut rocks
- ☐ Rock sieve
- ☐ Strainer
- ☐ American Whitewater (AW) safety code
- ☐ AW river classifications
- ☐ AW river signals

Use the whitewater kayaking skills and knowledge checklists as additional tools to assess skills learned throughout this unit.

From M. Wagstaff and A. Attarian, 2009, *Technical skills for adventure programming: A curriculum guide* (Champaign, IL: Human Kinetics).

eddy line—The divide between current flowing upstream in an eddy and current moving downstream around the obstruction that is creating the eddy.

eddy turn—A stopping maneuver in which the kayak moves from the downstream current into an eddy.

ferries—Used to maneuver a boat laterally across the current. The two types of ferries are upstream ferries and downstream ferries.

foot pegs—Point at which feet contact the kayak. Foot pegs are adjustable to accommodate different leg lengths among paddlers.

front surfing—The most common form of wave surfing; involves pointing the bow of the boat upstream and keeping the angle of the boat in line with the direction of the flow.

grab loop—Loops at both ends of the boat used primarily for carrying the boat but also for assisted rescues when on the river.

haystacks (backbreaking or cresting waves)—Waves that surge upward into an unstable mass of whitewater.

hip pads—Padding that helps to ensure a snug fit, keeping the paddler from shifting around in the seat of the kayak, thus making it easier to tilt, edge, or lean the boat.

hip snap—Movement of the hips from one side to another to initiate the C-to-C.

hole surfing—Performed when the kayaker enters a hydraulic and keeps the kayak perpendicular to the direction of flow. Gravity holds the kayak in the hole, aided by the circular flow of the water.

horizon line—On a river, the line at which the surface of the water meets the sky from the perspective of the paddler. Horizon lines are created when the river suddenly drops over ledges or falls or disappears around bends.

horizontal pins (or broaches)—Occur when a kayak broaches sideways against a rock, strainer, or other obstruction in the river. In a horizontal pin, the force of the current applies hundreds of pounds (kilograms) of pressure against the kayak, trapping it against the obstruction.

hull—The bottom of the boat.

hydraulics, or holes—A horizontal whirlpool created by water dropping over a ledge and being recirculated at the base of the ledge.

kayak roll—Technique used to maneuver a kayak from an upside-down position to an upright position without assistance.

keeper hydraulics—Hydraulics that can hold debris, boats, and people in their recirculating currents. Being able to distinguish between friendly and unfriendly hydraulics is essential in whitewater kayaking (see lesson 5 for further details).

log jams—Created when trees fall into the river and collect all sorts of debris and flotsam on their upstream sides. Paddlers should avoid them. They pose the same risk as undercut rocks and strainers. If you find yourself underneath one, rescue is extremely difficult if not impossible.

low-head dams—Human-made contraptions found on most rivers throughout the United States. Many were created to divert water into canals, irrigation ditches, and hydropower plants. Water flows over the tops of these dams, typically creating keeper hydraulics at the base of the dams. These are particularly dangerous river features and must always be avoided by conducting a portage.

objective risks—Risks that arise from the natural environment (for example, extreme weather; high water; animals; level of challenge presented by the river; and specific river hazards such as strainers, undercut rocks, and keeper hydraulics).

paddler's box—An imaginary box within which hands and arms should be kept when performing nearly all kayak strokes.

peel-out—A starting maneuver in which the kayak moves from the eddy into the current.

pillows—Formed by the current being forced over the top of a stationary obstacle such as a rock. From upstream they look like glassy mounds of water that have a small horizon line on the downstream side of the obstacle. These should be scouted before traveling over, or they should be avoided.

planing hull—Kayak hull that is flat.

rescue curve—Concept that posits that four steps intervene between participating in an outdoor adventure activity and winding up dead as a result of an accident during the activity: (1) accident prevention, (2) self-rescue, (3) rescue from within the group, and (4) rescue from an outside party. As the amount of time in responding to an incident increases, the victim's chances of survival decrease. Learning proper accident prevention and rescue techniques is essential to minimizing the risk of death because of an accident in an adventure activity.

rescue loop—Point to which carabiners and ropes can be attached to the boat for rescue purposes.

rescue PFD—A specialized PFD equipped with a harness and tether that can be used in rescue situations.

river classification—River difficulty is rated on a scale from class I to VI, I being the easiest and VI being the most extreme. See the International Scale of River Difficulty (figure WK5.6) for a description of the six river classifications.

river gradient—The average rate of descent for a river over a particular distance.

rocker—The curvature of the hull from bow to stern.

rock sieves and strainers—Jumbled piles of rocks or downed trees that act like strainers when debris, boats, and people become caught in them. They are considered as dangerous as undercut rocks.

seat—One of five primary points of contact with the kayak.

spinning—Maneuver performed by turning the kayak 360 degrees on the face of a wave or in a hydraulic.

spray skirts—Neoprene skirts used to seal the cockpit of the kayak to keep water out of the boat.

stern—The back of the boat.

subjective risks—Risks that arise from people and can be controlled by people (for example, ability level relative to the level of challenge presented by the river, horseplay, alcohol or drug use, knowledge of and preparedness for weather conditions).

thigh brace—The point at which the thighs contact the boat.

towline—A line used to tow a swimmer's kayak.

undercut rocks—A rock that is settled on an uneven kilter in the river. The upstream side is hollow underneath and can trap debris, boats, and people that are washed beneath them. Undercut rocks are one of the most dangerous features on a river. They should always be avoided.

upstream V—Unlike a downstream V, signifies that an obstruction is just beneath the surface of the water. The current is being diverted to either side of the obstruction, creating the V shape. The paddler should avoid these points in the river.

vertical pins—Occur when the bow of a kayak becomes trapped in a crevice as the kayak drops over a ledge or a waterfall.

wall—The foam wall along the centerline of the kayak. The wall gives structural integrity to the kayak.

waterfall—A point in the river where water drops or falls over a ledge. Waterfalls can range from only a few feet (a meter) in height to showering cascades that drop from hundreds of feet (meters) above.

watershed—Sometimes referred to as a drainage basin, a region in which all precipitation and groundwater in the region drains into one river course as it progresses toward sea level. Watersheds are separated by geographic divides, such as continental divides.

waves—Created in rivers where a change occurs in the velocity or speed of the current. A wave consists of a peak (or crest), a trough, a face, and shoulders on either side.

wave surfing—Performed by paddling a kayak onto the face of a wave and remaining there. Friction and gravity counteract one another to keep the kayaker on the face of the wave.

wave trains—A series of standing waves with short intervals between them. Waves are separated by troughs.

REFERENCES AND RESOURCES

REFERENCES

Gullion, L. (1987). *Canoeing and kayaking: Instruction manual.* Springfield, VA: American Canoe Association.

Kauffman, R., & Carlson, C. (1992, March). The rescue curve: A race against time. *American Canoeist*, pp. 10–13.

Martin, B., Cashel, C., Wagstaff, M., & Breunig, M. (2006). *Outdoor leadership: Theory and practice.* Champaign, IL: Human Kinetics.

U.S. Environmental Protection Agency. (n.d.). What is a watershed? Retrieved from www.epa.gov/owow/watershed/whatis.html

U.S. National Park Service. (n.d.). Geology fieldnotes. Retrieved from www2.nature.nps.gov/geology/parks/neri/index.cfm

Vaske, J.J., Donnelly, M.P., Whittmann, K., & Laidlaw, S. (1995). Interpersonal versus social value conflict. *Leisure Sciences*, *17*, 205–222.

Vaske, J.J., Dyar, R., & Timmons, N. (2004). Skill level and recreation conflict among skiers and snowboarders. *Leisure Sciences*, *26*, 215–225.

RESOURCES

Bennett, J. (1999). *The essential whitewater kayaker: A complete course.* Camden, ME: Ragged Mountain Press. Overview: Provides a comprehensive overview of whitewater kayaking. Excellent resource for beginner and intermediate paddlers. Includes topics such as paddling techniques, equipment, river reading, rescue techniques, and more.

EJ's play boating basics [Instructional video]. (Available from Jackson Kayak, 325 Iris Drive, Sparta, TN 38583; www.jacksonkayak.com). Overview: World freestyle kayaking champion and owner of Jackson Kayak, Eric Jackson, and Team Jackson Kayak offer lessons on performing basic play-boating techniques.

EJ's river running basics [Instructional video]. (Available from Jackson Kayak, 325 Iris Drive, Sparta, TN 38583; www.jacksonkayak.com). Overview: Eric Jackson, founder of the World Kayak Federation and Olympic champion, teaches basic river running skills and safety, accompanied by world squirt boat champion Clay Wright. This DVD represents a comprehensive instructional program that addresses equipment, trip logistics, safety, river running skills, and more. Five well-known rivers of the southeast United States are featured as the classroom.

EJ's rolling and bracing [Instructional video]. (Available from Jackson Kayak, 325 Iris Drive, Sparta, TN 38583; www.jacksonkayak.com). Overview: World freestyle kayaking champion and owner of Jackson Kayak, Eric Jackson, offers lessons on performing the sweep roll.

Give us a river [Promotional video]. (Available from Performance Video and Instruction, Inc., 550 Riverbend, Durango, CO 81301; www.performancevideo.com). Overview: This video gives a sense of the heritage of whitewater kayaking, portraying both contemporary whitewater kayaking and whitewater paddling in the 1960s and 1970s.

Hammitt, W.E., & Schneider, I.E. (2000). Recreation conflict management. In W. C. Gartner & D. W. Lime (Eds.), *Trends in outdoor recreation, leisure and tourism*. Cambridge, MA: CABI. Overview: This resource offers an overview of the nature of recreation conflicts that often arise because of interpersonal and values conflicts among multiple users of recreation resources. It offers a good framework for consideration of social impacts that result from recreational use of rivers and waterways. It relates specifically to the Leave No Trace principle "Be considerate of others."

Hampton, B., & Cole, D. (2003). *Soft paths: How to enjoy the wilderness without harming it* (3rd ed.). Mechanicsburg, PA: Stackpole Books. Overview: This text provides a comprehensive overview of Leave No Trace considerations related to outdoor adventure pursuits in general. Sections of the book address Leave No Trace principles and practices as they relate specifically to lakes and rivers.

Heads up: River rescue for river runners [Instructional video]. Available from the American Canoe Association, 7432 Alban Station Blvd., Suite B-232, Springfield, VA 22150; www.acanet.org). Overview: A 20-minute video that provides an excellent illustration of the concepts of self-rescue and assisted-rescue as they apply to whitewater kayaking, canoeing, and rafting.

Jackson Kayak 2006 promo video [Promotional video]. (Available from Jackson Kayak, 325 Iris Drive, Sparta, TN 38583; www.jacksonkayak.com). Overview: This video provides excellent footage of world champion kayaker Eric Jackson and Team Jackson Kayak performing a wide range of play-boating and river-running techniques on the Nile and Zambezi rivers in Africa. The well-made video is accompanied by a soundtrack that captures the flavor of the region.

The kayak roll [Instructional video]. (Available from Performance Video and Instruction, Inc., 550 Riverbend, Durango, CO 81301; www.performancevideo.com) Overview: World champion paddler, former U.S. junior national team coach, and former Nantahala Outdoor Center manager Kent Ford offers lessons on performing the sweep roll.

Kayaking with Eric Jackson: Strokes, concepts, and bombproofing your roll [Instructional video]. (Available from Jackson Kayak, 325 Iris Drive, Sparta, TN 38583; www.jacksonkayak.com). Overview: World freestyle kayaking champion, world slalom champion, and owner of Jackson Kayak, Eric Jackson, offers lessons on the basics of whitewater kayaking.

Lyons, B., & Pokorny, T. (2001). *Western river corridors*. In the Leave No Trace skills and ethics series. Boulder, CO: Leave No Trace. Overview: This booklet is designed to educate paddlers about how to minimize social and ecological impacts in river corridors. The booklet focuses specifically on western river corridors.

Nichols, R. (Filmmaker). (1989). *Cold, wet, and alive* [Instructional video]. Available from the American Canoe Association, 7432 Alban Station Blvd., Suite B-232, Springfield, VA 22150; www.acanet.org). Overview: This classic film provides an excellent illustration of a paddling adventure gone awry. The film looks at one of the primary risks in cold-weather paddling—hypothermia.

Podruchny, C. (2006). *Making the voyageur world: Travelers and traders in the North American fur trade*. Lincoln: University of Nebraska Press. Overview: This book recounts the history of French Canadian workers in the North American fur trade and their use of canoes as a primary mode of transportation in moving their goods to market.

Powell, J.W. (1997). *The exploration of the Colorado River and its canyons*. New York: Penguin Books. Overview: This book recounts in the words of explorer John Wesley Powell the first descent of the Colorado River through the Grand Canyon in 1874. This story gives a colorful account of river exploration in America in the 19th century. The book provides historical context for contemporary paddle sports such as whitewater kayaking.

Ray, S., & Bechdel, L. (1997). *River rescue: A manual for whitewater safety* (3rd ed.). Boston: Appalachian Mountain Club Books. Overview: This definitive resource provides a comprehensive overview of river rescue.

The river runner's edge [Instructional video]. (Available from Performance Video and Instruction, Inc., 550 Riverbend, Durango, CO 81301; www.performancevideo.com). Overview: World champion paddler, former U.S. junior national team coach, and former Nantahala Outdoor Center manager Kent Ford offers lessons on the basics of whitewater kayaking.

Taft, S.L. (2001). *The river chasers: A history of American whitewater paddling*. Mukilteo, WA: Flowering Water and Alpen Book Press. Overview: This book is an excellent source of information on the history of kayaking during the past several decades.

Walbridge, C., & Sundermacher, W.A. (1995). *Whitewater rescue manual: New techniques for canoeists, kayakers, and rafters*. Camden, ME: Ragged Mountain Press. Overview: This book is another excellent resource on river rescue. Charlie Walbridge, one of the authors, has been a leader in the field of river rescue for over 20 years.

Whitewater self-defense [Instructional video]. (Available from Performance Video and Instruction, Inc., 550 Riverbend, Durango, CO 81301; www.performancevideo.com). Overview: This instructional video offers an excellent illustration of key skills and techniques in river rescue.

Whiting, K., & Varett, K. (2004). *The ultimate guide to whitewater kayaking*. Beachburg, ON: Heliconia Press. Overview: Comprehensive guide to whitewater kayaking. Includes basic information, play-boating techniques, rescue information, tips for women, running big water, and overnight trips. An excellent resource for beginning and intermediate kayakers.

Canoeing

Laurie Gullion

▷ Introduction to Flatwater and Whitewater Canoeing

OVERVIEW

Understanding how people have traveled by canoe for thousands of years links the historic roots of canoeing to the modern recreational activity. In this lesson students learn the difference between solo and tandem canoeing on flatwater and whitewater. They also learn how different styles of canoeing have evolved in different regions of the world.

JUSTIFICATION

Understanding how modern canoeing is strongly tied to its aboriginal origins establishes a cultural context for canoeing. The student can see how the modern styles are re-creations of ancient activities.

GOAL

To develop students' understanding of the evolution of different styles of canoeing and to match each canoeist's desires and abilities to an appropriate type.

OBJECTIVES

At the end of this lesson, students will be able to

◆ identify the historical roots of canoeing (cognitive),

◆ understand the difference between solo and tandem canoeing (cognitive),

◆ understand the difference between flatwater and whitewater canoeing (cognitive),

◆ understand different styles of canoeing (cognitive), and

◆ appreciate how different styles of canoeing can enhance their enjoyment of canoeing (affective).

EQUIPMENT AND AREAS NEEDED

◆ Index cards that identify elements of canoeing history

◆ Index cards that identify different styles of canoeing

◆ One tandem touring canoe

◆ One solo whitewater canoe

RISK MANAGEMENT CONSIDERATIONS

◆ Select a teaching area that allows students to line up without hitting any equipment.

◆ Line up the two canoes so that students can walk between them and roll them over in an observational exercise.

LESSON CONTENT

Introduction

Use the following quotations as a way to engage the students' attention and introduce the main themes in this lesson:

- "The canoe is believed to be the oldest working boat in the world."
- "The canoe has been a boat for all peoples."
- "The canoe was termed a *poor man's yacht* when it gained popularity among the general public."
- "Only two concepts define canoeing."

Modern canoeing has its roots in ancient civilizations where it served as a primary mode of transportation on lakes, rivers, and oceans. Canoeing has had a timeless appeal among indigenous cultures, explorers, and modern travelers.

- The indigenous cultures of North America, Greenland, and Russia used the skins of seal, walrus, and caribou around wooden frames to create the **umiak**, or canoe. This large, undecked boat transported families over large distances. Propelled by paddling, rowing, or sailing, it was sometimes used to hunt whales. A circumpolar mode of transportation, canoes are believed to be the oldest working boats in the world (Snaith, 1997).
- Rock paintings in Norway from 3000 BC show illustrations of people paddling large vessels and hunting from what archaeologists believe to be skin boats.
- The basic design of these ancient craft was symmetrical and functional. Local materials were used in their construction; logs, bark, reeds, and animal skins are present in boats preserved in cold bogs or depicted in ancient pictographs (Snaith, 1997).
- Local needs are reflected as well; Polynesian cultures added outriggers to their canoes to explore thousands of miles (kilometers) of the South Pacific, and Asian peoples prized the stability of the canoe in exploring the New World (Kawaharada, n.d.).
- Canoeing as a modern recreational activity began in Canada in 1850 when Ontario craftsmen began to build plank-style canoes for wealthy explorers who wanted access to the interior of the country (Jennings, 2002).
- Interest in recreational canoe travel in the United States rose in the latter part of the century as "sports" hired guides for fishing and hunting on remote lakes and rivers (Bond, 1995).
- By the end of the century, craftsmen were able to produce canoes at a more affordable price, which led to an explosion of interest among the public in North America. This "poor man's yacht" made canoeing as popular as bicycling and led to the rise of canoeing clubs, regattas, national conventions, and organizations like the American Canoe Association (Jennings, 2002).
- Women's colleges like Smith and Wellesley believed that canoeing was a natural and healthy activity for young women, although "manless canoeing" still tended to be viewed with suspicion if vigorously performed (Gullion, 1999).

Two important concepts define canoeing:

◆ A canoeist sits or kneels in the boat, whether it is open or decked (covered).

◆ A canoeist uses a single-bladed paddle.

In any case, the canoeist must select and use appropriate equipment for different types of canoeing in different environments:

◆ A canoe with a sharply pointed **bow** will slice cleanly through the water and go straighter than a canoe with a wider bow that plows through flatwater.

◆ A canoe with rounded ends that is shaped more like a banana from front to back will turn quicker in **whitewater**.

Main Activities

Activity 1: Canoe History (10 Minutes)

Provide a quick introduction to canoe history by establishing that the activity is estimated to be 5,000 years old. Explain that all forms of canoeing today have their roots in ancient uses.

◆ Copy the canoeing history cards in figure CA1.1 (or print them from the CD-ROM) and distribute one card to each student. Encourage them to discuss the information on the cards. Explain that some facts can be from the same era.

◆ Ask students to cluster up in small groups that reflect the development of canoeing. Then create an overall order from the small groups.

Activity 2: Tandem Versus Solo Canoes (10 Minutes)

Line up a tandem flatwater canoe and a solo whitewater canoe next to each other. Have students in small groups examine each boat and ask them to define the difference between **tandem** and **solo canoeing**. Ask them to consider the effect of the seat positions on boat control when going straight and turning.

◆ The solo canoeist swings the paddle horizontally in a full 180-degree arc from front to back to explore the extent of her or his reach away from the center (pivot point) of the canoe.

◆ The tandem canoeists trace a smaller arc that shows the range of their paddling: the bow paddler uses a 90-degree arc from the hip forward to the bow, and the stern paddler uses a 90-degree arc from the hip backward to the stern. Discuss the tandem paddlers to consider the different responsibilities of the two positions. Ask the students to consider the different challenges and rewards of each craft.

◆ A solo canoeist sits near the middle of the canoe to have better control of both ends. The paddler must perform the functions of both the bow (front) canoeist and the stern (rear) canoeist, which can be physically and mentally challenging. A solo canoeist, however, can experience enormous satisfaction and confidence in mastering the canoe alone.

◆ Tandem canoeing divides the responsibilities between the bow and stern paddlers. Bow paddlers set the pace, and stern paddlers keep the boat on track and match their partners' pace. In whitewater, a bow canoeist has the additional responsibility of choosing a specific route through obstacles. Communication between partners can be challenging, but the cooperation required to canoe effectively is rewarding.

Canoeing History Cards

Umiaks, or canoes, transported large family groups to new settlements.	Umiaks were originally made from walrus, seal, and caribou skins.
Rock paintings in Norway show skin boats for transportation and hunting from 3000 BC.	Skin boats of 25 to 40 feet (8 to 12 meters) could be paddled, rowed, or sailed long distances.
Canoeing originated in circumpolar regions of the North.	Polynesian canoeists added outriggers to their boats for long-distance ocean travel.
Post-Victorian attitudes viewed the canoe as a means to healthy recreation.	Canoeing became a vehicle for cruising, camping, and courting.
Canadian boat builders modified fur-trapping expedition boats into sleeker, easily constructed canoes.	The canoe, viewed as the poor man's yacht, experienced explosive growth as a form of recreation in the United States and Europe after John MacGregor wrote a travelogue called *A Thousand Miles in the Rob Roy Canoe on the Rivers and Lakes of Europe.*
Women's colleges like Smith and Wellesley added canoeing to their physical education curriculum when post-Victorian attitudes viewed exercise as beneficial to women.	Urban canoe clubs grow in popularity at the turn of the 20th century as they attracted thousands of members, constructed elaborate boathouses, and sponsored major sporting events such as regattas and canoe races.

FIGURE CA1.1   Historical facts about canoeing.

From M. Wagstaff and A. Attarian, 2009, *Technical skills for adventure programming: A curriculum guide* (Champaign, IL: Human Kinetics).

Activity 3: Canoeing Styles (10 Minutes)

Ask the students to brainstorm the difference between flatwater and whitewater canoeing.

◆ Flatwater canoeing enables paddlers to move on the calm water of lakes and rivers, where current is not a variable.

◆ Whitewater canoeing lets paddlers explore moving water in rivers, where the current begins to speed up and flow around and over obstacles such as rocks to create interesting river features.

Copy the canoeing style cards in figure CA1.2 (or print them from the CD-ROM) and distribute one card to each small group. Ask them to determine whether either canoe is an acceptable choice for their style of canoeing.

Canoeing Style Cards

Freestyle Canoeing

Smooth, flowing, gymnastic maneuvers set to music; sometimes called canoe ballet or canoe dancing. Judges grade technical and artistic merit. The canoeist often leans the canoe aggressively on its side to turn it more easily.

Marathon Racing

A flatwater event in which canoeists race various distances from 5 miles (8 kilometers) to ultramarathon distances of 250 miles (400 kilometers). Some routes require portages. A whitewater variation called downriver racing requires that canoeists descend rapids and avoid obstacles. Longer boats that go straighter are best.

Canoe Poling

The canoeist uses a 12-foot (4-meter) pole to go upriver or downriver, often but not always in shallow water. A canoeist who poles can perform the same maneuvers as a whitewater canoeist. A flat-bottomed boat offers the best stability.

Whitewater Rodeo

Competition in which paddlers execute maneuvers in a river play spot characterized by waves and holes. Judges score the competitors on artistry and degree of difficulty. Short boats with lots of flotation bags to displace water are best.

Canoe Slalom

A style of recreational racing in whitewater where canoeists navigate a 25-gate (hanging pole) course in upstream- or downstream-facing positions. The fastest elapsed time wins, and touched poles result in added time penalties. Short boats that change directions quickly are best.

Outrigger Canoeing

A team style of canoeing in long, ocean-worthy boats with outriggers for enhanced stability.

FIGURE CA1.2   Six styles of canoeing.

From M. Wagstaff and A. Attarian, 2009, *Technical skills for adventure programming: A curriculum guide* (Champaign, IL: Human Kinetics).

Closure Activity

History Quiz (Five Minutes)

Divide the class into teams and ask whether they can connect a style of canoeing to its origins based on their new knowledge of canoeing history. The oldest activities are **marathon racing** and **outrigger canoeing**, which have their origins in the long-distance traveling of aboriginal cultures. **Canoe poling** is historically associated with Native American travel and later the fur trappers who hunted the interior waterways of North America. **Canoe slalom**, **freestyle canoeing**, and **whitewater rodeo** are modern inventions.

Follow-Up Activity

Styles of Canoeing (10 Minutes)

Ask students to identify a style of canoeing that interests them and to use the resources available on the Internet or identified at the end of this unit to obtain additional information about its modern form. They can focus on opportunities for participation and competition, which they can share with other participants later.

ASSESSMENT

- ◆ Check that students can identify the historic roots of canoeing by observing how they cluster the history cards into two groupings.
- ◆ Verify that students understand the difference between solo canoeing and tandem canoeing by listening to their discussion of the differences between the two types during main activity 2.
- ◆ Confirm that students understand the difference between flatwater and whitewater canoeing by observing their brainstorming discussion of characteristics during main activity 3.
- ◆ Check that students understand different styles of canoeing by observing how they determine whether the sample canoes are suitable for different styles of canoeing.
- ◆ Assess whether students appreciate how different styles of canoeing can enhance enjoyment by noting their desire to apply their canoeing skills and knowledge from the course to a particular style of canoeing.

TEACHING CONSIDERATIONS

- ◆ Keep the focus on the cultural context and general time periods rather than specific dates. Keep in mind that certain types of learners will want to know dates and more specifics. Have additional resources available for those learners.
- ◆ Your sample boats will probably not be representative of all canoeing styles. You can supplement your style cards with magazine and Web site photos that show the activity and the boats more clearly.
- ◆ Consider assigning homework related to researching boat types and styles instead of using class time to obtain this information.

▷ Canoeing Equipment and Use

OVERVIEW

Choosing the appropriate type of canoe and paddle is essential to paddling efficiently in flatwater and whitewater. In this lesson students learn the parts and function of canoes and paddles.

JUSTIFICATION

Understanding the functional performance of a canoe and paddle is essential for each student to paddle safely and enjoyably in a variety of water conditions.

GOAL

To instill an understanding of canoe and paddle design so that participants can select and use appropriate equipment for flatwater and whitewater canoeing.

OBJECTIVES

At the end of this lesson, students will be able to

* identify the basic parts of a canoe and a paddle (cognitive),
* understand how canoe design affects its function (cognitive),
* select and appropriately size a paddle (psychomotor),
* appreciate the difference between a flatwater canoe and a whitewater canoe (affective), and
* appreciate the use of an appropriately sized paddle (affective).

EQUIPMENT AND AREAS NEEDED

* One flatwater canoe
* One whitewater canoe with safety lines, flotation, knee pads, and thigh straps
* Straight-shaft paddle (one per student)
* Bent-shaft paddle (at least one paddle)
* Set of flash cards (with boat part names and definitions) for each team

RISK MANAGEMENT CONSIDERATIONS

* Check the outdoor teaching area for environmental hazards to running and take appropriate precautions. The canoe-part relay race involves running.
* The paddle-part game involves group action in a tight space. Encourage participants to be careful in swinging their paddles.
* Increasing the speed of the calls in the paddle-part game can create more energetic swinging of paddles. Determine whether your group can handle the activity responsibly.

LESSON CONTENT

Introduction

Use the following quotations to grab the students' attention and to introduce the main themes covered in the activities:

◆ "The paddle is your best friend, so grip the T but don't choke the throat!"

◆ "What spins faster on a flat surface—a banana or a cigar?"

◆ "What slices through butter more cleanly—a knife or a cigar?"

Selecting the appropriate canoe and paddle is essential for any canoeist. This equipment lesson focuses only on canoes and paddles. Additional necessary equipment for enjoyable outings is described in other water-based units. Figure CA2.1 shows a list of standard canoeing equipment.

Canoeing Equipment List

◆ One paddle per canoeist

◆ Spare paddle

◆ Canoe with safety lines tied to each end

◆ Personal flotation device (U.S. Coast Guard approved PFD)

◆ Helmet (whitewater)

◆ Flotation bags secured in canoe (whitewater)

◆ First aid kit

◆ Map and compass

◆ Weatherproof layers (raincoat or nylon jacket)

◆ Extra clothing (waterproofed inside a day pack or dry bag in case of capsize)

◆ Throw bag (whitewater)

◆ Dry bags

◆ Toilet kit with shovel

FIGURE CA2.1   Standard equipment that canoeists should always have.

Tell students to remember two important concepts about the paddle:

◆ Develop the habit of gripping your paddle as if it is your best friend, especially if you capsize. It is an important tool for finishing the trip!

◆ One hand holds the T in a relaxed but firm grip, and the other hand clasps the shaft rather than the throat to increase your reach with the paddle (figure CA2.2).

Two concepts are helpful for understanding how canoe design affects performance:

◆ A canoe shaped more like a banana will spin faster because its uplifted ends reduce drag against the water.

◆ A canoe with a sharply pointed bow will slice cleanly through the water and go straighter than a canoe with a wider bow that plows the water.

FIGURE CA2.2   Proper paddle grip.

Main Activities

Activity 1: Relay Race (10 Minutes)

Set up a flatwater canoe (figure CA2.3) and a whitewater canoe (figure CA2.4) in a straight line. Divide the group into two teams and have the teams gather on opposite sides of the canoes. Establish a starting line for each team, behind which the team has to conduct all group discussions.

◆ Give each team one set of cards that have the names of canoe parts (figure CA2.5) and one set of cards that have definitions of the same canoe parts (figure CA2.6). Some cards focus on the differences between a flatwater canoe and a whitewater canoe.

◆ Allow the teams an opportunity to inspect the boats. Encourage the students to examine all parts.

◆ When the relay race begins, teams can send only one member at a time to place the boat-part card and matching definition card on the appropriate part.

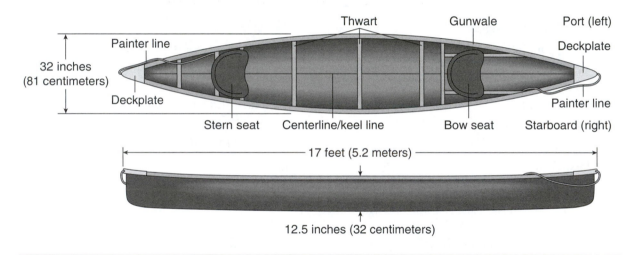

FIGURE CA2.3   Flatwater canoe.

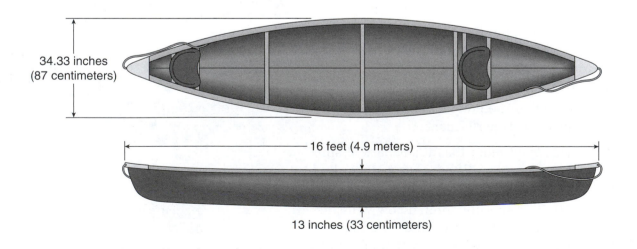

FIGURE CA2.4   Whitewater canoe anatomy.

Canoe Parts

Beam	Bow
Centerline	Deck plates
Flare	Gunwale
Hull	Painter lines
Port	Rocker
Starboard	Stem
Thwart	Tumblehome

FIGURE CA2.5   Teams will match these terms with the corresponding definitions in figure CA2.6.

From M. Wagstaff and A. Attarian, 2009, *Technical skills for adventure programming: A curriculum guide* (Champaign, IL: Human Kinetics).

Definitions of Canoe Parts

The maximum width of a canoe.

The front of a canoe.

An imaginary line down the middle of the canoe from bow to stern.

Plates attached to the gunwales at the bow and stern that shed water.

The upward and outward curve of a canoe side.

The rail along the top edge of the canoe that stiffens the canoe shape.

The body of a canoe.

The safety lines attached to the end of a canoe.

The left side of a canoe when facing the bow.

The curved shape of the hull when viewed from the side.

The right side of a canoe when facing the bow.

Upright part of the bow where the sides meet.

A crosspiece on a canoe that attaches to the gunwales and stiffens the canoe shape.

The inward sloping of the upper canoe sides.

FIGURE CA2.6   Teams will match these definitions to the terms in figure CA2.5.

From M. Wagstaff and A. Attarian, 2009, *Technical skills for adventure programming: A curriculum guide* (Champaign, IL: Human Kinetics).

Activity 2: Canoe Design (10 Minutes)

Ask each team to explain the functional design of a flatwater canoe and a white-water canoe.

◆ A flatwater canoe (figure CA2.7) is a longer, narrower boat, often with a straighter **stem**, that tracks straighter through the water and is more difficult to turn. It often has a flatter bottom that provides greater initial stability (when the canoe sits upright in the water). Sometimes it has **tumblehome**, which makes stroking near the canoe easier but adversely affects secondary stability (when the canoe is leaned on one side).

◆ A whitewater canoe (figure CA2.8) is a shorter boat with more rounded (rockered) ends that turns easier. It can have a more rounded or V-shaped **hull** that enhances boat lean. A whitewater canoe with a **flare** design will shed water more easily and stay drier in waves.

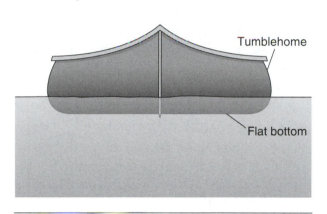

FIGURE CA2.7   Hull design of flatwater canoe.

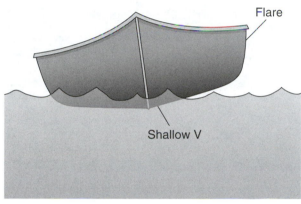

FIGURE CA2.8   Hull design of whitewater canoe.

Ask students to compare the two boats and find the similarities and differences. Follow up with these questions:

◆ How fast will each boat turn?

◆ How tippy is each canoe?

◆ How stable is the boat lean?

◆ How dry is each boat?

Activity 3: Introduction to Paddles (10 Minutes)

Divide the group into pairs and give each person a canoe paddle.

◆ Include at least one bent-shaft paddle in the pool of straight-shaft paddles. Briefly explain that a bent-shaft paddle slides faster into the optimal position for power application. Figure CA2.9 shows how the blade of a bent-shaft paddle sticks, or gets vertical, faster than the blade of a straight-shaft paddle does.

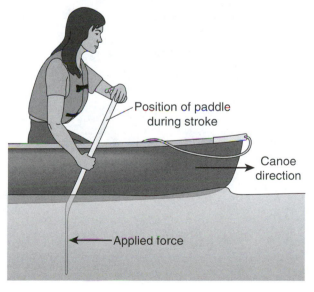

FIGURE CA2.9   Bent-shaft blade vertical at catch.

◆ Partners stand next to each other as the group forms a big circle. Ask partners to touch paddle parts together when a part is called out, and to be ready to move to another position in the circle (and to a new partner) when you call, "Paddle to paddle." When new partners greet each other, they have to hold their paddles in the high-five position and tap them together.

◆ Have students hold their paddles above their heads with the elbows at right angles (figure CA2.2). Let them know that this position is the best way to check their grip on the paddle before canoeing.

◆ Warm up by calling out parts slowly. Simplify the learning by calling out the same parts, that is, "Shaft to shaft" or "Blade to blade." Then increase the challenge by mixing up the parts, that is, "Tip to grip" or "Throat to grip." Call, "Paddle to paddle" about every fourth call. Gradually increase the speed of the calls.

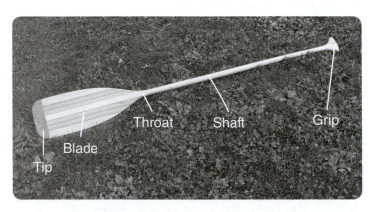

FIGURE CA2.10   Paddle parts.

Parts of a Paddle   The following terms identify basic paddle parts (figure CA2.10).

◆ Blade—the wider part of the paddle that is inserted fully into the water; the side pressed against the water is the **power face**, and the opposite side is the **back face**.

◆ **Shaft**—the section attached to the blade that a paddler will grip with one hand.

◆ Throat—the curved section of a blade where it attaches to the shaft. Paddlers should not grip the paddle at the throat because doing so compromises the ability to reach out.

◆ **Grip**—the handle of the paddle that a paddler grabs with one hand. The grip can be shaped like a T, a shape that allows greater control in changing the blade angle, or it can be pear shaped, a shape that is more relaxing for paddling on flatwater.

◆ Tip—the edge of the blade opposite the throat.

Activity 4: Paddle Use (Five Minutes)

◆ Ask each student to select a paddle that is properly sized for his or her torso and arm length. The simplest method is to place the **T grip** in the armpit and extend the arm along the paddle. The hand should rest on the shaft with clearance between it and the throat.

◆ Explain that when a canoeist takes a stroke with the blade fully inserted in the water, the grip should be about nose height. A simple check is to invert the paddle and place the grip on the floor. With the buttocks lowered to approximate seat height, the paddle throat should be between the chin and forehead (figure CA2.11).

FIGURE CA2.11   Sizing a paddle.

◆ Demonstrate a forward stroke with a straight-shaft paddle and with a bent-shaft paddle. Ask the students to watch when the blade assumes a vertical position in the water. Reinforce that a bent-shaft paddle reaches a vertical position more quickly, which means that it catches water faster at the optimal angle (90 degrees) to provide propulsion.

Closure Activity

Looking at Differences (10 Minutes)

Demonstrate the concepts discussed in the main activity section by demonstrating performance differences between flatwater and whitewater canoes.

◆ In a body of flat water, have a tandem team with paddling experience demonstrate boat **spins** in flatwater and whitewater canoes. Have the team perform boat leans as well.

◆ Have the group critique and compare the differences between the ways that the boats handle. This discussion will emphasize the importance of hull design and its function.

Follow-Up Activity

Reinforce Proper Paddle Size (10 Minutes)

After the closure activity is complete, provide the demonstration tandem team with paddles that are inappropriate in size. Have them conduct the spins a second time. Ask the students to critique body position and the effort required to paddle with inappropriately sized paddles. To accentuate the issues, try to obtain paddles with extremely long shafts for this exercise. This exercise flows well into lessons 5 and 6 when students learn basic **strokes**.

ASSESSMENT

◆ Check that students can identify the basic parts of the canoe paddle by observing how they identify the canoe and paddle parts during main activities 1 and 3.

◆ Verify the students' explanation of the functional design of each canoe and correct any incorrect explanations.

◆ Confirm that students understand how canoe design affects its function by listening to their comparison of the functional characteristics of the two boats, and confirm their analysis of similarities and differences.

◆ Check that students can select and appropriately size a paddle by confirming their paddle selections in main activity 4.

◆ Make sure that students appreciate the difference between flatwater and whitewater canoes by listening to their discussion of which canoes are appropriate for flatwater and whitewater activities, and check that they understand the differences in canoe design.

◆ Verify that students appreciate the use of an appropriately sized paddle by listening to their discussion of the issues regarding inappropriately sized paddles in the follow-up activity.

TEACHING CONSIDERATIONS

◆ Some terms can be confusing, and a team may not have the knowledge among its members. Depending on age, consider giving students hints to aid their problem solving or challenge them to continue debating answers within the group. Eliminate the more challenging cards, if needed, and use only the simplest definitions.

◆ Some students want more technical information about equipment. Determine whether enough group members are interested before fielding advanced design questions.

◆ Students can learn paddle parts quickly, so don't run the paddle activity too long.

UNIT 7, LESSON 3

▷ Transport, Carries, and Launches

OVERVIEW

Getting a canoe to the lake or river requires an understanding of how to lift a canoe, transport it on a vehicle or trailer, and carry it to the water. In this lesson students learn how to lift and carry a canoe safely. They also learn useful knots for tying a canoe to racks on a trailer. Finally, they learn how to stabilize and enter a canoe.

JUSTIFICATION

Carrying a canoe efficiently helps avoid back injury. Securing a boat properly to a vehicle is the responsibility of the driver. Stabilizing a canoe during entry helps avoid a common cause of capsizes.

GOAL

To develop participants' ability to transport, carry, and enter a canoe in preparation for learning to paddle.

OBJECTIVES

At the end of this lesson, students will be able to

◆ recognize unsafe body positions to avoid injury (cognitive),

◆ lift a canoe on and off a boat trailer (psychomotor),

◆ tie a canoe securely to a roof rack (psychomotor),

◆ use a tandem hand carry to transport a canoe to the shore (psychomotor),

◆ use an overhead carry to transport a canoe to the shore (psychomotor),

◆ stabilize and enter a canoe from a shore or dock (psychomotor), and

◆ enhance safety by consistently using the body effectively (affective).

EQUIPMENT AND AREAS NEEDED

◆ Canoes with two painter lines (enough for all students to be seated)

◆ Ropes or webbing for tie-downs (two ropes per canoe)

◆ PFDs (required for all on-water activities in all lessons)

◆ Boat trailer

RISK MANAGEMENT CONSIDERATIONS

◆ Use a teaching area that is large enough for partners to remove canoes from trailers and execute overhead carries without hitting other teams.

◆ Have students spot other teams who may need assistance with unloading or lifting canoes.

◆ Consider teams of more than two people if necessary to lift and transport canoes.

◆ Orient students to proper use of the back when lifting to avoid injury.

LESSON CONTENT

Introduction (Five Minutes)

Review the following with the students before beginning the main activity. These sayings will remind them to be conscious of safety when transporting canoes.

◆ "Lift and lower a canoe with your back and legs, not your arms!"

◆ "If one rope on a tie-down is good, then two are even better! If one knot is good, then two are better!"

◆ "Three points of contact with the canoe at all times when entering!"

◆ "Stay low and go!"

Remind students of these points when they are lifting and lowering a canoe:

◆ Bend your legs and keep your back straight when lifting and lowering a canoe. Don't bend over at the waist, which will stress the low back. Let your legs do the work of lifting and lowering.

◆ Communicate with your partner when lifting and transporting a canoe to improve balance and timing. Look at each other and be explicit with directions to be coordinated.

Main Activity

Practicing Essential Skills (One Hour)

You should model and have students practice the eight skills listed in the main activity at the appropriate time during the activity sequence. The specific situation, transportation resources, and paddling area will suggest a logical sequence for the instructional progression of carries, tie-downs, and entering the canoe properly.

Skill 1: Loading Canoe Trailers   Pairs of students carry boats to the trailer. They practice lifting and rolling canoes onto the racks. Teams that are waiting can spot the lifts by standing near enough to the canoe to grab a **gunwale** and help with the rollover if necessary. Load all canoes before teams begin their tie-downs. Have students work in pairs to tie the trucker's hitch and half hitch.

Skill 2: Auto Tie-Down   When tying down a canoe, use two lines or webbing to secure the canoe to a car or boat rack. The boat should not shift sideways nor should it slip forward or backward when tied to the racks. To prevent sideways slippage, use a minimum of two tie-down points that will be connected directly to the vehicle rack. The trucker's hitch is an effective method when using pieces of rope or webbing. Straps with buckles or camming devices are also effective. To prevent slippage from front to back, tie the stern and bow down. Having a bow line connected to the front bumper and stern line connected to the back bumper using trucker's hitches works well.

Skill 3: Initial Carry   With a partner, demonstrate a hand carry to take the canoe to the trailer.

◆ Stand on opposite sides of the canoe near the **deck plates** to distribute the weight equally.

◆ Grab the thwarts (if available) or gunwales, lift the canoe, carry the boat to the trailer, and line it up parallel to the trailer.

◆ Show how you can place four or six people at opposite points along the canoe to make the task easier.

Skill 4: Overhead Lift   With a partner, demonstrate an overhead lift to roll a canoe onto the racks (figure CA3.1). This is also known as the portage carry.

◆ Each partner stands in front of a canoe seat on the same side of the canoe.

◆ Both of you put your left hands on the same gunwale and your right hands on the other gunwale.

◆ Bend the legs and lift the canoe to the thighs.

◆ On the count of three, roll the canoe overhead with a little knee boost. Slide the canoe onto the car racks and center it.

Skill 5: Tie-Down   Demonstrate how to tie down a canoe using a trucker's hitch.

◆ Explain how the trucker's hitch creates tight tension for a secure tie-down and is designed to prevent loosening. An example of the trucker's hitch is found in unit 1, lesson 9.

◆ The system can be untied quickly.

◆ The **painter lines** can be tied to the racks to prevent the canoe from shifting forward or backward.

Skill 6: Upright Carry or Tandem Carry   After you reach the lake or river, have students untie the canoes and prepare to carry them to the shore. Demonstrate a simple upright carry that allows canoeists to transport some gear and make only one trip if the water is only a short distance away (figure CA3.2).

◆ This is a common two-person carry for short distances.

◆ Partners stand on opposite sides of the canoe near the stern and bow deck plates.

◆ Depending on canoe design, grab the canoe by the gunwale or by the deck plate hand grips.

◆ Carrying on opposite sides balances the weight of the boat and makes for a smoother carry.

◆ Remember to lift with the legs, not the back.

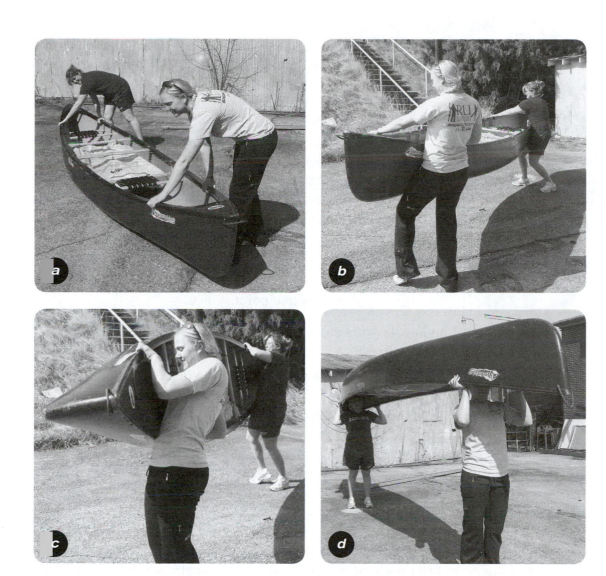

FIGURE CA3.1 Overhead lift and portage carry.

◆ If a canoe is too heavy for two people or the carry is long, discuss how four or six people can be equally spaced on opposite sides to lighten the load.

Skill 7: Overhead Carry Demonstrate the overhead, or portage, carry, which is suitable for longer distances or uneven terrain (figure CA3.1*d*).

◆ At the racks, you and a partner face in the same direction, each standing in front of a seat.

◆ Reach under the canoe to grab the opposite gunwale and slide the canoe off the racks and over your heads.

◆ Let the seat edge rest on the back of your neck and walk to the shore. The taller person should be in front to increase visibility.

FIGURE CA3.2 Upright carry or tandem carry.

FIGURE CA3.3 Entering a canoe.

Skill 6: Entering a Canoe The easiest way to enter a canoe from a dock or the shore is from the side. A partner can hold the gunwales and stabilize the canoe, while you demonstrate a side entry (figure CA3.3).

♦ Step carefully into the center of the canoe ahead of the seat, keeping your hands on the gunwales and your weight low.

♦ Sit quickly on the seat, and stay centered while your partner enters.

♦ Only one person at a time moves in a canoe.

♦ The most stable position is kneeling in the canoe with your buttocks resting against the seat for a solid three-point stance.

Also demonstrate how to enter a canoe from the end, a method that is helpful when entering from a brushy shore.

♦ A partner holds the gunwales, while you step over the deck plate and along the **centerline**.

♦ Keep your weight low and slide both hands along the gunwales to move to the opposite end.

Closure Activity

Skill Evaluation (15 Minutes)

Create teams of two boats, consisting of either two solo canoeists or four tandem canoeists. The team members work together to evaluate the new skills. Each team watches the other team perform overhead carries and boat entries. The observers check that the carrying team is being mindful of back health by lifting properly (with bent legs and a straight back) and that the entering team is using three points of contact.

Follow-Up Activity

Loading a Personal Vehicle (15 Minutes)

Have the students load and tie a canoe on a personal vehicle. Use a vehicle with a rack suitable for carrying a canoe. Typically, securing a canoe on a vehicle is a bit more problematic than securing a canoe on a trailer and requires some problem solving because of differences in vehicle designs.

♦ As mentioned earlier in this lesson, make sure that they tie two lines over the hull of the canoe—one affixed to the front rack and a separate line affixed to the rear rack.

♦ Use the canoe safety lines for tie-downs to the front and back bumpers to prevent the boat from shifting on the racks.

♦ Be sure that each line is taut to prevent shifting.

Canoeing ◆ **511**

ASSESSMENT

- Check that students recognize unsafe body positions that may cause injury by asking them to monitor whether other teams are safely lifting and carrying canoes.

- Confirm that students can lift a canoe on and off a boat trailer by checking to see whether teams can lift and roll a canoe onto a vehicle or trailer in one motion.

- Verify that students can tie a canoe securely to a trailer by jiggling the canoes to test the tightness of the tie-downs.

- Confirm that students can use a tandem hand carry by gripping the canoe on opposite sides. Require this to be the first carry that students perform as they practice the skills during the main activity.

- Confirm that students can execute an overhead portage carry as they practice the skills during the main activity by positioning themselves in front of the canoe seats and having the taller person in front for improved visibility.

- Check that students can stabilize a canoe from a shore or dock by monitoring whether the canoe rocks as they enter it.

- Confirm that students enhance personal safety by consistently lifting canoes with bent legs and a straight back.

TEACHING CONSIDERATIONS

- Pair up students of similar height so that the canoe is level for an overhead carry and thus easier to carry.

- During every segment, encourage students who complete tasks quickly to aid any teams who appear to be struggling.

- Offer students the option of receiving additional support to lift a canoe overhead, especially if your canoes are heavy. Some students may have difficulty rolling the canoe overhead but can carry it without difficulty after the canoe is in place.

- Check to make sure that students are not experiencing any back strain from lifts and carries.

- Consider modeling four-person or six-person carries to emphasize the concept of safety and teamwork.

- Pair up a student skilled with a trucker's hitch and half hitch with a student who is learning the knots.

- Encourage tandem carries because they promote sociability and enable a weaker person to contribute to the common good. Be aware that solo carries can create a competitive climate or a division within a group between those who are strong enough to solo carry and those who are not.

- Watch students carefully when they enter the canoes. Most capsizes occur at shore as people destabilize the canoe while stepping into it.

▷ Preparing to Paddle

OVERVIEW

Understanding basic body mechanics is essential to fluid paddling. Students learn in this lesson how to warm up their muscles for canoeing through fundamental body positions used in all strokes and maneuvers. They also learn optimum balance for leaning their canoes to execute various maneuvers during later lessons.

JUSTIFICATION

Knowing several key body positions not only helps canoeists become stronger paddlers but also protects their bodies from injury. Improving balance will also enhance canoeists' abilities to lean canoes appropriately and avoid capsizing.

GOAL

To develop students' ability to balance a canoe using efficient body dynamics.

OBJECTIVES

At the end of this lesson, students will be able to

- recognize unsafe body positions so that they avoid injury (cognitive),
- stretch core muscles to prepare for paddling (psychomotor),
- execute a controlled boat lean (psychomotor),
- enhance safety by consistently exiting the canoe safely (affective), and
- consistently practice and model efficient body positions that promote effortless canoeing (affective).

EQUIPMENT AND AREAS NEEDED

- Canoes for the entire group
- Paddles for each student
- Helmets, if using a whitewater canoe with thigh straps

RISK MANAGEMENT CONSIDERATIONS

- Monitor student body positions so that backs and shoulders are not overextended when practicing proper body movement.
- When capsizing boats, ensure that life jackets are properly fitted and worn at all times. Also, ensure safe distances between canoes.
- Be aware of swimming abilities and general comfort in the water before executing capsizing activities. Consider organizing a quick swim test to make this assessment.

LESSON CONTENT

Introduction

Most novice paddlers assume that the power and technique for a good canoe stroke is found in arm movement. Share the following important pieces of advice to rebut this false assumption:

◆ "Drive your paddle with your abdominal muscles!"
◆ "Lean a canoe with your lower body!"
◆ "Turn a canoe with your knees!"

Three important concepts related to body position and movement are keeping a straight lower arm, staying within the paddler's box, and doing a J-lean.

Straight Lower Arm   All strokes act as a brace against the water, which creates a more stable craft. Keep your lower arm relatively straight through all strokes, which forces your stronger abdominal muscles to rotate and power the strokes (figure CA4.1).

Paddler's Box   Always keep your hands and paddle in front of your torso within the paddler's box (figure CA4.2). When your torso rotates through a stroke, the imaginary box rotates, too.

J-Lean   Separate your upper body from your lower body. The legs and hips can then control boat lean, called a J-lean, while the torso remains relatively upright and can rotate more effectively through the strokes. This separation creates a J shape between legs and torso (figure CA4.3).

◆ In shallow water, present this demonstration to the students. Hold your paddle vertically with the blade on the lake bottom. Show how you can move the canoe toward the paddle by drawing the knees to the blade.

FIGURE CA4.1   Keep a straight lower arm.

FIGURE CA4.2   Paddler's box.

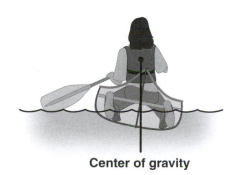

Center of gravity

FIGURE CA4.3   J-lean.

Reprinted, by permission, from American Canoe Association, 2008, *Canoeing: Outdoor adventures* (Champaign, IL: Human Kinetics), 143.

- Keep the paddle planted against the bottom and show how you can move the canoe back and forth by pulling and pushing with your lower body.
- Now lean the canoe. Demonstrate how leaning makes the steering easier by lifting the canoe ends and increasing **rocker**.
- Roll the canoe over and perform a wet exit to show students how to slide safely away from the thigh straps. Dropping your head down toward the centerline lets your thighs begin to move backward, which releases pressure against the straps. Slide away from the straps and swim to the surface with your paddle in hand.

Important Terms

The following terms establish a common language to learn correct body positions.

J-lean—A separation of the upper body and lower body to maintain boat balance; the lower body forms the curved J by one knee pressing down and the other knee lifting up; the torso remains upright.

paddler's box—An imaginary box in front of the canoeist's body plane that goes no higher than the forehead, stays in front of the torso and shoulders, and extends as far forward as the canoeist can comfortably reach.

torso rotation—The ability to swivel the upper body around the spine, allowing strong abdominal muscles to power a paddle stroke.

wet exit—An exit from a capsized canoe in which the paddler takes the head to the knees, releasing thigh tension against straps, and pushes away from the canoe. The head remains down until strap pressure diminishes.

Main Activity

Warming Up for Stroke Practice (30 Minutes)

Have students hold their paddles in front of their torsos, horizontal to the water.

- Have them rotate their torsos slowly from side to side, keeping the paddle horizontal.
- Ask them to note how far they can rotate their paddles by watching whether the paddle is parallel to the gunwale.
- Challenge them to stretch a bit farther to increase flexibility.

Have students try pressing up and down with knees and hips to lean the canoe.

- They should keep the paddles in the water initially to enhance stability. Then they hold the paddles in the air and horizontally to the water, and rock the lower body more vigorously.
- They should strive to keep the torso quiet by keeping the paddle stationary and horizontal to the water surface.

You can offer students a greater challenge with these exercises:

- They can slow the lean changes until they balance over each knee. Challenge them to hold the J-leans as long as they can.
- Students can try steering the canoe with their knees. They plant their paddles on the lake bottom in shallow water and move the canoe toward and away from the paddle by pulling and pushing with the lower body. The arms remain relatively straight, so the body core does the work.

Closure Activity

Simon Says (Five Minutes)

Use a Simon Says strategy with this activity. Call out different commands to the entire group: rock, rock faster, rock slower, and hold. Vary the calls by periodically not using the Simon Says preface.

◆ A canoeist who follows a command without the Simon Says preface must tip over.

◆ A variation when calling "Hold" is to count five seconds. Any paddler still moving strongly to hold the lean has to tip over.

◆ Your goal is to cause students to capsize during this activity. The last canoeist upright wins.

◆ If the weather is too cold for capsizing, award points for infractions. The person with the fewest points wins.

Follow-Up Activities

Activity 1: Stay Loose! (Five Minutes)

Return to balance drills at any time to loosen up students who have become tense.

Activity 2: Recognizing Safe Body Positions (10 Minutes)

Test the students' ability to recognize unsafe body positions by examining your demonstration of strokes outside the paddler's box and by troubleshooting solutions.

◆ Demonstrate such potential problems as having your top hand too high above your head and moving the paddle behind your body plane because your torso hasn't rotated through a stroke.

◆ Finish this exercise by having the students recall and discuss the important concepts related to body position and movement that you shared at the beginning of the lesson.

ASSESSMENT

◆ Check that students can recognize unsafe body positions that could cause injury by engaging them in a group critique and discussion of the improper technique that you demonstrated during follow-up activity 2.

◆ Verify that students stretch their core muscles to prepare for paddling by counting how many seconds they hold their leans on each side and noting whether an increase occurs as they practice. Students should determine whether they have a weaker side and strive to achieve balance.

◆ Confirm that students can execute a controlled boat lean by observing whether they attain an increase in the degree of lean with successive practice and can achieve a smooth transition from a flat canoe to a leaned canoe.

◆ Check that students enhance safety by being able to exit the canoe consistently and safely. Partners should watch each other's wet exits. Be sure to check that each paddler tucks the head and exits the canoe without struggling.

◆ Ensure that students consistently practice and model efficient body positions that promote effortless canoeing when partners watch each other during final practice of the activities.

TEACHING CONSIDERATIONS

- Students will vary greatly in flexibility. Encourage them to establish personal standards with the degree of J-leans and torso rotation. They should work to improve their personal standards.

- Some students are apprehensive about capsizing a canoe. If you are using boats with thigh straps, consider doing a demonstration on shore. Weather permitting, consider beginning the activities with the wet-exit drill so that apprehensive students can learn how to exit safely before other practice.

- A timid student can get a good feel for upper- and lower-body separation by holding a paddle horizontally to the water in front of her or him. Two partners can hold the paddle stationary by standing in the water next to the canoe, while the paddler uses hip and knee movement to lean the canoe from side to side. Holding on to the stationary paddle reinforces the paddler's command of a quiet upper body.

UNIT 7, LESSON 5

▷ Basic Tandem Strokes

OVERVIEW

Knowing turning and power strokes is necessary to perform tandem canoe maneuvers on lakes and rivers. In this lesson students learn how to execute basic strokes that allow them to paddle straight forward and turn the canoe. They also learn the responsibilities of bow and stern paddlers.

JUSTIFICATION

Knowing how to execute strokes efficiently will enhance tandem canoeists' ability to paddle effectively, successfully, and safely in a variety of conditions.

GOAL

To develop participants' ability to control a canoe by paddling cooperatively with a partner.

OBJECTIVES

At the end of this lesson, students will be able to

- recognize efficient elements of strokes to avoid injury (cognitive),
- execute turning strokes to spin a canoe (psychomotor),
- execute power and corrective strokes (psychomotor),
- enhance safety by consistently controlling the canoe (affective), and
- consistently practice and model efficient body positions that promote effortless canoeing (affective).

EQUIPMENT AND AREAS NEEDED

◆ Tandem canoes

◆ Paddles for each student

◆ Helmets, if using a whitewater canoe with thigh straps

◆ Natural features or buoys to maneuver around (six to eight points for a good practice sequence)

RISK MANAGEMENT CONSIDERATIONS

◆ Use a teaching area near the shore free of obstacles with water deep enough to immerse the blade completely during stroke practice. Students should be able to capsize without hitting underwater obstacles.

◆ Use a teaching area protected from wind and current during initial practice of maneuvers. Students will be able to understand more clearly the effect of their strokes and develop better boat control. You will be able to manage the group more easily as well.

◆ The American Canoe Association's suggested ratio for tandem canoe instruction is 1:6 on flatwater and 1:5 on whitewater (ACA, 2006). Determine the appropriate ratio for the environment and the characteristics of your students.

LESSON CONTENT

Introduction

Use the following quotations to stimulate the students' understanding of key concepts when tandem paddling:

◆ "Tandem canoeing can be a good marriage or a painful divorce."

◆ "Avoid a death grip."

◆ "One well-executed stroke is better than three hack jobs."

◆ "All strokes have three distinct phases."

Understanding the roles of each canoeist can be helpful in building a good partnership. Explain how the bow has real responsibilities in decision making, and the stern should not dictate the action from the back. Especially in whitewater, each partner must act quickly and independently in paddling the canoe. The best partnerships are those in which both canoeists contribute actively to the execution of various **maneuvers**. Proper technique dictates that each partner pick a side on which to paddle (opposite from each other) and stay on that side unless the bow paddler is executing a proper crossover stroke or both paddlers are executing a coordinated switch. This approach makes for a more stable canoe and more efficient paddling.

Paddling Responsibilities

Explain the following responsibilities when you teach the different maneuvers to promote efficient paddling:

◆ The bow paddler sets the pace, chooses the immediate route, initiates turns, and in current often provides power against the current.

◆ The stern paddler matches the pace, chooses the general route, keeps the canoe on the desired general course, and in current maintains the angle of the canoe against the current.

Efficient Strokes

Remember these basic tips for executing efficient strokes and use your body as the prop for demonstrating the points to students:

- Tight, white knuckles means tension in your grip. Wiggle your fingers to relax.
- Bending your arms weakens your stroke and promotes tendinitis. Keep the elbows relatively straight through all phases of the stroke.
- Keep your spine relatively upright during all strokes so that you can twist your torso for greater power. Centering your torso above your lower body also allows you to control the boat lean, which you can't do when hinged forward or sideways excessively from the waist. Hinging also tires your lower back.
- Keep the paddle in front of your torso to protect your shoulders. To do that, you have to rotate your torso to execute strokes.

Stroke Phases

Help students learn the strokes by dividing the technical elements into three phases:

- **Catch phase**—the beginning of the stroke, when the blade catches the water fully.
- **Power phase**—the part of the stroke when the paddler applies force against the paddle to move the canoe.
- **Recovery phase**—the part of the stroke when the paddler returns the blade to the catch position.

Paddle Blade Sides

When learning strokes, students can also benefit from understanding which side of the blade presses against the water:

- Power face—the side of the paddle pressed against the water during a forward stroke.
- Back face—the side of the paddle blade that has no pressure against it during a forward stroke; the side opposite the power face.

Practice

To practice initial paddling technique, line up canoes perpendicular to shore with the bows facing in the same direction. Ask students to pair up. One partner stands in the water holding the canoe, while the other partner practices the strokes. The observer can provide feedback on stroke execution while holding the canoe. The partners switch positions to complete the practice.

Main Activities

Activity 1: Turning Strokes (30 Minutes)

Three essential strokes for turning a canoe are the draw, cross-draw, and the pry. Use the following tips for teaching all phases of these strokes.

Draw Stroke   A **draw stroke** moves your end of a tandem canoe toward the blade.

◆ Place the paddle in the water opposite your hip and as far from the canoe as you can comfortably reach. Rotate your torso until your shoulders face the blade.

◆ Keep the top hand fairly stationary throughout the stroke and over the water. The paddle stays vertical to the water surface as a result.

◆ Move your hips toward the blade and stop before the blade strikes the canoe.

◆ Swivel your top hand by rotating your top thumb away from your body until the blade is perpendicular to the centerline. For the recovery, **slice** the blade back to the catch position and swivel your top hand until the blade is parallel to the centerline and ready for the next stroke (figure CA5.1).

Cross-Draw Stroke   A **cross-draw stroke** has the opposite effect of a draw; it moves the bow of a canoe the other way. Only the bow paddler does this stroke.

◆ In the bow, lift the paddle across the boat and rotate your torso as far your flexibility allows (but no greater than 60 degrees from the centerline). Your shoulders face away from the canoe.

◆ The paddle shaft should be more horizontal to the water surface, and the thumb of your grip hand points toward the sky (figure CA5.2).

◆ The shaft arm stays extended fully at the catch and throughout the stroke. The grip hand stays low between the hip and chest.

◆ Swivel your torso until your shoulders are perpendicular to the centerline, which will bring the bow to the blade.

◆ Lift the blade from the water before the canoe strikes it and recover the blade to the catch position.

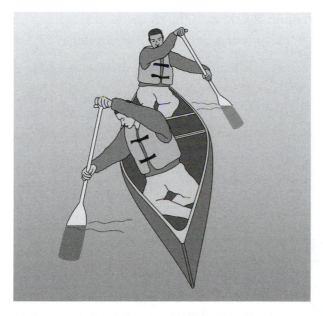

FIGURE CA5.1   Slice recovery for a draw stroke—bow and stern. The back face of the blade is oriented toward the bow during recovery.

FIGURE CA5.2   Catch position for a cross-draw—bow only.

Pry Stroke A **pry stroke** moves the stern of a tandem canoe away from the blade.

- Move the paddle into position by aligning it with the gunwale, more horizontal to the water. Rotate your shoulders around so that they face the paddle and gunwale. Now you can control the paddle more easily.
- Let the thumb of your shaft hand anchor the shaft to the gunwale. If you have small hands, use the heel of your hand on top of the gunwale to create a fulcrum (fixed point).
- Create this oarlock or leverage point behind your rear end so that the blade rests near the stern. Slide the shaft through your hand to get the blade fully in the water near the boat.
- Use the back face of the blade against the water by pulling in with your grip hand. Push the blade away from the stern about 6 inches (15 centimeters) for a short stroke (figure CA5.3).
- Lower your grip hand toward the gunwale so that the blade lifts free of the water and you can return it to the catch position.

Activity 2: Spinning With Turning Strokes (30 Minutes)

Students can combine the three strokes in different ways to turn the canoe in a spin (a tight turn in place). They can do onside spins and offside spins.

Onside Spin An **onside** spin turns the canoe toward the designated paddling side of the bow person (figure CA5.4). Launch the canoes away from shore and make sure that students practice the maneuvers in both bow and stern positions. Encourage them to remember their responsibilities: the bow sets the pace, and the stern matches the pace. Check for synchronized paddling. To encourage efficient and powerful strokes, challenge them to complete a 360-degree revolution in as few strokes as possible.

Offer these tips for onside spins:

- Both paddlers use draw strokes on opposite sides of the canoe.
- They execute the strokes simultaneously so that the boat spins smoothly rather than bobbles from side to side.

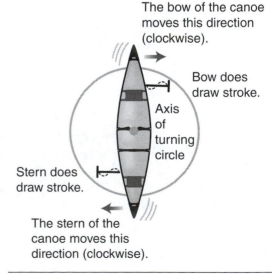

FIGURE CA5.3   Exit position for stern pry.

FIGURE CA5.4   Onside spin with draws.

◆ Encourage partners to reach out away from the canoe for big bites of water and to snap their hips toward the paddle for crisper turns.

Offside Spin   An **offside** spin turns the canoe away from the bow paddler's designated paddling side (figure CA5.5). Offer these tips for offside spins:

◆ The bow paddler uses a cross-draw, and the stern paddler uses a pry.

◆ The stern paddler executes about two pry strokes for every cross-draw taken by the bow paddler because the strokes are different lengths.

◆ The stern paddler should pry smoothly without cranking down on the gunwale to keep the canoe relatively flat as it spins. Ask them to see how fast they can spin before the pry becomes too jerky. They can then back off the speed to recapture smoothness.

Activity 3: Strokes for Paddling Straight (30 Minutes)

Two essential strokes for paddling a canoe in a straight line are the forward stroke and the J-stroke. Return to the shoreline teaching area to teach these new strokes, line up the canoes, and ask partners to hold the boats while others practice. Use the following tips for teaching all phases of these strokes.

Forward Stroke   A **forward stroke** propels the boat forward. Offer these tips for the forward stroke:

◆ Swivel your torso to slip the blade into the water at the catch (figure CA5.6). Extend the shoulder closer to the paddle comfortably forward as far as you can reach. Your shoulders should feel coiled around a central axis (your spine).

◆ Keep both hands over the water so that the paddle shaft is vertical to the water surface when looking from the front (figure CA5.7a).

◆ Uncoil your torso to propel the paddle through the water in an imaginary line parallel to the centerline of the canoe. Keep your arms comfortably straight so that your torso engages well.

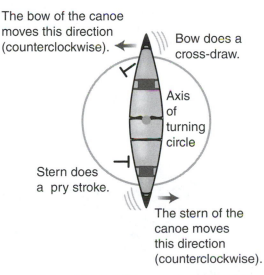

FIGURE CA5.5   Offside spin with a cross-draw and a pry.

Reprinted, by permission, from American Canoe Association, 2008, *Canoeing: Outdoor adventures* (Champaign, IL: Human Kinetics), 153.

FIGURE CA5.6   Forward stroke catch position (side view).

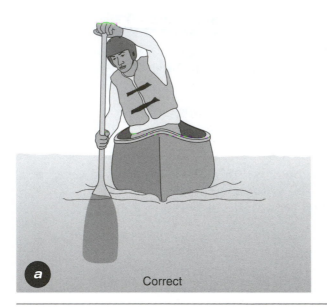

FIGURE CA5.7   Forward stroke catch position, front view: *(a)* the correct vertical orientation of the paddle and *(b)* the incorrect orientation.

Adapted, by permission, from L. Gullion, 1987, *ACA instructor's manual* (Fredericksburg, VA: American Canoe Association).

◆ Think of the paddle as a brace against the water and thrust your hips past the blade. The boat will move forward.

◆ Let your paddle slide sideways out of the water when the blade passes your hip. Return your paddle to the catch position by **feathering** or flattening it to the water surface.

J-Stroke   A **J-stroke** propels the boat forward and moves the bow toward the stern paddler's designated paddling side. Only the stern paddler executes it. You need to provide hands-on assistance to students when learning the J-stroke, because it is a challenging stroke.

Offer these tips for the J-stroke:

◆ Begin the J just as you do the forward stroke except the blade should be under the hull and your grip (top) hand should be out over the water (figure CA5.8*a*).

FIGURE CA5.8   J-stroke: *(a)* Start in a forward stroke position but with the blade under the hull; *(b)* slide the paddle past the knee and change the angle of the blade; *(c)* move the blade away from the canoe, using the side of the canoe for leverage.

◆ Uncoil your torso, keeping the blade under the hull through the beginning of the stroke.

◆ Slide the paddle along the hull and position it against the gunwale for good leverage.

◆ As the blade passes your knee, change the blade angle by rotating your grip hand away from your body and pointing your thumb forward. Keep a loose grip with the lower hand so that the paddle shaft can swivel to the correct position. Slide the blade into position slightly behind your hip (figure CA5.8b).

◆ Press the paddle grip into the canoe slightly, which moves the blade away from the boat in a J pattern. The paddle shaft against the gunwale provides good leverage. The blade stays less than a foot (30 centimeters) from the canoe at the end of the stroke (figure CA5.8c).

◆ Let the blade slide forward with no resistance from the water until it rises to the surface. Return it to the catch position for another stroke.

Activity 4: Paddling Straight (30 to 60 Minutes)

Launch the canoes and let students practice paddling in a straight line. Allow freeform practice at the beginning as students refine their strokes. Then ask them to perform a series of directed tasks before they switch positions for another round of practice.

Offer these tips for paddling forward straight:

◆ The bow canoeist should focus on setting a slow pace and using solid torso rotation during these activities. The stern canoeist focuses on directional control first and then adds momentum.

◆ First, paddle in a circle with the stern paddler doing continual forward sweeps. The bow will turn away from the stern paddler's stroke, and the boat will carve an onside circle. This task allows easy practice of the forward sweep.

◆ Then paddle in a circle with the stern paddler doing continual J-strokes. The bow will begin to turn toward the J-stroke in tighter and tighter circles, and the boat will carve an offside circle. The task allows unfettered practice of the J-stroke.

◆ Now pick a destination in the distance and paddle toward it in a straight line. Anticipate that the boat will veer off course and use a corrective stroke (usually a J) to bring it back on course. Execute the J before the boat veers greatly off course.

◆ Initially the stern paddler should focus on keeping the boat tracking in a straight line. Eventually the stern paddler needs to match the pace of the bow paddler while paddling straight forward.

Activity 5: Additional Strokes (20 Minutes)

Discuss two more strokes to assist in controlling the canoe and have students practice them. The forward and reverse sweeps serve to turn or spin the canoe. The stern paddler can also use the forward sweep as a correction stroke to keep the canoe in a straight line.

Forward Sweep　A **forward sweep** propels the boat forward and moves the bow away from the stern paddler's designated paddling side (figure CA5.9). Offer these tips for the forward sweep:

◆ Plant the paddle horizontally to the water surface opposite your hip at a 90-degree angle from the centerline when in the stern. Extend your arms fully and comfortably to reach away from the canoe and its pivot point. To extend your reach, keep your grip hand near the gunwale rather than your torso.

◆ Rotate your torso around, trying to get your shoulders parallel to the centerline. Let your eyes and shoulders follow the blade, which makes your torso apply force against the paddle.

◆ Keep your shaft arm straight early in the stroke to force the torso to be active. The arm may bend a little as the paddle exits the water.

◆ Before the blade strikes the canoe, lift it from the water and feather it back to the catch position.

◆ Bow paddlers begin the forward sweep by leaning forward and placing the blade toward the bow.

◆ The same principles apply as in the stern: Remember torso rotation, keep the shaft arm straight, and feather back to the catch position.

◆ Create a 90-degree arc and end at the hip when in the bow.

FIGURE CA5.9   Forward sweep in the stern: *(a)* Start at the hip and *(b)* finish at the stern.

Reverse Sweep   Emphasize that reverse sweeps and back strokes are inefficient strokes for maintaining a straight line and forward momentum. Inexperienced paddlers tend to use reverse sweeps as correction strokes when they have difficulty with J-strokes. This strategy is useful in reducing frustration and preventing the canoe from spinning off course.

Offer these tips for the **reverse sweep**:

◆ The stern paddler begins close to the stern by keeping the grip hand low and the shaft more horizontal to the water surface.

◆ Torso rotation is required to move the paddle into the correct position next to the stern.

◆ The back face of the blade pushes against the water. The grip thumb points up.

◆ Bend the arms slightly at the catch position and rotate the torso until the blade stops opposite of the hip at a 90-degree angle to the centerline.

◆ Let the shaft arm straighten at the finish so that it keeps the paddle farther away from the pivot point.

- The same principles apply in the bow: Remember torso rotation, start with the arms slightly bent, finish with the arms straight, and lift and feather back to the catch position.

- The bow stroke starts opposite the hip and arcs to the bow using the back face of the blade.

- Figure CA5.10 shows the sweep stroke sequence when tandem canoeing to execute both onside and offside spins.

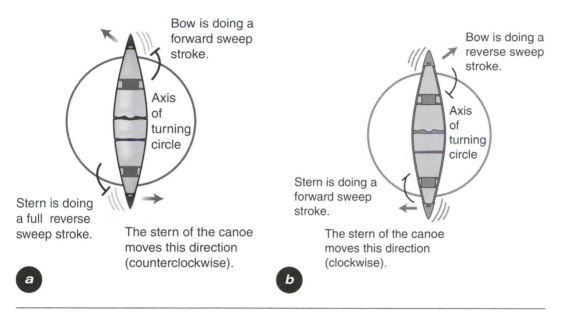

FIGURE CA5.10   Spinning with sweeps.

Reprinted, by permission, from American Canoe Association, 2008, *Canoeing: Outdoor adventures* (Champaign, IL: Human Kinetics), 71.

Activity 6: Preparing for River Paddling (30 Minutes)

Prepare the students for river paddling by setting up a course that combines a straight section with a turn, where the canoe completes a U-turn. These maneuvers form the basis for eddy turns (a U-turn into calmer current behind an obstacle) and peel-outs (a U-turn from an eddy back into the main current).

- Use fixed points on flatwater for students to turn behind—rocks, buoys, raft, or dock.

- Students use a count system (1-2-3-4) to stay coordinated with their partners. The stern paddler uses forward sweeps or J-strokes on 1-2-3 to get the canoe turning gradually in the desired direction; both paddlers then use turning strokes like draw or pry strokes on 4 to spin the canoe more sharply.

- Have students add an important element to the turning by leaning into the turn as a bicyclist would. This strategy prepares them for S-turns and C-turns in the river, where they must lean into turns to prevent the river current from flipping the canoe (figure CA5.11).

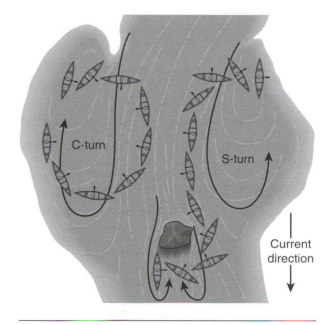

FIGURE 5.11   S-turns and C-turns.

Reverse, or Back, Stroke

You will note that the reverse stroke, or back stroke, is not included in this lesson. It was intentionally left out for several reasons. Novice paddlers tend to use the back stroke incorrectly by using it to steer or turn the canoe. In other words, they develop a poor habit. Consider teaching the back stroke much later in the progression or not at all in beginner classes. Attention to proper technique with the strokes outlined in this lesson will promote good technique.

Closure Activities

Activity 1: Obstacle Course Exercise (15 Minutes)

Set up an obstacle course with milk-jug buoys so that students can practice transitions between turns, particularly changes in boat lean. Remind them that they control boat lean with the lower half of the body. Return to reviews of specific strokes to clean up stroke efficiency.

Activity 2: Tag (20 Minutes)

Play a game of tag by designating one boat as "it." A legal tag occurs only when the bow of the "it" boat tags another boat anywhere from the midthwart forward. Establish boundaries and designate more than one "it" boat if the group is large or if the "it" boat is having difficulty. This activity forces students to integrate all strokes.

Follow-Up Activities

Activity 1: Moving Water Practice (One Hour)

Head to a river practice site with well-defined features such as shoreline eddies and midstream rocks to practice the U-turn and C-turn maneuvers (peel-outs and eddy turns, figure CA5.12). The current should be mild enough to allow students to paddle back upriver to repeat the moves and refine their execution.

Notice in the figure that the bow paddler is executing a Duffek stroke, which is covered in the solo strokes lesson. With more advanced students, cover the Duffek instead of the draw and cross-draw strokes for executing eddy turns and peel-outs. Note that a reverse sweep can be substituted for the stern reverse sweeping low brace until students develop more confidence with leaning a canoe in current. You can encourage them to make these adjustments to more aggressive strokes when they become comfortable with current.

Eddy Turn   Explain these steps for executing an eddy turn:

- Position the canoe near the target destination so that the current doesn't pull you away from it.
- Turn the canoe at an optimum angle against the eddy line (45 to 90 degrees) to enter the eddy.
- Paddle forward to cross over the eddy line.
- Lean into the turn.
- Execute the strokes necessary to turn the canoe.
- Paddle forward to stay in the eddy.

Use the same steps to leave an eddy and reenter the downstream current in a peel-out.

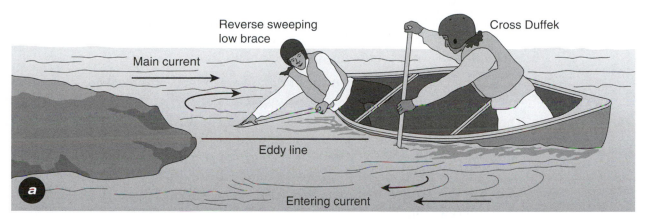

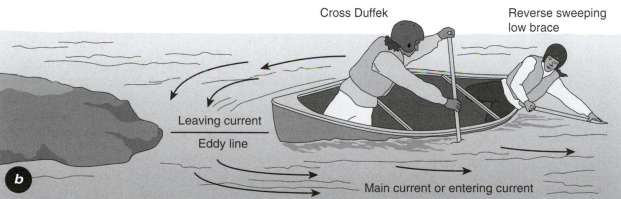

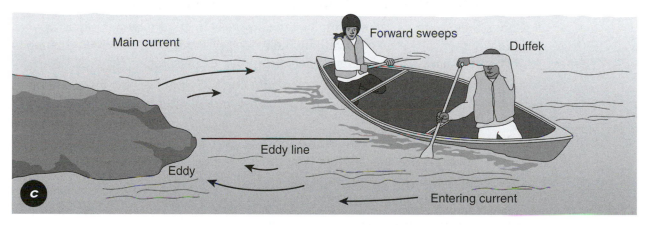

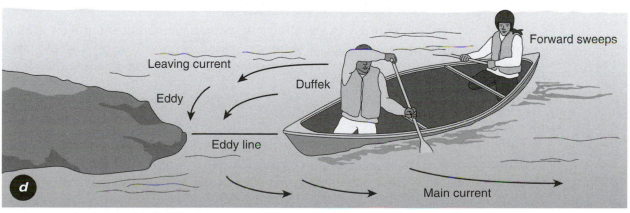

FIGURE CA5.12 Practice the U-turn and C-turn maneuvers: *(a)* offside eddy turn, *(b)* offside peel-out, *(c)* onside eddy turn, and *(d)* onside peel-out.

Reprinted, by permission, from American Canoe Association, 2008, *Canoeing: Outdoor adventures* (Champaign, IL: Human Kinetics), 71.

Ferrying   Students can also practice ferrying, a means of crossing from one side of the river to another, by using the concepts introduced in unit 5, lesson 10, and unit 6, lesson 6. Explain the following role responsibilities:

◆ The bow paddler provides power in the upstream end of the canoe, so that the boat doesn't lose power and position in the river.

◆ The stern paddler maintains the angle of the boat against the current and provides power against the current. Be ready to prevent the boat from spinning on the eddy line when the bow is in the downstream current and the stern is still in the eddy. Use a narrow angle of 5 to 15 degrees (pointed primarily upriver) until the entire boat is in the main current. Then you can widen the angle to 45 to 60 degrees to cross the river quickly.

Activity 2: Videotaped Critique (One Hour)

Videotape the practice session and show the tapes later for the group to critique. Videotaping is an effective method of promoting skill development and allows in-depth self-assessment and instructor assessment.

ASSESSMENT

◆ Verify that students can recognize efficient elements of strokes that help prevent injury by asking tandem canoeists to observe the maneuvers of another canoe team in a "human video" format. The observers describe to the paddlers what they saw and provide one tip for each paddler to improve technique. Be sure to listen to their analysis to ensure that correct information is exchanged.

◆ Check that students can execute turning strokes effectively by having them analyze whether they stroked simultaneously to spin a canoe by viewing videotapes of the practice session. Focus on synchronicity at the catch.

◆ Verify that students can execute power and corrective strokes by observing them paddle a straight course, change directions, and paddle a new straight course during the main activities.

◆ Assess whether students are enhancing safety by consistently controlling the canoe by observing the group at play during the tag activity. Note that students tend to let their guard down and allow their technique to falter, particularly if the game is fun and competitive.

TEACHING CONSIDERATIONS

◆ Students will vary greatly in the ability to focus on stroke development. Gauge the commitment of your group to technical paddling improvement. Use fun tasks and activities such as tag games, water soccer, and Frisbee games to break up technical talk.

◆ Begin with simple maneuvers like spins before working on more difficult challenges such as paddling straight.

◆ Some students will not learn the J-stroke quickly. If they are frustrated, make sure that they know how to use a forward stroke and a pry to keep the boat on a straight course. Going somewhere may be more important to them than mastering the J-stroke.

◆ An enjoyable finish to a program is bracing. See lesson 6, Basic Solo Strokes, for two bracing strokes useful to tandem canoeists.

◆ You can adjust the assessment process depending on students' needs. You can observe and coach the canoe teams, or each team can perform its own analysis, or you can have teams of two canoes watch each other under your supervision. Involving students in the analysis builds their analytical skills for improvements within and beyond the lesson.

UNIT 7, LESSON 6

▷ Basic Solo Strokes

OVERVIEW

Becoming a solo canoeist is a rewarding way to begin a paddling career or expand experience after learning how to tandem canoe. The solo canoeist is entirely responsible for the canoe and performs the combined functions of a bow and stern paddler. Knowing how to solo canoe makes students better tandem paddlers because solo paddling requires quick decision making. The skills are transferable between the activities, and students will experience satisfying improvements by participating in both. In this lesson students learn how to execute basic strokes that allow them to paddle straight forward, turn the solo canoe, and stabilize it.

JUSTIFICATION

Knowing how to execute strokes efficiently will enhance solo canoeists' ability to paddle effectively, successfully, and safely in a variety of conditions.

GOAL

To develop participants' ability to control a canoe when paddling solo.

OBJECTIVES

At the end of this lesson, students will be able to

◆ recognize efficient elements of strokes to avoid injury (cognitive),

◆ execute turning strokes to spin a solo canoe (psychomotor),

◆ execute power and corrective strokes to paddle a solo canoe in a straight line (psychomotor),

◆ execute bracing strokes to keep a solo canoe upright (psychomotor),

◆ enhance safety by consistently controlling the canoe (affective), and

◆ consistently practice and model efficient body positions that promote effortless canoeing (affective).

EQUIPMENT AND AREAS NEEDED

◆ Solo canoes (one per student)

◆ Paddles (one per student)

◆ Helmets, if using a whitewater canoe with thigh straps (one per student)

◆ Buoys (four to six create an effective practice area)

◆ Beach ball

RISK MANAGEMENT CONSIDERATIONS

◆ Use a teaching area protected from wind and current during initial practice of maneuvers. Solo canoes can spin around rapidly in wind and water currents, and a beginning student may have difficulty controlling the boat. You will be able to manage the group more easily as well.

◆ The American Canoe Association's suggested ratio for solo canoe instruction is 1:4 to enhance group management and improve the quality of instruction. You can adjust the ratios based on environmental conditions and student characteristics.

◆ During water soccer, warn participants of the dangers of swinging paddles and pinching fingers and hands between gunwales.

LESSON CONTENT

Introduction (15 Minutes)

Use the following quotations to emphasize key concepts related to solo canoeing:

◆ "You know who to blame in a solo canoe."
◆ "Solo canoes can dance on water."
◆ "Two roles are better than one."
◆ "A narrow boat is better."

Discuss how solo canoeists experience great freedom in making decisions and executing different moves, and experience profound satisfaction in controlling their own craft. If a maneuver fails, however, the solo paddler knows who is responsible, a circumstance that can create some frustration in the learning experience. Demonstrate how these responsive canoes create wonderful opportunities to glide or dance on water as the solo paddler slides easily between different maneuvers.

Review these basic concepts during the demonstration:

◆ You sit closer to the center in a solo canoe, so that you can be both bow and stern paddler. Show how your strokes send the boat off course more quickly, requiring faster execution of strokes.

◆ Expect to zigzag at the beginning when trying to keep the solo canoe on a straight course. You must supply the power of a bow paddler and the directional control of a stern paddler.

◆ Some canoes bulge outward at the midpoint, which makes solo canoeing more challenging. Use a narrower canoe so that you can reach the water more easily. Tilt the hull slightly toward your paddle to drop the gunwale and get it out of the way of your strokes.

Main Activities

Activity 1: Turning Strokes (15 Minutes)

A solo canoeist can use the same tandem canoe strokes in the bow and stern with some variations to create more stability, because solo canoes are often tippier with more rocker.

◆ If this lesson follows the tandem canoe lesson, review some strokes from lesson 5 (draw, cross-draw, forward sweep) as a warm-up and let students test the effect of those strokes on the solo canoe.

◆ If you are teaching solo canoeing as a stand-alone activity, begin with the strokes in this lesson.

You can launch the canoes and practice the strokes in a clustered circle in your teaching area. On a windy day, you may want to pair up students and have one partner hold or anchor the solo canoe while the other person practices a short series of strokes (for example, turning strokes). The partners then switch roles.

Two essential strokes for turning a solo canoe are the forward sweep and the reverse sweep. Begin with this exercise because it will be immediately successful.

Forward Sweep

◆ Use the basic progression in lesson 5 for teaching the forward sweep, with two modifications.

    – The catch position begins near the bow as far forward as you can comfortably rotate your torso.

    – The path of the paddle follows a 180-degree arc from bow to stern as far away from the canoe as you can reach. Follow the paddle with your eyes to make sure that your shoulders turn through the stroke, which will minimize strain on the shoulder joint (figure CA6.1).

◆ Executing forward sweeps will result in an offside turn, in which the boat spins away from your designated paddling side.

FIGURE CA6.1　Forward sweep path.

◆ Test the efficiency of your sweep by seeing how far around a 360-degree circle you can reach with one stroke. Then see how greater boat lean affects your ability to turn the boat. Lean to the outside of the turn (toward your stroke) at the beginning and to the inside of the turn from the midpoint of the stroke. You should feel as if you are sweeping water under the stern.

Reverse Sweep

◆ Reverse the path of the forward sweep (figure CA6.2).

◆ Make sure that you rotate your shoulders parallel to the gunwale and place the blade right next to the stern. Catch this water strongly because doing so will spin the boat quickly.

◆ Executing reverse sweeps will result in an onside turn, in which the boat spins toward your paddling side.

◆ Test stroke efficiency again by seeing how far one stroke will turn the craft. Increase boat lean to turn more completely.

◆ Flatten your blade against the water when reverse sweeping (press the back face of the blade against the water as if you are buttering bread). Lean toward the

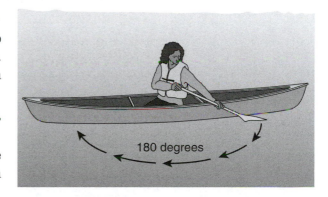

FIGURE CA6.2　Reverse sweep.

stroke at the beginning and away at the end, as if you are pushing water under the bow. After you feel comfortable with the support provided by the moving paddle, lean the canoe more dramatically to experience a faster turn.

Activity 2: Paddling Straight (One Hour)

The next step is paddling a straight course. Three essential and familiar strokes are the forward stroke, forward sweep, and J-stroke. Use the teaching progressions from lesson 5 for these corrective strokes and add some tips useful to the solo paddler. Also, teach the cross-forward because a solo canoeist can use it instead of a J-stroke to get the boat turning back toward the original paddling side.

Paddling a Straight Course

◆ Check to make sure that the paddle shaft is vertical to the water surface with forward strokes. Keep the grip (top) hand away from the chest and over the water so that you don't sweep the canoe off course. Leaning the canoe slightly toward the paddle can help keep the canoe turning toward your paddle and reduce the number of corrective strokes necessary, especially J-strokes.

◆ Keep the J-stroke blade under the hull during the early power phase so that the corrective J action stays near the canoe. If it strays too far from the canoe, the stroke will not turn the canoe effectively because it will encounter currents that are sliding around the boat. Leaning the canoe toward the paddle makes it easier to get the J-stroke under the hull.

◆ Paddle an outside circle using sweeps and an inside circle using J-strokes.

◆ Experiment with the path of a J-stroke while paddling an inside circle. Stroking right next to the canoe creates a tight circle, and stroking away from the boat (still in a straight line) creates a wider circle.

◆ If you have difficulty with the J-stroke, use a C-stroke to turn the boat back onto the desired course. Use a draw stroke ahead of the midpoint of the canoe to pull the canoe toward the blade. Then convert it into the J-stroke in one smooth, continuous action. This stroke tends to stall the momentum of the canoe; a cross-forward is a more efficient alternative.

Cross-Forward

◆ Lift the paddle from your original canoeing side and lean forward about 50 degrees from an upright position to place it in the water on the other side (figure CA6.3).

◆ Your arms are comfortably extended forward, and the paddle is vertical to the water surface at the catch.

◆ Lift your torso, pulling back on the paddle, to apply power against the water. Scoot your hips past the vertical paddle to move the boat forward.

◆ When the paddle approaches your knee, prepare to change the blade angle to return it to the catch position. Point your top thumb forward (away from you) to angle the blade parallel to the canoe.

◆ Slice the paddle underwater back to the catch, letting it rise to the surface if water pushes it around. Swivel the blade until it is perpendicular to the centerline to begin another stroke.

◆ Develop a quick back-and-forth rhythm by lifting and lowering your torso for several short strokes until the boat turns in the desired direction. Then return the paddle to your original paddling side.

FIGURE CA6.3 Cross-forward.

◆ Practice a jump start in which you quickly propel the boat forward using forward and cross-forward strokes from a stalled position. This exercise will build quick boat control and generate good momentum.

◆ Follow a zigzag course around markers or buoys, using a mixture of all corrective strokes to change directions.

◆ Follow a straight-line course for as long as you can keep it going.

Activity 3: Preparing to Paddle on the River (30 Minutes)

Now it is time to practice U-turns by combining straight forward paddling with turning. Students will have already learned all basic strokes, but some modifications are necessary to provide more stability with these maneuvers.

Modifying the Draw Into a Duffek   The Duffek promotes a snappier turn because the paddle provides a solid pivot point around which the canoe will spin (figure CA6.4). This is an effective stroke for catching an eddy.

◆ Change the catch position for the draw by moving the paddle inward and forward so that it is placed on a diagonal line from your knee.

◆ Change the angle of the blade so that the power face is oriented to face oncoming water and can brace against it.

◆ Keep the paddle shaft vertical, so that the paddle functions like a planted post around which you and the canoe will swing. When the water pressure leaves your blade (you will feel it), then convert the Duffek smoothly into a forward stroke.

◆ Some paddlers like to keep their forearms near their foreheads to keep the Duffek in front of the shoulder plane. This solid stance, in which you are looking through a frame created by your arms, protects your shoulder from dislocation.

◆ Choose an obstacle like a rock or the end of a dock and paddle toward it in a straight line. Then set up for an onside turn by using a J-stroke to initiate the turn and a Duffek to complete it.

◆ See Onside Spin in lesson 5 (page 520) for additional suggestions.

Modifying the Cross-Draw Into a Cross-Duffek

◆ Change the orientation of the cross-draw paddle shaft to more vertical in relation to the water surface. This change moves the blade nearer your body on a diagonal line off your knee. It also moves your grip (top) hand into a higher position at or above the shoulder. This is called a cross-Duffek (figure CA6.5).

◆ The vertical orientation of the paddle allows you to plant the cross-Duffek and hold it long enough for the boat to turn around it. As the canoe approaches the blade, convert the stroke into a cross-forward for a smooth finish.

FIGURE CA6.4   Duffek.

FIGURE CA6.5   Cross-Duffek.

◆ Choose an obstacle to turn behind and paddle a straight course toward it. Just before reaching the destination, initiate the turn with a forward sweep and use a cross-Duffek into a cross-forward to finish it.

◆ See Offside Spin in lesson 5 (page 521) for additional suggestions.

Activity 4: Bracing (15 Minutes)

Capsizing can happen quickly in a solo canoe, but some simple strategies can keep students upright. They can use the paddle as an outrigger to keep them upright by always leaving it in a resting position in the absence of other strokes. They let the paddle float gently in the water, where they can convert it easily to a bracing stroke when waves tip the canoe. Braces are essential to maintaining stability.

High Brace   A **high brace** is used to grab water when the canoe tips away from the designated paddling side.

◆ From the resting position, quickly punch your grip (top) hand away from the canoe until the paddle is vertical to the water surface (figure CA6.6).

◆ Keep the blade deeply immersed in the water so that it functions like glue.

◆ Push downward on the knee closer to the paddle to stop the canoe roll.

◆ Test its effectiveness by leaning slowly away from the paddle until you feel the need to grab water with the high brace. Arrest the flip.

FIGURE CA6.6   High brace.

Low Brace   A **low brace** is used like a beaver tail or outrigger when the canoe tips to the designated paddle side.

◆ Kneel in the canoe with the paddle in the resting position.

◆ Without changing your grip on the paddle, roll the blade over so that the back face presses against the water. Face your grip-hand knuckles down toward the water to roll the paddle over (figure CA6.7).

◆ Keep the paddle shaft perpendicular to the centerline for maximum bracing effect.

◆ Extend the paddle away from the canoe, so that your grip hand is near or in the water. A low grip hand keeps the blade near the surface and prevents it from sinking deeply into the water.

FIGURE CA6.7 Low brace.

◆ Press down on the knee closer to the paddle to move the gunwale out of the way and lean the canoe. This action simulates the capsize.

◆ Press the blade against the water and quickly use this pressure as a platform to change the lean of the boat with your knees and return upright in the canoe. Slide the paddle shaft across the gunwale and roll it over into the resting position. Remember to arrest the boat lean with knee pressure, which will stop you from pushing too hard off the paddle and straining your shoulder.

◆ Test the effectiveness of the low brace with increasingly aggressive boat leans.

Closure Activities

Activity 1: Obstacle Course Exercise (15 Minutes)

Set up an obstacle course with milk-jug buoys so that students can practice transitions between turns, including changes in boat lean. Return to reviews of specific strokes to clean up stroke efficiency. Have students observe one another and provide feedback with your assistance.

Activity 2: Water Soccer (20 Minutes)

Initiate a game of water soccer. Divide the class into two teams and create a playing field and goal lines with buoys. Students work in teams by using their paddles to manipulate the ball across their goal line to score points. You can modify the rules so that students can also throw the ball. Students must execute and practice all strokes and maneuvers.

Follow-Up Activity

Practice on Moving Water (One Hour)

Head to a river practice site with well-defined features such as shoreline eddies and midstream rocks to practice the U-turn maneuvers. A narrow section of river is useful for initial practice so that students don't have to cross large stretches of water where they can lose ground against the river. The current should be mild enough to allow students to paddle back upriver to repeat the moves and refine their execution. Encourage them to make the following adjustments to current:

◆ Shorten strokes and increase the tempo to generate momentum when entering and exiting eddies. This strategy will prevent stalling on the eddy line or sliding down it out of the eddy.

◆ Use the cross-forward to help maintain momentum. The J-stroke can interfere with generating speed because you may hang on it too long to correct your angle.

◆ Execute the strokes necessary to turn the canoe.

◆ Paddle forward to stay in the eddy.

Solo canoeists can also practice ferries by using the concepts in unit 5, lesson 10. Success with this move is enhanced by an ability to control a boat in a straight line on flatwater. In river current the solo canoeist needs to supply power as well as boat angle against the current to ferry across the river.

The solo canoeist should think and function like a stern paddler. A strong J-stroke and cross-forward are essential to developing momentum. A frustrated soloist who keeps losing the boat angle is wise to return to flatwater to practice maintaining a straight course when sprinting from a dead stop.

ASSESSMENT

- Check that students can recognize efficient elements of strokes to avoid injury by asking them to identify key elements of each stroke that will prevent injury during the student critique and feedback session in closure activity 1.
- Confirm that students can execute turning strokes to spin a canoe by watching them complete 360-degree revolutions during the main activity. You can also observe this during a game of water soccer.
- Verify that students can execute power and corrective strokes to paddle in a straight line by observing them paddle a straight course, change directions, and paddle a new straight course during the obstacle course closure activity.
- Check that students can execute bracing strokes to keep a solo canoe upright by asking them to lean their canoes progressively until they have to brace to return to an upright position.
- Ensure that students are enhancing safety by consistently controlling the canoe in activities such as water soccer or tag.
- Check that students consistently practice and model efficient body positions that promote effortless canoeing by dividing canoeists into teams of two boats and asking each canoeist to observe the other performing the different maneuvers in a "human video" format. The observers describe what they saw to the paddlers and provide one tip for each paddler to improve efficient modeling of technique.

TEACHING CONSIDERATIONS

- Students vary greatly in their ability to master the strokes. Be prepared to develop individual lesson plans so that each student practices independently rather than as an intact group.
- Begin with simple, successful maneuvers like spins before working on difficult challenges such as paddling straight.
- The cross-forward can be crucial in eliminating frustration that a solo canoeist might have in keeping a straight line. Spend some time on this stroke. Another option is teaching students how to use a forward stroke to a pry (a tandem stroke in lesson 5). Although this strategy will undermine momentum, it will allow them to move forward. Encourage them to pry quickly and return immediately to a forward stroke.
- Bracing is fun for students who don't mind swimming. Use it at any point in the program to lighten the learning and improve boat lean. Comfort with leaning can erase a host of inefficiencies with other strokes.
- Vary the types of observations depending on student needs. Some students will need more instructor feedback on stroke efficiency throughout their practice, because solo canoeing is more complex than tandem canoeing. Others may benefit from independent experimentation to refine strokes and maneuvers, which will ease the transition to paddling on their own after the lessons end.

▷ Rescues

OVERVIEW

A wise canoeist learns and practices self-rescues and group-assisted rescues to ensure that rescue skills keep pace with paddling ability. Knowing rescue priorities establishes basic principles that guide every unique rescue situation. Understanding how to complete a group-assisted rescue known as a T-rescue is necessary in the event of a capsize on flatwater. In rivers with current, students learn to perform a self-rescue as a primary form of rescue on which other rescues are based. They also learn a tow rescue to assist other canoeists in getting to shore.

JUSTIFICATION

Knowing how to rescue oneself and others is every paddler's responsibility. Canoeists' rescue skills need to match their paddling abilities so that they can manage individual and group safety in a variety of water and weather conditions. Group-assisted rescues work only if a canoeist understands basic rescue priorities and can execute an active self-rescue.

GOAL

To develop the students' ability to perform self-rescues and group-assisted rescues in calm water and in current.

OBJECTIVES

At the end of this lesson, students will be able to

- recognize appropriate rescue techniques for different situations (cognitive),
- execute efficient and effective T-rescues (psychomotor),
- initiate active self-rescue by swimming with a canoe in current (psychomotor),
- execute a tow rescue in current (psychomotor), and
- enhance safety by responding quickly and appropriately in different rescue situations (affective).

EQUIPMENT AND AREAS NEEDED

- Canoes with safety lines and flotation
- Paddles
- Helmets, when practicing rescues in current
- At least three rescue bags

RISK MANAGEMENT CONSIDERATIONS

- Use a calm-water, protected teaching area when practicing T-rescues to keep the group intact. Check water depth to make sure that students will not strike any obstacles when they tip over.

◆ Choose a practice site with moving water or class I features for river swimming and rescues. The main current should have few obstacles and a nearby shoreline eddy into which students can swim easily. The run-out below this practice site should be slow-moving water.

◆ You should demonstrate capsizes and self-rescue swimming before you ask any students to begin their practice. While doing this you can check for unforeseen hazards.

◆ Allow only one student at a time to swim in current and only one team at a time to capsize. This approach will focus the entire group on the rescue and allow you to supervise the scene effectively.

◆ Establish a communication system that alerts the entire group to the presence of swimmers and a rescue in progress.

◆ Before capsizing, encourage students to double-check security of PFDs and leave on shore any loose items in the canoes such as water bottles or sunscreen.

◆ Weather permitting, consider having students perform a swim test in flatwater before practice if you do not know the students and are unsure of their level of comfort in the water.

LESSON CONTENT

Introduction

Use the following quotations to emphasize the content covered in this lesson:

◆ "There are no rescue recipes, only ingredients."

◆ "All rescues are based on active self-rescue."

◆ "Do no harm."

◆ "Never stand up in current."

Remember that every rescue is unique and inherently chaotic. Rescues require quick decision making based on the situation. Some principles ("ingredients"), however, apply to all rescues:

◆ Rescue priorities shape the response: people first, then boats, and finally gear. Swimmers check whether their partners are OK.

◆ Swimmers must initiate an active self-rescue (figure CA7.1). This means that swimmers must be proactive by taking control of the situation and swimming the canoe and gear safely to shore or a rescue point. On flatwater, they immediately hold on to the canoe and paddles so that the gear doesn't drift away in the wind and waves. In current, each swimmer identifies a safe shore and immediately moves toward it in a safe swimming position. When swimming the boat, one swimmer can take the lead by grabbing a safety line while maintaining a position upstream of the boat and begin towing it toward shore. The second swimmer can follow behind and assist by pushing the other end of the boat using a strong scissors kick, always remembering not to place him- or herself downstream of the boat. Rolling the boat over so that the bottom is facing up will displace water and make the boat easier to manage.

◆ Group-assisted rescues cannot be executed until a person is ready to receive assistance from a safe swimming position. See lesson 3 in the rafting unit for a description of the correct swimming technique.

◆ Rescuers yell, "Canoe" to alert other boaters to a flip. They assess the overall scene and stand by if other boaters are assisting with the rescue. A rescuer has the responsibility to avoid complicating the situation.

◆ Canoeists never stand up in current; its power can knock them underwater if a foot becomes trapped in the rocks, and drowning is a possible outcome. Canoeists should always swim until they reach shallow water, which must be below the knees when standing. See the rafting unit, lesson 9, for more information on whitewater swimming and foot entrapment.

FIGURE CA7.1   Active self-rescue.

Main Activities

Activity 1: T-Rescue (30 Minutes)

Use a dry land demonstration of flatwater T-rescues so that students understand the roles of swimmers and rescuers in emptying a swamped canoe. Bring three canoes on to land and ask volunteers to assume the roles of swimmers and rescuers. The best T-rescues involve two rescue canoes side by side in a stable catamaran formation. The rescue obtains its name because rescuers paddle into position at one end of the swamped craft and form a T with it. If an appropriate site on land is unavailable, perform the demonstration in shallow water.

◆ Have the students walk the canoes into position and get into the canoes.

◆ The primary rescuers hold on to the swamped canoe, and the secondary rescuers hold on to the first rescue boat to create the catamaran.

◆ The bow paddler in the primary rescue canoe usually needs to turn around on the seat to grab the canoe.

◆ One paddler in the primary boat oversees the action and directs other canoeists when necessary.

◆ The swimmers can hold on to the capsized boat or come to the first rescue canoe and hold on to it.

◆ The primary rescuers lift one end of the overturned canoe and rest it on the gunwale of their boat. The primary rescuers slide the canoe across the gunwales and empty out the water. Figure CA7.2 shows an example using only two boats.

◆ After the overturned canoe is balanced equally across the catamaran, the primary rescuers roll the canoe over into an upright position. They slide it into the water and position it parallel to the catamaran, carefully avoiding the swimmers.

◆ The primary rescuers hold together the gunwales of the canoes before each swimmer kicks hard to reenter the canoe, one at a time.

FIGURE CA7.2   T-rescue with two boats.

After practicing on dry land, practice in the water. One canoe at a time may capsize. Continue the practice until every team has the opportunity to be swimmers, primary rescuers, and secondary rescuers.

Activity 2: Active Swimming (One Hour)

Active river swimming is the next step in a student's rescue practice.

- Analyze moving water or class I rapids with students. Identify any obstacles and lines of current that will affect their swim. Identify the safe shore (open shoreline with calm water) that students will swim toward.

- Review the river swimming position as described in the rafting unit and have them practice it on land: feet downstream to fend off obstacles, feet up and kicking near the surface, butt up, and body laid out flat on the back to slide over any underwater rocks and ledges.

- Demonstrate how to swim the rapid in the proper position, using an aggressive side stroke with strong kicking to swim toward shore.

- Establish a communication system so that only one swimmer descends the rapid at a time.

- Practice active self-rescue swim until canoeists are comfortable with it.

After practicing active river swimming, allow practice for students who want to flip over a canoe and self-rescue with the canoe.

- Tandem partners must check on each other when they surface after capsizing.

- Any paddler downstream of the canoe must immediately swim away from it.

- The swimmer on the upstream end holds on to the safety line about 4 to 5 feet (120 to 150 centimeters) away from the boat and uses an aggressive side stroke with strong kicking to swim the canoe to shore.

- If both canoeists end up swimming with the canoe, they should move away from each other on the safety line so that they do not kick each other.

Activity 3: Swimmer Assist (45 Minutes)

Use a dry-land demonstration on the river bank to show how a rescue boat can assist a swimmer (figure CA7.3).

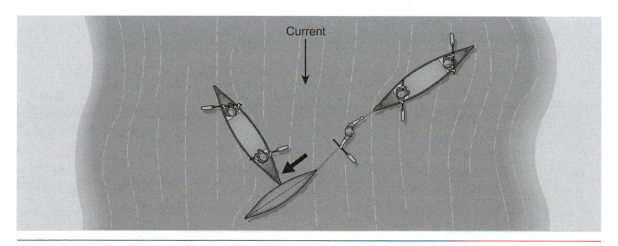

FIGURE CA7.3   Swimmer assist.

- Demonstrate how the rescue boat must spin quickly into position near the upstream end of the capsized canoe before the rescuer can hand the stern line to the swimmer.
- Emphasize that the rescuer must be very near the swimmer without hitting him or her to hand off the line.
- Show how the rescuer or rescuers must paddle hard straight toward shore, coaching the swimmer to kick hard while towing canoe in to shore.
- Continue the rescue practice on water until all canoeists have towed in a swimmer and boat.

> You may decide that your site requires that you review the use of throw bags and shoreline rescue before you practice swimming with canoes. If there is any chance that swimmers may not be able to get to shore with a canoe, add the shoreline rescue drills before the practice. See the rafting unit, lesson 8, for teaching throw-bag rescues from shore.

Closure Activities

Activity 1: T-Rescue Practice (10 Minutes)

Practice T-rescues until students can execute them smoothly and quickly. Record the elapsed times of several practice rounds and coach the teams to reduce their times until they are satisfied with their speed and efficiency.

Activity 2: Self-Rescue Practice (10 Minutes)

When swimmers are comfortable with a basic self-rescue, ask them to simulate the swimming pattern required in a rocky rapid, in which they remain on their backs but change directions by side stroking to the left and right to avoid obstacles. In subsequent practice have them flip over onto their bellies and swim aggressively toward eddies or shore with a freestyle stroke.

Activity 3: Tow Practice (10 Minutes)

Record the elapsed times of the tow rescues until canoeists improve their efficiency in towing paddlers and canoes to shore.

Follow-Up Activities

Activity 1: Increase the Challenge (30 Minutes)

When canoeists develop comfort with the exercises at a simple practice site, encourage them to practice the rescues in more challenging situations. Practice T-rescues in windy conditions and choose more technically complex rapids for self-rescue swimming.

You may have to give detailed instruction about how to empty water out of boats after towed boats make it to shore. Rolling the boat over, breaking the vacuum, and lifting from opposite ends is important.

Activity 2: Scouting the First Rapid (10 Minutes)

When scouting their first rapid on a trip, students should analyze all possible options for self-rescues and assisted rescues. Divide the students into small groups and ask them to discuss safe places to swim, safe shorelines, eddies to use, appropriate rescues for the site, and so forth. Have groups report back to the whole group and offer at least one or two options.

ASSESSMENT

◆ Check that students can recognize appropriate rescue techniques for different situations by having them analyze their first rapid and report their findings to the larger group.

◆ Verify that students can execute efficient and effective T-rescues by timing them and having them repeat the skill until times improve as described in the closure activity.

◆ Ensure that students can initiate active self-rescue by swimming with a canoe in the current as described in main activity 2. Assess by monitoring how efficiently the swimmers move the canoe to shore and how well they maintain the safe swimming position.

◆ Check that students can execute a tow rescue in current by watching whether they can efficiently spin into position near a swimmer and tow the person and canoe to shore.

◆ Confirm that students can enhance safety by responding quickly and appropriately in different rescue situations by watching their progress from the beginning to end of practice to determine whether they select appropriate strategies for each practice and increase their efficiency in executing the moves.

TEACHING CONSIDERATIONS

◆ Students will vary greatly in their comfort with rescues, particularly capsizing. Make the practice optional at each stage and encourage apprehensive students to be rescuers before they become swimmers.

◆ If some students are uncomfortable during T-rescue practice on flatwater, consider extending your flatwater program to increase comfort before beginning your instruction in current. Return to bracing activities near shore to loosen them up.

◆ If using boats with thigh straps, offer students the option to slide the straps off their thighs during initial practice.

◆ Sometimes students find that the hardest part of tow rescues is getting to the swimmer and swinging into position (not the actual towing). Consider some initial drills in which "swimmers" pretend to capsize but remain upright and drift in current, so that the rescuers can practice getting into position above the "swimmers."

UNIT 7, LESSON 8

▷ **Mechanical Rescues**

OVERVIEW

Pinning a canoe around a rock occurs when canoeists fail to anticipate the obstacle and do not paddle quickly away from it. When their canoe broaches or turns sideways against the rock, they need to lean downstream against it to prevent a pinning. After the upstream canoe gunwale sinks underwater, the canoeists need to exit the boat safely and consider how to extricate it from the river. In this lesson students learn how a mechanical rescue is useful in this situation.

JUSTIFICATION

Knowing how to use a mechanical rescue is useful in removing a canoe from a pinning situation. The canoe may be essential to your downriver travel in a backcountry situation, and it can present a hazard to other boaters if left in the river until the water subsides. Removing a pinned canoe is a paddler's responsibility.

GOAL

To develop students' knowledge of how to avoid a pinning situation and how to remove a pinned canoe using a variety of methods including a mechanical system.

OBJECTIVES

At the end of this lesson, students will be able to

- understand how to avoid a pinning situation (cognitive),
- learn how to leave the canoe safely when it pins (cognitive),
- learn how to remove a canoe without a mechanical system (cognitive),
- set up a simple mechanical system to retrieve a pinned canoe (psychomotor), and
- appreciate the danger and consequences of not handling a pinning situation appropriately (affective).

EQUIPMENT AND AREAS NEEDED

- Whitewater canoes with safety lines and flotation
- Two Pro rescue bags with rope rated at 4,500 pounds (2,000 kilograms) breaking strength
- Carabiner

RISK MANAGEMENT CONSIDERATIONS

- The mechanical system is best practiced on land until students are comfortable with the setup.
- In-water practice needs constant and close supervision, especially as students walk in current to the pinning site or handle ropes in the water. Encourage them to avoid slack ropes that can entangle rescuers.
- Retired plastic canoes are the best choice for in-water practice, because they have few sharp parts.

LESSON CONTENT

Introduction

Use the following quotations to introduce the main concepts covered in this lesson:

- "Always lean downstream; the rock is your friend."
- "When in doubt, paddle hard forward."
- "The Armstrong method is the first step."
- "A slack rope in water is a safety hazard."
- "Consider a rescue rope under tension as a firing line."

Canoeists can avoid a pinning by always being aware of obstacles downstream from their boat. Whenever canoeists are broached or perpendicular to the current, they must look downstream for upcoming rocks. Use a small model canoe and a rock to illustrate the following points:

- The initial strategy is to paddle hard forward away from any obstacles. But if the canoe floats toward a rock, lean downstream toward it to elevate your upstream gunwale. This action tilts the boat and prevents water from flowing into it. Then try to spin the canoe around the rock to float away from it.

- After incoming water pins the canoe against a rock, you must exit the boat safely to a downstream location. Lean over the downstream gunwale and crawl onto the obstacle (if the water is deep) or into shallow water on the downstream side of the canoe (figure CA8.1).

- In moving water and some class I rapids a small group of paddlers can roll the canoe off a rock without a mechanical system. This method, known as the Armstrong technique (figure CA8.2), works when paddlers stand below the canoe and roll it upstream, using the current to move the canoe away from the rock. One

FIGURE CA8.1   Exiting a pinning situation.

Current flow

FIGURE CA8.2   Armstrong technique.

person should hold on to a safety line to control the canoe when it rolls free and to swing it around in the current. You can attach a line around a **thwart** (crosspieces attached to the gunwales) to help roll the canoe.

◆ If the Armstrong method fails, the group should begin to set up a mechanical rescue such as a vector pull.

◆ All rescuers need to respect the hazard presented by ropes in water. A slack rope can trip rescuers or coil around their legs. Students should stand to the side of a rope under tension in a mechanical system in the event that a rope fails.

Main Activities

Activity 1: Dry Land Pinning Demonstration (15 Minutes)

Use an on-land site with a tree or rock to demonstrate the effect of a broach. Establish a direction for river current flowing toward the obstacle. A good simulation site will have another tree diagonally upstream of the pinning to use for the mechanical rescue.

◆ Ask two students to move a canoe into a broached position perpendicular to the obstacle.

◆ Show how boat lean can avoid a pin (tilted into the rock) and encourage it (tilted away from the rock).

◆ The canoeists can stand near their seats, and other students act like the current and hold the canoe to stabilize it. Then the canoeists show how they need to slide over the gunwales to step downstream of the canoe. Other students can assist the two canoeists from this downstream side to roll the boat upriver, overpowering the students acting as current.

◆ Use this opportunity to demonstrate what would happen if a swimmer becomes trapped and pinned between the canoe and the pinning object. You can simulate the pressure by placing a swimmer between the obstacle and the canoe and then have four or five other students press against the canoe without unduly stressing the victim. All should understand that the force of water against the canoeist is about a ton (900 kilograms) in a pinned canoe. Swimmers should always swim aggressively away from a potential pinning situation.

Activity 2: Dry Land Vector Pull (15 Minutes)

Reset the scene with a pinned canoe before beginning to set up the mechanical rescue.

◆ The first step is getting a rescue bag line from the tree on shore to the pinned canoe. Demonstrate river walking with teams of three canoeists in a train formation (figure CA8.3) or a triangle formation (figure CA8.4).

◆ Emphasize the importance of planting the feet sideways or facing upstream against current, a method that is less likely to result in feet getting stuck under rocks.

◆ Attach the rope to the canoe end nearer to the shore by tying it or clipping a carabiner to the grab loop. Walk back to the simulated shore.

◆ Run the rope back to the rescue tree and wrap it several times around the tree. Tie it off.

FIGURE CA8.3   In the train formation, the first person stabilizes with a paddle and the others hold on to PFDs.

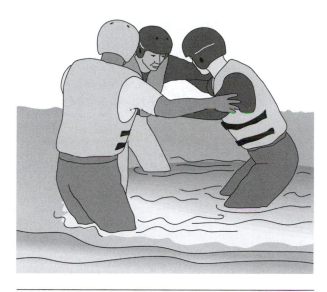

FIGURE CA8.4   In the triangle formation, two people face upstream while the third faces downstream, and the trio side-steps.

- The simplest rescue is a vector pull, in which rescuers attach the second rescue bag to the main line with a carabiner (figure CA8.5).

- Have several students pull directly back perpendicular to the main line. This force will begin to pull the canoe away from the rock.

- You can have some students act as current to test their strength against the mechanical system.

- Now consider what happens if the pulling crew stands on a simulated shore and the carabiner moves when they pull on the vector line (because they can't stand and pull perpendicular to the line). They may need to use a Prusik knot on the main line to create a stationary point to which they attach the carabiner, and then they can pull on the vector line.

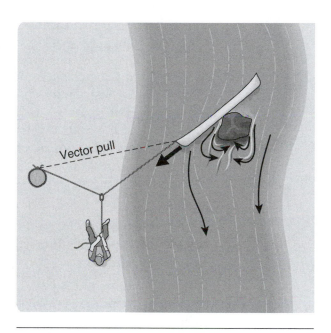

FIGURE CA8.5   Vector pull.

Activity 3: Pinning Simulation in the River (30 Minutes)

After students have practiced the setup on land, they can practice the rescue with a retired canoe against a rock in a simple moving water situation.

- Let them walk the canoe into position and broach it rather than paddle it into position against the rock, which can be hazardous to the swimmers.

- Make sure that students have an opportunity to experience a variety of roles during rescue practice until they feel comfortable with river walking, the rope setup, and positioning the webbing for the vector pull.

Closure Activities

Activity 1: Vector Pull Test (Five Minutes)

On dry land, students can test the superior strength of the vector pull by putting a small number of students on the webbing and a large number as current against the boat.

Activity 2: Walking Practice (10 Minutes)

In faster, deeper moving water, have students practice their walking techniques. Do this only in an area that is free of obstacles and has an appropriate run-out at the bottom of the rapid, such as a large eddy or calm pool, for the safety of students who lose their balance and swim.

Follow-Up Activities

Activity 1: Avoiding Pins (20 Minutes)

Have students review techniques and strategies to avoid a pinning situation by dividing them into smaller groups. Challenge them to create a five-minute presentation to teach or explain to others how to avoid pinning situations. Have one of the groups present their results. After the presentation, discuss and clarify issues.

Activity 2: Broaching Exercise (45 Minutes)

Using a retired plastic boat appropriate for pinning, pin the canoe in moving water against a single obstacle in a position known as a broach. Use a shallow-water site where students can walk easily in the water. Have the group determine the best techniques and methods to retrieve the canoe. Next, position the canoe against two rocks in a pinning known as a double-end broach and have the group modify their strategies to retrieve the boat.

ASSESSMENT

- Check that students understand how to avoid a pinning situation by asking them to identify strategies that will help them avoid being pinned as described in follow-up activity 1.
- Confirm that students have learned how to leave the canoe safely when it pins by asking them to describe safe exit strategies and demonstrate a proper exit in a simulation on land.
- Verify that students have learned how to remove a canoe without a mechanical system by asking them to describe how the force of water can help them remove a canoe using the Armstrong method and by having them simulate the removal on land.
- Check that students can set up a simple mechanical system to retrieve a pinned canoe by observing how smoothly they set up the main line and the perpendicular line in a vector pull.
- Assess whether students appreciate the danger and consequences of not handling a pinning situation appropriately by observing their behavior and level of respect when practicing exercises, particularly in moving water.

TEACHING CONSIDERATIONS

- Understanding mechanical systems can be challenging for people of certain learning styles. Avoid dry explanations of the physical forces and show how the system functions. Incorporate students in the demonstrations from the beginning.
- The simulation activities need a clear designation of current direction for some students to conceptualize the water force against the canoe. A good strategy is to set up the simulation next to the river and use the actual current direction in your simulation. Mark the current direction on the ground with a big arrow drawn in the sand or with paddles.

UNIT 7, LESSON 9

▷ Safety Considerations

OVERVIEW

Responsible canoeists plan wisely for paddling tours and trips, taking care of factors within their control so that they are prepared to handle uncontrollable factors such as adverse weather. Unfortunately, the number of canoeing accidents has risen with the increased popularity of the activity. In this lesson students learn the basic factors that have contributed to canoeing accidents. Managing a group effectively is an essential skill to prevent accidents. Students also learn how to choose appropriate environments and plan for local and backcountry travel.

JUSTIFICATION

Each canoeist has a personal responsibility to participate safely in the activity for his or her own sake and for the safety of other group members. A canoeist must prepare for tours and trips in a responsible way to prevent accidents. He or she also needs to show good judgment when traveling in a variety of environments.

GOAL

To develop students' understanding of accident prevention and safe travel for local and backcountry environments.

OBJECTIVES

At the end of this lesson, students will be able to

- identify common factors in canoeing accidents (cognitive),
- plan a local river tour or trip (cognitive),
- understand how to plan a backcountry river trip (cognitive),
- understand an international system of river communication (cognitive),
- organize a group on water (psychomotor), and
- confidently and accurately complete a self-evaluation of their abilities for a canoe trip (affective).

EQUIPMENT AND AREAS NEEDED

- Nine index cards that state common causes of accidents
- Criteria list for canoeing self-evaluation
- Checklist for trip planning
- Paddles for every group member
- Topographical maps of lakes and rivers (one for each pair of students or at least one for each group of three to four canoeists)

RISK MANAGEMENT CONSIDERATIONS

- Maintain spacing between participants when demonstrating the use of the universal signal system for communication.
- Use a philosophy of prevention rather than reaction in presenting information in this lesson.
- Find a small teaching area with the ground free of obstacles for a group game.

LESSON CONTENT

Introduction

Canoeing has long been an indigenous activity in the United States. Strong traditions have evolved from summer camp experiences. Familiarity may breed a lack of concern for the inherent hazards of the activities, from cold weather and water to changing weather and water levels. Share with students the research from the American Canoe Association's *Critical Judgment II* (2004) report:

- Fatality victims demonstrated little or no paddling skill.
- Fatality victims failed to execute even simple safety precautions.
- Fatalities often happen to people using the canoe for another activity such as hunting, fishing, or partying.
- Failure to use a **personal flotation device (PFD)** is the single greatest factor in paddle sport fatalities.
- Paddlers end up swimming from the craft for a variety of unexpected reasons: wind, waves, occupant movement, swift current, and overloading the craft.
- The combined effect of factors such as alcohol consumption, calm water (which can disguise the effects of cold water), and inexperience can contribute to a paddler's decision not to wear a PFD.

Consequently, the need for improved education around these issues is apparent. Beyond receiving instruction, beginning canoeists are wise to canoe with skilled paddlers who can maintain an intact group and follow an identifiable plan. Boating alone is not recommended, and having the support of experienced rescuers is an essential part of paddling safely.

Main Activities

Activity 1: Common Accidents (30 Minutes)

The American Canoe Association's *Critical Judgment II* (2004) identified key factors that contributed to fatalities from 1996 to 2001. Copy the cards that describe common causes of accidents from figure CA9.1 (or print them from the CD-ROM). Distribute the cards to small teams of students and ask them to prepare a one- to two-minute skit that portrays their cause. Have students read the information on the cards after their skit ends.

Activity 2: Trip Planning (30 to 60 Minutes)

Orient students to trip planning by asking them to complete the first step of the process—a self-evaluation of their canoeing abilities and trip needs (figure CA9.2). Trip planning begins with an honest evaluation of one's skills and personal needs. The selected river or lake should be within the ability of the least-skilled member of the party. A skilled recreational canoeist can paddle 3 miles per hour (5 kilometers per hour) without a break, but speed drops sharply with inexperience, lack of conditioning, hauling overnight gear, and adverse weather.

Each person should share the self-evaluation so that the group can choose a location that does not exceed abilities. Individual needs can affect trip distances, intensity (type of whitewater), routes (out-and-back or point-to-point), the need for alternate routes, and possible evacuation points.

Next, ask students to brainstorm a trip-planning checklist needed to prepare for a trip. Then check the list against a master list (figure CA9.3).

Activity 3: Group Management (15 Minutes)

A variety of factors influence management of a group on water. Rivers often lend themselves to a linear formation and a stay-to-the-right approach. Lake travel can benefit from a podlike formation to keep canoeists close together and protected from other boating traffic. Other factors include students' maturity (younger students may need a tighter organization) and ability (stay close to shore if people need breaks or additional instruction).

Review the linear and pod formations by asking students to assume different roles within a travel group and to grab the associated equipment. In a pod formation, the lead canoe may be to the side of the group as a barrier between the group and a high-traffic area. Assign the following roles:

◆ Lead canoe—knows the route, sets and adjusts the pace, carries a rescue bag for scouting rapids, communicates a plan to the group, and does not let anyone pass.

◆ Sweep canoe—makes sure that all canoes are ahead of it and carries first aid supplies, extra paddles, and rescue gear.

◆ Middle canoes—maintain the pace, pass messages between boats, and keep track of the boat behind.

Activity 4: Signal System (10 Minutes)

Review the international river signal system as a means of communicating with all canoes. See the rafting unit (lesson 3) for a description of paddle and hand signals.

◆ Test students' knowledge of signals by setting up a play area. You face the group about 20 yards (meters) away. Use a linear formation first and ask students to advance along the play area in response to paddle signals. Each paddler must pass back the signals.

◆ Repeat the activity in the pod formation and have students take different roles.

Common Causes of Accidents

Card 1

Eighty-three percent of drowning victims were not wearing a personal flotation device (life jacket).

Card 2

Occupant movement or weight shift played a major role in 50 percent of all accidents (switching positions, leaning over the side of the canoe, horseplay, standing up, casting a fishing rod).

Card 3

Fatal accidents were evenly divided between calm water and choppy or rough conditions.

Card 4

Inexperience was a contributing factor with 69 percent of fatalities having less than 90 hours of experience in the activity.

Card 5

Alcohol-related fatalities in canoeing made up more than 25 percent of the total, but alcoholic beverages were present in other accidents in which it was unclear whether they played a direct role. Alcohol does not appear to be an issue in kayaking fatalities.

Card 6

Approximately 90 percent of canoeing fatalities are male.

Card 7

Approximately 50 percent of fatalities were fishing when the accident occurred.

Card 8

Approximately 40 percent of fatalities were using aluminum canoes (for accidents in which information about boat type was available).

Card 9

Victims were generally using inexpensive canoe brands.

FIGURE CA9.1 Common causes of accidents.

From M. Wagstaff and A. Attarian, 2009, *Technical skills for adventure programming: A curriculum guide* (Champaign, IL: Human Kinetics). Adapted from the American Canoe Association's *Critical judgment II.*

Canoeist's Self-Evaluation Criteria

◆ Paddling ability—Can you paddle in a straight line? Can you control a canoe in windy conditions? Recreational canoeists with good boat control can paddle about 3 miles per hour (5 kilometers per hour).

◆ Rescue skills—Can you rescue yourself in the chosen environment (flatwater, whitewater, ocean)? Can you rescue other canoeists in your group?

◆ Pertinent medical conditions—Do you have appropriate medications? Have you accounted for a medical condition that affects your canoeing?

◆ Level of conditioning—Have you prepared your upper body for the duration and the intensity of the experience?

◆ Level of preparedness—How rested, relaxed, and well-fed are you?

◆ Group contribution—What knowledge, skills, and support can you offer the group?

◆ Personal needs—What knowledge, skills, and support do you need from the group to be an effective participant?

FIGURE CA9.2   Before planning a trip, students complete this self-evaluation to ensure that they select a destination that is within their abilities.

Trip-Planning Checklist

☐ Realistic self-evaluation and group evaluation

☐ Route research (maps, guidebooks, local canoeists, paddlers' chat groups, local paddling clubs, national paddling organizations in other countries)

☐ Local weather, water conditions, and climate (Internet resources, power company flow phones, local canoeists, daily scouting, prevailing weather and wind patterns)

☐ Permit and access clearance (private permission, public access, government permits, permitted camping and fees, parking permits and fees)

☐ Float plan (itinerary, time control including turnaround time, local emergency contacts, evacuation points, emergency contact at home who receives the float plan, emergency contact for each participant)

FIGURE CA9.3   This checklist will help ensure that students are prepared for their trip.

Closure Activity

Choosing a Route (30 Minutes)

Use topographical maps with large lakes and rivers so that small teams of students can identify possible routes and methods of organizing groups in a backcountry environment. Ask students to analyze the topography for prevailing winds, sheltered shores, and exposed stretches. Then ask them to choose a conservative route for a windy day and a more exposed route for calmer conditions. They can use the group management information to determine where the topography suggests linear or pod formations for organizing the group.

Follow-Up Activity

Developing a Trip Plan (One to Two Hours)

Assign small teams of students to develop a weekend canoe trip with a float plan and marked map that identifies the route. Ask students to use the self-questionnaires and group questionnaires to generate information about their group. Also, refer to the trip-planning information found in unit 1, lesson 2.

ASSESSMENT

- Check that students can identify common factors in canoeing accidents by engaging them in skits to role-play and discuss the major issues.
- Verify that students can plan a local river tour or trip by having them design a trip to a canoeing area using topographic maps and other trip-planning tools.
- Confirm that students understand how to plan a backcountry river trip by checking to see that their checklist for trip planning is complete.
- Check that students understand an international system of river communication by observing their ability to give and follow appropriate paddle signals on a trip.
- Confirm that students can organize a group on water by observing how they organize themselves in lead, sweep, and member roles in linear and pod formations.
- Assess whether students can confidently and accurately complete a self-evaluation of paddling abilities for a canoe trip by having them complete a self-evaluation. Structure peer and instructor feedback to determine whether those perceptions match.

TEACHING CONSIDERATIONS

- Maintain a matter-of-fact tone when discussing paddling fatalities and emphasize prevention to show students how they can take action.
- Emphasize that a canoeist's self-assessment at the specific time of the trip is essential. A person's abilities can vary from trip to trip if she or he is suffering from fatigue or emotional stress or has not practiced recently.

UNIT 7, LESSON 10

▷ Inclusion and Accessibility

OVERVIEW

Canoeing offers enormous freedom of movement to students who want to enjoy outdoor experiences but have difficulty with mobility on land. Canoeing can accommodate a variety of physical and cognitive abilities on flatwater and whitewater. Tandem canoeing in particular offers a student with a disability the help of a partner who can facilitate participation in the activity. Instructors will find that there are more similarities than differences in teaching students with disabilities and that they can manage the differences with some basic modifications of activities and equipment. Canoes can be adapted easily to improve seat outfitting and increase canoe stability, and paddle modifications can offer a person with impaired grip strength the ability to move the paddle. In this lesson you learn tips for inclusive canoe lessons and ways to achieve basic equipment modifications.

When implementing this lesson, keep in mind that you will be asking students to simulate disabilities such as blindness or deafness. Although this approach can be an effective training tool, you should preface this lesson with words of caution. Simulating a disability does not provide the student with the reality of what it would be like to have that disability, but it can offer insights into how to lead activities that accommodate a range of abilities. Whenever possible, incorporate people with disabilities into the students' training to provide a genuine inclusive learning experience.

JUSTIFICATION

Understanding how to modify lessons and equipment enables instructors to include students of all abilities in a canoe lesson. People with a range of disabilities are capable of experiencing the joy of canoeing with some simple adaptations in instruction and equipment.

GOAL

To develop students' ability to modify a lesson and equipment by working collaboratively with a person with a disability.

OBJECTIVES

At the end of this lesson, students will be able to

◆ understand how to modify a lesson for people with some common disabilities (cognitive),

◆ modify canoe seating for a person with lower-limb and torso impairments (psychomotor),

◆ modify a paddle grip for a person with upper-limb impairments (psychomotor), and

◆ enhance confidence with being able to teach a group with mixed abilities (affective).

EQUIPMENT AND AREAS NEEDED

◆ Canoes
◆ Paddles
◆ Blindfolds
◆ Ear plugs
◆ Parachute cord or small-diameter rope
◆ Duct tape
◆ Camp chairs, such as the style made by Crazy Creek or a Coleman seat back
◆ Closed-cell foam blocks and wedges
◆ Old closed-cell foam camping pads

- Flotation bags or beach balls
- Stiff plastic tubing (electric conduit)
- Old mountain bicycle inner tubes
- Old work gloves and mittens
- Zip ties
- Foam pipe insulation
- Knife (for cutting foam)
- Wrench
- Pliers

RISK MANAGEMENT CONSIDERATIONS

- Use a teaching area with a stable surface and gently sloping shoreline that is wheelchair accessible.
- Use additional instructors as needed to provide assistance and supervision when working with persons with disabilities.
- Consider whether two novice students with disabilities are capable of paddling in the same canoe. Alternatively, pair them with experienced students.
- Adapted seating and paddle grips should allow students to swim free of the canoe and paddle in the event of a capsize.

LESSON CONTENT

Introduction

When creating accessible canoeing programs, keep in mind four basic concepts: a paddler's interview, motivation, group or private lessons, and simple adaptations.

Paddler's Interview

An individual interview with a person with a disability can provide a wealth of information. The individual knows his or her abilities best, and you provide the expertise about canoeing. Together, you can strategize the best approach to the lesson, transfers into the canoe, and equipment adaptations. The American Canoe Association has curricula and resources available to facilitate adaptive paddling programs at www.americancanoe.org/GetGo/adaptivepaddling.lasso.

Motivation

Canoeing is a mental and physical activity, and people with a physical disability are powerfully motivated to canoe and are effective decision makers. In the paddler's interview, check the individual's needs and wants. In whitewater conditions some people benefit from paddling in the stern where they can follow the path or strategy initiated by the bow paddler. The rear position gives them an extra second of decision-making time, and they can read the body language of their partner. Some paddlers may want the reassurance of being paired with a skilled canoeist or a family member, which can relax them and increase enjoyment. Solo canoeing can provide a person with a disability with a feeling of independence and freedom. With information from you about the activity, they should determine the level of challenge they are willing to embrace.

Group or Private Lessons

The interview will tell you whether a person will benefit from a private or group lesson. If a person has the ability to participate with an equipment adaptation, inclusion in a group lesson is appropriate. The social nature of a group may be an important personal need. Another benefit is that many families and friends want to understand how to support the person with a disability in the activity beyond a lesson. Otherwise, a person may benefit from individual attention in a private lesson and may prefer it.

Simple Adaptations

Simple, inexpensive adaptations allow you to outfit a person for canoeing quite easily. Simplicity is best, because it increases the paddler's ability to separate from the adaptation quickly if necessary and it decreases preparation time before the program. Your goal is to develop an adaptation that provides enough support without compromising the ability to take efficient strokes, is secure enough to stay intact with movement, and is safe enough to allow a canoeist to exit the boat during a capsize. More expensive adaptations are available, but home-grown ingenuity allows you and your student to handle a variety of adaptations.

Main Activities

Activity 1: Paddling With Visual Impairments (30 Minutes)

In the paddler's interview, begin by asking the person what he or she can actually see. Glare on water can make it difficult for some paddlers to see landforms, river features, and current lines, but many can quickly sense changes in current speed in rivers and wind direction on flatwater.

Consider these teaching suggestions and adaptations:

◆ Pair the person with a partner who can see and ask the partner to provide oral coaching. Coaching can occur within a tandem canoe from either end of the canoe or in solo canoes with partners remaining in proximity to enhance conversation.

◆ Coaches can provide clear cues and directions that appeal to other senses (for example, go left or right, go straight, turn into the wind, spin toward the sun, shore is about 10 strokes away, the eddy line is coming in 3 strokes). Solo canoeing practice should occur at a mild practice site with a partner who can quickly and concisely communicate strategies for handling current and river features.

Pair up solo students and designate instructor and paddler roles. With tandem canoeists, have an instructor team and a paddling canoe. The paddlers will wear a blindfold or close their eyes, and the instructors will be sighted. The task is to follow a circuitous route at a flatwater site where the teacher coaches the paddler with oral cues. Establish a freeze command to control the activity so that paddlers do not bump into each other. Then switch roles. Have students share their perspectives in each of these roles.

Activity 2: Paddling With Hearing Impairments (30 Minutes)

Speak directly to a person with a hearing impairment and enunciate words clearly to allow lip reading. Visual demonstrations and cues are effective. Include the interpreter as a student if the person is expected to paddle a canoe as a group member. If the interpreter is along for the ride as third seat in a canoe, teach directly to the person with a hearing impairment.

Consider these teaching suggestions and adaptations:

- Establish simple signals for on-water communication that may go beyond the international signal system. Practice the signals so that they are clear. Advanced canoeists have created signals for challenging river features such as holes.

- Initial tandem practice is effective if the person with a hearing impairment paddles in the stern and can see signals from the bow. When the person switches to the bow, the stern paddler can tap on the canoe to create vibrations to get the partner's attention.

- Keep tandem canoeists together for a longer period if their communication system is working.

- Early practice on lakes and rivers is often effective when a person with a hearing impairment paddles immediately behind an instructor. He or she can see the desired route and receive signals without having them filtered through other students.

- After initial practice in solo canoeing, establish a buddy system for river trips in which the partner of a person with a hearing impairment paddles a rapid first so that he or she can communicate by sending visual signals upriver.

Pair up students or canoe teams and designate instructor and paddler roles. Give ear plugs to the paddlers. Ask the instructors to teach a basic stroke or direct practice of a maneuver through visual cues and demonstration. Then have students switch roles. They can share perspectives from each of the roles.

Activity 3: Paddling With Lower-Limb and Trunk Impairments (One Hour)

People with trunk and lower-limb impairments may have difficulty executing some canoe strokes, sitting unsupported on a canoe seat, maintaining balance when trying to lean a boat, and entering or exiting a canoe. Consider these lesson and equipment adaptations:

- Use a kayak paddle for greater and more uniform power.

- Lower the canoe seat several inches (centimeters) to increase stability. Buy longer bolts and create spacers between the seat and gunwales with stiff plastic tubing (for example, electrical conduit).

- Add back and side chest support to prevent the paddler from tipping over. Tie a Coleman seat back or Crazy Creek chair to the canoe seat and pad it with foam wedges (figure CA10.1). Cover the wedges with a neoprene pad to enhance skin protection. Be sure that the person can exit the boat easily if it capsizes.

  - Provide additional bracing for the feet by taping foam wedges, a flotation bag, or a beach ball into the bow. Make sure that the feet will float free if the boat capsizes.

  - Transfers from a wheelchair into the canoe can occur with a midpoint transition, such as lowering onto an upended plastic crate (covered with a closed-cell pad to protect the skin) at about the same height as the gunwale and then sliding over onto the seat.

  - Two people can lift a person into a canoe. One person lifts the torso, and the other person lifts the legs (figure CA10.2). The person being lifted will know how to direct the lift.

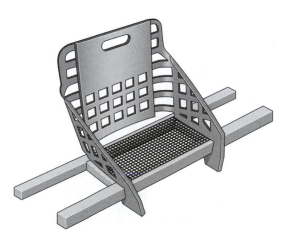

FIGURE CA10.1   Adaptive canoe seat.

◆ Practicing bracing strokes is essential so that the paddler can arrest any tipping of the upper body. More vertical strokes like Duffeks also provide additional support in turning if a person cannot lean the boat with the lower body.

◆ Padding the gunwales with a foam pad or pipe insulation can make wet-exit practice easier, especially if the person has little or no sensation in the legs. Rescuers can lower the canoe side, even slightly underwater, so that the swimmer can more easily slide over the gunwale into the canoe (figure CA10.3). They can help guide the swimmer's legs into the canoe if necessary. They then bail the canoe.

Provide students with seat adaptation materials and divide them into small teams. Assign these tasks to different teams: seat adaptation with Coleman seat back, seat adaptation with Crazy Creek, seat lowering.

FIGURE CA10.2   Transfer lift.

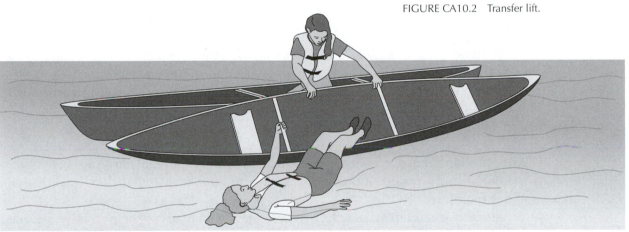

FIGURE CA10.3   Tilting canoe for reentry.

In addition, practice T-rescues with the scooping action (dropped gunwale) that allows a person to slide over the gunwale to reenter the canoe more easily. The swimmers should not use their lower legs to reenter the canoe.

Activity 4: Paddling With Upper-Limb Impairments (15 Minutes)

People with arthritis, neuromuscular disease, quadriplegia, and brain injuries may lack strength, have difficulty holding a paddle, lack range of motion, and be unable to swim. Consider these teaching suggestions and adaptations:

◆ Lighter boats and paddles are useful to reduce fatigue.

◆ Use a paddle with less surface area (narrower blade), which requires less strength to use.

◆ Use a kayak paddle for additional power.

◆ Use an adapted grip on the paddle with foam pipe insulation and bicycle inner tubes (figure CA10.4).

◆ Keep the paddle strokes lower to the water so that the canoeist does not have to lift the paddle as high.

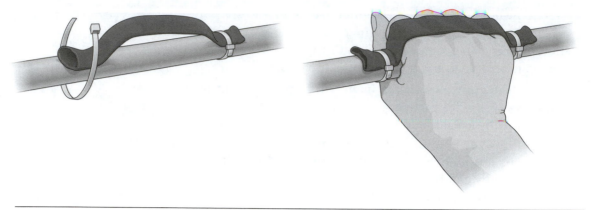

FIGURE CA10.4   Adapted hand grip.

Adapted, by permission, from A. Wortham Webre and J.A. Zeller, 1990, *Canoeing and kayaking for persons with disabilities, instruction manual* (Springfield, VA).

◆ A person may not have sufficient range of motion to use cross-strokes, so teach strokes that the person can execute on her or his strongest paddling side.

◆ If swimming ability is low or nonexistent, consider buying PFDs with greater flotation.

Provide hand adaptation materials and divide the group into small teams. Assign each team the task of creating a grip adaptation from the materials.

Closure Activity

Reflection (40 Minutes)

After students have coached paddlers with simulated sight and hearing impairments, lead a group discussion in which students share what they have learned about each role.

After the seat adaptation activity, have each team analyze their creation in terms of time required to construct, degree of stability achieved, functional performance, and ease of extrication.

After the grip adaptation activity, have each team analyze the final product for time required to construct, paddle control, and ease of extrication.

After scoop T-rescues, discuss the different ways in which rescuers and swimmers assisted with the modified rescue.

Follow-Up Activity

Paddler's Interview (20 Minutes)

The sighted and hearing activities can be taken to a moving water practice site so that students can experience what will occur in current. Manage the practice by creating distinct stations at the site that do not interfere with each other.

◆ Eliminate the blindfolds and ask people to close their eyes.

◆ Ask a local agency if people with disabilities would be willing to participate in parts of a lesson—a paddler's interview, outfitting session, and a lesson or tour. Assign small teams of students (two to three people) to work with each participant. Ask them to develop a list of questions for the paddler's interview and a content outline for the lesson that contains necessary modifications for their client.

ASSESSMENT

◆ Check that students understand how to modify a lesson for people with common disabilities by reviewing their paddler's interview questions and modified content outline for completeness.

◆ Confirm that students can modify canoe seating for a person with lower-limb and torso impairments by checking the modified seating for security, support, and ease of extrication.

◆ Verify that students can modify a paddle grip for a person with upper-limb impairments by checking the paddle grips for quickness of construction, paddle control, and ease of extrication.

◆ Assess whether students have gained confidence with teaching a group of mixed abilities by observing their effectiveness in teaching each other during mock activities for sight and hearing impairments or by observing how they teach a canoe lesson to a group with mixed abilities.

TEACHING CONSIDERATIONS

◆ Some students may be apprehensive about working with people with disabilities if they have had no previous exposure. Encourage them to relax and be open with a participant about what they know and do not know. Encourage them to treat the experience as a partnership.

◆ Encourage creativity with the adaptations. Methods are constantly evolving, and some students can develop entirely new functional modifications from a variety of scrap materials.

◆ Create a common area for supplies. The supply depot should have a well-defined area for tools, which can become lost in the grass.

◆ Clean up the area completely after the activity. Pieces of foam and tape will migrate into the landscape.

UNIT 7, LESSON 11

▷ Leave No Trace Considerations

OVERVIEW

Ecologically aware canoeists understand the topography of the landscape surrounding lakes and rivers and know how to apply Leave No Trace (LNT) principles to these environments. Canoeists should always work to minimize their impact on the water, shorelines, and surrounding terrain.

JUSTIFICATION

Many lakes and rivers traveled by canoeists experience a high number of visitors, and the lake and river corridors are showing increased signs of use. A variety of bird and animal life share these water corridors. Understanding their habitat needs is important.

GOAL

To develop students' understanding of how to apply LNT principles to water-based programs and environments.

OBJECTIVES

At the end of this lesson, students will be able to

◆ identify areas of impact around lakes and rivers (cognitive),

◆ analyze a map and identify potentially fragile areas (cognitive), and

◆ develop criteria by which a group will select rest breaks and campsites on a canoe trip (affective).

EQUIPMENT AND AREAS NEEDED

◆ Index cards with the seven LNT principles

◆ Topographical maps with lakes and rivers (one for each pair of students or at least one for each group of three to four canoeists)

◆ Field guides to trees, birds, and mammals for the region

◆ Internet access

RISK MANAGEMENT CONSIDERATIONS

None.

LESSON CONTENT

Introduction

Most environmental impact along a lake or river corridor happens within .25 miles (.4 kilometers) of the banks, where canoeists concentrate their activity during rest breaks and overnight camping. Especially in locales where vegetation is thick along shorelines, paddlers can find it difficult to get far enough from the shore to observe LNT practices. Also, campsites in well-traveled areas are often obvious, heavily impacted, and in locations that capitalize on an attractive view. The shoreline, which can quickly show evidence of erosion, is also home to plants and animals, including species with special status that should not be disturbed.

Main Activity

Topographical Map Review (30 Minutes)

Have students use the topographical maps to examine the ecological features within .25 miles (.4 kilometers) of a river stretch (bank elevation, likely soil stability, wetlands, likely vegetation, notable birds and animals). Ask students to consider the impact of the canoes on the riverine environment, noting especially the length, weight, and number of canoes in a group. Use the seven LNT principles to guide the decision-making process.

Have them develop a list of characteristics for suitable riverside stops for bio breaks, eating, and camping: stable banks, sandy soil, stony ground, ledges, lack of protected aquatic plants, and seasonal animal and bird considerations, such as nesting, birthing, and molting cycles. They can use field guides for the region to study the behavior of common species, such as beaver, otter, loons, osprey, eagles, and aquatic plants and shrubs. Internet resources offer information about state heritage programs and protected status for birds and mammals in the region. Also, they can check other government regulations or local practices that may influence use. For instance, catholes may be prohibited on small islands on well-traveled lakes.

Ask students to identify on the map prospective campsites that might meet acceptable practices. Also ask them to identify areas that would be inappropriate for stops. Initiate a discussion about the advantages and disadvantages of using heavily impacted, "sacrifice" sites and new campsites that adhere to LNT principles, and ask them to develop criteria for site selection that the group will use during a canoe trip. Ask them open-ended questions, such as the following:

◆ Should we use the existing heavily eroded path up from the shore, or should we find alternative paths?

◆ Should we use "sacrifice" campsites or use low-impact practices at new sites?

◆ In what situations or under what conditions might the group consider some impact to be acceptable?

Closure Activity

Facilitating Other LNT Activities (Time as Needed)

To emphasize LNT practices related to canoeing, consider facilitating activities found in the whitewater kayaking unit, lesson 11 and the rafting unit, lesson 10. The activities and information there apply directly to canoeing.

Follow-Up Activity

Raising Awareness (Time as Needed)

During a canoeing trip with the students, identify impacted areas along the way. Take time during the trip to analyze the area and discuss the issues. For example, identify areas where severe erosion has occurred because of boater use. Observe impacted campsites or parking areas and discuss the problems and solutions. In addition, challenge students to collect trash during the trip to raise awareness and to reinforce appropriate behavior.

ASSESSMENT

◆ Check that students can identify areas of impact around lakes and rivers by reading a topographical map and identifying likely areas of impact during travel.

◆ Verify that students can identify potentially fragile areas by describing the terrain revealed by the map along lake and river corridors.

◆ Confirm that students can develop criteria by which a group will select rest breaks and campsites on a canoe trip through a group discussion that results in a consensus about the criteria.

TEACHING CONSIDERATIONS

◆ Be ready to assist with interpretation of the map information. Some students have difficulty extracting this data because of their limited ecological knowledge or lack of map-reading skills.

◆ Avoid being the authority on ecological practices. Encourage students to develop their own values in applying the LNT principles.

Canoeing Skills Checklist

☐ 1. Understand different types and styles of canoeing.

☐ 2. Select appropriate equipment for flatwater and whitewater canoeing.

☐ 3. Efficiently transport, carry, and enter a canoe.

☐ 4. Balance and lean a canoe using efficient body dynamics.

☐ 5. Perform efficient turning strokes in the bow and stern positions to spin a canoe.

☐ 6. Perform efficient power and corrective strokes in the bow and stern positions to travel in a straight line.

☐ 7. Control a tandem canoe from the stern in windy conditions on flatwater.

☐ 8. Control a solo canoe in windy conditions on flatwater.

☐ 9. Understand river features in class I–II whitewater.

☐ 10. Choose appropriate routes in class I–II whitewater.

☐ 11. Execute ferries, eddy turns, and peel-outs from the bow and stern positions in whitewater.

☐ 12. Execute ferries, eddy turns, and peel-outs from a solo position in whitewater.

☐ 13. Perform an effective T-rescue.

☐ 14. Swim a rapid and perform a self-rescue.

☐ 15. Tow a swimmer to a safe shore.

☐ 16. Tow a canoe to a safe shore.

☐ 17. Remove a pinned canoe with a mechanical rescue.

☐ 18. Know common factors in canoeing accidents.

☐ 19. Plan and complete a local canoe trip.

☐ 20. Plan a canoe program that accommodates a student with a disability.

☐ 21. Develop an emergency response plan for a river trip.

☐ 22. Organize and lead a group on water.

☐ 23. Understand and use a signal system for on-water communication.

☐ 24. Know LNT practices for a river corridor in your region.

☐ 25. Plan and complete a multiday canoe trip.

☐ 26. Accurately complete a self-evaluation of knowledge and skills.

Use the canoing skills checklist as an additional tool to assess the skills learned throughout this unit.

From M. Wagstaff and A. Attarian, 2009, *Technical skills for adventure programming: A curriculum guide* (Champaign, IL: Human Kinetics).

GLOSSARY

back face—The side of the paddle blade that has no pressure against it during the forward stroke; the side opposite the power face.

beam—The maximum width of a canoe.

bow—The front of a canoe.

canoe poling—A type of canoeing in which the canoeist uses a 12-foot (4-meter) pole to go upriver or downriver, often but not always in shallow water. A canoeist who poles can perform the same maneuvers as a whitewater canoeist.

canoe slalom—A style of recreational racing in whitewater in which canoeists navigate a 25-gate (hanging pole) course in upstream- or downstream-facing positions. The fastest elapsed time wins, and touched poles result in added time penalties. Short boats that change directions quickly are best.

catch phase—The beginning of the stroke, where the blade catches the water fully.

centerline—An imaginary line down the middle of the canoe from bow to stern.

cross-draw stroke—A stroke that has the opposite effect of a draw; it moves the bow of a canoe away from the paddler's designated paddling side.

deck plates—Plates at the bow and stern that attach to the gunwales and shed water.

draw stroke—A stroke that moves the canoe toward the blade.

feathering—A recovery of the blade so that the paddle is above the water and flattened to the water surface to minimize wind resistance.

flare—Progressive widening of the hull from the waterline to the gunwales to deflect water and increase stability in rough water.

forward stroke—A stroke that propels the boat forward.

forward sweep—A stroke that propels the boat forward and turns it away from the paddler's designated paddling side.

freestyle canoeing—Smooth, flowing, gymnastic maneuvers set to music; sometimes called canoe ballet or canoe dancing. Judges grade technical and artistic merit. The canoeist often leans the canoe aggressively on its side to turn it more easily.

grip—The top of the paddle shaft where the canoeist grabs it.

gunwale—The rail along the top edge of the canoe that stiffens the canoe shape.

high brace—A stroke used to grab water when the canoe tips away from the designated paddling side.

hull—The body of a canoe stripped of any additional parts.

J-lean—A separation of the upper and lower bodies to maintain boat balance; the lower body forms the curved J by having one knee pressing down and the other knee lifting up; the torso remains upright.

J-stroke—Propels the boat forward and moves the bow toward the stern paddler's designated paddling side.

low brace—A stroke used like a beaver tail or outrigger when the canoe tips to the designated paddling side.

maneuvers—The effects of paddle strokes on a canoe.

marathon racing—A flatwater event in which canoeists use longer boats to race various distances from 5 miles (8 kilometers) to ultramarathon distances of 250 miles (400 kilometers). Some routes require portages. A whitewater variation called downriver racing requires that canoeists descend rapids and avoid obstacles.

offside—The direction of a maneuver in which the boat moves away from the bow canoeist's designated paddling side.

onside—The direction of a maneuver in which the boat moves toward the bow canoeist's designated paddling side.

outrigger canoeing—A team style of canoeing in long, ocean-worthy boats with outriggers for enhanced stability.

paddler's box—An imaginary box in front of the canoeist's body plane that goes no higher than the forehead, stays in front of the torso and shoulders, and extends as far forward as the canoeist can comfortably reach.

painter lines—The safety lines attached to the end of the canoe.

personal flotation device (PFD)—A vest-style jacket filled with foam panels that provide buoyancy.

port—The left side of a canoe when facing the bow.

power face—The side of the paddle blade pressed against the water during a forward stroke.

power phase—The part of a stroke in which the paddler applies force against the paddle to move the canoe.

pry stroke—A stroke that moves the canoe forcefully away from the blade.

recovery phase—The part of a stroke in which the blade is returned to the catch position.

reverse sweep—A stroke that pulls the canoe bow toward the paddle blade and pushes the canoe backward.

rocker—The curved shape of the hull when viewed from the side; greater rocker increases turning ability but decreases tracking ability.

shaft—The narrow neck on a paddle between the grip and the blade. A straight shaft has no angles from grip to blade; a bent shaft creates a 5- to 17-degree angle between blade and shaft.

slice—A recovery of the paddle below the water surface to the catch; the blade is usually parallel to oncoming water to minimize water resistance.

solo canoeing—A style of canoeing in which one person controls the boat.

spins—A maneuver in which the boat turns in tight circles.

starboard—The right side of a canoe when facing the bow.

stem—Upright part of the bow where the sides meet; similar to the prow of a ship.

strokes—Actions with a paddle that cause a canoe to maneuver.

tandem canoeing—Canoeing in which two people control the boat; the bow paddler controls the front, and the stern paddler controls the back.

T grip—A paddle grip shaped like a T that offers precise control of the blade angle.

thwart—A crosspiece on a canoe that attaches to the gunwales and stiffens the canoe shape.

torso rotation—The swiveling of the upper body around the spine; the use of the strong abdominal muscles to power a paddle stroke.

tumblehome—The inward sloping of the upper canoe sides from its widest point to the gunwales.

umiak—A large skin boat used by indigenous cultures primarily to transport people and goods.

wet exit—An exit from a capsized canoe in which the paddler brings the head to the knees, releasing thigh tension against straps, and pushes away from the canoe.

whitewater—Turbulent, aerated water.

whitewater rodeo—Competition in which paddlers execute maneuvers in a river play spot characterized by waves and holes. Judges score the competitors on artistry and degree of difficulty. Short boats with lots of flotation bags to displace water are best.

REFERENCES AND RESOURCES

REFERENCES

Bond, H. (1995). *Boats and boating in the Adirondacks.* Blue Mountain Lake, NY: Adirondack Museum/ Syracuse University Press.

Gullion, L. (1999). *Canoeing: A woman's guide.* Camden, ME: Ragged Mountain Press/McGraw-Hill.

Jennings, J. (2002). *The canoe: A living tradition.* Buffalo: Firefly Books.

Kawaharada, D. (n.d.). The settlement of Polynesia, part I. Retrieved from http://pvs.kcc.hawaii.edu/migrationspart1.html

Snaith, S. (1997). *Umiak: An illustrated guide.* Eastsound, WA: Walrus & Hyde.

RESOURCES

American Canoe Association and National Safe Boating Council. (2004). *Critical judgment II: Understanding and preventing canoe and kayak fatalities 1996–2002.* Newington, VA: Author. Overview: An in-depth source of statistics and analysis of common boating accidents, their causes, and prevention.

Bechdel, L., & Ray, S. (1997). *River rescue: A manual for whitewater safety* (3rd ed.). Boston: Appalachian Mountain Club Books. Overview: A comprehensive rescue handbook for canoe, kayak, and raft that explains and diagrams beginner and advanced techniques.

Conover, G. (1991). *Beyond the paddle—a canoeist's guide to expedition skills: Poling, lining, portaging, and maneuvering through the ice.* Gardiner, ME: Tilbury House. Overview: A comprehensive instructional book for wilderness canoe poling with crossover application to paddling a tandem whitewater canoe.

Davidson, J., & Rugge, J. (1983). *The complete wilderness paddler.* New York: Vintage Books. Overview: The bible of wilderness canoeing and still relevant to canoe trippers, this artful, humorous book follows two men from the initial stages of trip preparation through their journey down the Moisie River in Quebec.

Ford, K. (1991). *Solo playboating I & II* [Videotape]. Durango, CO: Performance Video and Instruction. Overview: Two instructional videotapes with practical, enjoyable tips for whitewater solo canoeing.

Ford, K. (2004). *Whitewater self-defense* [DVD]. Durango, CO: Performance Video and Instruction. Overview: An informative rescue DVD for recreational paddlers who want simple approaches to everyday river safety and rescue.

Foster, T. (2006). *Solo open whitewater canoeing: An instructional video with the focus on carving* [DVD]. Outdoor Experience Media Productions. Overview: An in-depth instructional DVD that provides beginner and advanced tips for technically precise solo canoeing.

Gullion, L. (1996). *The American Canoe Association's kayak and canoe games.* Birmingham, AL: Menasha Ridge Press. Overview: A small resource that offers quick games and fun-filled activities for teaching kayaking and canoeing with kids and adults.

Jacobson, C. (2005). *Expedition canoeing: A guide to canoeing wild rivers in North America* (20th anniversary ed.). Helena, MT: Falcon Guides. Overview: A how-to book filled with a myriad of practical and humorous tips about outfitting and executing canoe trips.

Mason, B., & Mason, P. (1995). *Path of the paddle.* Minocqua, WI: NorthWord Press. Overview: A revised and updated version of Bill Mason's classic instructional canoe book that profiles the Canadian style of wilderness canoeing.

Walbridge, C., & Sundmacher, W. (1995). *Whitewater rescue manual: New techniques for canoeists, kayakers, and rafters.* Camden, ME: Ragged Mountain Press. Overview: A helpful handbook with step-by-step directions for a variety of technical rescues.

Webre, A., & Zeller, J. (1990). *Canoeing and kayaking for persons with physical disabilities, instructionmanual.* Menasha Ridge Press. Newington, VA: American Canoe Association. Overview: Still the definitive handbook with practical advice on specific disabilities, effective teaching strategies, and equipment adaptations.

Rafting

Christopher R. Pelchat and Michael L. Kinziger

UNIT 8, LESSON 1

▷ Introduction to Rafting

OVERVIEW

Having working knowledge of the history of any given recreational sport breathes life into the experience. In this lesson students learn the key historical points of reference that led to the development of the sport of whitewater rafting.

JUSTIFICATION

Having knowledge of the history of rafting creates a greater appreciation of the sport and the natural environment in which we travel.

GOAL

To develop students' awareness of the roots and current status of whitewater rafting as a recreational sport.

OBJECTIVES

At the end of this lesson, students will be able to

- identify the historical roots of rafting (cognitive),
- summarize current facts and issues related to rafting (cognitive),
- appreciate the valor that went into the first whitewater river adventures (affective), and
- share personal rafting experiences and relate them to the historical endeavors of river exploration (affective).

EQUIPMENT AND AREAS NEEDED

- Index cards with historical events on them
- Name tags for each student
- Rafting video or DVD (e.g., Warriner's *Journey Into the Great Unknown*)

RISK MANAGEMENT CONSIDERATIONS

- Check the outdoor teaching area for environmental hazards and take appropriate precautions.
- Ensure that participants remain hydrated during extended periods of instruction.

LESSON CONTENT

Introduction

The way in which whitewater adventure sports came into existence is an exciting and evolutionary tale. Since the beginning of time people have been using rivers as routes of travel. The rivers that we now use as recreational outlets were once highways that connected distant villages.

Main Activities

The history of paddle crafts is covered thoroughly in lessons in the canoeing and kayaking units. To enhance this learning experience, incorporate the activities from those lessons. Rafting is relatively new compared with the other forms of water travel.

Activity 1: History (10 Minutes)

Put the historical events listed here on index cards without the dates. You can also copy the cards from figure RA1.1 or print them from the CD-ROM. Hand out the cards and have the group discuss the events. The students should attempt to put the cards in chronological order. This activity works well as an icebreaker to get the lesson started. Using information from lessons in the previous units will enhance this exercise.

- 1842: Lieutenant John Fremont explored the Platte River in a rudimentary square Horace Day army raft.
- 1869: John Wesley Powell led a team of explorers through the Grand Canyon section of the Colorado River in decked wooden oar boats that required looking upstream when traveling downriver.
- 1896: Circumstantial evidence indicates that Nathaniel Galloway, a hunter and trapper from Utah, first used the stern-first, face-forward technique against the current, to increase maneuverability.
- 1909: Julius Stone ran what is considered the first commercial rafting trip down the Grand Canyon with five participants, one of whom was Nathaniel Galloway. After completing the trip Galloway was the first to have boated the Grand Canyon twice.
- 1938: Amos Burg used the newly designed rubber army rafts to run the Middle Fork of the Salmon River in Idaho.
- 1952: Bus Hatch received the first commercial rafting concession in the country for rivers in Utah.
- 1965: Bryce Whitmore built a craft that looks similar to modern catarafts.
- Early 1980s: Self-bailing rafts became popular, reducing the need to bail water from boats with buckets.

Activity 2: Rafting Today (15 Minutes)

Lead a discussion of current facts and issues related to rafting. Use the following to spark discussion ideas. Depending on your knowledge and the knowledge of the students, you may need to assign the following items for students to research as a homework assignment to enrich the discussion. Use the resource list found at the end of this unit as a place to begin the research process.

- Current status of the industry such as number of commercial operations, examples of popular rafting rivers, state licensure requirements, and operations
- Popularity as indicated by permits issued, use numbers, and so on
- Professional associations and groups and ways to receive further training (for example, American Canoe Association, America Outdoors, state outfitter associations)

Rafting History Cards

Lieutenant John Fremont explored the Platte River in a rudimentary square Horace Day army raft.

Amos Burg used the newly designed rubber army rafts to run the Middle Fork of the Salmon River in Idaho.

John Wesley Powell led a team of explorers through the Grand Canyon section of the Colorado River in decked wooden oar boats that required looking upstream when traveling downriver.

Bus Hatch received the first commercial rafting concession in the country for rivers in Utah.

Circumstantial evidence indicates that Nathaniel Galloway, a hunter and trapper from Utah, first used the stern-first, face-forward technique against the current, to increase maneuverability.

Bryce Whitmore built a craft that looks similar to modern catarafts.

Julius Stone ran what is considered the first commercial rafting trip down the Grand Canyon with five participants, one of whom was Nathaniel Galloway. After completing this trip Galloway was the first to have boated the Grand Canyon twice.

Self-bailing rafts became popular, reducing the need to bail water from boats with buckets.

FIGURE RA1.1   Historical facts about rafting.

From M. Wagstaff and A. Attarian, 2009, *Technical skills for adventure programming: A curriculum guide* (Champaign, IL: Human Kinetics).

◆ How rafting differs now from the original trips in the 1800s—gourmet trips, full-service guiding, technology, equipment

◆ Paddle rafting versus oar rigging; one-day experiences versus multiday wilderness trips

Closure Activity

Sharing Experiences (10 Minutes)

Have participants share personal rafting experiences to broaden the group's perception of the activity. If participants have no rafting experience, obtain a rafting video that demonstrates the nature of the sport, such as Castillo and Rypins' *Let's Get Wet*.

Follow-Up Activity

Searching for Diverse Opportunities (15 Minutes)

Have students identify rafting opportunities on the Internet, either in class if access is available or as homework. Have groups share their findings by discussing the variety of trips, rivers, companies, and opportunities.

ASSESSMENT

◆ Confirm that students can identify the historical roots of rafting by appropriately placing the index cards in chronological order.

◆ Check that students can summarize current facts and issues related to rafting by discussing issues and trends in whitewater rafting and assimilating information.

◆ Verify that students appreciate the valor that went into the first whitewater river adventures by discussing and acknowledging the dramatic changes in the sport since its inception.

◆ Check that students share personal rafting experiences and relate them to the historical endeavors of river exploration by storytelling and referring to historical facts outlined in this unit and other water-based units.

TEACHING CONSIDERATIONS

◆ Students with no rafting experience will benefit from a video or visual images of the activity.

◆ A number of states such as Idaho, Colorado, Maine, and New York regulate the whitewater rafting industry in their states. Use the information provided by those states and others to obtain outfitter and guide requirements.

◆ Refer to the American Canoe Association for curriculum and instructor training requirements related to whitewater rafting.

UNIT 8, LESSON 2

▷ Equipment and Use

OVERVIEW

Students learn to identify a variety of rafting equipment including variations in boat design. Proper use of equipment is explored including an introduction to rigging and loading rafts.

JUSTIFICATION

Water sports have evolved a great deal over the years, and rafting technology has followed suit. Whitewater rafts and accompanying equipment continue to change and improve; the changes provided stronger, more durable, more capable, and more versatile rafts. As the equipment changes, participants need to stay familiar with trends, styles, and ideas.

GOAL

To develop students' ability to understand, identify, and appreciate essential equipment and its proper use.

OBJECTIVES

At the end of this lesson, students will be able to

◆ identify proper equipment for a specific application (cognitive),

◆ describe the equipment and its function (cognitive),

◆ demonstrate the correct placement and use of the equipment (psychomotor),

◆ develop their own opinions and preferences with the equipment choices (affective), and

◆ value the importance of proper equipment maintenance (affective).

EQUIPMENT AND AREAS NEEDED

◆ Several types of inflatable whitewater crafts (paddle rafts, oar rigs, and catarafts of various sizes)

◆ Rafting accessories (paddles, oars, frames, lashing material, bow lines, dry bags, thwart bags, electric and hand pumps)

◆ Safety equipment (flip lines, throw bags, rescue gear, spare PFD, spare paddle or oar, medical kit, hypothermia kit, and repair kit)

◆ Personal equipment (helmet, PFD, wet suit or dry suit, foot protection, whistle, and river knife)

◆ Sample equipment list

RISK MANAGEMENT CONSIDERATIONS

◆ Ensure that students use caution when carrying or moving large heavy objects such as the rafts and frames.

◆ Be sure to emphasize proper care of equipment such as not overinflating rafts or leaving them in direct sunlight, which can cause rupturing of the internal baffles.

◆ See lesson 1 for additional considerations.

LESSON CONTENT

Introduction

Equipment plays a vital role in safety and enjoyment during the rafting experience. A significant number of gear choices (brands, makes, models) are available. The main activities discuss the essential equipment and the associated knowledge needed to run a safe and enjoyable trip.

Main Activities

Activity 1: Equipment Identification and Construction (30 Minutes)

Stage all the equipment listed here in an orderly fashion to facilitate a lecture and hands-on activity for each topic area. Provide a handout (figure RA2.1) for note taking and as a reference for a quiz on the subject matter.

Rafting Equipment

Raft Types
- Raft (self-bailing and non-self-bailing)
- Cataraft

Basic Raft Anatomy
- Tubes
- Panels
- Seams
- Valves and covers
- Thwarts
- Floors
- D-rings
- Rubbing strakes
- Foot cups
- Baffles
- Chafe pads

Oars (Wood, Composite, Aluminum)
- Handle
- Shaft
- Throat
- Blade

Raft Frame
- Aluminum
- Wood

Pumps
- Electric
- Manual

Additional Equipment
- Spare paddle
- Nylon throw rope
- Hypothermia kit (hypo kit)
- Spare PFD
- First aid kit, perhaps stored in a thwart bag
- Pump, stored in the rescue kit
- Flip lines or belly strap
- Repair kit
- Rescue kit consisting of items that you are trained to use
- Cam straps

FIGURE RA2.1   General equipment list for rafting.

Identify each piece of equipment and its construction. Allow students the opportunity to handle each piece of equipment. Discuss advantages and disadvantages of the variations available.

Rafts
- Basic raft anatomy (figures RA2.2 and RA2.3)—**tubes, panels, seams, valves and covers, thwarts,** floors, **D-rings, rubbing strakes, foot cups, baffles,** and **chafe pads**.
- Materials—base fabrics and coatings (**Hypalon, PVC,** and **urethane**).
- Raft design characteristics—length, width, tube size, and floors (self-bailing and non-self-bailing). Self-bailing rafts have an inflatable, floating floor that allows water to flow out when the raft takes on water. Non-self-bailing rafts are constructed with noninflatable floors and require paddlers to bail water out with buckets or pumps when the raft takes on water. Table RA2.1 lists standard and unique design characteristics of select makes and models.

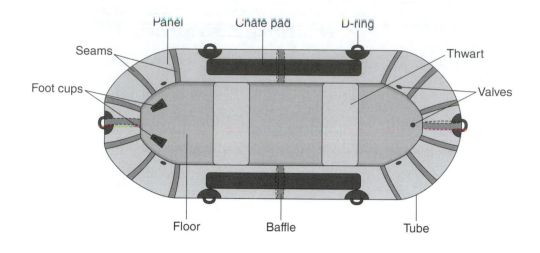

FIGURE RA2.2   Raft anatomy, top view.

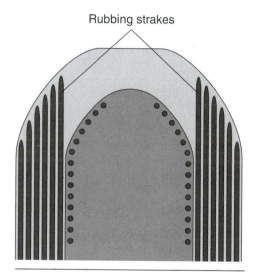

FIGURE RA2.3   Raft anatomy, bottom view.

Rafts come in all shapes and sizes. A basic raft design as seen in figure RA2.4*a* can be used as a paddle raft or an oar rig. A cataraft (figure RA2.4*b*), another popular style of watercraft, is a multitubed craft held together by a frame. As with rafts, tube size, length, and width affect the performance of the craft. Catarafts with longer tubes give a more buoyant ride and can carry larger volumes of equipment. Shorter tubes offer a sportier ride and allow more play boating opportunities. Catarafts are primarily used as oar rigs.

Frames   Frames provide a stiff, secure platform from which to row the raft down the river using a single person as the oarsman. Frames are typically crafted out of aluminum to reduce weight. There are several types of raft frames: center and stern mount, cataraft frames, and cooler frames. The key things to remember when selecting a frame so that it properly fits the raft are the following:

◆ Width between the center points of the outside tubes of the raft

◆ Distance between the thwarts

◆ Tube size

◆ Size of accessories such as coolers and dry boxes

◆ Distance from the top of the tubes to the top of the floor

The frame width should not be greater than the width of the raft, the frame accessories should not touch or interfere with the floor, and the frame crossbars and floors should fit properly between tubes and thwarts.

Oars

◆ Oars fall into three categories: wood, composite, and aluminum. For aluminum and composite oars, the blade may be removable for ease of maintenance or packing. Wood requires more maintenance, tends to be heavier, but is warmer to the hands in cold weather. Composite oars tend to be lightweight and strong but expensive. Aluminum oars are lightweight and less expensive but not as durable.

TABLE RA2.1   Raft Design Characteristics

Load capacity	Raft type	Length	Size	Other facts
1,697 pounds (770 kilograms)	Avon Scout Self-bailing	12 feet, 3 inches (3.7 meters)	Width: 5 feet, 11 inches (1.8 meters) Tube: 18 inches (46 centimeters) Weight: 95 pounds (43 kilograms)	Four chambers Two removable thwarts
1,150 pounds (522 kilograms)	AIRE 130 E Self-bailing	13 feet, 2 inches (4 meters)	Width: 6 feet, 2 inches (1.9 meters) Tube: 19.5 inches (50 centimeters) Weight: 115 pounds (52 kilograms)	Three chambers Two removable thwarts
2,003 pounds (909 kilograms)	Avon Ranger Self-bailing	14 feet, 2 inches (4.3 meters)	Width: 6 feet, 6 inches (2 meters) Tube: 20 inches (51 centimeters) Weight: 141 pounds (64 kilograms)	Five chambers Two or three removable thwarts
2,428 pounds (1,101 kilograms)	AIRE 156 E Self-bailing	15 feet, 7 inches (4.7 meters)	Width: 7 feet, 1 inches (2.2 meters) Tube: 21.5 inches (55 centimeters) Weight: 159 pounds (72 kilograms)	Five chambers Two or three removable thwarts
2,800 pounds (1,270 kilograms)	Maravia Tempest 2 Self-bailing	16 feet, 10 inches (5.1 meters)	Width: 7 feet, 6 inches (2.3 meters) Tube: 22 inches (56 centimeters) Weight: 180 pounds (82 kilograms)	Four chambers Two removable thwarts
3,505 pounds (1,590 kilograms)	Avon Superpro Self-bailing	17 feet, 11 inches (5.5 meters)	Width: 8 feet, 2 inches (2.5 meters) Tube: 22 inches (56 centimeters) Weight: 205 pounds (93 kilograms)	Five chambers Two, three, or four removable thwarts
3,500 pounds (1,588 kilograms)	Hyside 240 ASBU Self-bailing	20 feet (6.1 meters)	Width: 8 feet, 6 inches (2.6 meters) Tube: 24 inches (61 centimeters) Weight: 184 pounds (83 kilograms)	Five chambers
980 pounds (445 kilograms)	AIRE Cataraft Ocelot	14 feet (4.3 meters)	Tube: 22 inches (56 centimeters) Weight: 71 pounds (32 kilograms) without frame	Four chambers Two pontoons
2,273 pounds (1,031 kilograms)	AIRE Cataraft Jaguarundi	16 feet (4.9 meters)	Tube: 24 inches (61 centimeters) Weight: 84 pounds (38 kilograms) without frame	Four chambers Two pontoons

FIGURE RA2.4   Raft designs: *(a)* a basic design that can serve as a paddle raft or an oar rig; *(b)* cataraft.

◆ An oar has four parts, as does a paddle: handle, shaft, throat, and blade. The difference between an oar and a paddle typically confuses the novice rafter, so remind them that oars are for rowing and paddles are for paddling. Students understand this concept after you introduce an oar rig and a paddle raft.

◆ The two common ways to support an oar on a frame are pins and clips or oarlocks. Both types are popular, but oarlocks offer the most versatility.

◆ Paddle design and anatomy are discussed in the canoeing unit, lesson 2.

Activity 2: Raft Inflation (10 Minutes)

Demonstrate proper raft inflation using both electric and manual pumps. Discuss improper inflation and the potential for baffle damage by providing the following information.

Raft manufacturers typically describe the best order in which to inflate the tubes of their specific craft. These suggestions are found in the manual provided at the time of purchase. A general rule is to fill compartments in a clockwise direction until taut and then to travel around the raft a second time to top them off. If tubes are overinflated out of order, a baffle can be damaged by excessive pressure being exerted on just one side. Ideally, a raft struck with the hand produces the same sound as a basketball being dribbled on the ground. Remember that a fully inflated tube exposed to direct sunlight will continue to expand, so monitor tightness to prevent damage.

Activity 3: Rigging a Frame (10 Minutes)

Demonstrate proper frame lashing to the particular craft or crafts that you will be using. Secure frames so that they do not shift or move. Movement stresses the D-rings and could pinch passengers' hands. A loose frame can also throw the rower off balance when trying to maneuver. In general, the rigger wants all four corners to be secure. After the corners are secure, use available D-rings to secure the frame down the length of the raft. The rigging technique or design depends on the number of D-rings available.

Commercial cam straps provide a quick and efficient way to secure a frame to the raft. A useful tip is to make sure that all the straps have the cam facing the guide to allow speedy adjustments while on the river. Short straps (1 to 3 feet, or 30 to 90 centimeters) tend to be the most efficient length for cam straps when D-rings are abundant and provide multiple tie-down points. Again, this will vary depending on the raft design and D-ring placement. If cam straps are not available, an option is to use a series of trucker's hitches to ensure tension. The trucker's hitch is described in unit 1, lesson 9.

Securely fasten all loose ends of straps or rope to reduce the potential for entanglement of passengers.

Activity 4: Loading Accessories (20 Minutes)

Discuss the accessories required to be present in each craft, their proper locations, and how to lash them to the craft using the following outline for boat setup. Ideally, have a raft on hand to demonstrate options for proper storage.

- Spare paddle—tuck a spare paddle on the floor under the thwarts. Carry one spare for each boat on the water.
- Nylon throw rope—fasten this rope close to the guide's seat for easy access.
- Hypothermia kit (hypo kit)—this kit should contain a sleeping bag, spare clothes, stove, fuel, and a pot.
- Spare PFD.
- First aid kit—thwart bags are handy for storing the first aid kit.
- Pump—stored in the rescue kit.
- Flip lines or **belly strap**—these items are used to right a raft. If you are using flip lines, have at least one on each side to make finding them easier in the event of a flip. If you choose to use a belly line, it must be easy to release if necessary.
- Repair kit—items will vary based on the equipment used. Make sure that you have enough material to make field repairs on common problems.
- Rescue kit—bring rescue equipment that you are trained to use and keep it in a location that you can access quickly and easily.

Closure Activity

Rig a Raft (45 Minutes)

Divide the students into small groups and have each group rig a specific craft on their own based on the discussion and demonstrations. When the groups have finished, have each group move to another craft to evaluate the work of another group. Review any inconsistencies or problems with the entire group at the conclusion of the exercise.

Follow-Up Activity

Practice Makes Perfect (Time as Needed)

As you progress to water days, you will be rigging boats each day. Use this time to have students review proper boat-rigging strategies through physical execution. Make sure to cycle students through each craft type on different days to increase their understanding of equipment use and maintenance. As the instructor, you can use this time to evaluate retention and improvement.

ASSESSMENT

- Verify that students can identify equipment for a specific application by having them stage the setup for a specific craft as described in the closure activity.

- Ensure that students can describe the equipment and its function by reviewing the gear after main activity 1 or by having them complete a written quiz with pictures of each item.

- Confirm that students can demonstrate the correct placement and use of equipment by observing them rig boats after the lesson and each day on the river.

- Check that students develop their own opinions and preferences about equipment and assess their critical thinking by discussing with them their reasoning for deviating from the suggested methods.

- Assess whether students value proper equipment maintenance by observing the care, time, and effort that they put into equipment setup and takedown at the beginning and end of each day of activity.

TEACHING CONSIDERATIONS

- Cover equipment thoroughly at the beginning of the unit. Respond to future questions and comments regarding gear with information from the initial lesson.

- Discuss the equipment in an environment with few distractions.

- You can teach this lesson as a lecture–demonstration in which you display your own gear, describe your system, and set up the rafts in a specific way. After the lecture and demonstrations, the students need a chance to practice and run through the full scenario of boat rigging.

- You do not need to cover all the equipment described earlier. Assess what is important to your specific situation and cover that thoroughly. If you want to show more equipment than you have on hand, local outfitters may be a good source for borrowing equipment.

UNIT 8, LESSON 3

▷ Rafting Safety Considerations

OVERVIEW

Every raft guide must have a thorough understanding of the safety considerations that go into planning a trip and floating a river. This lesson covers preplanning information, participant safety briefings, and guide paddle commands.

JUSTIFICATION

Students need to know what information they should gather before a rafting experience as well as pertinent participant safety information. On the river, guides must be able to communicate outside a verbal context using guide paddle commands. Paddle commands allow communication at a distance and in noisy environments such as rapids.

GOAL

To increase students' awareness of preplanning considerations, safety briefings, and paddle commands.

OBJECTIVES

At the end of this lesson, students will be able to

- apply basic pretrip safety considerations (cognitive),
- understand the components and organization of a quality safety briefing (cognitive),
- deliver a well-organized safety briefing (psychomotor),
- demonstrate each guide paddle command (psychomotor),
- consistently demonstrate proper signaling commands (affective), and
- differentiate between a poor and excellent safety briefing and understand the effect of each on a group (affective).

EQUIPMENT AND AREAS NEEDED

- An assortment of guidebooks and river maps for rivers in your region
- Internet access if possible
- A PFD and helmet for each student
- Rafting paddles (enough for each student), throw rope, and a kayak

RISK MANAGEMENT CONSIDERATIONS

- When executing guide paddle commands, make sure that students have adequate room to swing paddles through the air.
- See lessons 1 and 2 for additional considerations.

LESSON CONTENT

Introduction

To ensure a safe day on the river, rafters must have up-to-date information on river conditions. You want to provide experiences that force students to use various resources to broaden their ability to search for this critical information. The process of searching for river conditions and water levels varies from river to river. Your job is to direct them to the most common resources discussed in the main activities. Then, on the river, all rafters practice the ritual of giving safety briefings to all passengers not familiar with safety systems commonly practiced on rivers.

Main Activities

Activity 1: Pretrip Safety Considerations (45 Minutes)

Use the resources listed here as a starting point to direct students in their search for information regarding the rivers rafted in their region. If your region provides several rafting opportunities, consider dividing the students into small groups and assign a river to each group. Then have students research their assigned river by answering the following basic questions:

- What are the appropriate sections to raft?
- What is the level of difficulty?
- How much experience is needed to run the river?
- What is the approximate time on the water?
- What issues are associated with water level?
- What are the rules and regulations for the run?
- What are the documented hazards?
- What are the logistics required to put in and take out?
- Is the river free flowing or dammed?
- Is severe weather predicted?
- Are specific items of equipment or supplies needed for the run?

Share the following resources with the students as tools to answer the preceding questions:

- www.americanwhitewater.org—This site is an excellent resource to learn what rivers are running by region and at what level throughout the United States. The site focuses on the popular rivers.
- http://water.usgs.gov/local_offices.html—This excellent site provides current water levels for many rivers throughout the United States. After the water level is determined, this information can be compared to information found in the guidebooks.
- Various weather sites—Check local weather sites for weather predictions. Some sites even provide local river conditions.
- Guidebooks—Numerous guidebooks exist for popular rivers. These are available at local outfitting stores, online, or at local bookstores.
- River maps—Boating maps exist for popular rivers. Your local land management agency or guidebooks possess these maps.
- People with experience—Experienced boaters can be one of the best sources of information. Be careful, however, because people claiming to be experts can pass on misinformation.
- Topographic maps—USGS maps are excellent resources. Access points, emergency evacuation points, and river gradient can all be determined from topographic maps.

As with all adventure sports, trip planning involves a number of factors. Unit 1, lesson 2 (on backpacking), describes a trip-planning process that can be applied to any paddling trip. In particular, rafters should be aware of the following questions before making their run:

- How do different river levels affect the difficulty of the run?
- Is severe weather expected?
- What is the level of difficulty?
- How much experience is needed to run the river?
- Approximately how much time will be spent on the water?
- What are the rules and regulations for the run?
- What are the logistics required to put in and take out?
- Is the river free flowing or dammed?
- Are any specific pieces of equipment or supplies needed for the run?

Activity 2: Safety Briefing (20 Minutes)

A safety briefing is necessary at the beginning of each on-river experience. Briefings can be done in several ways. Some commercial rafting companies give the briefing to the participants at the meeting point before going to the boat launch. Some companies run them at the put-in. The goal is to train new guides to be able to conduct a safety briefing within 10 minutes to avoid exceeding the participants' retention levels. Review the following with your students and discuss the components and sequence of a quality outline.

Get Everyone's Attention

- Introduce yourself and other staff.
- Note the floating order and the purpose of each craft.
- The safety briefing is not intended to frighten anyone. The situations that we are about to cover are not necessarily going to happen today. We are merely making everyone aware of what *can* happen. That way we are prepared to handle the situations if they *do* occur.

Provide the Following General Information

- You must wear a PFD that fits snugly.
- Do not tie yourself to the raft—doing so could cause entrapment if the rafts flips or becomes pinned.
- Wear foot protection—it's best to have toes protected, but it's not mandatory. But shoes such as flip-flops are unacceptable because they don't stay on your feet in moving water.
- Keep lines coiled so that they are handy and so that you will not become entangled in them.
- Glasses need safety straps.
- Wash your feet before getting into the boat to avoid bringing debris into the boat, which can be detrimental to the longevity of the raft.

Explain Proper Swimming Techniques in Case of an Unexpected Swim

- Stay calm.
- Remember to breathe. Let your crew know that you want assistance. Time breaths between waves!
- Try to hang on to the boat.
- Extend a paddle to the boat. Look for extended paddles from the boat.
- A throw rope may be coming in your direction. Listen for "Rope!"

◆ Stay out of strainers and holes (described in detail in the whitewater kayaking unit, lesson 5).

On dry land, describe and demonstrate proper techniques for both passive and aggressive whitewater swimming.

◆ Passive techniques are best for shallow water and obstructed rapids:
- Roll onto your back.
- Hold your feet up high and pointed downstream to avoid foot entrapment and to fend off objects.
- Use your arms to maneuver away from obstacles.
- Do not stand until you reach shallow or slow-moving water.

◆ Aggressive techniques are best for deep and powerful rapids:
- Roll over onto your belly and swim aggressively.
- Search for eddies and slow water.
- If possible, execute an upstream ferry to shore to avoid being washed into dangerous situations.

All paddlers must not rush to the aid of the swimmer. The guide will need assistance in moving the boat around. Generally, the person opposite the swimmer performs the rescue. Listen to the paddle captain's instructions.

Explain How You Will Handle a Pinning or Wrapping Situation

◆ If the raft ends up against an object in the river, such as a rock, the "High side!" command will be used.

◆ The crew should move quickly to the tube that is downstream (against the object). This is known as the high side (remember to tell the crew, "The rock is your friend—go hug it!").

◆ The object is to get all weight off the upstream tube so that it does not sink, causing the raft to pin or flip.

Explain How You Will Handle Unintentional Flipping of a Watercraft   When the raft flips, the most important issue to focus on involves handling yourself in the water in relationship to the raft and the other crew members.

◆ Remember the swimming instructions!

◆ When surfacing, get your hand above your head to feel for floating objects and the raft.

◆ Get out from underneath the boat.

◆ Hold on to the boat and stay to the upstream side.

◆ Let the guide and others know where you are.

◆ Help the guide if necessary.

Kayak Rescue   A whitewater kayak often accompanies a rafting trip for added safety. The highly maneuverable safety boat can easily pick up swimmers. If a safety boat is present on the trip, explain these techniques:

◆ Hold on to the grab loop on the stern of the kayak only. The kayaker can more easily pull a swimmer through the water than push a swimmer who is holding on to the bow grab loop.

◆ Help by kicking and working with the kayak to maneuver to the shore or another raft.

◆ If the kayak flips over, let go! It is difficult for the kayaker to execute a roll for a self-rescue with a swimmer hanging on to the boat.

◆ If the kayaker tells you to let go, do so immediately! A dangerous situation may otherwise arise.

Activity 3: River Signals (15 Minutes)

Explain and demonstrate the signals used for nonverbal communication on the river. Begin with the international signals and continue with more specific commands. Remember to emphasize that signals should be repeated until acknowledged and passed on to other boats if needed. These signals apply to all paddle craft, as seen in figure RA3.1.

After the initial demonstration, spread out the students so that they are at least two paddle lengths from one another. Make sure that all students have a single-blade paddle. Challenge students to execute the command quickly as you call out the signals at random.

International Signals

◆ Stop: Potential hazard or a problem; do not proceed until the all clear is given. Hold arms outstretched to form a horizontal bar or hold a paddle overhead horizontally (figure RA3.1*a*).

◆ All clear: Come ahead if you are ready. Hold a paddle or one arm straight up in the air. The response to this signal is the same and should be used only when ready to move ahead (figure RA3.1*b*).

◆ Help or emergency: Need assistance immediately. Wave a paddle, one arm, or any object such as a PFD or helmet. Three blasts of a whistle can be used in combination with this movement (figure RA3.1, *c-e*).

◆ Go this way: Used to signal a preferred course or direction. Point in the direction of preferred travel by extending an arm or a paddle in that direction. Never point toward the obstacle to be avoided (figure RA3.1*f*).

◆ Are you OK?: Used to ask others if they are OK. Tap three times on your head while pointing to the person you are questioning. If the person responds with three head taps, he is OK. Otherwise, he needs help (figure RA3.1*g*).

Additional Useful Signals

◆ Increase spacing: With your palms facing toward the receiver, motion as if you are pushing something back.

◆ Come closer or decrease spacing: With your palms facing toward you, motion as if you are clutching something ("come here" motion).

◆ Eddy out or group together: Wave a paddle or hand in a circular motion above your head, pointing in the direction of the eddy with the other hand.

◆ Raft damage; need repair kit: Form a circle with both thumbs and forefingers and place your hands over your head like a halo.

◆ First aid: Cross your forearms with one forearm vertical and the other horizontal.

◆ A boat has flipped: Starting with a forearm horizontal and pointing to one side with fingers flat and extended, swing the forearm up and overhead 90 degrees.

FIGURE RA3.1   International paddle signals: (a) Stop; (b) all clear; (c-e) help; (f) go this way; and (g) are you OK?

◆ Item overboard: Place and hold one hand on top of your head and point to the object in the water with the other hand. Do not get mixed up with the OK command of patting your head and pointing to the person you are questioning with the other hand.

Closure Activity

Trip Planning (One to Two Hours)

Have students plan a rafting trip on an unfamiliar river by applying critical pretrip planning considerations. After they complete their research, have them share their results. Use the findings to discuss issues that they encountered.

Follow-Up Activity

Briefing Practice (10 Minutes)

As students progress to actual trips, have a different student give the safety briefing each day. Safety briefings are usually given on shore before entering any craft. This approach allows the students to continue to practice. Allow time for peer feedback and to cover any missed items.

ASSESSMENT

◆ Check that students can apply basic pretrip safety considerations by having them research and report the specific considerations of using a river of their choice.

◆ Confirm that students can organize a thorough safety briefing by having them design an outline of their preferred style of safety briefing. Ensure that they include all pertinent information.

◆ Verify that students can deliver a well-organized safety briefing by having them perform a paddle captain briefing to their peers.

◆ Check that students can deliver each guide paddle command by having them execute each command called and assessing their recall as outlined in main activity 3.

◆ Confirm that students can consistently demonstrate proper signaling commands by having them execute the needed commands. Additionally, assess their recall each day on the river.

◆ Check that students can differentiate between a poor and an excellent safety briefing by having them give peer feedback at the conclusion of each safety briefing.

TEACHING CONSIDERATIONS

◆ A good tip is to create a crib sheet for your students that outlines the safety briefing. Put the paddle captain briefing on the back and laminate it. This way your students can always have the information in their PFD.

◆ Rafting companies, guiding services, paddling clubs, and land management agencies are practical resources to draw on when researching safety considerations for specific rivers.

◆ Practice and use signals consistently on the river so that their use becomes second nature.

UNIT 8, LESSON 4

▷ Transporting a Raft

OVERVIEW

Students learn proper raft carrying techniques in this lesson through demonstration and practice. River access varies significantly in distance and difficulty. Knowledge and ability in this area ensures a safer and more enjoyable rafting experience.

JUSTIFICATION

Whitewater rafts are heavy and awkward, especially when loaded with accessories. Transporting these crafts using proper carrying techniques reduces the risk of injury, especially to the neck and back.

GOAL

To develop students' ability to transport inflated whitewater rafts using a team approach.

OBJECTIVES

At the end of this lesson, students will be able to

- identify the potential risks of poor transportation and carrying technique (cognitive),
- demonstrate the correct technique for transporting and carrying rafts safely (psychomotor), and
- value the correct transporting techniques to ensure the safety of self and others (affective).

EQUIPMENT AND AREAS NEEDED

Multiple types of inflatable whitewater crafts loaded with accessories (traditional rafts of various sizes and catarafts)

RISK MANAGEMENT CONSIDERATIONS

- Check to make sure that all students have adequate foot protection.
- You should carefully monitor the first few lifts in this lesson to ensure proper technique. Remind students to use straight backs, squat, and use their legs to lift.
- See additional considerations in lessons 1 and 2.

LESSON CONTENT

Introduction

Every raft guide must be able to get the boat to and from the water in a safe manner. Because of the uneven terrain of most river entry and exit points, guides should know how to manage a group carry, especially when guiding people who have never been rafting before.

Main Activity

Raft Carries (30 Minutes)

The two most common raft carries are a straight arm carry and a fireman's carry.

Straight Arm Carry   Each carrier holds on to a D-ring, a handle, or the **perimeter line**. Bending at their knees and keeping their arms straight, they lift the boat in unison, keeping the boat at knee level. An equal number of people should be on each side of the craft (figure RA4.1).

Fireman's Carry   First, demonstrate a carry. Each carrier holds on to either a D-ring or a handle. Bending at their knees and keeping their arms straight, the carriers lift the boat in unison.

After the boat is in the air the carriers continue to lift the boat until it reaches shoulder height. The carriers can rest the boat on the shoulder that is closer to the craft. To avoid neck injury, carriers should not place the raft on their heads. Have the same number of people on each side of the craft. Staggering people by height increases efficiency and safety (figure RA4.2).

Group Practice   Divide your group into smaller groups. In each group, establish who is in charge of the movement of the craft. This person gives commands for moving the boat, such as left, right, stop, and so on. Establish some type of oral command and ensure that everyone is aware of what it is. Use a numerical audible such as "1, 2, 3, lift" to start the lift. Usually, someone at the front commands because she or he has a clear view of the path ahead.

Set up a small obstacle course with rocks, driftwood, and trees that simulates a riverbank. Try to find a place that has these features naturally to reduce impact and the amount of equipment needed. If possible, find an area that includes a slope, narrow passageways, narrow trails, low-hanging branches, and so on.

Have each student take the leadership role to get a feel for what it is like to move a group while carrying a raft. Afterward, have the groups self-critique their performance. Make sure that the discussion includes the potential risks encountered in this exercise.

FIGURE RA4.1   Straight arm carry.

FIGURE RA4.2   Fireman's carry.

Closure Activity

Securing Rafts for Transport (30 Minutes)

Besides carrying the raft from a parking area to the entry point, rafters must transport the raft by vehicle to the parking area. Rafts are often transported while deflated and are then inflated in a parking or staging area. At other times, inflated rafts are transported on roof racks, trailers, or bus tops to the staging area. Transporting principles learned in other units (unit 7, lesson 3) can be applied. Depending on your situation, have students practice securing an inflated raft on a roof rack or trailer.

Follow-Up Activity

Folding the Raft (30 Minutes)

Practice folding and rolling rafts for storage or transport. The manufacturer's suggestions are helpful, but lots of practice is needed to accomplish this task effectively. Demonstrate and explain the folding process. Then allow students to practice the skill.

◆ Hold team competitions for the best deflated and rolled raft.

◆ Remember to discuss cleaning out the rafts if this lesson occurs after a trip. All dirt and sand should be washed from the raft before deflating and folding it.

ASSESSMENT

◆ Check that students can identify the potential risks of using poor carrying technique by having them critique their performance and discuss the issues that they encountered when practicing their first carries as outlined in the main activity.

◆ Verify that students use the correct technique for transporting and carrying rafts safely by having them carry rafts through an obstacle course and to and from the river during the unit.

◆ Confirm that students consistently take the time and care necessary to lift and carry rafts safely in a team-oriented process.

TEACHING CONSIDERATIONS

◆ Cover transportation and carries at the beginning of the course.

◆ Discuss the equipment in an environment that has few distractions.

◆ You can teach this lesson as a demonstration in which you show the proper technique for lifting and group management during a carry. The first day on the river may be a good time to teach the lesson.

◆ Be sure to check the students' placement of others around the raft for equal strength to ensure safety.

◆ Pick a location that presents the challenges of an actual river if a river location is not available.

◆ In addition to the rafts, the remainder of the gear must be carried to the put-in. Discuss systems to do this efficiently. Discuss the concept of having one person in charge of sweeping the area to make a final check for any gear that may have been forgotten. The group can wear PFDs and helmets to reduce the bulk being carried in a raft or by hand. This practice also ensures that individuals have personal gear accounted for.

▷ Preparing to Paddle

OVERVIEW

To ensure a quality whitewater rafting experience, the guide or paddle captain must inspect the boat for river readiness and be able to give a thorough and well-organized paddle briefing to the crew. A unique aspect of rafting is that a group of people must function as a team. The paddle captain is responsible for providing guidance and leadership to maneuver the craft safely down the river.

JUSTIFICATION

The guide must quickly gain the trust of the crew. To do that, the guide must be precise in language and well organized in the presentation of information. This lesson provides students with opportunities to practice giving a thorough paddle captain briefing. Students receive feedback before they assume an actual leadership position. This lesson also covers the importance of a final craft check to ensure river readiness.

GOAL

To develop students' ability to articulate a paddle captain briefing in a public-speaking forum and to perform a quick evaluation of a craft for river readiness.

OBJECTIVES

At the end of this lesson, students will be able to

- identify the key elements of a thorough craft evaluation (cognitive),
- develop and organize a thorough paddle captain briefing (cognitive),
- deliver a well-organized paddle captain briefing (psychomotor),
- detect an improperly rigged craft (psychomotor),
- appreciate the value of performing a thorough craft evaluation (affective), and
- appreciate the difference between a poor paddle captain briefing and an excellent one and understand the effect of each on a crew (affective).

EQUIPMENT AND AREAS NEEDED

- Several inflated paddle rafts rigged with the necessary accessories outlined in lesson 2 (at least one raft for each three students to speed up the experiential component of the lesson)
- Rafting paddles
- Premade note cards that contain the prebriefing paddle captain speech
- Dry land or lake

RISK MANAGEMENT CONSIDERATIONS

- Emphasize during initial paddling practice that both hands should be kept on the paddle and that paddlers must be careful not to hit others while executing strokes or when swinging paddles to splash others for fun. Paddles can glance off the water uncontrollably and strike others in the face.

◆ See lessons 1 and 2 for additional considerations.

LESSON CONTENT

Introduction

As a guide, you must gain the trust of your participants as soon as possible. The best way to do this is by clearly articulating what you expect of them. The quality of the briefing given before the activity starts directly affects overall participant safety throughout the trip.

Main Activities

Activity 1: Final Raft Check (10 Minutes)

When setting up the rafts, improperly rig a couple of the accessories or rig the boat backward. Have your students work in teams of three to identify what is wrong with each craft. After the groups have looked at each craft have them choose a raft and rig it correctly. Use the following examples of what to include in a final check:

◆ The tubes should be inflated correctly and valve covers secured.

◆ All bow and stern lines should be neatly coiled. Any loose lines or straps should be neatly coiled or wrapped up to prevent possible entanglement.

◆ Flip lines should be secured.

◆ Any cargo such as dry bags or water bottles should be strapped down.

◆ A neat raft is a safe raft.

Activity 2: Instructor Paddle Captain Briefing (15 Minutes)

Although this activity is oriented for paddle rafts, much of the information applies to oar rigs as well.

Participants immediately start forming opinions about guides as soon as they set eyes on them. You are a leader and, at times, a role model. Keep in mind that you are being watched and evaluated constantly. Having an upbeat, confident attitude and attending strictly to safety protocols reassures your crew of your expertise. A paddle captain who shows signs of indecisiveness or fear might lose the confidence of the crew. Hold your chin high, make a decision, and follow through. Sometimes a paddle captain may need to provide additional encouragement and motivation to keep a crew going.

Using the following information, model a comprehensive briefing.

Introduction　Introduce yourself and give a little background about your experience.

◆ Be excited, friendly, and knowledgeable.

◆ Remember that the paddle captain affects the quality of the trip.

◆ As you execute the briefing, you will describe and demonstrate much of the information that follows, such as how to hold the paddle, strokes, and maneuvers.

◆ Note that some spacious, uncrowded river launch areas are conducive to a lecture–demonstration format. Have the crews enter the rafts to practice. Some situations require the paddle captain to do the entire briefing from the back of the raft. For this activity, you should focus on modeling the lecture–demonstration method.

Safety

◆ Review what to do if someone falls out.
  - River swimming positions (aggressive and passive)
  - T grip rescue and paddle control
  - Throw rope rescue
  - Boat flipping and pinning information

Paddle Use

◆ Hold the paddle by gripping the grip and shaft.
◆ Keep the paddle close to the body and hold it with both hands to avoid injuring others.
◆ Use your entire body for forward and backward strokes.
◆ Try to keep your body and paddle in control.

Pace (Bow) Person

◆ To ensure smooth paddling, everyone should key off the pace person. Designate that person at this time.
◆ Emphasize that teamwork is critical in paddle rafting.
◆ When beaching, the bow person is the first to jump out and secure the boat on the paddle captain's command. (Remind the bow person to survey the scene before blindly jumping out.)
◆ Remind the bow person to brace forward to grab waves and pull the boat over the waves.

Balanced Crew

◆ Balance the crew so that one side does not overpower the other.
◆ Switch the crew around in the boat as needed to match power on the port and starboard sides.

Commands

◆ To grab the crew's attention and to avoid having to repeat commands, use a pre-command cue (for example, "On the job . . . forward paddle!" or "On the job . . . back paddle!").
◆ Make your precommand cues consistent, so that the crew automatically anticipates that a command will follow the cue.
◆ Make sure that everyone in the boat can hear your commands. A loud, crisp, and confident command works best.

Strokes Practice on flatwater with your new crew as much as possible before entering any major rapids. Give your crew a good description of the route that you will use to go through the rapid. Practice the following strokes before hitting the first rapid.

◆ Forward stroke:
  - Maintain the cadence of the pace by following the designated pace setter in the bow.
  - The forward stroke is the most powerful stroke.

        – Lean forward and pull with the entire body.

        – Avoid using only the arms because you will fatigue quickly and be unable to supply enough power to move the raft.

◆ Back paddle:

        – The back paddle allows more time to maneuver.

        – Use your entire body as in the forward stroke.

        – The grip thumb points up when executing a back paddle.

◆ Rest:

        – Rest means removing the paddle from the water.

        – Resting gives the crew a break and slows the craft to maintain proper spacing between rafts.

◆ Turning:

        – For a right turn, call "Right back" during a forward stroke. The left side of the raft continues to paddle forward while the right side back paddles.

        – For a left turn, call "Left back" during a forward stroke. The right side of the raft continues to paddle forward while the left side back paddles.

High Side

◆ Used to avoid a pinning situation.

◆ All crew members quickly move toward the pinning object so that the upstream tube of the raft does not become submerged.

◆ Consider performing an unannounced practice before encountering potential pinning situations.

Water Fights

◆ Use squirt guns instead of paddles to get other crews wet.

◆ Ask permission of paddle captains.

◆ No boarding of other crafts unless the paddle captain gives the OK.

◆ Hold on to equipment.

◆ If the paddle captain says "Stop," please comply.

◆ Be sure that crew members are careful if using paddles to avoid injuries, or consider not allowing the use of paddles.

◆ No water fights above or in rapids.

While in the Boat

◆ Wash off the feet before getting into the raft.

◆ Be aware of bare skin touching tubes that get hot in the direct sun.

◆ Discourage excessive use of sunscreen, which causes difficulty sitting on tubes because greasy skin and rubber make a slippery combination.

Bracing

◆ Lean to the inside of the boat when in turbulent water.

◆ Don't kneel or sit in the bottom of the raft to avoid injury from objects such as rocks. Also, paddling properly from the floor is not possible.

◆ Keep your feet inside.

◆ Avoid getting your leg or foot trapped under a thwart.

◆ Keep the paddle in the water and use it as a source of support—explain the concept of the paddle brace (see unit 7, lesson 6).

Final Words

- Leave the river better than you found it. Explain what to do with trash.
- Explain what needs to happen if someone needs to use the bathroom.
- Have a fun and safe day!
- Take time to answer any questions about the safety talk and paddle briefing.
- Keep PFDs on and fully secured at all times unless otherwise stated.

Take-Out Orientation   At the end of the trip, a paddle captain should provide direction by orienting the crew to proper take-out procedures.

- Make sure that the crew gets out on the shore side to avoid hazards in deeper water.
- Have the crew organized with a preplan that includes what to do with helmets, PFDs, paddles, and other gear.
- Wash the raft of debris, especially sand. Do this before beaching or afterward.
- Try to keep the raft as clean as possible. Avoid dragging it to the loading area.
- Weather permitting, leave the raft inflated to dry before deflating and rolling.

Activity 3: Student Paddle Captain Briefing (30 Minutes)

Divide the students up into crews. Have a volunteer paddle captain in each group. The paddle captain gives a comprehensive briefing to the crew while in the boat. Note that this is different from the method demonstrated in activity 2 of this lesson. After the briefing ends, have the crews critique the briefing. Make sure that they identify components that were missed or not clear. Providing note cards with an outlined speech for reference will help paddle captains remember the important components.

Closure Activity

Briefing Practice (10 Minutes)

As you progress to water days, have different students give the paddle captain briefing each day. Paddle captain briefings can be given in an eddy or in slow-moving water. Alternatively, the captain can give the briefing on shore to the whole group and then practice on the water. The goal of this activity is to have all students practice giving the briefing at least once.

Follow-Up Activity

Delivery Improvement (30 Minutes)

After all students have had the chance to give a briefing speech, come together as a large group. Discuss who demonstrated unique, creative, and entertaining ways to share specific pieces of information. Use this discussion as a preface to brainstorm other creative techniques to execute a paddle briefing. Then have a volunteer demonstrate a briefing by modeling what was discussed. Alternatively, divide the students into small groups and have them create an engaging, entertaining briefing. Have a group demonstrate their product. This activity will help all students improve their delivery.

ASSESSMENT

◆ Check that students can identify the elements of a thorough craft evaluation by having them orally describe the proper location of key rafting equipment.

◆ Verify that students can develop and organize a thorough paddle captain briefing by having them design an outline of their preferred style of briefing. Be sure that they include all pertinent information.

◆ Confirm that students can deliver a well-organized paddle captain briefing by having them perform their briefing for their peers to be critiqued.

◆ Check that students can detect improperly rigged crafts by having them assess a rigged craft and point out any misplaced or improperly rigged equipment.

◆ Assess whether students appreciate the value of performing a thorough craft evaluation by having them assess a rigged craft, point out any misplaced or improperly rigged equipment, and discuss potential problems.

◆ Check that students appreciate the difference between a poor paddle captain briefing and an excellent one and understand the effect of each on a crew by having them give peer feedback at the conclusion of each paddle captain briefing.

TEACHING CONSIDERATIONS

◆ Run these exercises on dry land to ensure that students can focus on the quality of their paddle captain briefing. Doing their first briefing on moving water can be overstimulating, and the focus on the briefing will be lost.

◆ If the first paddle captain briefing must be done on water, set up the students for success by using a large eddy or a large section of flatwater.

◆ The paddle captain briefing outlined in this lesson is for paddle crafts. If you plan to use only oar rigs, simply cut out the unneeded information. All items in the outline found in activity 2 starting with high side would be included in an oar rig briefing. All paddling commands and maneuvers discussed before the section about high side are not applicable unless the oar rig uses paddlers in the bow of the raft. In oar rigs, paddle captains should review the best places on the raft to grab and hang on to avoid being pinched by the frame.

UNIT 8, LESSON 6

▷ Maneuvering an Oar Rig

OVERVIEW

Understanding and being able to execute the proper rowing strokes and oar rig maneuvers in whitewater environments is an essential function of a river guide. This lesson covers rowing strokes as well as strategies for moving an oar rig downriver.

JUSTIFICATION

Knowing how to execute strokes and maneuver an oar rig efficiently will enhance a raft guide's ability to row successfully and safely in a variety of conditions.

GOAL

To develop students' ability to control and move an oar rig in whitewater environments.

OBJECTIVES

At the end of this lesson, students will be able to

- understand the proper rowing techniques (cognitive),
- analyze moving water and pick appropriate maneuvers to navigate a variety of river conditions (cognitive),
- demonstrate the proper rowing techniques (psychomotor), and
- appreciate how specific strokes relate to desired maneuvers (affective).

EQUIPMENT AND AREAS NEEDED

- Personal river equipment for each student (PFD, wet suit, booties, and so on)
- Raft for each crew with appropriate frame
- Oars for each boat with one spare
- Spare PFD for each boat
- Two throw bags for each boat
- Two flip lines or a belly strap
- First aid kit
- Rescue kit (enough to build a Z-drag, which is covered in lesson 9)
- Buoys

RISK MANAGEMENT CONSIDERATIONS

- Always check river and weather conditions before embarking on any river trip, even if you were on the river the day before. Rivers are dynamic in nature and can change quickly.
- Always leave your trip itinerary with another person. In an emergency that person will be able to help you organize outside help while you focus on the incident.
- Choose an appropriate river classification for the lesson. No instructor should be teaching at the threshold of his or her own skill level. If you are a class IV boater you should be teaching class III and lower. Introductory rafting classes usually run class II to III whitewater according to the American Whitewater International Scale of River Difficulty (see unit 6, lesson 5, and figure WK5.6 on page 449).
- The desired student-to-instructor ratio for rafting with oar rigs is 3:1 because of space constraints.
- See lessons 1 and 2 for additional considerations.

LESSON CONTENT

Introduction

Rivers are dynamic in nature, always changing. A river guide must be able to initiate the needed strokes to maneuver the raft at a moment's notice. To attain this skill level, practice and time on the water are essential.

Main Activities

Activity 1: Strokes (45 Minutes)

Oar strokes follow the same school of thought as paddle strokes, covered in the canoeing unit, when it comes to the reach, catch, power, and recovery phases of the stroke. The basic rowing strokes and maneuvers covered in this section are as follows: back rowing, portegee, turning, and shipping.

For this activity, demonstrate the basic strokes in a calm body of water. After the demonstration, have students board their rafts and practice their strokes. Set up an obstacle course of milk jugs or buoys. Challenge students to make tight turns, spin their rafts, and so on. A game of Follow the Leader works well in this situation.

Back Rowing   Back rowing is initiated by pulling back on the oars with equal pressure on both oars.

- To begin the stroke, start with the reach phase by lifting the oar blades out of the water and pushing forward.
- After the reach phase is complete, move to the catch phase by lifting up on the oars to drop the blades into the water.
- After the oar blades are behind you and in the water use the power phase to propel your boat backward. Pull straight back on the oar shafts until your hands are close to your chest.
- You complete the stroke in the recovery phase by pushing down on the oars to lift the blades from the water.
- You are now ready to begin another cycle.
- Tips: Back rowing is your strongest stroke. Use your larger muscle groups such as your back and legs. Ensure that your foot bar or rest is close enough that you can use your leg muscles.

Portegee, or Forward Stroke   The portegee, or forward stroke, is the opposite of back rowing. You initiate it by pulling back on the oars with equal pressure.

- To begin the stroke, start with the reach phase by lifting the oar blades out of the water and pulling backward.
- After the reach phase is complete, move to the catch phase by lifting up on the oars to drop the blades into the water.
- After the oar blades are in front of you and in the water, use the power phase to propel your boat forward. Push forward on the oar shafts until you are completely leaned forward.
- You complete the stroke in the recovery phase by pushing down on the oars to lift the blades from the water.
- You are now ready to begin another cycle.
- Tips: The portegee is your weakest stroke. To maintain your energy during flat-water sections, you should vary your strokes. A handy variation of the portegee is to do one cycle at a time varying from your left arm to the right.

Turning   You can perform single-oar turns using a back row or a portegee. Use the previously described technique for either stroke but use only one oar.

- Pushing forward on your right oar turns the boat left.
- Pushing forward on your left oar turns the boat right.

◆ Pulling back on your right oar turns the boat right.

◆ Pulling back on your left oar turns the boat left.

◆ Do double-oar turns using a back row and portegee simultaneously.

◆ To turn right, portegee with your left hand and back row with your right (figure RA6.1*a*).

◆ To turn left, portegee with your right hand and back row with your left (figure RA6.1*b*).

◆ Tips: The double-oar turn is more powerful and versatile than the single-oar turn. Mastering it, however, can be challenging. The easiest way to remember which way your boat will turn using the double-oar technique is that the back stroke is the strongest stroke and will turn your boat that direction.

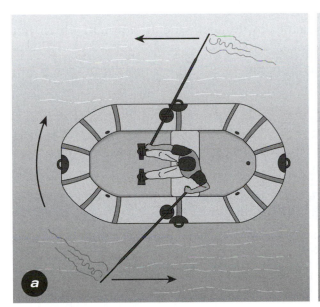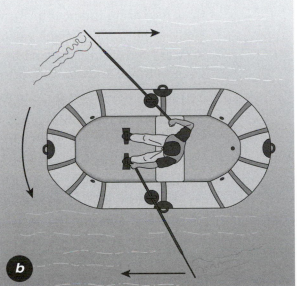

FIGURE RA6.1   Double-oar turns: *(a)* right turn and *(b)* left turn.

Adapted, by permission, from J. Bennett, 1996, *The complete whitewater rafter* (New York: McGraw-Hill). Adapted with permission of the McGraw-Hill Companies.

Shipping   When traveling through narrow channels your oars may be too long to pass through without damaging them. In this case you will need to ship your oars to pass through safely.

◆ When using frames with oarlocks, shipping your oars is easy work. Pull straight across your chest with both arms at the same time. This action will quickly reduce the length of your oars.

◆ When using frames with pins and clips or stationary oars, your options are to ship forward or backward. To execute this maneuver, complete the reach phase of either the back stroke or the portegee with a little more exaggeration.

Activity 2: Maneuvering (Time as Needed)

Running a raft down a river requires the ability to read water at a distance. Rafts are much larger than canoes or kayaks and require more time to set up for a desired route. Beginning rafters may have difficulty staying in the main current.

You can teach maneuvers in a variety of ways, depending on the students' background knowledge. Students with little knowledge benefit from discussion and demonstration of maneuvers using toy boats and mock rivers drawn in the sand. After giving explanations, the ideal progression is to find an appropriate place in moving current to practice ferries, eddy turns, and so on. You should row on the first moving-water experience to allow students to begin to use their river-reading skills to identify river features and the habits of the current. Allow students to get on the oars during flatwater sections or in an eddy to practice the strokes. Maneuvers such as eddy turns, ferries, and peel-outs are discussed in other water-based units. Specific tips for maneuvers are discussed here because they are the most common and needed maneuvers.

Ferrying   Ferrying is used to get from one side of the river to the other while losing minimum ground. The technique is also used to avoid danger.

◆ Back ferries are initiated by turning the bow opposite the direction in which you want to travel and using a back stroke.

◆ Forward ferries are initiated by pointing the bow in the direction in which you want to travel and using a portegee.

◆ Maintain a 45-degree angle to the current when using either ferrying technique.

Eddy Turns and Peel-Outs   Eddy turns and peel-outs refer to entering and exiting the water feature known as an eddy, covered in earlier units. Eddies provide places to stop or slow the pace of your group.

◆ The angle of entry into an eddy is critical, as explained in other water-based units. Power is needed to break through strong eddy lines.

◆ Warn passengers that the upstream tube may be sucked under if a tight eddy turn is needed in powerful current.

◆ The upstream tube may be sucked under and flush passengers out during a peel-out in strong current.

◆ Back rowing is the most effective method for breaking strong eddy lines.

◆ The best place to enter and exit an eddy is often farther downstream in the eddy where the eddy line is typically not as strong.

Paddle Assists   Under certain conditions, such as extremely technical water, participants may need to assist the rower by paddling in the bow of the raft with a raft paddle.

◆ For example, smaller oar rigs that navigate technical water benefit from paddle assists. In this case, the raft is commonly rigged with stern frames. This setup provides more room in the bow for paddlers and reduces the likelihood that the oars will hit the paddlers.

◆ Center frames are more common on multiday trips in which large, heavy loads are carried and must be balanced in the center of the raft.

Closure Activity

Maneuver Practice (Time as Needed)

Find a challenging place on the river where the current is powerful. Practice various maneuvers in challenging water as the students' skills develop. Have students take turns executing the maneuvers. An ideal location would be where students can easily recover and row back into the eddy for multiple attempts. Consider placing students downstream to practice throw-bag throwing to assist rafts in moving back into eddies.

Follow-Up Activity

Running Rapids (Time as Needed)

Each day on the river, cycle through your students to allow them to take challenges when they are comfortable. Take advantage of all flatwater opportunities for practicing. The American Canoe Association recommends 14 hours of on-river experience before becoming certified as a raft guide.

ASSESSMENT

- ◆ Check that students understand specific rowing techniques by having them explain the strokes needed to move the raft to the desired location.
- ◆ Confirm that students can analyze moving water and pick appropriate maneuvers to navigate a variety of river conditions by consulting with them on the routes that they wish to take and the reasoning behind those choices during a trip.
- ◆ Verify that students can demonstrate proper rowing techniques by observing them practice each of the rowing techniques during the obstacle course exercise and while on the river.
- ◆ Check that students appreciate how specific strokes relate to desired maneuvers by observing their improvement as they face more challenging situations.

TEACHING CONSIDERATIONS

- ◆ Using stern frames allows you to teach oar strokes as well as crew management. If you have many students on a course, stern frames allow more room with fewer rafts on the water.
- ◆ Before you teach this lesson, cover river reading and boat placement for executing maneuvers such as ferries, eddy turns, and peel-outs. Lessons on these topics are found throughout the paddling units, such as in lessons 5 and 6 of unit 6.
- ◆ Rafting on several rivers allows students to experience different currents and rapids, which builds the knowledge that they need to make informed judgments on future river trips.

UNIT 8, LESSON 7

▷ Maneuvering a Paddle Raft

OVERVIEW

Understanding and being able to execute the proper paddling strokes and paddle raft maneuvers in whitewater environments is an essential function of a river guide. This lesson covers paddling strokes for the crew and guide as well as strategies for moving a paddle raft downriver.

JUSTIFICATION

Knowing how to execute strokes and maneuver a paddle raft efficiently enhances a raft guide's ability to paddle successfully and safely in a variety of conditions.

GOAL

To develop students' ability to control and move a paddle raft in whitewater environments.

OBJECTIVES

At the end of this lesson, students will be able to

◆ understand and identify the proper paddling techniques for both guide and crew (cognitive),

◆ analyze moving water and pick appropriate maneuvers to navigate a variety of river conditions (cognitive),

◆ manipulate the raft using both guide-specific maneuvers and crew control to maneuver the raft to the desired location (psychomotor), and

◆ appreciate how specific strokes relate to desired maneuvers (affective).

EQUIPMENT AND AREAS NEEDED

◆ Personal river equipment for each student (PFD, wet suit, booties, and so on)

◆ Raft for each group

◆ Paddles for each group with one spare for each boat

◆ Spare PFD for each boat

◆ Two throw bags for each boat

◆ Two flip lines or a belly line

◆ First aid kit

◆ Rescue kit (enough to build a Z-drag, which is covered in lesson 9)

RISK MANAGEMENT CONSIDERATIONS

◆ Always check river and weather conditions before embarking on any river trip, even if you were on the river the day before. Rivers are dynamic in nature and can change quickly.

◆ Always leave your trip itinerary with another person. In an emergency that person will be able to help you organize outside help while you focus on the incident.

◆ Choose an appropriate river classification for the lesson. No instructor should be teaching at the threshold of his or her own skill level. If you are a class IV boater you should be teaching class III and lower. Introductory rafting classes usually run class II to III whitewater according to the American Whitewater International Scale of River Difficulty (see unit 6, lesson 5, and figure WK5.6 on page 449).

◆ The desired maximum student-to-instructor ratio for paddle rafting is 6:1. As the instructor, you will sit directly next to the student while he or she is guiding to correct any misjudgments in maneuvers.

◆ See lessons 1 and 2 for additional considerations.

LESSON CONTENT

Introduction

Rivers are dynamic in nature, always changing. A river guide must be able to initiate the needed strokes and corresponding commands to maneuver the raft at a moment's notice. This skill is an integral part of leading a team of paddlers. To reach this skill level, practice and time on the water are essential.

Main Activities

Activity 1: Paddle Raft Strokes (20 Minutes)

Demonstrate and discuss the basic paddle strokes used in rafting. You can do a dry land demonstration and practice before entering the water. On the water, having one crew in a raft to demonstrate is ideal. Use the following information to discuss paddle strokes.

Strokes for running a paddle raft are the same as those described in the canoeing unit. They include the forward stroke, the back stroke, and the draw stroke. All guides should know a high brace and low brace. Information on the brace can be found in the canoeing unit, lesson 6. Braces help the guide stay in the raft in rough water when leaning out to execute steering strokes. Crew members should be taught that a draw stroke can serve as a high brace.

A guide should learn to guide from a single side at a time. Knowing how to guide on both the port and starboard sides is handy, but switching back and forth while in rapids is inefficient. Any time the guide's paddle is out of the water, no guide is on duty!

The only additional stroke essential for guides is the rudder stroke.

◆ Place the paddle blade behind the stern and keep it in line with the axis of the raft.

◆ As the raft moves forward, the guide can sweep the paddle left or right to change the direction of travel.

Activity 2: Basic Commands (15 Minutes)

The basic commands outlined here are based on a syllable concept. When paddlers are in whitewater, hearing one another is difficult. By having each command made up of different syllables, paddlers will more easily know what they need to do.

Review the following commands with the class. You can do this as a dry land demonstration or in flatwater with the rest of the class watching from the bank.

After the demonstration, have all crews enter their rafts. Space the rafts apart and allow crews to choose a paddle captain. You call out commands, and all crews execute the strokes. Observe and critique each crew's performance.

◆ On the job: Having a command that alerts your crew members that you are about to need their assistance will ensure that your paddlers are ready when you need them. Call this command a few seconds before you call any other command.

◆ Forward: All crew members initiate a forward stroke.

◆ Back paddle: All crew members initiate a back stroke.

◆ Turning commands:

– Paddlers have a tendency to become confused between their right and left when they have their backs to the captain and are engaged in the thrill of paddling whitewater. Practice these commands before entering a rapid and during the captain's briefing. The following commands are called during a forward stroke to promote simplicity.

– Left back: Paddlers on the left side of the raft initiate a back stroke, while the paddlers on the right continue with their forward stroke. This action initiates a left turn (figure RA7.1*a*).

– Right back: Paddlers on the right side of the raft initiate a back stroke, while the paddlers on the left continue with their forward stroke. This action initiates a right turn (figure RA7.1*b*).

– Rest: Paddlers take their paddles out of the water.

– Stop: At times you may need people to stop immediately, so save this command for emergencies.

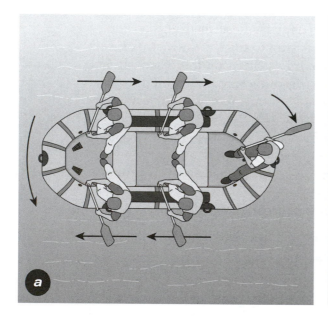 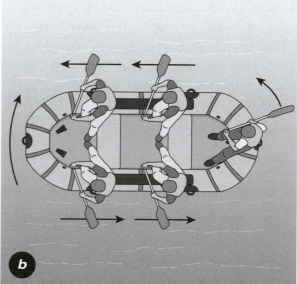

FIGURE RA7.1   Paddle raft turns: *(a)* left turn; *(b)* right turn.

Adapted, by permission, from J. Bennett, 1996, *The complete whitewater rafter* (New York: McGraw-Hill). Adapted with permission of the McGraw-Hill Companies.

Activity 3: Maneuvering (Time as Needed)

Running a paddle raft or oar rig down a river requires the ability to read water at a distance. Rafts are much larger than canoes or kayaks and require more time to set up for a desired route down the river. Beginning rafters may have difficulty staying in the main current.

Refer to the whitewater kayaking unit for specifics on maneuvering in moving water. The same techniques apply to rafts, although execution requires more time and occurs on a larger scale. The following are brief reminders about maneuvering a paddle raft:

◆ Ferries—Angle the bow of the raft in the direction of travel. Use the forward command. The paddle captain must maintain the angle with a rudder stroke and corrective strokes. The faster the current is, the more upstream the angle needs to be to cross the current.

◆ Eddy turns—Remind the crew to lean into the turn. Aim to catch the eddy high. The paddle captain should use left and right turn commands to obtain the proper angle. Speed may be needed to cross a strong eddy line. In challenging situations, the bow paddler can extend the paddle over the eddy line and assist by drawing her or his side of the raft into the eddy.

◆ Peel-outs—The raft will need speed to break the eddy line. Remind the crew to lean downstream after the raft crosses the eddy line.

◆ For more information on eddy turns, ferries, and peel-outs, refer to the following lessons: unit 5, lesson 10, for information on ferries; and unit 6, lesson 6, for information on ferries, eddy turns, and peel-outs.

At this point, running a day trip on a local river is the best way for students to assimilate this information. For the first on-river experience, you should guide the students but allow them to begin to use their river-reading skills to identify river features and the habits of the current. Allow students to get on the oars during flatwater sections or in an eddy to practice the strokes. As mentioned in lesson 6, when executing eddy turns and peel-outs in strong current, upstream tubes may be sucked under, possibly flushing crew members. Also, before running rapids and while scouting, have students articulate what maneuvers are needed and what commands or strokes should be used.

Closure Activity

Practice for Rapids (15 to 20 Minutes)

On a sandy beach or flat ground, simulate a river by creating obstacles using rocks, rope for downstream Vs, and so on. Have paddle groups take turns doing dry land runs around these obstacles. You direct the crew down the simulated river by pointing where to go. Students take turns as paddle captains. They must think on their feet, call out appropriate commands, and execute maneuvers to negotiate the staged rapids. Crew members and paddle captains mimic being in a raft and air paddle as they walk to simulate what they should be doing.

Follow-Up Activity

Individual Practice (Time as Needed)

Each day on the river, cycle through your students and allow them to take challenges when they are comfortable. Take advantage of all flatwater opportunities to practice. The American Canoe Association recommends a minimum of 14 hours of on-river experience as a paddle captain before becoming certified as a raft guide. Many state licensing agencies require significantly more hours or a specified number of trips.

ASSESSMENT

◆ Check that students understand and identify the proper paddling techniques for both guide and crew by watching them practice each of the paddle techniques as explained in main activity 2.

◆ Confirm that students can analyze moving water and pick appropriate maneuvers to navigate a variety of river conditions by consulting with them on the routes that they wish to take and the reasoning behind those choices during a trip.

- Verify that students can manipulate the raft using both guide-specific maneuvers and crew control to maneuver the raft to its desired location by assessing the previous criteria and seeing whether students can put it all together to have a successful rowing experience.
- Ensure that students appreciate how specific strokes relate to desired maneuvers by having them explain what techniques they will use to get to the desired location before running a rapid.

TEACHING CONSIDERATIONS

- Before you teach this lesson, cover river reading and boat placement. Lessons on these topics are found in the whitewater kayaking unit.
- Rafting on several rivers allows students to experience different currents and rapids, which builds the knowledge that they need to make informed judgments on future river trips.

UNIT 8, LESSON 8

▷ Basic Rescue

OVERVIEW

Having a foundational understanding of rescue and the ability to execute basic rescue maneuvers is a crucial raft guide competency. This lesson includes throw-bag demonstrations and opportunities for students to practice. The lesson also covers rescue procedures for a swimmer or swimmers in the river and procedures for dealing with a capsized raft.

JUSTIFICATION

Even the most experienced and skilled guide may have a participant slip out of the raft or even flip a raft while traveling on the river. To ensure the safety of everyone in the group, guides must know how to deal with these incidents before they happen.

GOAL

To develop students' ability to execute two important rescue skills: retrieving swimmers using a throw rope and manually flipping capsized rafts using multiple techniques.

OBJECTIVES

At the end of this lesson, students will be able to

- understand basic rescue procedures for recovering a swimmer (cognitive),
- execute two techniques for righting a flipped raft (psychomotor),
- execute two throw-bag rescues within 20 seconds (psychomotor), and
- value the importance of the speed and emotional support in safely recovering a swimmer (affective).

EQUIPMENT AND AREAS NEEDED

- Raft, with no frame to reduce risk of injury while practicing
- Flip lines and belly straps
- Throw bags
- PFDs
- Hula hoops
- Bucket of water for soaking throw bags during dry land practice

RISK MANAGEMENT CONSIDERATIONS

- This lesson can be done in a pool, in a lake, or in an eddy on the river. Make sure that space is adequate to prevent head injuries on rocks or on the edge of the pool.
- If you do this lesson on the river, make sure that the students are adequately outfitted for conditions.
- Helmets are not an industry standard for rafting but are recommended when flipping boats.
- Check to make sure that all students have adequate foot protection.
- Carefully monitor rope-throwing practice. Students can easily be pulled off balance or become tangled in ropes.
- See lessons 1 and 2 for additional considerations.

LESSON CONTENT

Introduction

Rafting is an inherently dangerous sport, but with proper training and practice of basic rescue procedures, guides can manage much of the risk associated with the activity. Guides must master two basic skills before they move on to advanced techniques.

- First, they must learn how to use a throw bag properly. They should practice the technique from both the raft and the riverbank. The throw-bag rescue is one of the most effective and efficient ways to retrieve a swimmer who has moved beyond reach of a crew member's hand or paddle.
- Second, guides must be able to deal with a capsized raft. Rafts capsize in a variety of situations. Guides must be able to react based on sound training to deal with this often chaotic situation.

Main Activities

Activity 1: Throw Bags (Two Hours)

One piece of equipment that every raft guide should have on hand while on the river is a throw bag. A throw bag is a simple, inexpensive piece of rescue equipment. Despite its simplicity, however, a guide needs training and practice to develop proficiency in its use.

General Tips
- Before starting a trip downstream, always check the status of throw bags. Deploy throw bags to ensure that they are not tangled or that other objects have not been inadvertently stuffed in the bag.

FIGURE RA8.1 Pendulum swimmer with rope.

◆ Position yourself with stable footing for the throw. Have the rescue bag in your throwing hand and the standing end of the line in the opposite hand.

◆ Aim the line to land across the swimmer's torso. Because the surface water that the rope is floating on is moving slower than the immersed swimmer, aim a little downstream to ensure that the swimmer can recover the line if your throw is off target. Throw with a smooth underhand action. You can also throw overhand to release the throw bag, but underhand is the better starting technique.

◆ Brace in a crouched stance with one foot forward to keep your center of gravity low so that you are not pulled off balance. Having a partner hold your PFD works well when rescuing heavier swimmers or boats full of water.

◆ From a raft, reel the swimmer in as you would a fish. From shore, pendulum the swimmer to shore using the current to your advantage (figure RA8.1). The guide in figure RA8.1 chose to anchor the rope higher across the back, anticipating very light resistance. For heavy resistance, find a partner or anchor the rope low around the hips in a belay stance to keep the center of gravity low.

◆ After you deploy the throw bag, restuffing for a second throw is inefficient. A coil comes in handy here. As you are pulling the bag back in from the first throw, use the butterfly coil to manage the rope. Using a split-fingered butterfly coil technique reduces the chance that the rope will become tangled after release. Another option to manage the rope is a classic mountaineering coil. This can also be split into two coils for rethrowing.

◆ When throwing a coil, a side-armed technique allows the coil to release naturally, reducing the chance that the rope will become tangled.

◆ Bag throwing should be completed in two phases to enhance effectiveness. This first phase is a dry land trial. The second phase is practice in moving water.

Phase 1: Dry Land Trial

◆ Have participants pick partners and form two parallel lines. Partners are in opposite lines directly across from each other, 25 feet (8 meters) apart. Place a hula hoop between the partners.

◆ Equip each student with a throw bag that has been dipped in water to replicate the weight of the bag in a river environment. Have the students throw the rescue bags toward the hula hoops. The goal is to place the throw bag just beyond the hula hoop, laying the rope directly over the center of the hoop.

◆ Have the students complete several bag tosses as well as coils at that distance. During the exercise, increase the distance by 10 feet (3 meters) until they reach the limit of the throw bags.

◆ After the students have practiced their throws, have some fun by organizing a single-elimination tournament for accuracy. Offer some piece of rescue equipment as a prize.

Phase 2: Practice in Moving Water   The ideal spot is a section of river where students can safely swim in class II water. The fast-moving current should be no more than 15 feet (5 meters) from shore to guarantee a positive experience for the students.

◆ Establish two groups: swimmers and throwers. The swimmers travel upstream to a place where they can enter the water safely. The throwers split into several groups, depending on your group size. Each group of throwers should consist of several members and be at least 15 feet (5 meters) from other groups. You should be 15 feet (5 meters) beyond the throwers as a safety thrower in case a swimmer gets by the throwers.

◆ A swimmer raises a hand to signal that she or he is ready. You blow one blast on a whistle to signal that the throwers are ready. The swimmer enters the water and gets into the downstream swimming position. As the swimmer passes each station of throwers, one thrower deploys a throw bag.

◆ Make sure that each thrower yells, "Rope" to gain the attention of the swimmer. The swimmer grabs the rope only from the last station and is pendulumed to shore. However, remind them that in a real situation they should always grab and hold the first rope that is deployed to them if possible. Remind them that the activity is only a simulation. Then a new swimmer should begin, and new throwers should be ready.

◆ The throwers should practice both bag and coil throws. After all throwers have had an adequate number of throws, have them switch with the swimmers. Begin the activity again. The goal is for a thrower to be able to make two throws in 20 seconds starting with a bag toss and then performing a coil throw.

◆ As students progress, increase the distance and difficulty of the throws. Discuss strategies as a group to increase effectiveness.

Activity 2: Righting a Raft (30 Minutes)

Every boat on the river should be equipped with either flip lines (figure RA8.2) or a belly strap (figure RA8.3). These devices are used to right a raft in the event of a flip.

The first task after a boat has capsized is to get back on top of it. The most difficult part of righting a boat is climbing back into the boat. That is why righting a raft is an essential skill to practice.

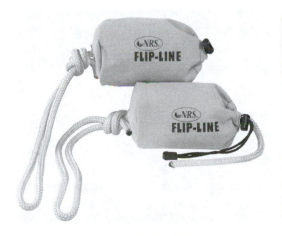

FIGURE RA8.2   Flip lines stuffed in bags.   FIGURE RA8.3   Raft rigged with a belly strap.

Explain these tips for using flip lines:

- The flip lines must be deployed and stretched across the bottom of the raft.
- The guide must then stand on the tube of the raft opposite the side of the flip lines.
- The guide applies pressure to the tube that he or she is standing on by pulling on the flip line and leaning back using body weight as leverage to get the raft over (figure RA8.4).
- With two flip lines, two guides can work together to make the job easier.

Explain these tips for using belly lines:

- Using a belly line is a more efficient method for righting a raft.
- The line must be applied to the raft using a releasable tension system such as a trucker's hitch tied off with a half hitch (figure RA8.5). This release is necessary to reduce the chance that the belly line will be caught on river debris.
- The belly line can make it easier to climb up onto the boat.
- The guide grabs the belly line and uses body weight as leverage to right the raft (figure RA8.6).

FIGURE RA8.4   Righting a raft with flip lines.

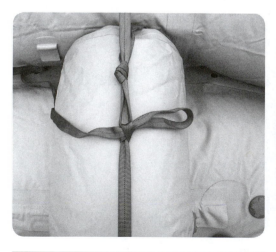

FIGURE RA8.5   Belly line with releasable tension system.

FIGURE RA8.6   Using a belly line.

After the raft is righted and the guide is in the boat, the next step is to get the participants back in the boat.

- Have the participants put their backs to the raft tube to reduce the potential of snagging buckles and other objects on the front of PFDs as they are pulled back into the raft.
- The guide grabs the PFD at the shoulder and bobs the participant up and down using the flotation of the PFD to assist with momentum.
- The guide then leans back using body weight as leverage to get the participant out of the water.

Have the crew of each raft flip their boat. They can use the flip lines or belly strap to capsize the boat. Allow each member of the crew to use both methods to right the boat. After each crew member has done it individually, have each crew work as a team. You can do this activity in a pool or on the river.

Closure Activity

Up the Challenge (One Hour)

Practice more challenging rescue scenarios such as deploying throw bags from the shore to rafts full of water. Students can then experience the challenge of managing a heavy object. Make sure that others serve as backup anchors to ensure safety.

Also practice a two-swimmer rescue using the split coil technique. Throw one side of the coil to the first swimmer and the second coil to the second swimmer. Again, be sure to back up the thrower.

Spend time discussing the judgment that goes into finding a suitable place to deploy the throws and strategies to avoid being pulled into the water, such as bracing against a rock while using a hip belay. Practicing these situations will increase the students' confidence and skills.

Follow-Up Activity

Daily Practice (10 to 15 Minutes per Practice)

During the remaining river days have the students practice deploying throw bags and righting boats while on the river. Use the flatwater sections of the river as the training area for rescue procedures. Stress practice, practice, practice!

ASSESSMENT

- Check that students understand basic rescue procedures for recovering a swimmer by having them peer critique the throw-bag efforts.
- Verify that students can execute two techniques for righting a flipped raft by having them practice the flips as described in main activity 2.
- Confirm that students can execute two throw-bag rescues within 20 seconds by timing their throws during a throw-bag practice session after they have had ample opportunity to practice.
- Assess whether students value the importance of speed and emotional support in swimmer recovery by observing their management of the swimmers with whom they are working.

TEACHING CONSIDERATIONS

◆ The key with this lesson is group management. Make sure that all students understand your commands—oral, body, and whistle—while participating in the activities.

◆ Use flatwater time to test the students' skills repeatedly and reevaluate those who may have been unable to execute two successful throws in 20 seconds.

◆ Folks who have a challenging time throwing a heavy, waterlogged throw bag can take rope out of the bag and create coils in the nonthrowing hand so that they are throwing a lighter bag that will pull the coils to achieve a maximum throw.

◆ Spend ample time explaining and demonstrating how to stuff throw bags using two techniques. The over-the-shoulder technique consists of stacking the rope on the ground. The guide stands with her or his back to the pile. The guide places the rope over the shoulder and stuffs the bag. The pinch method consists of using one hand to hold the bag and the other hand to stuff the rope. With the hand that holds the bag, the guide uses two fingers to pinch the rope after putting a coil into the bag to keep it from coming back out.

◆ Rafts full of water (non-self-bailing rafts) can be emptied using a team approach against the shoreline. The crew must work as a team to lift one side of the raft to empty the water. The team members must use proper lifting technique and communicate well.

UNIT 8, LESSON 9

▷ Advanced Rescue

OVERVIEW

Advanced rescue techniques are additional skills that a raft guide must possess when leading whitewater trips. This lesson focuses on foot entrapment rescue, rescuing a swimmer from a hydraulic, and recovering a pinned raft. Although certain conditions related to foot entrapment and raft pinning require advanced skills beyond the scope of this lesson, the basic principles will be covered to develop a foundational skill set. Resources found at the end of this unit provide advanced information that can be accessed for additional lessons and training.

JUSTIFICATION

Foot entrapments, swimmers being recirculated in hydraulics, and pinned rafts are serious situations that guides must be able to handle. With proper training, guides can deal with these situations effectively and efficiently under average conditions.

GOAL

To develop students' ability to execute rescue procedures for foot entrapment, swimmers in hydraulics, and pinned-raft scenarios.

OBJECTIVES

At the end of this lesson, students will be able to

◆ identify proper strategies in sequential order for dealing with foot entrapment, swimmers in hydraulics, and pinned-raft scenarios (cognitive);

◆ select appropriate equipment and apply it for a given rescue scenario (cognitive);

◆ execute foot entrapment and pinned-raft rescues through a series of practice scenarios (psychomotor); and

◆ appreciate the complexity of rescue situations in a whitewater environment by consistently managing these situations through prevention (affective).

EQUIPMENT AND AREAS NEEDED

The following equipment is required for each group of three:

◆ Raft

◆ Two throw bags

◆ Three carabiners

◆ Two pulleys

◆ Three Prusik cords

◆ Four 15-foot (5-meter) pieces of 1-inch (2.5-centimeter) tubular webbing

RISK MANAGEMENT CONSIDERATIONS

◆ Mechanical advantage systems create a lot of force. Take time to select appropriate areas. Make sure that students are aware of hazards such as drop-offs, unstable riverbanks, broken glass, and so on.

◆ These scenarios are best done as dry land exercises to avoid additional hazards.

◆ If practicing exercises in actual rapids, check for hazards and choose sites that have plenty of run-out at the bottom. Always discuss hazards with the group and create contingency plans for potential problems.

◆ See lessons 1 and 2 for additional considerations.

LESSON CONTENT

Introduction

The sport of rafting holds inherent hazards, but with proper training and practice, guides can mitigate much of the risk associated with the activity. Being able to execute rescue skills is an important competency for those serious about leading whitewater rafting experiences. After mastering basic rescue skills, a committed student should practice advanced skills to become a more well-rounded raft guide.

Main Activities

Activity 1: Foot Entrapment (20 Minutes)

A swimmer becomes entrapped by putting his or her feet down on the riverbed while in moving water. Feet are typically wedged between rooks or caught in debris. Maintaining the downstream swimming position is essential, but most novice river travelers instinctively walk to stand if possible to control the situation. What they don't realize is that the force of the water can be to their detriment if they become entrapped with the head forced down by the current.

To rescue an entrapped swimmer, follow the steps of the Bechdel–Ray one-line method. This method is also known as a tag line.

◆ Get a single rescuer to each side of the river, each equipped with a throw bag and a carabiner.

◈ One of the rescuers must deploy a throw bag across the width of the river to the other rescuer.

◈ The second rescuer, with both bags now in hand, then attaches the bags together with a carabiner.

◈ The second throw bag can be emptied of its rope and packed with a few rocks to help the bag sink after it is placed in the water.

◈ The rescuer who deployed the first throw bag then begins to pull the rope, with the connected bags, back across the river, keeping the rope out of the water as much as possible to reduce drag.

◈ After the bags are directly downstream of the victim, the rescuers lower the bags into the water (figure RA9.1).

◈ Both rescuers simultaneously walk the line upstream, pulling the victims' feet out. The objective is to place the rope so that it creates a U shape around the ankle of the pinned foot (figure RA9.2).

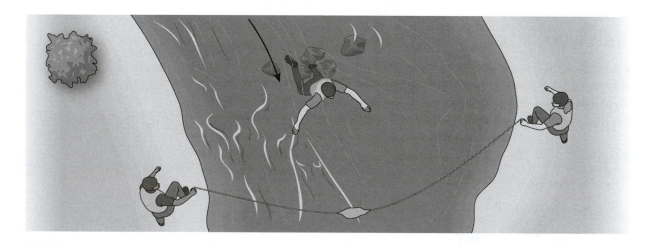

FIGURE RA9.1   Bechdel–Ray one-line method—tag line.

Reprinted, by permission, from Rescue 3 International, 2001, *Whitewater rescue technician for the river professional,* V.01.2 (Wilton, CA: Rescue 3 International), 111. © Rescue 3 International. The leaders in water rescue training. (800)457-3728.

FIGURE RA9.2   Bechdel–Ray one-line method—freeing the victim.

Reprinted, by permission, from Rescue 3 International, 2001, *Whitewater rescue technician for the river professional,* V.01.2 (Wilton, CA: Rescue 3 International), 111. © Rescue 3 International. The leaders in water rescue training. (800)457-3728.

For this activity you need to create a foot entrapment scenario. Have the students work in groups of three. One person serves as the victim, and the other two as rescuers. Set up a mock river by using throw bags to mark the edges of the riverbank. Have students run through the skill set. Rotate students through so that each student has a turn at being a rescuer.

Activity 2: Assisting a Swimmer Caught in a Hydraulic (20 Minutes)

Basic rescue information covered in lesson 8 also applies to assisting a swimmer caught in a hydraulic.

There are two basic ways to use a throw rope to assist a swimmer caught in a hydraulic.

- The rope can be thrown to the swimmer so that the swimmer can grab the rope and be pulled to safety.

- The rope can be used as a tag line by extending it across the hydraulic at water level, giving the swimmer something to grab onto. After the swimmer has grabbed the line, he or she can pull himself or herself to safety along the tag line. Alternatively, rescuers on one shore can take in the tag line to pull the swimmer to safety.

If a swimmer is too fatigued to assist in his or her rescue, rescuers will need to apply more advanced rescue techniques. In this case, a rescuer will likely need to enter the hydraulic to retrieve the victim.

- A rescuer should enter the hydraulic only when tethered to the tag line, using a rescue PFD or some other tethering device, so that he or she does not become a victim.

- Such a rescue is risky for the rescuer because of the possibility of becoming tangled in the rescue rope and the difficulty of remaining afloat in the aerated water of a hydraulic; nevertheless, this may be the only way to rescue a fatigued or unconscious victim caught in a hydraulic.

- When rafts and additional resources are available, more advanced rescue techniques can be used to minimize the risk of rescuers becoming victims in a rescue.

Using the mock setup described in the foot entrapment activity, simulate rescuing a swimmer from a hydraulic. Dry land practice like this builds confidence and facilitates discussion as well as in-depth learning.

Activity 3: Unpinning a Raft (One Hour)

A raft becomes pinned when it becomes stuck upstream of any obstacle. After the raft comes to rest it becomes part of the obstacle and the water transfers its force to the raft. This is commonly called a wrap because the water forces the raft to assume the shape of the obstacle, making the raft difficult to remove.

This situation is first combated with a high side command to force the downstream tube down in front of the object, letting the water carry the raft around the obstacle. If the high side command fails, the boat may become pinned and require technical rescue.

Follow these steps to construct and use a Z-drag system to extract a pinned raft. The Z-drag is one of the most common and least complicated mechanical haul systems to execute.

◆ Account for all crew members to determine the severity of the situation. A crew member may be trapped in or under the raft, a circumstance that would require quicker extraction.

◆ Assess the situation. You need to determine the direction of pull. To pull the boat free, you need to have your pulling force on the shore opposite the side of the raft the rope will be attached to (figure RA9.3). Note that rescue lines are attached to D-rings.

◆ Getting the rescue line out to the raft is a task in itself. For this lesson we assume that the boat is easily accessible. In some cases it may be more efficient under extreme force to attach rescue lines to the tubes by creating webbing anchors using a lark's foot (girth hitch). This scenario assumes that you are using a self-bailing raft and a carabiner (figure RA9.4). Then get the line to the appropriate shore either by tossing the line or by having a group member throw the rescuer a throw bag to attach the line to and then haul the line to shore.

◆ After the line is on shore apply the line to an anchor (rock or tree) built out of webbing with a figure-eight on a bight. See the rock climbing or caving units for anchor-building options.

◆ After the line is secure try a vector pull to see whether the raft will come free with that amount of force. The vector pull is described in the canoeing unit, lesson 8.

◆ If the vector pull does not free the raft, you will have to use a mechanical haul system called a Z-drag to free the boat. The Z-drag is a three-to-one haul system, which means that for every one pound (kilogram) of force you put into the system, you get three pounds (kilograms) of force out of it (figure RA9.5).

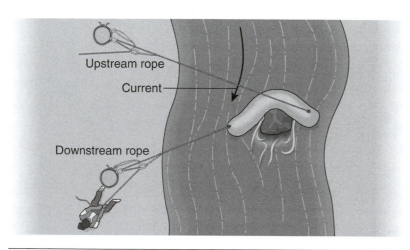

FIGURE RA9.3 Three-to-one hauls using two rescue lines.

Reprinted, by permission, from Rescue 3 International, 2001, *Whitewater rescue technician for the river professional*, V.01.2 (Wilton, CA: Rescue 3 International), 123. © Rescue 3 International. The leaders in water rescue training. (800)457-3728.

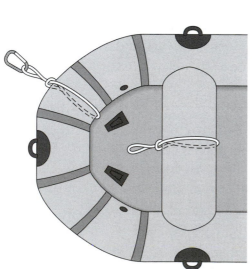

FIGURE RA9.4 Attaching lark's foot (girth hitch) to tubes.

Reprinted, by permission, from Rescue 3 International, 2001, *Whitewater rescue technician for the river professional*, V.01.2 (Wilton, CA: Rescue 3 International), 123. © Rescue 3 International. The leaders in water rescue training. (800)457-3728.

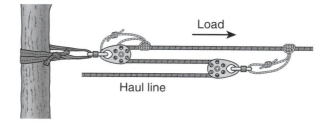

FIGURE RA9.5 Three-to-one haul system (Z-drag) connected to webbing anchor.

Reprinted, by permission, from Rescue 3 International, 2001, *Whitewater rescue technician for the river professional*, V.01.2 (Wilton, CA: Rescue 3 International), 106. © Rescue 3 International. The leaders in water rescue training. (800)457-3728.

◆ To set up a Z-drag you need two pulleys, two carabiners, and two Prusik cords. For more information on the use of Prusik cords, see the rock-climbing unit.

◆ To apply the Z-drag to the haul line, follow the diagram in figure RA9.5. You must have an unquestionable anchor.

◆ Apply force to the line using several rescuers. Make sure that bystanders are not in the danger zone (figure RA9.6). If the haul system were to fail, flying debris could seriously injure anyone in that area.

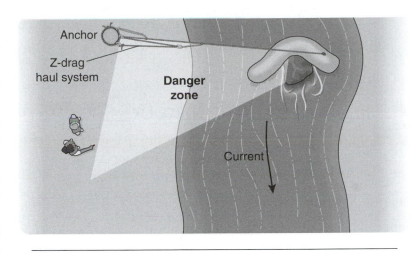

FIGURE RA9.6   Danger zone when applying a Z-drag.

For this activity you need to create a pinned-raft scenario. Have the students work in groups of three. On dry land, mark riverbanks with throw bags and place the raft in the middle of the imaginary current. Have students run through the skill set. Allow enough time for each student to apply the Z-drag to the haul line. The best place to do this activity is where trees are present to use as anchors.

Closure Activity

Raft-Pinning Scenario (One Hour)

Choose an appropriate site in moving water to pin a raft. As a group, formulate a plan to unpin the raft. Choose a group leader to oversee the exercise. Monitor the process carefully. Discuss as a group all potential hazards before initiating the activity. Debrief the activity afterward and brainstorm ways to improve the process.

Follow-Up Activity

On-Water Simulated Foot Entrapment (45 Minutes)

Choose an appropriate site in class I or II moving water to practice a foot entrapment rescue. Choose a group leader to oversee the exercise. Monitor the process carefully. Discuss as a group all potential hazards before initiating the activity. Have a student in the rapid to simulate a foot-entrapped victim. Debrief the activity afterward and brainstorm ways to improve the process.

ASSESSMENT

◆ Check that students can properly sequence the steps required to deal with foot entrapment, swimmers in hydraulics, and pinned-raft scenarios by listening to them formulate a plan of attack for the given activities.

◆ Confirm that students can select the proper equipment for a given scenario by having them lay out the equipment necessary for the scenario for your inspection.

◆ Verify that students can execute the techniques required in foot entrapment and pinned-raft scenarios by evaluating the performance of each in the role of incident leader as she or he handles the scenario from start to finish.

◆ Check that students appreciate the complexity of rescue situations in a whitewater environment by consistently managing those situations through prevention when engaged in moving-water scenarios as described in the closure and follow-up activities.

TEACHING CONSIDERATIONS

◆ To complete this lesson, the students must have knowledge of knots. Lessons for these can be found in other units. The knots necessary are the water knot, the figure-eight on a bight, and the Prusik knot (all three are discussed in unit 2, lesson 3) and the girth hitch (discussed in unit 1, lesson 9).

◆ These basic rescue strategies will work only in certain scenarios. Encourage the students to seek further training by participating in a whitewater rescue technician course.

◆ Emphasize prevention of rescue situations.

◆ Emphasize that a foot entrapment victim who cannot keep his or her head above water is in an extremely serious situation. Time is critical, and practice is the only way to improve the odds of a successful rescue.

UNIT 8, LESSON 10

▷ Leave No Trace Considerations

OVERVIEW

Leave No Trace (LNT) principles are covered throughout this manual, and each unit highlights specific applications. This lesson focuses on multiday rafting trips and how to minimize impact in a river corridor environment. Rafters are able to haul large amounts of gear and accompanying garbage for days on end. Multiday rafting requires specific knowledge and skills to ensure practice of sound environmental stewardship.

JUSTIFICATION

Specific LNT knowledge is required to maintain the integrity of sensitive river ecosystems. Rafters should develop an ethic that responsibly guides their decisions and associated behaviors.

GOAL

To increase students' awareness and skills concerning minimum-impact travel techniques in river corridors.

OBJECTIVES

At the end of this lesson, students will be able to

◆ summarize the key practices of minimum impact in river corridors with special focus on land management regulations (cognitive),

◆ execute minimum-impact practices on a daily basis (psychomotor), and

◆ willingly conform to regulations that serve to protect the land and the concept of wilderness experience (affective).

EQUIPMENT AND AREAS NEEDED

◆ Multiday kitchen equipment (stove, screen floor, tables, dry boxes, coolers, tarp, and miscellaneous cooking equipment)

◆ Groover and cleaning supplies

◆ Boat stakes

◆ Campfire equipment (fire pan, fire blanket, ash can, and shovel)

RISK MANAGEMENT CONSIDERATIONS

◆ When preparing the groover for a lesson make sure that it is clean so that students can have a close look at how your specific human waste disposal system works without being exposed to any contagious bacteria.

◆ Exercise care when dealing with campfires.

◆ Emphasize that thorough hand washing is the most effective way to prevent sickness and illness while living outdoors.

◆ See lessons 1 and 2 for additional considerations.

LESSON CONTENT

Introduction

Leave No Trace is a national, nonprofit, outdoor educational program that aims to inform all outdoor recreationists about minimum-impact skills and responsible backcountry behavior. By following some basic guidelines on multiday rafting, canoe, or kayak trips, groups make only a small mark on the land and water and foster the health of our water resources and the surrounding ecosystems. Another important objective is to leave no trace so that other river travelers enjoy their visit.

Main Activities

Activity 1: Kitchen Setup (30 Minutes)

A well-planned and organized kitchen is essential to minimizing the impact of multiday river trips (figure RA10.1).

Have the group members assemble the kitchen to your specifications. After they finish, do a walk-through of the kitchen to explain where equipment is located and how your kitchen setup is planned to meet the minimum-impact regulations of the area

FIGURE RA10.1 Well-planned kitchen.

where you are traveling. Have the group members prepare a meal and see how much waste is caught by the **screen floor**. Discuss these topics:

◆ Using a fire pan and choosing a location

◆ Setting up a convenient area to wash dishes

◆ Organizing food preparation tables for easy access

◆ Arranging coolers for easy access

◆ Establishing a garbage disposal area

◆ Establishing a hand-washing area

Activity 2: Groover Setup (15 Minutes)

Disposal of human waste while traveling in river corridors can be a daunting task, but if your method of carrying and disposal is well thought out the job can be relatively easy.

◆ A simple system for hauling and disposal is the River Bank Toilet System. This commercially made system is available through most whitewater equipment companies.

◆ Many portable toilet systems are on the market, but homemade systems work well too.

◆ Most systems are designed for solid waste only.

◆ Many rafters carry lime or other chemicals to manage the odor of toilets that sit in the sun for several days.

Walk the group through the setup of the toilet system. Emphasize these key areas:

◆ Pretreatment: Before first use, add a half cup (.25 liters) of Ridex or some other septic treatment solution. This chemical helps break down the waste. Install the rubber gasket around the tank lid. For obvious reasons make sure the gasket is on completely. Try to have several examples of commercially made, portable toilets to show students. Homemade groovers can be made out of military rocket boxes or 5-gallon (20-liter) plastic buckets.

◆ Use: Keep needed toilet materials near the **groover** in zippered plastic bags or other weatherproof bags. If the odor becomes intolerable you can use borax to cut the smell. Just sprinkle in a little after each use. To prevent sloshing, avoid urinating in the toilet. You can use a urine bucket that sits in tandem with the toilet for those who are too modest to use the edge of the river. After use, pour the contents of the urine bucket into moving current above flows of 500 cubic feet (15 cubic meters) per second.

◆ Clean up: Seal the lid. Ensure a tight seal and store in an upright position.

Activity 3: Fire Pan Setup (Five Minutes)

Most heavily traveled river corridors now require the use of a fire pan. Many commercial fire pans are on the market. Homemade pans such as large metal trash can lids or metal boxes work as well. The pan should have lips or sides to contain the ashes. Down and dead is a good rule of thumb when collecting wood. Using driftwood is acceptable in most river environments.

Walk the group through the setup of the fire pan. Use Leave No Trace practices to collect wood and build a fire within the fire pan. An additional requirement for river corridors is to pack out all burned wood and ash. An old ammo can works great for transporting ashes.

Closure Activity

LNT Research (One to Two Hours)

Have students research various river corridors to discover specific Leave No Trace applications required by the governing land management agency. Students will discover that specific practices, equipment, and behaviors will be mandated or recommended. In some cases, river runners are expected to attend a pretrip briefing sponsored by the resource management agency. Have students report their findings to the group.

Follow-Up Activity

Individual Setup Practice (Time as Needed)

After covering each of the topics outlined in this lesson, turn over the responsibilities of setup to the group members. Have each student rotate through the different setups to ensure proper execution of minimum-impact strategies.

ASSESSMENT

- Check that students can summarize the key practices of minimum impact in river corridors with special focus on land management regulations by having them explain the justification for the specific camp setups and how they meet the prescribed standard.
- Be sure that students can execute minimum-impact practices on a daily basis by demonstrating the ability to set up camp using minimum-impact philosophy.
- Confirm that students consistently conform to regulations that serve to protect the land and the concept of wilderness experience by adhering to the planned camp setup design during trips.

TEACHING CONSIDERATIONS

- You can easily teach these lessons while in the field at the beginning of a multi-day rafting trip.
- Have a preplanned kitchen setup in mind before the trip. Having the specific regulations for the river corridor that you will be traveling on most of the time will be helpful in guiding your equipment purchases. If you travel to other rivers you can modify your equipment to meet those regulations.

Rafting Skills Checklist

Equipment and Use

- ☐ Knowledgeable of proper equipment identification
- ☐ Proper equipment application and raft rigging
- ☐ Ability to properly maintain equipment

Safety Considerations

- ☐ Capable of creating a pre-trip safety plan
- ☐ Proficient at executing a thorough safety briefing
- ☐ Ability to demonstrate each paddle command
- ☐ Ability to demonstrate signaling commands

Transporting a Raft

- ☐ Proficient at transporting a raft from vehicle to the water's edge

Preparing to Paddle

- ☐ Proficient at executing a thorough paddle captain briefing
- ☐ Ability to evaluate crafts for water readiness

Maneuvering an Oar Rig

- ☐ Ability to execute the following strokes:
  1. Back rowing while tracking in a straight line
  2. Portegee
  3. Left turn
  4. Right turn
- ☐ Proficient at ferrying a raft across the river
- ☐ Able to enter an eddy
- ☐ Capable of exiting an eddy

Maneuvering a Paddle Raft

- ☐ Ability to execute the following strokes:
  1. Forward
  2. Back
  3. High and low brace
  4. Draw
  5. Rudder
- ☐ Capable of tracking forward in a straight line using the crew
- ☐ Proficient at turning the boat right using the crew
- ☐ Proficient at turning the boat left using the crew

Basic Rescue

- ☐ Ability to deploy a throw bag twice in 20 seconds
- ☐ Ability to right a flipped raft
- ☐ Proficient at assisting swimmers back into the raft

Advanced Rescue

- ☐ Proficient at setting up a foot entrapment rescue
- ☐ Competent at setting up a mechanical advantage system to unpin a raft

Leave No Trace Considerations

- ☐ Knowledgeable of setting up a minimum-impact camp environment
- ☐ Proficient at dealing with the health and sanitation of human waste disposal
- ☐ Competent at fire pan use and fire waste removal

Use the rafting skills checklist as an additional tool to assess skills learned throughout this unit.

From M. Wagstaff and A. Attarian, 2009, *Technical skills for adventure programming: A curriculum guide* (Champaign, IL: Human Kinetics).

GLOSSARY

baffles—The material that separates two chambers on the inside of the perimeter tube.

belly strap—A piece of 1-inch (2.5-centimeter) tubular webbing that runs around the width of the raft. It must be tied to release as needed and be placed over the thwart closest to the guide.

chafe pads—Pads located on the top of the perimeter tube to reduce the amount of abrasion that can occur between a frame and a raft.

D-rings—The D-shaped metal rings attached to the raft at various locations to aid in the attachment of frames or accessories.

foot cups—Welded or glued to the inside of a raft floor to give paddlers added purchase while navigating the river.

groover—A slang term for river toilet. The name developed from the common practice of using ammo cans as river toilets. When users would stand after sitting on the edges of the ammo can, grooves were left in their skin.

Hypalon—A lightweight rubber coating with a long shelf life. Hypalon rafts have the advantage of being able to withstand storage in rolled form.

panels—Welded or glued together to form tubes.

perimeter line—A cord that runs around the perimeter of the raft through the D-rings. This line must be secured so that the guide can release it if needed. This line should be kept free of slack to reduce the possibility of entanglement.

PVC—Similar in durability to Hypalon, but much lighter and stiffer. PVC rafts should be stored partly inflated or at least flat to reduce cracking.

rubbing strakes—An additional piece of durable material that is welded or glued in place around the perimeter of the raft to protect the chambers.

screen floor—A plastic mesh floor placed in the kitchen area that catches bigger particles of garbage but allows dirt and water to pass through.

seams—The place where two panels come together.

thwarts—Inflated tubes that run perpendicular inside a raft to give it torsional rigidity. The number of thwarts in a given raft depends on the size of the raft and the preference of the guide. Some thwarts are removable.

tubes—Inflatable chambers that make up the body of the raft.

urethane—A material that combines the best attributes of PVC and Hypalon. Urethane is extremely durable and long lasting. Urethane rafts should be stored partly inflated or at least flat to reduce cracking.

valves and covers—The control point where air is added to or expelled from the chamber of the tube. Valves may have a cover to protect them from the environment.

RESOURCES

American Canoe Association, www.acanet.org. Overview: The American Canoe Association (ACA) is a nationwide, not-for-profit organization that is in service to the broader paddling public by providing education on matters related to paddling, supporting stewardship of the paddling environment, and enabling programs and events to support paddle sport recreation. Since its founding in 1880, the ACA has actively promoted paddle sports across the United States by providing programs and services to its members and the American public. The ACA is uniquely qualified to help individuals and organizations understand how paddle sports can contribute to the quality of life through enabling safe and positive paddling experiences. The objective of the ACA is to be the recognized, primary resource to individuals, organizations, agencies, and regulators for information and guidance on all aspects of paddling. The ACA is the leading source of water-based education courses for certifying instructors.

American Whitewater, www.americanwhitewater.org. Overview: The mission of American Whitewater is to conserve and restore America's whitewater resources and to enhance opportunities to enjoy them safely. Their work breaks down into three focuses: river stewardship, safety, and outreach. American Whitewater works to protect and restore rivers, maintains and provides real-time flow information for a national inventory of whitewater rivers, monitors potential threats to whitewater river resources, publishes information on river conservation, works with government agencies to protect the ability of the public to have a voice in the management of federal and state rivers and environs, and provides technical advice to local groups regarding river management and river conservation. The American Whitewater Web site is an excellent resource for finding information about local rivers as well as environmental conservation and access issues.

Bennett, J. (1996). *The complete whitewater rafter*. Blacklick, OH: Ragged Mountain Press. Overview: This manual is endorsed by professional guides, instructors, and recreational river runners everywhere. With comprehensive step-by-step coverage starting with the first run, it includes tips from top guides, outfitters, and instructors, as well as the most complete guide to class V rafting techniques ever assembled.

Castillo, P., & Rypins, B. (1997). *Let's get wet.* Paddle Videos. Overview: This video teaches the ABCs of whitewater rafting. It provides novices with the techniques they need to row and paddle down class I, II, and III whitewater, yet it appeals to river runners of all abilities. International class V guides Paulo Castillo and Beth Rypins combine their vast knowledge of river running with their expertise in media production in this fast-paced, informative DVD. Detailed instruction combined with never-before-seen footage of the world's most exciting rivers make this DVD a must for the rafting enthusiast. "*Let's Get Wet!* is pumped tight with easy-to-follow instruction and dazzling rafting footage. A must for any rafter's video library." —Jeff Bennett, author, *The Complete Whitewater Rafter* (45 minutes).

Nichols, R. (1989). *Cold, wet, and alive.* American Canoe Association. Overview: Besides covering the traditional topics, this video documents the process of a person getting hypothermia in a recreational setting by making a series of judgmental mistakes. The video uses stop-action computer-enhanced diagrams of thermograms that graphically show the physiological changes in the body occurring from hypothermia (23 minutes).

Nichols, R. (1993). *Heads up! River rescue for river runners.* American Canoe Association. Overview: A wide variety of safety and rescue techniques are shown. Emphasizes the importance of self-rescue as the front line of defense on the river. Footage includes a number of real-life entrapments (none fatal) and rescues (29 minutes).

Rescue 3 International. (2001). *Whitewater rescue technician for the river professional.* Elk Grove, CA. Overview: This is the textbook for whitewater rescue technician certification courses offered by Rescue 3 International, an organization that provides rescue training to individuals and organizations.

Rescue 3 International, www.rescue3.com. Overview: Rescue 3 International is an organization focused on providing practical, real-world experience. To this end, all of Rescue 3's instructors are professionals working in the disciplines that they teach. They include paramedics, firefighters, law enforcement officers, search and rescue team members, as well as river guides and military personnel. Although Rescue 3's instructors come from a variety of fields, they all share the drive to save lives and teach others life-saving techniques. Rescue 3 International is the leading source of whitewater rescue courses for river professionals as well as people that use rivers for recreation.

USGS Water Resources for the United States, http://water.usgs.gov. Overview: The USGS manages water information at offices located throughout the United States. Although all offices are tied together through a nationwide computer network, each collects data and conducts studies in a particular area. This Web site shows river gauge readings for rivers all around the country. To use this Web site you need to know which gauge is relevant for the section of river that you are running. This information can be easily attained from the land managers from the specific region. Some of the gauge readings from this Web site are linked to the American Whitewater Web site for the more popular rivers.

Walbridge, C., & Sundmacher, W. (1995). *Whitewater rescue manual: New techniques for canoeists, kayakers, and rafters.* Blacklick, OH: Ragged Mountain Press. Overview: This book is for all whitewater paddlers, beginner to expert. The book presents the best techniques for self-rescue and rescue of companions on the river.

Warriner, G. (Producer). (n.d.). *Journey into the great unknown.* Camera One Productions. Modern-day explorers retrace the wild-water route of the Green and Colorado Rivers, first explored in 1869 and 1871 by the expeditions of John Wesley Powell. Powell's own journal entries, and photos from the 1871 expedition, invite scenic comparison with today's landscape, revealing a century of changes in the Grand Canyon environment (80 minutes).

PART III

Snow- and Ice-Based Units

The presence of snow and ice can transform the outdoors into an almost mystical environment, providing unique mediums for introducing additional adventure activities into your program. Snowshoeing, mountaineering, nordic skiing, and ice climbing, some of the common snow- and ice-based activities practiced by outdoor adventure programs, are the focus of this part. Snow and ice activities allow students to learn new skills or transfer previously learned skills to new situations and environments. For example, many of the knots, equipment, and practices found in rock climbing can be used in ice climbing and mountaineering. The skills learned in backpacking can be transferred to mountaineering.

Many of these activities are becoming more popular among outdoor programmers and enthusiasts. For example, the popularity of snowshoeing has increased over 300 percent since 1994 because smaller, lighter, maintenance-free aluminum frames, and a more versatile binding system are available (Schneider, Porcari, Erickson, Foster, et al., 2001). Nordic skiing is a diverse activity that includes ski touring, trail (or track) skiing, and cross-country–downhill. Like snowshoeing, nordic skiing has grown in popularity since the 1980s because of improvements in technology and design of equipment and clothing. The popularity of mountaineering and ice climbing can be attributed to the greater availability of equipment, visibility in the media, easier access to remote areas, and advances in clothing, technology, and skill.

The benefits associated with participation in snow and ice activities are many. The most obvious are improving physical and cardiovascular fitness as well as burning calories through aerobic exercise. Nordic skiing and snowshoeing are lifetime activities in which almost anyone can participate, no matter their age, fitness level, or expertise. These are also great activities to do with family and friends. Ice climbing and mountaineering (like rock climbing) have the potential to enhance both muscular and cardiovascular strength and endurance, flexibility, coordination, and balance. Important but less obvious benefits of ice and snow activities include improving personal confidence and self-esteem, improving team-building skills, enhancing self-reliance, reducing stress, learning to appreciate nature, and learning how to conduct oneself in a cold environment. Judgment and decision-making skills are also enhanced.

Inclusion

Unit 11, lesson 12, introduces a four-step process that aids the instructor and her or his students in identifying potential activity modifications. This useful model for working with people with disabilities can be applied to any adventure activity. Unit 9, lesson 8, shares a series of games to help participants with diverse abilities improve balance and coordination on snowshoes.

Leave No Trace

The Leave No Trace practices for the activities in this unit are similar, especially for snowshoeing (unit 9, lesson 7), skiing (unit 11, lesson 11), and ice climbing (unit 12, lesson 8). The authors for each of these activities focus primarily on LNT principles for winter environments, with subtle differences noted for each activity. Similar LNT principles are practiced for mountaineering (unit 10, lesson 9), but to avoid redundancy, that unit's authors emphasize LNT principles for alpine and subalpine environments—the primary settings for mountaineering activities.

Connecting Units

Throughout this and other parts of this book, you will find that the authors refer to other units if a topic was found elsewhere. For example, ice climbing, mountaineering, and rock climbing all use similar types of equipment, knots, skills, techniques, and so on.

A final note relates to stretching and warm-ups. Make sure that you stress to students that they should warm up before participating in any physical activity. This may include traditional stretching or simply engaging in the activity at a slow pace initially. Stretching and warming up is explained in detail in unit 9, lesson 4.

References

Schneider, P., Porcari, J.P., Erickson, J.D.A., Foster, C., Brice, G., & Freeman, A. (2001). Physiological responses to recreational snowshoeing. *Journal of Exercise Physiology Online, 4*: 45–52.

Snowshoeing

Briget Tyson Eastep

UNIT 9, LESSON 1

▷ Introduction to Snowshoeing

OVERVIEW

Knowledge of **snowshoeing** helps students appreciate and respect the activity. Students learn in this lesson the history and progression of snowshoeing, from its origin as a survival skill for Native Americans and early North American explorers to its current status as a varied recreation pursuit that allows people access to our wild lands for winter adventures.

JUSTIFICATION

Knowledge of the history and progression of snowshoeing provides students with a foundation from which their interest in this activity may progress. This lesson helps explain the increased popularity of snowshoeing in recent years.

GOAL

To give students an understanding of the history and progression of snowshoeing.

OBJECTIVES

At the end of this lesson, students will be able to

- describe the history of snowshoeing (cognitive) and
- appreciate and respect the sport of snowshoeing (affective).

EQUIPMENT AND AREAS NEEDED

One pair of snowshoes

RISK MANAGEMENT CONSIDERATIONS

- This lesson is designed to be presented indoors.
- If you conduct this lesson outdoors, check the teaching area for environmental hazards.
- Ensure that students have appropriate clothing for the setting.

LESSON CONTENT

Introduction

Adventure, fitness, and fun are three words that describe the sport of snowshoeing today. Yet 100 years ago **snowshoes** were used primarily for survival in cold-winter climates. By understanding the history of snowshoeing, students can better understand and appreciate this cold-weather activity.

Main Activity

History and Progression of Snowshoeing (30 to 45 Minutes)

Begin by sharing the following information with your students: Between 4,000 and 6,000 years ago, ancestors of Alaska's Inuit migrated from Asia to North America across the Bering Strait, bringing the first snowshoes to North America. These hardy people relied on snowshoes to explore new territory, hunt for food, and gather other raw materials needed for survival (Tucker, 2006). Early snowshoes were modeled after animals' paws (the paws of snowshoe hare and bear) and were up to 7 feet (2 meters) long. As bands of Native Americans moved east and south, they used snowshoes to travel and hunt through the winter months. Tribes adapted their snowshoes to serve them in different terrain. For example, those who lived in the Yukon wore long snowshoes to create optimal surface area to tread through the Northwest's deep snowpacks, whereas those who moved to what is now the Midwest and East Coast of the United States made shorter snowshoes in the shape of beaver tails to increase their maneuverability in thick forests.

- The earliest snowshoes were made from slabs of wood. These evolved into wood (ash being the most common) frames with rawhide lacings. Early European explorers, trappers, and hunters adopted these traditional snowshoes from the Native American tribes whom they encountered.

- For thousands of years people relied on snowshoes with wood frames and rawhide lacing for employment and survival. But after people began to use snowshoes for recreation in the 1960s and 1970s, the snowshoes evolved in shape and size because many recreational snowshoers found the traditional snowshoes to be awkward for walking and to have unreliable bindings.

- In addition, recreational snowshoers began using snowshoes to access the mountains in winter and found that they needed traction devices in the steep terrain. For those reasons, snowshoes began to be made out of aluminum with neoprene decking, and traction claws were added to increase control and stability in steep terrain.

- Today snowshoes are made out of aluminum or hard plastics with rubber decking and technologically advanced bindings that securely attach the snowshoe to the boot or shoe but allow for easy attachment or removal.

- The latest trend in snowshoe development is binding systems made for specific boots that fit like crampons.

- Winter clothing now includes synthetic base layers that wick moisture away from the skin and nylon or Gore-Tex outer layers that are windproof and waterproof.

- These technological advances have helped millions of people enjoy winter sports in style and comfort.

- Many people favor snowshoeing because the gear needed is relatively simple: snowshoes, winter boots and clothing, and the option of poles to aid balance.

Ponder what the first snowshoers would think about the sport of snowshoeing today.

- Because of the advances in clothing and equipment since the 1970s, snowshoeing grew to include over 5 million participants in 2005 (Outdoor Industry Foundation, 2006).

- In the early days when snowshoes were used as survival tools, men were the predominant users. Today 50 percent of people who buy snowshoes are women, and one-third of participants are between the ages of 16 and 24.

- Instead of using snowshoes for hunting and trapping, people today use snowshoes for racing (from 5Ks to marathons and triathlons), mountaineering, backpacking, day hiking, and exploring.

FIGURE SS1.1 "If you can walk, you can snowshoe."
—Carl Heilman, snowshoe enthusiast.

- Outdoor enthusiasts who love hiking use snowshoes to reach the wild areas that they love in the summer when the winter delivers snow. The difference is the magical, adventurous, and enjoyable experience of float walking through a field of fresh powder. Snowshoeing under a full moon offers an even more amazing experience.

- If you haven't tried snowshoes, now is the time. Snowshoeing is as straightforward as walking, but it is more fun and will deliver you to enchanted winter landscapes (figure SS1.1).

Closure Activity

History Review (10 to 15 Minutes)

Ask students to take approximately 10 to 15 minutes to reflect on the history of snowshoeing by responding to the following questions.

- Which snowshoeing period are you most interested in and why?

- What shape and size of snowshoes did Native Americans and early explorers use in your area?

- How are snowshoes today different from the snowshoes used 100 years ago?

- Why do you want to participate in this activity?

Follow-Up Activity

Snowshoeing Review (15 Minutes)

After the activity, bring students together in a circle.

- Initiate a conversation about snowshoeing, past and present.

- Encourage students to speculate how much time a snowshoer needs to practice to become proficient in the activity.

- Discuss what their goals are for learning about snowshoeing and how they intend to apply the knowledge and skills gained in the lessons to their personal recreation activities.

ASSESSMENT

- Check that students can describe the history of snowshoeing by having them identify a particular period in snowshoeing history and discuss some of the developments that occurred during that time.

- Assess whether students appreciate and respect the sport of snowshoeing in their discussion of its history.

TEACHING CONSIDERATIONS

This lesson is most likely a lecture-style presentation, but you can share the information by having students read the description in groups or on their own.

▷ **Snowshoeing Basics**

OVERVIEW

In this lesson students are introduced to snowshoes and snowshoeing. Students learn the different parts of snowshoes, practice walking with snowshoes, and participate in a playful activity designed to help them become comfortable maneuvering with snowshoes.

JUSTIFICATION

Many say that snowshoeing is just like walking, yet it is walking with shoes that are 10 times larger than standard shoes. Doing this takes some practice. By experimenting with snowshoes, students can gain the maneuvering skills that they need to become comfortable when hiking over longer distances.

GOAL

To give students confidence in maneuvering on flat terrain and through obstacles wearing snowshoes.

OBJECTIVES

At the end of this lesson, students will be able to

- identify the different parts of snowshoes (cognitive),
- be able to put snowshoes on securely (psychomotor),
- demonstrate maneuvering on flat ground and around obstacles wearing snowshoes (psychomotor), and
- appreciate the opportunities for winter hiking that snowshoes offer (affective).

EQUIPMENT AND AREAS NEEDED

- One pair of recreational snowshoes for each participant
- An open field (with or without snow)
- Obstacle course materials (below are suggestions, but the elements are limited only by your imagination)
  - Ten to 12 cones (to slalom through)
  - Jump rope (to jump)
  - Three or four hula hoops (to step through)
  - Tarp (to jump over)
  - Sled with sturdy pulling rope (to pull someone in)
  - Broomstick or mop handle (for limbo)
  - Two or three sections of 6- to 10-foot (1.8- to 3-meter) rope (to designate backward and sideways lanes)
  - Whistle

RISK MANAGEMENT CONSIDERATIONS

◆ You can do this activity in any season. If you are outside be sure that students are hydrated and dressed appropriately for the weather and season.

◆ The obstacle course involves running, jumping, and other maneuvers. Check the area for tripping hazards or other hazards. Clear the area of any hazards found.

◆ Sequence the movements to warm up before full exertion.

LESSON CONTENT

Introduction

Begin by asking students to imagine what would happen if they tried walking through 3 feet (1 meter) of snow. The answer is that they would sink up to their thighs and create "postholes" in their path. **Postholing** is strenuous, inefficient, no fun, and the whole reason that snowshoes were invented. Snowshoes were designed to help people float on top of snow instead of posthole through it.

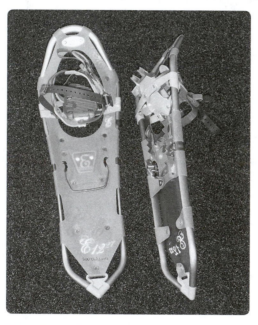

FIGURE SS2.1   Modern snowshoe.

◆ Floating allows a person to conserve energy and travel efficiently in deep snow.

◆ To float, snowshoes increase the surface area of the foot and distribute the person's weight over a larger surface area. The amount of surface area that a person needs to float depends on the person's size and the type of snow.

◆ To float, heavier people need larger snowshoes than smaller people do. To float in light, dry snow, people need larger snowshoes than they do in heavy, wet snow.

◆ Modern snowshoes are relatively simple with four major components: frame, decking, bindings, and **traction device**. (See figure SS2.1.)

Main Activities

Review the basic concepts mentioned earlier by first pointing out the different components. Next, demonstrate walking through snow with snowshoes. Then ask students how each part of the snowshoe helps a person float or travel through snow. Instruct students to put on their snowshoes, emphasizing that the binding should be snug for increased control of their new big feet.

Activity 1: Learning the Basics (10 Minutes)

Learning to walk, jump, and run short distances with snowshoes in flat, snowy terrain can be done intuitively, but by learning and practicing some techniques, students' efforts will be more graceful and efficient. Demonstrate each of the following:

◆ Walking: Lift up your feet and be careful not to place one snowshoe on top of the other. Try to keep snowshoes level.

◆ Jumping: Point your toes down so that the heel is the last piece to touch the ground.

◆ Running: Practice walking first and stay in control.

After demonstrating each technique, have students try each action by wandering from one end of the field to the other by walking, jumping, or running. You can make a game out of this practice.

◆ Inform students that the sequence of actions is walking, jumping, and running. Every time they hear the whistle they need to change actions.

◆ If they hear two whistle blows, they need to do the action in slow motion. Three whistle blows means walk backward, and four whistle blows means walk sideways.

◆ Spend five to eight minutes blowing the whistle to guide students' movements. Be sure to observe students' energy levels and body language and change actions often to keep students interested and moving.

Activity 2: Obstacle Course Challenge (15 to 20 Minutes)

After everyone in your group appears to be comfortable walking, jumping, and running with snowshoes, inform them of the obstacle course challenge. Have students complete a preset course. Use your imagination for stations and include stations that challenge students to maneuver using different actions with their snowshoes. Some of the activities on the course could include the following:

◆ Running a slalom course through cones

◆ Jumping rope (requiring each student to complete five jumps)

◆ Stepping through hula hoops that are held up (tied to a tree or pole), without touching the hoop

◆ Stepping through a number of hula hoops lying on the ground spread out side by side but slightly offset, using the rule that only one snowshoe can be in a hula hoop at a time

◆ Jumping over a tarp (controlling the difficulty by making it a wide or a narrow jump)

◆ Pulling a sled (with a person or a snowman in it) from one point to another

◆ Limboing with a broomstick or mop handle

◆ Having a backward lane

◆ Having a sideways lane

◆ Performing a team activity by dividing students into groups and having them run the course as a relay

Closure Activity

Snowshoe Analysis (Five Minutes)

In small groups of three or four, have students analyze which part of the snowshoe (the frame, decking, or binding) is most important in the various actions that they just used in the activities.

* Walking
* Running
* Jumping
* Going backward

Be sure to ask why they chose each part. Summarize by having each group determine how each part of the snowshoe helped them maneuver. For example, the decking increases the surface area of their feet so that they float. The binding system allows for foot movement, and the frame gives the snowshoe the rigidity that it needs.

Follow-Up Activity

Exploring With Snowshoes (Five Minutes)

Gather students into a circle and ask them to think of a place that they would like to explore with snowshoes. To help them, make a list of nearby areas—local nature parks or centers, open space areas, county parks, state parks, national forests, wildlife refuges, and national parks or monuments. Look for places that offer trails that are 2 miles (3 kilometers) or longer. You can also help students understand how different people use snowshoes. Find a local activity guide to find out whether any snowshoe races are held in your area or whether any lighted trails are open to snowshoers. Other ways that people use snowshoes include winter backpacking and mountaineering on one extreme to recreational day hiking or exploring on the other.

ASSESSMENT

* Assess whether students can identify the different parts of snowshoes by having them draw snowshoes and label the parts in their notebooks or journals.
* Check that students can demonstrate maneuvering on flat ground and around obstacles wearing snowshoes by observing them maneuver through the obstacle course.
* Confirm that students are able to put on snowshoes securely by observing them do this in each of the activities.
* Assess whether students appreciate the opportunities for winter hiking that snowshoes offer by having them tell about a place that they would like to explore with snowshoes.

TEACHING CONSIDERATIONS

* Snowshoeing is more strenuous than walking or running. Be sure to sequence activities to warm up, have a period of peak exertion, and then cool down.
* Boots are recommended for footwear in these activities.

▷ Equipment for Recreational Snowshoeing

OVERVIEW

Compared with other winter sports, recreational snowshoeing requires little equipment, yet the type of snowshoe and ancillary equipment needed varies according to a person's body size, the snow conditions, terrain, and the activity. Because snowshoeing is a winter activity, wearing appropriate clothing becomes a key safety issue. In this lesson students learn to choose the right clothing and equipment to be safe and comfortable on outings lasting up to a day.

JUSTIFICATION

Being able to choose safe and effective clothing and equipment will give students self-reliance and confidence to snowshoe safely and comfortably on daylong outings in the future.

GOAL

To give students the knowledge to choose the appropriate clothing using the VIP system and to analyze body size, snow conditions, and terrain to select the appropriate equipment for a daylong outing.

OBJECTIVES

At the end of this lesson, students will be able to

◆ select the appropriate snowshoe equipment according to body size, snow conditions, and terrain (cognitive),

◆ select the appropriate clothing using the VIP system to be safe and comfortable for a daylong outing in winter (cognitive),

◆ put on and properly use snowshoe equipment (psychomotor),

◆ layer and unlayer clothing to maintain comfortable body temperature while snowshoeing (psychomotor), and

◆ feel confident in selecting and using clothing and equipment (affective).

EQUIPMENT AND AREAS NEEDED

◆ One pair of recreational snowshoes per person (various sizes and types if available)

◆ One pair of telescoping trekking or ski poles per person

◆ Hiking baskets for poles

◆ Powder baskets for poles

◆ Winter activity clothing for each person (V = ventilating layer, I = insulating layer, P = protecting layer):
   – Head: fleece hat (I), balaclava or neck gaiter (I), sunglasses (P), goggles (P)
   – Torso: synthetic (for example, polypropylene) undershirt (V), two fleece or wool sweaters (I), water-resistant or waterproof shell (P)

- – Legs: synthetic (for example, polypropylene) long underwear (V), fleece or wool pants or leggings (I), waterproof shell pants (P)
- – Hands: insulated and waterproof gloves or mittens (I and P), glove liners (V)
- – Feet: synthetic liner sock (V), wool blend sock (I), sturdy boots (P)
- – Optional, but recommended for wet snow conditions: Neos or another snug-fitting waterproof overshoe (P)

◆ Ten essentials for safety (a systems approach)

◆ Day pack with hip strap

◆ High-energy food (for example, Power Bars, gorp, hot cocoa, peanut butter, bagels, cheese)

◆ Two to four quarts (liters) of water

◆ Collapsible snow shovel

◆ A "sit upon" Ensolite (closed-cell) square or a three-quarter-length Therm-a-Rest pad

◆ A snowshoe trail or route 1 to 3 miles (2 to 5 kilometers) long

◆ Copies of equipment descriptions from activity 3

RISK MANAGEMENT CONSIDERATIONS

◆ Winter conditions require precautions to keep students warm, dry, well fed, and hydrated. Prepare your students before heading outside for extended periods.

◆ When sizing snowshoes, weight is a consideration. Be aware of participants who do not want to share their weight and be able to generalize in a compassionate manner.

◆ Avoid avalanche territory.

LESSON CONTENT

Introduction (Two to Five Minutes)

While snowshoeing, the goals are to stay warm, dry, and on top of the snow. Brainstorm with students different ways to meet those goals. End by integrating their ideas into the main activity, which follows.

Important Terms

VIP clothing system (adapted from Nichols, 2002):
- – Ventilating (V) layers are worn next to the skin and wick moisture away, keeping skin relatively dry. Synthetic fabrics such as Capilene, polypropylene, or a polyester blend work best for this layer.
- – Insulating (I) layers are the middle layers designed to trap warm air radiating from the body. Synthetic fleece or pile and wool fabrics work best for this layer.
- – Protecting (P) layers are windproof and are made of water-resistant or waterproof (recommended) layers to protect the wearer from rain, snow, and wind. Gore-Tex, Event, and coated nylon fabrics are all effective for this layer. Protective layers must also protect the person from the sun, so include sunglasses, goggles, and hats with brims.

Main Activities

Activity 1: Layering System (Five Minutes)

Introduce students to the VIP clothing system and to the concept of layering to maintain a comfortable body temperature. Remind students that the key to effective layering is to anticipate becoming hot or cold. Add layers before you get cold and take off layers before you get hot. Anticipating how your body will feel will keep you comfortable because you will not have to warm up from getting cold and you will not have to cool down if you get too warm. You will also stay drier and warmer if you unlayer to avoid excessive perspiration with increased activity.

Activity 2: Versatility of VIP (10 Minutes)

Simulate a day of snowshoeing by having students dress appropriately for changing conditions.

- Begin by having students select a full system of VIP clothing.
- Next, take the students through an imaginary day of snowshoeing by having them layer and unlayer as the day progresses. In doing this, describe the various temperatures and weather that they are likely to encounter, but also include the extremes. As you talk, students will be putting on and taking off layers.
- To conclude this portion of the lesson, inform students that you will ask them to use the VIP clothing system and layering techniques to stay comfortable for the remainder of your time together.

Activity 3: Introduction to Snowshoeing Equipment (10 Minutes)

Introduce students to the following equipment. To make this part interactive, give each piece of equipment and its description to a group of two or three students. They have the task of introducing the piece of equipment to the class as if it were a person whom they were introducing to their friends. For example, a group receives a set of telescoping poles and a copy of its description from the following section. They discuss the characteristics of the poles as being sturdy, a great "friend" to lean on, adaptable to different situations, someone who adds balance to their lives, and, of course, short and skinny.

- **Bindings** secure your foot to the snowshoe. You want a binding that is simple to use and holds your foot securely in place. Bindings in modern snowshoes typically have a platform and either a lacing system or a ratchet system to secure the straps to your foot. Most bindings accept a variety of footwear, so you don't need specific shoes for snowshoes. Sturdy hiking boots are recommended.
  - Rotating bindings pivot where they attach to the decking of the snowshoe. The pivoting makes the tails of the snowshoes fall down with each step. This action sheds snow and promotes a more efficient stride to reduce fatigue in legs. Rotating bindings make it easier to kick steps into steep slopes, but they can be awkward when stepping over obstacles or backing up.
  - Fixed bindings are connected with rubber or neoprene bands and have little pivot. Snowshoe tails stay parallel with the foot on each step. Stepping over obstacles and backing up with these bindings is easy. The drawback to fixed bindings is that they kick up snow.
- **Decking** in modern snowshoes is made of either a synthetic rubber that is flexible or composite plastic, which is rigid. Both are effective, so choosing one over the other is a matter of personal preference.

◆ Frames in modern snowshoes are most commonly made of lightweight aluminum. Frames typically come in three sizes: small, medium, and large (table SS3.1).
  – Bearpaw frames have curved heels (figure SS3.1).
  – Teardrop frames have slim tails (figure SS3.2).

◆ Crampons, typically located under the ball of the foot, allow the snowshoer to dig into ice or hard snow crusts. Some snowshoes also have V-shaped traction devices on the heel decking that snow becomes stuck in on descents to slow descending speed.

◆ Poles are used for balance and to establish a walking rhythm. Telescoping poles can be adjusted to a variety of heights and can be compacted to strap easily on a daypack. Ski poles can also be used, but they are not adjustable. When holding a pole, the forearm should be parallel to the ground on flat terrain when holding the handle.

◆ Powder baskets are wide-pole baskets that will not sink as deeply in snow as smaller pole baskets.

◆ A snowshoe repair kit includes nylon packing straps, bailing wire, duct tape, a multitool with blades and tools, and extra screws, washers, and pins specific to the type of snowshoe being used.

TABLE SS3.1   Snowshoe Frame Sizes

Snowshoe size	Dimensions	Surface area	Weight capacity
Small	8 × 25 in., or 20 × 65 cm	170 sq in. (1,100 sq cm)	< 170 lb, or < 77 kg
Medium	9 × 30 in., or 23 × 75 cm	220 sq in. (1,400 sq cm)	170–220 lb, or 77–100 kg
Large	10 × 36 in., or 25 × 90 cm	275 sq in. (1,800 sq cm)	220–275 lb, or 100–125 kg

Note: Snowshoes made specifically for women are slightly smaller than these sizes and have contoured frames and bindings made to fit female shoe sizes.

Data from C. Heilman (2006) and G. Prater (2002).

FIGURE SS3.1   Bearpaw frames.

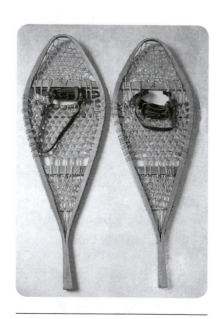

FIGURE SS3.2   Teardrop frames.

◆ Ten essentials for safety (a systems approach; figure SS3.3)

◆ Day pack with hip strap

◆ High-energy food (Power Bars, gorp, hot cocoa, peanut butter, bagels, cheese)

◆ Two to four quarts (liters) of water

◆ Collapsible snow shovel

◆ A "sit upon" Ensolite (closed-cell) square or a three-quarter-length Therm-a-Rest pad

Activity 4: Snowshoe Size Review (Five Minutes)

Review rules for deciding what size of snowshoe you need.

◆ Rule 1: You want the smallest snowshoe that will meet your needs. Smaller shoes are easier to manage than larger ones.

◆ Rule 2: Determine whether you need small, medium, or large snowshoes according to the frame chart (table SS3.1). Be sure to include your pack weight in your weight calculation.

◆ Rule 3: The lighter the snow is, the more surface area you want. Assess the snow conditions. If the snow is very light and dry, consider using a larger snowshoe.

◆ Rule 4: The steeper the terrain is, the more aggressive you want your crampon to be. For flat or rolling terrain a traction device is helpful, but on steep terrain an aggressive crampon under foot is necessary to help you hold your footing.

◆ Rule 5: Any well-designed snowshoe will work, so the shape of the snowshoe is a personal preference.

Activity 5: "Try It, You'll Like It" (15 to 20 Minutes)

Ultimately the best way to determine what size and type of snowshoe works best is to try out different sizes and shapes. Each student in your group should have a pair of snowshoes and a pair of poles. The goal of this activity is for students to try different snowshoes and poles to analyze how they will perform for them in different snow conditions and in different terrain. Students trade snowshoes periodically and have the goal of testing three different types by walking with their daypacks 25 to 50 yards (meters), in packed and unpacked snow if possible. They then analyze each one using the worksheet (figure SS3.4):

Ten Essentials for Safety

1. Navigation—map and compass
2. Sun protection—sunglasses and sunscreen
3. Insulation—extra clothing
4. Illumination—headlamp or flashlight
5. First aid supplies

6. Fire—fire starter and matches or lighter
7. Repair kit and tools, including knife
8. Nutrition—extra food
9. Hydration—extra water
10. Emergency shelter

FIGURE SS3.3   Items in these 10 equipment categories are essential for snowshoers' safety.

© 2003. The Ten Essentials reprinted with permission from *Mountaineering: The Freedom of the Hills*, 7th edition, edited by Steven M. Cox and Kris Fulsaas, Mountaineers Books, Seattle, Washington.

Snowshoe Analysis Worksheet

Trial I (With Poles and Powder Baskets)

Snowshoe brand and make: _____

Shape of snowshoe: bear claw   teardrop   other _____

Decking: synthetic   rubber   composite   hard   plastic   other _____

Binding crampon: not aggressive   moderately aggressive   aggressive

Heel traction device: yes   no

Size of snowshoe:

    small (8 × 25 in., or 20 × 65 cm)   medium (9 × 30 in., or 23 × 75 cm)

    large (10 × 36 in., or 25 × 90 cm)   other _____

My size with a pack:

    small (< 170 lb, or < 77 kg)   medium (170–220 lb, or 77–100 kg)

    large (220–275 lb, or 100–125 kg)

Snow conditions:

extremely light and dry   0   1   2   3   4   5   6   extremely dense and wet

Performance notes: _____

_____

_____

Trial II (Without Poles)

Snowshoe brand and make: _____

Shape of snowshoe: bear claw   teardrop   other _____

Decking: synthetic   rubber   composite   hard   plastic   other _____

Binding crampon: not aggressive   moderately aggressive   aggressive

Heel traction device: yes   no

Size of snowshoe:

    small (8 × 25 in., or 20 × 65 cm)   medium (9 × 30 in., or 23 × 75 cm)

    large (10 × 36 in., or 25 × 90 cm)   other _____

My size with a pack:

    small (< 170 lb, or < 77 kg)   medium (170–220 lb, or 77–100 kg)

    large (220–275 lb, or 100–125 kg)

Snow conditions:

extremely light and dry   0   1   2   3   4   5   6   extremely dense and wet

Performance notes: _____

_____

_____

continued ▶

FIGURE SS3.4   This worksheet will help you determine what size and type of snowshoe works best for you.

From M. Wagstaff and A. Attarian, 2009, *Technical skills for adventure programming: A curriculum guide* (Champaign, IL: Human Kinetics).

Trial III (With Poles and Hiking Baskets)

Snowshoe brand and make: _____

Shape of snowshoe: bear claw   teardrop   other _____

Decking: synthetic   rubber   composite   hard   plastic   other _____

Binding crampon: not aggressive   moderately aggressive   aggressive

Heel traction device: yes   no

Size of snowshoe:

      small (8 × 25 in., or 20 × 65 cm)   medium (9 × 30 in., or 23 × 75 cm)

      large (10 × 36 in., or 25 × 90 cm)   other _____

My size with a pack:

      small (< 170 lb, or < 77 kg)   medium (170–220 lb, or 77–100 kg)

      large (220–275 lb, or 100–125 kg)

Snow conditions:

extremely light and dry   0   1   2   3   4   5   6   extremely dense and wet

Performance notes: _____

_____

_____

Summary of the Three Trials

Snowshoe size preference: small   medium   large

For each circumstance indicate the snowshoe that you would prefer and why:

    Present snow conditions: _____

    Light and dry snow conditions: _____

    Heavy and wet snow conditions: _____

    Flat or rolling terrain: _____

    Steep terrain: _____

Pole preference: no poles   poles with hiking baskets   poles with powder baskets

FIGURE SS3.4   *(continued)*

From M. Wagstaff and A. Attarian, 2009, *Technical skills for adventure programming: A curriculum guide* (Champaign, IL: Human Kinetics).

Activity 6: Equipment List Review (15 Minutes)

This final activity addresses the complete equipment list for daylong snowshoeing excursions.

◆ Hand out a copy of the complete equipment list.

◆ Have groups of four to five students review the list and refine it for their needs. Would they exclude anything on this list? Why?

◆ Would they include anything not on the list? Why?

Closure Activity

Which Do You Prefer? (10 Minutes)

After the students analyze three different snowshoes, have them gather in a circle and explain to the group which snowshoe they prefer and why.

◆ During this discussion ask students if they would change their choice if the snow conditions were different or if the terrain was significantly different.

◆ Ask students to report how the VIP clothing system and layer strategies are working for them.

◆ Ask students what items they would exclude from the equipment list if they were going out only for an hour rather than all day.

Follow-Up Activity

Shakedown (One Hour or Longer)

Take a 2- to 4-mile (3- to 6-kilometer) hike with students to give them the opportunity to practice using the VIP clothing system and to try out their snowshoe and pole selections.

◆ After the hike ask students (in a circle again) to report about one thing (clothing or equipment) that worked extremely well and one thing that they would change the next time they go out.

◆ On the back of the worksheet or in their journals, have students report how confident they are about selecting snowshoe equipment and using the VIP system to select clothing.

◆ You can use a rating system in which 0 indicates that the student is unsure about making choices and 10 indicates that the student is extremely confident about making choices.

ASSESSMENT

◆ Assess whether students can select appropriate snowshoe equipment according to body size, snow conditions, and terrain by having them discuss how they selected snowshoe equipment according to those considerations.

◆ Check that students can select appropriate clothing using the VIP system to be safe and comfortable for a daylong outing in winter by having them explain their clothing selection using VIP terminology.

◆ Verify that students can layer and unlayer clothing to maintain comfortable body temperature while snowshoeing by observing students go through the process.

- Confirm that students can put on and properly use snowshoe equipment by observing students throughout the lesson.
- Assess whether students are confident about selecting and using clothing and equipment by having them report in their journals how confident they are in their clothing and equipment selection and use.

TEACHING CONSIDERATIONS

- Snowshoeing is more strenuous than walking or running. Be sure to sequence activities to warm up, have a period of peak exertion, and then cool down.
- Boots are recommended for footwear in these activities.
- Select a hike that you are familiar with, is not in avalanche territory, and is in relatively moderate terrain.
- When guiding students to layer and unlayer, you will determine the speed and mood of the activity. Keep students moving and having fun.
- Requiring students to have all the necessary equipment can be difficult and expensive. One way to approach this lesson is to discuss the alternatives to buying expensive high-tech clothing and gear. Thrift and army surplus stores often have a good variety of inexpensive insulating clothing and sometimes have ventilating and protective items as well. Borrowing is another good option. Having two or three complete sample sets of clothing and equipment is helpful for students.

UNIT 9, LESSON 4

▷ Basic Techniques

OVERVIEW

In this lesson students learn snowshoe techniques to maneuver safely up and down hills and through deep snow. The lesson begins with a guide to stretching to encourage students to make stretching part of their snowshoeing routine.

JUSTIFICATION

Students benefit from this lesson by learning efficient techniques for walking through deep snow, ascending, and descending with snowshoes.

GOAL

To help students gain confidence in their ability to snowshoe through varied terrain.

OBJECTIVES

At the end of this lesson, students will be able to

- describe at least three techniques to use when snowshoeing on level ground (cognitive);
- select the best technique for ascending a steep hill and a moderate hill (cognitive);

- soloct the better technique for descending a steep hill and a moderate hill (cognitive);
- explain how to break trail through powder (cognitive);
- move efficiently on level ground by striding, stamping, turning, breaking trail, and using poles correctly to aid balance (psychomotor);
- move uphill in snowshoes using the rest step, switchbacking, scrambling, kick stepping, and herringbone stepping (psychomotor);
- move safely downhill by glissading and using a controlled descent (psychomotor);
- properly stretch the calves, hamstrings, quadriceps, hips, and shoulders before snowshoeing (psychomotor);
- get up using poles after falling in powder (psychomotor); and
- participate in a snowshoe hike and express confidence in their skills (affective).

EQUIPMENT AND AREAS NEEDED

- One pair of recreational snowshoes per person
- One pair of telescoping trekking or ski poles with powder baskets per person
- Winter activity clothing for each person (V = ventilating layer, I = insulating layer, P = protecting layer):
    - Head: fleece hat (I), balaclava or neck gaiter (I), sunglasses (P), goggles (P)
    - Torso: synthetic (for example, polypropylene) undershirt (V), two fleece or wool sweaters (I), water-resistant or waterproof shell (P)
    - Legs: synthetic (for example, polypropylene) long underwear (V), fleece or wool pants or leggings (I), waterproof shell pants (P), and gaiters (optional but work well to keep snow out of boots) (P)
    - Hands: insulated and waterproof gloves or mittens (I and P), glove liners (V)
    - Feet: synthetic liner sock (V), wool blend sock (I), sturdy boots (P)
    - Optional but recommended for wet snow conditions: Neos or another snug-fitting waterproof overshoe (P)
- Day pack with hip strap
- High-energy food
- Two or three quarts (liters) of water
- Ten essentials for safety (see figure SS3.3 in lesson 3, page 637)
- A hill at least 50 yards (meters) long
- A snowshoe trail or route 1 to 3 miles (2 to 5 kilometers) long with hills to ascend and descend
- First aid kit
- Snowshoe repair kit (extra nylon straps, a multitool, bailing wire)

RISK MANAGEMENT CONSIDERATIONS

- Winter conditions require precautions to keep students warm, dry, well fed, and hydrated. Prepare your students before heading outside for extended periods.
- Avoid avalanche territory.
- Know the trail and terrain before you take students out into it.

LESSON CONTENT

Introduction

Snowshoeing can be a strenuous activity. It can contribute to cardiovascular fitness, muscle strength, flexibility, and coordination. To attain these benefits, a snowshoer must do more than short strolls on level terrain. Yet leaving level terrain requires use of particular techniques to ascend and descend rugged terrain efficiently and safely. Taking a snowshoe excursion into difficult terrain is taxing on the body; therefore, begin with a thorough stretching session.

Orchestrate an interactive stretching session by assigning each person a major muscle or joint to stretch. If they do not know a stretch, they can use one of the stretches described here.

◆ Neck: Reach your right ear toward your shoulder and roll it slowly forward until your left ear is reaching toward the left shoulder. Repeat without rolling the head backward.

◆ Shoulders: With your left hand grab your right triceps and pull it across your chest. Hold for 10 seconds without bouncing. Repeat with the left arm.

◆ Triceps: With your left hand grab your right elbow over your head and gently pull back on it. Hold for 10 seconds without bouncing. Repeat with the left arm.

◆ Hips: Sit on the ground with your knees bent and the soles of your feet touching each other (legs will look like a butterfly). Slowly push down on your knees and hold for 10 seconds without bouncing.

◆ Hamstrings: Sit on the ground with your legs straight in front of you, reach for your toes, and hold for 10 seconds without bouncing.

◆ Quadriceps: Stand and bend your right knee so that your heel is up behind your buttocks. Grab your right ankle behind you with your right hand and gently pull, holding for 10 seconds without bouncing. Let your foot slowly return to the ground. Repeat with the left knee.

◆ Calves: Put your body in a push-up position and then create a V with your body with your buttocks at the point. As you bend your right leg, you should feel the stretch in your left calf. Hold for 10 seconds without bouncing. Then bend your left leg, feeling the stretch in your right calf.

◆ Ankles: Write your whole name in cursive (even your middle name) with your right foot and then with your left foot.

As you stretch, prompt students to review the snowshoe basics that they learned in the first two lessons.

Main Activity

Snowshoe Techniques (30 to 40 Minutes)

Snowshoeing can be broken down into three types of travel: forward on level ground, ascending, and descending. In each case, to travel safely and efficiently, snowshoers can use a few variations on walking. This lesson is a demonstrate–do lesson. Afterward, students have an opportunity to try the different techniques in varied terrain on a snowshoe excursion.

Begin by demonstrating the different techniques below. Organize the techniques into a demonstrate–do pattern.

- Begin on level ground and move to a moderate hill where students have the opportunity to try all the techniques by going up and down the hill.
- You may also select particular students to demonstrate each technique.
- Be sure to observe each student practicing each technique and give feedback as necessary.
- Be sure to teach the technique of getting up after a fall.
- After the demonstrate–do, give students a well-defined boundary and have them practice moving through snow on level ground, ascending, and descending.
- Challenge students to practice each technique and identify the ones that they would use in steeper terrain.
- Make a copy of the snowshoe technique checklist on page 649 for each student so that they can track their progress.

Level Ground Techniques

Striding

- With symmetrical snowshoes, as your back foot swings forward, you must adjust your stride to allow for the width of the shoe to clear by swinging the foot out and around in a semicircular arc to clear the ankle. See figure SS4.1.
- If you don't mind accentuating the snowshoer's waddle, just keep your feet apart and you won't need to swing them around as much.
- If you are using asymmetrical snowshoes, you can walk naturally with no outswing and no waddle.

Stamping

- Stamping produces changes in snow structure. With each succeeding step on the same footprint, the snow hardens and forms a firmer base.
- When you stamp your feet, you should step lightly, pause, and then apply your weight.
- If you try to stamp and place all your weight on the shoe simultaneously, you will sink deeper than if you had not tried to stamp at all.
- The pause is the key. As you move forward, you'll find that a slight pause at the end of each step allows the snow to consolidate even more for the trailing shoers.

FIGURE SS4.1   Striding.

Turning

◆ Called kick or step turns, this turning technique allows you to reverse direction as you would if you were skiing.

◆ Plant your pole alongside the binding of your forward snowshoe, shift your weight onto the forward snowshoe and pole, then lift and swing the back shoe around 90 to 180 degrees to face the new direction. Make sure that you don't cross tails or step on the back of the front snowshoe with the rear one.

◆ Swing the front shoe around to point in the new direction and stamp it into the snow.

◆ Plan your path in advance. Choose the easiest route and the gentlest places on the slope to navigate your turns. See figure SS4.2.

FIGURE SS4.2 Turning: *(a)* Plant the pole alongside the binding of the forward snowshoe, shift your weight onto the forward snowshoe, and turn the back shoe 90 to 180 degrees; *(b)* swing the front snowshoe around, pointing in the new direction, and stamp it into the snow.

Breaking Trail

◆ When breaking trail, keep your stride lengths short and start steps with the tail of the shoe to prevent the toe from collecting snow.

◆ Because trailbreakers exert nearly 50 percent more energy than those following in their footprints, the lead should be rotated.

◆ Usually the trailbreaker leads for two to five minutes and then steps aside to fall into the rear.

◆ Taking turns breaking trail allows the entire party to move faster over the trail.

◆ The most difficult trail breaking occurs in relatively flat countryside, where the snow might be soft and powdery, 6 to 10 feet (2 to 3 meters) deep, and with consistently cold temperatures.

◆ Breaking trail here, even with the longest and widest snowshoes, means postholing, or sinking into the snow.

Using Poles

◆ Place the poles to your side, not in front, and don't use them to push off as a cross-country skier does.

◆ Instead, use your poles to give you better balance, to provide a more strenuous cardiovascular workout, and to strengthen your arms as they give your legs some assistance.

◆ Telescoping or variable-length snow poles work best.

◆ On hills, you can shorten the pole on your uphill side and lengthen the one on your downhill side.

Getting Up After a Fall

◆ When you fall, use your poles to help you get back on your feet.

◆ If the powder is so deep that you can't get your footing, lay your poles out horizontally on top of the snow, grab them around the midpoint, and use them to push off. See figure SS4.3.

◆ If this method doesn't work, simply loosen your bindings and pull yourself free from the shoes, stand up, and then reconnect yourself to your snowshoes.

FIGURE SS4.3   Getting up after a fall.

Ascending Techniques

◆ In general, going uphill in the fall line is better than traversing because snowshoes don't traverse well. (The fall line is the line that a snowball would take as it rolls down a slope.)

◆ To avoid slipping backward, take short steps, keep your head up, and place your weight on the balls of your feet for traction.

◆ Check out the crampons on the snowshoes and make sure that they have lateral points or teeth in front of the pivot rod. If the points are behind the pivot rod, you won't get as much traction.

The following ascending techniques are reprinted, by permission, from S. Edwards and M. McKenzie, 1995, *Snowshoeing* (Champaign, IL: Human Kinetics), 39-44.

Rest Stepping

◆ Rest stepping lets you maintain an aerobic workload while allowing your leg muscles to recover.

◆ First, plant or stamp firmly with one shoe to condense the snow. Then transfer your weight onto that leg and lock the knee in place.

◆ This stance puts the weight momentarily on your bones and joints and allows the working muscles to rest.

Switchbacking

◆ In open forest with widely spaced trees, snowshoers can climb a slope by breaking trail at 45-degree angles to the fall line.

◆ Do short switchbacks only for steep and narrow slopes. Use long zigzags on wider expanses.

◆ Remember that neither new recreational snowshoes nor traditional snowshoes perform well during lateral stepping or traversing because they lack lateral traction.

Scrambling

- This free-for-all ascending style is common in areas where the trees are so close together that the best solution is often to scramble over the crust by the shortest route possible.

- When scrambling, use a technique called walking on your toes, in which you stamp the front foot to dig in the crampon and force the lateral points into the snow.

Kick Stepping

- In steep terrain use the kick step. When you kick step, you take the front of the shoe and kick it straight into the side of the slope about 6 to 10 inches (15 to 25 centimeters). See figure SS4.4.

- You may have to make several kicks to dig deep enough to plant the claw and shoe so that they will hold weight.

- If the snow is unconsolidated, the steps can be fragile. The trailbreaker will often have less difficulty than the followers, because the steps that were cut will break out.

FIGURE SS4.4   Kick stepping.

- The line of steps may also become an ever-deepening trench, requiring more work for those in the back.

- Where the snow is not deep, a better approach may be to go without your snowshoes and do a bare boot kick step.

Herringbone Stepping

- Use this technique to climb moderate slopes.

- With each step, land toe out so that your shoe forms a V angle with the pitch of the slope. See figure SS4.5.

- Keep your knees well bent and straddle the fall line with your shoes in a reverse snowplow position.

- This stance is not comfortable for long, but it will provide traction when you are starting to backslide.

FIGURE SS4.5   Herringbone.

Descending Techniques

◆ Downhills are the ultimate test of the quality of the snowshoe binding because all your weight is driven forward into the toe piece.

◆ If the binding is an open-toe piece and the strap isn't tight enough, the toe will slide under the crosspiece and you'll fall face first.

◆ If you have good bindings, snowshoeing downhill is a delight.

The following descending techniques are reprinted, by permission, from S. Edwards and M. McKenzie, 1995, *Snowshoeing* (Champaign, IL: Human Kinetics), 43, 44.

Controlled Descent

◆ Use poles for balance and stability, keep your weight back on your heels, and walk down slowly. See figure SS4.6.

Glissading

◆ Lean back and draw back on the claws, forcing the toe upward. You can almost glissade down the slope with long striding, gliding steps.

◆ Some shoers prefer riding the tails of the snowshoes down a slope.

◆ You can also ride your shoes with one foot in front and the other trailing to adjust for braking.

◆ Leaning on your poles turns them into a rudder or a brake when you need to turn slightly or slow down. See figure SS4.7.

Closure Activity

Tips and Techniques (10 Minutes)

Have each student select one technique to review. The student should add any tips that she or he learned by practicing it. At the end of the practice session, direct students to describe in their own words each technique on the checklist (figure SS4.8) in their journals.

FIGURE SS4.6   Controlled descent.

FIGURE SS4.7   Glissading.

Snowshoe Technique Checklist

For the techniques listed, check the ones that you can do with confidence and describe each technique in your own words.

On Level Ground

☐ Stride

☐ Stamp

☐ Turn

☐ Break trail

☐ Use poles

☐ Get up after falling using poles

When Ascending

☐ Rest step

☐ Switchback

☐ Scramble

☐ Kick step

☐ Herringbone step

When Descending

☐ Controlled descent

☐ Glissade

FIGURE SS4.8   Checklist for assessing and describing basic snowshoeing techniques.

From M. Wagstaff and A. Attarian, 2009, *Technical skills for adventure programming: A curriculum guide* (Champaign, IL: Human Kinetics).

Follow-Up Activity

Terrain Challenge (Two to Four Hours, Depending on Group Goals and the Terrain)

Take a 2- to 4-mile (3- to 6-kilometer) hike in varied terrain and challenge your students to use all 13 techniques. Have them indicate on their checklists each technique that they use by putting a check next to it.

At the end of the hike, have students answer the following questions as they stand in a circle. Alternatively, have them write the answers on the back of their checklists.

◆ Which ascending technique is best for steeper climbs? For moderate climbs? Why?
◆ Which descending technique is better for steeper descents? For moderate descents? Why?
◆ Which is the most useful technique for ascending? For descending? Why?
◆ Why is it important to switch the lead position when breaking trail?
◆ Which is your favorite technique? Why?

ASSESSMENT

◆ Check that students can describe at least three techniques to use when snowshoeing on level ground by having them refer to the snowshoe technique checklist used for tracking their experience.

◆ Verify that students can select the best technique for ascending a steep hill and a moderate hill by listening to or reading their selections of the best technique at the end of the hike.

◆ Confirm that students can select the better technique for descending a steep hill and a moderate hill by listening to or reading their selections of the best technique at the end of the hike.

◆ Check that students can explain how to break trail through powder by having them articulate this during the hike.

◆ Verify that students can move efficiently on level ground by striding, stamping, turning, breaking trail, and using poles correctly to aid balance by observing them throughout the lesson.

◆ Confirm that students can move uphill in snowshoes by rest stepping, switchbacking, scrambling, kick stepping, and herringbone stepping by observing them using these techniques throughout the lesson.

◆ Check that students can move safely downhill by glissading and by using a controlled descent by observing them engage in these skills during the hike.

◆ Verify that students can properly stretches their calves, hamstrings, quadriceps, hips, and shoulders before snowshoeing by observing them during the warm-up phase of this lesson.

◆ Ensure that students can get up using their poles after falling in powder by observing them engage in this technique as it presents itself throughout the lesson.

◆ Check that students can participate in a snowshoe hike and express confidence in their skills by counting the students who participate in a hike.

TEACHING CONSIDERATIONS

Pairing up students to take turns coaching and practicing the techniques is a way to get students to interact and hold one another accountable for trying all the techniques.

▷ Cold-Weather Safety

OVERVIEW

This lesson introduces the most common cold-weather injuries and illnesses and ways to prevent them. Students pack a well-prepared day pack and participate in solving a series of scenarios to apply their newfound knowledge.

JUSTIFICATION

Students benefit from this lesson by learning the most common injuries and illnesses that occur in the backcountry in winter and how to prevent them. Students also have the opportunity to pack a day pack for a daylong winter excursion.

GOALS

To help students learn to identify and prevent hypothermia, frostbite, altitude sickness, dehydration, sunburn, and sunblindness; learn how to pack essential safety equipment; and solve problems in scenarios to demonstrate their understanding and judgment.

OBJECTIVES

At the end of this lesson, students will be able to

- identify hypothermia, frostbite, frostnip, altitude sickness, dehydration, sunburn, and sunblindness (cognitive);
- explain how to prevent the most common cold-weather injuries and illnesses (cognitive);
- respond to being cold so that they avoid hypothermia (psychomotor); and
- respect the risks associated with backcountry excursions in winter (affective).

EQUIPMENT AND AREAS NEEDED

- A list of clothing and equipment for a daylong snowshoe excursion (from lesson 3) for each student
- Copy of the three sets of cards for every three or four students: Cold Illnesses and Injuries, Symptoms, and Preventions

RISK MANAGEMENT CONSIDERATIONS

If you are teaching the lesson outside, make necessary arrangements to keep students warm, dry, hydrated, and well fed.

LESSON CONTENT

Introduction

Begin this lesson with a story about a cold-weather injury or illness. If you don't have a story you can ask students to share their experience or read them "Thanksgiving Weekend Death in the High Peaks" found at www.princeton.edu/~oa/safety/hypdeath.shtml.

- After listening to a survival story, have students discuss in small groups of four or five what went wrong.
- Accidents usually occur from a combination of human factors (for example, inexperience, fatigue, or not expressing one's needs) and environmental factors (for example, cold temperature, rugged terrain, or wet weather).
- Even cold-weather injuries and illnesses can be linked back to a combination of these two types of factors.
- Guide students to categorize their list of what went wrong in the story told or in "Thanksgiving Weekend Death in the High Peaks" according to the human and environmental factors.

Main Activity

Matching (20 to 30 Minutes)

In this activity students learn about common cold-weather illnesses and injuries by matching three sets of cards: Cold Illnesses and Injuries, Symptoms, and Preventions.

- Be sure to shuffle the cards before giving them to the student groups. Encourage students to take notes as they match the cards.
- Review the correct matches and ask whether students have any questions or comments regarding these common cold injuries and illnesses. The cards are listed in figure SS5.1.

Closure Activity

Choosing the Right Equipment (20 Minutes)

Give students the list of equipment needed for a daylong snowshoe excursion.

- Have students, in groups, review the list. On a blank piece of paper in their journals, have them write which items they can use to prevent the previously discussed injuries or illnesses.
- Each item may work to prevent several cold injuries and illnesses.
- Another option for this closure activity is to have the clothing and equipment on site. Hand out all the items to students and have each student explain how the items they have can prevent cold injuries or illnesses.
- Next, have students respond to the following questions in their journals: Is the backcountry dangerous in the winter? Can you make it less risky? If so, how? If not, why not?
- Finally, to add muscle memory to the lesson, have students act out how they would respond to becoming chilled (increase physical activity, remove a wet layer of clothing, eat high-energy food, drink warm liquids).

Cold Illnesses and Injuries

Frostbite

Occurs when skin is exposed to cold and freezes.

Frostnip

Occurs when skin is exposed to cold and turns white.

Hypothermia

Occurs when the body's core temperature falls below 95 degrees Fahrenheit (35 degrees Celsius). Hypothermia affects a person's ability to make sound decisions, so it can lead to more injuries.

Dehydration

Loss of water through sweating, urinating, defecating, and breathing.

Altitude Sickness

At higher altitudes the amount of oxygen in each breath decreases, reducing the amount of oxygen in the bloodstream. Most bodies acclimatize with time.

Sunburn

Occurs to skin exposed to the sun. Can also occur because of sun reflecting off snow, affecting ears, the area under the chin, eyes, lips, and inside the nose.

Sunblindness

Occurs when eyes are exposed to ultraviolet light reflecting from the snow.

Symptoms

Cold, white or gray, hard, and numb skin. Can become blistered or blotchy when reheated and can be painful. Most commonly occurs on the nose, toes, fingers, cheeks, or ears.

Firm, cold, white skin, usually on the face or extremities.

Chills, shivers, fatigue, loss of motor skills and coordination. The person may appear drunk, slurring and stumbling. The person is unable to warm up. In extreme cases a person stops shivering.

Rapid pulse, fatigue, headache, nausea, dark urine, thirst.

Headache, loss of appetite, fatigue, difficulty sleeping, and unusual shortness of breath.

Red skin. Can include blisters.

Swollen eyes, pain, tears, and swelling. Can cause temporary blindness.

continued ▶

FIGURE SS5.1 Matching cards for common cold-weather illnesses and injuries.

From M. Wagstaff and A. Attarian, 2009, *Technical skills for adventure programming: A curriculum guide* (Champaign, IL: Human Kinetics). Based on Edwards & McKenzie (1995); Schimelpfenig & Lindsey (2000); Tilton (2002).

Preventions

◆ Avoid exposing skin to the cold (wear face masks, gloves, and wool socks).	◆ Avoid exposing skin to the cold (wear face masks, gloves, and wool socks).
◆ Keep face and extremities relatively dry.	◆ Keep face and extremities relatively dry.
◆ Stay hydrated.	◆ Stay hydrated.
◆ Increase circulation through exercise or movement.	◆ Increase circulation through exercise or movement.
◆ Wear ventilating, insulating, and protecting layers and add or subtract layers to stay warm and dry. ◆ Stay hydrated. ◆ Eat high-energy food frequently. ◆ Avoid overexertion and keep a comfortable pace. ◆ Stay moving actively so that the body continues to create heat. ◆ Keep track of companions.	◆ Drink a minimum of four quarts (liters) of water or sport drinks throughout the day. ◆ Drink enough liquids to keep urine clear. ◆ Avoid ingesting diuretics such as nicotine and caffeine.
◆ Avoid going above 8,000 feet (2,400 meters). ◆ Drink lots of water. ◆ Eat carbohydrates. ◆ Exercise lightly.	◆ Cover the skin. ◆ Wear sunscreen.
	Wear polarized sunglasses or other eye protection that blocks the ultraviolet and infrared rays.

FIGURE SS5.1   *(continued)*

From M. Wagstaff and A. Attarian, 2009, *Technical skills for adventure programming: A curriculum guide* (Champaign, IL: Human Kinetics). Based on Edwards & McKenzie (1995); Schimelpfenig & Lindsey (2000); Tilton (2002).

Follow-Up Activity

First Aid Scenarios (15 to 20 Minutes)

- Students can research wilderness first aid courses in their area on the Internet.
- Students can create scenarios in which they identify and react to someone with the previously discussed symptoms in a backcountry situation. Creating these scenarios can help students develop judgment about cold injuries and illnesses.

ASSESSMENT

- Check that students can identify hypothermia, frostbite, frostnip, altitude sickness, dehydration, sunburn, and sunblindness by reviewing their journal entries and observing them match cards.
- Confirm that students can explain how to prevent common cold-weather injuries and illnesses by listening to them describe how they would use the clothing and equipment list to address each of these concerns.

◆ Check that students respect the risks associated with backcountry excursions in winter by reading their journal responses to questions.

◆ Assess whether students can respond to becoming chilled by observing their reaction and response to the question posed to them in the closure activity.

TEACHING CONSIDERATIONS

◆ The cards can be laminated to increase their durability.

◆ Treatments for these illnesses are not included. Certified first aid instructors must teach treatments.

▷ Emergency Survival Techniques and Prevention Steps

OVERVIEW

In this lesson students learn how to build an emergency snow shelter, what to do if they become lost, and what steps to take to prevent having to build an emergency shelter or getting lost.

JUSTIFICATION

Winter conditions and weather are unforgiving. Even with the best plans, something can go wrong. Planning properly for a daylong winter excursion means being prepared to spend the night out if necessary. This lesson prepares students to react in an effective manner to stay warm and dry if something goes wrong—if, for example, they become lost or a storm comes in unexpectedly and they are forced to stay out in the backcountry overnight because they can't make it safely back to the trailhead.

GOAL

To give students the knowledge and skills to respond to emergencies in the backcountry on daylong outings in the winter and an understanding of the best practices to avoid emergencies.

OBJECTIVES

At the end of this lesson, students will be able to

◆ generate three best practices for avoiding emergencies and explain them (cognitive),

◆ understand seven goals to guide those lost or stranded in the backcountry in the winter (cognitive),

◆ identify a place to build an emergency shelter (cognitive),

◆ understand the mechanics of a quinzee and be able to apply these to other emergency shelters (cognitive),

◆ build a quinzee as an emergency snow shelter (psychomotor), and

◆ respect the risks involved with backcountry travel in the winter (affective).

EQUIPMENT AND AREAS NEEDED

- A field or other location with snow
- Clothing and equipment to stay warm and dry (see the clothing and equipment list in lesson 3)
- A snow shovel for at least every two students
- Optional: a tarp to help excavate snow
- A journal (or blank paper and a solid writing surface) for every student
- Two colors of pens or other writing tools for every student
- A whiteboard and two or three dry erase markers (a whiteboard can be made by placing a Mylar or trash compactor bag over a Therm-a-Rest pad)

RISK MANAGEMENT CONSIDERATIONS

- This lesson involves building a snow shelter, which means that students are likely to get wet from digging and excavating. Prepare students by insisting that they have appropriate clothing and dry clothes to change into after they finish.
- When building snow caves or quinzees, there is always the chance that one will collapse on the builders. Each excavator needs a buddy on the outside who can help pull or dig her out if needed.
- Snow caves and quinzees are excellent ways to provide protection from the elements, but snow shelters without proper ventilation can lead to asphyxiation. Stress to students the importance of creating vents and having a door cover that allows air to move through it. Do not cook in a snow shelter because of the risk of carbon monoxide poisoning.
- Avoid building in avalanche terrain.
- Destroy the quinzees after the lesson ends. They can become unstable and a safety hazard if not maintained.

LESSON CONTENT

Introduction (Time Varies Depending on Length of Hike)

Begin by having students prepare for a snowshoe excursion. Prepare the group by having them take all that they would for a daylong winter excursion. This excursion will go to the place that you've designated to build quinzees. This place can be a field or school yard if you are in civilization or a place in the backcountry. The hike can take a few minutes or a half hour.

- The idea is to go to a remote location or to simulate going into the backcountry.
- After you have reached your destination, create a simulation by announcing in a dramatic way that the group is lost (or a storm has blown in and you can't make it back to the trailhead safely).
- Inform your students that the activity is a simulation, but do your best to put the group into the mind-set that they have an emergency to contend with using only what they have brought with them, their skills, and their judgment.
- Divide the students into groups of four or five and have each group come up with a plan. Instruct each person to write down their group's plan in a designated color.

◆ After they have their plan, instruct them to hold on to the plan and adjust it throughout the lesson using the content presented but making changes and additions in the second designated color.

◆ The students will submit their final plans to you at the end of the lesson for additional feedback.

Main Activities (Two to Three Hours for All Activities)

Begin by making a transition from being in an emergency simulation to being in a class. Inform the class that you will return to their plans but that you will be building snow shelters called quinzees first. Snow shelters are effective because snow is an excellent insulator. A well-built structure will be warmer on the inside and block falling snow and wind.

Activity 1: Building a Snow Shelter

The snow shelter that students will build is a quinzee (figure SS6.1). A **quinzee** is a practical snow shelter that can be built even in an area with a low snow pack. Building one requires only a shovel or even an improvised shovel. A quinzee is a good shelter to begin with because students learn what elements make a good snow shelter, but it may not be a good shelter to use in an emergency because it can take a few hours to build. Still, if students have built a quinzee, they can keep it in mind when improvising a quicker emergency shelter (like a snow shelter created out of a tree well or a downed log).

In groups of four or five, have students follow these steps:

◆ Begin by planting a pole or branch in the center of what will become the quinzee.

◆ Pile snow at least 6 feet (1.8 meters) in diameter and at least 4 feet (1.2 meters) deep around the center pole to create a dome.

◆ Tamp down the snow pile and let it settle for at least an hour (longer if the snow is dry and powdery). The snow crystals bind together with time, making a cohesive and strong building material. See figure SS6.2. You can use this hour to complete activity 2.

◆ After waiting at least an hour, have students return to finish their quinzees.

◆ Designate the leeward side (the side opposite the wind) and begin excavating the cave from what will be the door.

◆ Dig around the center pole until you have enough room to get in and curl up. Be sure to leave the ceiling at least 6 to 8 inches (15 to 20 centimeters) thick.

◆ Try to make the room big enough to sit in so that a person can change clothing inside rather than out in the elements.

FIGURE SS6.1   Quinzee.

FIGURE SS6.2   Tamping the snow pile.

FIGURE SS6.3   Vent hole with the pole still in place.

* After excavating the main room, remove the pole to create a vent hole. If snow is falling, keep the pole in place and move it periodically to keep the vent open. See figure SS6.3.
* Flagging tape or another kind of marker can be tied to the top of the pole for increased visibility.

Excavating Tips

* Use a tarp to pull large amounts of snow out of the growing shelter at one time.
* For speedier excavating, dig from two sides of the pile.
* When done, patch up one door to keep it warmer inside.

Tips for Staying Dry

* Digging out a quinzee is strenuous work. Take off all insulating layers and be sure to have dry insulating and ventilating layers to put on when done.
* Wear protecting layers to keep dry.

Safety Tips

* Have the person (or persons) excavating designate a buddy on the outside to help move snow out of the structure and, more important, to track the excavator's position so that if the structure collapses, he or she can help the excavator out of the snow.
* To prevent asphyxiation, be sure to have a good vent and some air moving through the door to keep the air flowing through the quinzee.
* Do not cook in a snow shelter. Doing so can lead to carbon monoxide poisoning.

Activity 2: What Can Go Wrong in the Backcountry in Winter

Begin this activity by having students brainstorm what can go wrong in the backcountry in the winter. Steer the conversation to include a review of lesson 5, because emergencies often begin with a cold injury or illness.

Besides having someone become injured or ill, a group can become lost if new snow or wind covers their tracks, if they become disoriented in a whiteout, or if they get stranded miles from the trailhead overnight because of an unexpected storm or because they must care for an injured person.

Next, guide students from discussing what can go wrong to determining their priorities in an emergency. If an emergency occurs, the group's priorities change from recreating to surviving.

When in a survival mode in the backcountry in winter, use these seven goals to guide decisions:

1. Stay dry and warm. Use your layers wisely.
   - If you are embarking on a strenuous activity, take off layers so that you do not soak yourself in sweat.
   - If you are staying relatively still, wear all your layers and continue moderate exercise and movement to keep blood circulating.
   - Change into your spare dry clothing, mittens, and hat if yours become wet.
2. Stay together. Chances of surviving alone are less than the chances of surviving in a group.

- Huddling together is a way to share body heat. Group members can help others by sharing a positive attitude.
- If you send a party for help, send at least two. The optimal size is four people who are prepared to withstand the elements and have all the supplies they would need to create an emergency bivouac.

3. Stay calm. Anxiety leads to panic, and panic leads to poor decision making. Staying calm and keeping an optimistic attitude can make a world of difference for a group in an emergency.

4. Create a shelter to protect your group from the elements. A quinzee is one possibility, but there are other options (Fey, 2001): A tree well can be quickly excavated to block the elements. See figure SS6.4. Snow banks or the snow under a downed tree are other good options for excavation. See figure SS6.5.

5. Keep drinking water and eating. Don't drink and eat all that you have at once, but consistently consume the food and water that you have.
   - Build a fire (outside the shelter) and use a water container to catch melting snow. Many choose to carry a metal cup for just this reason.
   - Eating snow is an option, but some snow holds little water and does a better job of cooling your core temperature than hydrating you.

6. Make a plan with contingencies for the worst-case scenario—that your group will be stranded in this emergency for a few days. How do you plan to keep the group dry and warm? How do you plan to keep drinking water? How will you send for help if needed? How will you keep a positive attitude?

7. If lost or expecting help, create a marker so that others can find you. Use your whistle (three blasts will be recognized as a distress call), flagging tape, or a brightly colored tarp. If snow is falling, wait so that your marker does not become buried. Note that a whistle being blown in a snow shelter may not be heard outside because of the insulating properties of snow. Likewise, whistles may not be heard in high winds or in areas where there is plenty of snow on the ground and on trees.

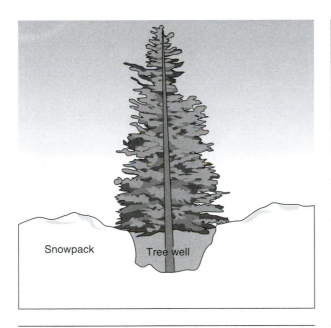

FIGURE SS6.4 Tree well.

FIGURE SS6.5 Snow banks.

After reviewing these seven goals, have students revise their plans to include these goals.

◆ Encourage students to return to their groups to discuss how to revise their plans.

◆ Next, redirect students to consider how emergencies can be avoided.

◆ Organize a "think, pair, share, quad" activity in which you first ask each student to create a list of what he or she would consider the best practices to prevent emergencies in winter.

◆ After students have written down their lists, instruct them to find a partner and compare lists. Let them know that they are free to add to their lists at any point during this activity.

◆ After pairs have shared their lists, instruct pairs to find another pair and compare lists again. At this point, challenge the quads to condense their multiple lists into one list with two or three best practices to follow.

◆ Have each group write their best practices on the whiteboard. Review all the best practices with the entire group. Be sure that the following practices are included and stressed in the closing discussion:

  – Leave a detailed itinerary with a realistic estimated time of return with a reliable person at home. Make sure that the person knows how to contact help if you do not return. Stick to the itinerary that you leave.

  – Use a map and compass to avoid becoming lost. Realize that the snow can alter the terrain but keep track of prominent landmarks as you go. Do not rely solely on being able to follow your tracks back out.

  – Stay on a trail or become familiar with an area.

  – Mark your trail with flagging or wands if you have concerns. Be sure to collect these markers on your way out.

  – Be prepared. Take the equipment and clothing necessary. Know how to use the equipment and clothing—and use it.

  – Expect the unexpected. If in the back of your mind you are expecting to bivouac, then it won't be such a shock if it happens.

  – Travel with one or several companions. There is safety in numbers. Stay together.

◆ Have students revise their lists of what they consider the best practices to follow to avoid winter emergencies.

Closure Activity

Quinzee Completion (Time as Needed)

Return to completing the quinzees.

◆ When all quinzees are complete, have each group give a tour of their structure.

◆ Choose a separate group to evaluate the strengths and weaknesses of the quinzee being toured.

◆ Unless the group is planning to spend the night in the quinzees, destroy them. Leaving them intact could lead to a stranger's investigation when they are not sound. That person could possibly become buried.

- Complete the lesson by encouraging students to continue discussing what they would do in an emergency and how they would avoid emergencies in the future.
- Have each person identify a place (a tree well, snow bank, or downed log) where they could build an emergency structure if needed. The idea is to motivate students to assess the landscape for possible options.
- You can do this by having students write down and draw their emergency shelter idea in their journals.
- At the trailhead, gather the students into a circle and have each student share the most valuable bit of information that they learned. Collect the lists that the students created so that you can give further feedback.

Follow-Up Activity

Quinzee Overnight Experience

If you have the time, knowledge, and resources, spend the night in the quinzees.

ASSESSMENT

- Check that students can explain the three best practices to avoid emergencies that they generated by having students write these practices in their journals.
- Check that students understand seven goals to guide those lost or stranded in the backcountry in winter by listening to them discuss the goals and then list them in their journals.
- Confirm that students can identify a place to build an emergency shelter by reviewing their ideas in their journals.
- Verify that students understand the mechanics of a quinzee and can apply them to other emergency shelters.
- Check that students can build a quinzee as an emergency snow shelter by observing them during the activity.
- Assess whether students respect the risks involved with backcountry travel in winter by listening to their responses to questions asked about the risks presented and the related discussion during the hike.

TEACHING CONSIDERATIONS

- To add a team challenge to the introduction, you can advise the group that everyone in the group must agree with the plan before they can consider it done.
- Sequencing the activities in this lesson depends on the weather and the comfort of the students. The goal is to keep students warm, dry, and comfortable.
- Having a discussion after piling snow can work well, but be aware of people who are wet from sweat or snow after creating their piles.
- Encourage students to use their layers to stay warm and dry. If the weather is snowy or windy, it may be beneficial to keep students active so that they stay warm.
- Use your judgment and check in with students. Take breaks as necessary to exercise, eat, and hydrate.

▷ Leave No Trace Considerations

OVERVIEW

This lesson gives students the opportunity to compare winter Leave No Trace (LNT) principles to general LNT principles and to apply the principles on a snowshoe excursion.

JUSTIFICATION

Over the past decade the number of people recreating in the backcountry during winter has increased. Although winter is a magical time to visit and explore natural areas, the increased use has led to recreation-related impacts. User conflicts, inappropriate disposal of human and pet waste, vegetation damage, and considerable impacts on wildlife are becoming more common. Although a thick covering of snow decreases impacts on soil and vegetation, uninformed or incautious users can still cause damage to vegetation, wildlife, and the experiences of others. To protect the natural areas used for winter recreation, backcountry visitors must follow Leave No Trace principles, even in the winter.

GOAL

To develop students' knowledge of LNT principles in the winter and the differences between LNT principles and LNT winter principles.

OBJECTIVES

At the end of this lesson, students will be able to

◆ discuss how LNT winter principles are different than LNT general principles (cognitive),

◆ plan and execute (in their imaginations) a snowshoe outing that incorporates LNT winter principles (psychomotor), and

◆ voluntarily practice LNT winter principles in and out of class (affective).

EQUIPMENT AND AREAS NEEDED

◆ A copy of LNT principles for each student

◆ A copy of LNT winter principles for each student

◆ A blank piece of paper for each group of three or four students

RISK MANAGEMENT CONSIDERATIONS

◆ You can teach this lesson inside or outside.

◆ If you are teaching outside, take the necessary precautions to keep students warm, dry, hydrated, and fed.

◆ Choose a place out of the direct sun to have the lesson.

LESSON CONTENT

Introduction (15 Minutes)

Begin by taking a poll. Have students raise their hands if they enjoy natural areas.

- Break students into groups of three or four and have them discuss what benefits they receive from visiting a natural or wild land area.
- Have each group designate a spokesperson to report their conclusions.
- Next, ask students whether they based their answers on visiting in summer or in winter (or one of the other seasons).
- Direct the students to discuss how visiting a place in winter is different than visiting it in summer. Again, have spokespeople report their conclusions.
- After you have established that students enjoy the backcountry and that visiting a natural area in winter is different from visiting in summer (yes, you're leading the group to these conclusions), move the conversation to a discussion of recreation impacts.
- Have student groups brainstorm all the ways that a natural area and the animals that live there can be affected by recreation users—in summer and in winter.
- After student groups have a list, generate a class list and compare winter and summer impacts.
- After this list is on the board, ask students if they know of ways to minimize or even eliminate these impacts. This discussion should lead you to introduce the LNT principles.

Main Activity

LNT Review: Winter Versus General (20 Minutes)

Give each student a copy of the general LNT principles (from appendix A) and a copy of the LNT winter principles listed here.

- Direct the groups to review both lists. For each principle, have them write down how the winter principles are similar and different from the general principles. You may want to guide students to create two columns, one titled "Similarities" and the other titled "Differences."
- Review each group's answers in class discussion.

LNT Principles (Leave No Trace, 2006)

Refer to the explanation of the Leave No Trace principles in unit 1, lesson 14.

- Plan ahead and prepare.
- Travel and camp on durable surfaces.
- Dispose of waste properly.
- Leave what you find.
- Minimize campfire impacts.
- Respect wildlife.
- Be considerate of other visitors.

LNT Winter Principles (Leave No Trace, 2002)

◆ Plan ahead and prepare.

– Familiarize yourself with the area you plan to visit.

– Always check avalanche and weather reports before departure.

– Check with local land managers about high-danger areas, safety information, and special regulations for the area that you plan to visit.

– Prepare for extreme weather, hazards, and emergencies.

– Monitor snow conditions frequently and carry and use an avalanche beacon, probe, and shovel. If necessary, take a course about winter backcountry travel.

– Always be sure to leave your itinerary with family or a trusted friend.

– For overnight trips, remember to repackage your food to eliminate the amount of trash that you are carrying into the backcountry and to save weight!

– Use a map and compass or a GPS to find your way to eliminate the need for tree markings, rock cairns, or flagging.

◆ Travel and camp on durable surfaces.

– While on the trail, stay on deep snow cover whenever possible. If you're out in the shoulder seasons and conditions are muddy, stay on snow or walk in the middle of the trail to avoid creating new trails and damaging trailside plants.

– In winter, you should travel and camp well away from avalanche paths, steep slopes, cornices, and unstable snow.

– When choosing a campsite, look for a durable surface such as rock or snow, not tundra or other fragile vegetation.

– Campsites should be in a safe location, out of view from heavily traveled routes and trails.

– Camps should be located at least 200 feet (60 meters) from any recognizable water source; consult your map.

◆ Dispose of waste properly.

– Pack it in, pack it out. Pack out everything you brought in with you. Do not bury trash and litter in the snow or ground.

– Be sure to pick up all food scraps, wax shavings, and other litter. Bring along an extra trash bag to pack out litter left behind by others.

– Solid human waste should be packed out. If packing human waste out is not an option, disguise it in deep snow well away from travel routes and at least 200 feet (60 meters) from water sources.

– Snow makes a great natural alternative to toilet paper. If you do use toilet paper, use it sparingly and pack it out.

– When washing dishes, use small amounts of biodegradable soap if necessary.

– Strain dishwater into a sump hole after removing any food particles, which you should pack out.

– Before you leave, inspect your campsite for trash or other evidence of your stay. You should dismantle all snow shelters, igloos, or windbreaks to naturalize the area.

◆ Leave what you find.

– Leave all plants, rocks, animals, and historical and cultural artifacts as you found them.

– Be sure to let the sounds of nature prevail by keeping loud voices and noises to a minimum.

◆ Minimize campfire impacts.
  – Campfires cause lasting effects in the backcountry. Winter backcountry users should always carry a lightweight camp stove for cooking.
  – If you determine that having a fire is safe and responsible, use only dead, downed wood, if you can find any.
  – When gathering wood, never cut or break limbs off live, dead, or downed trees.
  – Completely put out the fire and break up any chunks of coals into ashes. Scatter the cool ashes widely.
◆ Respect wildlife.
  – Winter is an especially vulnerable time for wildlife.
  – Observe wildlife from a distance and never follow or approach animals.
  – Feeding wildlife is particularly bad and should never be done. Take special care to secure food and trash properly.
◆ Be considerate of other visitors.
  – Winter recreationists should be considerate of other users by sharing the trails, yielding to downhill and faster traffic, and being courteous.
  – When taking rest breaks, move off the trail to allow others to pass by easily.
  – Whenever possible, set your snowshoe track separate from an existing ski track. Also, avoid hiking on ski or snowshoe tracks.
  – If you decide to take your pet with you, educate yourself about local regulations regarding pets. Be considerate of others by keeping your pet under control at all times.
  – Remember to pack out or bury all pet waste.

Leave No Trace principles—Copyright: Leave No Trace Center for Outdoor Ethics. www.LNT.org.

Closure Activity

LNT Challenge (15 to 20 Minutes)

After students have discussed the differences between the general LNT principles and the LNT winter principles, they should have a good understanding of how they can practice LNT skills. Their final challenge will be to plan a half-day snowshoe excursion for their group using the LNT principles. Have them write the report in the past tense, relating in detail how they applied each LNT winter principle throughout the excursion. Make sure that they include in the description how they planned the day.

Follow-Up Activity

Snowshoe Outing (Time as Needed)

Encourage students to participate in the excursion that they plan. To make this happen, challenge your students to plan a snowshoe excursion to a local area and apply the skills and knowledge that they've learned. Give students feedback on their hypothetical report, especially on the safety concerns they took into consideration as they planned the day. Discuss local areas such as county parks, open space, state parks, national parks, and local forest service areas.

ASSESSMENT

- Check that students understand how LNT winter principles are different from LNT general principles by listening to them discuss these differences.
- Confirm that students can plan and execute (in their imaginations) a snowshoe outing that incorporates LNT winter principles by reviewing their written plans or oral report.
- Verify that students voluntarily practice LNT winter principles in and out of class by having them enter into their logbooks or journals each time they practice an LNT principle over the course of a winter.

TEACHING CONSIDERATIONS

Another way to obtain buy-in from students is to discuss the ways in which significant impacts resulting from recreation use in a particular area changes their experience.

UNIT 9, LESSON 8

▷ Inclusion and Accessibility

OVERVIEW

Snowshoeing is an activity that is open to people with diverse abilities. The one requirement is that a person be able to use independent leg action. Poles are tools to use for increased balance, but no special prosthetic devices are necessary. Snowshoes can help people improve their balance, strength, coordination, and spatial awareness. All the lessons in this unit can be adapted to meet the diverse needs of people with differing abilities. When planning activities with people with diverse needs, consider and adapt distances, speeds, and accessibility to learning locations. The following lesson is simply a series of games that people can play on snowshoes. The goal is to promote inclusion and help people with diverse abilities improve their balance, coordination, and spatial awareness. You can use it as a warm-up lesson to a snowshoe excursion with people of diverse abilities.

JUSTIFICATION

Snowshoes allow people to maneuver through snow. Practicing movement can help people of all abilities feel more comfortable on snowshoes and with moving in general. At the same time, snowshoes make the snowshoer's feet 10 times larger, so playing games that inspire different types of movement and speeds can help players develop balance, coordination, and spatial awareness.

GOAL

To give people with diverse abilities the opportunity to play in snow, to have fun, and to improve their balance, coordination, and spatial awareness.

OBJECTIVES

At the end of this lesson, students will be able to

◆ learn the rules to at least one new game (cognitive),

◆ move forward, backward, sideways, fast, and slow on snowshoes (psychomotor),

◆ practice movement that develops balance, coordination, and spatial awareness (psychomotor),

◆ feel more confident in their ability to move with and without snowshoes (affective), and

◆ have fun in snow with a group of people (affective).

EQUIPMENT AND AREAS NEEDED

◆ A flat, open field of snow free from hazards (stumps, trees, gullies)

◆ Snowshoes for each participant

◆ Poles for participants who need extra balance

◆ Clothing appropriate for the weather for each participant (see lesson 3 for a list)

◆ Boundary markers that won't blow away (flagging with stakes, cones, or ropes)

◆ Place markers for each person (rubber spots or participants' hats work unless cold or snow forces students to be wearing them)

◆ Minefield obstacles: 20 to 50 tennis balls, beanbags, cups, plates, rubber shapes, and any other objects you have that can be placed outside on the ground

◆ An open space about 8 feet (2.5 meters) wide by 30 feet (10 meters) long

RISK MANAGEMENT CONSIDERATIONS

◆ You can do these activities in any season. If you are outside, ensure that students are hydrated and dressed appropriately for the weather and season.

◆ Clear the area of any found hazards.

◆ Sequence movement to aid warming up before full exertion. For example, use slow motion before using fast forward speeds in the games.

◆ Set the appropriate tone to encourage safety and inclusion.

◆ Remind students that having snowshoes on will lead to added challenges in moving.

◆ Be cognizant of the different movement abilities in your group. Encourage group members to participate to their best ability. Adapt the games' boundaries, speeds, challenges, and movements as appropriate.

LESSON CONTENT

Introduction (15 Minutes)

Gather the group into a circle and explain that it's game time. Review the rules of the first game. Remind the group that they are wearing snowshoes and must move with care. Begin with the group moving in slow motion if you are concerned with the students' agility. As the activity continues, slowly have the group move faster. This first game is an icebreaker and energy booster. It requires participants to maneuver around each other, so they are practicing balance, coordination, and spatial awareness.

Main Activities

Activity 1: All My Neighbors (Time Varies)

Ask participants to form a shoulder-to-shoulder standing circle and then have each person take three steps back. Give each participant a placeholder such as a rubber spot, which they should place at their feet. As the facilitator, you take a place in the center of the circle.

From here, this activity will remind you of the popular childhood game Musical Chairs. First, after the participants form the circle, everyone will have a spot, a placeholder, except the person (usually the facilitator) in the middle. The task of the person in the middle is to find a spot in the circle and have someone else end up without a place. The way the person in the middle makes this happen is by making a statement that is true for themselves and others in the circle. If the statement is true for a player, he or she must move to another space. For example, if the person in the middle is wearing mittens, she may say, "All my neighbors are wearing mittens." After the statement, all players wearing mittens move from their spaces to another space. This leaves one person without a space, and he or she becomes the middle person and starts the next round by making a true statement: "All my neighbors. . . ." Players may not move immediately to their right or left, and they may not move off a space and return to it in the same round. For safety, no running, body checking, kicking, or pinching.

When you think people have had enough, simply say, "OK, this is the last round." Give a round of applause to the person who ends up in the center (Aon, 2006).

Activity 2: Minefield (Time Varies, at Least 20 Minutes)

This game is traditionally a communication and trust exercise, but because it requires one person to cross a field of obstacles in snowshoes and using poles, it gives each player an opportunity to practice balance, coordination, and spatial awareness in a fun and challenging manner.

To begin, set up the minefield with your participants. Create a boundary (using stakes, markers, or ropes) about 8 feet (2.5 meters) wide by 30 feet (10 meters) long. Ask the participants to scatter the items that you've brought for the minefield randomly. You can also set up the minefield before your participants arrive, but it is often more fun for participants to create their own minefield.

Rules

1. Use more or fewer obstacles to increase or decrease the difficulty of getting to the end of the minefield. Because participants are wearing snowshoes, however, make sure that they have enough room between objects to get across the minefield.

2. Have participants operate in pairs. One participant is blindfolded and located within the minefield enclosure. The second member of the pair is sighted and must stay outside the obstacle enclosure. Only oral clues are allowed; the sighted player cannot touch the blind player. Allow all the blindfolded players to enter the obstacle course simultaneously to increase the difficulty

of moving and being heard. The level of difficulty for each pair depends on the pair's disabilities.

3. A blindfolded player who touches any obstacle must return to the beginning and try again or simply count the touches for later comparison.

4. After a successful traverse or at the end of a reasonable length of time, ask the players to switch roles.

5. As an added challenge, ask two blindfolded players to attempt a hand-in-hand traverse. Other challenges include taking as few steps as possible and traversing as quickly as possible.

6. For people with disabilities, maneuvering through the minefield fully sighted may be sufficient challenge. If being blindfolded is too much of a challenge, or listening to directions is too much of a challenge, challenge the person to work with a partner to cross the minefield without touching any of the objects. This is a useful game because the challenges can be individually catered (Rohnke & Butler, 1995).

© Project Adventure by permission.

Closure Activity

Mirror Image Progressing Into Follow the Leader (15 to 25 Minutes)

Mirror Image is an excellent game that involves nonthreatening interactions and stimulates many types of movements, as well as cooperation. Begin by pairing up your students. Then demonstrate by inviting a volunteer to face you, standing about 3 feet (1 meter) away. Initiate an action while your partner becomes your mirror image. The intention is to make your movements interesting and slow enough for the other person to mime as if she or he were a full-length mirror. The more exaggerated and silly the movements are, the more fun this game is.

Finish your demonstration by encouraging your group to be innovative and have fun. For example, act out a visit to the toilet (yes, with your snowshoes still on). Now, give your pairs a turn to be mirror images. Be sure that pairs are swapping roles, or direct the group so that each partner has a turn.

For a variation or advanced version, ask the pairs to try to mime the anti-image, in which the follower tries to perform movements opposite those of the partner. For example, if partner B is facing partner A and partner A lifts the left hand, partner B also lifts the left hand so that it appears to be moving with partner A's opposite hand. This game can lead to confusion and laughter.

This activity can help people develop coordination, balance, and spatial awareness because it requires them to practice movements that they don't normally do on their own.

When your group is done mimicking each other in pairs, redirect the group to form a line for a good old-fashioned game of Follow the Leader. You can begin as the leader to set the tone and speed, but having everyone get a turn at being the leader increases the fun. Encourage many different movements (sideways, backward, squatting, circles), but be considerate of the movement abilities of people in the group. Give students positive feedback as you go. Again, the goal is have participants improve their coordination, balance, and spatial awareness by practicing different movements with snowshoes on.

When everyone has had a turn being the leader, have the group form a circle again and bring closure to the activity by having each person report the favorite movement that he or she performed in the past hour (Project Adventure Australia, 2006).

Follow-Up Activity

Activities on Snowshoes (Time as Needed)

Play other games with your students. A simple game of Tag is not as straightforward with snowshoes. If you ask students to play in slow motion, those with disabilities have more opportunity to be involved. The sites in the resources list at the end of this unit are useful for finding more games.

ASSESSMENT

◆ Check that students learn the rules to at least one new game by observing them play by the rules for each game.

◆ Verify that students move forward, backward, sideways, fast, and slow on snowshoes by observing them perform each of those motions while playing games.

◆ Assess whether students feel more confident in their ability to move with and without snowshoes by observing them move.

◆ Confirm that students have fun in snow with a group of people by monitoring the laughter among the group as they interact with one another.

TEACHING CONSIDERATIONS

◆ Monitor your students and adapt the speed of the activities to ensure that everyone is able to play. You can adapt speed by using a whistle and establishing that one blast means slow motion, two blasts means fast motion, and three blasts means normal motion.

◆ If you have questions about the abilities of a student, talk with the student or his or her parent to find out what he or she is comfortable doing.

◆ Local ski areas with adaptive programs can be a useful resource for finding more information about working with people with disabilities and snowshoes.

◆ If you have a person who is visually impaired, assign that person a buddy who can offer voice commands throughout the activities. Keep the games in slow motion.

Snowshoeing Skills Checklist

☐ I can name the three parts of a snowshoe.

☐ I can walk comfortably on flat ground with snowshoes.

☐ I can list the equipment needed for a safe day of snowshoeing.

☐ I can describe the seven goals to guide me if I get lost in the backcountry in the winter.

☐ I can draw a quinzee and describe the steps to build one.

☐ I can describe the seven principles of winter LNT.

On level ground, I can (check all that apply):

☐ Stride

☐ Stamp

☐ Turn

☐ Break trail

☐ Use poles

☐ Get up after I fall

Ascending, I can (check all that apply):

☐ Rest step

☐ Switchback

☐ Scramble

☐ Kick step

☐ Herringbone step

Descending, I can (check all that apply):

☐ Control my speed

☐ Glissade

I know how to prevent and identify the symptoms of the following illnesses and injuries:

☐ Frostbite

☐ Frostnip

☐ Hypothermia

☐ Dehydration

☐ Altitude sickness

☐ Sunburn

☐ Sunblindness

Use the snowshoeing skills checklist as an additional tool to assess skills learned throughout this unit.

From M. Wagstaff and A. Attarian, 2009, *Technical skills for adventure programming: A curriculum guide* (Champaign, IL: Human Kinetics).

GLOSSARY

bindings—Secure the boot to the snowshoe.

decking—Made from hard plastic or a rubberlike material. The decking allows the snowshoe to float in snow.

postholing—Sinking past the knees in deep snow.

quinzee—A winter shelter made by excavating a large (6 feet by 4 feet, or 1.8 meters by 1.2 meters) mound of snow.

snowshoeing—A winter sport in which the participant wears snowshoes to stay afloat (rather than sink) in deep snow.

snowshoes—Made from aluminum, a hard plastic or rubberlike deck, and bindings. Creates a large "foot" with increased surface area that allows the wearer to float (rather than sink) in snow.

traction device—Metal claws found on the underside of snowshoes to aid control in steep terrain. Can be extremely aggressive, almost like a crampon.

VIP clothing system:

- Ventilating (V) layers are worn next to the skin and wick moisture away, keeping skin relatively dry. Synthetic fabrics such as Capilene, polypropylene, or a polyester blend work best for this layer.
- Insulating (I) layers are the middle layers designed to trap warm air radiating from the body. Synthetic fleece or pile and wool fabrics work best for this layer.
- Protecting (P) layers are windproof and are made of water-resistant or waterproof (recommended) layers to protect the wearer from rain, snow, and wind. Gore-Tex, Event, and coated nylon fabrics are all effective for this layer. Protective layers must also protect the person from the sun, so include sunglasses, goggles, and hats with brims.

REFERENCES AND RESOURCES

REFERENCES

Aon Consulting Management. (2006). *Pecos River Resources: Team activities*. Retrieved from www.pecosriver.com

Cox, S.M., & Fulsaas, K. (2003). *Mountaineering: The freedom of the hills* (7th ed.). Seattle, WA: The Mountaineers Books.

Edwards, S., & McKenzie, M. (1995). *Snowshoes (Outdoor Pursuit Series)*. Champaign, IL: Human Kinetics.

Fey, T. (2001, February). Emergency winter shelter. *North Country Trail Association Newsletter*. Retrieved from www.northcountrytrail.org/news/winshel1.htm

Heilman, C. (2006). *Snowshoes*. Retrieved from www.carlheilman.com/snowshoe11.html

Leave No Trace. (2002). *Tracker newsletter*. Boulder, CO: Leave No Trace.

Leave No Trace. (2006). *Leave No Trace principles*. Retrieved from www.lnt.org/programs/principles.php

Nichols, K. (2002). *Dressing for the outdoors* (PowerPoint®). Salt Lake City: University of Utah, Department of Parks, Recreation, and Tourism.

Outdoor Industry Foundation. (2006). *Outdoor Industry Foundation outdoor recreation participation study*. Retrieved from www.outdoorindustry.org/images/researchfiles/ParticipationStudy2006.pdf?27

Prater, G. (2002). *Snowshoes: From novice to master* (5th ed.). Ed. D. Felkley. Seattle, WA: The Mountaineers Books.

Project Adventure Australia. (2006). *Archive of activity ideas*. Retrieved from www.paa.org.au

Rohnke, K., & Butler, S. (1995). *Quicksilver: Adventure games, initiative problems, trust activities and a guide to effective leadership*. Dubuque, IA: Kendall/Hunt.

Schimelpfenig, T., & Lindsey, L. (2000). *NOLS wilderness first aid*. Mechanicsburg, PA: Stackpole Books.

Tilton, B. (2002). *Backcountry first aid and extended care*. Guilford, CT: Globe Pequot Press.

Tucker, J. (2006). *Snowshoes*. Retrieved from www.snowshoeracing.com/history.htm

RESOURCES

Adaptive Sports Center, Crested Butte, CO. www.adaptivesports.org. Overview: This center offers events, training, and resources for those interested in adapting winter sports for people with disabilities.

O'Bannon, A., & Clelland, M. (1996). *Allen & Mike's really cool backcountry ski book, traveling & camping skills for a winter environment*. Missoula, MT: Falcon Guides. Overview: A fun and valuable resource for survival in cold conditions.

Snowshoe Magazine. www.snowshoemag.com. Overview: This site is a wellspring of information on snowshoes. The goal of the magazine is "to promote the ongoing worldwide growth of the snowshoes sport and remain steadfast in its future. The *Snowshoe Magazine* team is proud to provide original content (online and print) and a consistent presence in the snow sports industry."

United States Snowshoe Association (USSSA). www.snowshoeracing.com. Overview: The purpose of the USSSA is to educate and promote the sport of snowshoeing. This Web site has information on racing, the history of the sport, gear, a newsletter, and links to other snowshoes resources.

Snowshoe Manufacturers

These manufacturers have information on buying snowshoes as well as links to places to go and other resources to prepare people to snowshoe safely.

Atlas, Berkeley, CA. www.atlassnowshoe.com

Crescent Moon, Boulder, CO. www.crescentmoonsnowshoes.com

Faber, Loretteville, Quebec, Canada. www.fabersnowshoes.com

GV Snowshoes, Wendake, Quebec, Canada. www.gvsnowshoes.com

Mountain Safety Research (MSR), Seattle, WA. www.msrgear.com/snowshoes/

Northern Lites, Wausau, WI. www.northernlites.com

Red Feather, La Crosse, WI. www.redfeather.com

Tubbs, Vashon, WA. www.tubbssnowshoes.com

Wilderness Medicine Resources

These leading wilderness first aid organizations offer many resources and further training.

Solo. www.soloschools.com/wfa.html

Wilderness Medicine Institute. www.nols.edu/wmi/

Wilderness Medicine Training Center. www.wildmedcenter.com

Mountaineering

Mat Erpelding and Scott Schumann

▷ Introduction to Mountaineering

OVERVIEW

By introducing mountaineering history and discussing its evolution as a valued pursuit, this lesson helps students understand and value the innovations and commitment of varied facets of the sport. An understanding of history will help students as they explore the varied philosophies in mountaineering as it has grown, evolved, and changed.

JUSTIFICATION

An exploration of mountaineering history can promote students' development as educated and adept adventurers. Through the study of mountaineering, students learn that current techniques and practices have evolved over 200 years. This lesson also helps students choose which mountaineering style and approach is most likely to provide them with an enjoyable backcountry experience.

GOAL

To develop students' awareness and knowledge of the history and evolution of mountaineering techniques and practices.

OBJECTIVES

At the end of this lesson, students will be able to

- describe the major mountaineering periods and the technological advancements that occurred in each (cognitive),
- identify some of the major personalities and their contributions to the sport of mountaineering (cognitive),
- understand the advantages and disadvantages of each type of mountaineering (cognitive),
- select the mountaineering techniques or approaches that they identify with most (affective),
- appreciate the development of modern mountaineering equipment (affective),
- appreciate the evolution of mountaineering as an ever-changing and developing adventure activity (affective), and
- qualify their reasons for pursuing mountaineering through journaling and discussion (affective).

EQUIPMENT AND AREAS NEEDED

- Articles on at least five mountaineers from 1850 to present. Consider personalities such as Oscar Eckenstein, Conrad Kain, George Mallory, Tenzing Norgay, John Roskelly, Willi Unsoeld, Reinhold Messner, Alex Lowe, Mark Twight, Wanda Rutkiewicz, Stacy Allison, Allison Hargraves, Lynn Hill, Steph Davis, Walter Bonatti, Arlene Bloom, David Brower, John Muir, and others. You can use articles from *Climbing Magazine* or *Rock and Ice Magazine* or simply go to the library and find autobiographies or biographies of famous mountaineers.

- Ten or 15 photos of mountaineering equipment from 1850 to present. You can use articles from *Climbing Magazine* or *Rock and Ice Magazine* or simply go to the library to find photos.
- An 8-foot-by-5-foot (2.5-meter-by-1.5-meter) whiteboard for students to generate a timeline
- Paper and pen for each student for individual notes and the reflection exercise
- Scotch tape

RISK MANAGEMENT CONSIDERATIONS

You can do this activity in an indoor classroom or an outdoor classroom that is considered safe.

LESSON CONTENT

Introduction

By understanding the history and evolution of mountaineering, students can better understand and comprehend the activity.

Important Terms

alpine mountaineering—A method of mountaineering used by a small party who attempts a route by carrying their supplies and operating without permanently established camps.

expedition mountaineering (siege tactics)—A method of mountaineering used by a large group of climbers who "lay siege" to a mountain using multiple camps, fixed ropes, and large amounts of supplies.

Main Activities

Activity 1: Introduction to Mountaineering (15 Minutes)

This lesson is presented in lecture format to provide students with a brief overview of mountaineering and a philosophical underpinning of why people climb.

Why Do People Climb?   Begin this lesson by asking students why people climb. Possible answers include the following:

- Personal challenge
- Experience wilderness
- Experience risk
- Personal freedom
- Recreation

History of Mountaineering From 1800 Through 1850
- The Swiss Alps was a popular vacation spot for western Europeans.
- Guide culture developed into a profession through an apprenticeship process much like that practiced in metal smithing, carpentry, and culinary fields.

♦ Equipment of the time included hemp ropes, hobnail boots, and devices for cutting steps.

♦ During this period, most mountaineering occurred on snow, but climbers occasionally ventured onto moderate ice slopes.

♦ Major peak ascents began to occur later in the 1800s.

History of Mountaineering From 1850 Through 1900

♦ During the late 1800s the British began to develop rock climbing as an offshoot of mountaineering because gritstone cliffs were readily available but alpine opportunities were not.

♦ In the United States, mountaineers began to climb the major peaks of the Cascades, Rockies, and Sierra.

♦ John Muir documented his ascents of Mt. Whitney, Mt. Shasta, Mt. Russell, and a host of other mountains in the Sierra and Southern Cascades.

History of Mountaineering From 1900 Through 1940

♦ Siege expeditions began to rule the mountaineering community as climbers attempted the world's highest peaks.

♦ Climbers such as George Malory, Sandy Irvine, Edmund Hillary, Kirt Diemberger, Herman Buhl, Paul Petzoldt, and Heinrich Harrer attempted the major peaks of the Himalayas including Nanga Parbat, K2, Annapurna, and Everest.

♦ In 1908 Oscar Eckenstein devised the first 10-point crampon. This innovation began to change the speed by which climbers could ascend and the types of terrain that they could travel over because the crampon reduced the need to cut steps.

♦ As early as 1906, a patent for a carabiner was granted, although carabiners were not popular until the 1920s. They became prominent only during World War II after advances occurred in aluminum forging techniques.

♦ In 1932 Grivel added front points to the crampon, allowing climbers to climb much faster and to take direct lines up extremely steep slopes.

History of Mountaineering From 1940 to the Present

♦ During the 1960s Yvonne Chouinard introduced a radical departure from standard axes by modifying the angle of the pick, which ushered in the sport of modern ice climbing.

♦ As first ascents of the major peaks were completed, climbers turned to more difficult routes, and siege climbing ended.

♦ Climbers such as John Roskelly, Mark Twight, Steve House, and Barry Bishop applied **light and fast** techniques to the extreme.

♦ Further development in synthetic fabrics removed wool from most climbers' backpacks. Today, new materials provide superior warmth, durability, and drying capability.

Activity 2: Why Climb?

Part 1—Why Do You Want to Be a Mountaineer? (10 to 15 Minutes) Begin by facilitating a discussion on why students want to become mountaineers. What are their personal reasons for taking the risks to summit a mountain?

Through discussion, distill the students' reasons into similar groupings. For example, some students climb for the adventure, the physical challenges, the aesthetic beauty of mountains, the recognition. This activity has no right answer. If students do not include reasons that you (the instructor) see as valid, be sure to engage in discussion on those reasons as well.

Part 2—Mountaineering Timeline (30 Minutes)   Explain and discuss the two major types of mountaineering addressed in this lesson.

* Draw a timeline on the whiteboard from 1800 to the present.
* Divide the class into small groups of three or four.
* Give each group two or three biographies and readings on the evolution of mountaineering.
* Include several printed photos of old and new equipment for each group.
* Allow 10 minutes for the group to read and summarize the major points of the articles.
* Have students present a biography of the climbers in their articles to the larger group. Each presentation should note the years in which the mountaineer was in his or her prime, the climber's personal philosophy or approach to climbing, major accomplishments, and technological advancements that occurred during the person's era.
* After each presentation, have each student group place the climber and equipment photos in the appropriate place on the timeline (students may use scotch tape to place the equipment photos in the proper location).
* Provide additional insight on each climber when necessary to ensure that his or her major contributions to the sport are adequately addressed as they fit the context of the unit.
* Allow time for discussion.

Closure Activity

Reflections (15 Minutes)

Ask students to take approximately 15 minutes to reflect on the history of mountaineering.

* Which climber and climbing era are they most interested in and why? Encourage them to think about their philosophy of mountaineering.
* Encourage students to discuss their reasons for enrolling in the course.
* What are their goals for the course, and how do they intend to apply the knowledge gained in their personal lives?

Follow-Up Activity

Mountaineers, Past and Present (15 to 20 Minutes)

* After students have learned about the history and philosophy of mountaineering, bring them together in a circle.
* Initiate a conversation about famous mountaineers of the past and present.
* Encourage students to speculate how much time a mountaineer needs to practice to become an expert.
* Encourage students to write in their journals about their strengths as mountaineers and the skills that they believe they need to practice in depth to feel comfortable traveling on mountains.

ASSESSMENT

- Check that students can describe the major developments and advancements in mountaineering history and evolution by observing them participate in the timeline activity.
- Verify that students can describe the major mountaineering periods and the technological advancements that occurred during each.
- Confirm that students can identify some of the major personalities and their contributions to the sport of mountaineering by listening to them discuss famous mountaineers of the past and present.
- Check that students understand the advantages and disadvantages of each type of mountaineering by asking them to discuss this issue during the follow-up activity.
- Verify that students can select the mountaineering techniques or approaches that they most identify with by having them share journal entries.
- Assess whether students appreciate the development of modern mountaineering equipment by observing them as they progress in skill development and knowledge throughout the unit.
- Confirm that students appreciate the evolution of mountaineering as an ever-changing and developing adventure activity by observing them as they progress in skill development and knowledge throughout the unit.
- Check that students can qualify their personal reasons for pursuing mountaineering through journal writing and discussion.

TEACHING CONSIDERATIONS

- This lesson is essentially a precursor to the instructor pack check. Do this lesson around the same time as lesson 2, to help students understand the need for adequate gear and realize how far equipment has evolved.
- Each instructor has personal climbing heroes, but selection of climbers should be well rounded and include a few climbers from all eras. It would be unfortunate if all the mountaineers were from the 1970s.
- Women have an important and diverse history within mountaineering. This lesson should include major female mountaineers and discussion about the barriers that many of them faced in pursuing mountaineering.
- Encouraging students to develop interest in the past may spark their interest in their climbing future and set you up for several checks of understanding during equipment selection, crampon instruction, and ice axe instruction. For example, during crampon instruction, you could ask, "Who invented the 10-point crampon?"

▷ Equipment and Use

OVERVIEW

The selection and use of equipment is an important consideration when planning a mountaineering trip. Having the proper equipment often means the difference between success and failure. By learning about the 11 equipment categories and scrutinizing one another's equipment, students learn the value and importance of selecting the appropriate equipment for a three-day alpine climb involving significant snow travel.

JUSTIFICATION

Formal instruction in the selection of equipment for an alpine climb will advance the students' development into becoming self-reliant climbers responsible for their own success. This lesson also increases students' confidence in the functionality of their equipment, allowing them to focus their efforts on the climbing objective, social goals, and safety when necessary.

GOAL

To develop students' awareness and knowledge of the most appropriate and modern equipment available.

OBJECTIVES

At the end of this lesson, students will be able to

- explain their rationale for including or excluding particular pieces of equipment (cognitive),
- distinguish between necessary and unnecessary equipment for a climb (cognitive),
- organize equipment into the 11 equipment categories (psychomotor),
- qualify the inclusion or exclusion of particular pieces of equipment (affective), and
- appreciate the value of using modern equipment for satisfying other goals such as the climbing objective, safety, and social aims (affective).

EQUIPMENT AND AREAS NEEDED

- Instructor backpack completely prepared for a three-day alpine climb (food, fuel, gear, clothing, referring to the 11 equipment categories as a guide)
- Various models of crampons—rigid, semirigid, step-in, and pneumatic
- Antiquated or inappropriate equipment (given modern equipment choices) such as:
  - Handheld flashlight
  - Denim or wool jacket
  - Large cotton sleeping bag
  - Oversized sleeping pad
  - Ball-lock carabiner as an example of an inappropriate carabiner for alpine climbing (figure MN2.1)

FIGURE MN2.1 A ball-lock carabiner is a poor choice for mountaineering because operating the gate
mechanism is difficult while wearing gloves in cold conditions.

* Examples of mountaineering boots (plastic shelled, leathers, and synthetic three-quarter shank)
* Whiteboard and dry erase markers
* Paper and pens for individual notes

RISK MANAGEMENT CONSIDERATIONS

You can do this activity in either an indoor classroom setting or in a stationary location outdoors that is considered safe.

LESSON CONTENT

Introduction

The following section introduces the 11 equipment categories. The activity will get your students thinking about why they are taking the equipment by placing it in a category and what they are doing to satisfy the equipment category and be well prepared. An amusing anecdote about a time that you or a student forgot an essential piece of equipment can start things off. For example, I had a climbing partner who forgot his climbing shoes on a trip to climb El Capitan in Yosemite.

UV Protection

This category includes items that provide protection from the harmful rays of the sun.

* Sunglasses with side shields—the sun's glare rebounding off the surface of the snow unchecked by sunglasses and side shields for as short as one hour can cause snow blindness, a problem that results from burning of the cornea (Auerbach, 1999).
* Zinc sunscreen—to protect the nose from being burned.
* Sun hat with a brim.

Navigational Tools

This category includes any items that assist in route planning and route finding.

* Route description photocopied from a guidebook or dictated from another climber.
* Topographic map.
* Compass.
* Altimeter—essential for finding one's location in a whiteout or when triangulation is difficult. Models that include a wristwatch and alarm work well in this application.
* **Wands**—Bamboo sticks approximately 3 feet (1 meter) in length with flagging tape attached to the tips. Wands are used to mark the route in the event of a whiteout (see figure MN2.2).

FIGURE MN2.2 Wands.

Emergency Supplies

Many climbers compromise this category because they have had the good fortune of not needing these items thus far in their climbing careers. In the event of an accident, these supplies will prove crucial in the swift treatment of injuries, preventing further injury, infection, or discomfort.

◆ First aid kit appropriate for dealing with medical issues in a backcountry setting

◆ Space blanket

◆ Knife or scissors

Clothing

This category was covered extensively in unit 1 (lesson 6). Layers should be appropriate for conditions. Keep in mind that carrying unnecessary clothing will slow a group down. The focus should be on having several layers rather than one or two thick layers. This head-to-toe category includes a warm hat, long underwear, socks, and Gore-Tex or soft-shell layers.

Nutritional Needs

This category includes items necessary to nourish the rope team or individual cook groups, including food, water, purification system, stove, fuel, and pots. Lesson 3 of unit 1 covers nutrition in detail.

Footwear

Footwear gives mountaineers freedom. Taking care of the feet and having effective footwear systems allows climbers to go faster and farther.

◆ Climbing boots—Various models of footwear are available. Care should be taken to choose the appropriate shank length. Three-quarter shank boots work extremely well on moderate terrain where front pointing is not necessary and traveling on a trail is likely. Plastic boots have a full shank and are designed to be waterproof, warm, and rigid (figure MN2.3). A climber venturing onto Mount Rainier (14,411 feet, or 4,392 meters) during early June in Washington may choose to climb in plastic mountaineering boots, whereas a climber in mid-August on Bear Creek Spire (13,713 feet, or 4,180 meters) in California's Sierra Nevada may choose a lighter synthetic boot with Gore-Tex because conditions are generally not as wet or cold.

FIGURE MN2.3 Various climbing boots: *(a)* lightweight, *(b)* three-quarter shank, *(c)* plastic.

FIGURE MN2.4   Gaiters.

- Gaiters—Gaiters come in a variety of models and should be chosen based on conditions. If traveling in deep snow is likely, a calf-high gaiter is appropriate. If conditions do not involve deep snow, ankle-high gaiters will keep snow out of the boot top and are lighter and cooler than calf-high gaiters (figure MN2.4).
- Down camp booties—a luxury item that doesn't add much weight.

Specialized Personal Climbing Equipment

This category involves technical equipment specifically sized to the climber.

- Crampons—metal points that attach to a climber's boots to provide purchase on hard snow and ice. Crampons should have a minimum of 10 points with 2 front points and fit securely to the climber's boots so that they don't come loose while climbing. Various types exist, including rigid (specific to water ice), hinged, step-in, and pneumatic.
- Axe—When sized appropriately, the spike (the base of the shaft) will hang just about level with the bottom of the ankle when the climber holds the adze in her or his hand. The axe will be discussed further in lesson 4.
- Alpine climbing harness—An alpine or mountaineering harness should be as trim as possible with little padding (because the climber's clothing will provide plenty) and have a pair of equipment loops. Leg loops with buckles are essential because they facilitate getting in and out of the harness and make it possible to use the restroom without having to remove the harness.
- Backpack—Most modern backpacks function well in mountaineering applications, but a few features may make things easier on the mountain. These are an ice axe loop to attach the ice axe and a removable lid that converts to a hip pack, which may come in handy on summit day. Some climbers choose to carry a small summit pack specifically for this purpose. In most cases the summit pack is nothing more than a stuff sack with shoulder straps.

Team Technical Equipment

These items are what the team will collectively use to climb its objective. Proper inquiry and assessment regarding route conditions (see lesson 3, Preparing to Climb) will dictate the equipment selected. Lessons 6 and 7 provide instruction on how to use each of these pieces of equipment. This lesson focuses on introducing the equipment.

- Snow pickets—lightweight, T-shaped aluminum stakes with clip-in points spaced along the spine. Recently, climbing rangers on Mount Baker in Washington have started modifying full-length pickets by cutting them in half for use in the heavy Cascade snowpack, taking light and fast to an ingenious new level (figure MN2.5).
- **Flukes**—wedge-shaped aluminum plates with a cable attached as a clip-in point. When placed, the fluke will sail deeper into the snowpack. Care should be taken in placing the fluke to ensure that it does not bottom out if it hits a layer of ice or the ground, which will cause it to slice outward toward the load and fail. Lesson 6 discusses appropriate placements, but note here that different-sized flukes are appropriate for particular snowpack densities (figure MN2.6).

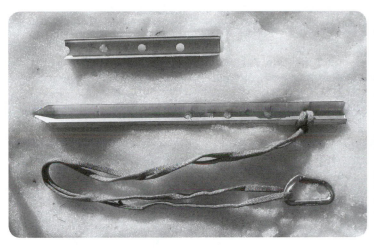

FIGURE MN2.5   Snow pickets.

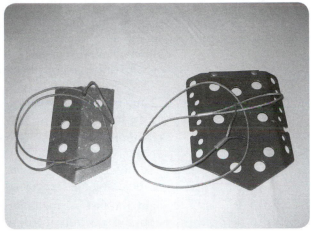

FIGURE MN2.6   Snow flukes.

◆ Rope—Falls in mountaineering generally do not generate forces like those that occur in rock climbing. For this reason, the diameter of mountaineering rope does not need to be as large as the diameter of ropes used in rock climbing. Modern climbers who do not expect their rope to be running over sharp rocks or edges climb on a single dry 8- to 10-millimeter rope (depending on the size of the loads that they are carrying). A dry rope is one that is coated or impregnated with a waterproof substance that protects the core from becoming wet, much heavier, and possibly frozen solid.

◆ Carabiners—locking and nonlocking. Be sure that climbers are able to manipulate the locking carabiners with gloves on. Many self-locking carabiners, such as the Petzl ball-lock carabiner, are difficult if not impossible to open without removing gloves (see figure MN2.1).

◆ **Sewn runners**—Varying lengths of webbing up to 36 inches (90 centimeters) long help with equalizing snow anchors. They are also used to wrap rock horns that can be used as anchors.

◆ Belay devices—optional. Many climbers use the Munter hitch or hip belay, depending on the application. Generally, two belay devices per rope team are adequate.

Night Needs

These items are what the mountaineer needs to make it through the night. Keep in mind that these items will vary depending on the style of climbing chosen. For example, a team that decides to climb with an extremely light and fast style may take bivouac bags rather than a tent with a fly and poles to save weight. Other items include a sleeping bag, sleeping pad, and headlamp.

Personal Effects

These items include toiletries, journal, camera, and so on.

Skills and Training

This category includes probably the most valuable pieces of "equipment" needed for climbing. These intangibles, such as experience, practice, and medical training, form the foundation for making sound judgments.

Important Terms

alpine climbing harness—An alpine or mountaineering harness should be as trim as possible with little padding (because the climber's clothing will provide plenty) and have a pair of equipment loops. Leg loops with buckles are essential because they facilitate getting in and out of the harness and make it possible to use the restroom without having to remove the harness.

crampons—Metal points that attach to a climber's boots to provide purchase on hard snow and ice. Crampons should have a minimum of 10 points with 2 front points and fit securely to the climber's boots so that they don't come loose while climbing. Various types exist, including rigid (specific to water ice), hinged, step-in, and pneumatic.

light and fast—A method of climbing that modern climbers take to varying levels. One end of the spectrum involves intentionally not taking equipment that usually provides comfort or safety (sleeping bag, tent, stove, extra food, extra clothing). Climbers take this approach in exchange for the ability to climb a route quickly and reduce exposure to the objective hazards inherent in alpine climbing. With this style, failure can be fatal. The other end of the light and fast spectrum refers to taking nothing more than is needed to climb a particular route while still allowing for significant comfort and minimal consequences in the event of failure. This lesson refers to light and fast as the latter approach.

snow pickets—Lightweight, T-shaped aluminum stakes with clip-in points spaced along the spine (figure MN2.5).

Main Activity

What's in the Bag? (60 Minutes)

Have your prepared instructor backpack available. Begin this activity by writing the first 10 of the 11 equipment category titles across the whiteboard. Place a "?" next to item number 11.

- Have students, one at a time, take any item out of the pack, describe its use, and write the item into the appropriate category on the board.

- As items are removed from the backpack, add to the descriptions and uses, which the students provide. Be sure that the equipment use and purpose are thoroughly explained.

- When a student pulls out a piece of inappropriate equipment such as a cotton sleeping bag or denim jacket, use this opportunity to illustrate the difference between the modern item and the antiquated item.

- Allow time for discussion.

Closure Activity

The 11th Category (20 Minutes)

Ask students to explain the 11th category. Explain to them that their equipment will not make them successful in the mountains unless they have the experience and sound judgment to use it. They are in the class for that reason—to learn, ask questions, and build skills.

- Using their journals, have students identify both the benefits of selecting proper equipment and the potential pitfalls of selecting poor equipment.

◆ Have students brainstorm where they might find the equipment that they will need to participate in a mountaineering experience. The list should include local retail stores, second-hand clothing stores, online sources, rental shops, and friends whom they can borrow from.

◆ As homework or extended practice, have students create their own equipment list for a three-day alpine climb. Students should list the category number (1 through 11) next to each piece of equipment. Collect the lists during the next class period to check their understanding or to answer any questions.

Follow-Up Activity

Pack-Check Party (45 Minutes or More)

Dedicate the next class period to a pack-check party to which the students bring their fully packed backpacks containing their personal and group equipment.

◆ Read the equipment list to the students and have them unpack their packs. Observe the items that they take out of their packs.

◆ The students can cook food for the party using their cookware and stoves, which they have unpacked. This is an opportunity for students to practice cooking meals and to discuss final preparations before the field experience.

ASSESSMENT

◆ Check that students can explain their rationale for including or excluding particular pieces of equipment by reviewing the equipment lists that they developed.

◆ Confirm that students can distinguish between necessary and unnecessary equipment for a climb by having them discuss their rationale for creating their equipment lists.

◆ Ensure that students can distinguish between necessary and unnecessary equipment for a climb by listening to their comments about the usefulness of modern versus antiquated equipment.

◆ Assess whether students appreciate the value of using modern equipment to achieve additional goals such as the climbing objective, safety, and social aims by facilitating discussion throughout the lesson as they describe the use for each item of equipment.

TEACHING CONSIDERATIONS

◆ This lesson is primarily a structured pack check by the instructor. Conduct this lesson at the beginning of the unit to give students time to buy, rent, or otherwise acquire equipment that they will need to participate in a multiday climb with the class or on their own.

◆ Many students will need to rent or borrow some of the equipment outlined in this lesson. Use this need as an opportunity for them to create their own equipment list.

◆ Passing equipment around for students to inspect will aid in their retention of details.

▷ Preparing to Climb

OVERVIEW

Accurate planning and preparation are hallmarks for successful alpine climbs. This lesson introduces students to the knowledge and content areas that they must address to prepare for alpine climbing.

JUSTIFICATION

Preparing to climb increases the likelihood of a successful climb. By being equipped with the necessary equipment, resources, and information, students are more likely to enjoy the mountains while leaving a minimum impact.

GOAL

To develop students' awareness and abilities to prepare for an alpine climb.

OBJECTIVES

At the end of this lesson, students will be able to

- describe the social importance and implications of planning (cognitive),
- describe the physical importance and implications of planning (cognitive),
- demonstrate the ability to plan sequentially for a climb (cognitive),
- justify taking the time to prepare for a climb (affective), and
- appreciate the contribution of thorough preparation to the overall enjoyment of the climb (affective).

EQUIPMENT AND AREAS NEEDED

- One 15-minute USGS topographical map for each group of three students with a clearly defined route or trail. These maps can be purchased at local outdoor stores or through the land manager of the area (National Park Service, Bureau of Land Management, U.S. Forest Service, state park).
- 4-foot-by-3-foot (120-centimeter-by-90-centimeter) sheets of paper
- One set of three colored markers for each group of three students
- Paper and pens for individual notes

RISK MANAGEMENT CONSIDERATIONS

You can conduct this lesson in an indoor or outdoor classroom. If you conduct the lesson outdoors, choose a site free from any objective dangers.

LESSON CONTENT

Introduction

Have you ever stood somewhere wishing that you were better prepared? For example, perhaps you have gone to watch a football or soccer game outside and halfway through the game, it begins to rain and you think to yourself, "I wish I had brought an umbrella." Or maybe you've gotten into your car to go to a party at a friend's new house and as you find yourself driving up and down streets that you thought your friend lived on, you realize, "I don't really know exactly where my friend's house is." Imagine those things happening while you are in the mountains. This potential exists and is the cause for the need to prepare sufficiently to climb.

Planning a climb includes three sequential parts: route research, groundwork, and final preparations.

> Planning a climb is living the good and the bad before it happens.

Route Research

Climbers should gather enough information about a particular route so that they can understand their objective and be willing to make alternative plans based on their findings. This route research may be as simple as talking with someone who has recently done the route or it can become more involved and include

- researching guidebooks and journals,
- searching the Internet for trip reports (good sources include www.summitpost.com for the Rocky Mountains and http://cascadeclimbers.com for the Cascade Range),
- contacting land managers,
- gathering maps and photos, and
- finding road maps and access information.

> Over time, routes change, glaciers recede, rivers braid, and climbers' memories fade. When doing route research, climbers should maintain a cautious approach and continually assess the reliability of the resource.

Groundwork

Groundwork includes preparing for all the physical actions that the climber will do while on the climb, assembling the equipment and logistics needed, and establishing the social constructs that the group will operate under while on the climb. The following are some of the tasks involved:

- Establish goals and define what success is on the trip.
- Establish a list of equipment needs (length and type of rope, hardware, first aid, emergency space blanket, and so on).
- Inspect and prepare equipment (for example, size crampons to boots before leaving home, sharpen crampons and axes, inspect cables and swages on flukes).
- Clearly establish a leader (many avalanche fatalities are the result of groupthink and not having a clearly defined leader who is responsible for the group).
- Create a route plan.

◆ Make a food plan of logical meals and establish fuel needs (note that some meals are better than others are for certain situations, such as pancakes at base camp or instant oats for an alpine start at 1 a.m.).

◆ Obtain permits if necessary.

◆ Consider methods to reduce potential environmental impacts (reduce food packaging, take natural-colored webbing for retreating off routes, take a poop system, and so on).

Final Preparations

Because of the dynamic nature of alpine environments, climbers must take several essential steps as final preparations both on and off the mountain, such as checking current snowpack stability or taking snowshoes on the summit bid if conditions of the day warrant.

> Thorough preparation off and on the mountain increases the likelihood of a safe and successful climb.

Off the Mountain Immediately before beginning the trip and climb,

◆ check the weather forecast,

◆ check the avalanche report and forecast,

◆ ask local climbers about latest route conditions and weather events,

◆ use the latest information to modify the route plan if necessary, and

◆ modify equipment selection based on the latest route conditions, such as choosing longer pickets, choosing smaller or larger flukes, and determining whether rock protection is needed.

> **Special tip:** Make a photocopy of your route description and other routes in the immediate area to help with route finding and provide alternatives if your objective is not in good condition or the presence of other parties forces you elsewhere. Reduce the size to make it more packable and accessible.

On the Mountain

◆ Choose a clothing system for current and potential conditions that will allow swift and efficient movement and create a comfortable temperature for you to climb in. (Tip: Avoid combinations of layers that create high friction, such as fleece layered under Schoeller, which feels like Velcro.) Keep additional layers near the top of your pack so that they are easily accessible. For example, keep your down jacket on the very top of your pack so that you can throw it on during rest breaks if conditions are cold.

◆ Stretch after warming up. Most mountain climbs start when it's dark and cold. Start slow and stretch in the first 30 minutes.

◆ Before beginning to travel, do a final team gear check, listing the personal items needed for the climb—sunscreen, glasses, helmet, harness, food, water, and so on.

Important Terms

final preparations—The final steps in the sequential planning process. Because of the dynamic nature of alpine environments, climbers must take several essential steps both on and off the mountain, such as checking current snowpack stability or taking snowshoes on the summit bid if conditions of the day warrant.

groundwork—Includes preparing for all the physical actions that the climber will do while on the climb, assembling the equipment and logistics needed, and establishing the social constructs that the group will operate under while on the climb.

route plan—An organized method of breaking a climbing route into segments or stages (trailhead to camp, stream crossing to a moraine, saddle to a ridgeline or particular terrain feature). A route plan also includes a time plan that establishes a turnaround time, planning for any objective hazards, and noting safe zones on the route.

route research—Includes the specific aspects of looking into a climbing route to learn what to expect while climbing, such as likely route conditions, equipment needed, access points from glacier to rock, and route-specific hazards such as rockfall during a section of the climb.

Main Activities

Activity 1: Imaginary Climb (10 Minutes)

Begin this lesson by asking students to close their eyes and imagine themselves, dressed as they currently are, standing on the lower flanks of Mount Rainier. Encourage them to focus on their surroundings: the temperature, the wind, the snow or soil under their feet, their location on the mountain (are they on a ridge, in a bowl, in an open snowfield?).

◆ Now tell them that they are going to climb the mountain.

◆ Have the students independently list on a piece of paper the items that they think they need, what they should have done, or what they want to know before they begin the climb. Be prepared for many clarifying questions but refrain from answering. Encourage students to write their questions on their lists.

Activity 2: Sequential Trip Planning (40 Minutes)

Introduce the concepts of the three sequential steps in preparing to climb without listing all examples of each step.

◆ Give students another opportunity to add to their individual lists.

◆ Break up students into groups of three and have them compile their lists on the 4-foot-by-3-foot (120-centimeter-by-90-centimeter) sheets of paper. They should list each item under one of the broader planning steps.

◆ Have each group post their lists in front of the class and expand on one preparation below each of the broader planning steps.

◆ After all groups have posted their lists, note the differences and similarities between groups.

◆ Allow time for discussion and rationalization of lists.

◆ Fill in and clarify any content missed by student lists.

Closure Activity

Creating a Route Plan (25 Minutes)

Introduce the idea of creating a route plan.

◆ Using the USGS maps provided, have the groups of three calculate the time needed to approach and climb the same predetermined route. Secretly time the groups and stop the clock when the last group finishes. You will use this information to reinforce the relatively small amount of time needed to plan a trip.

◆ Close by asking students how long it took to make their route plan. Move the discussion into how much time it might take to prepare thoroughly for a climb of two days, three days, one week, or longer.

Follow-Up Activity

Trip Planning: The Real McCoy (25 Minutes)

◆ Have the class plan a trip for their actual climb or a particular climb.

◆ Create a list of preparations necessary and assign preparations to individual students, such as sharpening crampons, acquiring or creating poop bags so that they leave no human waste on the mountain, searching the Internet for trip reports, doing a route plan, and so on.

ASSESSMENT

◆ Check that students can summarize positive physical consequences of thorough preparation and negative physical consequences of not being prepared by having them state three of each consequence in their journals.

◆ Confirm that students can summarize positive social consequences of thorough preparation and negative social consequences of not preparing by having them state two of each consequence in their journals.

◆ Ensure that students demonstrate an understanding of preparing to climb by listening to each group explain their list to the rest of the class.

◆ Confirm that students can justify the need for thorough preparation by observing discussions between members of small groups to validate their reasons for a particular preparation. If discussion is not forthcoming, pose a question such as, "How long do you think preparation x, y, or z will take? Is it worth the time?"

◆ Assess whether students appreciate the contribution of thorough preparation to the enjoyment of a climb by asking them, "Now that you've prepared, do you think that you will experience success on this trip?" and then observing responses.

TEACHING CONSIDERATIONS

◆ Before having each group of three list their preparations under one of the three broad planning stages, put an example sheet of 4-foot-by-3-foot (120-centimeter-by-90-centimeter) paper in front of the class. Ask students to use the corresponding colored markers as shown in the example. Route research is in blue, groundwork is in red, and final preparations off and on the mountain are in green. The color coding will help students track and compare group lists with one another.

◆ Some students may not know where to begin planning. If you think that students need some scaffolding to begin with, you may want to take them on a longer experience during your introduction. You can do this by reading an excerpt from a mountaineering journal or book such as *Touching the Void*, *Deborah and the Mountain of My Fear*, or *The White Spider*.

◆ Any book that has a short scene in which the climber is dealing with conditions, gear, and route finding should provide sufficient context for later discussion.

◆ Introduce mountaineering math to your students to help them develop a time plan for their three-day expedition (figure MN3.1).

Mountaineering Math

The following equation is suitable for a fit and efficient group of four climbers on moderate low-angle terrain:

Climb time in hours = (linear miles [kilometers] traveled × linear pace) + elevation consideration + break consideration

Linear miles (or kilometers) (LM) = Distance to be traveled or climbed

Linear pace (LP) = 1 / miles (kilometers) able to travel on flat nontechnical terrain in 1 hour (LP should be adjusted for route difficulty, other parties on the route, visibility, and conditions [hard-packed snow versus deep powder or breakable crust])

Elevation consideration (EC):

◆ Add 1 hour for every 1,000 feet (300 meters) of elevation gained
◆ Add 30 minutes for every 1,000 feet (300 meters) of elevation lost

Break consideration (BC) = Add total time for any instruction, meal breaks, and rest breaks

The following is an example time plan for climbing from Boston Basin to the summit of Sahale Peak in the North Cascades in Washington. The climb is 2 miles (3.2 kilometers) long and involves an elevation gain of 3,000 feet (900 meters). The route is 35 degrees at most with a short class 4 scramble to the summit. In 1 hour the team travels about 1 mile (1.6 kilometers). The group plans to spend 3 hours on anchor instruction, lunch, and rest breaks during the day.

(LM [2] × LP [1]) + EC (3) + BC (3) = 8 hours from camp to summit

---

FIGURE MN3.1   Mountaineering math will help students develop a time plan for the expedition.

▷ **Traveling on Snow**

OVERVIEW

In this lesson students learn through instruction and practice the various methods of traveling on snow with and without ice axes and crampons. Students also learn the limitations of their equipment and the importance of strong foot technique and balance.

JUSTIFICATION

Teaching the fundamental techniques for walking on snow gives students confidence in themselves and trust in each other as members of a rope team. Surefootedness and efficient ice axe use allows teams to travel faster and more efficiently, reducing their exposure to the objective hazards inherent in mountaineering.

GOAL

To develop students' ability to employ efficient and proper foot techniques and ice axe positions while climbing.

OBJECTIVES

At the end of this lesson students will be able to

◆ choose the appropriate foot technique for slope angle and snow conditions (cognitive);

◆ describe the parts of the ice axe (cognitive);

◆ describe the appropriate ice axe technique for a particular purpose (cognitive);

◆ execute the principal snow climbing techniques—flat foot, duck walk, diagonal ascent, and letter box (psychomotor);

◆ demonstrate appropriate step kicking for subsequent climbers to follow (psychomotor);

◆ execute the principal ice axe positions of cane, cross-body, and ice axe sleeve (psychomotor); and

◆ justify kicking steps for subsequent climbers to conserve the energy of the rope team (affective).

EQUIPMENT AND AREAS NEEDED

◆ One mountaineering axe per student

◆ One set of hinged, step-in, or strap-on crampons per student appropriate to the student's boot size and compatible with it

◆ Paper and pen for each student for individual notes

RISK MANAGEMENT CONSIDERATIONS

◆ Choose a stationary site for this lesson. Find a gradual slope with varying steepness and a flat run-out so that a failure to perform the skills taught will not result in injury.

◆ Ice axes used in this lesson should not be fitted with leashes. Leashes on this type of terrain are more dangerous than helpful. Losing hold of the axe in a fall creates a tethered weapon that could injure the student. Leashes are reserved for steep terrain.

◆ This lesson assumes that students do not know how to self-arrest. Not being skilled in self-arrest will emphasize the importance of sound technique and self-belay as a priority over the dubious safety net of the self-arrest.

◆ The location of the lesson should not result in consequences if a fall occurs.

◆ Students should never climb above one another, where a slide or fall could cause a student to collide with another student.

LESSON CONTENT

Introduction

The following section provides content on foot, crampon, and ice axe techniques. These techniques can viewed as a quiver of tools that a climber can use during a climb. These activities are designed to be fun and push students to failure in a safe environment. It will likely take a brave soul (possibly you) to try walking up a steep slope with a particular technique until failing and sliding down the slope into the run-out to encourage others to push their comfort zone with the activities. Remember that snow is soft and people like to roll around in it!

Foot Techniques

Flat-foot walking is usually intuitive to most climbers. The technique basically involves walking flat footed on level snow. Note that the three following techniques (the duck walk, diagonal ascent, and letter box step) may require kicking steps into the snow to create a platform to stand on. While kicking steps, the focus should be on shearing or slicing the snow and displacing it forward rather than compressing the snow from above. Students can imagine their foot swinging forward like a pendulum from the knee.

Leaders who are kicking steps should bear in mind that subsequent climbers will follow. They should avoid creating large, spaced-out steps.

Duck Walk   Climbers employ the duck walk when the slope steepens.

◆ Students should walk with the toes turned to the outside and the feet splayed apart (figure MN4.1).

◆ The climber should keep the feet flat and avoid weighting only the front of the feet, which will tire the calf muscles.

◆ Students should focus on walking upright. They should avoid leaning forward, which places the center of gravity in front of rather than over the feet.

FIGURE MN4.1   Duck walk.

Diagonal Ascent   Eventually, the climber will encounter a steeper slope that causes duck walking to become inefficient or unbalanced. Diagonal ascent is then the appropriate technique.

◆ Diagonal ascent provides improved balance when compared with the duck walk and disperses the climber's weight over the entire foot.

◆ Facing sideways, the climber trends diagonally. Each step is slightly higher than the last, and the climber places equal weight on each foot (figure MN4.2).

FIGURE MN4.2   Diagonal ascent.

◆ Diagonal ascent provides the opportunity to point out the in-balance position, when the inside foot is placed uphill and forward (figure MN4.3), and the out-of-balance position when the climber's legs are crossed and the outside foot is placed uphill (figure MN 4.4). Resting and moving the ice axe forward (discussed later in the lesson) should be done while in balance.

FIGURE MN4.3 In-balance position.

FIGURE MN4.4 *(a)* Out-of-balance position and *(b)* close-up of crossed legs.

FIGURE MN4.5 Letter box step.

Letter Box Step The letter box technique is used when the slope steepens or a direct ascent is preferred. The term *letter box* comes from the shape of the hole left behind, which resembles a mailbox (figure MN4.5).

Descending Descending with these foot techniques is similar to ascending. The major difference is that the letter box becomes plunge stepping if it is possible to drive the heel of the foot into the snow to make a suitable platform with each step.

Crampon Techniques

The first manufactured crampons were developed by Oscar Eckenstein in 1908 (American Alpine Institute, 2003). Crampons are used for climbing snow and ice when kicking steps is not possible (discussed further in unit 12).

The previously described foot positions can be employed on hard snow while wearing crampons. When these and other techniques are used with crampons on ice, they are referred to as French technique.

Ice Axe Techniques

While traveling on snow, the ice axe can be used as a third point of balance, as a self-belay tool, or for **self-arrest**.

- The ice axe is used and carried most comfortably in the cane position, which involves grasping the adze and using the shaft and spike as a cane.
- Grasping the pick is considered preparation for self-arrest and is less suitable for self-belay (figure MN4.6).
- Whenever possible the climber should move the axe when in balance. The climber can then take two steps, going from out of balance to in balance. The climber then repeats the sequence, beginning with placing the axe.
- The ice axe sleeve is a technique done by driving the spike and shaft into the snow; this technique works well as a self-belay. Done correctly, this technique will leave a hole for the next climber to place her or his axe into (figure MN4.7).
- Changing directions requires the climber to place the axe high directly above (not in front of) himself or herself, take a final step forward, take a step to put the feet into duck walk position, switch hands on the axe, and finally step through in the new direction to achieve an in-balance position.
- The cross-body ice axe technique is useful when traversing steep snowy terrain. The climber places the spike horizontally next to himself or herself with one hand on the adze and the pick facing away from the climber. For balance, the climber can put weight on the lower end of the shaft close to the spike.

FIGURE MN4.6 Grasping the pick in preparation for self-arrest.

FIGURE MN4.7 Ice axe sleeve technique. Drive the spike and shaft into the snow for an effective self-belay.

Important Terms

cane position—An ice axe technique in which the climber grasps the adze and uses the shaft and spike as a cane.

cross-body ice axe technique—Useful when traversing steep snowy terrain. The climber places the spike horizontally next to himself or herself with one hand on the adze and the pick facing away from the climber. For balance, the climber can put weight on the lower end of the shaft close to the spike.

diagonal ascent—Facing sideways, the climber trends diagonally. Each step is slightly higher than the last, and the climber places equal weight on each foot (figure MN4.2).

duck walk—Walking with the toes turned out and the feet splayed apart, the climber keeps the feet flat and avoids weighting only the front of the feet, which will tire the calf muscles.

front points—The two horizontally oriented points located at the front of the crampon.

ice axe sleeve—An ice axe technique done by driving the spike and shaft into the snow; this technique works well as a self-belay. Done correctly, this technique will also leave a hole for the next climber to place her or his axe into (figure MN4.7).

letter box technique—Used when the slope steepens or a direct ascent is preferred. The term *letter box* comes from the shape of the hole left behind, which resembles a mailbox (figure MN4.5).

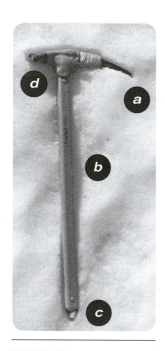

FIGURE MN4.8 Anatomy of the ice axe.

Parts of the Ice Axe

See figure MN4.8.

- **Pick (a)**—the narrow pointed end on top of the ice axe. Used for gaining purchase while performing self-arrest or ice climbing.
- **Shaft (b)**—the long tubular portion of the axe, ranging in length from 40 to 70 centimeters.
- **Spike (c)**—the pointed end at the base of the shaft, at the end opposite the pick and adze. Most often placed in the snow when the axe is used in cane position.
- **Adze (d)**—used mainly for chopping, this flat, shovel-like feature is opposite the pick on the head of the axe. Usually the most comfortable platform to hold while carrying the axe.

Main Activities

Activity 1: Footwork (60 to 90 Minutes)

This activity is designed to build an appreciation of sound footwork, beginning with the fundamentals of walking on low-angle terrain without an ice axe. Each subsequent skill relies on a solid understanding of the previous one. Allow time for practice and feedback. Preface the activity by pointing out that footwork is the primary focus and that the axe and crampon points are used only to augment good foot technique.

- Have students put down their axes and focus on their feet inside their boots. They begin by being aware of where their feet are.
- Demonstrate flat-footed walking and illustrate how you are positioned over your feet with the soles of your boots in complete contact with the snow.
- Have students walk flat footed on a flat run-out area (this will seem too simple but will warm them up).
- Demonstrate the duck walk and discuss the fine points of kicking steps by actively shearing snow forward (rather than stomping straight down) with your boots.
- Have students practice duck walking up the slope for about 30 feet (10 meters). Then have them descend using the plunge step.
- Demonstrate the diagonal ascent while describing the technique to students.
- Have students practice the diagonal ascent up the slope for about 20 feet (6 meters).
- Gain the students' attention by telling everyone to freeze. Use two students as examples—one to point out the in-balance position and the other to show the out-of-balance position. Have them move around and feel the difference as they continue to climb another 20 feet (6 meters). Have them descend using the diagonal or plunge step.
- Move to a steeper angle on the slope and demonstrate the letter box step while pointing out the disadvantage of creating big steps for smaller people who may follow.
- Have students do a lap using the letter box and then descend facing inward, reversing their own steps.

Activity 2: Ice Axe (40 Minutes)

Introduce the ice axe and its parts.

- Demonstrate moving the axe in the cane position while in balance as students follow behind you in a diagonal ascent.
- Stop the group and demonstrate changing directions with the axe. Then have students practice changing directions several times.
- Demonstrate the ice axe sleeve (self-belay) while using any of the foot techniques. Have students practice.
- By now you should be about 100 feet (30 meters) or so above the flat run-out. Have the students descend by plunge stepping or by reversing their steps using the self-belay (no glissading yet; you will teach it in conjunction with self-arrest in lesson 5).
- After you reach the bottom of the slope, have students climb again, employing all the techniques that they just learned. Call out the various techniques. They should combine foot techniques and ice axe techniques.

Closure Activity

Follow the Leader (20 Minutes)

Close by playing Follow the Leader. Give several students the opportunity to lead the group by calling out foot techniques as they combine the techniques over varying terrain. Positively reinforce the leader if she or he chooses the appropriate techniques for the slope.

Follow-Up Activity

Hard Snow Cramponing (30 Minutes)

* Following this activity, snow conditions will likely not be conducive to practicing these techniques using crampons because of warming temperatures as the day continues. You may need to wait until the following morning when conditions harden.
* Get out early the next day or hold class in an area with harder snow conditions to introduce crampons and the modifications of foot techniques. Crampon technique is thoroughly discussed in unit 12.

ASSESSMENT

* Confirm that students can execute the principal snow climbing techniques of flat foot, duck walk, diagonal ascent, and letter box by observing them as they practice the skill laps.
* Check that students can execute appropriate step kicking for subsequent climbers to follow when they are in the leader role.
* Verify that students can justify further improving kicked steps for subsequent climbers to conserve the energy of the rope team by observing their participation in a facilitated discussion about the value of well-made steps.
* Confirm that students know the parts of the ice axe by quizzing them by pointing to each part one at a time, going progressively faster.
* Check that students can execute the principal ice axe positions of cane, cross-body, and ice axe sleeve by observing them during skill laps and the closure activity.
* Verify that students can identify the most appropriate foot and ice axe techniques for particular applications by observing them in the leader role during the closure activity.

TEACHING CONSIDERATIONS

Students' comfort levels will vary greatly. Teach to the lowest ability in regard to the pace and height of the skill laps.

UNIT 10, LESSON 5

▷ Self-Arrest Techniques

OVERVIEW

A self-arrest is a technique used to stop a fall on moderately steep snow slopes or in the event of a crevasse fall on a glacier. Self-arrest may involve either a solo climber or a climbing team traveling roped together. As mountaineering has developed and advanced, self-arrest has remained relatively constant. In this lesson students learn arrest techniques as a last resort and learn to apply evasive maneuvers in the event of a slip or fall.

JUSTIFICATION

Although surefootedness and well-developed foundation techniques are the basis for mountaineering, in some cases a climber may need to arrest a fall on a slope or arrest a partner in the event of a crevasse fall. Self-arrest is a technique that should be ingrained in the student's subconscious as a reaction that requires little conscious thought.

GOAL

To develop students' ability to engage in evasive maneuvers designed to arrest a fall either by themselves or by a member of the rope team.

OBJECTIVES

At the end of this lesson, students will be able to

- identify the conditions when a self-arrest or team arrest is a plausible option (cognitive);
- describe the systematic steps needed to initiate an arrest when a fall occurs (cognitive);
- execute the principal self-arrest positions of sitting on the butt, lying on the belly with the head downhill, lying on the back with the head downhill, and various positions without an ice axe (psychomotor);
- demonstrate the appropriate holding position after the arrest (psychomotor); and
- appreciate the terrain and snow conditions, and know how to implement other safety measures in addition to the self-arrest (affective).

EQUIPMENT AND AREAS NEEDED

- One mountaineering axe per student (60 to 70 centimeters, or 24 to 28 inches, in length)
- Depending on conditions, a waterproof layer (Gore-Tex or a waterproof–breathable layer)
- Paper and pens for individual notes

RISK MANAGEMENT CONSIDERATIONS

- Choose a stationary site for this lesson. Find a site where failure to perform the skills taught will not result in injury. A moderate slope with varying steepness and a flat run-out for beginning each sequence is ideal.
- Students should not be wearing crampons for self-arrest practice.
- In the event that a natural stationary site is unavailable, you can improvise a stationary site by using a backup system known as a J-line (see the sidebar on page 702).
- Review ice axe anatomy. Talk about the sharp points that are likely to cause damage in a failed arrest or when poor technique is applied.
- Students should not use wrist loops or other attachment points for their axes. Instead, they should learn to hold on to the axe. Additionally, in the event of a failed arrest, the axe becomes a weapon. Losing an axe is better than allowing it to cause further harm.

LESSON CONTENT

Introduction

A common accident in mountaineering that can result in death or injury is an uncontrolled fall on snow or ice. Thus, no unit on snow climbing would be complete without a review of the self-arrest.

J-Line

- A **J-line** requires each student to have a harness, a long piece (approximately 4 feet, or 120 centimeters, in length) of webbing, and a locking carabiner.
- At the top of the slope build a snow anchor and attach a rope using a figure-eight on a bight.
- You must then assess the fall line by sliding down the slope and creating a slide track. Do this only if you are confident that you can successfully arrest your own slide.
- At the base of the slide, hike back uphill, away from the slide path.
- Build a second snow anchor at least 15 feet (5 meters) away from the line of travel. Attach the rope using another figure-eight and allow the line to hang below the bottom anchor, thus forming the shape of a J (see figure MN5.1).
- The J-line looks like the letter J. It has an anchor at the top and an anchor at the end of the curve.
- The bottom anchor needs to be well away from the slide line. Students who slide down the hill and lose control of an arrest will be caught between the two anchors where the rope becomes tight.

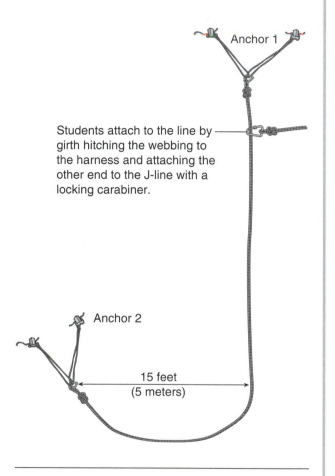

Anchor 1

Students attach to the line by girth hitching the webbing to the harness and attaching the other end to the J-line with a locking carabiner.

Anchor 2

15 feet
(5 meters)

FIGURE MN5.1   J-line setup.

Conditions That Make Self-Arrest Possible

- Personal arrest is possible on steep snow slopes when the pick of the axe is able to bite into the snow.
- Arresting a rope team is possible on moderately steep snow or in the event of a crevasse fall on a glacier with a low to moderate slope.
- Slopes in which a climber is approaching his or her personal limit may warrant using additional safety precautions.
- Self-arrest is nearly impossible on ice.
- A real arrest may occur with crampons on. Therefore, the self-arrest must be initiated quickly before momentum develops. Otherwise, the crampons are likely to throw the person into a tumble and may cause additional injury or thwart a complete arrest. Self-arrest must be an immediate reaction, not an action that requires contemplation.

General Concepts

- All self-arrests start with a common motion. The person must gain control of the axe with both hands. The hand holding the head of the axe maintains control, and the free hand grips the axe at the ferrule.
- Depending on how the axe is being held, it must be rotated into self-arrest position.
- Generally, students should hold the ice axe with the pick forward. Therefore, they need to learn how to rotate the pick in their hands to prepare for the arrest.
- The axe is held across the trunk with the adze slightly above the shoulder, and the ferrule is held at the base of the ribs.
- The elbows should be close to the body to maximize strength. After momentum has been generated and the pick bites into the snow, the axe can easily be ripped out of the climber's hands.
- The next step is to place the pick of the axe in the snow. The person always rolls the body toward the head of the axe and away from the spike.
- The finished arrest position is the same in all cases. The climber presses down on the pick and lifts the shaft slightly up, which drives the pick into the snow. The body should be flat and just slightly off the snow. The feet should be buried in the snow if possible, acting as anchors. Finally, the person should turn the head to look down the shaft of the axe away from the adze. This position prevents injury to the climber's face and teeth (see figure MN5.2).

Specific Positions

- A sitting slide downhill is the basic starting position for self-arrest. The student gains control of the axe, rotates the axe head into self-arrest position, rolls onto the pick, and digs the feet into the slope.
- Emphasize the position of the climber's head during this skill. The climber should be looking down the shaft of the axe away from the adze.
- Head first on the belly is the next progression. The climber takes the axe above the head, gains control with the free hand, rotates into self-arrest position, and places the pick in front of the body at arm's length and to the side, depending on which hand holds the head of the axe. The body will rotate away from the fixed point. Kicking the feet aids the process. Once on the belly, the climber moves into the finish position.
- Head first on the back is the most difficult position to arrest. The climber controls the axe, rotates into self-arrest position, and takes the pick of the axe to the snow at about the hip. This action may require the climber to sit up slightly. The pick enters the snow on the side of the body that holds the head of the ice axe. As the body rotates toward the pick, the climber moves into the finish position.

Self-Arrest With No Axe

Many instructors teach self-arrest without the use of an axe, but the important concepts remain the same.

- In the event of a fall, the climber uses the hands or elbows to initiate the rotation and goes through the same motions to get on the belly.
- Depending on snow conditions, once on the belly the climber tries to drive the elbows and feet into the snow to stop the fall. In soft snow the climber can try to scoop snow with the hands to create a pile of snow to stop the slide.
- The finish position is the same.

Main Activities

Activity 1: Understanding the Parts of an Ice Axe and Their Applications (10 Minutes)

Review axe anatomy and the various ways to hold an axe.

Activity 2: Self-Arrest (60 Minutes or Longer)

Introduce the concept of self-arrest by discussing in depth the uses and limitations of self-arrest. Begin by showing students how to gain control of the axe and hold it across the body.

◆ Walk around and lightly tug on the axe to demonstrate how much strength is required to maintain the position. Students should be holding axes in the self-arrest position.

◆ Demonstrate and highlight the importance of the finish position. Have students practice and provide them with individual feedback.

◆ As systematically as possible, demonstrate the sitting slide. Position students slightly downhill but out of your path. After the demonstration, encourage students to practice until they think that they have it. Students should practice while holding the axe first in one hand, then in the other hand.

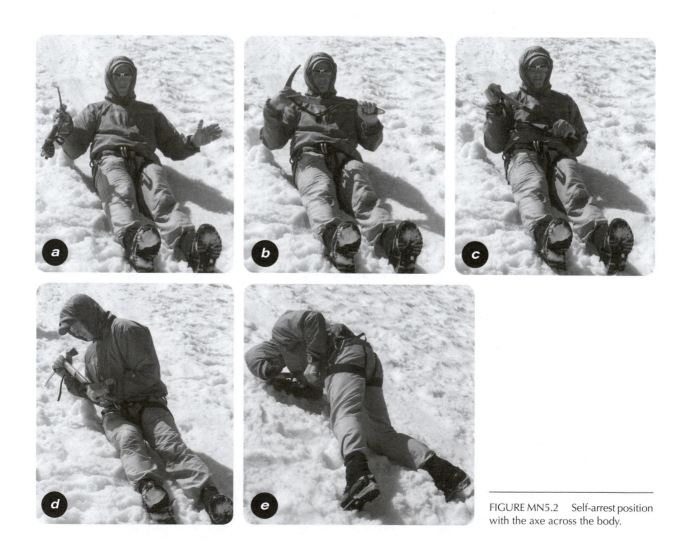

FIGURE MN5.2 Self-arrest position with the axe across the body.

- Introduce head downhill on the belly. Demonstrate the process and encourage students to practice until they are comfortable. Have them practice with the head of the axe in each hand.
- Introduce head downhill on the back. Demonstrate the process and encourage students to practice until they are comfortable.
- Have students practice without axes or choose a steeper slope.

Closure Activity

Self-Arrest Review (15 Minutes)

Reiterate the need to arrest a fall before momentum develops. Review the few situations in which a self-arrest is a viable form of snow safety and begin discussing what to do when self-arrest is not enough.

Follow-Up Activity

Are You Ready? Falling! (30 Minutes or Longer)

- While teaching rope travel, encourage students to initiate unannounced falls on climbing partners. As partners fall, they will begin to recognize the need to arrest the fall before any momentum develops.
- During the glissading lesson, review self-arrest by encouraging students to articulate the process as if they were teaching it.

ASSESSMENT

- Verify that students can identify the conditions when a self-arrest or team arrest is a plausible option by asking them to identify those conditions.
- Confirm that students can describe the systematic steps required to initiate an arrest when a fall occurs by having them orally review each step after completing the self-arrest practice session.
- Check that students can execute the principal self-arrest positions of sitting on the butt, lying on the belly with the head downhill, lying on the back with the head downhill, and various positions without an ice axe by observing them practice self-arrest in these positions and providing feedback.
- Verify that students can demonstrate the appropriate holding position after the arrest by observing them go through the procedure as they practice.
- Assess whether students appreciate the terrain and snow conditions and implement other safety measures by applying their self-arrest skills and knowledge to new situations.

TEACHING CONSIDERATIONS

- Self-arrest is a skill that most students really want to learn. It is also one in which injury can easily occur.
- Use a slope where you can stand downhill of the participants to watch technique and provide immediate feedback.
- Do not make arrest practice mandatory. As an instructor, you are responsible for the safety of your students. If students are not excited about sliding down a slope, then employ your skills to help them ascend the planned route safely.

- You should feel comfortable tying yourself to students who are incompetent or challenged by the environment.

- You have the choice of teaching students to arrest with their feet up or down. In any case, if momentum develops, an arrest is unlikely to be successful. Therefore, putting the feet down immediately may be best, even when wearing crampons.

- Self-arrest on the belly is particularly dangerous. You should be aware of the hazards and provide an opportunity for a student to choose not to do it.

UNIT 10, LESSON 6

▷ # Snow Protection and Anchor Building

OVERVIEW

Snow protection and anchor building is the foundation for safe climbing. The ability to place and construct secure anchors in a variety of situations is the hallmark of a capable climber. In this lesson students learn when snow protection is necessary, how to place various types of artificial protection, and how to use multiple pieces to build an anchor. Students learn through lecture, demonstration, practice, and self-discovery the holding strength of snow protection and how environmental conditions improve or compromise the placement. Improvised techniques for improving safety are also introduced and practiced.

JUSTIFICATION

Understanding when self-arrest techniques are not adequate and how to utilize snow protection techniques will develop students' abilities to recognize and adapt to the mountain environment and remain safe. Students further their experience by venturing into different snow environments, recognizing that the variability of snow conditions is the largest contributor to snow protection applications. Students finish the lesson with the ability to build quality snow anchors and place quality snow protection.

GOAL

To develop students' awareness of snow protection, its uses, placement methods, techniques for grouping to create anchors, and limitations.

OBJECTIVES

At the end of this lesson students will be able to

- identify the different types of snow protection available for use (cognitive),
- recognize snow conditions and apply the appropriate snow protection technique (cognitive),
- describe ways to improvise protection using mixed techniques (cognitive),
- build equalized anchors using a variety of snow protection (psychomotor),
- place pickets and flukes correctly (psychomotor),
- build T-slots, improvised deadmen, and bollards appropriately (psychomotor), and
- justify the need to study snow conditions as a part of the trip-planning process (affective).

EQUIPMENT AND AREAS NEEDED

- Harnesses for every student
- Four pickets for each group of three students
- One fluke for each group of three students
- Ice axe
- Three double-length runners for each group of three students
- One cordelette for each group of three students
- One 24-inch (61-centimeter) sling per picket
- Carabiners
- Weatherproof notepads for students to take notes while in and on snow
- One climbing rope for each designated climbing team
- Additional supplies for burying, including stuff sacks, backpacks, and so on
- Two or three snow shovels

RISK MANAGEMENT CONSIDERATIONS

- Conduct this lesson on a short slope of 35 to 45 degrees with a safe run-out. Assume that students have no snow protection training.
- Students should be able to move comfortably on the slopes without concern for objective hazards such as crevasses, falling rock or snow, or avalanche.
- Students should work across from one another, not above or below each other. That way, if a slip or slide occurs, the slider does not take out another student.
- Snow protection and anchors should be tested to failure by having one student at a time tie into the rope and bounce. Add students as needed to the line below the placement, about 5 feet (1.5 meters) from each other.
- You should attach a rope or cordelette to the piece with a hard knot (figure-eight or similar knot). Then attach the rope to the harness with a Munter hitch. In the case of well-placed gear, failure will be unexpected and can be catastrophic with the potential to hit someone.
- Attaching a backup line to yourself will act as a damper for the piece without pulling you, the students, and the protection piece.
- When testing placements, make sure that the run-out below is free of hazards and that students do not have their axes or sharp items attached to their harnesses.
- Pickets, in particular, become hazardous the more they are used. They develop sharp edges; students should handle them with care.

LESSON CONTENT

Introduction

The snowpack is dynamic. It can vary from very hard, or boilerplate snow, to hard crust over soft snow, fresh powder, fresh heavy wet snow, or soft spring snow.

- Snow anchor solidity depends on snow stability and strength, anchor materials, placement of the attachment point, and how the anchor is used (Bogie, 2005).
- Snow protection should be able to hold a falling climber who has generated force.

◆ All snow protection should be placed in the intended direction of pull.

◆ It is possible to age harden snow and build anchors in it. This time-consuming process may not be an option in time-challenged environments.

Climbers use two different types of snow protection. Natural protection involves using the existing environment to protect the mountaineer from an accident. Examples of natural protection include making bollards or wrapping the rope around a rock or tree. Artificial protection involves carrying additional supplies that are placed in the terrain to protect mountaineers from accidents. Artificial protection includes pickets, flukes, and T-slots.

Important Terms

age-hardened snow—Snow that has been manually compressed and given time to settle.

artificial anchors—Include pickets, T-slots, flukes, ice screws, and deadmen. Used in appropriate environmental conditions, artificial anchors are extremely versatile.

bollard—A teardrop-shaped pile of snow that has been cut into the slope. Generally, a trench is dug to create the bollard. The size of the bollard depends completely on snow conditions. The trench can be 1 to 1.5 feet (30 to 45 centimeters) deep and the teardrop mound can be 2 to 6 feet (60 to 180 centimeters) in diameter (figure MN6.1).

ERNEST—An acronym used to describe how to build anchors. Equalized, redundant, no extension, solid and timely are the terms that make up ERNEST. This anchor-building concept is discussed in detail in unit 2, lesson 7.

flukes—Specially shaped pieces of aluminum that resemble the head of a spade shovel and generally have two cables extending from them, one from the top and one from the bottom, which come together at a single clip-in point. When placed correctly, a fluke acts as a dynamic placement and will dive deeper into the snowpack as it is weighted (figure MN6.2).

natural anchors—Use of existing environmental mediums such as snow or ice to provide a placement without using artificial materials. Examples include bollards or seracs.

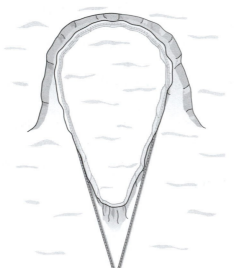

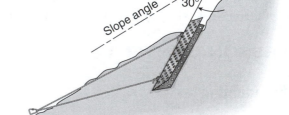

FIGURE MN6.1   Snow bollard.

FIGURE MN6.2   Snow fluke placement.

continued ▶

Pickets

- Snow pickets are placed vertically into the snow. Review several important concepts with students.

- Pickets need to be placed in well-consolidated snow that is of sufficient depth, hardness, and consistency.

- Pickets should be placed between 80 and 85 degrees to the angle of the slope. A guideline is to hold the picket perpendicular to the angle of the slope and adjust slightly uphill.

- Teach students to hammer in the picket without destroying the top of the picket. To avoid extensive picket damage, use the head of the axe. Avoid using the adze. Using the shaft is possible, but damage to the shaft may occur if attachment rivets are compromised.

▶ **continued**

picket—The most versatile type of snow protection. The picket is shaped like an oversized stake. The most common size is 2 feet (60 centimeters) long, although larger sizes are used if snow conditions warrant. They can be placed vertically into the snow like a fence picket (figure MN6.3) or horizontally in a trench.

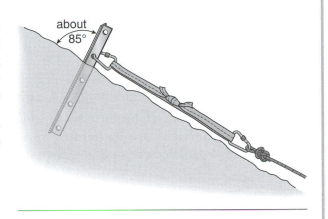

FIGURE MN6.3   Snow picket placement.

T-slot—Two trenches are created. One is horizontal to the direction of pull and longer than the linear object being placed in it, such as an ice axe, picket, or ski. The vertical trench is oriented from the center of the horizontal trench down toward the direction of pull. A sling or webbing is attached to the center of the buried object, which coincides with the vertical trench (figure MN6.4).

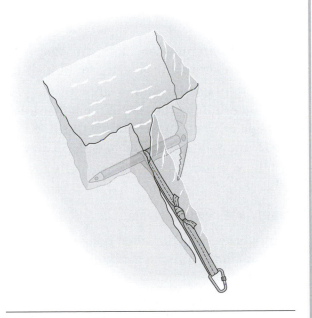

FIGURE MN6.4   T-slot.

◆ A good picket placement needs to be hammered into place. A guideline for students is that at least four to six solid hits with the head of the axe are required for a good placement. If the picket requires several strikes, but drops in quickly, then the snow stability is questionable and a different placement may be required.

Flukes

◆ Flukes should be angled back from the direction of pull by about 30 degrees.

◆ A guideline is to hold the fluke perpendicular to the slope and angle it away from the pull by about 30 degrees (see figure MN6.2).

◆ The top cable should be parallel with the slope before placement and with the direction of pull.

◆ The fluke will dive deeper into the snow as it is weighted. Its holding power depends on a consistent snowpack and proper placement.

◆ If the angle is too steep the fluke will slide out of the snow like a spatula. Varying snow layers such as a layer of ice can cause this phenomenon.

◆ Houston and Cosley (2004) recommend evaluating the need to take flukes if other anchors can be used.

T-Slots

◆ Items used in a T-slot include pickets, axes, skis, or other long objects.

◆ A perpendicular trench needs to be dug deep enough to bury the item completely and provide enough snow for holding power. Climbers should avoid compromising the snowpack located on the side that will be pulled.

◆ A perpendicular slot allows the attachment point of the buried item to pull with the slope. This arrangement minimizes the tendency to pull the item up and out of the trench.

◆ To strengthen the placement, climbers should fill in the trench with snow from the uphill side and stomp the item in place.

Bollards

◆ Bollards are time consuming to construct but extremely strong. The rope can be wrapped around the bollard for rappelling.

◆ A bollard can be reinforced by placing axes at pressure points. Climbers begin by determining the size of the bollard necessary and then dig the trench in the shape of a large upside-down teardrop.

◆ The strength and size of the bollard depend on snow conditions. In some cases a bollard will not hold, but generally the bigger the bollard is, the stronger it will be.

Improvised Anchor Techniques

Improvised protection often involves a variation or combination of natural and artificial anchors. A number of guidelines are listed here to enhance students' ability to improvise techniques in the field.

◆ Improvised protection includes burying virtually any object, including a backpack or a stuff sack filled with snow. Objects like these are universally referred to as deadmen. Improvised anchors resemble a T-slot but usually need a custom hole and attachment trench.

- Many anchors can be reinforced by placing an ice axe directly in front of the T-slot or deadman as a picket (figure MN6.5).

- Building an anchor may require at least two separate placements and an equalized system in the direction of pull.

- Anchors built in a linear fashion in which one placement is placed directly above another are excellent. The top placement supports the lower placement.

- Anchors with multiple placements should be extended so that the attachment point, or master point, is at an angle of 60 degrees or less. The smaller the angle between the pieces, the better the protection is (figure MN6.6).

Main Activity

Constructing and Setting Anchors (Time as Needed)

Get students' attention by presetting an anchor and encouraging them to test it to failure. After they have struggled to take it to failure, introduce each artificial piece and its appropriate placement.

- Discuss how important snow conditions are for choosing snow anchors.

- Have students work in teams of two or three as they practice placing gear.

- Inspect each placement, provide feedback, and test it to failure.

- Gather students together and introduce natural anchors and improvised placements.

- Encourage students to build natural anchors in their small groups.

- Gather the students to evaluate each group's anchor and predict how many participants will be needed to take the anchor to failure.

- Demonstrate ERNEST anchors and have each participant build one. (ERNEST principles are also discussed in unit 2, lesson 7, on page 194.)

- Build an ERNEST anchor and a poor anchor. Have students compare and contrast the two.

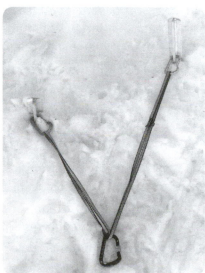

FIGURE MN6.5   Placing an ice axe directly in front of the T-slot or deadman as a picket reinforces the anchor.

FIGURE MN6.6   Master point angle.

Closure Activity

Determining Snow Conditions (10 Minutes)

Initiate a discussion about the day's snow conditions. Was it wet, consistent, powdery, dry?

Ask students to speculate about different geographic regions and different types of equipment necessary for those regions. Remember that the security of a snow anchor depends on the type and conditions of the snowpack. For example, the Pacific Northwest of the United States generally has a consistent, firm snowpack because of its maritime climate. Pickets work particularly well there. Conversely, the Rocky Mountains of North America have a much lighter and fluffier snowpack in winter because of colder conditions. Pickets may not work there because of unconsolidated snow conditions, so other anchoring techniques may be needed. As spring thaws come to the high country, the snowpack changes again. Late-season snowfields are generally consolidated, so pickets, bollards, and T-slots work extremely well. Flukes may not work because snow stratification may create an ice layer, which a fluke may bounce off of.

This discussion is designed to encourage students to think about what techniques are appropriate for particular conditions. Thus it is less about right answers and more about considering the implications of incorrectly applying the techniques. Fill in as needed.

Follow-Up Activity

Reinforcing Anchor Techniques (30 Minutes or Longer)

- After you introduce rope team travel and belay skills, reinforce anchor techniques because they are an integral part of the overarching system.

- Constantly evaluate students' gear placements and use of natural anchors.

- Use teachable moments to teach anchor concepts. Do not teach rules. Each situation, and consequently each anchor, is different.

- During rope team travel lessons, initiate a discussion on the need for anchors and their applications. With guidance, students should be able to discuss when to fix lines to an anchor, set up hand lines, use running belays, and set belay anchors.

- Discuss the importance of using placements before the situation becomes hazardous.

- Discuss why assessment and gear placement can help mountaineers avoid having to employ arrest skills.

ASSESSMENT

- Confirm that students can identify the various types of snow protection available for use by asking them to name each.

- Check that students can recognize snow conditions and apply the appropriate snow protection techniques for selected or current snow conditions.

- Verify that students can describe ways to improvise protection using mixed techniques through discussion during teachable moments.

- Confirm that students can build equalized anchors using a variety of snow protection by providing them with these items and observing them construct anchors.

- Check that students can place pickets and flukes correctly by observing them do this during the lesson and the climb.
- Verify that students can build T-slots, improvised deadmen, and bollards appropriately by observing them do this during the lesson and the climb.
- Confirm that students can justify the need to study snow conditions as part of the trip-planning process by requiring them to include this information in a trip plan.

TEACHING CONSIDERATIONS

- Anchors and anchor building should be exciting for students. Maintain a safe and fun atmosphere when students are testing placements to failure.
- If you are camping on snow, you may be able to apply the concepts for staking down a tent because they are similar to those used for placing snow anchors. This circumstance may allow extensive student input into the introduction and may change the way that you present the lesson.

▷ Rope Travel and Belaying

OVERVIEW

In some situations, mountaineers must travel together attached to a single rope. This practice is referred to as rope travel or a rope team. In this lesson students learn techniques for dispersing themselves evenly on a rope and walking together as a rope team. Students also apply their snow anchor skills as they learn when they must apply different types of belaying techniques. Throughout this lesson students lead rope teams and practice this important and necessary skill.

JUSTIFICATION

Traveling in the mountains requires that mountaineers use multiple techniques to maintain speed and safety. By practicing these techniques students develop teamwork and confidence in their ability to decide when to travel roped together, what belays to use, and how to incorporate previous lessons into this dynamic skill.

GOAL

To develop students' understanding of rope travel as it applies to terrain, team members' skills, snow conditions, and techniques that enhance safety.

OBJECTIVES

At the end of this lesson students will be able to

- identify the safest and most efficient methods of rope travel for various conditions (cognitive);
- demonstrate the ability to implement different techniques for belaying on varied terrain including running belays, body belays, anchor belays, and dynamic versus static applications (psychomotor);

◆ demonstrate the proper coiling of rope by using the mountaineer's and Kiwi techniques (psychomotor); and

◆ appreciate the appropriate use of snow anchors, rope travel, belay techniques, and ice axe and crampon use for mountaineering applications (affective).

EQUIPMENT AND AREAS NEEDED

◆ One ice axe and set of crampons per student

◆ One helmet per student

◆ One belay device per student, preferably including several types

◆ One 30-meter (100-foot) rope with the middle marked for each group of three students, who make up a rope team

◆ Four pickets for each rope team

◆ One harness per student

◆ Two locking HMS carabiners per student

◆ Four double-length slings for each rope team

◆ Short description of a Kiwi coil with a photo

◆ Short description of a mountaineer's coil with a photo

◆ Short description of the techniques used to space climbers evenly on a rope, including a description for three-person rope teams and four-person rope teams

◆ Additional snow protection as available for students to practice with

◆ Weatherproof notepads for students to take notes while in and on snow

RISK MANAGEMENT CONSIDERATIONS

◆ Conduct this lesson in the field at a site containing slopes with varying degrees of steepness.

◆ A safe zone should be present at the top and bottom of the slopes.

◆ If possible, practice without crampons.

◆ Because this activity divides the class into small moving groups, a student-to-instructor ratio of 6:1 or smaller is preferred. This will allow you to manage two rope teams by walking to the side of the teams. You will remain unroped for the exercises in this lesson.

◆ You need to have a keen eye for detail. Students will be applying the skills learned from each of the previous lessons. Constructive feedback is essential to making sure that students are applying the correct techniques during the learning process.

◆ Finding slopes as steep as those of the upper mountain is difficult. Students should recognize that they should be practicing the skills as if they are on a real slope. This mind-set will prepare students for success when they need to apply previously learned skills in a challenging situation.

LESSON CONTENT

Introduction

Rope travel should be taught following the introduction of basic snow skills, anchor building, placement practice, and self-arrest. Rope travel involves the same language, and students who understand the other lessons will pick up rope travel quickly.

Students should understand that if terrain requires a rope, additional precautions should be used so that the team is not jeopardized if one person slips or falls.

When presenting rope travel to students, focus on these key points and concepts:

◆ Traveling in small roped teams increases group safety when used correctly.

◆ Disadvantages include slower travel and the potential for misuse, resulting in unsafe practices and situations.

Prerequisites

A word of caution is appropriate here. Students who are learning roped techniques should already have some basic skills so that they can apply the new travel skills. From an instructor's perspective, you use the rope to keep your students safe. Thus, if you choose to climb a peak with students tied to your rope, you should have all the skills necessary to manage their lack of competence. Nonetheless, a logical progression exists in teaching mountaineering skills, and students should meet prerequisites before you teach rope travel.

◆ Students must be able to use ice axes, crampons, and snow protection materials.

◆ To be ready for this lesson, students must be able to apply snow anchors, knots, and techniques to ascend on snow.

Setup Considerations

◆ If traveling on snow slopes with potential for a slip or fall but insufficient potential to use running protection, the lead climber may choose to tie group members close to each other, spaced approximately 10 to 15 feet (3 to 5 meters) apart. This technique is useful only if the lead climber is comfortable on the slope and is confident that she or he can hold the fall alone without the help of running protection.

◆ If traveling on snow slopes with running protection, mountaineers should travel close enough to each other that they can communicate but far enough apart that they can still have a snow anchor placed between them and the lead climber when needed. Climbers should be spaced approximately 30 feet (10 meters) apart.

◆ To set up a three-member rope team, (1) find the middle of the rope, (2) tie a figure-eight on a bight at that point (the butterfly knot can also be used for this application, but the figure-eight is more common and the benefits of a butterfly knot are not sufficient to warrant making it mandatory), and (3) measure 10 to 30 feet (3 to 10 meters) from the center knot.

◆ Remember that the distance separating the group members depends on the skill of the lead climber, the skills of other group members, the terrain (snow slope or glacier), and the techniques employed (running belays or short roping).

◆ A guideline for determining how much rope is enough is to have students find the average of their wingspans (the distance from fingertip to fingertip when the arms are outstretched to the sides; much like the measurement from wingtip to wingtip on a bird). Most groups will average 5 or 6 feet (150 to 180 centimeters). Distances on the rope don't have to be perfect.

◆ For four climbers, find the middle of the rope and measure half the distance to be used between climbers on both sides of the middle mark. Add two knots (figure-eight on a bight) at these points and measure 10 to 30 feet (3 to 10 meters) from each knot, depending on the type of terrain expected.

When to Use the Mountaineer's Coil or the Kiwi Coil

◆ Coil the extra rope into either a mountaineer's coil or a Kiwi coil.

◆ The mountaineer's coil is more comfortable and stores the free rope. In some cases, mountaineers put the extra rope in their packs or over their shoulders.

◆ The mountaineer's coil should be constructed so that it fits comfortably over the shoulder without interfering with the harness or slipping off the shoulder (figure MN7.1).

◆ The Kiwi coil can be less comfortable, but it allows the team to extend distances between each other quickly when they encounter technical or glaciated terrain.

FIGURE MN7.1   Mountaineer's coil.

◆ The Kiwi coil begins at the end of the rope by having the end climber tie directly into the rope with a figure-eight follow-through. The climber begins coiling the rope to a marker knot located at the appropriate distance from the next climber. With a bight of rope, the climber ties the coil directly into the harness using a large overhand on a bight (figure MN7.2).

Guidelines for Moving Together as a Rope Team

◆ When walking together as a rope team, mountaineers keep the rope extending to other climbers on the downhill side. They do this because the ice axe is always in the uphill hand and so that a team member's fall will not cause the rope to pull their legs.

◆ Traverses should be as long as possible to minimize rope management problems for the climbers downhill and should ascend the slope at a moderate angle.

◆ The most challenging aspect of traveling as a rope team is at the turn for a traverse. In this situation, students should use the duck walk, execute the ice axe sleeve, and step over the rope without slipping, taking too long, or being pulled by the uphill climber.

◆ Using running belays will save time and protect team members through challenging terrain or areas with fall potential. Running belays include placing a piece of snow protection and clipping through it (figure MN7.3).

◆ In more challenging terrain a climber may choose to belay the other rope team members using a quick belay off the body.

◆ The most common quick belay is a hip belay from a seated position.

◆ Mountaineers may look for places to stand that will reduce the chances of being pulled down the slope. For example, they can use a small moat (where the snowfield and rock meet to create a hole), the back of a large flat ledge, a spot behind a solid rock, or the far side of a ridge (see figure MN7.4).

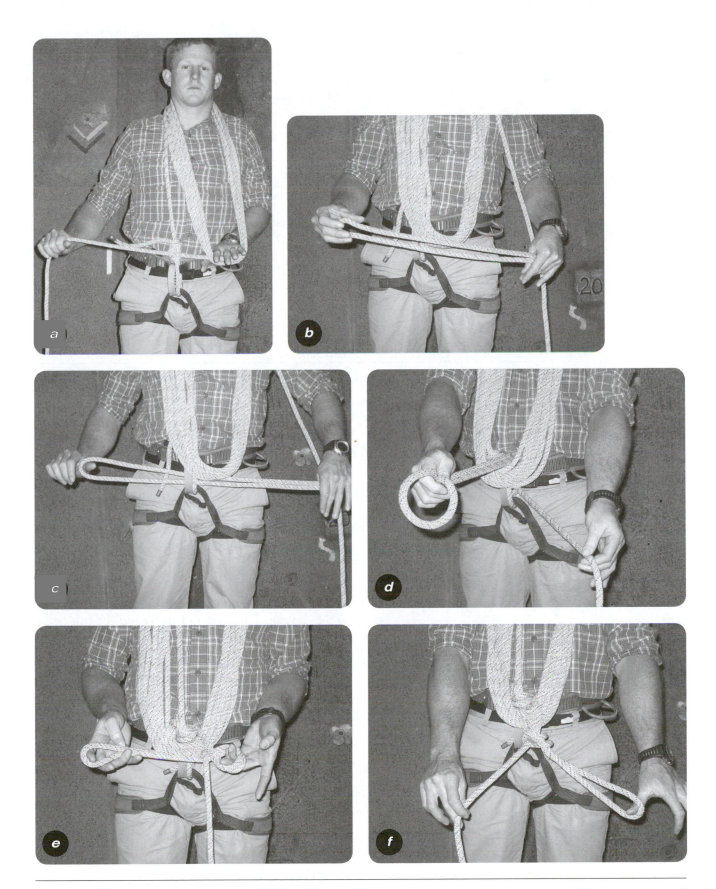

FIGURE MN7.2 Kiwi coil: Start by tying into the end of the rope as you normally would for climbing. *(a)* Start coiling the rope over your neck and around your hand. Continue coiling once the desired distance between the climbers is achieved. *(b)* Create a long bight (about 18 to 24 inches [46 to 61 centimeters]) with the strand leading away from the coils. *(c)* Thread the bight first through the belay loop or a locked carabiner, then *(d)* behind all of the coils including the figure-eight knot, and lastly out the center of the coil. *(e-f)* Finally, with the bight of rope, tie a complete overhand around the rope leading to your partner.

FIGURE MN7.3   Running belays save time and protect team members through demanding terrain.

FIGURE MN7.4   Hip belay from a good stance or snow seat.

- Students should test unanchored hip belays, because a failed hip belay can be catastrophic.

- If a climber is concerned about being able to hold a fall, an anchor must be built and the belay should be directly off the anchor. This can be accomplished with a Munter hitch (see figure MN7.5) or an auto-locking belay device such as a Petzl Reverso. Standard belay devices should not be used directly off the anchor for belaying. They are not designed for this technique and could result in a serious accident.

- If the anchor is suspect or a stance for the belay is challenging, a climber may choose to tie into the anchor and belay directly off the body using a belay device (figure MN7.6).

Main Activities

Begin with a global review of the past lessons, including basic axe skills, self-arrest position, knots, anchors, and equipment use.

Activity 1: Managing the Rope and Climber Spacing (30 Minutes or Longer)

- Provide students with descriptions of coiling and rope spacing. Provide enough time for students to look over the information (figure MN7.7).

- Break the students into small groups of three or four. Ask them to prepare the rope for travel and include coils on both ends if possible. If that is not possible, a coil should exist on one end.

FIGURE MN7.5   A Munter hitch used to belay directly off the anchor.

FIGURE MN7.6   Tie into the anchor and belay directly off the body.

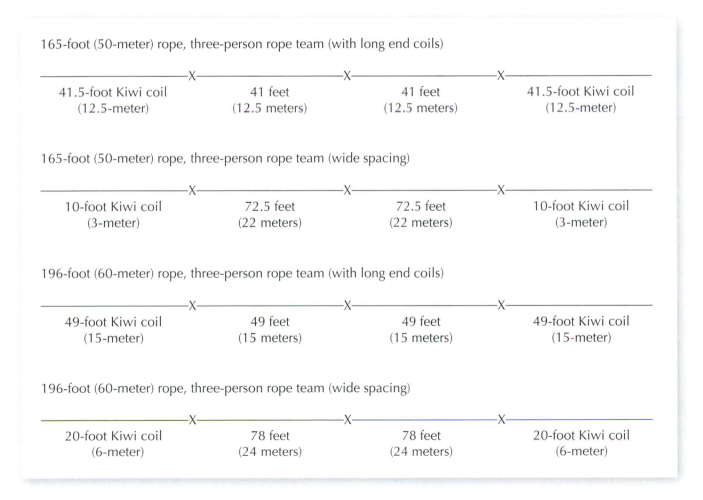

FIGURE MN7.7   Coiling and rope-spacing descriptions. X = climber

Data from M. Strong, E. Doerry, and R. Ojerio, 2001, *Glaciers: The art of travel and the science of rescue* (Guilford, CT: The Globe Pequot Press).

Important Terms

anchor belay—Using any fixed anchor as the belay point. In most cases, an anchor belay on snow will be directly off the anchor.

belay—Holding or arresting a fall by using friction to bind the rope. A belay can be static or dynamic. Static belays use friction to stop the rope. Dynamic belays use friction to slow the rope.

body belay—Belaying off the body. This technique includes wrapping the rope around the hip of the belayer or could incorporate the use of a belay device off the harness of the belayer.

friction—Multiple objects rubbing together such as a rope, belay device, and carabiner. Friction is important to belaying.

group arrests—Occurs when all able members of the rope team assume the self-arrest position if another team member falls.

running protection—Natural or artificial anchors placed by the lead climber and attached to the rope to aid the group in the event of a fall. Running protection is a common technique used when rope travel is necessary but simple self-arrest techniques will not stop a fall.

◆ Debrief the activity and demonstrate the techniques if needed to the whole group.

◆ Demonstrate effective methods of coiling the rope quickly with well-measured, even coils.

Activity 2: Traveling Together—Learning and Applying the Appropriate Techniques (30 Minutes or Longer)

◆ Introduce traveling together on a rope team and provide a course for the teams to take. Be sure to include critical information in the briefing such as rope location.

◆ Take the group to a section with traverse opportunities. Introduce traversing.

◆ Introduce the self-arrest position while traveling roped. Encourage students to stage a fall on their team members in appropriate locations.

Protecting the Team   Introduce placing protection in the form of a running belay. Discuss the need to make sure that placements are in the direction of the potential fall. Extend runners to avoid pulling out protection.

Choosing a Belay

◆ Take students to an area conducive to body belays such as the top of a hill, a moat, or another secure location.

◆ Discuss with students the differences between static and dynamic belays.

◆ Demonstrate a hip belay and variations. Be sure to include demonstrations of a faulty hip belay and a correct hip belay. Encourage student participation in a discussion about how to use a hip belay.

◆ Encourage students to change places on the rope to practice hip belays. Students will realize quickly that climbers in the center of the rope have some challenges when setting up for a quick hip belay.

- This progression should build on previous skills and may include a large amount of walking. If this is too much for students, you can introduce all the skills in a demonstration.
- Move the students to a steeper slope and introduce anchors with a fixed belay.
- Demonstrate an equalized anchor with a climber tied in and belaying off the harness.
- Demonstrate belaying directly off the anchor with a Munter hitch and with an auto-locking device. Discuss why a typical belay device cannot be used in the same way.
- Encourage students to practice all belay techniques.

Closure Activities

Activity 1: Prioritizing Safety, Critically Assessing the Terrain, and Choosing the Appropriate Technique (30 Minutes)

- Discuss the assessment process that contributes to determining which technique to use.
- Discuss how each system is used on slopes of varying degrees, snow conditions, and anchor strength.

Activity 2: When to Belay (15 Minutes)

- Engage students in a discussion about how and when to apply different belay techniques.
- Encourage students to point at different places on the mountain and speculate about what techniques are needed.
- Provide feedback as necessary.

Follow-Up Activity

You Be the Leader (Time as Needed)

Have each group of students decide who will be the leader during the activity. You then lead the students on another imaginary climb.

- As the students come up to you, you give them a scenario. They then choose how to proceed using the newly learned techniques. For example, as the leaders arrive, you describe a scenario: "You are on a 50-degree slope of hard snow and are going to continue climbing up to a rock band where you will need to bring the group together. How will you get your team to the rock band safely and efficiently?"
- Evaluate the students' choices. Did they use running protection? Did they build an anchor or use a hip belay? Why?
- Continue providing simulations until all rope team members have had the opportunity to be the leader, make decisions, and apply their skills.

ASSESSMENT

- Check that students can identify the safest and most efficient methods of rope team travel for various applications by observing their participation in challenging scenarios.

◆ Confirm that students can demonstrate the ability to implement different techniques for belaying on varied terrain, including hip belays, terrain belays, body belays off an anchor, and belays directly off an anchor, by observing them practice the skills and apply correct techniques during the simulations.

◆ Verify that students appreciate the appropriate method of travel for specific applications by observing their participation in discussions after each simulation.

TEACHING CONSIDERATIONS

◆ Spend time in advance to find a location where the simulations are not contrived.

◆ The rope team travel simulations require significant site management.

◆ Use a low student-to-instructor ratio.

◆ Do not teach dogma. For example, in areas where glaciers are not a concern and the group has chosen to climb without the use of running protection, traveling 30 feet (10 meters) apart is not a good idea. Thus, avoid teaching rules for distances on ropes and be sure to teach concepts on the positives and negatives of traveling roped together. Students may make different decisions. As long as the technique used works, it is OK. Rarely is a single answer the only correct one.

◆ Support students during the simulations. Allow the experience to be fun, not an assessment process. They are still in a learning situation. To maintain creative tension, students should understand and believe that making mistakes is OK.

◆ Discuss different solutions when necessary. For example, a student may climb to a stopping location and build an anchor with two pickets. After the anchor is built, he or she may choose to belay the group up to the anchor using an auto-locking device. This is a great solution!

◆ As the instructor, you might notice a moat that is shallow and safe to climb into. A hip belay from the moat would also suffice. Whenever you can provide your students with technique alternatives, you will further develop their critical assessment skills. The effectiveness of this approach depends on your skill mastery.

UNIT 10, LESSON 8

▷ Descending

OVERVIEW

Summiting a mountain is only half the adventure; the other half is getting back down. Students learn in this lesson that they can use a variety of methods to descend technical terrain in a mountain environment. After learning how to glissade and reviewing foot techniques, students are presented with various descent scenarios during which they will need to draw on prior knowledge and improvise to descend safely.

JUSTIFICATION

A planned or unplanned descent (backing off a route) may require a climber to use multiple techniques to descend safely. By practicing these techniques climbers will become more self-reliant and confident in their ability to retreat on a route or choose multiple routes of descent after successfully completing an alpine climb on snow.

GOAL

To build students' confidence by providing them safe opportunities to practice descending techniques and apply existing skills to various situations.

OBJECTIVES

At the end of this lesson students will be able to

- identify the safest and most efficient methods of descent for a variety of situations (cognitive);
- demonstrate different techniques for descending varied terrain including plunge stepping, diagonal descent, glissading (sitting, crouching, and standing), rappelling off a bollard, and down climbing facing in with or without protection (psychomotor); and
- appreciate the appropriate method of descent for specific applications (affective).

EQUIPMENT AND AREAS NEEDED

- One ice axe and set of crampons per student
- Four pickets for each group of three students
- One 30-meter (100-foot) rope for each group of three students
- One 30-meter (100-foot) rope and two pickets or flukes for setting up a backup belay if necessary
- Weatherproof notepads for students to take notes while in and on snow

RISK MANAGEMENT CONSIDERATIONS

- Conduct this lesson on a site containing slopes with varying degrees of steepness.
- A safe zone should be present at the top and bottom of the slopes.
- Because this activity breaks the class into small groups or stations, a student-to-instructor ratio of 6:1 or smaller is preferred. This approach will allow you to manage two groups simultaneously.
- You may need to provide a backup belay for scenarios 3 and 4 depending on snow conditions and student abilities. The students' belay should be above and to the side of the lead climber in the event of falling snow and ice.

LESSON CONTENT

Introduction

A primary option for descending climbers is to down climb using the foot and axe techniques discussed in lesson 4 (plunge stepping, duck walking while facing downhill, facing in with the letter box technique, and diagonal descent). But walking off the mountain is not always an option. Relate to the students a circumstance in which the planned walk-off descent on the south side of the peak is socked in. Glacier travel would be dangerous and route finding nearly impossible. An east-side descent down the way you came, though more technical, may present less risk because you won't be descending into the unknown.

◆ The foot techniques should be employed specific to the climbers' comfort level.

◆ Facing in is generally more comfortable and safer for climbers who are uncomfortable or on steep terrain where a slip could easily develop into a significant fall.

Glissading

Climbers should always glissade cautiously and use the technique only where a safe run-out is present and the consequences of getting out of control would not result in injury. On a glacier, for example, climbers rarely use long glissades because of the risk that the entire team may slide into a crevasse or, if unroped, because a climber may slide into a crevasse with no safety of a belay from the rope team.

◆ Never glissade with crampons on.

◆ Clothing manufactured with Gore-Tex slides the best (so climbers must be careful).

◆ Hard, packed snow is ideal for sliding but can be difficult to stop on, as are steeper slopes. Climbers must find the right combination.

◆ Safe glissading depends on snow conditions. Ideal conditions present themselves when snow is hard enough to allow a person to slide easily and soft enough to allow an ice axe pick to gain purchase during a self-arrest or to allow use of the adze simply to slow down.

Sitting Glissade   The sitting glissade is done with knees slightly bent, sitting straight up, and holding the spike of the axe in the snow to act as a brake to the side or behind to regulate speed (figure MN8.1).

Standing Glissade   The standing glissade involves standing with knees slightly flexed, feet flat, and the axe head in one hand to the side similar to the cane position. The climber can change directions by angling the feet in the desired direction. Stopping should only require weighting the heels and digging them into the snow.

◆ The standing glissade allows the person to stay dry, see obstacles ahead, and change directions as in downhill skiing (figure MN8.2).

◆ The person must be prepared for changes in snow conditions that may pitch him or her forward or backward as the feet cross the transition point.

FIGURE MN8.1   Sitting glissade.

FIGURE MN8.2   Standing glissade.

Crouching Glissade   The crouching glissade is generally awkward and less advantageous than sitting or standing. It is similar to the standing glissade and involves using the spike of the axe as a brake.

Important Terms

glissading—A technique used by alpine climbers to slide on the snow by standing, sitting, or crouching while maintaining control and speed.

Main Activities

Using foot and axe techniques, ascend to the top of a slope suitable for practicing glissading (approximately 100 feet, or 30 meters, tall with a safe run-out).

◆ Glissading is useful for descending snow slopes with a safe run-out.

◆ The technique is not recommended for glaciated terrain because of the risk that an entire team may glissade into an unexpected crevasse.

Activity 1: Sitting Glissade (30 Minutes)

◆ Begin by demonstrating the sitting glissade. Stop by using the spike.

◆ Next, demonstrate the sitting glissade and stop by using the self-arrest to show why it is a useful technique if the glissade gets out of control. Self-arrest should be considered a last resort if the person is going too fast to stop by using the spike and digging in the heels.

◆ Have the students practice in a conveyor belt style. This method involves one student at a time glissading while students who just slid walk up a boot-packed trail to the side with a good view of those glissading.

◆ Provide feedback as necessary.

◆ Provide a forum for students to critique each other and point out the characteristics of good or poor technique.

Activity 2: Standing Glissade (30 Minutes)

◆ Demonstrate the standing glissade.

◆ Have students practice on the conveyor belt, which is now wider because they will likely need to change directions during the descent.

Activity 3: Crouching Glissade (30 Minutes)

◆ Demonstrate the crouching glissade.

◆ Discuss the advantages and disadvantages compared with the other techniques.

Activity 4: Descent Scenarios (60 to 90 Minutes)

This activity requires students to apply their newly acquired knowledge and experience about anchors, rappelling, and descending with an axe and crampons.

◆ Move students into an area that contains a slope that varies in steepness and has a safe zone at the top and bottom.

◆ Set up four scenarios that require different methods of descent.

◆ Have students cycle through each of the scenarios while you manage any safety concerns that may develop from the students' decisions. This is structured discovery, and you should play a minimal role.

Scenario 1 The slope is safe to glissade.

Scenario 2 The slope is safe to down climb using the ice axe as a self-belay but too steep to glissade in control.

Scenario 3 Students have no snow protection, and the terrain is too steep to down climb safely. The ideal solution is to rappel off a bollard and continue to the bottom with a glissade. This approach leaves no gear behind in true Leave No Trace fashion.

Scenario 4 Ask students how they can descend and not leave gear behind (ask students not to chop a bollard but to use snow protection and the rope to descend). Ideal solution: The first two climbers rappel off the anchor and place protection on the way down, into which they clip the rope. The last climber cleans the rappel anchor completely, down climbs on lead, and cleans the subsequent snow protection as the climbers below provide a belay.

Closure Activity

Descending Scenarios (30 to 45 Minutes)

Have a group of three students create a descent scenario for another group. The challenged group then discusses their plan and presents their idea to you. If the plan can be safely executed, the challenged group performs their descent. If the plan needs a backup belay for safety, establish one. If neither of these options is safe, encourage the two groups to discuss and create a descent in which risk can be managed. The group who presented the challenge may have an ideal method in mind or may realize that their challenge was too difficult to overcome.

Site selection for this closure activity is extremely important. A small manageable location is preferable to a large site that spreads out the students or creates unnecessary consequences in the event of failure.

Follow-Up Activity

More Scenarios (20 to 30 Minutes)

◆ Have the students create four new scenarios that would require different descent techniques.

◆ The scenarios should consider time of day, snow conditions, run-out of the slope, group gear, energy level of the group, and descent techniques used.

◆ Students should use their journals to record their scenarios.

ASSESSMENT

◆ Check that students can identify the safest and most efficient methods of descent for a variety of situations by observing the methods that they choose during the descent scenarios.

◆ Confirm that students can demonstrate the ability to implement different techniques for descending varied terrain including plunge stepping, glissading (sitting, crouching, and standing), rappelling off a bollard, and down climbing with protection by observing them practice these skills during the glissade conveyor belt and descent scenarios.

◆ Verify that students appreciate the appropriate method of descent for specific applications by soliciting feedback and facilitating discussion (using journal entries) after students complete their descent scenarios.

TEACHING CONSIDERATIONS

◆ Spend time in advance to find a practice area where the scenarios are not contrived.

◆ The descent scenarios require significant site management and a low student-to-instructor ratio.

◆ Be flexible with the individual scenarios and allow students to design their own solutions. Monitor the level of frustration to maintain an environment of creative tension.

◆ Sound judgment and assessment play an essential role in choosing the most prudent method of descent.

◆ Students develop judgment and the ability to make safe decisions as they build on their personal experiences and reflect on the outcomes of their decisions.

◆ Discuss the ideal solutions after the students complete the scenarios.

UNIT 10, LESSON 9

▷ Leave No Trace Considerations

OVERVIEW

Knowing how to prevent environmental impacts in alpine and subalpine environments is necessary to protect natural resources. Students learn through discussions, challenges, research, and peer presentations about minimizing impact in alpine environments.

JUSTIFICATION

As mountaineering and alpine travel increase in popularity, human impacts have become increasingly evident. Environmental ethics and practices are therefore increasingly important in mountaineering to protect the natural environment. Besides protecting the natural environment, making a conscious decision to leave no trace helps in planning and preparing for expeditions or trips.

GOAL

To raise students' environmental awareness, develop their desire to support and protect the environment, and foster their ability to minimize impacts in alpine environments.

OBJECTIVES

At the end of this lesson students will be able to

- identify and describe the flora and fauna present in alpine environments (cognitive),
- summarize the seven principles of Leave No Trace (cognitive),
- understand the importance of local regulations regarding environmental care (cognitive),
- demonstrate the ability to integrate trip-planning concepts with minimum-impact techniques (cognitive),
- engage other students in discussions about mountaineering and environmental ethics (affective),
- appreciate the skills learned to help protect the natural environment (affective), and
- choose appropriate locations and techniques for minimizing impact in alpine environments (affective).

EQUIPMENT AND AREAS NEEDED

- Information about the specific mountain and surrounding environment
- One flora identification book or handout for the specific environment
- One fauna identification book or handout for the specific environment
- One geologic history book or handout for the specific environment
- One natural and cultural history book or handout
- One *Leave No Trace North America Skills and Ethics* booklet (LNT, n.d.)
- One set of seven colored markers
- One easel with paper
- Paper and pens for individual notes and the reflection exercise

RISK MANAGEMENT CONSIDERATIONS

This activity can be done in a stationary indoor or outdoor classroom that is considered safe. An outdoor stationary site is one in which students are free to move within a specific set of boundaries and where a reasonable opportunity for challenge can be provided (Nicolazzo, 2003). If the challenge results in failure, that failure will not be hazardous to the physical or emotional well-being of the students.

LESSON CONTENT

Introduction

Teaching students Leave No Trace principles follows a logical progression. It starts during the preparation phase of the unit and continues throughout the unit in methodical and well-placed discussions about options and choices that minimize impact. Leave No Trace ethics require students to understand terminology, develop an interest or attachment to the environment, and apply practical skills.

Important Terms

Mountaineers should be able to understand the difference between three distinct terms.

ethics—A set of moral values held by a common group.

principles—Guidelines established to help guide those who subscribe to a particular set of ethics.

regulations—A set of rules set forth by land managers for a specific management area.

Mountain-Specific Considerations for the Seven Principles

The seven principles are the guidelines established to help guide those who subscribe to minimum-impact ethics (Alpine Ascents International, 2007).

Plan Ahead and Prepare

- Define your trip itinerary and objectives by researching relevant information including route conditions, avalanche danger, weather forecasts, and local permits and regulations.
- Prepare for extreme weather, hazards, emergencies, and self-rescue.
- Determine the strategy for your team's food and fuel consumption, and for waste disposal.
- Choose an appropriate route that suits your team's size, ability, and experience. Leave a copy of your itinerary with family or friends.
- Repackage your food into reusable containers or bags.
- Carry and know how to use a map, compass, altimeter, route markers, and, possibly, a global positioning system (GPS) unit.

Travel and Camp on Durable Surfaces   On the trail:

- Focus your activities on durable surfaces, including established trails, deep snow, rock, or inorganic soil. Avoid vegetation, thin snow cover, and organic soils.
- Establish an appropriate route up the mountain, taking into consideration the team's safety and Leave No Trace principles. Plan your route with the idea that others will follow.
- Whenever possible and safe, remove route markers during your descent.

At camp:

- In high-use areas, use established campsites. In pristine areas, minimize your impact by breaking down constructed snow walls and windbreaks.
- Use manmade tent anchors (ice screws, axes, poles, and so on) whenever possible. Replace any rocks or other natural anchors where found.

Dispose of Waste Properly

- Pack it in, pack it out. Pack out everything that you carry with you including garbage, trash, and extra fuel. Trash left at altitude or in crevasses does not biodegrade. Whenever possible, remove others' discarded waste from the mountain.
- In high-use areas, use established restroom facilities. Otherwise, pack out solid human waste with "blue bags," Wag Bags, or other techniques. If packing out all solid human waste is not possible because of trip duration, refer to local protocols about how to dispose of human waste.

◆ Designate a clean snow area (upslope from camp) to serve as your water source. Focus your activities and waste disposal sites away from that area.

◆ Consolidate liquid human waste in a designated urinal downslope from camp and away from the designated water (snow) source. Consider using a pee bottle in camp to facilitate disposal. When traveling, step off the trail to urinate so that others won't have to hike through yellow snow.

◆ Dispose of gray water (dishwater) in a designated sump hole downslope from camp. Strain the dishwater and pack out all leftover solids.

Leave What You Find   Leave all rocks, plants, animals, and historical or cultural artifacts as you find them.

Minimize Campfire Impacts   Always carry a lightweight camp stove. Adequate wood is generally unavailable on mountaineering expeditions so making fires is infeasible and inappropriate.

Respect Wildlife

◆ Observe wildlife from a distance. Do not follow or approach them.

◆ Never feed wildlife or leave food behind to be eaten.

◆ Protect wildlife and your food by storing rations and trash securely. Anticipate changing weather conditions by marking your cache.

Be Considerate of Other Visitors

◆ Communicate and cooperate with other teams.

◆ Yield to uphill climbers by stepping off the route onto a durable surface.

◆ Avoid unnecessarily clustering campsites whenever possible.

◆ Take rest breaks off the route, away from other campsites, and on a durable surface.

◆ Let nature's sounds prevail. Keep loud voices and noises to a minimum.

Leave No Trace principles—Copyright: Leave No Trace Center for Outdoor Ethics. www.LNT.org.

General Tips

◆ Mountaineers are more likely to embrace and support environmental ethics if they have special knowledge about, an attachment to, or an interest in preserving the area. Special environments have a rich background including specific fauna, flora, natural history, geologic history, and cultural history.

◆ If mountaineers have an interest in their environment, they will be more likely to practice specific techniques designed to support each principle. But in mountaineering a few principles need to be weighed for safety versus minimum impact. For example, it is advisable for a mountaineer to use a bright yellow tent for safety concerns, but Leave No Trace recommends using colors that blend into the surrounding environment. In light of this, mountaineers constantly need to exercise their best judgment when determining how to maintain a balance between safety and minimum impact.

Main Activities

Activity 1: Our Leave No Trace Operational Language (20 Minutes)

Break the group into small groups of three and initiate a discussion. Challenge each group to define and differentiate ethics, regulations, and principles. Have them give examples of each concept.

Activity 2: Mountaineering LNT (50 Minutes)

◆ Introduce the seven principles of Leave No Trace by describing each principle with a general overview.

◆ Focus the group's attention on the need to prevent unnecessary impacts in alpine environments because of specific geologic formations, flora, fauna, and environmental conditions.

◆ Provide time for students to research the location of the route or trip (done in small groups).

◆ Provide supplies that help direct their research into specific areas of study.

◆ Encourage each group to research specific human impacts on mountains.

◆ Allow 30 minutes for each group to gather, prepare, and organize a presentation on their specific area of expertise or interest.

◆ As the instructor, be sure to introduce additional ecological concepts or organisms that may be used in the field as a reference. In particular, identify historical or geologic areas of interest, or specific flora located near or around a planned campsite.

◆ Provide an opportunity for each group to present their information to the large group and include a short question-and-answer session after each presentation.

> Knowing about a specific location beforehand makes the experience even more valuable afterward.

Closure Activity

LNT and the Alpine Environment (20 Minutes)

Bring closure to the previous activity by reviewing the vulnerability of the alpine environment to human impacts.

◆ Have students return to their small groups and discuss how they can apply each principle to help prevent impact to the topic that they researched.

◆ Place seven pieces of paper around the room with one principle written on each piece.

◆ Have students place their specific application under the appropriate principle and give their reasons for the placement.

◆ Close by asking students what they were not aware of and how their view of the alpine environment has changed.

Follow-Up Activity

The LNT Challenge (30 Minutes or Longer)

Say to your students, "Adhering to an ethic can be difficult. Can we do it?" Leave No Trace may be approached by increasing awareness. Review each principle during other field activities by engaging students in challenges that require thoughtful reflection, challenging choices, ethical dilemmas, and decision-making opportunities.

◆ For example, discussions about campsite selection could center on finding a balance between choosing a site that minimizes impact and one that maximizes safety.

◆ Encourage students to challenge themselves by drinking gray water to minimize impact and maximize hydration rather than disposing it in a sump. Gray water is produced when pots, bowls, and other items are cleaned with hot water. Soap is not needed in the field, and gray water can be ingested by adding a drink mix or just drinking it plain.

◆ On lower slopes, discuss route selection and encourage students to determine the best route, taking safety and impact into account.

◆ Maximize reflection by referring to the classroom activity to expand their knowledge about specific organisms or geologic impact.

ASSESSMENT

◆ Check that students can identify and describe the flora and fauna present in alpine environments by asking them to find and identify a new plant or animal for the class during a mountaineering trip.

◆ Confirm that students can summarize the seven principles of Leave No Trace by asking them to write in their journals about the principles and the specific challenges that they faced while on course.

◆ Verify that students understand the importance of local regulations regarding environmental care by having them investigate those regulations during trip planning and sharing them with the larger group.

◆ Check that students can demonstrate the ability to integrate trip-planning concepts with minimum-impact techniques by identifying travel routes on durable surfaces, disposing of waste properly, and avoiding wildlife while on course.

◆ Confirm that students can engage other students in discussions about mountaineering and environmental ethics.

◆ Assess whether students appreciate the skills learned to help protect the natural environment.

◆ Verify that students can choose appropriate locations and techniques for minimizing impact in alpine environments.

TEACHING CONSIDERATIONS

◆ Choose the books that you present to your students by researching the trip location.

◆ Some students may have sacred cows or previous training that is unlike the environmental ethic that you are teaching. Validate their training and challenge them to view environmental ethics from another perspective.

◆ Some students may not know where to begin their research. If you think that students need some scaffolding to begin with, you may want to take them on a longer experience during your introduction. You can do this by introducing an impressive alpine organism or geologic formation to help them grasp the concept of researching a specific item.

◆ Students interested in mountaineering may not see the need to learn about their microenvironment. Encourage those students to find metaphors that relate the specific study to a mountaineering application.

▷ Avalanche Awareness and Safety

OVERVIEW

This lesson is designed to instill in students an awareness of the dangers associated with traveling in avalanche-prone terrain. By reviewing and reacting to a series of case studies, students learn about the destructive potential of avalanches. Students also learn through lecture, structured discovery, and demonstration why avalanches occur, how to travel safely in avalanche terrain, what equipment they need to carry, and what to do if they are caught in an avalanche.

JUSTIFICATION

Understanding the hazards of traveling in avalanche terrain develops students' ownership of furthering their avalanche education before they venture into the back-country on their own. Knowing how to travel properly in avalanche terrain increases group safety and develops cohesion among group members. Students should finish the lesson motivated to seek further avalanche education.

GOAL

To develop students' awareness of how destructive avalanches can be, how to avoid an avalanche, what to do if they are caught in an avalanche, and where to receive further avalanche education.

OBJECTIVES

At the end of this lesson students will be able to

◆ state the recommended equipment to carry in avalanche terrain (cognitive),

◆ identify the appropriate techniques and methods for traveling in avalanche-prone terrain (cognitive),

◆ identify the physical consequences of not preparing for travel in avalanche terrain,

◆ identify the social consequences of not preparing adequately for travel in avalanche terrain, and

◆ justify spending the time and money necessary to further their avalanche education (affective).

EQUIPMENT AND AREAS NEEDED

◆ Three avalanche case studies resulting in fatalities or significant trauma, available in accident summaries posted by various avalanche centers throughout North America (www.avalanche.org)

◆ One transceiver, shovel, and probe for each group of three students

◆ Weatherproof notepads for students to take notes while in and on snow

◆ A list of providers of avalanche training such as guide services, ski resorts, land management agencies, parks and recreation departments, and outdoor programs

RISK MANAGEMENT CONSIDERATIONS

◆ Conduct this lesson in the field with visible avalanche-prone terrain but in a safe zone. Assume that students have no avalanche training.

◆ Developing extensive knowledge of avalanche hazards in one lesson is not possible. Entire courses are devoted to this skill set. This lesson is intended to heighten the students' awareness of the destructive potential of avalanches and the importance of obtaining comprehensive avalanche education if the intention is to travel in avalanche terrain after completing this unit.

◆ To make educated and sound decisions regarding avalanche hazards, mountaineers must be knowledgeable about pretrip preparation, snow observations and stability tests, travel techniques, and rescue skills.

◆ You have the responsibility to reiterate ad nauseam that knowing how to use a transceiver, shovel, and probe during a rescue is not sufficient knowledge to travel independently in avalanche terrain.

LESSON CONTENT

Introduction

A snowpack is dynamic. Make the analogy to an enormous layered ice cream cake sitting in the sun, cold, wind, and rain. Obviously, the cake will behave slightly differently than snow will, but think of how the cake would change. Some layers might become saturated with water from rain. If the weather turns warm the ice cream might begin to melt out and shift the cake layers above it. If the temperature falls not much would change because the cake would be frozen. If rain then fell the upper layers of the cake might begin to melt first. Then slowly the lower layers not exposed on the surface would begin to melt. An extended period of warm weather might cause the whole cake to congeal into one solid mass. Now imagine how things would change if the cake were on an angled slope.

◆ Over time the layers and crystals of snow metamorphose (change). At any time you can have wet layers, ice layers, fragile crystalline layers, and thick slabs.

◆ How these layers interact with each other and change as a result of weather, temperature, wind, and other factors, such as a climber standing on top of them, will dictate whether the layers remain in place or slide off one another. Has anyone ever seen a cake slide off to the side if it sits in the sun too long, or seen taffy crack in the cold?

McCammon and Schweizer (2002) noted that avalanches can occur because of variances within the snowpack. Avalanche forecasters and experienced backcountry users dig pits in the snow to study the individual layers. After exposing the layers, they perform various compression tests, shear tests, and in some cases examine snow crystals through a handheld lens to understand the destructive potential of the current conditions and the level of danger to potential users.

There are two major types of avalanches: loose-snow avalanches and slab avalanches.

◆ Loose-snow avalanches can occur on wet snow as a result of snow melting throughout the day or snow melting off rock faces and falling on slopes below. For this reason, mountaineers should travel early in the day and be off the route by the time loose-snow avalanches can occur.

◆ Slab avalanches occur when a cohesive slab of snow sets into motion beginning at a fracture line. Eventually, as the slab slides over a harder surface, it will break into smaller pieces until it comes to rest in a pile called the debris pile (figure MN10.1).

◆ Start zones are places where either type of avalanche (slab or loose snow) may begin. Trigger points are specific locations within start zones where localized snow failure occurs. These places include convexities, concavities, shallow or exposed rocks, protruding trees, cliffs, and loaded slopes below cornices. Avalanches have the potential to begin at any of those points.

FIGURE MN10.1   Note the debris pile at the bottom of the mountain.

◆ Climbers are generally caught in avalanches less often than skiers are because climbers often travel on ridges or steep faces that typically do not hold loaded snow well.

◆ Traveling below avalanche slopes late in the day or moving across avalanche-prone terrain such as convexities or concavities in the 30- to 45-degree range are the primary circumstances in which climbers are caught in avalanches.

◆ Although often poorly defined, avalanche terrain can sometimes be characterized by
  - slopes that are unvegetated or have only small shrubs and trees,
  - slopes with trees that are lacking branches on the uphill side (known as flagged trees) because of previous avalanches,
  - slopes ranging from 30 to 45 degrees,
  - slopes that have piles of avalanche debris at the base, and
  - places where avalanches are currently occurring or have recently occurred.

◆ If climbers believe that they are in avalanche-prone terrain, they should use these travel techniques to avoid being caught:
  - Stay on ridge lines.
  - Avoid convexities and concavities by choosing a route that links low-angle benches.
  - Choose routes that contain many trees close together (which act collectively as an anchor for snow, in contrast to one tree, which may be a trigger point).
  - Travel with some distance between team members to avoid having several people be caught in a slide, but always stay in sight of each other to spot one another if a slide occurs.
  - Avoid going out of sight of your party.
  - Descend using a buddy system to keep an eye on each other.
  - Special note: Don't travel over that rollover or rise; if your party can't see you, they won't know whether you are buried.

◆ If you are caught in a slide, try to get to the side of the slide by skiing or running out of the sliding snow. If you can't get out of the slide and find yourself cascading down with the avalanche, fight for the top! "Swim" or roll to stay on the surface. If wearing skis or snowshoes, kick them off because they will drag you downward, but keep your pack on because it will help you float higher in the slide debris.

◆ If you are buried, fight for the top! Partial burials have resulted in survival because the buried people were able to free themselves.

◆ Avalanche debris can set up fast and hard. Try to create an air pocket around your face if you are not able to reach the surface. Many avalanche survivors explain, however, that doing this was nearly impossible because their arms were cemented into the snow and they could not move them toward their mouth before they became entrapped.

◆ Travelers in avalanche terrain should carry transceivers, shovels, and probes. This equipment is essential in the event of an avalanche and can mean the difference between life and death! Don't be caught without it!

◆ The transceiver (aka beacon) transmits and receives signals from other transceivers. They are used to locate a buried person who is also wearing a transceiver. Using a transceiver is not intuitive, and practice is required to become efficient and thus effective.

◆ The **probe** is used to pinpoint the exact location of the victim after the general location of the buried person has been determined.

◆ The shovel is used aggressively to dig out a buried person (figure MN10.2).

◆ The faster you can find and dig out a person, the greater their chance of survival.

◆ Knowing how to use a transceiver, shovel, and probe will not decrease the likelihood of being caught in an avalanche. Awareness and avoidance are the primary skills that should be used in avalanche terrain. Rescue skills are extremely important, but they should not be relied on as a safety net.

◆ Avalanche education is essential training for anyone traveling independently in avalanche terrain.

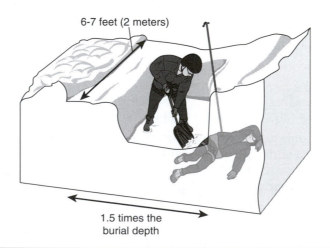

6-7 feet (2 meters)

1.5 times the burial depth

FIGURE MN10.2   Find and dig with intent. First, rescuers pinpoint the victim with a transceiver and probe. Then rescuers dig. The optimal length of the hole is 1.5 times the burial depth. The width of the hole should be 6 to 7 feet (about 2 meters), depending on the number of shovelers.

Reprinted, by permission, from B. Edgerly and D. Atkins, *Stategic shoveling: The next frontier in companion rescue* (Boulder, CO: Back Country Access), 4.

Important Terms

concavity—The inward-curving portion of a slope; similar to a bowl.

convexity—A slope that curves outward rather than inward.

flagged trees—Trees missing branches on the uphill side because of previous avalanches.

isothermic snow—A consolidated mass of snow that contains no variation in temperature, hardness, or water content. It may contain no notable layers.

loose-snow (point release) avalanches—Avalanches that usually start from a single point and gather mass as they flow down the slope, often forming a triangle from the trigger point (figure MN10.3).

probe—Used to pinpoint the exact location of the victim after the general location of the buried person has been determined. Typically composed of aluminum sections that connect like tent poles to create a uniform pole 2 to 3 meters (6.5 to 10 feet) in length.

slab avalanche—A cohesive slab of snow set into motion, beginning at a fracture line. Eventually, as the slab slides over a harder surface, it breaks into smaller pieces until it comes to rest in a pile called the debris pile (figure MN10.3).

start zone—The region of a slope where an avalanche begins.

transceiver (aka beacon)—Transmits and receives signals from other transceivers. They are used to locate a buried person who is also wearing a transceiver.

trigger points—Specific locations in a start zone where localized snow failure occurs, initiating an avalanche (Klassen, Murphy, Zacharias, Schwarz, et al., 2002) (see figure MN10.4).

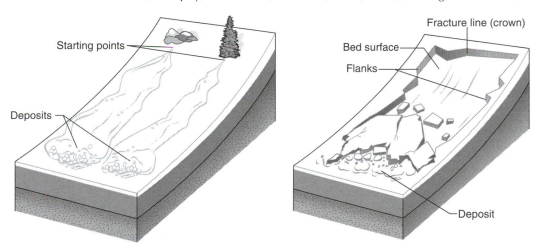

FIGURE MN10.3   Loose-snow (point release) and slab avalanches.

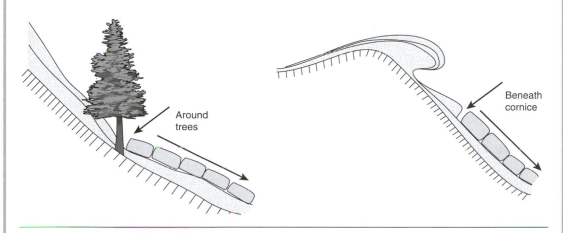

FIGURE MN10.4   Trigger points.

Main Activities

Activity 1: Context of Avalanches (30 Minutes)

◆ Read accounts of a few incidents involving fatalities or traumatic injuries resulting from avalanches to gain students' attention.

◆ Ask students to hypothesize how these incidents occurred or could have been avoided to start a discussion about the various causes and types of avalanches and why people are caught in them. This discussion should identify a number of pertinent points to clarify later in the lesson.

◆ Explain why you are not starting the lesson by discussing transceivers, shovels, and probes. Instead, emphasize why avalanches occur and how to avoid them. You will introduce and explain the equipment later.

◆ Discuss layers in the snowpack and how weaknesses can persist or develop over time.

◆ Expose a cross-section of the snowpack to show the layers (have the students use their shovels to dig).

◆ Describe the two major forms of avalanches: loose snow and slab.

◆ Show trigger points using figure MN10.4 or a drawing on a whiteboard. If possible, physically identify common trigger points where avalanches can begin.

◆ Ask students to point out avalanche paths they see in front of them and describe the characteristics. Add additional information that students miss. Introduce a situation where you are traveling and find yourself in avalanche-prone terrain.

◆ Ask the students what the group can do to reduce their risk. Fill in content as necessary.

Activity 2: Mini-Avalanche Scenarios (90 Minutes)

◆ Have students pair up. Locate a miniature slope where they will be able to use various travel techniques to ascend the slope.

◆ Have them use four sticks or other small items to illustrate spacing and the path of ascent for the group.

◆ Move to larger terrain and have students (in the same groups) chose a route after you give them a high point to achieve.

◆ Then have them pretend to be caught in an avalanche because of inadequate training, poor assessment, ego, or plain old bad luck.

◆ Ask them to explain what they would do if they were caught in a slide or buried.

Activity 3: Introduction to Avalanche Equipment (15 Minutes)

◆ Introduce the transceiver, shovel, and probe.

◆ Pass the items around so that students can manipulate them.

Closure Activity

Continuing Education (10 Minutes)

Explain to students that what they have learned in this lesson is just enough to get them caught in an avalanche and that having a basic understanding of avalanches does not qualify them to travel independently in avalanche terrain. Now that they have an awareness of avalanches, they need to continue learning how to avoid them and perform a rescue.

- Have students brainstorm where they can find further avalanche training.
- Encourage students to take a level 1 avalanche course from an outdoor program, ski resort, guide service, or land management agency (see the resources list).
- Close the lesson by providing students with a list of organizations that offer avalanche education (see resources).

Follow-Up Activity

Reinforcing Avalanche Knowledge (10 Minutes)

Follow up in subsequent meetings by asking students whether they have furthered their avalanche education. Positively reinforce the students who have done so by recognizing them formally for proactively increasing their outdoor skills.

ASSESSMENT

- Verify that students can state the recommended equipment to carry in avalanche terrain by asking them to recite in unison the three necessary pieces of equipment to carry in avalanche terrain.
- Check that students can identify the appropriate techniques and methods for traveling in avalanche-prone terrain by observing what routes they chose in the miniature and full-scale terrain scenarios.
- Confirm that students can identify the physical consequences of not preparing for travel in avalanche terrain by having them list and briefly describe in their journals three negative physical consequences of not preparing for travel in avalanche terrain.
- Verify that students can identify the social consequences of not adequately preparing for travel in avalanche terrain by having them list and briefly describe in their journals three negative social consequences of not preparing for travel in avalanche terrain.
- Check that students can justify spending the time and money necessary to further their avalanche education by facilitating a discussion with them about the risks of inadequate avalanche training.

TEACHING CONSIDERATIONS

- If you are digging in isothermic snow—a consolidated mass of snow that contains no variation in temperature, hardness, or water content—you may not find notable layers.
- Use that circumstance to illustrate the stability of the snowpack. Avalanches that occur in that type of snowpack are typically sluffs (or loose-snow avalanches) that result from radiation warming the snow on the surface, increasing the moisture content and weakening the bonds with the snow below.
- Be aware that students in the group may have lost a friend or family member in an avalanche. Monitor humor surrounding death by an avalanche while maintaining a fun and educational atmosphere.

Mountaineering Skills Checklist

Lesson 1

- ☐ Describe the major mountaineering periods and the technological advancements that occurred during each.
- ☐ Identify some of the major personalities and their contributions to the sport of mountaineering.
- ☐ Understand the advantages and disadvantages of each type of mountaineering.
- ☐ Select the mountaineering techniques or approaches that you identify with most strongly.
- ☐ Appreciate the development of modern mountaineering equipment.
- ☐ Appreciate the evolution of mountaineering as an ever-changing and developing adventure activity.
- ☐ Qualify your reasons for mountaineering through journal writing and discussion.

Lesson 2

- ☐ Comprehensively pack a backpack for a three-day trip including the 11 equipment essentials:
    1. UV protection
    2. Navigational tools
    3. Emergency supplies
    4. Clothing
    5. Nutritional needs
    6. Footwear
    7. Specialized personal climbing equipment
    8. Team technical equipment
    9. Night needs
    10. Personal effects
    11. Skills and training
- ☐ Explain your rationale for including or excluding particular pieces of equipment by developing an equipment list.
- ☐ Distinguish between necessary and unnecessary equipment for a climb by explaining your rationale for creating your equipment list.
- ☐ Distinguish between necessary and unnecessary equipment for a climb by comparing the usefulness of modern and antiquated equipment.
- ☐ Appreciate the value of using modern equipment to achieve additional goals such as the climbing objective, safety, and social aims by describing the use of each item of equipment.

Lesson 3

Demonstrate the ability to plan for a climb by performing the following steps:

- ☐ Route research
- ☐ Groundwork
- ☐ Final preparations
- ☐ Accurately complete a route-planning equation using mountaineering math
- ☐ Summarize positive physical consequences of thorough preparation and negative physical consequences of not being prepared by stating three of each consequence in your journal.
- ☐ Summarize positive social consequences of thorough preparation and negative social consequences of not being prepared by stating two of each consequence in your journal.
- ☐ Demonstrate an understanding of preparing to climb by listening to other groups explain their lists to the rest of the class.
- ☐ Justify the need for thorough preparation in discussions in small groups.
- ☐ Appreciate the added benefit of being able to enjoy a climb by preparing thoroughly.

Lesson 4

- ☐ Demonstrate the duck walk.
- ☐ Demonstrate diagonal ascent.
- ☐ Demonstrate the letter box.
- ☐ Practice appropriate step kicking for subsequent climbers to follow when in the leader role at the end of the activity.
- ☐ Justify further improving kicked steps for subsequent climbers to conserve the energy of the rope team.
- ☐ Demonstrate cane position.
- ☐ Demonstrate ice axe sleeve.
- ☐ Demonstrate cross-body ice axe technique.
- ☐ Demonstrate in-balance position.
- ☐ Demonstrate out-of-balance position.
- ☐ Identify the anatomy of the ice axe—pick, adze, shaft, spike.
- ☐ Identify the most appropriate foot and ice axe techniques for particular applications when in the leader role during the closure activity of Follow the Leader.

continued ▶

Use the mountaineering skills checklist as an additional tool to assess skills learned throughout this unit.

From M. Wagstaff and A. Attarian, 2009, *Technical skills for adventure programming: A curriculum guide* (Champaign, IL: Human Kinetics).

Lesson 5

- ☐ Identify the conditions when self-arrest or team arrest is a plausible option.
- ☐ Describe the systematic steps needed to initiate an arrest when a fall occurs.
- ☐ Demonstrate the ability to perform self-arrest from the principal positions of sitting on the butt, lying on the belly with head downhill, lying on the back with the head downhill, and with and without an ice axe.
- ☐ Demonstrate the appropriate holding position after the arrest.
- ☐ Appreciate the terrain and snow conditions, and know how to implement other safety measures in addition to the self-arrest.

Lesson 6

- ☐ Identify the different types of snow protection available for use including natural anchors (bollards and seracs) and artificial anchors (pickets, flukes, T-slots, improvised techniques).
- ☐ Recognize different snow conditions and apply the appropriate snow protection technique.
- ☐ Describe ways to improvise protection using mixed techniques.
- ☐ Build equalized anchors using a variety of snow protection.
- ☐ Place pickets and flukes correctly.
- ☐ Build T-slots, improvised deadmen, and bollards appropriately.
- ☐ Justify the need to study snow conditions as part of the trip-planning process.

Lesson 7

- ☐ Identify the safest and most efficient methods of rope travel for various conditions.
- ☐ Demonstrate the ability to implement different techniques for belaying on varied terrain including running belays, body belays, anchor belays, and dynamic versus static applications.
- ☐ Demonstrate the ability to tie a group into the rope with appropriate spacing.
- ☐ Demonstrate the proper coiling of rope using the mountaineer's coil and Kiwi coil.
- ☐ Appreciate the appropriate use of snow anchors, rope travel, belay techniques, and ice axe and crampon use for mountaineering applications.
- ☐ Demonstrate traveling with the rope and ice axe in the appropriate locations.

Lesson 8

- ☐ Demonstrate the standing glissade.
- ☐ Demonstrate the crouching glissade.
- ☐ Demonstrate the sitting glissade.
- ☐ Identify the safest and most efficient methods of descent for a variety of situations by choosing the correct methods during the descent scenarios.
- ☐ Appreciate the appropriate methods of descent for specific applications by making notes in your journal.

Lesson 9

- ☐ Identify and describe the flora and fauna present in alpine environments.
- ☐ Summarize the seven principles of Leave No Trace.
- ☐ Understand the importance of local regulations regarding environmental care.
- ☐ Demonstrate the ability to integrate trip-planning concepts with minimum-impact techniques.
- ☐ Engage other students in discussions about mountaineering and environmental ethics.
- ☐ Appreciate the skills learned to help protect the natural environment.
- ☐ Choose appropriate locations and techniques for minimizing impact in alpine environments.

Lesson 10

- ☐ Identify a convexity.
- ☐ Identify a concavity.
- ☐ Demonstrate how to dig to find a buried team member.
- ☐ State the recommended equipment to carry in avalanche terrain.
- ☐ Identify three negative physical consequences of not preparing for travel in avalanche terrain by listing them in your journal.
- ☐ Identify three negative social consequences of not preparing for travel in avalanche terrain by listing them in your journal.
- ☐ Justify spending the time and money necessary to further your avalanche education by discussing the risks of inadequate avalanche training.

(continued)

From M. Wagstaff and A. Attarian, 2009, *Technical skills for adventure programming: A curriculum guide* (Champaign, IL: Human Kinetics).

GLOSSARY

adze—Used mainly for chopping, this flat, shovel-like feature is opposite the pick on the head of the axe. Usually the most comfortable platform to hold while carrying the axe.

age-hardened snow—Snow that has been manually compressed and given time to settle.

alpine climbing harness—An alpine or mountaineering harness should be as trim as possible with little padding (because the climber's clothing will provide plenty) and have a pair of equipment loops. Leg loops with buckles are essential because they facilitate getting in and out of the harness and make it possible to use the restroom without having to remove the harness.

alpine mountaineering—A method of mountaineering used by a small party who attempts a route by carrying their supplies and operating without permanently established camps.

anchor belay—Using any fixed anchor as the belay point. In most cases, an anchor belay on snow will be directly off the anchor.

artificial anchors—Include pickets, T-slots, flukes, ice screws, and deadmen. Used in appropriate environmental conditions, artificial anchors are extremely versatile.

belay—Holding or arresting a fall by using friction to bind the rope. A belay can be static or dynamic. Static belays use friction to stop the rope. Dynamic belays use friction to slow the rope.

body belay—Belaying off the body. This technique includes wrapping the rope around the hip of the belayer or could incorporate the use of a belay device off the harness of the belayer.

bollard—A teardrop-shaped pile of snow that has been cut into the slope. Generally, a trench is dug to create the bollard. The size of the bollard depends completely on snow conditions. The trench can be 1 to 1.5 feet (30 to 45 centimeters) deep and the teardrop mound can be 2 to 6 feet (60 to 180 centimeters) in diameter.

cane position—An ice axe technique in which the climber grasps the adze and uses the shaft and spike as a cane.

concavity—The inward curving portion of a slope; similar to a bowl.

convexity—A slope that curves outward rather than inward.

crampons—Metal points that attach to a climber's boots to provide purchase on hard snow and ice. Crampons should have a minimum of 10 points with 2 front points and fit securely to the climber's boots so that they don't come loose while climbing. Various types exist, including rigid (specific to water ice), hinged, step-in, and pneumatic.

cross-body ice axe technique—Useful when traversing steep snowy terrain. The climber places the spike horizontally next to himself or herself with one hand on the adze and the pick facing away from the climber. For balance, the climber can put weight on the lower end of the shaft close to the spike.

diagonal ascent—Facing sideways, the climber trends diagonally. Each step is slightly higher than the last, and the climber places equal weight on each foot.

duck walk—Walking with the toes turned out and the feet splayed apart, the climber keeps the feet flat and avoids weighting only the front of the feet, which will tire the calf muscles.

ERNEST—An acronym used to describe how to build anchors. Equalized, redundant, no extension, solid, and timely are the terms that make up ERNEST. The anchor-building concept is discussed in detail in unit 2.

ethics—A set of moral values held by a common group.

expedition mountaineering (siege tactics)—A method of mountaineering used by a large group of climbers who "lay siege" to a mountain using multiple camps, fixed ropes, and large amounts of supplies.

final preparations—The final steps in the sequential planning process. Because of the dynamic nature of alpine environments, climbers must take several essential steps both on and off the mountain, such as checking current snowpack stability or taking snowshoes on the summit bid if conditions of the day warrant.

flagged trees—Trees missing branches on the uphill side because of previous avalanches.

flukes—Wedge-shaped aluminum plates with a cable attached as a clip-in point. When placed, the fluke will sail deeper into the snowpack.

friction—Multiple objects rubbing together such as a rope, belay device, and carabiner. Friction is important to belaying.

front points—The two horizontally oriented points located at the front of the crampon.

glissading—A technique used by alpine climbers to slide on the snow by standing, sitting, or crouching while maintaining control and speed.

groundwork—Includes preparing for all the physical actions that the climber will do while on the climb, assembling the equipment and logistics needed, and establishing the social constructs that the group will operate under while on the climb.

group arrests—Occurs when all able members of the rope team assume the self-arrest position if another team member falls.

ice axe sleeve—An ice axe technique done by driving the spike and shaft into the snow, this technique works well as a self-belay. Done correctly, this technique will also leave a hole for the next climber to place her or his axe into.

isothermic snow—A consolidated mass of snow that contains no variation in temperature, hardness, or water content. It may contain no notable layers.

J-line—A safety technique that uses a fixed line to protect students during self-arrest practice in areas without an ideal run-out.

letter box technique—Used when the slope steepens or a direct ascent is preferred. The term *letter box* comes from the shape of the hole left behind, which resembles a mailbox.

light and fast—A method of climbing that modern climbers take to varying levels. One end of the spectrum involves intentionally not taking equipment that usually provides comfort or safety (sleeping bag, tent, stove, extra food, extra clothing). Climbers take this approach in exchange for the ability to climb a route quickly and reduce exposure to the objective hazards inherent in alpine climbing. With this style, failure can be fatal. The other end of the light and fast spectrum refers to taking nothing more than is needed to climb a particular route while still allowing for significant comfort and minimal consequences in the event of failure. This lesson refers to light and fast as the latter approach.

loose-snow (point release) avalanches—Avalanches that usually start from a single point and gather mass as they flow down the slope, often forming a triangle from the trigger point.

natural anchors—Use of existing environmental mediums such as snow or ice to provide a placement without using artificial materials. Examples include bollards or seracs.

pick—The narrow pointed end on top of the ice axe. Used for gaining purchase while performing self-arrest or ice climbing.

picket—The most versatile type of snow protection. The picket is shaped like an oversized stake. The most common size is 2 feet (60 centimeters) long, although larger sizes are used if snow conditions warrant. They can be placed vertically into the snow like a fence picket or horizontally in a trench.

principles—Guidelines established to help guide those who subscribe to a particular set of ethics.

probe—A pole used to pinpoint the exact location of the victim after the general location of the buried person has been determined.

regulations—A set of rules set forth by land managers for a specific management area.

route plan—An organized method of breaking a climbing route into segments or stages (trailhead to camp, stream crossing to a moraine, saddle to a ridge line or particular terrain feature). A route plan also includes a time plan that establishes a turnaround time, planning for any objective hazards, and noting safe zones on the route.

route research—Includes the specific aspects of looking into a climbing route to learn what to expect while climbing, such as likely route conditions, equipment needed, access points from glacier to rock, and route-specific hazards such rockfall during a section of the climb.

running protection—Natural or artificial anchors placed by the lead climber and attached to the rope to aid the group in the event of a fall. Running protection is a common technique used when rope travel is necessary but simple self-arrest techniques will not stop a fall.

self-arrest—A technique used to stop a fall on moderately steep snow slopes or in the event of a crevasse fall on a glacier. Self-arrest may involve either a solo climber or a climbing team traveling roped together.

sewn runners—Varying lengths of webbing up to 36 inches (90 centimeters) long that help with equalizing snow anchors. They are also used to wrap rock horns that can be used as anchors.

shaft—The long tubular portion of the axe, typically ranging in length from 40 to 70 centimeters.

slab avalanche—A cohesive slab of snow set into motion, beginning at a fracture line. Eventually, as the slab slides over a harder surface, it breaks into smaller pieces until it comes to rest in a pile called the debris pile.

snow pickets—Lightweight, T-shaped aluminum stakes with clip-in points spaced along the spine.

spike—The pointed end at the base of the shaft, at the end opposite the pick and adze. Most often placed in the snow when the axe is used in the cane position.

start zone—The region of a slope where an avalanche begins.

transceiver (aka beacon)—Transmits and receives signals from other transceivers. They are used to locate a buried person who is also wearing a transceiver.

trigger points—Specific locations in a start zone where localized snow failure begins and becomes an avalanche.

T-slot—Two trenches are created. One is horizontal to the direction of pull and longer than the linear object being placed in it, such as an ice axe, picket, or ski. The vertical trench is oriented from the center of the horizontal trench down toward the direction of pull. A sling or webbing is attached to the center of the buried object, which coincides with the vertical trench.

wands—Bamboo sticks approximately 3 feet (1 meter) in length with flagging tape attached to the tips. Wands are used to mark the route in the event of a whiteout.

REFERENCES AND RESOURCES

REFERENCES

Alpine Ascents International. (2007). *Leave No Trace alpine mountaineering principles*. Retreived from www .alpineascents.com/lnt.asp

American Alpine Institute. (2003). *Guides manual*. Bellingham, WA: Author.

Auerbach, P.S. (1999). *Medicine for the outdoors*. New York: Lyons Press.

Bogie, D. (2005). *Snow anchors*. Retrieved from www.alpineclub.org.nz/documents/activities/instruction/snow%20anchor%20report.pdf

Houston, M., & Cosley, K. (2004). *Alpine climbing: Technique to take you higher.* Seattle, WA. The Mountaineers Books.

Klassen, K., Murphy, T., Zacharieas, C., Schwartz, H., Anderson, V., Carter, T., et al. (2002). *A field method for identifying structural weaknesses in the snowpack.* Presented at the International Snow Science Workshop, Penticton, British Columbia, Sept. 30–Oct. 4.

Leave No Trace (LNT). (n.d.). *Leave No Trace North America skills and ethics.* Boulder, CO: Leave No Trace Center for Outdoor Ethics. Available as a PDF at www.lnt.org

McCammon, I., & Schweizer, J. (2002). A field method for identifying structural weaknesses in the snowpack. In J.R. Stevens (Ed.), *Proceedings ISSW 2002* (pp. 477–481). Victoria, BC: International Snow Science Workshop Canada Inc., BC Ministry of Transportation, Snow Avalanche Programs.

Nicolazzo, P. (2003). *The site management handbook.* Winthrop, WA: Wilderness Medical Training Center.

Strong, M., Doerry, E., & Ojerio, R. (2001). *Glaciers: The art of travel and the science of rescue.* Guilford, CT: The Globe Pequot Press.

RESOURCES

American Institute for Avalanche Research and Education (AIARE). http://avtraining.org. Overview: Currently one of the leaders in avalanche education, science, and research in the United States and international mountain community.

American Mountain Guides Association (AMGA). www.amga.com. Overview: Currently leading the United States in mountain guide training. A member of the International Federation of Mountain Guides Association (IFMGA), AMGA offers trainings that meet the professional peer-reviewed international standards.

Brugger, H., & Falk, M. (2002). *Analysis of avalanche safety equipment for backcountry skiers.* Translation of a paper from JAHRBUCH 2002. Published by the Austrian Association for Alpine and High Altitude Medicine. Overview: Using published rescue data, the authors evaluate and compare avalanche safety equipment for downhill and backcountry skiers.

Cascadeclimbers.com. Overview: A Web forum for conditions, route descriptions, and access for the Cascade Range.

Cox, S.M., & Fulsaas, K. (Eds). (2003). *Mountaineering: Freedom of the hills* (7th ed.). Seattle, WA: The Mountaineers Books. Overview: A comprehensive introduction to mountaineering currently in its 7th edition. Considered by many to be the most useful single resource for any aspiring mountaineer. Includes illustrations and text explaining skills from map and compass to technical alpine rescue systems.

Harrer, H. (1959). *The white spider.* London: Rupert, Hart-Davis. Overview: An excellent piece of mountaineering literature. Ideal for pulling excerpts for prefacing lectures.

Klassen, K. (1998). *Technical handbook for mountain guides.* Golden, CO: American Mountain Guides Association–Association of Canadian Mountain Guides. Overview: The technical manual for modern alpine, rock, and ice guiding in North America. The current standard for guiding techniques and approaches explained in text and illustrations. Not for the layman but useful for experienced recreational climbers seeking further knowledge.

Roberts, D. (1991). *Deborah and the mountain of my fear: The early climbs.* Leicester, England: Cordee. Overview: Modern climbing escapades and epics. A great piece of literature for illustrating the importance of equipment, planning, judgment, and other mountaineering concepts.

Schell, S., & Svela, D. (2005). *Level 1 student manual.* American Institute for Avalanche Research and Education (AIARE). Overview: The course manual used during an AIARE level 1 avalanche course. The manual covers the integral knowledge for a backcountry user to travel in avalanche terrain including decision making, snowpack, terrain, classification of avalanches, preparation, rescue, and stability tests. When used in conjunction with formal field instruction and practical field experiences, this manual is a valuable reference for users of the backcountry when avalanche awareness is necessary.

Simpson, J. (1988). *Touching the void.* New York: HarperCollins. Overview: A tale of pain in the mountains. Ideal for discussing the pros and cons of methods of descent.

Wilderness Medicine Training Center (WMTC). www.wildmedcenter.com. Overview: A leader in the provision of wilderness first aid for mountain guides, university outdoor programs, outdoor educators, and anyone who enjoys traveling in the backcountry. Publisher of *The Art and Technique of Wilderness Medicine* and *The Wilderness Medicine Handbook* (a small, spiral-bound, waterproof, tearproof field manual).

Nordic Skiing

Reid Cross

UNIT 11, LESSON 1

▷ Introduction to Nordic Skiing

OVERVIEW

This lesson is an overview of the evolution of skiing, from its beginnings in the far north of Scandinavia to its current use in the backcountry. This lesson also provides students a greater appreciation of the sport and shows the relationship between the different styles of skiing that have emerged in the present day.

JUSTIFICATION

Understanding the history of skiing provides students with a foundation for a greater understanding of the sport, from the time of hunter–gatherers to its use by the military to move men to the recreational sport that it is today.

GOAL

To develop students' appreciation of the commonalities and differences between nordic and alpine skiing.

OBJECTIVES

At the end of this lesson, students will be able to

◆ understand the origins of skiing (cognitive),

◆ explain the major differences between alpine and nordic skiing (cognitive), and

◆ appreciate the beauty and grace of both types of skiing (affective).

EQUIPMENT AND AREAS NEEDED

◆ Notebooks

◆ Pen or pencil

RISK MANAGEMENT CONSIDERATIONS

◆ This lesson should be covered before going into the field.

◆ Because this lesson takes place in an indoor classroom, no risk management considerations other than those appropriate to a traditional classroom setting should be considered.

LESSON CONTENT

Introduction

The origins of the ski go back to prehistoric times when people were hunter–gatherers and the sole purpose of the ski was to allow a person to move across snow with less effort and more efficiency. This lesson provides an overview of this activity from its inception as a utilitarian activity to the recreation activity that it is today.

Important Terms

alpine skiing—A type of skiing in which the entire boot is attached to the ski.

backcountry skiing—A type of nordic skiing in which the skier goes off trail and seeks out difficult terrain, usually for several days at a time.

cross-country skiing—Another name for nordic skiing that has come to mean a type of skiing in which the skier sticks to trails and moderate terrain.

lurk—A single long pole that was used in early ski history for braking, steering, and as an outrigger for balance and propulsion.

nordic skiing—A type of skiing in which the heel of the boot is not attached to the ski and the toe is attached at the ball of the foot.

randonee skiing—A type of skiing in which the boot can be detached at the heel or attached at the heel. The toe of the boot is attached in front of the toe, not at the ball of the foot.

track skiing—A type of nordic skiing in which the skier stays on prepared tracks.

Main Activity

A History Lesson (15 Minutes)

"Of all the sports of Norway, skiing is the most national and characteristic. As practiced in our country, it ranks first in the sports of the world. Nothing hardens the muscles and makes the body so strong and elastic; nothing gives better presence of mind and nimbleness; nothing steels the willpower and freshens the mind as skiing. This is something that develops not only in body but also soul—it has a far deeper meaning for a people than many are aware of and a far greater national importance than is generally supposed."

Nansen, 1890, p. 35

The origins of the ski go back to prehistoric times when people were hunter–gatherers and the sole purpose of the ski was to allow a person to move across snow without sinking too deep. Most archeologists agree that the ski originated in the Scandinavian countries as a means of following the hunt. Survival in northern Scandinavia depended on hunting and gathering. The primary source of food was the reindeer, and the hunters followed the reindeer on skis.

Although no one knows for sure when skis were first used, the oldest ski, uncovered in a peat bog near Hoting, Sweden, dates back to 2500 BC. The ski is short and wide, has an indentation in the center for the foot, and has holes in it to lace straps around the foot (Bays, 1985). Petroglyphs of skiers that are twice as old were discovered at Rodoy, Norway.

Many other skis have been discovered ranging in age from 1,500 years old to 4,500 years old (Abraham, 1983). The skis differ somewhat—some are short and wide, others are long and thin with upturned ends. Some pairs were of different lengths with a short one for kicking and a long one for gliding (Parker, 2001).

The first mention of skis in literature appears in the writings of Jordanes, a gothic monk, in AD 555. He mentioned a group of people called Screrefinns, which translates to the gliding Finns, referring to people who hunt animals on pieces of curved wood (Bays, 1985). Paul the Deacon (AD 720–790) wrote, "The Finns are the furthest people of the North. . . . They are skilled hunters whose abode is uncertain, and they settle where they may find game. Borne on bent boards, they traverse the heights covered with snow" (Bays, 1985, p. 21).

Scandinavian Developments Historically, skis became a common part of Scandinavian culture. By 1535 the Norwegian postal service incorporated skis in delivering mail (Bays, 1985). In 1718 Norway formed a ski troop, led by Lieutenant Jens Henrik Emahusen. Fifteen years later, as a colonel, Emahusen wrote the first ski manual. The skis at this time were different lengths. One was 320 centimeters long and the other 190 centimeters. The long ski was hardened and waxed for gliding, and the shorter one was used for traction. The skier would kick on the short ski and glide on the long one. Most skiers at this time only used one pole, called a lurk, to aid in balance, propulsion, and braking (figure NS1.1).

By the 1800s skis changed. Both skis were the same length, and in most cases two poles were used instead of the lurk, although the lurk would remain in use for another 100 years. By this time, skiing had spread beyond the Scandinavian countries. The military used skis in central Europe to aid the defense of high mountain passes. This development was significant because skiing was then being developed in two distinct geographic areas—the gentle rolling hills and highlands of Scandinavia and the steep couloirs and high mountain passes of the Alps.

In the North two historical figures had a major influence on skiing. The first was Sondre Norheim, who did two things that changed skiing and still have influence to this day. First, he changed the way that the boot was attached to the ski by adding a heel binding. Up to that time the bindings consisted of leather that was wrapped around the forefoot. Norheim added thin birch roots that he had soaked in water and woven into a cablelike binding that went around the heel. This configuration gave the binding more torsional stiffness but left the heel free to move (figure NS1.2).

Norheim also introduced the world to the telemark turn. At a competition near Oslo he astounded spectators with a 76-foot (23-meter) jump and stopped himself with a telemark turn at the end. This turn became a viable technique for the long, thin skis used by the Scandinavians. Their skis were designed for travel over flatland and gentle hills; they did not have the side cut that is found on modern skis. The telemark turn was a great breakthrough because it gave the skier more control of the skis in steeper terrain.

FIGURE NS1.1 Mathias Zdarsky, considered the father of the alpine technique, skis using a lurk.

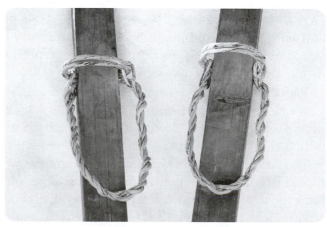

FIGURE NS1.2 Norheim's bindings.

The second historical figure was Fridtjof Nansen. Nansen was an explorer who shocked the world by skiing across Greenland in 1888. Nansen became a national hero and internationally famous. This trip did a great deal to introduce skiing to the rest of the world. Soon, people recognized the recreational and sport opportunities that skiing offered.

Developments in Central Europe   At this time parallel development in ski technique was happening in the central European countries. Although skiing was introduced as a method of transportation of military troops in the high mountain passes, it soon became a recreational activity. Because the terrain in the Alps is much different from the terrain in the Scandinavian countries, the progression of skiing took a different route. For the steep couloirs and high mountain passes, short-radius turns and quick stopping methods were needed. To accommodate these needs, shorter, wider skis began to be developed.

The leading historical figure in the development in the Alps was Austrian Mathias Zdarsky, considered the father of the alpine technique. Zdarsky developed a binding that held the boot to the ski at the toe of the boot (figure NS1.3). This type of binding would not allow the skier to perform a telemark turn, so Zdarsky and others developed the stem christie style of turning, which was better suited for the short-radius turns that they needed.

A bitter feud developed between proponents of the two types of skiing. An Austrian colonel, Georg Bilgeri, further developed the alpine techniques and began to publish his methods. One of Bilgeri's students, Hannes Schnieder, developed a method for teaching alpine techniques and introduced it to ski schools in 1912. At this point the telemark turn began to fall out of favor at ski areas, and the stem christie became the turn for downhill slopes. The split between the two types of skiing began. The style developed by Zdarsky, Bilgeri, and Schnieder was known as the alpine technique, and the style developed by Norheim and Nansen became known as the nordic technique.

Innovation and Change   The innovations in the sport slowed for a time, and little changed in skiing until after World War II. After the war, downhill skiing began to increase in popularity, especially in the United States. Eventually, the equipment went through major modifications. The boot became attached to the ski and offered no heel lift at all. This setup eliminated the use of skis for traveling across the flats and uphills; skiers depended on mechanized ski lifts to get them to the top of the hill so that they then could ski down. Although nordic skiing lost much of its popularity, it never went away. Small groups of people continued to practice it, but its development was slowed by lack of innovation in equipment and the popularity of downhill skiing. Most of the nordic equipment at that time was designed for ski racing. The extremely skinny and lightweight skis were designed for easy day tours on flat or gently sloped terrain.

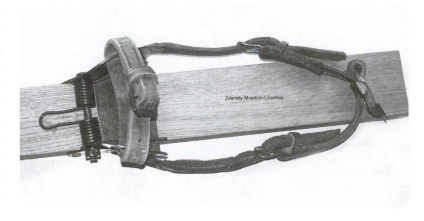

FIGURE NS1.3   Mueller binding.

In the 1970s groups of adventurers in different pockets of the world grew tired of the crowds at ski resorts and began to seek skiing opportunities in the less popular backcountry areas. Thus the rebirth of nordic skiing began. In the beginning, the revival was a rediscovery of old techniques. Eventually, new equipment was developed to fit the techniques better.

Styles of Nordic Skiing   Over time, nordic skiing has developed its own schools and styles. They can be broken down into four main categories: (a) ski racing, (b) ski touring, (c) backcountry skiing, (d) nordic downhill.

Ski racing uses lightweight, skinny skis and running shoe–type boots. This equipment is designed to produce long, smooth glides on flat and gently rolling terrain. Ski racers rarely encounter major changes in the snow because the races are on tracks designed and prepared for that purpose. The skis do not turn as well as wider skis on steep downhill slopes.

Ski touring uses slightly wider skis. They are designed to be used mostly on flat and rolling terrain, but because they are wider, they do not have to be skied on prepared trails. These skis glide well, although they do not produce the long, smooth glides of racing skis. Their advantage is that they turn adequately on moderate slopes.

Backcountry skiing uses skis that are very wide, are slightly shorter, and have metal edges. They are designed to be used off trails and in steep, mountainous country. They turn extremely well on steep slopes but do not glide far or smoothly. The term *backcountry skiing* also implies that the skier is out for extended trips lasting several days, carrying a pack, and often pulling a sled. The rest of this chapter continues to explore the equipment, technique, and styles that make up nordic skiing, in particular backcountry skiing. Figure NS1.4 shows how backcountry skis have developed since the 1950s.

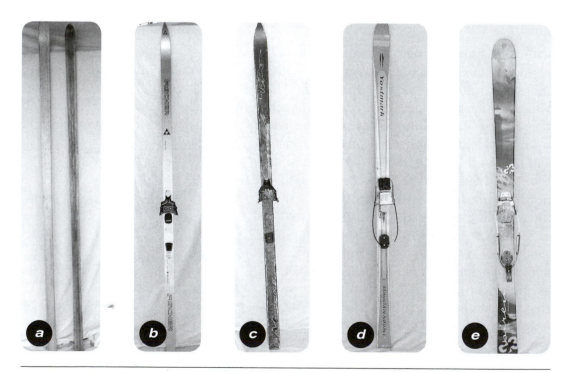

FIGURE NS1.4   Backcountry ski styles of *(a)* the 1950s–1960s, *(b)* the 1970s, *(c)* the 1980s, *(d)* the 1990s, and *(e)* today.

Nordic downhill resembles alpine skiing; it is limited to skiing and turning with free-heel skis at downhill ski areas. The equipment is specialized for making turns on these types of slopes.

Closure Activity

Conference Debate (20 Minutes)

Create a historical ski conference in which Sondre Norheim and his students debate Mathias Zdarsky and his students. Divide the class into two groups. One group can be the students of Sondre Norheim, proponents of the nordic ski movement. The other group can be students of Mathias Zdarsky, proponents of the alpine ski movement. Using information and resources from class, the two groups develop their material and then come together for an international debate on the "right" way to ski. Given enough time, the students can scour used-clothing stores and create period costumes.

Follow-Up Activity

Ski Shop Visit (Time as Needed)

Have your students visit a local ski shop and identify the various types of skis by their characteristics. They should also be able to explain the various construction differences and their uses. This activity is a great review for students who are not that familiar with the various ski types.

ASSESSMENT

- ◆ Verify that students understand the origins of skiing by having them outline the history of the sport in journals.
- ◆ Confirm that students know the history of skiing by administering a written exam covering the material in this section.
- ◆ Check that students can explain the major differences between alpine and nordic skiing by comparing and contrasting the two styles in their journals.
- ◆ Assess whether students appreciate the beauty and grace of both types of skiing by observing their progress throughout the course.

TEACHING CONSIDERATIONS

- ◆ Do this brief overview of skiing as a lecture to introduce the unit.
- ◆ Alternatively, you could provide the information at teachable moments throughout the unit instead of delivering it in one lecture.

UNIT 11, LESSON 2

▷ Backcountry Ski Equipment

OVERVIEW

With the confusing array of gear available today, knowledge of skiing equipment is essential. This lesson focuses on the types of skis and equipment intended for backcountry wilderness travel and aids the student and program provider in selecting the proper equipment.

JUSTIFICATION

Choosing the correct equipment for the type of skiing that a person is going to do is critical to successful skill acquisition and can be considered a risk management decision. Skis are made differently for different types of terrain and environments.

GOAL

To develop students' understanding of the major differences among various kinds of backcountry skis and equipment and to develop their ability to choose equipment appropriate for the intended use.

OBJECTIVES

At the end of this lesson, students will be able to

- understand the differences between the various types of nordic skiing equipment (cognitive);
- understand the need for equipment appropriate for backcountry skiing (cognitive);
- choose a ski of appropriate length for their height, weight, and skiing situation (cognitive);
- understand how to choose and size poles (cognitive);
- understand the safety considerations of ski equipment for the particular type of skiing and ski conditions (cognitive); and
- appreciate the differences in the types of skis and skiing equipment (affective).

EQUIPMENT AND AREAS NEEDED

- Notebooks
- Different types of skis
- Adjustable poles
- Three-pin bindings
- Cable bindings
- Plastic ski boots

RISK MANAGEMENT CONSIDERATIONS

- Cover this lesson before going into the field.
- Because this lesson takes place in an indoor classroom, no risk management considerations other than those appropriate to a traditional classroom setting should be considered.

LESSON CONTENT

Introduction

Different skis serve different purposes, and as the previous lesson explained, there are many types of skiing. Choosing the correct ski equipment is important to learning the skills, having the right ski for the terrain, and in gaining pleasure from the activity.

Important Terms

bindings—Attachments that hold the boot and consequently the foot to the ski.

camber—The amount of curve a ski has along its length.

poles—Aid in balance and in propulsion.

side cut—The difference in width between the tip of the ski and the waist of the ski. The more side cut a ski has, the easier it turns; less side cut means that the ski will run straighter and glide longer.

waist—The portion of the ski directly under the boot.

Main Activity

Getting Familiar With Your Equipment (One Hour)

Equipment decisions should be based on program goals, the type of terrain, and the ski conditions most often encountered. For example, wide skis are made for deep snow and variable snow conditions found in mountainous terrain. They are designed for maximum flotation and superior turning on long descents. By contrast, thin skis with flexible boots allow the skier to ski fast and glide far on flat or gently rolling terrain, but such skis lack turning potential. If a skier is using skinny skis with flexible boots, skiing in mountainous terrain would be difficult and probably a safety concern because those types of skis and boots do not support the ankles, increasing the potential for athletic injury.

Choosing the appropriate skis can be confusing because of the many opinions on the subject. From a program standpoint, the logical approach is to choose skis according to the types of courses most often taught. An outdoor program in the flat and gentle rolling terrain of Minnesota would choose a different type of ski than a program that operates in the steep ups and downs of the Rocky Mountains.

As described in lesson 1, the two main types of skiing are alpine and nordic.

- In alpine skiing the toes and the heels of the boots are locked down. This setup gives superior control while going downhill but makes skiing uphill or across flat terrain difficult.

- In nordic skiing the heel lifts off the ski and does not latch down, and the toe of the boot has some flexibility at the ball of the foot. This setup permits the skier to flex the foot and ankle, allowing the skier to push with the toes and move across flat terrain and up hills easier.

A third type of skiing, randonee, allows the heel to be locked down for downhill travel and released for flat terrain and going uphill.

- In this system the toe pivots where the toe of the boot is attached to the binding.
- This method gives the downhill control of alpine skiing and allows movement for the skier to go uphill and across the flats. The movement with the boot hinged at the front of the boot, however, is not an efficient method for fluid movement because it does not allow the skier to flex the foot and ankle.
- Randonee skiing is suited for mountainous terrain in which the goal is to ski up a slope and then ski down the slope. It is not as well suited for mixed terrain where flat ground is interspersed with ups and downs.

This lesson focuses solely on nordic skiing, skiing in which the heel is never locked down. It focuses on one type of nordic skiing called backcountry skiing.

- Backcountry skiing implies multiday trips traveling off beaten paths, away from groomed trails.
- In this type of skiing the skier usually carries a backpack and often pulls a sled.

Terrain   The terrain is the first thing to consider when choosing equipment for backcountry skiing.

- If the terrain is flat or gently rolling, the type of equipment chosen will resemble the equipment found in traditional ski touring.
- If the terrain is more mountainous like the Rocky Mountains, the equipment will closely resemble that found in nordic downhill.

Length   As a general rule the longer the ski is, the faster and farther it will glide. The disadvantage is that length sacrifices downhill turning efficiency.

- A short, wide ski turns well but is slower and less energy efficient on the flats and up hills.
- For less steep terrain, where normal skiing is flat with low hills, the skier should pick a ski based on his or her height.
- A good way to do this is for the skier to take his or her height in centimeters and add 25 to determine the ski length. For example, a person who is 5-feet-7 would be 67 inches tall, or 170 centimeters. Adding 25 centimeters gives the length of the ski as 195 centimeters.
- If the skier is carrying a heavy pack or the terrain is exceptionally flat, the skis could even be longer.
- For steep mountainous terrain the skier will want to sacrifice some kick and glide for turning ability.
- Nothing is more miserable than falling at every turn with a pack on. At this point the selection of skis leans towards shorter, wider skis with more side cut. With these types of skis the skier is more concerned with weight.
- Skis do not come in as many lengths as they did in the past, so a medium-sized male should choose a medium-sized ski in that make and model. A larger skier should select a slightly longer ski, and a smaller person should choose one that is slightly smaller.
- Many ski manufacturers make skis specifically designed for women. If a women's model is not available, women can follow the recommendations for men by downsizing the men's models.

Width

◆ The wider the ski is, the better it floats in powder snow. A wider ski still turns well, but it suffers in the gliding department.

◆ In steeper terrain a wider ski is better, and in less steep terrain a narrower one is preferred.

Camber   Camber is the curve built into the main body of the ski and relates to stiffness and flex of the ski. Skis have different cambers for different purposes. For backcountry skis both a nordic camber and an alpine camber are available.

◆ Skis with a nordic camber have a portion directly beneath the foot that does not touch the ground under normal body weight (figure NS2.1). The skier waxes that particular part of the ski. Under normal gliding conditions the waxed portion does not make contact with the snow. Instead, the skier must perform a forceful downward kick to get the waxed portion to make contact with the snow. This setup translates into longer glides and faster skis, but it results in less efficient turning because getting the whole ski on the snow to carve a turn is difficult.

◆ A ski with an alpine camber makes contact with the snow under body weight (figure NS2.2). With the whole ski on the snow, glides are shorter and the skis are slower. But these skis turn much easier because the whole ski bottom makes contact with the snow during the turn.

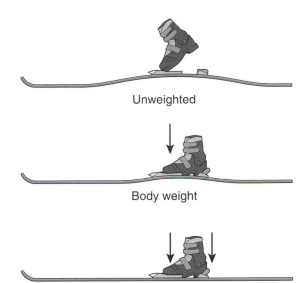

Unweighted

Body weight

Body weight plus extra downward force

FIGURE NS2.1   Nordic camber.

Reprinted, by permission, from Omer & Bob's Sportshop, Hanover, NH.

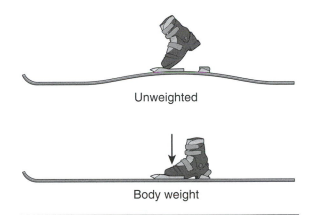

Unweighted

Body weight

FIGURE NS2.2   Alpine camber.

Reprinted, by permission, from Omer & Bob's Sportshop, Hanover, NH.

Edges

◆ All backcountry skis have metal edges that aid in holding to the surface in icy conditions (figure NS2.3).

◆ The metal edges help in turning because they cut into the surface snow, but they are not a substitute for proper technique.

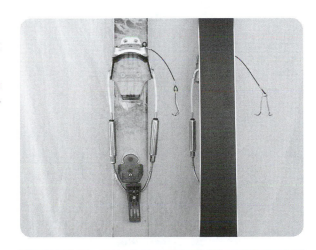

FIGURE NS2.3   Metal edges.

Side Cut

- Side cut (figure NS2.4) used to be referred to as side camber.
- In the 1860s Sondre Norheim cut an arch into the waist of his skis to make a side cut. This feature increased the ability of the ski to turn because when the tips and tails are wider than the waist, an arc is formed when the ski is pushed into the snow (Parker, 2001).
- Skis with less side cut run straighter with less energy than skis with more side cut.
- A skier can glide farther with less energy on skis with little side cut. But these skis do not turn easily, making them less suitable for steep terrain.
- Skis with a lot of side cut turn easily, but getting them to go straight is sometimes difficult. These skis are better suited for steeper terrain, because they will turn quickly with less effort.

Poles

- Adjustable **poles** are desirable (figure NS2.5). When a skier is skiing on the flat and up hills, longer poles aid in propulsion. Long poles may get in the way on downhill runs, however, forcing the skier's arms and upper body up out of the turn.
- If adjustable poles are not available, the skier should pick a medium-length pole for backcountry use.
- A good way to size poles is to stand on flat ground, turn the poles upside down, and grab them just below the baskets (figure NS2.6). The elbow should be bent at a 90-degree angle.

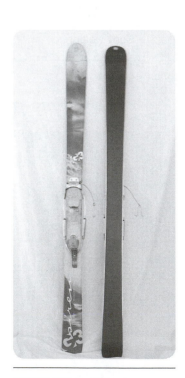

FIGURE NS2.4   Side cut.

FIGURE NS2.5   Adjustable pole.

FIGURE NS2.6   Sizing poles.

Bindings   Two common types of **bindings** are on the market today for backcountry skiing: the three-pin binding and the cable binding.

The three-pin binding has three pins affixed to it. Three holes in the boot fit onto the pins. A bail that fits over the toe and clamps to the ski holds them in place (figure NS2.7).

- The problem with three-pin bindings on extended trips is making sure that the holes and the pins stay securely seated. If they do not, the holes in the boots erode and become useless. Another issue during multiday tours is that the holes ice over.
- This binding is quickly becoming outdated because of a variety of problems, and new types of bindings are being introduced.

The most common binding today is the cable binding that secures the ball of the foot to the ski with a cable that wraps around the heel to provide more torsional rigidity, much like the ones that Norheim invented over 100 years ago (figure NS2.8). Cable bindings offer two distinct advantages over the traditional three-pin binding.

- The problem of pinholes in the boots icing up is eliminated because they are not needed for the binding to work properly.
- The extra torsional rigidity allows for more control over the ski, which transfers to more turning power.

Manufacturers have created a variety of new step-in bindings that allow the skier to step into them much like an alpine ski. They have added a safety feature that allows the binding to release under a predetermined amount of pressure. This feature is worth the investment if the skier has knees susceptible to injury or if she or he skis only at ski areas.

FIGURE NS2.7   Three-pin binding.

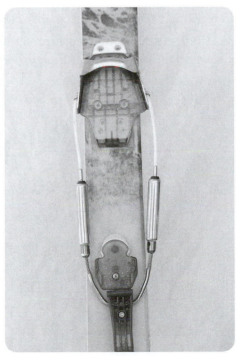

FIGURE NS2.8   Modern cable binding.

Boots Boots are the most important part of the ski system.

◆ Today, most backcountry boots on the market are double plastic.

◆ A double plastic boot has a plastic outer shell and an insulated liner that can be removed for ease of drying (figure NS2.9).

◆ Shells come in different flexibilities. The softer ones are better for gentler terrain, allowing the skier to flex his or her foot more to get a solid kick off the snow, thus allowing a longer glide.

◆ The drawback is that a softer boot loses some stiffness for turning.

◆ Stiffer plastic aids in the turn by transferring more power to the ski but tends to be too stiff for easy kick and glide.

◆ As a rule, the skier needs a stiffer boot for steep backcountry terrain. Not too long ago all ski boots were leather, but good leather boots are difficult to find today.

◆ Leather boots work just as well as plastic boots, but they cost more to manufacture, so most new boots are plastic. Boots that are mixture of leather and nylon are not stiff enough for backcountry use.

Waxless Skis To kick and glide, the bottom of the ski has to grip the snow to provide traction for a push-off. The three ways to do this are to use wax (discussed in lesson 5), climbing skins (discussed in lesson 8), or a ski with a waxless base (discussed here).

◆ Waxless skis have a system of ridges that are angled in a way that gives purchase on the kick and allows smooth movement during the glide (figure NS2.10).

◆ In some spring skiing conditions when snow temperatures and conditions change quickly, these types of skis are easier to use than skis that require waxing and rewaxing.

◆ Many skiers choose these skis because they think that waxing is too complicated, although waxing is not as difficult as many think (discussed in lesson 5).

◆ Waxless skis do not perform as well as waxable skis, because the scales on the bottom slow the ski on the glides and turns.

FIGURE NS2.9 Double plastic backcountry ski boot.

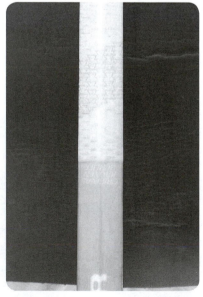

FIGURE NS2.10 Base of a waxless ski.

Closure Activity

Boot Bonanza (Time as Needed)

Have students try on different types of boots and walk around in them. The plastic backcountry boots will feel extremely stiff compared with some of the ski racing boots, which will feel almost like tennis shoes.

Work with a local outdoor retail shop to obtain examples of all types of skis and boots. I arranged to visit a shop after hours so that students could try on the boots and walk around the store.

Follow-Up Activity

Demo Day (Time as Needed)

Make arrangements with a local ski area to do a demonstration day with your students. Make sure that the area has both a cross-country center as well as a downhill area.

* Outfit the students with lightweight cross-country ski gear and have them ski on the prepared tracks and on the beginning slopes of the downhill area. This way they can see how the equipment works in two different situations—one that they were designed for and one that they weren't.

* Next, do the same thing with the heavier ski gear designed primarily for downhill use. Have the students ski on the beginning ski hills and on the cross-country trails.

* The problem with this activity is the cost involved. Most ski areas will charge a fee for this kind of demonstration.

ASSESSMENT

* Verify that students understand the differences between the various types of nordic skiing equipment by having them explain the differences and by having them discuss the advantages and disadvantages of side cut, camber, length, and width.

* Confirm that students understand the need for having appropriate equipment for backcountry skiing by having them discuss how terrain dictates the type of ski to choose. For example, if the terrain is flat or gently rolling, what are the advantages of a long, skinny ski with a stiff camber compared to a short, wide ski with no camber?

* Check that students can choose a ski of appropriate length for their height, weight, and skiing situation by observing them go through the fitting process.

* Confirm that students can choose and size poles by observing them go through the fitting process.

* Confirm that students understand the safety considerations of ski equipment for the particular type of skiing and ski conditions by observing them during the follow-up activity.

* Evaluate whether students appreciate the differences in the types of skis and skiing equipment by observing their actions during the closure and follow-up activities.

TEACHING CONSIDERATIONS

- Any time the subject of equipment comes up, some controversy and confusion will surface.

- The suggestions in this lesson are guidelines for extended backcountry use away from maintained trails.

- Having examples of different types of skis while giving this lesson aids in understanding. Local outdoor shops may loan equipment to use as examples.

- I have had success with following up this lecture with a prearranged visit to a retail store before or after normal store hours. Students could then inspect equipment without interfering with store operations.

- An important advantage of arranging an in-store session is that you do not have to transport the equipment because it is all at the shop.

UNIT 11, LESSON 3

▷ **Preparing to Teach Backcountry Skiing**

OVERVIEW

This lesson focuses on items that you, as the instructor, should know before beginning to teach a unit in backcountry skiing. The emphasis is on skills and preparation that are indirectly related to teaching skiing.

JUSTIFICATION

Backcountry skiing is a strenuous activity that takes place in the winter environment. To keep students safe, you must have experience and education in several areas.

GOAL

To provide the instructor with information associated with teaching backcountry skiing.

OBJECTIVES

At the end of this lesson, you will

- understand the dangers associated with snow avalanches and where to gain the training needed to teach in the winter (cognitive),

- understand the dangers associated with cold-weather environmental injuries (cognitive),

- understand the importance of clothing selection and layering in the winter environment (cognitive),

- understand the importance of physical conditioning for backcountry skiing (cognitive), and

- understand the importance of warming up before and cooling down after any skiing activity (cognitive).

EQUIPMENT AND AREAS NEEDED

- ◆ Notebook
- ◆ Pen or pencil

RISK MANAGEMENT CONSIDERATIONS

- ◆ This lesson should be covered before going into the field.
- ◆ Because this lesson takes place in an indoor classroom, no risk management considerations other than those appropriate to a traditional classroom setting should be considered.

LESSON CONTENT

Introduction

People should not participate in any backcountry skiing activity until they know the basics and the dangers associated with it. However, many people participate without considering the environment in which these activities take place. When teaching in a snow environment, you should focus a significant amount of your effort on managing risk and keeping students safe and comfortable. This lesson presents a number of topics relevant to backcountry skiing. Where appropriate, relevant lessons found elsewhere in this book are noted.

Main Activity

Risk Management Review (20 Minutes or Longer)

For many, exploring the backcountry on skis in winter is an amazing experience. At the same time, you must teach your students that the environment can be dangerous. To have a safe and rewarding trip, proper planning, leadership, and the right equipment are important. In addition, you should consider the following important safety and risk management issues as you prepare to teach backcountry skiing.

Avalanches Avalanches pose the greatest physical threat to the backcountry traveler. If you are teaching winter wilderness travel, you must understand how to travel safely in avalanche terrain, know how to dig test pits and evaluate snow conditions, and carry and know how to use avalanche transceivers. This subject is covered in unit 10, lesson 10, but there is no substitute for actual avalanche training. The American Avalanche Institute Web site (www.avalanchecourse.com) lists providers of avalanche training in the United States and Canada.

Cold-Related Injuries Instructors working in snow and ice environments should be able to detect and treat hypothermia, frostbite, and other cold-related conditions.

- ◆ Hypothermia is an abnormally low body temperature. It needs to be treated when the body temperature drops below 95 degrees Fahrenheit (35 degrees Celsius), and it becomes life threatening when body temperature drops below 90 degrees Fahrenheit (32 degrees Celsius). Signs and symptoms of hypothermia depend on the body temperature. The initial sign is a decrease in mental function, which eventually leads to impaired ability to make decisions. Tiredness or lethargy, changes in speech, and disorientation are typical. These symptoms can give the appearance that the victim is drunk.

- Frostbite is a serious cold-weather injury and occurs when there is freezing of the affected area, usually the hands, feet, nose, or ears. Other parts of the body may also be affected. This type of injury results from decreased blood flow and heat delivery to body tissues, resulting in damaging ice crystal formation.

- Chilblains is a common cold-weather condition that can develop several hours after exposure to extreme cold. Chilblains are itchy, painful, reddish or purplish areas of swelling that usually affect the fingers, toes, nose, or ears; other areas of the body may also be involved.

- Trenchfoot develops after prolonged exposure to a wet, cold environment. Trenchfoot (also known as *immersion foot*) is a medical condition caused by extended exposure of the feet to damp, unsanitary, and cold conditions, usually above 32 degrees Fahrenheit (0 degrees Celsius).

You can find more information on cold-weather safety by reviewing unit 9, lesson 5.

Other Medical Injuries   A variety of other injuries are associated with backcountry skiing (Brewster, 2008). The most common injuries involve the lower extremities, often the knee, and include sprains, fractures, and bruising. Skier's thumb, an upper extremity injury, occurs when the skier falls and the ski pole causes the thumb to extend, stressing the ligament. Nordic skiers also may be susceptible to overuse injuries because of the repetitive nature of the activity. Risk factors for injury consist of a variety of objective (natural environment) and subjective (the skier) factors and may include poor terrain, unsuitable equipment, poor balance, and skiing technique.

Here are some tips to consider for injury prevention:

- Be sure students properly warm up and stretch before skiing. Preseason conditioning and training are also important.

- Students should choose boots that are appropriate for the nordic skiing activity they plan to participate in.

- First-time skiers should get help from a professional when choosing their equipment.

- Pay particular attention to equipment, waxing skis, tread patterns on nonwaxing skis, and snow conditions, which are important factors in reducing injuries.

- Be on the lookout for hazards such as deep tracks, ruts, iciness, and sharp bends.

- Always leave a trip plan with someone.

- Rest, nutrition, hydration, and energy replenishment tend to enhance performance and reduce the likelihood of injury.

It is beyond the scope of this lesson to include treatment and care for all types of injuries. A list of organizations offering wilderness first responder training is included in appendix B.

Clothing   Cold poses a significant danger to anyone participating in snow and ice activities. The best defense is to dress properly and use the right equipment. Even if the day is mild, you should have warm clothes with you in case of trouble. Clothes that work for active exercise in the afternoon may not be warm enough when the weather changes. The time-tested approach to dress for cold-weather activities such as nordic skiing is layering. This system suggests that layers of clothing are better than one thick piece of clothing. Multiple layers provide more insulation and allow you to add or remove items as the exercise level and outside conditions vary. A highly aerobic activity such as nordic skiing can leave your students soaked in sweat. Wet clothing is much less effective in keeping them warm than dry clothing. The beauty of the layering system is that you can remove one or more layers of clothing based on activity level to control your temperature, preventing excessive sweating. Always watch for signs of frostbite on the ears, face, hands, and feet. For additional information on clothing and the layering system, refer to unit 1, lesson 6, and unit 9, lesson 3.

Physical Conditioning, Warm-Ups, and Stretching   Nordic skiing is a demanding activity that burns a lot of calories and requires superior cardiovascular fitness. Having a moderate level of fitness before going into this unit will aid in skill acquisition because you will be able to handle the demanding workload more easily.

- A good warm-up and cool-down are important components of exercise:
  - The warm-up is a low-level activity, such as a slow ski or jog, that should be completed before stretching and more strenuous exercises. The objective of the warm-up is to raise body and muscle temperature, preparing the body for more demanding activities. The warm-up period prepares the cardiovascular, respiratory, nervous, and musculoskeletal systems for more strenuous activity by gradually increasing the demands on these systems.
  - The cool-down period is just as important as the warm-up and provides a number of benefits to the body. These include returning the heart rate to normal, preventing blood from pooling in the muscles, and preventing muscle pain.
- Encourage your students to drink plenty of liquids during and after your sessions to help them stay hydrated or to rehydrate.
- Nordic skiing is a demanding activity that burns a lot of calories. Refer to unit 1, lesson 4, for more information on food and nutrition.
- For ideas on stretching, refer to unit 9, lesson 4.

Closure Activity

Review and Report (30 Minutes)

Have students work in pairs. Each pair selects a risk management concern, reviewing and reporting on their chosen risk. They should highlight the risk, discuss ways to reduce the risk, and explain where students can receive further information and training.

Follow-Up Activity

Fashion Show (20 Minutes)

Bring several items of clothing to class (including cotton, wool, synthetic, and high-tech) that cover the head, legs, and torso. Place the items in a pile on the floor. Have a student wearing a T-shirt and shorts volunteer to be a model. Challenge the other students to dress the model with the right clothing for participating in a backcountry ski outing.

ASSESSMENT

◆ Understand the dangers associated with a snow avalanche and where to gain the training needed to teach in the winter by evaluating students' performances in the closure activity.

◆ Understand the dangers associated with cold weather environmental injuries by evaluating students' performances in the closure activity.

◆ Understand the importance of clothing selection and layering in the winter environment by evaluating students' performance in the follow-up activity.

◆ Understand the physical conditioning in backcountry skiing by asking students what they have been doing to prepare for participation.

◆ Understand the importance of warming up and cooling down before and after skiing activity by having students articulate the importance of the warm-up and cool-down.

TEACHING CONSIDERATIONS

◆ It is beyond the scope of this lesson to delve deeply into each of the areas presented. Certified first aid instructors must teach treatments.

◆ It is your responsibility as an instructor to seek additional training in these areas.

UNIT 11, LESSON 4

▷ Applying the Base Wax

OVERVIEW

Knowledge of waxing is essential in traveling effectively and efficiently in the backcountry on skis. Students learn to apply a basic base wax to their skis, a task that encourages care for the equipment.

JUSTIFICATION

The proper base wax allows skis to glide more efficiently and gives the skier more control over the ski while turning. The base wax also increases the working life of the ski base and allows kick waxes to adhere to the ski. All that students need to know is how to apply the base wax using an iron. Students benefit from having more ownership in the learning process, and they develop an appreciation for care and maintenance of equipment.

GOAL

To develop students' ability to apply a base wax to the bottom of the skis.

OBJECTIVES

At the end of this lesson, students will be able to

- demonstrate the procedure for removing old wax (psychomotor),
- describe the purpose for applying a glide wax to the ski base (cognitive),
- describe the appropriate procedure for applying a glide wax to the ski base (cognitive),
- demonstrate the application of a glide wax (psychomotor), and
- appreciate and value the importance of caring for and maintaining equipment (affective).

EQUIPMENT AND AREAS NEEDED

- Commercial wax remover or denatured mineral spirits, which is less expensive and works well
- Wide-mouth container (for example, an old, clean peanut butter jar)
- A 2- or 3-inch (5- or 7.5-centimeter) paint brush (not an expensive brush)
- Two sawhorses or a long table to lay the skis on
- Plastic sheets or newspaper to place under the skis
- Shop rags
- Vinyl gloves (the kind used when applying finishes to woodwork)
- Safety glasses
- Ski scrapers
- Electric iron (the type used for ironing clothes, preferably with adjustable settings)
- Paraffin or glide waxes
- Ski corks (or corks from wine bottles)

RISK MANAGEMENT CONSIDERATIONS

- Proper ventilation is important when using mineral spirits.
- Safety glasses should be worn to protect the eyes when handling mineral spirits.
- Water should be available for flushing skin or eyes if they come in contact with the mineral spirits.
- Students must exercise caution when handling a hot iron because it will become hot enough to cause burns to the skin.
- Electrical appliances should be grounded and not used in damp or wet areas.
- Scrapers can be sharp and should be used appropriately. Gloves may be in order.
- This lesson involves melting wax with a hot iron. The hot wax can burn the skin.

LESSON CONTENT

Introduction

The base wax serves three purposes:

- It protects the base of the ski and keeps it from becoming brittle, thus increasing the useful life of the ski.
- It allows the ski to glide more efficiently on the snow, thus giving the skier more control over the ski.
- It allows the kick wax to adhere better.

Important Terms

base wax—The wax that is applied to the base of the ski. It serves three functions:
- Allows the ski to glide with less friction over the snow, which gives the skier more control of the ski
- Provides an adherent surface for the kick wax that is applied later
- Protects the base of the ski from oxidation, which increases the functional life of the ski

P-tex—A polyethylene material used to make the base of skis. There are two types: sintered and monolithic. Sintered bases are used on most backcountry skis. They are porous, hold wax better, and can be repaired in the field with candle wax. Monolithic P-tex is nonporous and does not hold wax well.

Main Activities

Activity 1: Strip the Old Wax (10 to 15 Minutes per Pair)

First, strip the old wax from the base of the ski. There are two ways to do this.

- Use the wax scraper to scrape off the wax.
- Apply mineral spirits (or a commercial wax remover) to the base of the ski, let it sit for 30 to 45 seconds, and then scrape off the wax with a scraper and rag.

Scraping works, but getting all the old wax off without damaging the **P-tex** ski base is difficult. Applying mineral spirits removes all the old wax and removes the wax from the pores of the P-tex base.

Follow these steps to remove the old wax:

1. Assure that ventilation is sufficient for handling mineral spirits.
2. Put on the appropriate safety equipment (safety glasses and vinyl gloves).
3. Spread plastic or newspaper under the sawhorses or on the table.
4. Lay the skis with the base up on the sawhorses or table.
5. Pour 1 ounce (30 milliliters) of mineral spirits into the wide-mouth container.
6. Take the 2- or 3-inch (5- or 7.5-centimeter) paintbrush and apply the mineral spirits to each ski base (figure NS4.1a).

7. Apply it liberally so that the mineral spirits stand on the skis, but don't apply so much that it runs all over the floor. Wipe off the excess with a rag (figure NS4.1b).

8. Allow the mineral spirits to sit on the ski for 30 to 45 seconds. It will thicken as it dissolves the wax.

9. Using the plastic ski scraper, scrape the softened wax off the ski base, wiping the scraper frequently on a shop rag (figure NS4.1c).

10. Dry the base of the ski with a shop rag or paper towel.

11. Repeat steps 6 through 10 as needed to remove all the wax.

12. Remember to do both skis.

FIGURE NS4.1　Strip the old wax by (a) applying mineral spirits, (b) wiping off the excess, and (c) scraping off the softened wax.

Activity 2: Apply the Appropriate Base Wax (25 to 35 Minutes per Pair)

Many possibilities are available here. A good deal of time and energy may be spent on deciding which base wax will provide the best performance.

◆ You can buy and apply specially formulated glide waxes to the ski base, but this approach may be cost prohibitive for a program.

◆ An alternative method is to use paraffin. Paraffin can be purchased in the food canning section of most grocery and hardware stores. It provides a hard base that protects the ski bottom, glides smoothly across the coldest snows, and provides good adhesion for the kick wax.

Follow these steps to apply the base wax:

1. Spread the plastic or newspaper under the sawhorses or on the table.
2. Lay the skis with the base up on the sawhorses or table.
3. Plug in the electric iron and set it on the wool setting. If your iron does not have a wool setting, set it at a temperature that melts the paraffin but does not cause it to start to smoke.
4. Take a stick of paraffin and hold it to the base of the hot iron.
5. Hold them both over the base of the skis with the front of the iron 1 to 2 inches (2.5 to 5 centimeters) above the ski base (figure NS4.2a).
6. Dribble the wax on the entire length of the ski.
7. Put the paraffin down and iron the bottom of the ski just as you would a shirt (figure NS4.2b).

8. Keep the iron moving so that the wax becomes spread evenly across the ski base. You do not want to melt the bottom of the ski.
9. After the wax is spread evenly, set the skis aside and allow the wax to harden completely.
10. After the wax has hardened, use the wax scraper to scrape away the excess wax (figure NS4.2c). This is a messy procedure, and wax shavings will go everywhere. It will appear as if you are taking all the wax off.
11. After scraping off the excess wax, take the cork and rub it vigorously over the bottom of the ski (figure NS4.2d). The rubbing assures that the wax adheres to the ski base and spreads it evenly across the base of the ski.
12. Remember to do both skis.

FIGURE NS4.2 Apply the base wax by (a) dribbling melted wax on the ski base, (b) ironing the base, (c) scraping off the excess, and (d) corking the base.

Closure Activity

Waxing Inspections (10 Minutes)

Have students inspect other students' skis for adequate waxing. Have them focus on the smoothness of the wax.

◆ The ski bottom should appear somewhat glossy and should not have splotches of wax.

◆ Another thing to look for is too much wax. The goal is to have just a thin layer of base wax. One way to check for this is to scrape a fingernail against the base; the fingernail should remove just a very thin layer of wax.

Follow-Up Activity

Waxing Tests (10 Minutes)

If snow is on the ground where this lesson is taking place, have one person put on a pair of skis and have another pull the skier around with an old rope.

◆ If the skis glide across the snow, the base wax has been applied well.

◆ If the skis stick to the snow, more scraping and corking is necessary.

ASSESSMENT

◆ Check that students can demonstrate the procedure for removing old wax by observing them go through the appropriate steps to remove old wax from their skis.

◆ Confirm that students can describe the purpose of applying a glide wax to the ski base by having them outline this process in their journals.

◆ Verify that students can describe the appropriate procedure for applying a glide wax to the ski base by observing them go through the appropriate steps to prepare their skis.

◆ Check that students can demonstrate the application of a glide wax by observing them apply the glide wax to their skis.

◆ Assess whether students appreciate and value the importance of caring for and maintaining their equipment by observing how they treat and maintain it.

TEACHING CONSIDERATIONS

This lesson gives the students a sense of ownership in their equipment. The activities can be time consuming, however, and if sufficient materials are not available some students may end up standing around. You can prevent this from happening in several ways:

◆ Have students pair up and share equipment.

◆ Irons can be found at secondhand stores at modest cost.

◆ Paraffin is inexpensive.

◆ Demonstrate on a pair of skis in class, then have students meet with you outside regularly scheduled class time to wax their skis.

▷ Applying the Kick Wax

OVERVIEW

Proper waxing is essential for effective and efficient travel in the backcountry on skis. In this lesson the students learn about various waxing systems and how to choose and apply the appropriate one for their particular situation. Knowing how to wax a ski makes skiing in the winter backcountry more enjoyable and efficient.

JUSTIFICATION

Many people are mystified and slightly apprehensive about waxing their skis, so they tend to use waxless skis or climbing skins. Although both methods work, they limit the backcountry traveler's choices and do not allow optimum efficiency. Knowledge of waxing allows the backcountry skier more flexibility in the terrain to cover and more efficient skiing. All that the skier really needs to know is the temperature of the snow and how to apply the appropriate wax.

GOAL

To develop students' ability to choose and apply the appropriate kick wax based on current snow conditions.

OBJECTIVES

At the end of this lesson, students will be able to

- describe the purpose of applying a kick wax to the ski base (cognitive),
- differentiate between the types of waxes for skis (cognitive),
- compare and contrast different waxing systems and chose the appropriate one for the current conditions and situation (cognitive),
- decide on the appropriate wax for the current conditions (cognitive),
- decide on the appropriate wax technique for conditions and situation (cognitive),
- demonstrate the procedure for removing old wax (psychomotor),
- demonstrate the appropriate application of kick waxes (psychomotor), and
- appreciate and value the independence and flexibility that knowledge of waxing provides (affective).

EQUIPMENT AND AREAS NEEDED

- Journal and pen
- Ski scrapers
- Small piece of chamois cloth
- Ski corks (corks from wine bottles will work)
- Kick wax kit
- Stem thermometer (not a necessity but does make it easier to determine the appropriate wax)

RISK MANAGEMENT CONSIDERATIONS

- Take appropriate precautions for environmental hazards at the teaching site such as dead trees and tree limbs.
- Because skiing is a winter activity and waxing is not a task that generates much warmth, pay extra attention to air temperature and wind exposure. Make sure that all students are warm and wearing adequate clothing.
- Be sure that students are properly nourished and hydrated for extended class time.
- Wax scrapers and most ski edges are sharp, so students must use caution to avoid cutting their hands.
- Ensure proper spacing between students. Skis are long, and students can easily hit a person behind them with a ski.

LESSON CONTENT

Introduction

To apply kick wax properly, students must know about the parts of the ski: tips, tails, and kick zone.

- The ski tip is the front of the ski where guide wax is applied.
- The ski tail is the back of the ski where glide wax is applied.
- The kick zone is the area beneath the binding where kick wax is applied.

Because of the camber (curve) of the ski, skis glide when the skier's full weight is not put on the ski. When the skier's full weight is applied, the kick wax sticks to the snow, increasing traction.

Explain these important items to consider when waxing:

- For cold, new snow with sharp crystals, use a harder (colder) wax.
- For warmer or older snow with rounded crystals, use a softer (warmer) wax.
- Warmer waxes can be applied to colder waxes, but cold waxes cannot be applied to warmer waxes. (To make the point, mention that you can put jelly on peanut butter but you can't put peanut butter on jelly.)
- If you start with a warmer wax, you must scrape it off before applying a colder wax.
- Wax skis as much as necessary to create efficient movement.
- Proper waxing allows the ski to grip the snow when it needs to and to glide when it needs to. This circumstance makes skiing more energy efficient and pleasurable.

Important Terms

tail—The end of the ski that is flat against the snow.

tip—The front of the ski that has a slight upward curve.

wax pocket—A place on the ski bottom right below the foot where the skier places wax. The weight of the foot on the ski engages the wax with the snow.

◆ Ski waxes are a mixture of hard paraffin and softer resins. More paraffin in a wax makes it harder. The wax therefore sticks less and glides more. More glycerin in the wax lets it stick to the snow and allows for a better kick (push-off) with the ski.

◆ Waxes are made for different snow temperatures.

◆ Waxes for cold, new snow have more paraffin and are harder. The new snow crystals are sharp and can penetrate the wax just enough to allow the skis to grip the snow.

◆ For warmer or old snow, the waxes have more resin and are softer. The snow crystals are not as sharp, but they can penetrate the softer wax.

◆ If you use a warmer wax on a cold day, the snow will stick to the base of the ski and turn them into glorified snowshoes.

◆ If you use a colder wax on warm snow, you will feel as if you are walking on ice in a pair of smooth-soled shoes; you will have no traction and do a lot of slipping and sliding.

◆ To make it easier, wax manufacturers have color coded the wax to correspond to respective temperature ranges (table NS5.1). Colder colors like green and blue correspond to colder snow temperatures. Warmer colors such as red and purple correspond to warmer snow temperatures.

TABLE NS5.1   Wax Chart

Wax	Hardness	Temperature	Snow
Green	Hardest	+5° F (−15° C)	New snow—cold with sharp crystals; very dry (will not make a snowball).
Blue	Medium	+23° F (−5° C)	New snow—cold with sharp crystals; it is still dry but can be compressed (but will not make a snowball).
Purple	Soft/Sticky	+32° F (0° C)	Old snow—warm with rounded crystals (makes a great snowball).
Red	Softer/Stickier	+37° F (+3° C)	Old snow—rounded crystals; very wet (makes a very slushy snowball).
Klister	Softest/Stickiest	+41° F (+5° C)	Old, very wet snow and slush—round grains; very wet (more suitable for making a slushee, not a snowball).

Main Activities

Activity 1: Choosing the Wax (5 to 10 Minutes)

◆ How cold is the snow? If possible, take its temperature using a stem thermometer. If that is not possible, you can use other methods to determine snow temperature. For example, can you make a snowball? Does the snow make a squeaky sound when squeezed? If you can make a snowball, the snow is warm snow; if not, it is a colder snow.

◆ How new is the snow? If snow is falling or has fallen recently, it will have sharper crystals and require a harder wax. If the snow has been on the ground for a few days, it will have round points and require a softer wax.

- Start with the coldest wax that will work, because starting with a hard wax and moving to a softer wax is easier than going the other way.
- If you start with a wax that proves to be too soft, you will have to scrape it off the ski before you apply the harder wax.
- How much grip will you need? The heavier the load is, the more wax you will need.

Activity 2: Waxing the Ski (15 to 20 Minutes)

After considering all this information, apply the wax.

- Starting with the hardest wax, set your ski so that the tail is in the snow and the tip is pointing in the air.
- Start by waxing the part of the ski that is directly under your foot. This part of the ski is often called the wax pocket. On some skis an area is actually marked as the wax pocket.
- If you are carrying a heavy load or pulling a sled, wax the ski farther up and down toward the tip and tail.

Many methods can be used to apply the wax.

- Start by rubbing the wax all over the bottom of the ski, much in the way that a young child would use a crayon in a coloring book (figure NS5.2a).
- After waxing the ski, take the cork and rub it vigorously up and down on the wax (figure NS5.2b). This action heats the wax and allows it to stick to the base of the ski. After corking, the wax heats up and becomes soft.
- Most backcountry skiers do not consider corking an important step. They just put on the ski and take off. The thinking is that the snow will smooth down the kick wax and that because the conditions are variable in the backcountry, corking does not accomplish much in the way of performance.
- After corking, put the skis in the snow and let the wax reach snow temperature before putting on the skis and taking off.
- If the ski is slipping underfoot, you applied a wax meant for colder snows. If this happens pick a wax that is slightly softer (meant for warmer snows) and apply it just as before.
- On the other hand, if snow is sticking to the ski and prohibiting glide, you applied a wax that is too soft for the snow. To fix this problem, scrape off all the old wax and then apply a harder one for the conditions. Refer to lesson 4 for more details about stripping off wax.
- After scraping off the old wax apply the harder wax just as before.

FIGURE NS5.2   Apply the kick wax by *(a)* rubbing the wax all over the base and *(b)* rubbing the cork vigorously over the wax.

Closure Activity

Wax Test (10 Minutes or More)

Ski a while to get a feel for how the wax is performing.

◆ If the skis are slipping underfoot when weighted, you need a softer wax.

◆ If the skis are sticking or the glide is limited, a harder wax is in order.

Follow-Up Activity

Beginning Ski Techniques (Time as Needed)

When the skis are waxed correctly, go right into the next lesson on beginning ski techniques.

ASSESSMENT

◆ Verify that students can describe the sequence of waxes from hard wax to soft wax by outlining the sequence in their journals.

◆ Confirm that students can explain the differences between the types of kick waxes for skis by randomly picking students and asking them to explain the differences between the various types of kick waxes.

◆ Check that students can describe when and why a skier would increase the area of the wax pocket of the ski by randomly picking students and asking them to describe the reasons for increasing the ski's wax pocket.

◆ Confirm that students can compare and contrast different waxing systems by having them outline each of the waxing systems presented.

◆ Verify that students can demonstrate the appropriate application of kick waxes by observing them choose the appropriate wax and apply it to the ski.

◆ Check that students can select the appropriate wax for the current conditions by observing them make choices.

◆ Confirm that students can decide on the appropriate wax technique for conditions and situations by observing the wax technique that they use to meet current snow conditions and situations.

◆ Assess whether students demonstrate the ability to choose the appropriate wax for current conditions by observing them go through the process.

◆ Check that students have the ability to apply wax to the bottom of the ski by observing them wax their skis.

TEACHING CONSIDERATIONS

◆ You can demonstrate the bulk of this class in the classroom the day before the field session. A quick review before the students start skiing minimizes the amount of time standing around in the cold.

◆ Watch technique closely. Skis slipping underfoot can be the result of poor technique, not improper wax.

◆ Have a selection of each type of wax on hand, so that more than one student can wax at one time. That way, no one will not have to stand around too long in the cold.

▷ **Beginning Skiing Techniques**

OVERVIEW

Knowledge of proper skiing techniques is essential for safe, efficient travel in the winter wilderness. In this lesson students learn and practice fitting of skis and poles, balancing on skis, standing turns, and getting up from falls.

JUSTIFICATION

Many people who try skiing in the backcountry give up quickly because they find the activity difficult. By learning the proper techniques in a logical progression, beginning students avoid frustration and build a strong foundation that allows them to move to the next level.

GOAL

To develop students' ability to perform proper foundational skiing techniques.

OBJECTIVES

At the end of this lesson, students will be able to

* summarize the purpose of achieving competency in basic balance and falling skills (cognitive);
* describe how to grip the poles (cognitive);
* explain why they grip the poles in a particular way (cognitive);
* demonstrate (psychomotor) the correct way to
    - put on the skis,
    - grip the poles,
    - get up from a fall,
    - assume an athletic stance for skiing,
    - do a wheel turn on skis,
    - do a kick turn on skis, and
    - perform the shuffle method of skiing;
* develop confidence in standing and balancing on skis (affective and psychomotor); and
* appreciate and value the independence and flexibility that proper technique provides (affective).

EQUIPMENT AND AREAS NEEDED

* Skis, boots, and poles for each participant
* Appropriate waxes for the conditions

RISK MANAGEMENT CONSIDERATIONS

- Take appropriate precautions for environmental hazards at the teaching site such as dead trees and tree limbs.

- Because skiing is a winter activity, devote extra attention to air temperature and wind exposure. Make sure that all students are warm and are wearing the proper clothing.

- Be sure that students are properly nourished and hydrated for extended class time.

- The teaching area should be flat and free of obstructions. Beginning skiers fall frequently and tend to have little control over their skis. A flat area eliminates the need to know uphill and downhill techniques.

- Ensure proper spacing between students. Skis are long, and students can easily hit a person behind them with a ski. In addition, beginning skiers fall frequently.

LESSON CONTENT

Introduction

A useful teaching ploy is to introduce an experience that you had when learning a particular skill. Here is an example of one that I use. When I was in second grade I checked out a library book about famous people of the American West. In it was a short story about Snowshoe Thompson, who carried the mail across snow-covered mountains wearing skis. I was fascinated by this story and the idea of gliding across the snow on skis. The next Christmas my family went to visit my grandparents in Chicago. It was cold there and the snow was deep, especially to someone just 4 feet (120 centimeters) tall. My grandpa had a keg of nails sitting on his back porch, and I noticed how the wooden slats of the keg curved like Snowshoe Thompson's skis. I dumped out all the nails and dismantled the keg. When I got the slats apart I took two of them, tied them to my rubber snow boots, and headed out to the snow. I tried to ski down into a small ditch and sunk in up to my waist. I was stuck solid and couldn't move at all. I finally started to cry, and my grandpa came and pulled me out. My new skis and rubber boots stayed in the ditch, because we couldn't get them out!

The basic points of this lesson are the following:

- Putting skis on correctly
- Gripping the poles correctly
- Becoming familiar and comfortable with skis
- Getting up from a fall
- Basic step standing turns

Main Activities

Many students are apprehensive about skiing for the first time. This lesson helps students gain confidence in their ability to control their skis in a safe learning environment.

Activity 1: Orienting and Putting on the Skis (10 Minutes)

- There is a right ski and a left ski.
- When bindings are mounted on a ski, they are measured and mounted with the boot in place so that the inside edge of the binding is more closely parallel with the inside edge of the ski.

- Most bindings indicate a right and a left. Sometimes the indicator is just a hole in the binding that is used to attach a safety strap that goes from the ski to the skier, so that the ski will not slide down a hill if it comes off. This hole is always on the outside edge of the binding.
- Sometimes the indicator is an arrow on the ski that points to the outside edge. Sometimes a footprint on the binding indicates the right or left ski.
- When inserting the boot into the ski, be sure to line up the toe of the boot properly with the binding.
- Make sure to remove all snow and ice from the binding and the boot.
- Place the toe of the boot as far up into the binding as possible before closing the cable device.
- If your students have three-pin bindings (as discussed in lesson 2), make sure that the pins in the bindings are lined up with the holes in the boots before engaging the bail.
- After putting on the skis check for excessive play between the boot and the binding. Do this by leaving the ski flat on the ground and trying to force the heel of the boot sideways. If the boot moves in the binding it needs to be tightened because excessive play between the boot and binding reduces control over the ski.

Activity 2: Putting on the Poles (Five Minutes)

- Each pole has an adjustable strap that can be tightened or loosened depending on hand size or for accommodating gloves or mittens.
- Putting the poles on properly is somewhat counterintuitive. Start by bringing the hand up from the bottom of the strap. The hand then grips the pole with the strap resting between the thumb and forefinger.
- The straps must fit securely around the wrist to allow the poles to be used properly.

Activity 3: Warm-Up and Stretching (10 to 15 Minutes)

The goal of these initial activities is threefold:

- To familiarize students with the feel of the skis and how to control them
- To serve as warm-up and stretching exercises
- To introduce the concept of weighting and unweighting the skis

These warm-ups and stretches are a good way to start each of the skill-based lessons because they aid in the development of fundamental skills.

- With the feet about shoulder-width apart and the poles planted in the snow next to the feet (that is, with the right pole about 6 inches, or 15 centimeters, from the right ski and the left pole 6 inches, or 15 centimeters, from the left ski), slide one ski forward about 8 to 12 inches (20 to 30 centimeters) and then back. Alternate from one ski to the other, performing 10 to 15 slides with each.
- Starting with the skis shoulder-width apart, move the right ski forward until the left knee is touching the left ski. Then come back to a standing position. Alternate from one ski to the other, and perform this 10 or 15 times for each leg. Point out to the students how much fore and aft stability they have in this position.
- Now the leg muscles should be warmed up. Repeat the previous exercise but push the forward leg as far as possible and hold the stretch for 15 to 20 seconds. Muscles obtain a more useful stretch after they are warm. Do this stretch three times on each side.

◆ This next warm-up serves two purposes. First, it warms up the muscles in preparation for skiing. Second, it introduces the concept of unweighting the ski, a technique that will be used in later lessons. Place both poles in the snow to the side. With the skis on flat ground, flex at the knees and then stand up again. Do this several times. Start slow and then gain speed, doing the exercise faster and more powerfully.

◆ As students gain speed and power, some of them will jump high enough to take their skis completely off the ground. At this point have all the students jump off the ground with both skis leaving the snow surface.

◆ Using the poles for balance in all the activities is OK.

◆ Then repeat the entire sequence without poles.

Activity 4: Falling and Getting Up (10 Minutes)

Falling is inevitable. Students should know how to fall and how to get up from a fall.

◆ On steeper slopes, knowing how to fall properly is helpful because falling with control is almost always safer than continuing to ski out of control and crashing.

◆ Learning to fall correctly can help prevent injuries that often result from skiing out of control.

◆ If at all possible, the best way to fall is in a sitting position just off to one side, preferably the uphill side.

◆ Practicing falling eases some of the anxiety that students might feel when they realize how close to the ground they can get before they fall.

◆ Getting up can be tricky with 5-foot (150-centimeter) skis attached to the feet, especially on a hill or in deep powder. Getting up can also be difficult if skis are tangled.

Have students practice both falling and getting up.

◆ Starting with the skis about shoulder-width apart, bend your knees until you are squatting over your skis. Then just fall to the side.

◆ Concentrate on falling onto the snow, not onto your skis.

◆ To practice getting up, roll over onto your back and get the skis in the air to untangle them. Then roll to the side (the downhill side if on a hill) and bring your legs underneath you so that your center of gravity is over the skis. Stand up, using the poles if necessary.

◆ In deep, powdery snow, follow the same procedure, but cross your poles in the snow so that they form an X (figure NS6.1). Push up on the center of the crossed poles, which provides a solid platform to push on and allows you to get your center of gravity over the skis.

Activity 5: Standing Turns (30 Minutes)

Practicing standing turns aids in balance and control over the skis, increases flexibility, and continues to build a foundation for more advanced skills.

Tip Wheel Turns

◆ With the tips of the skis together but not touching, pick up the right ski and move the tail about 6 to 8 inches (15 to 20 centimeters). Then pick up the left ski and move it to the right one, always keeping the tips together.

FIGURE NS6.1   After a fall in deep, powdery snow, *(a)* cross your poles, *(b)* push up on the center of the crossed poles, and *(c)* stand back up.

◆ Continue to do this until you have made a complete circle and are facing the way you started. The pattern that you made in the snow looks somewhat like a wagon wheel.

◆ Do this several times in each direction. (This exercise aids in becoming accustomed to controlling skis and develops a foundation for teaching a basic snowplow, or **wedge**, turn).

Tail Wheel Turns   This turn is done the same way as the tip turn except that the tails stay together while the tips move in a circle. (This exercise aids in becoming accustomed to managing skis and develops a foundation for teaching the herringbone method of climbing short hills).

Kick Turns

◆ This invaluable backcountry skiing skill is often used when traversing steep hills and negotiating descents that are beyond a skier's abilities.

◆ When turning to the right, place both poles on the left side of the skis, one at the tip and one at the tail.

◆ Bring the right leg up so that the ski is perpendicular to the ground. The tail will be resting on top of the snow, but do not let it sink into the snow.

◆ Now swing the tip of the right ski so that it is facing the opposite direction. The tail of the left ski and the tip of the right ski should be facing the same direction.

◆ Now swing the left ski around until the two tips are facing the direction that you want to go.

◆ You will have to lift your poles from the snow at the same time or you will hit them with your skis.

◆ Practice the kick turn going right and left until you can perform it without falling.

Shuffle   The shuffle is actually the beginning movement of the diagonal stride, though not as refined. The technique involves simply weighting one ski and then sliding the other ski forward. Students will build additional skills on this foundational skill.

◆ Students weight the left ski by shifting the center of gravity to that ski and sliding the right ski forward.

- ◆ They then transfer their weight to the right ski and slide the left ski forward.
- ◆ Have the students try to walk in a straight line by shifting their weight from one ski to the other without lifting their skis from the ground.
- ◆ Practice this until most people can move around without falling down too much.

Closure Activity

Giants, Wizards, and Elves (15 Minutes)

A fun closure activity for this lesson is a game of Giants, Wizards, and Elves, an old elementary school playground game used as team-building exercise. The game involves chasing and fleeing on skis and includes a lot of falling. The beauty of this game is that students can practice all the skills that they worked on in the lesson in a gamelike situation. A great deal of laughter always ensues.

The important thing to remember is spacing. Participants need to be about one and a half ski lengths apart.

Setup

- ◆ Draw a line in the snow to divide your meadow into two areas.
- ◆ Divide the class into two teams and have one team on each side of the line.
- ◆ Mark a line in the snow on each side about 50 feet (15 meters) from the middle line.
- ◆ Teach the actions for a giant, a wizard, and an elf (see the following section).
- ◆ Have the two teams stand with their skis about 5 feet (150 centimeters) from the line.
- ◆ Demonstrate the three signs that students will need to know. Explain that giants chase wizards, wizards chase elves, and elves chase giants. Be sure that the class understands this progression. The goal of the activity is for each group to win members from the other groups until only one group remains.

Rules

- ◆ A giant stands on tiptoes, keeps arms raised overhead, and gives loud roars. Demonstrate and have students practice.
- ◆ A wizard stands on one foot, puts his or her hands in front of him or her, wiggles his or her fingers, and says, "Shazaam!" Demonstrate and have students practice.
- ◆ An elf squats down, puts his or her hands behind his or her head, and yells, "Tweedle, tweedle, tweedle." Of course, an elf uses a squeaky voice.
- ◆ Demonstrate, and have students practice.
- ◆ Each group huddles together and decides which sign they will make, indicating their group (either a giant, a wizard, or an elf). All members of each team agree to make the same sign. Give them 45 seconds to do this.
- ◆ Have the students return to within 5 feet (150 centimeters) of the middle line. On the count of 3, the two groups show their signs simultaneously.
- ◆ The group that becomes the chasers (based on their sign and the sign of the other group) tries to tag those fleeing before they ski to safety behind their line.

- If tagged, those fleeing join the chasing group. For example, group A shows wizards as their sign, and group B shows elves. Group A becomes the chasers and group B becomes those fleeing. Any of the group B students who are tagged must join the A team.
- If the groups give the same sign, they return to their safety zones and select another.
- After each round, groups should reassemble behind their lines to pick another sign. The game continues until only one group remains or it is time to stop.

Follow-Up Activity

Ski Tag (20 Minutes)

- Have students play a game of tag while on their skis (no ski poles).
- Remember to set and enforce boundaries.
- This is a great aerobic activity and a good way to lead into the next lesson.

ASSESSMENT

- Have students explain in course notebooks or journals, in written exams, or through class dialogue the importance of learning to fall correctly.
- Have students explain in course notebooks or journals, in written exams, or through class dialogue why these foundational skills are important in learning to ski.
- Check that students can demonstrate the correct way to put on skis by observing them during the lesson.
- Verify that students can demonstrate the proper way to grip the poles by observing them during the lesson.
- Confirm that students can demonstrate an athletic stance on skis by observing them during the lesson.
- Ensure that students can demonstrate how to get up from a fall by observing them during the lesson.
- Check that students can demonstrate the wheel turn with the tips together in both directions by observing them during the lesson.
- Verify that students can demonstrate the wheel turn with the tails together in both directions by observing them during the lesson.
- Confirm that students can demonstrate the kick turn in both directions by observing them during the lesson.

TEACHING CONSIDERATIONS

- This first lesson on skis generally lasts from 60 to 90 minutes. After allowing the students a short break, I usually move on to the diagonal stride (the next lesson in the progression).
- Keep a close watch on spacing. Skis and poles are on the feet and in the hands of inexperienced skiers, and people could be hurt by an errant ski or pole.

- Keep the atmosphere light and humorous. These skills may seem basic to adult learners, and they may become bored. To keep their interest, go fast, laugh, and emphasize that these are important foundational skills.

- Think of other simple games that incorporate the skills. I often play Simon Says with the part of the class that deals with turns and falling down.

- This lesson introduces several important concepts. The most important is the weighting and unweighting of skis. This concept is critical for more advanced techniques. Taking the time to practice these basic skills builds the foundation for future success.

UNIT 11, LESSON 7

▷ **The Diagonal Stride**

OVERVIEW

Knowledge of proper skiing techniques is essential for safe and efficient travel in the winter wilderness. In this lesson students build on the foundation of the previous lesson and learn the diagonal stride, an efficient way of traveling on skis in winter.

JUSTIFICATION

The diagonal stride, the classic method of skiing in the backcountry, is an efficient means of traveling long distances carrying a pack or pulling a sled.

GOAL

To develop students' ability to use the diagonal stride and ski efficiently over flat terrain.

OBJECTIVES

At the end of this lesson, students will be able to

- summarize the purpose of achieving competency in basic balance and falling skills (cognitive);

- explain how the diagonal stride technique allows for micro rests with each stride (cognitive);

- explain why the diagonal stride technique is critical in developing efficient movement in the winter backcountry environment (cognitive);

- appreciate the beauty and efficiency of the diagonal stride (affective); and

- demonstrate (psychomotor)
    - the proper kick with the weighted ski,
    - the proper glide that begins with the unweighted ski,
    - shifting weight from one ski to another,
    - contralateral poling while skiing, and
    - the step turn while moving on skis.

EQUIPMENT AND AREAS NEEDED

- Skis, boots, and poles for each student
- Appropriate waxes for the conditions

RISK MANAGEMENT CONSIDERATIONS

- Take appropriate precautions for environmental hazards at the teaching site such as dead trees and tree limbs.
- Because skiing is a winter activity, pay extra attention to air temperature and wind exposure. Make sure that all students are warm and are wearing the proper clothing.
- Be sure that students are properly nourished and hydrated for extended class time.
- The teaching area should be flat and free of obstructions. Beginning skiers fall frequently and tend to have little control over their skis. A flat area eliminates the need to know uphill and downhill techniques.
- Ensure proper spacing between students. Skis are long, and students can easily hit a person behind them with a ski. In addition, beginning skiers fall frequently.

LESSON CONTENT

Introduction

Students usually enjoy hearing about your personal experiences. Here is an example of a story from my past that I use to help students feel comfortable about learning these complex psychomotor skills. As a student at Southwest Missouri State University, I was trying to figure out how to expand my backpacking to the winter months. I stumbled upon an old pair of wooden cross-country skis, bamboo poles, and funny-looking boots at a garage sale. I bought them, figuring that this equipment was just what I needed to explore the Ozarks in the winter. The boots were big, but with three pairs of socks they would work. Being young and invincible I did not even consider trying them out before I went on a trip. Following the first good snowfall I headed to Arkansas and the Buffalo River. Arriving at the trailhead I put on my skis and backpack, grabbed the poles and took off. I got a few feet from the car before falling flat on my back. I rolled over to my side and attempted to stand up. As I was getting up I put all my weight on one of the poles. It snapped in half, and down I went again. With some tape and the aid of an aluminum can, I repaired the pole and started off again. But my skis wouldn't cooperate. They were sliding all over the place. If not for the poles, I would have been on my face! I struggled across a flat area and started up a small hill, with disastrous results. I've never felt so helpless. Skiing uphill was impossible. If not for the poles, standing up would have been equally impossible. Eventually, I broke the other pole, got frustrated, took the skis off, and walked back to the car. As I drove away I thought that I would try snowshoes next!

The basic points of this lesson are the following:

- Progressing from the shuffle to the **diagonal stride**
- The step turn
- Using poles effectively

> ## Important Terms
>
> **glide**—The restful part of skiing. The skier leaves the ski on the snow and allows it to glide after kicking off with the other ski.
>
> **kick**—Weighting one ski so that the wax pocket makes contact with snow, giving traction to push off.
>
> **unweighting**—Shifting the center of gravity to take weight off the ski temporarily.
>
> **weighting**—Shifting the center of gravity to place pressure on the ski.

Main Activities

In this lesson, students progress from the shuffle technique of lesson 6 to the diagonal stride. The goal is to gain efficiency in kicking and gliding with the skis. Kicking and gliding are the foundational aspects of the diagonal stride; the technique is often referred to as the kick and glide.

- The kick is the forceful weighting of the ski that engages the wax, which permits enough purchase to push off the snow and allows the glide to happen on the other ski.

- When a skier kicks with one ski, the motion transfers the weight to the opposite ski, which initiates the glide, causing the ski to slide smoothly over the snow. The more powerful and efficient the kick is, the longer the glide is.

- The glide has two important functions: (a) It allows the skier to cover long distances with less energy expenditure, and (b) it gives the skier a micro rest between each stride.

- The length of the glide varies and depends on many variables such as snow conditions, wax, ski type, and technique. The length of glide can be anywhere from 4 to 10 feet (1.2 to 3 meters) or sometimes even longer.

- The micro rest allows a skier to cover greater distances while expending less energy. These rests add up toward the end of the day and can mean the difference between being exhausted or having energy when reaching camp.

Activity 1: Creating a Teaching Site (10 Minutes)

Find an area that is free from ski tracks, relatively flat, and free from obstructions such as trees. The idea is to create a rectangular practice track that is approximately 50 yards (meters) by 20 yards (meters).

- An easy way to do this is to have the students get in a single file behind you and use the shuffle to create the track. This activity has the bonus of serving as a warm-up for the lesson.

- The dimensions are not rigid, just guidelines. You just need enough room to allow the students an adequate ski run and to provide enough space between skiers to be safe.

- Leave the center of the rectangle unmarked by skis because it will be used later in the lesson.

Activity 2: Review (10 Minutes)

If more than a few hours have passed since lesson 6, review the important points from that lesson, ending with the shuffle. Doing this provides an adequate warm-up, incorporates stretching, and provides cognitive and psychomotor reinforcement of the skills.

Activity 3: Kick and Glide (20 Minutes)

The kick and glide is the basic technique that propels the skier forward.

◆ Leave the poles behind for the beginning of this lesson.

◆ Start with the shuffle step and create a steady rhythm of transferring your weight from the right to the left.

◆ During the weight transfer, place your weight down hard on the right ski, kick backward, and then transfer the weight to the gliding (left) ski. The result will be a longer glide than that gained in the shuffle.

◆ A key point to remember is that the initial weighting of the ski must be down, not back. Placing your weight down allows the wax to make solid contact with the snow, providing traction for the backward kick. If the initial weighting is back, the weighted ski will slide out from under you.

◆ Let yourself glide until you come to a stop. Then kick with the left ski and glide to a stop. Repeat this sequence until you get a solid feel for the movement.

◆ Once you get the idea of the kick and glide, initiate the kick before you come to a complete stop.

◆ Keep skiing around the track until you develop a sense of rhythm in the movement.

Activity 4: Step Turn (15 Minutes)

The step turn is a simple moving turn and an essential skill. The step turn is used to maneuver around objects in the trail and to descend slopes that are too steep for the skier's ability. The skier simply step turns slightly uphill while traversing the slope.

◆ Practice turning left by shifting all your weight to the right ski, lifting the left ski up, and placing it in the direction that you want to go.

◆ Next, place all your weight on the left ski, pick up the right ski, and place it next to the left one.

◆ Practice by picking one ski up off the ground and skiing briefly on the other one. Start with one ski and then the other without trying to turn, just to become accustomed to the balance required.

◆ After gaining some balance, try using the step turn at each corner of the rectangle track, an action that will turn it into an oval track.

Activity 5: Arm Swing and Telemark Stance (20 Minutes)

The next part of the lesson is designed to implement the arm swing, increase the glide with each kick, and introduce the telemark position.

◆ The arm swing in skiing is much like the arm swing used in walking. When the right leg moves forward, the left arm swings slightly forward, and when the left leg moves forward, the right arm moves slightly forward. This action is called contralateral movement.

FIGURE NS7.1 In the exaggerated telemark position, your front arm is parallel to the ground.

- The skier exaggerates this movement to increase the glide by aiding in the weight transfer and by throwing the body into a forward motion.
- Start by doing the kick and glide movement practiced earlier and then add exaggerated arm swings.
- When weighting your right ski, throw your left arm out in front of you, taking it up to your shoulder and gliding in that position until your next kick.
- Repeat this movement to each side. Exaggerate the arm throw so that the arm is parallel to the ground at shoulder height and the fingers are pointing in the direction of travel (figure NS7.1).
- Then add an exaggerated telemark stance to each gliding movement. Do this by flexing your back leg down until the knee almost touches the ski. Your heel will come off the ski.
- The front leg is also flexed, but the foot remains flat on the ski and the thigh is almost parallel to the ground.
- This position, the original telemark stance, provides both fore and aft balance.
- The telemark stance may feel a little shaky at first, but once mastered, it offers a comfortable, balanced position while moving on skis.

Activity 6: Single Poling (10 Minutes)

Now it is time to add the poles to the mix.

- Hold the poles as described in the previous lesson.
- Hold the poles loosely so that your shoulders don't tense up. Ski the rectangular track with poles in hand using the techniques described earlier.
- When you swing your arm forward, plant the pole near your foot and push on it when you glide.
- Follow through with the pole plant so that you get as much push as possible. At the end of the stride, you should be holding the pole loosely and almost let go entirely. The wrist strap then pulls the pole from the snow.

Activity 7: Diagonal Stride (20 Minutes)

Combine the single poling exercise and the exaggerated telemark–diagonal stride and practice them together as you ski a few times around the track (figure NS7.2).

Closure Activity

Fox and Geese (20 to 30 Minutes)

This game involves chasing and fleeing on skis and gives both chasers and those fleeing additional practice with the diagonal stride.

- Transform the rectangle into a giant wagon wheel by making trails across the center so that all the trails lead directly through the center and then extend to the other side.

FIGURE NS7.2   Diagonal stride.

- Designate one or two people as the foxes. The other students will be geese.
- The object is for the foxes to catch the geese. When a fox catches a goose, the goose becomes a fox and helps catch the other geese.
- The only rule is that everyone must stay in the tracks.

Follow-Up Activity

Stride Practice (30 Minutes or Longer)

The next step is to go on a short- to medium-length tour through relatively flat terrain to gain more practice with the diagonal stride.

ASSESSMENT

- Check that students can demonstrate the proper method of kicking by observing them go through the process. The foot is flat, and contact is made down before kicking backward.
- Verify that students can demonstrate gliding on one ski until they stop by observing them go through the process.
- Confirm that students can demonstrate the movement of kicking and gliding in a rhythmic fashion by observing them go through the process.

- Check that students can demonstrate the diagonal stride without poles by observing them go through the process.

- Assess whether students can demonstrate weighting one ski and lifting the other off the ground by observing them go through the process.

- Verify that students can demonstrate the proper step turn by observing them go through the process.

- Check that students can demonstrate the diagonal stride with the single pole technique by observing them go through the process.

- Ensure that students can explain the importance of these basic skills as the foundation of future skills either through dialogue or by writing in journals or class notebooks.

- Confirm that students can explain why these foundational skills are important in learning to ski either through dialogue or by writing in journals or class notebooks.

TEACHING CONSIDERATIONS

- If more than a few hours have passed since the last lesson, review the skills covered in that lesson.

- The skills in this lesson are important for building skills that are more advanced.

- Learning to kick downward, not backward, is a fundamental skill related to weighting and unweighting the skis.

- The exaggerated movements required to hit the telemark position teach the type of dynamic balance needed in skiing and learning the telemark turn later.

- The step turn is used all the time in skiing but is often overlooked. It is an important skill to perfect because it is useful in a variety of situations.

- Carefully select the tour route at the end of the lesson so that it does not contain steep uphill and downhill sections. The idea is to work on the balance and handling of skis and to build basic skills. Convince students of the importance of building foundational skills to make the more difficult skills easier to learn.

UNIT 11, LESSON 8

▷ Uphill Ski Techniques

OVERVIEW

Knowledge of uphill skiing techniques opens up new ways and areas of travel. This lesson concentrates on the techniques that allow the skier to ascend short and long slopes.

JUSTIFICATION

This lesson builds on the flatland foundational skills and adds uphill techniques that open up a greater variety of choices in wilderness travel. A person cannot ski in the backcountry for long without encountering some hills, so knowledge of uphill techniques is a critical skill for backcountry skiing. Besides learning the uphill techniques for their intended use of going uphill, students practice the skill of weighting and unweighting skis, which transfers to the downhill techniques covered in later lessons.

GOAL

To develop students' ability to use efficient uphill skiing techniques.

OBJECTIVES

At the end of this lesson, students will be able to

◆ explain how proper poling technique with the herringbone aids in the movement (cognitive);
◆ demonstrate (psychomotor)
  – uphill diagonal technique,
  – herringbone technique,
  – proper use of poles in the herringbone technique,
  – sidestepping technique,
  – traversing technique with the kick turn, and
  – use of climbing skins;
◆ explain why it is important to lay a good uphill track in less obvious spots (affective); and
◆ appreciate the freedom from motorized lifts at ski areas that the skier gains by learning the uphill techniques (affective).

EQUIPMENT AND AREAS NEEDED

◆ Skis, boots, and poles
◆ Proper waxes

RISK MANAGEMENT CONSIDERATIONS

◆ Take appropriate precautions for environmental hazards at the teaching site such as dead trees and tree limbs.
◆ Because skiing is a winter activity, pay extra attention to air temperature and wind exposure. Make sure that all students are warm and are wearing the proper clothing.
◆ Be sure that students are properly nourished and hydrated for extended class time.
◆ Ensure proper spacing between students. Skis are long, and students can easily hit a person behind them with a ski. In addition, beginning skiers fall frequently.

LESSON CONTENT

Introduction

Sharing your personal experience with your students can be a useful teaching tool. Here is an example of a story from my past that I use to help students feel comfortable about learning these complex psychomotor skills. While I was working for the

Forest Service on the Oregon coast, a coworker named Jack asked me whether I wanted to try a winter ascent of Mt. McLoughlin in southern Oregon. He had a pair of skis and a pair of snowshoes, so we set off on a long January weekend to climb the mountain. I had little experience on skis, but Jack assured me that with the proper wax I would be able to ski to the summit, where we would trade and he would ski down. The skis had randonee bindings that we could adjust to fit my mountain boots. At the trailhead Jack gave me a tube that looked like toothpaste. He said that it was klister and that I was to spread it on the bottom of my skis so that I could ski up the mountain. With the aid of a putty knife, I got my skis coated with this sticky, messy stuff. Then, with my pack on my back and skis on my feet, I took off after my friend. I had imagined that I would just ski gracefully behind Jack as he broke trail in his snowshoes. Instead, it seemed as if my skis stuck in the snow and would not glide. I plodded along about 100 feet (30 meters) behind Jack, noticing that my skis were becoming heavier. When we stopped for a break, I took off the skis and found that I had a 3-inch (7.5-centimeter) layer of snow stuck to the bottom of them. When we got to the summit, Jack took out his putty knife, scraped off the snow, and shot down the mountain like a rocket. I put on the snowshoes and walked down the same way I walked up, just plodding along.

The lessons I learned from my experience on Mt. McLoughlin were that I had little or no uphill technique and that I relied too much on the klister I placed on my skis. (To this day, I don't know if I put too much klister on my skis or if I chose the wrong color klister for the temperature!) Over the years, I became a good nordic skier and in the process developed an efficient uphill technique.

The basic points of this lesson are the following:

- Climbing with the herringbone technique
- Proper poling with the herringbone technique
- Sidestepping up a hill
- Traversing with kick turns
- Putting on climbing skins
- Skiing with climbing skins

Important Terms

climbing skins, or skins—Devices made of nylon, mohair, or rubber that either strap or glue to the base of the ski, allowing the skis to go uphill without sliding backward.

fall line—The direction in which the slope is running. A good way to picture the fall line is to imagine the path that a snowball would take if you rolled it down the hill.

herringbone—Technique for going uphill in which the tips of the skis are pointed outward and the tails are close together.

sidestepping—Stepping up a hill with the skis perpendicular to the slope.

traversing—Going across a slope somewhat perpendicular to the fall line. If ascending, the uphill ski leads slightly off the perpendicular to the uphill side.

Main Activities

In this lesson, students progress from flatland techniques to uphill techniques. Being able to travel uphill easily is one of the beauties of backcountry skiing. Because the heels on nordic skis are not locked down, the skier can move uphill easily and efficiently.

First, find a teaching site. A low-angle hill (15 to 18 degrees) works well for this lesson. The same hill will work for teaching the downhill techniques in the next lesson.

Activity 1: Uphill Diagonals (15 Minutes)

When the going becomes steep, the uphill diagonal technique is the most efficient means of ascending. This technique is similar to the flatland technique, but it includes some minor adjustments to the stance and movements. The principle is to keep the wax pocket of the ski in contact with the snow.

- To initiate this technique, lean slightly forward from the hips. This moves your weight forward, keeping the weight over the wax pocket of the ski. Note that you do not bend at the waist; you use just a slight lean.
- The kick is quicker, and the glide is shorter. Remember that you are trying to keep your weight over the wax pocket. Kick down and then back, not just back. Never allow the skis to slide backward.
- Poling uphill is similar to poling on flat ground (refer to lesson 7).
- Be conscious when going uphill that you want the poles to aid in pushing you uphill, not off the hill.
- A common mistake is pushing poles perpendicular to the slope, which in turn pushes the wax pocket of the ski slightly off the snow, causing the pocket to lose contact with the snow. When this happens, the kick is lost.
- Angle the poles behind you.
- Sometimes it is helpful to go into a slight jog uphill, slapping the skis onto the snow. Do this by lifting the skis off the snow and bringing them down flat onto the snow. This action ensures good contact between snow and ski.

Activity 2: Herringbone (20 Minutes)

When the steep section is longer and the uphill diagonal no longer works, the herringbone is the next technique. The herringbone uses the edges of the skis to form platforms to stand on while ascending the hill (figure NS8.1).

- Angle the knees inward and angle the tips of the skis out to form a V. Do not allow the tails to cross. Lean into the hill slightly and place each ski carefully onto the snow.
- Poling is important in the herringbone technique. Pushing straight down instead of angled back pushes the ski off the snow, causing the ski to lose its grip. Beginners often make this mistake.

FIGURE NS8.1   To do the herringbone technique, alternate lifting your skis while pushing back with the poles.

Activity 3: Sidestepping (15 Minutes)

The sidestepping technique (figure NS8.2) is used when the slope becomes too steep for the uphill diagonal or the herringbone technique. Sidestepping is a slow technique used mostly for short sections.

◆ Turn the skis perpendicular to the fall line of the slope. The tips should point slightly uphill but not enough that the skis slip backward.

◆ With each step, the uphill edges of the skis bite into the snow.

◆ As you step uphill, keep your feet flat on your skis. Bending the knees slightly into the slope engages the edges of the skis, providing a better grip.

◆ When sidestepping, the entire ski should make contact with the snow. If the entire edge of the ski does not make contact with the snow, the chances of slipping increase.

◆ Sidestepping works well in steep gullies or narrow places where traversing is not an option.

FIGURE NS8.2   When sidestepping uphill, keep your feet flat on the skis.

Activity 4: Traversing (30 Minutes)

Traversing requires making long, low-angle switchbacks across steep slopes. If slopes are too long for herringboning and sidestepping, traversing is a viable option.

◆ Place the skis across the fall line with the tips pointed uphill, but not so far that they slip backward.

◆ Traversing is a series of sidesteps combined with a forward motion.

◆ When you reach the edge of the traverse, kick turn and go the other direction.

Deciding whether to do an uphill kick turn or a downhill kick turn depends on the steepness of the slope and the weight of your pack.

◆ When executing a kick turn with the downhill ski, your back is turned toward the slope, making it easy to put your poles in the snow behind you to gain a solid, balanced stance (figure NS8.3). But the downhill kick turn causes you to lose elevation on the turn.

◆ Uphill kick turns are more difficult because you have to raise your legs higher with your back pointed downhill (figure NS8.4).

◆ If you fall while making an uphill turn, you fall on your back headfirst. The advantage is that you gain some elevation on the turn.

◆ The uphill kick turn is the only kick turn that you can use if you are pulling a sled.

FIGURE NS8.3 Executing a downhill kick turn.

FIGURE NS8.4   Executing an uphill kick turn.

Activity 5: Climbing Skins (15 Minutes)

The final method for going uphill is to use climbing skins—devices that attach to the bottom of your skis with glue, buckles, or both (figure NS8.5).

◆ Climbing skins were originally made from sealskin, hence the name. Today, skins are made out of nylon or rubber.

◆ Skins allow you to climb extremely steep slopes with fewer switchbacks.

◆ On long, steep climbs when you are carrying a heavy pack or pulling a sled, skins are necessary. They do not glide well, however, and they are incredibly inefficient in terrain that is rolling or moderately steep.

◆ Skins turn your skis into long, expensive snowshoes.

FIGURE NS8.5   Climbing skin.

Learning flatland and uphill techniques takes time, and many people want to concentrate on downhill techniques because they consider downhill skiing the most thrilling aspect of the activity. In this era of immediate gratification, people turn too early to skins because using them requires little or no skill. But learning flatland and uphill techniques will open up deeper areas of wilderness to the participant. Learning this aspect of skiing is worth the time and effort.

Closure Activity

Obstacle Course (20 to 30 Minutes)

Set up a small course that has some gentle uphill and downhill sections and requires some maneuvering between and around obstacles. Have the students complete the course as you watch. Incorporate into this course sections that require students to use a little bit of each skill so that they can practice without becoming exhausted.

Follow-Up Activity

Practice (20 to 30 Minutes)

Practicing these skills on a slope is helpful, but after students have practiced the skills, it is time to go and ski a while. Areas that are mostly flat or gently rolling are good choices for practice.

ASSESSMENT

- Confirm that students can demonstrate the uphill diagonal without slipping backward by observing them go through the process. Look for a slight forward lean and kicking down into the snow.
- Check that students can demonstrate the herringbone technique without crossing the tails of the skis and without slipping backward by observing them go through the process. Ensure that the inside edges of the skis are making contact with the snow and that the knees are rolled inward slightly.
- Verify that students can demonstrate uphill poling without lifting the bottoms of the skis from the snow by observing them go through the process.
- Check that students can demonstrate sidestepping by observing them go through the process. Be sure that the outside edges of the skis are making contact, that the skis are perpendicular to the fall line, that the skiers' feet are flat on the skis, and that the knees are rolled slightly into the hill.
- Confirm that students can demonstrate a sidehill traverse by observing them traverse a slope.
- Verify that students can demonstrate putting on skins by observing them go through the process.
- Check that students can explain how the previous skills have provided a foundation and progression for learning the uphill techniques through dialogue, by writing in journals or class notebooks, or by written exam.
- Confirm that students can explain why learning uphill techniques is more beneficial to overall skill growth than just learning to use skins through dialogue, by writing in journals or class notebooks, or by written exam.

TEACHING CONSIDERATIONS

◆ This lesson is usually taught immediately before the beginning downhill lesson.

◆ A gentle slope of about 15 degrees works well for this lesson and the subsequent beginning downhill lesson. In the process of practicing uphill techniques, students will pack the slope with their skis in preparation for the beginning downhill lesson.

◆ Students sometimes resist learning these skills because if they put on skins they can go just about anywhere. They subscribe to the mentality that the only fun in skiing is the downhill part. Learning uphill and flatland techniques opens up skiing farther from the road, offering access to greater winter wilderness experiences.

◆ Again, the skills in this lesson build on the skills from the previous lesson. Much of skiing is learning to weight and unweight the skis.

◆ Pay close attention to poling on the uphill, because many beginning skiers mistakenly use their poles to push their skis off the snow.

UNIT 11, LESSON 9

▷ Beginning Downhill Techniques

OVERVIEW

Knowledge of downhill skiing techniques is essential for safe travel in the wilderness. This lesson concentrates on techniques that allow the skier to descend slopes and come to a safe stop.

JUSTIFICATION

This lesson continues the nordic skiing progression and adds basic downhill techniques to the skills previously learned. Just as uphill is inevitable in the backcountry, so is downhill. To travel safely in the backcountry on skis, the skier must be able to negotiate downhill turns and be able to stop while traveling downhill.

GOAL

To develop students' ability to use basic downhill skiing techniques.

OBJECTIVES

At the end of this lesson, students will be able to

◆ explain how the wedge position controls descending speed (cognitive);

◆ explain why the telemark position provides superior balance in varied snow conditions (cognitive);

◆ demonstrate (psychomotor)
    – traversing a hill in a straight running position,
    – the step turn on a downhill traverse,
    – the basic wedge stance (nonmoving),

- the basic wedge position while traversing a slope,
- stopping using the wedge technique,
- the telemark position (nonmoving), and
- a running telemark position while traversing a hill; and

◆ appreciate the beauty and freedom of being able to travel on skis anywhere in the backcountry (affective).

EQUIPMENT AND AREAS NEEDED

◆ Skis, boots, and poles

◆ Proper waxes

RISK MANAGEMENT CONSIDERATIONS

◆ Pick a hill with a gentle slope to start; too much speed is not conducive to good learning.

◆ The hill should have a good run-out at the bottom so that if the students cannot stop themselves, they will stop at the bottom naturally.

◆ In this lesson students will be moving up and down the hill at the same time. To prevent collisions, designate an uphill track that is out of the way of the downhill skiers and insist that all students travel uphill on that track.

◆ Take appropriate precautions for environmental hazards at the teaching site such as dead trees and tree limbs.

◆ Because skiing is a winter activity, pay extra attention to air temperature and wind exposure. Make sure that all students are warm and are wearing the proper clothing.

◆ Be sure that students are properly nourished and hydrated for extended class time.

◆ Ensure proper spacing between students. Skis are long, and students can easily hit a person behind them with a ski. In addition, beginning skiers fall frequently.

LESSON CONTENT

Introduction

Backcountry skiing is a combination of many complex motor tasks. Learning the necessary skills requires a lot of repetitions and practice. Adult learners sometimes become frustrated with themselves faster than children do. Telling stories like the following lets them know that everyone has to go through a long learning process.

During the early 1980s I learned how to ski and how to wax. I could kick and glide and manage uphills. The skill that eluded me, however, was going downhill while maintaining control of my skis. I could not turn or stop. If something was in my way or if I had to turn, I would simply sit down and fall over, an effective but cumbersome technique. While living in Colorado I had a pair of 225-centimeter skis that I bought during a gear swap. They were too long for me, but they had metal edges and were genuine mountain skis. I bought a season pass at a nearby ski area and was determined to teach myself how to telemark. So armed with skis, a lift pass, and a Sierra Club book titled *Backcountry Skiing*, I embarked on a new learning experience.

I spent a lot of time getting up from falls instead of skiing. After a few weeks, I was standing at the top of the hill by the lift building when the lift operator came out to talk to me. He told me that my skis were too long, making them difficult to control. I asked him for advice on something that I could change. He told me not to bend at the waist, to squat straight down, and to keep my back knee tucked right behind my front knee. I listened and eventually started to pull off some rudimentary turns that looked like a telemark.

The basic points of this lesson are the following:

◆ Traversing hills in a straight running position
◆ Traversing a hill with the step turn
◆ Traversing the hill with a wedge position
◆ Stopping with a wedge turn
◆ Turning with a wedge turn
◆ Traversing a hill with the straight running telemark position

Important Terms

fall line—The direction that the slope is running. A good way to picture the fall line is to imagine the path that a snowball would take if it were rolling down the hill.

straight running telemark—Assuming the telemark position and "running" (not turning) in a straight line.

wedge—Also known as the snowplow. This technique is used to slow down and stop. The tips of the skis are together, and the tails are apart. The pressure is on the outside edges, which slows the descent.

Main Activities

In this lesson, students practice beginning downhill techniques. Being able to negotiate downhill sections and being able to stop are essential to safe skiing in the backcountry.

First, find an appropriate teaching site. Choose a low-angle hill with a safe run-out zone at the bottom. The type of hill used in teaching the uphill techniques (lesson 8) works well.

Activity 1: Traversing in a Straight Running Position (20 Minutes)

The first goal is to get students comfortable with the feel of going downhill. To do this, pick an angle across the slope that is steep enough to move without kicking but not so steep that students lose control.

◆ Keep the skis parallel and about 8 inches (20 centimeters) apart, bend your knees, and put your hands on your knees.

◆ When you come to a natural stop, kick turn and continue in the same fashion until you reach the bottom of the hill.

◆ Repeat this until you get the feel for traversing the slope perpendicular to the fall line.

Activity 2: Traversing With a Step Turn (30 Minutes)

This combination of skills already learned is an important skill to know. This skill combines the step turn with the straight running traverse.

◆ Start with a straight running traverse as in the previous exercise. Pick an angle that is steep enough to move without kicking but not so steep that you lose control.

◆ While moving across the slope, lift the uphill ski and step uphill. Then lift the downhill ski and place it parallel to the uphill ski.

◆ The key is to weight the downhill ski so that you can move the uphill ski freely. Then transfer all your weight to the uphill ski so that you can move the downhill ski freely.

◆ The uphill step should be approximately 6 to 8 inches (15 to 20 centimeters). Match the step with the downhill ski.

◆ Repeat this sequence until you come to a stop. If you stop midslope, pick a downhill angle, continue to the end of the slope, and then kick turn and repeat until you reach the bottom of the slope.

◆ This important skill will serve the backcountry skier well. When skiing down a slope that is beyond your ability level, when skiing with a heavy pack, or when pulling a sled, traversing a slope is a great way to manage downhill slopes safely and in control.

Activity 3: Traversing With a Wedge Position (30 Minutes)

The best approach to teaching the wedge or snowplow is to have students learn the body position on flat ground before proceeding to a slope. This step is often overlooked in ski lessons, but developing muscle memory is critical when learning motor skills.

◆ Assume the wedge position, a stance in which the tips are pointed inward and the tails are pointed outward (figure NS9.1).

◆ Keep the back straight and the arms relaxed at the sides.

◆ Flex your ankles to put pressure on the inside edges.

◆ Your knees should not be together, nor should your ski tips. Parker (2001) suggests that skiers keep a distance of the width of a soccer ball between the ski tips and between the knees.

◆ Practice moving from the parallel stance to the wedge stance while standing still.

◆ Now move back up the hill and practice traversing the hill in the wedge position.

◆ After you reach the opposite side, come to a stop, kick turn, and continue down the hill in the same manner.

◆ Practice going from the flats of your skis to the edges of your skis and back.

◆ To slow down, push the tails wider; to go faster, bring the tails closer together.

FIGURE NS9.1　The wedge or snowplow position.

Activity 4: Stopping With a Wedge Turn (30 Minutes)

- Begin with a traversing wedge stance.
- Rotate the upper body in the direction that you want to turn. In this case it will be uphill.
- Rotating the upper body will weight the downhill ski, causing it to turn uphill and bring you to a stop.

Activity 5: Turning With a Wedge Turn (30 to 60 Minutes)

Using the same techniques for the wedge turn, the skier can turn at the end of the traverse and continue down the hill without stopping.

- This time when traversing the slope, rotate your body downhill in the direction that you want to travel, causing the uphill ski to turn downhill.
- Keep weighting the uphill ski until you cross the fall line and are traversing in the other direction.
- Practice this until you can link wedge turns all the way down the hill.

The wedge turn and stop are good techniques but do not work well in soft powder snow, where the step turn is more effective. The telemark turn, invented over 100 years ago in the Telemark region of Norway, is another backcountry technique useful for turning in soft snow (see lesson 10).

Activity 6: Traversing With a Straight Running Telemark Position (30 to 60 Minutes)

FIGURE NS9.2 The modified telemark position is used when traversing the slope.

The telemark position was introduced in lesson 7. Here it will be modified to traverse the slope as the straight running telemark (figure NS9.2). Have students start in a flat area so that they get the feel of the position before attempting to do it on a slope. As with the wedge, you want students to develop some muscle memory before starting to move.

- Assume an athletic stance with the back straight. Lean slightly forward but do not bend at the waist. The position should be relaxed and ready for movement.
- Bend the knees so that the front foot slides forward and the rear foot slides backward.
- Position the front knee directly over the toes of the front foot. If you place the shaft of a ski pole against your knee, the tip should be on your toes.
- The hip of the back leg should be directly over the toe of the back foot. Again, if you place the shaft of a ski pole on your back hip, the tip should extend to the toes of your back foot.
- The front foot should be flat, and the back foot should be up on the ball of the foot.
- Your weight should be evenly distributed over both skis.
- Your arms should be relaxed at the sides with the hands about waist high.
- Return to the top of the practice slope and traverse the slope in the telemark position. When traversing, the downhill ski should be pointing forward.
- Ski across the slope in this position until you come to a stop. Then kick turn and traverse in the other direction.
- The goal is to become comfortable with the straight running telemark.

Closure Activity

Oral Review (20 Minutes)

This is an active lesson, and students are generally tired by the time it ends. A good closer for this lesson is a simple oral review of the important aspects of the techniques. Have a student demonstrate the techniques while you talk and point out the important body positions in each technique.

Follow-Up Activity

Practice (20 to 30 Minutes)

This physical lesson usually lasts five or six hours. After taking a break and making sure that students are hydrated and properly nourished, let them practice on the hill without formal instruction.

ASSESSMENT

- Check that students can demonstrate the straight running position to traverse a downhill slope by observing them correctly perform the technique during practice.
- Confirm that students can demonstrate a step turn while traversing a slope in both directions by observing them correctly perform the technique during practice.
- Verify that students can demonstrate weighting and unweighting skis while doing the step turn by observing them correctly perform the technique during practice.
- Check that students can demonstrate the wedge position on flat terrain by observing them correctly perform the technique during practice.
- Confirm that students can demonstrate traversing a downhill slope in the wedge position by observing them correctly perform the technique during practice.
- Verify that students can demonstrate rotating the body uphill from a wedge position, weighting the downhill ski, and coming to a stop by observing them correctly perform the technique during practice.
- Check that students can demonstrate rotating the body downhill from a wedge position, weighting the uphill ski, turning down the hill across the fall line, and skiing back across the slope by observing them correctly perform the technique during practice.
- Confirm that students can demonstrate the correct telemark position on flat terrain by observing them correctly perform the technique during practice.
- Verify that students can demonstrate the straight running telemark position to traverse across the slope in both directions by observing them correctly perform the technique during practice.
- Check that students can explain how the telemark position provides balance in varied snow conditions through dialogue, by writing in journals or course notebooks, or by written exam.
- Confirm that students can explain how the preceding lessons have provided a foundation for this lesson through dialogue, by writing in journals or course notebooks, or by written exam.

TEACHING CONSIDERATIONS

◆ Teaching beginning downhill techniques, especially when combined with the uphill lesson, creates a long, tiring day of skiing.

◆ Make sure to monitor students closely and encourage them to take breaks.

◆ Practicing skills when overtired is not productive. Remember that practice does not make perfect. Instead, perfect practice makes perfect.

◆ Students will not progress through this lesson at the same rate. You may have students still working on the straight running traverse.

◆ Try to have everyone skiing at the same time. Avoid having one student skiing and everyone else watching.

◆ The latter method makes it easy for you to observe but puts the spotlight on one student, which could be embarrassing.

◆ Pair up skiers of similar ability to help each other. Have one partner ski while the other watches and provides feedback.

◆ Adult learners tend to have little patience with themselves and can give up quickly. Assure them that skiing has a learning curve. Encourage them not to become frustrated.

◆ Again, the skills in this lesson build on the skills from the last lesson. Flatland and uphill techniques transfer to the downhill techniques.

◆ Going downhill frightens some students and thrills others. Be sure that all students understand that they work at their own pace and naturally progress at different rates.

UNIT 11, LESSON 10

▷ Beginning Telemark Turns

OVERVIEW

The telemark turn, one of the oldest turns in skiing, was invented specifically for the long skis used in early skiing. The turn affords the skier exceptional fore and aft balance. Today, Olympic ski jumpers use the telemark turn when they land. The focus of this lesson is learning the beginning telemark turn.

JUSTIFICATION

One of the beauties of skiing in the backcountry is the ever-changing snow conditions. The skier can encounter hard-pack snow in the shade and a moment later be in soft, mushy snow in the sun. To be an accomplished backcountry skier, a person must know a variety of techniques. The wedge turn, step turn, kick turn, and wheel turn are valid and valuable techniques, but they don't work well in all snow conditions. The telemark turn should be part of every backcountry skier's skill base.

GOAL

To develop students' ability to use a beginning telemark turn.

OBJECTIVES

At the end of this lesson, students will be able to

◆ explain the reason the unique ski position (one ski forward and one back) is an important factor in the telemark turn (cognitive);

◆ explain why equal weighting of both skis is important in the telemark turn (cognitive);

◆ demonstrate (psychomotor)
  – the telemark position,
  – the straight running telemark,
  – the beginning telemark turn,
  – a smooth lead change,
  – uphill garlands, and
  – turning across the fall line with a telemark turn; and

◆ appreciate the beauty and effectiveness of a properly executed telemark turn in a backcountry setting (affective).

EQUIPMENT AND AREAS NEEDED

◆ Skis, boots, and poles for each student

◆ Proper waxes for the conditions

◆ Climbing skins for each student

RISK MANAGEMENT CONSIDERATIONS

◆ Pick a hill with a gentle slope to start this activity. Too much speed is not conducive to good learning.

◆ The hill should have a good run-out at the bottom so that if the students cannot stop on their own, they will stop at the bottom naturally.

◆ In this lesson students will be moving up and down the hill at the same time. To prevent collisions, designate an uphill track that is out of the way of the downhill skiers and insist that all students travel uphill on that track.

◆ Take appropriate precautions for environmental hazards at the teaching site such as dead trees and tree limbs.

◆ Because skiing is a winter activity, pay extra attention to air temperature and wind exposure. Make sure that all students are warm and are wearing the proper clothing.

◆ Be sure that students are properly nourished and hydrated for extended class time.

◆ Ensure proper spacing between students. Skis are long, and students can easily hit a person behind them with a ski. In addition, beginning skiers fall frequently.

LESSON CONTENT

Introduction

The telemark is a complex motor movement that requires a lot of time to learn. Using stories about your own learning experience helps put the students at ease and may reduce the pressure that they put on themselves to be successful.

In 1986 I participated in an expedition to Baffin Island to climb several previously unclimbed peaks. To gain access to the peaks, we used skis as our primary method of transport. The mountains were beautiful, the terrain was rugged, and the weather was mostly misty and gray. The conditions were not great for climbing, but they were good enough for skiing. Of the 45 days we spent on Baffin Island, we climbed for 10 and spent the remainder of the time skiing the long, beautiful glaciers. One of our members, an exceptional telemarker, taught me how to turn. With a few pointers, I was linking turns down the glaciers for hours and quickly developed a new addiction.

The basic points of this lesson are the following:

- Traversing a hill with the straight running telemark position
- The transition, which requires weighting and unweighting the skis from the telemark position
- Turning uphill with a telemark garland
- Turning across the fall line with a telemark turn

Important Terms

angulate—To angle parts of the body in relation to other parts of the body; most commonly refers to the position of the knees in relation to the rest of the body.

garlands—Long turns across the slope.

lead change—The point in the telemark turn when the skier switches which ski is forward.

straight running telemark—Assuming the telemark position and "running" (not turning) in a straight line.

transition—The point before the lead change when the skis are unweighted.

Main Activities

In this lesson, students will develop the beginning telemark turn.

First, find an appropriate teaching site. Choose a low-angle hill with a safe run-out zone at the bottom. The hill used in teaching the uphill techniques (lesson 8) works well.

Activity 1: Warm-Up (15 to 20 Minutes)

As with all previous lessons, warming up and stretching is essential. A good warm-up is to review the basic skills covered in the previous lessons, starting with the stationary movements learned in lesson 6; refer to that lesson as necessary.

Activity 2: Traversing Hills in a Straight Running Telemark Position (30 to 60 Minutes)

After the warm-up, review the beginning downhill techniques of lesson 9. Take time to review the telemark position while stationary. Remind students that correct body position is crucial.

- After the review, begin with the straight running telemark with the downhill ski in the lead, or forward, position.
- When you come to a natural stop, kick turn and continue in the same fashion until you reach the bottom of the hill.
- Repeat this until you get a feel for traversing the slope perpendicular to the fall line.

Activity 3: The Transition (60 to 90 Minutes)

The transition is the point in the telemark turn when the skier shifts the position of the lead ski (figure NS10.1).

◆ The transition is done by standing up and then shifting the position of the skis. When you stand up, the upward motion of the body takes the weight off the skis momentarily.

◆ At that point, you slide the lead ski back and the back ski forward, performing a lead change. You then sink back down into the telemark position.

◆ This sinking motion puts weight onto the skis, causing them to seek a new direction.

◆ Start with the straight running telemark with the downhill ski forward, just as before.

◆ While traversing the slope, practice weighting and unweighting the skis. Do this by standing up, bringing both skis parallel, and then shifting the lead ski; bring the back ski forward and drop the lead ski back.

◆ Do not stay in the transition for long because, unlike the telemark position, it is not a position of balance.

◆ Practice the transitional phase as many times as possible while traversing the slope.

FIGURE NS10.1   Telemark transition.

Activity 4: Turning Uphill With a Telemark Garland (60 to 90 Minutes)

The telemark turn works by creating an equally weighted turning arc out of both skis.

- Imagine one long ski with the tip being the downhill ski and the tail being the uphill ski. This is a critical difference between the telemark turn and an alpine turn. In alpine turns, in which the entire foot is locked to the ski, the skier weights the downhill ski more than the uphill ski.
- In this exercise you are attempting to turn uphill and come to a stop. In the telemark turn you angle your knees in the direction that you want to turn.
- Also, remember that you are turning on the lead ski, so if your left ski is forward you will be initiating a right turn. The opposite is true if the right ski is forward.
- Start with the straight running telemark position.
- When you come to the end of the traverse, angulate your downhill knee toward the midline of your body. This action puts pressure on the inside edge of your downhill ski.
- At the same time, angulate your uphill knee to the outside. This action puts weight on the outside edge of your uphill ski.
- This technique will turn you uphill and bring you to a stop. Then kick turn and do the same thing to the other side.
- Practice these uphill garlands until you can initiate an uphill turn and come to a stop.

Activity 5: Turning Across the Fall Line With a Telemark Turn (60 to 90 Minutes)

Now you will have students attempt to link two traverses with the telemark turn. To do this, they must remember the lessons on weighting and unweighting.

- Start with the straight running telemark, with the downhill ski out front.
- Now unweight your skis by standing up. Perform the transition to shift the position of the skis. When you weight your skis again, your uphill ski will be out front.
- At this point several things begin to happen simultaneously.
  - Rotate your upper body in the direction that you want to turn (downhill). You did this previously in the wedge turn.
  - Angulate your knees into the turn. Both knees will be pointed downhill, in the direction that you want to turn. By doing this, the inside edge of the lead ski and the outside edge of the trailing ski will be weighted, and you will be able to hold your position to perform a turn downhill across the fall line and into the next traverse without stopping.

Closure Activity

Oral Review (20 to 30 Minutes)

This is an active, long lesson. Students may need several eight-hour days to learn the telemark. They will progress at different rates, and you should allow them to self-regulate. Some students will not be able to participate for the whole day. Some will become physically fatigued, and others will become mentally fatigued.

As a teacher I watch for this. When I see the focus start to wane, I pull all my students together and orally review the main points of the telemark turn. While doing this, you may want to have a student demonstrate each position while you explain the purpose and main points.

Follow-Up Activity

Ski Tour (20 Minutes or Longer)

If I have enough assistant instructors, I send the students who are too tired to practice on a short but not strenuous ski tour, or back to camp if the class format is a multiday trip.

Allow the other students to continue skiing but have them pair up. One student skis, and the other analyzes the technique and provides critical feedback.

ASSESSMENT

- Verify that students understand the reason the unique ski position (one ski forward and one back) is an important factor in the telemark turn by asking them for an explanation during main activity 3.
- Verify that students understand why equal weighting of both skis is important in the telemark turn by asking them for an explanation during the follow-up activity.
- Confirm that students can demonstrate the telemark position by observing them throughout the lesson.
- Confirm that students can demonstrate traversing a hill in a straight running telemark position by observing them during the follow-up activity.
- Confirm that students can demonstrate a smooth lead change by observing them in main activity 3.
- Confirm that students can demonstrate an uphill turn with a telemark garland by observing them in main activity 4.
- Confirm that students can demonstrate turning across the fall line with a telemark turn by observing them in main activity 5.
- Verify that students appreciate the beauty and effectiveness of a properly executed telemark turn in a backcountry setting by having them write a one-page entry in their notebooks on their telemark ski experience, emphasizing the setting and newly acquired skills.

TEACHING CONSIDERATIONS

- The goal is to have students learn a rudimentary telemark turn, not to link multiple turns down endless slopes of powder.
- The telemark is a complex psychomotor skill that requires many repetitions to master. As a teacher I sometimes spend several days on the skills presented in this lesson.
- Monitor students closely and encourage them to take breaks. Practicing skills when overtired is not productive. Remember that practice does not make perfect. Instead, perfect practice makes perfect.
- Introduce new skills at the beginning of the day, not the end. People need to learn new skills when the body is fresh, not fatigued.
- Students will not progress through this lesson at the same rate. At the end of the day some students will still be working on the straight running traverse while others will be starting to make the beginning telemark turns.

- Try to have everyone skiing at the same time. Avoid having one student skiing and everyone else watching. The latter method makes it easy for you to observe but puts the spotlight on the student, which could be embarrassing, especially with adult learners.

- Pair up skiers of similar ability to help each other. Have one partner ski while the other watches and provides feedback.

- Adult learners tend to have little patience with themselves and can give up quickly. Assure them that skiing has a learning curve. Encourage them not to become frustrated.

- Again, the skills in this lesson build on the skills from previous lessons. Flatland and uphill techniques transfer to the downhill techniques.

- Consider teaching this lesson at a downhill ski area. By using mechanized ski lifts, the students will be able to perform a greater number of downhill repetitions.

- Constantly remind students to weight both skis equally. They can forget to do this if the slope is packed. On packed slopes the skier can complete a telemark turn by weighting the forward ski more, but in the backcountry the snow is rarely packed. If the skier does not weight the skis evenly on an unpacked slope, the momentum will throw her or him over the forward ski.

- Allow students to sit out when appropriate and to push when appropriate. As a teacher you need to be alert for signs of fatigue. Suggest changes such as going back to beginning skill practice such as weighting and unweighting.

UNIT 11, LESSON 11

▷ Leave No Trace Considerations

OVERVIEW

Wilderness is a diminishing resource. As outdoor educators, we must do everything within our power to minimize our impact while traveling. This lesson reviews the Leave No Trace principles and focuses on special considerations for the winter environment.

JUSTIFICATION

Limiting our impact when we travel in a wilderness environment helps preserve our wild areas and safeguards the experience of other visitors.

GOAL

To increase students' awareness of Leave No Trace principles in the winter environment.

OBJECTIVES

At the end of this lesson, students will be able to

- compare Leave No Trace practices in winter and nonwinter environments (cognitive),

- know and follow Leave No Trace principles for a winter environment (cognitive), and
- appreciate the beauty of the winter wilderness and strive to leave as little impact as possible when traveling in the winter (affective).

EQUIPMENT AND AREAS NEEDED

None

RISK MANAGEMENT CONSIDERATIONS

- Because skiing is a winter activity, pay extra attention to air temperature and wind exposure. Make sure that all students are warm and are wearing the proper clothing.
- Be sure that students are properly nourished and hydrated for extended class time.

LESSON CONTENT

Introduction

Leave No Trace in the winter is not much different than Leave No Trace in any other season. People just have to apply the seven principles in a logical and rational way to the winter environment. I have listed the seven principles and commented on the aspects appropriate for winter.

Main Activity

Winter Aspects of LNT (Time as Needed)

In this lesson students gain understanding of the unique practices of Leave No Trace in a winter environment. See appendix A for the general Leave No Trace principles.

Plan Ahead and Prepare   The biggest difference here is being aware of the avalanche danger before going skiing.

- If the avalanche danger is high, the trip may need to be postponed or the type of skiing may need to be modified.
- Understanding avalanches is imperative before venturing out in the winter. Having and knowing how to use rescue equipment is also important.

In addition, time and daylight are factors are different in winter.

- The hours of daylight are much shorter. Having headlamps and extra batteries is important.
- On longer trips, think about carrying lanterns to save the number of batteries needed in a dark wilderness environment.

At first glance these considerations may not seem relevant to Leave No Trace principles, but if an accident occurs and a search and rescue operation commences, a large impact on the environment will occur, an impact that might have been prevented with adequate planning.

Travel and Camp on Durable Surfaces Leave No Trace principles do not change in this category. Because we are traveling and camping on snow, a resistant surface, we will not leave permanent impacts. But the visual impact of a camp or trail will remain most of the winter, so avoid camping in the middle of the trail and in popular ski areas. Find places off the main trails to set up camps.

Dispose of Waste Properly This category has only a few modifications for winter travel.

◆ Catholes are difficult to dig in the winter. The soil is often several feet (a meter or more) below the snow surface, or it is frozen solid. Skiers will need to use other methods to dispose of human waste.

◆ One method is to bury the human waste 1 to 2 feet (30 to 60 centimeters) below the surface of the snow. The freezing and thawing may aid in the decomposition of the human waste.

◆ Another viable method in the winter is to pack out all human waste. This method works well if using a product such as Restop 2 or Wag Bags designed for this purpose, especially when pulling sleds. Sleds take much of the weight off the back and make pulling the extra load of human waste less burdensome. A bonus in winter is that human feces freezes, reducing the odor problem.

◆ Urination in winter is more of a visual issue. Urine is readily visible on white snow, so travelers should ski away from the trails to urinate and then cover up the marks with snow.

Leave What You Find Nothing is uniquely different in this category during winter.

Minimize Campfire Impacts Fires are difficult to build in winter and are not an efficient means of cooking or staying warm. If a fire is built, however, follow LNT principles.

Respect Wildlife One of the unique things about wildlife in winter is being able to see tracks and follow them. Care must be taken when doing this to avoid disturbing the wildlife in their natural habitats by getting too close.

◆ In winter, water in liquid form is often scarce. Camping and taking breaks near water sources can disrupt the patterns of wildlife. Avoid lingering at those areas. Obtain the water that you need and then move away to camp or take a break.

◆ Being careful with food scraps in winter is important. Spilled food is easily lost in the snow, so take great care not to spill.

Be Considerate of Other Visitors No matter where you go in winter, you will leave a trail in the snow. Skiers need to be extra careful about taking breaks off the main trails, but being considerate of others is the same in winter as it is in other seasons.

Leave No Trace principles—Copyright: Leave No Trace Center for Outdoor Ethics. www.LNT.org.

Closure Activity

Plan an Excursion (15 to 20 Minutes)

After students have discussed the differences between the general LNT principles and the LNT winter principles, they should have a good understanding of how they can practice LNT skills. Their final challenge is to plan a half-day cross-country skiing excursion for their group using the LNT principles. Have them write a report in the past tense relating in detail how they applied each LNT winter principle throughout the excursion. Make sure that they include in the description how they planned the day.

They should address these items in the trip report:

◆ Current conditions in the area that they plan to visit. Avalanche conditions are easy to find by contacting state avalanche centers (www.avalanche-center.org).

◆ The five-day weather forecast.

◆ The type of fauna common in the area and their winter habits.

◆ The level of visitor use that the area normally receives in winter and speculation on how the group will affect others.

◆ A list of emergency equipment for the trip.

Follow-Up Activity

Participate on an Excursion (One-Half to One Full Day)

Have students participate in the half-day trip they planned. Make sure you review the plan to be sure that it can be logistically carried out, and make sure participants are sufficiently informed and prepared for the activity. Trip planning should focus on the following:

◆ Location suitable for students' skill level

◆ Routes and scheduling

◆ Appropriate group size

◆ Staffing

◆ Proper equipment and clothing

◆ Adequate food and water

◆ Transportation to and from the site

◆ Communication in the event of a serious accident

◆ Budget

◆ Safety and risk management concerns

ASSESSMENT

◆ Assess whether students understand how LNT winter principles are different from LNT general principles by listening to them discuss the differences.

◆ Check that students can plan and execute (in their imaginations) a ski tour that incorporates LNT winter principles by reviewing written plans, listening to a report that they develop, or observing their LNT practices during the half-day outing.

◆ Verify that students voluntarily practice LNT winter principles in and out of class by having them write in a logbook or journal each time they practice an LNT principle over the course of a winter.

TEACHING CONSIDERATIONS

Have students discuss how an area that is significantly affected by recreation use changes their experience.

▷ Inclusion and Accessibility

OVERVIEW

Outdoor and adventure education have an underlying theme of challenge by choice, cooperation, and teamwork. These values extend to all people. This lesson focuses on including persons with disabilities in backcountry skiing experiences.

JUSTIFICATION

Inherent in the philosophy of adventure education is the acknowledgment that it is OK to experience the activity in different ways. This is the basis of the challenge by choice philosophy, which is a foundational value for adventure education. Typically, challenge by choice is interpreted as allowing each participant to set his or her own goals and decide for himself or herself how much effort to put toward those goals. Extending this value also means aiding others in meeting the challenge of their choice. With this philosophy, failure is impossible. The major barrier for effective programming for persons with disabilities lies with the teacher or the facilitator (Cross, 2005).

GOAL

To adapt an existing inclusion model to backcountry skiing. Describing every conceivable adaptation for backcountry skiing would be cumbersome. Developing a perspective on looking for ways to adapt is more effective than focusing on particular adaptations.

OBJECTIVE

At the end of this lesson, students will be able to understand the functional approach for modifying movement experiences (FAMME) and apply it to backcountry skiing (cognitive).

EQUIPMENT AND AREAS NEEDED

◆ Notebook
◆ Blindfolds
◆ Skiing harness like those designed for teaching children to ski. They can be purchased for adults or easily made out of 1-inch (2.5-centimeter) tubular webbing and a chest harness. The student wears the chest harness, and two 20-foot (6-meter) pieces of webbing are attached to the back and held by the teacher like a pair of reins on a horse. The teacher uses the webbing to indicate a direction for turning and to slow a skier.

RISK MANAGEMENT CONSIDERATIONS

◆ This lesson should be covered before going into the field. Because the lesson takes place in an indoor classroom, no risk management considerations other than those appropriate to a traditional classroom setting should be considered.
◆ Some of the activities require a student to wear a blindfold. In these situations, conduct the activity in a slow, controlled manner.

LESSON CONTENT

Introduction

The first step in effectively including all people in backcountry skiing is to use good problem-solving skills. The teacher, with the aid of the student or students, must be able to assess the skill and decide what can be modified to cultivate increased participation and success of all students.

The functional approach to modifying movement experiences (FAMME) provides a conceptual framework that can be used for multiple types of physical skills (Kasser & Lytle, 2005). Instead of just dictating modifications for an activity, the FAMME model uses a four-step process that aids the leader and the participants in considering a range of possible modifications based on the skills involved in a particular activity (figure NS12.1). The FAMME model emphasizes matching modifications to ability differences.

Step 1: Determine underlying components of the skill.

Step 2: Determine current capabilities of the individual.

Step 3: Match modification efforts to capabilities.

Step 4: Evaluate modification effectiveness and revise if necessary.

FIGURE NS12.1   FAMME model.

Adapted, by permission, from S.L. Kasser and R.K. Lytle, 2005, *Inclusive physical activity: A lifetime of opportunities* (Champaign, IL: Human Kinetics), 138.

Main Activity

Encouraging Participation (Time as Needed)

As a class, use the FAMME model in a brainstorming session to modify backcountry skiing for a person with a disability. Remember that when brainstorming, all ideas are recorded and not discussed. Discussion occurs after the brainstorming session ends.

1. Determine the underlying components of skiing. Have someone write these components on a whiteboard or easel paper.

2. Determine current capabilities of the person. The person with the disability can do most of this step, but the class should also be able to participate. The modification involves everyone, not just the person with the disability. Have someone write these capabilities on a whiteboard or easel paper.

3. Match modification efforts to capabilities. As a class, decide which modifications are likely to work and how to accomplish them. This part of the class is when the ideas from the brainstorming session are evaluated for their effectiveness. The modifications are then matched to the capabilities.

4. Evaluate the success of modifications and modify again if appropriate. Do this evaluation in discussion or, if possible, in the phase when the modifications are actually attempted.

Refer to table NS12.1 for a list of skills and modifications needed for backcountry skiing.

Closure Activity

Experience the Modifications (One Hour)

A good closer for this lesson is to have students experience the modifications. For example, have a temporarily able-bodied (TAB) skier in a cross-country ski for persons with disabilities. This scenario will create better understanding of the situation.

◆ Using blindfolds and a skiing harness, have the student skiers go down an easy slope one at a time. You should ski behind them, holding the reins and giving verbal cues for turning and stopping. At this point, the reins and harness can be used to aid in slowing the skier with visual disabilities.

◆ Go slow and in short spurts, taking the blindfold off often. It is very disconcerting to be traveling downhill without being able to see where you're going.

◆ Increase the time and distance traveled with the blindfolds on.

◆ Progress to using no harness and just verbal cues.

TABLE NS12.1 Skills and Modifications for Temporarily Able-Bodied Skiers

Functional component	Modification

Muscular endurance	◆ Route modification to accommodate the skier's endurance level
	◆ Scheduled rest breaks during the day
	◆ Close attention to hydration and nutrition
	◆ Snowmobile accompaniment so that a person can rest while the group continues to move forward
	◆ Dog sled accompaniment so that a person can rest while the group continues to move forward
	◆ Alternate methods of carrying weight on extended trips
	  – Sleds
	  – Temporarily able-bodied skiers (TABs) to carry the person's weight
	  – Snowmobile accompaniment
	  – Dog sled accompaniment
	◆ TABs tethered to sit skis to aid the skier by pulling

Muscular strength	◆ Route modification, such as choosing a route that does not have fresh powder and thus would require less muscular strength
	◆ Preparing the trail in advance by packing it down
	◆ Modified cross-country skis
	◆ Support systems to carry equipment
	  – Sleds
	  – Snowmobiles
	  – Dog sleds

Balance and postural control	◆ Shorter, wider skis ◆ Poles with outrigger skis attached ◆ Cross-country skis for persons with paralysis or partial paralysis ◆ Skiing without a pack (see methods listed earlier for carrying the person's equipment)
Sensory perception	◆ Guide animals ◆ Guide people
Concept understanding	◆ Oral cues
Attention	◆ Skiing partner ◆ Shorter routes and shorter days

Follow-Up Activity

Service Project (Full Day)

Contact a local ski area and set up a service project for your students. The service project allows your students to volunteer to work with skiers with disabilities. With the help of your students, skiers with disabilities, along with their families and friends, can experience the joy of skiing.

ASSESSMENT

Assess students' understanding of the FAMME model through dialogue, by writing in journals or course notebooks, or by written exam.

TEACHING CONSIDERATIONS

- Instead of having a brainstorming session, divide the class into groups and have them go through the FAMME model on their own. Have each group present the model to the class.
- Contact a nearby ski area (most areas have a disabled skiing program) and arrange a tour of the area and the equipment used for skiers with disabilities.
- If possible have a skier with a disability come to talk with your students.
- Have able-bodied skiers try as much of the special equipment as possible. I have found this activity the most useful of all because students can experience what is possible for persons with disabilities.

Nordic Skiing Skills Checklist

Listed below are the skills covered in this unit. It is your responsibility to practice and master these skills. This checklist will be used to assess your progress.

Lesson 1 Introduction to Nordic Skiing

☐ Understand the origins of skiing.

☐ Explain the major differences between alpine and nordic skiing.

Lesson 2 Backcountry Ski Equipment

☐ Describe the different types of nordic skiing.

☐ Choose an appropriate length ski for your height, weight, and skiing situation.

☐ Be able to choose and size poles.

Lesson 3 Preparing to Teach Backcountry Skiing

☐ Be able to recognize the danger signs of snow avalanches.

☐ Be able to describe the dangers associated with cold weather environmental injuries.

☐ Describe the clothing system (layering) used in the winter environment.

☐ Describe (and demonstrate) the importance of warming up before beginning activity.

Lesson 4 Applying the Base Wax

☐ Correctly remove old wax from the ski base.

☐ Correctly apply glide wax to the ski base.

Lesson 5 Applying the Kick Wax

☐ Differentiate between the types of waxes for skis.

☐ Choose the appropriate wax for current conditions and situations.

☐ Correctly apply kick wax to the ski base.

Lesson 6 Beginning Skiing Techniques

☐ Grip ski poles properly.

☐ Put skis on correctly.

☐ Demonstrate a suitable way to get up from a fall.

☐ Demonstrate the appropriate method of doing a wheel turn.

☐ Demonstrate a kick turn.

continued ▶

Use the nordic skiing skills checklist as an additional tool to assess skills learned throughout this unit.

From M. Wagstaff and A. Attarian, 2009, *Technical skills for adventure programming: A curriculum guide* (Champaign, IL: Human Kinetics).

Lesson 7 The Diagonal Stride

- ☐ Demonstrate the diagonal stride.
- ☐ Demonstrate the proper kick with a weighted ski.
- ☐ Demonstrate the proper glide with an unweighted ski.
- ☐ Demonstrate shifting weight from one ski to another.
- ☐ Demonstrate contralateral poling while skiing.
- ☐ Demonstrate the step turn while moving on skis.

Lesson 8 Uphill Ski Techniques

- ☐ Demonstrate uphill diagonal technique.
- ☐ Demonstrate herringbone technique.
- ☐ Demonstrate proper use of poles in the herringbone technique.
- ☐ Demonstrate sidestepping technique.
- ☐ Demonstrate traversing technique with the kick turn.
- ☐ Demonstrate using climbing skins.

Lesson 9 Beginning Downhill Techniques

- ☐ Demonstrate traversing a hill in a straight running position.
- ☐ Demonstrate the step turn on a downhill traverse.
- ☐ Demonstrate the basic wedge stance while not moving.
- ☐ Demonstrate the basic wedge stance while traversing a slope.
- ☐ Demonstrate stopping using the wedge technique.
- ☐ Demonstrate the proper telemark position while not moving.
- ☐ Demonstrate a running telemark position while traversing a hill.

Lesson 10 Beginning Telemark Turns

- ☐ Demonstrate the straight running telemark.
- ☐ Demonstrate the beginning telemark turn.

Lesson 11 Leave No Trace Considerations

- ☐ Summarize the seven principles of winter Leave No Trace.
- ☐ Understand the importance of local regulations regarding environmental care.
- ☐ Demonstrate the ability to integrate trip-planning concepts with LNT principles.

Lesson 12 Inclusion and Accessibility

- ☐ Describe the functional approach for modifying movement experiences (FAMME).
- ☐ Apply the FAMME model to a backcountry ski setting.

(continued)

From M. Wagstaff and A. Attarian, 2009, *Technical skills for adventure programming: A curriculum guide* (Champaign, IL: Human Kinetics).

GLOSSARY

alpine skiing—Term used to distinguish downhill from nordic skiing. Alpine skis have bindings that fix both the toe and the heel to the ski.

angulate—To angle parts of the body in relation to other parts of the body; most commonly refers to the position of the knees in relation to the rest of the body.

backcountry skiing—A type of nordic skiing that takes place off trail, usually on difficult terrain and for several days at a time.

base wax—Wax applied to the base of the ski to allow the ski to glide with less friction over the snow. Provides an adherent surface for the kick wax that is applied later and protects the base of the ski from oxidation, which increases the functional life of the ski.

bindings—The attachments that hold the boot, and consequently the foot, to the ski.

camber—The curve built into the main body of a ski to allow an even distribution of the skier's mass over the whole ski in contact with the snow.

climbing skins, or skins—Devices made of nylon, mohair, or rubber that either strap or glue to the base of the ski, allowing the skis to go uphill without sliding backward.

cross-country skiing—A term generally used to describe only the track-skiing aspects of nordic skiing. Sometimes used to include off-track skiing, XCD, and ski touring.

diagonal stride—A stride in which the skier's opposite arm and leg move simultaneously, as when walking on foot. Each stride achieves a gliding phase when executed efficiently.

fall line—The direction that the slope is running. A good way to picture the fall line is to imagine the path that a snowball would take if you rolled it down the hill.

garlands—Long turns across a slope.

glide—The restful part of skiing. The skier leaves the ski on the snow and allows it to glide after kicking off with the other ski.

herringbone—A method of ascending by alternately lifting one ski and placing it ahead of the other, and placing them in a divergent position to each other on the snow.

kick—Weighting one ski so that the wax pocket makes contact with snow, giving traction to push off.

lead change—The point in the telemark turn when the skier switches which ski is forward.

lurk—A single long pole used in early ski history for braking and steering, and as an outrigger for balance and propulsion.

nordic skiing—Type of skiing in which the heel of the boot is not attached to the ski and the toe is attached at the ball of the foot.

P-tex—A polyethylene material used to make the base of skis. The two types are sintered and monolithic. Sintered bases are used on most backcountry skis. They are porous, hold wax better, and can be repaired in the field with candle wax. Monolithic P-tex is nonporous and does not hold wax well.

poles—Held in the hand and used to balance or to propel the skier.

randonee skiing—A type of skiing that can have the boot either detached or attached at the heel. The toe of the boot is attached in front of the toe, not at the ball of the foot.

side cut—The difference in width between the tips of the skis and the waist of the ski. The more side cut a ski has the easier it turns; less side cut means that the ski will run straighter and glide longer.

sidestepping—Stepping up a hill with skis perpendicular to the slope.

straight running telemark—The skier assumes the telemark position and "runs" in a straight line.

tail—The end of the ski that is flat against the snow.

tip—The front of the ski that has a slight upward curve.

track skiing—A type of nordic skiing that stays on prepared tracks.

transition—The point before the lead change when the skis are unweighted.

traversing—Going across a slope somewhat perpendicular to the fall line. If ascending, the uphill ski leads slightly off the perpendicular to the uphill side.

unweighting—Shifting the center of gravity to take weight off the skis temporarily.

waist—The portion of the ski directly under the boot.

wax pocket—A place on the ski bottom right below the foot where the skier places wax. The weight of the foot on the ski engages the wax with the snow.

wedge—Also known as the snowplow. This technique is used to slow down and stop. The tips of the skis are together, and the tails are apart. The pressure is on the outside edges, which slows the descent.

weighting—Shifting the center of gravity to place pressure on the ski.

REFERENCES AND RESOURCES

REFERENCES

Abraham, H. (1983). *Skiing right*. Boulder, CO: Johnson Books.

Bays, T. (1985). *Nine thousand years of skis: Norwegian wood to French plastic*. Ishpeming, MI: National Ski Hall of Fame Press.

Brewster, B. (2008). Conditioning for cross country skiing. Retrieved from www.portagehealth.org/index.php?p=contentlist&clid=ARTICLES&cliid=705

Cross, R. (2005). Adventure and outdoor programming. In S.L. Kasser & R.K. Lytle (Eds.), *Inclusive physical activity: A lifetime of opportunities* (pp. 207–218). Champaign, IL: Human Kinetics.

Kasser, S.L., & Lytle, R.K. (2005). *Inclusive physical activity: A lifetime of opportunities*. Champaign, IL: Human Kinetics.

Nansen, F., & Gepp, H.M. (Translator). (2003). *The first crossing of Greenland*. New York: Random House. (Orig. pub. 1890.)

Parker, P. (2001). *Free-heel skiing: Telemark and parallel techniques for all conditions*. Seattle: The Mountaineers Books.

RESOURCES

American Avalanche Institute. www.avalanchecourse.com. Overview: This Web site lists all providers for avalanche training in the United States and Canada. Contact information: P.O. Box 308, Wilson, WY 83014; 307-733-3315 (telephone) or 307-733-3315 (fax).

Cazeneuve, B. (1995). *Cross-country skiing: A complete guide*. New York: Norton. Overview: An excellent book for the beginning cross-country skier, it provides a good overview of classic track skiing, skating, and backcountry skiing. The text contains beautiful color photos and diagrams that help the skier learn different techniques. In addition, historical stories give an enjoyable perspective on cross-country skiing. Technique and equipment are also reviewed.

Hindman, S. (2005). *Cross-country skiing: Building skills for fun and fitness*. Seattle, WA: The Mountaineers Books. Overview: An excellent primer to nordic skiing. The author starts from scratch, describing the types of skis and bindings, and shows how to get started. This is followed by a gradual progression to the more advanced techniques of efficient and enjoyable cross-country skiing. Common problems receive sidebars of easily accessed information, and technique is surveyed for different terrain and snow conditions. The book includes games, health concerns, and tips on selecting skis and clothing.

Lovett, R., & Petersen, P. (1999). *The essential cross-country skier*. Camden, ME: Ragged Mountain Press. Overview: A good resource for beginner skiers. An easy read that covers choosing equipment, getting started, and good tips on technique.

Meloche, L., & McMahon, D. (2000). *Tao of skiing: Aide memoire for cross-country skiing aficionados (the way to learn to cross-country ski)* (CD-ROM). Xzone: Canada. Overview: The CD-ROM is complete with advice (text, images, and small movies) in an easy-to-read format. Each teaching point stands on its own. The viewer can take one point at a time without having to wade through pages of verbiage. Thousands of hints and ideas, photos, diagrams, and a dozen QuickTime videos keep the reader engaged.

Ice Climbing

Thomas Stuessy and John R. Kascenska

▷ Introduction to Ice Climbing

OVERVIEW

A subset of mountaineering, ice climbing enjoys a rich history that evolved from forays across snow and ice slopes in the Alps to the extreme vertical ice columns of North America. This lesson provides an introduction to and overview of the history of ice climbing.

JUSTIFICATION

To understand the evolution of this growing outdoor adventure activity, students should be aware of the historical developments of ice climbing.

GOAL

To develop a historical understanding of ice climbing.

OBJECTIVES

At the end of this lesson, students will be able to

- identify the key historical figures responsible for the development of ice climbing (cognitive),
- identify the major geographic areas involved in the development of ice climbing (cognitive),
- describe the major developments in ice climbing (equipment, technique, and so on) (cognitive), and
- appreciate the history of ice climbing and how it contributes to the activity (affective).

EQUIPMENT AND AREAS NEEDED

A variety of images (photos, DVDs, and so on) that depict the history and evolution of ice climbing. You can obtain images from regional guidebooks, texts such as Yvonne Chouinard's *Climbing Ice* (1978), and recent publications such as Andy Selter's *Ways to the Sky: A Historical Guide to North American Mountaineering* (2004).

RISK MANAGEMENT CONSIDERATIONS

- This session is normally part of the introduction on the first day and frequently occurs indoors where no special risk management considerations are present.
- Should this discussion occur outdoors, check for environmental hazards specific to the teaching site and take appropriate precautions.

LESSON CONTENT

Introduction

Ice climbing in the United States has enjoyed a rich history, especially in northern New England. Although many of the classic ice climbs were first climbed during the "Ice Revolution" of the early 1970s, new ice-climbing areas continue to be discovered. The following selected timeline of people, activities, and climbs provides a sense of that history:

- Jacque Balmat and Dr. Michael Paccard were the first to stand on the summit of Mont Blanc in 1786.

- Hazard Stevens and Philemon Von Trump ascended Mount Rainier in 1870.

- Green and Swanzy ascended Mount Bonney in the Selkirk Range of Canada in 1888.

- The headwall of Tuckerman Ravine on Mt. Washington was first climbed in 1894 by Dr. R.C. Larrabee, Herschel C. Parker, and a Mr. Andrew.

- The first 10-point crampons were created by Oscar Eckenstein in 1908.

- Konrad Cain ascended the Northeast Face and Upper Southeast Ridge of Mount Robson in 1913.

- The first technical winter ascent of Central Gully in Huntington Ravine was achieved by A.J. Holden and N.L. Goodrich in 1927.

- Samuel A. Scoville and Julian Whittlesey made the historic first ascent of Pinnacle Gully on Mt. Washington in 1929.

- Beginning in the late 1960s a series of significant ice climbs in New England marked the beginning of the "Ice Revolution."

  - Jim McCarthy, Bill Putnam, Rick Wilcox, Rob Wallace, and Carl Brandon made the first ascent of Pinnacle Gully without cutting steps. That same winter season, Sam Streibert and Al Rubin discovered the fantastic ice-climbing potential of Frankenstein Cliff. Both events occurred during the winter of 1969–1970.

  - John Bouchard made a solo first ascent of the Black Dike on Cannon Cliff in 1971.

  - John Bragg and Rick Wilcox made the first winter ascent of Repentance on Cathedral Ledge in 1973.

  - Michael Hartrich, Al Rubin, and Henry Barber ascended Twenty Below Zero Gully on Mt. Pisgah to begin development of the Lake Willoughby area in Vermont in 1974.

- Yvonne Chouinard introduced the first American-designed rigid 12-point crampons, alpine hammers, and ice axes with a curved pick during the winter season of 1969–1970.

- By 1972 Chouinard Equipment became the leader in the distribution of American-designed ice-climbing equipment, providing climbers across the country with crampons, ice screws, and ice axes that opened ice-climbing possibilities where none seemed to have previously existed. Other equipment manufacturers soon followed.

- In the Tetons, cousins Greg and Jeff Lowe ascended the Black Ice Couloir in 1971, making a significant statement of success on a long alpine ice route.

- Allan and Adrian Burgess, Bugs McKeith, and Charlie Porter made the first ascent of Polar Circus in 1976, a 1,000-meter climb.
- Bridal Veil Fall, near Telluride, Colorado, was climbed by Jeff Lowe and Mike Weis in 1974.
- Jeff Lowe and Mike Weis teamed up again to ascend the 1,000-meter Grand Central Couloir on Mount Kitchener in the Canadian Rockies in 1975.
- The ascent of steep icy pillars continued, as new climbs began to open up across North America, from the Canadian Rockies to New England (1970s and 1980s).
- Mixed climbing (climbing on ice and rock) entered the climbing scene in the 1990s and continued into the new millennium as a new wave of techniques and radical designs in ice-climbing equipment surged and climbing in general gained popularity.
- As in rock climbing, grades of difficulty were assigned to ice climbs to take into account the general steepness and length associated with them (1980s).
  - Grade 1—Low-angle water ice less than 50 degrees in steepness.
  - Grade 2—Low-angle water ice routes with short bulges up to 60 degrees.
  - Grade 3—Steeper water ice of 50 to 60 degrees, with short 70- to 90-degree bulges.
  - Grade 4—Short vertical columns interspersed with rests on 50- to 60-degree ice. This fairly sustained climbing requires good technique and stamina.
  - Grade 5—Generally multipitch ice climbs with sustained difficulties and few opportunities for rest. The steepness and length of these routes require uppermost preparation in terms of climbing knowledge, skills, and experience.
  - Grades 6 and 7—Grades of this nature are generally found on the long and steep routes characteristic of the Canadian Rockies and the alpine ranges of Europe.

Main Activity

History Report (30 Minutes)

Divide students into small teams to choose two significant developments in the history and evolution of ice climbing to report to the class.

Closure Activity

Area Ice Review (30 Minutes)

- Have students pair up and investigate the history and ice climbing routes of an ice climbing area of their choice.
- Have students report their findings to the class.

Follow-Up Activity

Ice Climbing Investigation (Time as Needed)

Give students an opportunity to research additional text and materials (especially guidebooks) on the history and development of ice climbing.

ASSESSMENT

◆ Check that students can identify the key historical figures responsible for the development of ice climbing by orally identifying three major figures and their contributions to the development of ice climbing.

◆ Confirm that students can identify the major geographic areas involved in the development of ice climbing by describing three major ice-climbing areas in North America.

◆ Verify that students can describe the major developments in ice climbing (equipment, technique, and so on) by having them prepare a short in-class presentation on a selected piece of ice-climbing equipment or technique.

◆ Assess whether students appreciate the history of ice climbing and how it contributes to the activity through group discussions.

TEACHING CONSIDERATIONS

◆ The amount of time that you spend on this lesson depends on the depth of understanding that you want students to have about the history and evolution of ice climbing.

◆ Consider providing local histories to highlight the development of ice climbing and climbing ethics prevalent in your particular climbing area.

◆ Consider placing text materials on reserve for students to research before and following initial ice-climbing introductions.

◆ Slide or PowerPoint® presentations depicting historical characteristics can add to student development and appreciation of the roots of climbing.

UNIT 12, LESSON 2

▷ Equipment and Use

OVERVIEW

The evolution of ice-climbing equipment continues through development of new designs that keep the traditional characteristics of tools fresh and new. This lesson provides an overview of crampons, ice tools, and ice protection and shows students how to recognize, use, and maintain this equipment (ropes, harnesses, slings, and cordelette are covered in unit 2).

JUSTIFICATION

Students should learn how to choose and use ice-climbing equipment to ensure their own safety and to maintain the integrity and longevity of their equipment.

GOAL

To develop students' understanding of ice-climbing equipment.

OBJECTIVES

At the end of this lesson, students will be able to

◆ identify and describe the parts of ice tools, crampons, and ice screws (cognitive);

◆ conduct the appropriate maintenance on ice tools, crampons, and ice screws (psychomotor); and

◆ value the importance of proper equipment maintenance (affective).

EQUIPMENT AND AREAS NEEDED

◆ Examples of the various types of ice tools and crampons (possibly with images)

◆ An assortment of ice screws

◆ One pair of tools, crampons, a helmet, and a harness for each student

◆ A pair of plastic or leather boots for each student

◆ Files for sharpening ice tool picks and crampons

RISK MANAGEMENT CONSIDERATIONS

◆ Putting on and walking in crampons is tricky for the beginner. Provide each student with adequate space to fit and stand. Initially, take a walk among obstacles on a flat surface such as in the woods. Emphasize the dangers associated with crampons. If they are not careful, students can tear clothing or injure themselves, especially the lower legs. Be sure to highlight that crampons will unnecessarily damage the environment if not used appropriately.

◆ Ice tools are dangerous. Be sure to set clear boundaries and give everyone plenty of space before distributing ice tools. Tell students why they need this space, because people have a natural tendency to swing ice tools once in hand.

◆ Ice climbers are always at risk of falling from ice. They should always wear a helmet when participating in any ice-climbing activity. Again, clear and well-established physical boundaries are a must.

◆ The ice tool leash should be used only when climbing. Prevent accidents by keeping tools facing the ice as much as possible.

◆ Place the belayer in a position that allows for some movement and protection from falling ice.

◆ When a climber is being lowered, be sure that the climber is in control and has the ice pick facing away from herself or himself.

◆ Anyone who instructs ice climbing should have a thorough knowledge of the physical environment and characteristics of ice, anchor systems, and vertical rescue techniques.

LESSON CONTENT

Introduction

This lesson identifies the parts and uses of an ice-climbing tool and how its design has evolved. The lesson also covers the characteristics, uses, and evolution of ice-climbing boots and crampons. The appropriate use of ice screws and tool leashes will be also be presented and discussed through several methods of instruction. Equipment maintenance is the final topic.

Important Terms

crampons—Tempered steel shaped to fit the bottom of boots to provide traction in snow or ice terrain. The two most common designs are rigid (no flex) and hinged (flexible).

front points—The front one, two, or three points on modern crampons.

ice screws—Hollow, threaded, toothed alloy tubes of varying lengths used as protection and in anchor systems while climbing.

ice tools—Evolved out of a need to cover vertical ice. Traditional ice axes are too long; thus a shorter, more ergonomic tool was developed. Tools have six main parts: spike, grip, shaft, pick, adze, and leash.

ice tool leash—A piece of material attached to the tool midshaft that connects the tool to the climber by wrapping around the wrist.

Main Activities

Activity 1: Gear Introduction (15 Minutes)

When introducing equipment, you should have on hand examples of the items that you will be discussing. Although photos may be used, having each item of equipment creates a more meaningful learning experience.

Activity 2: Presentations (10 Minutes per Presentation)

Give groups of two or three students the responsibility for researching and then presenting a specific piece of equipment to their peers. Fill in areas when the presentations lack relevant information.

Each student presentation should include the following information for each item of equipment:

◆ History

◆ Purpose

◆ Design features

◆ Maintenance

◆ Cost

◆ Manufacturers

◆ Storage

◆ Environmental impact of production and possibly local options

Ice Tools Ice tools designed to climb vertical ice evolved from the traditional mountaineering ice axe. The ice axe was an instrument used to cut steps in steep (not vertical) ice before the creation of crampons.

◆ After crampon front points were created and vertical terrain was attempted, these long step-cutting axes became cumbersome.

◆ In response to a new role of facilitating the climbing of vertical ice, "axes" became "tools" and were designed to be short and ergonomically suited for use on vertical terrain. Tools range from 35 to 70 centimeters (about 14 to 28 inches) in length. The longer, more traditional tools are effective while mountaineering to cut steps, to use as a cane for balance, or to assist with belays. Shorter tools are used mainly for vertical ice because the shorter shaft is easier to swing.

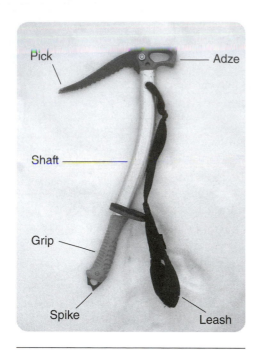

FIGURE IC2.1   Parts of an ice tool.

Tools have six parts: spike, grip, shaft, leash, pick, and adze (or hammer) (figure IC2.1).

◆ The spike is used for balance like a cane while approaching climbs or to assist in creating tool belays.

◆ The grip is where the climber holds the tool. The grip is an important feature for those with smaller hands because squeezing a large grip may be fatiguing. The grip on a traditional tool is in line with the shaft.

◆ The bend in the shaft of a tool serves multiple purposes: First, straight shafts cause a climber's knuckles to meet the ice far too often, resulting in sore or cut fingers. Second, when bent, the shaft allows a more ergonomic, free-swinging motion and produces much less damage to the climber's hands, especially the knuckles. Third, because of the clearance that the bent shaft provides, the climber can engage different types of terrain. Fourth, to meet the requirements of mixed climbing, gear manufacturers are developing tools to be used without leashes.

◆ A leashless tool (figure IC2.2) offers a distinct change of direction opposed to the shaft. A more progressive design allows the climber to employ more features on both rock and ice. Leashless tools offer two separate grips so that climbers can double grip one tool.

– Climbers choosing to climb with leashless tools must understand "grip shift." Grip shift is the swing of the bottom half of the tool in response to gripping high on the tool. If a significant amount of swing is encountered, the tool should be reconsidered.

– Climbers who are considering leashless tools should get out and climb with them in a variety of terrain.

◆ Picks are manufactured in three primary designs: straight, classic, and recurved (figure IC2.3). Classic pick designs are used more for the mountaineering axe and

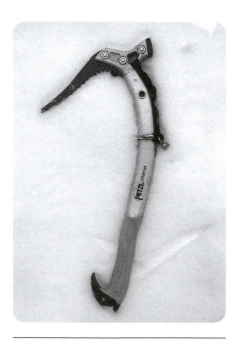

FIGURE IC2.2   Leashless tool.

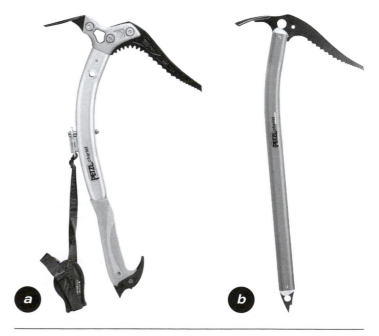

FIGURE IC2.3   Pick designs: (a) recurved and (b) classic.

seldom, if ever, used for vertical ice. For vertical ice, the recurved pick is the most common, because it allows good ice penetration and holding power.

◆ The final portion of the tool is the adze (or hammer), which, along with the pick, is attached to the shaft at the area called the head. The adze found on longer mountaineering axes was used to cut steps. The adze on a tool is still used to break away ice of poor quality or as a small shovel to sweep away crusty snow. The hammer is used for gear placement, but vertical ice climbers have rarely used it in the last decade. Mixed climbing (climbing done on routes that cover both rock and ice) has seen new and creative ways of using the adze and hammer, such as jamming in cracks to aid in upward progression on rock.

Picks can be sharpened as a maintenance measure or altered for better ice penetration. Altering the tool, however, may weaken the pick and will negate any warranty associated with it. Understanding how the pick is manufactured can be useful in the sharpening process. Three common parts of a pick can be sharpened (figure IC2.4).

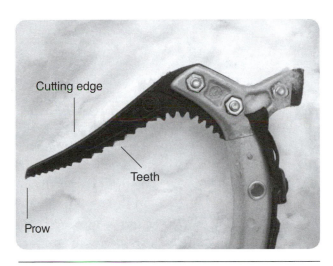

◆ First is the cutting edge, or the top edge of the pick. The manufacturer's angles should be followed when sharpening this portion of the pick.

◆ Second, the front point of the pick, the prow, should be sharpened. Aggressive sharpening at this point will ensure good penetration but weaken the pick when rock is encountered.

FIGURE IC2.4   Three parts of a pick can be sharpened.

◆ Third, the teeth on the pick can be sharpened. The teeth should be slightly beveled to ensure good holding performance when planted in ice. Most hanging or holding performance from a tool is on the front tooth of the pick. If a tool is difficult to extract from the ice, the front tooth has been sharpened too aggressively or the steps between the teeth are too deep.

To teach participants how to swing a tool, first give them an opportunity to try with little instruction. After students have had an opportunity to experiment, ask questions to obtain feedback. By doing so, students may bring your attention to a nuance of learning that you had not considered. After students have had a chance to experiment, break down the swing into the following parts:

◆ Properly position your hand on the grip.

◆ Be sure that the leash is an appropriate length (a full wrist snap should produce no pressure from the leash).

◆ Bring your hand back to your ear (tool shaft parallel to the shoulder blade).

◆ Keep your elbow in front of your body.

◆ Visually find the target.

◆ Swing the tool at the desired target and snap the wrist just before the pick makes contact with the ice.

A variety of manufacturers produce ice tools, ranging in price from $130 to $270. Tools should be stored in a dry place because the metal will rust and weaken if stored improperly. An additional storage strategy is to wipe down the picks with a lubricant such as WD-40.

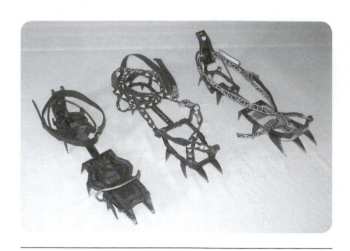

FIGURE IC2.5 Crampons.

Crampons   Before ice-climbing tools took on shorter and bent shafts, mountaineers placed crampons on their feet. Crampons are metal spikes that cut into and grip the ice to prevent falling (figure IC2.5). As an early mountaineering tool, crampons were simple but effective for covering a variety of terrain.

◆ Crampons are manufactured for both mountaineering and vertical ice climbing.

◆ Crampons come in a variety of shapes and sizes.

◆ The two main design features are the orientation of the front points and the distinction between rigid and hinged crampons.

– Historically, rigid crampons were popular because they offered a stable platform for climbers to stand on. As boot design developed, so did the crampon. As a result, two-piece and hinged crampons became the favorite and are the common choice today.

– Rigid crampons are still used, however, and are most common on rigid plastic boots.

◆ The front points of crampons may be configured in a variety of ways. Mono, dual, and three-pointed crampons can be seen at most crags today.

◆ Mono points offer an advantage when ice is thin or brittle, whereas dual points provide the beginner climber a more stable base to work from as opposed to a wobbly single point of contact.

◆ Three-pointed crampons have dropped out of favor in the last five to seven years. Having three points on crampons forces the climber to surrender sensitivity and often leads to overkicking in an effort to set the shorter points (the middle point is typically longer than the other two).

◆ Highlight the orientation of the front points. Mountaineering points are oriented parallel to the ground, whereas points for vertical ice climbing are oriented perpendicular to the ground.

Ice Screws   Ice screws (figure IC2.6) have been in use since the mid-1960s and were used to test vertical terrain in the 1970s. Because of the development of reliable ice screws and other technologies, ice climbing has seen tremendous growth in the last 40 years.

◆ Ice screws currently range in length from 10 to 22 centimeters (4 to 9 inches) and are approximately 8 to 10 millimeters in diameter.

◆ Made from alloys, screws are useful tools for climbers.

◆ The two purposes for screws are for leading protection and setting anchors. Ice screws require specific features to be effective.

◆ Placing an ice screw improperly or attempting to use poor ice is worse than not placing a screw at all.

◆ Placing a screw takes time and energy, two things that a good ice climber conserves.

◆ A poorly placed screw may instill a false sense of security, take precious time, and will likely fail in the event of a fall.

◆ Placing an ice screw is an art and begins with the feet.

◆ Without a stable platform to push against, placing the screw will take extra time and considerably more effort.

Break down ice screw placement into the following steps:

◆ After establishing a base, hold the screw like a gun (the hanger is at the base of your palm).

◆ Begin by putting the cutting edge of the screw on the ice at waist level and rotating your wrist back and forth cutting a groove in the ice.

◆ After a groove is cut, push in firmly while turning the screw to the right. Slowly, release your hand and quickly regrip the screw, continuing this motion.

◆ After the screw has bitten the ice, proceed until it is set properly in the ice.

The angle in which the screw is placed is important.

◆ Testing has shown that an upward angle of approximately 15 degrees is optimal in good ice (figure IC2.7).

◆ The strength of an ice screw is not in the tube but in the threads cut into the sides of the tube.

◆ Placing screws at a downward angle causes the climber to rely on the lateral strength of the screw, which is much less effective at holding a fall than are the threads.

◆ In some circumstances a straight or downward-angle placement must be used.

◆ If the ice becomes soft or slushy because of a change in weather, the strength of the threads cannot be trusted. Instead, and not ideally, the lateral strength of the tube must be relied on, and a downward angle may be the best option.

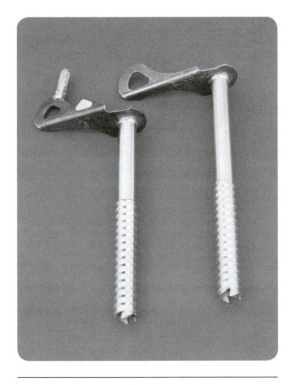

FIGURE IC2.6   Ice screws.

FIGURE IC2.7   Ice screw placement.

How strong are ice screws?

◆ The two most documented ice screw studies are the Harmston and Black Diamond study (1998) and the Luebben (1997) study.

◆ These studies showed that a properly placed ice screw should hold approximately 8,000 pounds (3,600 kilograms) of force. The word *should* is used in a literal sense.

◆ Ice is a changing medium, and leading on ice is an activity that must follow years of experience on a top rope.

Closure Activities

Allow students to manipulate gear so that they can learn how to handle and maintain it.

Activity 1: Picks and Crampons (20 Minutes)

Initiate this activity by demonstrating how to sharpen picks and crampons.

◆ Give students the opportunity to use a file on the picks in a controlled setting. Inquire about how filing the picks into certain shapes would help or hinder climbing specific routes.

◆ At this point, inquiry learning may be an appropriate teaching method.

◆ Ask students what each surface of the pick and crampons is designed to do.

Activity 2: Ice Screws (15 Minutes)

Only expert climbers or the manufacturer should sharpen ice screws. Each tooth of an ice screw has three or four surfaces. Given the small surface area on the teeth of screws, it would be easy to oversharpen one surface, rendering the screw in a less-than-optimal condition.

◆ Give each student an ice screw and ask students to find placements from the ground.

◆ After each student has placed a screw, take the class to a selected few to evaluate the placement.

◆ At this point introduce the ice features that they should be looking for to achieve good placement.

◆ Emphasize that solid ice is ideal, that concave surfaces hold better than convex (bulging) surfaces, that a downward angle is stronger, and that proximity to other screws is important in the event of ice fracture.

Follow-Up Activity

Student-Designed Evaluations (20 to 30 Minutes)

◆ Ask students to create two quiz questions to share with the class.

◆ Assign specific pieces of gear to each student to ensure that all the gear introduced in this lesson is covered.

◆ After each student has the opportunity to share quiz questions, review the quiz as a group to ensure that students understand all information.

◆ Be sure that all students have had an opportunity to interact with the gear in the field. Simple quizzing will not be enough to reach a real understanding. During this field time, you should be in a position to provide clear and immediate feedback.

ASSESSMENT

◆ Verify that students can identify and describe the parts of ice tools, crampons, and ice screws by observing their presentations in the main activity.

◆ Check that students can conduct the appropriate maintenance on ice tools, crampons, and ice screws by supervising and observing each student sharpen an ice axe pick and crampon during the follow-up activity.

◆ Confirm that students value the importance of proper equipment maintenance by having them climb first with poorly maintained equipment and then with well-maintained equipment on ice they can reach from the ground. Ask them to compare their performance with the two sets of equipment.

TEACHING CONSIDERATIONS

◆ You can present this lesson in two parts if the meeting time does not extend for an entire day.

◆ This lesson requires that students be prepared to be outside to access nearly vertical ice. Further, much of the gear being handled is sharp and dangerous.

◆ Students may need something to write on that the rest of the class can see. A portable whiteboard may be useful.

◆ You should be cognizant of the temperature and local weather to help ensure the safety of the group.

◆ You should also be wary of icefall at all times. Select a site where you can set clear boundaries and be able to stop or shift the activity quickly should it become necessary to do so.

UNIT 12, LESSON 3

▷ **Preparing to Climb**

OVERVIEW

Ice climbing requires participants to be well prepared for a day of strenuous physical activity in cold weather. Their physical comfort relates directly to wearing proper clothing and being physically prepared. This lesson provides a set of principles that you can apply to the participant group with whom you are working.

JUSTIFICATION

Knowledge and application of the proper dress for ice-climbing activity are essential to participants' comfort and enjoyment. Physical preparedness is equally important, because ice climbing is generally a more strenuous activity than other forms of climbing.

GOAL

To develop the students' knowledge of appropriate dress for participation in ice climbing and awareness of the principles that will aid in physical preparedness.

OBJECTIVES

At the end of this lesson, students will be able to

- identify the key components of being properly dressed for ice climbing (cognitive),
- identify the key components of physical preparedness associated with ice climbing (cognitive), and
- appreciate the contribution of thorough preparation to the overall enjoyment of ice climbing (affective).

EQUIPMENT AND AREAS NEEDED

Materials and supplies for this lesson include a full complement of clothing typically used in ice-climbing activity:

- Long underwear (tops and bottoms—lightweight to expedition weight)
- Liner socks
- Heavyweight insulated socks
- Soft-shell fabric (Scholler type) pant
- Soft-shell fabric zip jacket
- Fleece jacket
- Insulated jacket (down or synthetic)
- Gore-Tex (or similar) wind or rain pants or bibs
- Insulated gloves and mittens
- Gore-Tex shell jacket with a hood large enough to fit over a helmet
- Ski hat and balaclava
- Gaiters

RISK MANAGEMENT CONSIDERATIONS

- Students who are not outfitted with proper clothing run the risk of contracting a range of cold-related signs and symptoms, including mild hypothermia and frostbite.
- Participants who are constantly fighting against the cold will not be able to maintain focus on the essential elements of ice climbing, which are directly related to personal safety.

LESSON CONTENT

Introduction

It is not mandatory for ice climbers to experience being cold during the actual activity. Emphasize this point to students so that they arrive on the day of their first ice-climbing trip with the proper clothing.

◆ The range of temperatures and weather-related phenomena can vary dramatically from day to day.

◆ Temperatures that hover around the freezing mark are often the most difficult to dress for because students need to wear enough layers to ward off the cold but not so many layers that they overheat (and dampen underclothing) while climbing.

◆ Besides employing appropriate clothing items and layering, a key element to warding off cold is to strike a balance concerning nutrition, hydration, and pacing.

Equipment Preparedness

Offer these tips about staying warm:

◆ Wear fabrics that stay warm when wet. No cotton!

◆ Stay as dry as possible by applying appropriate layering principles.

◆ Be attentive to yourself. If you are getting cold, add an additional layer and stay active.

◆ Snack often on foods that are high in quick-burning carbohydrates.

◆ Stay hydrated; pack hot drinks such as tea in a thermos.

◆ Carry a minimum of two pairs of hand wear (insulated gloves and mittens). Some ice climbers carry more than two pairs, knowing that hand wear can become wet from constant contact with snow and ice.

Physical Preparedness

◆ Start the ice-climbing day with a few warm-up activities to allow students to ease into the physical demands of the activity and minimize any overstretching or straining of muscle groups.

◆ Most ice-climbing sites require a short approach (some are longer) that may afford students an opportunity to warm the core and extremities.

◆ Encourage students to engage in stretching activities on days when they are not climbing to enhance flexibility and range of motion.

◆ Daily stretching activities should take place for a minimum of 10 minutes. Taking a few minutes to engage in gentle stretching after reaching the climbing site will help muscle groups warm up through increased blood flow.

◆ Refer to the figures to develop a series of stretches:
  – Shoulders and upper back (figure IC3.1)
  – Arms and upper torso (figure IC3.2)
  – Knee to chest (figure IC3.3)
  – Calf (figure IC3.4)

Main Activities

Activity 1: Warming Up (10 to 15 Minutes)

Engage students in a demonstration and practice of the stretching exercises illustrated in the figures.

Activity 2: Trip Planning (20 Minutes)

Have students work together to generate an equipment and clothing list relevant to all participants and the weather that they are likely to encounter.

FIGURE IC3.1   Shoulders and upper-back stretch.

FIGURE IC3.2   Arms and upper-torso stretch.

FIGURE IC3.3   Knee-to-chest stretch.

Closure Activity

Clothing and Equipment Shakedown (30 Minutes)

Conduct an equipment and clothing check of all students before advancing to ice-climbing activities in the field. You need to ensure that students have the appropriate type and amount of clothing layers.

Follow-Up Activity

Group Stretch (10 to 15 Minutes)

◆ Lead the group in a stretching session or ask a student to lead. Ask individual students to share a favorite stretching or warm-up exercise.

FIGURE IC3.4   Calf stretch.

◆ Encourage students to keep an exercise and climbing journal throughout the unit. They should record any training activity and ice-climbing outings in which they participate.

ASSESSMENT

◆ Check that students can identify the key components of being properly dressed for ice-climbing activity by asking them to generate a list of the clothing items necessary for a comfortable ice-climbing outing.

◆ Confirm that students can identify the key components of physical preparedness associated with ice climbing by asking them to demonstrate a favorite stretching exercise during the follow-up activity.

◆ Verify that students appreciate the contribution of thorough preparation to their enjoyment of ice climbing by asking them whether they will experience success during ice-climbing outings and then observing their response.

TEACHING CONSIDERATIONS

◆ You can provide a show-and-tell presentation of clothing items typically used in ice-climbing activities. This activity will provide a literal hands-on teachable moment for all students to see what they need before going into the field.

◆ A review of the stretching activities listed earlier with full class participation will help students adopt this activity as a regular practice.

◆ Consider assigning a couple of students to lead the class in stretching activities before each field day session.

◆ Always carry extra articles of clothing in your pack, including hats, gloves, and socks, to share with students who may be inadequately prepared.

UNIT 12, LESSON 4

▷ The Anatomy of Ice

OVERVIEW

"Ice can be formed directly from water freezing, or indirectly through the continuing metamorphosis of neve, whereby the snowpack becomes more dense. The medium is called ice when its mass becomes airtight."

Chouinard, 1978

An understanding of how ice is formed and what forces cause it to change is critical to safe and enjoyable ice climbing. This lesson teaches students how to assess ice conditions utilizing color, weather, and shape.

JUSTIFICATION

The inherent danger of ice climbing makes reading ice conditions a critical skill for climbers. The ability to read and assess ice conditions accurately will enable students to develop confidence and independence regarding route choices.

GOAL

To develop participants' ability to read and assess ice conditions independently and accurately.

OBJECTIVES

At the end of this lesson, students will be able to

- understand how ice is formed (cognitive);
- recognize the characteristics associated with colors of ice (cognitive);
- understand how changing weather influences ice conditions (cognitive);
- use the shape of the ice as a determining factor regarding tool, crampon, and protection placement (cognitive);
- use equipment properly given the characteristics of the ice (psychomotor); and
- confidently assess ice characteristics on their own when climbing (affective).

EQUIPMENT AND AREAS NEEDED

- As many different types of ice as possible or photos of many different types of ice
- Ice tools, screws, crampons, harnesses, and helmets
- A site that can comfortably accommodate the number of participants in your group (ideally all will have access to ice at ground level)

RISK MANAGEMENT CONSIDERATIONS

- Sufficient space must be available for each participant to swing tools.
- Crampon placement should be done only on a tight belay that will compensate for rope stretch. Landing on uneven terrain can be challenging and possibly unsafe for climbers new to wearing crampons.
- Take time throughout this lesson to set clear boundaries for students. With boundaries, you can pause the action quickly and position yourself where you can provide immediate feedback.
- Do not use spotting as a safety precaution if students are stepping up on crampons, even just 1 or 2 feet (30 to 60 centimeters) off the ground. Tools may flail around or an awkward fall may lead to a spotter being kicked with crampons.
- The pick will displace ice on impact. Eye protection is recommended.

LESSON CONTENT

Introduction

Ice conditions influence the use of tools, crampons, and ice screws. By learning how to read the changing medium of ice, students will be able to use each of these pieces of gear appropriately and safely.

Main Activities

You will need to support this portion of the lesson with photos because no site will have all forms of ice covered here.

Important Terms

blue ice—Solid, stable, and often hard ice.

bulge—A convex piece of ice.

cauliflower ice—Resembling the vegetable cauliflower, this ice often forms near the bottom of ice climbs and is the result of water splashing and freezing. More often than not, it is stable and strong ice, good for hooking or absorbing a good swing (figure IC4.1).

chandelier ice—Multiple icicles in close proximity to one another typically offer unstable climbing until their diameters are large enough to hold the weight of a climber. This type of ice is often found early in the season (figure IC4.2).

verglas—Smooth, rock-hard sheets of thin ice, often found in midseason.

white ice—As in whitewater, the white appearance indicates the presence of air. White ice should be climbed with caution because aerated ice is weak. White ice is most frequently seen in the early and late parts of the season.

yellow ice—The yellow color indicates that the flow of water is transporting minerals. Yellow ice should not be a deterrent to climbing, but it indicates recent flow, which usually comes with warmer temperatures. Climbers should be careful.

FIGURE IC4.1   Cauliflower ice forms at the base of ice climbs.

FIGURE IC4.2   Chandelier ice is made up of icicles in close proximity to one another.

Activity 1: Identifying Ice Features (45 Minutes)

Ice features help determine what techniques a climber needs to use. The combination of understanding ice features and being able to execute climbing techniques is what enables a climber to be successful.

◆ Have small groups of students provide a topographical assessment of a portion of ice, approximately 6 feet across and 7 feet high (1.8 meters across and 2 meters high). Next, have them analyze what portions of the ice will be able to absorb a tool placement. Allow them time to read the ice under controlled conditions

- Provide each student with enough space and protective equipment to test assumptions about the ice features by swinging a tool at the ice.

- Students can offer an assessment of successful placement features. You can provide reasons why some placements were successful and others were not.

- Moving effectively on ice is often a matter of employing the proper technique in changing situations. The way that the ice reacts and your clear and immediate feedback will help students learn about varying ice conditions.

- To ensure an understanding of ice features, have students provide an explanation of what technique to use for each ice feature.

- Encourage students to explore different features found in the ice. For example, they can swing a pick at a bulge, or convex section, of ice. Then they can swing at a concave section and note the different outcomes.

- Have them repeat this experiment with chandelier, cauliflower, and different colors of ice.

Activity 2: Ice Formation (30 Minutes)

The mechanics of ice formation should be an ongoing lesson for participants. Early, midseason, and late-season ice all have distinct characteristics that climbers should understand.

When teaching about ice formation, use whatever conditions you have as a baseline. For example, if a group of climbers were to arrive in Vermont in mid-December, the teaching topic would be the characteristics of early season ice.

Early Season Ice
- Early season ice should be approached with extreme caution.
- Early season ice is often at the mercy of fluctuating temperatures.
- Early season ice is often aerated (white in color), full of chandeliers, and typically not well bonded to the rock.
- Good ice forms slowly from low volumes of water in mildly cold temperatures of 10 to 30 degrees Fahrenheit (–12 to –1 degree Celsius).
- Keeping safety as a priority over excitement for the upcoming season is tough, but express this warning to participants often.

Midseason Ice
- Midseason ice can easily be recognized by lateral ice growth.
- After ice forms in relatively warm weather, the flow is forced in new directions to create a climb that becomes well bonded and has more width.
- Often, midseason ice is still growing, leaving large holes in the middle of some routes. These holes are an excellent place to investigate the bond to the rock.
- Routes that are not forming completely typically result from climbers being on the route too soon and breaking off ice or from heavy water flow that causes melting or creates fragile chandelier ice.
- Midseason ice is more of a result of consistent temperatures than it is of ice features.

◆ In most regions of the country, temperatures below 30 degrees Fahrenheit (–1 degree Celsius) for an extended period ensure a strong bond between ice and rock.

◆ Midseason fluctuations in ice temperature regularly bring changing color to the ice. Yellow ice is an indication of recent flow. This new water flow carries with it mineral deposits from the soil that have been frozen.

◆ Cold temperatures also bring new colors. Blue ice is typically solid and well bonded to the rock, indicating that the temperature has been relatively stable and that new ice is not highly aerated.

Late-Season Ice

◆ Late-season ice holds many opportunities. Typically, temperatures are warming up, which leaves ice relatively soft and often stable.

◆ Many routes that were extremely difficult during the middle of the season will take picks and screws more easily, offering climbers a chance to test the skills that they have acquired throughout the season in a more forgiving environment.

◆ But the warmer temperatures and good climbing are not a secret. Climbers often appear in larger numbers during this time of year, so walking or standing near the base of a route is a more risky endeavor because of falling ice or gear. Climbers should have fun but be careful.

Closure Activity

The Perfect Model (10 Minutes or Longer)

After identifying a volunteer to climb, critique the volunteer's choice of route, features used, and technique.

◆ A discussion of ice features can follow. Be sure to answer students' questions.

◆ During the discussion, you should ask participants about specific ice features, colors, and weather conditions.

◆ Encourage students to climb a route without swinging. A no-swing climb slows the beginner climber just enough to break the pattern of looking only straight up.

Follow-Up Activity

Peer Evaluation (Time as Needed)

◆ Give each participant an opportunity to critique the climb of a peer. The critique should include an assessment of the route selected, features used, and how efficiently the climber moved.

◆ Have students participate in the single-swing test.
  – The single-swing test was developed to illustrate the mind-set required for each swing of the tool while climbing.
  – Give each student a tool and instruct the students to examine the ice for the best feature for a tool placement.
  – Each participant is allowed only one swing at the ice.
  – Assess how well each student placed the tool. After you evaluate each participant's placement, explain that climbers should use a similar focus for every swing while keeping in mind that good ice climbers keep moving.

◆ Have students keep an ice-conditions diary throughout the unit.
  – They should include data for ice climbs done in class and on their own.
  – The record should include date, location, ice climbs climbed or attempted, air temperature, weather and ice conditions, and color as the season progresses.
  – At the end of the ice season, they should draw some conclusions based on an analysis of the data. For example, was this a good ice season? A bad ice season? Why?

ASSESSMENT

◆ Check that students understand how ice is formed by asking them questions about the development of ice during their topographical assessment.

◆ Confirm that students recognize the characteristics associated with colors of ice by asking them to describe these through a short written quiz.

◆ Verify that students understand how changing weather influences ice conditions by looking at their analyses of the data generated from their ice conditions diaries.

◆ Check that students can use the shape of the ice as a determining factor regarding tool, crampon, and protection placement by observing them practice placements during the follow-up activity.

◆ Confirm that students can use equipment properly given the characteristics of the ice by observing them use equipment during the follow-up activity.

◆ Check that students can assess ice characteristics on their own when climbing by looking at the information generated from their ice conditions diaries.

TEACHING CONSIDERATIONS

◆ Make an effort to visit ice-climbing sites during early, mid-, and late season to allow your students to see how ice is formed and to familiarize them with the sites. Visit these same sites after warm spells, rain, heavy snow, or a hard freeze to examine how these factors affect the formation of ice.

◆ In some cases, some of this assessment can be done from a roadside with a good pair of binoculars.

◆ When doing site visits, be wary of icefall. Select an area where you can set clear boundaries and be able to stop or modify the activity quickly should it become necessary to do so.

◆ Remember to have the appropriate safety equipment with you when making these site visits.

UNIT 12, LESSON 5

▷ # Low-Angled and Vertical Ice-Climbing Techniques

OVERVIEW

Most beginning ice-climbing students are capable of moving from low-angled ice to more vertical ice in a relatively short period. The key to coaching students through this transition is to focus instruction and student practice on the use of a few critical skills that will allow them to attempt more difficult and challenging climbs with each outing. This lesson provides an overview of those key elements.

JUSTIFICATION

Students must learn the essential elements of low-angled and vertical ice climbing techniques. The use of proper technique will make the activity more enjoyable for the participant and enhance personal safety.

GOAL

To introduce students to techniques associated with low-angled and vertical ice-climbing techniques.

OBJECTIVES

At the end of this lesson, students will be able to

- identify and apply principles associated with the swing (planting the ice axe) (cognitive),
- identify and apply principles associated with the kick (planting front points) (cognitive),
- identify the principles associated with upward movement (cognitive),
- demonstrate the correct planting of the ice axe (psychomotor), and
- demonstrate the proper use of crampons (psychomotor).

EQUIPMENT AND AREAS NEEDED

- Ice axes
- Crampons
- Harness
- Helmet
- Climbing rope

RISK MANAGEMENT CONSIDERATIONS

- Students attempting to climb steep ice terrain are more likely to become fatigued than they were when working on low-angled ice slopes.
- Although students may expect to become fatigued higher up on a climb, failing to use good technique can cause falls low to the ground. As such, tight belays must be maintained throughout the climb to minimize fall potential.
- Catching a crampon point during a fall, even while on top rope, can result in anything from a sprained or broken ankle to a soft-tissue injury.
- Joint injuries are more likely to occur during vertical ice-climbing practice, particularly when a student's crampons sheer out from the ice, leaving a fatigued student hanging from the wrist loops.
- You should be familiar with techniques to provide the climber with a short-haul assist that will relieve pressure in those situations.
- Ice falling from above can be a hazard for belayers and other climbers, so you must employ appropriate climbing site management techniques.
- Dropped tools, as well as crampons becoming undone, can also be an issue.
- Students moving from using flat-footed techniques on low-angled ice to using front-pointing methods on vertical ice will find themselves pressed closer to the ice surface with the arms positioned overhead, all leading to increased fatigue.

LESSON CONTENT

Introduction

The heart of this lesson is instruction in the art of foot placement with crampons and tool placements as the ice terrain increases in steepness.

Main Activities

Activity 1: Foot Placements (10 to 15 Minutes)

- Remind students to keep their heels low to the point that the bottom of the boot surface is perpendicular to the slope of the ice. This position allows maximum penetration of the front points into the ice surface.
- Repeated kicks into the ice rarely improve crampon security.
- When encountering places to rest, students should stand on the right foot with the leg extended and arms hanging straight. The left foot is used to stabilize the diagonal.

Activity 2: Tool Placements (10 Minutes or Longer)

- Emphasize to students that they should maximize pick penetration and minimize the number of swings to produce solid ice tool placement.
- Point out that swinging with the whole arm will generate greater force and ensure solid ice placement on the first (ideally) or second swing.
- Point out that tool placements should be tested, meaning that students should weight the tool by pulling downward to ensure that the pick is stable in the ice before moving upward.
- Students can practice ice tool placements on the ground along the bottom of a vertical ice section.
- Most students will be challenged with using two tools, one in the dominant hand, and one in the nondominant hand.
- Students should understand the importance of not driving the pick of the ice axe too far into the ice. If they do this, pick removal can become difficult and add to fatigue, especially if the student is poised on the ice in a position that does not allow sufficient rest.

Closure Activity

Ice Bouldering (Time as Needed)

- Finish the lesson by having students engage in ice bouldering.
- Emphasize good axe technique and footwork.
- Encourage peer-to-peer critique of climbing techniques.

Follow-Up Activity

Practice What You Preach (Time as Needed)

Following your demonstration of vertical climbing techniques and practice by students (swinging the ice axe and ice bouldering), have students engage in a series of ice climbs. They should strive to use proper footwork and ice axe placements over the length of an entire ice climb.

ASSESSMENT

◆ Verify that students can identify and apply principles associated with the swing by asking them to review this skill orally with one another.

◆ Confirm that students can identify and apply principles associated with the kick by asking them to review this skill orally with one another.

◆ Check that students can identify the principles associated with upward movement by asking them to critique one another during the ice-bouldering activity.

◆ Verify that students can demonstrate correct planting of the ice axe by observing them during the ice-bouldering activity.

◆ Confirm that students can demonstrate the proper use of crampons by observing them during the ice-bouldering activity.

TEACHING CONSIDERATIONS

◆ Students can practice individual swing technique on vertical ice sections at the base of the ice-climbing site using both the dominant and nondominant arms without having to leave the ground.

◆ This procedure allows you to provide suggestions to students in an efficient manner.

◆ This activity can double as a good warm-up session for students before they advance into a roped climbing situation.

◆ Teaching proper crampon placements can be more challenging. Instructor demonstration is important. Placing students in a location where they can see the effect of proper foot position will help emphasize the importance of keeping the heels low in vertical climbing situations.

◆ Students will need individual coaching on crampon placement.

UNIT 12, LESSON 6

▷ Anchors for Ice Climbing

OVERVIEW

This lesson incorporates anchor demonstrations, anchor building, and anchor assessment techniques. Students have opportunities to rehearse setting anchors in a controlled setting.

JUSTIFICATION

Understanding how to construct an effective and safe anchor is a foundational skill for continued involvement in ice climbing. Practicing this critical skill promotes climbing independence and increases awareness of climbing systems among new climbers.

GOAL

To develop an ability to set top-rope, belay, and lead-climbing ice-climbing anchors.

OBJECTIVES

At the end of this lesson, students will be able to

◆ understand how to use natural and artificial protection for anchors (cognitive),

◆ demonstrate the appropriate edge behavior when setting anchors (psychomotor),

◆ demonstrate the use of natural and artificial protection for anchors (psychomotor),

◆ develop independence through learning how to build anchors on their own (affective),

◆ conduct a site assessment to determine what type of anchor system is most effective (cognitive), and

◆ perform an accurate assessment of a site and the resources therein (cognitive).

EQUIPMENT AND AREAS NEEDED

◆ Two cordelettes approximately 20 feet (6 meters) long for every two participants

◆ One static line approximately 100 feet (30 meters) long for every two participants

◆ Six ice screws, each no less than 12 centimeters (5 inches), for every two participants

◆ Four Prusik cords for every two participants

◆ Six locking carabiners per participant

RISK MANAGEMENT CONSIDERATIONS

◆ Manage the base (or staging area) of an ice climb by making sure that participants have adequate room for gearing up and are protected from icefall. Pay close attention for the signs and symptoms of hypothermia and dehydration.

◆ Maintain attention to weather patterns and temperature throughout the day.

◆ At the top of climbs, select a site that can safely accommodate the size of the group. People should be able to move around some, and the site should allow you to maintain clear and consistent edge protection.

◆ Do not attempt to bring a large number of people to the top of any climb, a circumstance that often leads to inadequate demonstrations and ineffective communication. Recall that the goal is to provide students with anchor information.

◆ Depending on the type of anchor being constructed, setting an anchor may include using artificial protection on the vertical face of a climb in the event that natural protection is not present near the top of the route. In this event, you must use a backup belay until participants demonstrate the ability to self-protect adequately over the edge while setting anchors.

LESSON CONTENT

Introduction

This lesson focuses on how to employ materials used to set anchors. Additionally, site assessment and decision making regarding systems and edge behavior will be developed.

Important Terms

cordelette—Cord of smaller diameter and 15 to 20 feet (4.5 to 6 meters) in length used for constructing anchors.

dynamic rope—Rope manufactured to stretch when force is applied.

edge culture—How people conduct themselves on a cliff edge.

fall factor—Formula used to determine the energy put on a system in the event of a fall.

kilonewton—1,000 newtons, or 224.8 pounds of force.

master point—The point at which the anchor is equalized and meets the carabiners holding the rope.

pounds of force—The climber's weight multiplied by the length of rope (in feet) extended beyond the last piece of protection.

screamer—An extending and shock-absorbing piece used to connect the rope to protection with two carabiners.

static rope—Rope that has little stretch, less than 3 percent.

Main Activity

Anchor Building (Two Hours or More)

The first portion of the lesson should be viewed from an outdoor skills perspective. To build students' outdoor skills, you should balance directive and experiential methods. In doing so, maintain challenge and encourage students to self-assess their abilities regarding anchor building. An effective lesson will ensure that students establish good anchor-building techniques and accurate self-assessment.

Technical Functions   First, break down the skill into its basic technical functions. Build on knowledge slowly while coaching anchor building. Set up the lesson for easy and early success. Be sure to empower your students. A good way to do this is to be in a physical position where you can provide immediate feedback. Anchor building is a competence and confidence builder among new climbers.

To get started, students should master knots and hitches. See unit 2, lesson 3, on knots and their applications.

Anchor Physics   After students master knots and hitches, you can address the physics surrounding anchors. Strong anchors are derived from three primary factors: materials, type of protection used, and the system chosen.

◆ Apply the ERNEST principle (equalized, redundant, non-extending, solid/simple, timely) for building anchors. This anchor-building concept is discussed in detail in unit 2, lesson 7.

  – Being timely with anchor construction in an ice-climbing environment is important in maintaining student comfort, but it should never exceed the goal of safety.

  – Taking a half hour to set an anchor during the winter typically means that a cold group will be standing or wandering around at the base of a route waiting to climb.

◆ As in rock climbing, natural anchors use the natural environment for protection. Artificial anchors for ice climbing incorporate ice screws. If placed properly, ice screws offer ease, safety, and multiple options for ice-climbing anchors.

◆ Begin anchor coaching at ground level ("ground school"). Use a progression that allows participants to employ previous knowledge while balancing directive and experiential challenges.

◆ What follows is a progression designed to use natural anchors as a first means of protection, followed by a combination of natural and artificial protection. Finally, lacking natural protection, artificial protection will be used.

Natural Protection   Find a large "bomber" tree, 12 inches (30 centimeters) or larger in diameter, and appropriately close to the edge. Use a cordelette with a wrap and figure-eight. This and other natural anchors are discussed in detail in unit 2, lesson 6 (see figure RC6.1 on page 189).

Combination of Natural and Artificial Protection   Using two types of protection is often necessary for ice climbing. Typically, a tree or boulder will be used with the assistance of one or more ice screws. ERNEST principles still apply.

Artificial Protection   Ice screws are fast, light, and strong pieces to use for anchors. But as with other pieces of equipment introduced in this unit, there is a right and a wrong way to use them.

Although studies have shown that a well-placed screw can hold more than 8,000 pounds (3,600 kilograms) of force (Leubben, 1999), this figure should not be taken at face value. Testing of ice-climbing equipment is done by professionals in controlled research conditions. The typical ice climber is far better served using knowledge gained through experience than the results of a piece of research.

What makes a well-placed screw?

◆ First, what is the ice quality? Like the pick of a tool placed into ice, screws require ice that is hard, well bonded to the rock, deep, concave, and able to accommodate the correct angle for the placement.

◆ The strength of an ice screw comes from the threads on the tube, not the tube itself (although certain types of ice may rely on the tube for strength).

◆ The lateral strength of a screw should rarely be relied on. Instead, as the studies suggest, the screw should be placed at an upward angle somewhere between 15 and 5 degrees, with the hanger down.

◆ Note several things in figure IC6.1. First, none of the screws are placed on the same horizontal or vertical plane. This arrangement is used so that an ice fracture will not affect all screws. Ice often fractures either vertically or in a slight frowning fashion laterally.

◆ The saying "70, 20" means that the top screw is at least 70 centimeters (28 inches) above the lowest screw and that the bottom screws are no closer than 20 centimeters (8 inches) and not on the same plane (figure IC6.2).

Closure Activity

Site Assessment (Time as Needed)

◆ If time and pace allows, divide students into groups of three.

◆ Have students conduct a site assessment to determine the appropriate anchor to use.

FIGURE IC6.1   Pre-equalized ice screw anchor.

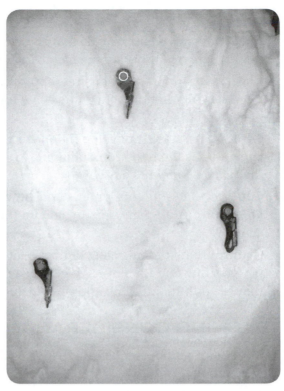

FIGURE IC6.2   Typical ice screw formation for an artificial anchor.

- Each group sets up a top-rope climb while maintaining edge protection. After you check each anchor, ask each group to set up an additional anchor at the same location.
- Be sure to place yourself in a position where you can stop the activity at a moment's notice if the site becomes unsafe.

Follow-Up Activity

Building Anchors (Time as Needed)

Building simple and effective anchors is an art that takes practice and must be done in a variety of settings.

- After you have taught the basics of anchor building and are sure that students understand proper edge behavior, make students responsible for setting all the anchors (checked by you).
- After students have more practice, you can offer additional information about topics such as multidirectional anchor points and vertical anchors (those that are over the edge of an ice climb).
- As climbing continues, students will be exposed to different kinds of anchor-building situations.
- Use each new situation as an opportunity to expand knowledge, including mixing natural and artificial protection, using static line or cordelette, and protecting the person building the anchor.

ASSESSMENT

- Confirm that students can demonstrate the use of natural and artificial protection for anchors by observing them construct both types of anchors.
- Check that students demonstrate appropriate edge behavior when setting anchors by observing them practice this behavior while constructing anchors at the top of each climb.
- Verify that students develop independence in building anchors on their own by encouraging them to keep a climbing log for each climbing site visited and noting the types of anchors employed.
- Confirm that students understand how and when to employ the appropriate knots for building anchors by conducting a site assessment during the closure activity.
- Confirm that students can conduct a site assessment by observing them as they perform one and then by asking them a series of questions about the criteria that they used to identify the appropriate anchors.

TEACHING CONSIDERATIONS

- Conduct reconnaissance on all sites to be used for teaching before the time of instruction.
- You should be in a physical position to stop the activity at a moment's notice to ensure safety of students at all times.
- You should be in a physical position to provide clear and immediate feedback to students.
- Use concepts that are inherent to the activity while using practical teaching progressions.
- Balance directive and experiential teaching methods to accommodate all learning styles.
- Include techniques that allow students to self-assess skills critically in an emotionally safe environment.

UNIT 12, LESSON 7

▷ Safety Considerations

OVERVIEW

Safety is a common thread that instructors must emphasize across every lesson associated with ice climbing. The medium in which the activity takes place demands it. The consequences of not maintaining safety management are significant (Nicolazzo, 2002).

JUSTIFICATION

Students must understand the essential elements of safety as it applies to ice climbing.

GOAL

To develop safety awareness among ice-climbing students.

OBJECTIVES

At the end of this lesson, students will be able to

◆ identify the elements of safety associated with ice climbing (cognitive),

◆ describe the various cold-related injuries associated with ice climbing (cognitive),

◆ identify the common objective dangers (environmental) related to ice climbing (cognitive),

◆ identify the common subjective dangers (human related) associated with ice climbing (cognitive), and

◆ appreciate the dangers of ice climbing and act accordingly (affective).

EQUIPMENT AND AREAS NEEDED

None.

RISK MANAGEMENT CONSIDERATIONS

None.

LESSON CONTENT

Introduction

Many hazards are associated with participation in ice climbing. Exposure to hazards can be mitigated by observing the considerations outlined in previous lessons of this unit and in the unit on mountaineering. The following is a selected list of common hazards that you can review with students before each ice-climbing trip, thereby planting a seed of safety management to be applied in the field.

Main Activity

Hazard Review (30 Minutes)

Review the following list of hazards with students before engaging in an ice-climbing session. You could challenge students to generate a list of hazards that they perceive are associated with ice climbing.

◆ Cold injuries and illnesses—Exposure to cold temperatures for extended periods can have devastating effects on students *and* instructors. Additional information on cold-related injuries can be found in unit 9, lesson 5, and unit 11, lesson 3.

◆ Temperatures below 0 degrees Fahrenheit (–18 degrees Celsius) will add greatly to the challenge of maintaining adequate warmth. Lowering of the body's core temperature below 98.6 degrees Fahrenheit (37 degrees Celsius) will cause a person to enter the beginning stages of hypothermia, which will require immediate action on your part to remove the person from immediate danger and further exposure.

◆ Helping students continue to generate body heat while preventing them from losing that heat to the environment are the two principles that must be followed.

◆ Localized cooling or freezing of soft tissue from exposure to cold can result in superficial to deep levels of frostbite. The extremities (fingers and toes) are most susceptible, although exposed areas of the face and ear lobes should be closely monitored as well. Proper clothing and footwear, proper nutrition and hydration, and proper pacing during the activity will ward off the adverse effects of the cold.

◆ Ice that falls on climbers and belayers can result in soft-tissue and other physical injuries that are difficult to treat in a cold environment. Keeping belayers and spectators in more protected areas out of the fall line of the climber will reduce this hazard. Establishing and maintaining a well-respected helmet zone is essential.

◆ Moderately angled snow slopes leading to the base of popular ice climbs are susceptible to avalanches when they are loaded with snow that contains weak bonds between the layers. You should be aware of this hazard and know how to use weather and field information to make avalanche assessments in the field. You should also be aware of approaches to and from ice-climbing sites that are safe in the existing environmental conditions.

◆ Freeze and thaw cycles can change ice conditions. As a result, ice ratings found in a guidebook may not match with what is found on a given ice-climbing day.

◆ Fatigue that develops from a long day of climbing can pull students' attention away from the all-important descent from the climbing area.

◆ Remind students to focus on safety while descending to terrain that is more level. Before the descent from the climbing area, make sure that all ice-climbing gear is properly stowed into packs (no dangling crampons or ice axes).

◆ Establish and maintain appropriate student-to-instructor ratios. Ratios of 4:1 are appropriate for basic top-rope programs. Smaller ratios (2:1) are required for multipitch climbing situations.

◆ If group size exceeds the recommended ratios, you may be unable to perform the periodic check-ins necessary to ensure the proper care, comfort, and safety of students.

Closure Activity

Summary Safety Review (15 Minutes)

To strengthen the focus of this lesson, provide a summary of the most common safety issues that students may encounter on their next ice-climbing outing.

Follow-Up Activity

Safety Reminder (Time as Needed)

◆ Provide gentle reminders to students regarding safety practices while in the field. An overbearing approach will likely result in increased student anxiety.

◆ Quizzing students about safety considerations will help them develop a healthy and appropriate level of safety awareness.

◆ Have students do a hazard assessment on their next ice-climbing outing.

ASSESSMENT

◆ Verify that students can describe the various cold-related injuries associated with ice climbing by asking them to state each of the injuries presented.

◆ Check that students can identify the common objective dangers related to ice climbing by quizzing them.

◆ Confirm that students can identify the common subjective dangers associated with ice climbing by quizzing them.

◆ Verify that students appreciate the dangers of ice climbing and act accordingly by observing them and providing feedback when they are engaged in any ice-climbing activity.

TEACHING CONSIDERATIONS

◆ Always review the basics of safety with students before heading to the ice-climbing site.

◆ Consider using teachable moments while in the field to point out objective hazards as they are encountered.

◆ Encourage buddy checks when students are participating in an ice-climbing outing.

▷ Leave No Trace Considerations

OVERVIEW

Ice and snow offer unique and challenging environments to practice Leave No Trace (LNT). This lesson encourages students to discuss and implement ways in which the principles of LNT can be practiced to improve the ice-climbing experience.

JUSTIFICATION

Most parks and natural areas are realizing an increase in visitors, including winter environments beyond the ski slopes (Manning, 1999). Ice-climbing areas have become more popular. Students should understand the proactive measures that they can take to ensure the sustainability of ice-climbing areas. These measures include being a role model to beginning climbers, being considerate to other climbing parties, volunteering for area cleanups and maintenance projects, and following the rules and regulations of the sponsoring land management agency. Invite dialogue with land managers and find solutions together. Further, encourage students to join or start a local climbing organization. This proactive step assists climbers in communicating with managers and private landowners, helps them learn about sustainable climbing, and will help ensure that future climbers can enjoy the ice-climbing experience.

GOAL

To develop students' understanding of the principles of LNT while ice climbing.

OBJECTIVES

At the end of this lesson, students will be able to

- identify the basic principles of LNT (cognitive),
- understand how LNT can be utilized in an ice-climbing environment (cognitive),
- demonstrate LNT principles effectively and accurately (psychomotor), and
- develop an appreciation for the natural environment by incorporating LNT into ice climbing (affective).

EQUIPMENT AND AREAS NEEDED

- Whiteboard
- A popular ice-climbing site

RISK MANAGEMENT CONSIDERATIONS

Depending on where the lesson is conducted, use the edge protection strategies and cold-weather precautions mentioned in previous lessons.

LESSON CONTENT

Introduction

This lesson provides an overview of the Leave No Trace ethic throughout the ice-climbing season (Center for Outdoor Ethics, 2001). Share with students that sensitivity to the natural environment is an important dimension of ice-climbing participation. A lack of sensitivity may lead to unnecessary damage to an area. Incorporating thoughtful interaction with the natural world into every lesson can lead to an enhanced ice-climbing experience (Center for Outdoor Ethics, 2004).

Seasons

Each ice-climbing season has three distinct phases: early season, midseason, and late season. This lesson will address LNT for each phase.

- Early season may be met with muddy trails, unsafe ice conditions because of temperature fluctuations, and many people eager to get out on the ice. During this time of the season, climbers should wear crampons only when necessary because they are hard on trails. Keep groups small to reduce the potential for trail damage.
- Midseason often means cold temperatures and brittle or hard ice. In these conditions, climbers may take chucks of ice off routes. In consideration of others, use caution when sharing a route with other parties.
- Late season typically brings out climbers in large numbers because of the stable ice and warmer temperatures. During this phase, climbing parties should be selective in choosing a climbing site in an effort to be considerate of other climbers and to avoid overusing smaller sites.

LNT Principles

The Center for Outdoor Ethics has established seven principles of LNT. The following section applies those principles to ice climbing:

Plan Ahead and Prepare Check the weather, have extra clothing, select an appropriate site, and follow an itinerary.

Travel and Camp on Durable Surfaces

* Snow and ice are durable surfaces, but LNT is still relevant in popular climbing areas.
* Optimal conditions for ice climbing are frozen and snow-covered conditions.
* The cliff should have a winter appearance with snow, hoarfrost, rime ice, or verglas covering the rock, not just snow covering ledges.
* Vegetation as a climbing medium is best when it is frozen or covered in snow or neve. In this condition it is least likely to be dislodged.
* Rock-climbing routes that are considered classic climbs should be attempted in winter only when fully coated with snow and ice to prevent damage to the underlying rock.

Dispose of Waste Properly

* Human waste can be left to freeze and then carried out. A cathole is often not an option because the ground will be frozen. Leaving excrement on the snow or ice surface is not considerate of others. A pack it in, pack it out mentality should apply.
* Another option is to use a Wag Bag or Restop. These chemically treated bags are made specifically for disposing of human waste directly into a bag. The user then packs out the bag.

Leave What You Find Climbers should not take any plants, rocks, or interesting-looking artifacts from the site. If something strikes a participant's fancy, encourage the person to take a picture instead (either mentally or with a camera).

Minimize Campfire Impacts If a fire ring is present (a rarity in winter), use it. If not, discuss among the group whether a fire is really needed. If it is, follow LNT principles.

Respect Wildlife While climbing and camping, provide a wide buffer between your party and wildlife. If you are seeking backcountry ice, store food in canisters.

Be Considerate of Other Visitors This LNT point is by far the most applicable to ice climbing. Large groups should avoid early or late-season ice. This ice is unstable and least likely to recover quickly, leaving one fewer route for others to climb.

Main Activity

LNT Review (Time as Needed)

The initial portion of this activity requires a fairly busy ice-climbing location.

* Have participants circle up and provide each with an outline of the LNT principles. Discuss each one.
* After you believe that students have a grasp of LNT ice climbing, observe climbers in the area and make note of at least one positive and one negative LNT behavior.
* After giving students time to reflect on their experiences, share your observations on site or in the classroom.

Closure Activity

Creating a Leave No Trace Culture (Time as Needed)

After sharing all observations, provide participants an opportunity to create a class norm regarding LNT. In essence, the class will describe a Leave No Trace culture that participants want to be a part of.

Follow-Up Activity

Reinforce LNT (Time as Needed)

◆ Practicing LNT is an ongoing issue among all groups that use the outdoors for learning.

◆ Follow-up regarding LNT behavior can be done in a variety of ways.

– You can stop and take time at each site to determine the students' appraisal of what LNT factors influence the climbing area.

– Several students can be chosen in advance to identify LNT issues throughout the day.

– At the end of the climbing day, those students can provide a summary of what the group did well and what the group did poorly regarding LNT, and seek feedback regarding each issue.

ASSESSMENT

◆ Check that students can identify the basic principles of LNT by having them recite each. When the ice season has ended, assess this topic with a written examination.

◆ Verify that students understand how LNT can be applied in an ice-climbing environment by having them identify LNT issues throughout the day and come up with appropriate practices to reduce those concerns.

◆ Confirm that students demonstrate LNT principles effectively and accurately by observing them during climbing outings and monitoring their LNT practices. Provide feedback when needed.

◆ Assess whether students develop an appreciation for the natural environment by incorporating LNT into their ice climbing by asking them questions that provoke thought and reflection.

TEACHING CONSIDERATIONS

◆ Basic teaching considerations include the availability of different sites, number of students participating, group composition, and amount of time allotted for the activity.

◆ You should also take into account different learning styles. For example, you can use the site for hands-on activities as well as discussion.

◆ Ensure that transfer occurs by explaining that LNT applies to all environments.

Ice Climbing Skills Checklist

Listed here are the ice-climbing skills that will be introduced in this unit. You are responsible for learning these skills. Periodically review this checklist to assess your knowledge and ability to perform the skills. When you are comfortable with a skill, have the instructor test your ability to perform it.

All skills must be initialed and dated by the instructor to be valid.

(Items from the rock-climbing skills checklist can be incorporated into this list to make it more complete. See unit 2, page 226, for more information.)

Climbing skills	Completed	Needs more work
Set up top-rope belays and anchors		
Hold falls and carry out lowers		
Demonstrate basic ice-climbing movement skills		
Properly place an ice screw		
Properly sharpen an ice axe pick		
Properly sharpen crampon points		

Use the ice climbing skills checklist as an additional tool to assess skills learned throughout this unit.

From M. Wagstaff and A. Attarian, 2009, *Technical skills for adventure programming: A curriculum guide* (Champaign, IL: Human Kinetics).

GLOSSARY

blue ice—Solid, stable, and often hard ice.

bulge—A convex piece of ice.

cauliflower ice—Resembling the vegetable cauliflower, this ice often forms near the bottom of ice climbs and is the result of water splashing and freezing. More often than not, it is stable and strong ice, good for hooking or absorbing a good swing.

chandelier ice—Multiple icicles in close proximity to one another typically offer unstable climbing until their diameters are large enough to hold the weight of a climber. This type of ice is often found early in the season.

cordelette—Cord of smaller diameter 15 to 20 feet (4.5 to 6 meters) in length used for constructing anchors.

crampons—Tempered steel shaped to fit the bottom of boots to provide traction in snow or ice terrain. The two most common designs are rigid (no flex) and hinged (flexible).

dynamic rope—Rope manufactured to stretch when force is applied.

edge culture—How people conduct themselves on a cliff edge.

fall factor—Formula used to determine the energy put on a system in the event of a fall.

front points—The front one, two, or three points on modern crampons.

ice screws—Hollow, threaded, toothed alloy tubes of varying lengths used as protection and in anchor systems while climbing.

ice tools—Evolved out of a need to cover vertical ice. Traditional ice axes are too long; thus a shorter more ergonomic tool was developed. Tools have six main parts: spike, grip, shaft, pick, adze, and leash.

ice tool leash—A piece of material attached to the tool midshaft that connects the tool to the climber by wrapping around the wrist.

kilonewton—1,000 newtons, or 224.8 pounds of force.

master point—The point at which the anchor is equalized and meets the carabiners holding the rope.

pounds of force—The climber's weight multiplied by the length of rope (in feet) extended beyond the last piece of protection.

screamer—An extending and shock-absorbing piece used to connect the rope to protection with two carabiners.

static rope—Rope that has little stretch, less than 3 percent.

verglas—Smooth, rock-hard sheets of thin ice, often found in midseason.

white ice—As in whitewater, the white appearance indicates the presence of air. White ice should be climbed with caution because aerated ice is weak. White ice is most frequently seen in the early and late parts of the season.

yellow ice—The yellow color indicates that the flow of water is transporting minerals. Yellow ice should not be a deterrent to climbing, but it indicates recent flow, which usually comes with warmer temperatures. Climbers should be careful.

REFERENCES AND RESOURCES

REFERENCES

Center for Outdoor Ethics. (2001). *Teaching Leave No Trace.* Boulder, CO: Author.

Center for Outdoor Ethics. (2004). *The Leave No Trace training cookbook: Training recipes for educators.* Boulder, CO: Author.

Center for Outdoor Ethics. (2006). *Welcome to Leave No Trace.* Retrieved from www.lnt.org

Chouinard, Y. (1978). *Climbing ice.* San Francisco: Sierra Club Books.

Harmston, C. (1998). *Myths, cautions, and techniques of ice screw placement.* Internal Black Diamond study. Salt Lake City, UT: Black Diamond Equipment.

Luebben, C. (1997). The cold truth . . . How strong is ice protection? *Climbing,* pp. 106–115.

Luebben, C. (1999). *How to ice climb!* San Ramon, CA: Falcon.

Manning, R.E. (1999). *Studies in outdoor recreation: Search and research for satisfaction.* Corvallis, OR: Oregon State University Press.

Nicolazzo, P. (2002). *The site management handbook.* Winthrop, WA: Wilderness Medical Training Center.

Selter, A. (2004). *Ways to the sky: A historical guide to North American mountaineering.* Golden, CO: American Alpine Club Press.

RESOURCES

Grivel. www.grivel.com. Overview: One of the best climbing Web sites focused on climbers and climbing. The history link is exceptionally informative.

Lowe, J. (1996). *Ice world: Techniques and experiences of modern ice climbing.* Seattle, WA: The Mountaineers Books. Overview: A thorough overview on a variety of topics including nutrition, crevasse rescue, group travel, and vertical technique. Also includes a description of the classic ice climbs around the world.

Raleigh, D. (1995). *Ice: Tools and techniques.* Carbondale, CO: Elk Mountain Press. Overview: A slightly dated book that provides timeless advice from a well-versed climber on topics such as ice movement, mental preparation, training, and history.

Appendix A:
Leave No Trace Principles

Each of the seven Leave No Trace principles is listed and briefly described here (LNT, 2006). The authors have modified these principles to address each of the activities presented in this curriculum guide.

1. Plan Ahead and Prepare.

- Know the regulations and special concerns for the area that you'll visit.
- Prepare for extreme weather, hazards, and emergencies.
- Schedule your trip to avoid times of high use.
- Visit in small groups. Consider splitting larger parties into smaller groups.
- Repackage food to minimize waste.
- Use a map and compass to eliminate the use of marking paint, rock cairns, or flagging.

2. Travel and Camp on Durable Surfaces.

- Durable surfaces include established trails and campsites, rock, gravel, dry grasses, or snow.
- Protect riparian areas by camping at least 200 feet (60 meters) from lakes and streams.
- Good campsites are found, not made. Altering a site is not necessary.
- In popular areas,
  - concentrate use on existing trails and campsites,
  - walk single file in the middle of the trail, even when wet or muddy, and
  - keep campsites small and focus activity in areas where vegetation is absent.
- In pristine areas,
  - disperse use to prevent the creation of campsites and trails, and
  - avoid places where impacts are just beginning.

3. Dispose of Waste Properly.

- Pack it in, pack it out. Inspect your campsite and rest areas for trash or spilled foods. Pack out all trash, leftover food, and litter.
- Deposit solid human waste in catholes dug 6 to 8 inches (15 to 20 centimeters) deep at least 200 feet (60 meters) from water, camp, and trails. Cover and disguise the cathole when finished.
- Pack out toilet paper and hygiene products.
- To wash yourself or your dishes, carry water 200 feet (60 meters) away from streams or lakes and use small amounts of biodegradable soap. Scatter strained dishwater.

4. Leave What You Find.

- Preserve the past: Examine, but do not touch, cultural or historic structures and artifacts.
- Leave rocks, plants, and other natural objects as you find them.
- Avoid introducing or transporting nonnative species.
- Do not build structures or furniture, or dig trenches.

5. Minimize Campfire Impacts.

◆ Campfires can cause lasting impacts to the backcountry. Use a lightweight stove for cooking and enjoy a candle lantern for light.

◆ Where fires are permitted, use established fire rings, fire pans, or mound fires.

◆ Keep fires small. Only use sticks from the ground that can be broken by hand.

◆ Burn all wood and coals to ash, put out campfires completely, and then scatter cool ashes.

6. Respect Wildlife.

◆ Observe wildlife from a distance. Do not follow or approach them.

◆ Never feed animals. Feeding wildlife damages their health, alters natural behaviors, and exposes them to predators and other dangers.

◆ Protect wildlife and your food by storing rations and trash securely.

◆ Control pets at all times, or leave them at home.

◆ Avoid wildlife during sensitive times: mating, nesting, raising young, or winter.

7. Be Considerate of Other Visitors.

◆ Respect other visitors and protect the quality of their experience.

◆ Be courteous. Yield to other users on the trail.

◆ Step to the downhill side of the trail when encountering pack stock.

◆ Take breaks and camp away from trails and other visitors.

◆ Let nature's sounds prevail. Avoid loud voices and noises.

References

Leave No Trace Center for Outdoor Ethics (LNT). (2006). *Leave No Trace principles.* Retrieved from www.lnt.org

Appendix B:
Professional Associations

This section lists a variety of professional organizations that you may find useful as you and your students plan and pursue some of the activities in this curriculum guide. Professional associations publish journals, host Web sites, and hold conferences. They also keep members updated on issues and developments, are a great source for networking with other professionals, and provide information about conferences, workshops, seminars, and trainings.

General

American Alliance for Health, Physical Education, Recreation & Dance

> 1900 Association Drive
> Reston, VA 20191-1598
> Internet: www.aahperd.org

Description: The American Alliance for Health, Physical Education, Recreation and Dance (AAHPERD) is the largest organization of physical education, leisure, fitness, dance, health promotion, and education professionals in specialties related to achieving a healthy lifestyle.

Association for Experiential Education

> 3775 Iris Avenue, Suite #4
> Boulder, CO 80301-2043
> Phone: 303-440-8844
> Toll free: 866-522-8337
> Fax: 303-440-9581
> Internet: www.aee.org

Description: The Association for Experiential Education (AEE) is a nonprofit professional membership association dedicated to experiential education and the students, educators, and practitioners who use its philosophy. The AEE endeavors to

- unite educators in practical ways so that they have access to the growing body of knowledge that enhances their growth and development;
- publish and provide access to relevant research, publications, and resources;
- increase the quality and performance of experiential programs through its accreditation program; and
- raise the recognition of experiential education on a global scale.

Association of Outdoor Recreation and Education (AORE)

> AORE National Office
> 6511 Buckshore Drive
> Whitmore Lake, MI 48189
> E-mail: nationaloffice@aore.org
> Internet: www.aore.org

Description: The Association of Outdoor Recreation and Education (AORE) is an organization developed by and for outdoor recreation and education professionals and students. It is the only organization dedicated to serving the needs of recreation and education professionals in nonprofit settings.

Training and Certifications– Education

National Outdoor Leadership School

284 Lincoln Street
Lander, WY 82520-2848
Phone: 800-710-NOLS
Internet: www.nols.edu

Description: Focuses on wilderness skills, leadership, and environmental ethics; is the leader in wilderness education.

Outward Bound–USA

100 Mystery Point Road
Garrison, NY 10524
Phone: 845-424-4000
Fax: 845-424-4121
Internet: www.outwardbound.org

Description: Outward Bound Wilderness is the nation's leading nonprofit adventure-education organization, offering a variety of course activities in many of the beautiful parks and natural areas throughout the United States and internationally. Outward Bound courses emphasize personal growth through hands-on experience and challenges. Students develop self-reliance, responsibility, teamwork, confidence, compassion, and environmental and community stewardship.

Wilderness Education Association

900 E. 7th Street
Bloomington, IN 47405
Phone: 812-855-4095
Fax: 812-855-8697
Internet: www.weainfo.org

Description: The Wilderness Education Association is an organization whose purpose is to educate the general public and outdoor leaders in the appropriate use of wildlands and protected areas by developing and implementing educational curricula and programs and by forming alliances with federal land management agencies, conservation groups, and organizations that benefit from using wildlands.

Training and Certifications– Stewardship

Access Fund

P.O. Box 17010
Boulder, CO 80308
Phone: 303-545-6772
Fax: 303-545-6774
Internet: www.accessfund.com

Description: The Access Fund has been the only national advocacy organization that keeps climbing areas open and conserves the climbing environment. It does this through five core national and local programs: public policy, stewardship and conservation (including grants), grassroots activism, climber education, and land acquisition.

Leave No Trace Center for Outdoor Ethics

P.O. Box 997
Boulder, CO 80306
Toll free: 800-332-4100
Phone: 303-442-8222
Fax: 303-442-8217
Internet: www.lnt.org

Description: The Leave No Trace Center for Outdoor Ethics is a national nonprofit organization dedicated to promoting and inspiring responsible outdoor recreation through education, research, and partnerships. Leave No Trace (LNT) builds awareness, appreciation, and respect for the nation's wildlands. LNT offers a variety of courses to train individuals to become comprehensive Leave No Trace educators or master educators.

Training and Certifications– Safety and Medical Training

Wilderness Medical Associates

189 Dudley Road
Bryant Pond, ME 04219
Phone: 207-665-2707
Toll free: 888-WILDMED (945-3633 within the United States)
Fax: 207-665-2747
E-mail: office@wildmed.com
Internet: www.wildmed.com

Description: Wilderness Medical Associates offers courses for both medical professionals and active outdoor people without a medical background.

SOLO

Stonehearth Open Learning Opportunities
P.O. Box 3150
Conway, NH 03818
Phone: 603-447-6711
Fax: 603-447-2310
E-mail: info@soloschools.co
Internet: www.soloschools.com

Description: Stonehearth Open Learning Opportunities offers education, research, and conference centers to both the internation outdoor rescue and emergency medical communities as well as the local rural communities of New England.

NOLS (Wilderness Medical Institute)

284 Lincoln Street
Lander, WY 82520-2848
Toll free: 800-710-NOLS
Phone: 307-332-5300
Fax: 307-332-1220
Internet: www.nols.edu/wmi/

Description: Provides the highest quality education and information for the recognition, treatment, and prevention of wilderness emergencies.

National Association for Search and Rescue

Phone: 703-222-6277
Fax: 703-222-6277
Toll free: 877-893-0702
Internet: www.nasar.org

Description: The National Association for Search and Rescue offers a course, Introduction to Search and Rescue (ISAR), to provide information on the general responsibilities, skills, abilities, and the equipment needed by individuals participating in a search or rescue mission.

Training and Certifications— Rock Climbing

American Mountain Guides Association

1209 Pearl Street, Suites 12 and 14
Boulder, CO 80302
Fax 303-271-1377
Internet: www.amga.com

Description: The American Mountain Guides Association (AMGA) offers a course, Top-Rope Site Management, which focuses on learning and applying technical skills for top-rope climbing. The course is intended for recreational climbers proficient in top-rope climbing and who, preferably, have lead climbing experience. The course is designed to benefit outdoor instructors, aspiring guides, and climbers who facilitate or seek to facilitate top-rope climbing programs in outdoor or human and leisure service agencies or organizations.

American Alpine Club

710 Tenth Street, Suite 100
Golden, CO 80401
Phone: 303-384-0110
Fax: 303-384-0111
E-mail: getinfo@americanalpineclub.org
Internet: www.americanalpineclub.org

Description: The American Alpine Club is the leading national organization in the United States devoted to mountaineering, climbing, and the issues facing climbers. The emphasis is on adventure, scientific research, and education.

Professional Climbing Instructors Association (PCIA)

P.O. Box 784
Bishop, CA 93515
Internet: http://pcia.us/pro/

Description: The PCIA provides education and instruction for new and existing climbing instructors who primarily teach basic skills or facilitate climbing experiences. In addition, the PCIA Accreditation Program helps assure land managers, insurance providers, and the public that employees of PCIA-accredited schools have been peer reviewed and demonstrate core competencies appropriate to the climbing venue.

Training and Certifications— Caving

National Speleological Society

2813 Cave Avenue
Huntsville, AL 35810-4431
Phone: 256-852-1300
Internet: www.caves.org

Description: The National Speleological Society (NSS) is made up of individual members. Local chapters (or grottos) sponsor outings, offer training, teach and practice cave conservation, and provide a framework for enjoying and studying caves.

Training and Certifications— Mountain Biking

The International Mountain Bicycling Association

> IMBA
> P.O. Box 7578
> Boulder, CO 80306
> Phone: 888-442-4622
> Fax: 303-545-9026
> Internet: www.imba.com

Description: The International Mountain Bicycling Association (IMBA) is a nonprofit educational association whose mission is to create, enhance, and preserve trail opportunities for mountain bikers worldwide. IMBA encourages low-impact riding, participation in volunteer trail work, cooperation among different trail user groups, grassroots advocacy, and innovative trail management solutions.

Training and Certification— Paddle Sports

American Canoe Association

> 7432 Alban Station Boulevard, Suite B-232
> Springfield, VA 22150
> Phone: 703-451-0141
> Fax: 703-451-2245
> E-mail: aca@americancanoe.org
> Internet: www.americancanoe.org

Description: The American Canoe Association (ACA) is a recognized leader in the fields of paddle sport instruction and education and keeps participants informed about paddle sport opportunities and activities. It also has an active Conservation and Public Policy department and an Events and Programs department. Funding for various projects is available through stewardship grants from corporate sponsors to help local paddle sport clubs preserve waterways.

American Whitewater

> P.O. Box 1540
> Cullowhee, NC 20723
> 866-BOAT-4-AW
> Internet: www.americanwhitewater.org

Description: The mission of American Whitewater (AW) is to conserve and restore America's whitewater resources and to enhance opportunities to enjoy them safely. AW activities fall into five main areas: education, conservation, events, safety, and river access.

American Red Cross

> American Red Cross National Headquarters
> 2025 E Street NW
> Washington, DC 20006
> Phone: 202-303-4498
> Internet: www.redcross.org

Description: The American Red Cross offers a series of training courses for the paddling enthusiast, some of which are Canoeing—Whitewater; Kayaking Fundamentals; Sea Kayaking; and Basic River Weekend.

Training and Certifications— Snow and Ice

Professional Ski Instructors of America, Eastern Division, and American Association of Snowboard Instructors

> 1-A Lincoln Avenue
> Albany, NY 12205-4907
> Phone: 518-452-6095
> Fax: 518-452-6099
> Internet: www.psia-e.org

Description: The Professional Ski Instructors of America, Eastern Division, and the American Association of Snowboard Instructors provide training and education certification for members (alpine, snowboarding, nordic, and adaptive teaching). Specialized programs for children's educators, seniors, and racing enthusiasts are also available.

Appalachian Mountain Club

AMC Main Office
5 Joy Street
Boston, MA 02108
Phone: 617-523-0636
Fax: 617-523-0722
Internet: www.outdoors.org

Description: The Appalachian Mountain Club offers over 8,000 trips each year for every ability level and outdoor interest, including hiking, climbing, paddling, snowshoeing, and skiing. Training programs are also offered for children, teens, and adults, as well as outdoor leaders.

Sierra Club

National Headquarters
85 Second Street, 2nd Floor
San Francisco, CA 94105
Phone: 415-977-5500
Fax: 415-977-5799
Internet: www.sierraclub.org

Description: The Sierra Club chapters throughout the United States and Canada offer opportunities for local involvement, activism, and outings.

Index

About the Editors

Mark Wagstaff, EdD, is professor of recreation, parks and tourism at Radford University in Radford, Virginia. Dr. Wagstaff has taught outdoor leadership and adventure education courses in the college setting since 1995 and has been a professional river guide since 1981. In addition to being an Outward Bound instructor, he has been a Wilderness Education Association (WEA) instructor since 1986 and has led outdoor adventures in Costa Rica, Ecuador, and Nepal.

Dr. Wagstaff is a master instructor trainer for Leave No Trace and is an instructor and member of the WEA, the American Canoeing Association, and the Association for Experiential Education. He has coauthored two other titles in the field of outdoor leadership. When he's not instructing or writing about outdoor adventures, he's taking part in them: He enjoys whitewater canoeing and kayaking, rock climbing, and traveling abroad in his leisure time.

Aram Attarian, PhD, is an associate professor in the department of parks, recreation, and tourism management at North Carolina State University at Raleigh. His teaching focuses on adventure recreation, outdoor leadership, and park and recreation facility and site management. His enthusiasm for teaching has earned him five teaching awards. Dr. Attarian's research interests center on outdoor leadership, adventure programming, and the impact of rock climbing on the environment. Recently he was named director of the State Park Leadership School, which emphasizes the training and development of future state park managers.

Dr. Attarian has spent over 30 years in the field of adventure education and outdoor leadership, where he has worked with a variety of populations and settings, including adjudicated youth, college and university programs, businesses, and camps. His most significant contributions have been with the North Carolina Outward Bound School, where he worked as an instructor, climber, and course director since 1978. He currently serves on the school's board of directors where he chairs the safety committee.

About the Contributors

Reid Cross received his doctorate in outdoor education from the University of Northern Colorado and is currently an associate professor of outdoor education and the outdoor education coordinator at California State University, Chico. Every year that goes by, he is amazed at how much he has yet to learn. His professional goals are to start a bachelor of arts degree in outdoor education at Chico and to keep the majority of the teaching and learning in a wilderness setting (out of the traditional classroom).

Mick Daniel has been involved in adventure education since 1992 when first introduced to the field on a North Carolina Outward Bound School (NCOBS) course. After working in the field for many years, Mick finished a bachelor's degree in wilderness leadership and experiential education at Brevard College. During this time he returned to NCOBS to instruct. Mick moved to Oklahoma and finished a master's degree in leisure services at Oklahoma State University in 2002. Mick is currently the director of student life, recreation, and adventure programs at Adams State College in Alamosa, Colorado.

Briget Tyson Eastep is the coordinator of the outdoor recreation in parks and tourism program at Southern Utah University in Cedar City, Utah. Briget enjoys getting her students outside to learn and recreate in southern Utah's mountains and deserts throughout the year. As an outdoor educator for the past 16 years, Briget has led wilderness education experiences for the Student Conservation Association, the Wilderness Education Association, the University of Utah, St. Cloud State University, and Southern Utah University. Her new favorite pastime is exploring the natural world around the neighborhood with her 2-year-old and her husband.

Mat Erpelding is an experienced outdoor educator and guide. He earned his MA in adult education from the University of Idaho and has worked internationally as a program consultant, educator, and trainer. As an independent contractor, he works for the Wilderness Medicine Training Center, American Alpine Institute, and Boise State University. He co-owns a leadership consulting company, World Leadership Solutions, which specializes in corporate, educational, or outdoor leadership development programs. Mat lives in Boise, Idaho, where he enjoys immediate access to the best trails in the country.

Shayne Galloway, PhD, is a lecturer in outdoor education in the school of physical education at the University of Otago. He completed his master's and doctoral degrees at Indiana University in adventure and outdoor education programming. Dr. Galloway served as assistant professor in recreation and program coordinator at Utah Valley State College (Orem, Utah) prior to moving to New Zealand. Dr. Galloway's major research interests center on factors influential in the naturalistic decision-making (NDM) environment in outdoor leadership contexts.

David Goodman graduated in 1999 from Radford University with an undergraduate degree in recreation and leisure and is currently completing a master's degree in student services. David serves as a certification instructor for the Wilderness Education Association and a trainer for Project Underground (a national initiative to educate the public about caves). He worked for several years as the adventure programming coordinator for the Southern Indiana Recreation Corporation and as a full-time professional caving guide. He is currently the assistant director for campus recreation at Radford University and RU outdoors director. He is a member of the National Speleological Society and a member of several grottos.

Laurie Gullion has completed 11 whitewater canoeing expeditions to Arctic and sub-Arctic rivers in the United States, Canada, Norway, and Finland—paddling almost 10,000 miles since 1980. Laurie has authored seven books on canoeing, kayaking, and nordic and alpine skiing. Her most recent book, *Canoeing: A Woman's Guide,* includes the reflections of more than 100 women. Laurie is the coordinator of the outdoor education option at the University of New Hampshire in Durham. She teaches water-based and winter adventure programming classes, leadership development, and program administration courses. Laurie is an instructor trainer for the American Canoe Association and a nordic examiner for Professional Ski Instructors of America. She is currently the editor of the ACA's upcoming adaptive paddling guide for people with disabilities.

Tommy Holden, PhD, completed his doctor of philosophy degree with a concentration in adventure recreation from North Carolina State University, department of parks, recreation and tourism management, in May 2004. He has been instructing sea kayaking courses since 1998 and has worked as a seasonal instructor for the North Carolina Outward Bound School since 2001, instructing both mountain and sea kayaking courses in North Carolina and the Bahamas. He has made numerous presentations at the East Coast Canoe and Kayak Festival and the West Coast Sea Kayak Symposium. Currently, Tommy is a teaching assistant professor and co-coordinator for the outdoor leadership minor at North Carolina State University in the department of physical education, teaching a variety of adventure recreation activity and theory courses.

John R. Kascenska, PhD, is the associate academic dean at Lyndon State College of Vermont. Before moving into his current administrative role, John founded the adventure-based program management degree program at Lyndon. John has been climbing since 1979 and has 25 years of outdoor adventure program experience, teaching courses in rock climbing, ice climbing, mountaineering, avalanche education, wilderness medicine (SOLO), outdoor leadership, risk management, and research. He is an American Mountain Guides Association (AMGA) certified top-rope site manager, an AIARE level I avalanche course leader, and member of the board of directors of the American Alpine Club.

Michael L. Kinziger received a PhD from the University of New Mexico in 1992. He now teaches at the University of Idaho in the department of health, physical education, recreation, and dance. Dr. Kinziger's areas of interest lie in effective leadership techniques for team building, game and activity instruction, tournaments and creative play, and the emergence of wilderness education programs in remote settings across the United States in relation to (a) effective wilderness therapy applications, (b) managers' perceptions of the use of wilderness, and (c) future use of wilderness or peripheral wilderness in the recreation field.

Bruce Martin, PhD, is an assistant professor in the school of recreation and sport sciences at Ohio University, specializing in outdoor education and recreation. He has been a whitewater kayak instructor trainer for the American Canoe Association since 1999. He was first certified as an ACA whitewater kayak instructor in 1995. He has actively promoted the sport of whitewater kayaking through his teaching ever since. Martin's other paddling experiences include numerous seasons working as a raft guide on the New and Gauley Rivers in West Virginia; two years living and working in southeast Alaska, where he occasionally taught open-water coastal kayaking; and a lifelong affinity for canoeing, which he has also taught over the years. His first swim from a whitewater kayak occurred on the Nantahala River in 1989. He performed his first combat roll while surfing at Swimmer's Rapid on the Lower Youghiogheny River not too long after.

Christopher R. Pelchat obtained a BA double major in outdoor recreation and recreation management, as well as a master's in education with a certificate in college instruction, from Eastern Washington University. Mr. Pelchat is now attending the University of Idaho where he is working on a PhD in health, physical education, recreation, and dance. He is currently teaching at Ithaca College in the department of recreation and leisure studies. Mr. Pelchat also holds instructor certifications in kayaking and rafting through the American Canoe Association and whitewater rescue through Rescue 3 International.

Scott Schumann, MA, possesses a diverse background in rock and ice climbing, whitewater paddling, sea kayaking, and canoe expeditioning. Scott combines his technical experience with his commitment to education to create effective and memorable experiences. He is an active instructor with the Wilderness Medicine Training Center (WMTC), the American Alpine Institute, and the Wilderness Education Association. Scott's research interests include freshman wilderness orientations, academic self-concept, teaching methodologies, and the mechanisms that affect the outcomes of adventure-based programs. He currently lives in Salt Lake City, Utah, with his wife, Joan, where he is pursing his PhD in recreation with an emphasis in adventure education.

Tammie L. Stenger-Ramsey enjoys spending time in the outdoors with her family, friends, and her dog, Chief. She likes to backpack, hike, canoe, and kayak. As an assistant professor in the recreation administration program at Western Kentucky University, she teaches in the outdoor leadership semester. She is a Wilderness Education Association national standards program instructor and a Leave No Trace master educator. Tammie's professional experience includes challenge course facilitation and facilitator training, environmental and adventure education instruction, and serving as a camp manager and a program director for a residential outdoor education center. She completed a BA and an MS from Western Kentucky University and an EdD from Oklahoma State University.

Thomas Stuessy, PhD, received his BA in 1997 from Western State College of Colorado and his MS from Aurora University in 1999. Since 2003, Tom has taught in the adventure recreation program at Green Mountain College in Poultney, Vermont, while completing his PhD at Indiana University. Beyond Green Mountain College, Tom is the proud co-owner of Know the Earth Institute and Guides.

Josh Whitmore currently serves as the director of outdoor programs at Western Carolina University. Previously, he worked extensively as a field instructor for NOLS and the North Carolina Outward Bound School. Before committing to a career in outdoor education, Josh had a brief stint as a professional bicycle racer, twice representing the United States in the World Championships. Even now, when not instructing a university outdoor trip, Josh can be found roaming the mountainous trails and roads of North Carolina on his bicycle.

You'll find other outstanding recreation resources at
www.HumanKinetics.com

In the U.S. call 1.800.747.4457
Australia 08 8372 0999
Canada. 1.800.465.7301
Europe . . . . . +44 (O) 113 255 5665
New Zealand . . . 0064 9 448 1207

HUMAN KINETICS
The Information Leader in Physical Activity
P.O. Box 5076 • Champaign, IL 61825-5076

How to Use the CD-ROM

System Requirements

You can use this CD-ROM on either a Windows-based PC or a Macintosh computer.

Windows

- IBM PC compatible with Pentium processor
- Windows 98/2000/XP/Vista
- Adobe Reader 8.0
- 4x CD-ROM drive

Macintosh

- Power Mac recommended
- System 10.4 or higher
- Adobe Reader
- 4x CD-ROM drive

User Instructions

Windows

1. Insert the *Technical Skills for Adventure Programming: A Curriculum Guide* CD-ROM. (Note: The CD-ROM must be present in the drive at all times.)
2. Select the "My Computer" icon from the desktop.
3. Select the CD-ROM drive.
4. Open the file you wish to view. See the "00Start.pdf" file for a list of the contents.

Macintosh

1. Insert the *Technical Skills for Adventure Programming: A Curriculum Guide* CD-ROM. (Note: The CD-ROM must be present in the drive at all times.)
2. Double-click the CD icon located on the desktop.
3. Open the file you wish to view. See the "00Start" file for a list of the contents.

For customer support, contact Technical Support:

Phone: 217-351-5076 Monday through Friday (excluding holidays) between 7:00 a.m. and 7:00 p.m. (CST).

Fax: 217-351-2674

E-mail: support@hkusa.com